GunDigest 2022

76th EDITION

EDITED BY

Philip P. Massaro

Published by

Gun Digest® Books, an imprint of Caribou Media Group, LLC

Gun Digest Media
5600 W. Grande Market Drive, Suite 100
Appleton, WI 54913
www.gundigest.com

To order books or other products call 920.471.4522
or visit us online at www.gundigeststore.com

CAUTION: Technical data presented here, particularly technical data on handloading and on firearms adjustment and alteration, inevitably reflects individual experience with particular equipment and components under specific circumstances the reader cannot duplicate exactly. Such data presentations therefore should be used for guidance only and with caution. Caribou Media accepts no responsibility for results obtained using these data.

ISBN-13: 978-1-951115-34-0

Edited by Phil Massaro and Corey Graff
Cover Design by Gene Coo
Interior Design by Jon Stein and Dave Hauser

Printed in the United States of America

10 9 8 7 6 5 4 3 2 1

John T. Amber
LITERARY AWARD

The John T. Amber Literary Award is named for the editor of *Gun Digest* from 1950 to 1979, a period that could be called the heyday of gun and outdoor writing. Amber worked with many of the legends in the business during his almost 30 years with the book, including the great shooting and hunting writer Townsend Whelen. In 1967, Amber instituted an annual award, which he named for Whelen, to honor an outstanding author from the previous year's *Gun Digest* edition. In 1982, three years after Amber's retirement, the award was renamed in his honor.

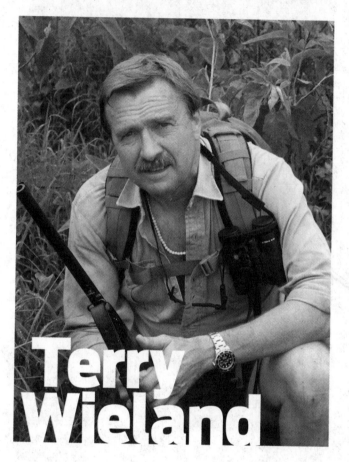

Terry Wieland

about admitting that I'm a big fan. His biography of the late, great Robert C. Ruark, *A View From a Tall Hill*, is perhaps the most fitting tribute penned to the great dangerous game author.

With that glowing introduction, I am pleased to announce that Terry Wieland is the recipient of the 40th Annual John T. Amber Literary Award for his feature article, "Echoes of Valhalla." The treatise on German Schüetzen rifles appeared in the 75th Edition of the *Gun Digest* annual last year.

Terry's storied literary career includes eight books, a massive volume of articles in numerous different hunting and shooting publications, and several literary awards, including the John T. Amber Literary Award in 2007.

I'll let Terry describe the journey which has culminated in his time behind the keyboard.

"I'm a Canadian, raised in Ontario. My earliest memories, circa four years old, involves a toy pistol, and I have never lost interest. When I was 13, my family moved to the country where I went to work on the farm next door, got my hands on a .22, and was delegated to control the woodchuck population.

Shortly afterwards, I started buying gun magazines, fell under the spell of Jack O'Connor and, a little later, John Taylor.

When I was 16, I read Robert Ruark's The Honey Badger, *and that decided me that my destiny was to write. I also became enthralled with Africa. In 1968, I got a job as a copy boy on the local daily newspaper, and got my first reporting job in 1969.*

In 1971, having decided I wanted to be a war correspondent, it seemed the best way to do that was to find a war and correspond. I left for Africa with a one-way ticket to London and C$210. in my pocket, crossed Europe, ended up in Uganda and then in the southern Sudan where the never-ending war was, well, never-ending. I came back to Canada in early 1972, wrote an article for The Toronto Star *about the Sudan, and later that year the Star sent me back to Africa to cover the expulsion of the Asian population from Uganda by Idi Amin.*

I have been a full-time freelance writer ever since. I made my first hunting trip to Africa in 1990, with back to back safaris in Tanzania and Botswana, fell in love with Cape buffalo, and have killed seven so far. If I could do just one more hunt before I called it quits, it would be for Cape buffalo."

I couldn't agree more with that last sentiment. Terry is a regular contributor to this book and stays busy as the Shooting Editor of *Gray's Sporting Journal*. Wieland currently resides in Fenton, Missouri.

Gun Digest proudly presents this Literary Award, named in honor of John T. Amber, the long-time editor of this book, to Terry Wieland, a significant figure in the history of hunting, firearms, and the literature which surrounds it all. Congratulations, Terry!

Phil Massaro, Editor-in-Chief

All gun writers are passionate about firearms, but few have the passion of Terry Wieland. An unabashed *aficionado* for all things African hunting, Terry's classic book, *Dangerous-Game Rifles*, holds a special place on my bookshelf; if you have an interest in the pursuit of dangerous game on any continent, this volume is a must-have. Having read the ink off the pages of that book, plus following Terry's writings in several different publications — his contributions to the A-Square *Any Shot You Want* reloading manual remain a particular favorite — I have no qualms

GunDigest® 2022

Photo: Weatherby, Inc.

WELCOME TO
Gun Digest 2022
76th Edition

PHILIP P. MASSARO
EDITOR-IN-CHIEF

Hello all, I'd like to welcome you to the 76th Edition of the *Gun Digest Annual*. It's difficult to imagine that it has been a year since I wrote the introduction for the 75th Edition, but it has, and to say it's been a strange year may be the biggest understatement I've ever put in print. There was an ammunition shortage and millions of new shooters joined our ranks. We endured quarantines, masks, canceled trade shows, virtual product releases, travel bans, postponed hunts, vaccines; all of these were issues we didn't have to deal with until recently. Bottom line: our lives have changed, and I'm not sure whether or not it will ever return to what we knew as normal.

But, life goes on. And looking at the bright side of things, statistics have shown that the number of hunters has increased — and that's a good thing. With firearm sales continuing to hold steady, more folks are embracing the gun culture and enjoying their Second Amendment rights than we've ever had before. The increase in new shooters creates a renewed need for training and information; the histories, designs, and performance of firearms, cartridges, and shotshells are, perhaps, more relevant than ever.

INSIDE THE 76TH EDITION

We've got lots of good stuff piled between the covers of this book, from choices for those looking to ring distant steel on a budget, to the history of Weatherby Magnum cartridges (big congratulations to Weatherby on its 75th anniversary), to modern single-action revolvers to the sordid histories of the Chinese SKS, Colt Python, and Colt Walker. In addition, Phil Bourjaily takes us on a tour of non-toxic shot choices for the shotgunner, Nick Hahn tackles his favorite snipe shotguns, and Dave Campbell discusses a lifelong love of .44-caliber revolvers.

There are also some wonderful cartridge profiles in this edition, starting with Mike Dickerson's feature on the .257 Weatherby Magnum (if you ever meet Mike, you'll quickly understand how passionate he is about that cartridge). Next, Dick Williams shows us just how underrated and overlooked the .41 Remington Magnum is, and Steve Gash discusses the merits of one of my favorites — the .280 Ackley Improved. Finally, Stan Trzoniec casts an eye upon the 6mm BR Norma, and Yours Truly sheds some light on the new Winchester-Browning collaboration known as the 6.8 Western.

Joe Coogan shares his insight on the rifles used by African Professional Hunters — Joe spent years as a PH in Botswana, hunting among legends — and Dave Fulson shares his experiences with and history of the revered double rifle. Finally, Alaskan Master Guide Phil Shoemaker recounts his famous experience with a big brown bear while armed with a 9mm pistol; there is plenty of excitement involved.

In an interesting feature article, the father and son team of Lek and Mark Nazi of Double Eagle Tactical Training explores what happens when a hollow-point handgun bullet strikes the walls of a residence. And we're not just talking about sheetrock, but both interior and exterior walls, not to mention siding and brick construction. I was as surprised by the results as Mark and Lek were, and these guys spend a considerable amount of time with a pistol in hand.

Our Reports from the Field section highlights a considerable number of new products related to the shooting industry. Our TestFire department has some in-depth reviews, from rifle and handgun designs of the 19th Century to the latest releases. And, as always, our Catalog compiles a comprehensive overview of firearms available to the shooter.

And, in what may be my favorite section of the *Gun Digest*, the One Good Gun section covers all sorts of exciting topics. When a writer is passionate about a gun they've spent time with — whether it is an entry-level firearm or a highly sought-after vintage piece — I feel they deliver their best work. Shane Jahn takes us on his customized .41 Magnum Ruger BlackHawk journey, and Jim House tells the tale of his .45-70 single-shot Handi-Rifle. Tyler Freel's well-worn Remington Model 710 .30-'06 Springfield has a story of its own to tell,

all over the 49th State. My friend Simon Barr uses his vintage Rigby Rising Bite 12-bore to complete the fabled 'Macnab,' and Jay Leyendecker recounts the tale of his prized Winchester Model 70 in .375 H&H Magnum, a special gift from his grandfather.

We may be stuck in a rut as Covid-19 complications pose an issue to traveling sportsmen and those who enjoy the simplicities of a trip to the range or a gun club meeting. But as the old saying goes: "*this, too, shall pass.*" We have witnessed the breakup of Remington, an absolute American icon. Still, like a phoenix rising from the ashes, Big Green and its sister companies have been picked up by several different organizations. For example, Remington's ammunition division is now a part of Vista Outdoor (parent company of Federal Premium, Speer, and CCI) and is up and running in its Alabama plant. Not only that, Barnes Bullets is now a part of Sierra Bullets and Marlin Rifles now hangs its hat under Ruger's roof; so, though there are inevitable changes in the firearms industry, not all of them are for the worst.

Our cartridge technology continues to develop, and with that comes advancements in bullet technology; not far behind, you'll see the changes in optics and so on down the line. But, just as the *Gun Digest* is steeped in the history of the firearms industry (this publication has been around longer than the .308 Winchester, .223 Remington, and .300 Winchester Magnum), many shooters, hunters, and readers still embrace blued steel and fine walnut, chambered in a classic cartridge. So, no matter what your passion in the firearms realm is, there is something in here for you. I hope you enjoy this, the 76th Edition of *Gun Digest*. **GD**

GUN DIGEST STAFF

JIM SCHLENDER | Group Publisher
PHILIP P. MASSARO | Editor-In-Chief
COREY GRAFF | Features Editor

DEPARTMENT CONTRIBUTORS

Wayne van Zwoll | Rifles
Todd Woodard | AR Rifles
Robert Sadowski | Semi-Auto Pistols
Max Prasac | Revolvers & Others
Kristin Alberts | Shotguns

Luke Hartle | Muzzleloaders
Joe Arterburn | Optics
Jim House | Airguns
Philip P. Massaro | Ammo, Reloading & Ballistics
Tom Turpin | Custom & Engraved Guns

The Mossberg Patriot LR Hunter

FEDERAL

6.5 PRC

O.F. Mossberg & Sons, Inc. has long produced firearms that represent a great value in the American market. That's true, from rimfire rifles to shotguns, to the highly popular centerfire rifles Mossberg manufacturers. New for 2021, the Mossberg Patriot LR Hunter is all business, being developed for the serious long-range shooter and hunter.

The newly designed polymer stock is specifically packed with features that the long-range shooter will enjoy: a Monte Carlo comb, which will aid in the proper alignment of the eye and larger riflescopes, dual forward sling swivels to facilitate the simultaneous use of a bipod and a sling, and machined aluminum pillar bedding to keep the action securely in place for consistent accuracy with even the hardest recoiling cartridges. The stock is Spider Gray, with a light microtexture to afford a firm grip in any weather, with gloved or bare hands. The fore-end of the stock is flat, much like a benchrest rifle, to give good stability when leaning upon any number of different surfaces. The fore-end width narrows toward the muzzle to provide a good purchase when wearing gloves or for those shooters with smaller hands.

The button-rifled, fluted barrel is free-floated, threaded for a suppressor or muzzle brake, and features an 11-degree match-grade crown at the muzzle. Mossberg has opted to include a Picatinny rail on top of the receiver for mounting your chosen optic. Like the standard Patriot models, the Patriot LR Hunter features the proprietary LBA ("Lightning Bolt Action") adjustable trigger, which you can adjust for a pull weight between 2 and 7 pounds. Other standard features include a detachable drop magazine and spiral-fluted bolt with an oversized handle for a positive hold, whether bare-handed or wearing gloves.

The Patriot LR Hunter is available in 6.5 Creedmoor and .308 Winchester, each with 5+1 capacity and 22-inch

barrels. You can also get it in 6.5 PRC (shown on the cover) with 4+1 capacity and a 24-inch barrel, and in .300 Winchester Magnum with 3+1 capacity and a 24-inch barrel. All models have a 13 ¾-inch length of pull and feature a matte blue finish on the receiver and barrel. The standard push-feed, twin-lug bolt face typical of the Patriot line is present here, and you can quickly push a two-position safety on the rear right side of the receiver into the fire position with your right thumb. For the long-range shooter looking for a lot of rifle and minimal investment, it will be difficult to beat the Mossberg Patriot LR Hunter.

The Leupold VX-3HD
4.5-14x40mm Riflescope

Leupold & Stevens is another name synonymous with tremendous value, as the company has a well-deserved reputation for rock-solid products at a fair price. The VX-3 and VX-3i line of riflescopes have long been a favorite of hunters and shooters worldwide, as they represent a perfect blend of necessary features and affordability. In 2021, Leupold has given the VX-3 product line a revamp and introduced the VX-3HD series of riflescopes. The lineup includes models suitable for nearly any application, from the low-powered dangerous game scopes with their wide field-of-view to the models well-suited to target work and hunting at longer ranges, where precise shot placement is paramount. The Leupold VX-3HD 4.5-14x40mm (shown here) is a natural choice for a long-range hunting scope, as it offers enough magnification to make a shot at any sane hunting distance, yet you can dial it down to perform in the deer woods. A 30mm main tube gives plenty of room for elevation adjustments, and the side parallax knob keeps the image crisp at any distance.

The VX-3HD 4.5-14x40 is — like other Leupold scopes — tough as nails, yet weighing in at a mere 16 ounces will not destroy the delicate balance of your favorite hunting rifle. The Elite Optical System offers the optimum performance in any light, and there is plenty of eye relief for even the hardest-kicking magnum cartridges. Elevation and windage adjustments are ¼ MOA with a positive click. The elevation turret has a zero lock to ensure you return to zero after every adjustment; push the button and twist to make an elevation adjustment, and upon return to zero the unit stays locked in the field. Leupold offers the CDS (Custom Dial System), which correlates to your chosen load's trajectory. Once you provide Leupold with the necessary ballistic data, you can swap a secondary elevation dial for the standard MOA graduated turret, which Leupold marks in yardage for your specific load. Range the target, dial the elevation turret to the proper distance, and squeeze the trigger. It couldn't be any more practical or straightforward.

The Wind-Plex reticle even further enhances the performance of the VX-3HD. The horizontal crosshair of the reticle is graduated in one-MOA hash marks, making wind adjustments on the fly easy. There is 10 MOA of graduation on either side of the crosshair, offering all the wind adjustment any shooter should need. Quality optics are a worthwhile investment, and Leupold has packed an awful lot of high-quality features into an affordable riflescope that will give a lifetime of service. Backed by Leupold's Lifetime Guarantee, this riflescope is designed, machined, and assembled in the USA and, with an MSRP of $749.99, you probably won't find a scope of this quality, with all of these features, at a price point this low. Serious shooters have always equated the famous Gold Ring with quality and dependability, and the VX-3HD is no exception. **GD**

BE RELENTLESS

VX-6HD
RUGGED PERFORMANCE.
RELENTLESS CLARITY.

LIFETIME
GUARANTEE

LEUPOLD

The .257 Weatherby Magnum, combined with today's lighter, weather-resistant Weatherby rifles, is an excellent choice for hunting big country where shots are long. Photo: Weatherby

.257 WEATHERBY MAGNUM:
The Once and Future King of the Quarter Bores

› MIKE DICKERSON

It may seem hard to believe now, but there was a time when Southern California was a hotbed of innovation and activity in the shooting sports. For many decades following World War II, before anti-gun politicians in Sacramento started legislating away gun rights, the old-Hollywood A-list elite counted many accomplished hunters and shooters among their ranks. Los Angeles was home to several top hunting and shooting publications. L.A. had numerous custom gun shops, like Pachmayr, and famed gunsmiths, including Jim Hoag, a competitive shooter who became known as the gunsmith to the stars. Other notable locals included legendary big game hunters Elgin Gates and Jack Lott — Lott was the inventor of the .458 Lott. In the 1960s, Col.

Jeff Cooper was holding court — and shooting matches — in the mountains above L.A., teaching the Weaver stance, which L.A. County Sheriff's deputy Jack Weaver developed. Later, Kim Rhode, who would become America's greatest female Olympic trap and skeet shooter, trained as a youngster at Mike Raahauge Shooting Enterprises, where I often shot pheasants and saw Kim training on clays with her father.

Long before then, during World War II, a car insurance salesman and wildcatter named Roy Weatherby spent his nights and weekends experimenting with handloads. He would develop cartridges that would forever change the industry and influence ammo and gun makers alike. One of the first of these cartridges was the .257 Weatherby Magnum.

IT ALL BEGAN WITH A FAILURE

Roy's historic journey of invention began with a failure when he wounded and lost a deer on a hunt in Utah using a rifle chambered in .30-'06 Springfield. The experience led him to develop his theory of what we would today call hydrostatic shock. Roy believed that if he could get a bullet moving fast enough to disintegrate inside the animal's body, the shock would cause instant death even if the animal was not hit in a particularly vital area.

The first cartridges Roy developed, including the .257, .270, 7mm, and .300 Weatherby Magnums were all based on the .300 Holland and Holland Magnum case. Roy blew out the cases, increasing powder capacity while reducing the parent case's taper, and gave the shoulder the iconic Weatherby double radius. That,

along with the case's brass belt, made Weatherby magnum cartridges readily identifiable at a glance. The belt, incidentally, was not needed for strength, as many people believe. Its purpose in the British parent cartridge was a means of proper headspacing.

For the .257, Roy necked the case down to .25 caliber and shortened it to about 2.5 inches. That worked best with the slowest-burning powders of the time and allowed the cartridge to fit in standard-length actions. There had been other .25-caliber cartridges before Roy's design, but the .257 Wby. Mag. blew them all out of the water. They included the .25-20 Winchester, a short-range round; the limited-range .25-35 Winchester; the obsolete .250-3000 Savage, which was the first .25 to crack the 3,000 fps barrier with light bullets; and the .257 Roberts, which pushed a 100-grain bullet along at slightly more than 3,000 fps. Even the newer .25-06 Rem., which Remington standardized in 1969, propels bullets substantially slower than the .257

Wby. Mag. for given bullet weights.

The .257 Wby. Mag. was then — and remains today — the king of the quarter bores. When Roy first trotted the cartridge out, shooters were astonished. The cartridge drove an 87-grain bullet at 3,825 fps. Numbers were equally startling for heavier bullet weights: 100-grain bullets blazed along at about 3,600 fps, 117-grain bullets stepped out at 3,400 fps, and 120-grain Nosler Partitions (my personal favorite for hunting) launched at 3,300 fps.

"As many people know, the .257 Weatherby Magnum was known as my grandfather's favorite cartridge," says the company's third-generation leader, Adam Weatherby, "I think it really demonstrated what he was all about … high velocity." Noting that the .257 Wby. Mag.

is still touted as the fastest .25 caliber today, Adam says he has a .257 in his personal safe that harvested four deer last year, including one his high school-aged daughter took. "It is a cartridge that has a cult-like following for those looking for something fast and flat. There truly is nothing else like it out there," Weatherby noted.

THE NEED FOR SPEED

Apart from those of us who have a profound need for speed, there's a certain

Roy Weatherby tested his magnum cartridges — including his personal favorite, the .257 Wby. Mag. — extensively in Africa. He killed many plains game with the cartridge and even used it on one occasion to kill a Cape buffalo to prove he could do it.

The differences between the .257 Wby. Mag. right, and its closest competitors, the .257 Roberts and the .25-06 Rem., are clear at a glance. For nearly 80 years, the .257 Wby. Mag. has ruled as the most potent quarter-bore cartridge.

The author says his personal favorite .257 Wby. Mag. rifle, a much modified Weatherby Vanguard, has likely accounted for more game than any other rifle in his collection.

smug self-satisfaction to be had when someone asks you what you're shooting, and you reply, ".257 Weatherby." Owning one is a bit like being the guy who shows up driving a Ferrari to a car rally where everyone else is driving a Prius. I once sat next to a rancher in a Texas blind who had just watched me shoot a whitetail at a couple of hundred yards. He was watching the deer with binoculars when I touched off the shot. "Holy Mother of God," he mumbled under his breath as he slowly lowered the binoculars. He immediately made me an offer on the rifle. Yes, performance can be that impressive — also, rifles in .257 Wby. Mag. also have relatively little recoil. Anyone who can shoot a .270 Winchester can comfortably shoot a .257 Weatherby.

Roy would later write that he couldn't pinpoint an exact date when he created the cartridge, but he was sure that it was in 1944. He once wrote that the .257 was his favorite for almost everything, and he had shot animals with it up to 300 yards away with dynamic success. "He himself was amazed at the killing power of the .257 Wby. Mag.," says Roy's son, Ed Weatherby, who led the firm from 1983 until 2017. "He used that caliber more often than any other, including the .300 Wby. Mag." Roy reportedly preferred to use the 100-grain bullet over the 117 grainers because he found that it did more damage within reasonable ranges.

While there was always some merit in the hydrostatic shock theory, its effects are not always guaranteed. There are limits to its application in the field, particularly with larger animals that are considerably more shock-resistant than deer-sized game. In those early years, Roy was working with relatively light cup-and-core bullets, and he didn't have the improved, controlled-expansion bullets that we take for granted today.

That changed in the 1960s. That's when Weatherby began loading .257 Weatherby Magnums with Nosler Partition bullets — or, more accurately, when Norma started to load them. Norma has manufactured Weatherby ammunition since the 1950s and was Nosler's first commercial loader. In any event, this made Weatherby one of the first to offer premium-grade ammo with

controlled-expansion bullets, and in the case of the .257, it proved to be a game-changer. Hunters still got the benefits of speed-induced shock — and uber-flat trajectories — but with bullets that would hold together and penetrate deeply.

Weatherby currently offers seven loads for the .257 with the following bullets: a 100-grain spire point, a 100-grain Hornady Interlock, a 100-grain Barnes TTSX, a 110-grain Nosler Accubond, a 110-grain Hornady ELD-X, a 115-grain Nosler Ballistic Tip, and the 120-grain Nosler Partition. Today's Weatherby ammo is multi-sourced and includes some loaded by Weatherby in Wyoming. Factory offerings don't stop there.

Hornady makes 90-grain GMX and 110-grain ELD-X loads. Nosler makes a 110-grain AccuBond offering in its Trophy Grade line and no fewer than five different loads in its Custom line with

bullet weights ranging from 100 to 120 grains. Federal's custom ammo shop will create loads for you using a 100-grain Barnes TTSX, a 110-grain Nosler Accu-cuBond, or a 110-grain Sierra MatchKing bullet. DoubleTap produces three .257 Wby. Mag. loads. Choice Ammunition has three, including one with a 115-grain Berger VLD Hunting bullet. HSM makes one load with the same bullet, plus another with a 117-grain SBT GameKing bullet. Norma currently lists only .257 brass for sale.

MATCHING THE CARTRIDGE TO THE GAME

Campfire discussions about the .257 Wby. Mag. often revolve around a single question: What can you kill with it? The answer, as demonstrated throughout the 77-year life of the cartridge, is just about anything. In North America, hunters

Many large hogs and blacktail deer fell to the author's .257 Weatherby during several decades of hunting the central California coastal range. Those were primarily spot and stalk hunts, and shots could be rather long, making the .257 perfect for the job.

The Weatherby Mark V line got a makeover in the last few years, as evidenced in this Mark V First Lite model, and the result is an updated take on an iconic American rifle design. In testing, this rifle chambered in .257 Wby. Mag. shot sub-MOA groups with all four tested loads, demonstrating both the cartridge and the rifle's accuracy potential.

The author used the .257 Weatherby Mag. loaded with a 120-grain Nosler Partition bullet to take this bruiser of a Texas whitetail.

The .257 Wby. Mag. also accounted for the author's best pronghorn to date, from New Mexico.

The Mark V rifle had radical styling when Weatherby introduced it, with Monte Carlo combs, fancy inlays, spacers, and high-gloss finishes. The rifle, and numerous other versions of the Mark V, were chambered for the .257 Wby. Mag. from the beginning.

have killed grizzly bears with the .257. Roy Weatherby was fond of telling the story about how he killed a Cape buffalo in Africa with the .257 — just once — to prove the cartridge could do it. Details of that hunt are lost to the mists of time, but as the story goes, he shot the buff while it was quartering away, and it dropped in its tracks.

Of course, the fact that you *can* do something doesn't necessarily mean that you *should*, and I'm not about to suggest that anyone who isn't in a hurry to meet their maker take up hunting large and dangerous game with the .257. As Roy and his hunting companions demonstrated in Africa many times, however, the cartridge is perfectly capable of downing

plains game as big and tough as zebra.

Some will tell you that the cartridge is inadequate for elk and moose, and that may be true with less-than-optimal shot placement, as it is with many other cartridges. Still, plenty of hunters have killed elk and moose with the .257. They had to wait for the right shot opportunity and sent their bullets where they needed to go. It is, after all, not the size of the hole that matters, but where you place it. The .257 works fine on black bears, and it's hard to imagine a more perfect cartridge for pronghorn.

Most North American hunters use the .257 for hunting mule deer and white-tails, and the cartridge shines in that role. As one fellow die-hard .257 fan puts

it, "There is no finer cartridge for deer than the .257 Wby. Mag." He is not alone in that belief. It has a fanatically loyal following, and with good reason. The critical thing to remember is that it's all about matching the bullet to the game and distance — no matter what you hunt with it.

The cartridge isn't without its critics. Some are quick to point out that it is seriously overbore, and so it is — but so are many other great cartridges with large case volumes and relatively small diameter bullets. Ah, they say, but burning that much powder will shorten barrel life. Again, that's true, but most owners of a .257 Wby. Mag. rifle aren't going to shoot it enough to wear out a

barrel in their lifetimes. The actual use of my .257 is limited to checking zero, being sure to let the barrel cool between shots, and taking shots on game. If you do the same, you should have no problem. But the ammo is expensive, say detractors. That's also true, but most people who buy Weatherby rifles in Weatherby magnum chamberings do so knowing that, and you can always cut costs by loading your ammo.

MY LOVE AFFAIR WITH THE .257

My love affair with .257 Weatherby Magnum began more than 30 years ago when I occasionally visited the old Weatherby retail store in South Gate, a Los Angeles suburb. In those days, my tastes ran toward racy and aesthetically pleasing rifles and cars, among other things, but my tastes often exceeded my budget. Happily, the store had a "blem rack," holding guns with slight cosmetic blemishes that it sold at a discounted price, and I sometimes found a gun there with no significant imperfections. My credit card came out so fast it smoked, and the store salesmen were happy because they didn't have to follow me around to prevent me from drooling all over the beautiful Weatherby rifles.

One of those guns was a Weatherby Vanguard chambered in .257 Wby. Mag. It did not long stay in its original con-figuration. I replaced the factory trigger with one from Timney and swapped the stock for a pillar-bedded Weatherby Fiberguard in an attractive tan color with a black spiderweb finish. I quickly realized why the .257 was Roy Weatherby's fa-vorite as I used the rifle to take a lot of hogs and blacktail deer on spot-and-stalk hunts in Central California in those years.

Since then, I have primarily fed the rifle Weatherby factory loads with 120-grain Nosler Partition bullets, which group around ¾ MOA out of that rifle. Launching those bullets at 3,300 fps, the load hits hard and shoots flat, and it's the one I would choose to handle just about everything that walks on the North American continent and several others. Using the old-school trick of zeroing the rifle to place bullets three inches high at 100 yards, it is dead on at 300 yards and hits a little more than three inches low at 350 yards. Within that range, there's no need to waste time calculating holdover or turning turrets. You get a good rest, hold dead-on, and shoot. The bullet, incidentally, is still packing nearly 1,750 ft-lbs of energy at 350 yards.

With that load, the rifle has always been nothing less than a death ray, and over time it has probably accounted for more game — and made more great memories — than any other rifle in my collection. That rifle was with me when I shot my first pronghorn in Wyoming, and it was the one I used to take a New Mexico record book pronghorn. With that gun, I've taken mule deer in several Western states, and it was the one I used to take my first javelina and my first axis deer. It has killed many whitetails, includ-ing my best to date — a barrel-chested 11-pointer nudging the 160 B&C mark from Texas. I killed a running whitetail with an offhand shot in Kentucky, and the list goes on.

Almost every animal I've shot with that rifle dropped in their tracks. A few ran a short distance, but none have ever required any tracking to recover. Mind you, that's not because I shot any of the animals through the shoulders to anchor them. I don't particularly appreciate wast-ing meat. I took all those animals with heart/lung shots, and when people saw the rifle perform in the field, they offered to buy it from me. For any of my friends

Inset: The .257 Wby. Mag. cartridge and guns like the Weatherby Mark V Weathermark LT are genuinely go-anywhere, do-anything combinations for most North American game. Today, Weatherby chambers all Mark V and Vanguard rifles in .257 Wby. Mag., except the Camilla models.

Left: The author spends more time testing and hunting with new rifles these days, but he still sneaks his .257 Wby. Mag. out occa-sionally for the pure joy of hunting with it.

Above: This axis deer, the first of many the author has taken, fell to the .257 Weatherby.

Right: The author also took his first javelina with the fast little cartridge.

who still haven't gotten the message, it's not for sale. That gun is going to remain in my family.

THE WEATHERBY MYSTIQUE

Of course, no discussion of Weatherby cartridges would be complete without touching on Weatherby rifles, for the two go hand-in-hand. Shortly after Roy developed his early cartridges, he began rechambering guns for people in his garage. He then started building rifles on just about any type of action he could get. These included FN Belgian Mauser, Enfield, Schultz & Larson, Brevex Magnum Mauser, and FN Sako Mauser actions. In 1957, he introduced the Weatherby Mark V rifle and thoroughly shook up the shooting industry, which produced rather bland products. Mark V rifles were radical designs by the day's standards, featuring Monte Carlo combs, fancy inlays, spacers, and high-gloss finishes. They were hot rod rifles for hot rod cartridges, and from the beginning, Weatherby chambered them in .257 Wby. Mag.

Ever the savvy salesman and promoter of his rifles and cartridges, Roy had a talent for accessing some key influencers in the entertainment business, including John Wayne, Gary Cooper, and Roy

Rogers. As he told one interviewer long ago, there were "damn few" important big game hunters who could afford a Weatherby rifle who didn't own one. The list included Ernest Hemingway, former president of Mexico Miguel Aleman, Prince Abdorreza Pahlavi of Iran, Air Force generals Curtis LeMay and Nate Twining, the presidents of Volkswagen and Gulf Oil, the owners of May Company and Ohrbach's department stores, several professional athletes and a few Indian maharajahs.

The prototypical Weatherby rifle is the Mark V Deluxe, which the company still makes. Weatherby added many other Mark V models to the lineup over the years, including the more affordable

Vanguard rifle line. Production has been both overseas and in the U.S. at different times, but where Weatherby made the guns mattered little because the company always exercised a high level of quality control.

Today, rifles chambered in .257 Wby. Mag. remain top sellers for Weatherby, ranking second only to rifles chambered in .300 Wby. Mag. According to Ed Weatherby, the .257 has historically always been one of Weatherby's top four calibers in sales. That may diminish a bit with the introduction of new Weatherby cartridges such as the 6.5-300 and 6.5 RPM, he says, but it will always be one of the most popular for medium-sized game like antelope, deer, and sheep.

As of this writing, Weatherby, now based in Sheridan, Wyoming, offers 18 different Mark V and 21 Vanguard models, and — except for the Camilla models — all of them include the .257 chambering.

Several custom rifle makers have produced guns in .257 Wby. Mag. You can find some other factory guns chambered for the cartridge over the years, but that begs the question: Why would you want to? A big part of the appeal of shooting Weatherby cartridges is shooting Weatherby rifles. Despite Roy's talent for getting his rifles into the hands of famous people, the guns were never just the bone-crushing playthings of wealthy Texans, as one writer described them long ago.

There has always been a certain mystique associated with owning and shooting Weatherby rifles and the Weatherby magnum cartridges. That's especially true of the .257, and its popularity shows no sign of slackening despite the current trend toward cartridges with long, heavy-for-caliber bullets and higher ballistic coefficients. The .257 Weatherby Magnum has been putting trophies on the wall and meat on the table for nearly 80 years now, and it's a pretty safe bet that it will continue to do so, with style, for a long time to come. ⌖

The ultimate catch for the collector is a Vietnam bringback such as this well-used Type 56 captured during the Cambodian Incursion in June 1970. Shown is a communist Khmer Rouge-checkered neckerchief jammed into the butt trap where the cleaning kit is typically stored. Note also that the stock was repaired and sanded down to remove a split or crack in the pistol grip. The sling even shows a repair! Though it is in used condition, its owner, SKS authority and Vietnam veteran Howie Bearse, once told the author, "I like such guns that have been there, done that!" Howie Bearse Collection

The Puzzle of China's SKS Carbine

Enigma of the Bamboo Curtain

> GEORGE LAYMAN

What became the most prolific copy of Sergei Simonov's world-renown semi-automatic military carbine was the near 30-plus-year production run of those manufactured in the People's Republic of China. These easily outnumbered all others in variety and distribution throughout the world, including the United States!

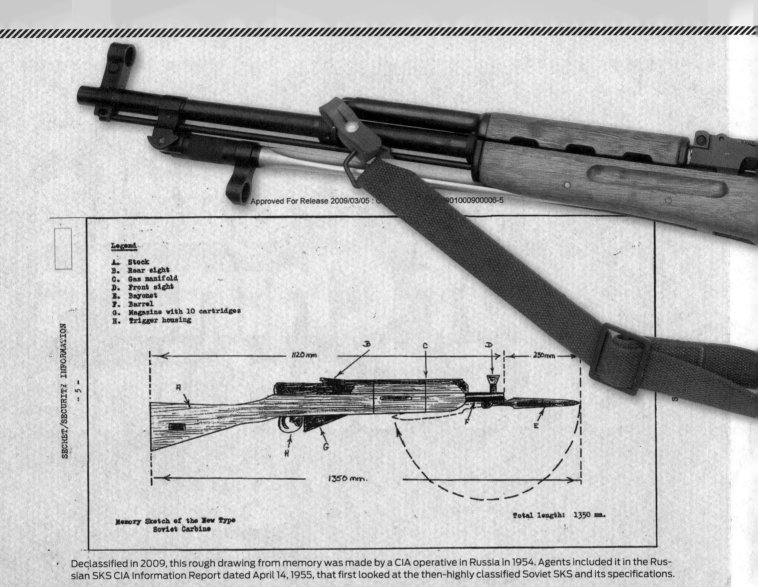

Legend

A. Stock
B. Rear sight
C. Gas manifold
D. Front sight
E. Bayonet
F. Barrel
G. Magazine with 10 cartridges
H. Trigger housing

SECRET/SECURITI INFORMATION

— 5 —

1120 mm   230mm

1350 mm.

Memory Sketch of the New Type
Soviet Carbine

Total length: 1350 mm.

Declassified in 2009, this rough drawing from memory was made by a CIA operative in Russia in 1954. Agents included it in the Russian SKS CIA Information Report dated April 14, 1955, that first looked at the then-highly classified Soviet SKS and its specifications.

The development behind the SKS carbine began five years before the German invasion of the Soviet Union in June 1941. Sergei Gavrilovich Simonov was getting close to nearing completion of a basic prototype of his semi-automatic infantry carbine. These were the dark, prewar days of the Nazi juggernaut, which would soon roll across Russia's seemingly endless western frontier. The details of Simonov's returning to the drawing board in 1943, and eventual perfecting of his famous SKS carbine, is well known among arms historians. However, the 8 1/2-pound, ten-shot semi-automatic gas-operated carbine wasn't finalized until late 1945 — too late to be issued to the Red Army during the Great Patriotic War. The Soviet Union would not officially adopt it until 1949.

The SKS-45 or *Samozaryadn'ye Karabin Sistemi Simonova 1945* (Simonov Semi-Automatic Carbine), did not enjoy a genuinely long service life. The Soviets selected Mikhail Kalashnikov's soon-to-be-fielded AK-47 for adoption in 1949. The Russian SKS became a stopgap weapon but did remain in official issue until 1958, when production terminated. It is, however, still an active participant in ceremonies and special functions. The world got its first glimpse of the still-classified SKS during the Hungarian Revolution of 1956. By that time, the Soviet Union offered its satellite states the opportunity to license and manufacture the SKS. Yugoslavia, Romania, and East Germany are three Eastern European countries that domestically produced the SKS. The fourth was Al-

bania, which formed a unique affiliation with the most prolific manufacturer of the Russian-designed SKS — the People's Republic of China (PRC).

The PRC was the first Soviet ally to receive licensing to manufacture the SKS, but in the beginning, it experienced a hint of reluctance that came with a hefty price. After Mao Tse Tung's People's Liberation Army drove the rightful Nationalist Chinese Government out of China's mainland to Taiwan in October 1949, chairman Mao quickly partnered his regime with Soviet Premier Joseph Stalin. Following a half-baked reception by the aging Russian leader, the Soviets allocated some standard Soviet weaponry quantities to Mao. Most of China's post-war ordnance consisted of countless surrendered Japanese military hardware and ammunition.

A full-length view of a Type 56 made at rectangle Factory/Plant 0141, located in Hebei, China. The rectangle factory guns appear in the early 1970s, and this T56 is sure to be a 1973 production gun given the 73 prefix, followed by 3,025, the actual number of guns made up to that point by this facility. Many rectangle guns have a line from the center of the box leading to the serial prefix. The characters "Five–Six Type" begin at the far left and are neatly done in a block print style. Adrian Van Dyk Collection

Over time, when satellite factories and sub-plants expanded, China cleverly devised methods to insert three and four numbers into a limited space. The triangle with a 3 inside a smaller triangle is Factory 6336. Studying this closely, one can understand how this reads compared to the more straightforward Factory 326, which is not difficult to interpret. Why many triangle markings end with the number "Six" is unknown; however, the author feels there is a connection to the Jianshe Factory 26. The location of most of these numbered plants is also unknown, aside from a small percentage. Factory 326 is in Anhui Province, with 6635 located in Guangdong Province. As numbers increase to four digits, many triangles are like puzzles and are challenging to decipher. All photos by author unless noted

Within a year of assuming power, Mao Tse Tung sent thousands of volunteers at the request of ally North Korea, four months after the South's invasion on June 25, 1950. This action resulted in China pleading with the USSR for substantial quantities of Soviet weaponry. The Chinese received 375,000 World War II-era, Russian small arms, and 250,000,000 rounds of ammunition in November 1950.

In June 1951, Mao sent a group of military emissaries to Moscow to purchase and request licensing for tooling and machinery to build small arms domestically. Stalin suspected that providing China with an inch would eventually result in many miles. He was right. China's ulterior motive was to obtain SKS technology, a subject yet to be brought up. China financially sacrificed a substantial price, paid to the Russians for World War II-era obsolescent ordnance, along with tooling, drawings, and spare parts. Thus, China obtained most on its wish list; however, it all arrived 14 months later than promised. Regressing to the June 1951 arms talks, Mao was incensed that his chief negotiator, Marshal Hsu Hsang Chien, had yet to acquire the

This refinished Sino-Soviet, Type One SKS is one of the 2,050 made as test and evaluation guns by the Chinese students at the Tula Arsenal in Russia. Its serial number of 1789 is over the 1,410 mark that indicates it is one of the 540 guns completed at Factory 26 between January and March 1956. Less than a dozen of its kind are known. They feature a four-digit number to 2,051 and a star at the right. The humidity-resistant fiberglass/phenolic stock is a replacement, but these can run beyond the $1,800 mark in any configuration. Adrian Van Dyk Collection

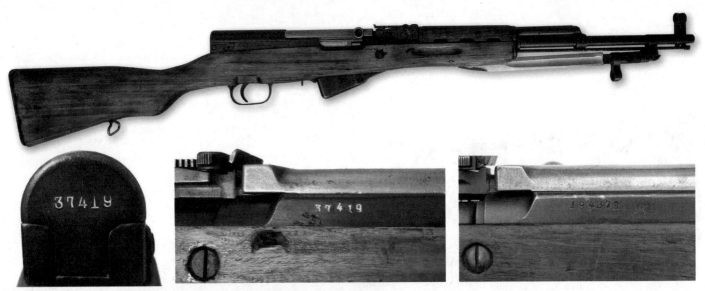

This Type Two was once another difficult-to-locate Chinese Type 56 SKS until the Albanian imports of the last ten years arrived and were completely original, as a matching numbered Type Two variant as shown. With nothing but a serial number from 2,052 to 215,000, these were not common during the 1980s and 1990s surplus SKS boom. Though rusting in places, this example has its original finish. It seems to have experienced more storage time than shooting and handling, given most of its original finish is remaining. Without its import marks stating CHINA as the origin, you could easily misidentify it as another country's product. The buttstock is a very distinctive grain of Arctic Birch. Pictured with it is a closeup of a 194,000-range, six-digit Type Two, and an extremely desirable North Vietnamese "Project One" Star at the end of the serial number. It is likely among the earliest Chinese Type 56 carbines given or sold to communist Vietnam early in the war. Photos by the author and the Adrian Van Dyk Collection

This 11-million prefixed Type 56, approximating 1967, is an excellent representation of Factory 26 guns made during the Vietnam era. It arrived with the last known batch of Type 56 guns from Albania in 2019 and, as is the norm, features everything from mixed up parts and incorrect bayonets to badly cracked stock. However, this example matches completely, with solid wood and 90 percent finish showing minimal use. The Triangle 26 at far left is a model number in characters followed by the prefixed serial number, representing the later majority. The chamber shows the shorter barrel collar/lug introduced by this time. In the 1970s, factories eliminated the short collar in favor of a more economical, press-fit, and pinned barrel. However, the Factory 26 guns' reappearance in 1979 retained the short collar and threaded barrel. This condition is desirable among collectors.

A disassembled view of one of the rare, 2,275 Russian Code K SKS guns, s/n K0811. This SKS was the first SKS Chinese model the military had a chance to familiarize itself with while students were in Russia training from 1954 to 1955. Arriving from Albania in the 2010s, it's the only one of its type reported thus far, and you can find the abundant Russian inspection markings in numerous locations. Jude Steele Collection

SKS part of the deal. Marshal Hsu also had not received Stalin's blessing to provide the SKS package and Russian technical advisors' schedule to move on the SKS project. It would be two more weeks of negotiating before a frustrated Marshal Hsu would finally convince Stalin and the Politburo with a hefty payment using the old Soviet bartering system.

As late as August 1953, however, China had yet to receive any word on the SKS equipment transfer. Thirteen months after Stalin's death in March 1953, China's long obsession with the SKS carbine slowly became a reality. The new Russian Premier Nikita Krushchev was informed through diplomatic channels that China had received nothing regarding the SKS equipment previously paid and agreed upon during the 1951 Second Sino-Soviet Agreement. Krushchev learned that Stalin's general mistrust of others had delayed the SKS program. In the original July 7, 1951 agreement, Marshal Hsu grudgingly concurred with Soviet demands that China should send apprentices to Russia's Factory 26 for SKS training before equipment transfer.

Krushchev got the ball rolling from late 1953 to Fall 1955, and China's Jianshe Fac-

Two views of the experimental stamped steel Type 56 SKS. This right front angle quickly identifies it by the square-contoured frontal frame and the cross bolt's presence. This gun made at rectangle Factory 0138 also has the "70" prefix found on cast steel guns. Whether 70 is a code or the production year is unknown. Another unique feature is the rounded area where the receiver cover meets the frame. Very few had the large, visible electro-penciled import markings of NORINCO, as shown. Norinco was a People's Liberation Army front organization operating in the United States as an arms importer. You cannot rule out a possible link to espionage. Jude Steele Collection

The early, one-piece gas tube (top) and the two-piece modified gas tube (bottom) appeared in 1967. Production-wise, the latter was far more inexpensive to produce than the former and eliminated expensive machining steps.

tory sent 95 Chinese apprentices to build SKS carbines on a rotational evaluation basis. The Chinese requested only 2,050 guns. The shrewdly astute Krushchev decided to formulate a Third Sino-Soviet Agreement in 1954. In part, it stipulated Russia would additionally supply 2,275 pre-issue SKS carbines for China's military to train with while the students were in Russia. These specially numbered SKS carbines are identified in the archives as the *Kitayets Otsenka Serii Kod Bukva' K' Programma* or Chinese Evaluation Series Code Letter K Program. Albania exported one known example in 2013; these SKS variants are quite rare. Furthermore, the Joint Sino-Soviet 1954 Agreement (officially known as the Lin/Kovalyov Signing) saw Russia providing substantial quantities of SKS components in addition to tooling,

drawings, and machinery, which China readily agreed would expedite production. This agreement was yet another separate payment, again using the bartering system.

The Chinese apprentices were schooled at Russia's Tula arsenal until December 1955, with the last group returning to China with the 67 Soviet technicians. In addition to the previous agreement in 1951, this payment went towards some 3,120,000 unfinished SKS carbines in various completion stages, about 812,000 yet-unidentified components, 10,500,000 bayonet blades, and 11,220,00 rear leaf sights, all shipped to China over two years. Oddly, the 2,275 "K Code" guns were separate and cost-free. However, the 2,050 SKS test carbines were chargeable commodities. Of these guns, Russia completed 1,640, with the remaining 410 finished in

China in March 1956. In this agreement, the materials bartered included natural resources such as tungsten, vanadium, salt, lead, and other minerals needed by the Soviets. Adding insult to injury, Krushchev ensured that Russia also demanded a quantity of refined gold, an added resource that rankled Mao Tse Tung to no end. The amount is still classified as Secret. The 67 Russian technicians were compensated monthly by China for their services on the Soviet wage scale. Thus, China paid a heavy price to acquire SKS technology. Soon after, the Chinese received the AK technology[1].

Both the Chinese SKS and AK-47 are identically christened the Type 56. By 1958, the original 67 Russians were replaced by 75 newly selected advisors who would be the "go-to" people when

The Chinese used four types of leaf sights on the Type Two SKS. The earliest, which lasted until the early 1970s, was one of the 10,500,000 purchased from the Soviet Union purchased per the 1954 Agreement. The base has a Cyrillic "P," which to English speakers appears as a square-topped "U." There are two abbreviations for this Cyrillic "P," the first is "Pritsel," meaning Rifle Sight, and "Postoyanyy," or Permanent; another means the standard position of the sight at 100 meters. The second early sight is a Latin "D" marking at the base, which, as a PLA soldier explained to the author, stands for "Di wei" or low position. The D-marked sight leaf is seen as early as 1964 and was in use through the 1970s. Many early Chinese M 21 carbines featured it. The next is a number "3" stamped leaf. The exact meaning is unknown, but you will find it on many 1980s and 90s imports. The final and latest sight leaf is like a Roman numeral III lined over the top and bottom. You'll see many of the later Public Security guns with this stylized leaf marking.

This DP-marked carbine has the prefix of Baicheng City behind the Type 56 markings in front of the serial number. One of 11 different city prefixes on DB/DP guns, this example was neatly marked. Assume that the 24 heading in the serial number on this non-Factory 26 Type 56 SKS indicates the 24th year of manufacture, 1981, with 1,192 representing the production number. Note the later press fit and pinned barrel lacking a collar. There is no known record of how many guns carried this vexing set of city prefix markings.

The lower forearm of the later Type 56 spike bayonet stock (top) had a far wider and lengthier inlet as opposed to the narrow and shorter channel (bottom). This feature accommodated the thinner width of the blade bayonet. The changeover occurred in late 1964. The forearm ferrule seen at the top is considerably more open to accompany the spike bayonet's width.

China required high-grade Russian steels and other materials not available in China proper. These early 2,050 guns are coined by collectors as the Sino-Soviet Type 56, along with SKS carbines built from 1956 into late 1960, as they consist of Chinese- and Russian-made parts. I have classified this first group as Type One. You identify these by a four-digit serial number and a small star at the right indicating receivers were made at Tula Arsenal. Fewer than a dozen are known, making them the scarcest Chinese Type 56 SKS carbines. Type Two continues from serial number 2,051 to about 214,000. These have five to six serial numbers, with no identifying markings to distinguish them. The Type Three variant of the Chinese T56 SKS is the first Factory 26-marked gun that appeared, with serial numbers 215,000 to 218,00.

The entire range of Type Threes runs from approximately 215,000 to about 1,820,000. In essence, China produced Type One through Type Three models from 1955 to 1959.

Following the Sino-Soviet Split in 1960, China independently produced the SKS as both countries had serious ideology issues. Hereafter, all assistance from the Soviets had halted. About this time, Factory 26

A left-hand closeup of a six-digit Type Three, made well beyond the time the triangle 26 markings appeared in the 218,000 serial number era. Adrian Van Dyk Collection

A seven-digit, Type Three SKS in the 2-million range that dates about 1958. The Russian-type long barrel lug or collar is visible, and note that it stops just before the rear sight base. Courtesy Howie Bearse

Another difficult-to-locate T-56 marking is that having an oval 9186. Some dyed in the wool Chinese SKS aficionados collect these based only on factory markings. Imports of many of the factories have never occurred in the United States, and you may never encounter one. This rarity all adds up to the thrill of the hunt.

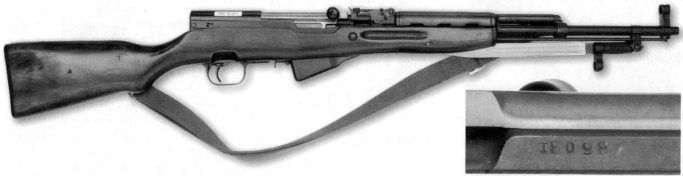

The letter gun period began in 1959. This example has the "I" prefix ahead of its four-digit serial number. Minus the side-mounted sling swivel, this gun is difficult to discern from a Russian-made SKS given its well-preserved, arctic birch stock. Unless worn, letter guns in this condition have a star cartouche on the right-rear buttstock. Most appear built from the one-million-plus serial range, with Russian components held in reserve. Adrian Van Dyk Collection

expanded operations by establishing satellite factories and assembly plants. Almost at once, China faced political and climatic catastrophes. Thus the so-called "Letter Guns" appear. In 1955, lead Russian technician Yuri Kuznetsov suggested a letter prefix serialization to throw off western intelligence sources.[2] China remembered this. Reaching approximately 3,820,000 SKS carbines, using what has been termed the "millionth placement numbering system," suddenly disappeared in 1959. Hence, the production of the Letter Guns starts that same year. Thus, Latin letters A to Y, minus Q and Z, prefixed a four- or five-digit serial number.

With China experiencing numerous internal problems, it squirreled away those earlier 3,120,000 Russian-made components in anticipation of a nationwide crisis. From 1959 to 1961, Factory 26 downsized its workforce to be utilized in other capacities. Thus, with a minimal crew, assembly of the prefabricated Russian components could be accomplished. Many letter guns display numerous Russian inspectors' markings and the arctic birch stocks, received cost-free in 1955. The side-mounted rear sling swivel appears in the 3,000,000 serial range (about 1958) and is standard to the letter guns, the triangle 26 lightly stamped at the right of the serial number.

From late 1961 to early 1962, complete Chinese manufacture began in

the 6,000,000 vicinities. The triangle 26 marking was visible at the left of the "Type Five-Six" stamping in Chinese characters, followed by a seven-digit serial number. The estimated 674,000 to 800,000 letter guns disappeared, and Factory 26 guns returned to the original "Millionths Placement" numbering system. Between 1964 to 1967, T-56 SKS production underwent several modifications to maximize the economy of scale. Historically, Spring 1957 saw Factory 26, known previously as Jianshe Arsenal, re-named "Jianshe Tool and Machine Factory," indicating other products produced at that location. Considering other plants' establishment during the 1960 to 1961 period, we don't know how many were operational. Presently, some 150 different locations identified by multi-numbered geometric symbols, including triangles, rectangles, ovals, circles, and diamonds, appeared on guns imported during the 1980s to 1990s SKS boom.

Previously, most SKS carbines in the U.S. were trophies from the Vietnam War and were the only SKSs typically seen in this country. The rare SKS cartridge, the 7.62x39mm, was completely unavailable. It has only been in the last 35 years that we've been able to sort out and compare large numbers of China's SKS inventory through networking, solving the Chinese SKS puzzle, and understanding its estimated production periods. Space permits only a fraction of the nuances in differ-

entiating the countless details relevant to the Chinese SKS. To the unfamiliar, any SKS is merely an "SKS," but details such as markings were once very evasive in China's case.

ESTIMATED ANNUAL ANALYSIS OF THE TYPE 56

1955–1956 Type One: Excluding the 2,275 "K" coded guns, the Sino-Soviet variation saw 1,640 of the original 2,050 manufactured in the Soviet Union, with the remaining 410 completed at China's Factory 26. A Tula star to the right of the serial number identifies these.

1956–1957 Type Two: Production continues at Factory 26 from late 1956 to Spring 1957, from serial number 2,051

Factory 26 Type 56 SKS

by Serial Range, Estimated Production Year, and Period of Importation

Import Batch Legend:
1st: 1984–1994
2nd: Albanian Imports 2012–14/2018–19

Type One: 1st import batch. All marked with Russian Tula Star following four-digit serial number 0001–2,050. None yet observed imported from Albania.

Type Two: The Factory /26\ marking is not present. The serial number ranges are five to six digits starting at 2,051 through 214,000. 1st and 2nd import batches. Note: Serial range 60,000 to 114,000 rare. Possibility of loss in Vietnam or destroyed in Albania during the Project ALBA Demilitarization Program, from 1997 through 2000.

Type Three: The first appearance of the Factory /26\ serial range approximately 215,000 to 216,000 to about 1,820,000 or slightly higher, 1st and 2nd import batches. Note: Factory /26\ triangle appears between 218 to 220,000 serial range

Letter guns: 1st and 2nd import batches. Most feature light Factory /26\ markings. Double-lettered examples numerically prefixed ahead of the letter are very scarce. The most common letters are I, J, M, and O, with some having a "stylized" Serif like C and a backward J with a line across the top. Aside from the side-mounted sling swivel, those having arctic birch stocks are practically identical to the Russian-made SKS.

Factory /26\: Here, Type 56 Chinese characters appear within the 6,xxx,xxx serial range. 1st and 2nd import batches. Note: Thus far, the first to have Type 56 markings in Chinese characters-serial numbers overlap in approximation between 1961 and 1962.

FACTORY /26\

SERIAL NUMBER RANGE	APPROXIMATE YEAR	IMPORT BATCHES
7,xxx,xxx	Serial range estimated at 1963	1st and 2nd
8,xxx,xxx	1964	1st and 2nd
9,xxx,xxx	1965	1st and 2nd
10,xxx,xxx	1966	1st and 2nd
11,xxx,xxx	1967	1st and 2nd
12,xxx,xxx	1968	1st and 2nd
13,xxx,xxx	1969	1st and 2nd
14,xxx,xxx	1970	1st and 2nd

to approximately 215,000, with no other identification present.

1957–1958 Type Three: Mid 1957 to late 1958. Between serial numbers 215,800 to 218,000, the triangle /26\ appears to the serial number's right. The production runs to the end of 1957 to approximately 1,820,000. From late 1958 to Fall 1959, the production ends near 3,800,000+ using the 1957 "millionths serial place holder."

1959-Late 1961 Letter Guns: An overlap of the above final number(s) is highly likely, but it is currently unknown when it exactly stops. From Spring 1959 until late 1961 or early 1962, it is considered the letter gun period. Total production surveys run from about 600,000 to 1,000,000 guns. This information is heavily veiled by the Chinese to this day and surrounds all obsolete ordnance in general.

From late 1961 to early 1962, the 6,000,000 serial number range began, and the "1957 Millionths Placement Formula" reappeared. Though workable, this formulated method is not written in stone. SKS collectors base it on statistical surveys and mathematically compiled figures, which equal one million guns per year. The Bureau of Alcohol, Tobacco, Firearms, and Explosives (BATFE) concurs with the formula regarding importing Chinese SKS carbines meeting the fifty-year Curio and Relic ruling that also includes the letter guns. A proscribed country since 1994, China's Factory 26-marked SKSs imported from neutral countries, and stored over the 50-year mark, has allowed importation. The below format estimates Chinese SKS serial numbers headed with a single or double millionth-placement prefix and joins the seven- or eight-digit number. In the case of Type One and Type Two, allowable import entry is without issue. Regarding Albanian imports, the prefix of 13 (1969) was officially the final year China had shipped the Type 56 accorded by the 1964 Sino-Albanian Agreement. The proof of meeting legal requirements, however, rests on the importer.

Listed are serial ranges, approximated years, and modifications of the T-56.

1961–62: 6,xxx,xxx serial range. Note: Type 56 markings appear this year.

1963: 7,xxx,xxx

1964: 8,xxx,xxx serial range. Note: This serial number range eliminates the

A left-hand closeup of the made for export M 21 version of the Type 56. This gun is also a Vietnam capture. Note that the underlined "No." marking is present ahead of the serial number.

long, Russian barrel collar/ lug in favor of the short lug. Also, the spike bayonet replaced the blade bayonet at this time. The lower forearm bayonet inlet was widened and lengthened to include enlarging the front stock ferrule.

1965: 9,xxx,xxx serial range. Note: The side-mounted, rear sling swivel reverts to the stock's bottom in this numerical serial range.

1966: 10,xxx,xxx serial range

1967: 11,xxx,xxx serial range. Note: Late into this range of numbers, an easier to produce, two-piece gas tube appears, and the lightening cuts on the bolt carrier and the bayonet lug are eliminated. The stamped triggerguard gradually replaces the milled one.

1968: 12,xxx,xxx serial range. Note: Though not marked Factory 26, between 1968 and 1970, both the experimental and supposedly cost-efficient stamped steel and cast steel receivers begin to appear. Made in limited numbers, they were not as economical as planned. Stamped steel guns also required a buttstock of different dimensions and weren't interchangeable with standard SKS wood. Also, they were prone to cracking adjacent to the receiver cross pin. Both experimental SKS carbines are of interest to collectors. The known hardness and brittle nature of these cast

The cast steel DB-marked versions of the Type 56 are relatively uncommon. This carbine seems chaotically marked as the Chinese city character prefix of Lushun is stamped in reverse, not to mention the serial numbers and DB were not carefully applied. The receiver's porosity quickly shows the nature of cast steel, for which the hardness or brittleness is challenging to determine. The 70 prefix is common to both the stamped steel and cast steel T-56 carbines. Note the side-mounted sling swivel — no parts on this rifle match. Sought by collectors, regular shooters should avoid these.

steel receivers are dubious at best. Some believed they were produced as late as 1980, which is peculiar.

1969: 13,xxx,xxx serial range.

1970: 14,xxx,xxx serial range. Note: This is the last year Factory 26 production was seen until its reappearance at serial range 23,xxx,xxx, around 1979. Interestingly, the ribbed-phenolic Bakelite handguard appears during this time.

You may find some Factory 26 guns with a 25 prefix (1981), but most 25

Factory 106 is among the earlier of the satellite triangle factories. This gun omits the Type 56 characters, which could be for a variety of reasons.

Any Type 56 SKS carbine having a diamond geometric symbol of plant or Factory 6614 is seldom encountered and is very scarce. These are of significant interest to the serious collector. The 23 prefix seems to indicate 1979, 23 years from 1957, with a mere quantity of four guns manufactured up to this point shown. The author believes this was a low-output assembly plant.

Classification of
Scarcity and Collector Desirability Listing of the Chinese Type 56

The two Chinese characters on the right frame are "Kong An" in Chinese, an abbreviation for the Public Security Bureau. The left receiver flat shows Triangle 416, with the 18 prefix possibly indicating 1975 as the production year. Keng's Firearms Specialties of Atlanta is the sole importer known to have brought limited quantities into the United States. In this condition, prices are easily double or more than standard Type 56 carbines in identical condition. Adrian Van Dyk Collection

A s of late, obscure factory markings do not influence price factors, aside from personal demand.

K Code Soviet pre-issue familiarization guns: With but a single example known to the author, this is by far the rarest SKS affiliated with the People's Republic of China.

Type One in all condition grades: Only twelve examples are known thus far. All reap premiums in any condition or modification.

Vietnam bringback Type 56- and M 21-marked variants, with Star One marking on left frame: Capture paper deter-

mines solid provenance. The Star One marked M 21 fetches higher prices. The M 21 variation having an M 21 No. or underlined No. were only brought back from Vietnam or Central America and never conventionally imported. The import M21 carbines have an N or NA prefix ahead of the serial number, with some having "296," another code indicating "Factory 26."

Stamped steel and cast steel guns: The Type 56 SKS variants were an experimental venture SKS production cost-cutting, as noted earlier. The stamped steel guns, however, are nearly double the price of the more common specimens. The cast steel

prefix guns had a different factory number. Chinese SKS production for the military stopped in 1984, at an estimated 25,000,000 to 28,000,000; however, collectors can stumble across a 32. What transpired at Factory 26 between 1971 and 1977 is still unknown. It's feasible that they concentrated on small arms of a different type, while other numbered factories as triangle /416\, /106\, /326\, rectangle [0136], [0147], etc., took up T-56 manufacturing during this interim period

— a plausible *modus operandi*. Those non-Factory 26 guns having prefixes of 15 through 22 and 25 through 32 appear to indicate an annual sequence from 1957. Their succeeding numbers are the actual production quantity on a per gun basis, i.e., 32 equals 1992.

I've shown a small sampling of the various markings other than Factory 26 as examples. Space does not allow listing them here in their entirety. There are a limited number of books on the subject that

display known factory markings. Another unique example of Type 56 SKS markings are those sans geometrical symbols. Such specimens include the M 21, a sanitized version of the Type 56 primarily intended for export without revealing national origin evidence. Laughably, it's not difficult to hide the obvious as no other country exported the SKS in quantities as large as China! The M 21 first appeared in the 1964 to 1968 period during the Vietnam War, with some marked with a "Star One"

A comparison of the later bolt carrier (right) and the earlier type with lightening cut (left) modified in the 11-million serial range, estimated as 1967. The right photo shows the solid carrier flat, dispensed with another machining step: the carrier's slotted countersunk portion (left).

models yield a slightly lower price than those mentioned above but will reap a 25 percent premium over the more common Factory 26 guns of the late 1960s.

Letter guns in original un-refinished condition: These are much scarcer than refinished guns. Recent Albanian-imported letter guns with all-matching part numbers are desirable in very good condition. The double-letter examples, such as the TO or NO, and numerical prefix versions such as the 2M, or 2I, are believed to indicate a second serialization run of particular letters and are very scarce examples that yield a premium.

Public Security Model: This Type 56 has long been a collector favorite for those with a bizarre fascination with secret police such as the KGB, Romanian Securitate, and other similar communist security organizations. Imported exclusively by Keng's Firearms Specialties in Atlanta, Georgia, all are marked with the abbreviated Public Security characters "Kong An" in Chinese on the right-center receiver. Earlier versions marked Factory 26 are a coup of the first order. The more common Factory /416\ of the late 1960s, 1970s, and 1980s versions with rectangle [0140], [0141], and [0144], are all desirable acquisitions.

Type Two five- and six-digit guns: Importers refinished almost all 1980s and 90s import guns. The all-matching Albanian imports with the original finish from the 2010s saw collectors scrambling.

DB- and DP-marked guns: There are 11 different Chinese city names with the first prefix of the city's Chinese character stamped on the left frame. The Chinese Pinyin Latin letters of DB and DP to the left of the character are among the Type 56 SKS's great enigmas. China produced them for domestic issuance and did not export them. It is apparent they left the Chinese mainland for the first time when the surplus boom began in the mid-1980s. Not considered rare, they are also not easily found. An uncommon find among these guns is those with cast steel frames, which yield a higher premium and may genuinely be a scarce find.

Triangle-numbered factories — Late Factory 26, oval, circle, rectangle, and diamond numbered guns: There are 92 known triangle markings at present. Aside from Factory 26, to say which of them built the Type 56 SKS from scratch is known only to the Chinese. For example, to multiply the estimated production total of 28,000,000 Type 56 carbines times the 92 known triangle facilities alone would

equal 2,576,000,000 guns! This figure is statistically impossible and completely defies logic. The point is, aside from Factory 26, we have no idea if these other triangles, and subsequent geometrically numeric locations, represent merely a parts production facility or an assembly plant for the Type 56. Another anomaly is that many of these triangle-numbered symbols end with a number 6. The Chinese used this last digit in the identification process of several locations. In any case, many of the obscure triangle-numbered plants have seen very few guns imported on their behalf. Again, the answers lie with China's defense ministry and may never be known. Ironically, various factories, including the DB/DP-marked guns, lack the "Type 56" characters, with some having "56" written in plain Arabic numerals. Speculation has it that guns marked with Type 56 characters were explicitly intended for the People's Liberation Army (PLA). In any case, there is much more to this story of which space will not permit.

For those wishing to delve deeper into the saga of China's SKS and other variants produced in Europe, I recommend my latest book, *The SKS and Its Variations,* as well as *The SKS Carbine 5th Edition* by Steve Kehaya and Joe Poyer.

symbol representing "Program, or Project One." China signed a bilateral agreement in 1957, by which North Vietnam became China's first communist client state to participate in a military support program. Within four years, the Star One guns were both the standard Type 56, the later M 21, and similarly stamped North Vietnamese-assembled SKS guns known as the "Type One." Collectors highly prize all, and even more so when accompanied by DD Form 603-1 capture papers.

By 1964, the other satellite factory numbers began appearing, such as triangle 306, 66, and several others. As mentioned earlier, these prefixed, non-Factory 26 guns having single or double digits arguably may be counted as the number of years dating from 1957. Only the Factory 26 guns represent both years and one million. Again, the lack of hard documentation means this is speculative. Some reliable former import sources assured me that Chinese SKS carbines

refurbished for the American market arrived on U.S. shores to the tune of 25,000 guns a month between 1989 and 1994. It was then that SKS collecting became a specialty, and the study of Chinese SKS manufacturing patterns was slowly undertaken and began making a semblance of sensibility with collectors drawing very workable conclusions. An example of such discoveries was sorting out the Type One, Type Two, Type Three, and letter gun series, all of which, at times,

The author firing at 20 yards with a now scarce, Navy Arms "Cowboys Companion," a short 16.5-inch barrel version of the Type 56 made without provisions for a bayonet for the U.S. market. About 960 were imported. The shorter-than-usual barrel accounts for the large muzzle flash of unburned powder. You must inspect and remove all Cosmoline before shooting any surplus Chinese SKS carbine, the bolt especially. The free-floating firing pin can be caked with the dried, gummy substance, leading to slamfires if the pin sticks in the forward position. Disassembly of the bolt to clean out pockets is best, or place the entire bolt into boiling water for twenty minutes, dry, and then thoroughly lubricate the bolt with oil. Finally, inspect to ensure smooth firing pin movement.

and Type Three variants of the Type 56. Still, thousands of the later versions of the 1963 to 1969 period were sold or bartered to Enver Hoxha's communist Albanian government over time.

In Albania, the 1990 end of communism saw hundreds of thousands of weapons of all categories stored in half a million concrete bunkers nationwide. Fifteen years after the 1997 Albanian civil uprising — 2012 to 2014, and again in 2018 and 2019 — it was a replay of the past. A moratorium of the ongoing destruction of thousands of Chinese SKS carbines halted their eventual demolition. It was more profitable to sell them to European export companies like Limex in Stral, Austria, who sold them to American importers. The result? After a 19-year hiatus, American collectors could again purchase surplus Chinese SKS carbines! Here, you'll find the scarcer, earlier guns in more significant numbers during the 2013 to 2014 and 2018 flow of surplus Chinese SKS carbines than earlier.

As mentioned, though China was a proscribed nation since 1994, a relaxing of BATFE rulings stipulated that import-eligible Chinese guns had to be retained in a neutral, disinterested country for more than 50 years. This ruling met C&R (Curio and Relic) status, and entry was allowed into the United States. This unexpected loophole provided a second chance for beginning shooters and collectors that missed out on the SKS boom years earlier. Seasoned collectors even welcomed this second surplus invasion of the Type 56, an unseen variant in the past. The Albanian im-

provided clues to a Russian connection by Soviet inspection markings on various parts and other details that disappeared over time. The big bonus for collectors and shooters who missed out on those $95 to $275 Chinese SKS carbines from the past two-plus decades had a second chance when, at varying intervals, the arrival of Chinese Type 56 SKS carbines imported from Albania occurred with an array of many unseen markings.

A once staunch ally of China in the early 1960s, the Sino-Albanian love affair lasted until 1978 when both countries had a falling out and parted ways. The very first Type 56 SKS carbines and some leftover Russian versions arrived in this small Balkan state in 1961 in limited quantities. Still, after Chou En Lai visited Albania in 1964, over 265,000 Chinese SKS carbines were exported to Albania until 1969. China also supplied tooling and machinery that led to the manufacture of a domestically produced version, the Type 56-1, with modifications different from any other SKS. Many of the Chinese Type 56 carbines supplied to Albania were older, well-used hand-me-down Type Two

ports in "as is" condition with original finish and heavy wear made little difference. In essence, none of these later Albanian imports had a facelift like those refinished in the past. The bot-

tom line: what you saw was what you got. Collectors have seen anything and everything — from fair condition with cracked stocks, mismatched numbers, higher-grade specimens having had minimal use, to all matching numbers. These are now long gone from distributors. Whether importers will bring in more is a good question, as 2019 was the last time importers brought in a batch.

From 1999 to 2000, a U.S. contractor employed me in the Albanian Kosovar region during the Balkan War scale down, and I am still in touch with several colleagues in Albania. Two had reliably informed me in 2020 that there are about 25,000 to 30,000 more serviceable T-56 SKS carbines remaining in storage bunkers near Erdesek and Kukres. All of those that arrived in the past nine years were thickly preserved in Cosmoline, requiring thorough cleaning. The below listing of Chinese SKS carbines provides a chronology of Factory 26 guns with serial number ranges and import periods.

The SKS makes for a great semi-auto rifle for hunting medium-size game, general shooting, and even self-defense for shooters. Once rarely available, the 7.62x39 cartridge has become a gun shop staple in the last 20 years, with most ammunition produced in Russia, Yugoslavia, the Czech Republic, and even in the United States. All of this commercial fodder is, of course, non-corrosive. However, you cannot say the same for the vast amounts of Chinese, Yugoslavian, and other surplus ammo that remain from the Cold War.

Many former communist nations continue to produce military ammunition in 7.62x39 caliber for their AKs and export. Commercial-wise, my preference is Tulammo's 122-grain full metal-cased ammo, made at the famous Ulyanosk ammunition factory in the Russian Federation. I have found that both it and Barnaul's steel-cased 123-grain loads provide shot grouping satisfactory with the SKS carbine's open sights. Experience finds barrel length is not a critical factor. The standard 20.5-inch and 16.5-inch barrels of the modified "Paratrooper Models" shoot anywhere from 2-1/2 to 3-inch groups on average, offhand at 50 yards. The sights on most SKS carbines are a standard adjustable leaf and hooded post

front sight; these are typical of military iron sights, intended for general center mass shot placement.

Militarily considered a stopgap measure or a "second player" to the selective-fire AK, the SKS has often been a standard military arm for troops of limited experience. Military planners viewed it as ideal, given its attached folding bayonet and fixed magazine that precludes loss of components during firefights. It remains in limited use within Third World militaries issued to second-line troops. From the Hungarian Revolution, the Vietnam War, and numerous conflicts right up to the civil war in Syria, China's Type 56 has outlasted all others of its type in countless wars of liberation. Though utilized in China's numerous capacities, it has become one of the most popular surplus military arms in the United States.

The only disappointment for collectors is that its entire story has yet to be told. However, rest assured, China never expected American collectors to analyze its Type 56 SKS carbine's historical details. As the pieces fall into place, this most puzzling of firearms stakes its clearer place in the annals of military rifle history. **GD**

Author's note: I wish to thank military arms authority Jude Steele, and SKS specialists Adrian Van Dyke and Howard "Howie" Bearse, for their photographic contributions and assistance.

Bibliography

The SKS and Its Variations, George Layman, Mowbray Publishing, 2021

The SKS Carbine CKS-45, Fifth Edition, Steve Kehaya, and Joe Poyer, North Cape Publications 2014

The author test-fired a standard 20.5-inch-barreled Type 56 SKS using non-corrosive, Tulammo with 122-grain FMJ projectiles on a full-size upper torso silhouette target (right) at 50 yards offhand. The SKS shot extraordinarily low, producing 2- to 3-inch groups. The half-size upper torso silhouette target (left) was shot offhand at 50 yards. The 123-grain full metal jacketed Russian Barnaul cartridges printed 2-inch groups and surprisingly a five-shot group in the 10 ring! Russian Wolf brand ammunition grouped nearly identical to the Tulammo on the larger target with shot placement hitting lower into the 6 and 7 rings with three flyer shots outside the measured center mass. Though the author preferred Tulammo with the shorter, 16.5-inch-barreled Paratrooper Model, the results show the Barnaul brand producing far more satisfactory shot placement with the full-length SKS. Barnaul is also more expensive than the Tulammo. All ammo tested was steel-cased and Berdan-primed.

Endnotes

1 The above information concerning the Type One, Type Two, and Type Three, and the K Code SKS, was obtained by my Russian colleague, Pavel Lukashenko, a former Soviet-era GRU (Main Intelligence Directorate) foreign service officer whom I befriended after the Cold War in 1995. As a retired employee of the Russian-Soviet government, he has permissive access to acquire historical data from varied historical archives that have restricted access and are off limits to foreigners. Contained here are brief excerpts from my book, *The SKS and Its Variations*, which is the first time any detailed information regarding the Chinese SKS from the Third Sino-Soviet Agreement has been publicly shown in the United States. Thus, at the now re-designated Kirov Archive in St. Petersburg, Russia (formerly Leningrad), Pavel acquired information from the 1954 agreement, much of which had been missing or displaced. There are other portions of the Agreement that are unavailable due to their sensitive sources, and remain classified information in the Russian Federation to the present.

2 Pavel Lukashenko, St. Petersburg, Russia 3rd Sino-Soviet Agreement, Leaf 9 Archive 2017

44 Years With .44 Revolvers

Some cartridges and guns are a lot like potato chips; you can never settle for just one.

> DAVE CAMPBELL

The forty-four: The term seems to coat your mouth with a syrupy charred-oak elixir with just enough burn in it to satisfy, much like 10-year-old, 100-proof bourbon. Perhaps that is why — despite what the actual bullets measure in diameter — forty-four, or .44, was chosen for several caliber names. If you haven't figured it out yet, American cartridge designations are often more about marketing than anything truly factual regarding the cartridges' measurements or capabilities.

.44 HISTORY

One of the first .44-caliber centerfire cartridges, the .44 Smith & Wesson American, featured a 205-grain round-nose lead bullet that measured .434 inch in diameter. Another early .44 was the .44-40 Winchester Central Fire — now called the .44-40 Winchester Center Fire or WCF, which launched a 212-grain, flat-nose lead bullet measuring .427 inch. Still later, Smith & Wesson made revolvers chambered in .44 S&W Russian with a 246-grain, .429-inch bullet. Today, thankfully, if you are a handloader, Smith & Wesson settled the issue for modern .44s — the .44 Smith & Wesson Special and .44 Remington Magnum — with bullets measuring approximately .429 inch. I say "approximately" because there have been slight tolerance variations over the years, with some throats running a tight .427 inch, others a rather loose .430 to .431 inch. Nonetheless, forty-four sounds a whole lot better than keeping track of

This Colt Single Action Army is one of a consecutively numbered pair the author uses in cowboy action shooting. It is chambered in the traditional .44-40 WCF and is fed exclusively with blackpowder ammunition.

all these actual fractional numbers. And there is no denying the allure of a ".44."

I fell hard for .44-caliber revolvers some 44 years ago as I write this. In 1976, I was a gun-struck, wannabe *pistolero* with three handguns, not much money, only a humongous desire to have the siren .44 revolver. Hollywood complicated the matter more because, in late

1971, the movie *Dirty Harry* starring Clint Eastwood and co-starring a Smith & Wesson Model 29 in .44 Magnum, burst onto the silver screen. Regrettably, as now, Hollywood had a significant impact on modern culture, especially among the great unwashed. The movie featured Eastwood as a San Francisco police inspector who dispatches .44-caliber justice with flair. Special effects engineers gave the revolver and cartridge such melodramatic characteristics that many ignorant theatergoers took it as Gospel. Handgun blast blew the bad guys back at least three feet from where they were standing. Sound engineers substituted the revolver's report with that of a major-caliber rifle in an echo chamber. But by golly, every wannabe had to have one of these revolvers.

However, I did some research — reading the popular gun magazines of the day — and found there was a little brother to the mighty .44 Magnum, one that had nearly the same punch and much less punishment to the shooter, plus it was a bit lighter. Writers such as Skeeter

Skelton, George Nonte, and Jeff Cooper had plenty of good things to say about the .44 Special cartridge. It was accurate and hit like a sledgehammer. The trouble was, Smith & Wesson discontinued making .44 Special revolvers in 1966 and, along with Colt, had no plans to revive it. Prices of .44 Special sixguns were more than the scalper prices of Model 29s. I looked for more than a year for a .44 Special Smith & Wesson. I eventually found one, and the price tag on it was $750, which would be like $3,411 in today's money.

During that period, a close friend needed some cash. He had a brand new 6 1/2-inch-barreled Model 29 with which he was willing to part. I gave him $350 and forgave a prior loan, and I had my first .44.

Like nearly everyone else, my first few rounds shot out of it impressed me greatly — and it was not a pleasant impression. A couple of years before, I had been sending about 500 rounds a week downrange from my Smith & Wesson Model 27 in .357 Magnum (more-or-less evenly split between .38 Special wadcutters and magnum loads) and several hundred rounds of .45 ACP from a 1911 pistol. I was progressing along OK with these handguns — not yet proficient, but getting there — however, the .44 Magnum was a whole different kettle of fish. So, I put the .44 Magnum in the closet as I continued to develop my skills with the other handguns. But I kept my eyes peeled for a .44 Special.

Toward the end of 1976, I found a brand new, unfinished Smith & Wesson 1950 Target barrel marked ".44 Special Cartridge." Further dredging produced a Model 28 Highway Patrolman, .357

Lew Horton Distributors did a limited run of Smith & Wesson Model 24 revolvers with 3-inch barrels. The author snapped up one of the first, and carries it often.

Smith & Wesson Model 24s in .44 Special with 4-inch barrels are relatively rare and sought by collectors. This one is a regular companion of the author on backcountry trips.

The author built this, his first .44 Special, from a Model 28 Highway Patrolman and a new 1950 T barrel. The 5-inch barrel is just about a perfect compromise of portability and shootability.

The author's .44 is marked "Colt Single Action Army .44 Special."

After replacing the original black hard rubber grips with a one-piece, pre-ban ivory, the author's first Colt Single Action Army is retired from general field duty. However, it still goes along with him on outings when the risk of damaging the stock is minimal.

Magnum as a donor gun. I found a gunsmith who would marry the two for me, although he did not finish it. It seemed to take forever, but after several months I had my .44 Special.

As part of the conversion, I had the gunsmith shorten the barrel from 6 1/2 to 5 inches and refit the ramp and front sight. Fortunately, the barrel's roll marks centered after the bobbing, which looked like a factory gun. He removed about half of the forcing cone during the transformation, requiring him to time the cylinder to the barrel carefully. The revolver shot very well: groups of less than 2 inches at 25 yards were easy with my then-young eyes and steely nerves. But there was a problem: it was ugly as hell. More scrounging and dredging produced a gunsmith who specialized in polishing and bluing. He did a great job on it. Regrettably, after some 44-plus years, I no longer recall the names of these gentlemen.

So, I had incorporated the .44 Special

Frames with this roll mark are relatively rare. The turning ring on the cylinder and holster wear indicate the author carried this revolver regularly.

Lipsey's has made some limited edition runs of Ruger's New Model Blackhawk revolvers chambered in .44 Special. Among collectors, it is known colloquially as the Flat Top model. This sturdy single action is not only pleasing to the eye but accurate, too.

into my regular rotation of shooting activities. I moved to Wyoming from southern California in 1979 and soon found a position as a part-time police officer in Afton. At that innocent time and remote location, an officer could carry about anything he or she wanted, provided that it was .38 Special or better, and they could qualify with it. My .44 Special immediately accompanied me in a Don Hume Jordan Trooper holster and River Belt. Handloads held a Lyman 429421 semi-wadcutter weighing 245 grains in front of 7.5 grains of Hercules Unique. (The current Alliant iteration of Unique has a slightly different burn rate and energy-per-grain content, making this load obsolete.)

I also found some employment at a local gun shop. One of the perks of that was when sellers brought in unique guns to sell. I often got the first crack at owning them, including a new Colt Single Action Army. You guessed it — .44 Special. Its price was well above my pay grade, but I negotiated a trade for a Ruger No. 1 in .30-'06. I had my first SAA, and it was in the best chambering. Not long after that, Lew Horton Distributors had a limited run of Model 24 Smith & Wesson revolvers with the K-frame round butt and a 3-inch barrel. I snapped up one as soon as it hit the store.

The bobbed-nose Smith alternated with my 1911 as an everyday carry gun — something I still do to this day. My .44 Specials shoot the same bullet and powder but a different charge. Since the loading manuals do not list that charge, I won't

divulge it here. In my revolvers, it is safe, but your mileage may vary.

Response to the limited run of Model 24s was robust enough to spur Smith & Wesson and a few other makers such as Freedom Arms, Taurus, and Ruger to give the cartridge another whirl. Smith brought out another limited run of Model 24s, a mere pittance with 4-inch barrels and many more with 6 1/2-inch barrels. A few years later, I acquired a 4-incher. In 1996 Smith released a Model 696, L-frame stainless steel, five-shot .44 Special with a round K-frame-size butt cloaked in Uncle Mike's rubber Combat Grips and a 3-inch barrel. Since I already had a 3-inch .44 Special, I didn't get one when I should have. The run of Model 696s lasted but five years. Now it's tough to find one. I recently perused GunBroker. com and found but a single Model 696, no dash (the most desirable because it is pre-lawyer designed) with an opening bid of $1,699.

In 2001, Smith & Wesson parleyed its then-cutting-edge technology in light-weight metals to produce the Model 396, another L-frame five shooter but made from its proprietary Scandium alloy. At 18 ounces with a 2 1/2-inch stainless steel barrel, the recoil was certainly stiff but not unmanageable for an experienced shooter. This run lasted just

three years. Now, on the "vintage" market, a .44 Special Model 396 will eat four figures out of your wallet. I missed out on this as well. Smith also made a Model 296 with a shrouded hammer. Some say it's the ugliest .44 Special ever made.

Ruger, via Lipsey's, made some limited edition Flat Top Blackhawk revolvers in .44 Special. They have been available in blue, stainless, 4 5/8- and 5 1/2-inch barrels, standard and Bisley configurations. I have one each of the classic blued revolvers. The 5 1/2-inch model is the more accurate, but the 4 5/8-inch one is an excellent knock-around revolver for the boondocks.

Happily, I have never had to shoot someone, but a couple of fellas have seen the muzzle of one of my .44 Specials. Fortunately for both of us, they listened to my commands. My .44s have been primarily field guns and I've taken several wild pigs with them. One afternoon at a ranch on the Sierra Nevadas' west slope, a friend and I were on a walkabout for *chislers*, a.k.a. ground squirrels, when a pair of 80-pound sows came boiling out of a cut 40 yards ahead. I drew the Colt SAA, swinging the muzzle through one sow's body and ahead of her nose. When the trigger broke, she collapsed and slid several feet, stone dead. Another time I was hunting on a Texas ranch when some white-tail

In 2006, Ruger made a 50th Anniversary Flat Top chambered in .44 Magnum. This one dotes on 20.0 grains of Alliant 2400 pushing a Lyman 429421, 245-grain semi-wadcutter at 1,196 fps.

This latest addition to the author's .44 collection is a Performance Center Model 629. It has no problem dumping its shots into 2 inches at 50 yards.

The author's first .44 is now 44 years old. Although intimidating to him as a young and inexperienced shooter, he finally got the hang of it, taking several deer and wild pigs.

does came in. One shot was all I needed.

Now lest you think I jettisoned the Magnum for the little brother, think again. That first Model 29 has accounted for a couple of deer, perhaps a half dozen wild pigs, and a pile of small game, including a pair of blue grouse that I took the heads off from at 10 yards one time. The magnum herd has grown a little as well. Currently, in addition to that first Model 29, a Ruger 50th Anniversary Flat Top and a Smith & Wesson Performance Center Model 629 are in my safe as well. Neither has yet drawn blood, but I am working on that.

.44 AMMUNITION

While the guns attract the most attention, feeding them is equally important. We have come far in bullet and propellant technology, no longer tying ourselves to blackpowder — which is pretty fun itself — and soft lead balls. Today's smokeless powders and jacketed bullets seem to define the modern-day *pistolero*. Yes, I have used a few factory jacketed bullets on game. Like any other bullet, when they go where they're supposed to, critters tip over, reduced to possession. If the bullets don't go where intended, problems invariably occur.

After 44 years of fooling with .44s, jacketed bullets are at their best in the .44 Magnum, in my not-so-humble opinion. You need velocity to expand — or more appropriately, rivet — a bullet to impart its energy into a live target. The .44 Special does not have that level of velocity to expand a bullet reliably unless you load it to near-magnum speeds and use light bullets, which often fail to penetrate. Lots of shooters like to push their guns to the velocity limit. Since I'm blessed to own both .44 Special and .44 Magnum revolvers, I can shoot the more pleasant loads in .44 Special guns and reserve the big stuff for my magnums.

About a dozen years ago, the cowboy action shooting bug bit me. And to that end, I splurged and ordered a

The First Colt Single Action Army in .44-40 WCF

This is the first Colt Single Action Army to leave the Colt factory on April 26, 1877. Along with two others, they were sent to Turkey for trials by way of London.

A Colt Single Action Army revolver, serial number 36xxx, was shipped to the Colt Patent Fire-Arms Mfg. Co., London Agency, London, England on April 26, 1877. Colt sent three there that day, but this revolver had the lowest serial number. It also happened to be the first SAA chambered in .44-40 WCF to leave the Colt factory.

Ultimately, however, its destination was not to be Britain. Colt had sent it and the two other .44-40s as trial revolvers for the Turkish army. Mistakenly, the word was the Turkish army was equipped with Winchester Model 1873 rifles in the same chambering. It turned out that there was some miscommunication because the Winchester rifles the Turks had were Model 1866s chambered in .44 Henry Rim Fire. Nonetheless, the London Agency quickly shipped the revolvers to Turkey. We know that it was a quick turn-around in London, as there are no British proof marks on these revolvers.

When the revolvers arrived in Turkey, a skilled armorer set about converting the revolvers to the rimfire cartridge by modifying the recoil plate and firing pin, the cylinder was left unaltered. After fir-

pair of consecutively serial-numbered Colt SAAs from the Colt Custom Shop. With the desirable 4 3/4-inch barrels and 3 1/2-pound triggers, I specified them chambered in a traditional cowboy cartridge, the .44-40 WCF. I completed the ensemble with a Uberti copy of the

1873 Winchester in the same chambering. These are fun guns. I shoot them with blackpowder handloads exclusively, and they are accurate and a kick in the pants to shoot. Bullets are from a Lyman 427666 mold and drop out at 212 grains using my alloy. I seat them over 33 grains

of FFFg Goex blackpowder. Nope, it's not a full load, but it's pleasant to shoot and a snap to clean up after shooting. There's no leading, and a little soap and hot water followed by a healthy squirt of brake cleaner to help dry everything up, and then finished with some Ballistol to

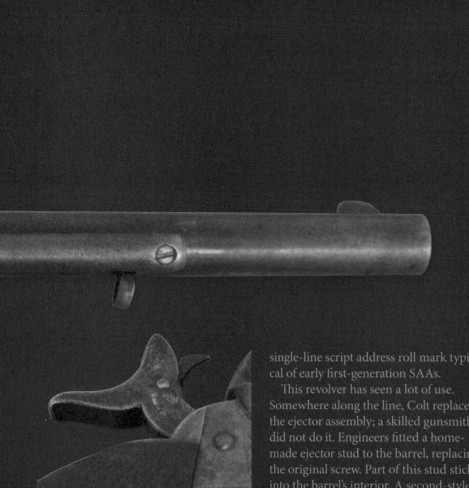

Because of a misunderstanding, the three Colts had to be modified by a gunsmith to fire .44 Henry Rimfire cartridges. A new firing pin had to be constructed from scratch and installed after modifying the recoil shield to accommodate the new pin.

A pair of .44-40 Single Actions belonging to the author are carried in this custom shuck by Blue Mountain Saddlery. Good guns rate good leather.

ing probably thousands of .44 RF ammo — which is shorter than the .44-40 cartridge — a distinct ring about halfway down the cylinder became visible.

The 7 1/2-inch barrel has six wide lands and grooves. It is not the standard gain twist seen in many of the pre-Frontier barrels from the army contract of 1873. Colt marked the barrel with the single-line script address roll mark typical of early first-generation SAAs.

This revolver has seen a lot of use. Somewhere along the line, Colt replaced the ejector assembly; a skilled gunsmith did not do it. Engineers fitted a home-made ejector stud to the barrel, replacing the original screw. Part of this stud sticks into the barrel's interior. A second-style ejector tube replaced the original. Another mutilation occurred when someone stamped "U.S." on the left side of the frame to portray the revolver as a U.S. marshal pistol disingenuously.

Overall, this revolver has a brown patina, but you can see traces of the barrel's original bluing. The grips are one-piece walnut, and if you examine it closely with a magnifying glass, you can see some of the original varnish.

How this revolver returned to the United States remains a mystery, but it eventually became part of a New England man's collection. It was sold at auction about 25 years ago to another collector who lives near me in Wyoming. A few years ago, he asked me if I wanted to see the first .44-40 SAA shipped from the Colt factory. You can figure my reply. He showed me a factory letter and provenance proving the history of this scarce Colt.

Amazingly, he let me examine this remarkable piece of history, including cocking it to photograph the modified firing pin. The safety and half-cock notches are gone, and as I approached full cock, I noticed the effort straining the mainspring as it stacked. I was scared to death that it may have crystallized to the point of shattering under strain, but my concerns were unfounded.

Recently, he put this piece of history up for auction, and, of course, it went well beyond my pay grade. It's probably best. Knowing me, I'd have tried to figure a way to shoot it.

prevent rusting, keeps them at the ready.

I chose the .44-40 WCF because it is a traditional cowboy cartridge. Most cowboys could not afford one cartridge for their revolver and a different one for their rifle, so .44-40 was what usually got the nod. The cartridge, while technically obsolete, isn't something to be sneezed at. At full-load capacity (38 grains of Goex FFFg), I get 970 fps from my Colts. A friend uses 8.3 grains of SR 7625 smokeless powder to achieve similar results.

Today, many shooters tout the 9mm cartridge; others wax about .40 calibers and 10mm. Some still like revolvers in the ubiquitous .357 Magnum — of which I am also a fan. There's no doubt that any of them will do in a given situation. However, after nearly a half-century experience, when I carry a revolver, it's most likely a .44. **GD**

THE 6.8 Western

Good Things Come in Small Packages

PHIL MASSARO

The 6.8 Western is a collaboration between Winchester and Browning. The cartridge gives you near .300 Win. Mag. performance in a short-action .277 (6.8mm) designed for heavy 150- to 175-grain bullets.

C olorado is supposed to be beautiful in the fall, or so I've heard. I've seen photos of the quakies, with their leaves all golden in the sunshine and slightly blurred from the breeze moving them, but it wasn't exactly like that when I arrived. The last week of October had turned nasty, with a front moving in and delivering a half-foot of snow and causing temperatures to drop well below zero. It was par for the course when it comes to my hunting luck. Inclement weather aside, the group that gathered at Ivory Tip Outfitters was both optimistic and eager to hunt, as we all had tags for elk and mule deer. And, perhaps most importantly, we had the opportunity to test the new Winchester 6.8 Western cartridge.

I stood on a ridgeback, watching two elk cows about 200 yards off and a decent mule deer buck thrice that distance, with my feet covered in snow and just enjoying the majesty of those frosted hills. The rifle over my shoulder was the Winchester XPR, an underrated bolt-action rifle topped with a Leupold VX-6HD 3-18x44mm riflescope, replete with a CDS dial calibrated for the 6.8 Western's trajectory. The shots in northwestern Colorado can range anywhere from "how-was-that-buck-right-in-front-of-us?" to "you-want-me-to-shoot-that-far?" And, as the terrain runs the gamut from wide-open fields with little or no cover, to cedar breaks and thick coulees, all the way to the brushy hilltops choked with live oak, carrying a do-all cartridge makes all sorts of sense. The 6.8 Western is a do-all cartridge.

Looking closer at the new cartridge, 6.8mm translates to our .277-inch bore diameter (much like the 6.5mms, it refers to the land diameter, not the groove or bullet diameter), and to my mind, that bore belongs to Winchester. The .270 Winchester has been with us since 1925 and has become an irrefutable classic. Winchester upped the ante when it introduced the .270 Winchester Short Magnum in 2002. Giving a velocity increase of almost 250 fps over the .270 Winchester, the .270 WSM is undoubtedly a speed demon but still uses the same bullet weight range as the .270 Winchester.

Roy Weatherby saw the benefits of a speedier .270 cartridge much earlier, and his double-radiused .270 Weatherby Magnum was among his earliest designs, which he introduced to the shooting world in 1945. Despite the impressive speed generated for that era, it never came close to the popularity of the .270 Winchester. And while the 6.8 SPC made a bit of a splash in the MSR community, it wasn't a hugely successful hunting cartridge. The 27 Nosler is a definite game-changer — pushing a 165-grain Nosler AccuBond at almost 3,160 fps — but its velocity will show its effects on the throat before long. That Nosler case is based on the .404 Jeffery, blown out in the body, shortened to 2.59 inches to fit in a standard long-action receiver, and necked to hold .277-inch diameter bullets. The 27 Nosler uses a 1:8.5 twist rate to stabilize the 165-grain bullets, as they are longer and heavier than the standard 1:10 twist rate used in the .270 Winchester and .270 Winchester Short Magnum.

The 6.8 Western is the result of a Winchester-Browning effort to design a short-action cartridge that could handle the high ballistic coefficient bullets that have become so popular recently, deliver-

Above: The author's Browning X-Bolt rifle prefers the Winchester 165-grain Nosler ABLR load, printing groups well under MOA.

Lower Left: The Expedition Long Range load from Winchester uses the 165-grain Nosler AccuBond Long Range bullet at a muzzle velocity of 2,970 fps.

Below: Browning's Long Range Pro Hunter load for the 6.8 Western uses a 175-grain Sierra Tipped GameKing bullet.

Left: With two Winchester offerings, the 6.8 Western can easily take most big game animals.

Above: Massaro with a Colorado mule deer, neatly dispatched with the 6.8 Western.

ing a good trajectory without excess barrel wear or recoil. The twist rate plays an essential role in bullet stabilization; the 1:10 twist of the .270 Winchester and .270 WSM preclude the use of bullets much heavier than 150 grains. Years ago, as a young hunter, I couldn't understand

how the smaller 6.5mm (.264-inch diameter) cartridges could use the 156- and 160-grain bullets and the slightly larger 7mm (.284-inch diameter) could handle projectiles weighing up to 175 grains. Yet, the .270 and its ilk could only take ones weighing 150 grains. Short answer: the twist rate.

There are more than a few instances of this among popular cartridges. I believe it is, in part, because the designers couldn't have envisioned the excellent (and utterly reliable) optics we have today. Considering that Winchester released the .270 Win. in 1925 in the Model 54 (which it designed for use with iron sights), a bullet that showed its benefits past 500 yards probably wasn't a high priority.

You'll see the same problem in the .22-250 Remington, with its 1:12 twist rate preventing the use of bullets heavier than 55 or 60 grains, and the .308 Winchester's 1:12 twist rate is the reason it can't use the 220-grain bullets. The times have changed, and our optics have never been better. Modern rangefinders can quickly and accurately determine distances to the target, and our ballistic calculators can predict both trajectory and wind deflection in an instant. The extreme long-range target shooting community wants cartridges and rifles capable of handling the bullets with the highest B.C. values possible. If you hunt in an area where shots are on the longer side yet still in the realm of sanity, a high B.C. bullet is most

definitely an advantage.

So, let's look at what makes the 6.8 Western more than just another pretty face. The engineers started with the .270 WSM case, keeping the .535-inch rim diameter and the 35-degree shoulder. Being forced to work within the confines of the short-action rifle magazine and wanting to use heavy bullets, the engineers shortened the case, reducing the datum line (the distance from the base of the cartridge to the shoulder, where headspacing begins) to 1.5835 inches, as opposed to the 1.664-inch datum line

of the .270 WSM. They reduced the cartridge length to 2.02 inches yet retained the neck length of the .270 WSM (.276 inch) to maintain proper neck tension. Browning and Winchester chose some very effective bullets for the 6.8 Western: Winchester factory ammo features the 165-grain Nosler AccuBond Long Range and the 170-grain Ballistic Silvertip bullet in its Expedition Big Game Long Range line. The Browning Long Range ProHunter load uses the 175-grain Sierra Tipped GameKing made for Browning and features a gold polymer tip. Brown-

ing needed to stabilize those long bullets, so it used a 1:7.5 twist rate; Winchester rifles use a 1:8 twist.

Though there is no 'magnum' in its name, the velocities generated by the 6.8 Western are at magnum levels. The 165-grain AccuBond load has a stated muzzle velocity of 2,970 fps, which equates to an attractive trajectory with good wind deflection values and retained energy. It was this load that we took hunting in Colorado, and which made an immediate impression on my colleagues and me. With a G1 Ballistic Coefficient of .620 and a Sectional Density value of .307, the AccuBond Long Range features a polymer tip, a jacket chemically bonded to the lead core, and a boattail to maximize downrange performance. If you haven't used the Nosler AccuBond — either in the standard variety or the Long Range version — you should; it is wonderfully accurate and utterly reliable. The bonded core slows expansion and holds

The Winchester XPR rifle shot the 165-grain Winchester load very well, printing three-shot groups just over ½-MOA.

Winchester's 170-grain Ballistic SilverTip is a perfect choice for any deer at any sane hunting range.

The author used a Leupold VX-6HD 3-18x44 with a range-compensated elevation turret, making longer shots much more manageable.

things together should you strike bone, and the bullet's shape makes it effective at any sane hunting distance. Even in lighter bullet weights — such as the 140-grain AccuBond in my petite Tikka T3X Lite in 7mm-08 Remington — it expands significantly and penetrates deeply. Use the heavier bullet weights with the higher sectional density, and you can reach the vitals from nearly any angle. Professional Hunters who pursue dangerous game often recommend a bullet with an S.D. value of 0.300 to ensure penetration, and the 165-grain .277-inch diameter AccuBond Long Range exceeds that value. I'm not saying that this is a bullet for buffalo or brown bears, but there is plenty of bullet for the deep penetration required on elk, moose, and larger African plains game species.

Leupold's Shawn Skipper and I were high-stepping after our guide, Eric T. Fleming, who was

The 6.8 Western (on the left) has a shorter datum line and case length than the .270 WSM (on the right).

The Browning Long Range ProHunter comfortably nestled in the X-Bolt's polymer magazine.

in high gear pursuing a mule deer herd shortly before sundown. Two days of climbing, descending, floundering, and slogging in those hills, through the mixture of melting snow and fresh mud had begun to take its toll on us, but one of the bucks at the rear of the herd renewed our resolve. As the does worked their way down the grass-covered slope, the bucks followed suit, and we

Right: The author's Browning X-Bolt rifle shot the 165-grain Nosler ABLR very well, especially when handloaded over a suitable charge of IMR 8133 in Winchester component cases.

hustled to get into a position where the lead does would draw the bucks into an area where we could get a shot. Fleming spread the shooting sticks, I got the Leupold's crosshair steady, and when the larger of the bucks came clear and stood broadside at just over 200 yards, the Winchester's trigger broke. The 4x4 mulie fell out of the scope and never even twitched;

the AccuBond took him just behind the shoulder's point, and he went down as if poleaxed. There was no chance to recover the bullet, as it passed clean through the deer.

Two days later, on the last morning of the hunt, I'd have another opportunity to test the terminal ballistics of the 6.8 Western and that 165-grain load when a spike elk made the fatal mistake of offering a shot at just over 100 yards. The 6.8 Western put it down quickly and humanely with a single shot, and shortly after returning home, I learned why people rave about elk venison.

The story repeated itself among all my colleagues, with shots ranging from 75 to 475 yards. We only recovered one bullet among six hunters, but sadly I didn't have the opportunity to weigh it. Considering that elk are tough animals and that the .270s have been considered marginal for hunting them in the past, the 6.8 Western proved that it is adequate for elk, even the biggest-bodied bulls. Whether the distances were short and impact velocities high or the distance long and the bullet slowed, penetration was excellent, expansion adequate.

Upon my return from the hunt, I asked the folks at Winchester/Browning to send a test rifle to have some range time with the new cartridge, and they shipped a Browning X-Bolt, topped with the same Leupold VX-6HD 3-18x44 we'd used on the Colorado hunt. With a 24-inch barrel tipped with a muzzle brake, the rifle had an adjustable comb and a sweet trigger, which made work at the bench a pleasure.

I had an ample supply of the Winchester 165- and Browning 175-grain loads, so I grabbed the Oehler 35P chronograph and headed to the backyard

Above Left: Redding offers excellent full-length resizing die and seating die for the 6.8 Western in its Custom series of reloading dies.

Left: With its bonded core and sleek profile, the .277-inch-diameter 165-grain Nosler AccuBond bullet will retain its velocity downrange and its weight after impact.

range. With the rifle rested on sandbags, I got to see exactly how the 6.8 Western performed on paper, and I wasn't disappointed in the least. Based on the cartridge's velocity, I felt three-shot groups were adequate to assess accuracy so that barrel heat wouldn't skew results. The Browning X-Bolt printed three 165-grain AccuBonds in an average group of just under ½-inch at 100 yards and three of the Browning bullets just over ¾-inch. Quite like the Winchester XPR I'd used in Colorado, recoil was more than manageable (especially with the muzzle brake), and the report was minimal compared to the velocities generated. In all honesty, I'd sooner hand a new shooter a rifle chambered in 6.8 Western than the majority of rifles I've owned or shot chambered in .270 Winchester.

Nosler AccuBond Long Range load will give a trajectory on par with both the 6.5 PRC with a 143-grain ELD-X and the .300 Winchester Magnum with a 180-grain Swift Scirocco II. With all three zeroed at 200 yards, the 6.8 Western and 6.5 PRC are within .3 inch out to 500 yards, with velocities so close it's not funny, though the 6.8 Western has over 250 ft-lbs more energy at 500 yards. And though it is very difficult to quantify with energy figures alone, it is not difficult to envision the penetration advantage of an additional 22 grains of bullet, as the 165-grain .277 has an S.D. of .307 vs. the 6.5mm 143-grain's .293 figure. Looking

"What we then have is a cartridge housed in a lighter, short-action receiver (the 6.5 PRC is too long to be properly housed in a short-action rifle), which gives a minimal amount of recoil while very nearly mirroring the performance of the venerated .300 Winchester Magnum in every manner, save frontal diameter."

6.8 WESTERN AMMO

As far as current factory ammunition goes, I tested the 165-grain bonded core at 2,970 fps and a 175-grain cup-and-core bullet (Sierra bullets have a stellar reputation) at a muzzle velocity of 2,830 fps. Let's look at how these two bullets fare downrange and how they compare to other popular cartridges.

The 6.8 Western with the 165-grain

to the highly popular .300 Winchester Magnum and the 180-grain Swift Scirocco II, as loaded by Federal to a muzzle velocity of 2,960 fps, you'll see the trajectory nearly identical to the 6.8 Western. At the 500-yard mark, the .300 Winnie hits only 2.5 inches lower than the 6.8 Western, though the larger cartridge has a bit less energy at that distance. If you are a holdover-type shooter, think of the trajectory like this: with a 200-yard zero, you'll need 6 inches of holdover at 300

Loading the 6.8 Western with 150-grain Sierra GameKing spitzer boattail bullets on the Redding T7 turret press.

TABLE 1. 6.8 WESTERN - BROWNING X-BOLT RIFLE - WINCHESTER BRASS CASES

BULLET	POWDER	CHARGE WEIGHT (GRAINS)	PRIMER	C.O.L. (INCHES)	AVERAGE VELOCITY (FPS)	GROUP SIZE (THREE-SHOT GROUP, INCHES)
130-grain Hornady GMX	IMR 4451	57.0	Win WLRM	2.870	3,128	0.95
130-grain Hornady GMX	H414	55.2	Win WLRM	2.870	3,096	0.80
130-grain Hornady GMX	IMR 7977	64.3	Fed GM215M	2.870	3,178	0.74
136-grain Federal Terminal Ascent	IMR 4451	57.5	Fed GM215M	2.840	3,120	0.98
136-grain Federal Terminal Ascent	IMR 7977	63.7	Fed GM215M	2.840	3,143	0.55
136-grain Federal Terminal Ascent	H4831 SC	61.0	Win WLRM	2.840	3,140	0.78
150-grain Sierra Game King SBT	IMR 4451	54.2	Fed GM215M	2.809	2,928	1.05
150-grain Sierra Game King SBT	IMR 4955	57.0	Fed GM215M	2.809	2,940	0.88
150-grain Sierra Game King SBT	IMR 7977	62.0	Fed GM215M	2.809	2,968	0.76
165-grain Nosler AccuBond Long Range	H4831SC	55.4	Win WLRM	2.900	2,805	0.68
165-grain Nosler AccuBond Long Range	IMR 7977	59.5	Fed GM215M	2.900	2,785	0.90
165-grain Nosler AccuBond Long Range	IMR 8133	62.2	Fed GM215M	2.900	2,865	0.82

Left: Federal's 136-grain Terminal Ascent bullet printed very well when seated over a Federal GM215M primer and a suitable charge of IMR 7977; this would make an excellent load for lighter species of big game.

Right: The Sierra 150-grain boattail spitzer has a shorter ogive than the other bullets the author tested and needed to be seated slightly deeper to avoid contacting the rifling. It shot well when mated with IMR 4955.

case of switching to the lighter-recoiling 6.8 Western. You get more bang for the buck (pun intended), though ammunition availability is a factor, especially in our current environment.

But, while the heavy bullets are great for bigger game species and for shooting at longer ranges, will the 6.8 Western also cover the same ground as the .270 Winchester and .270 WSM? Let's take a look at handloading for the 6.8 Western, with both the heavy bullets and with the standard 130- through 150-grain bullets so popular and readily available.

RELOADING THE 6.8 WESTERN

Grabbing a set of Redding 6.8 Western reloading dies and some Winchester component brass, I set out to develop a few handloads that would maximize the new cartridge's capabilities. With load data provided by Hodgdon — covering the Hodgdon, IMR, and Winchester trio of powder brands under its roof — and a versatile selection of .277-caliber bullets that would cover almost all North American game species, I cooked up a variety of test loads. For projectiles, I grabbed a quartet I felt would cover the gamut of species you'd possibly take with the 6.8 Western. The 165-grain Nosler AccuBond Long Range would be the heavyweight choice, but the 150-grain Sierra GameKing spitzer boattail, 136-grain Federal Terminal Ascent, and 130-grain Hornady GMX would complete the range of bullet weights.

To spark the 6.8, I used Winchester's WLRM and Federal's GM215M Gold Medal Match large rifle magnum primers in Winchester cases. Several powders would have been suitable for the 6.8 Western, but certain ones stood out as the best choices for my particular rifle. Hodgdon's H414 and H4831SC were excellent choices, and the IMR Enduron powders, including IMR 4451, IMR 4955, IMR 7977, and the slow-burning IMR 8133, gave terrific results. The 6.8 Western likes powders on the medium to

yards, 18 inches at 400 yards, and 36 inches at 500 yards.

Comparing the three cartridges' energy at 500 yards, you see the 6.8 Western delivering 1,863 ft-lbs, the .300 Winchester Magnum 1,796 ft-lbs, and the 6.5 PRC 1,604 ft-lbs. The numbers for the 175-grain load drop off a bit, with the heavier bullet hitting 4.5 inches lower than the 165-grain at 500 yards, and at that distance, the heavier bullet retains about 100 ft-lbs less than the lighter load. Comparing the three cartridges' felt recoil, I will confidently say that the 6.8 Western has the least felt recoil by a large margin in my experiences with them in different rifles.

I tested the two factory loads' velocities on my chronograph and found them consistent, though slightly lower than advertised. The Browning X-Bolt drove the 165-grain load to an average muzzle velocity of 2,918 fps, 52 fps slower than indicated, and the 175-grain load left

the muzzle at an average speed of 2,770 fps, 60 fps slower than advertised. I've seen worse deviations, so I wasn't overly concerned; the extreme velocity spread was inside of 20 fps, and that consistency is indicative of the accuracy I observed.

What we then have is a cartridge housed in a lighter, short-action receiver (the 6.5 PRC is too long to fit in a short-action rifle), which gives a minimal amount of recoil while very nearly mirroring the performance of the venerated .300 Winchester Magnum in every manner, save frontal diameter. It is no surprise that I saw the terminal effects as I did in Colorado. I'm a huge fan of the .300 Winchester Magnum, as well as the .30-06 Springfield and .308 Winchester, but unless you plan to use the 200- and 220-grain bullets, you could make the

The author took this spike elk on the last day of his Colorado hunt with a single shot from the 6.8 Western.

slow burn rate from IMR 4350, H4350, and Winchester's StaBall 6.5, all the way up through Hodgdon H1000 and RETUMBO.

Though I had good results with several, were I forced to pick the powder which performed best in my test gun, I'd look to IMR 7977. It wasn't always the fastest, but it was the most consistent in both accuracy and velocity. With the 165-grain Nosler AccuBond Long Range bullets, IMR 8133 gave the highest velocities, as it is the slowest burning of the powders tested. The factory stuff was a bit faster than my handloads — as expected — but I would still be satisfied with the speeds my handloaded ammunition generated. I used a 2.900-inch cartridge overall length for the 165-grain ABLRs, as the rifle seemed to like that length best, but the other bullets required a bit shorter C.O.L. The Nosler AccuBond Long Range and Federal Terminal Ascent bullets produced the best accuracy. They would be my choice for

shots at longer ranges, letting the species' size and tenacity dictate the choice.

What I ended up with were handloads perfectly suited for hunting nearly all game species you'd want to use the 6.8 Western for; though it would work, I suppose the cartridge might not be considered a sound choice for prairie dogs and other small varmints. The 130-grain bullets will handle whitetails without issue. With the 136-grain Terminal Ascent, you've got an excellent choice for pronghorns, sheep, and other similar species. The 165-grain Nosler AccuBond could handle the bears, larger cervids, and a wide selection of African game species as well.

CONCLUSION

Considering that the .270 Winchester and .270 WSM cannot stabilize the longer projectiles without a replacement barrel and having seen the effects of the heavier projectiles on game animals,

the 6.8 Western's ability to mimic the terminal effects of the larger 7mm- and .30-caliber cartridges make it a viable design. In a saturated market with excellent cartridges, the 6.8 Western brings a unique sense of balance, performance, and versatility usually reserved for classic designs. I have never been overly enthusiastic about the Winchester Short Magnum cartridges, and the 6.8 Western is undoubtedly a part of that family, even if the name doesn't reflect it. But there is something different and unique about this one. I had none of the feeding issues I've experienced with the .300 WSM and .270 WSM; perhaps that slightly relocated shoulder is playing a part in that.

Where the 7mm WSM and .325 WSM have lost the shooting public's attention, and the WSSM cartridges have all but faded into obscurity, I feel the 6.8 Western will prove to be a popular choice, as it fills a niche which, in my opinion, has long been needed. GD

GUNS of the African Professionals

> JOE COOGAN

Above: Harry Selby (left) and Robert Ruark with Ruark's first buffalo taken with a .470 Westley Richards double rifle during his 1951 safari in Tanganyika, East Africa that he featured in his best-selling book, *Horn of the Hunter*.

Right: In the 1967 British film, "The Last Safari," Stewart Granger plays the PH carrying a double rifle on a hunt for an elephant that killed his friend. The client next to him has a heavy magazine rifle. Granger was a keen hunter and came on several safaris using a very fancy engraved .577 Westley Richards double rifle.

Paramount Pictures presents
"THE LAST SAFARI"
Starring KAZ GARAS • STEWART GRANGER • GABRIELLA LICUDI
Technicolor®

Copyright © 1967 by Paramount Film Service Limited. All rights reserved. Permission granted for newspaper and magazine reproduction. (Made in U.S.A.) **67/288**

A pproaching a bull elephant within spitting distance commands your full attention and will have your heart pounding like a jackhammer. Merely closing with an elephant in thick bush can trigger a charge before you ever fire the first shot. And if he charges, you'd better have a reliable big-bore rifle at the ready that's capable of stopping seven tons of angry animal determined to crush you — and an experienced hunter at your side with a heavy rifle to back you up.

Common sense dictates that you include two capable rifles when hunting dangerous game. Any of Africa's Big Five — elephant, rhino, buffalo, lion, and leopard — can inflict severe injury or death. As Ruark's quote above suggests, a balance of emotion enables you to face an angry elephant or track a wounded buffalo into the thick bush — and, of course, having a big-bore "stopper" in your hands and the second one in your partner's.

A current-production .470 Westley Richards boxlock double rifle with scroll-engraving, color-casehardened receiver, and a walnut stock selected for strength and beauty.

To hunt dangerous game you should be scared enough to be cautious and brave enough to control your fear — and use enough gun!
— **Robert Ruark**

Originally, East African PHs were called "white hunters" until the early '60s when political correctness in newly independent Africa ended its use. Pictured here is Kenya PH Bill Jenvey with a massive tusker taken in the Tana River region of NE Kenya — the heavier tusk weighed 122 lbs. Jenvey's rifle is a .500/465 NE Holland & Holland sidelock double.

Wally Johnson with a giant Mozambique tusker taken sometime in the 1930s. Wally is holding a rare rifle by Imman Meffert in 11.2x72 Schuler. Cartridges for this rifle were hard to find, so his use of it was limited. Once he acquired his Winchester Model 70 in .375 H&H Magnum around 1938, it became his most used and favorite working rifle.

In most African countries that allow hunting, a licensed professional hunter (PH) must accompany non-residents to hunt big game. Professional hunters carry rifles on which the lives of many people depend and, when necessary, he'll bring that rifle into play to keep close calls from becoming radio calls for help. With few exceptions, a PH's rifle is a big bore of .400 caliber or larger.

My family lived in Kenya during the '60s. As residents, we were able to hunt on our own after satisfying strict game department requirements that included having rifles of sufficient caliber to hunt specific species. We began by obtaining permits for importing our firearms into Kenya; based on the game we planned to pursue, these included a Remington Model 721 in .300 Holland & Holland Magnum and a Winchester Model 69-A in .22 LR. And with some excellent bird shooting in mind, we included my father's trusty Winchester Model 12 pump-action 12-gauge shotgun.

In the mid-1950s, Westley Richards introduced a new no-frills model of its boxlock double rifle called the "White Hunter." The idea was to keep the cost down and appeal to the African professional hunters who could not afford a double gun.

Side view of the Westley Richards with double triggers and basic engraving.

Top view of the Westley Richards "White Hunter" with express sights and tang-mounted safety.

After a couple of years spent learning the ropes of African big game hunting and gaining valuable experience, we were eager to step up to the challenges of hunting dangerous game. For that endeavor, we added a couple of big-bore rifles to our safari battery — two post-'64 Winchester Model 70s chambered in .458 Winchester Magnum.

When finally licensed for dangerous game, my father and I each carried a .458 and focused mainly on hunting buffalo and elephants, taking several buffs and up to four elephants per year for several years. As poaching became more and more prevalent in Kenya, the future of hunting there became dubious. In 1972, I was extremely fortunate to be offered a safari job in Botswana, where I served an apprenticeship with Ker, Downey & Selby (KDS) Safaris for my professional hunter's license.

When I began conducting hunting safaris, I worked alongside some of the industry's giants, respected men, including Harry Selby. He managed KDS and guided Robert Ruark on his many safaris during the 1950s. Other renowned PHs working for the company included Lionel Palmer, Wally Johnson, Walt Johnson, Jr., Soren Lindstrom, and John Kingsley-Heath, to name just a few. I had plenty of opportunities to compare notes with these legends of Africa and reap the benefit of the many exciting tales they told and opinions they shared sitting around the campfire.

BACKUP RIFLES FOR DANGEROUS GAME

Two time-proven platforms serve as the basis for the unfailing reliability that a PH's big-bore stopper must have — either a bolt-action magazine rifle or a double-barreled side-by-side. During the first half of the 20th Century, doubles were the primary rifle of choice for

PH Derrick Dunn and client, Paul Deutz with a northern Tanzania buff that measured 59 3/8 inches, qualifying it as the World's Record up until 2000 when a pair of horns picked up in the Lake Manyara NP measured 62 3/4 inches.

Syd Downey, a founding partner of Ker & Downey Safaris, established right after World War II, was a highly respected hunter who relied on his double .500 NE.

most East African professional hunters, which coincided with the golden age of the British double rifle. Famous names of the best-known doubles are primarily British and include Holland & Holland, John Rigby & Co., Westley Richards, James Purdey & Sons, William Jeffery, and William Evans. Double rifles of Eu-

ropean origin include Kreighoff, Merkel, Sauer & Son, Chapuis Armes, Heym, Ferlach, and Hartman & Weiss.

Double rifles are generally shorter than a magazine-fed rifle because they lack the added receiver length that contains the bolt and magazine. Double gunners also believe there's a distinct advantage to hav-

ing two certain shots without having to cock and reload the gun over the possible three or four shots from a magazine rifle that requires cycling the action with each shot. Those proficient with double rifles find them quick to point and very handy when working close in thick bush.

Quality double rifles feature either

Harry Selby with his .416 Rigby rifle and a Botswana elephant taken by his client, Frank Lyon, in 1995. Lyon bought Selby's rifle before the hunt to use it for hunting an elephant with Selby.

PH Mark Selby with a .450/400 Jeffery double his Godfather Robert Ruark gave him, shortly after Mark was born. Mark used the double for several years during his early years as a PH but switched to a .416 Rigby later in his career.

a sidelock or boxlock action. A hand-detachable sidelock action, developed by Birmingham gunmakers W&C Scott & Son, is featured on the higher-end rifles. Many consider the sidelock to be a strong and certainly attractive action, and it requires hours of hand-fitting to make, which dramatically increases the cost of the gun. Just as strong, minus the distinctive side metal, is the more economic boxlock action Westley Richards employees William Anson and John

HUNTING • SHOOTING • ADVENTURE

Guns

SPECIAL
SAFARI
ISSUE

JANUARY 1965 50¢

BIG GAME AROUND THE WORLD!

In 1964, when Winchester introduced a new line of rifles and shotguns, it featured Kenya PH David Ommanney, who tested the new guns on safari in Tanganyika, East Africa. Winchester called Ommanney "Our Man in Africa." Several gun magazine covers featured him.

Winchester's "Our Man in Africa," David Ommanney, with a lion he took in Tanganyika with Winchester's new post-'64 Model 70 "African" rifle.

Deeley developed. The Anson & Deeley boxlock action has proven itself a robust and reliable one for many years.

Double rifles typically incorporate express-style iron sights with the rear sight dovetailed into a quarter-rib and utilizing a leaf or blade cut with a wide "V" and a front sight featuring a brass bead. Although double rifles sometimes accommodate scopes, the extra weight affects the balance and feel, interrupting the gun's clean lines and sleek look. As a backup gun, PHs rarely, if ever, fit a scope to their double.

Makers normally chamber doubles in one of the big-bore Nitro Express (NE) calibers that include the .450/400 NE, .450 NE, .500/.465 NE, .475 Jeffery, .470 NE, .500 NE, .600 NE, .577 NE, and the behemoth .700 NE. You can chamber double rifles for rimless cartridges such as the .375 H&H Mag. and .458 Winchester Magnum, but it takes a spring-loaded extractor to lift the cartridge from the chamber, which some consider a weak point if not kept meticulously clean and clear of any dirt, grime, or grit.

Most NE big-bore calibers produce a muzzle velocity of between 2,000 fps and 2,400 fps, with many falling in the range of around 2,150 fps. These velocities are not intended for long-range shooting but can be devastating for close work on dangerous game. Suppose the maker correctly regulated the barrels to a particular load. In that case, an accurate double rifle should print shots from both barrels to under five inches at 100 yards — considered the maximum distance for a double.

The other unique feature of a double rifle is a two-trigger system, one on the right-front side firing the right barrel and the other on the left-rear firing the left barrel. The two triggers operate independently of each other, so if in the unlikely event that one fails, the other is still operational. Because of the big-bore doubles' stout recoil, many shooters pull the rear trigger first, which fires the left barrel and prevents the trigger finger from slipping off the front trigger with recoil and firing the second barrel unintentionally and in quick succession. Whichever method you choose, I

In 1962, Robert Ruark thanks a native Samburu girl who directed Harry Selby to this impressive tusker in Kenya's Northern Frontier District, where Ruark's final safari in Kenya took place. Note Selby's .416 Rigby rifle lying on the elephant's side.

In 1964, Winchester initiated a magazine ad campaign featuring PH David Ommanney testing the new line of rifles and shotguns on safari in East Africa. Winchester's timing coincided with Kynoch suspending ammo production for the double gun calibers, which thrust the .458 Winchester Magnum into prime position to become the leading cartridge for dangerous game.

recommend plenty of practice with snap caps.

For those who learned to handle and shoot a double-barrel side-by-side shotgun, the transition to a double rifle is smoother than for those who are more accustomed to shooting magazine rifles. The feel, balance, and sight picture of a double gun are unique and take practice to become comfortable and confident. Quick reloading is another advantage double gunners point out. Still, it takes practice to perfect the method of holding

TURNING THE TABLES

FROM THE GAME ART COLLECTION
OF THE
REMINGTON ARMS COMPANY, INC.

Artist Bob Kuhn had a particular fondness and respect for the Cape buffalo, which, when wounded, is extremely dangerous. As depicted in his painting, a hunter hastily reloads his double while a gun bearer aims a bolt gun at a wounded buff charging a tracker.

two cartridges between your fingers supporting the fore-end and not dropping them during recoil.

By the mid-1950s, the rising cost of high-priced doubles and dwindling ammo sources caused many young up-and-coming professional hunters to gravitate to the more economical and available magazine rifles. Like the pump or lever action, bolt actions were more robust, more accurate, and cycled ammunition more reliably than other repeating actions. They also came chambered in a wide variety of big-bore cartridges ranging from the .404 Jeffery up through the .500 Jeffery and .505 Gibbs.

A good rule to follow when hunting dangerous game is to use as much gun as would be suitable for following that animal if it were wounded — in other words, a rifle/caliber combination capable of stopping that particular animal in a charge. There are accepted minimum calibers determined by common sense or as legally required in some countries. The .375 H&H Magnum, classified as a medium-heavy cartridge, is perhaps the most universally accepted caliber for hunting the world's big game, including most dangerous species. But its stopping power is considered marginal against Africa's

DANGEROUS GAME

700   600   577   500   470   375

Popular and romanticized double gun Nitro Express cartridges designed for hunting the world's most massive game.

most giant game — a role better suited to the .400 and larger calibers designed to penetrate thick skin and heavy bones of buffalo, elephant, and rhino. Although you can kill these animals with lighter calibers under ideal circumstances, using enough gun makes good sense. And because they must deal with "worst-case scenarios," a professional hunter's rifle needs to be more than enough gun.

Choosing bullets for a professional hunter's rifle is straightforward — you use non-expanding, full-metal-jacketed bullets, commonly called solids, exclusively for the thick-skinned, heavy-boned game. However, you can employ expanding bullets or soft points for thin-skinned game such as lions and leopards. When it comes to buffalo, there's varying opinion regarding the use of soft-points or solids. Penetration is all-important on the heavy game, but there's a chance that a solid from a side-on shot might pass through the buffalo and hit another animal. A compromise in the soft/solid debate is to use a soft point for the first shot and follow up with solids when you need greater penetration.

Most of the old school PHs loaded solids exclusively for the thick-skinned dangerous game, and some even for the cats, if they were hunting elephants at the same time. But their era did not enjoy the technological advancements in bullet construction and manufacturing from which we benefit today, making the use of a soft point on buffalo an effective option. For elephants and rhinos, solids remain the only option.

ESSENTIAL FEATURES

The late gun writer, Finn Aagaard, a former Kenya professional hunter himself, believed a PH's rifle should be strictly utilitarian. Aagaard wanted an imminently portable rifle — that is, short enough to use in thick cover, but still with enough heft to be steady on longer shots. He wanted sights that were usable from 15 feet to 100 or more yards, and the rifle would have to withstand rugged country and rough service, but above everything else, it had to be reliable. Aagaard described reliability as

Winchester's Model 70 was first chambered for the .458 Winchester Magnum cartridge in 1956 and called the "African." This pre-'64 magazine ad features the M70 African, which became the "go-to" rifle and cartridge for PHs when ammo for doubles became scarce.

unfailing mechanical functioning. "It must go bang without fail every time the action is operated and the trigger pulled," he wrote. "But reliability also includes consistent grouping ability and the dependable maintenance of zero."

His bolt-action choice for the ideal professional's magazine rifle was the Mauser Model 98, which combined reliability with accuracy. Aagaard was not alone in his opinion. Most knowledgeable shooters still believe the Mauser Model

LON PAUL Custom .416 Rigby

Working with Harry Selby in Botswana for many years, I gained great respect for his .416 Rigby rifle. Several years ago, I initiated a gun project with Tanglewood gunsmith Lon Paul. He incorporated all the features I consider necessary for the ideal professional hunter's rifle, using Harry Selby's .416 Rigby as a model — a rifle Selby carried for more than 40 years.

Besides my admiration for Harry's rifle, I selected the .416 Rigby chambering because of its excellent Africa success. From the time John Rigby & Co. first introduced its new heavy bolt-gun caliber in London in 1912, it quickly gained respect in Africa. There the caliber proved to be one of the most effective magazine rifle cartridges ever designed for dangerous game. The .416 enjoyed that status up through the early 1960s when Kynoch began cutting back on sporting cartridges and eventually quit producing factory cartridges for the .416. Thirty years later, Federal Cartridge Co. picked up the ball and began producing .416 Rigby ammo again in the mid-1990s. Federal utilizes premium-quality 400-grain solids and soft-nosed Trophy Bonded bullets, as

Tanglewood gunsmith Lon Paul understands and appreciates the classic "look and feel" of a London best bolt gun. The author's .416 custom-built rifle features a beautiful straight-grain English walnut stock, selected for strength and beauty and shaped to Rigby-style dimensions. The stock exhibits fine-line checkering on the wrist and fore-end and a cap of polished Cape buffalo horn.

well as 400-grain Nosler Partitions for its loads.

A vintage Brno ZKK 602 action with an integral pop-up aperture sight built into the receiver provided a solid and robust foundation for my rifle project. While the Brno action's double-square bridge configuration with integral dovetails will accept a scope, I designed my rifle to be used exclusively with iron sights.

Lon fitted a 24-inch Douglas premium barrel to the action and then attached a quarter-rib, barrel-band front sight with an ivory-beaded pop-up low-light sight

98 to be one of the finest, if not *the finest* action for a big game rifle ever designed. Included among the M98-style actions are Winchester's pre-'64 Model 70 action (currently available in post-'94 production) and the Czech-made Brno ZKK 602 magnum-length action. These actions employ a non-rotating claw extractor for positive feed and extraction, and they are plenty strong to handle the heaviest calibers.

Some perceive it as a fault that the M98 bolt only picks up and feeds cartridges from the magazine. Because the extractor will not snap over the cartridge's rim, you cannot drop a cartridge directly into the chamber and close the bolt over it. It's possible to alter the extractor by changing

The vintage Brno ZKK 602 double-square bridge magnum action has an M70 wing-type safety. The rear-square bridge incorporates an integral spring-loaded aperture sight that you access with a right-side button, but when not required, can be pushed down flush with the square bridge and out of the way. Both square bridges have integral dovetails to allow easy scope fitting.

A spring-loaded aperture sight makes this vintage Brno ZKK 602 double-square bridge action distinctive. The rear-square bridge houses it. The push of a button on the receiver's right-rear side pops the aperture sight up and into view.

and barrel-band sling swivel. The quarter-rib accommodates three shallow-V express-style leaves that all fold down and out of the way. These allow the use of the spring-loaded aperture sight, positioned with the push of a button on the receiver's right-rear side.

There is a barrel-band front ramp sight at the muzzle and a barrel-band sling-swivel 2½ inches in front of the fore-end. The metalwork has been rust-blued, the action polished smooth as oiled glass, and the crisp trigger breaks at exactly 3½ pounds. Like an original Rigby, the magazine holds four rounds with a cartridge loaded in the chamber. Paul replaced the Brno's safety with an M70 wing-type safety.

Lon gave great attention to the stock design and dimensions to achieve the original Rigby's handling and pointing qualities. Tapping his taste for English guns, he fitted the barreled action into a beautiful stock cut from straight-grain English walnut he selected for strength

and beauty. The stock exhibits traditional fine-line checkering on the wrist and fore-end and is shaped to Rigby-style dimensions, thus achieving a classic "look and feel." Rifles properly set up with "quick-to-acquire" iron sights demand somewhat more drop at the heel than most modern rifles with high or sight-combed stocks designed for scope use.

A hinged steel grip cap hides a spare front sight wrapped in oilcloth that you store in a small hollow in the bottom of the pistol grip. A Pachmayr Decelerator recoil pad tames recoil, and Paul capped the fore-end with a fine-grained section of Cape buffalo horn that exhibits the look of polished marble.

"You rarely find modern stock designs possessing the 'bird gun' pointing qualities that one is immediately aware of when handling a vintage Rigby, Jeffery, or London-designed firearm," Lon pointed out.

A skilled and talented gunsmith, Lon Paul transformed the sturdy and rugged

Brno-actioned rifle into a handsome dangerous game gun, which now embodies all the best features required of a gun on which your life may depend. I do not doubt that when called upon, this rifle will provide the kind of reliable insurance that's necessary to stop Africa's largest and toughest game.

the bevel on the hook's front face so that it will snap over a cartridge rim, but this is very tricky to do without shortening or weakening the hook, thus compromising the gun's reliability. If you attempt this type of alteration, only a very competent gun-

smith familiar with the work must do it.

John "Pondoro" Taylor, noted African hunter and author of *African Rifles and Cartridges*, stated in no uncertain terms that he was opposed to any alteration of the original Mauser bolt design. "Person-

ally, I consider it an exceedingly dangerous habit (loading directly into the chamber), and have repeatedly said so…" he wrote. "Not only do you run the risk of breaking your extractor without knowing that you have broken it, which would

Harry Selby's .416 Rigby rifle rests in a place of honor after serving for more than 50 years on safari. This rifle is unique in that it had a standard commercial-grade Mauser action.

Harry Selby acquired his .416 Rigby in Nairobi in 1949, after his double .470 Rigby was damaged beyond repair when a vehicle accidentally drove over the barrels. After using the Rigby bolt gun on a couple of safaris, Selby never considered going back to a double.

result in your being unable to fire a quick second shot should you want it, but there is also a very real risk of giving yourself a dangerous jam in a tight corner."

When judging the merits of a particular bolt gun for backup work with dangerous game, consider first and foremost the smoothness of action for the bolt to work quickly and reliably. Placement, position, and angle of the bolt handle all determine how accessible it is — again, important for rapid cycling of cartridges. Concerns about the distance of bolt travel on magnum-length actions should be secondary to the action's smoothness.

Professional hunters' rifles almost always sport iron sights, either with express-style shallow-V blade sights or aperture-style peep sights. Iron sights are sturdy, virtually damage proof, and completely weatherproof. An aperture sight with a large opening referred to as a ghost ring is possibly the fastest sight of all. Which type of sight you use is a matter of personal preference — they

both work well. Scopes generally offer a slight advantage during close work in thick cover but can hinder you, snagging on the brush.

The position of safety catches varies from sliding tang-positioned safeties to Winchester M70-style wing safeties located on the back of the bolt sleeve. Mauser's three-position leaf safety rotates laterally 180 degrees across the bolt's back. All these safeties are efficient but require complete familiarity and awareness to master, flicking them off as you engage the rifle for shooting.

Bearing in mind that an animal is only dangerous when at close quarters, a professional hunter's rifle must shoot precisely to the point of aim at close range and function flawlessly in the heat of the moment. Long before an aspiring professional hunter will have to brain a charging elephant or down a Cape buffalo at 15 paces, he should be so familiar with his rifle that it comes up as quickly and as naturally as pointing his finger. **GD**

Selby fit his .416 Rigby with a wider trigger shoe, which he preferred to the Mauser action's slim trigger. The rear sight is express style with one standing and two folding leaves featuring a shallow "V" cut.

Thoughts on the Professional Hunters' Choice

During the planning phase of Joe's article, we decided that a list of Professional Hunters' rifles — or at least those we could accurately confirm — would be an asset for both the scope of his feature and for posterity as well. So, Coogan, PH Jay Leyendecker, and yours truly put our heads together to come up with a list of the choices of Professional Hunters who regularly pursue dangerous game from the last century-and-a-quarter. I'm the first to admit that this list is incomplete — as you could spend a lifetime trying to fill in the blanks — but rather is based on the personal experiences of the three of us, information hunters themselves offered, and that which we could find through research. The lineup is broad, representing several eras of safari, but the inevitable conclusions are there: a certain level of terminal performance is preferred, and availability of both rifles and ammunition. The .458 Winchester Magnum and .470 Nitro Express have the most entries — both drive a 500-grain bullet to 2,150 fps — followed by the .500 Nitro Express. I believe that the performance level of the first two, combined with the reliable terminal ballistics and wide-scale availability, plays an important role in the popularity of those cartridges. And, undeniably, the added horsepower of the .500 NE is a boon to those who clean up wounded animals for a living. As a client,

I've personally seen all sorts of cartridges in the hands of my Professional Hunters, from the .375 H&H Magnum and .416 Rigby to the .458 Winchester Magnum, .450, .470, and .500 Nitro Expresses. But, for the best insight, I'll turn it over to the Professionals. – Phil Massaro

JOE COOGAN ON THE PROFESSIONALS:

Shortly after the end of World War II, when safari hunting resumed in East Africa, a new crop of white hunters stepped forward to enjoy the benefits of the first four-wheel-drive vehicles, improved medicines, and effective anti-malarial prophylactics, more reliable radio communications, and ice in the clients' sundowners. But what changed very little were the guns and ammo used on safari — up, until 1956, that is.

In East Africa, there was never any formal training available to anyone hoping to become a professional hunter, so the only chance of being signed on by a safari outfitting company as a "stooge," or if a currently licensed professional hunter took you under the wing, depended mainly on the prior hunting experience the hopeful aspirant had accumulated as a youngster growing up on his family's farm. Those accepted as aspiring "learner" hunters would be expected to supply their rifle, likely a family gun or one that had been handed

down to him. It might be a double gun or a magazine rifle, whatever was at hand, but it had to be capable of dropping an elephant or stopping the charge of a rhino, buffalo, or lion.

There were seldom opportunities for trying different rifles to see what best suited the aspiring PH. And because of the expense and scarcity of ammo, rifle practice was usually out of the question. A youngster could only sharpen his eye and improve his shooting skills by his time spent in the field and the actual hunting he did.

Sometime during the early 1950s, Kenya game laws established parameters for the calibers considered acceptable for hunting dangerous game. Simply put, the thick-skinned dangerous game (elephant, rhino, and buffalo) required rifles of .400 caliber or larger, and the thin-skinned game (lion and leopard) required a .375 H&H Mag. or larger. These limitations applied to those who were hunting on a game license, while a professional hunter assisting a visiting sportsman, at a minimum, carried a .404 (considered marginal) or larger, in a magazine rifle and a .450 NE or larger in a double rifle.

In 1956, big game hunters welcomed Winchester's introduction of the .458 Win. Mag. cartridge intended for the Winchester Model 70 "African" rifle. This development came about when the double gun cartridges, and even many magazine rifle calibers, became more and more scarce. Now, there was finally a big-bore rifle and cartridge combo that was affordable and here to stay. With little or no competition from other guns and ammo manufacturers at the time, the success of Winchester's African and the .458 Win. Mag. cartridge was assured and well established by the 1960s. – Joe Coogan

JAY LEYENDECKER:

Looking at this compilation, you can see a certain level of experimentation among the PHs, but based on the prevalence of the .458 Win. Mag. and .470 NE, it's easy to see that there's a common thread.

The basic formula of the .450 NE (which evolved into a 500-grain bullet at ~2,150 fps) is a perfect choice for stopping dangerous game. Couple that with the availability of the .458 and .470, and it's no real wonder that they went on to become so popular.

I prefer the additional horsepower of my .500 Jeffery, but always took great care to make sure I brought a supply of quality ammo from the U.S. Finding ammo for my rifle in Botswana was nearly impossible.

Many PH rifles are acquired by circumstance, whether through dealer promotion, a retiring professional hunter letting go rifles, a gift from a client, or inheritance.

These factors often dictate the caliber someone shoots. My .500 Jeffery came by way of a friend who could no longer handle the recoil and wanted to sell it. He offered me the rifle at a price I could not refuse. Ultimately, he wanted me to have it more than he cared about the money. This is a common occurrence as to how a professional hunter acquires the rifle and caliber that becomes synonymous to him.

– Jay Leyendecker

AFRICAN PROFESSIONAL HUNTER GUN LIST

LAST NAME	FIRST NAME	COUNTRY HUNTED	PREFERRED RIFLE/CARTRIDGE
Aagaard	Finn	Kenya, Tanzania	Win M70 .458 Win. Mag.
Adams	Derek "Gomez"	Zimbabwe	Manton .470 NE
Allen	Bunny	Kenya, Tanzania, Uganda	.470 Rigby double
Alonso	Javier	Central African Republic, Botswana, Tanzania	.458 Ferlach
Ambrose	Gerard	Kenya, Tanzania	.458 Win. Mag.
Anderson	G.H. "Andy"	Kenya	.577 NE, .470 NE, .318 Westley Richards
Angelides	George	Tanzania	.500 Ferlach
Angelides	Michael	Tanzania	.500 Ferlach
Aniere	Johnny	Kenya, Tanzania, Uganda	.458 Win. Mag.
Archer	Tony	Kenya, Tanzania, Uganda, Botswana	.500
Baldry	Andrew	Zambia	.500 NE
Banks	Frederick "Deaf"	Uganda	.577 NE
Batchelor	Ian	Tanzania, Zimbabwe	.505 Gibbs
Blunt	Nicky	Tanzania, Kenya, Uganda	.416 Rigby
Bothma	Piet	Zambia	.500 NE Krieghoff
Branham	Mike	Kenya, Tanzania, Uganda	.458 Winchester M70, .416 Rigby, .470 Chapuis, .450 No. 2 Jefferys
Brar	Harpreet	Tanzania	.577 Ferlach
Broome	Geoff	South Africa, Zimbabwe, Tanzania	Westley Richards .375 (Belted) double, .500 NE (seldom used)
Broome	Rusty	South Africa, Zimbabwe, Zambia	Pre-'64 Model 70 .375 H&H, Evans .500 NE, Army & Navy .470 NE
Calavrias	Terry	Tanzania	.375 H&H, .416 Rem Mag, .470 NE
Calitz	Johan	Botswana	.460 G&A* ; .500 NE; .470 NE; .416 Rigby
Carr	Adrian	Zambia, Sudan	.416 Rigby
Cedegren	Sten	Kenya, Tanzania, Uganda, Zimbabwe	.500 NE Westley Richards, Win. Model 70 .458 Win. Mag.
Chadwick	Kevin	Botswana, Tanzania	.458 Win. Mag.
Charlton	Buzz	Zimbabwe	.416 Rigby
Cheffings	Joe	Kenya, Tanzania	Win. M70 .458 Win. Mag.
Chipman	Peter	Zambia, Tanzania	.470 NE, .458 Win. Mag.
Clements	Adam	Tanzania	.470 NE
Coenraad	Vermaak	South Africa	.458 Win. Mag.
Coleman	Bryan	Kenya, Tanzania, Uganda	.577 NE
Collins	Chris	Botswana	Win. M70 .458 Win. Mag.

LAST NAME	FIRST NAME	COUNTRY HUNTED	PREFERRED RIFLE/CARTRIDGE
Collins	Dougie	Kenya, Tanzania, Uganda	.458 Win. Mag.
Coogan	Joe	Botswana, Tanzania	Win. M70 .458 Win. Mag.; Mauser 98 .458 Win. Mag.; BRNO 602 .458 Win. Mag. Lott: Lon Paul Custom .416 Rigby
Cottar	Glen	Kenya, Tanzania, Uganda	.500 NE Rigby
Cottar	Mike	Kenya	.470 NE
Coupe	Franz	Zambia, Tanzania, Sudan	.458 Win. Mag.
Crous	Ronnie	Botswana	.470 NE
Cundill	Gordon	Botswana	.500 NE Manton
Curtis	Paddy	Zimbabwe, Tanzania	.470 NE
Dafner	Peter	Tanzania	.500 NE Heym 88B
Dandridge	Daryl	Botswana	.458 Win. Mag. Win. M70
Dandridge	Chris	Botswana	.470 NE
Dandridge	Colin	Botswana	.458 Win. Mag.
Dawson	Andrew	Zimbabwe	.470 NE
De Bodd	Dirk	Namibia	.470 Wm. Evans
DeBono	Edgar	Kenya, Sudan	.500 NE H&H
Destro	Reggie	Kenya, Tanzania, Uganda	.500 NE H&H
Doria	Craig	Zambia, Tanzania	.458 Westley Richards, .450 Dakota
Downey	Syd	Kenya, Tanzania, Uganda	.470 NE double rifle
Du Toit	Joekie	Botswana, South Africa	.470 NE
Duckworth	Barry	Zimbabwe	.505 Gibbs, .458 Win. Mag.
Dugmore	John	Kenya, Tanzania, Uganda, Zambia, Botswana	.470 NE William Evans
Dunn	Derrick	Kenya, Tanzania, Uganda	.500 H&H
Dyer	Tony	Kenya, Tanzania, Uganda	.416 Rigby
Eaton	Clive	Botswana	.470 NE
Englebrecht	Willy	Tanzania, Botswana	.458 Win. Mag., Ferlach double rifle
Fabris	Mauro	Botswana, Tanzania	.470 NE, .500 Jeffery
Fell	Michael	Tanzania	.500 Jeffery, .416 Rigby, .470 NE, .577 NE
Finch-Hatton	Denys	Kenya, Tanzania, Uganda	.450 NE Lancaster , .350 Rigby Magnum
Fletcher	John	Zambia, Kenya, Tanzania, Uganda	.500
Friedkin	Tom	Zimbabwe, Botswana, Tanzania	.505 Gibbs
Frylinck	Athol	Zambia	.500/465 NE H&H Royal
Gibson	Ian	Zimbabwe	.458 Win. Mag.
Goosen	Adam	Zimbabwe	.416 Wby. Mag.
Haldane	Mark	Mozambique	.470 NE Heym 88B
Hallamore	Lou	Zimbabwe	.470 NE, .458 Win. Mag.
Harland	Richard	Zimbabwe	.458 Win. Mag., .500 Jeffery
Harvey	Charlie	Zambia	.470 NE Westley Richards
Henley	Tony	Kenya, Tanzania, Uganda, Botswana	.500/465 H&H Royal, .375 H&H
Hibbs	Murray	Botswana	.500 NE
Hoffman	George	Tanzania	.416 Hoffman
Holbrow	Peter	South Africa, Botswana	.470 NE
Holmberg	Andrew	Kenya, Tanzania, Uganda, Botswana	Rigby .470 NE
Hunter	John A.	Kenya	.416 Rigby, .500 NE, .505 Gibbs
Hurt	Robin	Kenya, Tanzania, Uganda, Zambia, Sudan, Botswana	.416 Rem. Mag., .470 NE, .500 NE

LAST NAME	FIRST NAME	COUNTRY HUNTED	PREFERRED RIFLE/CARTRIDGE
Hurt	Derek	Tanzania	.470 William Evans
Hurt	Roger	Tanzania	.470 William Evans
Illum Berg	Natasha	Tanzania	.458 Lott
Jamieson	C. Fletcher	Zimbabwe	.500 Jeffery
Johnson	Wally	Mozambique	.375 H&H
Johnson	Walter	Mozambique, Botswana	.458 Win. Mag.
Judd	Bill	Kenya	.577 Westley Richards, .450 Army & Navy, .350 Rigby
Kelly	Garry	South Africa	.470 NE Webley Scott
Ker	Donald	Kenya, Tanzania, Uganda	.500 H&H
Kibble	Mike	Namibia, Caprivi	.500 NE Verney-Carron
Kidson	Ron	Zambia	.458 Westely Richards, .458 Dumoulin double
Kingsely-Heath	John	Kenya, Tanzania, Botswana	.470 NE Westley Richards
Kok	Marthinus	Zimbabwe	Custom .500 Jeffery, Heym .500 NE
Kyriacou	Mark	Botswana	.458 Win. Mag.
Kyriacou	George	Botswana	.470 NE
Labuschagne	Divan	Namibia	.470 NE, .500 Jeffery
Lamprecht	Jofie	Namibia	.500 NE Heym 88B
Lawrence-Brown	Stan	Tanzania	.470 NE H&H
Lefol	Alain	Zambia, Sudan, Tanzania, Central African Republic	.458 Win. Mag.
Leyendecker	Jay	Botswana	CZ550 .500 Jeffery
Lindstrom	Soren	Kenya, Tanzania, Uganda, Sudan, Botswana	Ferlach double .458 Win. Mag.
Lovemore	Russell	Mozambique	Ruger RSM .416 Rigby, Heym 500 NE
Lowe	Kevin	Zambia	.458 Lott
Manners	Harry	Mozambique	.375 H&H
Mantheakis	Michel	Tanzania	.450 Dakota
Marsh	Brian	Zimbabwe, Botswana	.404 Jeffery
Marx	Wilhelm	Tanzania	.500 Wheeler, .500 Heym
Mauladad	Iqbal Bali	Kenya, Tanzania, Uganda, Sudan	.470 NE, .475 NE, .416 Rigby
McCallum	Danny	Kenya, Tanzania, Uganda, Zambia, Sudan	.470 NE
McDonald	Alex	Mozambique, South Africa	.458 Lott
McNeil	Douglas	Tanzania	.500 Jeffery double rifle
Miller	Gerard	Kenya, Tanzania, Uganda	Rigby in .460 Wby. Mag.
Moore	Tony	Sudan, Tanzania, Uganda, Zimbabwe, Zambia	.458 Win. Mag.
Murray	Mike	South Africa, Botswana	458 Lott, 577 NR
Nel	Martin	Zimbabwe, Tanzania	.458 Win. Mag.
Newgass	Richard	Zimbabwe, Tanzania	.470 NE Westley Richards
Ommanney	David	Kenya, Tanzania, Uganda, Sudan, Zambia	.470 NE Rigby, Win 70 .375 H&H
Oosthuizen	John	Zambia, Tanzania, South Africa	.505 Gibbs
Palmer	Lionel	Botswana, Kenya	BSA .458 Win. Mag.
Palmer	Terry	Botswana	.458 Win Mag.; .470 NE*
Palmer-Wilson	Clary	Kenya, Tanzania, Uganda	.450 No. 2 Jefferies, .450 Ackley
Paul	Simon	Botswana, Kenya	Pre '64 Win M70 .458 Win. Mag
Percival	Phil	Kenya, Tanzania, Uganda, Sudan	.450 No. 2
Ramoni	Lorene	Tanzania	.577 NE

LAST NAME	FIRST NAME	COUNTRY HUNTED	PREFERRED RIFLE/CARTRIDGE
Rann	Jeff	Botswana	.500 NE, .577 NE
Ray	Bunny	Kenya, Tanzania, Uganda	.500
Read	Adrian	Zimbabwe	.416 Rigby
Reitnauer	Robert	Kenya, Tanzania	.416 Rigby
Riggs	Cecil	Botswana, Kenya	.458 Win. Mag.
Robertson	Kevin	Zimbabwe	.505 Gibbs Dumoulin
Robinson	Garth	Botswana	.470 NE
Rogers	Dudley	Zimbabwe	.500 Jeffery
Rundgren	Eric	Kenya, Tanzania, Uganda, Botswana	.450 NE, .577 Westley Richards, .470 NE
Ryan	Bill	Kenya, Tanzania, Uganda	Westley Richards .470 NE (single trigger)
Salmon	Roy "Samaki"	Uganda	.416 Rigby, .470 NE
Samaras	Luke	Tanzania	.416 Rigby, .470 NE
Sanchez-Arino	Tony	Numerous	.416 Rigby, .500 Jeffery
Sandenberg	David	Botswana	.458 Win. Mag.
Selby	Harry	Kenya, Tanzania, Uganda, Botswana	Rigby Big Game .416 Rigby; Win M70 .458
Selby	Mark	Botswna, Tanzania	.450/.400 Jeffery; .460 Wby. Mag.; Rigby BG .416 Rigby
Selous	Frederick C.	Tanzania, Zimbabwe	Various Blackpowder rifles, .461 No. 1 Gibbs
Seth-Smith	Tony	Kenya, Tanzania, Uganda	.500 H&H
Shallom	Ryan Eric	Tanzania, Uganda	.470 NE
Sharp	John	Zimbabwe; Tanzania	.470 NE, .458 Win. Mag.
Smith	Steve	Kenya, Tanzania, Uganda	.416 Rigby
Stanton	Lindon	Zimbabwe	Ruger RSM .458 Lott, Heym .500 NE
Stumpfe	Karl	Namibia	.577 NE
Sutherland	Jim	Mozambique, Tanzania, Congo	.577 NE, .318 Westley Richards
Sutton	John	Kenya, Tanzania, Uganda, Sudan	.500 NE H&H
Thiessen	Nigel	Tanzania, Zimbabwe	.416 Rigby custom
Torrence	Kevin	Kenya, Tanzania, Uganda	.500 NE
Traut	Jamie	Namibia	Win. 70 .458 Win. Mag., Kreighoff .470 NE
Vallaro	Mark	Zimbabwe	.470 NE Heym 88B
van Blerk	Brian	Zimbabwe, Tanzania	.500 NE, .416 Rem. Mag.
van Zyl	Poen	Mozambique	.416 Rigby Ruger RSM
Vermaak	Hans	South Africa	.500 NE Kreighoff
Voigt	Robin	Zambia, Tanzania	.458 Win. Mag.
von Blixen-Fineke	Bror	Tanzania, Kenya, Uganda	W.J. Jeffery .600 NE, .350 Rigby
Walker	Cliff	Tanzania, Zimbabwe	.577 Ferlach
Webley	Mike	Kenya, Tanzania, Uganda,	.458 Win. Mag.
Whitehead	Quintin	Tanzania	.450 Watts
Wightman	Nicky	Zambia	.458 Win. Mag. (Browning Rifle)
Williams	Dave	Kenya, Tanzania, Uganda	.500/.465 H&H
Wincza	Laddy	Kenya, Tanzania, Uganda	.458 Win. Mag.
Wright	Dougie	Botswana, Kenya	.458 Win. Mag.

The .300 Weatherby Magnum was designed for days like this: A fantastic Altai argali, taken in Mongolia in 2018, using a .300 Weatherby Magnum with 200-grain ELD-X.

75 Years of Weatherby Magnums

Fifteen fast cartridges … from .224 to .460!

> CRAIG BODDINGTON

R oy E. Weatherby (1910–1988) was a good old American gun tinkerer and wildcatter from Kansas. He was also a zealot who believed fervently in his concepts of velocity, cartridge design, and sporting rifle stocking and style. He would become a marketing genius, with his ideas and company now passed to the second and third generation. Not all of us use Weatherby Magnums, but it's unlikely there's a serious shooter in the world who doesn't associate the name "Weatherby" with speed and performance!

There are now fifteen Weatherby Magnum cartridges, in bullet diameter from .224 to .458 inch. The "original" Weatherby Magnums were probably finalized in Roy's garage shop after he and his wife Camilla relocated to California in 1944, with Weatherby's Sporting Goods established in 1945. Although it's unknown exactly how many cartridge designs he considered, between 1945 and 1968, Roy Weatherby would "go commercial" with 10 Weatherby Magnum cartridges. After his passing, son Ed Weatherby would add four more. In 2019, grandson Adam Weatherby added another, the unique 6.5mm Weatherby Rebated Precision Magnum (RPM).

Roy E. Weatherby (1910–1988).

Ed and Roy Weatherby, in the office at the old South Gate, CA facility.

Working up loads for Mark V in 7mm Weatherby Magnum. The author has never understood why the 7mm Remington Magnum took off so quickly in 1962, when the superior 7mm Weatherby Magnum had been on the market for 18 years.

Left to right: .257 Weatherby Magnum, .270 Weatherby Magnum, 7mm Weatherby Magnum, shown with .375 H&H. The .257, .270, and 7mm, all three original 1945 Roy Weatherby cartridges, are based on the H&H case shortened, necked down, with body taper removed.

Covering *15* cartridges in one article is a daunting task; the first dilemma being finding the most logical approach. The typical approach would be caliber progression, but the two smallest, the .224 and .240 Weatherby Magnums were Roy Weatherby's final cartridges (1963 and 1968). I have chosen to group the Weatherby Magnums by parent case and case design, with a separate chronological listing.

SHORTENED H&H CASE

Roy based his "original" cartridges on the belted .375 H&H (or .300 H&H) case. Numerous "Improved" versions were in use, but Weatherby added his distinctive "double Venturi" shoulder. When necking down the long (2.8-inch) H&H case, going over-bore capacity was a concern, especially with 1940s propellants. So, Roy developed his original cartridges from the H&H case shortened to 2.549 inches. This design gave the tremendous advantage of housing these cartridges in standard (.30-'06-length) actions. My guess, however, is that Roy was more concerned with performance than action length.

.257 Weatherby Magnum: Able to propel a heavy-for-caliber 120-grain bullet to 3,300 feet per second (fps), the .257 Weatherby Magnum is the fastest commercial .25-caliber cartridge. It was Roy's personal favorite; he loved to tell about dropping a Cape buffalo in its tracks with the .257. While exact circumstances are unknown (I never thought that Roy considered using the .257 for buffalo a good idea), he often told the story as a perfect example of his "hydrostatic shock" theory.

.270 Weatherby Magnum: Which shoots flattest, the .257 or .270 Weatherby Magnum, is arguable, but both are among the flattest-shooting of all commercial hunting cartridges. Depending on the load, the .270 Weatherby Magnum runs a couple of hundred fps faster than the .270 Winchester, with a resultant energy increase that I have always believed can be seen in the impact on larger game.

The recoil remains mild, and accuracy is usually superb. Over the years, the .270 Weatherby has been the second-most-popular Weatherby Magnum cartridge.

7mm Weatherby Magnum: In the 1950s, respected pundits such as Les Bowman and Warren Page were screaming for a fast 7mm cartridge, culminating in the 7mm Remington Magnum later in 1962. Honest, I never understood this, because there was already an excellent and fast 7mm on the market, precisely what they were looking for: The 7mm Weatherby Magnum! Roy's 7mm Weatherby was one of his initial 1944 developments, although factory ammunition didn't exist until a few years later. Dimensions are very similar to the 7mm Remington, but Weatherby's double-radius shoulder allows more powder capacity. The 7mm Weatherby Magnum outruns the 7mm Remington Magnum by as much as a couple of hundred fps, depending on the load.

FULL-LENGTH H&H CASE

Four Weatherby Magnum cartridges use the full-length H&H case. These

Above: Boddington and Finn Aagaard, with a mouflon taken with a .257 Weatherby Magnum in about 1980.

Left: The full-length Weatherby Magnums based on the H&H case are, left to right: 6.5-.300 Weatherby Magnum, .300 Weatherby Magnum, .340 Weatherby Magnum, .375 Weatherby Magnum, shown with .375 H&H parent case. The .300 and .375 were original 1945 cartridges; the .340 was introduced in 1962; the 6.5-.300 by Ed Weatherby in 2016.

Below: A good mid-Asian Ibex, taken in Kyrgyzstan with a .300 Weatherby Magnum, since 1945 a common choice among serious mountain hunters.

Above: Below: The mountain hunter's Holy Grail, a fine Suleiman markhor from Pakistan's Torghar Hills, taken (of course) with a .300 Weatherby Magnum.

cartridges all require a full-length (.375 H&H) action, always standard in the Mark V Magnum action. Only two of the four were among Roy's original introductions: .300 and .375 Weatherby Magnums; the .340 followed in 1962, the 6.5-.300 Weatherby Magnum in 2016.

6.5-.300 Weatherby Magnum: Roy Weatherby considered a 6.5mm Weatherby Magnum in the 1950s, probably following the .264 Winchester Magnum's initial success. According to legend, he decided against it because 6.5mm bullet selection was poor and, with existing powders, over-bore capacity would have been a significant issue. Times change! Thanks to the amazing success of the 6.5mm Creedmoor and other developments, the 6.5mm (.264 inch) is "in." Bullet selection has expanded tremendously, and new slow-burning propellants make the 6.5-.300

much more viable than in Roy's day. Roy's son, Ed, introduced the 6.5-.300 Weatherby Magnum in 2016. It is still slightly over-bore capacity and limited in acceptable propellants. It is still the fastest and flattest-shooting of all 6.5mm cartridges, providing superb long-range performance without the recoil of larger calibers.

.300 Weatherby Magnum: The .300 is the line's flagship, long the most popular Weatherby Magnum. The long, tapered .300 H&H case with a gentle shoulder is ripe for "improvement." With body taper removed and his signature double-radius shoulder, Roy's cartridge is just one of several versions that achieved popularity in the 1940s and is the only one that made it into factory form and has lasted for 75 years. The .300 Weatherby Magnum is no longer the fastest production .30-caliber, surpassed by

the .300 Remington Ultra Magnum and Weatherby's own .30-.378. However, it is still extremely fast and powerful, exceeding the .300 Winchester Magnum by about 200 fps, depending on the loading. From inception, it became a favorite of international hunters seeking a variety of game on unfamiliar turf because of its tremendous versatility. I started using the .300 Weatherby Magnum in 1982 and continue to use it today. It has been my choice on most Asian mountain hunts and near-perfect for the full run of non-dangerous African game. I have found it extremely accurate and easy to load for, still one of the world's greatest hunting cartridges.

.340 Weatherby Magnum: Roy Weatherby introduced the .340 Weatherby Magnum in 1962. About 1980, I asked him about his cartridge designa-

tions. Instead of taking offense, he just laughed. "Well," he said, "The .458 was getting popular, so I thought I'd suggest hunters were getting a bit more and call mine the .460. Likewise, the .338 seemed to be catching on, so I rounded mine up to .340." Using the full-length H&H case (2.85 inches), the .340 Weatherby Magnum was an unabashed improvement on the shorter-cased .338 Winchester Magnum, which was introduced in 1958. The .340 is a significant improvement, with a velocity increase of about 200 fps, making it noticeably more powerful and flatter-shooting (and thus more versatile). Recoil is also considerably sharper. I used the .340 quite a lot in the 1980s and 1990s, finding it wonderfully effective on both grizzlies and coastal brown bears. It was the only rifle I took on several African safaris, and it performed wonderfully on the full range of African antelopes up to eland.

.375 Weatherby Magnum: As with the .300 Weatherby Magnum and .300 H&H, there were various improved versions of the .375 H&H. Finalized in 1944 and introduced in 1945, Roy's cartridge removed the body taper to increase powder capacity, and, of course, added his unique shoulder. The velocity increase over the .375 H&H was about 200 fps. This increase takes the .375 into a slightly different class, producing well over 5,000 ft-lbs of energy (about 25 percent more than the H&H). War- ren Page of *Gun Digest* and *Field & Stream* fame was a devout "fast 7mm" proponent. From a historical standpoint, I find it odd that he

never latched onto the 7mm Weatherby. He was, however, a staunch proponent of the .375 Weatherby. Although Page did little sheep hunting, he had much more international experience than his counterpart at *Outdoor Life*, Jack O'Connor. Page wrote that he used his .375 Weatherby Magnum for elephants, buffaloes, rhinos, lions, leopards, tigers, gaur, and much more — shooting out two barrels in the process! I used the .375 Weatherby Magnum as my only rifle on several safaris in Cameroon and the Central African Republic, finding it versatile and hard-hitting. In 1953, Weatherby replaced it with the faster, larger-cased .378 Weatherby Magnum. Since then, it has been removed and reintroduced to the Weatherby lineup. It is not as fast or powerful as the mighty .378 Weatherby Magnum but has the advantage of being housed in a .375 H&H action, and, although recoil is considerably more than the .375 H&H, it is much less severe than the .378.

.378 WEATHERBY FAMILY

To my knowledge, Roy never precisely admitted it, but the .378 Weatherby Magnum case is essentially a belted version of the .416 Rigby case, which would have been obscure in the early 1950s. That fact became im-portant a decade later when Kyn- och

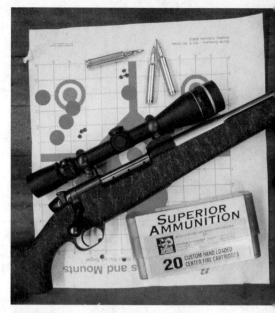

Initial groups from Boddington's Mark V AccuMark in 6.5-.300 Weatherby Magnum. This rifle wants to shoot!

ceased loading the big Nitro Express cartridges. Owners of .416 Rigby rifles (including Jack O'Connor) solved the ammo problem by merely turning the belts off .378 or .460 Weatherby Magnum cases. The five cartridges based on the .378 Weatherby Magnum are all the fastest in their respective caliber classes. Aside from generous blast and recoil, their primary disadvantage is (like the .416 Rigby itself), you must house them in an extra-large or true "magnum" action.

.378 Weatherby Magnum: In-troduced in 1953, the .378 Weatherby Magnum is the fastest and most powerful factory .375 cartridge. Also, the flattest-shooting, able to propel a 300-grain bullet close to 3,000 fps. All the cartridges in the .378-based family are hard kickers, but the .378 hits hard and *fast*, with severe re- coil velocity and crushing ft-lbs of

The author used this Mark V AccuMark in 6.5-.300 Weatherby Magnum with 127-grain Barnes LRX to take this excellent barren-ground caribou on the Alaskan Peninsula in 2019.

Weatherby Magnum Lineage:

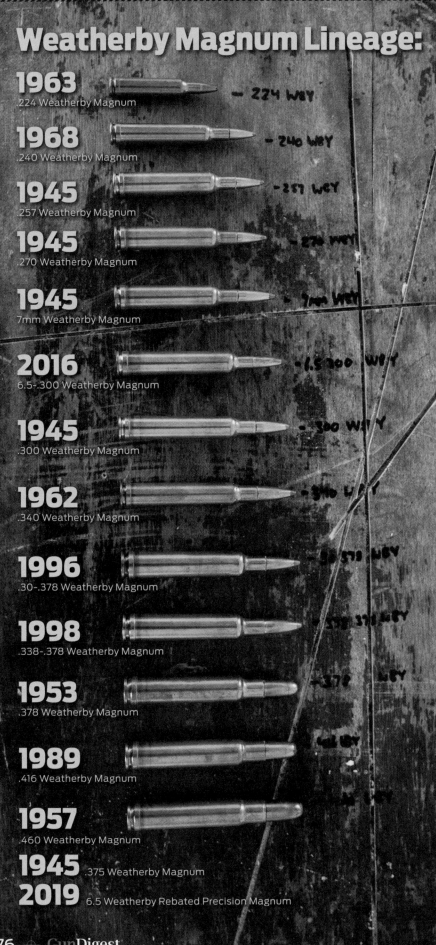

1963
.224 Weatherby Magnum

1968
.240 Weatherby Magnum

1945
.257 Weatherby Magnum

1945
.270 Weatherby Magnum

1945
7mm Weatherby Magnum

2016
6.5-.300 Weatherby Magnum

1945
.300 Weatherby Magnum

1962
.340 Weatherby Magnum

1996
.30-.378 Weatherby Magnum

1998
.338-.378 Weatherby Magnum

1953
.378 Weatherby Magnum

1989
.416 Weatherby Magnum

1957
.460 Weatherby Magnum

1945 .375 Weatherby Magnum
2019 6.5 Weatherby Rebated Precision Magnum

energy. It had a reputation for premature expansion in its early days (like many Weatherby cartridges) because bullets of the day couldn't handle such high velocity. Today, with tough bonded-core and homogenous-alloy bullets, the .378 is dramatically effective on the largest game, but that recoil level isn't for everyone.

.30-.378 Weatherby Magnum: The .30-.378 was created by an obvious and simple necking-down of the .378 Weatherby Magnum case to .30 caliber. It was developed in 1959 to fill specifications for a military contract. Though never adopted by the military, it languished as a wildcat cartridge until Ed Weatherby put it into the Weatherby Magnum factory lineup in 1996. It set accuracy records in long-range competition as a wildcat, including the first "10X" perfect score in a 1,000-yard benchrest competition. Although John Lazzeroni's proprietary .308 Warbird may be slightly faster, the .30-.378 Weatherby Magnum is by far the quickest factory .30-caliber cartridge, propelling 180-grain bullets above 3,400 fps.

.338-.378 Weatherby Magnum: In a previous generation, it seems that the prominent gun writers all had a "gimmick" caliber. For O'Connor, it was the .270; for Page, the 7mm; for Colonel Askins, the 8mm. For Elmer Keith, it was the .33 caliber, first the British .333 diameter, later the .338. The .338-.378 was wildcatted in the 1960s by Elmer Keith and Bob Thomson as the .338-.378 Keith-Thomson. It was Elmer's idea of the "ultimate" .33 caliber. Although their version shaved a quarter-inch off the case, the .338-.378 remained a wildcat cartridge until 1998. That's when Ed Weatherby took it into the line as the .338-.378 Weatherby Magnum. The case length of the Weatherby factory cartridge is 2.913 inches, the same as the .30-.378 Weatherby Magnum. It is the fastest .33-caliber factory cartridge, propelling 250-grain bullets above 3,000 fps, slightly faster than the .338 RUM or the .338 Lapua Magnum. Recoil is severe, but the .338-.378 Weatherby Magnum is powerful and flat-shooting, clearly an awesome choice for large game such as elk and moose at long range.

.416 Weatherby Magnum: The .416

A good Central Africa savanna buffalo from northern Cameroon, taken with a Mark V in .375 Weatherby Magnum, the only rifle Boddington brought on this safari.

Weatherby Magnum was Ed Weatherby's first proprietary cartridge, introduced in 1989, just a year after his father's passing. Although the case capacity of the .416 Rigby and .416 Weatherby Magnum is almost identical, the Weatherby cartridge is loaded to full potential, with a 400-grain bullet at about 2,700 fps. Thus, it's the fastest and most potent of the .416s. When Weatherby introduced the cartridge, I went to Botswana with Ed Weatherby, where we "wrung it out" on several Cape buffaloes. The performance was spectacular! Between 1988 and 1989, Federal introduced the first modern .416 Rigby load, and Remington introduced the .416 Remington Magnum. In a short time, we went from the .416 being a rare bullet diameter to multiple cartridge choices, but in 1989, bullet selection was

limited. Bullet manufacturers responded quickly. A short while later, Chub Eastman, then of Nosler Bullets, and I took Nosler's new .416 Partition to Australia, again seeing the devastating performance from the .416 Weatherby Magnum. Today, great .416 bullets are readily available, and to some extent, the "compromise" .416s have taken market share from both the .375s and the true big bores.

.460 Weatherby Magnum: Winchester introduced the .458 Winchester Magnum in 1956. Although the exact date is uncertain, about this time, the East African Professional Hunters Association established a minimum of .40 caliber for thick-skinned dangerous game. Although the .378 Weatherby Magnum produced 6,500 ft-lbs of energy and was more potent than most of the

The 6.5 Weatherby RPM is the first Weatherby cartridge not to feature a belt or the signature double-radius shoulder.

Above: A fine Botswana buffalo, taken in 1989 when the .416 Weatherby Magnum was brand new. One shot, one buffalo.

The .378 family is based on a belted version of the .416 Rigby. Left to right: .416 Rigby (parent); .30-.378 Weatherby Magnum; .338-.378 Weatherby Magnum; .378 Weatherby Magnum; .416 Weatherby Magnum; .460 Weatherby Magnum. The .378 was introduced in 1953; the last, the .338-.378, by Ed Weatherby in 1998.

Over the years, Weatherby has produced some real showstoppers, such as this Wyoming Silver Model with attractive engraving.

old big-bore Nitro Express cartridges, this left the .378 technically illegal for dangerous game in some African jurisdictions. Roy wouldn't let this stand, so in 1957 he necked up the .378 case to take a .458-inch bullet. Producing about 7,500 ft-lbs of energy, for nearly thirty years, the .460 Weatherby Magnum reigned as the world's most powerful sporting rifle cartridge. Today, the massive .700 Nitro Express technically eclipses it. However, with low velocity and massive frontal area, the .700 doesn't penetrate well. The .460 does! With tough bonded cores, homogenous alloy expanding bullets, and modern solids, it performs wonderfully.

In hunting, everything depends on shot placement and bullet performance. Still, the .460 Weatherby Magnum is among few shoulder-fired cartridges that can drop Cape buffalo to the shot — not always, but consistently. Because recoil velocity is lower, many fans of both the .416 and .460 Weatherby Magnums find it easier to shoot than the fast-recoiling .378. However, the .460 remains a hard-kicking cartridge: It is impossible to generate 50 percent more energy than the .470 Nitro Express without paying the price in recoil.

UNIQUE CASE DIMENSIONS

As we have seen, the dozen Weatherby Magnums discussed so far are based on the .300 or .375 H&H case or the .378 Weatherby case. There are three more Weatherby Magnum cartridges with unique case dimensions:

.224 Weatherby Magnum: Initially introduced in 1963 in a scaled-down Mark V, the .224 was first called the Varmintmaster, later renamed to the .224 Weatherby Magnum. It is the only .22 centerfire based on a belted case and has a unique .429-inch rim (and belt) diameter between the .222/.223 Remington and the .22-250. In the 1940s, Roy Weatherby experimented with multiple fast .22-centerfire wildcats, but the .224 Weatherby Magnum is and remains Weatherby's only .22-caliber cartridge. The .224 Weatherby Magnum is an extremely capable cartridge, with good handloads slightly faster than the .22-250. Despite the performance, it has not been

Left to right: .244 Weatherby Magnum, 6.5 Weatherby RPM and .240 Weatherby Magnum. Unlike the rest, these three Weatherby cartridges have unique case dimensions, without a parent cartridge from which you can size cases.

popular, almost certainly because of the wider availability of other .22 centerfires. It was removed from the Weatherby line but reinstated in 2002.

.240 Weatherby Magnum: With a .473-inch rim belt and 2.5-inch case length, the .240 Weatherby Magnum is essentially a belted version of the .30-'06 case, distinctly narrower than cartridges based on the H&H case. In 1968, it would be the last cartridge introduced by Roy Weatherby. It is extremely fast and powerful, propelling a 100-grain bullet as much as 300 fps faster than the .243 Winchester. It requires a standard action, and its popularity has probably also been hampered by a single-source (Weatherby) for brass and ammo. The .240 Weatherby Magnum is a fast, flat-shooting, hard-hitting cartridge with very light recoil.

6.5mm Weatherby Rebated Precision Magnum (RPM): Introduced in 2019, the 6.5 RPM is Adam Weatherby's first cartridge introduction as President of Weatherby, Inc. The concept is unusual but sound. Building on the newfound popularity of the 6.5mm (.264-inch) bullet diameter, plus today's search for efficiency as well as range, the 6.5 RPM is based on the excellent 6.5-.284 Norma case, lengthened to 2.570 inches. The rebated .473-inch rim means it matches

Adam Weatherby used his new 6.5 RPM to take this big black bear, the first animal to fall to the new cartridge.

the ".30-06 family" bolt face and will fit into a standard-length action. Weatherby designed it to chamber in Weatherby's standard (and lighter) six-lug Mark V action. With a 140-grain bullet at 3,050 fps, it's faster than the 6.5-.284 and, although similar in velocity to the 6.5mm PRC, you can chamber it in a lighter, trimmer rifle. The 6.5 RPM is a departure: It's the

first unbelted Weatherby cartridge, the first with a rebated rim cartridge, and it does not have a double-radius shoulder. Weatherby rifles so chambered do not have the freebore common to Weatherby rifles since the beginning. Time will tell if this is the beginning of a new family of Weatherby cartridges, but the potential is undoubtedly there! **GD**

How to Tune Your AR-15

› PATRICK SWEENEY

What's the "best" AR-15? It's the one you've tuned to maximize reliability — and which gives you the most confidence!

I commonly get asked, "What's the best AR-15?" Invariably, the asker has some expectation, a particular type or variant, a specific manufacturer, or just the most expensive in mind. Often, they want validation, not information. Sometimes, the question is, "What did the guy who won the latest 3-Gun match use, or what do the Navy SEALs use?" These questions can be interesting, but they are not relevant if you are looking for the AR-15 equivalent of a truck gun.

But now and then, someone wants to know how to make their AR-15 the best it can be. And they want to do it without spending a house payment or two on a premium barrel, or a free-float handguard made of *unobtainium*, or a super-slick coating that removes any need for cleaning.

To bring your AR-15 to its potential, you need to do six things: Stake, spring, gauge and ream, buffer, paint, and graph.

STAKE

Things that gun makers have tightened are supposed to stay put. There are two main culprits here. One is the gas key on the carrier, and the other is the castle nut on the telestock assembly. The gas key is that tube on top of the carrier that receives the gas sent back from the gas port. If it leaks, your system will be sluggish, or it could short-stroke. The preliminary test is to hold the carrier in one hand and grasp the key with your other hand. Try as hard as you can to move the key. Don't worry; no one among us has strength enough to damage it with bare hands alone. If there is any movement at all, reset it. Look at the base of the key. If you see gas jet out from the key seat's edges, you should reset it. If your rifle has been working sluggishly, even with proper ammo, you need to reset it.

You'll need a narrow file, fine-grit sandpaper or crocus cloth, cleaning materials, and a good grade of Loctite. Me, I use the dark green 680 Shaft and Bearing goo, as it sets up quickly and solidly. You'll also need a MOACKS. More on that in a bit.

The only way to be sure it is tight and not leaking is to take it off and re-attach it. You can re-use the screws if you wish, but you may want to use fresh ones since the proper torque limits for these screws are close to their tensile strength, and you might already have ready-to-break screws.

Remove the carrier assembly and take the bolt out of it. Scrub the carrier assembly clean inside and out. Clamp the carrier in a padded vise and remove the screws. Scrub the key base and the carrier slot it rides in, even scraping clear the corners of the slot. Use your narrow file and a fine grade of sanding cloth (220 works well, finer is better) to scrub the surface clean and level. Put some cloth sanding-side-up on a flat surface or a larger file and rub the key back and forth on the surface to scour the key's bottom the same way you did the slot. You want to reduce the high spots on each of the mating surfaces, so you have as flat a pair of surfaces as you can get — thus eliminating leaks.

Degrease the surfaces. Spread a small amount of Loctite on the carrier slot flat and place the key in the slot. Insert

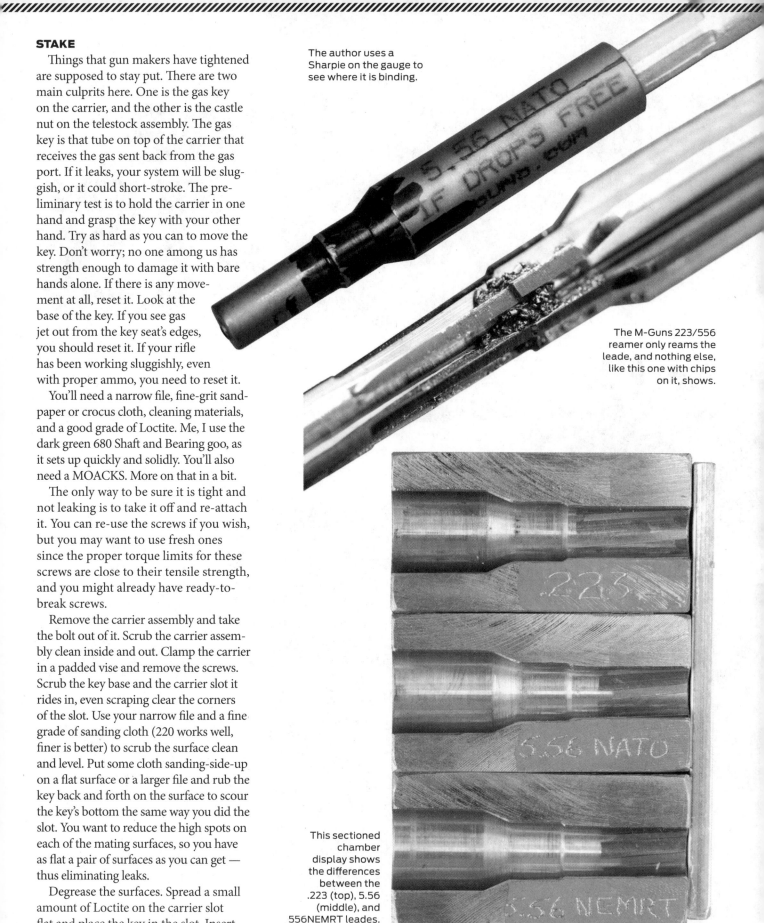

The author uses a Sharpie on the gauge to see where it is binding.

The M-Guns 223/556 reamer only reams the leade, and nothing else, like this one with chips on it, shows.

This sectioned chamber display shows the differences between the .223 (top), 5.56 (middle), and 556NEMRT leades.

Just because it says "556" on it doesn't necessarily mean it is. You should check to be sure.

If you bust your buffer or discover someone incorrectly assembled it, replace it.

Someone locked this gas block in place; paint indicates the locking screws.

the screws, and torque them down. The acceptable range is 50-55 in-lbs. These screws can fail at 70-80 in-lbs, so you want to either use a solid but not overly tight touch or a torque wrench.

Take a Q-tip or other cotton-tipped swab, and reach into the bolt tunnel and wipe off any Loctite that may have found its way down into the bore.

Next, stake the screws. This step is where the MOACKS comes in. Named by law enforcement trainer Jeff Chudwin, and invented by gunsmith Ned Christiansen, the MOACKS (mother of all carrier key stakers) removes the need for a chisel, hammer, and steady hand. Ned makes several variants of the MOACKS, but they all work the same way: You slide the carrier with the key into the MOACKS, position it, and tighten the staking screw until it stops. Repeat as necessary. How important is the staking of the gas key? It is so crucial that, if you own more than one AR-15, you should buy a MOACKS from M-Guns.com and use it. If you only own one AR, you should find the guy in your gun club who does own a MOACKS and borrow it one day at the range. It's that important.

Those who have a belt-and-suspenders approach to life can now use a spring-loaded machinists' marking punch to counter-punch the head of the screw for more engagement against the MOACKS staking. In this instance, the rock and roll motto certainly holds: Some is good, more is better, too much is not enough.

I know what you're thinking: What do I do when I've worn out the gas key? (Oh, you optimist, you.) Simple: you grind the staking off, use a torch to burn the Loctite, pry off the remnants of the old key, and clean the carrier and repeat all this with a new key. Carriers, short of a *ka-boom*, are a lifetime part — several lifetimes. Keys currently cost $25, and the screws are $2 each. If your barrel only lasted you 5,000 rounds and you replaced the key along with the new barrel and gas tube (a new gas tube is not always needed), you will have burned through thousands of rounds before needing to replace a worn key.

When should you not stake the key? Every carrier key gets staked except those installed by Yankee Hill. For some

The MOACKS stakes screws on the gas key like there's no tomorrow. It's the single best tool for ARs you can have.

SPRING

While you have the bolt out of the carrier, remove the extractor. The AR-15 (and the M-16 as well) is historically under-sprung for extractor tension. The extractor spring should stay stuck in the extractor, with a small synthetic drum inside the spring. If it is missing or the drum is not blue or black (indicating the strength of that material), you need to get one of those colors. If the extractor falls out, it was either installed upside down or is otherwise damaged. Replace it.

The Army adopted an increased-power spring, which it had plated to appear gold in color. Your existing spring is probably good enough, but if you have a gold spring, install it.

With a good spring in place and a dark-colored synthetic booster inside the spring, you need to add more. The best is the D-Fender, a D-shaped wedge-angled booster that rides around the outside of the spring. The Army went cheap and bought a bazillion o-rings. Both work, provided you purchase the o-rings that are strong enough (they come in a variety of strengths) and of a material that will stand up to heat, oil, and powder residue. Brownells can help you here.

It will be more work to get the extractor installed in the bolt with the boost of the D-Fender or o-ring, but you want the extra tension. Many malfunctions ascribed to various other causes were a result of insufficient extractor tension. The Army says the M4 (carbine) needs both its gold spring and o-ring and that rifles need only the gold spring. The Army is wrong. Some guns do, some don't. Your AR will tell you which it needs.

Can you have too much extractor tension? Yes. Here's how to tell, but you have to do this at the range. Start with a clean rifle. Lock your bolt back. Drop a loaded round into the chamber. Now grab the charging handle, control and unlock

reason, Yankee Hill doesn't stake and tells people not to stake, or it voids their warranty. So don't stake an already assembled carrier and key from YHM. But if it comes loose, be sure to tell them about it.

The other thing requiring staking is the castle nut on the stock assembly. Do this by applying a spring-loaded marking tool (a standard tool used by machinists) to the receiver retaining plate at two of the castle nut staking slots. The big slots on the nut are for the wrench and face the butt-stock. The smaller ones are towards the muzzle, and that's where you stake. Kick a spur of steel into at least two slots. This stake keeps the castle nut from loosening under vibration. You will find that some hardened receiver plates are not mil-spec — you will not be able to stake them. This situation is one of the rare times when I use Loctite on the castle nut. The castle nut must not be allowed to move. If staking isn't an option, then bring on the Loctite. Otherwise, stake away.

Above: Your extractor needs an inner polymer part that is blue or black, a good spring, and a booster such as a D-Fender, or here, an o-ring.

Right: This Colt barrel isn't marked. That's because when Colt purchased its barrels in the 1960s and 1970s, it never used a .223 leade.

Don't assume that your AR is ready to run just because it's new. Follow the author's six-step method outlined here to ensure every-thing runs optimally. Photo: Jorge Amselle

the bolt, and ease it forward. When you feel the bolt bump into the case rim, gently let go of the charging handle. The buffer spring should finish closing the bolt and cam the extractor over the rim of the case. If your rifle completely closes, you're good to go. If it won't cam over the rim, you may be over-tensioned. There could be other causes, but they are rare and require a skilled armorer or gun-smith to diagnose.

GAUGE AND REAM

Do you have a .223 or a 5.56 chamber? Trick question: they are the same, at least as far as headspace is concerned. What we are looking at is called the leade. (pronounced "leed.") The leade is forward of the case neck. It's the ramp's angle of the rifling as it begins and in front of the bullet. The .223 is short and steep. The 5.56 is longer and shallower. If you have a .223 leade and shoot 5.56-rated ammuni-tion in your rifle, you will have excessive pressure. Not may, not might, but *will*.

Here's the catch: the markings on your barrel may not be what you think. (Cue the Spaniard from the Princess Bride.) I have seen rifles with barrels marked "5.56" with .223 leades. The earliest Colts

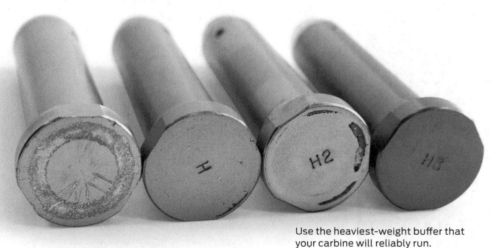

Use the heaviest-weight buffer that your carbine will reliably run.

This buffer is the most *craptastic* thing that the au-thor has ever seen. Someone made it using conduit, and it split along the seam when you attempted to use it. Of course, you ditch stuff like this.

didn't even have such markings because there was only the 5.56. Now, there are barrels made across America, and you must be careful.

To find out which chamber you have, use the .223/5.56 gauge from M-Guns.com. This tool is a precision-ground gauge for 5.56 leade dimensions. To use it, scrub your chamber clean. Install the gauge on its handle. Insert it into the chamber. If it sticks in place, you have a .223 leade. If it turns freely, you have a 5.56 leade. I routinely use a Sharpie to blacken the gauge. That way, if there is any resistance to the gauge, I can see where the chamber has rubbed it off. This information prevents me from reaming a .223 Wylde chamber, which is unneces-

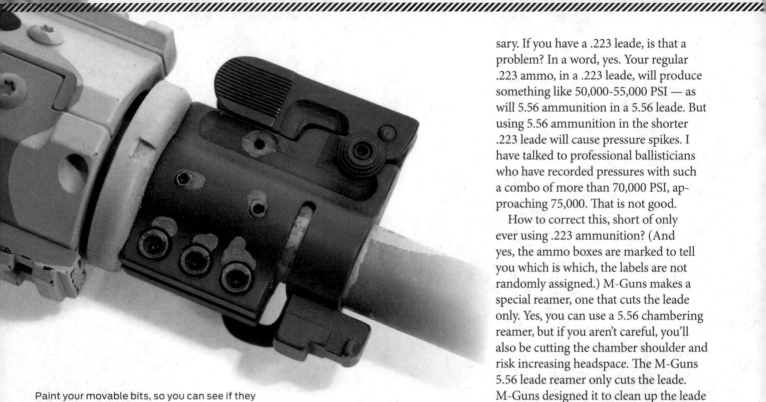

Paint your movable bits, so you can see if they shifted, like this GG&G front sight assembly.

This Ballisticker from M-Guns gives you the drop to distance for a given load. Stick it on where you can easily reference it.

sary. If you have a .223 leade, is that a problem? In a word, yes. Your regular .223 ammo, in a .223 leade, will produce something like 50,000-55,000 PSI — as will 5.56 ammunition in a 5.56 leade. But using 5.56 ammunition in the shorter .223 leade will cause pressure spikes. I have talked to professional ballisticians who have recorded pressures with such a combo of more than 70,000 PSI, approaching 75,000. That is not good.

How to correct this, short of only ever using .223 ammunition? (And yes, the ammo boxes are marked to tell you which is which, the labels are not randomly assigned.) M-Guns makes a special reamer, one that cuts the leade only. Yes, you can use a 5.56 chambering reamer, but if you aren't careful, you'll also be cutting the chamber shoulder and risk increasing headspace. The M-Guns 5.56 leade reamer only cuts the leade. M-Guns designed it to clean up the leade and produce a freebore length that is a bit more than most 5.56 leades to clean up the leade as much as possible (there are many "556" leade dimensions out there).

One caveat: as tough as the reamer is — it can ream even a chrome-plated chamber — it will not cut a leade in a barrel that has been Melonite treated. You'll dull the reamer. And those objecting to reaming off the chrome plating? What part do you think burns off first? After a thousand rounds or so, your leade doesn't have much chrome left, and having reamed it, you now have controlled pressures when using 5.56 ammunition.

If you're worried about accuracy loss, I was too, so I did a test with a bolt-action rifle in .223. I shot groups before (.223 leade) and after reaming (5.56NEMRT leade) and could not see any accuracy difference. And it was — and still is — an accurate rifle.

BUFFER

Buffers used to be easy; then they got ugly, now they are easy. The easy early days gave you two choices: rifle or carbine. The ugly days saw a proliferation of carbine buffers made God knows where. If it isn't a USGI carbine buffer, ditch it. The Colt plastic ones with the lead shot? Awful and need to be swapped out, pronto. I even saw buffers made from sections

What is the best AR-15? The author suggests one that runs reliably.

of conduit tubing in the ugly days, and the seam would split. Now, if the carbine I am working on or bought (rifle buffers never changed, never needed to, and are always good) has anything but a USGI one in it, I toss it. I run with the heaviest buffer that will reliably cycle the gun, as many of the "commodity" level carbines are over-gassed and benefit from the change to an H, H1, or H2 buffer. And obviously, if the buffer is damaged or improperly assembled, fix or replace it.

PAINT

Once parts are tight, how do you make sure they stay tight? You could use Loctite, but too much of that, and you have other problems, especially if you used the wicking formulations. Instead, use a dab of paint on a screw head and an adjacent part of the firearm. The paint is both an impromptu Loctite (as much as the Loctite people might hate me saying it) and an indicator. If the paint line you created breaks, the screw has moved.

You can use whatever color combinations you like, and any paint will serve, as long as you degrease the surface, so it has a chance to adhere. I routinely paint in the screws for handguards, scope mounts, gas blocks, and anything else that needs to stay put.

GRAPH

We've all seen hand-scribbled notes on paper, taped to a rifle, concerning trajectory and drops. I saw one rifle where the owner put down a coat of camo paint, then used a fine-point Sharpie to write the data, and then matte clear-coated over the writing. That's a lot of work when a simple sticker will do the job. Again, from M-Guns.com (and no, I don't get a commission, I think Ned makes a lot of very cool stuff), the Ballisticker offers a trajectory chart for various loads. Pick a bullet weight and velocity, and attach it to your rifle in a place you can readily see. Once zeroed, you now know your drops/hold-overs to your effective range.

These are essentials, and they are also the details you'll most likely need to address for an AR-15 to work its best.

You can take one of the "hobbyist" or "commodity-grade" AR-15s, and if you do all these steps to it, it will work reliably and shoot up to the level the ammo and barrel quality is capable. More than once, I have done just these steps to a student's rifle in an LEO class, and took what had been an unreliable pile of parts, and turned them into a reliable gun. I might not put on the Ballisticker because not everyone feels the need to know their drop to 300 or 400 yards. Many LEOs consider a Buick's length to be the expected engagement distance and across the parking lot to be a long-distance shot.

Your rifle or carbine might not bear an elite brand status name, and it may lack the current-high-speed-low-drag parts. And you may not have topped it with a super-scope. But it will work, it will work reliably, and it will get you through a class, a match, or a predicament. If a snooty name is more important to you than reliability, well, good luck with that.

Either as a bought gun or a built AR, this is how you make your AR reliable. And reliability is always best. **GD**

SAKO SAFARI: WEST for MULE DEER!

The Sako Finnlight II Brings European Elegance to Montana's Mule Deer Mecca

> COREY GRAFF

At least since the advent of indoor plumbing, the thrill of adventure has compelled man to trade comfort for the West's bitterly cold wind-whipped hills. And so it was as we left the gravel road and entered Gumbo Land, somewhere east of the Continental Divide. We roll slowly past an emaciated ranch house where the only signs of life are the sharptailed grouse packed onto shrub oak branches and bobbing around in the frozen ditches like chickens. A road sign, riddled with bullet holes, reads: "Road Impassable When Wet." We drive on. Soon we arrive at a little BLM section, and, before long, I'm trudging into unforgiving horizontal sleet that lashes exposed skin like an industrial sandblaster. I'm gazing upon an alien landscape of chiseled gorges, steep breaks, and giant rock goiters that form a bizarre mouse maze of Paleozoic and Precambrian rock. The locals call it the Badlands. Here live strange, Dumbo-eared mule deer that hide like rabbits amid sagebrush and vanish into the gray expanse. After a year of planning and a lifetime of dreaming, we have arrived: Eastern Montana — the ideal place for a mule deer safari and to test the Sako Finnlight II!

**

The adventure begins earlier that year when the benefit of time and easy summer living tint all things rosy red and make every far-flung dream seem plausible. I wanted to take a mule deer buck by fair chase on public land, and *of course*, needed a lightweight, laser-accurate bolt rifle chambered in a flat-shooting cartridge to do it. Like all desperate middle-aged men staring the crisis of time in the face, you desire the best. To me, that meant Sako.

If the Colt Python is the Cadillac of Revolvers, then the Sako Model 85 Finnlight II is the Audi R8 of bolt-action big game rifles. From the moment you pick it up, you instantly understand how the Finnish maker can claim to "demand perfection" as its slogan and command such high prices and loyal following. What you're buying are refinement and gilt-edge precision.

The Finnlight II is the luxury class upgrade of the first model Finnlight, which sports an unpainted stainless barrel and action, and has a more straightforward stock. The Finnlight evolution goes back further, starting in 1997 with the Sako 75, which had an injection-molded synthetic stock. It was still a mainstay in 2000 when Sako upgraded to the 85 series

Sako builds the Finnlight II around the 85M action, which cycles rounds effortlessly. Sakos are known for glassy actions, and this one didn't disappoint.

Miikka Tamminen of Sako developed the Sako Finnlight II as a refined mountain rifle.

action. The first-gen Finnlight would remain unchanged through most of the 2000s. In 2009, Sako hired an ambitious young industrial designer named Miikka Tamminen, who began work on the then-existing generation Finnlight and later became a project manager. By 2018, Tamminen began the Finnlight upgrade, and this new model rifle — Sako named it the Finnlight II and released it officially in 2019 — would become the sports car of the lineup. The main attraction was its proprietary stock and other refinements.

"The idea was that we wanted something more solid, and we wanted to go away from injection molding altogether," said Tamminen. "Back in 2016, we had already introduced the Carbonlight, so we had a technology to make composite stocks that are solid inside and out … combining fiberglass in 80 percent of the stock in the critical parts such as inlets and behind the recoil pad. We reinforce that with carbon fiber so we could have a lightweight stock which is very sturdy and wouldn't be super expensive as if we would have used full carbon fiber."

That hybrid stock construction method, Tamminen explained, employs Resin Transfer Molding, or RTM technology like BMW uses in its A330 chassis, so it literally incorporates European sports car DNA. The action is bedded with carbon fiber as well, which not only provides a rock-solid platform for the recoil lug, but there are carbon-fiber areas within the stock "where the recoil forces are traveling from the sides of the stock to your shoulders," Tamminen said.

Tamminen devised a way to accent the stock on the fore-end and pistol grip using a polyurethane-based rubber material that is scratch-resistant and impervious to gun cleaning solvents. It also sticks to your hand like glue. That's an advantage for rifle shooters facing precip that can thrash you and your gun raw on any hunt. The cheekpiece is of the same space-age rubber material. Sako painted the stock with a tough, industrial paint that improves purchase and shrugs mud and dirt; practical benefits for a mountain rifle. Sako has since upgraded the stocks of its other high-end hunting rifles using the same construction methods, including the Model 85 Carbonlight and Carbon Wolf and the Tikka T3X UPR.

The stock's push-button adjustable cheek riser is a showstopper, giving you perfect alignment and an ergonomically correct view through any optic. Tamminen said that many European hunters are using red-dot sights, which tend to run higher.

Sako machined the action from a forged preform to create an extremely robust bolt construction. The 85 series bolt has three locking lugs, a controlled-round feed in the Mauser style, and typical so-reliable-it's-boring mechanical extraction. It's available in small (S) for standard .308 and 6.5 calibers; (SM) for the short magnums; medium or (M) for the .30-06 and .270 chamberings; and large (L) for the magnums, handling the .300 Win. Mag. and 7mm Rem. Mag. You can also get it in left-handed versions. A word here about Sako action smoothness needs to be said: Rifle connoisseurs know Sako's actions for their slickness. That frictionless feel characterizes each new round you feed. It gives you confidence in the hunting fields to run that bolt

The Finnlight II's adjustable cheek riser and easy-to-grip rubberized surfaces on the pistol grip, fore-end, and cheek riser are well thought out. These refinements make you want to shoot and practice with this rifle.

fast. It runs on air rails. What's Sako's secret?

"It's hard work. But it's clever design," Tamminen revealed. "And also hard work in the matter of how we treat the surfaces. But there is actually one, (I don't know if you'd call it the secret sauce) … it's also at the same time an expensive one because how we make the internals of the receiver. We use the broach method, so we don't drill our receivers inside when you take the bolt off when you look inside it's not round — it's actually the shape of the locking lugs. The locking lugs are the carrying surfaces for the bolt totally. We don't use this oversized bolt design where the whole bolt body is basically gliding against the receiver; we use the locking lugs … making contact with the [receiver]. It's quite different from everybody else."

Other differences include the Finnlight II's double-staggered magazine that combines steel with an aluminum follower. It has a clever dummy-proof feature known as the "Total Control Latch" (patent pending), in which you depress upward on the mag to actuate the tang to release. No depression, no release. That means no accidental mag droppage. You can load the mag from the top — so-called "top-loading" — a feature that Europeans tend to use more than American hunters.

The Sako's match-quality single-stage trigger is the stuff of dreams. Mine broke at a cat's whisker more than two pounds after adjusting it down from three using an Allen wrench. It is as good as any honed trigger on custom rifles I've had. There is a set trigger option, but that is also more popular in Europe than here in the States.

You can get the Finnlight in multiple barrel lengths, all fluted to shave ounces, and it's available with or without a threaded muzzle. I ordered mine in .270 Winchester, no threads. The barrel is Cerakoted gray, as are the action and bottom metal, including the trigger-guard. It shrugs Montana mud, which is saying something. Calibers range from .22-250 to .300 Win Mag. And you can get it chambered in 6.5X55 Swede, which is not an easy chambering to find here in the USA.

True to its namesake, the Finnlight

Tipping the scales at eight pounds with optic and ammo, the Finnlight is indeed a mountain rifle you can carry all day. It's the ideal weight for lugging through thin air over ridges and draws — and it handles recoil from the .270 Win. like a custom-stocked target rifle.

The Finnlight II has a very good single-stage trigger. It's adjustable down to about two pounds using an Allen wrench. The author mounted the Swarovski Z8i scope to the 85M action using Low Talley rings, which proved not only solid but classy-looking.

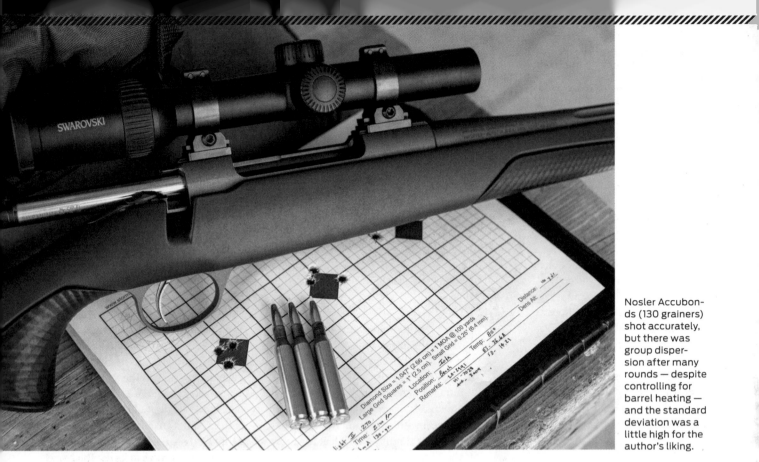

Nosler Accubonds (130 grainers) shot accurately, but there was group dispersion after many rounds — despite controlling for barrel heating — and the standard deviation was a little high for the author's liking.

II registers a couple of ounces over six pounds on a precision bathroom scale and eight pounds on the mark when loaded with 5+1 rounds of .270 Win. and topped with a scope. Speaking of scope, I topped her with the best Austrian glass a la Swarovski, opting for the Z8i 1-8x24mm. The more experience I get, the more convinced I become

of the superiority of low-power optics. I wanted a setup to dial down to genuine 1x magnification for still hunting the dark timber or popping over western draws and catching big mulies dozing at stone's throw.

The Swaro Z8i 1-8 gives you a massive field of view on 1x and, as you'd expect, the glass is brilliant and sharp to the edges; the Z8i sports illumination and a 4A-IF red dot, which is the business when the sun sinks early, as it does when

the mountains rise all around you. Not only that, its FLEXCHANGE reticle allows you to switch to an encircled dot, which is handy for quick running shots that are so common in European driven boar hunts. Its 30mm tube and Austrian glass vacuums every drop of available light, giving you a stunningly brilliant image. I mounted the

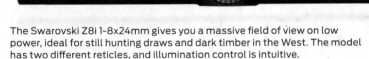

The Swarovski Z8i 1-8x24mm gives you a massive field of view on low power, ideal for still hunting draws and dark timber in the West. The model has two different reticles, and illumination control is intuitive.

Z8i to the Sako with Talley 30mm Low Detachable Rings, which proved not only perfectly concentric in alignment for a rock-solid mount but also attractive on the rifle.

***

The ultimate test with any rifle is how well it behaves on the range, and the Finnlight shines there. Of course, like any rifle, there were some ammo choices it shot lights out, others it didn't favor. All Sakos have a five-round, 1-MOA accu-

racy guarantee. I had no trouble finding several loads that proved that precision. I tried three factory .270 Win. options — Federal Non-Typical 130 grain, Federal Terminal Ascent 136 grain, and Hornady Superformance 130 grain. The Non-Typical load shot OK, but my chrony was having fits then, and I didn't capture velocity data. The Federal Terminal Ascent load averaged 2.35 inches. With an average velocity approaching 3,000 fps and a 136-grain bullet, it's evident that Federal has a pretty hot load in the Ascent line. As I would come to learn, the little Sako liked milder loads.

And then there was the outlier: The Hornady 130-grain Superformance load. Good Lord! That round set the Earth on fire and scorched the skies red. It averaged 3,166 fps over the chronograph, which is screaming from a 22-inch barrel. Accuracy was MOA, which for a pencil-barreled bolt gun is about what you want. I was committed to hunting with reloads, though, so I kept the Hornady load in the

The 130-grain Sierra GameKings had the lowest standard deviation, under 10 fps.

back of my mind as a factory alternative.

Reloading allows you to see what a rifle can do, and I shot my right shoulder black and blue proving it. I hoped the Sako would shoot a partitioned hunting bullet well, so I started with the 130-grain Swift A-Frame and the 4831 powders. But no amount of wishful thinking or confirmation bias could force it, at least not with IMR 4831 or H4831. The Nosler Accubond bullet was another head-scratcher: It just wouldn't shoot, except for one H4831 load, which turned in respectable groups. However, it seemed that the barrel was fouling with the Accubonds — each successive group would open, even when factoring in a controlled half-hour barrel cool-down period.

Next, I tried some Berger VLDs, again 130-grainers, and these shot like laser beams — 3/4 MOA groups all day long. Now, I have taken many whitetails with the Bergers, and they kill like the Wrath of God.

The author ran handloads in the test rifle. The Sako liked Nosler brass, Federal primers, H4350 powder, and 130-grain Sierra GameKings.

Even so, I wanted to try a more traditional hunting bullet, so I gave some Sierra GameKings a whirl behind H4350. And suddenly the heavens opened, the angels sang, and the rifle came into its own. The accurate load was doing 2,883 fps — far from the top end of the .270's range — but I could tell the rifle was happy: The recoil lost its harshness, and the standard deviation dropped to 9.94. The universe was in harmony, and I'd found my load. Using Jack O'Connor's infamous 3-inches high at 100 yards sight-in, I zeroed the Sako at 260 yards, which kept that GameKing in the vitals to 300 yards with a dead-center hold.

***

Back in Montana, the mid-November

Spotting Scope or 15x Binos?

On any western hunt, good optics are critical. Getting a good look at your quarry can prevent an unproductive full day's hike. The ability to ascertain details while peering at distant game can make or break your hunt. I came to rely upon the Swarovski SLC 15X56mm binoculars for my western adventure. The benefit over a spotting scope? Eyes-open glassing and less eye strain. The 15x magnification is plenty to examine game on distant slopes, and using Swaro's tripod adapter means you can secure the big binos to a tripod for rock-steady observation. As with all Swarovski glass, the focus is sharp to the edges, and the light transmission lets you see well past sundown.

The Swarovski 15X56mm SLC binos enable you to peer into the dark canopy of distant timber or assess game on a distant ridge. Sharpness is typical Swarovski — best in class.

The author prefers the Swarovski SLC 15X56mm binos to a spotting scope. Magnification at 15x is tremendous, and using the tripod adapter means you can lock it to a stable support system for relaxed, all-day both-eyes-open glassing.

Sako Celebrates Its 100th Anniversary (1921–2021)

> MICHAEL SHEA

T he Finnish people have long been precision-minded. Much of that bore from historical and geographical necessity. A country about the size of New Mexico, Finland shares an 832-mile border with Russia. That has led to many conflicts over the generations and a mid-20th-century need for accurate shooting. This is the legacy of Sako, Tikka, and Lapua.

From the middle ages, the Catholic and crusading Kingdom of Sweden dominated the Finn lands until the 1809 Finnish War when most Finnish-speaking landmass ceded to the Russian Empire. Under the Russians, the Tikkakoski factory was established in 1893 in the northern city of Jyväskylä to produce sewing machines and other household goods. Very quickly after Finland declared independence in

sako
100
SINCE 1921

Finnish troops marching with skis.

1917, the factory converted its production lines to gun parts. Sako — an acronym for *Suojeluskuntain Ase-ja Konepaja Osakeyhtiö* that translates to "Firearms and Machine workshop of the Civil Guard" — was established in 1921 to build rifles for the new and independent country.

During World War II, Finland fought a series of wars against the Soviets and the Germans, armed mostly with updated and improved Mosin-Nagant rifles from Tikkakoski and Sako. During the 105-day Winter War of 1939 and 1940, they beat back the Russians with a fraction of the troops, tanks, or air support of their numerically superior rival. The Finns took 70,000 casualties to the Soviets'

days began to warm as the Mule deer rut kicked into overdrive. Flatlanders notice many peculiar things in this corner of the Great Plains, such as Golden Eagles, Greater Goshawks, and other great raptors of the Rockies, perched everywhere on overwatch and ready to dispatch the rodents with chilling efficiency. Indeed, we are a long way from the boreal forests of Finland, and the factory *Suojeluskuntain Ase- ja Konepaja Oy* — aka Sako — in Riihimäki.

Half the time, it is impossible to tell if we are staring at cow pasture or prime muley draws, so we don our packs and walk. You appreciate the "light" part of

the Finnlight II by each passing mile. All hikers know that ounces equal pounds, but backpack hunters are keenly aware of how ounces can equal crushing pain if you get lucky and need to pack meat out in an already heavy pack. A lightweight rifle is a Godsend.

Eventually, we spot a good, mature muley buck two nights in a row tending his baker's dozen harem of hot does. But his whereabouts from one day to the next suddenly becomes challenging to pinpoint. However, across a massive valley, a bachelor group of five bucks lounge under a miles-long ridgeline as the sun sinks. I think we can access them from

a southerly direction, and a game plan takes shape.

The morning sun rises early, and the cold night has frozen the Montana mud. A pair of hunters has beaten us to the area, but they glass the draw, see nothing, and turn around and leave. We stick with the plan — on go the heavy packs, and the long hike begins. I set the Swaro Z8i on 1x as we sneak crosswind, popping carefully over each draw, careful not to skyline ourselves, hoping to catch the bucks unawares. They could be anywhere, and I'm expecting a close shot. Random beef cows dot the landscape, glaring at us, appearing happy to have company. Some follow us,

estimated 320,000 or more. Much of that success was due to the Finns' guerrilla tactics, dividing the Soviet lines, then picking them apart with sniper fire in the frigid below-zero conditions. (In early January, temperatures on the battlefield dipped below -45 degrees.) The Finns knew their country, how to stay warm, and often skied into position through the thick snow-strewn woodlands to strike, then vanish back into the trees. The Sako bolt-action rifle dealt more death than the young country's ineffective fleet of tanks and airplanes.

The Finnish sniper Simo Häyhä, nicknamed "The White Death," killed between 505 and 542 Russian soldiers with his Sako-produced Mosin-Nagant. The Model M/28-30 shot the accurized Finnish variant 7.62x53mmR and was widely used for target shooting before the war by the Civilian Guard. It had iron sights with a rear micrometer marked from 150 to 2,000 meters. Much later, Lapua's radar

trajectory tested the round and the sight markings. It found it remarkably accurate at all distances. Many remember Häyhä as the deadliest sniper in world history — a distinction almost lost to time. Decades after the war, someone discovered his journals hidden in an old drawing box and only then did the full scale of his remarkable war record fully come to light.

Accurate rifles kept modern Finland independent. After the Winter War, the Russians came at the Finns again, with the Continuation War of 1941 to 1944. Unfortunately, Finland was helped considerably by Nazi Germany this time before turning on the Germans in the Lapland War of 1944 and 1945. During this highly volatile time in Europe, Finland is something of a wonder. Russians were pressing in from the East, Germans from the North through occupied Norway, yet neither occupied Finland. Like Norway, the country wasn't taken over or complicit in Nazi war production, like Sweden whose iron ore fields fed German foundries. The Finns held their land from all-comers with skis and bolt-action ri-

A worker at the Sako factory during World War II.

fles. Look at a list of the most deaths by the percentage of the population in World War II by country, and Finland doesn't even make the top 20 — and unlike most other countries, it shared long, hostile borders with Soviet Russia and the Third Reich.

After the war, the arms factory Tikkakoski was considered a German-owned company by the Allied Powers. Its assets were confiscated for the Soviet Union in 1947, discontinuing firearms production and focusing again on sewing machines. Sako remained independent after the war, owned by the Finnish Red Cross. Finnish businesspeople bought Tikka from the Soviets in 1957; in 1962, they sold it into private hands. Rifle production continued, and in 1983 Sako bought Tikka. In 1986, the arms manufacturing division of the government-owned Valmet conglomerate purchased the combined company. The state relinquished ownership in a 2000 sale to the Italians, Beretta Holdings Group.

This sidebar is an excerpt from the newly released book Rimfire Revolution, *available at GunDigestStore.com.*

White Death, Simo Häyhä, is credited with the most sniper kills in combat ever recorded. Most of them unfolded over the 10-month Winter War.

TYPE	LOAD	VELOCITY (FPS)	ENERGY (FT-LBS)	100-YARD GROUP AVG. (IN.)	100-YARD GROUP BEST (IN.)
Factory	Federal Non-Typical 130 gr.	-	-	.99	-
Factory	Federal Terminal Ascent 136 gr.	2,956	2,639	2.35	1.97
Factory	Hornady Superformance 130 gr.	3,166	2,894	1.09	.91
Reload	Swift A-frame 130 gr./IMR 4831	2,868	2,375	1.10	-
Reload	Swift A-frame 130 gr./H4831	2,909	2,443	2.11	1.90
Reload	Berger VLD Hunting 130 gr./H4831	2,918	2,458	.81	.73
Reload	Nosler Accubond 130 gr./H4831	3,009	2,614	.73	.52
Reload	Nosler Accubond 130 gr./IMR 4350	2,874	2,385	1.23	.45
Reload	Nosler Accubond 140 gr./H4350	2,864	2,550	1.79	.81
Reload	Sierra GameKing 130 gr./H4350	2,883	2,400	.65	.44
Reload	Sierra GameKing 130 gr./H4350	2,861	2,363	1.04	.62

The author measured velocities with a Shooting Chrony chronograph 10 ft. from the muzzle.

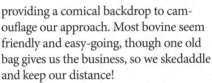

The author took this good Montana mule buck fair chase. A fine rifle such as the Sako Finnlight II is like icing on the cake to a successful hunt.

The Sako Finnlight II and the little Swarovski safari-style optic point as a natural extension of your hand-eye coordination. The setup is right at home chasing Montana's public land muleys.

providing a comical backdrop to camouflage our approach. Most bovine seem friendly and easy-going, though one old bag gives us the business, so we skedaddle and keep our distance!

That's when I spot the bucks: Some are bedded, the rest milling around. I range them — 660 yards. There are two 3-year-olds, the other bucks all younger. The stalk is on. We slip in like cats. As the sun beats down, the temps warm, and the winds slow to a puff. Warming air transforms the hard ground underfoot into gumbo slop, which sticks to our expensive mountaineering boots like industrial epoxy. By this time, six inches of mudgrease packed with field straw, sagebrush parts, and cow pies had turned boots into pancake batter-crusted stilts and made me glad there were no cowboys around to poke fun. Even so, we make our way to the nearest knoll and take a reading — 350 yards. I can make this shot, I think.

I manage to sneak my pack onto the top of the muddy knoll for a rifle rest and get prone behind the Sako. Dialing the Swaro to 8x, I take a deep breath. It's at moments like these when you appreciate good glass. I'm looking at a tack-sharp image of the muley bucks from better than three football fields distant. There is no reason to rush the shot. I put my head down, try to relax, and breathe a few more deep breaths of the cool, clean Montana mountain air. I think about the two road hunters from that morning who completely missed that these deer were in the area. And then I think: *If I kill this buck, I'm going to have to carry its meat a long damn way.*

Finally, it is time. The crosshair bisects the biggest buck — the trigger breaks. The rifle cracks, thundering through the valley — the muley drops. Its amigo jumps up and locks antlers, thrashing the downed leader around like a wet noodle. There is more to this story, of course — the quartering of the deer, and the trudging of heavy meat-filled packs through Montana mud, and the happy memory of long-subsided aches and pains.

***

Big Sky Country is home to some 33 million acres of public land, much of which lies safely east of killer grizzly bear territory. Here in the vast, endless

SAKO FINNLIGHT II SPECS

Actions: S, SM, M, L

Length: 1030-1145mm (40.55-45.08 in.)

Barrel Length: 510, 620mm (20.07-24.40 in.)

Overall Weight: 2.8-3.1kg (6.17-6.8 lbs.)

Caliber/Twist Rate:

5+1 magazine: .22-250 Rem/14 in. | .243 Win/10 in. | 6.5 Creedmoor/8 in. | 7mm-08 Rem/9.5 in. | .308 Win/11 in. | 6.5x55 SE/8 in. | .270 Win/10 in. | .30-06/11 in.

4+1 magazine: .270 Win. Short Mag./10 in. | .300 Win. Short Mag./11 in. |

7mm Rem. Mag./9.5 in. | .300 Win. Mag./10 in.

sako.fi/en-us

SWAROVSKI Z8I 1-8X24 SPECS

Weight: 18.2 oz.

Length: 11.9 in.

Magnification Range: 1-8x

Scope Objective Diameter: 24mm

Scope Tube Size: 30mm

Turret Adjustment (Click Value): 1 mrad

Reticle Position: Second Focal Plane

Reticle Details: 4A-IF Reticle

Field of View: 127.5-15.9ft/100yds

Exit Pupil: 8.1-3.0mm (.32-.12 in.)

Eye Relief: 95mm (3.74 in.)

Light Transmission: 93%

Illuminated Reticle: Yes

swarovskioptik.com

hiding place known as Eastern Montana, the state's rifle season is long, giving an inexperienced western hunter time to slow down, relax, and find the game. I would carry the Sako Finnlight II uphill and downhill, and over yonder, and it proved to be an ideal mountain rifle — not too heavy to carry all day, but not so lightweight that it knocks your teeth out when you squeeze a round off. I would later hunt with the little Sako back in my home state of Wisconsin, and by that time, it had already become my favorite bolt gun. Indeed, Sako has a long history of building high-end firearms, which it has used historically to defend its homeland, and the nation has rich hunting history to boot. It may very well be that the Finnlight II ends up ranking as a pinnacle of hunting guns in every way, capable of whatever type of safari you may dream. **GD**

THE Walker Colt

How the Walker Colt Changed the World

❯ TERRY WIELAND

ON A CREEK NOT FAR FROM SISTERDALE...

Sisterdale, Texas, is a village — a hamlet, really — on the Guadalupe River northwest of San Antonio. It's a cluster of old buildings, many dating from the 19th Century, and even the newer buildings try to look older than they are. There's a dance hall, another that used to be a general store, a third has a hitching post. Sisterdale's main claim to fame is a vineyard that offers wine-tasting tours in the shade of the live oaks that line the road. Even at its liveliest, it's pretty peaceful.

Driving into Sisterdale from any direction, the view is the same: Broken Texas hill country ravines, creek bottoms, bluffs, distant rocky peaks, live oaks, and thick cedars — lovely, to be sure, but with a certain sameness. That sameness accounts for one of the minor puzzles of modern history. Not far from Sisterdale — no one is sure where — in early June of 1844, on what was then called Walker's Creek, a battle took place that changed the world.

The Guadalupe, a mile south of Sisterdale, Texas. Historians believe The Battle of Walker's Creek took place not far from here, but they have never confirmed the exact location.

Cimarron Arms' Walker Colt reproduction, one in a series of 1,000 that replicates the original military series, produced to commemorate the 200th anniversary of the Texas Rangers.

As pivotal battles go — Waterloo, Gettysburg, Stalingrad — Walker's Creek was not much. It pitted 15 Texas Rangers under Captain Jack Hays against 75 Comanches, commander unknown. It was accidental — what the tactics manuals call an "encounter" battle — in the sense that the Rangers bumped into a band of Comanches they didn't know were there. But, in a larger sense, it was deliberate that they rode out of San Antonio, up into the hill country, looking for trouble. And, they found it.

Throughout a day-long running battle, the Rangers killed or wounded more than half the Comanches, for the loss of one Ranger dead and four wounded. What set the encounter apart was the fact that, for the first time, the Rangers armed themselves with revolvers. Instead of the usual tactic of dismounting and forming a defensive position, they fought on horseback, employing their reckless and soon-to-be-legendary aggressiveness to deadly effect. The revolver made this change of tactics possible, and it was to transform the character of Indian warfare on the Texas frontier.

***

Thus begins the story of the Walker Colt, itself one of the direct results of the Battle of Walker's Creek. (The similarity of name is purely coincidental, as far as anyone knows.) As a class, Walkers are the most valuable guns in the world. No ultra-serious Colt collection is complete without one. But the story of the Walker, and how it came to be, is a historical Gordian Knot. There are many strands, and they stretch in every direction, back through the centuries and down through the years.

The story involves larger-than-life personalities such as Sam Colt, Captain Hays, Samuel Walker, and Texas legend Sam Houston, and there are the Texas Rangers and their arch-enemies, the Comanches. Mexico plays an important part, as does the Washington bureaucracy and even the short-lived Texas Navy. The pioneering manufacturer, Eli Whitney, Jr., is involved. If we wanted to, we could throw in the armaments collection in the Tower of London, where Sam Colt reputedly — accounts are mixed — saw an exceedingly early repeating firearm

The Cimarron reproduction, cased with accouterments that replicate those of the "Danish sea captain," the only known Walker in its original case with fittings.

with a revolving cylinder.

Historians wrote entire accounts about all the above, each from their own viewpoint, emphasizing (and sometimes ignoring) some of the facts. As a result, there is, even today, considerable difference of opinion about what did or did not, or may or may not, have happened. For example, in his history of the

Texas Rangers, published in 1935, Walter Prescott Webb does not even mention the Battle of Walker's Creek by that name or any other. He makes a vague reference to an encounter between the Rangers and the Comanches "on the Pedernales" and dates it to the late 1830s, not 1844. Webb is one of the most respected historians of the American West, and collectors have

only recently discovered some facts of the battle in the 85 years since he wrote his landmark work. Still, many quote reputable historians without cross-checking, and as a result, many questionable "facts" find themselves being repeated as gospel long after being disproven or corrected.

That being the case, it behooves us to take the essential elements one at a time, look at their histories, and tie them all together. The story begins sometime in the 1600s in the mountains of western Wyoming.

Thanks to a steady diet of western movies, there is a broad misconception about the Plains Indians and the horse. We assume all native people were natural horsemen when only a few put the horse to maximum use, and only one tribe — the Comanches — habitually fought on horseback.

The Comanches originated in the Wind River Range and were a minor and downtrodden offshoot of the Shoshones from farther west. However, once introduced to the horse, they developed an immediate bond, learning not only to catch, tame, and ride horses but eventually to breed them selectively — the only Indian tribe to do so. It was like Romeo

Cimarron's reproduction Walker powder flask, identical to the one originally found in the case of the Danish sea captain.

meeting Juliette, and they developed an affinity for the horse that was mystical. Within a century, they had become the finest irregular light cavalry in the world.

Once mounted, the entire character of the tribe changed, and from 1650 onward, they expanded steadily east and south, defeating everything in their path. Neighboring Indian tribes were terrified of them. They became known as the Lords of the Southern Plains, dominating an area that includes eastern Colorado, Oklahoma, Kansas, New Mexico, and Texas, and across the Rio Grande into Mexico. This area was also the great southern buffalo herd territory, which became the tribe's mainstay. Inevitably, the Comanches came up against the Spanish as they expanded north.

Unlike many plains tribes, the Comanches were never farmers and never lived in settled villages. They were constantly on the move and always at war, both with other tribes and encroaching settlers — the Spanish from the south, Americans from the east. There were never many of them; at the absolute most, 30,000 individuals divided into half a dozen main subgroups, each with its territory. Comanche warriors could ride 400 miles at a time, sleeping on horseback and striking deep. They made a specialty of raiding remote homesteads, burning, looting, killing, scalping, and kidnapping. They took captives and turned torture into an artform worthy of the Spanish Inquisition and maintained a reign of terror on the plains.

In his superb history of the Comanche wars, *Empire of the Summer Moon*, historian Sam Gwynne calls the Comanches "the most powerful Indian tribe in American history," and it's difficult to question that. Even the Iroquois Confederacy at its height commanded only a fraction of the territory.

The Comanches had a loose alliance with the Kiowas, a sub-branch of the Apaches whose lands lay farther west and who had followed a path like their own. Physically, Comanches tended to be short and blocky and made themselves seem taller by wearing a headdress made from a buffalo head. The image of buffalo horns silhouetted against the summer moon — the dreaded "Comanche moon" — became as frightening a nightmare to settlers on the Texas frontier as anything to emerge from Dracula's Transylvania.

The Comanches were the most feared of all the Indians that opposed European expansion into the American West. They were the reason Mexico allowed Americans to settle in Texas in the first place, hoping the Anglo barbarians would provide a buffer. Of course, it did not turn

out quite as planned (the Alamo, Battle of San Jacinto, and so on), but it seemed to be working for a while.

After Texas gained its independence from Mexico in 1836, the stream of white settlers became a flood. The Americans came west mainly on foot, armed with muzzleloading rifles and shotguns, and such horses as they had were primarily for pulling wagons. They were ill-equipped to face the hard-riding Comanches, who attacked from horseback, firing well-aimed arrows. Comanche horses were agile, quick, and durable, able to go long periods without water and live on almost nothing. Since the horses could live on nothing, and the Comanches could live on horseback, it created a long-range threat almost independent of conventional logistics.

When attacked, the settlers' usual tactic was to form a defensive position. The Comanches then responded with the infamous "Comanche wheel," circling them at a gallop and peppering the defenders with arrows while hanging from their

heels on the far side of the horse, shooting from under its neck, and slowly tightening the circle like a grinding wheel. A Comanche on horseback with a quiver of 20 arrows he could loose with astonishing speed and accuracy was a fearsome opponent — and fear them they did.

As early as the 1820s, the Texans formed groups of irregulars known as "ranging companies" to fight back. These evolved into the Texas Rangers, but they had no permanence or formal organization until after independence. In the early years, they provided horses and weapons, wore whatever they liked, and drifted in and out of service as money was, or was not, available to pay them.

Sam Gwynne: "The Rangers were a rough bunch. They drank hard and liked killing and fistfighting and knife-fighting and executing people they deemed criminals or enemies. As time went by, and so many of them were killed, creating a sort of natural selection in their ranks, they got even rougher, more brutal, and more aggressive. Seen from the more civilized

parts of nineteenth-century America, they occupied a place in the social order just this side of brigands and desperados. They were not whom you wanted to pick a fight with in a frontier saloon."

In 1838, a young Tennessean named John Coffee Hays arrived in San Antonio. He was slim, quiet, and looked even younger than his 21 years. He found work on a surveying crew, mapping out homesteads. The Comanches particularly hated surveyors, who they saw as land thieves. Surveyors had a high mortality rate, and they learned to fight Indians or die. Jack Hays learned to fight Indians. He was one of those men who don't look the part but seem born to do just one thing. He was a natural leader and soon recognized as such among the Rangers.

Under Hays's leadership, the Rangers gradually changed, acquiring horses similar to the Comanche mustang. They adopted Comanche ways, from tracking, to sleeping rough, to living on practically nothing. They also learned Comanche methods of fighting on horseback, shoot-

Colt's third-generation Walker, produced in 1994.

ing and fighting while mounted. Here, however, Hays encountered a seemingly insuperable problem. The Comanches had short bows and quivers full of iron-tipped arrows; he and his men still had only muzzleloading pistols and rifles. This inequality accounts in part for the Rangers' insane aggressiveness. When they fired their two or three shots, and their guns were empty, death-defying audacity was all they had, and they proved it was better than nothing.

The turning point came in 1843. For reasons that are lost to history, the short-lived Texas Navy on the orders of then-Texas president Mirabeau Lamar had purchased, in 1838, 180 of Samuel Colt's five-shot Paterson revolvers. Returned to office, Sam Houston disbanded the navy. Somehow (no one knows how), the Patersons found their way to Jack Hays, who was commanding the Ranger station in San Antonio. Captain Hays and his men seized upon these novel weapons, recognizing that while they were smaller caliber compared to their muzzleloading horse pistols (.36 vs. .58 or greater) and intricate and fragile, they gave the user five shots without reloading. *Five shots!* Here was the key — the possible equalizer to counter the mounted Comanches' firepower advantage.

Hays's Rangers practiced with the revolvers, learned to shoot them accurately even while riding at full gallop (Hays had instituted formal training sessions), and had such faith in them by the time of Walker's Creek that they carried no other weapons. That decision almost turned out to be a grave error. Each man carried two Patersons and four spare cylinders for a total of 30 shots. The cylinders were difficult and tricky to change, and soldiers could not recharge them quickly, but by the standards of 1844, they were guns that "never ran dry."

By the end of the day at Walker's Creek, only about 35 Comanches remained, but Hays and his men were out of ammunition. Once the Comanches realized this, the Rangers were dead. Hays asked if anyone had a single round

Sister Creek near its confluence with the Guadalupe River.

left. Robert Gillespie replied that he did, and, as the Comanche chief rode towards them, Hays ordered Gillespie to dismount and pick him off. Gillespie did, and, as their chief toppled from his horse, the Comanches withdrew. Although that part of the story is not widely known, it deserves to be. Killing a man at "30 long paces" with a Colt Paterson was as phenomenal as Billy Dixon's 1,526-yard kill on a Comanche at the later Battle of Adobe Walls (1874) and, in the final analysis, vastly more influential. Had Gillespie missed, all of what followed might never have happened.

***

The Colt Patersons (as they came to be known) came from Samuel Colt's Patent Arms Company in Paterson, New Jersey, but they were anything but a success. The U.S. government had no interest in them, the Texas Navy purchase had been one of the few nibbles, and by the time of Walker's Creek, the company had gone

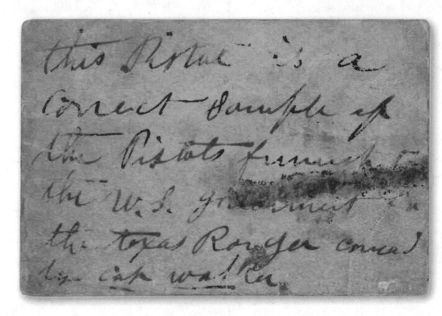

Original note found with the Danish sea captain: "This Pistol is a correct sample of the Pistols furnished to the U.S. government [and] the Texas Rangers, carried by Cap Walker." Historian Charles Pate believes Samuel Colt himself wrote it. Photo: Rock Island Auction Company

A Cimarron reproduction of the Walker Colt, aged to look original and numbered like the first military-issue Walkers. Most replicas, including Colt's second- and third-generation models, have minor undisclosed differences that allow experts to identify them as non-original — a critical consideration when originals change hands for a million dollars or more.

The reverse side of the note: "Sold by Blunt & Syms 44 Chatham New York." This script is in different handwriting, probably written by an employee of Blunt & Syms. Photo: Rock Island Auction Company

under, and Samuel Colt was living in poverty with nothing left but his patents. He did not possess even one example of his invention.

At this point, the story of the invention of the Walker Colt becomes confused, controversial, and vague. The exact details of how it came about — who wrote to whom, who suggested what, and how the revolvers were ultimately issued and to whom — are vague at best. Colt historians — including genuine experts — are still debating it. A new book by Charles Pate, *The Walker Army Revolver*, deals with all these questions and is, as of right now, the authoritative source.

Here is what we know for sure: In 1845, the Union admitted Texas, and a boundary dispute with Mexico led almost immediately to the Mexican War of 1846-48. Captain Jack Hays and his Texas Rangers enlisted en masse, forming units of the "U.S. Mounted Rifles." General Zachary Taylor employed them as scouts and skirmishers, a role for which they were supremely suited. Although Taylor complained of their "lawlessness," they

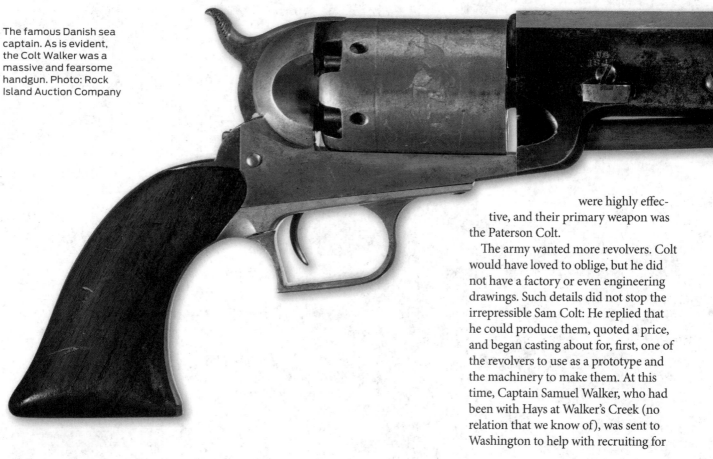

The famous Danish sea captain. As is evident, the Colt Walker was a massive and fearsome handgun. Photo: Rock Island Auction Company

were highly effective, and their primary weapon was the Paterson Colt.

The army wanted more revolvers. Colt would have loved to oblige, but he did not have a factory or even engineering drawings. Such details did not stop the irrepressible Sam Colt: He replied that he could produce them, quoted a price, and began casting about for, first, one of the revolvers to use as a prototype and the machinery to make them. At this time, Captain Samuel Walker, who had been with Hays at Walker's Creek (no relation that we know of), was sent to Washington to help with recruiting for

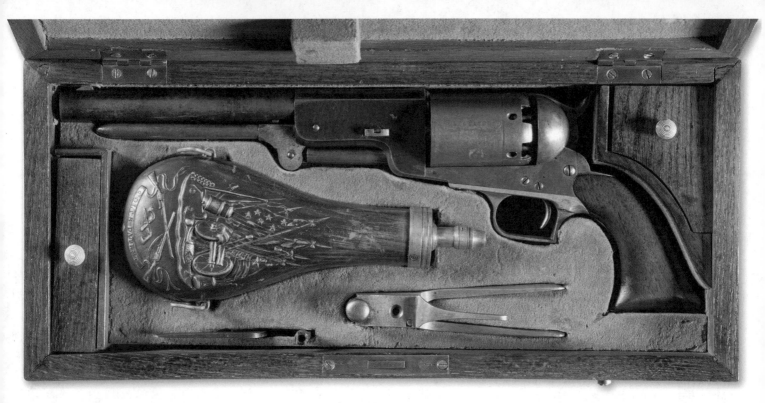

The Danish sea captain, in its case with accouterments. Somewhere along the line, the original Walker powder flask was removed and, presumably, sold separately, but it provided a pattern for companies to reproduce the original. Pictured is a later Dragoon flask. Photo: Rock Island Auction Company

a new mounted unit. He and Colt soon corresponded, with Walker suggesting ways in which they could improve the Paterson.

These improvements included a larger caliber (.44 instead of .36), a six-shot cylinder, a means of loading with the cylinder in place (although soldiers could still carry spare loaded cylinders), and replaced trigger. This drop-down affair only appeared when the hammer was cocked, with a conventional trigger and triggerguard. The pistol had a 9-inch barrel and weighed more than 4 1/2 pounds. As a final touch, Colt roll-engraved the cylinders with a scene of Rangers pursuing Comanches at Walker's Creek as a tribute to the men and the battle. Some of these changes were Walker's, others were

Colt's, but it was a collaboration that, quite literally, changed the world.

Sam Colt persuaded his friend and sometimes business associate, Eli Whitney, Jr., to produce the revolvers at his factory in New Jersey. They made 1,100 in the first run — 1,000 for the U.S. Mounted Rifles, numbered by the company ('A' Co. 1 to 220, 'B' Co. 1 to 220, and so on) plus 100 "civilian" models. The 'E' Co. series went only 1 to 120. This numbering system assumed that they were then issued to one formal military unit when they were shipped in several lots and distributed among different units.

The military sent a pair of civilian Walkers to Captain Walker, who was carrying them when Mexicans killed him at the Battle of Huamantla in 1847.

The massive Walker Colts made an immediate impact, not only on the

Mexicans but on the military thinkers in Washington. Until 1855, the United States Army did not have cavalry as we think of it today, for the same reasons the early Texans found it challenging to combat the mounted Comanches. Muzzleloading rifles and the old single-shot percussion horse pistols were not ideal for mounted combat. The cavalry in Europe carried lances and sabers, but lances and sabers were not especially useful against Comanche bows and quivers full of arrows. Such mounted units as the army possessed were dragoons (mounted infantry), who moved on horseback but usually fought, as infantry, on foot.

Once the military saw how (now Col.) Jack Hays and his men performed on horseback, first with the Patersons and then the Walkers, they became convinced. Sam Colt was on his way to fame and fortune, with orders pouring in, both military and civilian. The U.S. Army began forming the mounted units that would be the spearhead of military efforts in the American West for the next 50 years. The U.S. Cavalry, as we know it, was born.

The Walker Colts were not perfect by any means. Their weight and size limited them, practically speaking, to the traditional role of horse pistols, carried in holsters attached to the pommel. The means of fastening the Walker's innovative loading rod in place under the barrel was weak, and heavy recoil could snap it down, tying up the cylinder. The cylinders themselves proved to be weak, and many disintegrated when soldiers stuffed too much powder into them. The military supplied soldiers with bullet molds for cylindrical bullets; these were easier to load upside down, but this reportedly caused excessive pressures and more damaged cylinders.

Despite this, the soldiers liked them. Many did not turn them back in when they were disbanded, using them on the frontier and right through the Civil War. Samuel Colt noted the gun's weaknesses, set out to improve them, and produced the subsequent models — first the Transitional Walker, then the first-, second-, and third-model dragoons. He built a factory with the latest machinery in Hartford, Connecticut, and in 1849 began producing the pocket pistol bearing that designation which became his best-selling percussion revolver of all time. The almost equally popular 1851 Navy followed it.

Colt's Patent Firearms Manufacturing Company became a cornerstone of America's industrial transformation, using machinery and innovative mass-production methods. Colt himself became one of the wealthiest men in the country. Some insist that the basis for these developments properly belongs to the Patersons used at Walker's Creek. But, while they were undoubtedly the catalyst, it was the Walker that brought it all together.

Samuel Colt was a marketing and industrial genius. You could argue that he was the founder of modern marketing techniques, and his favorite method was to make up special guns, superbly engraved, as presentation pieces for influ-

Colt Walkers had their serial numbers stamped on all major parts. Pictured is 'E' Company No. 120, auctioned by Rock Island Auction Company in 2019. It was the last original military Walker that Colt manufactured. Photo: Rock Island Auction Company

ential people. He also established a collection of his revolvers, the cornerstone of what became a minor industry in itself: The collecting of Colts.

Since 1847, the Colt Walker has had a checkered and controversial history. Of the original 1,100 military and civilian guns, roughly 237 are known to have survived. The number changes because collectors have not accounted for all the missing ones. When collectors make a discovery, experts scrutinize it closely. That's because, as Walkers climbed in value, so did the incidence of counterfeiting. Philip Schreier, the Senior Curator at the NRA's National Firearms Museum, told me that counterfeiting Walkers became at one time, "practically a cottage industry."

"A list compiled in the 1930s and '40s came up with a total of about 125 genuine Walkers," he said. "Since then, the Internet and further research have revealed more."

Over the years, Walker owners replaced many parts on the surviving guns, and it's rare to find one that displays anything like conventional "collector" condition. In a way, this makes counterfeiting easier, but in another, more complex. It's relatively easy to produce something in "new" condition, but something that looks legitimately aged is trickier. Because of the distinctive numbering used on the 1,000 military revolvers, you

can track the survivors like thoroughbred stallions: what they lack in condition (one of the three pillars of collector value) they make up in provenance, and there is no question whatever about the historical association.

Of the genuine Walkers extant, six are particularly noteworthy — five from the 100 "civilians" and one military.

In 1847, Sam Colt sent a unique pair of civilian models with consecutive numbers to Samuel Walker, who was fighting in Mexico. Captain Walker was carrying them when Mexicans killed him, and supposedly, someone returned one of the guns (#1019) to Colt at Walker's request. It went into the Colt collection, eventually donated to the Wadsworth Atheneum in Hartford, where it resides. It was later joined by Walker #1020.

But were these Captain Walker's pair? Another pair with consecutive numbers later came to light — 1009 and 1010 — that the Walker family possessed for almost a century. Since there are some unresolved questions about the ones in the Wadsworth Atheneum, there are those, including Schreier, one of the country's acknowledged Walker experts, who believe 1009/1010 to be the genuine pair. A few years ago, these were sold privately to Bill Koch, a wealthy collector.

The price he paid in the private sale was between four- and five-million dollars.

Another famous Walker is a civilian, cased with almost all original accouterments, known to *aficionados* as the "Danish sea captain." In (probably) late 1847, Captain Niels Hanson went into the shop of Blunt & Syms, a New York gunmaker and dealer that produced the Walker prototype for Colt. He bought Walker #1022 and took it back to Denmark. In 1940, when the Germans occupied the country and seized firearms, the pistol's owner buried it in a garden. It was recovered in 1945 and returned to the U.S., in 1951, by Ray Riling of Ray Riling Arms Books. It eventually ended up in the collection of Robert M. Lee.

In 2018, after Bob Lee's death, Rock Island Auction Company consigned the gun for auction, where it brought an eye-watering $1,840,000. It's believed to be the most expensive gun ever sold at auction.

The notable military revolver is 'E' Co. 120, the last one made, which ended up in the collection of Colt historian R.L. Wilson. Rock Island sold it in 2019 for $1,035,000.

Kevin Hogan, CEO of Rock Island Auction Company, told me that being the auctioneer in such a situation is frightening and exhilarating.

"As an auctioneer, my ambition was always to sell a gun for a million dollars," he said. "For the first 20 years, I never had the opportunity, but I've now sold two, and both for more than a million.

"We knew the Danish sea captain had the potential. Of course, when the bidding is hovering around a million, you get nervous. The electricity in the hall was a hundred percent. Exhilarating? Absolutely!"

Hogan added that selling such a gun makes you a part of its history. "When it sells a century from now, we will be in the provenance."

Kevin Hogan is himself, a gun collector. He bought his first gun, an early Smith & Wesson, at an auction when he was six years old, and 19th-Century American guns remain his passion. He says Colt and Winchester have always been "the blue chips of gun collecting. I rank them equally."

Even in that rarified world, however, the Walker Colt occupies a unique niche. Hogan: "You have to have a Walker in order to put together a really fine 19th-Century collection. There are only a few, and very few of those are in great condition, so you look at original parts more than condition. Cylinder scene? Serial numbers matching? If there is any blue left on the barrel at all, you're looking at one of the top ten Walkers.

"And each Walker is different. Each one tells a different story."

***

The Walker exerted a spell on more than collectors. Anything billed as "most

Walker cylinders had a roll-engraved depiction of the Battle of Walker's Creek to honor the original engagement that led to the Colt Walker and the revival of Samuel Colt's fortunes. Photo: Rock Island Auction Company

powerful" is bound to attract attention, and until the advent of the .357 Magnum in 1935, the Walker was the most powerful American repeating handgun ever made. It fired a .454-diameter ball, weighing 140 grains, ahead of up to 60 grains of blackpowder, from a 9-inch barrel, and delivered muzzle energy of around 400 foot-pounds.

Although the later Dragoons were modifications of the Walker, they were all slightly smaller, lighter, and less powerful. Colt solved the problem of brittle cylinders in 1860 when it adopted the new "silver steel" alloy that allowed its revolvers to be smaller still, yet strong enough to withstand high pressures.

Naturally, in the 1950s, when interest began to develop in making replicas or reproductions of early percussion revolvers, the Walker was near the top of the list. However, producing an authentic replica Walker presented its difficulties, not least of which was getting an original Walker to duplicate.

In 1971, Colt Industries embarked on its Blackpowder Program, making reproductions of old models that would be genuine Colts. The nomenclature became an issue. After all, they were Colts, so they were not "reproductions." Most settled on calling them "continuations" or, later, Second Generation. The first one Colt produced was the 1851 Navy.

In 1980, Colt brought out the Walker, with serial numbers starting at 1200 — logical given that the originals ended at 1100. A year later, a second run began at

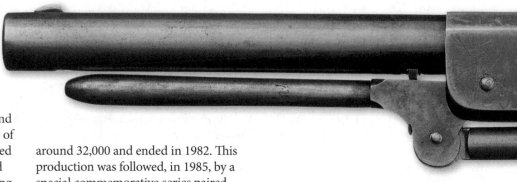

around 32,000 and ended in 1982. This production was followed, in 1985, by a special commemorative series paired with R.L. Wilson's newly published *The Colt Heritage,* with fitted presentation cases and matching numbers. There was a third-generation in 1994 and, finally, in 1997, a 150th-anniversary series.

Many companies, mostly in Italy, got into the reproduction business during this period, including such familiar names as Uberti and Armi San

Marco. Having completed its run of reproductions, continuations, and second and third generations, Colt spun off a company to continue on its own. The Colt guns had the advantage of being genuine Colts and have since become collector's items in themselves.

Colt designed some undisclosed minor details in its new guns to head

Cimarron makes its guns in Italy. With the 200th anniversary of the Texas Rangers approaching — 2023, more or less — Cimarron produced a series of 1,000 guns, aged to look original and numbered like the first thousand that went to the U.S. Army — 'A' Co. 1-220, and so on. The guns could be had with appropriate accouterments in a fitted case, not unlike the one housing the Danish sea captain. The series sold out quickly.

The Walker's impact extended beyond the military, the industrial, and the technology of firearms to have serious financial fallout. As Colt historian, Larry Wilson put it, "The Walker gave Samuel Colt the keys to the mint." Almost two centuries later, it is still generating dollars — *big* dollars.

***

As for the Battle of Walker's Creek, collectors don't mention it in the same breath as Gettysburg or Midway. For all the study and research that historians have devoted to the Walker Colt over the years, they are still hazy about locating Walker's Creek.

Among the irregular spider web of creeks around Sisterdale, some flowing into the Guadalupe, others running into other streams that flow into it, none is "Walker's Creek" nor has been for many years.

In 2020, a Texas historical society announced it would erect a plaque on the battle site — or what they believe is the site — but expects it will take until 2024 before it is sure enough to name a location. All the society is confident of right now is that it will be somewhere near Sisterdale. An odd fate, indeed, for one of the most significant battles in history. **GD**

A Colt Walker, 'E' Company No. 120 in remarkably good condition. Of the original 1,100 military and civilian revolvers, collectors believe only 237 have survived; of those, very few have all original parts due to cylinders bursting, parts breaking and replacing them, and general hard usage. It is evident from this photograph how closely Cimarron's "Texas Rangers" series resembles the originals. This Walker sold for $1,035,000 at Rock Island in 2019. Photo: Rock Island Auction Company

off any attempt by the unscrupulous to pass them off as originals. This modification would allow experts such as Larry Wilson to recognize a counterfeit immediately. It was one more move in the endless chess game among collectors, dealers, counterfeiters, and consultants to big-money buyers.

The "continuation" Walkers received a warm reception from the many Colt enthusiasts who wanted the experience of owning and shooting a Walker but could never hope to own an original. Today, the sum usually mentioned, when anyone suggests he wants a Walker, is $100,000 and up, and that's for an average specimen.

Cimarron Arms of Fredericksburg, Texas, introduced one of the most interesting of the Walker reproductions.

HANDGUNS AND BEAR PROTECTION: A Master Guide's Opinion

Will a 9mm handgun stop a charging grizzly? The author found out the hard way.

❯ PHIL SHOEMAKER

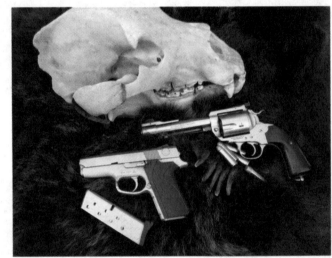

Immensely powerful handguns like this .475 Linebaugh are preferred for hunting but sacrifice portability and multiple rapid hits for self-protection.

Few animals on Earth excite our primitive emotions more than grizzly bears. Today, people with opinions and an Internet connection who have never laid eyes on a bear in real life will argue for hours about the best protection methods from them. As is usual with these soaring, pontificating arguments, they generate more heat than light and seldom touch down on the solid ground of experience or verifiable facts.

Nearly two decades ago, a pair of articles appeared in the March 2003 issue of *Handloader* magazine by men whom I know and respect for their depth and variety of knowledge about firearms. Both addressed the value of handguns for bear protection. The first was by Editor Dave Scovill, a lifelong historian, reloader, and technical guru on single-action Colt minutia. The other was Idaho rancher, hunter, and longtime gun scribe Brian Pearce, likely the most learned and skilled handloader and *pistolero* in the nation.

Brian's feature described the ballistics attributes and performance of various large-caliber handguns and his long and extensive experience using them while hunting massive animals. Dave pointed out that there are few situations where people need a firearm, and even if they have one, they were not likely to be effective using it.

Photo by slowmotiongli

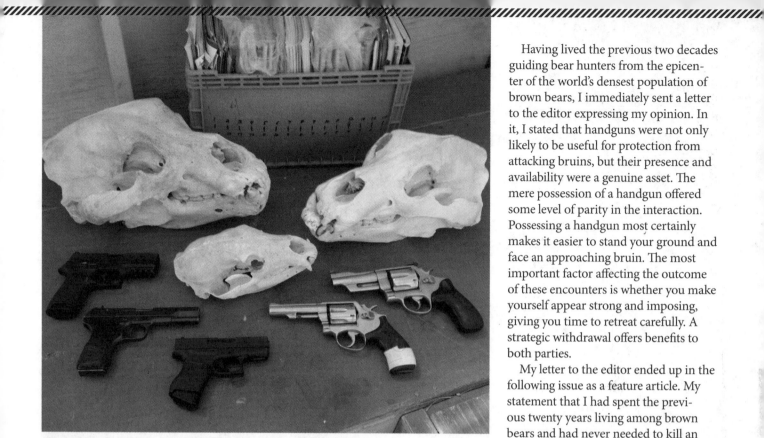

Brown, grizzly, and black bear skulls in front of the author's homemade bullet trap. Some handguns he tested include the Sig 250 9mm, .30-cal. Tokarev, 9mm Glock, and .357 and .44 Magnum Smith & Wesson revolvers.

Having lived the previous two decades guiding bear hunters from the epicenter of the world's densest population of brown bears, I immediately sent a letter to the editor expressing my opinion. In it, I stated that handguns were not only likely to be useful for protection from attacking bruins, but their presence and availability were a genuine asset. The mere possession of a handgun offered some level of parity in the interaction. Possessing a handgun most certainly makes it easier to stand your ground and face an approaching bruin. The most important factor affecting the outcome of these encounters is whether you make yourself appear strong and imposing, giving you time to retreat carefully. A strategic withdrawal offers benefits to both parties.

My letter to the editor ended up in the following issue as a feature article. My statement that I had spent the previous twenty years living among brown bears and had never needed to kill an unwounded one was not offered as proof that handguns were unnecessary. It would be another twenty years and many hundreds of close bear encounters later before I would have to put one to the test.

THE FATEFUL DAY

Strong winds are a common occurrence on the Alaska Peninsula any time of year. One summer, during our fishing season, the sound of increasing winds awakened me in the early morning hours. I rolled out of bed and stumbled out into the dark to turn the airplanes into the wind. I suspected we might need to reassess our morning fishing plans. A few hours later, Larry, a guest from many previous visits, arrived in the kitchen. His expert assistance in helping dispose of remaining slices of sweet potato pie from the evening's dinner is always appreciated. By the time we were finishing our last cup of coffee, his wife and two teenage daughters were drifting into the kitchen.

During the night, the winds had continually picked up to near gale strength and the possibility of flying that morning was not a reasonable option. As this was the second visit from the Walker family, we used the morning hiatus to catch up on the previous year's events. By mid-af-

The author shows where the charging bear first appeared when it lunged toward Larry and his wife.

ternoon, the winds had moderated. I was confident we could safely make a short flight to one of the closer creeks. The two daughters, Leah and Lynn, had by then become engrossed in some project and chose to remain in camp with my wife and daughter while Larry and his wife Nadine decided to fish. We looked forward to a couple of productive hours on the stream, gathered up rods, and loaded them into the plane.

Soon we arrived and landed on a short cinder bed. I taxied in close behind a protective patch of alders and tied down both wings of the plane. After removing daypacks and rods from the baggage compartment, I reached in to grab my favorite old Smith & Wesson M-629 .44 Magnum Mountain Gun that resides in the tail of the plane during fishing season. Lying alongside it was my double-action semi-automatic Smith & Wesson M-3953 9mm. The previous week, I had been testing some new 147-grain Buffalo Bore +P "Outdoorsman" 9mm ammunition that Tim Sundles, owner of Buffalo Bore ammunition, had sent for my opinion. He wanted to market it as viable defensive ammunition for owners of 9mm handguns who did not wish to purchase a larger gun.

After a few days of comparing the 9mm Buffalo Bore ammo's performance to my other loads, I concluded that it would likely work if necessary. Penetration-wise (in stacks of dry and wet magazines), it was not significantly different than a .30 Tokarev (86-gr. FMJ at 1,460fps) like I had used in Vietnam, my 4-inch-barrel .357 (180-gr HC at 1,400 fps), or .44 Magnum (Speer 240-gr. FMJ 1,250 fps and 270-gr. HC at 1,130 fps) revolvers.

Having spent most of my life guiding bear hunters and living surrounded by the densest population of brown bears in the world, I was under no illusion that any handgun cartridge would qualify as a "bear-stopping" round. Their primary value is more akin to a life preserver on a boat or a fire extinguisher in a home.

As I contemplated the weight difference and slimness between my familiar .44 Smith & Wesson Mountain Gun and the 9mm semi-auto, I decided to wear the 9mm in a thin, leather paddle holster.

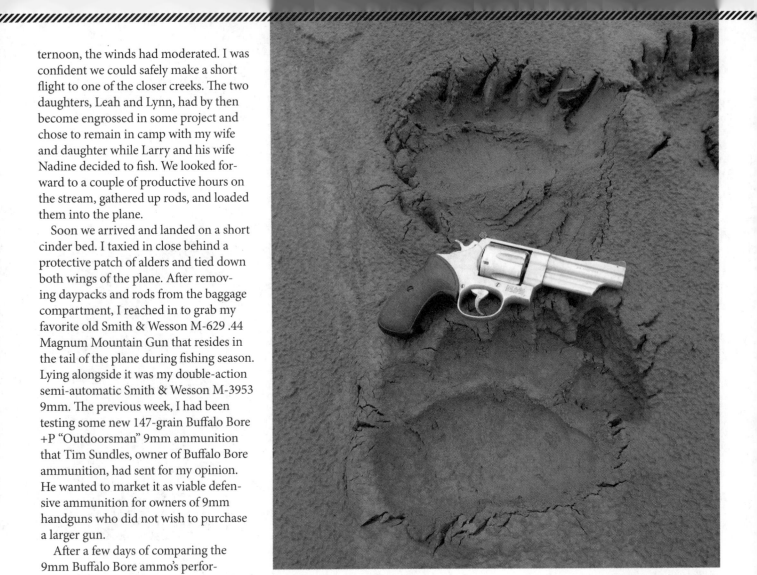

The author's S&W 629 .44 Magnum Mountain Gun compared to large bear tracks.

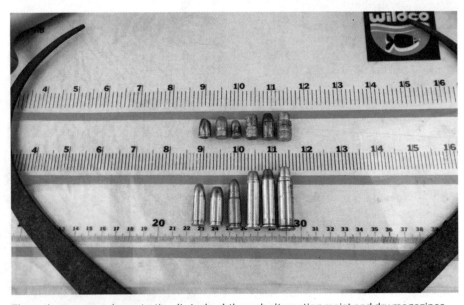

The author compared penetration (in inches) through alternating moist and dry magazines. The loads he tested included 9mm ball, 9mm Buffalo Bore 147-gr. Outdoorsman, military .30 Tokarev, .357 180-gr. Buffalo Bore Outdoorsman, handloaded 180-gr. .357 Magnum Sierra FPJ match, and .44 magnum 265-gr. Keith bullets.

Close encounters with brown bears during Alaska's salmon run are everyday events. Like many large males, this one was not paying attention.

It was only going to be a short day of fishing anyway. It was the first time I strapped on anything other than that .44 for the past 18 years. (Before that, I had worn a Smith & Wesson stainless M65 .357 but had given it to my daughter Tia when she turned 16. She has carried it ever since.)

It was a short 400-yard walk to the creek. Most of the distance was along an overgrown, meandering river channel. The wind was in our faces, so I tried to keep up a light banter with Larry and Nadine in the hopes we did not inadvertently bump into a bruin. They followed 10 to 15 feet behind. We approached the creek by descending into the tall grass and brush alongside the main channel.

Suddenly, a close, heavy huffing sound in the brush just off our right side brought us to a stop. My handgun always rides close behind my right hip and was in my hand immediately. From the low tenor and heavy crashing, I assumed we

The Walker family is enjoying a family stroll on a nearby stream during a previous visit. Bears are a constant presence along streams during salmon runs. This sow with two cubs was doing its best to avoid humans.

were dealing with a large boar. I could hear it moving in our direction, so I hollered to let it know we were human. It paused for a few long seconds, and then we could hear it crashing away back toward the creek. I looked back to check on Larry and Nadine and re-holstered my pistol. We were beginning to move again when our world switched into a slow-motion horror film.

From the dense brush behind and

downwind of us, I heard the heavy, deep grunts of an angry bear crashing directly toward us. It had circled to get our scent and, rather than running away, decided to deal with us.

We were standing in a narrow corridor of chest-high grass bracketed by dense thickets of willow and alders. The bear had us pinpointed, was coming at full speed, and would be within 10 or 12 feet of us before we would even be able to see

it. I remember consciously thinking that even with my .458 Winchester Magnum, which I desperately wished I had in my hands, we were in a terrible position. The best I could hope for would be getting off a single shot, and it would be close and would need to be quick.

I focused on the edge line of the pucker brush a dozen feet from my position. However, the tall grass concealed the charge more than I anticipated. I saw a quick flash of movement in the grass before a large, animated, and highly agitated boar appeared where Larry and Nadine had been standing. From my position just feet away, I could see the bruin seemed to be confused. It was stressed, drooling profusely, and rapidly swinging its head from side to side, searching for its opponent.

Two primary thoughts were going through my mind: The first was, where were Larry and Nadine? Whatever happened, I was aware that I needed to make sure of their position. I did not want a bullet passing through the bear and hitting them. The second thought was that the bear appeared confused, and I hoped that perhaps it would turn and run. I have seen that happen before when an

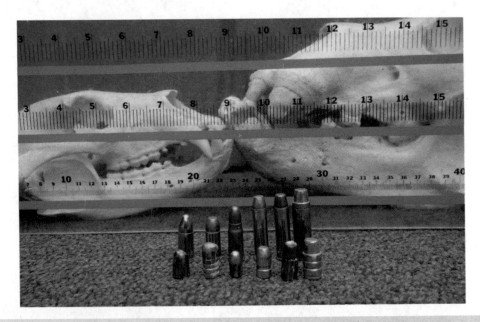

A sow with cubs fishing alongside a fly fisherman. This bear was not charging, as its ears are up, indicating an intent to catch fish.

aggressive bear realizes there are multiple people. But the realization that an adult boar had retreated, then circled downwind to get our scent, decided to attack, and was now likely standing over my friends, left me no choice.

Assuming that Larry and Nadine were laying close to where I had last seen them and were likely under the bear, I placed the first shot directly behind the bear's shoulder — it roared and spun to bite at the wound! I paused momentarily to assess its reaction. As it swung its head back, I placed a second shot close behind the first. The bear reacted the same by roaring and twisting to bite at the wound. At each hit, it moved a step closer to me. The following two shots elicited the same response, but I could see the bear was tiring of this game and looking for a way out. It turned away as I fired the fifth shot, and it bolted away back toward the creek. I vividly remember aiming for the root of its tail for the next shot, just as I have done on numerous escaping bears wounded by clients. As I pulled the trigger, I thought, "It is leaving, and there is no need to shoot again." I saw the bear go down about 20 yards away.

Larry and Nadine popped up out of the grass right where I had seen them last. Both appeared shaken but unharmed. Their reaction had been perfect. When they saw the bear coming, they grabbed each other and fell back into the tall grass. They also succumbed to tachypsychia, where time appears to slow down. They said the bear was close enough to have bitten them when they were on the ground and that they had heard my first warning shot before I began shooting in earnest. I doubt there was more than a second between my first and remaining shots.

Realizing they were unharmed, I turned my attention back to the bear. I saw it lying in an old overgrown channel but could also tell it was still moving and breathing. Reverting to four decades of old habits, I walked over and ended its misery. I double-checked my pistol and noticed I had but a single round remaining in the chamber. I decided not to walk up to a wounded brown bear with a single shot in a 9mm handgun.

The Alaskan brown bear that the author stopped mid-charge with a 9mm handgun and Buffalo Bore hardcast bullets. Rapid shots overcame the 9mm's lack of kinetic energy.

Nadine asked if we were still going fishing and, being the hospitable guide, I answered yes if they wanted. However, she expressed that she had lost interest in fishing, so we turned around and returned to camp.

My daughter Tia met us at the aircraft and recognized something was wrong. Her face reflected the seriousness of the situation when I told her we had a DLP — the acronym used by Alaska to kill an animal in defense of life or property. Having faced multiple bear charges herself and assisting another experienced guide after a nighttime DLP, she understood the implications fully.

As Larry and Nadine removed their fishing gear, Tia contacted our local Fish & Wildlife officer and local biologist to report the incident. At the same time, I grabbed a camera, a large backpack, assorted skinning knives, and my .458. Nadine, of course, was only too happy to remain in camp, but Larry wanted to do all he could to assist Tia and me to skin the bear.

Once we arrived back at the carcass, Tia used the camera to document the event while Larry and I moved to positions showing exactly where and how the story had unfolded. The three of us then removed the bear's hide, with claws intact, and the skull to turn into Fish & Game as the law requires. Besides inspecting the placement and extent of the bullet wounds on the bear, which we estimated to be a 9- or 10-year-old boar, we noticed the bear had multiple recent facial and neck wounds.

During the entire time, we could hear splashing from what sounded like another large bear, maybe 25 yards away, chasing salmon in the creek. We speculated that the bear we were skinning had, likely, recently fought over a favorite fishing hole, was napping, nursing its wounds, and when we disturbed it, it decided no one was not going to push it away again.

Back in camp, Larry, Nadine, and I filled out the required paperwork, including our statements. As we were not planning to fly to town until the end of the week, Tia and I salted the hide to preserve it the following morning. We flew into King Salmon the next week to turn the hide and skull over to Fish & Game. The first question the officer asked was to inquire about the ammo I had used. He said it was a common occurrence for state troopers to dispatch moose injured in highway accidents. Their currently issued .40-caliber handguns were not as effective as the .357 revolvers they had previously carried.

Both Tia and my wife asked what had ever possessed me to choose the 9mm over my .44. I could tell my explanation was not particularly compelling, so we all walked to our shooting range at my insistence. I placed half a dozen small scraps of 2x2 and 2x4 lumber on the ground in front of us.

I explained they were to shoot as many of them as possible, as quickly as possible, and only hits count.

In turn, they each fired six shots with my 9mm, followed by Tia's .357 with heavy loads, then my .44 Magnum Mountain Gun with heavy loads, and finally my son's Hamilton Bowen .475 Linebaugh. As the size, power, recoil, and muzzle blast of the handguns increased, so did their stress levels, and the hits came slower and less frequently. It quickly became evident that more power did not necessarily equal better performance.

WHAT IS THE BEST BEAR STOPPER?

There is little doubt that powerful, large-bore handguns can be effective and capable hunting tools. A few years previously, Tia had guided handgun hunter Darrel Harper on a fall brown bear hunt. Darrel used a .500 S&W revolver and, with a single, well-placed shot, had killed a massive boar with the finality of a rifle. But carefully stalking close and placing a single shot from a powerful handgun on an unwary game animal is not the same as using a side-arm for self-defense. There is, of course, no substitute for accuracy. But in a life-threatening self-defense scenario where time is of the essence, your adrenalin levels spike, reducing your fine motor skills. That is something for which the ability to make rapid, multiple shots can compensate.

Experience and practice will improve your performance, but everyone has limits. I like to use the late, legendary Bill Jordan as an example. I met him when he gave an impressive exhibition for my college pistol team. He had been a Marine Corps officer in World War II and retired after 30 years as a U.S. Border Patrol Agent and combat shooting instructor. He is considered one of the fastest and deadliest gunfighters in history. Towering over six and a half feet tall, Bill was an imposing figure who looked as if he should be able to handle any handgun. In his book, *No Second Place Winner*, he explains that the big magnums were better killers, but an involuntary reaction to recoil and noise impeded rapid shooting. His choice of calibers for making fast hits was the .357 Magnum revolver with lightweight bullets.

People often ask me if I now recommend the 9mm for protection from bears. My response is always the same: I ask what they own and what is most familiar and comfortable? Choosing the handgun with which you are comfortable and competent can be important to a hunter, but it is imperative for self-defense. GD

FIVE BUDGET
Long-Range
Rifle Rigs

> **THOMAS GOMEZ**

From a practical standpoint, learning the fundamentals of long-range shooting will make you an all-around better marksman — even if you don't want to spend your weekends shooting a National Rifle League Match or an F-class competition. A general knowledge level, where you can consistently hit targets at 1,000 yards, means attaining a solid grasp of optics, external ballistics, body position, trigger control, and ancillary gear like ballistics engines, chronographs, and anemometers (wind meters). Traditional hunting ranges, typically 400 yards and in, will begin to seem like a chip shot for sharpshooters with these skills. This proficiency leads to increased harvest for the hunter and more precise shots on game, which leads to more humane kills.

Before a prospective hunter or marksman even purchases or fires a rifle, consider a beginner long-range course. Increased familiarity with and understanding of gear from the beginning allows you to select a system optimized for how you will use it and prevents spending money twice to correct an uninformed purchase.

Long-range shooting used to be expensive. Accurate rifles, usually match-grade .308 Winchester or .300 Winchester Magnum, would cost north of $1,500 and require at least another $1,000 for a riflescope. Ballistics calculators were neither refined nor accessible, and if you wanted to push the distance, you had to handload your ammunition. With the increased interest in long-range shooting, there are now scores of good factory rifles and scopes available within the financial reach of most shooters. Affordable, match-grade hunting and precision rifle ammunition is now widely available, as are reloading components if you want to tune a load to your barrel and squeeze out that last bit of accuracy.

This article will look at five different budget rifle builds suitable for long-range shooting. Each build includes scope recommendations and some meaningful upgrades should you customize the gun in the future. With the proper optic and ammunition, these rifles can hit a 66 percent IPSC target, 20 inches tall and 12 inches wide, at 1,000 yards. Some consider these guns hybrid rifles, meaning that they will work for both hunting and long-range shooting. They base this distinction mainly on weight. The builds will increase in price as we go through the article. The higher-end builds might be more reliable in the long run or have a few more bells and whistles, but everything recommended will get the job done. I have owned or tested all the rifles in this article at some point.

CALIBER SELECTION

Before we discuss individual rifles, let's talk about ammunition and caliber selection. For each build, I recommend the 6.5 Creedmoor round. I have personally never seen a factory 6.5 Creedmoor rifle that was not accurate with factory ammunition. Hornady made the 6.5 Creedmoor for a high hit percentage at 1,000 yards and, once adopted by the shooting community, permitted a lot of people to join the "1,000-Yard Club" quickly. Ammo makers have released other "super calibers" like the 6.5 PRC, but they met a lukewarm response from the market. Love it or hate it, the 6.5 Creedmoor is here to stay, especially with adoption by the U.S. Special Operations Command and Department of Homeland Security.

From the standpoint of external and terminal ballistics, the 6.5 Creedmoor outperforms factory .308 Winchester. Any game animal that you can kill with

The last 15 years have witnessed an explosion in long-range shooting. Precision rifle competitions like PRS and NRL, and F-Class have driven the firearms Industry to offer match-accurate rifles and ammunition to meet these disciplines' demands.

Mossberg Patriot Predator. The author shot this rifle to 1,800 yards with Hornady 147-grain ELDMs. On a 24-inch steel target, he had a 40-percent hit ratio.

a .308 Winchester will fall to the 6.5 Creedmoor. The caliber is not expensive to shoot, is easy to handload, and companies like Hornady offer the ammunition in bulk.

MOSSBERG PATRIOT PREDATOR

The Mossberg Patriot Predator is an inexpensive rifle with a traditional form factor. The lightweight rifle features an adjustable trigger and threaded barrel. The ones I have shot were capable of sub-MOA accuracy with factory ammunition. Recoil was not bad, but you could mitigate it further with a muzzle brake or suppressor. If you intend to shoot a lot in the prone, plan on building up the comb height with a riser or foam and tape, or look at the Mossberg Patriot LR Hunter.

The only component that you may need to replace is the scope base. Mine kept coming loose, and I eventually swapped it out with the 20 MOA base from Evolution Gun Works.

For an optic, I recommend the Genesis 4-14 FFP from Blackhound Optics. These rugged scopes retail for around $300 and are available in Milliradians (MILs) and Minute of Angle (MOA) options. They have enough mechanical adjustment to get to 1,000 yards if you want to dial for a long-range shot. And, they feature a reticle with hash marks if you hold for elevation.

Want to customize in the future? Drop the Mossberg Patriot Predator into an Oryx chassis or composite wood stock from Boyds. I have used both, and they are fantastic. The Mossberg Patriot Predator is light enough for a backcountry hunt but is more than capable of getting consistent hits at long range. This model is a great all-around rifle that you can set up for around $700.

RUGER AMERICAN

Ruger offers two inexpensive models perfect for pushing a 6.5 Creedmoor round out to great distances: The Ruger American Predator and the Ruger Amer-

The author's father with a semi-custom Ruger American. This rifle has a Blackhound Genesis 6-24 riflescope and a Boyds Pro Varmint laminate stock.

Remington 700 SPS AAC.
Photo: Remington Arms

Ruger American Rifle Hunter.
Photo: Sturm, Ruger & Co., Inc.

A Boyds Pro-Varmint laminate stock is an excellent upgrade to the Mossberg Patriot Predator.

ican Rifle Hunter. The Ruger American Predator has a traditional style, synthetic stock that feeds from an AICS-style magazine, Ruger's Marksman Adjustable Trigger, and a threaded muzzle. Like the Mossberg Patriot Predator, it is a hybrid suited for long-range work and mountain hunting. Consider raising the comb if you intend to shoot a lot in the prone.

If you want a rifle to chase animals around the woods and prairie and still train on 1,000-yard targets, the Ruger American Predator is great. If you purchase this model and want to upgrade slowly, consider a muzzle brake and a stock or chassis system. Magpul, Modular Driven Technologies, and Boyds make excellent aftermarket stocks for the short-action Ruger American series. You can purchase the Ruger American Predator for around $470. When you pair the rifle with a Blackhound 4-14 Genesis scope, the setup will set you back $770.

If you want an affordable, dedicated precision rifle, get the Ruger American Rifle Hunter, which retails for around $700. It features a slightly heavier barrel than the Predator, a muzzle brake, and a Magpul Hunter stock. It's perfect as a tough, simple, dedicated long-range rifle. However, although fine for hunting, I am

Remington 700 SPS AAC attached to an MDT LSS-XL Gen 2 rifle chassis.

not sure I would carry it for a backpacking hunt in the Rockies, where I anticipate walking 10+ miles a day. If your hunt will not entail strenuous hiking, the Ruger American Rifle Hunter would work well, granted you have a good pack or sturdy sling with which to carry it. Pair it with a Blackhound Genesis 6-24 scope, and you'll have a complete rifle setup for about $1,000 — that's a buck a yard!

REMINGTON 700 SPS TACTICAL AAC

The Remington 700 family is where a lot of shooters started their long-range journey. A great and inexpensive rifle is

Remington 700 SPS AAC attached to The Legend from MC3. Awesome stock system.

the Remington 700 SPS Tactical AAC. It features a heavy 22-inch threaded barrel and Remington's adjustable X-Mark trigger. You'll need to purchase a scope base separately, and I recommend a 20 MOA MIL-STD-1913 Picatinny rail from Evolution Gun Works or Modular Driven Technologies. With factory ammunition, the Remington 700 SPS Tactical AAC is capable of sub-MOA accuracy. The rifle comes with a Hogue Overmolded stock, which is okay. Most people eventually upgrade the stock, although the rifles I have shot were insanely accurate right out of the box. A threaded muzzle allows you to affix brakes and suppressors. Because it is a Remington 700, there is an entire aftermarket of accessories such as triggers, barrels, stocks, bolts, and generations of

gunsmiths familiar with the platform. A Remington SPS Tactical AAC will cost around $700.

Want to customize the rifle? The first thing I would do is ditch the Hogue stock for a chassis from Modular Driven Technologies (MDT) or Kinetic Research Group (KRG). Both companies offer premium chassis systems at multiple price points. A chassis from either company allows for length-of-pull and comb height adjustments, along with better attachment points for ancillary gear such as tripods, bipods, and slings. If you want a traditional rifle stock, The Legend from MC3 is hard to beat.

I would pair this rifle with a Blackhound Genesis 6-24 FFP riflescope. Since the Rem 700 is a dedicated long-range setup, the more magnification, the better, especially when pushing past 700 yards. A Remington SPS

Tactical AAC, MDT scope base, and Blackhound Genesis 6-24 FFP scope would cost around $1,200.

When I wrote this article, Remington was going through bankruptcy and sold its various business components. Remington 700 rifles are still available online. When the dust settles, Remington will undoubtedly continue producing the 700 series. If you can find a used Remington 700 SPS AAC with a low round count, buy it, learn the fundamentals, and slowly upgrade as you gain experience. The Model 700 is an incredible platform and one of my personal favorites.

HOWA 1500 BARRELED ACTION WITH MDT CHASSIS

This next build starts as a series of components but ultimately leads to one of the most capable precision rifles at any price point. The build consists of a Howa 1500 Threaded Heavy Barrel Action, a Modular Driven Technologies chassis,

The author's primary training and testing rifle. He set this rifle up for shooting to one mile. It's not exactly a budget build but demonstrates the versatility of the Howa 1500 Heavy Barreled action.

A pair of Howa 1500 barreled actions attached to the ACC chassis system from Modular Driven Technologies. Note the Tract TORIC UHD riflescopes.

and a Tract Optics riflescope. In 2014, Howa started selling barreled actions, consisting of barrel, action, bolt, trigger assembly, action screws, box magazines, and bottom metal. The only thing an end-user must do is purchase a stock and assemble the rifle. Around 2015, Howa released a heavy barreled action chambered in 6.5 Creedmoor. The current models feature a threaded muzzle for suppressors and brakes.

Several years ago, Howa sent me a barreled action for testing, which I mated to a Kinetic Research Group chassis. After bore sighting, I fired three rounds at the center of a paper target. Looking through my spotting scope, I failed to see a group, so I walked downrange to inspect the target. I was stunned to see three rounds through the same hole. When paired with an MDT chassis, Howa barreled actions have been my preferred platform for all my precision rifle work, specifically hunting, training, and testing. I built a small fleet of them for Quiet Professional Defense, for use in its Precision Rifle courses, and they are available for students as loaner rifles. I also

take one with me on my annual journey to Clarendon, Texas, for the Advanced Precision Rifle course taught by Accuracy 1st.

How do you build one of these excellent rifles? Go to Brownells.com and purchase a Howa 1500 Barreled Action chambered in 6.5 Creedmoor. Purchasing a barreled action is essentially buying a firearm since the receiver is a serialized component. After you receive that barreled action, head over to the Modular Driven Technologies website to pick out a chassis system. Suppose you want a more traditional design. Then consider the XRS chassis. If you want one for competition, look at the ACC. For a general chassis, the LSS XL Gen 2 and ESS are perfect. The Howa 1500 Barreled Action does not include a scope base, so you will need to purchase one. I recommend a

20 MOA MIL-STD-1913 Picatinny rail from Evolution Gun Works or Modular Driven Technologies. Once you get all the components, mate the barreled action to the chassis system.

To maximize this rifle system's performance, I recommend getting a Tract TORIC UHD PRS Long Range Rifle Scope. This premium optic costs around $1,300 and features excellent SCHOTT High Transmission glass and a Christmas tree-style reticle. These scopes are some of the best on the market and are perfect for long-range, competition, or general precision work. If this scope is out of your price range, consider the Blackhound Genesis 6-24 FFP. Depending on what chassis and scope you choose, the package will cost $1,400 on the low end to around $2,500 on the high end. You can't go wrong with this rifle setup, and I would put it up against any custom rifle.

TIKKA T3X COMPACT TACTICAL RIFLE (CTR)

The Tikka T3x CTR is perfect right out of the box. The trigger is fantastic, the ac-

Tikka T3x CTR. Perfect right out of the box. Photo: Beretta USA Corp.

tion is smooth, the gun can shoot three rounds through one ragged hole, and it comes equipped with a threaded muzzle and scope base. The CTR is heavy enough for legit precision rifle work, but you can also carry it through the mountains on a hunt. These rifles require little in the way of customizations. End users who want to upgrade will swap out the stock with something from KRG or MDT.

The Tikka T3x CTR is a premium rifle, and I would go with a premium optic like

Kestrel 5700 with Applied Ballistics and a rear bag from Accuracy 1st.

the Tract TORIC UHD PRS Long Range Rifle Scope. If the Tract TORIC UHD is out of your price range, there is nothing wrong with a Blackhound Genesis 6-24 FFP riflescope. The Tikka T3x CTR retails for around $1,000.

MISCELLANEOUS LONG-RANGE GEAR

Long-range shooting is a blending of knowledge, skill, and gear. Achieving first-round hits past 400 yards requires specific technology. We have covered rifles and scopes; let us look at some other equipment you will need to be successful at long-range shooting.

BIPOD AND REAR BAG

Long-range shooters spend a lot of time in the prone position. Prone is where you zero, confirm data, and if you are lucky, take shots on animals when hunting. There are two critical pieces of gear when learning to shoot in the prone position: a bipod and a rear bag. A bipod facilitates getting into the optimal position and allows you to "load" your weight into the bipod to increase consistency and mitigate recoil. A rear bag enables you to raise or lower the buttstock to find a natural point of aim and negates the blood flow in your support hand, which is enough to disturb your reticle. I own some premium bipods but still use the Harris HBRS for most of my shooting needs. For rear bags, my current go-to is the Rear Shooting Bag from S2 Delta.

RANGEFINDER

Over the last decade, laser rangefinders have dropped in price, putting them in reach of most hunters and long-range shooters. To get a firing solution, you feed

Blackhound Genesis 4-14 riflescope atop the author's goddaughter's rifle, which she used to shoot a cow elk at 446 yards clean through the heart. The gun is a Howa 1500 hunting profile barreled action chambered in 6.5 Creedmoor. The Hornady 143-grain ELD-X round passed clean through the elk and completely exited.

the target's range and other variables into a ballistics calculator. The calculator will tell you how many Minutes of Angle or Mils to hold or dial in order to compensate for bullet drop. You could use your reticle for ranging the target, but laser rangefinders are faster and more accurate.

A recent experience highlighted the need for a laser rangefinder. I was hunting deer in my native New Mexico and spied a buck on the canyon's opposite side. To my naked eye, the animal appeared to be 300 yards away. My rangefinder said 128 yards, so I quickly deployed my tripod, steadied my rifle, and harvested the animal with a clean shot. When I hiked up to the buck and looked at my firing position, it appeared to be a paltry 60 yards away. Lesson learned: don't trust your eye; trust your rangefinder. Excellent laser rangefinders are available from Nikon, Vortex, Sig, Bushnell, and Leupold.

BALLISTIC SOFTWARE

Ballistics software is vital to long-range shooting. In the "old days," you would zero your rifle, get a known distance, and walk rounds on target until you got hits. You would record every piece of data

you could and add them to a shooting journal. There is nothing wrong with such practice of data gathering, but it takes a long time. Ballistics calculators streamline the process. You build a gun profile that accounts for barrel twist, twist direction, sight height, caliber, caliber weight, velocity, ballistic coefficient, and zero data. You plug in real-time data, specifically distance, density altitude, temperature, and wind data, and the calculator gives you holds for windage and elevation.

You can download a ballistics solver to a smartphone. I recommend Applied Ballistics and Hornady 4DOF.

KESTRELS AND HANDHELD WEATHER STATIONS

How do you gather wind and atmospheric data at your position? You use a handheld weather station — known as an anemometer — like a Kestrel weather meter. Kestrel has a broad product line, from simple weather meters that tell you the wind speed and atmospheric data to units with ballistics software that run Hornady or Applied ballistics. If you are on a budget, consider the Kestrel 5000 Environmental Meter and pair it with a ballistics calculator on your smartphone.

For most long-range shooters and hunters, this works just fine and costs around $350. If you want a weather meter with an integrated ballistics solver, look at the Kestrel 5700 series. Depending on features, these models can run anywhere from $500 to $850.

BLACKHOUND OPTICS AND TRACT OPTICS

For these builds, I overwhelmingly chose Blackhound Optics and Tract Optics. These companies are committed to customer support and have customer service that is second to none.

Tract Optics sells premium scopes with a direct-to-consumer model, which removes dealers and passes the savings on to the consumer. I have Tract scopes mounted on both hunting rifles and class guns, and they work. If money were no object, I would still choose Tract riflescopes over many other premium brands.

Blackhound Optics started in May 2019. Born out of a 40-year-old OEM manufacturer, Blackhound makes affordable riflescopes that perform like optics twice their price range. I had the opportunity to torture-test a Blackhound riflescope when it first hit the market, and I was stunned at the quality. Tracking and parallax calibrated correctly. The reticle was practical and not cluttered, and the image remained clear through all levels of magnification. I have class rifles and hunting rifles that I've equipped with these optics.

CLOSING THOUGHTS

A decent precision rifle does not have to be expensive. Recently, my 11-year-old goddaughter hunted elk in the Valles Caldera National Preserve. I trained her in long-range shooting and built her a lightweight Howa 1500, chambered in 6.5 Creedmoor. I attached the barreled action to an old Kinetic Research Group chassis and mounted a Blackhound Genesis 4-14 riflescope. During training, she achieved first-round hits out to 650 yards prone or off a tripod. Ultimately, she harvested a cow elk at 446 yards with a perfect shot through the heart. Preparation and training with a good rifle will win the day. You do not have to spend a ton of money to be successful in long-range shooting. GD

Five Favored CUSTOM Rifles

❯ TOM TURPIN

Based upon the author's experience with the composite-stocked .280, he had this more traditionally styled rifle commissioned, also a .280 Remington.

The year 2020 was one hell of a ride. In addition to the political upheavals of a hotly contested presidential election, the pandemic that the Covid 19 virus inflicted on the planet has caused more havoc than any other natural event in my lifetime. It is doubtful any in recorded history has been worse. Among the many others, one of the casualties has been the wholesale cancellations of scheduled events, large and small, including the annual Firearms

Engravers Guild of America (FEGA) Exhibition in Las Vegas.

I have, for several years, relied on the kindness of my good friend, Master Engraver Sam Welch, to provide much of the photography and information that I needed to compile my annual *Gun Digest* section, Custom & Engraved Guns. Alas, the cancellation of the 2020 FEGA Expo forced a different approach.

Those readers familiar with my byline will not be surprised that the custom

gun bug has stricken me longer than most have been out of diapers. I commissioned my first custom about 60 years ago and have the components for one last custom rifle in my safe. I have a maker in mind, one whose work I've admired for a very long time, and we've discussed the project. However, at my advanced age, I've not yet decided to proceed. Time will tell. The only hint at this stage is that we'll base the project on a Ruger No. 1 if

The second or third custom that the author had made. Much of the work was done in Germany in the late 1960s. He did the stock finishing and checkering. It is a pre-64 Model 70 in .270.

Above and Below: The only custom Turpin had made with a composite stock, and his first rifle chambered for the .280 Remington cartridge.

In the meantime, I thought I'd do some serious thinking and make a decision on five favored custom rifles from the 25 or so that are in my safe. I'll add a little history on each that influenced the decisions. Deciding the all-time favorite was easy. However, selecting two through five was considerably more difficult. I did not try to rate the remaining four numerically. I'll identify my overall favorite and list the other four in no particular order.

One rifle I chose is somewhat unique for me in a few aspects. First, while I've owned several customs chambered for the .270 Winchester, this was the first rifle that I've owned chambered for the .270's first cousin, the .280 Remington. Secondly, it is the only synthetic-stocked rifle in my top five and the first custom I've commissioned that was not walnut stocked. It is also the only push feed action I can recall

using for a custom project.

I'd long had the urge for a rifle chambered for the .280. There was a new Heym SR-20 standard length action, as well as a hammer-forged 7mm barrel blank from the same maker, in my parts stash. I'm not a fan of push feed actions, but I've owned several factory rifles using such actions and can't recall ever having a problem with any caused by an action glitch. I also came up with a synthetic stock that McMillan had made for a planned new Heym SR-20 model. I added it to the parts stash. (I was a consultant to Heym at the time, making parts a bit easier to come by.) I gave all the components to my pal Glenn Pierce, an Arizona riflesmith and talented rifle marksman.

Glenn tweaked the action, honing and polishing the parts until they functioned like a well-oiled machine. He fitted the barrel and chambered it for the .280 Remington, using competition specifications. I provided a set of Buehler two-piece mounts and a Schmidt & Bender 6X scope, which Glenn mounted for me. When he was satisfied, he delivered it. I couldn't have been more pleased.

A few range trips showed that it was as accurate as any rifle in my rack and considerably more accurate than most. Three-shot .5 MOA groups were the norm. I decided to use it for much of my hunting. There was a minor hiccup, though. The super-tight target chamber was very demanding on the ammo that it would flawlessly digest. Loading for it was a real chore.

Also, even though it functioned fine, I wouldn't say I liked the chintzy factory safety. I decided to

correct both issues and gave the rifle to Dave Miller and Curt Crum to modify for me.

They fabricated a new side-swing two-position type safety and fitted it to the action, solving the safety issue. Curt re-chambered the rifle, providing a bit more latitude in the chamber. That fixed the ammo issue. It wasn't quite as accurate as it had been, but it still delivered MOA and was much simpler to find loads. On the surface, it comes off as plain Jane personified. Perhaps so, but this Jane can cook!

I was so pleased with the Pierce/Miller/Crum rifle that I decided that another .280, but more traditionally crafted, was justified. I had a nice stick of European walnut that I got from Bill Dowtin of Old World Walnut. I came up with a pre-'64 Winchester Model 70 action from my parts stash, a set of Dave Talley mounts, a Kahles 3-9X42 scope, a Ted Blackburn bottom metal unit, and a few other odds and ends.

I gave the action to Danny Pedersen for one of his superb cut-rifled barrels, which he fitted and chambered to my action with a finished length of 22 inches. I then sent the barreled action and the Dowtin blank to my old friend and stock maker Gary Goudy. Gary is not only a fantastic stock maker, but he works fast, is reasonably priced, and delivers when he says he will, all qualities hard to find these days.

A few trips to the range

proved the rifle to be highly accurate with a variety of loads. As a result, I decided to retire my old Miller .270 and use one of the .280-chambered rifles for such hunting that I had left in me. Both .280s quickly became favorites.

A few years back, during a long talk with my pal and colleague Terry Wieland, the conversation quickly shifted to rifle chatter. After the initial pleasantries, Terry mentioned a project that he had begun but had lost interest in completing. It involved a pre-'64 Model 70 action, a Krieger barrel blank in .458 bore, and a Blackburn bottom metal unit. One of our best makers had partially metalsmithed the action.

At the time, plans were underway for a Cape buffalo hunt in Tanzania with Luke Samaras Safaris and my favorite PH, Nigel Theisen. Fortunately, the hunt was still a couple of years off as there was no suitable buffalo rifle in my rack that I was happy with. I don't recall the specifics, but I traded Terry something for his big-bore makings. I sent the components, including a stick of California English walnut, to Kentucky 'smith Craig Click to turn into a .458 Lott buffalo rifle. The blank wasn't a fancy stick but appeared to be excellent for this rifle.

In due time, I received a call from Craig. "Houston, we have a problem!" He had finished work on the rifle and, during a range session, detected a crack in the stock. He did several modifications to stop the cracking but couldn't eliminate it. The crack was due to an internal flaw in the blank that was undetectable

Above and Inset: A .458 Lott buffalo rifle with its original stock gave the author fits and ran up his liquor tab.

Above and Below: The author used this .338 on an Alaskan brown bear that was not happy with him and his guide. It is the only time he had to defend himself against an animal during a lifetime of hunting.

I had to use once to save my bacon, the only time in a long lifetime of passionate hunting. One of our best custom makers, Curt Crum, built it for me. I provided a pre-'64 Model 70 action, a stick of Circassian walnut,

until the cracking started. It had nothing to do with Craig's excellent work.

I had already sent the rifle details and serial number to the outfitter, so I couldn't easily switch out the rifles. It had to be this rifle going with me. Craig sent me the rifle, and when I received it, I gave it to David Miller and Curt Crum to see what they could do. Primarily, they added a muzzle brake that David had designed and fabricated. I'm not a fan of brakes, but in this case, it reduced the nasty recoil sufficiently to get me through the hunt with the rifle, taking three buffalo with it.

After the hunt, I sent the rifle and a nice stick of English walnut to Gary Goudy for a new stock. I'll not take another buffalo with it, nor anything else for that matter, but perhaps my sons or grandsons will take their first with it. Despite the stock issue, it earned my favorite custom big bore title.

The next rifle in my top five is a fantastic rifle that

a Heym hammer-forged stainless steel barrel blank with a .338 bore, a set of Blackburn bottom metal, a Canjar trigger, and a few other bits and pieces. Curt turned these components into a superb union of wood and steel.

He finished it just in time to take along on a combo moose and caribou hunt on the Alaska peninsula

with Chris Goll's Rainbow River Lodge. I planned to use my Miller .270 on the caribou and the new Crum .338 on moose. As it turned out, things didn't work out that way.

There were five of us in camp — two guides, two hunters, and a packer. My hunting compadre was Bob Hudson from Mississippi, also booked for a moose/caribou combo hunt. I tagged a record-class caribou on the morning of our second hunting day (we lost a few hunting days early due to torrential rains). Chris and I spent most of the remainder of the day packing out the meat and taking care of the trophy.

Bob and his guide also tagged a good caribou but late in the day. They didn't make it back to camp until around midnight. They brought the trophy head back with them but had to return the next day to the kill site to recover the meat.

The following day, we headed out in different directions, both looking for a good bull moose, plus Bob also had the meat recovery to contend with. Their plan was to moose hunt as they returned to the caribou carcass, then spend the rest of the day caring for the meat and tending to the trophy head they had left in camp.

Chris and I headed off in hopes of filling my moose tag. Moose were pretty

A superb Winchester Model 70 Featherweight that Gary Goudy stocked and a couple of other 'smiths had a hand in refining. It served as a plains game rifle on two African safaris in its original factory guise. It didn't quite make Turpin's 'top five,' but it is a lovely and useful rifle.

Main and Inset: A super-nice Dakota 76 in .257 Weatherby crafted by Don Allen and the Dakota Custom Shop crew. Turpin took a couple of pronghorn antelope with it.

The top rifle is a G33/40 action, Danny Pedersen barrel and Gary Goudy-stocked .25-'06. The bottom rifle is a pre-64 Model 70 action, Danny Pedersen barrel, and Gary Goudy-stocked rifle in 9.3x62. After being primarily dormant outside Europe and Africa, this wonderfully useful cartridge had a flurry of activity 10 or 15 years back in America.

CUSTOM RIFLES
I've Known Through the Years

Alas, the following are not my rifles but rather two wonderful customs from two exceptional makers. The first, James Anderson, I have known for at least 20 years and perhaps a bit longer. His work is outstanding. I've seen very few .22 rimfire custom rifles, and this one is as good as they come.

The second, Ben Piper, is a fellow Arizonan. His gunmaking artistry is new to me, but I hope to see a lot more of it.

This project began with a Dakota .22 rimfire that needed lots of TLC. Former Dakota employee James Anderson brought it back to life, and then some. As Dakota is presently defunct and hasn't made a .22RF in a very long time, no factory parts are available. It required extensive metalwork in the Anderson shop, including, but not limited to, fabricating a new bolt. When he finished the metals, Anderson carved out a lovely stock from a stick of English walnut. He checkered the stock at 32LPI. Jesse Kaufman, another former Dakota craftsman, cut the unique scroll engraving. Anderson then completed the project with an excellent rust blue job. They don't get any better than this 6-pound masterpiece. Photos: James Anderson.

scarce in our hunting area. We had seen only a handful, none of which were trophy quality. We figured on a hard and long hunting day, so I opted to take the .270 instead of the heavier .338. As it turned out, it wouldn't have mattered. We made it about a mile from the camp when we spotted a bull moose about a half-mile from us. It was no king of the mountain, to be sure, but was represen- tative of the species, would be excellent table fare, and was the biggest bull we had seen. The hunt was rapidly ending; I elected to go after it.

Getting through the thick under-

Gunmaker Ben Piper of Piper Rifles did the metal and stock on this superb .375 H&H. He began the project with a Granite Mountain Arms Mauser-style action, which he modified, including crafting a custom bolt handle and shortening the rear tang. He fitted a Lothar Walther 23-inch, 1:10 twist barrel machined to his custom contour. He made a 1/4 rib with rear sight insert and fitted a NECG Masterpiece front sight and hood. He crafted and fitted a buffalo horn fore-end tip and cross-bolt plugs covering the steel cross bolts. He custom-made the barrel band and rear sling swivel studs on the rifle. He finished the stock with 30 coats of hand-rubbed London's Best oil finish and color casehardened the metal surfaces. Master engraver Phil Quigley executed the lovely Germanic-style hand engraving, including a portrait of Ahmad Khan on the floorplate, using hammer and chisel. Finally, David Van Boxtaele of Get A Grip Checkering cut the checkering. This magnificent rifle is now ready for an African safari. Photos: Tom Alexander

brush covering the mountainside was a chore, but we managed to get within about 100 yards of the bull without spooking it. A couple of 130-grain Bitterroot bullets through the lungs, and

the real work began. That ended my hunt. We field dressed the bull, made the carcass as bear-proof as possible, and headed back to camp for a little celebrating. We had stashed a six-pack

in the ice-cold lake before leaving camp, just in case.

We returned prepared to celebrate; however, the first thing we noticed when getting to camp was that Bob's caribou

head was nowhere in sight. We had seen numerous bears during our hunt, so we immediately knew what had happened. Sure enough, we found evidence that a bear had visited the camp and left with Bob's caribou trophy.

Chris decided to track the bear to recover the trophy. I asked him to wait a couple of minutes while I got my .338 from the tent, only a few yards away. I grabbed the rifle, loaded it full of 210-grain Nosler Partition ammo, and sat at a field table at the edge of camp and watched Chris head off after the bear. I asked Chris to accompany him. However, he requested that I remain where I was. He told me that he wanted to turn and shoot at the slightest sound and didn't want the noise to

be me tripping over an alder bush. That made good sense to me. Chris lost the track after a couple of hundred yards and came back to camp. We were mulling over

what our next move should be when the bear decided for us — it came ambling along toward us, about 50 yards away. I heard Chris mumble, "Damn, I'm afraid we may have to kill this one!"

"Get outta here, you SOB!" he yelled, and the bear snapped its teeth and came! I put a 210-grain Nosler in the bear's chest, and Chris followed immediately with a 300-grain Bitterroot from his

.375 H&H. All told, the bear took 1,530 grains of lead before crying uncle. That fact made the .338 custom stand tall in my rack. A favorite? You bet!

Finally, we come to my absolute favorite custom rifle that I own or have ever owned. Although I've been fortunate enough to have quite a few rifles explicitly crafted for me, this one was not. The David Miller Co. in Tucson, AZ, built the rifle for a client.

Below: A factory pre-'64 Model 70 Winchester .375 H&H that Turpin had substantial metal work done in Germany. Jim Wilkinson of the Rifle Ranch in Prescott, AZ custom stocked it. One of Jim's stockers, Art Bowman, did the stock.

Above: "I must confess that I had forgotten this rifle and discovered it in the back of my safe as I was preparing this yarn," the author writes of this rifle. "I've forgotten who did the work on it, but both wood and metal are very well done. It's a .270, which one can't have too many of."

A bunch of folks had a hand in crafting this Mauser .416 Ruger. The author's close friend and custom rifle fanatic Bud Miller, with professional help and advice from Jules La Bantchni, did most of the metalwork. Alas, Bud passed unexpectedly, leaving the rifle to the author. Originally a .338, not a chambering Turpin needed, he asked Danny Pedersen to re-bore and re-chamber it for the then-new .416 Ruger cartridge. Gary Goudy stocked it with a stick of English walnut.

I relocated to SE Arizona in 1978 and learned of Dave and Curt Crum and the work they were doing perhaps a year later. After getting to know them, I visited their shop almost every time I was in Tucson. I was doing a fair amount of writing by that time, and I used the Miller shop for ideas, photography, and learning about custom crafting rifles. The more I learned about their work, the more I lusted after one of their rifles. Alas, they were well outside my price range.

A few years passed, and, in about 1985, as I was preparing for a combo moose and caribou hunt in Alaska,

The author's all-time favorite custom, a David Miller Co. .270. While David Miller didn't make it for him, it fits like a glove. Turpin retired it a few years back but hunted with it far more than any other rifle over the years.

Dave gave me a call. He asked if I could visit him before leaving for my hunt as he had something to show me. I rearranged my schedule and made a quick trip to Tucson. I had no clue about what David had up his sleeve.

We had some small talk in Dave's office when I arrived and then adjourned to the shop. David showed me a rifle he had just gotten in. He told me about building the rifle for a local attorney. After owning it for a while, the attorney took up competitive trap shooting and traded it to a Phoenix dealer on a high-grade shotgun. Dave found out about the deal and arranged to purchase the rifle from the dealer. He made me a price. It was still out of my price range, but I thought it less than what it might

fetch on the open market, should that become necessary. I bought it.

The rifle is the epitome of simplicity, having everything it needs and nothing that it doesn't. Miller scrutinized every part of the rifle. It began as a Browning factory sporter model. After a few range trips, David determined the factory barrel was exceptional and retained it. He cut and crowned it to 22 inches. Curt crafted the classic stock with an Arizona-aged blank of

California English walnut after they had gone over all the metalwork with a fine-toothed comb. He selected the blank for its ideal properties and not for fancy looks, although it is attractive, to be sure.

Assuming a .270 was adequate for the game sought, I used the rifle for all my hunting from that day until I retired the gun about five years ago. The only times that I didn't take it were on sponsored hunts when I had to use host-provided rifles. When I retired it, one had to work hard to shoot a 3-shot group *larger than* .75 MOA. Using its preferred load of 59.5 grains of H4831 and most any good 130-grain bullet, it delivers 3,150 fps.

It has accompanied me to Africa, Europe, Mexico numerous times, and all over the USA. A rifle doesn't get any better than this one. It always will be my favorite custom of all. **GD**

THE Versatile .41 MAGNUM

›DICK WILLIAMS

Freedom Arms' beautifully made and slightly downsized Model 97 in .41 Mag. and topped with a 2X Leupold pistol scope would thrill the heart of any handgun hunter.

In the mid-1960s, Smith & Wesson introduced the .41 Magnum to the handgun world, chambering it in its classic N-frame revolver. Writers of the day heralded the new cartridge by referring to it as the ultimate police round. Interestingly, some of the most famous writers, e.g., Elmer Keith, were not cops but rather serious outdoorsmen. It wasn't uncommon for law enforcement personnel who endorsed the new .41 for police work to have operated in the open country along the Mexican border.

Perhaps the new magnum would have fared better in the market had the writers focused more on the .41 Mag's outstanding capabilities as an all-purpose field handgun rather than a standard-issue gun for police departments that operated primarily in urban or suburban environments. These outdoor writers were all accomplished pistol shots and perhaps forgot that the average cop was neither a dedicated nor even accomplished marksman. The way to upgrade marksmanship is not by dramatically increasing felt recoil! Finally, the police world's surg-

ing interest in and ultimate domination by semi-auto pistols snuffed the .41 Magnum's potential legacy as the perfect police handgun.

As it turns out, the "middle magnum" is alive and reasonably well today because it generated some devoted followers in the outdoorsman's market. And it achieved this following because the well-balanced cartridge does almost everything a .44 Magnum will do without administering quite the same punishment to the shooter. Due to my lifelong passion for handgun hunting, I own several .41 Mag. revolvers. However, they are not particularly suitable for all-day carry and quick deployment. Still, they have all proved effective and deadly on a variety of game in the field.

For this kind of use, the all-time classic .41 Magnum has to be the Smith & Wesson Model 57 with its bright blue finish and 8.375-inch barrel. Its basic appearance convinces you that Smith made this gun for long-range shooting, a capability that caught the attention of more than a few handgun metallic silhouette shoot-

Two of the author's classic Smith & Wesson .41 Magnum revolvers evolved from the original Model 57: a 7.5-inch-barreled hunting model and a highly customized "belly gun" with all the nice touches from Ken Kelly at Magnaport. Combined with a Randall knife, a man can accomplish anything!

ers in the late 1970s and '80s. With its sub-.44-caliber barrel and chambers, the .41 Magnum Smith has more metal in the barrel and cylinder and can withstand full-power loads for a greater duration than the .44-caliber N-frames. It even has a slight edge when hunting since it shoots flatter than the .44 Magnum, as Elmer Keith noted in his writings. For larger (or more dangerous) game, the middle magnum is fully capable of launching heavy-

for-caliber bullets like the 265-grain hardcast loads from Buffalo Bore that ensure maximum penetration. It does all of this with slightly less felt recoil.

If you prefer stainless steel handguns for your outdoor adventures in inclement weather, I have a couple of quality candidates. Smith & Wesson's Model 657, a stainless version of its blued Model 57, features a 7.5-inch barrel with a full-length underlug. The underlug offers

excellent balance and stability when fired standing and adds a little extra front-end weight to help control muzzle rise and absorb felt recoil on the heavier/higher-velocity loads. While I like Smith's wood stocks' looks, I prefer Hogue's aftermarket rubber grips with finger grooves for magnum revolvers. Perhaps not as fast for presentation, but I'm more concerned with the precision achieved with the first shot on game. The slightly thinner

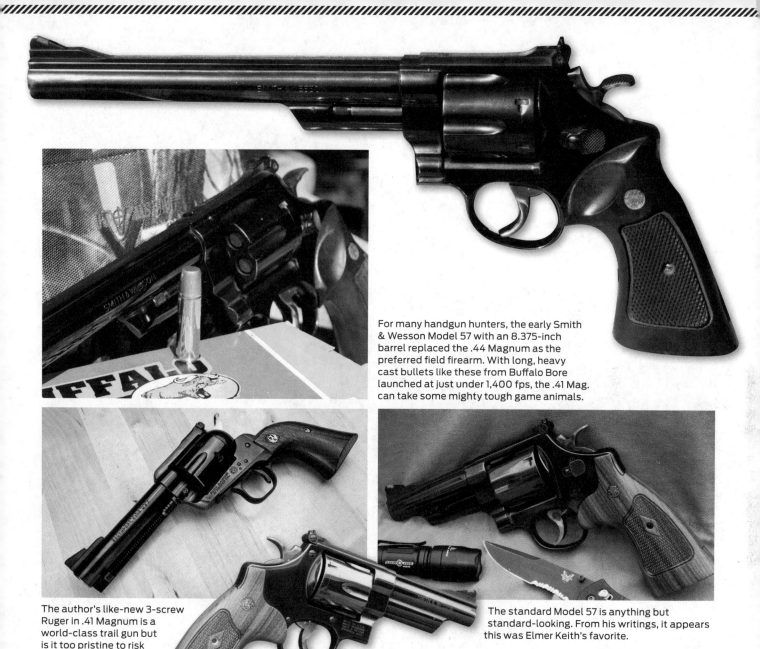

For many handgun hunters, the early Smith & Wesson Model 57 with an 8.375-inch barrel replaced the .44 Magnum as the preferred field firearm. With long, heavy cast bullets like these from Buffalo Bore launched at just under 1,400 fps, the .41 Mag. can take some mighty tough game animals.

The author's like-new 3-screw Ruger in .41 Magnum is a world-class trail gun but is it too pristine to risk afield? Nah!

The standard Model 57 is anything but standard-looking. From his writings, it appears this was Elmer Keith's favorite.

grips also fit my hand better than the oversize wood stocks provided on Smith's magnums.

For handgun hunting, there are two precision-made Freedom Arms single-action revolvers with 7.5-inch barrels. Freedom Arms designed and built the older and larger Model 83 to handle cartridges up through the mighty .454 Casull, so the milder .41 Mag. is no challenge to the gun's strength and durability. The Freedom Model 97 comes with a reduced-size cylinder (diameter and length) and grip frame, making the revolver user-friendly

for smaller hands. Equipped with optics, I've seen Freedom Arms revolvers produce 1- to 2-inch groups at 100 yards.

The benchmark .41 Magnum handgun is a blue S&W Model 57 in either 4- or 6-inch barrel for many shooters. Even so, I prefer the 6-inch barrel for handgun hunting as a good compromise between performance and portability. It packs nicely in a hip holster (my preferred method of carrying any handgun) but is easily accessed even when carried in a shoulder rig under a vest or jacket. I spent a few days at Gunsite carrying the slightly slimmer and lighter weight Model

57 4-inch Mountain Gun in a strong side, high-ride OWB belt rig. We went through several defensive scenarios and then tackled the more offense-oriented Scrambler where you have to deal with "attackers" out to distances of 75+ yards. What I sacrificed in reloading speed to the semi-autos I made up for in precise first-round hits. There's a reason the 4-inch-barreled revolver was the standard duty gun for police officers or for anyone who spent a great deal of time sitting in a car. In my opinion, the 4-inch .41 Magnum is a viable candidate for an all-purpose civilian carry or survival gun.

There are a couple of viable carry gun candidates for those who prefer single-action revolvers. Ruger offered its original, small-framed, 3-screw/no transfer bar Blackhawk in .41 Magnum. It was the first .41 Mag. I ever owned, which I purchased in late 1966 upon returning home from a tour of duty in the Philippines. Since it lacks the transfer bar, you should carry it with an empty round under the hammer, meaning you have a five-shot revolver. Freedom Arms also makes its Model 97 smaller-frame revolver (which holds five rounds in .41 Magnum,) but with its transfer bar system is safe to carry fully loaded. Somehow having quick access to only five rounds of .41 Magnum ammo instead of six does not leave me feeling diminished. Ruger offers several variants of its New Model Blackhawk with transfer bars chambered in this powerful middle magnum. Topped with a small pistol scope, it was an easy-to-carry handgun that could improve either a new or veteran handgun hunter's shooting skills.

If you think the .41 Magnum might make a great concealed carry gun, custom gunsmiths can make your dream a reality. Case in point, an S&W Model 657 with the barrel cut to three inches to facilitate concealment, Magnaported to minimize felt recoil and muzzle flip, and a deluxe action tune-up for improved trigger control when shooting double action. Ken Kelly at Magnaport did all of that to my gun, which I later took to Gunsite for a concealed carry event. Erik Little of Rafter L Combat Leather made a custom rig for the package that included holster, belt, and slide-on cartridge loops for extra ammo. The holster rides high on the right hip and, when covered with an open shirt or jacket, you can completely conceal the whole package, yet it's instantly accessible by sweeping the outer garment aside in the draw stroke. As much as I enjoyed it in the Combat Leather rig, I'll admit the gun is a bit too heavy for a pocket pistol!

SHOOTING THE .41 MAG.

At Gunsite, tactical or partial reloads

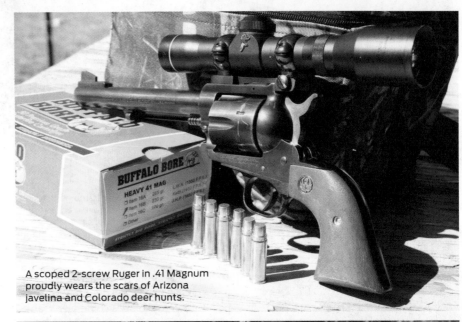

A scoped 2-screw Ruger in .41 Magnum proudly wears the scars of Arizona javelina and Colorado deer hunts.

Above: The author's Model 57 Mountain Gun, considered by some to be overly large for a concealed carry weapon, proved itself a great defensive weapon at Gunsite's testing fields. Inset: The Mountain Gun and two speedloaders carried all day comfortably in leather from Simply Rugged. An outstanding package for anyone hitting the trail.

went smoothly as long as I followed the instructors' techniques and "topped off" — replacing one or two rounds as I shot them. With a double-action revolver, partial reloads allow one to maintain a muzzle down orientation throughout the maneuver. Point the gun at the ground, push the ejector rod part way up, and then ease it back down. The unfired rounds will drop back into the cylinder chambers while (hopefully) the fired rounds will remain protruding from the cylinder and can be plucked from the gun one or two

at a time. Remove the required number of fresh cartridges from your belt loop, pouch, or pocket, and insert them into the empty chambers. If someone attacks you during the reloading procedure, drop the empties or fresh rounds, smack the cylinder shut and re-engage the threat with the rounds remaining in the gun. It's not as fast as a semi-auto, but the good

Above: In the new millennium, Smith & Wesson made a run of "classics," in this case a copy of the Model 58, originally envisioned as the "ultimate" cop gun, shown here with a couple of cop tools.

Left: A pair of .41 Magnums superbly suited for field carry with adequate power for anything encountered.

news is that there are no partially loaded magazines to deal with when the reload is complete. What makes it tricky is that a partial revolver reload requires considerably more dexterity and fine motor control than you need to work magazines in and out of a semi-auto pistol. These skills are difficult to maintain in a stressful situation, so practice the maneuver.

While working through the various drills on an earlier trip to Gunsite, I began to think maybe we missed out on a good thing in the 1960s by not issuing .41 Mag revolvers to all the cops. Given the ammo technology back then, my .41-caliber Mountain Gun was looking quite

good. It made big holes without depending on bullet expansion, its enhanced penetration capabilities could pierce an adversary's cover, and it surrendered little in speed, placing the first six shots where you wanted them.

But then I switched to the S&W Model 58, the smaller, lighter .41 revolver that Smith & Wesson designed to be the police-issue sidearm, and my conclusions went down the toilet. Recoil from the first six rounds caused the triggerguard to smack my knuckles hard enough that I benched the gun with its small factory grip and switched back to the Model 57 with the Hogues. The ammo I was using at Gunsite was a reasonably close duplication of the original Remington reduced load. Specifically, my reloads

used 7.0 grains of Hodgdon Universal power behind a 225-grain cast bullet. In a four-inch S&W, it generated 869 fps. You could easily manage it with the ergonomically friendly Hogue grips on the Mountain gun, but it was less friendly with the "police-duty issue" Model 58.

CUSTOM .41S

On my latest trip to Gunsite, I was accompanied by Magnaport's beautifully rebuilt compact Model 657 and experienced a double dose of gratification. First, I was thrilled by all the "oohs" and "aahs" generated by my peers when they tried the double-action trigger on Ken Kelly's creation. The second was the renewed availability of reduced (or practice) .41 Mag. ammo now being manufactured

Below: There are some unique aspects of a Bowen No. 5 conversion, such as the front sight, barrel treatment at the muzzle, differing front and backstrap of the grip frame, the cylinder pin, and rotating cylinder pin release latch.

Right: Considering that this is truly a "one of a kind" sixgun, the author was surprised and somewhat flattered that the gun's owner, David Sargent, was willing to take it hunting and allow pictures in the field.

Lower Right: Ruger's small-frame 3-screw .41 Magnum with a box of 210-grain JHP Federals; it worked for deer in the 1960s, and it still works today.

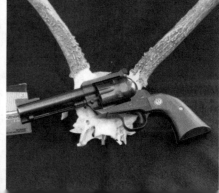

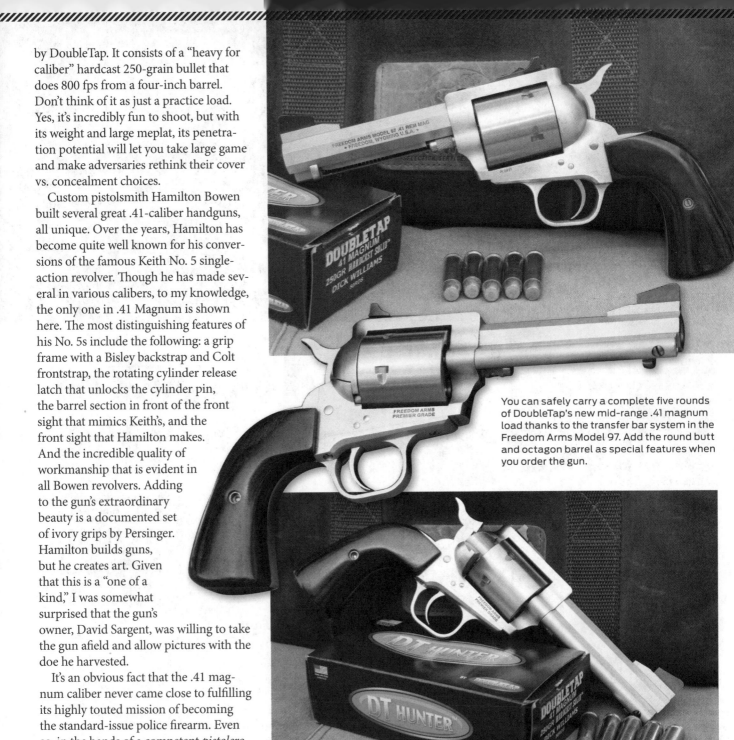

by DoubleTap. It consists of a "heavy for caliber" hardcast 250-grain bullet that does 800 fps from a four-inch barrel. Don't think of it as just a practice load. Yes, it's incredibly fun to shoot, but with its weight and large meplat, its penetration potential will let you take large game and make adversaries rethink their cover vs. concealment choices.

Custom pistolsmith Hamilton Bowen built several great .41-caliber handguns, all unique. Over the years, Hamilton has become quite well known for his conversions of the famous Keith No. 5 single-action revolver. Though he has made several in various calibers, to my knowledge, the only one in .41 Magnum is shown here. The most distinguishing features of his No. 5s include the following: a grip frame with a Bisley backstrap and Colt frontstrap, the rotating cylinder release latch that unlocks the cylinder pin, the barrel section in front of the front sight that mimics Keith's, and the front sight that Hamilton makes. And the incredible quality of workmanship that is evident in all Bowen revolvers. Adding to the gun's extraordinary beauty is a documented set of ivory grips by Persinger. Hamilton builds guns, but he creates art. Given that this is a "one of a kind," I was somewhat surprised that the gun's owner, David Sargent, was willing to take the gun afield and allow pictures with the doe he harvested.

It's an obvious fact that the .41 magnum caliber never came close to fulfilling its highly touted mission of becoming the standard-issue police firearm. Even so, in the hands of a competent *pistolero*, it does an outstanding job as a defensive handgun. Equally obvious, the caliber has made a successful crossover and has become a highly effective general-purpose handgun for the serious outdoorsman. Choose an application, and the .41 caliber will serve you well. Pick a particular model or make of .41 Magnum revolver, and you'll be able to find it in either the new or used gun market. For a caliber that nearly died, the middle magnum is and has been an enormous success. **GD**

You can safely carry a complete five rounds of DoubleTap's new mid-range .41 magnum load thanks to the transfer bar system in the Freedom Arms Model 97. Add the round butt and octagon barrel as special features when you order the gun.

Like all Freedom Arms single-action revolvers, this compact version loads (and ejects) one round at a time through the loading gate. Using DoubleTap's new 250-grain cast bullet at 800 fps, you get a lot of pop in a small package with minimal felt recoil.

.41 MAGNUM VELOCITIES IN S&W MODEL 57 WITH A 7.5-INCH BARREL

LOAD	VELOCITY (AVERAGE FPS)	ENERGY (FT-LBS)
Federal 210 gr. JHP	1,301	789
Federal 250 gr. Cast	1,196	794
Buffalo Bore 170 gr. JHP	1,574	935

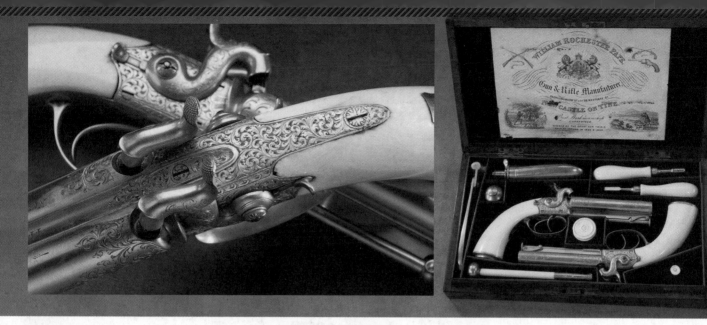

PHOTO ESSAY: Curiosa of Vintage Firearms

This article is an excerpt from *The Illustrated History of Firearms, 2nd Edition*, available at GunDigestStore.com.

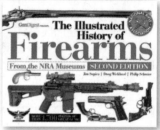

❯ JIM SUPICA, DOUG WICKLUND, AND PHILIP SCHREIER

Top: Cased Pair of W. R. Pape Double-Barrel Percussion Pistols - .50 caliber - circa 1858. With both guns fully loaded, the owner has a total of four shots before reloading. Gold plated with ivory grips and accessory handles and fine scroll engraving.

Left: British Four-Barrel Flintlock Pistol - .36 caliber - circa 1800 - The barrel cluster is rotated by hand to fire the second pair of shots. Each barrel has its own frizzen, which when closed keeps the priming charge from spilling.

H. V. Perry Three-Barrel Percussion Rifle - .45 caliber - circa 1845-1850 - The multiple-barrel concept begins to become heavy and cumbersome as additional barrels are added. Guns with more than two barrels in this era are scarce.

Right: Brackley Double-Barrel Tap-action Flintlock Pistol- .40 caliber - circa 1800 - A lever on the side adds a priming charge to the pan for the second shot. Spring-loaded bayonet.

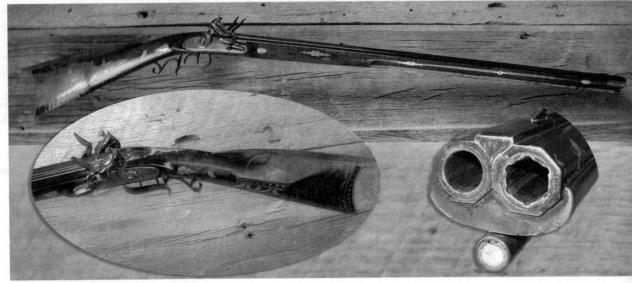

Kentucky Style Combination Gun - .44 rifled / .45 smoothbore caliber - circa 1800 - With one barrel rifled and one smoothbore, a combination gun makes a versatile hunting arm.

REPEATERS

The muzzleloading system was slow for repeat shots. After a round was fired, a fresh charge of black powder had to be poured down the barrel, a lead projectile rammed down on top of it, and either the priming pan filled with powder on a flintlock or a cap placed on the nipple on a percussion arm. In the early 19th century, experimentation in firearms design was often focused on development of guns that could fire multiple times without reloading. The earliest form of repeater—a gun with multiple barrels—is still popular today. Double-barrel shotguns are used for bird hunting and clay target shooting, and double rifles for heavy game.

Not every multi-barrel gun is a repeater. The firearms on the bottom half of this page fire all their barrels at the same time.

Above: Duckfoot pistols feature an array of splayed barrels which fired simultaneously, spreading the shots. Intended users were sea captains who might have to face down a mutinous crew, or bank guards and prison wardens where one man might have to face down multiple attackers. These two British examples are .60 and .50 caliber, circa 1800.

At left: The Nock Volley Gun was adopted by the British Navy in 1779 for repelling boarders. All seven .52 caliber barrels fired simultaneously. Only 500 were made, and the brutal recoil combined with a propensity to ignite the ship's rigging limited their utility.

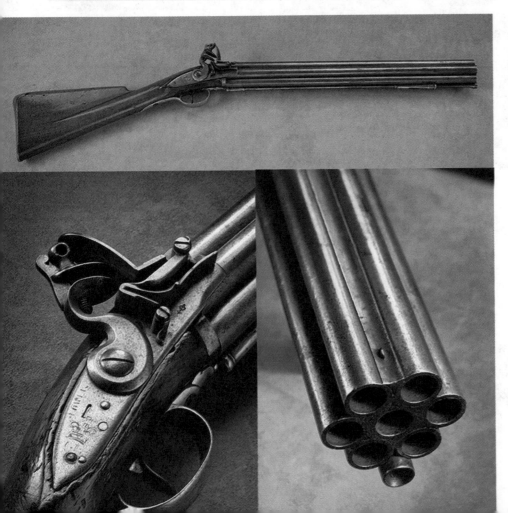

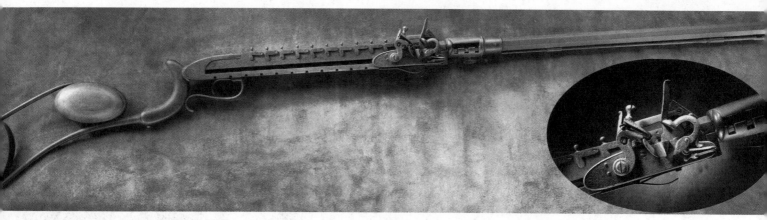

Isaiah Jennings Multi-Shot Flintlock Rifle - circa 1821 - This "Roman candle rifle" took superposed charges to extreme levels, accommodating 12 charges of powder and ball loaded one on top of the other in the barrel breech. A self-priming flintlock was slid back from the front charge to the next behind it as each was fired. Other innovative features include detachable barrel and detachable buttstock.

EARLY SUPERPOSED REPEATERS

One method of creating a repeating firearm was to stack multiple charges in the same barrel. Various methods were used to provide sequential shots, while some were designed to fire mutliple rounds with a single trigger pull.

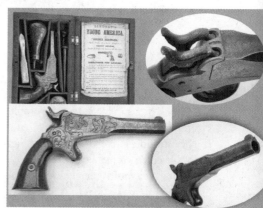

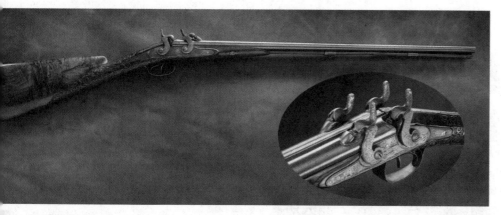

Above: Lindsay "Young America" Super-posed Charge Pistol - .41 caliber - circa 1860s - This handgun counterpart to the Lindsay double musket stacked two loads in a single barrel with two hammers.

Left: DeWalle Freres Superposed Charge Shotgun. 12 gauge - circa 1844-1862 - This Belgian-proofed shotgun was fitted with four hammers and the two forward hammers were intended to fire the upper loads first, then the lower loads would be dis-charged by the second set of hammers.

John Shaw Cookson-Type Flintlock Repeating Rifle - .57 caliber - circa 1690-1720 - This Cookson pattern repeater had a powder magazine and a magazine for seven lead balls inside the buttstock. A turn of the crank on the left side of the frame loads the chamber, cocks the hammer, primes the pan, and lowers the frizzen for firing, making for a very early seven-shot repeater. The original concept was developed by Lorenzoni of Italy about 1680.

Bennett & Haviland Many-Chambered Revolving Percussion Rifle - .40 caliber - circa 1838-1840 - This rifle has 12 individual chambers that can be rotated into position for successive shots by rotating a wheel on top of the action. Very rare, estimated that fewer than ten were made.

French/Persian Repeating Flintlock Musket - .65 caliber - circa 1800 - Rotating chambers allow for multiple shots. An early application of the revolver concept.

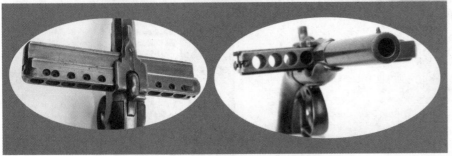

European Bar Magazine Harmonica Pistol - 9mm pinfire - circa 1880 - This ten-shot handgun requires manual advancing of the horizontal magazine for each shot.

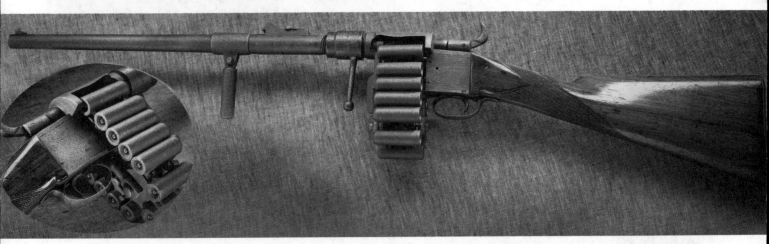

Treeby Chain Repeating Rifle - caliber .52 percussion - circa 1855 - Incorporating a 14-chamber chain that is advanced in a loop through the action by unbolting and re-attaching the barrel, this design was patented in England in 1855. A folding hand rest under the barrel is a surprisingly modern feature. Caliber: .52 percussion.

PEPPERBOXES

The earliest widely successful repeating handgun, the pepperbox used a rotating cluster of barrels. Introduced around 1830, most were manufactured in England, the U.S., and Belgium. They remained popular through the 1850s. However, they soon lost ground to Colt style percussion revolvers which were lighter, more compact, and more accurate.

While most pepperboxes were five or six shot, other configurations existed, such as the manually rotated four shot all brass British single action above, circa 1840, and the eighteen shot ring trigger double-action Belgian pepperbox below, circa 1850.

Top left to lower right: Allen & Thurber Double-Barrel Single-Trigger Pistol - .34 cal. - circa 1850s – A 2-shot predecessor to pepperboxes. British Pepperbox - .32 caliber - circa 1830s-1850s - six shot. Manhattan Firearms Pepperbox - .28 caliber - circa 1850s - six shot.

Collier's repeating flintlock design is one of the first true revolvers. Elisha Collier's invention in America of a manually rotated cylinder holding five chambers that was primed separately was manufactured in England by John Evans & Son, beginning in 1819. The .40 caliber Collier was seen by a young Sam Colt during his travels aboard the brig Corvo and it has been speculated that Colt's later Paterson revolver design was in part due to his exposure to the Collier. This example is believed to be a well-made reproduction.

The double-barrel LeMat system of a revolver cylinder rotating around a shotgun barrel was also applied to long guns. This LeMat carbine used 12mm and 28 gauge pinfire cartridges, circa 1867. The use of metallic cartridges in a revolving long gun minimized the danger of chain-fires. However, on most revolving firearms, bits of burning powder and small shavings of lead can escape the gap between the front of the cylinder and the rear of the barrel when fired. With a revolving cartridge rifle, this debris could painfully pepper the non-shooting hand if it is being used to support the barrel forward of the cylinder.

Belgian Pinfire Revolver - 7mm pinfire - circa 1870-1880 - This unusual high-capacity 21-shot revolver uses two rows of chambers in the cylinder and over/under barrels with a folding trigger.

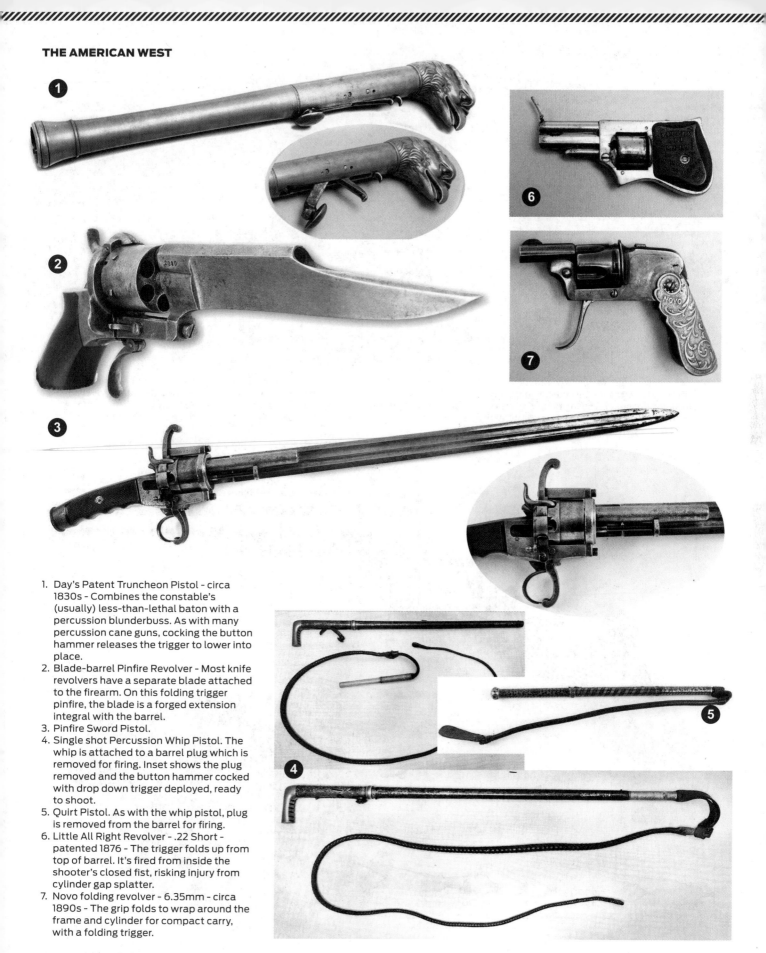

1. Day's Patent Truncheon Pistol - circa 1830s - Combines the constable's (usually) less-than-lethal baton with a percussion blunderbuss. As with many percussion cane guns, cocking the button hammer releases the trigger to lower into place.
2. Blade-barrel Pinfire Revolver - Most knife revolvers have a separate blade attached to the firearm. On this folding trigger pinfire, the blade is a forged extension integral with the barrel.
3. Pinfire Sword Pistol.
4. Single shot Percussion Whip Pistol. The whip is attached to a barrel plug which is removed for firing. Inset shows the plug removed and the button hammer cocked with drop down trigger deployed, ready to shoot.
5. Quirt Pistol. As with the whip pistol, plug is removed from the barrel for firing.
6. Little All Right Revolver - .22 Short - patented 1876 - The trigger folds up from top of barrel. It's fired from inside the shooter's closed fist, risking injury from cylinder gap splatter.
7. Novo folding revolver - 6.35mm - circa 1890s - The grip folds to wrap around the frame and cylinder for compact carry, with a folding trigger.

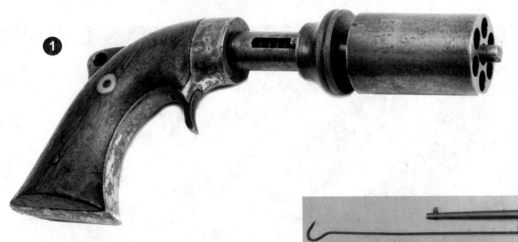

TRAP AND ALARM GUNS

Animal trap guns, alarm guns, spring guns, and booby trap guns have in common the disconcerting (and today highly illegal) characteristic of firing on their own when their trigger is tripped without a shooter's presence to confirm the legitimacy of the target. They were used for killing pest animals, harvesting furs, or sounding an intrusion alarm (or shooting an intruder!) The potential for tragic unintended consequences is obvious.

1. North & Couch animal trap gun - .31 caliber - circa 1890s - Six-shot percussion pepperbox fires all barrels when a baited string attached to the muzzle is pulled. Reportedly used in Australia for kangaroo control.
2. Reiff & McDowell - .22 blank rimfire alarm gun - circa 1900.
3. S. Coon Door Jamb Alarm Pistol - .28 cal. percussion - circa 1860s.
4. F. Reuthe Double-barrel Percussion Trap Gun - .44 percussion - circa 1860s. Bait is attached to the hooks. When the bait is pulled, both barrels fire.
5. Brass Cannon-Barrel Alarm Gun - 12 gauge pinfire blank - circa 1880s.
6. Never-Fail gopher trap gun- circa 1922 - Set at the entrance to a burrow, when the brass plate is pushed a .38 S&W blank is fired into the varmint's belly.
7. Taylor Fur Getter .22 rimfire - circa 1920s - The stake can be pressed into the ground. When the baited hook is pulled, the round is fired into the furbearer.

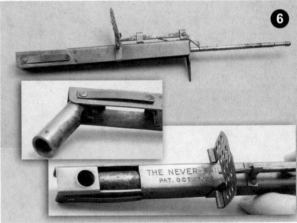

Hornady made Nitro Express-caliber ammunition available and affordable and played a considerable role in the resurgence of interest in double rifles.

I Dreamed of Double Rifles

❯ DAVE FULSON

"Every dream realized had to have, by definition, a starting place."
– Author unknown

That great truth hangs in a simple frame in my home office, a gift from a deep thinker of note, who also put in double-duty as my dad. I have contemplated it many times over the thirty or so years since he presented it to me.

From an early age, I dreamed of Africa. More specifically, I dreamed of stalking big game in the thick tangles of the Dark Continent's great spaces. That's a pretty ambitious dream for a blue-collar kid from Ft. Worth, Texas, who had yet to take his first whitetail.

But I was a voracious reader, and I still am. My inspiration was partly due to adventures I read about and photos that brought those stories to life in the pages of *Sports Afield* and *Outdoor Life* magazines. Later, there were books by Robert Ruark, Ernest "Papa" Hemingway, John Hunter, and the great hunter of man-eating cats in India, Jim Corbett, to name a very few. Their tales of danger and adventure further fanned the flames of interest in both the hunt and especially the double rifles they carried. Lord, but I coveted those worn-looking, bush-scarred two-barreled beauties I saw draped over broad shoulders or held in sweat-slick hands.

Proof of things to come, the author pictured with his first double rifle. This photo depicts the beginning of his life-long love affair with the two-pipe.

Theodore Roosevelt took this elephant bull with his Holland & Holland Royal Grade .500/.450 Nitro Express.

Gunsmiths designed the double rifle for the largest, most dangerous game at close range. The ability to instantly deliver two large-caliber bullets at some big ugly breaking cover at short range (coming or going) is where the double rifle truly comes into its own. It was true in Roosevelt's day, and it is true today.

In the mid-1830s, legends such as William Cotton Oswell and Roualeyn Gordon Cumming were tackling big game with blackpowder muzzleloaders. Pure lead balls — sometimes hardened by tin for deeper penetration — were the choice of the day. These early doubles had limited rifling, but even so, they were more accurate than the smoothbores that preceded them. Due to their excessive weight, the 2 bores and 4 bores were single-barrel designs, but later, the 8 bore became available in a double-barrel con-figuration. And even with these shoulder breakers, two quick shots were better than one!

These guys were lobbing quarter- and half-pound shells at the massive, danger-ous game, with the only available tool for the job. There is no doubt this period in big-bore rifles was the birthplace of *shooter's flinch.*

This article is by no means an attempt to chronicle the double rifle's full evolu-tion; there simply is not enough room

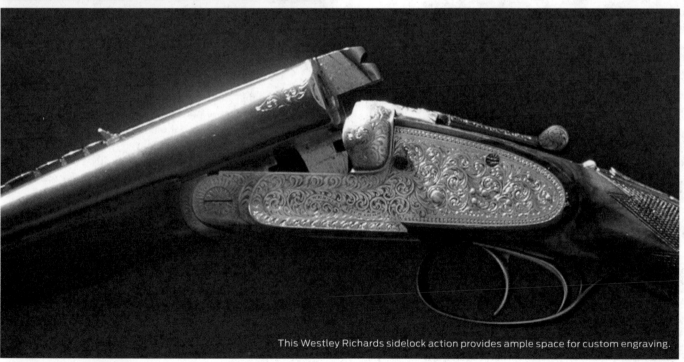

This Westley Richards sidelock action provides ample space for custom engraving.

here. But our trip back in time points out the continued need future hunters would have for improved, twin-barrel big-bore options as new generations of professional and client hunters continued their pursuit of dangerous game.

BRIEF HISTORY OF THE DOUBLES

In the early heydays of the double rifle, the British makers all but cornered the market. John Rigby, Holland & Holland, William Evans, Westley Richards, Joseph Lang, and James Purdy are just some of the manufacturers who would accept your King's ransom-sized deposit and build you a well-regulated double in a variety of newly introduced Nitro Express calibers. Indeed, there were other manufacturers producing doubles, but the Brits were getting all the press.

The Golden Age of African hunting saw the professional hunters (PH) using these fine double rifles, men who depended on the power of a real "stopper" when dangerous game was the goal. The Maharajas of India (and British officers who thrilled at the hunting India offered) were also generally armed with double rifles when after tiger, Indian elephant,

Legendary gun writer Elmer Keith used his Boswell .500 Nitro Express to take this big Kenya tusker. The .500 has long been a favorite caliber of many serious elephant hunters.

Ernest Hemingway bagged this black rhino on his 1953 safari with his beloved Westley Richards .577 Nitro Express. He cherished this rifle above all others.

leopard, gaur, sloth bear, or the Indian rhino.

Kynoch was the recognized manufacturer of Nitro Express ammunition for the day's vintage doubles, and it ruled the market until it closed its doors in the 1970s. The lack of available ammunition — combined with the cost of an entry-level English double — found most of these rifles relegated to the gun safe, sold,

or replaced with bolt rifles like the .458 Winchester Magnum, which Winchester built on its iconic Model 70 action. The Model 70 was a desirable option for young professional hunters in Africa who could now own a genuine 'stopper' rifle and needed readily available ammunition at a price they could afford.

Yet the allure of the double rifle remained, especially for those of us who

Once you've confirmed the point of impact from both barrels, you must get away from the bench and practice offhand and from shooting sticks. Big double rifles require time to master. Don't wait until your safari.

grew up fantasizing about owning one of our own some distant and wonderful day.

New life for the double rifle as we know it today began with Jim Bell and his introduction of newly-made .470 Nitro Express brass in the early 1980s. That interest has been growing ever since as ammunition companies such as Hornady, Federal, and Superior (to name just a few) ramped up production on some of history's most popular double-rifle cartridges.

Hornady Manufacturing of Grand Island, Nebraska, has been a sponsor of my company's flagship TV series, *Tracks Across Africa*, for fifteen years. I well remember 2008 as the year Hornady jumped feet first into the Nitro Express market. I was hunting with and filming Steve and Jason Hornady and Neil Davies and other Team Hornady members just about non-stop around Africa for several years as Hornady's lineup of double-rifle cartridges and bullet offerings expanded. Today, Hornady offers six Nitro Express cartridges in calibers ranging from .450-

400 up to .500 Nitro Express. Thanks in large part to Hornady, today's double rifle owner has access to a tremendous range of calibers, cartridges, and quality ammunition in both expandable and solid bullet options. Based on these offerings, new interest surfaced (seemingly overnight) in the mighty "two-pipe."

Thus, armed with both need and desire, I finally fulfilled a lifetime dream when I sprang for a Searcy double in the popular .470 Nitro. I had been shooting other folks' doubles long before that, but now I had 500 grains of *problem solver* at my fingertips anytime I wanted it. And I still recall the thrill of dropping those gleaming beauties into the chamber for the first time!

When I first started hunting seriously in Africa, any double in the camp was most likely the professional hunter's property. But today, especially on safaris targeting one or more dangerous game species, it is not surprising to see *several* clients show up with a double rifle as part of their safari battery. However, hunters

showing up with brand new doubles can be — excuse the pun — a double-edged sword. My years in the safari business have taught me many lessons. Some I learned by observing clients while filming their hunts. I learned others on my dime and my time. Most seasoned PHs will agree that the single biggest mistake their clients make is before the safari even begins, and that mistake is lack of practice with their rifle. And that goes double for hunters showing up with a new two-pipe in hand. Most Americans grow up shooting bolt-action rifles topped with scopes, not open-sighted Express rifles. And the vast majority of those spend too much time shooting only from the bench. Trust me on this: a shooting bench is not practical to carry afield in Africa!

Your new double rifle, however, will shock you if you intend to do most of your range time with it off the bench. A bench and padded shoulder brace will help you determine two important things: whether your rifle is well-regulated and if your sights are correctly adjusted. But you won't look back upon extended benchrest lessons fondly.

Once you've confirmed the regulation and you've made the necessary sight adjustments, now is the time to get off the bench and get comfortable using shooting sticks and shooting freehand. These techniques are how you will be taking shots while on safari, and you must master each long before you step foot on African soil. Aiming down a scope-less barrel using a rear V-shaped leaf sight and small front bead takes a lot of getting used to, as do the twin triggers of a double. I have filmed many, many hunters that have not mastered the trigger issue. The first barrel goes boom, and then they stand there trying to fire the other barrel while squeezing the hell out of the same trigger! They are generally in the danger zone of an elephant or buffalo hit with their first bullet, compounding the danger factor of their mistake. This little miscue can result in a wounded animal at best — or a body bag at worst.

Like most experienced double shooters, I sight, and fire with both eyes open most of the time. The rare exception is if an animal is at a more extended range and

unaware of my presence. I tend to close my left eye and pick an exact spot with my front bead in this situation. Then it is back to both eyes open on the follow-up shot. This method works for me, but practice until you discover what works best for you. Then practice it some more. It is common for new double shooters to throw it to their shoulder and let it fly in the heat and excitement of a close-up encounter with a buffalo or elephant. Picking an exact and lethal spot on an animal is every shooter's primary and most important job, regardless of action type.

I did *the same thing* on the first buffalo I tackled with a double rifle. I was already an experienced buffalo hunter, but I always shot bolt rifles. When a real beast of a Zimbabwe bull unexpectedly burst out of a thick patch of riverine bush 40 yards away, I just swung on the bull and gave him a bullet *somewhere* around the chest. The bush instantly swallowed him, and he headed for the boundary of Zimbabwe's Mana Pools National Park. Where I hit him *exactly,* I will never know because I did not aim precisely, and I knew the mistake I had made before I was out of recoil.

That mistake cost the buffalo physi-cal suffering, and it cost me emotional suffering. And to this day, it remains the only buffalo I have ever lost. Do not assume that a dangerous game animal will collapse at your shot just because you are toting an "elephant rifle" (the typical catchall phrase for double rifles). I have seen many elephants drop on the spot with an accurate shot from the smaller .375 caliber. Still, I have also seen elephant bulls ramp the horizon, never recovered, carrying slugs from the mighty .700 Nitro Express. Those shots were only slightly off-target brain shots. The more frequently I see big stuff shot, the less faith I put in the "shock theory" of even the most potent calibers. Accuracy, shot placement, and bullet penetration kill, kinetic energy alone does not.

DANGEROUS GAME SIMULATOR

When it comes to realistic practice, there are few places better than Barksdale, Texas, home to the world-renowned FTW Ranch, with its SAAM Safari and SAAM Precision Shooting Schools.

The author facing down one of the famous FTW SAAM Safari course chargers. Realistic situational shooting is the perfect double-rifle practice for the real thing.

During an elephant charge, the two in-stant shots delivered from a double gun can offer a life-saving advantage. Both the PH and client pictured are carrying doubles.

The author holds the great Jim Corbett's .450/400 Jeffery. Corbett used this rifle to kill the most lethal man-eating tiger on record, the dreaded Champawat tigress.

targets that await you on the dangerous game courses. Some are stationary, some moving, and some even charging — all life-sized. They include buffalo, elephant, lion, leopard, and even grizzly bear, all waiting to ambush you and your PH/instructor without a moment's notice. When you encounter them, he will tell you when and where to send your first shot. Then you better be ready for an automated, life-sized, big nasty bursting from cover and headed right at you! Throw in the insane scream of an enraged elephant bull or the bass bawl of a wounded buffalo (no, I'm not kidding), and it is the closest simulation to the *real thing* you can experience. And all the while, you are becoming more comfortable and competent with your double rifle.

SHOPPING FOR DOUBLES

So, you think a double rifle is in your future. There are many considerations to factor into your decision, including a budget, brand, action type, barrel length, ammo availability, resale value, side-by-side or over/under barrel configuration, stock fitting, and on it goes. Without writing the book that it would take to discuss each of these subjects at length, let's aim at the basics that will help you choose the right rifle for you.

A pre-owned rifle can be a great option, but does it fit? A critical factor to consider on a used rifle (especially an old one) is that the average British man in 1900 was only 5 foot, 5 inches tall. And the style of gun mount in that era was much different than it is today. The more erect shooting style from the early 1900s also required a lot of drop on the stock. Do you mount the rifle the same way? What about barrel length? Condition of the bores? Or are you buying a new rifle in caliber, fit, and price made just for you? Both are fine choices, and there is no right or wrong, but older rifles certainly have more variables.

Do you want a sidelock or boxlock action? Aficionados consider sidelock doubles 'fine rifles,' while boxlocks are a more affordable, less 'bells and whistles' option. If you desire fancy engraving, a sidelock certainly provides the engraver a much larger canvas on which to work.

Which is better? Well, historically

In this hunter's opinion, both are the finest marksmanship and hunter training programs to be found anywhere. FTW honcho Tim Fallon and his expert instructors' staff have developed the most realistic safari training course you could imagine. They offer a full, four-day safari course, as well as a two-day safari prep training program. I have attended, learned from, and thoroughly enjoyed both, and they can customize their training courses for the double-rifle shooter.

There is also a classroom element to the Safari program. You will learn about double rifle designs, shooting techniques unique to doubles, bullet designs, and discussions on solids vs. expandables, including the whys and whens for both. You will discuss the need to be prepared for backup shots, the dual-trigger issue, and much, much more.

In between classroom sessions, the shooting challenges waiting for you on

the general safari and dangerous game courses are practical and educational, and a lot of fun. It will challenge you, and you will learn at every turn. You will perfect the use of shooting sticks, which is an everyday reality in Africa. You will practice shooting, loading, and reloading, sometimes on the run, and this is something your local rifle range simply can't offer. Situational stations will make you choose between shooting a soft or a solid bullet first. The course forces you to remember which one rides in which chamber. It sounds easy on paper, but it's not. But if 'repetition truly is the mother of skill,' you will have the opportunity to do it so much that the lessons you are learning will become second nature.

Scattered among the hills and thickets of the sprawling 11,000-acre ranch, the cherry on top (and the talk of every SAAM Safari student) will be the time spent shooting the variety of realistic

speaking, many have argued that sidelock actions are stronger but with weaker stocks (gunsmiths must remove more wood to accommodate the lockwork attached to the sideplates). In contrast, the boxlock action is considered by some to be "weaker" than the sidelock. That's because more steel has to be removed from the action to accommodate the "locks" inside the "box." The reality? Each is sufficiently strong. The quality of steels available today could not have been imagined 100 years ago when many of these debates started. Regardless of your choice, each action type has worked well for more than a century, and they will continue to do so.

I believe automatic ejectors are worth the extra cost. Breaking the action and having two empty cases automatically flung from the smoking chambers is a time-saving benefit in the reloading process. The alternative is having to manually pull the empty brass out with your fingers, as is necessary with a basic extractor rifle. Fast reloads on the practice range are unnecessary. Still, if you find yourself in the middle of an angry elephant herd (involving multiple enraged animals), extra seconds can be a life-saving commodity. Indeed, this would be a rare instance, but it happens each year to *someone* on safari. What if it was you?

There are always older double rifles around, but the days of stealing them off uneducated

Bill Jones used Elmer Keith's .476 Westley Richards to take this Cape buffalo. The 'Jones Collection' of historic double rifles is a testament to Jones' passion for fine rifles and history.

sellers, who in days past were just family who inherited them from granddad or great-granddad and have no idea of their value, are as rare as 50-inch buffalo. If you are comfortable with the price and the rifle,

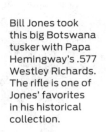

Bill Jones took this big Botswana tusker with Papa Hemingway's .577 Westley Richards. The rifle is one of Jones' favorites in his historical collection.

The Trijicon RMR does not compromise the classic lines of a double rifle. Still, it offers a red-dot aiming point that can significantly increase accuracy for most double shooters.

then a vintage double could be yours; they are still out there for you to find. Double triggers are the rule on most two-pipes, but there is the single trigger option if you feel that getting used to a double trigger is something you just can't do. But first, consider what you're giving up: A double rifle is, effectively, two independent rifles joined by a common stock. There are two barrels, two hammers, two sears, and two triggers. Think of it as a twin-engine airplane. If one engine goes down, you've got a backup to get you home. The same is true for the double rifle and, more specifically, double triggers. They allow you to choose which barrel (and bullet type) you want to fire first and represent a second rifle, ready to go if something goes wrong mechanically. That is the primary reason for getting used to double triggers, and it is a wise investment of your time.

Today, the well-heeled hunter can still

The author in full recoil after firing the eye-crossing .700 Nitro Express. The power it takes to push the 1000-grain bullet makes an impression — on both ends.

Heym USA President Chris Sells tested his company's model 89B in .470 caliber on this massive Australian water buffalo. It passed the test.

walk into Holland & Holland and order a Royal Grade dinosaur stopper if that is your desire. Several years ago, my partner Tim Danklef (a vintage double lover if ever there was one) and I strolled into the London Holland & Holland shop on a long layover en route to Africa. We dressed for comfort, not style, and I believe the folks behind the counters thought we bumbled in off the street looking for a bathroom! I still honestly believe that one lady would have reached beneath the counter for pepper spray if I had asked for her assistance in getting my ordinary American mitts on one of the beauties on display. We still laugh at that, and I often tease my safari companions and say, "That's the reason I am not a Holland shooter today!"

THE UNTOUCHABLES

I have had my hands on, shot, and even hunted with some excellent and very *famous* double rifles. The term *Africana* can cover many things. Sometimes it is a renowned hunting destination, a famous hunter, a piece of art, or even a vintage book. Sometimes, Africana is made of wood and steel.

Many vintage doubles became famous for the men who carried them. Others are historic because of notable game taken with them. Holding one of these treasures is a thrill and a step back in history. And the honor of firing one will be a memorable highlight of your shooting lifetime.

Because of my good friend Bill Jones of Birmingham, Alabama, I have experienced both over the years. Few men have devel-

oped a greater passion for fine, famous, and still functional double rifles than Jones. The "Jones Collection" of historic rifles is the finest of its kind. Not all are doubles, but since this is our topic, I will focus on them. See if any of these rifles or their owners ring a bell. Ernest Hemingway's Westley Richards .577, Elmer Keith's Charles Boswell .500 Nitro Express and .476 Westley-Richards, Phillip Percival's matched pair of Joseph Lang .450 Nitro Expresses, John Hunter's .500 Boswell, and Dave Ommanney's .470 Rigby.

To my eyes, the Holy Grail of all double rifles is Jim Corbett's .450-400 Jeffery. The most noted hunter of man-eaters of his day, or hell, *any* day, Corbett used this rifle to kill the dreaded Champawat tigress, among several other man-eaters

A great example of old and new doubles in action. PH Andrew Dawson (left) with his William Evans .470, and PH Paul Smith (right) with his Krieghoff .500 Nitro Express. Both are classic elephant calibers, as the picture proves.

The author pictured with his favorite 'safari tune-up' species, the feral hog. Porkers like these offer fun, affordable, and fast-paced double-gun practice.

Double Rifle Caliber Considerations

Today's double rifle shooter has many caliber options. Pictured (left to right) are the .450-400 3-inch, all the way up to the mighty .700 Nitro Express.

Double rifles in true dangerous game calibers range from .375 up to the mighty .700 Nitro Express. Today, the three most popular calibers used are the .450/400 3-Inch, .470, and .500 Nitro Express. The .450/400 with its 400-grain bullet in a 9- or 10-pound rifle offers plenty of penetration and light(er) recoil. It can be mastered by just about anyone. The .470, however, is a step up in rifle size and recoil. At 11 pounds, the .470 and its 500-grain bullet generate significantly more recoil and require serious practice to reach proficiency. The .500, of course, is a step above that as well. And even in a 12-pound rifle, the .500 will get your attention. That's not to say that you can't master the largest calibers, but they take more time and practice than the smaller ones.

in the Kumaon region of India. This most lethal man-eating cat on record holds the all-time mark for human kills at 436. Due to the remote area in which the tigress operated, Corbett believed the actual number was higher. The simple hill folk it so long terrorized often just accepted a human kill as part of their sad reality and did not officially report it.

I have shot many of Bill's doubles, including one of his two .700 Nitro Express eye-crossers, but none matched the thrill of my 2016 encounter with Corbett's double. Bill knew of my admiration for the great man and made me his first call upon his purchase of this priceless treasure, as he knew what it would mean to me to get it into my unworthy hands. Humble is an often overused word these days, but it

is the word that struck me as Bill gently handed me the rifle. As I slowly brought it to my shoulder and aligned the rear sight and front bead atop the twin barrels, I knew these were the same sights Corbett himself had lined up on when literal life and death were riding on a well-placed bullet. Laugh if you will, but it was an out-of-body experience that genuinely moved me for the hour or so that I held that piece of precious history. Even more pleasing, Bill and I have a hunt planned, and I will be carrying the Corbett rifle for what will be the *hands-down* highlight of my shooting career. Humble, in this case, really is the *only* word.

AFFORDABLE DOUBLES

The assurance of available ammunition

has led several firearms manufacturers to enter the double-rifle market. There are some fantastic and affordable options if you want to own a double without breaking the bank. Names like Heym, Searcy, Krieghoff, and Merkel, are just a few of the options a hunter can consider when looking for a reasonably priced double.

Common sense and observation have taught me that not all doubles are built to the same standards. You can dress up any rifle with beautiful wood, custom engraving, and even a perfect fit, and come up with a rifle that is not as accurate as it should be. The regulation process is complicated in the extreme to execute for even the most competent gunsmith. And it would eat the rest of my allotted word count if I attempted to explain it here.

Zimbabwe PH Andrew Dawson shows proper form on African shooting sticks. The rifle is his cherished and well-worn William Evans .470 Nitro Express.

In short, the term *double-rifle regulation* describes the time-consuming and challenging process of getting two independent barrels with a slight convergence to eventually print a four-shot grouping of softball-size at, say, 50 yards.

Craig Boddington's excellent book, *Safari Rifles II,* is a must-read for anyone thinking of purchasing a double rifle, new or vintage. It breaks down the subject from A to Z and tackles it thoroughly in book fashion. Included is the science behind the art of double-rifle regulation. It is the most thorough explanation of the process I have ever read.

A warning: I have seen and shot some exceedingly expensive doubles that did not shoot well. And I am talking recognized names here. I saved a safari client a small fortune when he asked me to help him check out a British double he had an option to purchase. I brought along my Searcy .470 for fun as the property owner designed double-rifle practice into his range. My friend knew how to shoot and was not

recoil sensitive, yet several hundred dollars in ammo and sore shoulders for both of us revealed that he was about to buy a classic, beautifully engraved, mint-condition *lemon*. It was 'minute of basketball' at 100 yards and all over the place. His mood did not improve when he started punching tennis ball groups with my American made, working man's double from Butch Searcy's California shop.

The lesson is: never, and I mean *never* buy a second-hand double rifle without shooting it first. The only exception is if you simply want it as a collector's item. If you are new to the double rifle buyers' game, find someone experienced with doubles to go with you to look at and test shoot a potential purchase. They will be in a better position to judge the quality of the rifle.

A well-regulated double is generally far more accurate than its shooter. Compared to today's customized bolt guns, it is a spear thrower, but consider the size of the bullet it is throwing and its purpose:

stopping dangerous game at close range.

But there are options to improve accuracy. I once heard a respected PH say, "By the time most hunters can financially spring for a good double, their best eyesight is behind them." So, what is the answer? A low-power scope can bring surprising accuracy to a well-regulated double, especially at the longer edge of your range.

Yet, many shooters, including myself, cannot warm up to a traditional scope atop the classic lines of a double rifle. A great option that does not clash with the rifle's classic look is the RMR (Ruggedized Miniature Reflex) from Trijicon. The RMR is compact and in no way alters the beauty or balance of the rifle. It allows swift target acquisition and still enables you to shoot with both eyes open because both eyes fixed on the red dot while picking an *exact* spot on the animal. I have found this sight especially useful on moving game in fast follow-up shot situations. Also, easy windage and elevation adjustments make it simple to sight in;

a welcome advantage when that process includes Nitro Express calibers.

DOUBLE-RIFLE PRACTICE

Regardless of the caliber, cost, name brand, or preferred sighting system, you must develop the habit of practicing with the double. Assuming you're not a PH specializing in dangerous game, what are your reasonable options?

I have taken bull elephants with a double, but my last recorded kill was a male bobcat in North Texas. I was hunting feral hogs on a friend's ranch, which just happens to be my favorite tune-up game, when I saw a large 'cat scoot across a dirt road 75 yards away. I instantly swapped my right barrel soft point for a solid, backed into a mesquite bush, and started making squeaking sounds with my hands

to attract it. Within seconds, Mr. Spots came back to the road and began trotting right to me. At about 6 yards, I raised my .470, which instantly brought the cat to a stop with an obvious, "This-can't-be-good" look on its face. Before it could move a whisker, 500 grains of Hornady DGS solid did the trick. It was a fun experience and provided a beautiful pelt, even if I was a bit over-gunned. In addition to the cats, feral hogs are the perfect training ground for the novice or veteran double shooter. They provide lots of running shots, are numerous around the country, taste great, and ranchers are generally happy to have their numbers thinned.

I well remember the days of my youth ghosting around overgrown fencerows and bramble patches with my .22 or 20 gauge trying to kick cottontail out of cover. I also

remember fantasizing that my hands held a beautiful double rifle and that the quarry that might charge me from close range would be a lion, Cape buffalo, or one of Corbett's man-eating tigers. My imagination still works like that at times. Eventually, some of those dreams of charges turned into gut-wrenching realities while hunting and during my filming career. Indeed, my life has been spared several times following a well-placed shot from a double rifle. I think about that a lot.

For some, the double rifle might be an investment opportunity; it may fill a serious hunting need for others. But for this hunter, the double rifle started as a dream that I chased, eventually captured, and with which I will forever have a love affair. Here's to small boys chasing big dreams. **GD**

The author pictured alongside a big Zimbabwe elephant bull taken with his Searcy .470.

Colt Python

The Gun,
The Myth,
The Legend

›BOB CAMPBELL

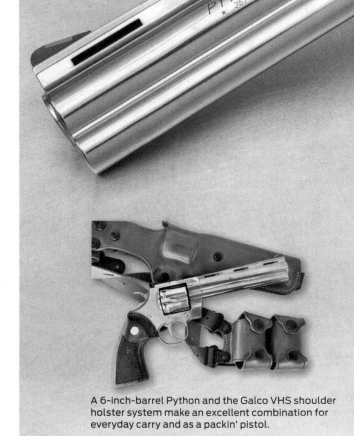

A 6-inch-barrel Python and the Galco VHS shoulder holster system make an excellent combination for everyday carry and as a packin' pistol.

Some firearms become classics because they have served in combat or police service. Others earn the title based on performance alone. The Colt Python has become both a classic and an icon, thanks to its superb accuracy, smoothness, and manufacturing quality. In other words, public accolades, and respect by sophisticated handgunners, have cemented its place in history. The Python has enjoyed much police service and has served in Vietnam, but it has seen only a fraction of the Colt 1911's or Smith & Wesson Combat Magnum's time in battle. The Python — known variously as the "Cadillac of Revolvers" — has always sported superb quality of manufacture and accuracy. It has never been inexpensive, but it just got more affordable by a considerable margin. Like the Single Action Army, the Python is now back in production. Yes, the Python is back. But does it stack up to the original, or is it a poor imitation?

Colt has been out of the double-action revolver business for some time. Recently, it introduced a quality revolver called the Cobra. The new .38 Special Cobra is not anything like the original. It is a more robust and rugged gun than its predecessor, and its action is newly designed. Based on pre-1900 guns, Colt incrementally upgraded its Classic Cobras over the years — first the New Police, then the Police Positive Special with its hammer block. Later came the Detective Special and the aluminum-frame Cobra. There were short-lived variants with a new action. I suppose Colt got its feet wet returning to the revolver market with the Cobra.

Colt had been hinting at the re-introduction of the Python for many years. The new wheelgun is quite impressive, even sensational. Colt introduced the Single Action Army or SAA in 1873. Other than modern steel, today's SAA is practically identical to the original. In contrast, the new Python isn't a makeover of the original. Thus, some purists will not be happy. But I am pleased with the new revolver as I am a shooter, not a collector. The new Python is a fine revolver — as well made as the original with notable improvements.

NEW 2020 PYTHON INTRODUCED

The differences in shooters, collectors, and accumulators are laid out plainly by the different camps' reactions to the 2020 Python. Shooters are happy to have an affordable Python at a $1,500 street price. Accumulators, without a specific goal in mind, want another type of Python to add to the pile. On the other hand,

You must understand the V-spring design of the Colt Python to get the best results. If you do not allow the Colt to reset completely, the trigger will feel locked up. It just needs a full reset. Not understanding its operation has led many people to assume the new model was defective.

collectors are concerned with the value of their collections. I don't think anyone who is holding an unfired New-in-Box 1967 Python needs worry. After all, these are the quintessential collector guns. Extensively fired specimens — or those that show excessive holster wear — are not collector pieces in any case. Pythons selling for $2,000-$3,000 will no doubt continue to go up in value. Understandably, some may question the cost and performance of a new Python that sells for half those prices. How can it be better than an original from 1977, they wonder. These questions miss the point. Few will argue that new 1911s are produced from better steel and have a laser-accurate fit; thus, they are superior to the old 1916 Colts. But are they worth a fraction of the originals? Consider those last-production Pythons that sold for $1,100. The new guns are reasonable. They are inexpensive compared to the collector pieces but remain the most expensive production American double-action revolver.

A fair question might be, what made the original Python the gun it was, and does the current model compare? The Colt Army Special .38 was a favorite of savvy shooters near the turn of the previous century. It eventually became the Colt Official Police, which featured an improved action and hammer block. Colt engineers gave the Official Police adjustable sights and target grips in some versions. The model is heavier than the Smith & Wesson Military & Police, and Colt built it on a .41-size frame. In the interim between the two World Wars, a great deal of development occurred in the handgun world. While the history of the National Match 1911 is well known, less understood is revolver upgrades. King's Gun Works and others perfected revolver sights, trigger actions, and

ribbed barrels. These modifications led to the new short-action Smith & Wesson revolvers after the war. Colt developed an even more extensive revamp based on custom revolvers of the day.

Colt released the Python in 1956. Shortly after, the heavy barrel and barrel underlug underwent a few design changes, but engineers maintained the distinctive Python profile. The revolver featured a lustrous finish and a super smooth hand-fitted action. The balance was superb. The Python's action differed from the Official Police and would go out of time more often than comparable Smiths. You couldn't dry-fire the

action extensively, or you'd risk breaking the floating firing pin. These trade-offs that allowed the shooter to own and fire one of the most accurate handguns of any type ever manufactured. Colt chambered it for the powerful .357 Magnum cartridge. Barrel lengths included the standard 4- and 6-inch

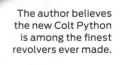

The author believes the new Colt Python is among the finest revolvers ever made.

Essential features of the new Python include a countersunk muzzle and an easily changed front sight.

The new Python is an all-stainless revolver that is similar but not identical to the original.

sizes, and later the 2 ½-, 8-, and 5-inch guns marked a small production run at one time. The Python was comparatively expensive, selling for about fifty percent more than Smith & Wesson's best revolvers. Indeed, the Python was among the smoothest and most controllable double-action revolvers.

Specifications are

not quite the same thing as tolerances. Most revolvers are only as tight as they need to be, and some are very good. It isn't profitable to hold tolerances as tightly as possible and try to sell the revolver at a price point that fits most budgets. The Python's tolerances ensure that it is accurate. The wheelgun is tight where it counts. Close tolerances result in less eccentric wear. Python's operating system transfers more recoil energy to the action than S&Ws, but it takes many thousands of shots before the revolver needs to be re-timed. Keep most of your shooting to .38 Special target loads, and the Python will last

The redesigned cylinder features recessed chambers for safety.

The new Python features a heavier topstrap and improved sights.

practically forever.

Ultimately, the Python became so expensive to manufacture it eventually was sidelined and then went out of production. Oddly enough, collectors began to pay exorbitant prices for the iconic snake guns, costs that many average shooters would not pay. Interestingly, such market fluctuations in a finite quantity hurt those of us who are shooters — collectors priced the Python out of most shooters' budgets. Few people understand condition grading, and I have seen shooter-grade Pythons for sale at ridiculous prices lately. The popularity of shows like *The Walking Dead* has raised the demand for Pythons, particularly 6-inch stainless steel versions. Despite the high value of Pythons in my collection, I do not wish to sell them. These fine revolvers will find their way into my heirs' safes someday.

Let's shift our thoughts to the present. I have to admit sometimes I thought twice before sticking my original Python in a holster and going hiking or camping or merely carrying it as I go about my daily chores. While the Wilson Combat and Les Baer handguns I often use are more expensive than the classic Python, they are replaceable. So, now with the new production Python, I have the opportunity to obtain a backup to my original 1977 model, and naturally, I had to have

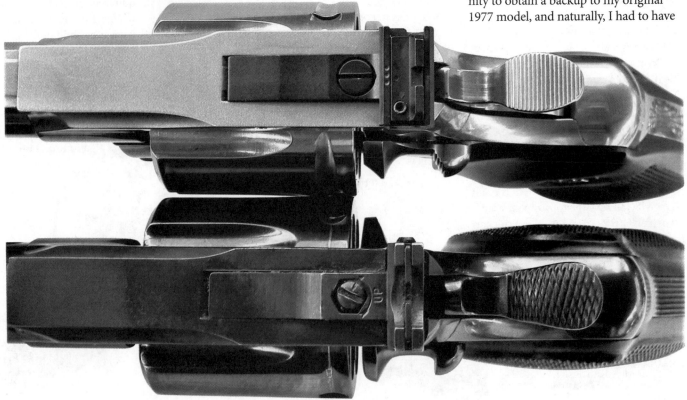

Subtle changes in geometry in the new Colt revolver result in an improvement in handling.

one. I found one at an MSRP of $1,500, one of the second or third guns available in my state. The new Python is a well-made revolver, but it is not the same as the older Colt. It's a better gun than the original, as you would expect. Colt has had a few years to look over the Python, and there has been some competition as well. I am not certain Colt looked at its old competitor Smith & Wesson as hard as it looked at Ruger. The Ruger GP100 enjoys an enviable reputation for ruggedness. The GP100 is not as smooth as the Python, but it takes a good shot to prove the Python is the more accurate revolver. The difference may be purely subjective.

Colt has beefed up the frame and modified the action. Today, CNC machines turn out Pythons. Throats, leades, and rifling are precise, and the action is precisely fitted. Detail changes are essential. For example, the barrel crown is now countersunk. The front sight is easily changed. Colt says the topstrap is about 30 percent stronger and mics out thicker than the original. It wasn't challenging to redesign the rear sight to make a sturdier unit while retaining a wide range of adjustments. The triggerguard changes the angle between the hand, fingers, and trigger, allowing greater

The Python may owe some of its sturdiness to design influence from the Ruger GP100.

leverage on an already smooth action.

The new production revolver is pure Python in feel. Cocking the hammer in single action results in a bit of perceived drag (as it seems the cylinder is not locked), but as you press the trigger, the Python locks up tightly indeed. The action is buttery smooth, something it has in common with the original. The double-action trigger breaks at only 9 pounds, well below the threshold I had expected to be necessary for reliable ignition. The new model is

smoother than the first generation, even though my original has been in use for more than 43 years. The improved action is slick, more robust, and uses fewer parts — we have no bone of contention to pick with it over the older revolver. With an improved geometry, we have a piece that handles and fits the hand better. The sights are more rugged. Engineers redesigned the cylinder.

Save for the grips, not a single piece is interchangeable with the original revolver. The grips, by the way, are practically artwork. Featuring stabilizing studs, they were so tight I was reluctant to remove them for photos. For an original look, Deer Hollow (deerhollowonline.com) offers reproductions of the classic Python grips. After years of use, I have replaced my 1977 Python grips with a new set from Deer Hollow. They would look great on the new production model as well. The new Python, so far, is offered only in stainless steel. Lighter wood looks excellent on this revolver.

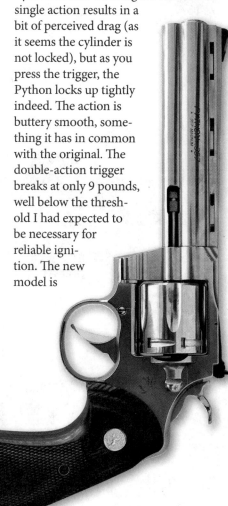

Before taking the new Python to the range, I dry-fired it extensively using snap caps. The action is smooth but requires attention to detail when handling. I use the proven method of firing a double-action revolver: line the sights up and press the trigger to the rear. As the revolver recoils, allow the trigger to reset and fire again when

Shooting from a braced position, the .357 Magnum Python becomes a rifle on the hip.

the sights are re-aligned. One difference between the Colt and the Smith & Wesson line of revolvers: The Colt V-spring powers the hammer and returns the trigger. The Smith features a separate trigger return spring. If you do not allow the Colt to reset completely, the trigger seems to lock up. On the contrary, it just needs a full reset.

SHOOTING THE PYTHON

The Colt Python is like any other revolver. Learn the trigger action and practice sight picture and sight alignment for best accuracy. You may believe you are a good shot, and you may think the pistol is accurate, but it is a tall order to shoot up to the Colt's potential. I have a consuming interest in accuracy. The means of achieving the best accuracy are indelible in my mind from long practice. The Python is an excellent revolver in offhand double-action fire. It comes on target quickly and gets hits more rapidly

If your Python doesn't get covered in a powder residue, you are not getting the most out of it.

Carrying the Python

I have used several holster combinations with good results. Use a high-ride holster for the 4-inch gun to keep it angled slightly forward for a rapid presentation. The Bullard Leather (bullardleather.com) pancake holster offers excellent all-around utility. With a covering garment, the 4-inch gun conceals well. For use under a concealed carry vest, I sometimes use the Bullard Leather belt slide, a nicely finished and stitched holster that keeps the revolver close to the body and aids in concealment. The Python is a big piece, and the Bullard Leather scabbard keeps it bearable on the hip.

Use a crossdraw holster to carry the 4-inch model for hunting or spelunking. The Galco Phoenix holster is perfect for this application and is among the finest factory-ready scabbards ever devised. However, the 6-inch version presents a more significant problem. I don't want to go to a chest holster or a low-riding field holster, so I prefer something versatile that allows wearing the long barrel revolver under a covering garment.

The Galco Vertical Holster System, or VHS, has recently been upgraded and is the right choice for a big sixgun. When wearing any holster, you need a sturdy gun belt, so don't neglect that part of the equation. Also, I have used Galco's 2 x 2 carrier, which holds six cartridges. I have also used the Speedloader pouch worn on the right front of the belt. The VHS shoulder holster balances the weight of the handgun against a pair of speedloader pouches. Compared to many 6-inch hunting revolvers, the Python is not excessively heavy, and the VHS holds it comfortably. The VHS spreads out the handgun's weight on your shoulders, more broadly distributing the load than carrying a 4-inch revolver on the belt. It takes a bit of acclimation to adapt to the shoulder holster. It is not for everyone. Don't waste time with a cheap holster combination. The VHS is pure class and well-designed.

Among the most comfortable means of carrying a 6-inch Magnum revolver is the Galco VHS shoulder holster. It fits the Python like a glove.

than almost any other double-action revolver. The addition of Deer Hollow grips has resulted in an improvement over the originals in handling. I can understand why Colt modified the original grips to allow speedloader use, but the cut on both sides doesn't allow the best hand fit. The nicely checkered grips are a significant improvement. In absolute accuracy, the single-action trigger allows a trained shooter to perform wonders off the bench.

Accurate loads are essential. The 178-grain semi-wadcutter (mattsbullets.com) and a stout charge of Titegroup in the .38 Special case breaks 1,060 fps — a sweet spot for Python accuracy. A solid inch for a five-shot group at 25 yards is not out of the question, but most groups print larger at 1.5 inches. The factory Black Hills 125-grain JHP load is superb for most uses, including personal defense. I have confidence in this loading at 1,440 fps in the 4-inch gun and 1,550 fps in the 6-incher, and the new 127-grain Honey Badger is a great performer with much to recommend. The Black Hills Ammunition 158-grain JHP load edged the 1,400 fps mark in the 6-inch revolver for outdoor use. Ammunition performance is a critical part of the picture with the Python and the .357 Magnum cartridge. Colt and Black Hills make a perfect combination.

FINDING THE 2020 PYTHON

While I still enjoy the older Colts, the big news is the new Python. No matter how we may wax poetic over its attributes, the original gun is not easily obtainable. At present, the 2020 Python is not in the usual channels, either. I have yet to see one for sale on the shelf in a showcase. All Pythons so far have been subject to preorder and are spoken for, so expect to look around. There is a waiting list. Most dealers are fair with buyers, while some are greedy and engage in price gouging. Take this into consideration when you spend your hard-earned money. If you want a new Python, get on a list and be patient; it is worth the wait. In my opinion, it is superior to the original, but then it should be. Materials and manufacturing have come a long way since 1956, and CNC machinery produc-

es consistency and close tolerances. You will not regret this purchase.

COLLECTING THE COLT PYTHON

If you are a collector rather than a shooter and are looking for some return on the dollar, the Colt Python may represent steady appreciation. The caveat: be prepared to wait at least five years for any return on investment. I don't believe the new revolver will hurt originals' value, as the older guns are authentic collectibles. Hard-used or refinished revolvers are just shooters. Guns without the original box or missing original grips are just shooters. Last I checked, the price for re-finishing a Python was upwards of seven-hundred dollars. The revolver will look good after refinish, but anyone who knows Pythons will be able to spot a re-finished handgun as opposed to the original Colt blue. When you begin to subtract the need to re-finish, find an appropriate box from a shooter-grade revolver to make it collectible, you may run up a total of more than the gun would be worth. I have seen quite a few Colts at fair prices. The overpriced ones are usually the shooter-grade types that sport funky grips or honest wear. You should shoot them, but folks are asking more than shooter price for them. It would be best if you avoided these. The new Python is a much better value as a shooter.

The first-gen Python was an upgraded Shooting Master. Colt built these target-grade .38 revolvers on the Official Police frame. Interestingly, the original Python was beefed up in certain areas to contain the energy and momentum of the .357 Magnum cartridge. The Magnum doesn't blow guns up, but small parts take a beating. So the original, like the current Python, was an improved version built for strength. When Colt ceased production of the Python in 1999, demand skyrocketed. The Python was not Colt's bestseller, or it would have kept it in production. A finite supply seems to

The Colt Python, top, is a very lovely shooter-grade revolver. The Colt Three-Fifty-Seven, below, is much rarer with a short production run. It brings a fraction of the price of the Python.

In rapid-fire or absolute accuracy, there is nothing quite like a Colt Python.

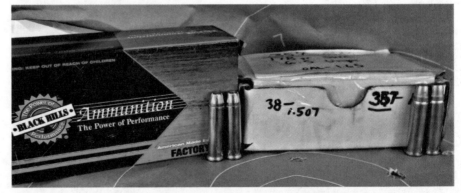

The author achieved excellent results from the new Python using factory ammunition. However, to save money and achieve ultimate accuracy, the author uses handloads, right.

2020 Colt Python Problems and Fixes

The author feels the new Python is a sensation, a great shooter well worth its price.

While the manual of arms is the same as most revolvers, the Colt trigger action demands special handling.

After the introduction of Colt's new .357 Magnum Python in 2020, there were several problems marring shooters' impression of the re-introduced snake. Today, with nearly 30,000 Colt Pythons shipped, the problem guns have been few and far between. There were legitimate problems with a few of the new revolvers. In my professional opinion, though, some of the issues, including one I witnessed, resulted from folks who did not know how to fire a Colt revolver correctly. Some reported light primer strikes. I admit I had that concern as well. The action is so light that I felt it wouldn't crack hard Magnum primers with reliability. Magnum primers, such as the CCI 550, feature a thicker or harder primer cup to withstand Magnum pressures. A pierced primer is a real possibility.

The two new model Pythons I have fired had very smooth trigger actions and were reliable with a wide range of loads. These include .38 Special and .357 Magnum factory ammunition, handloads, and magnum loads with the hardest magnum primers. But two guns are not the same as thousands. Colt reports that some foreign-produced ammunition might be off-spec and not function correctly. I have used quite a bit of ammunition produced overseas and, while it will not win a prize for match-grade accuracy, the loads are usually reliable. The new Python problem is the same issue seen with the older Colt Official Police and the original Detective Special. If you do not understand the specific operation pattern and don't allow the trigger to reset before you fire again, the action can lock up.

It is easy to demonstrate. In one case I examined, the shooter had failed to allow the Colt to reset. He panicked and kept pressing the trigger until he bent the hand, locking the revolver up. Even with the new linear spring, the latest Python is much the same gun. I am not saying some of the folks making the Internet noise don't know how to shoot. I am saying they don't know how to manipulate the Colt action properly. You can learn it and most shooters have no problem.

Those accustomed to the Smith & Wesson, Ruger, and Taurus actions may have a more difficult time adjusting. Others master the Python seamlessly. The usual shooter having a problem with the Colt Python is used to a long double-action-only automatic pistol. They press the trigger and then ride the reset. This technique isn't going to work with the Colt Python.

Colt announced that it would 'modify' the original action for a heavier strike. I inspected a Colt Python delivered to a local dealer. The action was within an ounce of my earlier new model Python. So, I am not concerned with light primer strikes. Don't spend the money for a Python unless you are willing to understand the action and its proper manipulation.

The second problem with the new Colt Python has been revolvers delivered with side plate screws that were either loose or worked loose. A simple tightening would seem to be the cure, but the issue certainly isn't something you would expect with a Colt. The company has elected to use a thread locker on the side plate screws to keep them secured. Colt recommends only experienced gunsmiths work with these handguns. If necessary, a gunsmith can easily break the thread locker to gain access. Colt has fixed this problem in current revolvers.

If your revolver has ever had a loose side plate, you should return it to Colt for repair and adjustment. The lockwork may have borne against the side plate, damaging small parts. Another complaint was 'cosmetic damage' around the muzzle. These are easily polished out, and if you own one, you should send it to Colt.

I have examined a number of the new model Pythons. I find the advantages over the original are apparent. The new generation is more rugged, can be dry-fired, is smoother, and perhaps more accurate. The teething problems are minuscule compared to many new introductions. I have no problem at all recommending the Python for any use.

The Python is the author's only Colt, but it may be the best example.

Colt's fit and finish are excellent. Perhaps a few early models were scuffed during manufacture. Colt designed them to be fired and used!

The elusive and highly sought-after new model 4.25-inch barrel Colt Python.

The Colt side plate screws may work loose in early model revolvers.

This is a very 1970s-looking Colt. The trigger and hammer are gold flash plated, and the grips are non-original. However, it is a great shooter.

With good ammunition, an original shooter-grade Python is an excellent all-around defense and hunting handgun.

Be sure that the sight screws are not touched at all. A tiny scratch will drive the price of a collector gun down. A shooter? Not so much.

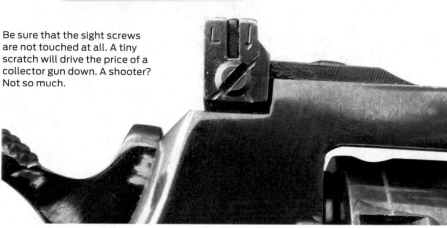

trigger something in the human mind. Overnight, demand priced the Python out of the reach of many shooters. By 2005, even Custom Shop production had ceased. The stainless steel guns seem particularly desirable.

If I could own any vintage Python, regardless of the price, it would be the stainless steel version for longevity. That said, the 4-inch blued version seems an all-business handgun worth its cost in slick eye appeal alone for pure classiness. If you are going to collect Pythons, be sure to learn the various nuances and desirability. For many, a specimen from 1960 and earlier is the most desirable. There are several generations of grips as well. An astute collector can spot the early grips without the step, which Colt added later. The step may be to accommodate speed loaders or as a superior thumb rest. I have seen excellent quality grips bring upwards of five-hundred dollars, average ones about half that. If you own an otherwise good-condition Python with replacement grips, the originals may get you up to speed for value. Be sure you obtain the correct generation. Again, Deer Hollow offers

superb-quality reproduction grips at a fair price. Quality is superior to the original in every way. It isn't a restoration replacement, but it is a way to make a nice shooter original.

I would recommend purchasing the *Standard Catalog of Firearms* and studying the details. Then, troll the Internet and prowl gun shows. There are several genuinely excellent Pythons for sale at shows, though some guns are practically junk. As an example, at one show, I spied a very lovely shooter-grade 4-inch-barrel blued finish 1977 Python for $2,000. Another seller priced a nickeled gun with plastic grips at $1,800, and it later sold for $1,600. Then I examined what had once been a decent 4-inch barrel Python. The frame was blue, the barrel and cylinder were devoid of finish. I could not imagine why anyone would desecrate a Python in that manner. The fellow was asking $2,000. I am confident that he took the gun home. Eight or nine hundred would have been fair considering the gun needed bluing. But then again, when I see something like this, I am suspicious of a firearm that someone has abused.

The 4-inch barrel seems most common. Six-inch revolvers are plentiful as well. The 8- and 2 ½-inch-barrel Pythons are the rarest. Colt made some 5-inch guns; the Florida State Patrol had some, and so did the royal guard in Kuwait. I have never seen one.

If you are buying for investment, you are a gunny person attempting to combine the retirement account and gun collecting. The problem is, you will not wish to part with the gun at any price! I am a shooter. I obtain guns that I fire, including my Pythons and an 1874 Colt Single Action Army. Colt made these to shoot. No one wants to pay too much. Spending a little too much for a shooter is OK; overpaying for a collector Colt that isn't as good as you thought it was is a disaster. Do your homework before shedding greenbacks. **GD**

Above: A beautiful original Colt Army Special with a professionally shortened barrel. A 6-inch Colt Three-Fifty-Seven and a 1964 Detective Special with a rare 3-inch barrel. Each is rarer than the Python but brings a fraction of the price.

Above: This is among the first Colt .357 Magnums: the New Service. Collector interest is small compared to the Python.

Right: Know your grips! That is a 1956 Colt-style grip on the left, 1969 on the right.

A 19th-Century snipe shooting scene, a lithograph by A. B. Frost. Hunters specially trained dogs, like the two setters in the picture, to handle snipe.

SNIPE, SNIPE GUNS, and SNIPERS

> NICK HAHN

A snipe in flight.

A popular prank called "snipe hunting" originated over a century ago in boys' summer camps in America. It involves unsuspecting (naive) boys dispatched into the woods with a gunnysack and flashlight — or a lamp in the older times — and instructed to hold the bag open, shining the light inside the bag, and whistle, supposedly to attract a snipe into the bag! Ironically, unlike the popular prank, real snipe hunting is possibly the least practiced form of upland hunting in America today. In Europe, the snipe is considered the premier game bird. In Japan, perhaps the only country in Asia where sport hunting took root in the early 20th Century, the faithful eagerly pursue the *shigi*, as the Japanese call the snipe, each season. The Japanese even make special equipment for snipe hunting, like snipe calls and other neat stuff rarely found elsewhere. For various reasons, in

Below: Snipe engraving is not common. Additionally, most snipe engravings are not particularly good, with birds appearing either as skinny woodcocks or sandpipers. These snipes, laser engraved on the Franchi Fenice, are surprisingly realistic and well done.

America, snipe shooting today has only a tiny following, although it is a very loyal and dedicated group.

Perhaps most people are unaware that the name "sniper" was coined sometime in the 19th Century when wing shooting, or "shooting flying," as hunters called it then, became popular. Hunters who shot game on the wing found that snipes were a challenging target. According to some sources, the British snipe hunters in India gave birth to this name. It could have just as easily started on the British Isles since "shooting flying" was popular at that time, and both terms, *snipe*, and *sniper*, are English in origin. Because snipes were considered a challenging target, anyone who could hit the elusive and speedy bird in the air was considered an expert shot and called a "sniper." However, through the years, the name "sniper" came to be associated with expert rifle shots in military or law enforcement circles, not bird hunters, as it originally meant. Many non-English speaking countries like Russia and others use the term "sniper" for their military and police marksmen. But the name was born in the marshes and fields of the British Isles and India, where sportspeople pursued feathered, winged targets with shotguns.

In America, the name snipe was

A pen and ink drawing by Eldridge Hardie, who illustrated the excellent little book by Worth Mathewson, *Reflections on Snipe*, published as a limited edition of 600 in 1995.

generally applied in broad terms to all shorebirds during the market hunting days of the 19th and early 20th Centuries. Market hunters and sportsmen engaged in shorebird shooting, taking various types of plovers and sandpipers in massive numbers for the market. Restaurants offered shorebirds on their menus along with waterfowl and other game. Shooting shorebirds for sport became popular. Some claim the sub-gauges — 28 gauge and the .410 bore — gained popularity in America with shorebird shooting before skeet made its appearance. Supposedly, well-heeled sportspeople would arm themselves with dainty sub-gauge Parkers or other similar classic American doubles to make shorebird shooting more sporting. Be that as it may, the market hunters preferred larger bore sizes that carried more shot, such as 12- or 10-gauge shells they loaded with a fine shot like No. 10. They would hide in blinds with a decoy spread and lure the birds with calls until flocks landed, then ground sluiced them to get as many as possible. There was nothing "sporting" about it, of course. But, they were shooting for the market, not for sport, and it was more feasible to

Early 1950s artwork shows a surprised hunter on a snipe hunt. Like many similar pieces, it illustrated an article that promoted snipe shooting, which had just reopened in 1953.

do it that way rather than trying to knock down one bird at a time with a small-bore gun, as the well-heeled did with their 28s and .410s.

Whatever the case may be, the bottom line is that wingshooters took an awful lot of shorebirds — including snipes — during that era. The high-volume shooting of waterfowl and shorebirds by market hunters, combined with the destruction of habitat by draining wetlands for agriculture and urban sprawl, took a heavy toll and brought about a sharp decline in the population of migratory birds. In 1913, the U.S. banned the hunting of migratory birds in the spring. In 1918, the U.S., Canada, and Great Britain signed the International Migratory Bird Treaty, establishing additional conservation measures such as seasons and bag limits on migratory birds. But the migratory bird population continued to drop. In 1934, the U.S. passed stricter laws, imposed shorter seasons and bag limits, and required Duck Stamps. Most of these regulations involved waterfowl, but they covered shorebirds as well.

It was still not enough, and in 1941 game departments banned the shooting of all shorebirds, including snipes. Ironically, the snipe population was not in the same dire situation as the rest of the shorebirds, and the snipe population in North America did not suffer quite like the other species. The leading cause of the decline in the snipe population in North America was habitat loss, although overshooting did impact it. The closure of snipe season was in effect for only a dozen years, from 1941 until 1953, but it was enough to significantly affect the popularity of snipe shooting in America. In 1953, the U.S. Fish and Wildlife Service (USFWS) reopened the snipe season, while the ban remained for all other shorebirds, which has lasted to

The author's wife, Jo, with a pair of snipes she shot using a 20-gauge single-shot in Yonabaru, Okinawa, in 1967.

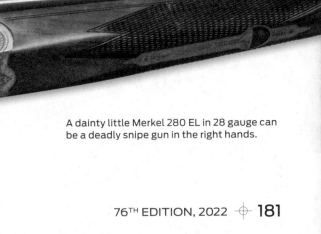

A dainty little Merkel 280 EL in 28 gauge can be a deadly snipe gun in the right hands.

The author's brother Jim with a snipe limit that he shot with a Beretta Model 303 20-gauge autoloader at Gray Lodge, Gridley, California, in 1988.

this day. A survey conducted by the US-FWS concluded that the snipe population was healthy enough to handle moderate hunting pressure, so they reopened the season.

When the USFWS lifted the ban in 1953, some who had hunted snipes before the ban rejoiced; however, most hunters, including the younger generation, had never paid any attention to the snipe and did not pursue it. To this day, the popularity of snipe hunting in America is virtually non-existent. There are many factors involved in the lack of interest in this bird. Some believe that the closure of the spring season in 1913 had the most significant impact. Others cite the small size of the bird and difficulty in identifying it. There isn't any apparent reason, but snipe hunting just never caught on after 1953.

Specially trained pointing dogs handled the very skittish snipes, which usually refused to sit tight. Spaniels and retrievers worked close to flush the cagey little bird. Market hunters rarely used dogs except for retrieving duties since they mostly hunted from blinds. Today, you'd have to look far and wide to find a true snipe dog in America. In England and Europe, where many still consider the snipe to be a premium game bird, hunters continue to train snipe dogs. The Irish setter, not the big, lumbering show variety, but the smaller, original type in Ireland, are reputed to be premier snipe dogs. Irish hunters have trained them for generations to hunt snipes. But in America, it seems to have become a dying art. Today, the most common snipe hunting method is "walking-up," slogging through flooded pastures or swampy areas, flushing snipes as you walk. In some places, in Asia or South America, you could conceivably hire boys to walk

The author's German shorthair, Smoke, with some snipes in 1970. Smoke learned to handle the little birds well, managing to pin them down on point about every third or fourth bird. The snipe gun is a Franchi 48AL 20 gauge.

A limit of snipe shot with a Browning Superposed Super Light 20 gauge in Petaluma, California, with Smoke's help in 1973!

in-line and flush the birds toward you. In other words, you could engage in driven snipe shooting. This technique was the form practiced by the British in India and other parts of the world during the British Empire's old days and still practiced on some of the UK estates for exclusive driven shoots. However, that is rarely done today in other places, perhaps only by some outfitters who specialize in bird shooting. But in most of the world, and indeed, in America, it is the

walk-up
shooting that is most practiced for snipe, unless, of course, you are lucky enough to have one of those rare old-fashioned snipe dogs.

In America, the late 19th and the early 20th Century were the peak years of snipe shooting. Aside from those who shot shorebirds with decoys from a blind, A. B. Frost's lithographs depicted dedicated snipe shooters, showing sportsmen with setters shooting the zippy little birds. There were, in fact, some who were addicted to snipe shooting. Perhaps the best-known snipe hunter of that period in America was J. J. Pringle, a wealthy and somewhat eccentric sportsman who seemed to have been obsessed with snipes. He traveled all over North America and owned property in Louisiana, where he shot incredible snipe numbers, averaging over a hundred daily. According to his detailed gamebook, he shot over 78,000 snipes during a 20-year span, which he documented in his book,

An incredible Belgian Dumoulin round-body 12 bore that weighs 6 pounds, 10 ounces, and is an excellent snipe gun. It is a graceful-looking and beautifully handling double.

Browning's long-discontinued model, the Double Auto "Twentyweight," made for an excellent snipe gun in 12 gauge.

Twenty Years' Snipe Shooting, published in 1899. Pringle's best single-day bag is recorded at 366, by far the highest number of snipes shot by anyone in a day ever recorded. In 1988, Worth Mathewson of Sand Lake Press republished the book.

Mathewson is perhaps the dean of snipe shooting in America today and has written numerous articles about it in many of the best-known sporting publications through the years, more so than any other current active outdoor writer. He also published a special limited edition (600 copies) of *Reflections on Snipe* in 1995. The book is a collection of various pieces written by different snipe shooters from all over the world, and it is wonderfully illustrated in pen and ink by Eldridge Hardie. Mathewson has shot snipes worldwide, but his primary sniping grounds have been the Oregon marshes near where he lives. Today, it seems he is the only known writer who is an avid sniper. The late Charles Waterman often wrote about snipe shooting and penned the forward for *Reflections on Snipe,* in which he lamented the fact that the little bird is so overlooked by hunters today. Few regularly wrote about the game bird during the last half a century. Exceptions included Waterman,

from the 1960s through the 1980s, and Mathewson, from the 1970s until today.

Occasionally an article will appear about the snipe by one of the few remaining aficionados of the trade, but those articles are few and far between. That's a pity because, before the snipe shooting ban in 1941, many in America actively pursued this wonderful sporting bird. Among those who loved to shoot snipes and eagerly sought it when the season reopened was Ernest Hemingway, the celebrated American author. Like his favorite 19th-Century Russian author Ivan Turgenev, Hemingway had a particular affinity for the snipe. Anyone who has read Turgenev's *Sportsman's Sketches* (also called *Hunter's Notebook or Hunter's Album* and other variations in some translations) has noted how often Turgenev mentions snipe hunting. Incidentally, throughout his life,

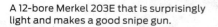

A 12-bore Merkel 203E that is surprisingly light and makes a good snipe gun.

A Jack snipe. Note that the smaller bird is stockier and has a shorter bill than the Common or Wilson snipe.

Hemingway always had a copy of this neat little book in his possession.

For several years now, the game departments in various states have actively promoted snipe hunting. Magazine articles by game biologists and other management experts have lamented that the snipe is an overlooked and under-hunted game species in America. I have seen some game department publications that published recipes for cooking snipes, encouraging hunters to take more interest. Periodically an article will appear on snipe shooting in one of the outdoor publications, showing that, however rare, there are indeed still those who avidly pursue this bird.

The snipe found in North America is the Wilson snipe, while the one found in the rest of the world is called the Common snipe. The difference between the Wilson and the Common (also called Eurasian snipe) is indistinguishable.

The main difference appears to be the number of tail feathers, one more for the Wilson type (eight versus seven), and a very slight difference in white edging on the wingtips. It wasn't until 2003 when the Wilson snipe was declared a separate species. Before that date, it was considered a sub-species of Common snipe. But whatever you call it, and wherever you find it, it is the same delightful game bird. The distinctive "scaiping" alarm call that it gives as it flushes, and the trademark erratic zig-zag pattern that it flies, cannot be mistaken for any other bird.

KNOW YOUR SNIPE

The Wilson snipe is often mistakenly called Jack snipe by some, but Jacks are a smaller, different bird. The Jack snipe is the smallest of all the snipe species and is a stockier bird with a shorter bill that is not native to North America, while the Giant snipe of South America the largest. There is the Double snipe in Asia and Europe, which is considered a great trophy by hunters and is about one-half times larger than the Common snipe.

Several other species are either smaller or larger than the Common type. The most often encountered and pursued is the "Common" or Eurasian snipe of Asia and Europe and the Wilson snipe of North America. The South American snipe is identical to the Eurasian or

Above: Ernest Hemingway, with his Browning Superposed and snipes shot in Sun Valley, Idaho, in the 1950s.
Below: A lovely 20-gauge round-action CSMC Inverness makes for a nice snipe gun.

Common snipe. Some South American species are a bit different, like the Andean snipe. But in general, you can find the South American snipe in boggy lowland areas, just like the Eurasian or Common. Except for some local variety, the snipes found in Africa are the Eurasian and Common variety, which migrated from Europe and other parts north. Those found in Australia migrated from Asia, particularly from South East Asia, called Java snipes.

THE SNIPE GUNS

Many snipes are shot incidentally by duck hunters using tightly choked 12 gauges with heavy duck loads. But that doesn't mean that a typical duck gun makes for a good snipe gun.   Ideally,

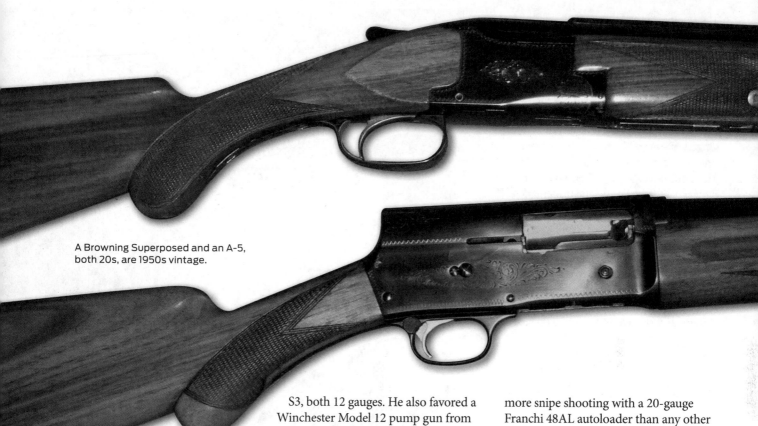

A Browning Superposed and an A-5, both 20s, are 1950s vintage.

a light, open-bored upland gun with small shot, #8s or #9s, is best suited for snipes. Although you can shoot them with a .410, you would be handicapping yourself using this small bore size. The sparse pattern of the .410 won't allow you to hit snipes consistently. As has been said many times by various shotgun writers, the .410 is an expert's gun and best left in the hands of a very good shot who knows its limitations. The 20 seems to be ideal for the snipe, not too small and not too big. A light, open-bored 20 loaded with 7/8 ounces of #8 or #9 shot makes for almost an ideal snipe gun. However, that doesn't mean that another bore size would not make a good snipe gun.

Among those who pursued the snipe passionately in the past, the vast majority used 12-gauge doubles, including Ernest Hemingway. Hemingway seems to have shot most of his snipes with either a 12-gauge Browning Superposed or a 12-gauge Winchester Model 21. However, he had several other guns, including a W. C. Scott (which he supposedly used to take his own life) and a Beretta

S3, both 12 gauges. He also favored a Winchester Model 12 pump gun from time to time.

J. J. Pringle seemed to prefer a Purdey, but he also shot other English Best Guns, including a Stephen Grant. But Purdeys appeared to be his favorite, and they were all 12 gauges. One of the most avid snipe hunters that I have known used an old Belgian double that had no maker's name. Despite the lack of the maker's name, it was a magnificent double, and yes, it was a 12. Another man, the best wing shot I have ever met, shot an old pre-war Browning humpback 12 gauge that was choked full. Of course, he hit all his game with that gun, and as I said, he was the best wing shot I ever met in my life.

I have shot snipes on five different continents and with all types of shotguns during some half a century of hunting. I've bagged North American Wilson snipes the most. Still, I've also taken many Eurasian or Common snipes in Europe and Asia and North Africa and South America, including the Giant snipe. I've taken snipes with everything ranging from a 28-gauge pump gun to 12 gauges in all categories; pumps, autos, side by sides, and over/unders. However, I probably shot more snipes and did

more snipe shooting with a 20-gauge Franchi 48AL autoloader than any other type of shotgun. It seems that the daily limit on snipes in America has remained the same — at eight — since 1953. I didn't always shoot my limit of eight, but I bagged the most snipe limits with the Franchi 20-gauge autoloader. After the Franchi, the 20-gauge double was probably the most often used for snipe shooting by me, both the side by sides and the over/unders. Lately, I have started to use the 28 gauge more often, probably because the little 28s are delightful to hold and shoot, not because I am shooting them any better.

SNIPERS HERE AND NOW

Hunters in Europe and other parts of the world will continue to pursue the snipe and consider it a premier winged target. Despite our game departments' attempts to encourage and raise interest in America, it is unlikely that it will ever become popular as it has in other countries. It is not in average American hunters' DNA to go after the relatively small bird when larger birds such as the ringneck pheasant are available. Like dove and quail, hunters pursue smaller birds because there is dog hunting tradition surrounding them. Ruffed grouse

hunting is one example so steeped in tradition and, in fact, like quail hunting, has had a cult following for generations. The same applies to the American woodcock (which usually goes hand in hand with grouse hunting) or any other bird that you can hunt with dogs.

On the other hand, doves have always been shot in large numbers and have become a tradition of sorts in many parts of the country as a "warm-up" for other hunting types since dove season is usually the first to open. Many hunters will shoot doves on opening day and pay them no more mind until early September of the following year. According to ammunition makers, they sell more shotgun ammo during dove season than any other time of the year.

It is a pity that more American hunters don't take advantage of snipe hunting in this country. But that is how it is and how it will be, at least for the foreseeable future. American hunters never established the snipe shooting tradition like wingshooters in Europe and other places.

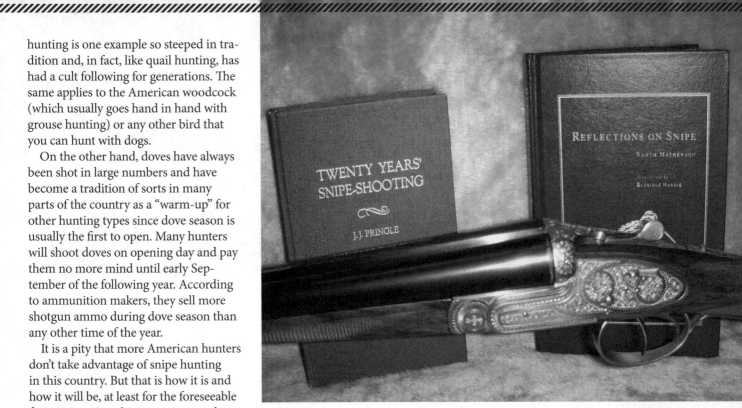

Two worthy books on snipe hunting, *Twenty Years' Snipe-Shooting* by J. J. Pringle and *Reflections on Snipe* by Worth Mathewson. The gun is a lightweight, 16-gauge Garbi, an excellent shotgun for this niche application.

The Franchi 48AL 20 gauge is perhaps an ideal snipe gun if you choose a repeater. It is light and points wonderfully for speedy targets like snipes. This one is the long-discontinued Eldorado Grade with the beautifully hand-engraved Arabesque scroll.

While tradition surrounds other game birds in America — most especially quail and grouse, and of course, waterfowl — snipe hunting is an orphan in this regard.

Still, though the numbers may be small, some — like Worth Mathewson today and Charles Waterman in the past — will continue to pursue the snipe and keep writing about the sport. However, although now a rare breed of wingshooter, new members will join the snipe hunting fraternity. New "snipers" will chase this wonderful game bird, and like the shotgunners of long ago, they too will pursue the snipe with passion. 🅖🅓

A Treatise on NON-TOXIC Shot

❯ PHIL BOURJAILY

Effective and economically priced, Kent Fasteel 2.0 offers velocities from 1,500 to 1,625 fps.

A flock of big Canadas — the largest weighed more than 13 pounds — backpedaled to land 30 yards from my layout blind. I sat up and shot three, each one falling just as dead as the three I'd shot the day before. Like that, my 2020–2021 goose season was over.

The hilltop where I loaded my birds, decoys, and blind into a sled for the drag out seems like an appropriate vantage from which to look back at thirty years of non-toxic shot. The performance of the shells I used — inexpensive, 3-inch 12-gauge, 1 ¼ ounce loads of Kent Fasteel 2.0 BBs — reinforced my opinion that the only people who complain about steel shot anymore are those who can't shoot or those who really can. The rest of us should shut up and go hunting. And, if you want better ammunition, or if you're

going to hunt with your Belgian Auto-5, you can spend more on bismuth or Tungsten-Matrix shells. It's not a perfect situation, but we're in a much better place now than we were thirty years ago when the U.S. Fish & Wildlife Service banned lead nationwide.

The author shot this limit of Canadas with Federal's 3-inch 20-gauge Meateater-branded bismuth shells.

ROUGH TRANSITION

In 1991, the USFWS dragged duck hunters, many of them kicking and screaming, into the non-toxic shot era. Depending on who you listened to, the lead ban was either necessary to save ducks and geese from ingesting poisonous lead, or it was an anti-hunting plot and backdoor gun ban. For the record, I have interviewed too many biologists who were also duck hunters to believe the lead ban was anything but a well-intentioned conservation measure. Nevertheless, we could all agree on this: if you wanted to hunt waterfowl legally, you hunted with non-toxic shot. In the early 90s, that meant steel.

The steel shot controversy existed long before the 1991 lead ban. As far back as the mid-19th Century, we knew lead shot poisoned waterfowl. References to steel shot appear as early as the 1940s, and the U.S. ammo industry was already experimenting with steel waterfowl loads in the early 1950s. Although several years of research predate its publication, you can trace the beginning of non-toxic shot

A pair of Canada geese fell to Rio bismuth shortly after the maker reintroduced it.

A heavy gas gun like the Remington Versamax helps tame the recoil of 1,700 fps Hypersonic ammunition.

requirements to the 1959 article, "Lead Poisoning as a Mortality Factor in Waterfowl Populations" in the *Illinois Natural History Survey Bulletin*. Biologist Frank C. Bellrose wrote that a switch to non-toxic shot nationwide would save 1.6–2.4 million ducks and geese annually. Steel's many critics countered, claiming that ineffective ammunition would cripple as many birds as it saved. They also worried that the price of steel and the necessity of buying a new gun to shoot it would drive hunters out of the sport.

Both sides were correct. The non-toxic shot did reduce the ingestion of lead pellets almost immediately in some places. Crippling rates also rose, and many hunters retired old guns for fear of damaging them with steel. Some hunters quit after seeing how badly early non-toxic ammo performed. Others didn't want to buy new guns, and some simply didn't like being told what to do.

There was collateral damage. Some gun clubs that shot over water, including the famous Remington Lordship Gun Club in Connecticut and the Lincoln Park Club in Chicago, were closed for depositing lead in the water. You can blame opportunists who took advantage of the lead ban to shut down noisy neighbors,

but an ammunition industry that stuck its head in the sand and didn't develop non-toxic target loads deserves a share of the blame. It's not as if they couldn't see lead bans coming.

MAKING THE BEST OF STEEL

Those of us who kept on hunting ducks and geese soon discovered steel wasn't just shiny lead. It had its advantages: hard, round, steel pellets patterned efficiently, with short shot strings. Steel didn't poison ducks, it was legal, and it was the only USFWS-approved lead alternative we had. That was about the end of steel's upside.

There were plenty of downsides. Steel pellets damaged gun barrels and Full chokes. Full was a lousy choice because steel patterned tightly, making it difficult for many hunters to hit. If you dunked the shells, pellets rusted. The slow powders required for safe pressures left barrels dirty and produced inconsistent velocities. Worst of all, steel pellets were light. Steel weighed 7.8 grams per cubic centimeter and lacked the density that made lead (11.34 g/cc) an effective shot material. The lower a pellet's density, the faster it sheds velocity and energy. Steel wasn't bad for birds over decoys, but it

didn't hit like lead, and a lot more birds required finishing shots on the water. Once you stretched your range past about 35 yards, steel lost its punch altogether. Never mind that many waterfowl hunters, and I include 1991 me in that group, have no business shooting past 35 yards. Steel still got the blame for every bird that flew off from a volley. Some of those complaints were justified.

Stuck with steel, ammunition makers worked to make it better and educate hunters on its use. We all learned the "rule of two" to choose shot sizes of two or even three sizes larger than lead to compensate for steel's lack of energy. That meant thinking of 2 shot — formerly a goose and fox pellet — as duck medicine and venturing into the alphabetical world of BB, BBB and T shot for geese.

Above: Blind Side's squared steel pellets allowed Winchester to fit more shot pellets into a hull.

Left: The author shot this limit of doves with Rio bismuth 7s in a B. Rizzini 28 gauge.

Guns changed. Three-inch 12s, once the big guns of goose specialists, became standard duck guns. Mossberg and Federal had already begun collaboration on a new cartridge, the 3 ½ 12 gauge. A more versatile gun than a 10, a 3 ½ 12 gauge offered 10-gauge payloads and higher velocities (it was spec-ed to higher pressures than the 10) without weighing a ton, nor confining you to heavy loads. Not long after, a little-known Italian maker called Benelli introduced the first 3 ½-inch semi-auto, and the big shells were here to stay.

Some hunters tried to cope on their own with dubious homemade solutions. When the lead buckshot pellets one of my neighbors liked to use for pass shooting geese were banned, he and his friends found a similar size steel ball bearing and loaded their own. But, he said, one shell's worth of ball bearings didn't have the pattern density to kill a goose by itself. "Two guys have to shoot at once," he told me. "We count to three." It's surprising they ever killed a goose at all, and even more surprising, they didn't blow themselves up with their homemade steel loads as there was little in the way of reloading data or components for steel available.

Steel didn't react to choke the same way lead did. Some hunters opened chokes, and some cut off gun barrels. A few experimented with drilling and tapping their guns' muzzles for set screws that extended far enough inside to grab and slow the wad and separate it cleanly from the shot charge. Like handloading ball bearings without data, that falls under the heading of "don't try this at home." It also led to the development of the Patternmaster and other wad-stripping chokes that perform well with steel.

Screw-in chokes became standard

Federal TSS Black Cloud 20 gauge combines steel 3 shot and TSS 9 to make the twenty a legitimate duck gun.

equipment in the 80s and 90s. It became much easier for gunsmiths to experiment with tubes, constrictions, and internal geometries. Hunters could try different chokes without having to buy a new barrel. Steel seemed to pattern best in more extended chokes, many of which extended beyond the muzzle, with a tapered section and a parallel section that helped stabilize the shot before it exited the muzzle. Hunters learned, too, that Full choke patterns were hard to hit with when you shot tight-patterning steel. Modified or even Improved Cylinder proved much a better all-around choice, and these days Light Modified, which splits the difference between the two, is deservedly popular.

Ammo makers improved steel wads, toughening them until barrel damage in modern guns was no longer a problem. They learned to lacquer seal steel shells around the crimp and the primer. On a media hunt back in the 90s, we writers

came down to breakfast to find all our shells — new Winchester DryLoks — in Ziploc bags of water to show off their waterproofing. Volume loading lowered the price of steel. New primers kept pressures down, and new powders burned cleaner and drove pellets faster.

"Faster" turned out to be the operative word. As hunters gained experience with steel, they noticed a correlation between velocity and birds in the bag. At first, steel came in two speeds: "slow" (1,375 fps) and "even slower" (1,260 fps). While the slower shells offered an extra ⅛ ounce of shot, speed seemed to help steel kill, even at pellet count expense.

Estate shells were among the first to boost steel to the then-screaming velocity of 1,450 fps in the mid-90s. Not long after, Winchester introduced a 1,450 fps load of its own. I took them hunting, saw the results, and was ready to declare the end of history and get on with killing ducks and geese. All these years later, steel at 1,450 fps, give or take 50 fps, is what I usually shoot.

DOES SPEED KILL?

Of all the improvements to steel, the most impressive engineering feat belonged to Remington, which reimagined the shotshell as, more or less, a

Left: Federal Speed Shok, a.k.a. Blue Box, is extremely popular among hunters who want a solid non-toxic load without a premium price tag.

two-stage rocket. Remington's Hypersonic shells contained a wad with a hollow stem inside that covered the primer. The powder inside the stem ignited first, pushing the wad forward far enough to create larger space for the rest of the powder to burn, thereby keeping pressures to a safe level. Hypersonic reached velocities of 1,700 fps with payloads up to 1 ⅜ ounces in a 3 ½ 12 gauge.

Unquestionably, though, speed does kill. Energy-wise, increasing the velocity of a load by 200 fps is the equivalent of using one size larger shot. However, that energy boost comes at the expense of more open patterns and lots more recoil. I look at it the other way around. Shooting one size larger increases energy without decreasing patterns nor increasing my pain. The more I hunt with steel, the less I care about speed. A few years ago, I hunted in Saskatchewan, where the only shells available were 1 ⅜ ounces of steel at 1,300 fps. Even I, not a huge velocity fan, thought, "What are we supposed to kill with these?" The answer turned out to be "everything." Ducks, geese, and cranes fell in large numbers. To be sure that it wasn't a fluke, I kept shooting slow steel all fall at home with good results. I especially remember ending that season on a cold January afternoon by turning a 40-yard-plus goose into a lawn dart with 1,300 fps BBs.

Besides the extra energy, manufacturers like to tout the shorter lead holds required when shooting with fast steel. The difference in your lead between two shells 200 fps apart is roughly eight inches on a true 90-degree crosser at 40 yards, which, frankly, is a shot most people miss by feet, not inches. Besides, most hunters shoot waterfowl at closer and less acute angles where the lead difference is even less. I have neither changed my leads nor did I ever feel the need to get "a feel for steel," as people recommended when we first made the transition. Experts advised leading birds less at close range to com-

pensate for steel's high speed and more at long range to make up for its rapid deceleration. In my opinion, if you're thinking that much about lead, you might as well take the shells out of your gun and throw them at the birds. I keep it simple, shooting right at close birds and in front of birds that are farther away, although I couldn't tell you how much lead I give them.

There may be improvements that

ammo makers will bring to steel. In the meantime, the steel shot we have is good enough. If you want better, we have that, too. You just pay more for it.

HEAVIER METALS

Even before the non-toxic mandate, people were studying their periodic tables, looking for a substitute. It would have to be dense, affordable, and, ideally, soft enough not to damage old guns. It

Above: The author shot this pattern using Hevi18, an 870 Super Magnum, and a turkey choke.

Left: Hevi18 is one of several TSS loads that extend the range of turkey guns to unheard-of distances.

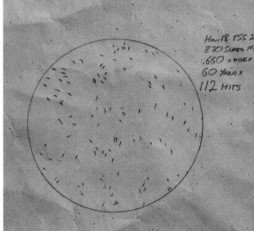

Hevi18. TSS 2~
870 Super Ma
.660 choke
60 Yards
112 HITS

Above: This Hevi18 load produced genuine 60-yard killing patterns in the author's tests.

would also have to garner USFWS approval as non-toxic. Finding a metal that checked all the boxes wasn't easy. Gold, for instance, checked three out of four. It's soft. It's dense. It's non-toxic enough for dental use, so it's likely safe for ducks to ingest. Affordable? Well, not really.

John Brown, a carpenter from Ontario who liked hunting ducks with old guns, was among the people looking for a new shot material. Looking at periodic tables at the library, he hit upon bismuth. It was dense but brittle. It wouldn't harm gun barrels. As the active ingredient of Pepto-Bismol, it was the opposite of toxic, and it was relatively affordable. Brown had molds made and started casting pellets.

He found a partner to bankroll his project in *Guns and Ammo* owner and gun collector Robert Petersen, who helped pay for an initial toxicity study. USFWS approved it around 1993. The bismuth-tin shot was safe in old guns, and, despite a tendency to shatter upon setback in the shell and upon striking

bone, it killed better than steel. It cost more, too, between one and two dollars a shell. It came packed in 10-round boxes to reduce sticker shock, and enough hunters bought it that the race to improve steel was on.

Tungsten was another metal that showed promise. It was very dense and extremely hard, and it could be alloyed with iron to make a kind of super-steel pellet. Federal offered the first tungsten-iron loads. They were almost as dense as lead and came loaded in a thick, two-layer wad to protect gun barrels. As a result, not many pellets fit inside, limiting loads to an ounce or 1 1/8 ounces at most, but they patterned tightly and hit hard. I handed out some early samples to the guides on a September goose hunt in Ohio in the mid-90s. One of the guides made a long backup shot on an escaping honker, dropping it dead. "That would have been two shots with steel!" he

Rio was the first ammo maker to reintroduce bismuth shot.

exclaimed.

English ammo maker Kent Cartridge went a different direction, blending powdered tungsten with polymer to create an unusual non-toxic pellet that was essentially a very dense nylon sphere. Tungsten-Matrix pellets hit hard yet were not soft enough for all gun barrels.

Because USFWS hadn't yet approved T-M in the United States, Kent took a

bunch of writers to Uruguay, where lead is legal. We shot ducks in the morning and, on a couple of days, pigeons in the afternoon. To save the precious T-M for morning ducks, we were issued lead field loads of 6 shot for pigeon. The lead 6s proved a little light for the *picazuro* pigeons, which are as tough a bird as I have ever shot. *Petersen's Hunting* Editor Greg Tinsley and I hit one bird solidly four times before Tinsley headshot it as it flew a dazed circle around him. The following afternoon, I snuck some of the heavier loads of T-M 5s into the pigeon field, and that day those tough pigeons dropped like doves.

T-M remains my all-time favorite non-toxic pellet, and I shoot my carefully hoarded supply at pheasants. It's just as deadly, responds to choke the way lead did, and it's safe for my bird guns. You shoot most pheasants going away, and inevitably pellets wind up in the meat. T-M hits birds hard, but it's so soft the pellets squish between my teeth if I bite one by accident.

In their Uruguay presentation, the Kent people had told us they designed their pellet to be almost as dense and lethal as lead. At the time, I thought, "Why didn't they make a pellet that was denser than lead? That would be a great marketing hook. Wouldn't people buy that?"

That is almost precisely what Frank Morse, a duck hunter with some money to invest, said to his old friend and hunting partner, Darryl Amick, in 1998. Amick happened to be the recently retired metallurgist who had developed Federal's tungsten-iron, and he approached Morse for backing for a new tungsten-iron project in the 90s. He blended enough tungsten into his pellet alloy to make it denser than lead at 12 gr/cc. HEVI-Shot pellets were deformed to the point that some looked like snowmen, and they were odd-sized, too, so that the joke about them was that instead of numbered sizes, HEVI-Shot came in Small, Medium, and Large. Sometimes you got all three in one shell.

But the stuff was no joke. HEVI-Shot

changed everything we thought we knew about shotshells. It was an article of ballistic faith that pellets had to be spherical to pattern tightly. Lumpen HEVI-Shot pellets proved that notion wrong by demolishing the lead competition at

the National Wild Turkey Federation's Still-Target Shoot, where you win by putting the most hits in a 3-inch circle at 40 yards.

HEVI-Shot wasn't just as good as the old lead loads. It was better. You could

Steel shot sidelined older guns like this 3-inch Model 12. Bismuth and Tungsten-Matrix brought them back to the blind.

Some 20-gauge Boss bismuth and a 12-year-old German shorthair helped the author bag these two wild ringnecks.

around if you want to pay for them, and ITX shot and Nice Shot, two tungsten pellets popular with reloaders, remain on the market, too, but ammo makers saw where the market was headed. They turned their attention away from tungsten and back to refining steel loads.

It seemed as if we were fated to go back to shooting steel and reminiscing about the good old days of tungsten-iron and bismuth, the way old-timers talk about lead. Then bismuth came back. It had faded away both due to Bob Petersen's death and competition from HEVI-Shot and other denser-than-lead pellets. Rio Ammunition was the first to offer bismuth again after parent company Maxam bought Eley, which made bismuth shot.

shoot at least one size smaller with HEVI-Shot than you could with lead. HEVI-Shot 4s became my favorite load for big Canadas at any range. Other ammo makers, seeing that hunters would pay for better-than-lead performance, came up with pellets of their own. What followed was a brief golden age of non-toxic ammo.

Federal introduced HeavyWeight. Winchester made Xtended Range. Remington named its tungsten-iron pellet Wingmaster HD, and they were all deadly. At the seminar Winchester held to introduce Xtended Range at Nilo Farms, we shot flighted ducks with Winchester engineers ranging the birds over our shoulders. The new ammo consistently stoned ducks at 55 yards.

Not long after, Remington took a few of us writers to a lodge that offered an elaborate flighted duck operation, with birds coming from three directions and half a dozen boats, each with a Lab on board to handle the retrieving. I shared a blind with a couple of people from Remington. For about half an hour, there were ducks everywhere. I chose only the longest shots and killed every bird I shot at, then realized I was the only one shooting. My partners had put their guns down to watch me. I guarantee that has never happened before nor since, but it happened that day, and it might not be a

Rio Bismuth 3s in 20 gauge accounted for these two geese.

coincidence that I was shooting Wingmaster HD when it did.

GOODBYE TUNGSTEN, HELLO AGAIN BISMUTH

In 2010 or 2011, the party ended when the price of raw tungsten skyrocketed. It hasn't come down, and it's not going to. Demand is high in part because there's a little tungsten weight in every cell phone to make it vibrate, and there are a lot of cell phones. Where some duck hunters had gotten accustomed to paying $2 or more per shell for better-than-lead performance, $5 per shell was too much. HEVI-Shot and Tungsten-Matrix are still

Kent, Federal, HEVI-Shot, Browning/Winchester, and newcomer Boss Ammunition all have bismuth loads, now, too. Not only is bismuth back, but it's also improved. The new pellets contain a little more tin than the old alloy did, and while they will still crack against bone, they don't turn into powder in the shell or upon impact as the old stuff sometimes did. I shoot the new bismuth frequently at ducks and upland birds, especially in my older guns. Bismuth is an upgrade over steel, but it's still halfway between lead and steel in density. To my way of thinking, a bismuth 3 equals a steel 2 equals a lead 4.

Where bismuth lost out to equally

expensive but denser tungsten-iron the first time around, this time it looked like a bargain by comparison. Manufacturers found ways to cut costs. Kent found a new method of making pellets and realized savings it could pass on to consumers by packing shells in 25-round boxes instead of 10-round packs. Boss sells only online, cutting out middlemen. HEVI-Shot offers not only all bismuth but bismuth/steel blends, and as of this writing, Browning ammo has just announced a similar bismuth/steel load that should fall closer in price to premium steel.

TUNGSTEN SUPER SHOT

If it weren't for HEVI-Shot and the other tungsten-iron pellets that followed it, Tungsten Super Shot probably wouldn't exist. TSS went mainstream in 2018, but if you paid attention to reloading, you already knew about these super-dense (up to 18.5 gr/cc) pellets that turkey hunters were loading into .410s and 28 gauges. A very few duck hunters were using it, too. TSS made a stir when it debuted in factory ammo. Did I mention the price of raw tungsten was high? The new shells from Federal and boutique maker Apex cost as much as $13 per shell if you wanted a 3 ½ inch magnum 12 gauge's worth of TSS to throw at a turkey. It was so dense that a TSS 9 had the same penetration as a lead 5, meaning you could sling clouds of pellets at birds from a 12 gauge or turn a .410 into a real 40-yard turkey gun. Despite the price, people lined up at the Federal booth to buy it when the maker debuted it at the National Wild Turkey Federation Show, and every last shell was gone in 45 minutes. Now, Browning and HEVI-Shot offer TSS turkey loads, too. Turkey hunters can get several seasons out of a box of shells, and a lot of them seem to think a few rounds of TSS is a sound investment.

While the number of waterfowlers willing to pay for pure TSS duck loads is small, there are a few. Those who like to get an inkling of how the other half hunts, Federal, Apex, and Migra add a spoonful of TSS shot to steel loads. The half dozen or so geese I've shot with Federal Black Cloud TSS seemed impressed.

THIRTY YEARS ON

The percentage of ducks and geese with lead in their gizzards is much lower than it used to be. In wetlands with muddy bottoms, old pellets eventually sank out of reach. Ducks and geese still have pellets in their gizzards, but now they're steel. Along the hard-bottomed sand bays of the Texas coast, a few birds can still find thirty-year-old lead pellets. Up to 10 percent of ducks on the coast once showed lead ingestion signs. That number is now about three percent. Non-toxic shot does save ducks and geese.

Crippling rates, which steel critics predicted would kill as many birds as non-toxic shot saved, rose during the years when regulations phased in steel shot. After that, as hunters adjusted to steel and ammunition improved, crippling rates fell, and they remained below the lead shot-era levels. Non-toxic ammunition is better. I am confident in steel at 40 yards and more, but the real change is hunting and hunters. Thirty years ago, pass shooting around refuges, especially for geese, was widespread. Long shots with any pellet will cripple birds. Perhaps partly of necessity, hunters adapted to steel by getting better at scouting, hiding, calling, and decoying birds. I enjoyed plucking birds out of the sky at 50-yards plus until I learned how much more fun it is to see them close. If that's an unanticipated side effect of the lead shot ban, it might be the very best one. ⒼⒹ

With muzzle velocities as high as 1,700 fps, Remington Hypersonic represents the fastest, hardest-hitting factory steel load.

Pocket PROTECTORS of the Past

Collecting Off the Beaten Path

❯JIM SUPICA

How to bring a knife to a gunfight. Left: Harrington & Richardson Model 3 with a folding knife blade. Handguns with folding blades were slightly more common in Europe than in the U.S. Right: Iver Johnson Safety Hammerless Automatic Revolver with knuckleduster grip. Swagger stick with a concealed blade. Bailey Brower, Jr., collection. Stoney Roberts photo

ollecting guns isn't usually an active choice. Most folks slide into it sideways. I remember being baffled as to why anyone would buy a beat-up, obsolete old gun, paying multiples of the price they'd pay for a cool, new shooter and several boxes of ammunition. However, one thing leads to another, and one gun leads to another. Before you know it, you've got a stack of guns that you don't shoot. Soon, you become curious about their predecessors and history. Eventually, you may start wondering about the old guy sitting along the back wall of your local gun show with the table full of oddball rust clusters.

Even once someone becomes a collector, some deny the title, modestly claiming to be a mere "accumulator." Face it: If you have more guns than you shoot, you're a collector. And once you accept the inevitable, the question occurs — what shall I collect next?

Collectors tend to use established collecting fields. You can get a modest starter set of Colt percussion revolvers or early Winchester lever actions for the low six figures. If your taste runs to more modern guns, you might be able to find a high-condition example of a Colt Python or a Smith & Wesson Registered Magnum, or a first-year 1911 for

From the 1860s through the early 1880s, the predominant type of repeating pocket firearm was the single-action spur-trigger, despite the tendency of the hammer spur to snag the clothing when drawn. Each shown here is serial number 1 of that model. Top to bottom: Marlin No. 38 Standard 1878, Victor No. 32, and Colt New Line 22. On the bottom is an unknown European tip-up folding trigger revolver, with fake Smith & Wesson markings to fool the unwary buyer. All photos by author unless noted.

under five figures. But what if you can't afford to spend the price of a new car or home on your "hobby"? And what if you don't want to follow the fields that collectors have extensively researched and published in minutiae for decades?

We'll take a look at some of the less-well-recognized old guns that can form a fascinating collection, including some areas where there is still research to be done. And we'll consider fields in which you can build an interesting collection without taking out a second mortgage.

DEVELOPMENT OF CONCEALABLE FIREARMS

One of the most significant, most visceral, most essential firearm roles has been personal protection throughout

history. These are concealable defensive tools that can be kept close at hand as a potentially life-saving equalizer. The first concealable firearm was the wheellock, introduced around 1500. Before this invention, attributed by some to Leonardo Da Vinci, a gun had to be carried with a lit smoldering "slow-match" to ignite the gunpowder and fire the charge. That design prevented tucking it under your cloak for quick accessibility. The wheellock was also responsible for the first gun-ban laws. European royalty was nervous at the thought of ordinary subjects invisibly arming themselves in their regal presence. In 1523, an Italian town reportedly issued a decree stating, *"An especially dangerous kind of firearms have come to be used, which are called wheellock, with*

which a homicide can easily be committed. His Excellency, knowing that these are devilish arms, prohibits their being carried without explicit authorization, under penalty of having a hand publicly cut off."

Official disapproval did not dampen the enthusiasm for concealable personal defense firearms. Small single-shot muzzleloaders that could be concealed in a gentleman's pocket or a lady's muff remained widely popular throughout the flintlock era, along with twist-off barrel single shots that facilitated more effortless loading. Later, in the percussion era, a prolific American gunsmith, Henry Deringer of Philadelphia, became synonymous with hideout guns — "derringers."

When Samuel Colt introduced his earliest version of a repeating percussion

"Papa says it won't hurt us." Iver Johnson Safety Hammerless Automatic revolvers. First Model, right side. Second Model, top left. The Third Model, bottom left.

handgun in the late 1830s, one of his first models was a small .28-caliber five-shot Pocket Model with a folding trigger, called the Baby Paterson by collectors today. Although his first New Jersey production facility failed, he came back strong with improved models featuring traditional triggerguards a decade later. Colts dominated the repeating handgun market through the end of the Civil War. Its most popular cap and ball revolver? The compact 1849 Pocket Model, with 340,000 manufactured. Admittedly, pants pockets were larger then, but it was still a compact handgun adaptable to concealed carry.

After their failed lever-action "Volcanic" pistol venture, Horace Smith and Daniel Wesson found their first success with an even smaller pocket revolver, the Model One seven-shot .22 spur-trigger, introduced in 1857. It offered the advantage of using self-contained metallic cartridges, making it much handier than the percussion revolvers that required blackpowder, lead balls, and caps to load. Pocket-size handguns remained a Smith & Wesson staple, although the .22 rimfire tip-ups were replaced in the product line by top-break .32 and .38 S&W revolvers by the late 1870s and early 1880s.

By this time, firearms industry leaders such as Remington, Marlin, Sharps, Stevens, and Whitney were also churning out concealable cartridge handguns for an eager market. But these prestigious American manufacturers were not the only entrepreneurs riding this hot-ticket bandwagon. And that brings us to the subject of this article — the millions of small personal defense handguns made in the U.S. and Europe in the late 19th through 20th century, especially some of those that are little known, unusual, and under-appreciated by most current gun collectors.

Identifying features of Iver Johnson Safety Hammerless Automatic revolvers. Left: The top two guns have the First Model single-post frame latch. The bottom two have the double-post latch of the Second and Third Models.

The Harrington & Richardson snag-free revolvers include .32-, .38-, and .22-caliber Hammerless Safety Models. The Young America Safety Hammer Model at far right has an exposed hammer with no hammer spur.

TARGETING COLLECTABLE FIREARMS

What makes a handgun concealable? Size and weight are obvious considerations, but not the only ones. The design must be compact, safe to carry, and snag-free when quickly drawn from a pocket or other hidden location. The hammer spur tends to be the prickly, grabby part of a small revolver, and eliminating this hang-up led to the popularity of hammerless double-action-only revolvers. Doing away with the single-action function also simplified operation. It eliminated the risk of accidentally cocking a revolver with a light single-action trigger pull when fumbling with the gun in a high-stress situation. These revolvers did not lack hammers; makers merely hid them within the frame. A more accurate description is "concealed hammer," but "hammerless" is the universally used term. The most common chamberings for American products were .32 S&W and .38 S&W, with some .22 rimfire models. Most weighed a pleasantly light 11 to 18 ounces.

AMERICAN HAMMERLESS REVOLVERS

Smith & Wesson introduced an early concealed hammer pocket revolver in 1887, marketed as the "Safety Hammerless" or "New Departure" model. Its grip safety also led to the nickname "Lemonsqueezer." Originally a five-shot .38 S&W, a smaller frame .32 S&W model soon followed. It wasn't the first hammerless revolver. Pettingill had made a double-action-only percussion hammerless revolver during the Civil War, although it was hardly pocketable in .44 caliber with a 7 1/2-inch barrel. However, the little Smith & Wesson opened a new market, and other American makers quickly adopted the concept.

Firms such as Iver Johnson, Harrington & Richardson, and Hopkins & Allen fed the demand for compact, affordable, reliable revolvers through-

American hammerless revolvers, top to bottom: Forehand Arms. What appears to be a spurless hammer is the break-open latch. Foehl & Weeks top-break hammerless revolver. Hopkins & Allen Acme solid-frame hammerless revolver. Forehand Arms top-break hammerless revolver.

Meriden hammerless and trade name revolvers by Meriden. The topmost has Meriden's unique push safety lever on the side of the frame. Trade names shown include Eastern Arms Co., Federal Fire Arms Co., New England Fire Arms Co., and Howard Arms Co. The only marking on the bottom example is "FOR 32 SMITH & WESSON CTG," presumably intended to take advantage of the Smith & Wesson name.

out most of the 20th century. These companies have been referred to as "Armorers to America's Nightstands," sometimes with a sneer, other times with genuine affection.

Of these, Iver Johnson was probably the most prolific. Like Smith & Wesson, it offered small-frame .32 or large-frame .38 five-shot top-break hammerless revolvers. Both firms also produced similar models of traditional double-action revolvers with exposed hammers. The Iver Johnson line went through three significant models during its 1894 to 1941 production run. The manufacturer produced the First Model Safety Hammerless Automatic revolver only in the initial year. You identify it by a single-post frame for the top latch. (A rotating lever releases that latch on the left rear of the topstrap.) It has a hammer shroud that is a separate piece from the rest of the frame. The Second

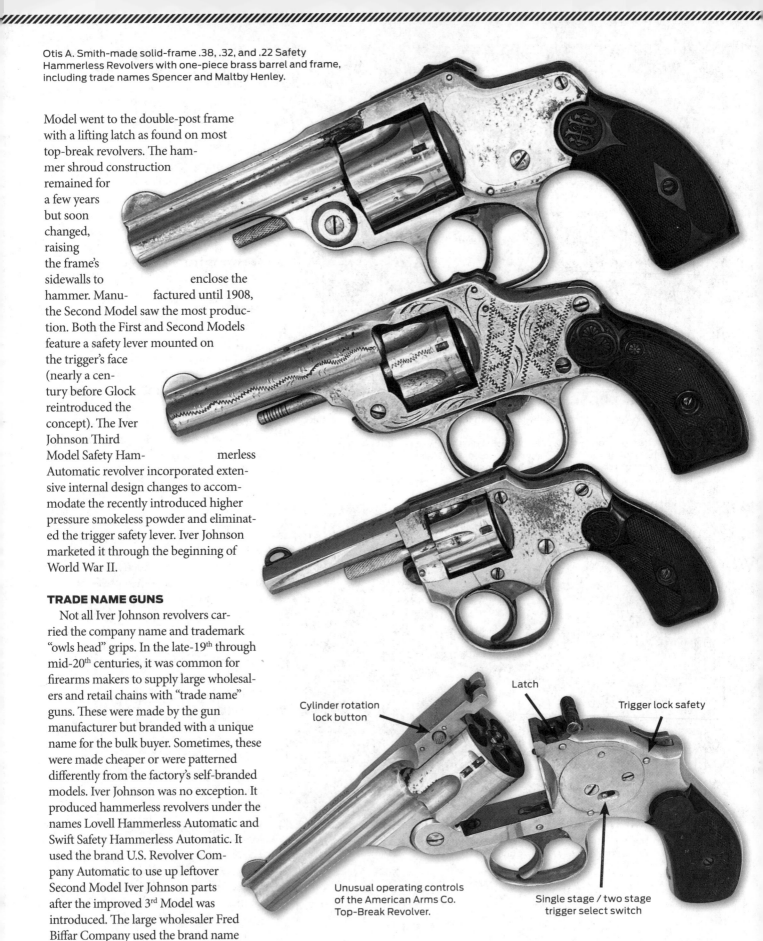

Otis A. Smith-made solid-frame .38, .32, and .22 Safety Hammerless Revolvers with one-piece brass barrel and frame, including trade names Spencer and Maltby Henley.

Model went to the double-post frame with a lifting latch as found on most top-break revolvers. The hammer shroud construction remained for a few years but soon changed, raising the frame's sidewalls to enclose the hammer. Manufactured until 1908, the Second Model saw the most production. Both the First and Second Models feature a safety lever mounted on the trigger's face (nearly a century before Glock reintroduced the concept). The Iver Johnson Third Model Safety Hammerless Automatic revolver incorporated extensive internal design changes to accommodate the recently introduced higher pressure smokeless powder and eliminated the trigger safety lever. Iver Johnson marketed it through the beginning of World War II.

TRADE NAME GUNS

Not all Iver Johnson revolvers carried the company name and trademark "owls head" grips. In the late-19th through mid-20th centuries, it was common for firearms makers to supply large wholesalers and retail chains with "trade name" guns. These were made by the gun manufacturer but branded with a unique name for the bulk buyer. Sometimes, these were made cheaper or were patterned differently from the factory's self-branded models. Iver Johnson was no exception. It produced hammerless revolvers under the names Lovell Hammerless Automatic and Swift Safety Hammerless Automatic. It used the brand U.S. Revolver Company Automatic to use up leftover Second Model Iver Johnson parts after the improved 3rd Model was introduced. The large wholesaler Fred Biffar Company used the brand name

Cylinder rotation lock button

Latch

Trigger lock safety

Unusual operating controls of the American Arms Co. Top-Break Revolver.

Single stage / two stage trigger select switch

These two Foehl & Weeks pocket revolvers are from the Smith & Wesson factory collection, presumably used to research competitors' products. The top-break version at the top has the unusual frontstrap grip safety found on some other Foehl & Weeks hammerless specimens. The solid-frame Double Action No. 32 model has a Smith & Wesson-style grip safety added to the backstrap, possibly as an experiment by Smith & Wesson.

European Velo-Dog and other hammerless revolvers, with .5.5 Velo-Dog cartridges compared to .32 and .38 S&W rounds. Stoney Roberts photo

Secret Service Special and manufactured by a string of firearms companies. Those included Meriden, followed successively by Iver Johnson, Hopkins & Allen, Harrington & Richardson, and an unnamed Spanish maker. Although all variations carried the Secret Service Special marking, each manufacturer kept their distinctive design features, and the configuration can identify the actual maker of an SSS revolver.

Harrington & Richardson, or H&R, a successor firm to Frank Wesson and then Wesson & Harrington, was the other leading U.S. maker of reliable, affordable handguns during the 20th century. H&R made .32- and .38-caliber top-break Hammerless Safety revolvers, each available in either a large-frame six-shot or small-frame five-shot configuration. The small frame came as a seven-shot .22 rimfire model. It also offered a small snag-free solid-frame revolver with an exposed hammer, but with no hammer spur, under the model names Vest Pocket Safety and Young America Safety Hammer. You could fire it quickly in double action, or, with focused attention, you could carefully cock the hammer for a single-action trigger release.

With Hopkins & Allen revolvers, the daisy-chain of successor firms and acquisitions becomes even more convoluted. The firm established itself in 1868 as a successor to Bacon Arms Co. Then, Hopkins & Allen acquired Forehand Arms, formerly Forehand & Wadsworth, in 1901, which was itself the successor to Ethan Allen & Company. Too, Hopkins & Allen was tangled up with Merwin Hulbert, building its high-quality revolvers in the same factory. Like Iver Johnson and Harrington & Richardson, Hopkins & Allen (and Bacon & Forehand, and Wadsworth & Hulbert, and Merwin & that other Allen) became known for making inexpensive functional firearms. H&A produced solid-frame hammerless revolvers, such as its Acme Hammerless No. 1, and top-breaks like the Safety Police Hammerless. Hopkins & Allen also made the latter under the Forehand brand. What's more, H&A came up with another approach to snag-free pocket guns by offering folding hammer spurs on both the H&A and Merwin Hulbert

double-action revolvers.

The Merwin Hulberts are some of the best-made revolvers of the late 19th century, with a unique twist-open mechanism that requires precise machining and fitting. While some of its double-action models incorporate the H&A patented folding hammer spur, no known hammerless revolvers exist. However, at least one .38-caliber Merwin Hulbert hammerless has surfaced with a Smith & Wesson-style grip safety.

In terms of quantity, Hopkins & Allen's biggest sellers were probably little single-action spur-trigger revolvers. This style of handgun was also widely popular as a hideout gun. They were made by many manufacturers, in addition to H&A, under a wide variety of trade names. Quality ranged from good to execrable, with the general type earning the nickname "suicide specials." Many, maybe the majority, of these were made with no indication of manufacturer. Instead, most bore a colorful and enigmatic trade name including such zingers as American Boy, Bull Dozer, Tramp's Terror, Senator, Blue Whistler, Dictator, Knockabout, Little Joker, Rattler, Earthquake, and Swamp Angel.

In many cases, using a tradename was likely an effort to hide the identity of a manufacturer of questionable goods. As far as we know, none were named Blow Your Finger Off. These colorful revolvers represent another fascinating and under-appreciated collecting field, although a more detailed discussion is beyond this article's scope.

Smaller less-known manufacturers also offered hammerless revolvers, some with unique design features. Otis A. Smith made a good-quality, solid-frame Safety Hammerless Revolver with both the frame and barrel produced from a single piece of brass under names such as Spencer and Maltby Henley. American Arms had a top-break revolver with a surprising number of controls on it, including a button on the topstrap that kept the cylinder from rotating during loading and unloading. It also sported a rocker latch on the backstrap knuckle that locked and unlocked the trigger as a safety device — and a sliding switch on the left side of the frame that let the

"That dog will never bark again!" American bicycle guns (clockwise from top left): Smith & Wesson .32 Safety Hammerless, Hopkins & Allen, Harrington & Richardson, Iver Johnson.

HAMMERLESS REVOLVER PRICES

YEAR	MODEL	PRICE	IN TODAY'S DOLLARS
1895	S&W .32 Safety Hammerless	$11.50	$358
	S&W .38 Safety Hammerless	$12.00	$373
	H&A Automatic Hammerless, .32 or .38	$4.90	$152
	H&A Acme, .32 or .38	$2.65	$82
	Forehand & Wadsworth Hammerless	$4.75	$148
1920	S&W .32 Safety Hammerless	$25.50	$331
	S&W .38 Safety Hammerless	$27.50	$357
	H&R Hammerless, .22, .32 or .38	$10.70	$139
	Iver Johnson Hammerless, .22, .32, or .38	$11.00	$143
	U.S. Hammerless, .22, .32, or .38	$10.75	$139
	Baby Hammerless .22 S&L	$5.00	$65

shooter select single- or two-stage trigger pull.

Although British-made and too large for pocket carry, the massive Kynoch Schlund .476-caliber hammerless revolver deserves mention with the hammerless oddities due to its unique stacked double-trigger operating system. The lower trigger rotates the cylinder and cocks the internal hammer, and the upper trigger fires the gun.

In addition to Forehand & Wadsworth, there is another F&W American manufacturer — Foehl & Weeks. Although the firm only lasted a few years, it did produce several hammerless top-break revolvers, including the Perfect and a grip safety model. It was succeeded by Columbian Firearms, which used a Foehl & Weeks patent to produce an even smaller hammerless revolver.

LI'L TINY BABIES

Baby Hammerless revolvers were probably first made by Columbian, with the bulk of production initially by Kolb and then Sedgley. The vast majority are small-frame six-shot .22 rimfire revolvers, with slightly larger .32-caliber models also produced. The Baby is the smallest widely produced American hammerless revolver and the only one to feature a folding trigger. The small-frame First Model weighs less than 4.5 ounces and is 4.5 inches in overall diagonal length, including a 1.25-inch barrel. Although they seem scarce on the market today, they enjoyed good popularity with around 250,000 produced from 1896 to 1930.

Many generalist collectors enjoy own-

Above: Rare large-frame hammerless revolvers. Top: Top-break .45-cal. Belgian-made with spurious Smith & Wesson barrel address, patents, and logo grips. Right: A pitted and engraved folding-trigger .44-cal. Belgian-made. Left: A Gilon folding-trigger .45 cal. with a unique release for the swing-out cylinder. Bottom: A Colt New Service .45 Colt gunsmith-modified with a shrouded hammer and shortened grip frame. Center: A Baby Hammerless revolver for scale.

Left: Top-break large-frame hammerless revolvers. Top: French Dumoulin Freres hammerless top-break .44 WCF revolver with S&W-style grip safety. Bottom: Unmarked Belgian .44 revolver with lever safety on the lower-left frame. Center: Smith & Wesson .32 Bicycle Gun for scale.

ing a Baby Hammerless as a curiosity and a size contrast to other guns in their collection. However, you could build an extensive and varied specialized collection of Babies due to many variations. Four major model groups are quickly identifiable in the more common small-frame version — solid-frame First Model, Model 1910, and Ejector Model, along with the top-break New Baby Model. Between the 1910 and Ejector Models, there is also a group of Transition Models distinguished primarily by markings and internal changes. The First Model is the smallest and features a round or bird's head butt. The Model 1910 introduced the square butt design. Unloading these early-type guns was peculiar. After removing the cylinder, you had to push out each cartridge or case from each chamber using the removable cylinder pin. The Ejector Model introduced a star extractor, like that used in today's familiar hand ejector double-action revolvers, to empty the removed cylinder. The New Baby is a top-break model and was made first with a round butt and, later, a square butt configuration. The square-butt adds automatic ejection of shells and cartridges when you open the gun.

The much rarer "large" frame model was still smaller than most other revolvers at 7.5 to 8.5 ounces and 6-inch diagonal overall length. The standard configuration was a five-shot .32 centerfire, but you could find an eight-shot .22 rimfire. It has two major model groups — the First Model and the Model 1910. Accordingly, a budding Baby collector could be proud of a representative collection of six total guns — four small frames and two large frames.

That's assuming he doesn't tumble into the "one of each variation" rabbit hole, a wonderland featuring 33 identifiable

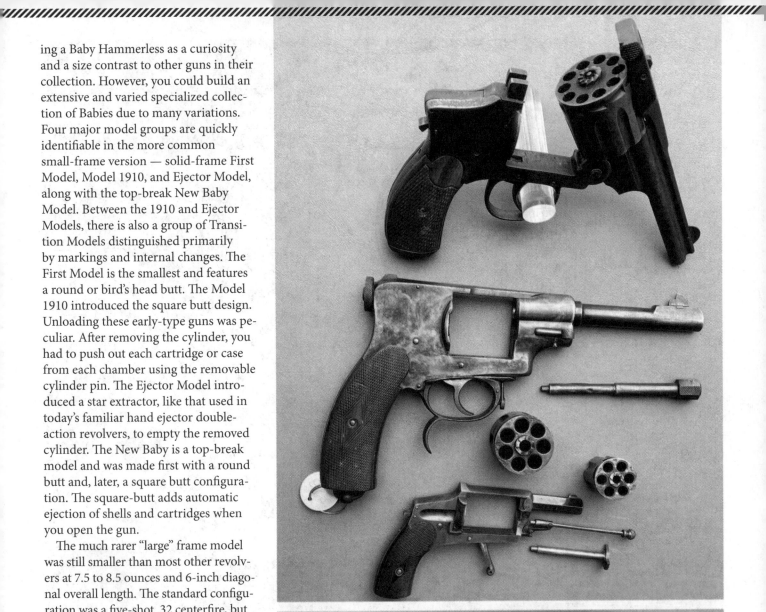

Top: Unmarked ten-shot 5.5mm Velo-Dog top-break hammerless revolver with switch-type safety on the top rear of grip knuckle. Middle: An unmarked German-made seven-shot .32 or 8mm solid-frame hammerless revolver with an unusual take-down system and case-colored frame. Bottom: Belgian six-shot 5.5mm Velo-Dog revolver.

Engraved European Velo-Dog revolvers.

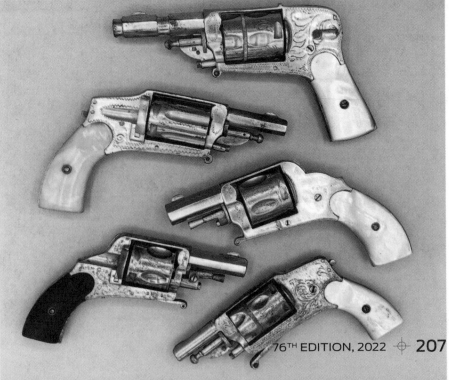

The five major Savage auto pistol models: Top left: Rare .45 ACP government trials pistol. Top right: Model 1907 with exposed hammer and rectangular grip. Bottom right: Model 1915 hammerless model with a grip safety, gold plated with rare "Tuxedo" pearl and black factory grips. Bottom left: Model 1917 with exposed hammer and flared trapezoidal grips. Center: Rare .25 ACP model. Bailey Brower, Jr., collection. Stoney Roberts photo

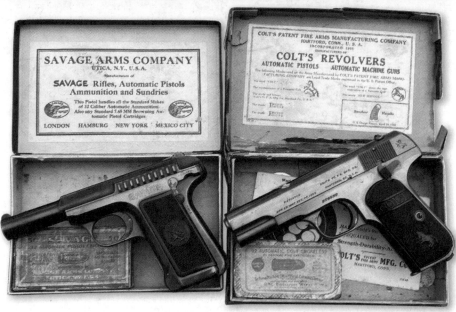

The Colt Model 1903 Hammerless Pocket Auto and Savage Model 1907 Pocket Auto competed in the early American market for .32 ACP auto pistols.

Early Pocket Autos. Center: Engraved Walther Model 9 Vest Pocket, .25 ACP, 1921–1945. The inner ring of .25 ACPs, clockwise from top: Jieffeco, Belgian made, imported by Davis Warner ca. the 1920s. Mondial, Spanish, 1920–1922. Salvaje, Spanish copy of Savage including similar grip logo, the 1920s. Liliput Model 1925. Harrington & Richardson Self-Loading caliber .25, 1912–1920, two examples are shown. Left side top to bottom, American .32 ACPs: Colt Model 1903 Pocket, Browning design, 1903–1946. Remington Model 51, 1918–1927. H&R Self-Loader, Webley design, 1912–1915. Right side top to bottom, misc. .32 ACPs: Fabrique Nationale Model 1900, Browning design, 1900–1914. Mauser Model 1914, 1914–1934. Savage Model 1907, Westley Richards marked, 1910–1917. Bottom center, left to right, .32 ACPs: Another Mauser Model 1914. Warner Infallible, 1917–1919. Bailey Brower, Jr., collection. Stoney Roberts photo

model variations — 23 small frames and 10 large frames — distinguished by configuration, caliber, markings, and internal design changes. These Babies were constantly improved and modified, with a new model name accompanying most changes. For example, the Transition variants include Models 1910, 1916, 1918, 1920 no screw, 1920 pull release, 1921, 1922, and 1924. Then there are cosmetic variations to add to the collection. Most Babies came with nickel finishes, but you could choose from a smattering of blued guns. Standard small-frame grips were hardened rubber, with a circled K for Kolb or S for Sedgley on most guns, and fancy pearl grips were a popular option, plus you could have the hard rubber version with four inlaid rhinestones on each panel. The few period-engraved specimens are prized by collectors and bring a stout premium.

WHY NOT A SMITH?

With the popular and well-made Smith & Wesson Safety Hammerless kicking off this market, what was the incentive to buy a hammerless revolver by the other makers? One word: price.

In other words, you could buy an off-brand hammerless revolver for about 20 to 40 percent of what you'd pay for a Smith & Wesson. You could get four *cheapos* for the price of one premier brand revolver. How did this work out for these "non-prestige" makers? During the full production run from 1887 to 1940, Smith & Wesson produced about 500,000 Safety Hammerless revolvers. From

Oddities. Left: Chicago Firearms Company Protector Palm Pistol, .32 extra short with an internal eight-shot disk magazine with the chambers pointing outward like wheel spokes. Rare blue finish. Scarce box illustrates correct holding method, with the handle pointing up; they are often held or pictured incorrectly upside down. Right: Manufrance Gaulois squeezer palm pistol, .32 extra short, five-shot internal box magazine. Bottom: Percussion cane gun. Bailey Brower, Jr., collection. Stoney Roberts photo

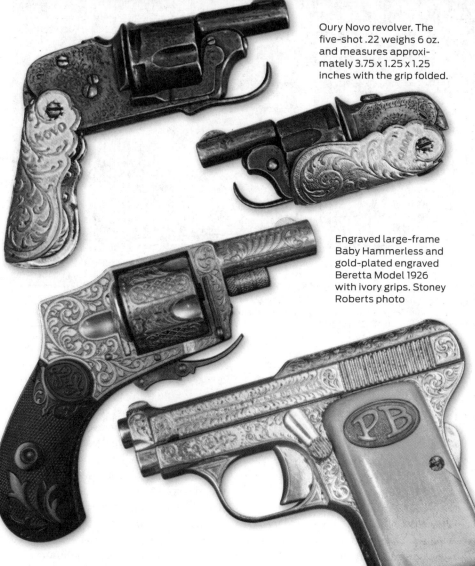

Oury Novo revolver. The five-shot .22 weighs 6 oz. and measures approximately 3.75 x 1.25 x 1.25 inches with the grip folded.

Engraved large-frame Baby Hammerless and gold-plated engraved Beretta Model 1926 with ivory grips. Stoney Roberts photo

1894 to 1941, Iver Johnson made almost 1,740,000 hammerless revolvers.

CANINES AND VELOCIPEDES

During the era in which hammerless pocket pistols grew in popularity, human-powered wheeled transportation was undergoing a similar development period. The first bicycle with pedals emerged in the mid-1850s. By the 1870s, the colorful high-wheel bicycle gained popularity among young men with a sense of adventure, good balance, and a certain disregard for its inherent dangers. However, it wasn't until the 1880s and 1890s that the pedal-chain rear-wheel drive "safety bicycle" velocipede found favor as an efficient form of personal transportation for the general public, with the advantage that you didn't have to feed it hay and oats.

During this time, Smith & Wesson and other gun firms began marketing short-barrel versions of their hammerless revolvers as "bicycle guns." Before this, most of these pocket revolvers had a barrel in the 3- to 4-inch range. The short 2-inch barrel on the bicycle model certainly made it easier to carry in a pocket while the legs were vigorously pumping pedals. It begs the question: exactly why did early velocipedists need to carry a gun? Some of the advertisements of the era made

one purpose explicit. Pre-leash-law free-roaming dogs hated the new-fangled gizmos and were wont to attack rider and vehicle alike! A .32 or .38 lead pill struck the marketers as the perfect prescription for persistent petulant pups.

The intended usage was even more explicit in Europe. That's where an entire genre of pocket pistols emerged explicitly for this purpose. They were christened "Velo-Dog revolvers," sometimes also called "Revolver de Poche" ("Poche" apparently meaning "pocket," not "pooch.") Some argue that the "dog" part of Velo-Dog references bulldog-style revolvers, but the similarity escapes me. They even had their own cartridge — the 5.5mm Velo-Dog (also variously called the 5.6, 5.75, 5.8, or 6mm Velo-Dog). Note that concealed carriers often loaded these cartridges with cayenne pepper or a hopefully less-lethal cork or wax bullet.

Initially, the term was probably applied exclusively to the revolvers chambered for that specific round. Today, the Velo-Dog term is used for a broad assortment of Euro pocket revolvers in various calibers by diverse (and often anonymous) makers, probably because no one can think of what else to call them. They all are pocket size. They all have one or more of three specific features — concealed hammer, folding spur-trigger, and manual safety. French manufacturer Galand introduced the first in the mid-1890s. Most came from Belgium, France, or Spain, with additional production in Germany, Italy, and Brazil, with nearly 50 different manufacturers identified. The most prolific production was from the turn of the 20th century to World War I. To the adventurous collector exploring this field, it can sometimes seem more challenging to find two alike than to find a new variation. Rarities that will generally bring a premium include large-frame hammerless revolvers and engraved specimens.

In 1997, Casull Arms introduced an updated and very well made version of the Velo-Dog revolver style in .22 LR, the Model CA2000. It is a hammerless double-action-only five-shot stainless steel revolver with a folding trigger and manual safety. Casull discontinued manufacturing of the model in 2005, with reportedly less than 1,000 made.

Fine scroll-engraved Iver Johnson .38 S&W Safety Automatic revolver.

RISE OF THE AUTO-PISTOL

During the hey-day of the hammerless revolver, a new type of concealable handgun was on the rise. In the late 19th century, the "Automatic" part of the model name of many of the pocket revolvers referred to automatic extraction of cartridges and cases when you opened the top-break. The term would soon come to be associated with the automatic loading and ejection feature of slim, handy, box-magazine-fed handguns in what we call semi-auto pistols today.

Before designing the all-time classic 1911 .45 ACP pistol, John Moses Browning had already introduced "Pocket Models" in .25 ACP, .32 ACP, and .380 ACP. Each of these cartridges had been developed specifically for the Browning pistols that chambered them. The pistols were initially produced by Colt in the U.S. and by Fabrique Nationale in Belgium. Model designations generally indicated the year of introduction, including 1903, 1905, 1907, and 1908.

SAVAGES!

The early Browning-designed Colt autos had a direct competitor — Savage Arms Company. The U.S. military,

Spanish gold damascene pocket autos. Bufalo .32 ACP and Astra .25 ACP, along with gold-engraved Liliput Model 1925, chambered for the small 4.25mm cartridge. Bailey Brower, Jr., collection. Stoney Roberts photo

seeking to adopt a new issue sidearm to replace the Colt and S&W .38 Special revolvers (which had recently replaced the .45 Colt Single Action Army), conducted an extensive series of trials between 1907 and 1911. The military rapidly narrowed the various guns submitted for consideration to two, both in .45 ACP — a Colt and a Savage. Each firm produced 200 pistols for field trials. The competitors made improvements and conducted a

Exceptional factory-engraved and cased pair of Savage Model 1907 pistols with pearl grips, one blue and the other gold-plated. The only other similar pair is in the NRA National Sporting Arms Museum at Bass Pro Shops in Springfield, MO. Bailey Brower, Jr., collection. Stoney Roberts photo

final grueling head-to-head 6,000-round shootout in March 1911. When the dust settled, the Colt 1911 was selected to arm American troops. The military returned the runner-up test pistols, and Savage refurbished them for sale to the public.

During this time, both Savage and Colt were making smaller versions for sale to the public, with success. Between 1907 and 1929, Savage sold approximately a quarter-million .32 and .380 ACP pocket pistols.

The Colt pocket autos of the early 20th century have become prestigious collectors' items, with high condition specimens bringing premium prices. The Savages are currently less vigorously pursued. They are worthy of serious consideration as a collecting specialty in high-quality historically significant

American-made auto-pistols from a century ago, with a wide range of variations and exciting history.

As with Baby Hammerless revolvers, you can start a Savage pocket pistol core collection with relatively few specimens. There are three basic models, each easily identified at a glance. The Model 1907 has an exposed hammer and a somewhat rectangular grip configuration. The Model 1915 is hammerless (concealed hammer) with a similar grip shape and the addition of a grip safety. The Model 1917 has an exposed hammer but a distinctive trapezoidal grip frame with a significant flare at the base and no grip safety. If you get one of each basic model in each of the two available chamberings — .32 and .380 — you have an instant representative collection.

However, there are many variations,

and the dedicated collector could happily spend decades building and adding to a collection. As with most new firearms technology, the design was frequently being modified and improved. There are 20 modification variations of the earliest 1907 Model alone. The finish changed over the years, beginning with a beautiful bright blue for most products, with a more matte finish offered later. Savage even experimented with a paint finish that turned out not to be durable, making high-condition specimens rare and valuable today. Grips vary as well, including changes in which direction the Savage Indian chief logo is facing and an era of blued metal grips.

Collecting options go far beyond mechanical and cosmetic production variations. There are military sales for Portugal

Colt Bankers Special revolvers in .22 LR and .38 S&W represent "snub nose" swing-out cylinder revolvers introduced in the late 1920s. Bailey Brower, Jr., collection. Stoney Roberts photo

and France and shipments to Canada and Britain, and police sales to Saskatchewan and Kingston. You could order special enhancements from the factory, including plated finishes in nickel, silver, or gold, and several varieties of pearl grips, including the extremely rare "tuxedo" grips — pearl plates on a black, hard rubber panel. Even so-called "target sights" were offered. As with all desirable collector arms, quality engraving can greatly enhance interest and value, with period factory engraving much more desirable than later non-factory enhancement.

The lucky collector can occasionally unearth a factory prototype or experimental model or a pistol with credible documented historic attribution to a particular individual. For the Savage pistol enthusiast, there are also rare,

larger, and smaller related models — the .45 government contract guns and the limited-production .25 ACP version. Like many other quality American handgun designs, there are European knock-offs of Savage pattern pistols, including a Spanish "Salvaje" pistol with a strikingly similar grip logo.

A WORLD OF POCKET AUTOS

In Europe, the development of semi-automatic pistols began in the early 1890s, with the Borchardt among the first to gain modest success in 1893. The Mauser "Broomhandle," introduced in 1896, was widely adopted by militaries and popular on the commercial market. Pocket-sized models by various European makers were not far behind. In addition to personal defense, European police

and some military generally considered .32-caliber handguns adequate for their applications.

The interwar period, including the Roaring Twenties, saw the ascendency of these pocket autos for convenient concealed carry, notwithstanding John Dillinger's admonition to "Never trust a woman or an automatic pistol." European makers, large and small, mostly catered to the self-loader market. The prestige brands, such as Walther, Mauser, and FN already enjoy significant established collector interest. However, there is a world of less-recognized and nearly anonymous early Euro pocket pistols to explore and acquire at reasonable prices for the adventurous. Spanish Ruby-style guns offer a diverse selection by a range of makers.

Small maker Chiefs Special-style revolvers, clockwise from top right: Security Industries Police Security Special .38 s/n AB1; INA Tiger .38 s/n 000001; FIE Arminius Titan Tiger .38 s/n N000001; Firearms International Corp. Regent, .32 s/n G00001.

The first Charter Arms gun manufactured, Undercover serial number 1, circa 1965, was remarkably similar in size and configuration to the Smith & Wesson Chiefs Special.

AND THEN IT GETS WEIRD

When discussing pocket protectors more than a century old, I would be remiss in failing to mention the oddities and curiosa. While most of these are well recognized by collectors and usually sell for significant premiums, they are fascinating and just plain fun. Combination weapons include revolvers incorporating folding knife blades or brass knuckles. There are squeezer repeaters such as the Chicago palm pistol and Gaulois that are barely recognizable as guns. The Novo revolver managed to make a package even smaller than the Baby Hammerless by incorporating not only a folding trigger but also a folding grip. Cane guns don't fit into a pocket, but you can disguise them, even if they are a somewhat impractical defense weapon that you can keep at hand without looking like a Victorian-era commando.

VALUE ENHANCERS

As with more widely recognized collecting specialties, the price of these overlooked pocket guns from a century ago can be significantly increased by unique features. Factory original boxes or cases are relatively rare for guns of this vintage, being fragile and disposable. Special non-standard features can bring a premium, assuming the model is well-researched enough to determine its standard configuration. And, of course, period engraving can significantly increase the value, with factory engraving especially desirable. Experts generally evaluate non-factory engraving by the intricacy, execution, and coverage, but even simple period line engraving will up the value. Gold damascene is an incredibly flashy and attractive form of decoration sometimes found on Spanish auto-pistols from this era.

THE REVOLVER EVOLVES

As the 20th century wore on, a new type of double-action revolver gained popularity for concealed carry — the solid frame swing-out cylinder hand-ejector style. The first of the kind was

introduced by Colt in 1889, with Smith & Wesson entering the market in 1896. The most common 4- to 6-inch barrels were too long to be considered pocket pistols. Colt initiated the snubnose revolver market with the 2-inch barrel Detective Special in 1927, a six-shot .38 Special. The next year, it introduced it in .38 S&W or .22 LR, as the Bankers Special.

It took Smith & Wesson a while to get into the spirit of things, but in 1950 it introduced the smaller frame Chiefs Special, a five-shot 2-inch .38 Special. Smith developed its hammerless (enclosed hammer) Centennial in 1952 and the shielded hammer Bodyguard in 1955. At the same time, it shaved weight off the models by offering alloy frame versions branded "Airweights."

Other firms followed suit. One successful American manufacturer, Charter Arms, was built on short-barrel pocket revolvers. In 1965, Charter introduced its first gun, the Undercover, basically a revised version of the Chiefs Special, which weighed just 16 oz.; Charter advertised it as "A Pound of Prevention." It was the lightest steel frame .38 Special. Its retail price was $55, about half that of a Chiefs Special. Charter followed with a slightly larger five-shot .44 Special and were early adopters of stainless steel manufacture.

Both Colt and Smith & Wesson early snubbies enjoy enthusiastic collector interest with commensurate prices. However, they also set the stage for a broad field of imitators and innovators that generally fly under the collecting radar.

FROM THE ROARING TWENTIES TO THE SWINGIN' SIXTIES

The market for affordable concealable defensive sidearms continued into the 1960s, 70s, and 80s with products by new manufacturers and distributors. Just like the wheellock nearly half a millennium earlier, they inspired a spate of bad-idea anti-gun legislation.

This time, the targets were "Saturday Night Specials." Gun banners used this sometimes-racist derogatory term to refer to cheap handguns. Gun control advocates attacked the guns on the grounds of being unsafe and the preferred arm

Pocket protector design concepts from over a century ago remain popular today. Clockwise from top right: Smith & Wesson Hammerless Model 642 .38 Special; Seecamp LWS .32 ACP pocket pistol; Freedom Arms spur-trigger single-action .22 revolver s/n MRL1, and Casull Arms .22 LR Model CA2000 s/n OTS1, which incorporates all three distinguishing features of the Velo-Dog revolvers — hammerless, folding trigger, and manual safety.

of muggers and robbers. Subsequent research has generally proven both assertions to be unfounded. Perhaps their real sin was that they were within the budget of poor folks — the peasant class that the elite wanted to be disarmed and disenfranchised. Congress passed the Gun Control Act of '68 to stem the "flood of cheap imports," establishing a "sporting purpose" test for firearms importation, a criterion never considered by the Second Amendment's drafters.

As with most anti-gun legislation drafted by ignorant pearl-clutching non-shooters, which focuses on guns' specific characteristics, manufacturers and importers immediately found ways to circumvent the legislative specs, such as adding target sights or slightly increasing the size of various models. Since the law only restricted imports, several makers of inexpensive models previously made abroad shipped their parts to American companies, who assembled them. The guns thus suddenly became non-import American-made firearms. As a result, Americans continued to enjoy affordable personal defense handguns with only some minor annoyance.

The wide variety of off-brand or small-maker defensive concealable handguns from this era offers a broad and affordable smorgasbord for the collector interested in more recent history or bored with the consensus about what is collectible. There are copies of classic designs and unusual innovations. Gun snobs might turn up their noses at these, but I think they're way neat. The best advice for an aspiring collector? Collect what you like. **GD**

REFERENCES:
Savage Pistols by Bailey Brower, Jr.
Iver Johnson Arms & Cycle Works Firearms, 1871–1993 by W.E. Goforth
Hopkins & Allen Revolvers & Pistols by Charles E. Carder
Flayderman's Guide to Antique American Firearms by Norm Flayderman
Suicide Specials by Donald B. Webster, Jr.
Rare Selections for Old Gun Catalogs 1880–1920 by Joseph J. Schroeder & Gun Digest
Sportsmen's Supplies of Character, Guns Catalog No. 87 by Schoverling, Daly & Gales
www.velodog.com

BACK TO THE WALL:
Handgun Bullet Penetration in Homes

❯ MARK NAZI

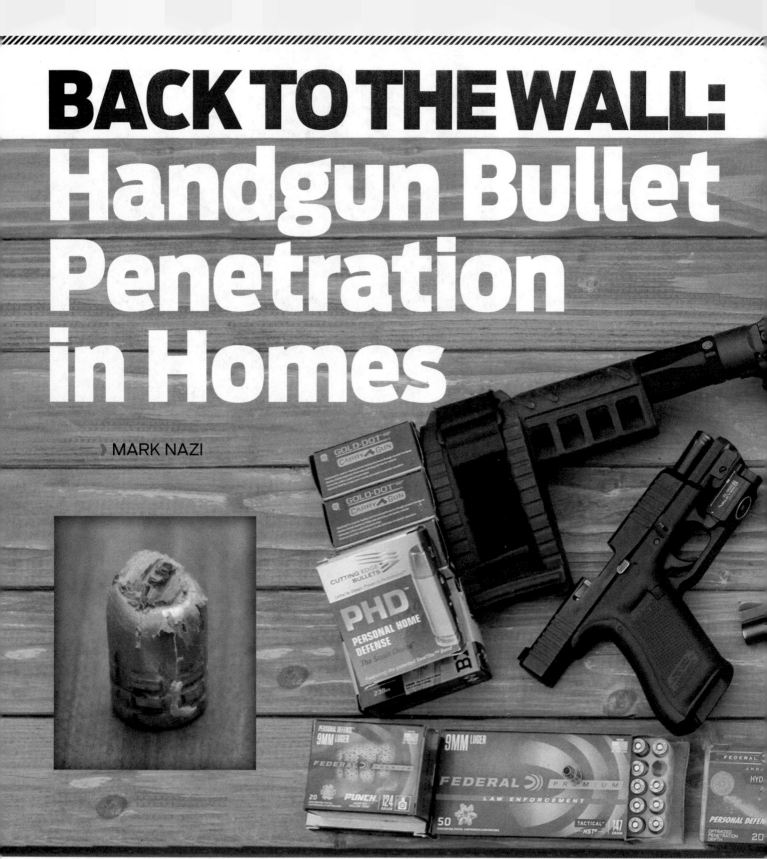

God forbid you ever must discharge a firearm within your home in self-defense. It pays to know what those bullets will do.

L ate one night, so hungry I could eat a horse, I dashed off to the Cask and Rasher, a local bar with a fantastic menu. Entering the place, I instantly noticed a man sitting at the bar in what I could only describe as a green safari shirt; it was Phil Massaro, editor of this publication. We ordered some goodies, and soon the debate swung to ammunition, specifically carry ammo. No one can talk with a mouthful like Phil can. We discussed and debated everything from caliber to bullet choice, magazine capacity, lethal force laws, and the damage caused by bullets designed to

mushroom upon impact versus ones that rely on hydraulic shock. Also on this list was an in-depth discussion of worst-case scenarios. For us, potentially having to discharge a firearm inside the home, for whatever reason, was near the top of the list. We found that we were both keenly interested in what happened to bullets that missed their intended target and hit a wall or hard obstruction in the home. Would our homes' walls provide any stopping properties of ballistic protection (especially since neither of us lives alone)? How would such obstructions affect the bullets — would they cause failures? Would bullets simply break apart?

The next day started with a phone call. It was Massaro. "Mark, I want you to test some bullets and do an article." Of course, I answered. "No, Mark, I want you to test the shit out of these bullets, shoot them at things, shoot them through things, really test them." Luckily for me, aside from working full-time in law enforcement, my father and I own and operate Double Eagle Tactical Training, Inc. It offers everything from basic firearms and self-defense to force-on-force simunition courses and advanced tactical training. Most importantly, we have a 10-acre range ideally suited for said testing.

As I write this, ammunition is practically non-existent, firearms sales are at record highs, and ammunition prices are the highest I've seen in my lifetime. We are seeing an entirely new group of shooters emerge on the scene. Part of me is thrilled to see more and more people embracing their Second Amendment rights. During the height of firearm sales, I was lending a hand at Country Armory LLC, a local gun store that always has what I need in a pinch. During my time helping around the shop, I also got to talk to a ton of new shooters. I had a lot of questions. I commonly asked things like, "What brings you in today?" or "What caused you to now become a firearm owner?" The answers I got were highly diverse, but the most common one was always "for home defense" or "just in case." I swear I saw people buy just about every type of firearm known to man in a wild variety of calibers for home defense — everything from AR-15s to .22 Derringers. Knowing full well I was going to write this article, I started asking about their dwellings. How many people did they live with, and what materials

Getting things in order before beginning the test.

did they use in construction, ranch-style versus multiple floors? I also asked them if they believed that their home walls would provide any ballistic protection from incoming rounds or their rounds fired in self-defense. Would their walls stop the caliber they had chosen? Most people told me they believed the walls of their home would have no issue containing the rounds. Even the guy with the AR-15 confidently said to me that he "sees no overpenetration issues."

Thanks to my owning a BB gun at a young age and thinking how cool it would be to target practice in my bedroom, I've had to learn how to repair sheetrock. I can tell you with confidence that sheetrock provides absolutely no ballistic protection. At any rate, I wanted to know what the walls of a modern home

afforded in ballistic protection. I was also interested in what these materials would do to the bullet itself.

HOLLOWPOINT BULLETS

The history of how the hollowpoint bullet came to be the defensive round we now know and love is intriguing. Today, the hollowpoint is the most popular bullet chosen by civilians as well as law enforcement. However, back in the 19th Century, bullets were non-jacketed lead, and blackpowder ruled the world. These early bullets did a decent job due to their soft lead construction and low velocity. The low speed and soft alloy caused expansion upon impact, but nothing like what came later. People began drilling holes in the projectile's face and removing material from the center to increase

velocity, following the theory that lighter is faster.

Ammo firms marketed early versions of these as "express bullets." Ammunition makers produce similar stuff today; cowboy action shoots use it primarily. The firearms are mostly single-action revolvers, and the ammunition is designated "cowboy load." Enter the advent of smokeless powder, which increased velocities. Counterintuitively, the new increased velocity was not cutting the mustard: solid lead or drilled lead bullets fragmented before impact and caused extreme lead fouling on the inside of the barrels due to lead fragments coming off the bullet while it was traveling down the bore. These all proved to be significant issues. Enter the jacketed round-nose bullet. With the increased velocity, man-

ufacturers needed a way to ensure the projectile's lead core would stay together and maintain accuracy and repeatability. Manufacturers encased the lead bullets in a copper alloy. Copper alloy is stronger than lead, and it ensured that the bullet remained in one piece as it traveled to the target.

Now we have the bullet moving faster than before and adding a copper alloy jacket so that the projectile stays together and does not separate. Still, we have lost expansion — and gained penetration — due to the hard jacket. No expansion and lots of penetration is never a good equation for stopping a human threat. This requirement led to the introduction of "soft-point" bullets. Ammo makers encased the lead core in copper alloy, leaving about a third of the nose exposed lead. Lead, being a much softer metal than copper, allows the bullet to expand and "mushroom" upon impact in soft tissue, combating overpenetration and soft tissue damage. Soft points are still a popular bullet choice today. I hunt with Speer 240-grain Hot-Cor bullets loaded in my .35 Remington lever gun. Soft points became wildly popular in the hunting community as the bullet's shape allowed high velocities. The exposed lead caused the bullet to mushroom upon impact, controlling penetration. When we look at handguns versus rifles, the former's velocities are substantially less than that of the latter, not only due to cartridge size but also because the longer barrel length of the rifle allows the powder charge to burn longer and more efficiently. Even so, when fired at handgun velocities, the soft points still penetrate more than desired and don't expand. That is why the drilled bullet cemented its place in firearms history.

Around the same time as their inception, the international community outlawed hollowpoint bullets for war. The Germans made the first-known complaint in 1889, noting that the use of these new bullets breached the "laws of war." This argument had merit: the Hague Convention of 1899 banned bullets designed to flatten or expand in the body. The St. Petersburg Declaration of 1868 outlawed exploding projectiles weighing less than 400 grams or any weapon designed to aggravate a soldier's injuries or cause inevitable death. Now, who or what weapon inspired such wording, I can only wonder.

So, as velocities increased with smokeless powder and the knowledge that lead bullets did not take this bump in speed very well, ammo makers needed a new solution. The first jacketed hollowpoints flooded the market, earning such names as "man stopper" due to their effectiveness in stopping a threat quickly and efficiently. How was this accomplished? Ammo producers encased a lead core in a copper alloy jacket, then drilled a hole through the jacket and into the core. When this hole impacted soft tissue, it aided the copper in expanding into a mushroom shape. The mushroom shape slowed the bullet down once it impacted its target, reducing overpenetration. It also caused a significant amount of soft tissue damage. Early hollowpoints were not drilled very deeply and did not reliably expand due to the very thick copper jacket.

Now let's inject a few decades of technology, research, and development into the hollowpoint's evolution. Today's hollowpoints come in a variety of shapes, sizes, colors, and forms. Multiple manufacturers have done their research and added tweaks over the years to give us some excellent options. If one were to do an online search of "hollowpoints," the results would take a lifetime to weed through. So, how do you select the best hollowpoint for your application?

When I'm selecting a hollowpoint, I first think of its intended use, followed closely by the environment in which I will be shooting it. Things to consider are penetration and what I'll call "method of damage," all while keeping accuracy and function as the highest priorities. Many hollowpoints rely on forcing the soft lead core against the thin copper-alloy jacket, resulting in a mushroom-like shape. Advancements in this category range from small slits cut into the jacket (providing a weak point for controlled expansion) to the addition of soft polymer inserts that aid in consistent expansion. Over the years, we've learned that certain materials like heavy clothing and jeans can clog a hollowpoint — essentially turning it into a jacketed round-nose bullet. So, now you see the addition of rods and different methods to ensure expansion in various materials, such as plating. Some new additions to the market are constructed totally from copper and contain absolutely no lead. Others rely on hydraulic shock to cause damage with solid copper

The authors assembled the test wall, making it as lifelike as possible to simulate a home's interior.

projectiles with fins and rifling to make the bullet spin.

Enter one of the few things the government is useful for: testing. Across the board, law enforcement people carry hollowpoints in their duty weapons. The government and its respective agencies did not just blindly choose hollowpoints. They did testing — and I'm talking *a lot of testing*. The good news is that the data is a public record, and you can easily find it. If you're having trouble choosing a hollowpoint to rely on, that makes a great starting point. Also included in this data are many of the same concerns involved in the home defense application — penetration, expansion, performance on ballistic gelatin, reaction to different materials, and of course, wound and damage data. I've found that many of these big companies will not only do their extensive testing but send their products out to be tested by independent parties. These tests are not overly complicated and are inexpensive to replicate.

TESTING THE HOLLOWPOINTS

To prevent any chance of my ammunition not functioning in the test guns, we ran two tests. The first is called the "digestion test." I make sure that the firearm will properly cycle when combined with the ammunition. Typically, I will load three or four magazines. I'll point downrange and squeeze the trigger rapidly for the first magazine, double taps for the second mag, single shots for the third mag, and a variety

The author performs the wall test.

of all for the fourth. What I'm looking for here is to see if the configuration will function properly. During this test, failures happened when the feed ramp's angle didn't match the hollowpoint's lip, jamming the gun. That does not mean that there is anything necessarily wrong with the firearm or ammunition; it just means that they do not function as a combination.

Secondly, once a gun and ammo combo passes the digestion test, you can move on to the "point of aim versus point of impact" test. For this test, use a target covered in 1x1-inch boxes, along with a shooting bench and rest. Start with your target at five yards and progress

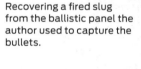

Recovering a fired slug from the ballistic panel the author used to capture the bullets.

to about 25 yards in increments of five yards. Pick one box, take five shots, seated off a rest. Your primary focus is keeping your point of aim the same for every shot and allowing the rest to remove as much human input as possible. After each five-shot string, inspect the target. You want to ensure that the hollowpoints consistently impact where you want. I strongly recommend a quality shooting rest. Shooting this test offhand will not yield the best results and may result in the "shoot low and to the left" type of data. If your rounds are impacting consistently, just not where you aim your sights, have a friend fire a few shots at a different box to confirm. Your sights may be off and need to be adjusted. Even so, out of thousands of guns that have passed under my instruction, I can count on one hand those requiring a sight adjustment.

For the test, I had to beg, borrow, and call in massive favors to get my hands on various hollowpoints over a range of popular calibers. To make sure this test was accurate, I took a close look at the construction of both interior and exterior home walls, comparing old construction versus new, siding versus brick or stone, and types of insulation used. I built two exterior walls consisting of 1/2-inch sheetrock, followed by fiberglass insulation, a 3/4-inch piece of plywood commonly used on exterior walls, 2x6 studs, and standard siding. I did not expect this to do a whole lot in the way of stopping a bullet, and I've noticed a lot of homes have a brick exterior, so I finished the bottom half of my wall with a sheet of EPS poly panel insulation and then a wall of building brick.

Also, I needed to ascertain how, if a bullet penetrated the wall, I would recover the slug without causing further damage to it from hitting the range's dirt berms. For this, I used expired bulletproof vests. I had a few expired Level-3 soft armor panels lying around. I didn't want to secure the panels to the wall because I didn't want the bullet hitting the panel to cause further

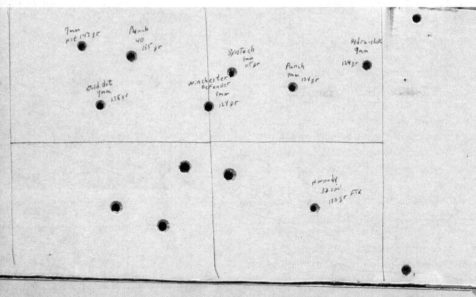

A variety of entry holes from tested ammunition.

Double Eagle Tactical Training Instructor Lek Nazi uses a Kimber TLE II 1911 to test the .45-caliber ammo.

The 9mm Gold Dot G2 bullet after penetrating the wall.

Right: Cutting Edge Bullets' .45 ACP 150-grain PHD, after impacting the wall's bricklayer.

deformation. I wanted to see the condition of the bullet as it left the wall. For this reason, I set the panels against the wall, leaving them loose and not secured to anything so that they would have plenty of room to capture the bullet as it left the wall. This setup would allow me to inspect the slug and any effects the wall materials had on it.

9MM TEST RESULTS

I shot a variety of 9mm, .38 Special, .40 S&W, and .45 APC. For the 9mm, I chose my Glock Model 45 for the delivery system. First up was the Winchester Defender 124-grain +P hollowpoint load. It claimed a five-yard velocity of 1,188 fps with a bullet "notched jacketed preprogrammed to expand." I also noted that on the rim of the cup, Winchester rounded the petals. As to be expected, this thing whistled through my siding wall like it was not there and sent the vest panels flying. I was able to recover the bullet without issue. The recovered bullet weighed 125.7 grains and expanded from 9mm to 17.62mm. It also had a large chunk of plywood embedded in the slug. When faced with the brick wall, the bullet shattered and did not affect the brick. I was able to recover 90.8 grains of material.

Next down the pipe was the Speer Gold Dot G2 135-grain load, claiming a muzzle velocity of 1,120 fps and boasting a "shallow dished, elastomer-filled nose," which Speer says prevents plugging by barrier materials. This bullet also had no issue passing through the siding wall. (In fact, to save a lot of repetition, I'll say

this: every bullet tested whistled through the exterior siding wall with no issue.) Once recovered, the slug weighed 133.1 grains and expanded to 15.61mm. As Speer claimed, I found no barrier materials embedded in the slug. Next up was the Federal Punch 124-grain jacketed hollowpoint, with a muzzle velocity of 1,150 fps. I had to dig this slug out of the vest panel with a knife — it hits hard! I firmly believe "Punch" is a well-earned name. Once recovered, the slug *gained*

some weight, weighing in at 126.8 grains and expanding to 14.00mm. It also had a large chunk of plywood lodged in the front. It did expand, but the petals did not open. When faced with the brick, the Punch bullet moved the brick and broke a chunk off. I was not able to recover any of that bullet.

Next into the gauntlet was the Federal Tactical HST 147 grain. This load uses a jacketed hollowpoint with slits cut down the slug side and claims a muzzle

velocity of 1,000 fps. Once recovered, it weighed 149.0 grains, and I could identify sheetrock in the core. It expanded to 14.24mm. I recovered most of the bullet once it hit the brick. Once I moved the brick away, I retrieved the jacket absent the core. The jacket had expanded to 29.15mm and weighed 39.2 grains. Again, the brick proved to be a good bullet stopper.

I acquired some of the new Syntech Range ammo from Federal. This load has a lead bullet jacketed with powder coating and came to me in the 115-grain variety claiming a muzzle velocity of 1,150 fps. Once recovered, it weighed in at 113.6 grains and showed minimal expansion of 11.34mm (Federal did not design it to expand). I wasn't able to recover the slug because it shattered when faced with the brick. Once again, the brick stands strong!

Next down the pipe was the Federal Hydra-Shok 125-grain jacket hollowpoint. (Federal claims a muzzle velocity of 1,120 fps.) In addition to cuts in the jacket, I also noticed a rod in the hollowpoint center. Federal introduced this to prevent the slug from clogging with clothing and barrier materials. Once recovered, the slug weighed in at 123.00 grains and expanded to 14.01mm. While this slug had good expansion, I did observe a small amount of sheetrock embedded in the core. Again, the bullets were

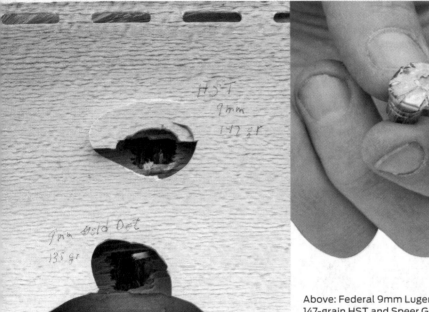

Above: Federal 9mm Luger 147-grain HST and Speer Gold Dot G2 135 grain exit holes.

Left: Federal 9mm 147-grain HST after passing through the wall.

A variety of recovered slugs.

shattering upon impact with the brick, and I could not recover any material.

.38 SPECIAL TEST RESULTS

After wondering how much punishment my brick wall was going to take, it was time to try a different caliber. For the next test, I dropped a round of Hornady Critical Defense .38 Special 110 grainers. This load comes with Hornady's FTX bullet with a small, red polymer ball inside the hollowpoint and cuts on the side for expansion. Hornady claims a muzzle velocity of 1,010 fps. The .38-caliber slug exited the wall with the least amount of force, bouncing off the vest panels and falling to the ground. Once recovered, the slug weighed 110.6 grains and expanded to 12.55mm. I noted that the red poly ball was still visible, but no material got into the slug. When faced with the brick wall, I recovered the core, absent the jacket, and the small red ball was nowhere to be found. The core weighed in at 86.2 grains and expanded to 26.09mm.

.40 S&W TEST RESULTS

Time to kick things up a bit. I switched my Glock Mod 45 out for my duty gun: a Glock Mod 22 chambered in .40 S&W. First to leave the pipe was the Federal Punch 165-grain jacketed hollowpoint, with a claimed muzzle velocity of 1,130 fps. Once recovered, that slug weighed in at 169.2 grains and expanded to 15.58mm. I also noted that the Punch had a big chunk of wood embedded in the slug. When faced with the brick, it caused damage but did not penetrate. After recovery, I noticed the core separated from the jacket, and it weighed 117.4 grains and expanded to 25.80mm.

.45 ACP TEST RESULTS

With newfound respect for brick, it was time to test the .45 ACP with a Kimber TLE 2 1911. The first shot was the Federal Hydra-Shok DEEP 210 grain (980 fps). Federal says this round will

Federal .45 ACP 210-grain Hydra-Shock DEEP after impacting the brick.

Federal .45 ACP 230-grain Punch slug after passing through the wall.

penetrate 15 inches of ballistics gel. The bullet has aggressive cuts on the jacket and a rod in the core. Once recovered, the slug weighed 212.3 grains, expanded to 12.95mm, and had sheetrock plugged in the core. Good thing I bought extra bricks! The .45 ACP was much more abusive to the brick wall but still did not penetrate it. Once recovered, the jacket completely separated from the core, and I measured 194.6 grains of material. The jacket expanded to 26.50mm.

Next up in the heavyweight division was the Federal HST 230 grain. It has slits cut down the length of the slug and a notable cup. Federal says it does 890 fps. Once recovered, the slug weighed in at 232.3 grains and expanded to 12.04mm. The recovered slug did have sheetrock embedded in the core. After retrieving the slug from the brick wall, it weighed 227.4 grains and showed massive expansion to 27.97mm. The only visible material was a chunk of plywood embedded in the slug.

Next was the Hornady Critical Duty 220-grain flex lock (990 fps). Again, we see slits cut into the jacket and the red poly ball inserted into the hollowpoint. The captured slug weighed 218.3 grains and expanded to 18.97mm. The red ball was no longer intact. When faced with the brick, the core separated from the jacket, but I found both. The recovered materials weighed 193.6 grains and broke into four separate fragments.

Next into the wall was the Federal Punch 230-grain bullet at 890 fps. I noted slits cut down the length of the projectile and a deep cup. The slug weighed 233.3 grains and expanded to 13.16mm. I made a note of sheetrock and insulation embedded in the core. I will say, this thing rocked the bricks. It did not penetrate, but it sure hurt a few of them. I was also able to recover the slug. It weighed 229.9 grains and expanded to a massive 25.91mm.

The pistol-caliber slugs proved no match for the last layer of brick.

RESULTS

		BEF RECOV	AFTER RECOV	BEF RECOV	AFTER RECOV	BEF BRICK	BRICK	BEF BRICK	BRICK
WINCHESTER DEFENDER		9mm	17.62mm	124 gr.	125.7 gr.	9mm	N/A	124 gr.	90.8 gr. Recoverd
SPEER GOLD GOT G2		9mm	15.6mm	135 gr.	133.1 gr.	9mm	14mm	135 gr.	126.8 gr. Recoverd
FEDERAL TACTICAL HST		9mm	14.24mm	147 gr.	149 gr.	9mm	29.15mm	147 gr.	39.2 gr.
FEDERAL SYNTECH		9mm	11.34mm	115 gr.	113.6 gr.	9mm	N/A	115 gr.	N/A
FEDERAL HYDRA-SHOK		9mm	14.01mm	125 gr.	123 gr.	9mm	N/A	125 gr.	N/A
40 S&W	FEDERAL PUNCH	10mm	15.58mm	165 gr.	169.2 gr.	10mm	25.80mm	165 gr.	117.4 gr.
45 ACP	FEDERAL HST	11.43mm	12.04mm	230 gr.	232.3 gr.	11.43mm	27.97mm	230 gr.	227.4 gr.
	HORNDAY CRITICAL DUTY	11.43mm	18.97mm	220 gr.	218.3 gr.	11.43mm	N/A	220 gr.	193.6 gr.
	FEDERAL PUNCH	11.43mm	13.16mm	230 gr.	233.3 gr.	11.43mm	25.91mm	230 gr.	229.9 gr.
	CUTTING EDGE	11.43mm	12mm	150 gr.	160.1 gr.	11.43mm	18.17mm	150 gr.	150 gr.
	BROWNING BXP	11.43mm	16.92mm	230 gr.	233.9 gr.	11.43mm	33.39mm	230 gr.	122.5 gr.
	CIG ELIETE PERFORMANCE	11.43mm	15.83mm	185 gr.	188.5 gr.	11.43mm	15.83mm	185 gr.	52.1 gr.
	FEDERAL HYDR-SHOK DEEP	11.43mm	12.95mm	210 gr.	212.3 gr.	11.43mm	26.50mm	210 gr.	194.6 gr.
38 SPECIAL	HORNADY FTX	9.1mm	12.55mm	110 gr.	110.6 gr.	9.1mm	26.09mm	110 gr.	86.2 gr.

From Cutting Edge Bullets, we have a 150-grain all-copper bullet. Cutting Edge claims extreme trauma, balanced penetration, and five penetrating wounds — after 1 1/2 to 2 inches of soft tissue penetration, four blades are designed to break off and create their wound channels. The reported velocity was 1,050 fps. On the siding wall, the recovered projectile weighed 160.1 grains and expanded to 12.00mm. I found the slug clogged with plywood and minimal expansion. When facing the brick, however, the recovered slug weighed 150.0 grains and expanded to 18.17mm. I did note that the recovered slug remained in one piece.

Next in line to hit the wall was the Browning BXP 230-grain BXP X-Point. This bad boy leaves the muzzle at 920 fps. It has some lovely slits at the top of the projectile, and inside the hollowpoint is what Browning calls its x-point technology. Once recovered, the bullet weighed 233.9 grains and expanded to 16.92mm. I observed a large chunk of plywood lodged in the projectile. When facing the brick, the core separated from the jacket, and I recovered 122.5 grains of material. The recovered jacket expanded to 33.39mm.

To finish out the test, the last con-

testant was the Sig Elite Performance 185-grain V-Crown jacketed hollowpoint. The slug weighed 188.5 grains and expanded to 15.83mm. Plywood and sheetrock were visibly present. When facing the brick, the core separated from the jacket, and I recovered 52.1 grains of material. The jacket expanded to 15.83mm.

CONCLUSIONS

Now on to the cool thing that happened while shooting the interior sheetrock wall. Every round that hit the sheetrock raised about three or four inches and continued its original direction. This phenomenon was so repeatable that we ended up mak-

ing an L-shaped piece off the wall to track what we call "skim hits." With practice, we could predict the impact of a bullet that we skipped off the sheetrock — something to keep in mind if you find yourself in a defensive situation.

What I learned was that the walls of homes (absent brick) would do next to nothing in the way of stopping bullets and, in most cases, will not even slow them down much. Bottom line? It's not a bad idea to build your house from brick. Barring that, remember your firearm safety rules, especially in a home defense situation: Be sure of your target and what lies beyond. **GD**

Federal .45 ACP 230-grain Punch slugs.
Left: Side exterior wall, no brick.
Right: Side exterior wall, brick.

Trappers!

Short-barreled lever guns are as rare as hen's teeth and the handiest working guns you'll ever find.

RICK HACKER

For any firearms fan who is fascinated by word association games — just as the mere mention of "Thompson" can invoke thoughts of the Thompson submachine guns of the Roaring 20s, and "snubby" conjures images of a private eye stuffing a Smith & Wesson .38 Special into his trenchcoat pocket — this article's title inspires vivid imagery. "Trappers" triggers Jack London-inspired visions of stubby-barreled lever actions that hunters, adventurers, and yes, even trappers carried as they trudged their way through thick, snow-encrusted forests of the far north. And by "stubby-barreled lever actions," I am specifically referring to those handy, lightweight carbines Winchester and Marlin made during the late 19th and early 20th Centuries that sported barrels noticeably shorter than the standard 20-inch cataloged saddle guns.

An officer of the Phoenix-based Arizona State Liquor & Narcotics Enforcement Division ordered this Winchester Model 1894 with a 15-inch barrel in 1931, carrying it on numerous bootlegging raids during Prohibition.

Indeed, as the late Harold M. Williamson noted on the Model 1892 carbine in his classic book, *Winchester – The Gun That Won The West,* "One interesting use of this gun was among the trappers in the northern United States and Canada. In running a line for traps for smaller animals these men would not infrequently catch a wolf or a bear, and a Model 92 with a fourteen-inch barrel was effective in dealing with these animals."

And as Williamson also wrote, "…The short barreled Model 92 also proved to be popular in the jungles of Brazil for use on the rubber plantations," which interestingly enough, is where a lot of these early trappers ended up, where they no doubt dispatched many a non-furbearing critter, such as pythons, vipers, and other venomous reptiles entwined throughout the thick growth of the Amazon rainforests. Light, compact, quick to get into action, and capable of fast repeat shots

Today, replicas such as this Uberti 1873 Trapper with its 16 ¼- inch barrel utilize a standard 1873 carbine forearm, which is proper for this barrel length.

with better sight radius and pointability than a pistol, the trapper-styled lever actions were ideally suited for the often dangerous jobs at hand. The only thing they sacrificed was magazine capacity.

Yet ironically enough, during their existence, these guns were never called or cataloged as trappers. Instead, Winchester, on the rare occasion when it cataloged them, referred to them as "Baby Carbines" or "Special Short Carbines." At the same time, Marlin called them "special lightweight carbines," often pairing their shorter barrels with half magazines

to further reduce weight. On the other hand, Winchester always fitted its trapper guns with full-length magazines unless the customer specified otherwise.

In his seminal book, *Marlin – A History of the Guns and the Company That Made Them,* author William S. Brophy, also Marlin's Senior Technical Manager, called them "baby carbines" — even though the company did not. According to rumor, Brophy reportedly hated the trapper term.

Collectors coined the "trapper" term — now universally adopted — to denote carbines with barrels shorter than the cataloged standard 20 inches. No one knows precisely when this terminology first appeared. Still, I guess that it was sometime after 1933 — the

last year Winchester cataloged its "Special Short Carbines," for the Models 1892 and 1894, which, up until then, you could special order with barrel lengths of 14, 15, and 16 inches. I have even encountered a factory original Model 73 Trapper with a 12-inch barrel. By that barrel length, it was on a par with the Buntline Special: another gun with a name that collectors have universally adopted (as well as Colt Firearms itself) after Stuart Lake first mentioned it in his 1931 biography of Wyatt Earp. But I digress.

The 1933 date notwithstanding, we know that the first trapper carbines, per se, were special order Winchester 1873s. There were no factory original Henry or Model 1866 "Trappers," despite current replicas suggesting so by firms such as Uberti, Cimarron Firearms, and Dixie Gun Works. But according to the late

George Madis, author of *The Winchester Book,* one out of every 1,600 Model 1873 carbines had special order short barrels, even though Winchester did not even mention the possibility of ordering shorter-than-carbine length barrels in its catalogs until 1920, with the introduction of a 15-inch barrel option.

Nonetheless, one of the earliest documented short-barreled Winchesters is a Model 1873 with a 17-inch

Cimarron's 1892 Trapper is a replica of an 1892 Short Rifle, as it features an octagon barrel and steel nose cap. Unfortunately, it utilizes a full-length rifle forearm, which looks out of proportion with a 16-inch barrel, in the author's opinion.

barrel and a serial number of 115139, which puts its date of manufacture at 1876. Even more interesting is a nickel-plated 15-inch barreled Model 1873 chambered in .32-20 and depicted on page 184 of *The Winchester Book,* which shows it outfitted with Express sights. With a serial number of 382027 (placing its date of manufacture at 1892), one can only imagine who ordered this unique baby carbine and for what purpose.

But by far, most Winchester trappers are to be found as 1892 and 1894 baby carbines. But "majority" is a relative term in this case, as all are rare. To put

it in perspective, Madis estimates that "…of a total of 215 Model 1892 baby carbines, two had twelve inch barrels; the rest had fourteen and fifteen inch barrels and the old Model 94 saw 159 carbines (Trappers) … These counts are only approximate, since a few of these special carbines do not have notations as to barrel lengths. Of the small number of "Special Short Carbines" made, many were sent to other countries."

Marlin, on the other hand, did not officially begin offering baby carbines with shorter-than-average barrel lengths until 1905, when it first listed 15-inch barrels as special order options for the 1893 carbines in .32-40 and .38-55 calibers and the 1894 carbines in .25-20, .32-20, .38-40, and .44-40 calibers. There are also rumors of a very few 1889 short-barreled Marlins, although I have yet to encounter any. Plus, in a letter dated April 1, 1980, from William Brophy to the AFT director, Brophy mentions that he had gone through all of the Marlin factory records from 1883 to 1906 looking for carbines with barrels shorter than 16 inches. All he could find were model 1893 and 1894 carbines, and all these had 15-inch barrels — nothing shorter.

However, since Winchester and Marlin were competitors and Winchester was already producing a few lever actions with shorter-than-standard barrel lengths, it makes sense that Marlin would be doing the same on special order. Back in the late 1980s or early 1990s, a small number of authentic Marlin 1893 and 1894 Trappers mysteriously surfaced on the collector's market; I first spotted more than one of these rarities at the old Beinfeld Las Vegas Gun Show at the Sahara Hotel.

Unfortunately, neither Winchester nor Marlin's records have detailed information about which of their total production of carbines were of the "baby" variety (as noted, Marlin seems to have some records of baby carbines). Still, the majority of trapper-style lever actions encountered — whether Winchester or Marlin — have 15-inch barrels. And as

In 2010, Winchester produced a limited run of its 1892 Trapper Takedown in .44 Remington Magnum, .357 Magnum, and .45 Colt. Its 16-inch barrel, pistol gripped and checkered stock, and takedown feature made it an interesting modern-day variation of the older Winchester Model 92 Trapper.

In 2010, Winchester produced a limited run of the 1892 Trapper in .44 Remington Magnum, .357 Magnum, and .45 Colt as a 16-inch version with a takedown feature.

extremely short ranges in close cover.

But these same attributes also appealed to several lawmen who had specialized needs for a short, fast-shooting, hard-hitting gun that wouldn't jam. Examples include two 15-inch barreled Winchester 94 Trappers, each in .30-30 caliber and purchased in 1931 through Southern Hardware in Phoenix, Arizona by the Arizona State Liquor & Narcotics Enforcement Division. That occurred during the height of Prohibition, so it should come as no surprise that law enforcement used them in numerous bootlegging raids, which had supplanted cattle rustling in the hidden desert canyons surrounding the Valley of the Sun.

far as the Winchester Model 1892 and Marlin 1894 are concerned, most are in .44-40 caliber, which is interesting, as a .25-20 Trapper would leave a much smaller bullet hole in a furbearing animal and thus preserve more of the prized pelt. This peculiarity, of course, brings up the possibility that trappers did not all use these guns. Simply by their shorter barrel length and lighter weight, they would appeal to anyone who had to carry a lever action over long distances or rough terrain and would only need it at

Interestingly, Arizona Liquor Enforcement continued to use both trappers until 1955, when Phoenix police Sergeant (later Lieutenant) Phil Morgan purchased the guns from the department for his duty use. Lieutenant Morgan later headed up the Arizona Liquor Enforcement Department before retiring in the 1970s. Years later, when I talked with him, he spoke glowingly of one of the trapper rifles that he used while on duty all those years.

"I liked that short barrel," Morgan recalled of his Model 94 Trapper, "because it was easy to store in the trunk of your car. I used to carry it with a full magazine of Remington 170-grain ammo and an empty chamber. I often had to throw down on someone with that rifle, and it made them realize you were serious. It wasn't like carrying a pistol; every-

The author commissioned the old King's Gun Works of Glendale, California, to make this 16-inch Trapper from a Browning B92 carbine in .44 Remington Magnum to use as a trail gun. The gunsmith duplicated the loop lever on the Winchester 92 Trapper that John Wayne used in the movie "Stagecoach." The Browning, which is factory-engraved with Hacker's name, is shown with the author's well-used Randall Model 4-7 Big Game and Skinner hunting knife.

"Nothing Doing" by renowned artist Sydney Laurence (1865–1940) is one of the few period paintings that depict the hard life of a trapper — in this case with a rifle in hand, dejectedly inspecting an empty snare the critter avoided, judging by the tracks in the snow. Laurence came to the Alaska Territory in 1904 to prospect for gold but found greater riches as one of Alaska's most important historical artists.

A 16-inch-barrel Winchester 94 Trapper (left) is 1929 vintage and shown alongside a Winchester 92 Trapper made in 1903 with a 15-inch barrel.

one carried a pistol. But if you had that Trapper, you didn't have to shoot anyone because it opened their eyes. When they saw that .30-30, they knew you meant business."

That might also have been the case with the very business-looking 14-inch barreled Winchester 94, serial #589609 (found on page 438 of *The Winchester Book*) that indicates Winchester manufactured it in 1911, which was still a rough and rugged time in the American Southwest. In fact, in some Arizona and New Mexico border areas, these baby carbines are still occasionally referred to as "Pancho Villa Models."

These were guns meant to be used. As Madis wrote, "Those who ordered these special guns probably intended to use them a great deal every day, in all weather and in any possible situation … Because of their handy size, these babies often saw much abuse and the majority has (sic) seen neglect and abuse." To be sure, they were hand-carried over long distances, shoved into saddle blankets on horseback, thrust between coarse canvas sacks on

An original Winchester 1894 saddle ring trapper in .30-30 caliber, with a 16-inch barrel. According to the Cody Firearms Museum, Winchester shipped it on August 27, 1929. Note that the forearm wood is the proper length for a standard '94 carbine.

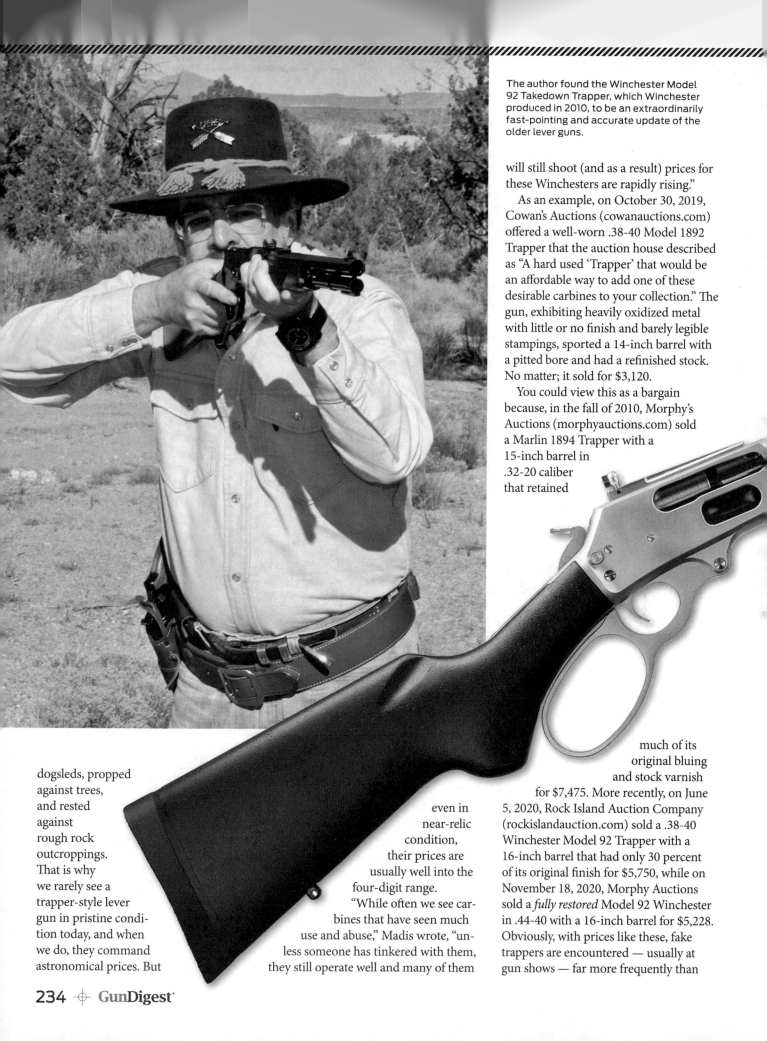

The author found the Winchester Model 92 Takedown Trapper, which Winchester produced in 2010, to be an extraordinarily fast-pointing and accurate update of the older lever guns.

will still shoot (and as a result) prices for these Winchesters are rapidly rising."

As an example, on October 30, 2019, Cowan's Auctions (cowanauctions.com) offered a well-worn .38-40 Model 1892 Trapper that the auction house described as "A hard used 'Trapper' that would be an affordable way to add one of these desirable carbines to your collection." The gun, exhibiting heavily oxidized metal with little or no finish and barely legible stampings, sported a 14-inch barrel with a pitted bore and had a refinished stock. No matter; it sold for $3,120.

You could view this as a bargain because, in the fall of 2010, Morphy's Auctions (morphyauctions.com) sold a Marlin 1894 Trapper with a 15-inch barrel in .32-20 caliber that retained much of its original bluing and stock varnish for $7,475. More recently, on June 5, 2020, Rock Island Auction Company (rockislandauction.com) sold a .38-40 Winchester Model 92 Trapper with a 16-inch barrel that had only 30 percent of its original finish for $5,750, while on November 18, 2020, Morphy Auctions sold a *fully restored* Model 92 Winchester in .44-40 with a 16-inch barrel for $5,228. Obviously, with prices like these, fake trappers are encountered — usually at gun shows — far more frequently than

dogsleds, propped against trees, and rested against rough rock outcroppings. That is why we rarely see a trapper-style lever gun in pristine condition today, and when we do, they command astronomical prices. But even in near-relic condition, their prices are usually well into the four-digit range.

"While often we see carbines that have seen much use and abuse," Madis wrote, "unless someone has tinkered with them, they still operate well and many of them

the real thing. Fakery is an unfortunate situation for the unwary, compounded by the fact that most authentic baby carbines are not identified in factory records by their serial numbers and barrel lengths.

Consequently, when contemplating acquiring a genuine trapper, always seek professional verification by a qualified collector or dealer (be prepared to pay an appraisal fee in many cases) or get a detailed written bill of authenticity and guarantee by the seller. And, of course, only buy from a reputable source. However, there are a few caveats to consider.

The biggest giveaway that a trapper isn't authentic is the forearm wood, which should measure 7 7/8 inches, approximately 1 3/8 inches shorter than the forearm wood on a standard 20-inch-barreled carbine. Authentic trappers with barrel lengths of less than 16 inches have their barrel address stamping on top of the barrel between the front sight and the forearm barrel band. There is not enough room to stamp on the barrel between the rear sight and the receiver. Trappers with barrels of 16 inches and longer will exhibit the normal barrel stamping position, which is on the side of the barrel and in the vicinity of the rear sight. Also, on ones made after 1916, the front sight bases were forged as part of the barrel, not dovetailed or soldered on, as were the earlier guns. Again, beware of fakes!

Due to the National Firearms Act of 1934, any trapper with a barrel length of shorter than 16 inches must be cleared — via letter — by the Bureau of Alcohol, Tobacco, Firearms, and Explosives (BATFE). The agency will certify that it has a factory-original short barrel, classifying it as a Curio & Relic. In many cases, a trapper will already be sold with this certification by the previous owner. Still, if not, you will have to physically send the gun to the BATFE firearms and technology division. Not a welcome endeavor, I grant you, and the process can take over a year to receive the proper certification, assuming the gun is indeed a genuine trapper. To my knowledge, there is no charge for this service but, as of this writing, it is a well-known fact that the current administration is not particularly gun-friendly.

That said, it is no wonder that many of today's hunters and shooters who want to experience owning a "Trapper" have turned to the replicas by firms such as Chiappa, Cimarron, and Uberti. These makers produce 16 ¼-inch-barrel 1873 and 1892 trappers, but they often use standard rifle- or carbine-length forearm wood, sometimes with a rifle nose cap, which visually looks off-balance and aesthetically makes me cringe.

That is why, back in 1979, when Browning introduced its non-limited edition B92 replica of the Winchester 92 carbine in .44 Magnum, I ordered one (Browning released a .357 Magnum version in 1982 but discontinued both models in 1987.) And I had the no-longer-existing King's Gun Works in Glendale, California, cut the 20-inch barrel down to 16 inches. I also had the place build and install a John Wayne-style loop lever, as seen in the 1939 motion picture, "Stagecoach," and trim off a small portion of the forearm wood to replicate better the original short wood found on period trappers. That was well before replicas even existed, so I was a little ahead of my time. I carried that little pseudo-baby carbine over much of West Texas and the gold rush hills of California on various jaunts and still have it today.

I was not alone in my fascination with trappers. In 1990, US Repeating Arms reintroduced a 16-inch barreled Model 94 Trapper Carbine in .30-30. It added .44 Remington Magnum and .45 Colt chamberings. Still, being a product of the times, it had Winchester's "improved Positive Side-Eject" version of the Angle Eject that had replaced the nostalgic pre-64's top ejection. Then, in 2010, Winchester produced a limited run of its 1892 Trapper Takedown. Winchester chambered this little gun — no longer available — in .44 Remington Magnum, .357 Magnum, and .45 Colt. With its 16-inch barrel combined with a unique takedown feature, it seemed a little redundant. I mean, why try to make an already small gun even smaller? Nonetheless, it was surprisingly accurate and quickly broke down into a compact two-piece package less than 24 inches long — perfect for transporting in the smallest car trunk or a locked suitcase, or even a bugout bag. Also, in 2017, Marlin introduced a modern-day stainless steel "Model 1995 Trapper" in .45-70 with a loop lever and a 16 ½-inch barrel, but, as good as it was, aside from its name, it had no direct lineage to Marlin's earlier "baby carbines."

Although authentic prewar trappers have become collectible rarities, I have, on occasion, taken my 1929-era 16-inch saddle ring .30-30 trapper deer hunting. Still, escalating values have recently caused me to limit its outdoor activities to the shooting range. There, the little gun never fails to draw admiring glances and occasional offers to purchase. And it still shoots reasonably well, despite a slightly bent front sight, the result of a tumble off a horse.

Whenever I pick it up and work the action, it functions and locks up with all the authority I'm sure it exhibited when it was new. It reminds me of what George Madis once wrote, "These rare Winchesters are a tribute to the people who designed them, made them and used them … and every Winchester collector would like to have at least one in his collection."

Amen to that. GD

In 2017, Marlin introduced a modern-day stainless steel "Model 1995 Trapper" in .45-70 with a loop lever, Skinner peep sight, and 16 ½-inch barrel; it is light years removed from Marlin's "baby carbines."

THE 6NormaBR FOR Competition OR Sport

Testing in benchrest and sporter rifles, the author proves the 6NormaBR is a well-rounded cartridge for any task.

› STAN TRZONIEC

Like everyone else in the shooting sports, my thoughts always shift to finding the "ideal" cartridge, rifle, or handload. If you dig further, the subject then broadens out to perhaps the limits of the discussion. Are you going to use it for varmints, general hunting, or delve deep into the competitive aspect? Additionally, do you want a lightweight sporter or something with more meat on the stock or barrel? Longer or shorter barrel, carbon or stainless, wood or a synthetic stock? Over the past few years, I've had the opportunity to try a little bit of each, all tied into a very unusual, uncommon little cartridge. It's called the 6NormaBR, aka 6mm BR from Remington.

6NORMABR BASICS

The 6NormaBR had its genesis in a cartridge with slightly different dimensions known as the 6mm BR. Around 1978, that cartridge was a competitive, long-range round suitable for distant 600-yard targets and very accurate for varmint hunting. Splitting hairs, the difference in physical size between the parent 6mm BR and the later 6NormaBR is only a mere forty-thousandths of an inch. You could find 6mm BR commercial ammunition with the option of unloaded, factory brass, all of which Remington based on a shortened .308 Winchester with a small rifle primer pocket. Later, Norma would upgrade the final 6Norm-

aBR cartridge to a longer neck dimension of 1.560 inches to restrict it from being used in one of the older wildcat chambers while making it the standard measurement today.

For this article, we will be dealing with the 6NormaBR. According to various sources, if it were not for Norma and its push for the cartridge, the 6mm BR would still be chambered in rifles available only through Remington's Custom Shop. Today, while the 6NormaBR is not a household word, the folks at Savage, Cooper, and Shaw still supply rifles in this caliber either off the shelf (Savage) or on a custom basis (E. R. Shaw or Cooper).

The Shaw Mark X rifle (top) and the Savage Benchrest rifle with some of the components that go into reloading the 6NormaBR. All photos by the author.

First, a bit of history about the 6mm Bench Rest Remington and the 6NormaBR, courtesy of Glenn Burroughs and his fine research. Essentially, both cartridges are the same. In short, while Remington machined its rifles to accept bullets up to 70 grains, Norma designed its version for rifles with longer throats to take bullets over 100 grains for longer-range shooting. Norma also changed the throat angle from 3 to 1.5 degrees for better overall performance and based it on the .308 Winchester case. Norma shortened and necked down the 6NormaBR to accept 6mm bullets and small rifle primers. If you can't purchase or locate the preferred Lapua brass, Remington 6mmBR brass will do fine for the 6NormaBR and will not affect the final results. Naturally, with all this going on, Norma chose to give the cartridge a new name — hence the 6NormaBR came to light.

Over time, the benefits of using the 6NormaBR surfaced among knowledgeable riflemen. Topping the list: It was one of the most accurate cartridges around, with the range to complement its very tight groups to 600 yards or more. My experience shows that out-of-the-box rifles at closer distances of 100 yards print .350-inch groups or smaller time and time again. The barrel's life is to 4,000-rounds-plus, much more than the .243 Winchester — almost double. If you are a handloader and have a rifle chambered for the parent 6mm BR Remington cartridge, you do not need

Left: With the same powder, charge, and 88-grain Berger bullet, the Shaw Mark X rifle printed this .250-inch group. Three shots are touching.

Below: Bedding on this gun consists of three stock screws pillar bedded under the receiver for uniform fit and equal pressure, all designed for accuracy. Take note of the hefty recoil lug cutout forward of the screws.

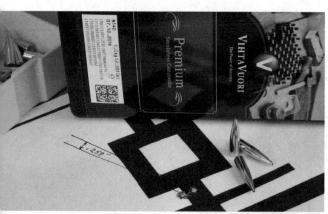

Topside from the rear of the Savage receiver, we see the tang safety, stylized bolt handle, and the bolt release at the receiver's rear bridge.

The Savage Benchrest's receiver is open on both sides. Using the right-side opening to eject, you can load the gun from the left for the next shot without moving the rifle from the rest.

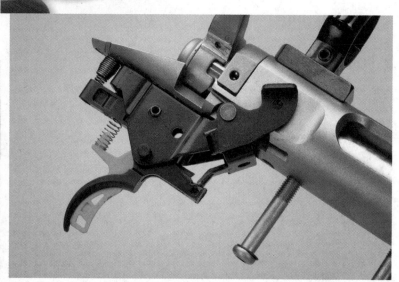

Savage installs a non-standard target trigger on the Benchrest rifle at the factory. With this mechanism, you can adjust the trigger pull to the light limits you need for long-range shooting.

to purchase a new set of dies for the 6NormaBR.

There is no question that the 6NormaBR is on a roll, something Remington and its version never accomplished. Remington was the first kid on the block to show this 6mm wonder to the world, but — except its custom 40X target rifle — never followed through. On the other hand, Norma popularized the cartridge, and now it is starting to show up in many venues. Of course, like any popular cartridge, there are going to be variants or "improved" versions that wildcatters will create. To date, these include the 6mm Dasher, 6 BRX, and the 6 BRBS. Me? I'll stick with the 6NormaBR and enjoy the availability of components, powders, and rifles.

6NORMABR RIFLES

6NormaBR-chambered rifles are limited. Savage has the Model 12 F Class with a 30-inch barrel and laminated stock. It has a long, wide forearm you can rest on a sturdy bench. For my testing, Savage provided a Model 12 Bench Rest rifle. It has a 29-inch long .890-inch diameter stainless barrel with a fast 1:8 twist. Indeed, Savage made the rifle for long-distance precision shooting. You can adjust its AccuTrigger to less than two pounds. The receiver has twin ports (left load, right eject), the bolt knob is oversized, and it has a laminated stock with a full, three-inch ventilated flat forearm for serious precision shooting. There is no cheekpiece and, with a classic-styled stock and pistol grip with palm swells

tailored to prone shooting, you have a gun set up to get the most out of the cartridge. The setup checked in at 15 pounds with a Bushnell 6-24 X 40mm scope.

While I set up this rig for benchrest-type shooting, moving it around in the field might be a problem (there is no sling swivel stud for a bipod, for example). Hence, as an alternative for this accurate cartridge, I looked for a sporter for my yearly varmint forays. Surprisingly, I came up with more than a few.

Cooper Arms of Montana offers several guns in 6 Remington Benchrest, and I believe the Remington Custom Shop once offered rifles in both cartridges. Still, with the company in bankruptcy, it's hard to find anything on its site. For a more definite order, I turned to E.R. Shaw in Bridgeville, Pennsylvania. Shaw sent a Mark X custom rifle at a very impressive price point. You can choose from nearly a hundred different chamberings — from the .17 Remington Fireball up to the more powerful magnums and some of the newer cartridges such as the 27 Nosler and .350 Legend.

From here, you choose the barrel contour and length (16 to 26 inches), stainless or carbon steel, polished or matte finish with a smooth or fluted finish. My choice here was the 22-inch length (the muzzle brake would lengthen it to 24 inches), polished stainless, sporter profile with no fluting, and a 1:10-inch twist. The older Shaw Mark VII rifles used the Savage

action, complete with the famed AccuTrigger. While the trigger is still part of the receiver assembly in today's models, the host receiver is now an authentic Shaw Mark X proprietary action with a Shaw-licensed trigger in cooperation with Savage Arms.

The receiver is available in either a short or long action, right or left bolt, and Shaw has machined flat sides with a Picatinny scope base making the mounting of a scope easy with only the purchase of scope rings. With the addition of a Leupold Freedom 3-9x40mm scope in matte rings, I was ready to move forward. The safety is tang-mounted with three-position detents denoting its position and a detachable magazine standard. (More details of the receiver at *ershawbarrels. com*.) Suppose you have a Remington Model 700 action rifle you are not using. Shaw can rechamber and rebarrel the action with the same profile as the original, so it fits into your factory stock with no inletting, cutting, or bedding.

I next focused on the stock to complete the Shaw. While you can have a laminated stock in pepper or nutmeg coloring, the standard fare is Grade 5 walnut with more than enough grain, figure, and color that looks to be worth more than the $1,400 price tag suggests. The stock is well-proportioned to the classic look with a semi-gloss finish, which brings out the

The Shaw Mark X rifle is custom-made to your specifications. You have a choice of dozens of options from the stock to the receiver and barrel. The author picked the Grade 5 wood for his rifle in combination with a highly polished barreled action.

best of the wood. The fine line checkering is in a point pattern on both the forearm and pistol grip, with a ribbon running through both areas. The pistol grip features a swell, and there is a moderate cheekpiece. The stock has a rubber recoil pad and sling swivel studs.

Working with the 6NormaBR is a pleasure, and that starts with the right barrel twist, especially for the lighter bullets. I chose a 1:10-inch twist on the Shaw and a 1:8-inch twist on the Savage. Since my forte is small game, this twist was a better choice for lighter, somewhat shorter bullets with the option of heavier ones when needed for larger game. I chambered the sporter in 6NormaBr instead of the 6mm Remington BR. The operative word here is versatility. Perhaps more importantly, I had no issues with this gun in operation, accuracy, extraction, or ejection of any spent cartridge. Could the 1:10 twist be ideal for the 6NormaBR? After all the work and testing, I believe it may be with the 88-grain Berger, as we'll soon see.

6NORMABR RELOADING

Let's start with a good foundation first — the brass. For my use, Lapua brass has superb uniformity right out of the box with no case prep. Neck runout on samples from Lapua shows less than .002 inch. Sure, you can use Remington brass, but right now, as the company is in the throes of reorganization, I'd hunt around for Lapua. Norma is another choice but is challenging to get and costs more. Next, acquire a large quantity of CCI 450 primers and stick with them. Changing primers during the testing will not prove much — if anything — as we've established the accuracy of this cartridge with the small rifle CCI primers.

With the accuracy potential of this cartridge, a good set of precision dies is the ticket. For this, I turned to the Redding Company (redding-reloading.com) and its Type S Match Die Set #38317. Included in the set is a body die you use to bump the shoulder back to factory specs. Do this if, for example, you purchase brass from an individual at a gun show or have fired it in another rifle. The second die is a bushing neck die, which uses bushings in increments of .001 inch that allow you to tailor your cases for your rifle and accuracy requirements. The bushings significantly improve the concentricity of the case, and they self-center on the case neck while sizing. Overall, the case length should come out to 1.550 to 1.560 inches.

To order the proper bushing, measure

You can choose from a wood or laminated stock in the Shaw Mark X line. On the wood model, the fit and finish of the gun is first class, complete with point pattern checkering along with color, grain, and figure, making the rifle worthy of any custom gun without the lofty price tag.

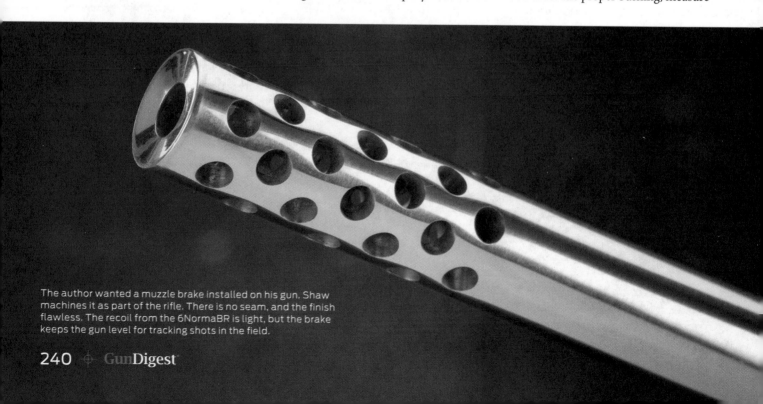

The author wanted a muzzle brake installed on his gun. Shaw machines it as part of the rifle. There is no seam, and the finish is flawless. The recoil from the 6NormaBR is light, but the brake keeps the gun level for tracking shots in the field.

the neck of a loaded cartridge with a micrometer. Subtract .001 inch to allow for the brass to spring back after sizing, resulting in a proper press fit for the bullet. With my tests, the .266-inch bushing did the trick for both rifles using out-of-the-box brass. Using the micrometer, outside neck dimensions (OD) came in at .268 inch. After firing, it was .270 inch; with sizing, the neck came in at .266 inch with the inside diameter at .242 inch. The third die is the micrometer-seating die. The micrometer allows you to keep a record of each bullet and its seating position in the case. It adjusts to increments of .001 inch; each complete revolution equals .050 inch. The novel floating seating stem centers and supports the bullet as it enters the case. Before seating, a very light touch with neck chamfering is all that's required to guide the bullet into each case.

After fireforming, the internal case capacity comes in around 38-39 grains of water. This capacity makes the cartridge a candidate for a long list of intermediate powders. Although I used a wide range of propellants for both guns, for those just starting, take a 75-grain bullet, drop 30.0 to 32.0 grains of Varget into the case, and have at it. Groups should be around or under 3/4 of an inch at 100 yards with little effort on your part.

For lighter bullets of around 55-58 grains, IMR 8208XBR powder is a good choice and gives the highest velocity. Moving up the scale from 70 to 75-grain bullets and, depending upon

the gun used (see my chart), Benchmark, Norma 201, Varget, and Vihtavuori N135 are suitable matches with Benchmark giving the highest velocity. The 80- to 88-grain bullets, especially the Berger Match Flat Base, liked the Vihtavuori N140 with velocities approaching 3,200 fps. 90-grain bullets showed Varget in the lead and, finishing up with the heavier 100-109 grain bullets, H-4895 was the all-time winner in group sizes.

Looking at the chart, you can see I used as many powders as needed to bring both guns to their full potential. To this end, I used the same loads, bullets, and overall length of each sample in both guns without getting overly technical. In that way, I'd have a strict record of comparing how each rifle shot with the same load, albeit different barrel lengths, diameters, and manufacturers. If you are looking for the best powder to use, I will not dwell on one brand or type since several performed well. For example, Vihtavuori N140, with a charge of 34.0 grains, filled the case halfway up the neck and

Left to right: A fired case, neck-sizing only, and finally, the case is cleaned and ready for loading. The author smoked the cases with a candle to track the progress of the die for neck sizing only.

turned out to be one of the best powders to use when it came to accuracy. Benchmark, 8208XBR, H-4895, and Vihtavuori N135 filled the case at the neck/shoulder area. Norma 201, Varget, and Vihtavuori N540 went to the bottom of the shoulder while H-335 filled the case a little below that. For those shooters who load a lot of ammunition for matches or varmint shooting, I found that H-335, Norma 201, and Vihtavuori N-135 were the best

Precision dies are the best way to get the most out of the 6NormaBR cartridge. A three-die set includes a neck-sizer only, a body die, and a micrometer die on the right.

Shown here is the bushing detail associated with the sizing die on the Redding set. The bushing brings out the full potential of the cartridge, especially around the neck area.

Recently, Shaw incorporated a new receiver design into the Mark X to include a new slab-sided look and Picatinny mounts topside. The magazine release is forward of the triggerguard. Shaw includes the famed AccuTrigger. Note tang safety.

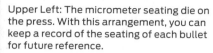

as did the Berger Varmint and Match FB bullets in 80 and 88 grains and the long, streamlined 109-grain Match bullets. Sierra was a good choice in the heavier weights with the Savage rifle (.185-inch groups), and depending upon the gun, component bullets from Winchester (.489 inch) and Remington (.546 inch) did well in the Savage Benchrest rifle. Nosler printed .650 inch and the Berger bullets did exceptionally well with the Shaw rifle, with groups coming in at .250 inch and .335 inch at 100 yards. Averaging all the groups, the Shaw had a mean of .841 inch, the Savage .849 inch. Digging even more, the best 3-shot groups averaged .463 inch for the Mark X; with the Savage, .413 inch. It seemed you could do no wrong with this cartridge, no matter the gun used.

When it came to reloading, I did everything with precision in mind. Although I had no complaints with the Lapua brass, it was checked seven ways to Sunday through all stages of loading with the Redding die set. The cartridge's overall length with the bullet inserted was arrived at with prior testing and so noted on the final chart. At the range, and to keep everything as equal as possible, I checked the weather for temperature and windless days by direct calls to the local forecasters. I even allotted five minutes between all groups to allow for a near-constant barrel temperature. I set up the guns to allow a direct line to each target at 100 yards with a minimum amount of movement at the bench and between shots.

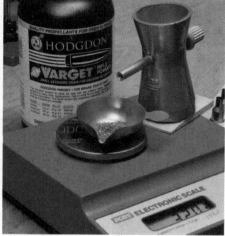

for volume loading without the need to trickle every load. However, it is still best to check every tenth round before seating the bullet. Nevertheless, I trickled all powders for every load to keep the results as precise as possible.

When it came to bullets, I put a lot of research into what I thought would be the best choice in the various weights. Hornady V-Max, Spire Point, and Boat Tail soft points gave good performance,

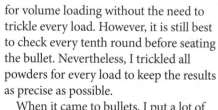

PRACTICAL USES OF THE 6MM CARTRIDGE

Final thoughts on the 6NormaBR? While this cartridge is not the fastest 6mm on the planet, it still has a lot going for it. Granted, you can use the .22-250 Remington or the newer 22 Nosler, but with 55- to 80-grain bullets, any varmint hunter worth their salt will see the advantages in economy and accuracy, all teamed with a pleasant recoil experience. The choice in rifles is far from overwhelming; however, for the serious target shooter, the Savage Benchrest is the one to beat; for walking around the north forty as I do, the Shaw Mark X fills the bill with power to spare.

The 6NormaBR is an excellent cartridge for a multitude of hunting tasks. This benchrest variant offers a modest challenge at the loading bench, but once tested and zeroed in your rifle, it will be your friend for life. **GD**

Long, thin bullets like these from Berger bring out the best in the cartridge downrange.

The best group came in at 0.340 inch for lighter bullets with 29.0 grains of Vihtavuori N-140 powder and an 88-grain Berger Match bullet.

The best group with the Savage was this .185-inch cluster at 100 yards. The author made this target. It has a circle in the middle to match the dot in the scope at that distance for shot-to-shot consistency.

TABLE 1. 6NORMABR HANDLOADS — SAVAGE AND SHAW RIFLES

BULLET (GRAINS)	POWDER	POWDER CHARGE (GRAINS)	CARTRIDGE OVERALL LENGTH (INCHES)	SAVAGE VELOCITY (FPS)	SAVAGE GROUP (INCHES)	SHAW VELOCITY (FPS)	SHAW GROUP (INCHES)
55 Nosler Spitzer	H-335	32.5	2.100	3,519	.975	3,286	.995
58 Hornady V-Max	8208XBR	33.0	2.100	3,546	.758	3,384	.575
70 Sierra BlitzKing	Benchmark	31.5	2.100	3,238	1.050	3,207	.850
70 Nosler Spitzer	Norma 201	31.0	2.100	3,252	1.100	3,105	.650
70 Hornady Interlock	N-133	28.5	2.100	3,119	1.020	2,991	.730
70 Nosler Match	H-4895	31.0	2.100	3,186	1.280	3,016	1.045
75 Hornady V-Max	Varget	32.0	2.115	3,184	.507	3,081	.845
75 Hornady Spire Pt.	N-135	31.0	2.100	3,135	.940	3,091	.735
80 Berger FB Varmint	N-140	34.0	2.100	3,283	.795	3,164	.335
80 Berger FB Match	N-135	30.0	2.115	3,106	.643	2,967	.590
80 Remington PLHP	H-4895	30.0	2.115	2,992	.546	2,840	1.225
80 Winchester PS	N-133	31.0	2.115	3,216	.489	3,172	.800
88 Berger FB Match	N-140	29.0	2.115	2,780	.340	2,730	.250
90 Sierra FMJBT	N-140	31.0	2.115	2,965	1.680	2,881	1.125
90 Speer FMJ	N-140	29.8	2.115	2,859	1.370	2,751	1.260
90 Swift BT Spitzer	Varget	30.2	2.115	2,909	.790	2,853	1.305
100 Hornady BTSP	Varget	28.0	2.100	2,616	.785	2,592	.830
100 Remington PSP	N-140	29.0	2.100	2,742	.892	2,638	1.125
100 Sierra Boat Tail	H-4895	27.0	2.100	2,656	.185	2,539	.568
109 Berger Match	N-540	32.1	2.100	3,004	.850	2,834	.985
		AVERAGE GROUP SIZE			.849		.841

Notes: All 3-shot groups fired from a benchrest at 100 yards. The author tested loads on various days and took the temperature and wind conditions under consideration in all sessions. He clocked velocities at 10 feet with an Oehler Model 33 chronograph.

Surviving THE Drought

Our once endless stacks of practice ammo can be burned through in a hurry when there are no replacements to be found.

Cope with ammo shortages and keep shooting when scarcity befalls the supply.

❯ RON SPOMER

The battles between the Texas Rangers and 19th-Century Comanches illustrate our current conundrum over ammo shortages. Perhaps we can learn and benefit from their clashes.

The Comanches ruled West Texas for 150 years and held back "civilization" with its guns, steel, and wheels. They regularly whipped Spanish, Mexican, U.S., and Texas military units sent to punish them.

They did it with clubs, spears, and bows and arrows.

How, you must wonder, could sticks and string defeat the power and reach of rifles? (And we're not talking flintlock muzzleloaders, but a combination of cap lock muzzleloaders and brass cartridge

buffalo rifles.) The answer is a combination of blitzkrieg-like attack and high-volume fire.

The Comanches were superb horsemen. They were the North American equivalent of Genghis Khan's Mongols, who swept across Asia to create the largest contiguous empire the world has ever known. The Comanche's empire was tiny by comparison, but they were no less the accomplished horse warriors. A fully trained Comanche warrior could ride full tilt while firing multiple arrows per minute at troops who had to dismount to fire and reload their rifles. While a soldier was sheltering behind his horse or saddle and reloading, his adversary was riding down on him. The tide began to turn only after Texas Rangers discovered

Samuel Colt's revolvers and combined them with Comanche-style horseback counter attacks. It turned out an accomplished horseman with a pair of six-shooters beat an equally competent horseman with a bow.

What does this history have to do with us and our frequent ammo shortages? It dramatizes our dependence as opposed to the Comanche's independence. We, like the Rangers, are dependent on an elaborate supply chain stretching around the world. The Comanches, on the other hand, could withdraw deep into the backcountry, rebuild their arsenals of spears and arrows, and be back in the fight. Endlessly.

Trying to find ammunition for virtually any modern rifle in recent months

Above: Finding enough hunting ammo these days can be a bear of an ordeal. Best cling to what you find.

Left: According to bullet and ammo manufacturers, they're still turning the stuff out by the barrels, but supply doesn't seem to be keeping up with demand.

Below: In times of tight supply, availability may force you to grab what you can while you can. A broad mix of bullets and brands isn't ideal for consistency in your shooting, but it beats not shooting at all.

has made me feel like a Texas Ranger west of the Pecos with an empty ammo pouch. Where can I find more? How will I procure more? More broadly, how can all of us guard against what is sure to be sporadic — if not frequent or even perennial — ammo shortages?

Retreating to our woodland redoubts to create more "arrows" would seem a sensible course of action. But can we? Short of reverting to bows and arrows, what can shooters do to remain active? Limited supplies and rising costs of base materials — combined with panic buying, increased demand, hoarding, and our increasingly chaotic times — mean ammunition shortages could become chronic. The following are ten options.

1. **Shoot less often.** This option is not ideal but a viable last-ditch effort. Were I down to my last 20 rounds of .270 Winchester, I wouldn't be burning them up on targets before the deer season.

2. **Order early and often.** If Mother Hubbard's shelves are bare, place an order for the next shipment. Do this at every local retail store and every online store. You never know who'll come through or when.

3. **Send a mass email to your friends.** Many retired hunters have old ammo supplies they might be happy to unload. Widows, especially, want or need to clear out the dearly departed's guns and ammo.

4. **Estate and garage sales.** You never know what you might find.

5. **Buy in bulk.** When you can — more detail on this below.

6. **Handload.** Of course, you still need to lay in supplies of brass, primers, powder, and bullets, but once you

have them, you can create all kinds of ammo. Details below!

7. **Buy rifles chambered for odd, uncommon cartridges.** Many have noted that when all the .223 Rem., 6.5 Creedmoor, and .308 Win. are gone, a few lonely boxes of .250 Savage, .280 Remington, or .338 Federal linger. Ah, but this cuts both ways. When ammo makers crank up to meet demand, they build .223, 6.5 Creedmoor, and .308 first (if they're not too busy making 9mm).

8. **Sell all your other guns and keep one all-around, do-everything firearm.** This way, you learn it inside and out, don't waste ammunition, and can stock up on lots and lots of cases. You'll be that oft-cited, deadly accurate shooter with one gun you know how to use. Except …

9. **Owning just one gun is less fun and more limiting.** I'm not crazy about hunting squirrels with a 7mm-08, although I've built reduced loads that can do it. If you suddenly discover there's no ammo for that particular rifle, you're out of options. No, I'd rather have a .22 rimfire, .17 rimfire, .22 centerfire or three, some .24, .25, .26, .27, .28, .30 calibers and keep going. Someone's bound to have a cartridge for one of them!

10. **Shop early and often.** Yes, preparing to survive our all too common ammo shortages comes down to planning ahead. Alas, as I'm writing this, "ahead" is already "behind." If you didn't fill the armory eight or 12 months ago, this is currently not a good option.

CRAZY IDEAS OR WORTH CONSIDERING?

The first option listed above, shooting less, has long been the standard operating procedure for many, perhaps most, casual hunters and gun owners. For decades, a badge of honor for rural folks has been getting 20 deer with a 20-round box of

Garage and estate sales often include bullets, cases, and loaded ammo. Snatch it up.

Right: Having rifles in a wide variety of chamberings means you're more likely to find ammo for at least one of them.

Below: Put the word out to older friends who might have unused and forgotten supplies of old ammo stashed away. If stored dry and away from extreme heat, it should be as good as ever.

ammo. The more extravagant need 40 because they like to zero the day before the opener.

Such frugality might suffice for ultra-conservative hunters, but most shooters enjoy using their guns too much to let them languish in a safe 360 days out of the year. Yet, time and money can be in short supply for them, too. How can any of us maintain and improve our shooting skills during price hikes and shortages?

By dry firing. Seriously. Just as baseball hitters visualize themselves seeing the stitching on a fastball, powering the bat through that ball, and driving it over the centerfield fence, so can shooters visualize the perfect hold and sight picture, the ideal trigger break, the flawless cycling of the action for the follow-up shot.

If this sounds too esoteric bordering on voodoo, please reconsider. Pre-visualization coupled with "going through the motions" works in all sports. It's especially effective in shooting because the shooter can move through every step of the operation except recoil. Think about what you do in a "dry run." You carry the unloaded rifle slung over your shoulder. Pretend a buck appears in the far corner of the room. How will you smoothly and quickly get the rifle on target, align the front post or reticle on its shoulder, snick off the safety, and drop that firing pin?

Just going through the motions of carrying, mounting, aiming, and dry firing your guns is remarkably effective at honing your shooting skills.

Minimizing your rifle collection to two or three common chamberings like these Savage bolt actions in .223 Rem and .30-06 simplifies bulk ammo buying. However, it doesn't give you many options when those two rounds are off the shelves.

Modern smokeless powder can remain viable for decades if stored cool and dry. Give it the sniff test and watch for rusty fumes that indicate degradation.

Shooters who handload for a variety of calibers have better odds of finding bullets for at least one of them.

And when you hear the "click," where was that sight? Still on the target? Or did you pull right and low?

Dry firing even works on the bench. Watching your sight picture as the hammer falls can be a real eye-opener. How did that reticle end up high and left? Champion competition shooters dry fire often and regularly. Everyday shooters discover that dry firing hones their muscle memory and trigger technique. And they can do this any day, every day, free. No need to travel to the range. No burning up ammo stocks. Just significant improvement in handling, target acquisition, trigger control, and follow-through. I've yet to meet a shooter who didn't shoot more precisely after dry-fire practice.

BULK PURCHASING

While the *click click click* of dry firing

will improve your skills, at some point, you need to see hits on targets. Ensuring sufficient ammo suggests buying in bulk when the buying is good — and when there's bulk to buy. It's an expensive option for most of us, but trying to scrounge up a box or two of your favorite loads when stores are empty and scalpers have jacked up prices by 100 percent — well, that's expensive too. It may be too late today, but you can begin saving for tomorrow. This fresh start could be like starting a piggy bank for that new rifle or scope. Except it's a case or two of ammo. Give up the daily beer, soda, or fancy coffee, and within a month or two, you'll have the cash to lure hundreds of rounds of your favorite cartridges into your safe. But beware …

I might be belaboring the obvious, but test before you leap. Any shooter beyond an amateur knows he or she must determine which bullet they need for a specific rifle, which brand or ammo featuring that bullet shoots it accurately, etc. You need to sample and test until satisfied, then make that bulk purchase. On the other hand, you can be like some shooters. They find a stack of ammo in a chambering they don't own, but the ammo, and go searching for a gun to shoot it!

The super cautious might insist on bulk buying ammo from the same lot lest the manufacturer changes its recipe. The challenge is getting the test box finished in time to catch the same lot in the store or online. I don't know if one can request a specific lot by the number from online retailers, but if you're picky, it might be worth a try.

THE HOARDING CONUNDRUM

If, and when, you identify the perfect load for your rifle, grab all you think you'll need for the next year — or lifetime. I realize this amplifies hoarding, but you can look at this another way: If today's hoarders had stocked up three, 10, or 20 years ago, they wouldn't be cleaning out the shelves now. Besides, stocking up for the cautious, one-deer-a-year hunter might mean two boxes, maybe three. For the serious shooter who hunts widely and practices more widely, a case a year might barely suffice. Assess yourself and your shooting honestly. And don't worry

The heady days of sending dozens of bullets downrange for training have been put on hold for many of us.

Quantities of reloading components that once seemed like more than enough start to look relatively thin when retailers put replacements on years-long back-order.

How quickly things change. Just a couple of years ago, you could find stacks and stacks of bullets in bigger retail stores.

If your ammo supplies are minimal, don't burn them all up practicing. Leave some for deer season.

Handloading has always been the perfect solution to factory ammo shortages, but only if you have adequate quantities of primers, powder, cases, and bullets.

This conundrum throws the reloader into the same hopper as the factory ammo shooter. You must buy ahead and stock up. Fortunately, components are as durable as fully loaded ammo. Bullets and brass don't go bad. They might tarnish, but that's just cosmetic, and you can polish it off. Primers are as durable and long-lived as powder if you store them similarly, so let's plunge into powder maintenance. Powder, if kept cool and dry, lasts for decades with little or no loss in power. But it doesn't remain viable indefinitely.

According to powder manufacturer Hodgdon, remnant acids used in smokeless powder break down the main ingredient, nitrocellulose. Left unchecked, this has led to self-ignition. Ka-boom in storage. To prevent a ka-boom, powder makers add stabilizing chemicals. These react with the acids to slow decomposition. Eventually, however, the stabilizers are consumed, leaving the acids to resume their degradation.

Acidic break-down accelerates with heat, so it's best to store the powder in airtight containers at comfortable room temperature or lower. Musty attics, dank basements, hot barns, and humid outbuildings are not good storage sites. Unopened canisters of new powder should last decades with little or no degradation in performance. Opened canisters aren't far behind, but keep lids closed and avoid opening them frequently in high humidity. The moisture probably doesn't degrade the powder so much as weaken it by raising its moisture content. Of course, you can dry it to regain its potential.

You can check powder by sight and smell. If you lightly shake an open can and any rusty fumes or vapors rise from it, that's bad. Advanced degradation. If the powder is colored red or rusty, also too far gone. It will still ignite, but it will not have its original potency or consistency in burning rate. More likely, you'll detect an acidic odor from degrading powder. Some say it smells like vinegar; others ammonia or muriatic acid. Fresh powder has a chemical, metallic odor too, of course, so if you have new stuff to compare against old, you'll have a benchmark.

Deteriorated powder is probably no

too much about not burning through all the rounds you buy. They could well be worth more 20 years down the road than they are today.

Don't worry about ammo longevity. The stuff is durable, stable, and viable for decades if you store it in a dry and cool place, or at least room temperature. Keeping it in plastic bags minimizes brass oxidation and tarnishing. As a hedge against flood, fire, and theft, spread it across two or three locations. Lock and key are an excellent idea, too.

But the best way to keep an ample supply of munitions fresh is to shoot from the back of the pile. Stack up your bulk supply, then every time you burn through a box or two, buy replacements as soon as they become available. Shoot your next rounds from the old stack and restock again. This program maintains a consistent supply of "hard times" ammo while maintaining longevity.

HANDLOADING TO HEDGE YOUR BETS

Handloaders have long gloated in times of ammo shortages. *No problem. I can make more.* But these days, even DIY has become challenging. Powder, bullets, and primers are scarce as loaded ammo. Everyone sold out of everything.

more dangerous than fresh, but its inconsistency could cause pressure spikes. Or lower pressures. Subtle powder decline could show up as weaker handloads. If the muzzle velocities of your newest handloads drop significantly from previous levels loaded with the same powder, suspect deterioration and put that powder to work growing corn.

Corn? Well, maybe. Standard wisdom for decades has been to sprinkle the old gun powder on lawns and gardens and water it in as fertilizer. There are nitrates in nitrocellulose. The cellulose part is usually from wood. All organic! However, some folks are concerned about traces of ethyl acetate, paraffin waxes, and deterrent chemicals like dinitrotoluene (carcinogenic). It might be wiser to sprinkle on the grass and water it in.

The alternative to fertilizing is burning. Yes, you can safely burn smokeless powder because it is not an explosive that detonates but deflagrates, i.e., burns. When you shoot a gun, burning under close confinement in the rifle barrel leads to what sounds like an explosion because the heat conversion of the solid to gas results in a massive expansion. It is this high-pressure gas escaping the muzzle that creates the loud blast of sound. It's like a glorified balloon pop.

However, out in the open air, a line of smokeless gun powder merely burns hot and progressively. To safely dispose of it, spread it in a shallow line well away from flammable materials (a driveway works well) and ignite one end.

VARIETY IN THE RIFLE LINE

Our final investigation returns us to

No. 9 above — multiple rifles in multiple chamberings. Storing a long-term supply of one or two cartridges does sound simple, but having many seems the better option for keeping at least some of them fed. When a run on the ammo banks depletes all the .308 Winchester, .223 Remington, and 6.5 Creedmoor, you might still find a scattering of .284 Winchester, 6.5x55 Swede, or .338 Federal.

Variety is the spice of life. Who wants to limit all their shooting and hunting to a .30-'06? Suppose you like to shoot gongs at extreme range, whitetails in heavy woods, feral hogs in large numbers, Cape buffalo now and then, or

sheep across a wide mountain basin. In that case, you'll likely want or even need several different rifles and cartridges to meet those situations. So don't let the fear of ammo shortages constrain your collection. Get the rifles you need or want for the shooting you desire, and then keep up with ammo needs as outlined above. When the pickings get slim, you're more likely to find something you can shoot if you have more options.

Say, is that a box of .257 Roberts I see on that shelf? **GD**

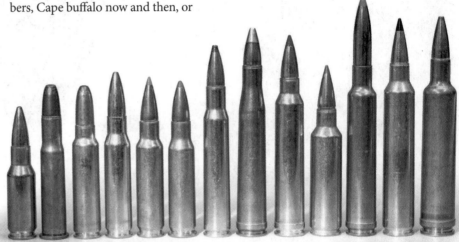
Owning rifles in multiple chamberings makes it easier to find ammo for at least some of them.

Instead of practicing in quantity, concentrate on quality. Shoot more precisely if you must shoot less frequently.

When ammo shortages hit, it's time to circle the wagons! And the greater variety of wagons you have, the greater the chance you'll find fuel to keep at least one running.

WALNUT,
Before
It's
Gone

The warm red-brown glow of carefully crafted American walnut enhances this lovely Ruger No. 1.

As polymers, fiberglass, and carbon fiber replace it, here's what you should know about walnut!

❯ WAYNE VAN ZWOLL

When I was a wee lad, Tom Frye was shooting for Remington. In 1959, after more than 140 years of stocking rifles with walnut, the company announced a .22 autoloader wearing lightweight nylon called Zytel. To give the new rifle street cred, Frye started using it on hand-tossed 2 ¼-inch wooden blocks. The marathon session would challenge the record of Winchester ace Ad Topperwein, who in 1907 hit 71,491 of 72,500 thrown. Undaunted, Frye passed the 43,725 mark with just two misses. After the 100,010th toss, he'd drilled 100,004. I can't recall how many Nylon 66s passed through Frye's capable hands during this exhibition. Still, Remington made a heap of commercial hay with it, so followed the autoloader with Zytel-stocked lever- and bolt-action rifles. Between 1959 and 1990, more than a million of these 4-pound .22s — initially priced at $25.75 to $49.95 — survived farm-truck dust, trapline dunkings, and all manner of rough handling to become the terror of Rodentia, from barn rats to cottontails. In '63, Remington applied Zytel to its XP-100 single-shot pistol in .221 Fireball.

Walnut lasts! The scarred, oil-blackened stock on this century-old Winchester 1894 has "character."

At Ruger, an inspector eyes a machine-checkered stock for a Hawkeye rifle. Plain American walnut.

"royal walnut," now varies in grain structure and color by region, but it has just one scientific name worldwide. Common names denote location, not genetic differences. So, English and French walnut are taxonomically the same trees, grown in different places. After arriving there, Californians adopted *J. regia* as "California English." The honey-and-black streaking of archetypal English walnut is evident in California English. But grown from nuts, the California variety is less apt to show the "marble cake" of high-grade English. Classic French typically boasts a warm orange hue. From a region in the northwest Caucasus on the Black sea, Circassian walnut has sultry, smoky character. Fiddleback figure can come from any region.

Claro walnut, *J. hindsii*, was discovered around 1840 in California. Relatively open-grained and ruddy, Claro, crossed with English, produces ornamental Bastogne walnut. Nuts from these shade trees are infertile, but Bastogne grows fast, and its tight grain makes it a favorite of gun makers. It handles recoil well and checkers more cleanly than Claro. These qualities, plus fetching color and figure,

Not that wood had graced every shoulder arm before 1950 or that walnut was always the favored timber. Earth has tree species enough to fill books on dendrology.

In the 13th Century, when Marco Polo allegedly brought walnuts from their native Persia to Italy, there was no demand for figured gun stock blanks. Still, nuts and seedlings found their way north to France and England, and other parts of Continental Europe. *Juglans regia*, or

have increased demand for Bastogne. It's becoming less common, more expensive. As with *J. regia*, the most seductive Bastogne comes from trees at least 150 years old.

American or black walnut, *J. nigra*, has been the mainstay of the firearms industry stateside since "Kentucky" rifles emerged from the shops of German 'smiths in Pennsylvania. Little appears so dark as to look black in sunlight, but the signature deep brown color can be strongly streaked with black. Like its close kin, American walnut can be plain or richly figured, depending on the tree's age and origin and the type of cut. Quarter-sawn walnut shows the tightest color bands because the blade runs across growth rings. Plane-sawn walnut has wider bands, as the saw moves tangent to growth rings. Either cut can yield a sturdy, attractive rifle stock, but many custom stockers and their customers prefer quarter-sawn walnut. Two-piece stocks for shotguns and nearly all rifles *except* bolt actions are easier to find if you're looking for color, figure, and perfect layout because you don't need wood 32 inches long.

Don Allen knew more about walnut than anyone else I can name. Before founding Dakota Arms, Don established a stellar reputation as a stock maker while finishing a career as a commercial pilot. He patterned his Model 76 rifle after the pre-war Model 70 Winchester, but with better walnut, impeccably shaped and detailed. Allen traveled the world to find superior walnut, later applying his talents in firearms design and stock making to produce a dropping-block Model 10, a "baby" Sharps, and another single shot on the Miller action. He also fashioned an exquisite double shotgun that he never commercially produced.

Not long before his untimely death, Allen lamented that walnut was becoming alarmingly scarce. "The truly fine wood is surely vanishing," he told me. "*Regia*

is hard to find in England and France. Some excellent wood comes from Turkey and Morocco, but it's being sawed into dollars at unsustainable rates. Trees felled in Turkey may be 400 years old!"

In other words, we're inletting wood from trees that may have been seedlings before the advent of metallic cartridges, before the Declaration of Independence. Pulp plantations can grow harvestable trees in little more than a decade, but high-quality walnut is the product of centuries.

Easier to apply than checkering, stippling improves your grip in rain and snow. (This rifle: a Mossberg.)

"In other words, we're inletting wood from trees that may have been seedlings before the advent of metallic cartridges, before the Declaration of Independence. Pulp plantations can grow harvestable trees in little more than a decade, but high-quality walnut is the product of centuries."

Wayne shot this fine buck with an early Ruger No. 1, noted then for figured walnut. Not so much now.

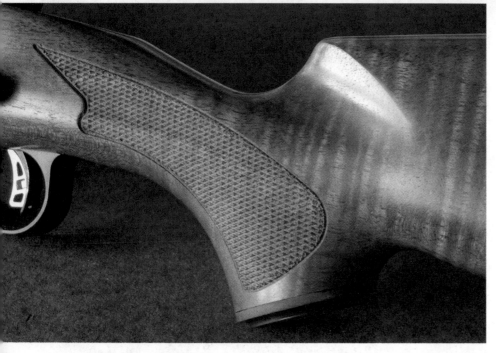

Walnut endures abuse, recoil. Pins in this plain stock ensure against splits from .458 Magnum kick.

Fiddleback walnut perfectly laid out distinguishes this Savage rifle. Note the fill-in checkering panel.

It was a relatively common wood during North American settlement; inexpensive, durable, warm to the touch, and amenable to checkering and stippling. Unlike oak and mesquite, walnut yielded easily to the saw and rasp. It had reasonably small pores, unlike pine and white fir, so it finished up nicely with clear sealants that repelled water. Walnut had strong, often striking figure. A single blank could show a range of colors: honey to red to black. Even brown had a fetching glow. On the U.S. frontier, settlers prized quilted maple, but it wasn't common, and its pallor begged a stain.

Harvesting walnut now is not as straightforward as when fallers dismissed waste or bucked it up for firewood. Old trees are costly, and you must cut them to yield as many blanks of proper length and layout as possible. There's much to plan before the saw bites and more to consider afterward to bring out the best in each stock.

Walnut growers in France steam logs before they cut them into slabs (flitches). Steaming kills insects and turns white sap to amber. Before further sectioning, sawyers bear in mind the shape and use of the finished stock.

You must dry walnut before you attack it with stock-making tools. "Immediately after a blank is cut," said Allen, "free water starts to escape. Think of a soaked sponge dripping. If water leaves too fast, the wood can crack and check. The surface can even crust, inhibiting movement of bound water from the core. Structural damage may result."

A kiln helps throttle the release of water. "Most drying damage happens soon after a slab is cut," Allen said. "Moisture

content will then stabilize at about 20 percent. The blank can then be air-dried or kiln-dried without damage."

He said that you don't need a special environment to air-dry wood brought to 20 percent moisture. "A cool, shaded place is best, away from humidity and temperature extremes. I weigh the blank periodically. When the weight stabilizes, the blank is dry enough to work." Some stock makers turn the blank to a rough profile at this juncture, then let it dry another six months before inletting.

In my youth, you could get a fancy American walnut stock blank for $25. I paid Herter's $7.50 for the plain semi-inletted stick I whittled on over winter to stock my first rifle, a Short Magazine Lee Enfield that had drained my pockets of $30. Raw slabs of *regia* now command much steeper prices.

Less costly woods like birch and beech are replacing walnut on some rifles that still wear wood. Laminates are affordable, too, offering strength, stability, and striking color options. Another path: stocks with naturally finished walnut slabs that, from the side, conceal a laminated core. These make economical use of planks too thin for one-piece stocks.

"I just paid $2,250 for an English *blank*!" groused the late Roger Biesen a few years back. "Not long ago, we sold finished rifles for that!" I'd visited the Biesens' Spokane, Washington shop often during the 1980s. After a long, celebrated career building rifles for Jack O'Connor and other notables like O'Connor's sheep-hunting pal Prince Abdorezza Pahlavi of Iran, Roger's father Al was still working then. Before his death in 2016, Al told me he had bought most of his walnut from Sacramento supplier Joe Oakley. After Joe passed, he and Roger shifted their business to Ed Preslik, also in California, then to his son Jim. Like Don Allen, Al Biesen was a wood enthusiast, with a basement vault full of dusty blanks awaiting draw knife and chisel.

The layout is the crucial first step in making a gunstock from a blank. Viewed from the side, grain in quarter-sawn

This O'Connor Tribute Rifle mirrors Cactus Jack's Biesen-built .270s, but with coarse machine-cut checkering.

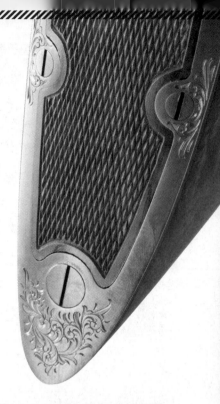

MNR gunmaker Matthew Roberts fitted this skeleton buttplate, cut small, clean, perfect diamonds.

The author patched a ding here by finding wood of similar color, fitting, gluing, then checkering over it.

Glass bedding in the recoil lug mortise nixes wood compression, prevents splits, aligns the receiver.

This "stick of fiddleback" shows fine checkering in progress on the cradle of ace stocker Gary Goudy.

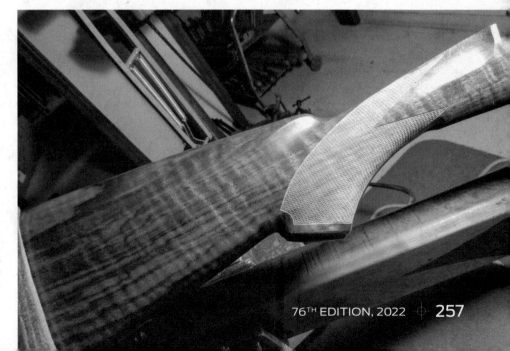

Laminated wood (here on a Volquartsen .22) is usually stronger, more stable than walnut, and heavier.

walnut should run parallel with the grip, so the narrow grip remains strong. From above, the grain should parallel a rifle's bore. Skewed grain in figured wood is no asset regarding strength and stability, even if that wood is very dense. The figure in the butt won't affect accuracy, but crotches and knots in the forend are less benign.

Glass bedding strengthens wood but doesn't eliminate warpage. I like glass or epoxy in the recoil lug mortise of bolt-action hunting rifles to prevent splitting through the magazine well and give the metal firm contact with the stock. A small bedding patch under the tang makes sense too. Some custom stockers dismiss glass as a fix for shoddy inletting. Even with expert inletting, however, the brutal kick of some magnums can test the integrity of bare walnut.

Checkering helps you grip the stock while dressing it up. As hand checkering became more and more costly, pressed panels appeared. On inexpensive rifles and shotguns of the 1960s, these impressions looked to be hammered in by a meat tenderizer. Machine-cut checkering followed and has improved.

Hand checkering can be as fine as 32 lines per inch (lpi), albeit such tiny diamonds require hard, uniform wood and are as much cosmetic as functional. They appear most often inside skeleton grip caps and buttplates. The grip and forend on production-class firearms typically have 18- to 22-lpi checkering, while 24-lpi work marks upscale and custom stocks.

Fleur-de-lis checkering has been around for as long as point-pattern panels. Oddly enough, the basic *fleur-de-lis* is easier to cut. That's because it is a fill-in job — you scribe a border, then cut grooves to it. A point pattern incorporates the border. If you err cutting a fill-in pattern, the border is unaffected; but one line off-kilter in a point pattern dooms you. The overall effect can suffer all out of proportion to the boo-boo. A skewed panel doesn't beg a magnifying glass! Of course, slim ribbons in a *fleur* pattern make a fill-in much more difficult. Only masters of the checkering tool can cut smooth, uniform fly-line ribbons unbroken by over-runs.

"Can you erase bad dings, freshen the wood, and make the finish look original?" The gun shop's proprietor had second-hand inventory that

This laminated "hunting stock" for a Patrick Holehan rifle complements a duplicate in fine walnut.

Wood Stock CENTRAL

Boyds has affordable, finished, checkered walnut stocks for drop-in fit, here for a Remington 700.

Ready to finish for drop-in fit. Boyds offers stocks of solid walnut, also varicolored laminates.

Stacks of dry walnut — and sheets of saw-ready laminates — fill Boyds warehouse near Mitchell, South Dakota.

These walnut blanks at Boyds await rough-shaping and inletting on multiple-spindle pantographs.

"**Y**ou might say this business took me by surprise," grinned Randy Boyd when we chatted years ago. But that aw-shucks routine veiled talent, drive, and enduring optimism.

The son of a gunsmith, Randy grew up in Geddes, South Dakota, 70 miles from Mitchell. He tells of trading an old Plymouth for two Mauser rifles, which he refurbished "and sold for a small profit." His father's heart attack put Randy "in the family shop: a grainery with a wood stove, in a Dakota winter." He bought a two-spindle duplicating machine and began turning gunstocks. "One a day."

In 1986, Boyds earned a contract to furnish stocks for Chipmunk Rifles. To make 100 stocks a week, Randy bought three high-volume duplicators. CNC machines followed. Now the biggest gun stock supplier in the U.S., Boyds is run

A knob on one arm traces the contours of a slave blank; cutters on other arms shape walnut blanks.

A sanding belt marries a recoil pad with the wood at Boyds, the biggest gun-stock house in the U.S.

The color of this rifle stock is in the laminates. The spray in this booth applies a weather-proof finish.

by Justin Knutson and his skilled staff in a 50,000-square-foot plant in Mitchell. Order a blank or finished stock. You'll find hundreds of style and laminate-color combinations drop-in ready for

your rifle. A long list of options too, all at surprisingly modest cost. Expect delivery not in months, but days. I've used Boyds stocks for decades on a variety of rifles. No gunsmithing is needed.

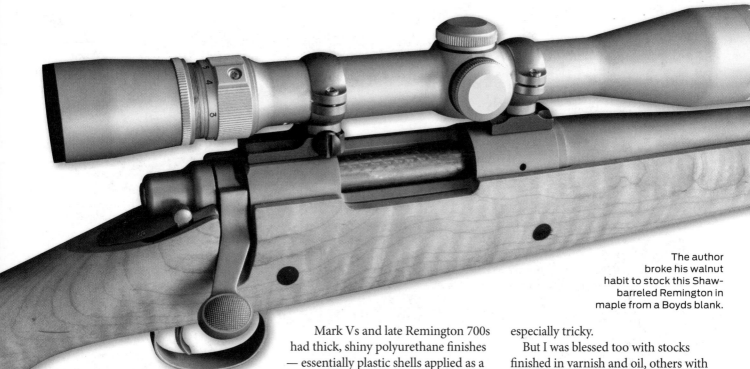

The author broke his walnut habit to stock this Shaw-barreled Remington in maple from a Boyds blank.

needed such attention. I needed work.

"Absolutely," I assured him.

The flood gates opened, and shortly rivers of weary rifles and shotguns washed up on my bench. Weatherby

Mark Vs and late Remington 700s had thick, shiny polyurethane finishes — essentially plastic shells applied as a liquid. They wouldn't "feather," so to rid them of even small scars, I had to hand sand all that waterproof, abrasion-resistant glitter down to the wood without leaving scratches, dishing flat places, or rounding edges. Sanding behind the grip cap and where metal met walnut was

especially tricky.

But I was blessed too with stocks finished in varnish and oil, others with finish worn off. While these assignments didn't hike my tax bracket, they taught me quite a bit about walnut and stock finishing.

Except for polyurethanes, chemical paint stripper will remove the stock finish to prep wood for a new look. You're

To finish bare walnut, seal pores with first coats of spar varnish or (here) a commercial equivalent.

Finish Options

Factory stock finishes have evolved. Winchester's first Model 70 stocks, in the late 1930s, wore a clear lacquer finish over alcohol-based stain and filler. The lacquers contained carnauba wax. You repaired minor flaws with stick shellac. But World War II drained supplies of carnauba wax, ushering in hard lacquers. Unlike shellac (whose Sanskrit root referencing tree or beetle secretions appears in both words), lacquers repel water and cure without imparting an amber hue.

"Oil" finish doesn't refer to petroleum oil but plant-based products like tung oil (from pressed seeds of tung tree nuts) and linseed oil. Oil finishes are the easiest to apply, renew, and repair. To keep drying time within the decade, you want *boiled* — not raw — linseed oil or, for faster results, commercial finishes such as George Bros. (GB) Lin-Speed and Birchwood Casey's Tru-Oil. I apply them after basecoats of spar varnish. Tung oil cures to a gloss that's a tad harder.

Custom stockers famously guard their pet finishes, but Curt Crum is graciously forthcoming. He treats the fine walnut on David Miller rifles to Daly's Teak Oil after filling pores with water-thin sealer.

wise to let stripper curdle on the surface, then scrape or, with coarse steel wool, scrub finish off. Use a toothbrush to clean checkering. Then mask the checkering before sanding.

Choose sanding grit just coarse enough to get results. Remember, you must remove all sanding marks with finer paper. I use a hard-rubber eraser as a sanding block to keep flat surfaces flat. Without the block, finger pressure can produce ripples. For curved surfaces, a section of dowel works well. Both keep edges sharp. Leave until last, the wood where it meets steel, to ensure you don't alter that junction. For final sanding, use wet-or-dry emery paper, 400-grit. Damp, it raises grain and "whiskers" — as does steaming out dents with an iron over a wet rag. Dry strokes remove those hairs.

Examine the stock often as you final sand, in good light. You want to find scratches that would otherwise grin at you under a coat of finish.

Unless I must match an existing look, I don't stain walnut or even light-colored woods. If you do, wipe it on evenly with a rag *after* final sanding.

Spar varnish can serve as a base for an oil finish. It's weather-resistant, thick enough to fill tiny pores. It dries fast. Cut buildup between coats with fine sandpaper or steel wool.

Before applying the finish, have a coat-hanger dangling upside down to hook through a guard screw hole. Rub in your chosen oil until the wood gets hot under the friction of your hand. Thinning the oil with turpentine enhances penetration in the wood. Let the stock hang until dry, then rub in more finish. Polish this off with a cloth (jeans denim works well) and let it dry again. You

The Walnut Men

As the North American frontier moved west, so did the demand for walnut. After World War I, Edward Cox Bishop saw a future in that market. In 1929, on the eve of the Depression, he moved to Warsaw, Missouri, and with his son John built a sawmill. His first stocks went to Remington shotguns. In 1935, he began turning out semi-finished rifle stocks. Four years later, Bishop invited Reinhard Fajen of nearby Stover to join his company. Fajen custom finished stocks for Bishop. The Second World War took the men in different directions, but both returned to working with walnut. In '49, John Bishop, who'd acquired his father's interest in the business, suggested to Reinhard Fajen that they merge. They did, for a couple of years; then Bishop sold out to Jack Pohl, a relative. Fajen started his firm and, by the 1990s, had 80 employees producing stocks for 200 models of rifles and shotguns. Warsaw had become the country's walnut capital! In 1992, Larry Potterfield bought the Reinhard Fajen Gunstock Company. Three years later, while building a new plant in Lincoln, just north of Warsaw, Potterfield also acquired Bishop. Hobbled by market forces that included increased use of synthetic stocks, the Fajen/Bishop venture shuttered in 1998.

may wish to cut first coats to wood with fine abrasive or steel wool. A slurry of rottenstone in boiled linseed oil removes slight imperfections.

The secret of a fine finish is multiple, very thin coats of oil. One ace stocker gave a gorgeous piece of walnut 25 coats! With boiled linseed oil, drying time can stretch from days to weeks and months. Make sure each coat is dry before adding

another. Finally, remove the masking tape from the checkering and brush oil lightly into it with a toothbrush. You're done.

Occasional light polish with boiled linseed oil, then a soft rag, can keep your stock looking fresh. GD

Its lustrous oil finish enhanced this plain, open-pored walnut stock, aftermarket for a 1917 Enfield.

Ruger Hawkeye African

The author tested the new Ruger Hawkeye African in .280 Ackley Improved. This rifle covers a lot of bases. Photo: Sturm, Ruger & Co., Inc.

Photo: William Davies

Meets
.280 Ackley

Ruger chambers a wildcat for a versatile plains game and whitetail rifle!

› STEVE GASH

The Ruger Hawkeye is the latest iteration of the Model 77 that debuted in 1968. In the intervening 53 years, there have been numerous improvements and design enhancements that made this fine rifle even better, with enough model variations to satisfy both hunters and collectors alike.

One specialized version was called the "African" and was available in .375 H&H Magnum, .416 Rigby, .458 Winchester Magnum, and a real sleeper — 9.3x62 Mauser. Ruger offered a fancy version with a Circassian walnut stock from 1976 to 1978, but discontinued the original African in 1991.

Thanks to a slim but steady demand for specialized arms, in mid-2020, Ruger partnered with distributor Lipsey's and offered another African. It is styled like the English "best" rifles of old and chambered for four cartridges worthy of a trip to Africa — or anywhere you hunt plains game. Two chamberings are real thumpers, the .375 Ruger and the .416 Ruger, and two others are stellar cartridges for plains game where you need to make a long shot, the 6.5x55 Mauser and the .280 Ackley Improved (AI). While the .375, .416, and 6.5mm are seasoned veterans, the .280 AI is relatively new to the realm of factory loads.

I received a new Hawkeye African in .280 AI in April 2020. We'll get to the details on the cartridge in a minute, but first, let me entice you with a rundown on this new Ruger African.

NEW HAWKEYE DESIGN DETAILS

Ruger based the new Hawkeye on the tried-and-true Model 77 action, all gussied up to fit the part. The stock is of nice American walnut, with rounded contours along the barrel and on top of the pistol grip. It has a satin oil finish, with plenty of nicely done checkering in a point pattern on each side of the pistol grip, which wraps around the fore-end. There is no Monte Carlo comb or cheekpiece, and there is almost no drop from the comb to the heel, so recoil doesn't cause the stock to come up and smack the shooter in the face. Ruger adorned the fore-end with a gen-u-ine ebony wood tip, and the pistol grip has the traditional Ruger cap. There are two cross-bolts at the front and rear receiver rings for added strength. The red buttpad is slightly concave in the middle and varies from ¼ to ⅜ inch in thickness. Note: It is just a *buttpad*, not a recoil pad. There is a swivel stud at the toe of the stock. The front swivel? Just hold your 'taters; we'll get to that later.

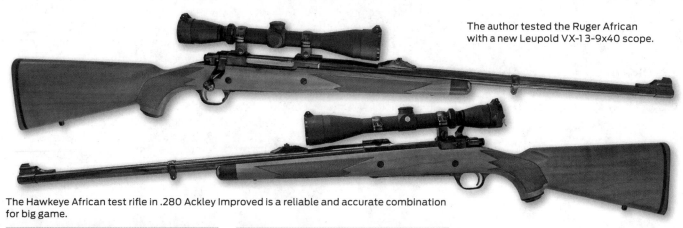

The author tested the Ruger African with a new Leupold VX-1 3-9x40 scope.

The Hawkeye African test rifle in .280 Ackley Improved is a reliable and accurate combination for big game.

The open sights are correct for this "stalking rifle." The rear is a folding express with a V-notch.

The front sight is a "gold" bead on an elevated barrel ramp.

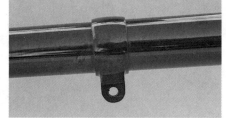

Another traditional feature is the barrel-band front sling swivel stud.

The action and the 24-inch barrel are subtle satin blue. The 5-groove rifling is cold hammer-forged, and the twist is a steep 1:8.5 inches, so it's all ready for today's long, high-tech bullets with high ballistic coefficients. The African has Ruger's new LC6 trigger with a crisp break, but the pull weight, as received, was a little heavy at 5 pounds, 2.1 ounces. I easily reduced it to 3 pounds, 5.2 ounces, by adding a Timney trigger spring.

The rifle's one-piece steel bolt has a Mauser-type non-rotating extractor that provides a controlled feed. A fixed blade-type ejector flips cases or loaded rounds out with zeal when you retract the bolt. Reloaders will quickly learn to stop the bolt travel just ahead of the ejector and pluck valuable empties off the extractor. The fixed box magazine holds four rounds, and the hinged floorplate has beautiful engraving with the Ruger name

and crest. The patented magazine latch is in the front of the triggerguard and is flush with the triggerguard to avoid accidentally releasing cartridges in the field.

And about that front sling swivel: It is mounted on a solid barrel band, three inches in front of the forend tip. You don't like a stud there? Not a problem. Positioned 2½ inches back from the forend tip is a cover screw. Removing it reveals a hole with a threaded steel escutcheon in the stock under the barrel. Ruger includes what it calls an "optional forend swivel stud" that you can install in the stock. Ruger includes an appropriately sized hex wrench. Like I said, first-class, all the way.

Ruger positioned the three-position safety at the right rear of the bolt. Pulling the safety back locks the bolt with the safety "on." The middle position unlocks the bolt, but the rifle is still on safe, so you can safely unload the chamber. Fully

forward is the fire position.

The open sights are also correct for the rifle. In the front is a .068-inch bead. Ruger calls it "gold," but it looks a lot like brass to me. Nonetheless, it is an appropriate front for the arm. The rear is a folding-leaf express-style with a V-notch. The sight dovetails into a base attached to the barrel with two stout screws, and the sight blade itself is adjustable for windage by loosening a tiny screw and drifting it right or left. However, while not many folks will probably hunt plains game with open irons, these sights fall under the "BUIS" (backup iron sight) category. But if the scope sight goes south, they'd be right handy in such a situation. And, they look the part.

You get a set of Ruger solid steel rings that attach to the cutouts machined directly into the receiver for mounting optics. Of course, aftermarket rings of various heights and diameters are available.

For testing, I mounted a new Leupold VX-1 3-9x40mm scope in the supplied Ruger rings. So equipped, the rifle-scope combo weighed 9 pounds, 7 ounces. Okay, I know what you're thinking. Isn't that a bit heavy for a mid-sized cartridge like the .280 Ackley? Well, yeah, but maybe there's a plan here.

INHERENT ADVANTAGES

Ruger's people didn't just fall off a cabbage truck; they think things through on new products. Consider this hypothetical. Let's say that Joe Blow from Kokomo

has finally saved enough money for a modest African safari. He needs a battery but doesn't want it to cost as much as the safari. So, our erudite hunter researches the various offerings (many chronicled in this august tome). He notes that the Ruger Hawkeye African comes in the calibers listed above. He knows Ruger's reputation for quality and accuracy. He surmises that a .375 or .416 Ruger will handle the big stuff, and either the 6.5x55 Swedish Mauser or .280 AI would be perfect for a variety of plains game.

And a significant advantage would be that these two rifles are as alike as two peas in a pod. The safeties, triggers, and other controls would all be the same. So, if he's familiar with one, he's familiar with both, so there's much less chance of a *faux pas* when the opportunity for a shot at a great trophy arises. As for the weight, well, perhaps that would be the gun bearer's problem, heh? In any event, a hunter heading to the Dark

Continent has prepared themselves for a wide variety of game with just these two rifles. That's my story, and I'm stickin' to it.

THE "IMPROVED CARTRIDGE" ALLURE

The .280 Ackley Improved is one of the dozens of "improved" cartridges developed by the famous gunsmith Parker Otto Ackley. "Improving" cartridges was an extremely popular and sometimes lucrative endeavor for gun cranks of various skill levels from about the 1940s on. In fact, with only a modicum of research, I was able to locate the names of 51 developers of "improved" cartridges! Doubtless, there are dozens more.

Rifle shots developed these wildcat cartridges in the heady days before an accurate chronograph graced every loading bench. They made

some wild velocity claims, and pressures were unknown. Also, the dimensions of cartridges with the same name from different gunsmiths could vary, as there were no standards for the wildcats. However, while the actual increases in velocity of many improved cartridges were minimal, there is a technical advantage. As P.O. Ackley proved decades ago, the decreased body taper of an improved case clings to the chamber wall better upon firing and reduces the back thrust against the firearm's locking mechanism.

Several excellent wildcats ultimately became factory cartridges. For example, Remington domesticated the .22-250, .25-'06, .260, 7mm-08, and .35 Whelen; Federal the .338, and there are many more.

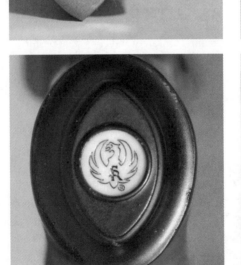

Left: The fore-end has a genuine ebony wood tip. Note the screw 2½ inches from the fore-end tip. Removing it reveals the provision for what Ruger calls an "optional fore-end swivel stud." The checkering is precisely cut.

Right: The floorplate features tasteful engraving with the Ruger crest and name.

Top left: The bolt has a traditional rotating Mauser-type extractor. The fixed ejector is at the left rear of the action.
Top right: Ruger reinforced the stock under the action with two cross-bolts.
Bottom left: The pistol grip cap also has the Ruger crest.
Bottom right: The pistol grip also has plenty of nicely executed checkering.

While fireforming cases is easy, Nosler and Hornady provide ready-made brass cases with the proper headstamps.

Two good factory .280 Ackley Improved ammo choices are Hornady's Precision Hunter with the 162-grain ELD-X bullet and Nosler's Trophy Grade with the 160-grain AccuBond. Both proved accurate from the bench.

You fireform the .280 AI (right) from the .280 Remington case (left). When fireforming, seat the bullet out to force the case head back against the bolt for proper forming.

THE INDUSTRY'S TRAFFIC COP

The Sporting Arms and Ammunition Manufacturing Institute (SAAMI) is a voluntary association of arms and ammo makers that develops specifications for cartridges and chambers that member companies must follow. SAAMI approval makes a cartridge a factory round. It is essential for safety and consistent performance.

The .280 AI has had a small, steady cadre of votaries, and in 2007, Nosler submitted the round to SAAMI for approval. The .280 AI finally became a factory round.

Chronographs and pressure-testing equipment festoon the labs of every powder, bullet, and ammo company, and many shooters and most handloaders have chronographs, as well. Based on its ballistics and history, I was incredibly anxious to try the round in my new Hawkeye African.

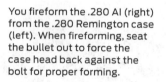

Handloading the .280 Ackley Improved is a snap. The author developed several excellent loads, including his "deer load," which uses VihtaVuori N165 powder and the Sierra 160-grain Spitzer Boattail.

.280 AI DESIGN FEATURES

The .280 Ackley Improved case follows the pattern of most improved rounds. Ackley reduced the body taper and made the shoulder sharper. All this increases powder capacity somewhat, and the cognoscenti think the new shape improves powder burn and aids accuracy.

Ackley increased the body diameter at the shoulder from .441 inch to .454 inch, and the shoulder angle changed from 17½ to 40 degrees. And for some reason, he reduced the overall case length from 2.540 to 2.525 inches.

Consistency is a benefit of SAAMI standardization. As a wildcat, the body taper, shoulder angle, and other dimensions of the cartridge could vary at the whim of its designer. All ammunition, reloading dies, and rifle chambers must adhere to these specifications as a factory round. This standardization is a major safety feature. And I think that cases last a little longer with such a shape.

Past velocities wildcatters claimed were dispelled with the advent of accurate and affordable chronographs. The .280 AI is a fine cartridge, but it isn't a 7mm Remington Magnum, nor should the handloader try to make it one. The only way one can increase velocities by very much is to load to much higher pressures — not a good idea. A velocity increase of about 100 fps is a good approximation of what the handloader can expect out of one.

Factory ammo for the .280 AI is not as available as, say, the .270 or .30-'06, but you can find some excellent high-tech loads. I obtained some Hornady Precision Hunter ammo loaded with the new 162-grain ELD-X big game bullet for testing. It lists at 2,850 fps. Out of my Hawkeye African, it registered 2,801 fps, pretty darn close to spec, and groups averaged .71 inch. Nosler loads its new Trophy Grade ammo with a 160-grain AccuBond bullet, listed at 2,950 fps. From the Ruger, it clocked 2,859 fps and averaged .75-inch groups. The accuracy of both loads is within "minute of kudu." Plus, they shoot flat, as their bullets sport high ballistic coefficients. The ELD-X's BC is .630, and for the AB, it's .531.

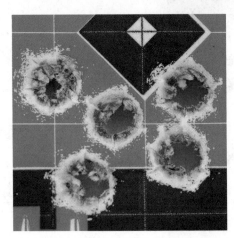

Above: The Hornady Precision Hunter load with the 162-grain ELD-X bullet was accurate and produced an average velocity of 2,801 fps.

Right: Thanks to the popularity of the many 7mm cartridges in use today, there is an excellent selection of bullets available that work well in the .280 AI.

HANDLOADING THE .280 ACKLEY

But what good is a cartridge if you can't reload it? So, it was with glee that I gathered up the necessary dies, bullets, and powders and set about to see if I could best the velocity and accuracy of the two factory loads. In a nutshell, I didn't, but I came close and had fun trying. I was able to work up several great loads, and (no surprise) I selected one for the 2020 Missouri deer season.

Slower powders, from the 4831s on up, perform best in the .280 AI. I ended up trying 10 different powders, with burning rates from Hybrid 100V through IMR 8133, and I found some accurate and powerful loads with each. I used Nosler and Hornady cases and Federal No. 210 primers for all handloads.

RANGE RESULTS

I shot for groups at 100 yards, firing off a Lead Sled DFT. When the dust settled, I was impressed with the accuracy of the new rifle but not surprised at the slight increase in the velocities of my handloads over factory ammo. The overall average of the 29 handloads tested was a delightful .75 inch, and several loads approached ½ inch. As this is a premier hunting round, I stuck with big game bullets. Here are some examples.

First, the speed burners. The two fast-

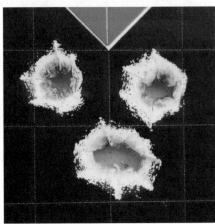

The Nosler Trophy Grade with the 160-grain AccuBond also shot within "minute of deer." Velocity was 2,859 fps.

est loads were with the Nosler 140-grain Partition bullet. With 62.0 grains of either Norma MRP or Alliant Reloder 22, velocities topped 3,000 fps. While groups with both were acceptable, the MRP load was slightly more accurate in my rifle.

Hornady makes the ELD-X bullet of 150- and 162-grain weights, and each shot well. The 150-grain version over 55.5 grains of IMR 4831 clocked 2,802 fps and averaged .63 inch. The 162-grain ELD-X was fastest with 58.0 grains of Reloder 22 but was slightly more accurate with 57.5 grains of VihtaVuori N560 (.57 inch). But they all were under an inch, so I'm not

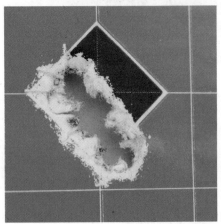

This 3-shot group was the final zero-check of the load selected for deer season: The Sierra 160-grain Spitzer Boattail over 60.0 grains of VihtaVuori N165. Velocity was 2,837 fps.

quibbling.

Sierra Spitzer Boattails in 150- and 160-grain weights have been a go-to bullet for my standard .280 Remington (a stainless synthetic Hawkeye), so I was not disappointed in the improved version's performance. The velocity of the 150-grain bullet with 52.1 grains of Hybrid 100V was 2,759 fps, with a .43-inch average. But if you can't find any of this powder, you can duplicate these ballistics with 55.5 grains of IMR 4831. With the 160-grain SBT, 60.0 grains of VihtaVuori N165 produced 2,837 fps and averaged a consistent .71 inch.

The African was as effective in the field as it was on the range. The author took this nice meat buck with one shot at about 80 yards.

Moving on from the "deer loads," the Speer 160-grain Grand Slam is suitable for larger deer, like elk. Here the same charge of VihtaVuori N165 registered 2,792 fps and grouped under an inch. Another good load with this bullet was with 61.5 grains of IMR 7977, one of IMR's new Enduron powders, which produced 2,759 fps and a .75 inch group average.

I found a bruiser load with the Swift 175-grain A-Frame. The star here was another Enduron powder, IMR 8133. A charge of 63.5 grains produced 2,623 fps and averaged 1.16 inches, and both bullets have a proven record of performance on big game.

FIELD RESULTS

The Hawkeye African is the quintessential hunting rifle, so it was only appro-priate that I use it in the upcoming deer season. But first, I had to pick a load; this was not easy, given the excellent accuracy of many of the combinations. I thought about using one of the two factory loads I had. Both the Hornady 162-grain ELD-X and the Nosler 160-grain AccuBond shot great, and the effectiveness of both is well known. But I am, after all, a handloader at heart, so I picked the load with the Sierra 160-grain Spitzer Boattails and 60.0 grains of VihtaVuori N165. My go-to bullet for my standard .280 Remington is the Sierra 150-grain SBT, a proven deer slayer. The die was cast.

Appropriate attire for the weather for the Missouri deer season can vary from a camo T-shirt to down parka and muck-lucks. But opening day dawned partly cloudy, a balmy 56 degrees, and light

An excellent assortment of 7mm bullets available for the .280 AI includes the following (from left): Sierra 150-grain Spitzer Boattail, Sierra 160-grain Spitzer Boattail, Sierra 150-grain GameKing, Sierra 160-grain MatchKing, Sierra 160-grain Spitzer Boattail, Federal 140-grain Trophy Bonded Tip, Swift 150-grain Scirocco II, Swift 160-grain A-Frame, Hornady 162-grain ELD-X, Nosler 150-grain AccuBond Long Range, Nosler 168-grain AccuBond Long Range.

RUHER HAWKEYE AFRICAN VELOCITY & ACCURACY

BULLET	POWDER (TYPE)	(GRS.)	CASE	PRIMER	COL (IN.)	VEL. (FPS)	S.D. (FPS)	RECOIL (FT-LB.)	M.E. (FT-LB.)	100-YD. ACC. (IN.)
						.280 ACKLEY IMPROVED				
Hornady 139-gr. SST	IMR 7977	63.5	Nosler	Fed 210	3.295	2,941	11	18.3	2,670	1.36
Hornady 150-gr. ELD-X	H 1000	59.5	Nosler	Fed 210	3.338	2,697	12	15.9	2,423	0.94
Hornady 150-gr. ELD-X	IMR 7828	58.0	Nosler	Fed 210	3.338	2,771	19	16.4	2,558	0.88
Hornady 150-gr. ELD-X	IMR 4831	55.5	Nosler	Fed 210	3.338	2,802	22	16.2	2,616	0.63
Hornady 162-gr. ELD-X	IMR 7828	56.3	Nosler	Fed 210	3.357	2,669	9	16.4	2,563	0.55
Hornady 162-gr. ELD-X	H 1000	59.0	Nosler	Fed 210	3.357	2,687	4	17.2	2,598	0.67
Hornady 162-gr. ELD-X	IMR 7977	61.0	Nosler	Fed 210	3.357	2,771	15	18.8	2,763	0.76
Hornady 162-gr. ELD-X	Viht. N560	57.5	Nosler	Fed 210	3.357	2,796	21	18.2	2,813	0.57
Hornady 162-gr. ELD-X	IMR 4831	55.3	Nosler	Fed 210	3.357	2,807	17	17.9	2,835	0.63
Hornady 162-gr. ELD-X	Reloder 22	58.0	Nosler	Fed 210	3.357	2,842	15	19.0	2,906	0.88
Nosler 140-gr. Partition	IMR 7977	63.5	Nosler	Fed 210	3.250	2,945	5	18.5	2,697	0.79
Nosler 140-gr. Partition	Norma MRP	62.0	Nosler	Fed 210	3.250	3,007	6	18.9	2,812	0.61
Nosler 140-gr. Partition	Reloder 22	62.0	Nosler	Fed 210	3.250	3,057	10	19.5	2,906	1.16
Nosler 150-gr. Partition	IMR 7977	62.5	Nosler	Fed 210	3.248	2,854	5	18.5	2,714	0.55
Nosler 150-gr. Partition	Reloder 22	59.2	Nosler	Fed 210	3.248	2,855	15	17.7	2,716	0.50
Nosler 150-gr. Partition	Viht. N165	61.0	Nosler	Fed 210	3.248	2,887	6	18.6	2,777	0.90
Sierra 150-gr. Spitzer Boattail	Viht. N165	61.0	Hornady	Fed 210	3.250	2,908	14	18.9	2,817	0.61
Sierra 150-gr. Spitzer Boattail	IMR 7828	57.5	Hornady	Fed 210	3.250	2,696	14	15.5	2,422	0.54
Sierra 150-gr. Spitzer Boattail	IMR 4831	55.5	Hornady	Fed 210	3.188	2,758	18	15.7	2,534	0.51
Sierra 150-gr. Spitzer Boattail	Hybrid 100V	52.1	Hornady	Fed 210	3.188	2,759	13	15.0	2,536	0.43
Sierra 160-gr. Spitzer Boattail	Viht. N165	60.0	Nosler	Fed 210	3.178	2,837	5	17.6	2,695	0.71
Sierra 160-gr. Spitzer Boattail	IMR 7828	57.0	Nosler	Fed 210	3.178	2,672	22	16.3	2,537	0.66
Sierra 160-gr. Spitzer Boattail	IMR 4831	54.4	Nosler	Fed 210	3.178	2,707	18	16.2	2,604	0.71
Sierra 160-gr. Spitzer Boattail	Hybrid 100V	52.0	Nosler	Fed 210	3.178	2,732	12	15.9	2,652	0.58
Speer 160-gr. Grand Slam	Viht. N165	60.0	Nosler	Fed 210	3.272	2,792	13	17.6	2,692	0.94
Speer 160-gr. Grand Slam	Viht. N560	58.0	Nosler	Fed 210	3.272	2,714	12	17.0	2,618	0.74
Speer 160-gr. Grand Slam	Reloder 22	58.5	Nosler	Fed 210	3.272	2,730	2	17.4	2,649	1.08
Speer 160-gr. Grand Slam	IMR 7977	61.5	Nosler	Fed 210	3.272	2,759	11	18.5	2,705	0.75
Swift 175-gr. A-Frame	IMR 8133	63.5	Nosler	Fed 210	3.207	2,623	26	19.1	2,674	1.16
								handload average acuracy:		0.75
Hornady Precision Hunter 162-gr. ELD-X	extruded	55.0		Factory Load	3.319	2,801	20	17.7	2,823	0.71
Nosler Trophy Grade 160-gr. AccuBond	extruded	57.0		Factory Load	3.243	2,859	28	18.7	2,905	0.75
								factory load average acuracy:		0.73

Notes: A Ruger Hawkeye African rifle with a 24-inch barrel and a 8.5-inch twist was used for all testing.
Sight was a Leupold VX-1 3-9x40 scope set at 8x. Velocity is at 10 feet. Accuracy is the average of three, three-shot groups at 100 yards from an indoor bench rest.
Range temperature was 77 to 88 degrees F.
Abreviations: SST, Super Shock Tip; ELD-X, Extremely Low Drag eXpanding; COL, Cartridge Overall Length.

winds. My wife and I hunt our acreage from ground blinds at the edges of some riparian timber. Unfortunately, the deer must have missed the memo that the season was opening, as they steadfastly refused to participate.

After a mid-day break that afternoon, we were once again situated in our blinds. Still, we saw no deer. Then, with only about 10 minutes of shooting hours left, a plump buck sauntered out of the timber and ambled across the pasture. I carefully aimed and fired. The buck collapsed and never moved.

I must report that the grilled venison was delicious. So, the Hawkeye came full circle and did its job perfectly. **GD**

The single-action revolver was a favorite of savvy lawmen, especially in the American Southwest. Shown here is an engraved Colt along with a set of engraved handcuffs.

THE Single-Action REVOLVER TODAY

A USFA single action in .45 Colt with a set of custom spurs.

> JIM WILSON

Despite being well into the 21st Century, the iconic American handgun is still the single-action cartridge revolver. Indeed, part of this is the frontier history that will forever be attached to this type of handgun. It reminds us of Wyatt Earp, Billy the Kid, Frank Hamer, and many Old West characters that we have all read about while growing up. And to be honest, those old sixguns are also a reminder of our cowboy movie heroes like John Wayne, Roy Rogers, Clint Eastwood, and Gene Autry, to name just a few.

But I would argue that history and nostalgia alone are not enough to keep the single action's popularity alive. And, since more than a dozen companies manufacture or import single actions in this country, it is a forgone conclusion that the popularity exists among American shooters. They are rugged guns, dependable guns, and they are available in just about every handgun caliber that a fellow would want.

In my case, with my love of history aside, I have to credit Elmer Keith for sending me down the single-action road. You see, I thought that Mr. Keith was just a pretty savvy handgunner and still do.

So, as a young man reading his works, I had to have a .44 Magnum revolver. Saving and scraping on a young policeman's salary, I bought my first Smith & Wesson Model 29, which was, indeed, an excellent handgun. The only trouble was that I didn't shoot it very well because the powerful revolver beat my hand up. The gun was not comfortable for me to shoot, and I started flinching badly, anticipating the recoil. I tried thick stocks, thin stocks, rubber stocks, hard stocks; in short, I tried them all and just had no luck.

I was right at the point of admitting I wasn't manly enough to handle the .44 Magnum when I had the chance to try an Old Model Ruger Flat Top .44 Magnum with a 6 1/2-inch barrel. The single-action grip shape allowed the gun to roll in my hand and absorb a good bit of the felt recoil, and it was just as accurate as the Smith & Wesson. Since then, I've never been without a .44 Magnum or a single-action revolver in that caliber.

One thing needs to be clear from the outset. Many of the early-style single actions, such as the Colt Single Action Army and the Old Model Ruger Blackhawk, do not have a safety feature that prevents the firing pin from resting

Adjustable sights are handy on a gun you use. Here is a pair of Colt New Frontier single actions in .45 Colt and .44 Special.

on a cartridge primer when the hammer is down. If dropped, such a gun will nearly always land on the hammer, and a loud noise will follow, often requiring medical attention for someone. Even Wyatt Earp learned this the hard way while he was a young Kansas lawman.

The old-style guns are fine, but you should carry them with an empty chamber under the hammer. Many of the newer single actions have a safety feature that prevents the firing pin from resting on a primer. If the individual shooter doesn't know which type he has, he should carefully read his owner's manual. Instead of an owner's manual, the next best move is to contact the manufacturer. Until one knows for sure, the smart thing is to make sure that there is an empty chamber under the gun's hammer.

Shooters of the old-style guns can follow the procedure that we used to call "Five Beans in the Wheel." To do this, you bring the hammer to the half-cock position. Load one chamber, skip one and load four more. Then the hammer is brought to full cock and let down easy. When done correctly, the firing pin will rest on an empty chamber. With a bit of practice, the shooter can reload in this manner in the dark or without taking his eyes off the target, whatever the target might be.

Since those days when Mr. Keith got me interested in the .44 Magnum, the single-action revolver has been my go-to hunting gun. I've taken squirrels, rabbits, wild turkeys, javelinas, whitetail deer, mule deer, feral hogs, and black bears with my single actions. And a handgun hunter can find a single-action revolver in just about any caliber that his little old heart desires, from .22 rimfire right on up to the .475 Linebaugh or one of the .50-caliber magnums. Matching the caliber to the game is not a problem if a man shoots a single action. The Colt New Frontier .45, the Old Model Blackhawk in several calibers, and the Freedom Arms .454 Casull are among my favored possessions and hunting tools.

Years ago, I was guiding some hunters on a feral hog hunt. One of them shot a hog late in the afternoon. When I got to their location, they told me that the pig, hit solidly, had run down into a deep, rocky ravine. It was now getting dusk, so

A pair of United States Fire Arms single actions in .45 Colt. Although this company is no longer in operation, you can find these guns on the used market. USFA made them exceptionally well.

Above: This custom Ruger .44 Magnum is about as handy a woods and hunting gun as any outdoorsman would want.

Left: The combination of adjustable sights and the popular .44 Special caliber make this Colt New Frontier a popular choice for most handgun chores.

I decided to go down there and bring the hog out since it was probably lying dead by that time, I figured.

Unlimbering my .357 Magnum Ruger Blackhawk, I eased down into the ravine and had to get on my knees to look under the cedar trees in that draw. Down on the ground and kind of bent over, I found the hog. Or, I should say the hog found me. It wasn't dead, and it appeared to be blaming me for its recent troubles. Fortunately, thanks to the Ruger, I was able to sort things out and drag the hog up to my hunters.

I found the hunters enjoying a good laugh, and I told them that I was glad that I could entertain them. "Oh, Sheriff," one of them said, "We weren't laughing at you. We just never had heard a single ac-tion go full-automatic before!"

Speaking of Ruger, one of my favorite handguns happens to be a Ruger single action. Ruger built it to honor lawman and gun writer Skeeter Skelton. Skeeter had worked with gunsmiths to convert Old Model .357 Blackhawks to his beloved .44 Special caliber, which made for a very handy and accurate big-bore revolver. Towards the end of his life, Skeeter visited with John Wootters and Bob Baer, explaining the conversion. At Wootters' urging, Bob Baer began a .44 Special conversion on a Ruger that was a surprise gift to Skeeter. Unfortunately, Skeeter died before they completed the gun.

Following this, John Wootters had Bob Baer complete the custom work. The gun, marked "SS 1," became John's favorite handgun. Ultimately, they showed it to John Taffin and me at one of the Shootists Holiday events, and we agreed that there ought to be more of the Skeeter Skelton Specials built. Once we had the Skelton family's permission, we engaged Bob Baer and Bill Grover (Texas Longhorn Arms) to do the conversions. Six more guns were completed for Taffin, Bart Skelton, Terry Murbach, Bob Baer, Bill Grover, and me. Texas Long Arms built all them on the Old Model .357 frame and rechambered them for the .44 Special. My gun is "SS 5" and has a 4 5/8-inch barrel, ivory stocks, a tuned action, and a King Mirror Ramp front sight. In keeping with Skeeter's enjoyment of using guns, it is certainly not a safe queen. I've packed it

many a mile and put many SWC cast bullets down the barrel.

You might be surprised to learn that quite a number of folks carry single-action revolvers for personal defense. This fact could be because a particular handgunner might live where two-legged and four-legged predators are a concern. It could also be that his hobby is cowboy action shooting, and he does most of his practice with single-action revolvers making this the type of gun that he can run without having to rethink the whole handgun thing. Or it could just be that he likes single actions and shoots them well.

Some of the Internet Commandos would have you believe that any single action is a horrible choice for personal defense. Those guys are all about gear and equipment. In the real world, several things are more important than what kind of gun you carry. Good defensive tactics are one of them. The determination to fight savagely, whether you are armed or not, is another. And your ability to place a fight-stopping center hit is critical. While the SA revolver is not my first choice for a fighting handgun, in the end, it is not about what you carry but what you can do with it that counts.

For gunfighting, the only real drawback to the SA sixgun is that it is slow to reload. Some think that this is a big mark against it, but, in reality, the first couple of shots fired in a gunfight are the most critical. If you correctly placed those shots, the whole affair will likely have come to a screeching halt.

In defensive situations, the SA revolver is much like the defensive shotgun, which also doesn't hold many shots. The key is to replenish what you have shot

Single actions are the first choice of many savvy hunters.

The author had this Old Model Ruger converted from .357 Magnum to .44 Special and customized to honor Skeeter Skelton.

I Remember Skeeter

Compiled by Sally Jim Skelton

continually. Now, if you are standing out in the open with an empty handgun and you haven't stopped the fight, your tactics stink. Cover is your friend, and it is much easier and safer to reload behind cover.

Captain A.Y. Allee was one of the great Texas Rangers, having worn the Ranger badge from 1932 until the late 1960s. For much of that time, he carried a 4 3/4-inch Colt Single Action Army in .45 Colt. Since he was no stranger to the smell of gunsmoke, I once asked him about using a single action in a gunfight. His reply was, "Son, if you can't get the job done with five .45 Colt cartridges, just throw it in the river and run." To my good knowledge, the captain never had to throw one of his guns in the river.

If the handgunner carries a single action for personal defense, a few techniques and suggestions will help immensely. The first is to get into the habit of placing the little finger of the shooting hand under the revolver's grip frame. This technique allows the shooter to manage recoil and pull the gun back down and get it back on target. It also

Positioning the little finger beneath the grip frame allows the shooter to control recoil.

Wilson finds single-action revolvers meet most of his handgunning needs.

This old Roy Baker pancake holster is a good rig for concealment or outdoors carry. Simply Rugged Holsters makes an excellent version of this holster.

gives the shooter a much more secure grip on the handgun.

The single action's draw stroke is no different than any other handgun except, of course, that you must cock the hammer for each shot. As the gun clears the holster and you level the muzzle at the target, the hands come together for a secure two-hand hold. At this point, the shooter uses the thumb of his support hand to cock the handgun. This method allows the shooting hand to maintain a secure shooting grip throughout without shifting. And, of course, the trigger finger should be straight and outside the triggerguard until the sights are on the target and you have made the decision to fire.

Big-bore single actions can also feel a bit heavy when carrying them for hours in a belt holster. It is critically important to use a quality holster fitted to the particular gun and have a stout belt made for carrying the rig. Fortunately, several companies build excellent concealment rigs for single actions, and my favorites

are Barranti Leather Company and Simply Rugged Holsters.

Finally, the defensive shooter who elects to carry a single action needs to get professional training. The Gunsite Academy, in Paulden, Arizona, offers a defensive school just for single-action shooters. The student will learn the proper draw stroke and firing technique, allowing him to shoot just as fast as he can with any other type of

handgun and get successful hits on the target. They will also teach the shooter the best technique for topping off his gun during a lull in the fight, and he can learn to do this without looking at his handgun. The SA revolver is no different from any other defensive handgun because proper, professional training is a life-saving endeavor.

But the single-action revolver, like all other firearms, is not just about killing

people and animals. It is also all about the simple fun of shooting. And nobody has any more fun with single actions than the folks who enjoy cowboy action shooting. Cowboy action shooters get into the history as well as the marksmanship. It's not just enough to be a good shot; you also need to wear an authentic outfit and be a good sport. I particularly enjoy the stages that feature big-bore revolvers and the authentic blackpowder loads of the old days.

Being a horseman, I also enjoy watching mounted shooting events. The contestant gallops into the arena, armed with two sixguns, and has to take out several balloons set in a pattern on wood stakes. Of course, for safety reasons, they are not shooting solid bullets at those balloons. Regardless, I invite anyone to try running two revolvers through the balloon pattern while horseback at a dead run.

The only time I ever tried shooting from horseback was when I came across a javelina in the middle of a brush-choked South Texas pasture. Luckily, I hit the critter with my first shot because that was the only shot that I fired. Promptly after that, I was dumped on my *como se llama*

by said horse who had taken an entirely dim view of the whole project.

But the cowboy shooters do have fun with their mounted shooting and the various shooting stages featuring single actions, lever-action carbines, and shotguns. Having fun at shooting; what a concept!

But you don't have to explain having fun while shooting to most avid plinkers, killers of bean cans and caliche rocks. And, once again, the single-action revolver will fit right into the program. A .22 SA is just about right for such work, although it is your day off, so you should shoot whatever caliber suits you. I particularly like to take out a sack of charcoal briquettes and just broadcast them across the shooting area. When hit, they make a nice black cloud that indicates success — and you don't have a mess to clean up when done. The charcoal powder washes right into the soil.

When my son was little and learning to shoot, we did a lot of that. He learned on a single-action .22 rimfire. Most importantly, he quickly understood how the gun functioned and how to load and

unload it. And, if the hammer was down, there was little or no chance of a negligent discharge. Not only did it start him on the shooting hobby, but he also still has that .22 sixgun, some 40 years later.

So, I think that the real reason that single-action revolvers are still around is that they are simply useful. The handgun hunter won't have trouble bringing home the venison if he will do his part in the stalking and marksmanship department. The defensive shooter is also far from being helpless if he learns proper defensive techniques and the skill to hit his intended target. And the fellow who shoots for fun, whether cowboy shooting or plinking, won't find any better choice than the single-action revolver.

Winter is about over in my part of the Southwest. I am ready to get out of the house and roam the hills and brush country. I don't know which boots I'll wear, and I'm not sure which hat to put on my head. But I know which gun I'll be packing. It's that Skeeter Skelton Special No. 5 in .44 Special. Single actions? Yeah, I like 'em. GD

An Old Model Ruger .44 Magnum (top) and a heavily customized one (bottom).

My Friend SAGE

The great cartridge developer Ned Roberts never failed to credit his shooting buddy and close friend, Fred Sage.

❯JIM FORAL

Mr. Sage had a flair for hiding behind a rifle when someone tried to take his picture. So here he is with a .25 Roberts Mauser in the Summer of 1933.

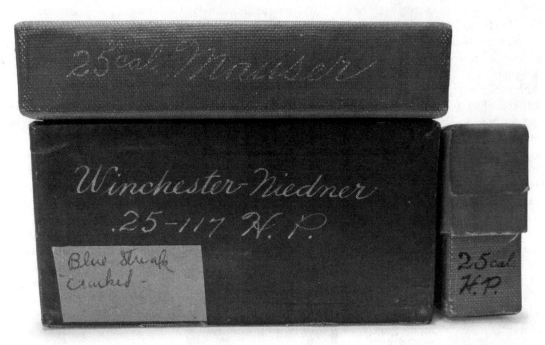

Ned Roberts liked to reinforce cartridge boxes with oilcloth and mark them in his distinctive and calligraphic hand.

Ned Roberts posing at the same bench on the same day and with the same gun.

There is no shortage of notorious sidekicks in our culture. Batman had Robin; the Lone Ranger had Tonto. Watson assisted Sherlock Holmes, and Robinson Caruso enjoyed the company of Friday. You generally think of these associates as subordinates; and expect them to remain in the background. Much progress in the field of firearms had come from individuals' endeavors, and everyone knows that the development of the .257 Roberts cartridge was the work of a named individual. Still, almost no one is aware of the sidekick involved. Here is that story — of one Fred Sage, sidekick to Ned Roberts of .257 Roberts fame.

Ned H. Roberts was a lifelong rifle enthusiast and an experimentally inclined rifle crank with a technical background. He owned many rifles, shot, and handloaded as much as any man in America. He was fully engaged in this avocation. Professionally, he was a schoolteacher. Mr. Roberts broke into the sporting magazines as a regular contributing presence in 1908. Unlike many of his con-

temporaries who broadcast their insipid opinions just for the sake of it, Roberts had something meaningful and authoritative to say, and publishers deemed him worthy of their magazine space. They came to expect, and to receive, a certain standard from him. His authority shined through in his unstilted, readable prose, and he further qualified himself as time went on.

Through the late 1890s, Ned Roberts wanted the optimum medium-bore target/woodchuck rifle, but the .32-40 was a little too common and a bit too big. When Stevens announced the .28-30 Stevens in the fall of 1900, Roberts thought it might fill the bill. He sent his pet Stevens Ideal #49 to Chicopee Falls to be factory re-barreled for the new straight shell. Despite his best efforts, hundred-yard groups were no better than a disappointing two inches. The rifle went back to the Stevens factory where F.C. Ross worked his magic on the tube. Afterward, it shot remarkably well until the soft Stevens action loosened and the lever drooped more and more.

Ned salvaged the good barrel and had it fitted to a new beefed-up Stevens action a few months later. At the same time, he gave it an upgraded #47 checkered pistol grip stock. He received the rifle in August 1909 at the Troy Conference Academy, a co-ed college at Poultney, Vermont, where he was a teacher. Ned and his friend Sage used the .28-30 cartridge for eight years and found it effective on woodchucks out to 400 yards. They agreed that it was capable of good target accuracy. Roberts owned four .28-30 rifles and was proud of a Stevens-Pope 44 ½ #52 Stevens with a half-octagon barrel. It would print ten-shot sub-MOA

groups with a breech-seated 136-grain Pope bullet.

The individual most frequently referred to by Roberts in his writing as "my friend Sage" owned a .28-30 rifle, too. Frederick J. Sage designed a 132-grain flat-point bullet that punched a hole "practically as large as a .30 caliber bullet," according to Roberts. The clean and defined hole produced could conceivably nick the scoring ring of the next higher value. The standard pointed, or round-nose .28-caliber bullets perforated a smaller-than-full diameter hole as it pushed the paper edges aside in their passage. This detail was a small but important consideration. A few thousandths of an inch could be the difference between a first and second place in a close match, a slight advantage that mattered. John Barlow at Ideal Manufacturing shaped the cherry and cut some molds for this Sage bullet but didn't include it in his regular catalog line. Ned Roberts used the Sage, Pope, and Ideal bullets but considered his friend Sage's most accurate.

Frederick Joyner Sage was born in New Marlboro, Connecticut, on April 14, 1869, descended from Welsh immigrants who'd arrived in the colony in the 1650s. His father was Francis Sage, and his mother was Emma A. Joyner. She died when Frederick was ten years old.

No one knows how or when Ned Roberts and Fred Sage crossed paths, but it must have occurred in the late 1890s. Mr. Sage wasn't the lackey who ran down range to shag Roberts' targets or be his shadow. Sage was himself a capable and skilled modern rifleman and thoroughly abreast of the trending times. In every sense, Roberts and Sage were contemporaries, peers, equals, and friends with shared passions and goals. As a team, they complemented and challenged each other in the 'two heads are better than one" fashion. Ned Roberts didn't hog the limelight. He was the one with the inclination

and the writing skills to record and communicate the results and progress of their various projects. Owing to his byline, many readers understandably perceived these as "his" projects. Over the years, both men moved around some, but for almost forty years spent the summer's school break months — July and August — together on the rifle range each day.

The .25-caliber bug bit both riflemen, and they abandoned the .28-30. Roberts had Stevens remove the latest .28-30 barrel and fit a #2 weight, 1:12-inch twist barrel chambered in the long, straight .25-25 Stevens to his #47. He ordered the hard nickel steel barrel option to handle any metal-cased bullets he might eventually try. It showed promise when he shot ten shots into a 1.5-inch square on the factory 100-yard test target. Roberts and Sage gave the rifle a thorough wringing out during the Spring and Summer of 1910. They tried black and smokeless powder and all manner of suitable cast and jacketed bullets. The best 200-yard group that they could coax from the rifle was twelve inches. That experience didn't sour either man on caliber .25. Roberts reasoned that the narrow shell didn't hold enough powder to give him the performance he expected.

Ned couldn't ignore the nagging yen developing for a more powerful .25 caliber for shooting long-range woodchucks. In his mind's eye, he saw an up-to-date, powerful rifle that met specific essential requirements. In an *Arms and the Man* article, N.H. Roberts broadcast the criteria for the .25 caliber he had in mind. He wanted the gun to be a solid single-shot rifle that would meet his lofty and uncompromising accuracy standards. He fully expected and demanded 100-yard ten-shot groups to stay within an inch. Secondly, the shell needed to be easily reloadable with affordable metal-cased bullets available on the open market.

Roberts deliberated options. Case volume — and as recent experience had shown, its shape — mattered. While he sifted through the possibilities available to him in those days, a necked-down Krag case seemed the best choice. However, the thought of a .30-40 Krag shell holding a .25-caliber bullet was not original to him. Dr. Mann had been working with several forms of it in his base-band bullet experiments since 1904. In May 1910, Roberts met A.O. Niedner at the Walnut Hill range and discussed rechambering the Stevens .25-25 barrel for the Krag case, using full-diameter .25-caliber bullets.

Niedner made the necessary reamers and dies, fitted and chambered Ned's barrel, and casehardened and vented the breechblock. He also furnished 200 formed cases and a straight line bullet seater. The December 2, 1910 entry in Niedner's shop books shows a total of $16 in charges. At the time, Roberts was living in Staunton, Virginia, likely teaching

More from the Roberts' estate is a line-up of his .25-caliber cartridges. Left to right, .25 Roberts, .257 Roberts, and .25 Niedner — all formed on Ned's loading bench.

From Ned Roberts' estate are some of his cartridge boxes and shells, together with his .25-caliber bullet pointing swage from 1909.

school. On December 10, the two men met at Walnut Hill to test the new gun on the club's machine rest. It was just another cold, windy day in Boston, but it was a banner day for Ned Roberts. The gunsmith had prepared an assortment of loads using the Winchester 86 grain ($3.50 per thousand) metal jacketed bullets. These preliminary loads approached their 1-inch group size goal, and both gun maker and customer were delighted with the results. Shortly afterward, Niedner built for himself a Krag .25 for use with base-band bullets.

Ned's enthusiasm gushed out across *Arms and the Man* and *Outers Book* pages when he wrote up the range results. He was looking for *the* rifle, he told his readers,"… and now, like Pythagoras, I can say 'Eureka, I have found it.' And It is the .25 caliber high power rifle." It was known to Robert's readers after that as the .25 H.P. Stevens-Niedner. As a schoolteacher, Roberts should have known, and the editor should have caught, that "Eureka" was the yelp of Archimedes, the Greek mathematician and scholar. Pythagoras was a 5th-Century B.C. Greek who reasoned out the relationship of the hypotenuse of a right triangle to its other sides.

At any rate, as pleased as he was with the rifle, Roberts sold it through a classified ad in the January 1913 number of *Outers Book*. Answering the ad was W.B.

Swan of Erie, Pennsylvania, a kindred rifle enthusiast and Roberts' senior by several years. Mr. Swan had seen enough to recognize the difference between fine and almost fine as they described rifles. A few months went by before Swan's ruling arrived in Roberts' mailbox: "I have owned many fine rifles and fine shooting rifles, but the Stevens-Niedner .25 Caliber High power is the very finest shooting rifle I have ever owned."

Sage was able to pursue his rifle interests and quirky preferences. In 1914, he fell for a Stevens Model 44 ½ rifle that Niedner had for sale. It was chambered for the .32-40 case necked to .22 caliber and shot 60-grain base-banded bullets to about 3,000 fps. This 1907-era concept was a holdover from the Mann/Niedner alliance, and Mr. Niedner regarded it as strictly a target cartridge. It was made momentarily famous by Linwood Lewis of Dorchester, Mass., who ordered a Stevens rifle, chambered ".22-40" from Niedner and wrote about this startling novelty in *Arms and the Man* in 1909. It was capable of tiny groups for a 6-pound rifle.

Niedners' shop book entries of 1914 show a replaced breechblock and Sage's purchases of .22-40 formed cases and repeated orders for bullets. At the time, Mr. Sage was headquartered in parts unknown and working as a clerk at a

postal sorting service that sorted mail en route to a destination and readied it for delivery upon arrival. By 1921, Sage's desire for the gun had worn off, and he sold it to Roberts. Ned recorded that this unusual Stevens-Niedner H.P. was 'absolutely the finest shooting, most accurate rifle at ranges of 100 and 200 yards that I have found to date during forty years of experience in rifle shooting."

Fred Sage had his own Winchester-Niedner and is pictured in Ned Roberts' article on Niedner's "Bolt action Single Shot Rifle" (the famous Hamburg rifle), which appeared in *Outers Book*, September 1912. Sage's rifle was a plain straight grip High Wall that Niedner re-barreled and chambered for the .25 Krag case. Niedner entered the work into his book on December 8, 1911, as "One .25 H.P. bbl, Win." It had a 1:14-inch twist and wore a Stevens' 8x scope. Roberts and Sage kept an accurate log of each shot exiting their rifles. By May 1914, the count from Sage's Winchester Niedner exceeded 3,500 rounds — more than enough to wash out a Springfield service barrel but was a long way from needing replacement.

In a November 11, 1934 letter mailed from Roberts' residence in Berlin, New Hampshire to Harvey Donaldson in Little Falls, New York, there is a casual mention that "my friend Sage uses the .25

Krag cartridge in a Springfield action." The mentioned combination is undoubtedly an unlikely and bewildering one. The Krag action was the logical and standard platform for a rimmed cartridge, and in those days, when a writer meant Krag, Krag was written. On the other hand, entries in Niedner's book fall short of explaining intriguing questions. On June 25, 1914, a gunsmith billed Sage $7.80 for "chambering Springfield." On March 8, 1917, Sage received an invoice amounting to $3.50 for "special work on a Springfield." This double-set triggered rifle with the 25-inch medium-weight Niedner barrel and a 13-inch twist became another one of Sage's .25-caliber woodchuck guns and mentioned by Roberts numerous times for the next twenty years.

In 1916, Niedner's .25 caliber on the .30-40 Krag case was superseded by the .30-1906 case necked to the quarter-inch bore. It was, for a time, the transitory rage whose primary claim was an eyebrow-raising muzzle velocity of 3,300 fps with the useful 101-grain bullet.

Ned Roberts didn't do things by halves. A local physician, Dr. Fred Walker, had asked him to test his 9.5-pound Springfield-Niedner with its tight-necked Mann-Niedner chamber (which Niedner built for him) and determine the best load for it. Ned saw the undertaking as an opportunity to put the gun through its paces and gain from experience. Roberts devoted himself to the task and later wrote of the project: "It has occupied my Saturdays for the last three months." Afterward, he was able to file a detailed report that took up eight pages of the *Outdoor Life* Arms and Ammunition

column in August 1917, where he made no mention of his friend Sage.

Meantime, Roberts got a .25 Niedner of his own. In late July 1916, a gunsmith billed Ned $5 for "chambering .25 H.P." with an extra charge of $1.50 for "necking down .30 shells." In April of the following year, Niedner had fitted the barrel to Roberts' Springfield action, provided the loading tool, fitted scope blocks, and an additional 100 ".25 Springfield" cases, together with a bill for $14.50. In 1917, N.H. Roberts served as Secretary of the New Hampshire State Rifle Association and qualified as an Expert on the Goffstown N.H. range rifle club. Curiously, in October 1916, the same club reported the recent expert qualification of Fred J. Sage.

The consensus of the era's rifle shots seemed to be that the .25 caliber had reached its zenith with the .25 Spring-

From *Outers Book* September 1912. Posed together are three like-minded rifle cranks. Left to right: A.O. Niedner with his bolt-action Single Shot rifle fitted with a Sabine scope, F.J. Sage holds his .25-caliber H.P. Winchester Niedner. Ned Roberts on the right is showing his .25 Hi-Power Stevens Niedner.

Some Niedner/Roberts .25 calibers from the 1912 era, 1) Special .25-caliber cartridge for the Niedner bolt-action Hamburg rifle. The cartridge is 3.5 inches long, with a charge of 48 grains of Lightning powder. 2) A .30-06 cartridge for perspective. 3) Dr. Mann's .25-caliber cartridge, 3 1/16th-in. length, .35-40 grains of Lightning with his 100-grain base band bullet. 4) Niedner .25 caliber cartridge, Krag case necked down, 35 grains of Lightning, and an 86-grain base band bullet. 6) Niedner special .32-40 necked to .22 caliber for a 70-grain base band bullet.

field Niedner. Roberts and Sage thought differently and challenged the notion that bigger is better. Due to its increased velocity, the Springfield Niedner's slight trajectory advantage didn't offset the resultant decreased average accuracy than the .25 Krag. Over the next ten years, the two men exhaustively tested the .250-3000 in a bolt action and determined that the case volume was too small to suffice, and that of the .25 Niedner and its early 1920s twin (the .25 Whelen) were too big. The .25 Krag continued to be ideal in all essential particulars.

Rifleman in America had accepted the demise of the single-shot rifle and acknowledged its bolt-action replacement, requiring a rimless shell, as the wave of the future. Roberts and Sage had laid the groundwork for a successful, up-to-date .25-caliber rifle cartridge. The obstacle of adapting the concept to a modern bolt-action rifle by duplicating the shell, less the rim, remained. In 1927, Roberts and Sage sifted through the selection of modern rimless shells to get close to the Krag's capacity. It narrowed to a choice of two: the 7mm Mauser and the 6.5mm Mannlicher. The Mauser shell was the more robust, better adaptable, more available, and the wisest choice. The two men necked the case to .25 caliber and proceeded to perfect it into what they hoped to become the rimless version of the flanged "it" of 1912 and awaited the beholding of its Eureka moment.

As he seemed prone to do, Roberts made a full-blown production of the project. Sage and he were at the task for ten years. They undertook several costly case shapes, adjustments, shoulder locations, powders, bullets, and upwards of 50,000 shots fired through many different barrels.

Roberts met Col. Townsend Whelen in August 1927 in Vermont, discussed the project cartridge face to face, and followed through with an exchange of letters. The Niedner Rifle Corp. and the Roberts/Sage alliance would share the costs involved in producing reamers, loading tools, and whatever they needed to get underway. Roberts credits Fred Sage as the individual who induced Niedner to bring out the new cartridge. Whelen agreed to provide the considerable support that his byline afforded and suggested a name for the new shell — the .25 Roberts.

Bringing the .25 Roberts cartridge to fruition far outpaced the crawl of its development. In May 1929, Ned Roberts provided *American Rifleman* readers with an update on the .25 Roberts still in the process of being wrung out. The Niedner Rifle Corp. and Griffin & Howe Rifles made barrels to order. There was no factory ammunition, just a limited selection of component bullets. In June, Ned motored to Dowagiac, Michigan, to spend two weeks at the Niedner Rifle Corp. range and machine rest. He spent his days chasing the one-inch ring with .25-caliber bullets. From mid-July to late August, just as they always did, Roberts and his friend Sage shot daily at the New Hampshire range and broke it up with some woodchuck shooting. Roberts' and Sage's 1929 .25 Roberts groups averaged 1.25 to 1.50 MOA. They were disappointed but expected to see better soon.

In two years, ten-shot groups at MOA were on track for the emergence of the 1931 title of "it." Ned credited the ammunition companies for turning out better bullets than before, coupled with a noticeable improvement in smokeless powder quality. The input of a growing number of experimentally minded .25-caliber converts with similar goals, sound techniques, and Griffin & Howe .25 Roberts rifles also contributed to lower average group size. In 1933, Griffin & Howe ads for its Mauser rifles chambered .25 Roberts claimed "woodchuck accuracy to 400 yards."

From the January 1913 *Outers Book*, we find Roberts' ad to sell his .25 H.P. Stevens-Niedner.

With its *American Rifleman* exposure, the .25 Roberts blossomed into a following and then demand. After tweaking the shoulder angle to facilitate production, Remington started churning out .25 Roberts cartridges in May 1934. A second lot of cartridges carried the headstamp .257 Roberts, another Remington idea. Remington added the chambering to its Model 30 in 1934, and Winchester sold .257 Roberts Model 70s by 1935.

The spokesman for the great 17-year .257 Roberts project was without question its principal. It makes sense to presume that the silent, scarcely-mentioned man shrinking in the background is to have a secondary, subordinate role. Ned Roberts substantiated Sage's importance in the .257 Roberts development when he wrote in the January issue of the *American Rifleman*, "As many of our readers know, the .25 Roberts cartridge was designed by my friend Fred Sage and myself with the assistance of our mutual friend A.O. Niedner." Sage had been involved and considered a friend, partner, and co-developer in the joint venture from start to finish.

For several years, Fred Sage lived in New Canaan, Conn. and was there as late as 1935. In 1940, the two friendly gun bugs were living in the same little village. Sage was renting a house in Goffstown, New Hampshire, while Roberts resided at his ancestral farm just outside of town. Professional educator, author, and renowned ballistic expert Ned Henry Roberts died at 82 years in Goffstown on July 20, 1948. Lesser-known Fred Sage's contribution to the history of arms and ammunition had never received its rightful recognition. He never took a bride. It is easy to picture him, married to a stack of rifles and going through life quite contented with the arrangement. F.J. Sage died December 22, 1955, at age 86 in Groton, Connecticut. **GD**

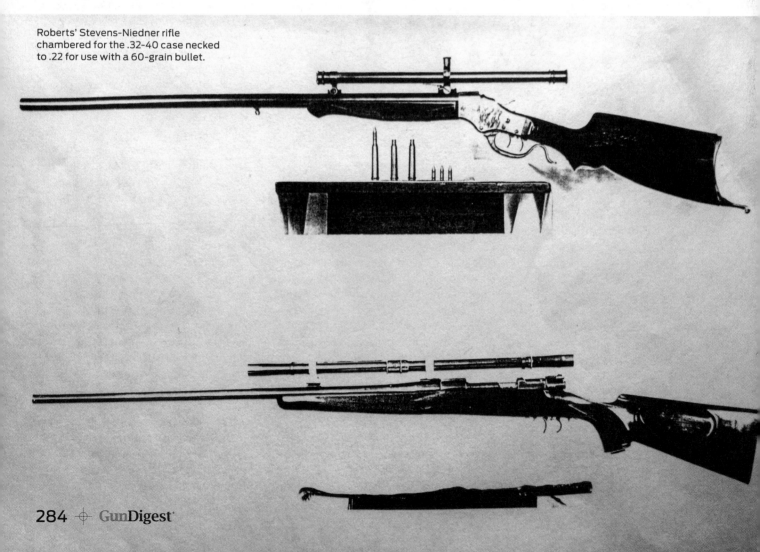

Roberts' Stevens-Niedner rifle chambered for the .32-40 case necked to .22 for use with a 60-grain bullet.

The New Uberti 1885 Courteney "Stalking Rifle"

› L. P. BREZNY

Frederick Courteney Selous.

Built when African big game hunting was king among the British royals and designed to fit the needs of the modest budget of the working man who wanted to take on the African bush, the 1885 Courteney was the tool to have. Now, Uberti offers a replica in its long line of historically accurate rifles.

First envisioned by Frederick Courteney Selous, hunter, explorer, and naturalist (1861–1917), he built the gun as a light stalking rifle that used blackpowder in the .303 British for Africa's big game. Rifles used in Africa were of the double gun design, but their cost was relatively high. The Courteney — with its single barrel, high wall design — fended off some of those production costs and still handled a popular military rifle cartridge.

I first observed the Courteney 1885 high wall single-shot at the 2019 Shot Show. The designers of this modern version yearned for something different as an addition to the Uberti line. To date, no one had pressed into production the design of the original Courteney "Stalking Rifle."

Uberti built it as a single shot on the robust 1885 high wall falling-block action. I found the rifle to be accurate with several factory .303 British ammunition brands. Today, there are not many options in factory loads from which to select. When I reached out to my friends at Hornady for solutions to the problem, they helped with a factory load consisting of a 150-grain Interlock bullet launched at 2,685 fps and some

The Uberti Courteney has attractive color casehardening in a high wall single-shot design.

handloading components including new Hornady .303 British brass and two bullet weights.

The Hornady handloads included the 150-grain Interlock and 174-grain Interlock, both in the .311 diameter (versus the .308 diameter of the American-based .308 Winchester). The .303 British favors the .310 through .312 bullet diameter.

To test the light stalking rifle, I took on steel targets from 100 to 400 yards. The initial zeroing process was easy, and the gun printed one-inch groups with Federal and Hornady 150-grain bullets. For optics, I used the Nikon ProStaff long-range scope. Uberti suggests a small, low-powered scope for the rifle, but South Dakota is not Africa with its heavy bush-style hunting. With the beautifully machined quarter rib and slotted rail designed for Weaver bases and rings, the Nikon dropped into place naturally.

Uberti fit the rifle with iron sights and a hooded ramp sight. If you are not interested in having a scope on the gun, it comes in a rib-free model. Save for hunting the Black Hills, the riflescope is a must in my part of the world and would bring out the best of the 303 British cartridge for big game.

This dream gun uses the Prince of Wales buttstock design, red rubber recoil pad, and slim-fitted forend with an African heartwood end cap. The stock setup and cut checkered pistol grip and forend held well against soft cotton gloves, as I shot from standing offhand at 100 to 150 yards and sitting with sniper sticks to 400 yards.

Testing began with Federal 150-grain Power Shok and Hornady 150-grain Interlock bullets. Later, I found a cache of PPU 150- and 174-grain Serbian ammunition. This Serbian ammo was not familiar, and I was unsure of its performance. Still, I found out quickly that it was capable when shot from the Uberti 1885 Courteney.

When shot to 300 yards and using a DOPE table that I derived from Hornady's ballistics programs, I owned the mid-range kill box.

The rifle makes use of the two-stage open hammer that is classic to the rifle (the first stage allows a safe position to carry off the firing pin, and the second-stage fire position). This design meant you needed to consider hammer drop time or lock time for accuracy. Since I have used my .45-70 Sharps in the field

on buffalo, and having shot .50-caliber blackpowder Hawken guns, T/C handguns, and carbines, controlling the Courteney's trigger was no trouble. The hammer on the Uberti Courteney travels almost a full inch forward from full cock to fire. In terms of fitting steel to steel, the gunsmiths at Uberti did their job quite well, indeed.

Using the Nikon with an open-adjustable top turret set to MOA graduations and a left-side parallax knob, I doped the rifle to 400 yards with nine one-MOA elevation clicks shooting the 150-grain bullet. In effect, the new rifle was ready for some field application on warm targets.

Shooting mostly Hornady handloads consisting of new Hornady brass and 43.9 grains of Alliant RL-15, I cranked a consistent 2,700 fps out of the .303

Detail wood to metal fit. Uberti chambers the classy reproduction in .303 British.

British round. That velocity gave me a solid 325-yard accuracy load when pressed against mountain marmot, the target of choice for summer gunning.

I managed some very workable shots on marmots from the sitting position and off shooting sticks. Over as many weekends into the Black Hills high country, seven hunts produced enough success with the Courteney that I felt ready to take on the Missouri River Dakota Breaks' whitetail population. The winds turned cool, and the first snows had come early.

With a boatload of pure luck, an old friend located near Mobridge, South Dakota, had cleared the way for me to hunt my very favorite spot on the river breaks. This area was an old, abandoned farmstead that almost no one ever took a serious look at for big game hunting.

After two days of sitting on stand, taking the time to admire the rifle's case-hardened receiver and well-crafted wood-to-metal fit, all hell broke loose. Below me, a pair of young bucks crossed under my elevated position, but they were just not shooters. The rifle felt good, and I trusted it entirely if a shooter buck showed up. No more had the thought crossed my mind when, at the 400-yard mark, a 4x5 buck walked out of some dark brush and stood broadside to my line of sight.

I had the DOPE marked at 9.1 clicks, and at once, I started turning turret settings. Now with the hammer back and a Hornady 150-grain chambered, I touched off the round. As the rifle's recoil settled, I could see the brush

BALLISTICS TABLE.
UBERTI COURTENEY | .303 BRITISH BIG GAME LOADS

Load (type/grains)	Powder (grains)	Velocity (fps)	3-Shot Group Avg. (in.)
Hornady 150Interlock SP	IMR 3031 38.1	2,600	1.767
Hornady 150 Interlock SP	H4895 36.7	2,600	1.627
Hornady 150 Interlock SP	Varget 40.8	2,600	1.015
Hornady 150 Interlock SP	Alliant RL-15 43.9	2,680	1.272
Hornady 174 Interlock RN	Varget 39.1	2,400	1.590
Hornady Interlock RN 150	Factory load	—	0.944
FMC BT 174	Factory load	2,400	1.313
SP FMC BT 150	Factory load	2,600	1.221
Federal 150 SP Power Shok	Factory load	2,600	.839

Best of two groups shot for accuracy and recorded. Benchrest over heavy sandbags. Temp 51 F. Wind following 5 mph. Altitude 3,000 feet. Cold bore.

explode behind the deer.

At the shot, the buck came straight at me, and I quickly chambered a second round. Getting back on the scope, the deer stopped at about 175 yards. I reset my zero to 100 yards and just pulled up into the white patch on the deer's neck, then sent round two downrange. When the 150-grain .303 British bullet hit, it was like the sound of a sack of wet grain being dropped off a bridge deck onto a freeway. I had taken that buck with a single-shot African rifle designed in the year 1885.

The Uberti Courteney is not a long-range target rifle or even a good sheep rifle in the high country. The design amounts to a high wall single-shot that balances like a dream, and if the shooter is confident enough to shoot a single-shot gun, an excellent choice as a medium-range big game rifle. Actual original Courteneys sell for many thousands if you can even locate one. This rifle is an affordable, classic reproduction of that original firearm and a solid working rifle. **GD**

The author with the first harvest from the .303 British cartridge and the Courteney rifle. This Uberti is a working field rifle.

(left) The author with game photo targets and shooting for real-world performance. (right) The first warmup targets "rock chipping" South Dakota mountain marmots.

PIG-POPPING PISTOL

Long Range in a Small Package with the Lantac 6ARC

› **DAVE MERRILL**

The folks at LANTAC first caught rumor of an exciting new round in development for the AR-15 back in 2018. They were part of a military research project looking for both a new rifle and corresponding intermediate caliber. In January of 2019, they were among a small, select group of companies handpicked to further develop the 6ARC and the rifle to go with it. Hornady, PROOF, and E-Lander were also a large part of this project.

Once they had their base design with Hornady supplying the ammunition, Lantac decided to invest a lot of

research and development on the capabilities of shorter barrels with 6ARC. Because some companies actually do the R&D, Lantac started with an 18-inch barrel with an extremely short gas system, then cut off an inch at a time while tracking ballistic results and capabilities. Once they hit the 15-inch mark, they began chopping off a half inch at a time. In particular, we were told that 14.5 inches was phenomenal in terms of increased range compared to its 5.56 brethren.

But they didn't stop there. Everyone involved was surprised at the

capabilities of the 11.5-inch barrel for its size, so they settled on that for a shorty. Thus, the impetus of this article: what we dub the Lantac 6ARC Pig/People Popper.

DESIGN

For the roots of this stubby 6ARC, Lantac started with their LA-SF15 UTP LAW Pistol and made modifications from there. You get the same receivers, SPADA-ML M-LOK handguard, LAW folder, and ambi controls; you just get a bit more to top it all off.

Our version came bundled with the

300BLK, 5.56, 6ARC, and 7.62N compared.

single-stage, 3.5-pound E-CT1 trigger. This co-branded Timney cassette-type trigger delivers a crisp and light break, especially when using the bottom of the bow.

An 11.5-inch 1:7.5 twist PROOF barrel is the heart of this rifle. Even with this diminutive barrel length, Lantac forgoed the traditional carbine-length gas system and went with a mid-length system for a smooth impulse. This is especially impressive when you consider a mid-length gas system can be finicky to dial in even on a 14.5-inch gun, but Lantac consistently uses longer gas system lengths than tradition dictates.

Aside from the caliber itself, the most innovative component here is Lantac's enhanced bolt carrier.

The Lantac E-BCG for the 6ARC is the most advanced that they've produced to date. Starting with a billet of 8629 steel, the carrier is machined then coated with nickel boron via the diamond NiB polish process for an extremely slick and slippery result. The bolt is Carpenter 158 and magnetically particle inspected, like we'd expect from any quality manufacturer. As with all other Lantac carriers, the 6ARC E-BCG features their domed head cam pin, designed to reduce wear both within the receiver itself as well as the cam-pin track in the carrier itself.

BALLISTICS

The 6ARC is initially available in 103-, 105-, and 108-grain loads. The most effective demonstration of the ballistic capability of the 6ARC is to directly compare the Lantac 11.5 with 108-grain ELD match to the Knight's Armament 20-inch barreled M110 7.62x51mm sniper rifle shooting 175-grain SMK.

Impressively, these two vastly different rifles diverge by no more than about 0.7 mil — and that's at 1,000 yards. You'll also note that when shooting the full kilo, 6ARC has more velocity than 7.62x51mm.

AT THE RANGE

Sometimes a particular combination of ammo, muzzle device, and silencer gave us good results, and other times the opposite; at first, we thought we were dealing with strange barrel harmonics. Ultimately, we found it to be a heat issue. From a cold bore, we'd get sub-MOA groups (just under 0.9 MOA), which would open up to nearly twice that once the barrel was heated over the course of two magazines. Keep in mind that this is a pre-production barrel, and the variation may not be as drastic with production models. Also remember this gun isn't intended for PRS competitions but to replace 5.56mm — even our largest groups were smaller than standard M855/A1.

We tried out several silencers, settling on the Dead Air Sandman-S with a 7.62 flash hider endcap. Not only did it consistently group well, the shift when attaching the silencer was exactly 1 mil low, making for incredibly easy adjustments when popping small targets at range.

We found it simple to engage MOA targets out to 800 yards. After it goes transonic, projectile flight becomes erratic. Still, we got hits on a 12x12-inch plate at 1,000 yards, with the main limiting factor being the center aiming point of the Vortex 1-10x reticle obscuring a target of that size.

This isn't a precision rifle capable of a combat role. This is a combat rifle capable of precision. **GD**

This TESTFIRE is an excerpt from RECOIL Magazine, Issue 51. Learn more at recoilweb.com.

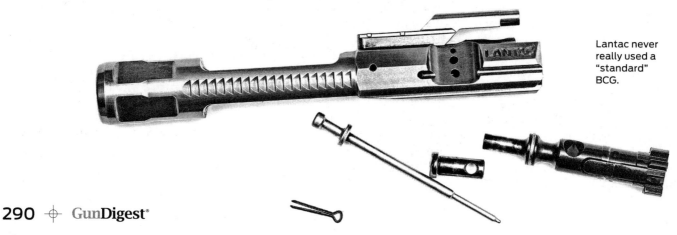

Lantac never really used a "standard" BCG.

A thick cloud of blackpowder smoke hides the author's big smile!

SNUBBY!

Taylor's & Company 1860 Army Snub Nose

› BOB CAMPBELL

Among the most important Colt revolvers is the 1860 Army. That Colt saw action during the Civil War and inflicted a deadly toll. The conflict was a handgun war more than any before or since. Cavalry troops carried two or more revolvers, often as many as six, to stay in the action. Adversaries respected the effect of the .44-caliber ball against men and horses. The soft lead ball deformed when it hit a living target, resulting in a severe wound. Early fixed cartridges were not nearly as effective. Only when we had the .45 Colt were we able to field a revolver as effective as the .44 Army.

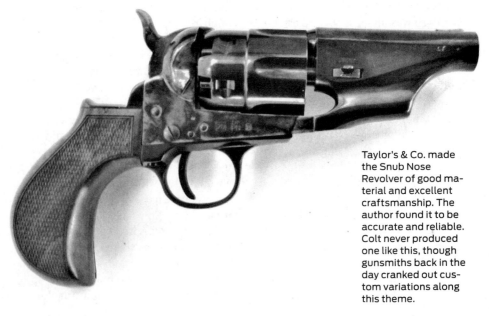

Taylor's & Co. made the Snub Nose Revolver of good material and excellent craftsmanship. The author found it to be accurate and reliable. Colt never produced one like this, though gunsmiths back in the day cranked out custom variations along this theme.

The Taylor's Snub Nose .44 (bottom) compared to the Taylor's & Co. Devil Anse revolver (top).

Among the more exciting conversions was the modification of the Colt 1860 into a snub nose revolver. The original long-barrel revolver was a fine holster gun but not so good when the owner worked in town. Lawmen, barkeeps, and merchants needed a concealable handgun. Small .32- and .38-caliber wheelguns lacked the wound potential necessary to put an attacker down with a minimum of shots. I suspect the older Colts were far less expensive and more readily available than a new Colt Sheriff's Model. Famous gunners carried some of the surviving handguns. Porter Rockwell owned a pair of modified Colt 1860 revolvers with special precision sights. Dallas Stoudenmire was carrying his modified Colt backup the night he was killed. The revolvers were the Fitz Specials of the day. A short-barrel big-bore revolver was a handy thing to have in the voluminous pockets of the day. Worn in a sash, they offered a fast draw. While accuracy may have suffered in the short-barrel version, the Snub Nose 1860 would be a fine defense gun across

the card table or a muddy street with proper sights.

Taylor's & Company has offered quality reproduction revolvers for many years. I have found good results with them as far as quality, fit, and finish. Taylors now offers a new gun based on the Colt 1860 Army. Colt never made this one, but enterprising gunsmiths modded similar ones. The 1860 Army Snub Nose is a beautiful handgun. The steel frame, color casehardening, and blue finish leave little to be desired. The action is tight and crisp, and you can lock the hammer between the percussion nipples for safety.

The Taylor's snubby features a front sight superior to any I have examined on period conversions. The originals used a simple brass screw (if they had a front sight), while some custom guns had a square piece of metal. Others used a half penny fixed in a dovetail. This front sight is lined up with a notch in the hammer as you cock the pistol to fire. It is a fast system and accurate enough for those who practice.

A conversion cylinder is available to

fire .45 Colt cartridges. The conversion cylinder is nicely finished and holds five cartridges. Since Colt built the original 1860 Army on a .36 frame, it could not fit six .45s into the frame window. The 1860 Army Snub Nose features a bird's head grip never offered on the original. I like this grip on several counts; it both looks good and is comfortable when firing this light-kicking revolver.

Since the Taylor's & Company Snub Nose doesn't have a loading ram, the company provides a loading rod for pressing the ball in place. This process isn't difficult, but a special standalone press for loading the cylinder is a neat item for cap and ball enthusiasts. I used a spent .45 ACP cartridge case to load 28 grains of FFG powder and the Speer 148-grain round ball. Be sure the ball gets a good, tight seal. I also run a bit of Crisco over the chamber to prevent chain fires. You cap the cylinder with No. 10 percussion caps. (I fired off six caps to clear the nipples of oil and packing grease before loading.)

Firing this little snubby is a joy. The sound and recoil impulse is different

than smokeless powder. There is plenty of smoke and, yes, that pungent smell. Unlike most cap and ball revolvers, Taylor's properly sighted this handgun for the six o'clock hold at 15 yards. With care in loading, accuracy is excellent. A 15-yard five-shot group of two inches is average. The velocities averaged 703 fps. I am confident I could beef up the charge for more power, but why bother?

The plentiful spent .45 ACP case measures out 28 grains for easy loading, and this is a fun revolver without any need for greater energy. Just the same, more velocity sometimes provides greater accuracy. I fired 30 balls and did not experience any binding or powder fouling.

The five-shot conversion cylinder is well-machined. A cap on the cylinder

TAYLOR'S & CO. 1860 ARMY SNUB NOSE

Barrel Length:	3-in. Round
Caliber:	.44, .36
Capacity:	6
Weight:	2.30 lbs
Finish:	Casehardened frame
Grip/Stock	Checkered walnut
Manufacturer:	Pietta
Sights:	Blade front sight, rear sight notch in the hammer
Overall Length:	9.3 in.
Action Version:	Taylor Tuning Not Available

taylorsfirearms.com

contains five firing pins struck by the hammer as you fire. You must load the cylinder with the barrel removed. Press those round balls into place and replace the barrel. After shooting, remove the cylinder to unload the spent brass. It's not a fast system but an innovation that makes for a more versatile revolver (Taylor's cautions to use standard loads only). Most cowboy action shooting loads average 750 fps, so this isn't a difficult loading to find. I used the Black Hills Ammunition 250-grain .45 Colt load primarily. This powder is a clean-burning load that has proven accurate in all my revolvers. The big bullet clocks 707 fps in the Taylor's short barrel, about 50 fps slower than a full-size wheelgun.

The sound and recoil are much different than the blackpowder cylinder. I very much enjoy blackpowder but like loading and cleaning less. I fired the revolver for accuracy and found that it is pretty accurate for the type — another 2-inch 15-yard effort. But don't think I fired the Snub Nose in static tests. Most action was in snap shooting, quickly bringing the sight to eye level and firing fast. The Snub Nose .45 is a hoot to shoot in such a manner. It fits the hand well, and, like most single-actions, it points naturally. Indeed, it will make a good backup to the SAA .45 I often carry when hiking or traveling. It has the right looks and is undoubtedly one of the fun guns of the new century. GD

(top) The author did much of his test firing offhand. The revolver proved reliable and accurate. (above) The cap and ball cylinder (left) and the ingeniously designed cartridge conversion (right).

RUGER'S .44 MAGNUM CARBINES

›ROBERT SADOOWSKI

The Ruger .44 Magnum Carbine created a legacy of compact and powerful long guns.

Here in the eastern part of North Carolina, about a mile into the Holly Shelter Game Land, one finds a meandering edge of oak trees that abut wetlands. The area is dense with both brush and deer. It is the perfect hunting spot to use a short, powerful, lightweight carbine. "When I'm fixin' to hunt the Ridge," my old-time hunting pal says, "I bring my old Ruger Model 44." He's not alone. I carry something similar. It's an often-overlooked little bolt gun from Ruger, the Model 77/44, also chambered in .44 Remington Magnum.

The .44 Magnum Carbine looks rugged and straightforward — like it is ready for hard hunting. Featuring an 18.5-inch barrel and plain hardwood stock with a curved metal butt plate and barrel band, it is a very traditional-looking carbine.

(top) The .44 Magnum Carbine is a handy and potent gun that offers a fast follow-up shot.

(bottom) Ruger equipped the 44RS variant with a receiver-mounted rear peep sight.

It uses a gas-operated system with a short-stroke piston. What's cool about this carbine is the internal four-shot tubular magazine; it's similar to the magazine tube on a semi-automatic shotgun. The loading port is forward of the trigger guard. You press the lifter latch with a cartridge and push it into the magazine with your thumb. It is a self-contained system with no magazine to drop in snow or tall grass, and it is lightweight at 5.75 pounds — and compact with an overall length of 36.75 inches.

RUGER 96/44

I ran the lever-action 96/44 with open sights at 50 yards. On the 77/44 bolt action, I mounted a scope and tested it at 100 yards.

The .44 Rem. Mag. loads I had on hand consisted of my go-to Black Hills 240-grain JHP, SIG V-Crown 240-grain JHP, and Grizzly Cartridge Company's 300-grain WFNGC (Wide Flat Nose Gas Check). The Grizzly round is a solid, cast lead bullet that uses a gas check. The SIG ammo averaged 199 fps faster than the Black Hills stuff and grouped higher at 50 yards. The Grizzly ammo also had an average increase in muzzle velocity of 214 fps over the Black

Hills load. Serious lead at serious speed.

The rifling twist rate in the two Ruger rifles is 1:20 inches, which stabilizes traditional .44 Mag. bullet weights like 240 grains and long, heavy bullets in the range of 300 to 325 grains. Some models have a 1:30-inch twist rate.

One of the first things you notice about the 96/44's lever throw is that it is much shorter and faster to manipulate than the typical lever action like a Winchester Model 1892 or Marlin 1894. There is no exposed hammer like there is on traditional lever-action rifles and carbines. The hammer is enclosed inside the receiver, making the gun more streamlined, plus there is little chance of debris getting caught in the action.

The 96/44 uses a cocking indicator that can be seen and felt. A small brass indicator pin protrudes from the rear of the receiver, letting you know the rifle is cocked and ready to fire. The lever is casehardened, adding a nice touch to the blued receiver and barrel. The cross-bolt safety button is located just forward of the trigger and can be a bit of a stretch to reach unless you have long fingers.

The plastic magazine is a supersized 10/22-style rotary type that is super easy to load and holds four cartridges. Even the slightly longer 300-grain bullet ammo loaded with ease, and there was plenty of room for the larger bullets

The 77/44 is a traditionally styled hunting rifle with good wood and appointments. The Bushnell PRIME series 1-4x24mm scope uses traditional hunting-style turret covers. Adjustment clicks were positive and precise.

in the magazine. When I pressed the magazine release button, the magazine dropped into the palm of my hand just like a 10/22 mag. Insert the magazine's front edge into the magazine well first and then rotate the rear until it clicks (similar to a 10/22). The 77/44 magazine is not comparable with the 96/44.

The two-stage trigger pull was more than I like at 6.6 pounds. The smallest three-shot group was 0.5 inch. Across all ammo, the 96/44 averaged 1.5-inch groups with open sights. I assume a scope would shrink those groups.

The 96/44 is a fast-shooting rifle with moderate recoil, good accuracy, and slick, fast action. If you see one on the used rack of your dealer, you might want to make an offer like I did.

An average group from the Ruger 77/44. The top hole is from two bullets using Black Hills ammo.

RUGER 77/44

Caliber:	.44 Rem Mag
Capacity:	4
Barrel Length:	18.50 in.
MSRP:	$999
ruger.com	

RUGER 77/44

The 77/44 sports a straight-comb stock of American walnut that is nicely checkered. Blued steel is standard. This model is a traditional bolt-action rifle tweaked to run on a pistol cartridge via a rotary four-round magazine that sits flush with the bottom of the stock.

The bolt is matte gray and has a 90-degree lift, which means the scope's eyepiece is close to the bolt knob when you lift the bolt knob. I could not run the 77/44 as fast as I could the 96/44. I found lifting the bolt with my trigger finger, racking it back with my trigger finger, then pushing forward with my thumb was fast, but I still needed to crank the bolt handle down to close the bolt. The 77/44 could not keep up with the lever-action for quick follow-up shots. The trigger was heavy at 6 pounds but had no creep.

You can easily remove the bolt from the receiver via a small bolt button; simply press it and pull the bolt free. I like the three-position safety, which allowed me to safely unload the 77/44

without removing the magazine when in the middle position. With the safety in the full rearward position, the bolt is locked.

The magazine does not drop free, which is good when in a treestand or the snow. You can also load the mag while inserted in the magazine well as if it were a fixed mag. I loaded single rounds by placing the cartridge on top of the magazine and pushing the bolt forward.

With SIG V-Crown 240-grain JHP, my best three-shot group measured

slightly more than the diameter of the .44 Mag. bullet. With the Black Hills load, groups were somewhat larger. I was driving tacks with the 77/44.

Ruger started building rifles with the .44 Magnum and, over the years, created a legacy of short, handy rifles that are plenty accurate and comfortable to shoot. The 77/44 continues that legacy. **GD**

TABLE 1. RUGER MODEL 96/44

.44 Rem. Mag. Load (grains)	Velocity (fps)	Muzzle Energy (ft-lbs)	Best Accuracy (inches)	Avg. Accuracy (inches)
SIG Sauer V-Crown 240 JHP	1,687	1,517	1.51	1.57
Black Hills 240 JHP	1,330	943	0.99	1.10
Grizzly Cartridge Company 300 WFNGC	1,481	1,461	0.53	0.82

Accuracy measured for best five-shot groups at 25 yards.

TABLE 2. RUGER MODEL 77/44

.44 Rem. Mag. Load (grains)	Velocity (fps)	Muzzle Energy (ft-lbs)	Best Accuracy (inches)	Avg. Accuracy (inches)
SIG Sauer V-Crown 240 JHP	1,669	1,482	0.45	0.48
Black Hills 240 JHP	1,245	924	0.61	0.76
Grizzly Cartridge Company	1,517	1,533	0.94	1.50

Accuracy measured for best five-shot groups at 25 yards.

The Savage Impulse:
Straight to the Point

For the hunter looking for rapid firepower in the field, a straight-pull rifle like the Savage Impulse is hard to beat.

Savage's new straight-pull Impulse brings fast cycling and tack accuracy to American hunters. ❯**PHIL MASSARO**

It was our first day on a late-season safari in Mozambique, and it was getting warm. Glassing the edges of the Zambezi flood plain, we caught sight of a herd of reedbucks, and as a part of the agreement with the local village, Zambeze Delta Safaris provides a half-dozen of the elegant little antelopes to the locals. So we made a plan, put a stalk on the herd, and got within 150 yards. "On the shoulder," commanded Poen van Zyl, my Professional Hunter. He was curt, and I followed his order. I settled the fore-end of the .300 Winchester — this rifle was a Heym SPPR — in the sticks and broke the trigger, putting the ram down immediately, but I quickly and smoothly reloaded the gun. This hunt was one of my first experiences with a straight-pull rifle, but it wouldn't be my last.

The Mauser Gewehr 98 of the late 19th Century pretty well defined the bolt action or turnbolt rifle. Watch almost any shooter pick up a bolt gun, and the first thing they'll do is lift the bolt, then pull it rearward. There's

no issue with a traditional design like the Mauser and its hundreds of clones, but a straight-pull rifle defies the conventional. For those who spend time on European-driven hunts, or any similar situation which requires rapid follow-up shots or presents multiple targets, the straight-pull rifle can be a true blessing. Companies like Blaser, Heym, Merkel, and others popular in the European market have great models, but Savage jumped head-first into the straight-pull rifle market with its Impulse this year.

Savage offers the Impulse in three different versions: Big Game, Predator, and Hog Hunter chambered in 6.5 Creedmoor, .308 Winchester, .30-06 Springfield, and .300 Winchester Magnum. My test rifle was the Hog Hunter in .300 Winnie, with the Savage AccuStock and AccuFit feature, which is customizable for comb height and length of pull, and the excellent AccuTrigger, long proven to be a winner. My Lyman Digital Trigger Scale

SPECIFICATIONS

Model:	Savage Impulse
Barrel Finish:	Matte
Barrel Length:	24 in.
Barrel Material:	Carbon steel
Caliber:	.300 Winchester Magnum
Magazine Capacity:	3
Length of Pull:	13.75 in.
Magazine:	Detachable box magazine
Overall Length:	44.25 in.
Rate of Twist:	1:10 in.
Receiver Material:	Aluminum
Stock Color:	OD green
Weight (unscoped):	9.1 lbs.
MSRP:	$1,379.00
savagearms.com	

showed that the Impulse's trigger broke consistently at 2 pounds, 5 ounces. A detachable magazine of steel and polymer construction sits flush against the bottom of the stock; the magazine for the test rifle holds three magnum

While it may look conventional, all bets are off once you work the action of the Savage Impulse.

cartridges. The rifle uses a barrel nut to set headspacing, and the barrel is free of iron sights, though the muzzle Savage threads it for a brake or suppressor (it comes with a threaded cap). The 24-inch hand-tuned barrel is well-suited to the .300 Winchester Magnum. These features are where the similarities to other Savage models end, and the unique aspects of the Impulse begin.

Instead of using fixed locking lugs as so many traditional bolt-action repeating rifles do, the patented Hexlock system has six retractable ball bearings on the bolt head to lock the action into battery. The ball bearings sit in a recessed channel in the barrel extension and are driven outward upon ignition of the powder charge, making for an exceptionally strong action. A plunger actuated inside the bolt body drives the ball bearings and pushes the bolt forward and into battery; you can only release them by firing the rifle or pressing the button at the back of the bolt. The bolt handle rotates fore and aft, which moves the bolt and cocks the rifle.

Savage has made the Impulse truly ambidextrous. You can switch the bolt handle to either side of the bolt, and it has a centrally located tang safety through the ejection port on the right side of the lightweight aluminum receiver. As a result, it is a very flexible package, down to the integral 20-MOA Picatinny rail on the top of the receiver.

AT THE RANGE

I mounted a Leupold VX-3HD 4.5-14x40mm scope with the CDS-ZL elevation turret in a set of Leupold Backcountry rings, tossed it on the bore sighter, and grabbed some ammo to test the Savage Impulse at the range. First, to measure velocities, I used the trusty Oehler 35P chronograph. Next, I wanted a selection of ammo brands and bullet weights, so I chose Federal's Fusion 165-grain load, the Norma American PH load with the 180-grain Oryx bullet, the Nosler Trophy Grade 190-grain AccuBond Long Range ammo, and the Federal Terminal Ascent 200-grain load. I zeroed the rifle in four shots and set to work printing three-shot groups on the 100-yard target.

I noticed the felt recoil first; between the AccuFit stock and 9.6-pound weight fully dressed, it felt more like a .30-'06, even from the seated position with the rifle on sandbags. I've long been a fan of the AccuTrigger, and it didn't fail to please on this range day. Like many .300 Magnums, the Impulse showed a preference for the longer, heavier bullets, yet even the shorter 165-grain Fusions gave acceptable hunting accuracy, putting three shots into groups averaging 1 MOA. The best of the lot — Federal's Terminal Ascent — ran at just over ½ inch at 100 yards, with the Nosler 190 ABLRs printing a bit wider. The 180-grain Norma Oryx, a vastly underrated bullet, put three shots on the target in just over a ¾-inch group. Velocities measured were well within the range of any deviation I've seen from a rifle using factory loads

The aluminum receiver and bolt of the Impulse; note the rotating bolt handle, tang safety, and bolt-release button at the bolt's rear.

spend most of your time stalking or sitting on a stand waiting to fill a single tag, the Impulse and its ilk may not present an advantage to you. On the other hand, if you routinely pursue feral hogs, coyotes, and other species that may offer multiple targets requiring rapid shooting, the Impulse might be your baby. Simply put, there is no other rifle of this style, of this quality, at this price point. The useable features Savage stuffed into this rifle warrant any shooter's attention, as you'll struggle to find its equal among American-made production rifles. Like the entire Savage line, it is an accurate rifle. It's packed full of very useable features to the average shooter — possibly to the point where the

The Impulse bolt head. Note the ball bearings in a radial pattern that locks the action.

and were consistent. The Impulse is a shooter. I had no issues with feeding or extraction during my range time and would happily take this rifle on any hunt suitable for a .300 Winchester Magnum.

WHY STRAIGHT PULL?

The conventional turnbolt rifle has worked perfectly, so why should you make the switch to a straight-pull rifle? The short answer is rapid firepower. Gaining popularity among European-driven hunters, where the possibility of multiple running targets is a reality, only autoloading rifles surpass the rate of fire of the straight pull, possibly only equaled by lever guns. Unfortunately, in many of those European countries, semi-autos aren't legal. Also, except for the Browning BLR, most lever guns can't handle high-pressure cartridges like the .30-'06 Springfield and .300 Winchester Magnum.

The Savage Impulse allows you to keep the rifle butt on your shoulder and remain focused on the target during a reload. But, unlike turnbolts, your cycling hand doesn't come into your field of view. Instead, it remains at the end of the bolt and below your line of sight — even with irons. If you've spent decades with a traditional-style

The Leupold VX-3HD on the Impulse's 20-MOA Picatinny rail gives all sorts of long-range flexibility.

turnbolt, you may find the transition to a straight-pull rifle a difficult one, but for a new shooter, the learning process is simple. In the time I've spent with a straight-pull, I've found it becomes second nature in a day's hunting. However, I'll admit that I inadvertently tried to lift the bolt handle at the shooting bench when concentrating on the shot. Old habits die hard.

If you hunt deer, elk, or bear and

shooting public has taken this level of performance for granted.

The Savage Impulse line offers fantastic accuracy and incredibly rapid follow-up shots in a package you can customize at a fraction of the cost of comparable models. The design may seem foreign to many shooters here in the U.S., but I have a strong feeling the Impulse will be around for quite some time. **GD**

TABLE 1. SAVAGE IMPULSE .300 WINCHESTER MAGNUM

Load/bullet (grains)	Avg. Group Size (in.)	Avg. Velocity (fps)
Federal Fusion 165	1.07	3,112
Norma American PH 180 Oryx	0.77	2,915
Nosler Trophy Grade 190 AccuBond Long Range	0.81	2,885
Federal Terminal Ascent 200	0.56	2,796

The author used an Oehler 35P Chronograph 15 feet from the muzzle to record velocities. 100-yard three-shot groups.

The author's Winchester Model 70 Safari Express .375 H&H with a few essentials.

The Winchester Model 70 Safari Express in .375 Holland & Holland

› JAY LEYENDECKER

The old man asked the boy, "Now explain to me, why exactly do you need a .375 Holland & Holland?"

"Because it is the single most versatile caliber ever created. It can easily handle hogs here in south Texas or duiker in Africa all the way up to elephant. I plan on being involved in Africa for many years to come, and it is the base rifle I would need to proceed in that direction," said the boy.

"Is there a brand or model you would want?" asked the old man.

"Yes, I would want a Model 70 Safari Express made by Winchester."

"Why is that?"

"Well, primarily due to the claw extraction. It ensures that from pick-up to release the cartridge will enter the chamber or be expelled from it. In other words, I won't short stroke it when in a potentially dangerous situation."

The old man thought and was silent for a second or two and said, "Well, young man, it sounds like you've done your research, and I don't see you dropping this Africa stuff anytime soon. I think this could be a good investment for you, but I'd like to buy it for you. You just have to make me

(top) Troy Calaway with a massive Kalahari Desert eland bull he took in Botswana. The eland was quartering hard away but was downed to a single .375 H&H 300-gr. Triple Shock after a grueling tracking job.
(above) An old buffalo taken in thick mopane scrub with the .375 H&H.

one promise."

Puzzled and wide-eyed, the boy asked, "Yes, sir?"

"For now," said that old man, grinning from ear to ear, "don't tell your grandmother."

That boy was me, and that rifle changed my life.

It remained our little secret and marked the beginning of my decades-long journey with the Winchester Model 70 .375 Holland & Holland Magnum. My late grandfather, Frank Leyendecker, purchased the rifle brand spanking new in 2000 for $600, just after my second jump across the pond to the African continent. Earlier that same year, I spent some time with my uncle and seasoned African hunter Evan Quiroz. He just about forced me to borrow a .375 H&H Sako that he had and made sure it was in my gun case before my departure. "It's the finest all-

around African cartridge invented," he said. "It's perfect cat medicine, buffalo too, when you need to thread the shot through brush or he's a little too far out for the irons. It's also good on elephant if you know what you're doing."

I vividly remember studying the ballistics charts on the rifle and the various bullet weights available. I had settled on the combination of 300-grain Federal Trophy Bonded Bear Claw soft points and Sledgehammer solids. The holdover was easy to remember; if you sight it three inches high at 100 yards, you will hit dead-on at 200 yards and 12 inches low at 300 — a piece of cake.

The .375 Holland & Holland Magnum was born in London in 1912. Originally, H&H designed the belted cartridge for use with cordite, and in turn, the case has a soft 15-degree shoulder, ensuring a smooth feed and extraction. The 300-grain Federal Trophy Bonded Bear

chance of an accidental short stroke (and resulting jam) by capturing the cartridge's rim as you feed it upward from the magazine. That helps control the cartridge into the rifle's chamber.

With a properly placed shot, the rifle can take the largest game animals: the African elephant. But, as with any cartridge and rifle combination, shot placement reigns supreme. The rifle's effectiveness is never really the question, but one's capability is the wild

(left) A big zebra stallion the author took with the Model 70.

(below) A mature whitetail buck the author took with the Model 70 Safari Express. Yes, you can use the .375 H&H Magnum for whitetails!

Claws generate just over 4,300 ft-lbs of energy, with a muzzle velocity of about 2,500 fps. It's not a heavyweight stopper, but it is one of the most useful cartridges on the planet.

The Winchester Model 70 Safari Express is a bolt-action rifle designed for the rough and tumble use one would expect of a dangerous game gun. It comes with a fixed magazine, and will hold one in the pipe and three down below. The stout American walnut stock has a pliable Pachmayer Decelerator Pad and is all one would need for the already mild recoil of the .375 H&H. There are two glass-bedded recoil lugs. The rearmost lug is machined into the front of the receiver and the second just four inches ahead of the receiver, and they do an excellent job of keeping the walnut stock in one piece. It has simple yet effective iron sights; this system is straightforward to use and rock-solid. The front sight is hooded, but you can easily remove the hood. Having the open-sighted option gives you the comfort of having a scoped rifle or making the trade and going with the open sights.

I've saved the best for last: the bolt. The bolt is the primary reason the rifle is so popular amongst dangerous game enthusiasts; it's based on the ultra-strong pre-'64 Mauser-style claw extractor. The claw extraction and controlled-round feed minimize the

card. Knowing your limitations is the key that determines wild success or gut-wrenching heartache.

My first hunt with the rifle was in the mountain country of South Africa. The landowner had asked me if I would cull a couple of zebras for him. Of course, I very gladly and willingly obliged. So, after a bumpy trek up a rough road, I took off on foot with a tracker. He believed the zebras were in the bowl of the mountain we were about to scale.

We crested a ridge and immediately spotted a herd of a dozen zebras across a mountainside, and they were in range. I determined the second from the right was the stallion, as its composition was much more masculine than the others, and I knew I could make the 300-yard shot. I found a semi-awkward position to take a rest, snuggled up next to a massive boulder with a crook in it, which perfectly fit my backpack for a rest. I placed the crosshairs just short of the stud's back and squeezed the trigger.

The zebra dropped to the shot and never moved again.

Another memorable experience with that rifle was in deep-South Texas with my good friend CJ Sibert on a water buffalo hunt. We heard about a particularly cantankerous bull that resided on this massive property, which had chased around border patrol agents, oil field employees, and ranch staff on various occasions. On top of its bad attitude, it was massive. There was no time to wait as the buffalo became more of a liability to the landowner. So, we made a plan.

We set off with my two most trustworthy rifles: CJ carrying my Model 70 .375 H&H and me with my CZ550 .500 Jeffery in pursuit of the bruiser buff. We would catch only glimpses before it moved off; we got on the sticks only once, but it didn't give us any time for the shot. Then on a scorching afternoon, I decided to go out and check a couple of the water sources.

The buffalo fed on a creek's edge along the cattails.

We disembarked the hunting truck, and I immediately checked the wind. We arrived at a giant mesquite tree I was steering for and found ourselves less than a hundred yards from the buffalo. At the last moment, it caught movement from our hunting party. However, CJ had the rifle up and the safety off. The buffalo shifted position just as he broke the trigger. CJ is an old hand in dangerous game hunting and put three more rounds into the buffalo before it thundered into the dense mix of mesquite, prickly pear cactus, and black brush thicket. From that moment, we took it slow, very slow. We had an animal weighing over one ton, known for its aggressive nature, potentially still alive in vegetation with less than five-foot visibility.

We went back to the truck to rehydrate and prepared for a track in the mid-day sun. Soon after the hunt

CJ Sibert with the .375, and the author with the big .500 Jeffery. The hunters stopped this formidable water buffalo with mere feet to spare.

any large-bodied animals weighing 300 pounds or more, I can guarantee the Winchester Model 70 will be with me. It has served me well over the last twenty years of international big game hunting, and it has long been a bridge between my grandfather and me. It will always be a treasure to me, not just because of the experiences I have enjoyed with it throughout the world, but how it came to be. **GD**

(left) The author aims with the two-decades-old .375 H&H Model 70 Safari Express.

(below) The author's grandfather Frank Leyendecker and the author's first kudu taken with the Model 70 Safari Express.

resumed, I picked up spoor. Suddenly, at 25 paces directly in front of us, we could see a black mass in the white brush beneath an ancient mesquite tree. We moved slowly; then the other bulls stood up, but still, we couldn't make out which was which. I took a baby step forward, and then it came — it sounded as though we had just unleashed a freight train without brakes. I shifted, spun left, and placed the ivory bead between the whites of its eyes, and fired. CJ and Rod followed suit. The buff didn't slow down. I chambered a second round and, at mere feet, pulled the trigger, striking it a second time in the head with a 570-grain Barnes Banded Solid. That turned the buff, but I had to jump back to avoid getting run over. Rod placed a .30-30 round just above the beast's right eye as it crashed past us. And then it was gone.

We reloaded, sure that if it came once, it would do it again. We took up tracks, found it bedded in less than 50 yards. The defiant bull faced us and tried to get up yet again. CJ delivered the *coup de grâce* with the Winchester .375 H&H.

That rifle has since traveled with me and has become a staple in my arsenal. I have made long-range pokes with it, threaded shots through tight vegetation, and even used it to defend my life. It's taken African animals ranging from steenbok to hippo and dozens of species in between. When guiding hunters for

› SHANE JAHN

TYLER GUN WORKS RUGER NO. 5

Two classics, the Tyler Gun Works Ruger #5 and Barranti Longhorn Companion holster.

I n 1928, a young bronc-riding six-gunner who would become a gun writing legend, Elmer Keith, sought out the skills of three gunsmiths named Houchins, O'Meara, and Sedgley to customize a Colt Single Action Army (SAA) revolver. Keith was an experimenter who wore a revolver as casually as he wore his big hat. Incorporating some ideas from Harold Croft's designs on previous revolvers, they transformed what many consider an ideal revolver into a work of art and pure handgun genius.

A watered-down description of the main alterations married the Colt with a Bisley backstrap and an SAA frontstrap, forming a unique grip in both purpose and appearance. Adjustable rear and front sights allowed for various loads to be fine-tuned to the preferred point of impact, and modifying the grip gave the revolver a functional and unique look. To those devoted to the revolver, Keith's "Number Five" is one of the most recognizable handguns ever made. The numbered nomenclature of "five" is since Croft had numbered four previously modified revolvers one through four. Keith incorporated his ideas into the full-size gun and branded it "#5," and that was what he considered to be "the last word." Keith chambered his #5 in .44 Special. His earlier

experiments with heavy loads had shown him the cylinder wall of the .45 Colt SAA was too thin for the pressures he was forcing upon those old handguns, so he went with the smaller caliber, hence thicker cylinder wall, for his pet gun.

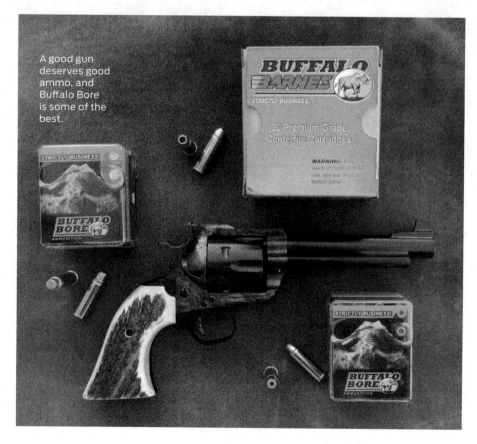

Elmer Keith's #5. Photo provided by John Taffin from John Taffin's *Book of the .44*.

THE .41 MAGNUM IDEA

Keith promoted the .41 Remington Magnum, but he wasn't alone. Bill Jordan of U.S. Border Patrol fame and esteemed lawman and gun writer Skeeter Skelton also evangelized it. Touted as something in between the 1956-designed .44 Remington Magnum and 1935's .357 Magnum, Remington marketed the .41 Mag. as an optimal round for law enforcement. With a recommended recoil-managing round of a 210-grain bullet at 950 to 1,000 fps, it filled the gap between the puny .38 Special loads of that time, which cops largely carried, and hot .44 Magnum rounds that caused shooters to flinch, convulse, and cuss, and which were far too ambitious for law enforcement use.

Unintentionally, the .41 Magnum and Smith & Wesson N-Frame combination were too heavy for some cops to carry for an entire shift, and even the "police" load was too much for the recoil-sensitive.

A CARTRIDGE FOR THE HANDGUNNER

While it faded from much of law enforcement, the .41 Magnum caught the eye of astute handgun hunters. Keith took the first game with the .41 Rem. Mag. when he shot a couple of caribou to supply fresh meat to a hungry Eskimo family while he was on a polar bear hunt. In the story, reprinted in *Gun Notes Volume II*, Keith recounts how flat the .41 shot when compared to his beloved .44 Magnum and — on the 11th shot — killed one at a range many of us could not make with a scope-sighted rifle! Heck, he *started* shooting farther than some folks should be shooting with a rifle, but that was Elmer Keith, and he could do it.

Legendary gun writer John Wootters described the .41 Magnum in an article titled *Big Iron…for Whitetails*. When comparing the .41 and .44 Magnums, he wrote, "I've found nothing it (.44 Remington Magnum) can do that the .41 Magnum can't do just as well, with less fuss and commotion." I do not mean to get the cartridge debate going around the proverbial campfire. It is simply to say that the .41 Remington Magnum is a relevant round. Although to be fair, Wootters lauds the old .45 Colt above both of them!

SELECTING THE .41 REMINGTON MAGNUM

The .41 Remington Magnum might not be the "cool" round of the day, but apparently, it works. There is something about the not-so-mainstream cartridge that draws me to it — dressed in its hunting clothes, the Big .41 can come out of the chute smokin' with factory loads at 1,350 to 1,650 fps!

I got a hankering for a good revolver chambered in the .41 Mag. a while back and came across a like-new pinned and recessed Smith & Wesson Model 57 with a four-inch barrel. A few months later, I bought a very slightly used, Old Model, three-screw Ruger Blackhawk.

A good gun deserves good ammo, and Buffalo Bore is some of the best.

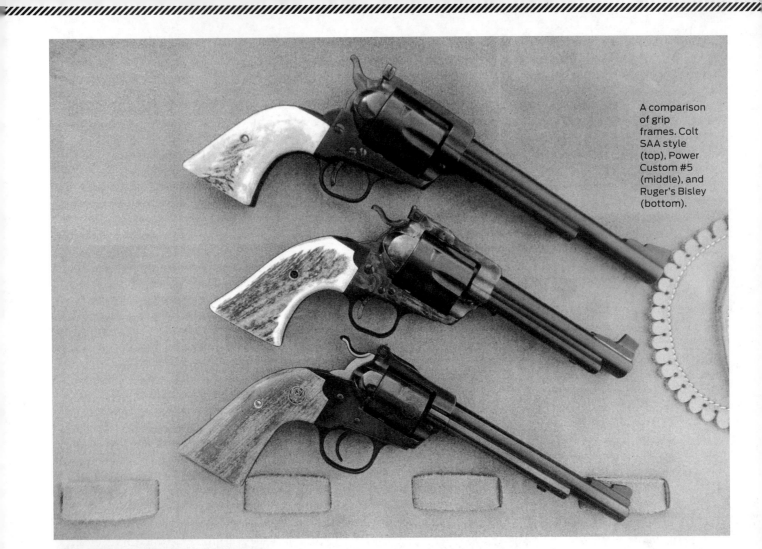

A comparison of grip frames. Colt SAA style (top), Power Custom #5 (middle), and Ruger's Bisley (bottom).

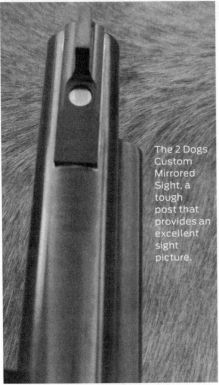

The 2 Dogs Custom Mirrored Sight, a tough post that provides an excellent sight picture.

This good sixgun would have been fine as-is, but I had other plans. I could see this gun transformed into a Keith-style #5 and quickly shipped it to Bobby Tyler.

Located on the high Texas plains once roamed by fierce Comanche warriors near Friona, Tyler Gun Works (TGW) offers custom work and finishes that are truly functioning works of art. Bobby and his crew turn out color-case finishes and bluing that are stunning, and they are good folks to boot.

THE RUGER GETS THE WORKS

The specifications I provided Bobby were to replace the original grip of the Ruger with a Power Custom Keith #5 grip frame and Bisley hammer. TGW cut the factory 6.5-inch barrel to 5.5 inches. That's the length of Elmer Keith's #5 and is an excellent choice for a field gun, combining the best of both

worlds for portability and shoot-ability. The TGW boys also did a superb job of crowning the shortened barrel.

For the front sight, TGW installed a 2 Dogs Custom Mirrored Sight. Sheriff Jim Wilson has an original King Mirror-Ramp sight on his Skeeter Skelton Special, and I have always admired it, so having a similar sight on my gun adds a little extra nostalgia.

Bowen Classic Arms has been turning out fine custom guns for decades, and its Rough Country rear sight finished out the aiming portion of my semi-custom sixgun.

I asked for a Belt Mountain #5-style base pin to replace the original and action tuning with a crisp trigger pull around two pounds. TGW did so and set the cylinder gap at 0.0025 inch. We were going to add a steel ejector rod, but none were available.

Looking at the Tyler Gun Works

website left me with a couple of dilemmas. Did I want the gun finished in one of the exquisite bluing options or add a bit of the color casehardening for which it is famous? Then there were the stocks. I have a Ruger Flattop Tyler Gun Works gun stocked in stag. Stag not only looks good, but it is also tough. But then, the dark, figured walnut stocks sure dress up a fine sixgun. When I originally ordered the gun, I was on the fence and wanted to discuss the options as we neared completion. Bobby called me when the time came, and I settled on stag stocks and color-cased frame, hammer, and trigger.

"WHERE PRETTY MEETS PERFORMANCE"

Finally, after months of waiting, the revolver I received in the mail was nothing less than spectacular! The stout sixgun looks and performs great in fit, finish, and function. TGW tuned the action to perfection, and the crisp trigger breaks cleanly at two pounds. The color casehardening of the frame, hammer, and trigger emit a "custom firearms look." The bluing is uniform. The stag stocks perfectly fit the grip frame, and this set has some nice bark on them. The base of the stocks is flat, even with the bottom of the grip frame.

AMMO, TEST FIRE, AND FUNCTION

Buffalo Bore produces quality ammunition and is one of the brands I purchase out of my pocket for my guns and serious use. It offers various good loads and bullets and provides shooters with loadings at the upper end of the power spectrum. For example, I ordered three different loads for my .41: The Heavy .41 Magnum Outdoorsman uses a 230-grain hardcast SWC Keith bullet at 1,450 fps, followed by a 180-grain Barnes XPB at 1,550 fps, and lastly, the 170-grain JHP at 1,650 fps. All are named "Heavy" for a reason! I shot the revolver at 25 yards from a sandbag rest, and the best group came from the 170-grain JHP load measuring 2.38 inches.

The #5 grip frame performed just as I had hoped it would. The shape of the grip gives excellent control of the revolver and distributes recoil into the hand, and makes it very manageable. I gambled choosing that grip frame since I had never actually handled a gun in that configuration. I had only seen pictures of Keith's gun, other customs, and the long out-of-production Improved Number Fives that the late Bill Grover of Texas Longhorn Arms once made. The verdict? It feels good in my hand, offering a full grip. There is no need to curl my little finger under the grip base as I do on traditional single actions. (I have a medium-sized paw, a big-handed shooter likely would have to drop their pinky.) It is similar in feel and appearance to Ruger's Bisley grip frame. The only difference I can see is the #5 flares more towards the base, and the Ruger Bisley grip is longer.

The 2 Dogs Custom Mirrored front sight provides a perfect sight picture with that big, bold Patridge-style post clearly against the target.

The #5 grip fits the hand, and the big revolver balances perfectly with the 5.5-inch barrel.

The Tyler Gun Works #5 Ruger, the author's new favorite.

CUSTOM HANDGUN HIDE

A good gun deserves a good holster, and when you buy one, get the best. Mike "Doc" Barranti is the builder of fine, quality leather gear. His holsters are second to none and will hold up to hard use. On top of all that, Doc is one heck of an artist when carving on leather. I wanted a holster that would carry this revolver high on my waist, preventing the barrel from hitting the ground when you sit. The Longhorn Companion does just that and allows you to wear the gun crossdraw. Doc recreated this holster from one Bill Grover initially designed. Another neat function is that you can remove the holster from the belt slide by simply unsnapping the strap, so you don't have to unbuckle your belt.

A NEW FAVORITE

My adventures have just begun with this revolver. In the coming days and weeks, I will be wearing it while hunting aoudad in the rugged mountains of the Big Bend. I will keep it stoked with Buffalo Bore and, if I can get close enough to an old ram, I will hopefully do what few have done. It is challenging to get within open-sight pistol range on free-range aoudads

in this country. Also, I have already made plans for next fall with hopes of taking a big whitetail and maybe even a pronghorn buck with it. The Tyler Gun Works Ruger #5 in .41 Remington Magnum is sure to become one of my favorite handguns. I'm confident Ol' Elmer would approve! GD

Tyler Gun Works, tylergunworks.com
Fermin C. Garza-Customized Shooter's Resources, fermincgarza.com
Grand Masters LLC, powercustom.com
Bowen Classic Arms, bowenclassicarms.com
Barranti Leather Co. LLC, barrantileather.com
Buffalo Bore Ammunition, buffalobore.com
John Wooters, johnwootters.com

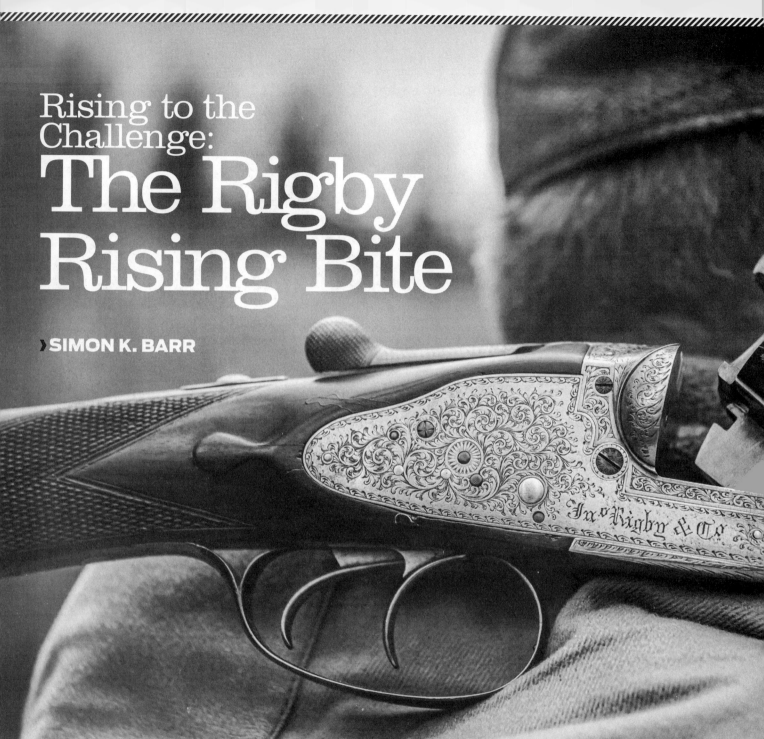

Rising to the Challenge: The Rigby Rising Bite

> **SIMON K. BARR**

Photos by Tweed Media

When you open your gun slip at the start of a day's shooting, it produces a visceral response for anyone with a remote passion for firearms. That smell of gun oil and anticipation of the day ahead conspire to excite. But, when you pull out a gun that hunters have used across three centuries, when you feel that familiar heft and weight, the cold metal with engraving that is faint from much handling, the slight edge of the hairline crack, and feel the ease with which it opens, the emotion is more than excitement, more than just anticipation of the sport that lies ahead.

I'm talking about a gun I don't even own (though, for the avoidance of confusion, I will call it "mine" throughout!), and as I write, flashes of some of my favorite experiences creep into my head.

The gun I'm writing about, the gun that means the most to me is a Rigby Rising Bite shotgun. Built in 1896, it belongs to the Rigby Museum. It was, according to the records, sold to Edward Carter Esq. on 20 August 1896. The description says "Best top lever ejector hammerless vertical bolt," which is better known as the Rigby Rising Bite. The book states its weight at 6 lb. 9 oz., with 30-inch steel barrels and a

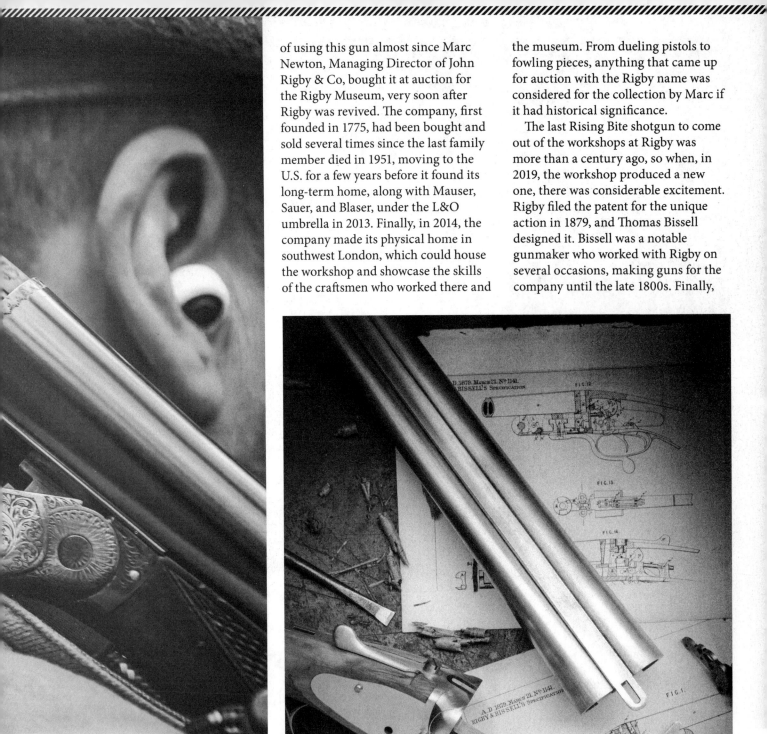

of using this gun almost since Marc Newton, Managing Director of John Rigby & Co, bought it at auction for the Rigby Museum, very soon after Rigby was revived. The company, first founded in 1775, had been bought and sold several times since the last family member died in 1951, moving to the U.S. for a few years before it found its long-term home, along with Mauser, Sauer, and Blaser, under the L&O umbrella in 2013. Finally, in 2014, the company made its physical home in southwest London, which could house the workshop and showcase the skills of the craftsmen who worked there and

the museum. From dueling pistols to fowling pieces, anything that came up for auction with the Rigby name was considered for the collection by Marc if it had historical significance.

The last Rising Bite shotgun to come out of the workshops at Rigby was more than a century ago, so when, in 2019, the workshop produced a new one, there was considerable excitement. Rigby filed the patent for the unique action in 1879, and Thomas Bissell designed it. Bissell was a notable gunmaker who worked with Rigby on several occasions, making guns for the company until the late 1800s. Finally,

stock length of 14 9/16 inches. Today, it is by no means perfect — resleeved with nitro-proof 28-inch barrels, it has a hairline crack on the pistol grip. The engraving is worn, the chequering is soft from handling, and the gun is not a particularly good fit for me, with its low rib and my eye dominance issues. Yet this gun has come to be my favorite companion in the field.

I've had the privilege and pleasure

third "bite." This engineering not only provides the gun with strength but adds an element of attraction: much like seeing the workings of a watch action or an engine, the combination of form and function is hugely pleasing.

The original bar action lock-plate has dipped edges. However, they do not serve any specific purpose. Another element is inherently recognizable as a Rigby feature — and of course, it carries over to the new shotgun.

There are machined components that use modern production methods in the new version, but this is not surprising: modern machinery has become increasingly sophisticated. Most guns today are made using only machinery. Still, Rigby uses machinery to produce fine tolerances and then finishes everything by hand, giving that traditional feel to the gun.

Like mine, the finishing is stunning and less worn: color casehardening, carved leaf fence actions, and scroll engraving. I have tried the modern version of "my" gun: it is lovely to use. Though, of course, it had none of the friendly worn-in feel that mine does, nor was it any better fitted, but there was no doubt whatsoever that it was a descendant and that it shot like one, too.

Back to my gun, however — no matter how stunning the new version is, at a price tag of £79,000 *(Editor's note: as of this writing this equates to*

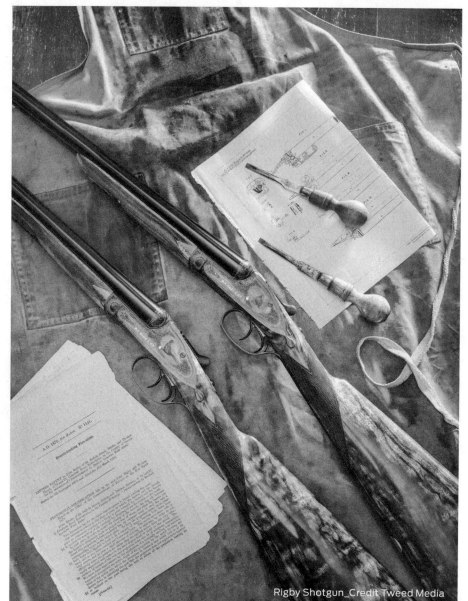

Rigby Shotgun_Credit Tweed Media

two years in the making, Nick Coggan, Rigby's "Rising Bite Executive," built the first pair of Rising Bite shotguns. With more than 30 years' experience, Nick started working in the gunmaking trade when he was 16 years old. He was passionate about antique arms and militaria, and horology, making him the perfect person to take on this unusual engineering challenge.

Working from the dimensions of the shotgun I so love, it was clear that a traditional Purdey patent double under-bolt holds the barrels on the face from below, using bites in the two lumps. Its unique vertical bolt rises from the top of the action and locks into a "bite" in an extension of the top rib, giving a

US$111,500) plus VAT, I'm unlikely to buy one any time soon. So would I buy a vintage one if it came up at auction? Possibly, but it still wouldn't be the same as mine, which I now know so well.

I never use this gun for high-driven birds. With its short barrels and vintage action, a full day of high-driven game with modern cartridges and propellants might be too much for the old girl, nor would it make the best of my shooting. However, this piece is the perfect gun for grouse and partridge, where you can use a lighter cartridge, where a shorter barrel means faster swing, where carrying extra weight can hamper you during a long day's hunt on foot if walking-up game.

Several times I have been lucky enough to borrow this gun from the museum, I've attempted a Macnab — a uniquely British challenge, born from a novel named John Macnab, written in 1925 by John Buchan. This event has become part of sporting legend. The challenge is to shoot a stag, a brace (pair) of red grouse, and catch a salmon on the fly, all in a day. I have made 11 attempts, every one a physically and mentally grueling experience, almost always an emotional rollercoaster, and always a learning experience. While some might question my sanity — "Insanity is doing the same thing over and over again and expecting a different outcome" — each failed attempt only renewed my focus and determination.

Perhaps to show that I wasn't insane, I did, a few years ago, try to change what I was doing. Traditionally, the Macnab participant starts trying to land the fish, as anyone who has cast a fly at a salmon knows, it is the most unpredictable element. So, a few years ago, I thought I'd start with arguably the easiest part, the stag. I managed to find and shoot a stag by mid-morning and, pausing only to switch from a rifle (a Rigby Highland stalker, of course) to my Rising Bite shotgun, and we set off to the top of a Munro (the Scottish term for a mountain, which must be more than 3,000 feet).

All this was on Auch, which is an unusual estate in Argyll, on the west coast of Scotland, where, while there are not huge numbers of grouse, there are decent numbers of ptarmigan, also part of the grouse family. So, rather than the usual red grouse, I'd attempt to shoot a brace of these beautiful birds found only above 2,000 feet. We hauled ourselves to the top of the highest hill (Scottish term for any mountain). As we summited, thinking we'd now be able to walk up a few birds, we flushed a covey of at least 30. I thought that was my chance blown, but we had to keep trying. Walking for several hours, I didn't think I stood a chance, but just as we started to head downhill, a brace

got up, and I managed a right-and-left on them. Not many shotguns would be light enough for walking up and down hills like this, but the Rising Bite is the perfect piece for the job.

By now, it was early afternoon, and we rushed back down the hill, found a beat on a river, but to no avail. No fish was forthcoming.

This year, despite all the Covid complications, I've been lucky enough to enjoy a few special days of shooting: grouse on the Lammermuirs, partridge in the Ettrick Valley, and, amazingly, another Macnab attempt in September in Caithness. The water conditions on the Thurso were appalling, with no rainfall to speak of since July, but there were fish. The fish, however, were bored of being teased with flies and seemingly uninterested in any activity at all. Day one saw me start early, knowing I had until midday to land one to allow enough time for the stag and grouse. Six hours later, I felt exhausted. I'd not paused for the entire time and had not a bite to show for my efforts. I gave up, rested, and resolved to try the next day.

We headed to lower pools, nearer the sea the following day, and, with the pools bubbling with activity, I felt hopeful. To my amazement and delight, just 20 minutes later, I had a salmon on my line. Four seconds later, I'd lost it.

Rage and hopeless despair brought up language to make a sailor blush, and I stamped and swore, showing a complete lack of sportsmanship. The ghillie, Jim Cameron, gave me a talking to, told me to compose myself, and move along the river. Mind overcame madness, and I calmed myself. And lo and behold, I landed a cock grilse of 4 lb.

There is, in the Macnab, no time to celebrate each element, so we raced to attempt the grouse. Here, I was lucky. We had a lovely and experienced English setter at our disposal, which made finding the birds so much easier than just walking them up. After just half an hour, the setter went on point and, on command, flushed a covey. The

Rising Bite went to my shoulder and, while nerves hampered my mount, I managed to shoot the first bird but missed a second. Luckily for us, the setter found us another covey, and this time I was settled, and the gun lifted smoothly, and I had my second. Yet again, my comfort and ease with the Rising Bite had paid off. After a few hours of stalking and a nerve-filled 90-minute prone position wait for the stag to stand, I shot. After ten unsuccessful attempts, I'd finally done it.

I'm so glad that it was the Rising Bite that I used. Sure, an over-and-under might be more efficient, more certain, and more manageable, but I feel that I have now added to the Rising Bite's story. I don't know if it ever took part in a Macnab before my numerous attempts. I have on many an occasion wished it was mine, truly mine. But these thoughts are soon banished; what a privilege to add to its history, to know that this lovely gun will remain part of the Rigby story and the museum.

It is a proper credit to the Rigby gunmakers of the late 19th Century that this gun is still functioning perfectly, well into the 21st Century. In the same year in which Rigby built this gun, Buffalo Bill founded the city of Cody. The first car ever was driven on the streets of Detroit, and Queen Victoria surpassed her great grandfather, King George III, as the longest-serving British Monarch. Since then, we have experienced two world wars, a man on the moon and the advent of the Internet. But this trusty old Rigby shotgun is still doing what Rigby designed it for. So, in my own little way, I hope I have added a little to the story of this fine vintage gun, and I'll always be grateful for the opportunity to have enjoyed it so. **GD**

The REMINGTON Model
710

The author took this excellent Alaskan caribou bull with his trusty Remington Model 710.

›TYLER FREEL

I paused, in somewhat of a daze, to wipe the blood running down my nose. Finally the bull moose at my feet gave its final kicks. It was my first bull moose and first big game animal, whose 60-inch antlers I have yet to best. In my excitement, the scope of my .30-'06 had notched the bridge of my nose. Like a rite of passage, that wound and rifle marked the first steps down a long path that has taken me places to which I could have only dreamed.

In the summer of 2001, I had one goal: to buy my first real hunting rifle. Like many young fellows, my first was a Ruger 10/22, which someone had stuck behind the Christmas tree the year before. That gun was certainly special, but I needed a big game rifle. Growing up in Colorado, I was obsessed with hunting, but we had meager means and even less time to hunt during the state's short rifle seasons. In my childhood, we primarily bowhunted and called coyotes in the winter, but I

The author's first big game rifle, the Model 710, is a budget rifle that brought home the venison.

longed for more. I knew I would have to save for my rifle, so I devoured every hunting magazine I could get my hands on, paying particular attention to each review and advertisement. It so happened that in that year, Remington released its model 710. So again, I studied reviews, revisiting each crinkled manuscript multiple times, and decided that it was the one I would buy.

It may purely be my perception, but the Remington 710 was the first "economy" model rifle that I ever remember seeing. It seems commonplace now, and each brand has its affordable models. I remember reading intently about the rifle's features that not only made it a dead-nuts shooter but also saved costs compared to the much more expensive Model 700. The recoil lug's design and the 3-lug bolt (which locked into the barrel) allowed a lightweight receiver with a nylon inner sleeve as the bearing surface with the bolt. This design would ensure a tight fit and virtually zero wear. The rifle came as a package with a Bushnell scope and was priced right at $350, very attainable for a kid working potato fields part-time all summer like me.

When the first one showed up in our local store's turnstile display, it was a rotisserie of dreams that I made sure to inspect during every trip to the store. Although Remington offered the 710 in .270 Win. and .30-'06, I wanted the '06. The only debate in my mind was between it and a particularly handsome stainless Ruger .25-'06.

The Remington Model 710 was also the catalyst to start me into handloading. At the time, I didn't realize or appreciate how meager my farmwork earnings were, and even at the prices back then, I couldn't afford much ammo. So I ordered a Lee Classic Loading Kit for about $20 and bought a box of 180-grain Nosler bullets, some primers, and a pound of IMR 4350. My dad had used a Lee Loader as a teenager himself, and it seemed a great way to roll my loads. The Lee Classic Loader is an entire reloading kit in a small box. It consists of a neck-sizing die, decapping rod, and primer and bullet seater. You use a plastic mallet, and although it

The author proves that experience and confidence in a well-used rifle are things you can't buy.

heard of a chronograph at the time, so I'd be lying if I was to give a velocity. Looking back, I have to roll my eyes at the crudeness and appreciate the access I now have to better equipment. But I loved that '06. I managed to kill quite a few coyotes with a little Speer 52-grain hollowpoint but learned that I had to make the first shot count. I soon found out that in cold weather, the nylon sleeve inside the rifle receiver would contract, adding resistance that made it almost impossible to cycle the bolt with any level of efficiency, with the feeling that you were pulling it through frozen molasses.

The real story of this rifle begins the following year when we packed up and moved to Alaska. My dad had grown up in Fairbanks, we had family there, and I couldn't have been more excited to go.

seems like a crude method, you can produce accurate loads. The process is slow, especially measuring each load down to the kernel of powder on a balance scale, but it worked, and the rifle shot pretty damn well.

I don't remember the first rifle season for elk that fall, only that I didn't kill one. What I do remember are coyotes. Since my dad was busy coaching and playing football in the early fall, he would spend his winter weekends calling coyotes with me. It took us a year or two to get good at it, but we did, and once I got that Remington, I wanted to use it on coyotes, being as my only other option was a .22 LR. Leading up to the winter, I had managed to find and order a package of .30-to-.22-caliber sabots. These were .30-caliber plastic sabots, in which you pressed a .22-caliber varmint bullet and load in a .30-caliber rifle. "Accelerators" were manufactured by Remington when I was a kid, and this seemed like the answer to turn my .30-'06 into a .22-250.

With that Lee Loader, I managed to work up acceptable loads, good enough to hit a coyote. I probably hadn't even

The author took this Alaskan sheep with a well-placed shot from the .30-'06. It was a big game trophy that hunters many years his senior dream about but never harvest.

I had heard about it my entire life, and this move was undoubtedly going to set me down a path of adventure that I could have only ever dreamed about in Colorado. Alaska is unlike anything I had seen or experienced, and I couldn't comprehend how much I had yet to learn, but I had my rifle.

I approached my first moose season as an Alaska resident with a similar level of vigor as our hunting in the lower 48, passive at best. We went out a few times, but I had no idea what I was doing. Then, with only a few days left in the season, my uncle took us on a duck hunting/pike fishing camping trip, and of course, I brought my rifle along because moose season was still open. Then, one afternoon, as we motored around the bends of a quiet slough on our way to a fishing hole, an enormous set of antlers exploded out of the water.

By the time I got my rifle out of the rack and got the boat topper open, the bull left nothing but a path of swaying alders in its wake. So we kept on our way. The slough continued to wrap around in a horseshoe manner.

Finally, we got out of the boat and walked through the alders to check for a clearing. There was, and right in the middle of it stood that bull. At that moment, my clunky Model 710 awarded my first shot at a big game animal with a dandy bull moose and a healthy scope cut. It took us well into the following day to cut a trail and pack all the meat from the bull back to the boat. Any amount of work couldn't have dampened my spirit at that point, but it was a valuable lesson that I have kept in mind ever since.

My luck continued later that year as I set out for my very first sheep hunt with my cousin. Opening day found us cresting a ridge, looking for a band of rams that we had located in the high bowl the previous evening. We had the drop on them and had determined that there was at least one legal ram in the bunch. I had spent the entire night replaying the sight in my head and dreaming of the morning to come. But, unfortunately, when we slowly peeked over the skyline, the rams appeared to be gone. My heart sank.

We began moving lower, cautiously exposing more of the terrain to our view when we saw them, and they saw us. We did our best to act disinterested, and it seemed to calm the sheep, but the rams slowly dispersed. One of the last rams remaining was the lead ram. I painstakingly examined it through the spotting scope to make sure it was legal. When I was satisfied, I rested my Model 710 on a rock and sent a 150-grain Hornady Interlock through its lungs. It was almost unbelievable walking up to that ram and putting my hands on those horns for the first time — a feeling for which every sheep hunter longs. A tough 20-mile pack out cemented the direction of my life. It was official: I would pursue the white sheep.

Although I killed more moose and white rams, the Model 710 quickly found itself passed over in favor of "better" and newer rifles. These days, rifles seem to come and go, and it's rare for me to develop an attachment to them. That old clunker Remington Model 710 is, by many points of criteria, a piece of junk and in no sense of the word "good." Although it's a rifle I probably would have to pay someone to take off my hands, it's one of very few that I can't imagine selling. It's been beaten up, neglected, and left in the closet, and I cringe at the thought of taking it hunting again, but it served its purpose — it ushered me into a life of adventure. In that sense, it indeed has been one good gun. **GD**

The H&R Handi-Rifle in .45-70 Government

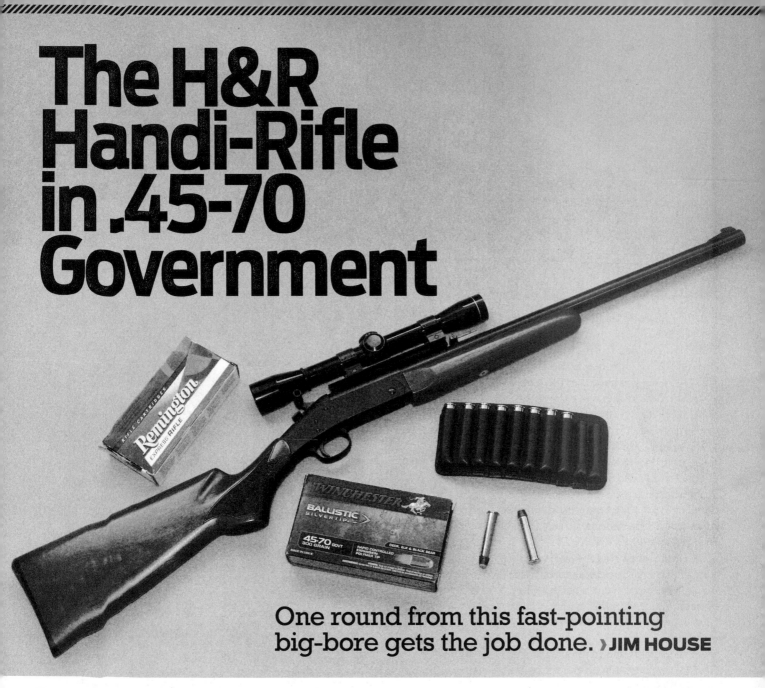

One round from this fast-pointing big-bore gets the job done. ›**JIM HOUSE**

The year 1873 marks the release of the first rifle that chambered the cartridge known as the .45-70 Government. That single shot has become known as the Springfield Trap Door model because of its hinged door that you lifted to insert a cartridge. To say that single shots are enormously popular would be a mistake, but it would be equally incorrect to say that such rifles are defunct. Single shots in one form or another have existed ever since someone poured in a charge of blackpowder and inserted a patched ball.

Many shooters are pleased with a single-shot rifle. If a hunter places the bullet carefully, one shot should bring the game to bag. Moreover, it is not particularly slow to open the action and insert another cartridge. It is interesting to note that African hunters Frederick Selous and John Taylor used single shots extensively. Taylor notes in his classic volume *African Rifles & Cartridges* that, in his opinion, the single-shot rifle is eminently suitable for hunting. He also states that "with a scope-sighted single-loader you should get your beast every time." Taylor also says that Frederick Selous did most of his hunting with a single-shot .450 Express and then had another chambered in .303 British.

My first rifle was a single-shot .22 bolt-action Stevens Model 15. One opened the bolt, inserted a cartridge, closed the bolt, and pulled back on the cocking piece to ready the rifle for firing. Most single shots follow these steps except for those that cock as you open the action. The elegant Ruger No. 1 and some other high-end single shots have an underlever that, when pushed downward, draws the locking block downward to expose the chamber.

To open the New England Firearms

Opening the action is as simple as pushing down on the latch button.

around a piece of tubing of appropriate diameter, I solved that problem. The checkering on the grip area and the overall finish of the wood were superb. My Handi-Rifle is now not only handy but also attractive.

(below) Shown here are (left to right) two .45-70 handloads that contain 350-grain Chey-Cast and 300-grain Hornady hollow-point bullets.

(bottom) A .45-70 works very well with cast bullets such as the (left to right) 320-grain Mt. Baldy, 350-grain Chey-Cast, or 350-grain Laser-Cast. The Chey-Cast bullet utilizes a polymer coating that serves as a lubricant and reduces airborne lead.

H&R Handi-Rifle's action, you depress a raised tab (it has a traditionally styled hammer). The Handi-Rifle utilizes a transfer bar that lifts behind the firing pin only when you cock the rifle. Thus, a blow to the hammer when the rifle is not cocked cannot cause an accidental discharge.

The original H&R Company was founded in 1871 but went out of business in 1986. New England Firearms Company resurrected the brand as H&R 1871. I got into Handi-Rifles just before Remington acquired New England Firearms. In 2015, Handi-Rifle production ceased, to the dismay of many. The rifles represented inexpensive but capable guns prized by beginners and traditionalists alike. Moreover, you could get them in centerfire calibers that ranged from the .22 Hornet to such thumpers as the .45-70 Government, with the entire list of calibers numbering 22. Both my .22 Hornet and .45-70 Gov't. rifles are real keepers, but I wish I had added a .30-30 Winchester along the way.

My .45-70 came with stock and forearm made of black polymer. Although nicely shaped and functional, I wanted to upgrade the rifle, make it elegant. So I installed a checkered Boyd's walnut stock and forearm. I was somewhat skeptical at first, but when the wood arrived, that feeling disappeared. The barrel channel in the forearm was not quite wide enough to accommodate the robust barrel of a .45-70. Still, by using sandpaper wrapped

H&R produced Handi-Rifles in several configurations. Some featured blued metal mated to synthetic or wood furniture; others employed stainless steel, usually with a synthetic stock. Some models featured open sights, whereas others did not, but the maker provided a scope rail. Both my .22 Hornet and .45-70 Gov't. have iron sights, just as rifles should. Some Handi-Rifles have extractors that manually move the case out of the chamber; others have an ejector that launches the case when you open the action. My .45-70 is of the latter type. The serial number indicates that this is a 2001-manufactured gun.

Although H&R Handi-Rifles are no longer available as new models, it is not uncommon to see them in used gun racks. Like many other discontinued things, they are becoming harder to find, and prices have escalated, particularly for those in more "connoisseur" single-shot calibers such as .22 Hornet, .30-30 Winchester, and .45-70 Government. The throat of my .45-70 Handi-Rifle is very short, and as a result, when I tried to chamber some cast bullet handloads (with bullets not rounded just ahead of the case mouth), some of the bullets engaged the rifling. I solved the problem by seating the bullets slightly deeper. Jacketed bullets have a more tapered profile, and seating them to the cannelure works fine.

All major ammunition companies produce at least one factory load in .45-70 caliber, with a good number offering a selection. Most utilize 300-grain hollowpoint bullets, but others have 405-grain jacketed flat-point bullets. Rifles in .45-70 caliber are of several types. The original Springfield Trap Door rifle chambered a cartridge that utilized a lead bullet propelled by blackpowder. Eventually, lever-action rifles such as the Winchester 1886 and Marlin 1895 appeared, and they have stronger actions. In more recent times, Ruger produced the No. 1 with a robust action that can easily handle the most powerful magnums. Ammunition manufacturers keep pressure low should someone fire their stuff in weaker rifles. The handloader can tailor loads to a particular type of rifle.

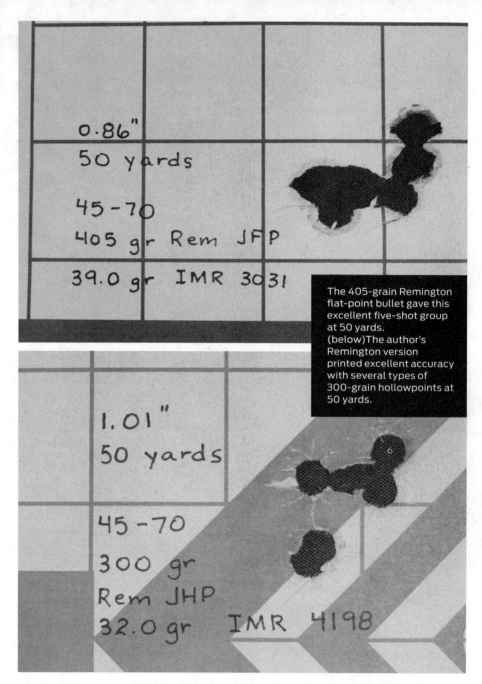

The 405-grain Remington flat-point bullet gave this excellent five-shot group at 50 yards. (below) The author's Remington version printed excellent accuracy with several types of 300-grain hollowpoints at 50 yards.

The .45-70 is a versatile cartridge. In Hornady's LEVERevolution line, a 325-grain bullet featuring a flexible tip gives the bullet a pointed profile and makes it suitable for use in tubular magazines. Hornady also has a 250-grain Monoflex copper bullet load. Remington, Fiocchi, Winchester, and others offer loads with 405-grain bullets for use in all .45-70s. I could get by fine with 300-grain jacketed hollowpoints from Hornady, Speer, Sierra, or other sources for handloading. Still, I confess to also having a fondness for the 300-grain Ballistic Silvertip Nosler and Winchester produce. That bullet is also available in factory ammunition from Winchester. Being a conservative loader, I keep my handloads at the level designated for trap door rifles. Even so, you can drive a 300-grain bullet at 1,600 to 1,800 fps. These speeds produce about 2,000 ft-lbs of energy at the muzzle, and that's with a heavy slug of large diameter. I don't need more power.

Reading what others have said about

In its original configuration, the Handi-Rifle performed well, but it had little eye appeal, and begged for an aftermarket stock.

Handi-Rifles shows that some owners do not like the feel and weight of the trigger. I may be fortunate, but the trigger on my .45-70 breaks with a pull of 3.4 pounds with no take-up. I have a few rifles that were much more expensive, which I wish had such good triggers. With the polymer stock and forearm, the gun weighs 6.4 pounds, but the Boyd's furniture increases that a few ounces. Overall, it is still an extremely comfortable, comforting, and handy rifle to carry in Wyoming's forests and elsewhere.

The performance of my Handi-Rifle is outstanding. I have shot a selection of both handloads and factory ammunition. At 50 yards, five-shot groups measuring around an inch are common. I tested the rifle with a 2.5x Weaver K2.5 Classic scope that is an excellent match for this classic rifle. There is no doubt that the rifle is sufficiently accurate for any appropriate game at ranges of 125 or 150 yards. With handloads using a 300-grain hollowpoint and muzzle velocity of approximately 1,600 fps, I zero the rifle at 100 yards, so the bullet path is about 1.3 inches high at 50 yards. To sight in at 150 yards, the point of impact needs to be about 3.5 inches high at 50 yards and about 4 inches high at 100 yards. This zero is adequate for species as large as deer or hogs but slightly too much deviation for coyotes.

Some factory loads with 300-grain bullets have muzzle speeds of about 1,800 fps, and you can zero such loads at 150 yards when the bullet path is 2.5 inches high at 50 yards and 3.2 inches high at 100 yards. The action of the Handi-Rifle is strong enough to shoot such loads easily, but for my uses, I prefer ammunition that is slightly less punishing (and less expensive) in a light rifle. With either the handloads or factory ammo, a 125-yard zero is just about right for the old cartridge.

Production of H&R single-shot rifles may have ceased, but many of us can hope that someone will reintroduce the line at some point in time. If it is, I will buy a couple immediately because a single shot serves very well for my type of shooting. **GD**

- REPORTS -
from the Field
AR-STYLE RIFLES

❯ TODD WOODARD

What a year for gun sales. According to National Shooting Sports Foundation (NSSF) figures, there were 21 million background checks for firearm sales in 2020. That topped 2019's totals of 13.2 million by 60 percent. It also shattered the previous record from 2016, when the DOJ conducted 15.7 million background checks on firearm sales. This year's 21 million total surpassed 2016 by 5.3 million, or 34 percent.

The Aero Precision Thunder Ranch Special Edition M4E1.

The Aero Precision Thunder Ranch Special Edition M4E1 is Clint Smith's "Ultimate Carbine," it includes key features requested by the Thunder Ranch founder.

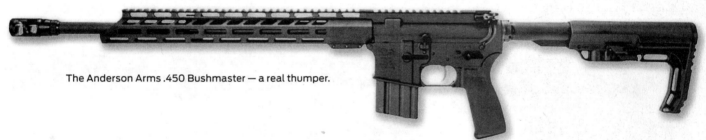

The Anderson Arms .450 Bushmaster — a real thumper.

Also, tucked into those massive numbers are very high sales of AR-15s and AR-10s, which aren't broken out into a separate category. But we can get an idea from previous years' sales. In most months, sales of handguns make up about 55 percent of sales, long guns 36 percent, and the other 9 percent. NSSF estimates that in 2018, approximately one-half (48 percent) of all rifles produced and imported (less exports) in 2018 were Modern Sporting Rifles, a broad category that includes AR-15s and AR-10s. So, let's call it 17 percent of total sales are AR-related types. When you apply this to the 21 million background checks in 2020, 17 percent of all sales approximately equal 3.57 million ARs sold in 2020 — apparently,

black rifles matter.

Also, that demand for ARs has made many companies turn off the sexy options and go to full-bore production of whatever they can complete.

Following are a few selections that may be worth looking for when availability returns.

AERO PRECISION

Aero Precision makes a well-made AR-pattern rifle called the AC-15 that's affordable, starting at $700. But there's also a sexy one, the M4E1, built as a partnership with Thunder Ranch. Aimed to achieve Clint Smith's "Ultimate Carbine," it includes critical features requested by Thunder Ranch founder Smith.

Chambered in 5.56 NATO, the

Thunder Ranch Special Edition M4E1 forged lower receiver has the Thunder Ranch "TR" logo with a MIL-A-8625F Type III Class 2 hardcoat anodized or Cerakote finish. The upper is also a branded Thunder Ranch part with no forward assist. Furniture pieces are a Magpul MOE SL stock, MOE grip, and Magpul MBUS sights, but the handguard is an Atlas R-ONE M-LOK model. Barrel choices are 14.5- and 16-inch mid-length styles topped with a VG6 Delta 556 Flash Hider that's pinned on the 14.5-inch tube. An ALG Defense QMS Trigger starts the fun. *aeroprecisionusa.com*

ANDERSON MANUFACTURING

When supplies become available, one of Anderson Manufacturing's new

The Brownells XBRN177E2 is a retro Special Forces variant.

CMMG's Endeavor rifles are now available in Hornady's new 6mm ARC (Advanced Rifle Cartridge).

chamberings is the .450 Bushmaster, built on the .284 Winchester case. The .450 BM runs at a 38,500 PSI max chamber pressure and develops 2,200 fps shooting a 250-grain bullet. The B2-K869-K000 unit has a list price of $1,003.29 and, importantly, comes with a muzzle brake and an 8-pound listed weight. It also has a Battlelink Minimalist buttstock, which you might want to change out for something with a rubber pad on it. That's because shooting the .450 Bushmaster with a hard-plastic or aluminum stock might not be too much fun.

The 18-inch heavy-contour barrel has a black nitride finish and a twist rate of 1:24, a slow spin suited to the .450 BM's stubby, heavy bullet. The gas system is a mid-length low-profile style with a .750-inch gas-block diameter. The handguard is M-Lok compatible. *andersonmanufacturing.com*

BROWNELLS

The Iowa-based parts powerhouse continues to roll out new "retro" models that consumers love. Among the more recent entries are the following models:

The BRN-PROTO 5.56 goes back to the beginning of the AR-15 — a faithful replica of Eugene Stoner's very first AR-15 prototype. Based on AR-15 Serial Number One, the Brownells BRN-Proto sports the distinctive trigger-like charging handle on top of the receiver and under the carry handle, just like the early AR-10 models. It has the uncluttered "slick-side" upper receiver of the early rifles — and the stock, handguard, and pistol grip of a brown reinforced polymer replicates the look of the original fiberglass furniture. The round cross-section handguard looks oversized because it was a "borrowed" AR-10 handguard. The matte-gray anodized receiver meets a skinny A1-profile barrel capped off with the early three-prong "duckbill"

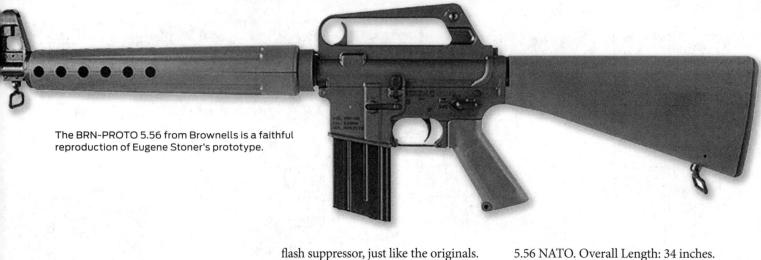

The BRN-PROTO 5.56 from Brownells is a faithful reproduction of Eugene Stoner's prototype.

flash suppressor, just like the originals. The BRN-Proto's front sight base mirrors that of the Number 1 prototype. The windage-adjustable A1-type rear sight drum is nestled right inside the carry handle. Each BRN-Proto comes with one 25-round steel-bodied magazine, a distinctive replica of the original, which Brownells designed and manufactured specifically for this rifle. 5.56x45mm NATO. 1:12 rifling twist. Barrel, 20 in. rifle-length gas tube. Internal dimensions conform to modern "mil-spec" standards. $1,625.

The XBRN177E2 Carbine is not as well-known as the iconic M16A1 used by thousands in Vietnam, but it was a less-cumbersome model based on the commonly used AR platform

The Colt XM177E2 Retro Carbine like the Original Colt Model 629 specifications from the 1960s.

issued to Special Operations forces during the war. The gun comes equipped with a true-to-form polymer CAR buttstock, XM177 flash hider, and a phosphate bolt-carrier group. The XBRN177E2 AR-15 Rifle also provides enthusiasts with the standard, gray-anodized receiver, as well as a 12.7-inch barrel with a pinned and welded muzzle device that meets BATFE regulations.

5.56 NATO. Overall Length: 34 inches. Weight: 5.8 lbs. $1,390. *brownells.com*

CMMG

CMMG's Endeavor line of rifles is now available in Hornady's new 6mm ARC (Advanced Rifle Cartridge). CMMG designed these for superior long-range accuracy, and the Endeavor line features a 20-inch barrel to squeeze every drop of ballistic performance from the new caliber. Each rifle ships with one 10-round magazine. This chambering has a 20-inch barrel made of 416 stainless steel with a 1:7.5 twist — the SV Brake screws on to 5/8-24 threads. The gas system is rifle-length with an SLR adjustable gas block protected by a CMMG RML15 M-Lok handguard. Furniture is a Magpul PRS stock and a Magpul MOE triggerguard. The trigger is the excellent Geissele Automatics SSA 2-Stage. It's a hog, though, at 9.1 pounds unloaded and measures 40.5 inches in OAL. *cmmginc.com*

COLT

The Rampant Pony is turning on the Wayback Machine with its XM177E2 Retro Carbine. Colt builds this Retro Classic Carbine to the Original Colt Model 629 specifications from the 1960s. The 11.5-inch barrel has an extended flash hider designed to replicate the original moderator that was so iconic for this model. This unit reproduces the original vinyl-acetate coated aluminum butt-

stock and has the U.S. Property Marked rollmarks. It is a true collectible that's as comfortable on the range as it will be in an enthusiast's display. $2,599.00. *colt.com*

DANIEL DEFENSE

Lost in the stampede to the 6.5 Creedmoor, AR-pattern rifle shooters seem to have forgotten about the .260 Remington, which most makers don't chamber. But Daniel Defense does in the DD5 V5, and the round provides users of its semiautomatic platform excellent long-range precision shooting capability. (Yes, it also comes in 6.5 CM). Gains in ballistic efficiency help the modern shooter stretch the effective range out to 1,000 meters or more in this highly accurate and durable rifle. An adjustable gas block allows for a consistent feel, whether shooting suppressed or unsuppressed. The perfected bolt carrier group reduces overall recoil impulse and is easy to maintain and operate in all conditions. The 20-inch chrome-lined barrel made of cold-hammer-forged proprietary steel has a four-bolt connection system to ensure greater accuracy. Daniel Defense designed the bolt with enhanced extractor geometry and dual ejectors for reliable cycling. The twist for the .260 Rem is 1:7. It accepts all SR-25 magazines. Weight: 8.9 pounds. Length: 38 3/8 to 41 5/8 inches. Daniel Defense includes a full-latch impact plastic case. $2,500. *danieldefense.com*

JP ENTERPRISES

JP Enterprises builds the LRI-20 Semi-Monolithic Long Range Precision Rifle for long-range competition or sniper duty. The LRI-20 upper receiver offers a stable, repeatable platform for a precision gas gun, the core of which is the new integral handguard nut, which counters the weak point of standard AR design by adding material to stabilize the barrel mount and the front pivot pin joint. Paired with the MicroFit Takedown Pins, the LRI-20 offers a unified chassis that helps tighten groups. Patterned on the lightened military-style upper design, the LRI-20 includes both dust cover and forward assist paired with a dedicated side-charging handle. The integral nut

The JP Enterprises LRI-20 Semi-Monolithic Long Range Precision Rifle for long-distance competition or sniper duty.

Mossberg MMR Pro now chambers the fast-stepping .224 Valkyrie. It trips with a JM Pro Drop-In Match trigger.

The Patriot Ordnance Factory (POF) Prescott Rogue is a lightweight (7 pounds) 6.5 Creedmoor.

design works with any iteration of the company's MK III handguard tubes. This nut is also internally undersized for the JP Thermo-Fit installation that produces a durable link between barrel and receiver. Complete guns are available either

Mossberg makes the receivers from 7075 T-6 aluminum, and they come with a dust cover, forward assist, and M4 feed ramp. The gun runs on a direct-impingement rifle-length gas system and has a full-length top rail. The trigger is

simple and easy. The triggerguard and pistol grip are Magpul's MOE models. $1,478. *mossberg.com*

PATRIOT ORDNANCE FACTORY

Patriot Ordnance Factory's Prescott Rogue is another effort to turn the platform into the lightest semi-auto rifle on the market. Built on the Rogue platform and weighing only seven pounds, the 6.5 Creedmoor Prescott is built to hunt. Among the features are the following: 3.5-pound straight POF drop-in trigger with KNS anti-walk pins; Micro-B muzzle brake, a nitride-heat-treated single-port design; rifle-length gas block for smoother shooting and enhanced reliability; match-grade stainless steel barrel with E2 dual extraction; Slim Renegade handguard with multiple QD points and patented heat sink barrel nut; 5.56 buffer, anti-tilt extension tube, and LUTH-AR MBA-4 stock. The Prescott has an MSRP of $1,866. *pof-usa.com*

SAVAGE

The Daniel Defense DD5 V5 now chambers .260 Remington!

as ready-to-ship Ready Rifles or custom spec'd in the online Rifle Builder. $3,499. *jprifles.com*

MOSSBERG

In 2016, Mossberg revamped its MMR line of AR-15 rifles and came out with the MMR Carbine. In 2018, Mossberg released the MMR Pro in 5.56 NATO. Now the line is chambered in the .224 Valkyrie, offering even more performance in a rifle priced at just under $1,500.

Mossberg keeps the MMR's weight right at 7 pounds, even with an 18-inch barrel and SilencerCo muzzle brake.

the JM Pro Drop-In Match, designed in conjunction with competitive shooter Jerry Miculek. It produces a four-pound trigger break with adjustable overtravel.

The narrow aluminum AXTS Raptor ambidextrous charging handle allows for rapid charges from either the strong or support side. Mossberg's six-position adjustable stock offers 3.25 inches of LOP adjustment, and the Flex TLS (Tool-less Locking System) makes recoil pad swaps

Savage has committed a rifle to the 6mm Creedmoor, an increasingly common long-distance chambering known for its slipperiness and low recoil. The MSR 10 Precision is "complete and ready to compete." It comes standard with a stainless steel heavy barrel and 5R button rifling. What also makes it competition-worthy right out of the box are upgrades like an 18-inch Arca handguard, Magpul PRS stock, and TangoDown Battlegrip Flip Grip, which quickly rotates from 24 degrees of rake to vertical. In addition, a +2 gas system that you can adjust for optimal

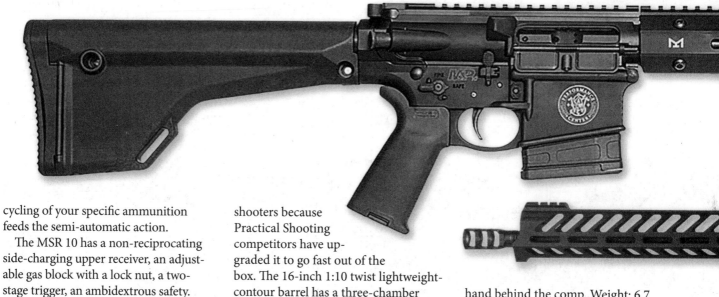

cycling of your specific ammunition feeds the semi-automatic action.

The MSR 10 has a non-reciprocating side-charging upper receiver, an adjustable gas block with a lock nut, a two-stage trigger, an ambidextrous safety. Savage chambers it in .308 Win. and 6.5 Creedmoor with basically the same appointments. It weighs 11.4 pounds and is 44 inches long, primarily due to the 22.5-inch 1:7.5 5R gain-twist rifling. The detachable box mags hold 20 rounds. *savagearms.com*

SIG SAUER

It might surprise shooters to know that one of Sig Sauer's most expensive rifles based on MSRP doesn't fire the 5.56 NATO round; instead, it is the Sig MPX Pistol Caliber Carbine (PCC) in 9mm at $2,799. The MPX PCC has found favor among top

shooters because Practical Shooting competitors have upgraded it to go fast out of the box. The 16-inch 1:10 twist lightweight-contour barrel has a three-chamber compensator to reduce further the 9mm carbine's already paltry recoil. A Timney single-stage trigger is the giggle switch, but it's not a low-gram precision unit. Instead, it breaks at around 4.75 pounds and has a crisp, fast, definable reset. A full-length M-LOK handguard is slim and long, 15.5 inches, offering a lot of out-front real estate for even long-armed shooters to clamp a C grip on or to mount lights, lasers, vertical grips, or stops. Helpful, too, in that last regard is the slight flaring at the muzzle end of the guard to keep the off-

hand behind the comp. Weight: 6.7 pounds. Length: 35.25 inches. Gas-piston operated. Stock: 5-position telescoping folding. *sigsauer.com*

SMITH & WESSON

Many shooters may not know that a common upgrade well known on S&W pistols — a Performance Center upgrade — is also available on the company's M&P 15 and M&P 10 rifles in 5.56 NATO, 6.5 Creedmoor, and .308

The Savage MSR 10 Precision comes standard with a stainless steel heavy barrel and 5R button rifling. Savage chambers it in 6mm Creedmoor.

Above: A Performance Center Edition (PCE) of the Smith & Wesson M&P 10 in 6.5 Creedmoor sports custom options right from the box.

Below: The Sig MPX Pistol Caliber Carbine (PCC) in 9mm is a favorite among Practical Shooting competitors.

SPRINGFIELD ARMORY

The Saint Edge rifle is the cream of the crop of Springfield Armory's ARs, with features like a multi-mode gas block for maximized versatility, a free-floating handguard for accuracy, and 6.4-pound curb weight. The Saint Edge is the product of elite engineering with premier components and upgrades comparable to custom-built ARs. Chambered in 5.56, the Edge has a Springfield Armory Modular Match Short Reset Single Stage trigger that paves the way for a trigger press with zero creep. The Edge's upgraded furniture includes a free-

Win. These are semi-custom versions of catalog guns that command a hefty premium. A base M&P 15 runs $1,189.00, and its Performance Center Edition (PCE) version goes for $1,599.00, a $410 upcharge. On the M&P 10, the PCE version costs up to $966 more. What you get for your money with the PCE upgrades is hand-fitted parts and higher-end components, such as a two-stage match trigger, 15-inch free-float Troy M-LOK hand-guard, a 2-inch aluminum M-LOK accessory rail panel, and Magpul MOE rifle stock. The barrel is free-floated inside the Troy handguard, and the aluminum handguard has a continuous top rail with T-marked rail slots and M-Lok mounting slots. A Performance Center rifle's two-stage match trigger is much better than the GI-style trigger components on a standard-catalog M&P rifle. They regularly break at less than 3.75 pounds. M&P 15 Performance Center Edition, $1,599. M&P 10 Performance Center Edition, $2,055. *smith-wesson.com*

float handguard, Bravo Mod 2 pistol grip, and six-position Bravo Mod 0 SopMod buttstock. The Edge's 7075 T6 machined billet lower receiver deploys a flared magazine well for better reloads. In addition, it has an ambidextrous safety and an integrated QD sling attachment system. The triggerguard is flared and enlarged for gloved hands. The low-profile gas block feeds a mid-length gas system that you can readily tune to optimize performance with different loads. The Edge comes with a built-in Accu-Tite Tension System, an adjustable setscrew that ensures there is no play between the upper and lower receivers. Housed within the forged Type III hard-coat anodized 7075 T6 aluminum upper receiver is an M16-pattern bolt carrier group shot-peened and MPI tested for reliability. Premium 16-inch 1:8-inch-twist Melonite-coated barrel. $1,350. *springfield-armory.com* **GD**

The Springfield Armory Saint Edge in 5.56 NATO.

- REPORTS - from the Field RIFLES

› WAYNE VAN ZWOLL

Iron sights, well-finished walnut stippled at wrist and fore-end sold Wayne on this Mossberg Patriot.

A virus-induced pause hasn't derailed tooling for new rifles — or choice 2021 models and line extensions!

The centerfire Anschutz 1780 hunting rifle (here) is now followed by the 1782, with a threaded muzzle.

Remington Arms, as we knew it, has disappeared. Savage no longer rides with Vista. Marlins will soon come from Ruger. The long months ending a forgettable year have treated us to corporate chess, the cancellation of SHOT and other key industry events, and travel strictures that nixed hunting in most of the world's great game fields. Beyond all that, political upheaval and shuttered shops tell of grim weeks that ran to months, then into another year. But, better times will surely come.

Meanwhile, the plans and production lines of companies that serve the shooting public have stayed busy. Many rifle makers have delayed new product introduction to meet the demand for existing models. Others have added to chambering rosters from a spate of fresh cartridges. Sub-models, with distinctive stocks, barrels, and finishes, extend familiar series. Can you believe Winchester now offers 16 variations of its Model 70?

Because 2020 applied the brakes to some roll-outs and limited production runs and field time for many rifles, a review of top offerings from last year is also in order. So, here's what's on fresh sell-sheets from America's rifle makers.

ANSCHUTZ

Long ago, an Anschutz 1413 carried me through four-position matches in Olympic trials to a state prone championship. More accomplished shooters than I favored rifles from this German firm — and still do. Afield, you won't find a more accurate rifle than the walnut-stocked Anschutz 1761 bolt-action in .17 HMR, .22 LR, and .22 WMR. Sharing the 1761's refined looks and handling, the centerfire 1771 comes in .17 Hornet, .22 Hornet, .204, .222, and .223, its action perfectly proportioned for these slim small-bore rounds. Big game hunters look to the 1780 and new 1782, in chamberings from .243 to 9.3x62. The 1782 has a threaded muzzle, no sights. *anschuetz-sport.com*

ASHBURY PRECISION ORDNANCE

Five rifle types comprise the Ashbury line: Competition rifles have features in common with the Multi-Sport series for long-range shooting. There's a lovely wood-stocked hunting rifle called the American Jaeger. The $2,750 Saber M700 Tactical Rifle in 6.5 Creedmoor and .308 was new in 2020. Ashbury adds useful features like a Rifle Basix trigger, also on the modular-chassis Saber Sport Utility. Given a supply of actions on hand to weather a hiatus in 700 production, Ashbury will continue to earn its reputation for bullseye accuracy with first-cabin refinements and workmanship. *ashbury-precisionordnance.com*

BERGARA

Last year, Bergara trotted out the B-14 Wilderness Series (from $899) in Sniper Grey Cerakote to bridge the B-14 and Premier series. In a broad range of chamberings, 6.5 Creedmoor to .28 Nosler and .300 Winchester, Hunter and Ridge

Bergara B-14 rifles have lightweight single-stack magazines. The straight-line feed is butter-smooth.

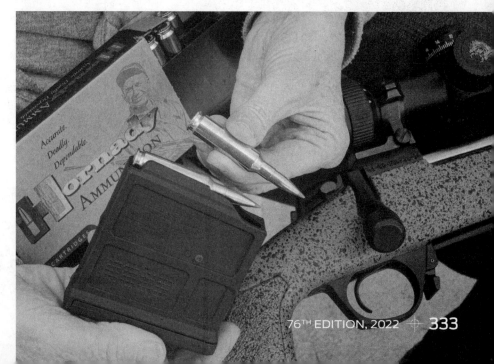

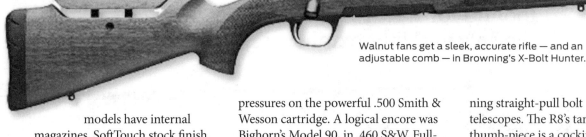

Walnut fans get a sleek, accurate rifle — and an adjustable comb — in Browning's X-Bolt Hunter.

models have internal magazines, SoftTouch stock finish. Wilderness Terrain and HMR rifles on "mini-chassis" feature brakes and AICS detachable boxes. *bergarausa.com*

BIGHORN ARMORY

A 400-grain bullet, powered by 41.5 grains of Hodgdon's H110, hurtled downrange. *Whock!* The steel disc lurched on its chain. Cycling fast, I emptied the .500. The pocked disc shuddered to a stop. So went my introduction to Bighorn Armory's Model 89, which builds on the best of John Browning's most celebrated rifles: the Winchester 1886 and 1892. Both introduced to lever guns the vertical locking lugs of the dropping-block single-shot rifle that brought his genius to Winchester's attention. The Bighorn cycles like an '86, but it boasts modern steels and machining to brook the breech pressures on the powerful .500 Smith & Wesson cartridge. A logical encore was Bighorn's Model 90, in .460 S&W. Full-house loads in either are a handful in a revolver. But Bighorn rifles bring recoil to heel while sending a ton and a half of punch out the muzzle. Models 90A and 90B, in .454 Casull and .45 Colt, followed. Bighorn carbines and rifles weigh 7 ½ to 8 pounds, with barrels 16, 18, and 22 inches long. All are of 17-4 stainless steel. Pick brushed or Hunger Black finish, the latter a product of salt bath nitriding. Bighorn prices run north of $2,500. *bighornarmory.com*

BLASER

After a recent change in leadership, Blaser headlines are rimfire. The switch-barrel R8 will now fire .22 LR ammo! Progeny of the Blaser R93, the R8 has a radial-head bolt with an expanding collet that locks into the barrel. The slick-running straight-pull bolt telescopes. The R8's tang-mounted thumb-piece is a cocking switch, not a safety, so you can carry the rifle safely with a loaded chamber. Plasma nitriding on hammer-forged barrels ensures a return to zero with Blaser's superb QD scope rings. Chamberings range from .223 to the .338 Lapua.

For 2021, the single-shot Blaser K95 rifle chambers a new cartridge: the 8.5x55 Blaser. Loaded by Norma, the slightly rebated case suggests .404 Jeffery heritage. The 8.5mm (.338) bullet diameter bridges a "caliber gap" between 7mm and 9.3mm cartridges popular in Europe. The 8.5x55 should see use in bolt rifles for its efficiency in short barrels. The use of suppressors has reduced the effective length of barrels, more noticeable in repeaters than in the K95 with its stubby breech. The 8.5x55 hurls 230-grain bullets from Norma loads at 2,960 fps for 3,696 ft-lbs of muzzle energy. *blaser-usa.com*

BROWNING

Consolidation seems the buzzword at Browning, whose "discontinued" list now includes A-Bolt rifles and several BAR LongTrac and ShortTrac versions. In rimfires, the BL-22 and BL-17 are on the skids — the good news: Browning's flagship X-Bolt centerfire bolt rifle is a fast-growing family. The Max Long Range Hunter with adjustable stock and heavy, fluted barrel appeared last year in 6.5 PRC and .30 Nosler, also in nine other chamberings. It joined the X-Bolt

Bighorn Armory builds beautiful big-bore lever rifles for powerful rounds like S&W's .500 and .460.

Western Hunter Long Range is new for 2021, with a 26-inch barrel in nine frothy chamberings, 6.5 Creedmoor to .30 Nosler, .300 Ultra Mag, .300 Winchester, .300 PRC. It retails for $1,100. An upscale Hells Canyon Long Range comes in at

replaced the 455, which had supplanted the 452. Like the 455, the 457 has easily interchangeable barrels. But its receiver is shorter, with new two-piece bottom metal, a fully adjustable trigger. A Scout model for young shooters lists for $365. Others, in .22 LR, .22 WMR, and .17 HMR, wear walnut, laminated and synthetic stocks (the 457 Varmint Precision Trainer boasts a Manners CF stock) and barrels of various contours. The new Varmint Precision Chassis has an alloy chassis, an

The stock on Blaser's R8 Carbon Success has racy form, feathery carbon-fiber heft, leather accents.

Max Varmint/Target, with a heavy, fluted stainless barrel in .204 Ruger to .28 Nosler and .300 Winchester. The X-Bolt Tungsten added 6.5 PRC, .30 Nosler, and .300 RUM. The Target McMillan A3-5 Ambush with its stiff, fluted, braked barrel in 6.5 Creedmoor, 6.5 PRC, .28 Nosler, and .300 Winchester lists from $3,140 to $3,200. Hell's Canyon Speed rifles chamber 15 popular fast-stepping cartridges, from $1,260. The walnut-stocked Hunter Long Range with adjustable comb was new in 2020. The Hunter costs $300 less at just under a grand, without comb adjustment or muzzle threads.

Entry-level prices begin in Browning's line with the AB3, now in four versions from $600. The X-Bolt

$1,430. New for the BAR series: five left-hand rifles from $1,300, .243 to .300 and .338 Winchester. The BLR clan has a new shine for 2021, with its Gold Medallion and Gold Medallion Maple, in chamberings from .243 to .300 Winchester. Either rifle costs $1,540. *browning.com*.

CZ

CZ's rimfire line changed last year when the 457

adjustable AR-type stock with M-LOK slots, and a threaded muzzle. A 457 Royal sporter in figured walnut features a 20 ½-inch threaded barrel. The 457 Premium, new in 2020, is a deluxe rifle of European profile in walnut, with iron sights on a 24 ½-inch barrel. The beech-stocked

In 16 versions, .17 HMR and .22 WMR, and .22 LR, the 457 is the new CZ rimfire bolt rifle.

crown blanks expertly, finished as barrels. Customers can spec their own Shaw custom rifles online. "We've trimmed delivery time to 10 weeks," Bud Shaw told me. "Turnaround should get even faster." Shaw sells accessories, including muzzle brakes. *shawbarrels.com*

trims ounces. By the way, H-S is the only custom rifle company I know that produces every major component of its rifles, down to its brakes and detachable magazines. Pick from 14 models of bolt-actions, including take-downs, in

457 Jaguar carries adjustable irons on a 28 ½-inch threaded barrel. *cz-usa.com*

Simple elegance. H-S rifles boast fine machining, with industry-leading barrels and synthetic stocks.

E.R SHAW

Known for its high-quality custom, replacement, and OEM barrels, family-owned E.R. Shaw now also fits barrels on custom rifles and builds its own. Shaw Barrels has two bolt actions that it barrels to dozens of popular cartridges. The Mark 7 mirrors Savage's 110; the Mark 10 hails from Shaw patents. As you'd suspect, barrel options are legion. My Shaw rifle is in .370 Sako. The action is slick, the trigger crisp, the barrel cleanly fluted under a deep, lustrous blue. The bore is very smooth; snug groups were no surprise. CNC machines at Shaw's three Pittsburg plants rifle, contour, and

H-S PRECISION

For 2021, H-S has unveiled its PLC Long Range Carbon Fiber Rifle. According to marketing VP Josh Cluff, "we wanted a lightweight rifle with the features and reach of the best long-range rifles. That is, we wanted a lighter version of our PLR." It could have used the PLR's stock, but H-S gave the PLC its own adjustable, prone-friendly model. The CF barrel has less resin than many, which

chamberings from .204 Ruger to .458 Lott. Stainless twin-lug actions are CNC-machined to onion-skin tolerances. H-S triggers adjust to a crispy 2 ½ pounds. Cut-rifled stainless barrels nestle in hand-laid CF stocks with alloy bedding blocks. *hsprecision.com*

HENRY REPEATING ARMS

Tapping the talents of B. Tyler Henry, Oliver F. Winchester and company built the Henry .44 rimfire rifle of Civil War fame. The current Henry is a series

Value! Henry rifles marry traditional lever-gun style with modern manufacturing. Here: a .45-70.

Kimber's 84M, perfectly proportioned for .308-length rounds, has sired actions for other cartridges.

of lever-action rifles chambered for a range of modern rimfire and centerfire rounds. Made in the U.S. and priced for the proletariat, they've become exceedingly popular. Henry Big Boy short-action rifles from under $875 arm hombres at Cowboy Action shoots. My .45-70, on a longer frame, cycles smoothly, punches tight groups and is much kinder to your cheek and clavicle than were its forebears. The box-fed Long Ranger has a rack-and-pinion bolt with a six-lug rotating head to brook pressures from high-velocity rounds like the .223, .243, and .308. Starting at under $500, the Frontier rifle in .22 LR and .22 WMR offers threaded barrels. Embellished and commemorative rifles are a Henry specialty. *henryrifles.com*

HOWA

Walnut stocks are on the wane and increasingly costly. But Howa gives them their due in its Walnut Series announced by Legacy Sports International at the 2020 SHOT Show. Howa fit the Walnut Hunter (from $619) stocks to stainless and blued actions. Pick from seven standard or four magnum chamberings in blued rifles. Stainless limits you to 6.5 Creedmoor and .308. I'm pleased to see a swing back to internal magazines on these Howas. (The Mini Action Walnut Hunter in .223, 6.5 Grendel, 7.62x39, and .350 Legend has a detachable box.) Also new: two rifles in 6.5 Creedmoor with carbon-fiber barrels and internal boxes. The H-S stocks have full-length alloy bedding blocks. MSRP: $1,819. Another fresh pair of Howas, with Cerakote "Tactical Gray" metal finish, feature pillar-bedded Hogue stocks in Verde and Vias camo. They sell from $759 in nine chamberings, .22-250 to .300 Winchester. New GamePro 2 models in gray and OD green boast these Hogue stocks and internal boxes. Threaded barrels come in 11 chamberings, including 6.5 and .300 PRC, at $699. All Howa centerfires are push-feeds with stout cylindrical receivers, twin-lug bolts, three-position safeties. Two new rimfire rifles in .22 LR, .22 WMR, and .17 HMR wear green and gray synthetic stocks and stiff 18-inch barrels. Howa includes a 3.5-10x44 Nikko Stirling scope in the starting price of $699. *legacysports.com*

KIMBER

For 2020, Kimber shaved 12 ounces from its Open Range rifles with stiffer fluted barrels in 6.5 Creedmoor and .308. Both Granite and Open Country camo versions wear threaded, carbon-fiber-wrapped barrels from Proof Research. Kimber's Hunter, the company's first rifle with a detachable box, is a bargain, with the 84M barreled action pillar-bedded to a well-shaped stock of molded polymer. First in .243, .257 Roberts, 6.5 Creed-

The Marlin brand recently sold. Rifles like this 1960s-era 336, if revived, will come from Ruger.

Mossberg's Blaze .22 rimfire series has included rifles of various forms — all for more fun shooting.

moor, 7mm-08, and .308, the 6 ½-pound Hunter now comes in a long-action version, for the .270, .280 A.I. and .30-06. Kimber's Traditional, Super America, and Caprivi rifles still feature walnut. *kimberamerica.com*

MARLIN

In September 2020, a U.S. bankruptcy court approved the sale of what remained of Remington's firearms business to Roundhill Group, LLC, all except Marlin. That asset would go to Sturm, Ruger in late November. The price paid has been listed at $28.3 million to $30.1 million. Regardless, Ruger CEO Chris Killoy announced that "the brand aligns perfectly with ours" and would add diversity to Ruger's already diverse and growing stable of sporting arms. By the time you read this, Marlin manufacturing will be well on its way to start-up at Ruger facilities. "We hope to begin production of Marlin firearms sometime in the second half of 2021," said a company spokesman. *marlinfirearms.com*

MAUSER

Sharing a campus in Isny, Germany, Mauser, Blaser, and Sauer are owned by the L&O Group, an organization keen to compete across a wide price range in the rifle market. Besides the posh Model 1898 sporter, recent Mausers include Models 12 and 18 (for debut years 2012 and 2018). "M" was removed from the designation of the M18; it's now simply the Mauser 18. An upscale entry-level rifle ($650 list) has a plain profile but excellent features: a well-shaped synthetic stock, adjustable trigger, three-detent safety, three-lug bolt head on a full-diameter body. Its receiver accepts Remington 700 scope mounts. The M12, stocked in walnut or synthetic, costs a bit more. The Model 03, a carriage-class modular rifle, allows you to switch barrel, bolt head, and magazine to suit different cartridge classes. *mauser.com*

MOSSBERG

The MVP LR has a prone-style stock with an adjustable comb. Without the adjustable comb, that profile graces the new Patriot LR Hunter in 6.5 Creedmoor and .300 Winchester. Patriot Predator rifles, with stocks in Flat Dark Earth and True Timber Strata camo, include a .450 Bushmaster with FDE stock and a threaded 16 ¼-inch barrel under iron sights. All feature Mossberg's LBA trigger, which adjusts down to 2 pounds. Priced from $396, the Patriot series seems to me one of the great bargains in hunting rifles. In .375 Ruger with walnut stock and iron sights, mine weighs only 6 ½ pounds but is surprisingly comfortable to fire. My first three shots went into a .7-inch knot. Would that all my rifles shot that tight! *mossberg.com*

NOSLER

Nosler's Mountain Carbon Ultra Lightweight and Long Range Carbon

Model 48 rifles, rumored in 2019, came to market last year. Both feature carbon-wrapped barrels.

The Ruger No. 1 is a "Distributor Special" rifle this year. Ruger reduced production, hiked the price.

The Nosler Mountain Carbon Ultra Lightweight weighs just 6 pounds in various chamberings.

The Mountain Carbon UL weighs just 6 pounds in its Aramid-reinforced stock. The Long Range Carbon scales a bit more, and its 26-inch barrel makes it two inches longer. The stock, shaped to help you hit distant targets prone, has more beef at the grip and fore-end and two front swivel studs. For 2021, Nosler has added the 6.5 PRC and .280 Ackley Improved to the Ultra Lightweight's chambering roster. Also available: the fast-stepping 26, 27, 28, and 30 Nosler. *nosler.com*

REMINGTON

In September 2020, U.S. Bankruptcy Court Judge Clifton R. Jessup, Jr. of the Northern District of Alabama approved the sale of the non-Marlin portion of the Remington Firearms business to Roundhill Group, LLC for $13 million. By some measures, that sale ended the 13-year struggle of America's oldest gunmaker since its acquisition by Cerberus Capital Management, later called the Freedom Group. On July 27, 2020, Remington filed for its second Chapter 11 bankruptcy in two years. The previous year, company sales had totaled $437.5 million, just half the total in 2016. Remington had not been profitable since 2018.

The dissolution of Remington included an $81.4 million sale of Remington ammunition to Vista Outdoor, Inc. (Federal, CCI, Speer). It was the biggest slice of a $155 million pie, proceeds of which the court applied to Remington's debt. Other corporate orphans included Barnes, bought by Sierra Bullets for $30.5 million, and Marlin, sold to Sturm, Ruger for a little less. Bushmaster, Harrington & Richardson, DPMS, and other brands went to three additional bidders. Roughly 700 employees at Remington's storied Ilion, New York plant, and others at the Lenoir City, Tennessee pistol barrel factory and the Dakota shop in Sturgis, South Dakota, are awaiting word. And work.

Jeff Edwards of Roundhill has worked in the shooting industry, notably at Easton, and assures the concerned faithful that the Group is "committed to keeping Ilion open." Optimists outside speculate the Model 700 bolt rifle, with 870 pump and 11-87 autoloading shotguns, and the R1 1911 pistol, will emerge first in any resurrection. At this writing, little else has been announced about the fragmented firm. *remington.com*

RIGBY

Before the Great War put England and Germany at odds, Rigby built from Model 1898 Mausers some of the finest magazine rifles of that day. Soon after young Marc Newton became Managing Director at Rigby short years ago, he moved to re-establish ties across the Channel. His visit to the current Mauser factory in Isny, Germany yielded the Rigby Big Game rifle, built on fresh 1898 actions barreled, stocked, and finished to prewar quality standards at Rigby in London. The double-square-bridge Magnum Mauser, re-introduced in 2015, is the heart of Rigby's new dangerous-game rifle in .375, .416, and .450. Rigby machined this stout, elegant action with a deep magazine and dual recoil lugs from steel billets. It was followed two years later by the slim, lightweight Highland Stalker in .275 Rigby (7mm Mauser). Now in chamberings to

Rigby has renewed ties with Mauser. Here: a fresh 1898 Magnum action in a classic Rigby in .416.

9.3x62 and stocked in figured Turkish walnut, the Highland Stalker has excellent iron sights, a scope-friendly safety, and an adjustable trigger. Rigby revived the "rising bite" action for double-rifle enthusiasts of means, developed in 1879, a century after the first John Rigby opened a Dublin gun shop. Rigby builds finished rifles to order. *johnrigbyandco.com*

ROCK RIVER ARMS

A chassis-based bolt-action rifle was Rock River's headliner in 2020, breaking with its tradition of AR-style self-loaders. Barreled to the 6.5 Creedmoor and .308, the RBG comes in two versions, both with proprietary stainless steel actions and Wilson fluted stainless barrels (20-,

Joining Sako's 85 series, the new "hybrid" S20 Hunter has a full-length chassis, V-block bedding.

22- or 24-inch), rifled 1-in-10. They're threaded, air-gauged and cryo-treated, and fed by Magpul-compatible AICS detachable boxes. Oversize bolt knobs, 20-minute rails, and Triggertech triggers are standard. The adjustable KRG stock comes in black or tan and brings rifle weight to about 10 ½ pounds. A "Tactical" version with McMillan A-6 stock is available. The RBG retails north of $4,100. *rockriverarms.com*

The Ruger No. 1 single-shot is listed only as a Lipsey's Distributor Exclusive — a lightweight "A" version in .475 Linebaugh/.480 Ruger (blued) and .30-30 (stainless), both with walnut stocks. Seven sub-models of the affordable American bolt-action come in chamberings from .223 to .300 Winchester. The Hunter has a Magpul stock, detachable box magazine, and muzzle brake. More traditional Americans start at just $489 and consis-

adjustable Marksman trigger for $599. Ruger offers its Scout rifle in .350 Legend. Ruger's crew will be busy later this year building new Marlin-branded rifles. *ruger.com*

SAKO

Sako announced a new rifle, the S20. The company bills it as a "hybrid," with elements of both

Savage's new Impulse is a straight-pull rifle, its bolt handle not rotating but pivoting to lock, unlock.

tently deliver eye-popping accuracy. My 6.5 Creedmoor is an ace! A growing list of chamberings now includes the .350 Legend and .450 Bushmaster for whitetail cover, the 6.5 PRC, and .25-06 for long shots on the prairie. Choose from five rimfire Americans in .22 LR, .22 WMR, and .17 HMR. The Long Range Target version in .22 LR has an adjustable comb, threaded bull barrel,

hunting and precision rifles. It's also "modular," as you have choices in all major components. Pick a Tactical Precision stock, with steep, full prone grip and M-Lok slots in the front, or a thumbhole Hunting stock. Both have a full-length aluminum chassis, QD sling pockets on the sides, and an adjustable comb. Spacers let you change the length of pull. Detachable double-stack polymer magazines, 5- and 10-shot, feed a three-lug stainless bolt. The receiver, "V-block-bedded" to the chassis, has an integral

RUGER

Ruger's 2021 roster includes magnum and 6mm Creedmoor chamberings in the Ruger Precision Rifle (RPR).

Wayne used Ruger's Hawkeye Long Range Hunter (in 6.5 PRC) afield: "Nimble, accurate, durable."

Picatinny rail. Barrels of blued carbon and Cerakoted stainless steel are cold-hammer-forged and threaded. The S20 is chambered in .243, 6.5 Creedmoor, 6.5 PRC, .308, .270, .30-06, and 7mm Remington and .300 Winchester Magnums. *sako.fi*

SAVAGE

Savage's big news for 2021 is its Impulse, a straight-pull rifle whose bolt head uses a ring of ball bearings

Springfield Armory's first bolt-action rifle, the Waypoint, is new for 2021. CF barrel. Smooth action.

in what Savage calls its Hexlock system to engage recesses in the barrel extension to lock up. Pushing the bolt handle forward moves a cam that forces the six bearings into the battery; pivoting it back frees them. A button on the bolt shroud releases the handle should you wish to cycle the cocked action to empty the chamber. The receiver's integral rail has 20 minutes of gain. Fluted, threaded, medium-weight barrels on the Impulse Big Game rifle come in .243, 6.5 Creedmoor, .308, .300 WSM, .30-06, and .300 Winchester Magnum. Cartridges feed from a flush detachable box. The carbon steel barrel and aluminum receiver wear Hazel Green Cerakote; the stock wears Kuiu's Verde 2.0 camo. Price: $1,449. The Impulse Hog Hunter (same chamberings save .243 and .300 WSM) and Predator (in .22-250, .243, 6.5 Creedmoor and .308, with AICS magazines) have different finishes and list

for $1,379. Savage's 2021 rimfire clan has the Rascal Minimalist .22 single-shot with an 11 ½-inch laminated stock in colors appealing to youngsters and a 16 1/8-inch threaded barrel. Another new version wears a red, white, and blue synthetic stock. Both feature AccuTrigger. *savagearms.com*

SPRINGFIELD ARMORY

Late in 2020, Springfield Armory announced its first bolt rifle, the Waypoint. Call it a hunting/match rifle. The pillar-bedded AG Composites stock is of hand-laid carbon fiber, with a steep, full grip and tall comb, M-Lok slots, and QD swivel pockets. But contemporary lines haven't made it heavy. That stock scales just under two pounds, half again

as much with an adjustable cheek rest. It comes in Evergreen, and Ridgeline Camo finishes. The stainless receiver has a Remington 700 footprint. Its fluted two-lug bolt glides in races cut by EDM. Bolt and receiver are machined *after* heat-treating to ensure uniformity of the finished steel. The nitride-treated bolt is easy to disassemble without tools. Dual-cocking cams boast an easy 90-degree lift. Unlike Remington 700 recoil lugs, the Waypoint's are integral with the receiver ring. Four 6-48 screws and two recoil pins secure a Picatinny rail. Receiver and barrel shank, bottom metal, and muzzle

Weatherby's svelte six-lug action accounts for about 50 percent of Mark V sales, up from 20 percent.

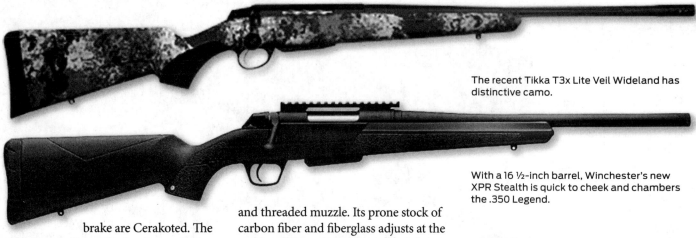

The recent Tikka T3x Lite Veil Wideland has distinctive camo.

With a 16 ½-inch barrel, Winchester's new XPR Stealth is quick to cheek and chambers the .350 Legend.

brake are Cerakoted. The TriggerTech trigger adjusts from 2 ½ to 5 pounds, a "free-floating roller" smoothing release. The Waypoint's 1.9-millisecond lock time is "up to 45 percent faster" than its competition's. A two-position thumb safety blocks the trigger only.

Twist rates accommodate the long, ballistically efficient bullets: one turn in 7 ½ inches for the 6mm Creedmoor, 1:8 for 6.5s, 1:10 for the .308. Barrels are threaded 5/8-24 for the included radial brake. Waypoint guarantees .75 MOA accuracy. The Waypoint I've tested, in 6.5 PRC, sent the first three Hornady 147-grain ELD Match bullets (at 2,910 fps) into a .62-inch slot. Three more groups measured .63, .70, and .82 — including the shot I pulled on the last series. Average: .69.

The Waypoint runs from $1,699 to 2,399. *springfield-armory.com*

TIKKA

In 2020 Tikka unveiled the T3x Lite Veil Alpine and Lite Veil Wideland, distinguished by stock camo and Cerakote colors on the steel. Braked 22 ½- and 24 ½-inch barrels come in 10 chamberings. The Lite Roughneck has blued steel, a Roughtech stock, tan or black, a close match in profile. To lure long-range shooters there's the UPR, or Ultimate Precision Rifle, in .260, .308, and 6.5 Creedmoor, with a 10-round magazine and threaded muzzle. Its prone stock of carbon fiber and fiberglass adjusts at the comb and butt. A 6 ½-pound Polyfade T3x in digital camo, with single-stage or set trigger, comes in 20 chamberings. *tikka.fi*

WEATHERBY

Carbon-fiber barrels in .300 and 6.5-.300 Magnums are increasingly popular in the Weatherby line. The use of lightweight materials has paid off in brisk sales of new Vanguard and six-lug Mark V rifles.

A current star: the six-pound Backcountry in 6.5 RPM (Rebated Precision Magnum) at $2,499. The RPM uses every bit of space in the six-lug action to send 127-grain bullets at over 3,200 fps, 140s at over 3,000.

With nearly a ton and a half of muzzle energy, they bring 1,500 ft-lbs nearly 500 yards! Unlike other Weatherby cartridges, the RPM has no belt or radiused shoulder, and it fits standard bolt faces. Absent too: "freebore" — the long throats Roy cut in rifle bores to keep a lid on breech pressures. Pro and Elite AccuMarks with prone-style CF stocks excel for long-range shooting. The Cerakoted Weathermark weds traditional barrels with fiberglass stocks for $1,499. The Camilla Deluxe, stocked for women, now comes in an Ultra Lightweight version. It weighs 5 ¾ pounds, costs $2,399. A Camilla Wilderness has joined other Howa-based Vanguard rifles at $799. *weatherby.com*

WINCHESTER

Winchester's XPR series now comprises 18 variations. All have a button-rifled barrel secured by a nut ensuring precise headspace. The full-diameter three-lug bolt is nickel Teflon-coated for slick travel in a receiver machined from bar stock and has a lug-mounted extractor and plunger ejector, a single-stack detachable box. Praise be, you can feed this rifle from the top! A two-detent thumb safety locks the bolt; a tab lets you unload safely. The adjustable M.O.A. trigger on my XPR in .325 WSM breaks cleanly. Line extensions in 2020 brought the XPR Hunter and Compact. This year, there's the 6 ½-pound XPR Stealth, chambered

Winchester's 4-pound, 10-shot Wildcat 22 Suppressor-Ready rifle has an adjustable ghost ring sight.

for nine cartridges, .223 to .300 WSM. It has a green composite stock, a threaded, 16 ½-inch matte-blue barrel, a Talley Picatinny rail. Finally, the .350 Legend is now on the cartridge roster for all XPRs.

For 2021, Winchester has announced a Wildcat 22 Suppressor-Ready rifle, with a threaded 16 ½-inch barrel fed from a 10-shot rotary magazine. An adjustable ghost ring rear sight pairs with a post front sight. This 4-pound carbine lists for $280.

Traditional 1866, 1873, 1885, 1886, 1892, 1894, and 1895 Winchester lever rifles (and the Model 71) re-produced by Miroku in Japan are still cataloged. Prices start at $1,070. *winchesterguns.com* **GD**

- REPORTS -
from the Field
SEMI-AUTO
PISTOLS

> ROBERT SADOWSKI

If you thought reflex sights on concealed carry handguns were a fad, think again.

Manufacturers are going all-in with optics-ready variants. Brands like Glock, FN, Springfield Armory, Smith & Wesson, and others all make it easy to add a reflex-style optic. While these may not have the traditional look of a semi-automatic, you can't stop evolution. There's no question the red dot provides an edge when it comes to fast aiming and quick follow-up shots. There are also several .22 LR rimfire pistols from Browning, Taurus, and Volquartsen to meet every budget. In addition, SAR, FN, and MasterPiece Arms are heating up competition with 9mm race guns equipped to perform.

The Ed Brown KC9-VTX brings together a combination of the most requested features in one optics-ready package.

Browning introduced several new .22 LR pistols, including new Buck Mark variations like this Contour Gray URX with 5 ½-inch barrel.

BROWNING

In need of a competition-ready .22 LR rimfire? The Buck Mark Contour Gray URX 5-½" (MSRP $579.99) features a — you guessed it — 5.5-inch contoured barrel. The thing has the heft for added stability and improved accuracy in timed and rapid-fire stages — or when marauding tin cans are the target. It also features a full-length Weaver optics base, so mounting a red dot is a piece of cake. The adjustable rear sight and Patridge-style front sight come standard. Browning's Ultragrip RX (URX) ambidextrous grips give you a secure, comfortable hold.

Want a more tricked-out competition gun? The Buck Mark Plus Vision UFX Black (MSRP: $719.99) weighs even less, thanks to an alloy-sleeved steel barrel that slashes weight

by nearly 9 ounces. In addition, it includes a fiber-optic front sight and adjustable rear, plus an integrated optics rail and muzzle brake. Another

The Browning 1911-22 A1 Compact Gray.

lightweight shooter is the Plus Vision UFX Blue (MSRP: $719.99), which checks many boxes for an accurate rimfire pistol. It has a fiber-optic front sight and adjustable rear, with optics rail, muzzle brake, and a blued finish alloy frame and barrel sleeve

with diamond cutouts.

The 1911-22 A1 Compact Gray (MSRP: $619.99) features a lightweight composite frame

The CZ-USA Tactical Sport 2 or TS 2, with redesigned and lowered frame and improved ergonomics.

with an alloy subframe. The 1911-22 Speed sports A-TACS AU Camo finish, alloy slide with Cerakote Burnt Bronze finish, composite grips, stainless steel barrel block, steel 3-dot sights. *browning.com*

CZ-USA

CZ competition guns are phenomenal, and the CZ Tactical Sport is now the TS 2 (MSRP: $1,699). The slide profile is as low as possible for better recoil management, and the redesigned frame improves ergonomics. All this translates into less muzzle flip. The TS 2 has front and rear slide cocking serrations, adjustable rear sight, and a fiber-optic front post. You'll like its magwell, which sucks in magazines during reloads. *cz-usa.com*

ED BROWN

Ed Brown expanded its EVO Series with the new KC9-VTX (MSRP: $2,495), combining the most requested features in one optics-ready package, and primed for daily carry. Features include a thinner slide with unique front and rear serrations. Mounted on top is a 6 MOA Vortex Venom red-dot sight. The frame has Ed Brown's Snakeskin treatment on the frontstrap and Bobtail for just the right amount of grip texture. *edbrown.com*

FN

The FN 509 LS Edge (MSRP: $1,499) is a long-slide striker-fired pistol chambered in 9mm and designed as the ultimate tactical/competition handgun. It comes equipped with a 5-inch hammer-forged barrel, crisp and flat-faced trigger, flared aluminum magazine well,

lightening-cut Long Slide, Low-Profile Optics-Mounting System, and fiber-optic sight package. Plus, it has the other features you expect in the 509 series, such as enhanced texture, two interchangeable backstraps, and Picatinny accessory rail.

Also new to the FN 509 family of striker-fired 9mms is the 509 Compact (MSRP: $1,499). This new

The Kel-Tec P50 gives you 50 rounds of retro-futuristic steampunk firepower.

configuration delivers the same reliability and high-performance but in a compact, highly concealable package. It has low-profile carry sights and comes with 12- and 15-round mags. Finishes include FDE and matte black. *fnamerica.com*

The FN 509 LS Edge carries a long slide and is a striker-fire pistol in 9mm. FN designed it as a tactical/competition handgun.

GLOCK

Who says the .40 S&W Auto is dead? Glock has released several new .40-caliber pistols in Gen5 configuration. The lineup includes the full-size G22 (MSRP: $599) and G22 MOS (MSRP: $599), compact G23 (MSRP: $599) and G23 MOS (MSRP: $599), as well as the subcompact G27 (MSRP: $647). All have Gen5 features like nDLC finish, flared

Glock rolled out a new family of Gen5 .40s!

mag-well, enhanced Glock Marksman Barrel (GMB), and ambidextrous slide stop lever. Plus, the competition-ready G35 (MSRP: $840) and G35 MOS (MSRP: $840) get the Gen5 treatment. *us.glock.com*

KEL-TEC

Kel-Tec's new P50 (MSRP: $995) is chambered in the hot and fast 5.7x28mm caliber and designed around the FN P90 50-round, double-stack magazine. (The P50 comes with two 50-round mags.) Overall length is 15 inches, and its weight unloaded is 3.2 pounds. The look of the P50 is retro-futuristic, if that makes any sense. Kel-Tec is positioning the P50 as a sport-utility pistol for plinking and personal/home protection. With 50 rounds of 5.7 ammo at hand, this pistol is high-intensity and

maximum firepower. *keltecweapons.com*

MASTERPIECE ARMS (MPA)

You know MPA for Chassis Rifle Systems, but now it offers the DS9 Hybrid Pistol (MSRP: $2,999), a wide-body, double-stack 9mm 1911 pistol line. The DS9 comes in a variety of finishes and configurations. They are competition-ready with incredible accuracy and reliability. Expect a 2-pound trigger, 5-inch stainless bull barrel, ambi' safety, and steel frame. You can order it with iron sights or optics-ready. *masterpiecearms.com*

The MPA DS9 Hybrid Pistol is a competition-ready double-stack nine.

MOSSBERG

Mossberg expanded its MC2c striker-fire series 9mm with a 10-round flush-fit magazine model.

The SAR9 Sport is like a tricked-out CZ 75.

It's available in five variants: standard (MSRP: $505) matte finish, cross-bolt safety version (MSRP: $505), two-tone finish (MSRP: $505), and a TruGlo tritium Pro sight model (MSRP: $613). *mossberg.com*

SAR

Sarsilmaz (SAR) is one of the world's largest firearms manufacturers and has introduced new striker-fired models based on the iconic CZ 75 platform. The new SAR9 Sport (MSRP: $549) 9mm is a tricked-out competition-ready semi-auto based on the SAR9 platform. Features include a longer forged steel slide with cooling ports and a lightweight black polymer frame, enhanced triggerguard, striker status indicator, changeable left or right magazine release button, ergonomic grip. Steel magazines come in 17- and 19-round capacities.

Another new addition to the SAR9 family is the 9mm SAR9 optics-ready (MSRP: $799). This optics-friendly SAR9 is the same platform proudly carried by NATO and elite forces worldwide. Features include a 4.5-inch hammer-forged barrel with recessed crown, optics-ready mount, and interchangeable backstraps for custom grip fit. *sarusa.com*

SIG

The P320 X Series now has an XCarry Legion and X5 Max (MSRP: $1,658). The XCarry Legion is a 9mm striker-fired pistol, with the TXG tungsten-infused heavy XCARRY grip module and attached magwell. It also wears a Legion Gray PVD Slide, 4.6-inch threaded barrel, and has XRAY3 adjustable tall sights. Not

The Springfield Armory Hellcat RDP (Rapid Defense Package) with HEX micro red dot, a single-port compensator, and a new Gen 2 Trigger.

STOEGER

Stoeger tricked out its STR-9 striker-fired 9mm pistol to create the STR-9S Combat (MSRP: $549). It combines high fiber-optic suppressor sights, threaded barrel, flared mag-well, optics-ready slide, three modular back-

The SIG X5 Max is optics-ready and comes standard with features we used to consider custom.

straps, and three magazines with 20-round capacities. Just add a red dot. *stoegerindustries.com*

only that, but it is also optics ready. SIG tricked the X5 Max out for competition with a 5-inch barrel, 21+1 capacity, and Romeo3MAX red-dot factory installed. Steel plates are scared. *sigsauer.com*

SPRINGFIELD ARMORY

The Springfield Hellcat has evolved into the Hellcat RDP (Rapid Defense Package) configuration. Think of it as the Roland Special treatment given to the Hellcat (MSRP: $899). Features include

a Springfield Armory HEX micro red dot, a single-port compensator, and a new Gen 2 Trigger. The trigger is re-contoured for enhanced ergonomics, giving you a more comfortable shooting experience, and the Wasp red dot has a 3.5 MOA reticle and 65,000 hours of battery life. Also, the compensator is self-indexing, which means installation and removal are easy. Two models are available; one with no manual safety and one with manual thumb safety.

TAURUS

I have had a lot of fun plinking with the Taurus TX 22. It has a comfortable, full-size grip, and the trigger is consistent. The only thing missing was the ability to add a red-dot optic. Well, the all-new TX 22 Competition (MSRP: $485) not only comes out of the box optics-ready but also has a slew of competition features like a 5-inch threaded bull barrel for match-grade accuracy, three 16-round magazines, and adjustable 3-dot sights. Taurus includes two adapter plates so you can mount a variety of red-dot sights. *taurususa.com*

VOLQUARTSEN

The Volquartsen Black Mamba-X (MSRP: $1,342) is a competition-ready .22 LR rimfire pistol combining features from the Scorpion .22 LR Target Pistol with the push-button takedown

New to the Ronin 1911 series is a full-size model chambered in 10mm (MSRP: $849). It features a full-size 5-inch barrel, a two-tone finish with a stainless steel frame, and blued carbon steel slide. Tactical rack rear and fiber-optic front sights guide 10mm rounds like lasers. *springfield-armory.com*

The Taurus TX 22 is now optics-ready, with the new Competition variant!

functionality of the Ruger MK IV 22/45 frame. Standard options include a threaded stainless steel 4.5-inch barrel with Volquartsen single-port compensator, 2.25-pound trigger pull, and DLC-coated Volquartsen Competition Bolt. It comes with Hogue grips and allows for numerous red dot mounting options. *volquartsen.com*

same barrel as the PPQ. The updated slide profile has course serrations that protrude. Walther calls it SuperTerran Serration, which is ideal with gloves. The slide is also optics-ready. Walther

slide serrations for optimal grip traction in severe and hard-use environments. In addition, expect a 3.5- to 4.5-pound trigger pull, contoured magazine well, high-ride Bullet Proof beavertail, and

The new Springfield Armory Ronin 1911 is a full-size model chambered in 10mm.

The Volquartsen Mamba-X competition-ready .22 LR.

WALTHER

Walther builds its new PDP (Performance Duty Pistol) series of 9mm striker-fired pistols (MSRP: $649) on polymer frames — with many innovative ergonomics and design features of the PPG steel frame guns. The grip is new and provides an aggressive texture yet is non-abrasive so that it won't chew the palm of your hand during extended training. The slide is entirely new but shares the

even refined the trigger and called it the PDT (Performance Duty Trigger). The PDT has shortened the length of travel and improved tactile feel. Three models are available: a Compact variant with a 4-inch barrel and two full-size models with 4- or 4.5-inch barrels. The Compact has a 15+1 capacity; the Full size holds 18+1. *waltherarms.com*

Battlesight rear sight with a fiber-optic front sight. It's available in Full-Size, Professional, Commander, and Compact versions.

The Walther PDP, or Performance Duty Pistol, has improved slide design, upgraded trigger, and is optics-ready.

The Wilson Combat X-TAC Supergrade in Commander size.

WILSON COMBAT

The X-TAC Supergrade 1911 models from Wilson Combat (MSRP: $4,795–$4,906 depending on caliber) are hand-built, making every Supergrade an heirloom-worthy collector's piece. Caliber choices include .45 ACP, 9mm, or .38 Super. Features include enhanced, bi-directional, X-TAC frontstrap and

The Limited Ten #4 is the next limited edition 1911 to pass through Wilson Combat's custom shop. Layne Zuelke hand engraves it. In addition, other features include a Professional-size polished stainless steel frame, 30 LPI checkered frontstrap, Commander hammer, flat-top slide, and 4.25-inch barrel. *wilsoncombat.com*

- REPORTS -
from the Field
REVOLVERS
& OTHERS

› MAX PRASAC

Welcome to the COVID Edition of Revolvers & Others. Political uncertainty has lit a fire under the hindquarters of the firearm industry, igniting sales and manufacturing.

Photo: T. Skougor

As this goes to print, gun and ammo sales continue to accelerate, leading to shortages. As a result, supply and demand have hit the handgun world particularly hard. That's not a bad thing unless, of course, you are the one unable to buy the revolver you want because it is on backorder, with no end in sight!

Positive takeaways? Revolvers remain exceedingly popular. They are timeless, considering their record sales this year.

Therefore, revolvers are here to stay.

COLT

Last year we were fortunate to get a new and improved Colt Python back in the lineup. This year, its big brother —

the all-new Anaconda .44 Magnum — has returned after a very long hiatus. This American icon is back, this time in

Colt's new Anaconda .44 Magnum is back and looking better than ever! Photo: Colt

stainless steel only, and better than ever. Originally debuting in 1990, Colt has not produced an Anaconda since 2003. This one is based on a scaled-up new Python action and is as smooth as ever. Like the first iteration, Colt chambered it in the ubiquitous .44 Remington Magnum. It is a six-shot and is available with a ribbed 6- or 8-inch barrel. I believe the new Anaconda will make for a great hunting handgun. *colt.com*

HERITAGE MANUFACTURING

Producers of classic-style single-action revolvers, Heritage Manufacturing, Inc., introduced the newest member of its family this year, the Barkeep. The 19th-Century Colt "Storekeeper" model inspired this pint-sized revolver. It is a compact, defensive six-shooter. The Barkeep comes chambered in .22 LR (six

Heritage Manufacturing introduced the Barkeep, a short-barreled .22 LR/.22 WMR, fixed-sighted single-action revolver in two finishes: black oxide or simulated casehardened. Photo: Heritage

shots) and either a 2- or 3-inch barrel. In addition, it is compatible with the more powerful .22 WMR; a .22 WMR cylinder is an available option for the Barkeep.

The Barkeep is a compact, concealable, and lightweight package boasting open sights for quick acquisition. Many grip options are available, and the sharp-looking little revolver comes in either the standard black oxide or simulated casehardened frame finish. It includes a stylish ejector pin with a turned wooden handle. *heritagemfg.com*

TAURUS

This year, a new Raging Hunter graces the Taurus lineup, chambered for the powerful .460 Smith & Wesson Magnum cartridge. In a nutshell, the Raging Hunter is a double-action five-shot revolver with integral Picatinny rail built into the top of the barrel shroud, making the addition of scope or red-dot sight simple. The .460 S&W version marks the return of Taurus's largest framed revolvers (recall that Taurus previously produced a .500 Smith & Wesson Magnum Raging Bull) to accommodate the 1.8-inch case length of the .460. So, is a .500 Smith & Wesson Magnum next? I like its design as you can equip it with an optic without disrupting the iron sights. If your optic dies for some reason in the field, you can remove it, and your irons are ready to go. In addition, the unique barrel system features a steel sleeve inserted into an aluminum housing that significantly cuts down on weight.

The cushioned insert grips and porting reduce felt recoil, enabling faster target acquisition when you require multiple shots. For the handgun hunter, this one appears to be a winner. Three barrel lengths are available — 5.12, 6.75, and 8.37 inches — so there is something for pretty much everyone. The Raging Hunter comes in two finishes, a positively sinister matte black and the two-tone matte stainless. *taurususa.com*

The all-new Taurus Raging Hunter in the mighty .460 Smith & Wesson Magnum chambering. Photo: Taurus

TAYLOR'S & COMPANY

New in Taylor's catalog is the Gunfighter model 1873 single action that features the large Army-sized grip frame, making it perfect for the shooter with larger hands. In addition, it's available with the additional Taylor Tuned action for a smoother, lighter trigger. The barrel comes in two lengths — 4.75 and 5.5 inches, with walnut grips (checkered or smooth) in .357 Mag-

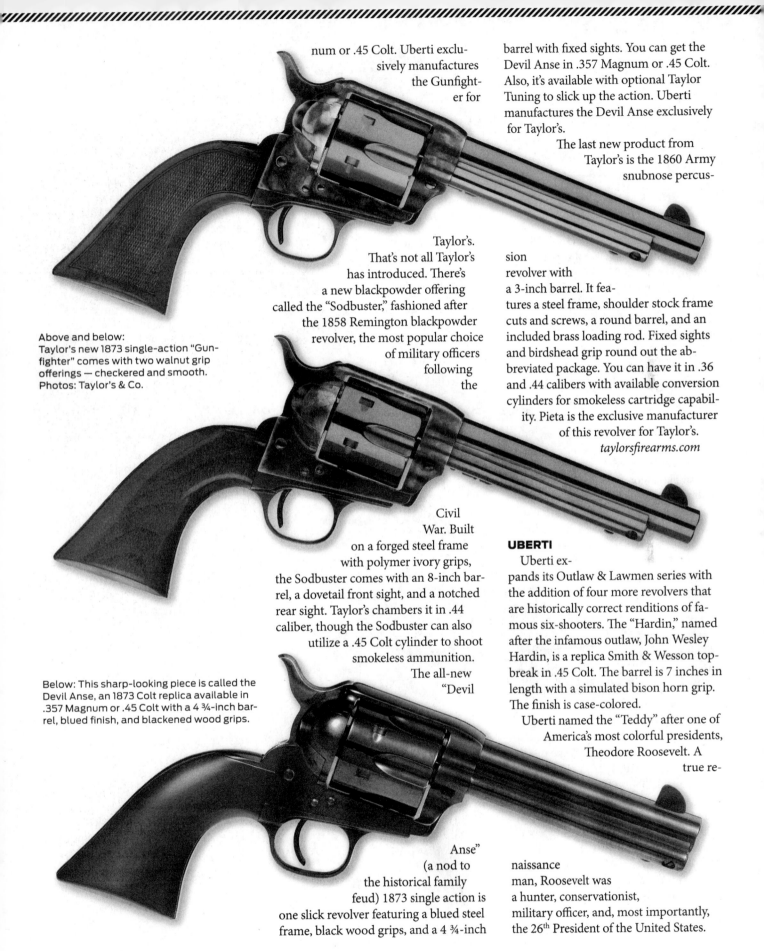

num or .45 Colt. Uberti exclusively manufactures the Gunfighter for Taylor's.

That's not all Taylor's has introduced. There's a new blackpowder offering called the "Sodbuster," fashioned after the 1858 Remington blackpowder revolver, the most popular choice of military officers following the Civil War. Built on a forged steel frame with polymer ivory grips, the Sodbuster comes with an 8-inch barrel, a dovetail front sight, and a notched rear sight. Taylor's chambers it in .44 caliber, though the Sodbuster can also utilize a .45 Colt cylinder to shoot smokeless ammunition.

The all-new "Devil Anse" (a nod to the historical family feud) 1873 single action is one slick revolver featuring a blued steel frame, black wood grips, and a 4 ¾-inch barrel with fixed sights. You can get the Devil Anse in .357 Magnum or .45 Colt. Also, it's available with optional Taylor Tuning to slick up the action. Uberti manufactures the Devil Anse exclusively for Taylor's.

The last new product from Taylor's is the 1860 Army snubnose percussion revolver with a 3-inch barrel. It features a steel frame, shoulder stock frame cuts and screws, a round barrel, and an included brass loading rod. Fixed sights and birdshead grip round out the abbreviated package. You can have it in .36 and .44 calibers with available conversion cylinders for smokeless cartridge capability. Pieta is the exclusive manufacturer of this revolver for Taylor's.
taylorsfirearms.com

Above and below:
Taylor's new 1873 single-action "Gunfighter" comes with two walnut grip offerings — checkered and smooth. Photos: Taylor's & Co.

Below: This sharp-looking piece is called the Devil Anse, an 1873 Colt replica available in .357 Magnum or .45 Colt with a 4 ¾-inch barrel, blued finish, and blackened wood grips.

UBERTI

Uberti expands its Outlaw & Lawmen series with the addition of four more revolvers that are historically correct renditions of famous six-shooters. The "Hardin," named after the infamous outlaw, John Wesley Hardin, is a replica Smith & Wesson top-break in .45 Colt. The barrel is 7 inches in length with a simulated bison horn grip. The finish is case-colored.

Uberti named the "Teddy" after one of America's most colorful presidents, Theodore Roosevelt. A true renaissance man, Roosevelt was a hunter, conservationist, military officer, and, most importantly, the 26th President of the United States.

On many of his adventures, he strapped an 1873 Colt revolver to his waist. This replica is nickel plated and features full laser engraving on the frame, cylinder, and 5 ½-inch barrel. The grips are simulated ivory. Uberti chambers the Teddy in .45 Colt.

Next is the new .357 Magnum version of the "Dalton" replica. It sports a 5 ½-inch barrel. The receiver, grip frame, cylinder, and barrel feature hand-chased engraving from the renowned Italian engraving company Atelier Giovanelli. Simulated pearl grips round out the package that accentuates the gorgeous color-cased frame.

Lastly is the .357 Magnum version of the "Frank" 1875 Remington replica revolver, named after the outlaw Frank James. It features a 7 ½-inch barrel, nickel plating, and simulated ivory grips fitted with a lanyard loop. *uberti.com* **GD**

This 1860 Army percussion revolver features a 3-inch barrel and birdshead grip frame. Taylor's chambers it .36 and .44 caliber.

Uberti's tribute to the infamous John Wesley Hardin, a historically correct replica of the S&W Top-Break revolver. The striking revolver features a case-color finish and simulated bison horn grips in .45 Colt. Photos: Uberti

Uberti's "Teddy" is named after the 26th President of the United States, Theodore Roosevelt. It is a replica of the 1873 Colt (in .45 Colt) that Roosevelt carried on many adventures. Laser-etched, nickel-plated, the Teddy is topped off with simulated ivory grips.

Uberti's tribute to the infamous Dalton Gang, a historically correct replica of the Single Action Army, only chambered in .357 Magnum. It's like the one found on killed Dalton Gang leader Bob Dalton.

- REPORTS -
from the Field
SHOTGUNS

❯ KRISTIN ALBERTS

What is driving the scattergun world this year? Numerous trends are arising, given increased demand not only in terms of personal defense but also in hunting and competitive shooting.

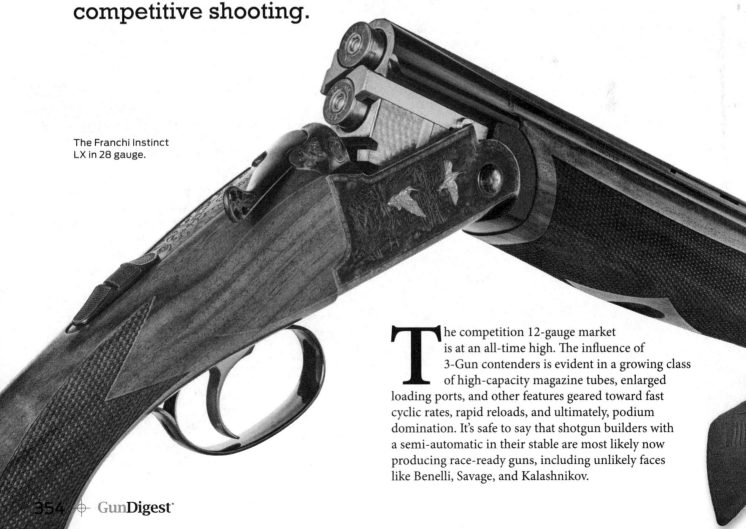

The Franchi Instinct LX in 28 gauge.

The competition 12-gauge market is at an all-time high. The influence of 3-Gun contenders is evident in a growing class of high-capacity magazine tubes, enlarged loading ports, and other features geared toward fast cyclic rates, rapid reloads, and ultimately, podium domination. It's safe to say that shotgun builders with a semi-automatic in their stable are most likely now producing race-ready guns, including unlikely faces like Benelli, Savage, and Kalashnikov.

The Browning Maxus II Sporting Carbon Fiber.

In this changing era with preparedness concerns at the forefront, security and defense firearms are almost certainly out of stock at both online and local gun retailers. Yet, companies including EAA, Stevens, Winchester, and Rock Island Armory charge headlong into that space with pumps and semi-automatics specifically for home security. Heck, even companies like western-centric lever-builder Henry Repeating Arms has initiated a Protect & Provide campaign bridging the divide between hunting and home defense in its shotgun series.

Still, the market is not all repeaters and home defense. No sirree! Fine doubles complete with intricate engraving and delightful color case finish grace many of the following entries.

We are blessed to enjoy an era of gun-building wherein hand-crafting by true artisans melds with the engineering magic of modern technology and machinery. Best of all, these pieces are not mere eye candy but useful tools of the trade.

The Benelli Ethos Supersport is a lightweight, competition-ready model that tips the scales at 5.4-pounds. You can have it in 12 or 20 gauge with either a 26- or 28-inch barrel.

BENELLI

The Inertia-Driven Ethos line of semi-automatics expands to include both a Cordoba BE.S.T. and Super Sport. And, the Super Black Eagle 3 (SBE3) line now offers three-inch chambered variants in the 12, 20, and 28 gauges.

The SBE3 3-inch models wear synthetic furniture with multiple finish options, including black synthetic, Realtree MAX-5, Gore OptiFade Timber, and Mossy Oak Bottomland. The other

The Benello Ethos Cordoba BE.S.T.

beloved SBE3 features remain the same. The retail price on the latest iteration of the SBE3 starts at $1,699.

High-volume shotgun hunters will immediately recognize the new Ethos bird buster's Cordoba namesake. Think South America, doves blackening the skies, and autoloaders so overworked they straight-up overheat and quit running. Not this time. The Ethos Cordoba BE.S.T. takes the best features of the Ethos line, adds the company's Benelli Surface Treatment (BE.S.T.) for extreme use, and tailors elements to serious shooting. Available in 12, 20, and 28 gauge, 3-inch with 28- or 30-inch barrel, the Cordoba is ready to hunt.

Though it sounds like all hunting, all the time, Benelli hasn't forgotten about the competition shooters and target breakers. The Ethos Super Sport is a lightweight, competition-ready model that is as light as 5.4-pounds. It comes in

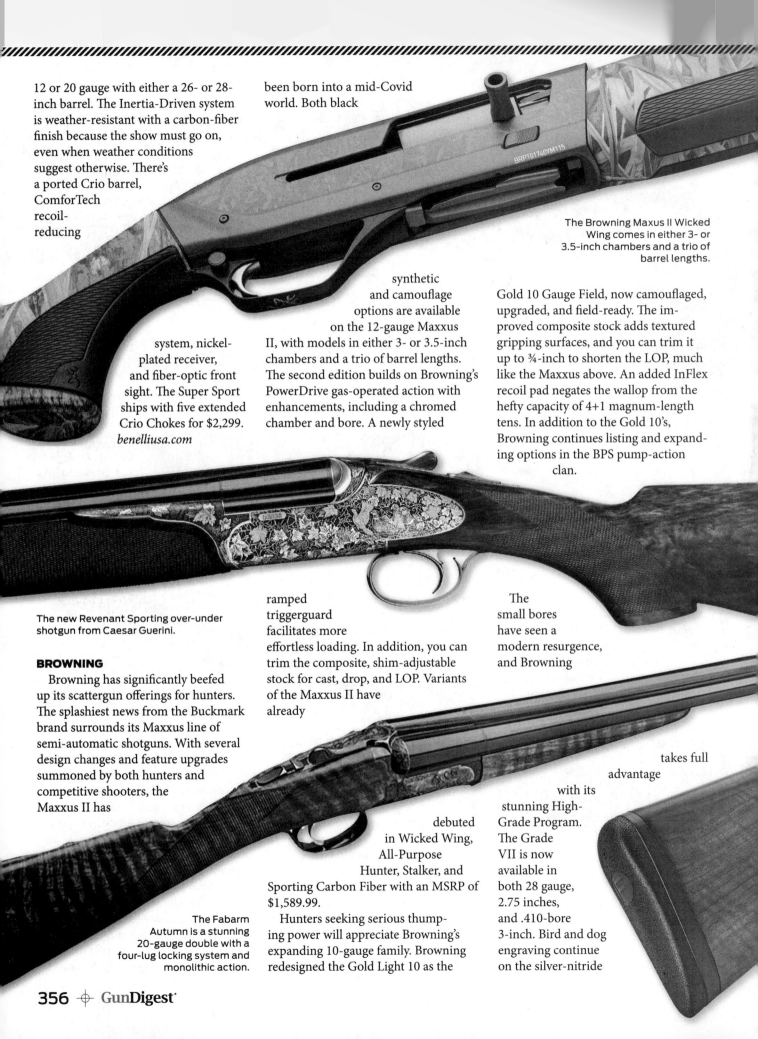

12 or 20 gauge with either a 26- or 28-inch barrel. The Inertia-Driven system is weather-resistant with a carbon-fiber finish because the show must go on, even when weather conditions suggest otherwise. There's a ported Crio barrel, ComforTech recoil-reducing system, nickel-plated receiver, and fiber-optic front sight. The Super Sport ships with five extended Crio Chokes for $2,299. *benelliusa.com*

been born into a mid-Covid world. Both black synthetic and camouflage options are available on the 12-gauge Maxxus II, with models in either 3- or 3.5-inch chambers and a trio of barrel lengths. The second edition builds on Browning's PowerDrive gas-operated action with enhancements, including a chromed chamber and bore. A newly styled

The Browning Maxus II Wicked Wing comes in either 3- or 3.5-inch chambers and a trio of barrel lengths.

Gold 10 Gauge Field, now camouflaged, upgraded, and field-ready. The improved composite stock adds textured gripping surfaces, and you can trim it up to ¾-inch to shorten the LOP, much like the Maxxus above. An added InFlex recoil pad negates the wallop from the hefty capacity of 4+1 magnum-length tens. In addition to the Gold 10's, Browning continues listing and expanding options in the BPS pump-action clan.

The new Revenant Sporting over-under shotgun from Caesar Guerini.

BROWNING

Browning has significantly beefed up its scattergun offerings for hunters. The splashiest news from the Buckmark brand surrounds its Maxxus line of semi-automatic shotguns. With several design changes and feature upgrades summoned by both hunters and competitive shooters, the Maxxus II has

ramped triggerguard facilitates more effortless loading. In addition, you can trim the composite, shim-adjustable stock for cast, drop, and LOP. Variants of the Maxxus II have already

The small bores have seen a modern resurgence, and Browning

debuted in Wicked Wing, All-Purpose Hunter, Stalker, and Sporting Carbon Fiber with an MSRP of $1,589.99.

Hunters seeking serious thumping power will appreciate Browning's expanding 10-gauge family. Browning redesigned the Gold Light 10 as the

takes full advantage with its stunning High-Grade Program. The Grade VII is now available in both 28 gauge, 2.75 inches, and .410-bore 3-inch. Bird and dog engraving continue on the silver-nitride

The Fabarm Autumn is a stunning 20-gauge double with a four-lug locking system and monolithic action.

receiver. Grade VII Black Walnut stocks are stunning with a gloss oil finish, 20 lines-per-inch (LPI) checkering, and the inclusion of an owner's initials nameplate remains. Both sub-gauges are priced the same at $6,539.99, slightly more than their 12- and 20-gauge counterparts. *browning.com*

CAESAR GUERINI

Some firearms are works of art, but the best are also fully-featured

and accurate shooters. That's Caesar Guerini, and in particular, the new Revenant Sporting over-under shotgun.

While there are many eye-catching Caesar Guerini models, the new Revenant Sporting holds our focus. The stacked double exudes class and is available in either 20 or 28 gauge with 28- or 30-inch barrels. There's a rubbed oil finish as well as a separate wood butt plate. To that end, overall wood-to-metal fitment is flawless. Checkering is 26 LPI. There's a solid-tapered rib and boss-style fore-end. The inertia trigger is not selective but instead fires the bottom barrel first. In an old-fashioned nod to customization, left-

handed furniture, 26-inch barrels, and English stocks are all available by special order. MSRP on the Revenant Sporting is $13,895.00, which the company advertises as one-fifth the price of its hand-built competitors. *gueriniusa.com*

CZ-USA

Two groups of shooters oft on the outside looking in are left-handers and teenagers, especially when it comes to doubles. CZ offers solutions to both with expansions in the Bobwhite side-by-side. The Southpaw will favor lefties, while CZ builds the Intermediate for teens or small-statured shooters. All the other features on the Bobwhite line remain, including double triggers, English-style straight stock, black chrome finish, and a full house of five flush chokes.

The most eye-brow-raising shotgun news is only yet whispers and hints at the time of publication. CZ has been running a crowd-sourcing campaign, compiling shooter and hunter input as it designs a pair of shotguns with help from the Project Upland community. Though we have yet to lay eyes on the newbies, rumor has it they'll feature upgraded wood and other features uplanders request. After folks had a chance to voice opinions directly influencing firearms design, a few things seem certain. Side-by-sides were by far the most popular platform, followed by the over-under. Case color finishing received the most votes, while high-grade wood scored off the charts. Engraving, choke style, and rib design remain fluid, but we fully expect the vote-getting 20 gauge with 28-inch barrels to be making an appearance soon. *cz-usa.com*

FABARM

Fine Italian shotguns seem like an oft-typed line these days. Yet, those words demand inclusion with mention of Fabarm, especially in conjunction with the surfeit of latest shotguns, which are at once lovely and practical.

The Autumn, a delightfully stunning and well-balanced double, steals the show. Curtain call on this baby. It's a side-by-side 20 gauge and a 3-inch

The Fabarm Elos N2 combo sports an adjustable competition trigger, a quick-release rib, and extended choke tubes.

chamber, with either 28- or 30-inch barrels topped in a textured top rib. A four-lug locking system drives the monolithic action. There are deluxe Turkish walnut stocks with a hand-oiled matte finish, available in either straight English or standard pistol-grip style. 'Tis the color casehardened receiver finish,

Both the Franchi Instinct LX and SLX over-under get downsized to a 28-gauge frame. Each uses the magnum 3-inch chamber, auto-ejectors, and features engraving and inlays.

though, with ornamental scroll engraving that melts eye-candy. A hand-fit walnut buttplate is icing on this uplander's dream cake. Throw in five InnerHP extended chokes, a single trigger, and auto-ejectors, and the $4,095 price seems perfectly reasonable. Heck, lefties can order one as well. Finally, some guns you don't need but just want. Put the Autumn on my list.

That's not all from Fabarm. Discerning over-under competitors and hunters alike will already be familiar with the company's Elos line. They have now

The Henry Single Shot Turkey chambers 3.5-inch magnum shells and has a 24-inch barrel with fiber-optic sights. Henry prepped it for optics mounts.

added both an Elos N2 Allsport Combo and Elos 2 Elite.

The former is a 12-gauge competition-ready set that partners O/U barrels with an Unsingle in several lengths and configurations. Custom orders for lefties are welcome, and there's also a Compact LOP version. All the Elos N2 Allsports

have an adjustable comb, adjustable competition trigger, Quick Release Rib (QRR), and extended choke tubes.

The latter Elos 2 Elite comes in either 12 or 20 gauge with 28-inch barrels. The deluxe-grade European Walnut plays well with the rich case-colored action

The Franchi Affinity Turkey Elite.

inlaid with gold sporting birds. Again, a left-handed stock option is available by special order. There's a single trigger, TriBore HP barrel, and Inner HP flush-fitting chokes. MSRP on both Elos additions is $3,325. *fabarmusa.com*

FRANCHI

Though much focus falls on its Momentum rifles, Franchi seriously bulks up shotgun offerings with a total of

five fresh offerings. The subgauge craze advances through Italian fronts with two 28-gauge Franchi additions. Both the Instinct LX and SLX over-under get downsized to a 28-gauge frame, and both doubles use the magnum 3-inch

chamber, auto-ejectors, engraving, and inlays. In addition, both wear lovely AA-Grade Walnut stocks and 28-inch barrels with extended choke tubes. The SLX joins existing 12, 16, and 20 gauges and carries an MSRP of $1,799.

The Henry .410 Side Gate Models wear 24-inch round barrels with Invector-style chokes.

Meanwhile, the LX becomes part of the 12- and 20-gauge roster with a 28-inch barrel, case color finish, and retails

for $2,099.

Shifting from classic looks, Franchi keeps with attractive guns but also utilitarian ones for turkey hunters. The Affinity Turkey and Turkey Elite are an exciting pair of autoloading gobbler getters springing from the company's successful Affinity group of Inertia-driven long guns.

Franchi introduced the Affinity Turkey in 12 or 20 gauge with a trim profile, 24-inch barrel, and full Mossy Oak Bottomland camouflage from butt to muzzle. A pistol grip adorns the Turkey-specific models for fast handling, while

extended turkey and extra-full turkey chokes are both included for quick, hunt-specific changes. MSRP lists at $1,129.

Choose the Elite Turkey in either 12 or 20 gauge with a 3-inch chamber and 24-inch barrel. OptiFade Subalpine camouflage coverage pairs nicely with Midnight Bronze Cerakote. The Elite also includes a pistol grip but adds a Picatinny rail and upgrades the chokes to Rhino extended turkey and extra-full turkey chokes along with precision cone patterning to put out lethal shot strings. MSRP is set at $1,249. Now, if we could only get the sub-gauge option on Franchi's Turkey guns, I'll be over the moon. *franchiusa.com*

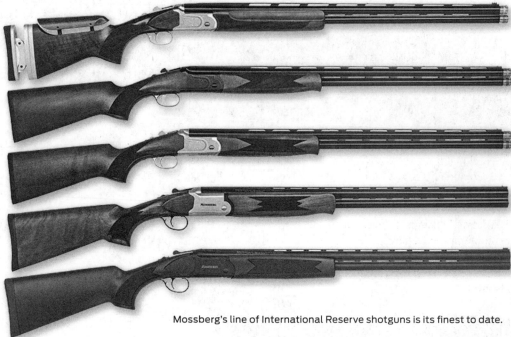

Mossberg's line of International Reserve shotguns is its finest to date.

HENRY REPEATING ARMS

Last year marked Henry's initial foray into the shotgun section of this book,

and let me tell you, the Made-in-America-or-Not-Made-at-All company has done anything but sit back on its haunches.

The Mossberg Gold Reserve.

Not only has it launched a bevy of fresh rifle designs, but it beefed up shotgun offerings to legit levels.

The wildly successful side-gate models — which added a side-loading gate to Henry's traditional tubular magazine feeding port — are now tooled over as a permanent design change on all lever guns rolling out the door of both the Rice Lake, Wisconsin and Bayonne, New Jersey plants.

The blacked-out X-Model continues its tactical growth, with demand in .410 bore still outstripping supply nearly a year after its announcement. A pair of .410-bore

Side Gate Models are built of blued steel, checkered American Walnut, and tipped with a rubber recoil pad. The former wears a 24-inch round barrel with Invector-style chokes, while the latter is a 20-inch fixed cylinder bore birdshot brush-buster. When beauty is paramount, the stunning yet practical brass side-gate .410 packs a six-round capacity along with delightful scroll-and-logo Walnut engraving. They are limited only by the 2.5-inch chambering and the shooter's imagination, where small game, birding, plinking, and even home defense are all in play.

After finding success with a limited line of single shots that

showed off both steel and polished brass options, the company continued with a youth-specific twenty. The Single Shot Slug in 12 gauge with a 3-inch chamber wears a 24-inch round barrel that is fully rifled. With fiber-optic sights and a receiver drilled and tapped for a Weaver base, the Slug hits a prime market for those in hunting areas limited to shotguns or alternate weapons. Blued steel and checkered American Walnut round out the whitetail-bagging package.

Longbeard chasers will appreciate Henry's first dedicated Turkey-specific hunting gun. The Single Shot Turkey is the company's only magnum 3.5-inch-chambered shotgun, fitted with a 24-inch barrel, fiber-optic sights, and prepped for optics mounts. An extended Turkey choke ensures tight, beard-busting patterns at a distance, while Mossy Oak Obsession camo coverage represents the National Wild Turkey Federation (NWTF)'s official pattern. *henryusa.com*

with a revamped lineup of over-under shotguns. Forget anything you've known previously about the company's doubles. The new International Reserve Series comes in two bases: Silver Reserve Field and Gold Reserve Sporting, purpose-built for a combination of upland hunting and clay busting. In addition, there are Field-specific models, good-lookers, a Bantam youth, and even a competition sporting design. While some higher-end design features and enhanced looks are part of the launch, Mossberg still manages to make and keep O/U's affordable and accessible to the masses.

The Silver Reserve utilizes shell extractors, select Black Walnut or synthetic stocks, and matte blue barrels. In addition, there's a company logo laser engraved into the receiver. You can order your receiver in either satin silver or matte blue. A flush-fitting set of five

Eventide variant retails for $632, with the rest set slightly higher at $692.

The Gold Reserve instantly be-

MOSSBERG

Though the pandemic seemingly dampened many presumed new introductions, Mossberg ventures onward

Field chokes comes standard. Available in 12, 20, and 28 gauges and .410 bore, there is also a Youth 20 gauge with a reduced LOP of 13.25 inches. A Black

The Savage Renegauge Competition marks Savage's first foray into race-ready 3-Gun shotguns.

The Rock Island Armory VR82 semi-automatic 20 gauge is the little brother of the VR80, weighing only 7.5-pounds with an 18-inch barrel.

comes Mossberg's finest shotgun offering to date with both internal and external improvements. Aesthetic receiver detail and wood fitment exude class. The guns wear Grade-A Black Walnut stocks, ejectors, ac- tion jew- eling, polished blue barrels, scroll-engraved receivers, and 24-Karat Gold inlay. In addition, they ship with a five-choke extended Sport Set. The base lineup is available

in 12, 20, and .410 bores. Pricing: $983. A Gold Reserve Black Label comes in a 12-gauge 30-inch configuration, as does the top-end Super Sport. The latter adds a high-profile ventilated rib and fiber-optic front sight, as well as a

buttstock that is adjustable for length of pull, cast, and comb height. Mossberg's Gold Reserve Super Sport lists at $1,221. *mossberg.com*

ROCK ISLAND

Rock Island Armory and Armscor have added two exciting shotguns: a purely tactical semi-automatic that builds upon the success of the company's VR-Series. The other is a new, ground-up pump platform that should appeal at once to hunters, home-defenders, and youngsters alike.

The All Generation slide-action shotgun solves a common problem in the firearms market for families with smaller-framed shooters. Those looking for one gun that can do it all — and still fit most family members — will want to get hands-on with the All Generation. The pump comes in various model variants available in 12, 20, and .410, each with a 3-inch chamber, including barrel options in 18.5, 26, and 28 inches. Stocks are black polymer, and the fit is what drives the namesake series.

Each shotgun ships with LOP spacers and adjustable cheek rest for a customized fit. All but the shortest-barrel model include three interchangeable chokes. The best news yet? The retail price on the flexible All-Generation Series shotguns is only $299, making them not only a practical but ultra-affordable option.

Shooters who already gravitate to the company's more tactically minded lines will appre- ciate the addition of Model VR82. Think of this semi-automatic 20 gauge as the little brother of the VR80, weighing only 7.5-pounds with an 18-inch barrel and built of 7075 T6 aluminum. It wears a thumbhole-style cutout stock. The magazine-fed VR82 repeater has a 5+1 round capacity out of the box and accepts VR-series 10- and 20-round mags. MSRP: $729 *armscor.com*

SAVAGE ARMS

Two new 12-gauge models join Savage's

The Stoeger M3500 Snow Goose with distressed white look.

Renegauge stable. First, a Renegauge Prairie expands the company's bloodlines in the hunting market. The Prairie wears True Timber Prairie camouflage stocks with color-matched Brown Sand Cerakote metalwork, and its 28-inch fluted carbon steel barrel includes three flush-mount Beretta/Benelli-style chokes. MSRP is $1,599 on the Prairie.

Meanwhile, the Renegauge Competition marks Savage's first shotgun foray into race-ready 3-Gun contenders. Performance, capacity, and balance are paramount in any such tete-a-tete, and the

The Stevens 320 Security Thumbhole caters to the home defense market.

Renegauge Competition ticks all boxes. An extended magazine tube grants a generous 9+1-round capacity. There's a competition-ready loading port, oversized controls, and a durable Melonite finish. The 24-inch fluted carbon steel barrel ships with specialty extended

chokes, including a Skeet2 Light Mod with .15-inch constriction. A snappy Red Cerakote-finish receiver and mag tube finish set the target-busting model apart from its sporting and hunting brethren. MSRP lists at $1,959.

The two new models join the stable of Renegauge Field, Turkey, and Waterfowl variants. After bagging a trophy tom turkey with the same Renegauge shotgun used to shoot trap and sporting clays, I'm hooked. *savagearms.com*

STEVENS

Local gun stores could not keep the affordable Model 301 single-shot Turkey Model on the shelf when hunters saw proof of its incredibly tight patterning performance and then flipped over the sub-two-bill price tag. So Stevens doubled down by adding an XP Turkey variant that ships with a bore-sighted red-dot optic and now a 301 Turkey Thumbhole. With a 26-inch barrel tipped in a proven Win-Choke Extra Full gobbler tube, this baby bore continues its line of Federal Premium Heavyweight TSS-optimized shooters.

The latest 301 Thumbhole Turkey is in .410 bore and wears its namesake stock in Olive Drab with an ambidextrous-cheek riser synthetic furniture. This baby is svelte, weighing only five pounds and measuring 41.5-inches overall length. But, don't let its small stature fool you. Folks who say hunters cannot ethically take big birds with the smallest bore have never paid the cash for tungsten shot and reveled in the joy of a one-shot clean harvest on Wild Turkeys.

Wallet-friendly Stevens models continue into the slide-action market with a pair of 320 pumps — the 320 Security Thumbhole and 320 Turkey Thumbhole. Continuing on the gobbler front, the 320 Turkey is a bigger bore, coming in either 12 or 20 gauge with a 3-inch chamber and 22-inch chrome alloy steel barrel. The Olive Drab synthetic thumbhole stock is upsized from the 301, though the ambidextrous cheek riser remains. Adjustable fiber-optic turkey sights bring those birds into rapid focus, while an extended Win-Choke Extra Full tube ensures dense shot patterns. Both pumps use dual-action bars and a rotary bolt for durability. The bottom-loading tubular magazine holds five rounds. The 320 Turkey Thumbhole lists for $323. *savagearms.com*

STOEGER

Specialty shotguns are becoming all the rage, but they usually come at a significantly increased cost. Nevertheless, Stoeger manages to continue finding new niches for firearms that fill a need and do so reasonably. Its two scattergun announcements do just that, customizing existing lines of the Condor over-under and semi-automatic 3500.

The Condor Field Synthetic substitutes black composite stocks for wood, a shift that grants worry-free durability and simultaneously cuts cost. This 12 gauge with a 28-inch barrel and 3-inch chamber includes two screw-in chokes. It lists for only $349, a sure bargain for those entering the double-gun market.

Stoeger's M3500 Snow Goose is a 3.5-inch-chambered magnum semi-automatic on the proven Inertia-Drive system. It combines the M3500 Waterfowl with Stoeger's 922R-Compliant extended magazine Freedom series to produce a high-capacity Snow Goose-dropping specialist. Distressed White Cerakote covers the gun from stem to stern to meld with wintry landscapes. The full 10+1 capacity ensures adequate firepower when those migrating whities lock wings into range. There's also a red bar fiber-optic front sight, paracord sling, and shim kit. The Snow Goose ships with five extended choke tubes for an MSRP of $899. *stoegerindustries.com*

SYREN

Is it a Caesar Guerini? Is it a Syren? Yes, on both counts. Syren is the name builder Caesar Guerini gives its shotguns for women. This pandemic's treasure? The Syren Julia Sporting. Named after the daughter of Julius

The Syren Julia is a looker. It sports competition chokes, has DuoCon forcing cones, and a ventilated tapered rib.

Caesar, the Julia is a competition-grade target over-under. Its engraving is like no other before, done in fantasy-style whereby a woman's countenance evolves from scattered floral scrollwork. Though stunning in appearance, the Julia sacrifices nothing in terms of features or practicality while catering to serious female hunters and shooters.

A rich, color casehardened finish on the elongated side plate receiver, paired with high-grade Turkish Walnut stocks, exudes elegance. This 12 gauge with 30-inch barrels ships with six competition chokes, has

TRISTAR

The self-proclaimed "Value Experts," TriStar creates a seismic market shift, not with its typical shotgun designs, but rather, inaugural side-by-sides. The Bristol family includes two distinctly styled doubles.

The first pairs a sweet case color finish with a straight, English-style buttstock. Meanwhile, a Silver variant tends traditional with a nickel-finished receiver accented with 24-Karat gold inlay and laser engraving, then fitted to a standard pistol grip-style stock.

These fresh doubles are available in four appealing

WINCHESTER

It's mostly quiet on the Winchester-front, in terms of shotgun headlines, that

is. Instead, the brand focus falls solely on the company's 6.8 Western centerfire launch, though The American Legend did work in a few 12- and 20-gauge model additions.

The semi-automatic SX-4 family of gas-driven repeaters, already a laundry list of variants, gets a few more. The Hybrid Hunter with its 26- or 28-inch barrel in multiple new finishes and the Waterfowl Hunter bring Mossy Oak Shadow Grass Habitat coverage. For smaller-framed sportsmen and women, the Waterfowl Hunter Compact shortens the length of pull 1.25 inches to 13 inches with options of 24-, 26-, or 28-inch barrels. MSRP on the latest Portugal-built SX-4s ranges

Duo-Con forcing cones and a ventilated tapered rib. The DTS trigger system allows for adjustments to overtravel and take-up, and length of pull. Whether busting clays or pocketing birds, Julia does it with a rare combination of class and performance in a feminine-specific platform. *syrenusa.com*

chamberings: 12, 20, and 28 gauges along with .410 bore. The 28-inch barrels are chrome-lined and ship with five Beretta-style choke tubes. MSRP on the Bristol line starts at $1,000, a legit bargain for upland hunters and sub-gauge clay shooters who have price-shopped doubles in the last decade. *tristararms.com*

The Winchester Waterfowl Hunter wears a Mossy Oak Shadow Grass Habitat camo scheme.

from $959.99 to $1,099.99.

Pump lovers will appreciate Winchester amping up slide-action offerings. Hunters gravitate to simple reliability and new faces like the SXP Hybrid Hunter and Waterfowl Hunter, both dressed in Mossy Oak's Shadow Grass Habitat camouflage. *winchesterguns.com* **GD**

- REPORTS - from the Field MUZZLELOADERS

> LUKE HARTLE

It wasn't long ago when the phrase "primitive weapons" could be used interchangeably with muzzleloaders. But those days are long gone, and they ain't coming back. Sure, you can buy a flintlock, a frilled leather jacket, and go as old-school as you like, but today's muzzleloading technology is keeping pace with the best of the centerfire world.

At its core, the art of shooting a muzzleloader is still a conscious decision to make life harder than it has to be. You get one shot, and although you can do a complete reload in as little as 15 seconds by seasoned hands and strategically placed speedloaders, that seems like an eternity when compared to how long it takes to run a bolt.

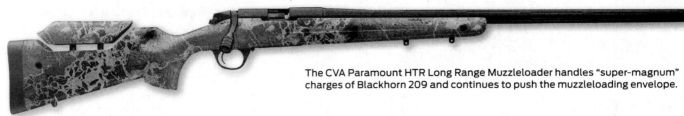

The CVA Paramount HTR Long Range Muzzleloader handles "super-magnum" charges of Blackhorn 209 and continues to push the muzzleloading envelope.

But "primitive" stops there. The best of the current muzzleloader class boasts accuracy and velocities that run parallel with a .308 Winchester. Read that last sentence again if you must, but it's entirely true.

CVA PARAMOUNT HTR LONG RANGE MUZZLELOADER

A few years ago, CVA kicked down

CVA's new Paramount Pro wears a custom-quality Grayboe fiberglass stock, TriggerTech trigger, and is Cerakoted. The Pro is available in .45- and .50-caliber models.

the barricades that defined how far a muzzleloader could accurately shoot — and it did so with the introduction of the Paramount. The Paramount HTR is the line's newest family member for 2021, and it will be offered in both .40 and .45 calibers.

Like all the Paramount models, CVA designed the HTR specifically to handle "super-magnum" charges of Black-

horn 209 (although it's not mandatory, CVA has designed all its Paramounts around Blackhorn 209). When using the maximum recommended propellant charges, the Paramount HTRs produce muzzle velocities comparable to centerfire rifles. Yes, read that again if you must.

When stuffed with PowerBelt ELR 225-grain bullets (the Paramounts are also designed around the PowerBelt ELR bullets, but shooting them is not required), the .40-caliber HTR can produce

muzzle velocities eclipsing 2,700 fps — that's challenging .30-06 speeds.

The HTR has a more hunting-focused stock design than the original Paramount model, featuring an adjustable comb and an internal aluminum chassis that provides a consistent shot-to-shot foundation for the action and free-floating barrel. MSRP: $1,225 *cva.com*

CVA PARAMOUNT PRO

Although technically released by CVA last year, the introduction of the Paramount Pro marked such a unique departure from all other muzzleloaders on the market that it certainly warrants an additional conversation. This "ol' smoke pole" was developed to handle super-magnum propellant charges (think 105

grains by weight), creating the velocities mandatory for making the muzzleloader a 300-plus-yard hunting tool.

The Paramount Pro is built on a custom-quality Grayboe fiberglass stock, wears a TriggerTech trigger, and is bathed in Cerakote. It's available in .45- and .50-caliber models and runs on the VariFlame breech plug system, which is sparked by a magnum rifle primer rather than the more traditional 209-style primers.

CVA also unveiled a .50-caliber Paramount Pro Colorado version that includes a set of Williams peep sights — for those behind-the-times states that still hold firmly to the definition of "primitive weapons season." MSRP: $1,699 *cva.com*

CVA ACCURA LRX

Fear not: CVA hasn't gone full space-

age with its muzzleloaders. Instead, the Accura LR-X continues the exceptional Accura tradition and is the longer-barreled muzzy in the line (the LR stands for "Long Range").

The LR-X boasts a 30-inch Nitride-treated stainless steel Bergara barrel (Bergara makes exceptional barrels) and a quick-takedown design for easy cleaning and compact transport. Like

The more traditional CVA Accura LR-X sports a 30-inch Bergara barrel to maximize velocity — and you know Bergara tubes are accurate!

the Paramount line, the new Accura LR-X comes with a carbon-fiber collapsible field rod, which you carry on your hip, a configuration that allows the barrel to be completely free-floated. The stock also wears a height-adjustable comb.

Unlike the Paramount series, the Accura LR-X utilizes the more traditional screw-in/out breech plug system and is available in .45- and .50-caliber options. MSRP: $675 *cva.com*

CVA MUZZLE BRAKE

A muzzle brake for a muzzleloader? Welcome to 2022! CVA designed its Paramount Muzzle Brake specifically for Paramount and Accura models. The brake is a three-port design, with a "larger" bottom port through which you can remove cleaning patches.

The newer muzzleloaders create faster ignition and more velocity from magnum charges — which makes more felt recoil. The muzzle brake, of course, mitigates that felt recoil but it certainly creates some bark.

It also creates some minor challenges that you need to overcome: A field funnel for pouring powder is mandatory. Plus, it's smart to use at least a 4-inch jag on the cleaning rod because of the additional length of the barrel with the brake installed. MSRP: $79 *cva.com*

The CVA Paramount Muzzle Brake slashes felt recoil in today's magnum-charged smoke poles.

CVA POUCH LOADER SET

The Universal speedloaders are simple enough: semi-translucent, florescent orange design that holds the bullet and the powder in separate compartments. Plus, CVA specifically designed the lid to hold either a 209 primer or a VariFlame adapter for the Paramount series. And, if you're not a fan of storing speedloaders in your pockets, you can wrap the Speed Pouch around the buttstock to hold two universal speedloaders for quick (at least by muzzleloading standards) follow-up shots. MSRP: $36/pouch with two universal speedloaders. *cva.com*

FEDERAL FIRESTICK 80-GRAIN EQUIVALENT

In 2020, Federal changed the muzzle-loading game with the introduction of the FireStick, which is essentially an element-proof capsule that loads from the breech while the projectile loads from the front. The goal was to give the shooter a more consistent powder charge via an easier-loading solution.

The caveat is that the gun must be specifically designed for use with the FireStick, and at present, only Traditions has jumped on board with its NitroFire model. In addition, the BATFE has determined that you must move the gun through an FFL, which of course, is not mandatory for most other muzzleloaders.

Federal first released FireSticks in 100- and 120-grain-charge equivalents. This year, you can get the FireStick 80-grain equivalent for an even lighter-recoiling experience. MSRP for a box of 10 is $27.99. *federalpremium.com*

HORNADY BORE DRIVER FTX

What's the biggest drawback to most muzzleloading bullets? Fumbling with sabots when trying to conduct a quick reload in the field with cold, adrenaline-charged fingers. Hornady has recently released a new solution. Without a sabot, the Bore Driver FTX seats

quickly and easily — and as muzzleloader shooters know, that seating consistency also aids in shot-to-shot accuracy.

In short, the polymer base (aka pre-fitted sabot) features a "post" that inserts into the bottom of the bullet that swells upon ignition, creating tight and consistent base-to-bullet connection and

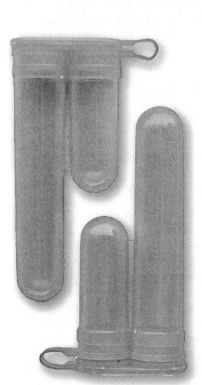

The CVA Pouch Loader Set uses handy universal speedloaders, a built-in lid for your primer, and powder in separate compartments. CVA designed the pouch to wrap around your buttstock for easy access and quick reloads.

improved base-to-barrel contact.

The FTX bullet sports Hornady's InterLock ring, which helps retain bullet weight upon impact. In

boasting a precise and accurate trigger pull, along with a rebounding hammer and manual cross-block trigger safety.

In addition, a Dual Safety System, Accelerator Breech Plug (the plug

mer found on most in-lines, allowing you to cock the muzzleloader with the push of a button. To de-cock, press the recessed de-cocking button — or open the action. This entire series features a Chromoly steel barrel, premium

The Traditions BuckStalker XT gives you 200-yard accuracy in a budget package.

conjunction with the tough copper alloy jacket of the FTX, that ring delivers deep penetration and rapid expansion. And, if you know Hornady, you know it loves the FlexTip, which initiates expansion at lower velocities, boosting terminal performance in front of lighter charges.

As of now, the BoreDriver FTX is available only in a 290-grain .50-caliber option, but let's hope Hornady expands that to include a .45-caliber variant soon. MSRP: $34.99 box of 20. *hornady.com*

Federal FireSticks now come in 80-grain equivalent for a lighter recoil option or chasing accuracy.

is removable by hand and allows the use of loose or pelletized powder), and what Traditions calls its Speed Load System.

The XT will be available in a pile of configurations, including G2 Vista camo or black, various finish options, as well as scoped and non-scoped versions. And, for hunters who pulled tags in Idaho and Oregon, the Buckstalker XT Northwest Magnum features the musket ignition, open breech, and open-sights. MSRP: $229 *traditions-firearms.com*

No more fumbling with sabots, thanks to Hornady's Bore Driver FTX muzzleloading bullet. Its polymer base is full-bore diameter, and these bullets hit hard on big game.

Traditions has upgraded the Vortek StrikerFire to a 1:24-in-twist configuration. This fast twist rate stabilizes long bullets, increases accuracy, and expands the range of projectile options for long-range muzzleloading.

TRADITIONS BUCKSTALKER XT

Traditions upgraded the Buckstalker XT to a premium-grade Chromoly steel barrel, making the muzzleloader lightweight yet solid and accurate. That also allowed Traditions to chase shooters seeking 200-yard accuracy from a very budget-minded package.

The Buckstalker XT got a trigger upgrade with the Elite XT trigger system,

Recently upgraded with a VAPR twist barrel, Traditions has upgraded the Vortek StrikerFire to a 1:24-in-twist configuration. This faster twist rate stabilizes long bullets, increases accuracy, and expands the range of bullet options fueling the current long-range muzzleloading trends.

The Vortek StrikerFire system replaces the conventional external ham-

Cerakote finish, Tac-2 Trigger System, Hogue Comfort Grip, Dual Safety System, Accelerator Breech Plug, and Speed Load System.

The Vortek StrikerFire is available in many new configurations, including a 28- or 30-inch barrel, a couple of camo options or black, as well as scoped and non-scoped versions. MSRP: $449. *traditionsfirearms.com* ⓖⒹ

REPORTS - from the Field OPTICS

›JOE ARTERBURN

The coronavirus pandemic may have slowed or shut down many aspects of the world, but it hasn't affected the continued advancements in the world of optics. Technology, design, and materials continue to evolve and push optical performance and capability beyond limits. The word *limit* doesn't seem to be in the vocabulary of optics designers and manufacturers.

Major manufacturers rolled out new developments, new models and continue to add to their lines of tried-and-true products. Here's a snapshot of what is out there now. Look fast. Optics are changing at the speed of light.

AIMPOINT

Aimpoint's CompM5b has interchangeable turrets to enable you to adapt using ballistic profiles of different calibers, essentially meaning customization for different ammunition. It's lightweight at only 9 ounces, it doesn't add much, and what it adds is well worth it. It allows for unlimited eye relief and is compatible with Aimpoint's 3XMag-1 and 6XMag-1 magnifiers and all generations of night vision devices. It features ten intensity settings of the 2 MOA red dot to match varying light conditions. It runs on AAA batteries. Available in two configurations, with either a 39mm or 30mm optical axis.

Aimpoint designed the Acro P-1 for use on pistols and other firearms requiring a small enclosed red-dot sight. The fully enclosed housing protects electronic compo-

The Aimpoint CompM5b allows for unlimited eye relief and is compatible with Aimpoint's 3XMag-1 and 6XMag-1 magnifiers and all generations of night vision devices.

GERMAN PRECISION OPTICS

German Precision Optics (GPO) has introduced its new second focal plane Spectra line of riflescopes in 4x, 6x, and 8x models and added a 2.5-20x50i model to the GPOTAC series of first focal-plane tactical riflescopes.

The Spectra 4x scopes, targeting hunters facing diverse conditions, feature GPObright high-transmission lens coatings, PASSIONdrop hydrophobic exterior lens coat, and double high-definition glass objective lenses. Some Spectra scopes feature GPO's microfiber optic dot iCONTROL illumination system, adjust-

sights. The RXS-100 and RXS-250 are budget-friendly options (MSRP: $99.99 and $249.99, respectively) of quality sights for pistols, shotguns, and rifles. Bushnell houses the sharp, bright 4 MOA dot reticle in a durable aluminum housing with an oversized hood for glare reduction and lens protection. Detented windage and elevation adjustments adjust with 1 MOA increments. Auto shutoff preserves batteries when not in use. It features eight brightness settings and comes with a low Weaver-style mount. You can pair the RXS-250 with night vision.

Bushnell's LMSS2 Elite Tactical Spotting Scope is the evolution of a lightweight modular scope designed for your choice of either the H322 or TREMOR4 reticle, both great for spotting with any MRAD-based riflescope reticle. Both feature 0.2-mil Horus Grid; the H322 has patented Rapid Range Bars for robust wind and drop compensation, range estimation, and follow-up shots. MSRP: $1,749.99. *bushnell. com*

The Bushnell RXS250 is a budget-friendly 4 MOA red-dot optic.

able for low light to bright conditions. The Spectra line also features a modernized turret system combining a low-profile bal-

nents and 1X non-magnifying optics. Designed as a primary sight for handguns, it can also serve on carbines, shotguns, and rifles, even used as a backup sight on magnified scopes or thermal imaging optics. A variety of mounting options are available. And it is parallax-free, so the 3.5 MOA red dot remains parallel to the bore no matter the angle you hold it, so you don't have to worry about centering the dot. Ten brightness settings (four of them compatible with night vision). It weighs only 2.1 ounces. MSRP is $599. *aimpoint.com*

BUSHNELL

Bushnell is producing high-quality, reliable, and affordable products with the RXS collection of reflex

listic turret with a protective cap. GPO includes a customizable blank turret.

For medium- and long-range hunting, both the Spectra 2-12x44i and 2-12x50i feature either the BRWi ballistic reticle or the G4i, with your choice of a 44mm or

The GPO Spectra 4x 2.5-10x44i with G4i Drop reticle.

50mm objective lens. For increased light transmission and low-light accuracy, the Spectra 3-18x56i features a massive 56mm objective lens, as well as the

The redesigned Hawke Sidewinder is lightweight and sports a 30mm tube with a 24-degree field-of-view.

GPO BRi reticle, a fully illuminated ballistic reticle with illuminated holdover markers. MSRPs are: 1-6x24i, $799.99; 1.5-9x32i $899.99; 1.5-9x44i $899.99; 2-12x44i $899.99; 2-12x50i $949.99; 3-18x56i, $1,099.99. *gpo-usa.com*

4-16x50 at $799 and 6-24x56 at $819. *www.hawkeoptics.com*

HI-LUX OPTICS

The Hi-Lux TD-3 (which stands for Tac Dot 3 MOA) is an open reflex sight for quick target acqui-

The Kahles K524i 5-25x56i first focal-plane scope features the Austrian maker's new SKMR4 reticle.

HAWKE OPTICS

Hawke Optics redesigned its best-selling Sidewinder riflescope making it lighter, stronger, and even better-performing. It features a 30mm tube and ultra-wide 24-degree field of view and has generous 4-inch eye relief. The new push/pull locking elevation turret has a "witness window" showing an internal scale that travels up or down as you dial so you can quickly glance to get back to zero — no need to count clicks. Instead, you have instant visual confirmation and help in eliminating second-guessing on longer shots. Eight second-focal plane variations are available, ranging from 4.5-14x44 at $619 to 8-32x56 at $689; and two first-focal plane models,

si-tion for optics-ready pistols and other firearms. Machined from lightweight, durable aircraft-grade aluminum and featuring reinforced electronic housing, Hi-Lux designed it to withstand heavy-recoil calibers. You select the reticle pattern of 2.5 MOA dot or 34 MOA circle, or both, and one of 10

brightness settings. (The two lowest are compatible with night vision.) The 28mm x19mm window provides a wide field of view. It comes with a Picatinny rail mount. MSRP: $279. *hi-luxoptics.com*

KAHLES

Kahles has introduced its SKMR4, the fourth variation of its SKMR reticle, available only on the K525i riflescope, the 5-25x56i first focal-plane scope popular with hunters, competitive shooters, and other shooters with a

The Leica Calonox thermal imaging camera produces high-contrast imaging at long distances, farther than 3,000 yards.

The new DeltaPoint Micro Red Dot Sight from Leupold is a fully enclosed, low-profile red dot explicitly designed for concealed carry.

penchant for fine optics. The SKMR4 reticle, developed in collaboration with Shannon Kay of the K&M Shooting Complex and owner of the Precision Rifle Series, has been fine-tuned with enhanced features, facilitating faster and more precise shooting. It provides greater hold precision with 0.2-mil holds while having 15 marker bars for longer-range capability and an increased number of marker bars (from 12 to 15) and solid (rather than hollow) windage bars for better visibility. MSRP: $3,721. *swarovskioptik.com*

LEICA

Hunters are going to dig Leica's Calonox, its first thermal imaging camera. The Calonox comes in two versions, a handheld unit or one that mounts directly to riflescopes, allowing you to search for game in the dark or tough light conditions — and video record the experience with high contrast and detail. It uses new Leica Image Optimization, which works in conjunction with the unit's large sensor and high-resolution OLED display to produce high-contrast imaging at long distances, farther than 3,000 yards in some instances. Operation is easy, with just three buttons to manipulate. The Calonox "Sight" is the version that you can mount on conventional riflescopes. It features 1x magnification (since the scope will provide magnification), but you can also use it as a stand-alone handheld unit. The Calonox "View" is the handheld version, with 2.5x magnification. Both have 42mm lenses and operate at least six hours on one charge of the rechargeable battery. MSRP: $3,999.

Leica has

The new mid-priced Leupold VX 3HD scope.

also launched a new line of premium riflescopes called Amplus 6. This scope features 6x zoom capability, sharp reticle illumination, and a 30mm tube design. The Amplus 6 series comes in eight models with various magnification ranges, objective lens sizes, and reticles, including its L-4a universal hunting reticle and the L-Ballistics reticle designed for precision shooting at long distances. Both are second focal plane reticles. Leica builds these scopes for everyday, all-around use and adverse conditions — and they feature the premium optical performance for which Leica is known. $1,599. *leicasportoptics.com*

LEUPOLD

Leupold's new DeltaPoint Micro Red Dot Sight is a fully enclosed, low-profile red dot explicitly designed for concealed carry and personal defense firearms. Compact and easy to hide, it mounts directly to the rear sight dovetail and sits at the same height as factory iron sights, so the red dot aligns with the front sight. The first models will fit non-MOS Glock models and Smith & Wesson M&P handguns. It measures 2.25 inches in length and 1.25 inches in height and weighs only 1.1 ounces. Other features include DiamondCoat II scratch-resistant lenses, fully enclosed LED and Leupold's Professional-Grade Optical System, plus Motion Sensor Technology that switches to sleep mode after five minutes of inactivity and reactivates upon movement. Leupold isn't listing MSRPs this year, they say, just "street/retail" prices, which for DeltaPro Micro is $399.99.

Leupold launched a new line of riflescopes as well, VX 3HD, designed to be tough, lightweight, and deliver performance in low light, pretty much everything hunters look for — at prices that won't stagger your bank account. Leupold's Elite Optical System provides excellent dawn-to-dusk light transmission for a bright image when it matters most, emphasizing low light periods when animals are most active. The new line includes an array of magnification ranges, objective lens sizes, main tube diameters, and elevation adjustment types. Illuminated reticle models are available, and all have Leupold's Custom Dial System (CDS), which eliminates the need for holdovers on longer shots. Also, the ZeroLock moves when you want it to and allows an accurate return to zero. Match-grade repeatability and ergonomic controls are easy to read and use, even when wearing gloves. Prices range from $499.99 to $999.99. *leupold.com*

MAVEN

This year, Maven produced its first range-finder, the RF-1, which boasts a ranging performance from 5 to 4,500 yards (to 2,700 yards on animals; 4,500 on reflective targets). It features a 25mm objective lens, an adjustable eyecup, and an impressive 7x magnification. It also gives you a choice of line of sight or angle-compensated measurement, as well as rapid acquisition times as fast as .25 seconds for instantaneous readings in scan mode. You can manually switch between modes: Field Mode, which ignores larger, more reflective objects in the background while reading a less reflective target closer to the use (think a deer standing in front of a tree row), or Forest Mode, which reads the farthest item that reflects, ignoring brighter (think snowbank), and dimmer (branches) targets in the foreground. Tech specs: aluminum housing, magnesium chassis, IPX7 waterproof rating, waterproof, fog-proof, and scratch-resistant multi-coated lenses. MSRP: $400.

Maven builds the new 5-30x RS.4 Long-Range Riflescope specifically for precision rifle-shooting competitors and other long-range enthusiasts, those who require precise, minute adjustments. This optic is a first focal plane scope with parallax adjustment, four-level red and

The Maven 5-30x RS.4 Long-Range Riflescope is a first focal plane scope with parallax adjustment, four-level red and green reticle illumination, and your choice of MOA- or MIL-based reticles.

green reticle illumination, and your choice of MOA- or MIL-based reticles. With easy-to-feel positive stops, the mechanical zero stop ensures you can get back to your original zero. Quality is evident, including ED glass for clarity, silky-smooth focusing, precision-milled adjustment, and durable anodized finish to the ele-

The Meopta Optika5 riflescope line features 5x zoom, zero-reset turrets, and advanced MeoBright lens coatings for edge-to-edge clarity.

ments and heavy use. Check with Maven about customization options. MSRP is $1,800. *mavenoptics.com*

MEOPTA

Meopta jumps into the laser-rangefinding binocular pool with its MeoPro Optika LR line, including a 10x42HD (MSRP $1,499) and 8x50HD ($1,849) models that can measure out to 2,600 and 2,950 yards, respectively. As always, Meopta loads them with its European optics, including high-definition glass and MeoLux lens coating for bright imaging in low light and high resolution and contrast, meaning clear,

Maven's first rangefinder, the RF-1, can range to 4,500 yards (to 2,700 yards on animals; 4,500 on reflective targets).

crisp viewing. They feature three modes: auto for continuous ranging of moving targets; near ranging, which ranges the object closest in the aiming circle—and far-ranging, which measures the farthest thing in the ranging circle. The near and far-ranging modes cut out the annoying tendency for unintended targets to grab your rangefinder's attention. They also compute angle compensation for uphill and downhill.

Meopta's newest line of riflescopes, the advanced one-inch Optika5 series, features 5x zoom, zero-reset tur-

The Nightforce NX8 F2 in 2.5-20x50 and 4-32x50 models sport wide magnification ranges while trimming weight and length, building on the F1 line's success.

rets, and advanced MeoBright lens coatings for edge-to-edge clarity and bright, sharp images. Six models — 2-10x42 RF (rimfire), 2-10x42, 3-15x44, 4-20x44, 4-20x50, and 4-20x50 RD — with second focal-plane models available. A nice touch is the rear-facing magnification display you can see from behind the scope. Multi-coated lenses, of course. MSRP ranges from $349.99 to $549.99. *meoptasportsoptics.com*

NIGHTFORCE

Building on its F1 NX8 models' success, Nightforce designed the NX8 F2 (in 2.5-20x50 and 4-32x50 models; MSRP: $1,900

The reasonably priced ZULU6 line of binos from Sig Sauer includes 10x30 and 16x42 models with image stabilization.

and $2,100, respectively) with wide magnification ranges while trimming weight and length. Though compact, these scopes are full-featured, including Nightforce's ZeroStop turret, Digillum reticle illumination, power throw lever, and purpose-built F2 reticles, including the new MOAR-CF2D and MIL-CF2D reticles with dual scale calibration, an open center with a dot and intuitive number-ing. The Dual Scale reticle system features numbering at both 16x and 32x and a calibrated mark on the power change ring. ED lenses for optical quality to allow for superb optical quality with an 8x zoom ratio and short overall length are among this new offering's best features.

Also, Nightforce's new ATACR 4-20x50 F1 scope is unique in that it offers 130 MOA of elevation adjustment with parallax adjustment down to 11 yards. It efficiently fills a magnification need in Nightforce's popular ATACR line. Smaller and lighter (but with a 25-per-cent im-prove-ment in magni-fication over the 4-16x42 F1, for you Nightforce fans), it features Digillum illumination, ZeroStop turret, power throw lever, and quality ED lenses. MSRP: $3,000. *nightforceoptics.com*

SIG SAUER

Sig Sauer brought stabil-ity to its popular ZULU series of bin-oculars with the ZULU6. Those binos feature Optical Image Stabilization (OIS) technology, which uses an electronically stabilized two-axis gimbal system to can-cel vibration caused by shaking hands, pounding heartbeats, heavy breathing, even buffeting wind, choppy waves, or rough roads. Sig introduced this image-stabilizing technology a few years ago in its OSCAR3 compact spotting scope, and now it's available in the new, reason-ably priced ZULU6 line, which includes 10x30 and 16x42 models. The idea is to eliminate the vibration and movement that can cancel part of the optics' resolu-tion and optical performance. Lenses are multi-coated with Sig's SPECTRACOAT, LENSHIELD, and LENSARMOR coat-ings. They also feature MOTAC motion-activated illumina-tion

The new NL Pure binos have Swarovski's largest field-of-view so far and a compact and ergo-nomic design that fits your hands. The FRP forehead rest adjusts to line up your view and provide stable three-point support for steady viewing.

and earned an IPX4 waterproof rating. MSRP: 10x30, $799.99; 16x42, $899.99. *sigsauer.com*

SWAROVSKI

Like many others, suppose you thought Swarovski's EL line of binoculars was pretty much it when it comes to quality and performance. You weren't giving Swaro's design and engineer teams enough credit. Now the NL family of binoculars, in the making for years, take *it* to another level. Let's jump in on the improvements, starting with things you'll notice right away, like Swarovski's largest field-of-view so far and a compact and ergonomic design that fits your hands, making long periods of viewing more relaxed and comfortable. Adding to viewing comfort is the new FRP forehead rest, which adjusts to line up your view and provide stable three-point support for steady viewing, especially useful when using a tripod at high magnification. As you'd expect from Swarovski, image definition, clarity, and color fidelity are top-notch. Other pluses include a smooth focusing mechanism and rugged and lightweight construction. These two models come in a 10x42 for an MSRP of $3,366 and a 12x42 for $3,443.

And Swarovski has added a new 115mm objective module to its popular modular spotting scope system. Yes, that's huge, Swarovski's largest, which adds to the 65mm, 85mm, and 95mm line of modules, all of which combine with three available modular oculars (ATX angled, STX straight, and BTX dual eyepiece) for a versatile spotting scope system tailored to your preferences. MSRP: $3,299. *swarovskioptik.com*

The Tract TORIC 34mm 4.5-x30x56 MOA ELR riflescope is for extreme long-range shooting.

TRACT

Tract targets extreme-range shooters — we're talking out to a mile and beyond — with its TORIC 34mm 4.5-x30x56 MOA ELR riflescope. It features a "Christmas-tree" style reticle designed so shooters can measure targets to determine the distance and then make corrections by either dialing or using windage and elevation marks for quick, precise compensation. Easy to quickly read, the reticle features 1 MOA and 5 MOA increments along the horizontal and vertical crosshair with larger hash marks indicating 5 and 10 MOA increments. The upper vertical and horizontal crosshairs also feature .5 MOA grids for precise target measurement. It's not as complicated as it may sound. The .14 MOA floating center dot does not obscure the target, and the first focal plane design means you can use the reticle at any magnification. MSRP: $1,694. *tractoptics.com.*

The new Vortex Fury HD 5000 10x42 Laser-Rangefinding Binocular lets you range targets, plus it pairs with the Applied Ballistics Elite Solver so that you can create custom ballistic profiles.

Trijicon downscaled its popular RMR red-dot sight in the new RMRcc, designed for smaller concealed carry handguns.

TRIJICON

Trijicon's new RMRcc, a down-scaled version of the popular RMR red-dot sight, is designed for smaller concealed carry firearms. The thinner, lower-profile design provides for comfortable concealed carry and reduces snagging risk during the draw. Trijicon has managed to keep all the larger version's popular features, including easy-to-use buttons, standard 2032 battery power, and various mounts to fit a boatload of carry pistols. A crisp illuminated aiming point, adjustable to 3.25 or 6.5 MOA, and eight brightness settings, centers focus on the target. A nicely-thought-out touch is that it stays on your chosen brightness setting until you change it, not every time you turn it off and on. The multi-coated lens provides wideband light transmission for minimal change to the target area color. Waterproof, rugged battery contacts and electronics to survive harsh use and elements are standard. MSRP is $699. *trijicon.com*

VORTEX

Binoculars aren't just binoculars anymore. Vortex's new Fury HD 5000 Laser-Rangefinding Binocular not only lets you see and accurately range targets, but it also pairs with onboard technology and connectivity to provide you with wind and drop solutions to shooting challenges. Pair it with the Fury HD app and onboard Applied Ballistics Elite Solver, and you can create custom ballistic profiles (or use one of three preloaded profiles of popular cartridges). It has an onboard compass and humidity, barometric pressure, temperature sensors, and two wind modes. Plus, it can link to your Kestrel weather unit or Applied Ballistic Garmin devices to put a full range of information at your fingertips. This new unit continues Vortex's use of

The new Vortex SPARC red-dot series harnesses solar energy to power what may be its smartest red-dot sight so far.

high-definition clarity with the XR lens coatings for crisp imaging. The range-finder can reach out to 5,000 yards on reflective targets in three ranging modes. MSRP: $1,999.99.

Solar-powered red-dot sight. How smart is that? Vortex's latest iteration of the SPARC red-dot series harnesses solar energy to power what may be its

smartest red-dot sight so far. Vortex says it'll get up to 150,000 hours of battery life. Auto D-TEC technology detects ambient light conditions and automatically switches from solar to battery power if the sun can't power the ultra-fine 2 MOA dot. There are 10 daytime illumination settings and two night vision-compatible settings. Motion activation keeps it ready, and auto-shutoff preserves battery life. Fully multi-coated glass protected by a tough, one-piece chassis. MSRP: $359.99. *vortexoptics.com*

ZEISS

Zeiss has added to its popular SF line of binoculars with Victory SF 32, an ultralight all-purpose binocular with an impressive field-of-view and unique ErgoBalance concept that shifts the center of gravity toward the eyepiece producing less muscle stress for less-fatiguing long-term viewing. The 8x model weighs 21.2 ounces; the 10x, 20.8. Both models deliver exceptionally wide field-of-view (465 yards at 1,000 feet, essentially 20 percent more observable area), which can be essential in covering large areas quickly and catching tell-tale movement at the edges of the sharp viewing field. Focusing is fast, taking just 1.6 revolutions of the focus wheel to adjust from 6.4 feet to infinity, an exceptional balance of speed and precision in focusing. MSRP on the 8x32 is $2,249.99; 10x32, $2,299.99. *zeiss.com* GD

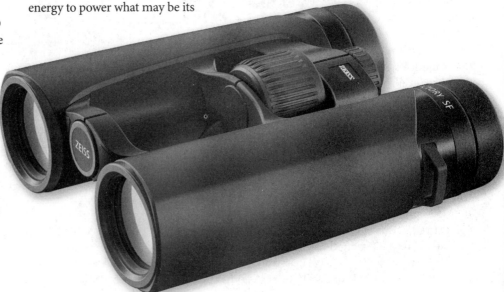

The Victory SF 32 is an ultralight all-purpose binocular with an impressive field-of-view.

- REPORTS -
from the Field
AIRGUNS

❯ JIM HOUSE

When doing background work for this piece, I was struck by the number of listed products out of stock at major airgun sellers. Moreover, the shelves in sporting goods stores have much less merchandise in the airgun section.

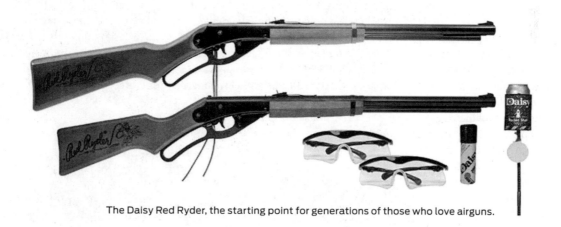

The Daisy Red Ryder, the starting point for generations of those who love airguns.

There are three major themes in airguns at this time. The first is full-auto models that fire BBs at a rate of 1,400 rounds per minute from a magazine containing 25-30 BBs. That means that the rate of fire is slightly over 23 BBs per second, so that you could empty a 25-round magazine in 1.07 seconds. I could not have inserted a single BB in the muzzle of my Daisy

100 that quickly. I suppose that such BB-firing guns provide a lot of fun for some shooters, but the possibility of ricocheting sprayed BBs dictates prudence in their use.

A second direction for airguns is toward large-caliber, pre-charged models in the range of .25 to .50 caliber. Some have enormous power for an air-powered rifle; others are repeaters. Such air rifles are

for hunting or silhouette shooting. Since compressed air from a reservoir powers them, it is necessary to fill the reservoir ("pre-charge" it, hence pre-charged pneumatic or PCP), which requires a special pump and compressor or a scuba tank. These are not "stand-alone" models that permit taking just the rifle and a supply of ammunition out for some shooting. It takes specialized equipment to

take advantage of the free air that is the propellant.

A third trend is CO_2 guns that are replicas of existing and popular firearms. From models that resemble the Colt Peacemaker to ones mimicking the Walther CP99, airgun makers imitate virtually every popular handgun. I don't know if there is an imitation of the Liberator single-shot pistol of WWII fame that fired the .45 cartridge, but I would not be surprised to see one sometime. Unfortunately, the realism in both appearance and function can — and has — lead to disaster. Therefore, one must use caution and discernment in when and how to display the realistic-looking guns.

Speed Sells.

There is no doubt that hunt-

lead pellet available. However, since lead airgun projectiles have a bad connotation in some places, lightweight alloy pellets are in vogue. As a result, some manufacturers advertise muzzle velocities with the light alloy pellets to have the highest possible velocity for their products. Unfortunately, advertised speeds may not always give a realistic indication of the velocities at which you can drive heavier hunting-type pellets. Even so, there are some very powerful airguns!

The Winchester 1911 looks like a Colt 1911 .45 Auto, but it fires BBs.

Closely resembling a Ruger SR22, Daisy intended this little 426 pistol for recreational shooting.

ing with powerful airguns is a sport that is on the rise. Several publications have regular columns and features on the sport. Some states officially recognize hunting with airguns. Advertisers have been quick to display their models in magazines. As new subdivisions arise to accommodate those who wish to escape urban areas, there is a place for this type of hunting and pest control.

When it comes to both airguns and firearms, it seems that velocity sells.

It used to be that manufacturers of airguns listed velocities with the lightest

AIRFORCE AIRGUNS

AirForce Airguns has a popular line of PCP models that includes the Texan, which is available in .257, .308, .357, .457, and .50 calibers. All have velocities up to 1,000 fps depending on pellet weight, with corresponding energies of 190, 300, 400, 600, and 600 ft-lbs as the caliber increases.

These list for $1,084.95. The Texan SS is a shorter model with a special shrouded barrel. Most features are like those of the standard Texan, except that it does not include a .50-caliber offering and top velocities list at 930 fps. The Texan SS costs $1,234.95. In .177, .20, .22, and .25 calibers, AirForce offers the Condor, like the Texan but with maximum velocities specified as 1,450, 1,250, 1,150, and 1,450 fps, respectively. MSRPs run $784.95 for all calibers.

CROSMAN

Although it may seem anachronistic, there is still a place for the single-shot pistol powered by either air or CO_2. Two models that occupy a special place in my memory are the Crosman 2240, a .22-caliber, CO_2 powered model, and the .22-caliber Crosman American Classic, a multi-pump. These pistols produce up to

The AirForce Texan is available in all popular calibers from .177 to .50 for hunting everything from pests to wild pigs.

460 fps, and in .22 caliber, are suitable for small pest control. By removing the grip panels, you can add a shoulder stock or scope, making them even more versatile. The Crosman 2300T is a target version with many of the features of the 2240, but with a longer barrel, adjustable sights, and a steel breech that is suitable for scope mounting. Crosman continues making an array of CO_2 powered pistols, some that launch BBs and others that use .177 pellets. Both revolver and autoloading configurations are available.

Gone are the .20-caliber Sheridan multi-pumps and the Benjamin .177 and .22 multi-pump models that were so popular for decades. However, information on Crosman's website and from reading comments on airgun forums

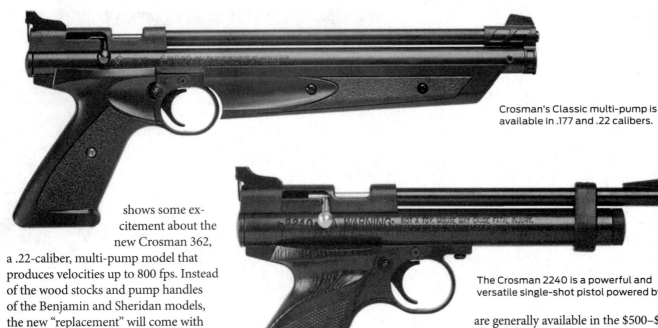

Crosman's Classic multi-pump is available in .177 and .22 calibers.

The Crosman 2240 is a powerful and versatile single-shot pistol powered by CO_2.

shows some excitement about the new Crosman 362, a .22-caliber, multi-pump model that produces velocities up to 800 fps. Instead of the wood stocks and pump handles of the Benjamin and Sheridan models, the new "replacement" will come with polymer furniture. If you find a Benjamin 392 or 397 still available, as I did while seeking information for this review, buy it. In .177 caliber, the Crosman 2100 is a multi-pump that gives excellent performance.

Also new from Crosman is the Model 2289 Drifter Kit, which includes stock and pistol grips and a bag for carrying and storage. This airgun is a short-barreled, multi-pump that utilizes the single-shot bolt action of Models 2240

hunting air rifles is the Marauder, a PCP model in .177, .22, and .25 calibers with velocities of 1,100, 1,000, and 850 fps, respectively. It utilizes a rotary magazine that holds 10 rounds (eight rounds in .25 caliber). Options include wood

and 2260. It is also a .22 caliber that has an advertised muzzle velocity of up to 550 fps. There is a place for these short, handy air rifles. They don't require air compressors, tanks, or CO_2 cartridges: You can pick your air rifle and some pellets and do some shooting.

The mainstay of the Crosman line of

or polymer stock, and some feature an adjustable comb. The .177 and .22 models are also available with an optional Lothar Walther barrel. For those who want a PCP air rifle in one of the smaller calibers (.25 or smaller), the Marauder is available with many options. It has established an enviable reputation over the years, and I have Marauders in .22 and .25 calibers that have impressed with their performance. The various Marauder models

are generally available in the $500–$600 price range.

Another Crosman product that should be of interest to pest and small game hunters is the Benjamin Maximus, a single-shot PCP available in .177 and .22 calibers. Muzzle velocities go 1,000 fps for the .177 caliber and 850 fps for the .22. As in other PCP rifles, the Maximus is potent enough for use on pests and small game. In addition, because of its reservoir design, you can charge it with

a hand pump. With retail prices in the $225–$300 range, the Maximus is one of the least expensive ways to get started with a PCP rifle.

DAISY

Long known for its most iconic product, the Red Ryder BB gun, Daisy specializes in airguns of low to modest power. Several BB guns that have been

The Benjamin Marauder is an excellent PCP rifle despite its moderate price.

Available in .177, .22, and .25 calibers, the Benjamin Maximus is a solid value.

staples in the product line for years are still available. A Red Ryder Heritage Kit includes both an adult-size Red Ryder and the standard youth model so that an adult and a trainee of small stature can have identical guns. Daisy markets several other BB guns, including the famous model 25 pump.

Daisy offers a rather extensive line of pistols that fire BBs or .177 pellets, most of which require CO_2 cylinders. Almost all the models indicate a velocity of up to 430 fps.

The model that intrigues me is the Model 426, a replica of the Ruger SR22 rimfire pistol (unlike the Ruger, it lacks a visible hammer). The grip section can be removed, exposing a 15-round magazine and the frame that holds a CO_2 cylinder. However, unlike the Ruger firearm, the rear sight on the Daisy is not adjustable. On the Daisy 426, the safety is a cross-bolt that passes through the frame just behind the trigger.

In contrast, Ruger located the dual safety levers on the SR22 on either side of the frame just below the slide. Even with those differences, the Daisy 426 closely mimics my favorite rimfire pistol. Daisy continues to market the Winchester Model 11 pistol that mimics a Colt 1911 in size, weight, and many functions. It has a magazine that holds 15 BBs with muzzle velocities of up to 410 fps by a CO_2 cylinder.

One of the most popular multi-pump rifles is the .177-caliber Daisy 880, which Daisy introduced in 1972. It is still available either alone or as part of a shooters kit. It is available with stock and forearm made of a brown polymer, and it is a classic air rifle with an advertised muzzle velocity of up to 800 fps. You can use the 880 as a single-shot pellet rifle or a repeater when used with BBs. However, its rifled barrel performs better with pellets. A similar airgun, dubbed the Winchester 1977XS, is available in combination with scope. In that configuration, the rifle has a neat thumbhole stock made of a black polymer.

HATSAN

Some of the most common and potent PCP rifles carry the Hatsan label, and suppliers such as Airgun Depot, Airguns Arizona, Pyramid Air, and Midway USA market them. The Hatsan Hercules is available in several calibers, including .30, .35, and .45, with maximum velocities of 1,070, 910, and 850 fps, respectively, and corresponding to these velocities, energies of 115, 150, and 290 ft-lbs. These energies correspond roughly to those produced by the .45 Auto, .380 Auto, and .32 Auto handgun cartridges. Such energies do not approach centerfire rifles in equivalent calibers, but they aren't weaklings. Even a .22 Short will

Weighing 295 grains and selling for about 70 cents per round, this Hatsan Vortex Supreme .45 pellet is not for casual plinking.

dispatch large animals under carefully controlled conditions. No airgun operating at 3,000 to 4,000 psi can duplicate the performance of a firearm that generates from 20,000 to 30,000 psi. However, for hunting with an airgun, a PCP rifle is the logical choice. Hatsan models generally fall in the $600–$1,000 range.

UMAREX

Umarex offers the Strike Point

The Hatsan Hercules is available in calibers from .177 to .45.

single-shot multi-pump in .177 and .22 calibers with velocities of up to 650 and 529 fps, respectively. When it comes to pistols that have realistic appearance and function, it's hard to outdo Umarex. Models are available in all forms at a wide range of prices.

Umarex has several PCP models. One is the Gauntlet, which shoots .22-caliber pellets up to 950 fps

Although the Walther Reign is a compact model, it is a powerful PCP for serious hunting.

or .25 pellets to 890 fps. The Umarex Origin is a .22 model that gives a velocity of 1,000 fps with alloy pellets. Priced in the $350–$400 range, the Origin and Gauntlet are moderately priced but effective.

WALTHER

The Walther Reign is a compact PCP model available in .22 and .25 calibers with velocities specified as 975 and 870 fps. The Reign is a bullpup design that measures only 34 inches in length and weighs just 5.4 lbs. Such a model would be a small game hunter's or pest shooter's delight. It sells for $600. GD

- REPORTS -
from the Field
AMMUNITION

› PHIL MASSARO

Ammunition? What ammunition? That may be the most asked question of the last year, and in many ways, events have warranted it.

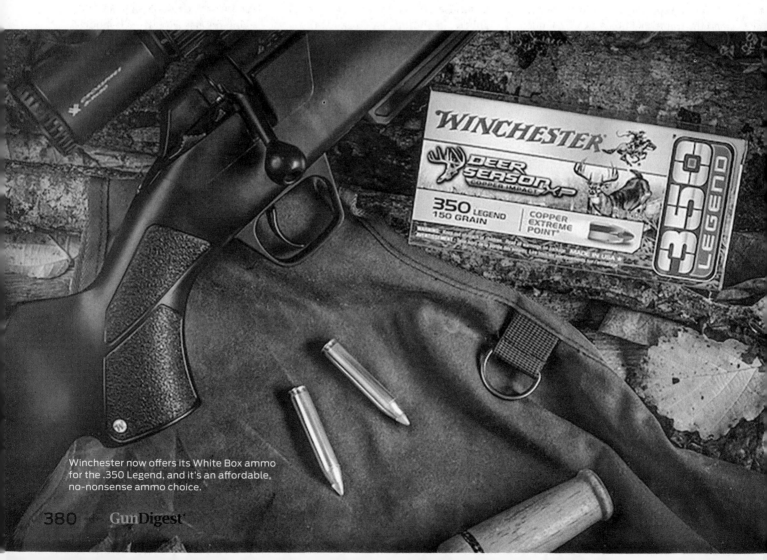

Winchester now offers its White Box ammo for the .350 Legend, and it's an affordable, no-nonsense ammo choice.

Berger's loaded ammunition line now includes a pair of great choices for the ever-popular .223 Remington.

223 REMINGTON 77 GRAIN TACTICAL

223 REMINGTON 73 GRAIN BOAT TAIL TARGET

Empty shelves, seemingly endless backorders, and too many canceled trips to the range have some folks a bit antsy. Still, I can assure you the ammunition companies are doing everything in their power to provide us all with the products we want. And despite — or perhaps even in defiance of — the current shooting supply issues, there are a healthy number of new products released this year. With a couple of brand new cartridges and many line extensions, there are plenty of innovative options coming. So, let's jump right in and take a look at the new ammo offerings.

BERGER

Berger, whose component bullets have been the favorite of handloaders for years now, extends its line of loaded ammunition for 2021 to include the .223 Remington. There are two new loads: the 73-grain boat-tail Target bullet at a muzzle velocity of 2,820 fps and the 77-grain OTM Tactical bullet at 2,750 fps. Both are heavy-for-caliber, with the former requiring a twist rate of 1:9 inches and the latter twist rate of 1:8. With G1 Ballistic Coefficients of .348 and .374, respectively, these make an excellent choice for target work, long-range coyotes and foxes,

as well as prairie dogs and woodchucks way across the town or alfalfa field. Packaged in boxes of 20. *bergerbullets.com*

BROWNING

The latest waterfowl shotshells from Browning, Wicked Blend, offer a blend of varying sizes of bismuth and steel shot. The mixed-metal payload is stuffed into Browning's Wicked Wad, using 30 percent bismuth and 70 percent steel, in a combination of BB (steel) and No.

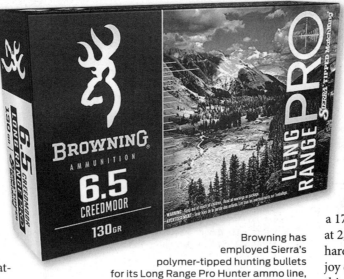

Browning has employed Sierra's polymer-tipped hunting bullets for its Long Range Pro Hunter ammo line, and it's a great combination.

1 (bismuth) or No. 2 (steel) and No. 4 (bismuth) in 12 gauge (3 ½ and 3 inches) and 20 gauge (3 inches). Available in 25-count boxes.

There are several excellent loads in Browning's new The Long Range Pro Hunter series for those who embrace

the standard cartridges. The series uses the proven Sierra Tipped GameKing bullet — a laser-accurate cup-and-core projectile with a jacket thick enough for good penetration yet soft enough upfront to open reliably — but with 'Browning gold' polymer tip instead of the traditional Sierra green tip. Browning uses nickel-plated cases for the Long Range Pro Hunter line, which resists corrosion from sweaty hands. Included in the line are the 6.5 Creedmoor and 6.5 PRC (130-grain TGK), .270 Winchester (140-grain TGK), .308 Winchester (165-grain TGK), .30-06 Springfield, .300 WSM, and .300 Winchester Magnum (180-grain TGK). *browningammo.com*

BUFFALO BORE

Though younger than its ultra-popular sibling, the .30-30 Winchester, there is still a strong if quiet following for the .32 Winchester Special. Buffalo Bore offers a pair of loads for the .32 Special; one features a 170-grain jacketed flat-nose soft point at 2,300 fps, the other is a 200-grain hardcast flat nose at 2,200 fps. If you enjoy carrying a lever gun chambered for this grand old cartridge, you'll be well served by Buffalo Bore ammo, as I've never been disappointed by its products. *buffalobore.com*

CCI

For 2021 CCI teams up with renowned camouflage company Realtree to introduce Clean-22 Realtree .22 Long Rifle

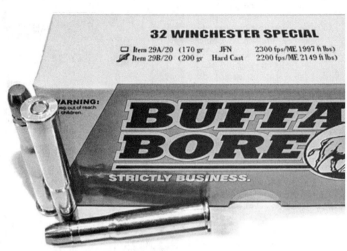

Buffalo Bore keeps the .32 Winchester Special alive with two new loads.

ammunition. It uses a 40-grain bullet at 1,235 fps muzzle velocity in a rifle barrel. The polymer-coating — tan, green, and black to make a sort of camo pattern within the bottle — reduces barrel fouling and will also keep your suppressor cleaner. Packaged in a 400-count bottle, Clean-22 is suitable for plinking, target work, and small game hunting alike. *cci-ammunition.com*

FEDERAL

The Federal Punch .22 LR ammo line extension for 2021 is one of the most unique, as Federal offers a 29-grain nickel-plated lead-core bullet optimized for performance in shorter-barreled handguns. While many shooters don't associate the .22 LR with defensive handguns, Federal's testing has shown the Punch's flat-nose bullet driving 12 to 16 inches of penetration in ballistic gel, beating some centerfire cartridges, like the .25

CCI has teamed up with Realtree to produce a signature look for its Clean-22, using three different colored projectiles.

Auto and .32 Auto. Punch .22 LR does 1,070 fps from a 2-inch handgun barrel and 1,650 fps from a 24-inch rifle barrel. Loaded in nickel cases to resist corrosion and packed in 50-count boxes, Federal's Punch .22 LR load makes a sound choice for a backup handgun or those shooters who are especially recoil sensitive.

The Swift A-Frame is one of the most

well-respected rifle bullets on the market, and the handgun version is equally revered. With its dual cores separated by a thick partition of copper gilding material, the A-Frame handgun bullet has a hollowpoint to initiate expansion. In addition, the separate cores ensure bullet integrity for deep penetration. While the A-Frame has long been a fantastic component bullet, Federal has also offered them in its handgun and rifle ammunition. However, Federal has now extended its lineup to include a 100-grain A-Frame load for the .327 Federal (a too-often overlooked cartridge) and a 200-grain load for the hefty 10mm Auto. This bullet takes both cartridges to a new level in the hunting fields, as I have often opined that the Swift A-Frame — in any iteration — is one of the most potent and reliable soft points ever produced. I can't recommend one better — equal, perhaps, but not better. Federal loads these with a high-performance primer in corrosion-resistant nickel cases.

Federal introduced its HammerDown line in 2020, with cartridge cases especially tuned for optimum performance in the lever guns. I can attest to the accuracy and potency of the ammo, as I used the 300-grain .45-70 Government load to take a mature eight-point whitetail

buck in the Catskill Mountains last season. With chamfered cartridge rims, nickel-plated cases, and a bonded-core flat-point bullet, HammerDown is an excellent choice for traditional lever guns at conventional ranges. Now, Federal extends the line to include three new cartridges. The first is the popular .35 Remington with a 200-grain bullet, which still has a large following, as it remains a popular choice in the Marlin Model 336 rifle. Among those who still carry a lever rifle afield, the rimless .35 Remington is probably second to the classic .30-30 Winchester, and the .35 Rem aficionados still cite the advantage of greater bullet weight and larger frontal diameter. The second cartridge is the .444 Marlin, offered with a 270-grain bullet; for those who enjoy carrying a big-bore lever gun, the .444 Marlin is a sound choice, even if it isn't as popular as the .45-70 Govern-

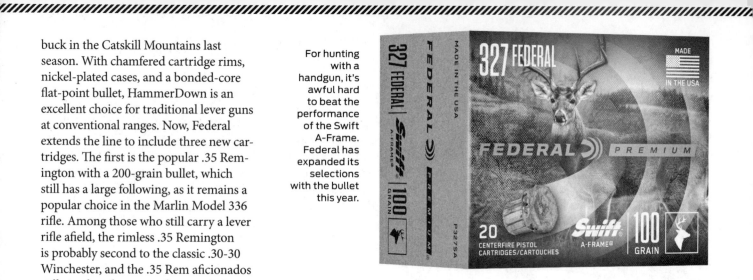

For hunting with a handgun, it's awful hard to beat the performance of the Swift A-Frame. Federal has expanded its selections with the bullet this year.

1.49 inches (just a tad shorter than the Grendel) and an overall cartridge length of 2.26 inches. The cartridge has a base diameter of .440 inch, the same as its parent, so it requires a unique bolt face. There are three loads available from Hor-

nady: the 105-grain BTHP in the BLACK line, the 108-grain ELD-Match in the Match series, and the 103-grain ELD-X in the Precision Hunter load. That ELD-X has a G1 B.C. of .512, and with a muzzle velocity of 2,800 fps and a 200-yard zero, you'll see that bullet strike 7.6 inches low at 300 yards and 21.8 inches low at 400 yards. At the 400-yard mark, the bullet still retains more than 1,000 ft-lbs of energy, making it a perfectly suitable deer cartridge.

Hornady also introduced a muzzle-loading bullet that doesn't require a patch or sabot. The Bore Driver FTX uses a hollow polymer base that expands upon ignition to seal the gases in the bore and the FlexTip (a pliable polymer tip) to initiate expansion, even at low velocity. The Interlock ring controls expansion. The .50-caliber bullet weighs 290 grains and comes in packs of 20. *hornady.com*

A .22 LR for personal defense? Federal says yes, with its new Punch load.

ment. Lastly, Federal now has a 250-grain HammerDown load for the .45 Colt, making that classic double-duty cartridge even more potent. Available in boxes of 20 cartridges. *federalpremium.com*

HORNADY

Hornady designed the new 6mm ARC (Advanced Rifle Cartridge) to optimize the performance of the AR-15 platform. Based on the 6.5 Grendel and sporting a 30-degree shoulder with minimum body taper, the 6mm ARC has a case length of

Hornady's 6mm ARC is destined to be a good choice for the AR platform.

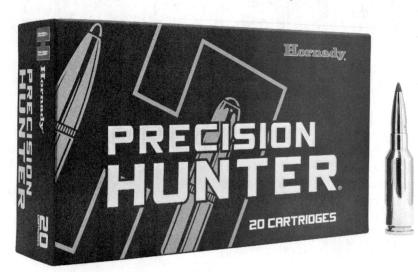

Winchester's Super X 16-gauge steel loads keep that great shotgun bore in the field and not in the cabinet.

REMINGTON

Remington Ammunition is back! Despite the turmoil of 2020, with the Remington brand's future being questionable, it is back and in good hands. Remington Ammunition is now a part of Vista Outdoors, which houses such names as CCI, Federal Premium, and Speer. And I can happily announce that the first product is a line extension, and a good one: The 6.5 Creedmoor loaded with the 130-grain Swift Scirocco II. Neither of these needs an introduction. The Creedmoor has a considerable following, and the Swift Scirocco II has been a solid performer for a couple of decades. With a muzzle velocity of 2,750 fps, the polymer tip and boattail retain energy and resist atmospheric drag, while the thick copper jacket and bonded core construction ensure the bullet retains close to its original weight. The polymer tip also acts as a wedge to initiate expansion. So, if you want to take your Creedmoor hunting, the 130-grain Swift Scirocco II is an excellent choice.

But that's not all. As Remington enters its newest stage of the journey, it extends the Premier Match line to include the 6.5 PRC cartridge, with a 140-grain Berger OTM. The 6.5 PRC is a stout cartridge, capable of fantastic long-range performance, and the Berger OTM is a perfect match (pun fully intended) to that case.

I'm looking forward to seeing the Remington line back in action. *remington.com*

WINCHESTER

Based on the .270 WSM case, with the case length and datum line shortened a bit, the 6.8 Western is a Winchester/Browning collaboration

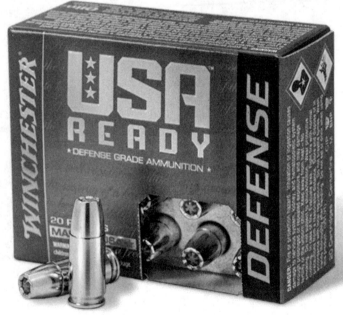

Winchester's USA Ready handgun ammo line; note the unique insert in the hollowpoint.

which uses a faster twist rate (1:8 or 1:7.5 inches, depending on the rifle) to launch 165-, 170- and 175-grain .277-diameter bullets at outstanding velocities. Housed in a short-action rifle, the 6.8 Western will send the Winchester Expedition Big Game Long Range load with the 165-grain Nosler AccuBond Long Range at a muzzle velocity of 2,970 fps. Moreover, the Winchester 170-grain Ballistic SilverTip screams at 2,920 fps, and the Browning Long Range Pro Hunter load (featuring the 175-grain Sierra Tipped GameKing) sends at a velocity of 2,830 fps. These effectively give you the trajectory and energy figures of the .300 Winchester Magnum with a 180-grain spitzer boattail at a reduced recoil level. The 165-grain Nosler ABLR bullet has a G1 B.C. of .620, and the 175-grain Sierra TGK has a G1 B.C. of .617; they both retain energy and resist the effects of wind deflection.

It seems the 16 gauge is making a comeback, and that would have made my grandfather and his brothers happy, as they enjoyed their sixteens. For 2021, Winchester offers its famous Super X shotshells in 16 gauge, with a 15/16-oz. payload of steel shot in a 2 ¾-inch shell at 1,350 fps. This load is a perfect choice for waterfowlers and those required to use the lead-free shot for upland and other game. In addition, Winchester offers this load with a thicker wad to prevent the steel shot from contacting your barrel. Available in 25-count boxes.

For handgunners, Winchester offers its USA Ready line of handgun ammunition, featuring its proprietary Hex-Vent insert in the bullet's hollow cavity. This unique polymer insert shields the bullet from obstruction (common among hollowpoints) while consistently expanding the bullet. Winchester loads these jacketed hollowpoints into nickel-plated brass and uses a match-grade primer for consistent ignition. Available in three highly popular cartridges: 9mm Luger +P (124 grains, 1,170 fps), .40 S&W (170 grains, 1,000 fps) and .45 ACP (200 grains, 1,200 fps), packaged in boxes of 20. *winchester.com* GD

- REPORTS -
from the Field
RELOADING

❯ PHIL MASSARO

Much like the ammunition scene, the last year left us reloaders scrambling to find supplies to keep our presses running.

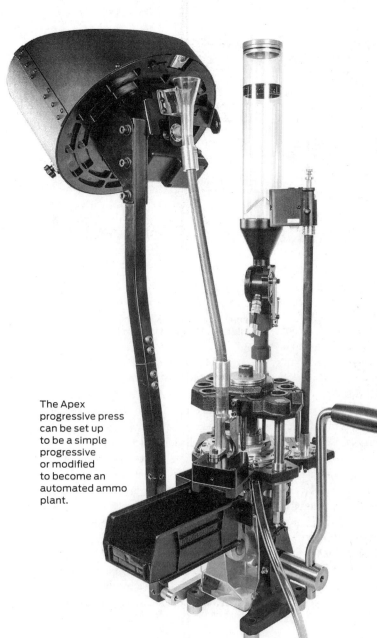

The Apex progressive press can be set up to be a simple progressive or modified to become an automated ammo plant.

B ut, despite the record number of new shooters coming to the market, there are still components available. And like ammo makers, those who produce reloading components and tools are doing their best to see that orders ship. Unfortunately, both RCBS and Redding have no new products to offer, as they concentrate on the production of back-ordered tools. But there are a significant number of new components and reloading tools — some more traditional, others a bit left of center — so let's take a look at what's fresh in the handloading world.

ALLIANT

Alliant introduced Reloder TS 15.5, a new temperature-stable powder with a burn rate between the company's excellent Reloder 15 and the more recent Reloder 16. Like its older sibling, Reloder TS 15.5 will work great in medium-capacity cases such as the .308 Winchester, .223 Remington (especially with heavier bullets), .22-250 Remington, and .35 Whelen. Still, it will also be a stellar performer in the large safari cartridges such as the .375 H&H Magnum, .404 Jeffery, .458 Lott, .470 Nitro Express, and .505 Gibbs. It contains a de-coppering agent to keep things tidy in your barrel, and the traveling hunter will appreciate the powder's consistency across a wide range of temperatures.

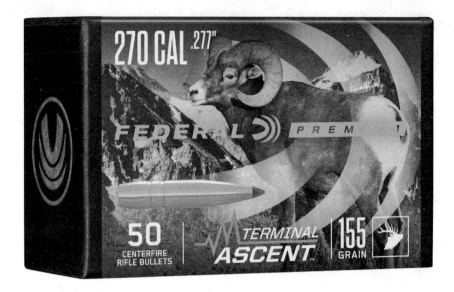

270 CAL .277"

FEDERAL PREM

50 CENTERFIRE RIFLE BULLETS

TERMINAL ASCENT

155 GRAIN

Federal's Terminal Ascent is a strong, sleek, and accurate bullet.

Federal has now extended the available choices in the Terminal Ascent line to include heavier bullets in three of our most popular bore diameters: .277, .284, and .308. The .270s will see a 155-grain T.A., the 7mms get a 175-grain T.A., and the .30s have the chance to launch the 215-grain T.A. If you appreciate fantastic terminal performance coupled with flat trajectories and high retained weight, this trio of Terminal Ascent bullets from Federal probably has something to make you happy. *federalpremium.com*

Available in 1- and 8-lb. containers. *alliantpowder.com*

BERGER

Berger has released two new quarter-bore bullets: the 133-grain Elite Hunter and the 135-grain Long Range Hybrid Target. The former is a heavy-for-caliber hunting bullet, requiring a 1:8-inch twist rate, with a G1 B.C. of .613, using the famous J4 jacket. The latter is a target bullet using the Berger MRT (Meplat Reduction Technology) to maintain a consistent B.C. value (a G1 of .650 in this instance), also requiring a 1:8 twist. The typical scheme of tighter twist rate/longer, high-B.C. bullet continues, and Berger answers the call for those wishing to extend the capabilities of the standard formulae of yesteryear. *bergerbullets.com*

FEDERAL

If you haven't had the opportunity to load up some of Federal's Terminal Ascent bullets yet, you truly are missing out. With their proprietary blue Slip-Stream polymer tip that resists heat, maintains a high B.C., and initiates expansion upon impact, the Terminal Ascent is an excellent bullet for hunting at just about any sane range. The AccuChannel groove in the bullet's shank reduces drag, and a short lead core chemically bonded to the jacket combined with a boattail makes it devastating on game. In addition, it has proven to be wonderfully accurate — my .280 Ackley Improved loves the 155-grain 7mm Terminal Ascent — and will reliably expand even down to low impact velocities, yet is rugged enough to hold together when delivered at high speed at a short distance, even from magnum cartridges.

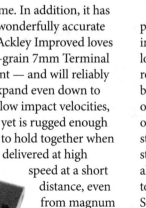

Berger is famous for its long, sleek hunting bullets and is now available in .257-caliber.

FRANKFORD ARSENAL

The Frankford Arsenal F1 Single Stage press is an ergonomic design incorporating some new features with a familiar look and feel. Constructed with steel rod frame pillars for strength without bulk, the F1 uses a steel ram that rides on ball bearings for an ultra-smooth feel on every press stroke. Designed to hold standard ⅞-14 reloading die bodies and standard shellholders, Frankford's F1 also comes with a switchable LED light to illuminate your work while reloading. Spent primers kick to a roomy, quick-detach bottle, or the user can convert to a

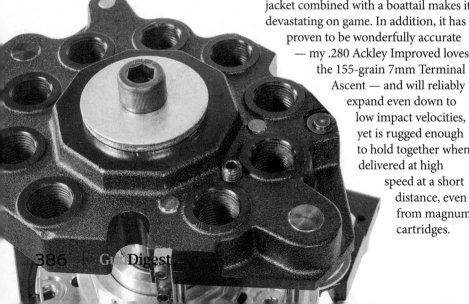

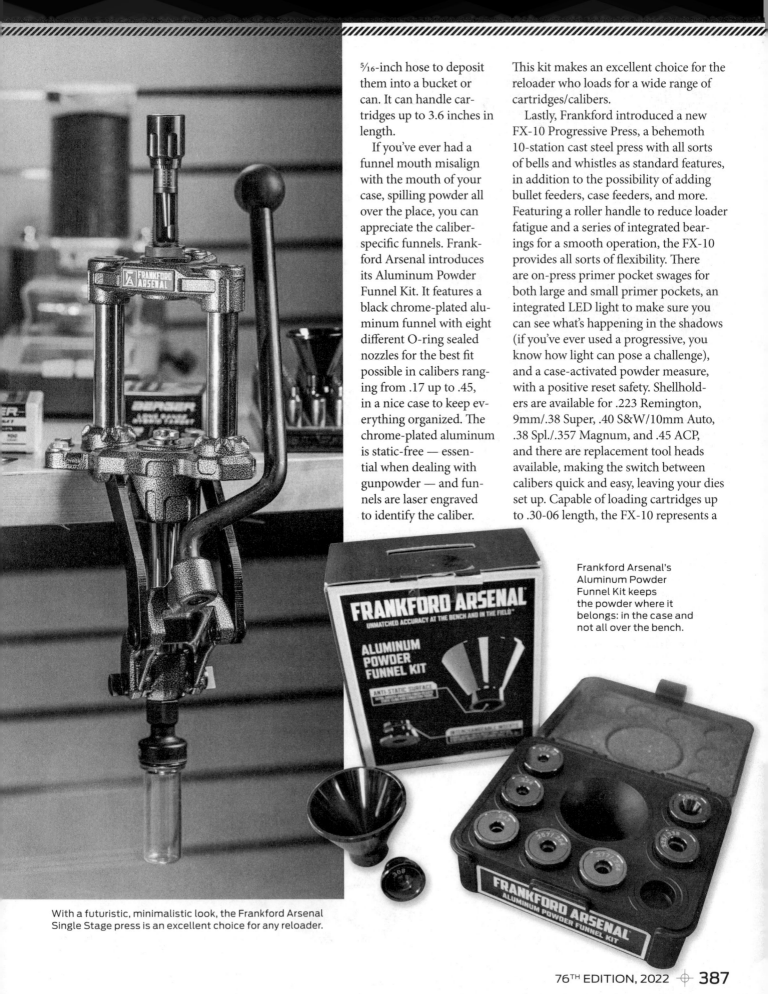

⁵⁄₁₆-inch hose to deposit them into a bucket or can. It can handle cartridges up to 3.6 inches in length.

If you've ever had a funnel mouth misalign with the mouth of your case, spilling powder all over the place, you can appreciate the caliber-specific funnels. Frankford Arsenal introduces its Aluminum Powder Funnel Kit. It features a black chrome-plated aluminum funnel with eight different O-ring sealed nozzles for the best fit possible in calibers ranging from .17 up to .45, in a nice case to keep everything organized. The chrome-plated aluminum is static-free — essential when dealing with gunpowder — and funnels are laser engraved to identify the caliber.

This kit makes an excellent choice for the reloader who loads for a wide range of cartridges/calibers.

Lastly, Frankford introduced a new FX-10 Progressive Press, a behemoth 10-station cast steel press with all sorts of bells and whistles as standard features, in addition to the possibility of adding bullet feeders, case feeders, and more. Featuring a roller handle to reduce loader fatigue and a series of integrated bearings for a smooth operation, the FX-10 provides all sorts of flexibility. There are on-press primer pocket swages for both large and small primer pockets, an integrated LED light to make sure you can see what's happening in the shadows (if you've ever used a progressive, you know how light can pose a challenge), and a case-activated powder measure, with a positive reset safety. Shellholders are available for .223 Remington, 9mm/.38 Super, .40 S&W/10mm Auto, .38 Spl./.357 Magnum, and .45 ACP, and there are replacement tool heads available, making the switch between calibers quick and easy, leaving your dies set up. Capable of loading cartridges up to .30-06 length, the FX-10 represents a

Frankford Arsenal's Aluminum Powder Funnel Kit keeps the powder where it belongs: in the case and not all over the bench.

With a futuristic, minimalistic look, the Frankford Arsenal Single Stage press is an excellent choice for any reloader.

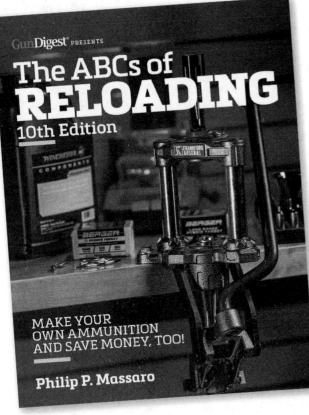

Gun Digest's *ABCs of Reloading 10th Edition*, penned by Phil Massaro.

HODGDON

The *Hodgdon 2021 Annual Manual* is a magazine-style reloading manual containing over 5,000 loads, and it includes feature articles. It is a simple manual, updated annually, and filled with plenty of information for classic and modern cartridges alike. In the 2021 issue, Hodgdon includes load data for the 6mm ARC, 6.5 Weatherby RPM, 27 Nosler, and .458 SOCOM. Of course, being Hodgdon's manual, the powder choices include those brands under its roof: Hodgdon, IMR, and Winchester. But that trio of powders covers an awful lot of ground. Included in the 2021 issue is a tribute to Hodgdon's own Ron Reiber — the resident wizard of powder at Hodgdon who's been there for nearly thirty years — who retired at the end of 2020. I enjoyed getting to know Ron while on a pheasant hunt in southeast Kansas (the man gave a clinic with his Perazzi .410 bore), and I know his presence in the industry will be missed. However, he assuredly deserves a happy retirement. Cheers, Ron! *hodgdon. com*

HORNADY

With a 1,500-grain capacity, the Hornady M2 Digital Bench Scale is a brilliant addition to any bench, as it will quickly and accurately measure the weight of all sorts of components, from powder to bullets to cases and even loaded ammo. With a large LCD (perfect for those of us with aging eyes) and 0.1-grain accuracy discrimination, Hornady ships the M2 with an AC power adaptor, two calibration weights, and a metal powder pan. In addition, Hornady builds the M2 with the same load cell used in its Auto Charge powder dispenser.

The Hornady G3-1500 Electronic Scale is a small, portable, battery-powered scale perfect for benches with little room or for the reloader who enjoys portability. Operating on two AAA batteries (not included), this unit is compatible with a

good value for the reloader looking to make a large volume of ammunition. *frankfordarsenal.com*

GUN DIGEST

Well, folks, it's shameless plug time. The 10th Edition of the classic reloading instructional manual *The ABCs of Reloading* is now available, penned by none other than Yours Truly. This series of books has been around for quite a while and has been authored by Dean A. Grennell, Bill Chevalier, and C. Rodney James; the 10th Edition is my effort. I wrote *The ABCs of Reloading* with the beginning reloader in mind, giving background and instruction on tools, components, and the techniques required to walk newbies through the steps needed to produce safe, reliable ammunition. If you're interested in reloading or know someone who is, I can proudly recommend it as a reference book that will guide them safely on their way. 288 pages, softcover, black & white format. *gundigeststore.com*

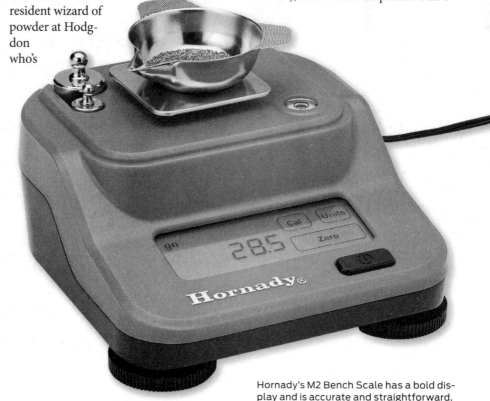

Hornady's M2 Bench Scale has a bold display and is accurate and straightforward.

Hodgdon's *2021 Reloading Manual* is a neat, concise, and welcome addition to any reloading bench.

The Frankford Arsenal FX-10 progressive press is one serious piece of gear, fully capable of generating a whole lot of ammo quickly.

that is computer-interfaced and automatically driven. Even the powder measure is motorized and programmable for different loads, and the unit features an onboard primer collator. Safety is paramount, and the Mark 7 sensors can cover all the bases, down to a Swage Sensor, which detects any primer pocket obstruction upon repriming the case. The Mark 7 Progressive Presses start at $2,995.00, and they go up from there. If you are serious about producing a lot of ammunition, look at the detailed YouTube videos showing the operation of the Mark 7 presses to decide if they are right for you. *lymanproducts.com/brands/mark-7-reloading/*

powder trickler and will give measurements up to 500 grains. With a large power button and a bold LCD, the G3-1500 uses a precise load cell with an accuracy of 0.1 grain. It comes with a scale weight for calibration and a dust cover to keep the unit clean. *hornady.com*

LAPUA

Lapua extends its line of excellent brass cartridge cases for 2021 to include four new cartridges. The pair of PRC cartridges (6.5 and .300) and the .284 Winchester, and the classic .300 Winchester Magnum are now available with the Lapua headstamp, and all are annealed for long cartridge life. That .284 Winchester is seeing a resurgence among F-Class shooters, obviously being popular enough to warrant Lapua producing its highly revered cases. *lapua.com*

LYMAN

Lyman announced that Mark 7 Reloading is now a Lyman brand and includes the Evolution line of progressive presses designed for the serious reloader. You can get various models, ranging from the manually activated Evolution to the commercial-grade Revolution, which is entirely digital-automated, and computer operated. Any option is available, from the case and bullet feeders to all sorts of sensors that will indicate anything from a lack of decapping to improper primer orientation to a bullet sensor that stops the process if it doesn't sense a bullet, to a digital powder check. At the top end of the scale, the Revolution is an automated, motorized system

Hornady's G3-1500 is a handy little portable scale, which runs on battery power.

6.5 PRC · .284 Win · .300 PRC · .300 Win Mag

NEW LAPUA® CASES FOR 2021!

Lapua has long made excellent brass cases, and for 2021 offers four new calibers.

tions for each from other industry folks (you might see a familiar face in there) as well as tips from the Nosler Lab crew. *nosler.com*

OK, this may not necessarily be a new reloading tool, but it's a rare occasion when the central focus of a book is about an innovator in the reloading industry. Bob Nosler, son of founder John Nosler, relates the tale of his life's experiences to Gary Lewis (who also worked with John on his book *Going Ballistic*) in a new release titled *Born Ballistic – The Life and Adventures of Bob Nosler*. Having worked in a family business since the age of 11, I can immediately relate to Bob's tale, and this book held my attention from cover to cover. Nosler's success story — now in the hands of Bob's son John — is a great one. If you've enjoyed the accuracy and terminal performance of any of Nosler's extraordinary designs, you'll feel a connection to this book. This book makes an excellent gift for the reloader in your life or addition to your reloading library. *shop.nosler.com*

NOSLER

A good reloading manual is an essential part of any reloader's library, and with the speed at which makers are releasing new cartridges, it can be challenging to keep up.

Nosler — which produces an imposing lineup of projectiles from rifle to handgun, target to hunting, from .17- to .458-caliber — has published its *Reloading Guide No. 9*, an 800-page hardcover book chock-full of excellent data, cartridge introductions and histories, and much more. With a message from company President John R. Nosler and a foreword by John B. Snow, No. 9 is a must-have for any reloader. Nosler includes 101 different cartridges in the Guide, with introduc-

Biographies of reloading component producers are few and far between, and *Born Ballistic* should have a place in your reloading library.

SHARPSHOOTER 22LR RELOADER

Sharpshooter 22LR Reloader offers the One Stroke Gas Check Die, a simple die that screws into your single-stage press with a punch that slides into the shell-holder groove. Using aluminum 'valley' flashing, a single stroke of the ram creates a gas check for cast bullets. Available in five of the most popular calibers — .38/.357, 9mm, .40, .44, and .45 — the One Stroke Gas Check Die makes gas checks for a fraction of a penny. For those into cast bullets

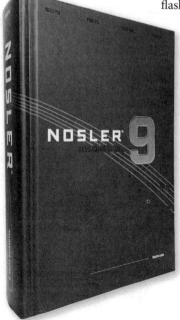

Modern, reliable, and most importantly, safe load data is imperative, and Nosler does a great job of delivering all that in its *No. 9 Reloading Manual*.

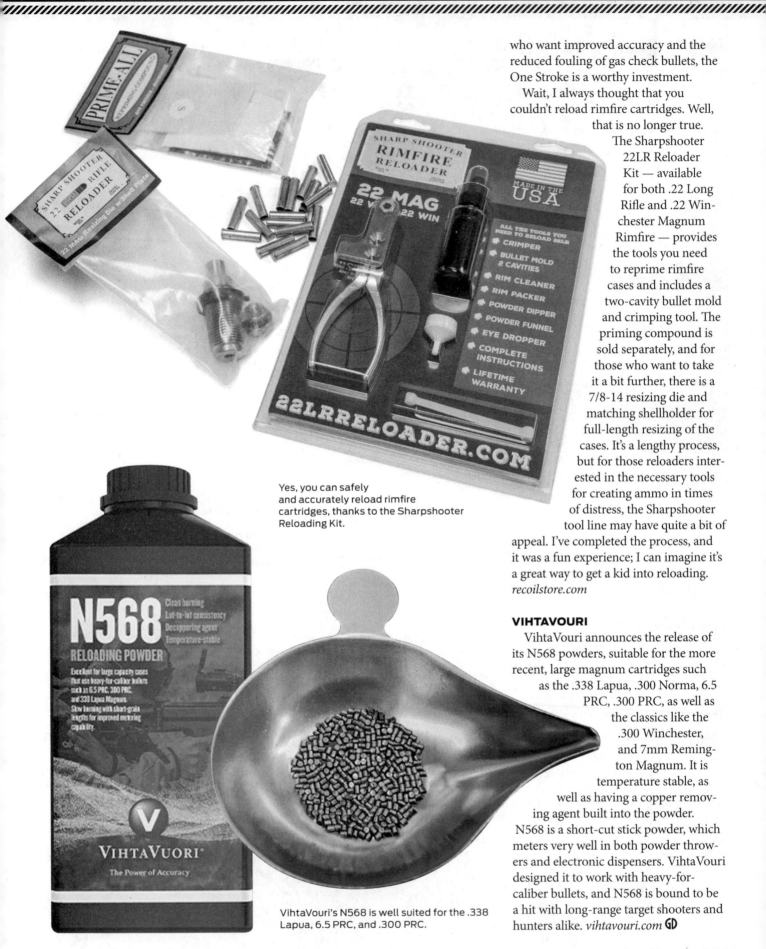

who want improved accuracy and the reduced fouling of gas check bullets, the One Stroke is a worthy investment.

Wait, I always thought that you couldn't reload rimfire cartridges. Well, that is no longer true. The Sharpshooter 22LR Reloader Kit — available for both .22 Long Rifle and .22 Winchester Magnum Rimfire — provides the tools you need to reprime rimfire cases and includes a two-cavity bullet mold and crimping tool. The priming compound is sold separately, and for those who want to take it a bit further, there is a 7/8-14 resizing die and matching shellholder for full-length resizing of the cases. It's a lengthy process, but for those reloaders interested in the necessary tools for creating ammo in times of distress, the Sharpshooter tool line may have quite a bit of appeal. I've completed the process, and it was a fun experience; I can imagine it's a great way to get a kid into reloading. *recoilstore.com*

Yes, you can safely and accurately reload rimfire cartridges, thanks to the Sharpshooter Reloading Kit.

VIHTAVOURI

VihtaVouri announces the release of its N568 powders, suitable for the more recent, large magnum cartridges such as the .338 Lapua, .300 Norma, 6.5 PRC, .300 PRC, as well as the classics like the .300 Winchester, and 7mm Remington Magnum. It is temperature stable, as well as having a copper removing agent built into the powder. N568 is a short-cut stick powder, which meters very well in both powder throwers and electronic dispensers. VihtaVouri designed it to work with heavy-for-caliber bullets, and N568 is bound to be a hit with long-range target shooters and hunters alike. *vihtavouri.com* GD

VihtaVouri's N568 is well suited for the .338 Lapua, 6.5 PRC, and .300 PRC.

AUTO-ORDNANCE 1927A-1 THOMPSON

Caliber: .45 ACP. Barrel: 16.5 in. Weight: 13 lbs. Length: About 41 in. overall (Deluxe). Stock: Walnut stock and vertical fore-end. Sights: Blade front, open rear adjustable for windage. Features: Recreation of Thompson Model 1927. Semi-auto only. Deluxe model has finned barrel, adjustable rear sight and compensator; Standard model has plain barrel and military sight. Available with 100-round drum or 30-round stick magazine. Made in USA by Auto-Ordnance Corp., a division of Kahr Arms.

Price: Deluxe w/stick magazine $1,551.00
Price: Deluxe w/drum magazine.....................................$2,583.00
Price: Lightweight model w/stick mag $1,403.00

AUTO-ORDNANCE CASE HARDENED THOMPSON

Calibers: 45 ACP. Capacity: 20-round stick magazine. Barrel: 18-in. finned. Weight: 13 lbs. Length: 41 in. Stock: Walnut, fixed buttstock with vertical foregrip. Sights: Blade front with open, adjustable rear. Features: Hand-machined semi-automatic example of the original Thomson submachine gun, using blued steel and hard wood stocks. The Case Hardened line of Tommy Guns are meant to be a work of art built around a 1927 pattern Thompson. American made.

Price: $1,872.00

AUTO-ORDNANCE 1927 A-1 COMMANDO

Similar to the 1927 A-1 except has Parkerized finish, black-finish wood butt, pistol grip, horizontal fore-end. Comes with black nylon sling. Introduced 1998. Made in USA by Auto-Ordnance Corp., a division of Kahr Arms.

Price: T1-C...$1,479.00

AUTO ORDNANCE M1 CARBINE

Caliber: .30 Carbine (15-shot magazine). Barrel: 18 in. Weight: 5.4 to 5.8 lbs. Length: 36.5 in. Stock: Wood or polymer. Sights: Blade front, flip-style rear. Features: A faithful recreation of the military carbine.

Price: $1,036.00
Price: Folding stock..$1,137.00

BARRETT MODEL 82A-1 SEMI-AUTOMATIC

Calibers: .416 Barret, 50 BMG. Capacity: 10-shot detachable box magazine. Barrel: 29 in. Weight: 28.5 lbs. Length: 57 in. overall. Stock: Composition with energy-absorbing recoil pad. Sights: Scope optional. Features: Semiautomatic, recoil operated with recoiling barrel. Three-lug locking bolt; muzzle brake. Adjustable bipod. Introduced 1985. Made in USA by Barrett Firearms.

Price: $9,119.00

BARRETT M107A1

Caliber: 50 BMG. Capacity: 10-round detachable magazine. Barrels: 20 or 29 in. Sights: 27-in. optics rail with flip-up iron sights. Weight: 30.9 lbs. Finish: Flat Dark Earth. Features: Four-port cylindrical muzzle brake. Quick-detachable Barrett QDL Suppressor. Adjustable bipod and monopod.

Price: $12,281.00

BERETTA CX4 STORM CARBINE

Calibers: 9mm, 40 S&W, .45 ACP. Barrel: 16.6 in. Stock: Black synthetic with thumbhole. Sights: Ghost ring. Features: Blowback single action, ambidextrous controls, Picatinny quad rail system. Reintroduced in 2017.

Price: $700.00

BROWNING BAR SAFARI AND SAFARI W/BOSS SEMI-AUTO

Calibers: Safari: .25-06 Rem., .270 Win., 7mm Rem. Mag., .30-06, .308 Win., .300 Win. Mag., .338 Win. Mag. Safari w/BOSS: .270 Win., 7mm Rem. Mag., .30-06 Spfl., .300 Win. Mag., .338 Win. Mag. Barrels: 22–24 in. round tapered. Weights: 7.4–8.2 lbs. Lengths: 43–45 in. overall. Stock: French walnut pistol grip stock and fore-end, hand checkered. Sights: No sights. Features: Has new bolt release lever; removable trigger assembly with larger trigger guard; redesigned gas and buffer systems. Detachable 4-round box magazine. Scroll-engraved receiver is tapped for scope mounting. BOSS barrel vibration modulator and muzzle brake system available. Mark II Safari introduced 1993. Made in Belgium.

Price: BAR MK II Safari $1,230.00
Price: BAR Safari w/BOSS $1,400.00

BROWNING BAR MK III SERIES

Calibers: .243 Win., 7mm-08, .270 Win., .270 WSM, 7mm Rem., .308 Win, .30-06, .300 Win. Mag., .300 WSM. Capacities: Detachable 4 or 5-shot magazine. Barrel: 22, 23 or 24 in.es. Stock: Grade II checkered walnut, shim adjustable. Camo stock with composite gripping surfaces available. Stalker model has composite stock. Weight: 7.5 lbs. Features: Satin nickel alloy with high relief engraving, stylized fore-end.

Price: ....$1,340.00–$1,440.00
Price: Left Hand ....$1,380.00–$1,480.00
Price: Camo...$1,380.00
Price: Stalker..$1,340.00–$1,440.00
Price: Left-hand BAR MK3 Stalker ....$1,380.00–$1,480.00

BROWNING BAR MK 3 DBM SERIES

Caliber: 308 Win. Capacity: 10-round "detachable box magazine," so named for the DBM series. Barrel: 18-in. fluted blued. Length: 40-1/8 in. Weight: 7 lbs. 6 oz. Stock: Choice of two model variants. DBM Wood uses Grade II Turkish Walnut with oil finish. DBM Stalker uses black synthetic. Features: Picatinny top rail for optics mounting. Other features comparable to standard BAR Mk 3.

Price: BAR MK3 DBM Wood $1,590.00
Price: BAR MK3 DBM Stalker $1,560.00
Price: Left-hand BAR MK3 DBM Wood $1,570.00
Price: Left-hand BAR MK3 DBM Stalker $1,540.00

CENTURY INTERNATIONAL AES-10 HI-CAP

Caliber: 7.62x39mm. Capacity: 30-shot magazine. Barrel: 23.2 in. Weight: NA. Length: 41.5 in. overall. Stock: Wood grip, fore-end. Sights: Fixed notch rear, windage-adjustable post front. Features: RPK-style, accepts standard double-stack AK-type mags. Side-mounted scope mount, integral carry handle, bipod. Imported by Century Arms Int'l.

Price: AES-10, From $450.00

CENTURY INTERNATIONAL M70AB2 SPORTER

Caliber: 7.62x39mm. Capacity: 30-shot magazine. Barrel: 16.25 in. Weight: 7.5 lbs. Length: 34.25 in. overall. Stocks: Metal grip, wood fore-end. Sights: Fixed notch rear, windage-adjustable post front. Features: Two 30-rd. double-stack magazine, cleaning kit, compensator, bayonet lug and bayonet. Paratrooper-style Kalashnikov with under-folding stock. Imported by Century Arms Int'l.
Price: M70AB2, From..**$480.00**

DSA SA58 STANDARD

Caliber: .308 Win. Barrel: 21 in. bipod cut w/threaded flash hider. Weight: 8.75 lbs. Length: 43 in. Stock: Synthetic, X-Series or optional folding para stock. Sights: Elevation-adjustable post front, windage-adjustable rear peep. Features: Fully adjustable short gas system, high-grade steel or 416 stainless upper receiver. Many variants available. Made in USA by DSA, Inc.
Price: From...**$1,700.00**

DSA SA58 CARBINE

Caliber: .308 Win. Barrel: 16.25 in. bipod cut w/threaded flash hider. Features: Carbine variation of FAL-style rifle. Other features identical to SA58 Standard model. Made in USA by DSA, Inc.
Price: **$1,700.00**

EXCEL ARMS X-SERIES

Caliber: .22 LR, 5.7x28mm (10 or 25-round); .30 Carbine (10 or 20-round magazine). 9mm (10 or 17 rounds). Barrel: 18 in. Weight: 6.25 lbs. Length: 34 to 38 in. Features: Available with or without adjustable iron sights. Blow-back action (5.57x28) or delayed blow-back (.30 Carbine).
Price: .22 LR **$504.00**
Price: 5.7x28 or 9mm...**$795.00–$916.00**

FNH FNAR COMPETITION

Caliber: .308 Win. Capacity: 10-shot magazine. Barrel: 20 in. fluted. Weight: 8.9 lbs. Length: 41.25 in. overall. Sights: None furnished. Optical rail atop receiver, three accessory rails on fore-end. Stock: Adjustable for comb height, length of pull, cast-on and cast-off. Blue/gray laminate. Based on BAR design.
Price: **$1,767.00**

HECKLER & KOCH MODEL USC

Caliber: .45 ACP. Capacity: 10-round magazine. Barrel: 16 in. Weight: 6.13 lbs. Length: 35.4 in. Features: Polymer construction, adjustable rear sight, ambidextrous safety/selector, optional Picatinny rail. Civilian version of HK UMP submachine gun.
Price: **$1,499.00**

INLAND M1 1945 CARBINE

Caliber: .30 Carbine. Capacity: 15 rounds. Barrel: 18 in. Weight: 5 lbs. 3 oz. Features: A faithful reproduction of the last model that Inland manufactured in 1945, featuring a type 3 bayonet lug/barrel band, adjustable rear sight, push button safety, and walnut stock. Scout Model has 16.5-in. barrel, flash hider, synthetic stock with accessory rail. Made in the USA.
Price: **$1,299.00**
Price: Scout Model **$1,449.00**

KALASHNIKOV USA

Caliber: 7.62x39mm. Capacity: 30-round magazine. AK-47 series made in the USA in several variants and styles. Barrel: 16.25 in. Weight: 7.52 lbs.
Price: KR-9 Side-folding stock **$1,249.00**
Price: US132S Synthetic stock **$799.00**
Price: US132W Wood carbine **$836.00**

RUGER PC CARBINE

Calibers: 9mm or 40 S&W. Capacity: 17 (9mm), 15 (40 S&W) pistol magazines. 10-round state-compliant versions available. Barrel: 16-in. cold-hammer forged, threaded, fluted. Sights: Standard model with iron sights; chassis models with Picatinny optics rail. Length: 32.25–35.5 in. Weight: 7.3 lbs. Stock: Choice of synthetic, fixed, or adjustable aluminum chassis furniture. Features: Aluminum alloy receiver, hardcoat anodized. Utilizes 10/22 trigger components with light, crisp pull. Ergonomic pistol grip with extended trigger reach for precise control. Interchangeable magazine wells for use with common Ruger and Glock magazines.
Price: **$649.00**
Price: With handguard...**$729.00**
Price: Adjustable Chassis **$799.00**
Price: State Compliant **$799.00**
Price: Distributor Exclusives ....**$779.00–$899.00**

RUGER MINI-14 RANCH RIFLE

Calibers: .223 Rem., .300 Blackout (Tactical Rifle). Capacity: 5-shot or 20-shot detachable box magazine. Barrel: 18.5 in. Rifling twist 1:9 in. Weights: 6.75–7 lbs. Length: 37.25 in. overall. Stocks: American hardwood, steel reinforced, or synthetic. Sights: Protected blade front, fully adjustable Ghost Ring rear. Features: Fixed piston gas-operated, positive primary extraction. New buffer system, redesigned ejector system. Ruger S100RM scope rings included on Ranch Rifle. Heavier barrels added in 2008, 20-round magazine added in 2009.
Price: Mini-14/5, Ranch Rifle, blued, wood stock **$999.00**
Price: K-Mini-14/5, Ranch Rifle, stainless, scope rings **$1,069.00**
Price: Mini-14 Tactical Rifle: Similar to Mini-14 but with 16.12 in. barrel with flash hider, black synthetic stock, adjustable sights **$1,019.00**

SIG-SAUER MPX PCC

Caliber: 9mm. 30-round capacity. Barrel: 16 in. Features: M-LOK handguard, 5-position folding telescoping stock. Weight: 6.6 lbs. Sights: none.
Price: From **$2,016.00**

SPRINGFIELD ARMORY M1A

Caliber: 7.62mm NATO (.308). Capacities: 5- or 10-shot box magazine. Barrel: 25.062 in. with flash suppressor, 22 in. without suppressor. Weight: 9.75 lbs. Length: 44.25 in. overall. Stock: American walnut with walnut-colored heat-resistant fiberglass handguard. Matching walnut handguard available. Also available with fiberglass stock. Sights: Military, square blade front, full click-adjustable aperture rear. Features: Commercial equivalent of the U.S. M-14 service rifle with no provision for automatic firing. From Springfield Armory.
Price: SOCOM 16 ....**$1,987.00**
Price: Scout Squad, From **$1,850.00**
Price: Standard M1A, From **$1,685.00**
Price: Loaded Standard, From **$1,847.00**
Price: National Match, From **$2,434.00**
Price: Super Match (heavy premium barrel) about **$2,965.00**
Price: Tactical, From ....**$3,619.00–$4,046.00**

Prices given are believed to be accurate at time of publication however, many factors affect retail pricing so exact prices are not possible.

76TH EDITION, 2022 ✛ **393**

ALEXANDER ARMS AR SERIES

Calibers: .17 HMR, 5.56 NATO, 6.5 Grendel, .300 AAC, .338 Lapua Mag., .50 Beowulf. This manufacturer produces a wide range of AR-15 type rifles and carbines. Barrels: 16, 18, 20 or 24 in. Models are available for consumer, law enforcement and military markets. Depending on the specific model, features include forged flattop receiver with Picatinny rail, button-rifled stainless steel barrels, composite free-floating handguard, A2 flash hider, M4 collapsible stock, gas piston operating system.

Price: .17 HMR **$1,097.00**
Price: 5.56 NATO **$1,155.00**
Price: 6.5 Grendel **$1,425.00**
Price: .300 AAC **$1,275.00**
Price: .50 Beowulf **$1,425.00**

ALEXANDER ARMS ULFBERHT

Caliber: .338 Lapua Mag. Custom-designed adjustable gas-piston operating system. Barrel: 27.5-in. chrome moly with three-prong flash hider. Stock: Magpul PRS. Length: 41.25 in. (folded), 50 in. (extended stock). Weight: 19.8 lbs.
Price: **$6,090.00**

ANDERSON MANUFACTURING AM-15 RIFLES

Calibers: 5.56 NATO, .300 Blackout, 7.62x39, .450 Bushmaster. This manufacturer produces a range of AR-15-type rifles and carbines. Barrels: 16, 18, 24 in. Models are available for consumer, law enforcement and military markets. Builds include CNC-machined 7075 T6 aluminum forgings for uppers and lowers, which are machined to military specifications and marked "Multi-Cal" to be used with multiple calibers on the AR-15 platform. The company offers its proprietary RF85 metal treatment on some rifles, which the company bills as needing "zero lubrication."
Price: AM-15 M4 Optic Ready 5.56 ....**$559.00**
Price: AM-15 M4 Optic Ready 5.56, RF85 .... **$800.00**
Price: AM-15 M4 Optic Ready 7.62x39 .... **$689.00**
Price: AM-15 M4 Optic Ready 7.62x39, RF85 .... **$862.00**

ANDERSON MANUFACTURING AM-10 RIFLES

Calibers: .308 Win., 6.5 Creedmoor. Barrels: 16, 18, 20, 24 in.
Price: AM-10 EXTSP-RT2, .308 Win.,18 in. **$1,100.00**
Price: AM-10 EXTSP-RT2, 6.5 Creedmoor, 20 in. **$1,222.00**

ARMALITE AR10 TAC 6.5

Caliber: 6.5 Creedmoor. Capacity: 25 rounds, windowed PMAG. Barrel: 22 in., med-heavy 1:8 stainless steel, black nitride finish. Stock: Magpul PRS with adjustable length-of-pull and comb height. Sights: Magpul MBUS front and rear. Weight: 10 lbs. Overall Length: 44 in. Features: ArmaLite Two-Stage Trigger, AR10 15 in. tactical handguard, ATB762 muzzle brake. New 6.5 CM chambering is superbly accurate for match shooting. Introduced 2020.
Price: **$2,099.00**

ARMALITE AR10 (3GN13/3GN18)

Caliber: 7.62x51/.308 Win. Capacity: 25 rounds, windowed PMAG. Barrel: 13.5 in., pinned and welded, or 18 in., stainless steel, 1:10 twist. Stock: MBA-1 Light Weight Precision with adjustable length-of-pull and comb height. Sights: Mil-Std 1913 top rail. Weight: 8.8-9.9 lbs. Overall lengths: 36.25, 40.25, 41.25 in. Features: Timney 4-lb. single-stage trigger, ArmaLite Tunable Competition Muzzle Brake, ambidextrous safety and Raptor charging handle, 12 in. free-floating, tactical Key-Mod handguard, ERGO wide grip. Introduced 2020.
Price: **$2,199.00**

ARMALITE EAGLE-15 VERSATILE SPORTING RIFLE – 15EAVSR

Caliber: .223 Rem., 5.56x45 (.223 Wylde chamber). Capacity: one 30-round Magpul PMAG. Barrel: 16 in., HB, chrome moly, 1:8 RH twist, flash suppressor. Stock: 6-position collapsible stock. Sights: Mil-Std 1913 rail section. Weight: 6.6 lbs. Overall Length: 31.1 in. collapsed, 34.5 in. extended. Features: Carbine length gas system, 15 in. Versatile Sporting Rifle Key-Mod handguard, forged flat top with Mil-Std 1913 rail, 7075-T6 aluminum upper receiver, forged 7075-T6 aluminum lower receiver.
Price: **$818.00**

ARMALITE M-15 LIGHT TACTICAL CARBINE

Calibers: .223 Rem., 6.8 SPC, 7.62x39mm. Capacity: 30-round magazine. Barrel: 16 in. heavy chrome lined; 1:7 in. twist, flash suppressor. (10.3 and 11.5 in. available. NFA regulations apply) Weight: 6 lbs. Length: 36 in. overall. Stock: Green or black composition. Sights: Standard A2. Features: Forged flattop receiver with Picatinny rail, 10-in. aluminum KeyMod handguard, anodize aluminum supper/lower receiver, flip-up sights. Introduced in 2016.
Price: ....**$999.00-$2,099.00**

ARMALITE AR-10 3-GUN COMPETITION RIFLE

Calibers: 7.62x1mm/.308 Win. Capacity: 25-round magazine. Barrel: 18-in. stainless steel. Weight: 8.9 lbs. Features: MBA-1 buttstock with adjustable comb and length of pull, 15-in. free-floating 3-Gun handguard, Raptor charging handle, Timney trigger, ambidextrous safety.
Price: **$2,199.00**

ARMALITE EAGLE-15 VERSATILE SPORTING RIFLE (VSR)

Caliber: .223 Rem/5.56x45 NATO (.223 Wylde chamber). Capacity: 30-shot Magpul PMAG. Barrel: 16-in. chrome moly with flash suppressor. Stock: 6-position collapsible with free-float rail system, rubberized grip. Weight: 6.6 lbs. Features: Carbine length gas system, 15-in. handguard with Key Mod attachments, forged lower and flat-top upper, Picatinny rail.
Price: **$800.00**

BRAVO COMPANY MFG. BCM M4 CARBINE MOD 0

Caliber: 5.56mm NATO. Capacity: 30 rounds. Barrel: 16 in., standard government profile, 1:7 twist, M4 feed ramp barrel extension. USGI chrome-lined bore and chamber. Mil-Spec 11595E barrel steel, manganese phosphate finish. Stock: BCM Gunfighter. Sights: Flat-top rail, post front. Weight: 6.3 lbs. Overall Length: 32.5 to 35.5 in. Features: Upper and lower receivers machined from aluminum forgings 7075-T6 and hard-coat anodized per

Prices given are believed to be accurate at time of publication however, many factors affect retail pricing so exact prices are not possible.

MIL-A-8625F, Type III, Class 2. Upper has M4 feed ramp flat top with laser T-markings. Standard carbine gas system. BCM bolt carrier group. Machined from Mil-Spec Carpenter No. 158 steel, HPT/MPI, shot peened, tool steel extractor w/BCM extractor spring, chrome-lined carrier (full auto profile).
Price: **$1,202.00**

BRAVO COMPANY MFG. BCM RECCE-16 KMR-A CARBINE
Caliber: 5.56mm NATO. Capacity: 30 rounds. Barrel: 16 in., USGI profile, 1:7 twist, M4 feed ramp barrel extension. USGI chrome-lined bore and chamber. Mil-Spec 11595E barrel steel, manganese phosphate finish. Stock: BCM. Sights: M4 feed ramp flat top with laser T-markings. Weight: 6.1 lbs. Overall Length: 32.5 to 35.5 in. Features: Upper and lower receivers machined from aluminum forgings 7075-T6 and hard-coat anodized per MIL-A-8625F, Type III, Class 2. Mid-length gas system. BCM bolt carrier group, Mil-Spec Carpenter No. 158 steel, HPT/MPI, shot peened, tool steel extractor w/BCM extractor spring, chrome-lined carrier (full auto profile).
Price: **$1,500.00**

BARRETT MODEL REC7 GEN II
Calibers: 5.56 (.223), 6.8 Rem. SPC. Capacity: 30-round magazine. Barrel: 16 in. Sights: ARMS rear, folding front. Weight: 28.7 lbs. Features: AR-style configuration with standard 17-4 stainless piston system, two-position forward venting gas plug, chrome-lined gas block, A2 flash hider, 6-position MOE stock.
Price: **$2,759.00**

BROWNELLS "WHAT WOULD STONER DO" 2020 RIFLE
Caliber: 5.56 NATO or .223 Rem (.223 Wylde chamber). Capacity: 30-round Magpul P-Mag. Barrel: 14.5 in., with titanium flash hider for OAL of 16 in., 1/2-28 tpi muzzle threads. Upper/Lower Receivers: KE Arms MK3 polymer receiver. Weight: NA. Trigger: SLT-1 Sear Link Technology. Overall Length: NA. Features: One-piece polymer lower with an improved mag well that's been optimized for use with Magpul P-Mags and D-60 drum mags. Ambidextrous selector, ambi mag release, ambidextrous charging handle, PDQ lever, JP Silent Capture Spring System, carbon-fiber handguard. The Mk3 lower will also be available separately either stripped or with Mil-Spec internals.
Price: **$1,700.00**

BROWNELLS BRN-10 RETRO RIFLE
Caliber: .308 Winchester. Capacity: one supplied 20-round Brownells aluminum magazine. Compatible with metal DPMS/SR-25 magazines. Barrel: 20 in., 1:10 RH twist, 5/8-24 tpi muzzle threads, QPQ Nitride finish, 3-prong Dutch-style flash hider, .750-in. diameter at the gas block. Direct impingement. Upper/Lower Receivers: Machined from 7075 T6 aluminum billet. Stock: Type D, no trap door. Sights: Rear enclosed by the carry handle. A2-style horizontal thumbwheel adjusts elevation. Windage is changed by loosening a setscrew and drifting the rear peep. Standard AR-15-style front sight base. Weight: 8.6 lbs. Trigger: AR-15 style. Overall Length: 40.5 in. Features: Re-creation of Eugene Stoner's original lightweight .308 caliber battle rifle, Armalite AR-10. Slab-sided lower with straight magazine well. Serrated takedown pins, selector lever, magazine release and bolt release. No forward assist and shell deflector. "Trigger"-style charging handle located under the carry handle. Carrier has flats and two stabilizing flanges at the rear found on early carriers, and the entire bolt/carrier group is chrome plated. Bolt machined from 9310 carbon steel and magnetic particle inspected (MPI). Functional heavy fluting on the barrel under the handguard. Brown furniture. Many components are compatible with modern DPMS/SR-25 parts or AR-15 parts. The BRN-10B is inspired by later export rifles and has a closed-prong, Portuguese-type flash hider, later-style black furniture, and a lightweight barrel. Weight: 7.8 lbs. Length: 40.75 in.
Price: BRN-10A **$1,260.00**
Price: BRN-10B **$1,186.00**

BROWNELLS BRN-605 5.56 CARBINE
Caliber: 5.56 NATO. Capacity: one 20-round metal. Barrel: 15.5 in.; 1:12 RH twist, A1-profile, standard 3-prong "duckbill" flash hider. Upper/Lower Receivers: Machined 7075 T6 aluminum receivers. XBRN16E1 lower has partial "fence" around the magazine release. Upper has forward assist, but no shell deflector. Stock: Fixed "Type D" buttstock. Sights: Windage-adjustable A1-type rear sight drum. Weight: 7.5 lbs. Overall Length: 34 in. Features: Colt's first carbine variant of the M16 rifle. The Model 605 reproduction is a standard M16 with 4.5 in. lopped off the A1 barrel, retaining the rifle-length gas tube. Chrome-plated bolt/carrier group. Enlarged gas port, M193-type ammunition with 55-grain bullets recommended. No steel case or underpowered ammunition. Black furniture of reinforced polymer, triangular cross-section handguard.
Price: **$967.00**

CMMG MK SERIES
Calibers: 5.56 NATO, .308 Win., 7.62x39, .300 BLK. This company manufactures a wide range of AR and AK style rifles and carbines. Many AR/AK options offered. Listed are several variations of CMMG's many models. Made in the USA.
Price: MK4 LEM .223..**$995.00**
Price: MK3 .308 ....**$1,595.00**
Price: MK47 AKS8 7.62x39 (shown)......................**$1,650.00**
Price: MK4 RCE .300 BLK **$1,500.00**

CMMG MKW ANVIL
Caliber: .458 SOCOM. Barrel: 16.1 in. CMMG SV Muzzle Brake. Weight: 7.5 lbs. Stock: M4 with A2 pistol grip, 6 position mil-spec receiver extension. Introduced in 2017.
Price: **$1,850.00**

CMMG MK4 DTR2
Caliber: .224 Valkyrie. Capacity: 10-round magazine (6.8 magazine). Barrel: 24 in. threaded. CMMG SV Muzzle Brake. Weight: 9.2 lbs. Stock: Magpul PRS with MOE Pistol grip4 with A2 pistol grip. Features: Model is engineered to deliver on this new cartridge's promise of long-range accuracy and high-energy performance.
Price: **$1,699.95**

CMMG RESOLUTE 100 RIFLES AND CARBINES
Calibers: 5.7x28mm (Conversion), 9mm (Conversion), .350 Legend, .458 SOCOM, .22 LR, .300 Blackout, .308 Win., .40 S&W, .45 ACP, 5.56x45mm, 5.7x28mm (FN), 6.5 Grendel, 7.62x39mm, 9mm (Colt), 9mm (Glock). Capacity: 30-round Magpul PMAG (5.56). Barrel: 16.1, 16.6, or 17 in. (varies by chambering), 1:7 twist, medium taper, 4140CM, SBN (5.56). Stock: CMMG M4 with 6-position receiver extension. Sights: Flat-top rail. Weight: 6.3 lbs. Overall Length: 32.5 to 35.5 in. Features: Forged 7075-T6 AL M4-type upper, AR-15-type lower, Type III hard-coat anodize finish, CMMG single-stage Mil-Spec trigger, integrated or CMMG triggerguard, Mil-Spec charging handle, A2-style pistol grip, CMMG RML15 M-LOK free-floating handguard, M4-style buttstock, salt bath nitride barrel finish, M4 Mil-Spec receiver end plate, A2 Comp, threaded 1/2-28, standard safety selector.
Price: .... **$950.00-$1,500.00**

Prices given are believed to be accurate at time of publication however, many factors affect retail pricing so exact prices are not possible.

76TH EDITION, 2022 ✛ **395**

CMMG RESOLUTE 200 RIFLES AND CARBINES

Calibers: 5.7x28mm (Conversion), 9mm (Conversion), .350 Legend, .458 SOCOM, .22 LR, .300 Blackout, .308 Win., .40 S&W, .45 ACP, 5.56x45mm, 5.7x28mm (FN), 6.5 Grendel, 7.62x39mm, 9mm (Colt), 9mm (Glock). Capacity: 30-round Magpul PMAG (5.56). Barrel: 16.1, 16.6, or 17 in. (varies by chambering), 1:7 twist, medium taper, 4140CM, SBN (5.56). Stock: CMMG Ripstock. Sights: Flat-top rail. Weight: 6.3 lbs. Overall Length: 32.5 to 35.5 in. Features: Forged 7075-T6 AL M4-type upper, AR-15-type lower, Type III hard-coat anodize finish, CMMG single-stage Mil-Spec trigger, integrated or Magpul MOE triggerguard, Mil-Spec charging handle, Magpul MOE pistol grip, CMMG RML15 M-LOK free-floating handguard, M4-style buttstock, salt bath nitride barrel finish, M4 Mil-Spec receiver end plate, CMMG SV muzzle device threaded 1/2-28, standard safety selector.
Price: .... **$1,125.00-$1,675.00**

CMMG RESOLUTE 300 RIFLES AND CARBINES

Calibers: 5.7x28mm (Conversion), 9mm (Conversion), .350 Legend, .458 SOCOM, .22 LR, .300 Blackout, .308 Win., .40 S&W, .45 ACP, 5.56x45mm, 5.7x28mm (FN), 6.5 Grendel, 7.62x39mm, 9mm (Colt), 9mm (Glock). Capacity: 30-round Magpul PMAG (5.56). Barrel: 16.1, 16.6, or 17 in. (varies by chambering), 1:7 twist, medium taper, 4140CM, SBN (5.56). Stock: CMMG Ripstock. Sights: Flat-top rail. Weight: 6.3 lbs. Overall Length: 32.5 to 35.5 in. Features: Forged 7075-T6 AL M4-type upper, AR-15-type lower, laser-engraved "Resolute" on lower receiver. Premier Cerakote finish (10 color options), Geissele SSA two-stage trigger, integrated or Magpul MOE triggerguard, CMMG ambidextrous charging handle, Magpul MOE pistol grip, CMMG RML15 M-LOK free-floating handguard, M4-style buttstock, salt bath nitride barrel finish, M4 Mil-Spec receiver end plate, CMMG SV muzzle device threaded 1/2-28, CMMG ambidextrous safety selector.
Price: Mk4 5.56 .... **$1,450.00-$2,000.00**

COLT LE6920 M4 CARBINE

Caliber: 5.56 NATO. Barrel: 16.1-in. chrome lined. Sights: Adjustable. Based on military M4. Features: Magpul MOE handguard, carbine stock, pistol grip, vertical grip. Direct gas/locking bolt operating system.
Price: .... **$849.00–$1,099.00**

COLT LE6940

Caliber: 5.56 NATO. Similar to LE1920 with Magpul MBUS backup sight, folding front, four accessory rails. One-piece monolithic upper receiver has continuous Mil-Spec rail from rear of upper to the front sight. Direct gas (LE6940) or articulating link piston (LE6940P) system.
Price: LE6940 .... **$1,399.00**

COLT L36960-CCU

Caliber: 5.56 NATO. Capacity: 30-round magazine. Barrel: 16-in. Stock: Magpul MOE SL with pistol grip. Weight: 6.7 lbs. Features: Combat Unit Carbine with 30-shot magazine. Aluminum receiver with black finish, mid-length gas system, optics ready.
Price: **$1,299.00**

COLT EXPANSE M4

Caliber: 5.56 NATO. Capacity: 30 rounds. Barrel: 16.1 in. Sights: Adjustable front post. Comes optics ready. Weight: 6.4 lbs. Flattop Picatinny rail. Stock: Adjustable M4 with A2-style grip. Economy priced AR. Introduced in 2016.
Price: **$799.00**

DANIEL DEFENSE DD5V3 RIFLE

Calibers: 7.62x51mm/.308 Win. Capacity: 20-round Magpul PMAG. Barrel: 16 in., 5/8x24 tpi muzzle thread, S2W barrel profile, 1:11 twist. Stock: Daniel Defense Buttstock. Sights: Full-length top rail. Trigger: Daniel Defense Mil-Spec. Handguard: Daniel Defense DD5 Rail 15.0, 6061-T6 aluminum, M-LOK. Weight: 8.3 lbs. Overall Length: 33.375 to 37 in. Features: Intermediate gas system, two-position adjustable gas block, DLC-coated bolt carrier group, cold hammer chrome-lined forged barrel, Mil-Spec heavy phosphate coated. 4-Bolt Connection System, ambidextrous controls (bolt catch, magazine release, safety selector, furniture, GRIP-N-RIP charging handle). Lower Receiver: Enhanced flared magazine well and rear receiver QD swivel attachment point. CNC machined of 7075-T6 aluminum, Type III hard-coat anodized. Upper Receiver: CNC machined of 7075-T6 aluminum, Type III hard-coat anodized. Daniel Defense Superior Suppression Device, 6-position Mil-Spec 7075-T6 aluminum receiver extension. Daniel Defense Pistol Grip, accepts all SR-25 magazines.
Price: DD5V3 .... **$2,499.00**
Price: DD5V4 (7.62mm, 6.5 CM, 18-in. barrel) **$2,499.00**
Price: DD5V5 (6.5 CM, .260 Rem., 20-in. barrel) **$2,499.00**

DANIEL DEFENSE AR SERIES

Caliber: 5.56 NATO/.223. Capacity: 20-round Magpul PMAG magazine. Barrels: 16 or 18 in.es. Flash suppressor. Weight: 7.4 lbs. Lengths: 34.75–37.85 in. overall. Stock: Glass-filled polymer with Soft Touch overmolding. Pistol grip. Sights: None. Features: Lower receiver is Mil-Spec with enhanced and flared magazine well, QD swivel attachment point. Upper receiver has M4 feed ramps. Lower and upper CNC machined of 7075-T6 aluminum, hard coat anodized. Shown is MK12, one of many AR variants offered by Daniel Defense. Made in the USA
Price: **$1,599.00**
Price: DD5VI 7.62/.308 .... **$3,044.00**
Price: DDM4V7 .... **$1,729.00**
Price: DDM4ISR .300 Blackout **$3,135.00**
Price: DDM4V11 .... **$1,729.00-$1,999.00**
Price: DDM4V9 .... **$1,826.00-$1,999.00**
Price: MK12 .... **$2,162.00**
Price: Ambush Camo **$1,946.00**

DSARMS AR15 ZM4 WARZ SERIES 5.56 RIFLE

Caliber: 5.56 NATO. Capacity: Magpul Custom G2 MOE 30-round magazine, black with Flat Dark Earth ribs. Barrel: 16 in., lightweight mid-length, 1:8 twist, M4 feed ramps on both barrel extension and upper receiver. Stock: B5 Systems Custom SOPMOD Stock, Flat Dark Earth, B5 Systems QD end plate. Sights: Full-length top rail. Weight: 6.9 lbs. Trigger: ALG Defense Advanced Combat Trigger. Overall Length: 33 to 35 in. Features: Premium match barrel machined from either 416-R Stainless Steel or 4150-11595 Mil-Spec material, 5.56 match chamber. Enhanced A3M4 upper receiver, upgraded fire control group, ambidextrous selector switch and WarZ triggerguard, bolt catch and charging handle. Low-mass sand-cut bolt carrier group with nitride finish. DuraCoat finish in Flat Dark Earth over the hard-coat anodized lower receiver, upper receiver and handguard. 4140-steel MK12-style low-profile, set-screw gas block, stainless steel mid-length gas tube. Midwest Industries 15-in. Combat Series M-LOK free-float handguard. Magpul Custom MIAD Modular Pistol Grip, Flat Dark Earth with black two-tone. DSArms Enhanced FDE alloy triggerguard, SureFire Pro Comp (1/2x28 tpi).
Price: FDE **$1,150.00**
Price: Titanium **$1,150.00**

Prices given are believed to be accurate at time of publication however, many factors affect retail pricing so exact prices are not possible.

DSARMS AR15 SERVICE SERIES 5.56X45 NATO BLOCK 1 CARBINE - KNIGHT'S ARMAMENT UPGRADES

Caliber: 5.56 NATO. Capacity: ASC 30-round gray alloy magazine. Barrel: 14.5 in., with permanently affixed A2 Bird Cage Flash Hider for 16 in. barrel OAL, M4-profile, chrome-lined chamber and bore, 4150 - 11595E Mil-Spec barrel steel, 1:7 twist. Stock: Mil-Spec, M4-style, 6-position Mil-Spec buffer tube. Sights: Top rail segments, forged front sight tower (F-Marked). Weight: 6.9 lbs. Features: Carbine-length gas system, M4 feed ramps on both barrel extension and upper receiver. Stainless steel carbine-length gas tube, Knight's Armament Co. M4 RAS carbine-length handguard assembly. Knight's forward vertical grip. DSArms forged A3M4 Mil-Spec upper receiver, DSArms forged lower receiver, both hard-coat anodized per MIL-A-8625F, Type III, Class 2 finish. Mil-Spec M16 complete bolt carrier group. Mil-Spec A2-style pistol grip.

Price: **$1,200.00**

F-1 FIREARMS BDRX-15 SKELETONIZED RIFLE

Caliber: .223 Wylde chamber for 5.56 NATO or .223 Rem. .300 AAC, 7.62x39mm, .224 Valkyrie. Capacity: 30-round magazines standard. Barrel: 16 (standard) or 18 in., light, medium, fluted contours, 1:8 twist, F-1 Firearms Flat-Face, Angle-Face, or F-1 Firearms Slay-AR compensator, 1:10 twist on 7.62x39mm, stainless and black-nitride finishes. Upper/Lower Receivers: 7075-T6511 BDRx-15 billet receiver matched set, skeletonized. Black Type III hard anodizing. Stock: Magpul MOE standard. Handguard: C7K 12.75-in., 7-series aluminum lightweight free-float rail system. Sights: None, scalloped partial top rail. Weight: 8 lbs. Trigger: Hiperfire EDT Heavy Gunner standard. Velocity and Geiselle brands available as options. Length: 33-37.5 in. Features: Introduced 2019. Modular build; user selects options on almost all components. 60-degree beveled mag well.

Price: **$2,050.00**

F-1 FIREARMS BDRX-15 RIFLE SPECIAL EDITION STEAMPUNK

Similar to BDRX-15, but with specific feature set. Barrel: 16-in., .223 Wylde Proof Research carbon-fiber barrel, Slay-AR brake in rose gold. F-1 Firearms grip and foregrip, minimalist stock, Hiperfire EDT2 trigger, ambi charging handle.

Price: **$3,410.00**

F-1 FIREARMS BDRX-10 SKELETONIZED RIFLE

Calibers: .308 Win., 6.5 Creedmoor. Capacity: 20-round magazines. Barrel: 16, 18, 20 in., 1:10 twist, medium contour (.308, 416 stainless steel), 22-in. Criterion (6.5 CM). Proof Research carbine-fiber barrels offered as upgrades (add .... $500). Upper/Lower Receivers: 7075-T6511 BDRx-15 billet receiver matched set, skeletonized. Large-frame DPMS High-Profile-style compatible, 60-degree beveled mag well. Black Type III hard anodizing. Stock: Magpul MOE standard. Handguard: C7K 14-in., 7-series aluminum lightweight free-float rail system. Sights: None, scalloped partial top rail. Weight: 8.4 lbs. Trigger: Hiperfire EDT Heavy Gunner standard. Length: 33-37.5 in. Features: Accepts all Mil-Spec (DPMS) patterned parts as well as SR25 patterned mags.

Price: **$2,950.00**

F-1 FIREARMS BDRX-10 RIFLE SPECIAL EDITION STEAMPUNK

Similar to BDRX-10, but with specific feature set. Barrel: 16-in., Proof Research, Slay-AR brake in black DLC. F-1 Firearms grip and foregrip, Magpul CTR stock, Hiperfire EDT2 trigger, ambi charging handle.

Price: **$4,255.00**

FN 15 SERIES

Caliber: 5.56x45. Capacity: 20 or 30 rounds. Barrels: 16 in., 18 in., 20 in. Features: AR-style rifle/carbine series with most standard features and options.

Price: Tactical II (also in .300 BLK) **$1,599.00**
Price: Standard rifle **$1,149.00**
Price: Sporting **$1,749.00**
Price: DMR II **$1,999.00**
Price: Carbine **$1,149.00**
Price: Competition **$2,240.00**
Price: Military Collector **$1,749.00**

FN 15 TACTICAL CARBINE FDA P-LOK

Caliber: 5.56x45mm. Capacity: 30-shot PMAG. Barrel: 16-in. free-floating and chrome-lined with FN 3-prong flash hider. Stock: B5 Systems buttstock and grip. Weight: 7.2 lbs. Finish: Flat Dark Earth. Features: P-LOK handguard, M-LOK accessory mounting system, hard anodized aluminum flat-top receiver with Picatinny rail, forward assist.

Price: **$1,499.00**

FN 15 SRP G2

Caliber: 5.56 NATO. Capacity: One 30-round magazine. Barrel: 11.5 and 16 in., 1:7 RH twist, alloy steel, button-broached, chrome-plated, A2-style flash hider. Stock: 6-position, collapsible. Sights: Low-profile, folding metal front and rear sights. Full-length 12 o'clock Picatinny rail with five built-in QD points. Weight: 5.6 lbs. (11.5 in.); 6.25 lbs. (16 in.). Trigger: FN Combat Trigger, 4.75-7.75 lbs. Overall Length: 27.5-30.75 in. (11.5 in.); 31.9-35.2 in. (16 in.). Features: Law-enforcement models have lightweight design, extended handguards and sight-ready configuration. Multiple M-LOK and quick-detach (QD) points, chrome-lined barrel with pinned low-profile gas block, MPI-inspected and marked M16-style bolt carrier. Free-floated handguard (10.5-in. long with 11.5-in. barrel, or 15-in. long with 16-in. barrel.)

Price: 11.5-in. barrel .... **Agency Request**
Price: 16-in. barrel .... **Agency Request**

Prices given are believed to be accurate at time of publication however, many factors affect retail pricing so exact prices are not possible.

76TH EDITION, 2022 ✦ **397**

FNH SCAR 16S
Caliber: 5.56mm/.223. Capacities: 10 or 30 rounds. Barrel: 16.25 in. Weight: 7.25 lbs. Lengths: 27.5–37.5 in. (extended stock). Stock: Telescoping, side-folding polymer. Adjustable cheekpiece, A2 style pistol grip. Sights: Adjustable folding front and rear. Features: Hard anodized aluminum receiver with four accessory rails. Ambidextrous safety and mag release. Charging handle can be mounted on right or left side. Semi-auto version of newest service rifle of U.S. Special Forces.
Price: **$3,299.00**

FNH SCAR 17S
Caliber: 7.62x51 NATO/.308. Capacities: 10 or 30 rounds. Barrel: 16.25 in. Weight: 8 lbs. Lengths: 28.5–38.5 in. (extended stock). Features: Other features the same as SCAR 16S.
Price: **$3,499.00**

FNH SCAR 20S
Caliber: 7.62x51mm. Capacities: 10. Barrel: 20 in. Weight: 11.2 lbs. Lengths: 40.6-42.5 in. (extended stock). Stock: Precision adjustable for LOP, adjustable cheek piece, Hogue rubber pistol grip with finger grooves. Features: Hard anodized aluminum receiver with four accessory rails, two-stage match trigger, Semi-auto version of newest service rifle of U.S. Special Forces.
Price: **$4,499.00**

FRANKLIN ARMORY 3 GR-L
Caliber: 5.56mm/.223. Capacities: 10 or 30 rounds. Barrel: 18 in. fluted with threaded muzzle crown. Weight: 7.25 lbs. Stock: Magpul PRS. Adjustable comb and length of pull. Features: Hard anodized Desert Smoke upper receiver with full-length Picatinny rail. One of many AR type rifles and carbines offered by this manufacturer. Made in the USA.
Price: **$2,310.00**

FRANKLIN ARMORY F17-L
Caliber: .17 Winchester Super Magnum Rimfire. Capacity: One 10- or 20-round magazine. Barrel: 20 in., full contour, 1:9 RH twist, 11-degree target crown. Stock: Magpul MOE. Sights: Optic ready 12 o'clock Picatinny rail. Weight: NA. Trigger: FN Combat Trigger, 4.75-7.75 lbs. Overall Length: 30.75 in. Features: Gas piston rimfire rifle, F17 Piston. Rotating locking bolt and piston design, 12-in. TML M-LOK Handguard/Upper, .17 WSN Salt Bath Nitride bolt carrier, Ergo Sure Grip. Libertas lower.
Price: **$1,900.00**

FRANKLIN ARMORY F17-SPR
Similar to F17-L. Barrel: 18-in., lightweight profile. Lower Receiver: FAI. Stock: MFS Battlelink Minimalist. Grip: MFT EPG16. Weight: 6.6 lbs.
Price: **$1,450.00**

FRANKLIN ARMORY F17-M4
Similar to other F17-Series models. Barrel: 16-in., M4 Contour. Lower Receiver: FAI. Handguard/Upper: 7-in. TML M-LOK. Stock: M4. Grip: A2. Weight: NA.
Price: **$1,380.00**

FRANKLIN ARMORY F17-VS4
Similar to other F17-Series models. Barrel: 20-in., full contour. Lower Receiver: FAI. Handguard/Upper: 12-in. TML M-LOK. Stock: A2. Grip: A2. Weight: NA.
Price: **$1,480.00**

FRANKLIN ARMORY F17-X
Similar to other F17-Series models. Barrel: 16-in., M4 Contour. Sights: Fixed front and MBUS. Lower Receiver: FAI. Handguard/Upper: Magpul MOE SL M-LOK Gray. Stock: Magpul SL. Grip: Magpul K2. Weight: NA.
Price: **$1,480.00**

FRANKLIN ARMORY BFS III M4
Caliber: 5.56 NATO. Capacity: One 10- or 20-round magazine. Barrel: 16 in., LTW Contour, 1:7 RH twist, A2 muzzle device. Stock: M4. Sights: Optics ready 12 o'clock full-length Picatinny rail. Weight: NA. Trigger: BFSIII Binary Trigger. Overall Length: NA. Features: Standard charging handle, low-profile gas block, 15-in. FST Handguard/Upper, salt bath nitride bolt carrier, A2 Grip. FAI-15 lower.
Price: **$1,000.00**

FRANKLIN ARMORY M4-HTF R3
Caliber: .350 Legend. Capacity: One 10- or 20-round magazine. Barrel: 16 in., M4 Contour, 1:12 RH twist, Aura XTD muzzle device. Stock: B5 Bravo. Grip: B5. Handguard: 15-in., FSR. Sights: Optics ready 12 o'clock full-length Picatinny rail. Weight: NA. Trigger: BFSIII Binary Trigger or custom tuned. Overall Length: NA. Features: .350 Legend was designed for use in a number of American states that have specific regulations for deer hunting with straight-walled centerfire cartridges. It has the same rim diameter as a 5.56 case (0.378 in.), so it can use the same bolt. Rounds will fit in a modified AR magazine. MFT EVOLV charging handle, mid-length gas system, low-profile gas block, salt bath nitride bolt carrier, FAI-15 lower.
Price: **$1,300.00**

HECKLER & KOCH MODEL MR556A1
Caliber: .223 Remington/5.56 NATO. Capacity: 10+1. Barrel: 16.5 in. Weight: 8.9 lbs. Lengths: 33.9–37.68 in. Stock: Black synthetic adjustable. Features: Uses the gas piston system found on the HK 416 and G26, which does not introduce propellant gases and carbon fouling into the rifle's interior.
Price: $3,399.00

HECKLER & KOCH MODEL MR762A1
Caliber: Similar to Model MR556A1 except chambered for 7.62x51mm/.308 Win. cartridge. Weight: 10 lbs. w/empty magazine. Lengths: 36–39.5 in. Features: Variety of optional sights are available. Stock has five adjustable positions.
Price: $3,999.00

HK-USA MR762A1 LONG RIFLE PACKAGE II
Caliber: 7.62x51mm. Capacity: 10- or 20-round magazines. Barrel: 16.5 in., four lands and grooves, right twist, 1:11. Stock: Fully adjustable G28 buttstock. Sights: Leupold 3-9VX-R Patrol 3-9x40 mm scope, base, mounts. Weight: 10.42 lbs. Trigger: Two stage. Overall Length: 36.5 to 40.5 in. Features: MR762 semi-auto rifle with LaRue/Harris bipod, new long 14.7-in. Modular Rail System (MRS) handguard, Blue Force Gear sling and sling mount, one 10-round and one 20-round magazine, OTIS cleaning kit, HK multi-tool, and Pelican Model 1720 case.
Price: $5,999.00

JP ENTERPRISES LRP-07
Calibers: .308 Win, .260 Rem., 6.5 Creedmoor, .338 Federal. Barrels: 16–22 in., polished stainless with compensator. Buttstock: A2, ACE ARFX, Tactical Tactical Intent Carbine, Magpul MOE. Grip: Hogue Pistol Grip. Features: Machined upper and lower receivers with left-side charging system. MKIII Hand Guard. Adjustable gas system.
Price: $3,299.00

JP ENTERPRISES JP-15
Calibers: .223, .204 Ruger, 6.5 Grendel, .300 Blackout, .22 LR. Barrels: 18 or 24-in. Buttstock: Synthetic modified thumbhole or laminate thumbhole. Grip: Hogue Pistol grip. Basic AR-type general-purpose rifle with numerous options.
Price: $1,999.00

JP ENTERPRISES SCR-11 RIFLE
Calibers: .223, 6.5 Grendel, .224 Valkyrie, .22 LR. Capacity: Magazines vary by chambering. Receiver: Machined from billet 7075-T6 upper/lower receiver set with left-side charging system on upper receiver. Matte black hard-coat anodizing on aluminum components. Barrel: JP Supermatch 416R air-gauged, button-rifled, cryogenically treated barrel Thermo-Fit to receiver, polished stainless, JP Compensator. Stock: Hogue OverMolded, Magpul MOE, Magpul CTR, LUTH-AR "Skullaton," or Mission First Tactical BATTLELINK. Handguard: JP MK III system. Grip: Hogue pistol grip. Sights: Optics ready top rail. Weight: NA. Trigger: JP Fire Control Package available in weights of 3.0 to 4.5 lbs. Overall Length: NA. Features: Scaled-down version of the LRP-07 available with the same caliber, barrel, handguard, metal finishing and stock options as the CTR-02. Exaggerated bevel on the magazine well. JP adjustable gas system; choice of JP Low Mass Operating System or JP Full Mass Operating System.
Price: $2,699.00

JP ENTERPRISES LRI-20 SEMI-MONOLITHIC LONG RANGE PRECISION RIFLE
Calibers: 6mm and 6.5 Creedmoor, .260 Rem. and .308 Win. Capacity: Magazines vary by chambering. Receiver: Machined from billet 7075-T6 upper/lower receiver set with left-side charging system on upper receiver. Matte black hard-coat anodizing on aluminum components. Barrel: JP Supermatch 416R air-gauged, button-rifled, cryogenically treated barrel Thermo-Fit to receiver, polished stainless, JP Compensator. Stock: Hogue OverMolded, Magpul MOE, Magpul CTR, LUTH-AR "Skullaton," or Mission First Tactical BATTLELINK. Handguard: JP MK III system (Signature or Rapid configuration). Grip: Hogue pistol grip. Sights: Optics ready top rail. Weight: NA. Trigger: JP Fire Control Package available in weights of 3.5 to 4.5 lbs. Overall Length: NA. Features: Scaled-down version of the LRP-07 available with the same caliber, barrel, handguard, metal finishing and stock options as the CTR-02. Exaggerated bevel on the magazine well. New integral handguard nut stabilizes the barrel mount and front pivot-pin joint. MicroFit Takedown Pins, lightened military-style upper design, dust cover and forward assist paired with dedicated side-charging handle. Thermo-Fit installation. LRI-20 upper assemblies pair with any existing LRP-07 side-charge lower. JP adjustable gas system; JP .308 Low Mass Operating System with JP High Pressure EnhancedBolt.
Price: $3,499.00

KEL-TEC RFB
Caliber: 7.62 NATO/.308. 20-round FAL-type magazine. Barrel: 18 in. with threaded muzzle, A2-style flash hider. Weight: 8 lbs. Features: A bullpup short-stroke gas piston operated carbine with ambidextrous controls, reversible operating handle, Mil-Spec Picatinny rail.
Price: $1,927.00

KEL-TEC SU-16 SERIES
Caliber: 5.56 NATO/.223. Capacity: 10-round magazine. Barrels: 16 or 18.5 in. Weights: 4.5–5 lbs. Features: Offering in several rifle and carbine variations.
Price: ....$682.00–$900.00

LARUE TACTICAL OBR
Calibers: 5.56 NATO/.223, 7.62 NATO/.308 Win., .260 Rem. Barrels: 16.1 in., 18 in. or 20 in. Weights: 7.5–9.25 lbs. Features: Manufacturer of several models of AR-style rifles and carbines. Optimized Battle Rifle (OBR) series is made in both NATO calibers. Many AR-type options available. Made in the USA
Price: OBR 5.56 ....$2,245.00
Price: OBR 7.62, .260...$3,370.00

LEWIS MACHINE & TOOL (LMT)
Calibers: 5.56 NATO/.223, 7.62 NATO/.308 Win. Barrels: 16.1 in., 18 in. or 20 in. Weights: 7.5–9.25 lbs. Features: Manufacturer of a wide range of AR-style carbines with many options. SOPMOD stock, gas piston operating system, monolithic rail platform, tactical sights. Sharpshooter Weapons System includes Harris Bipod and case, eight 20-shot magazines, FDE finish. Made in the USA by Lewis Machine & Tool.
Price: Standard 16 ....$1,649.00
Price: Comp 16, flattop receiver.......................................$1,685.00
Price: CQB Series $2,399.00
Price: Sharpshooter Weapons System $6,499.00
Price: Valkyrie..$2,299.00
Price: 6.5 Long Range $2,999.00

Prices given are believed to be accurate at time of publication however, many factors affect retail pricing so exact prices are not possible.

76TH EDITION, 2022 ◈ 399

LWRC INTERNATIONAL M6 SERIES

Calibers: 5.56 NATO, .224 Valkyrie, .6.5 Creedmoor, 6.8 SPC, 7.62x51mm, .300 BLK. Capacity: 30-shot magazine. Features: This company makes a complete line of AR-15 type rifles operated by a short-stroke, gas piston system. A wide variety of stock, sight and finishes are available. Colors include black, Flat Dark Earth, Olive Drab Green, Patriot Brown.

Price: M6-SPR (Special Purpose Rifle) **$2,479.00**
Price: REPR (Shown) **$5,139.00**
Price: SIX8 A5 6.8 SPC.................................. **$2,600.00–$2,750.00**
Price: IC-DI 224 Valkyrie **$1,995.00**

LWRC INTERNATIONAL IC-PSD

Caliber: 5.56 NATO. Barrel: 8.5 in. Capacity: Magpul PMAG 30-round magazine. Stock: LWRC adjustable compact stock. Sights: Low-profile, flip-up Skirmish Sights. Weight: 5.9 lbs. Trigger: LWRC Enhanced Fire Control Group. Overall Length: 25-28 in. Features: Part of the Individual Carbine series of rifles. NFA item. LWRCI Monoforge upper receiver with modular 7-in. rail system. Nickel-boron coated bolt carrier, LWRCI High Efficiency 4-Prong Flash Hider.

Price: **$2,396.00**

MIDWEST INDUSTRIES COMBAT RAIL SERIES

Caliber: .300 AAC Blackout. Capacity: AR-15-pattern magazines. Barrel: 16 in., Criterion 1:8 twist, stainless-nitride finish, A2 flash hider, .625 in. diameter. Upper/Lower Receivers: Forged 7075 aluminum, M16/M4 specs. Stock: Magpul CTR buttstock. Grip: Magpul MOE. Sights: Optics-ready top rail, laser engraved T-marks. Weight: 6.2 lbs. for MI-FC300CRM12. Trigger: NA. Overall Length: NA. Features: MI-CRM Combat series handguards, M-LOK compatible. Hard-coat anodized Mil 8625 Type 3, Class 2 finish, M4 feed ramps, .250-in. takedown pins, M16 bolt carrier group. Works with standard AR-15 components and magazines, receiver rear takedown pin detent hole threaded for a 4-40 set screw. Models denote handguard lengths.

Price: MI-FC300CRM12 .... **$1,225.00**
Price: MI-FC300CRM14 .... **$1,230.00**
Price: MI-FC300CRM15 .... **$1,235.00**

MIDWEST INDUSTRIES SLH FIREARMS

Caliber: .300 AAC Blackout. Capacity: AR-15-pattern magazines. Barrel: 16 in., Criterion 1:7 twist, stainless-nitride finish, A2 flash hider, .750 in. diameter. Upper/Lower Receivers: Forged 7075 aluminum, M16/M4 specs. Stock: Magpul CTR buttstock. Grip: Magpul MOE. Sights: Optics-ready top rail, laser engraved T-marks. Weight: 6.2 lbs. for MI-FN300SLH12. Trigger: NA.

Overall Length: NA. Features: MI-SLH 12-in. Slim Line Handguards, M-LOK compatible. Hard-coat anodized Mil 8625 Type 3, Class 2 finish, M4 feed ramps, .250 in. takedown pins, M16 bolt carrier group. Works with standard AR-15 components and magazines, receiver rear takedown pin detent hole threaded for a 4-40 set screw. Models denote handguard lengths.

Price: MI-FN300SLH12 .... **$1,125.00**
Price: MI-FN300SLH14 .... **$1,130.00**

MIDWEST INDUSTRIES MI-10F-16M

Caliber: .308 Win. Capacity: one Magpul 10-round magazine; accepts SR-25 pattern magazines. Barrel: 16, 18, 20 in., Criterion 1:10 twist, stainless-nitride finish. Upper/Lower Receivers: Forged 7075 aluminum. Stock: Magpul Gen 3 PRS buttstock. Grip: Magpul MOE. Sights: Optics-ready top rail. Weight: 8.2 lbs. for MI-10F-16M. Trigger: NA. Overall Length: NA. Features: Midwest Industries 308 bolt-carrier group, 12-in. M-LOK handguard, two-chamber-enhanced muzzle brake, mid-length gas system, .750 in. gas block, MI-HDEP heavy-duty quick-detach end plate.

Price: MI-10F-16M **$1,700.00**
Price: MI-10F-18M **$1,775.00**
Price: MI-10F-20M **$2,075.00**

MOSSBERG MMR SERIES

Caliber: 5.56 NATO. Capacity: 10 or 30 rounds. GIO system. Barrel: 16 or 18 in. with A2-style muzzle brake. Features: Picatinny rail, black synthetic stock, free-floating stainless barrel. Offered in several variants. Pro and Optics Ready have JM Pro match trigger. Optics Ready has 6-position stock with FLEX pad, Magpul MOE grip and trigger guard. Introduced in 2016.

Price: MMR Carbine...**$938.00**
Price: MMR Tactical Optics Ready...................................**$1,253.00**
Price: MMR Pro..**$1,393.00**

PATRIOT ORDNANCE FACTORY ROGUE

Caliber: 7.62x51mm NATO (.308 Win.). Capacity: one Magpul 20-round magazine. Barrel: 16.5 in., 1:8 twist, 5/8x24 tpi muzzle threads, match-grade stainless steel, Micro-B muzzle brake. Stock: Mission First Tactical. Sights: None, optics ready with top Picatinny rail. Weight: 5.9 lbs. Trigger: 4.5-lb. POF-USA drop-in trigger system with KNS anti-walk pins. Length: 34 in. Features: 11-in. M-LOK Renegade free-floating rail with four integrated QD sling mounts. E2 dual-extraction technology helps dislodge cartridge cases. One-piece, high-phosphorus nickel coated direct impingement bolt carrier with mechanical key built into the body and positioned behind the cam pin. Chrome-plated bolt, extractor and firing pin. Oversized heat-sink barrel nut, KNS Precision stainless steel non-rotating anti-walk pins. Mil-Spec aluminum anti-tilt buffer tube. Patented roller cam pin with NP3-coated roller head. Introduced 2020.

RADICAL FIREARMS .350 LEGEND

Caliber: .350 Legend. Capacity: .350 Legend magazine. Barrel: 16 in., 1:14 twist, 4140 chrome-moly vanadium steel, Melonite finish, Big Bore Contour, A2 flash hider, 5/8x32 tpi muzzle thread. Upper/Lower Receivers: Forged

Prices given are believed to be accurate at time of publication however, many factors affect retail pricing so exact prices are not possible.

7075 T6, M4 Mil-Std upper with oversized ejection port, forward assist and dust cover. Type III anodizing. Stock: B5 Bravo, 6-position. Handguard: Free-float M-LOK hybrid rail, 15 in. Sights: None, full length top rail. Weight: NA. Trigger: Mil-Std. Length: 33-37.5 in. Features: Carbine-length gas system, low-profile gas block, Mil-Std charging handle, carbine Mil-Std buffer tube.
Price: $850.00

RADICAL FIREARMS .308 WINCHESTER
Caliber: .308 Win. Capacity: 20-round, .308 magazines. Barrel: 18 in., 1:10 twist, 5/8x24 tpi muzzle threads, RF-MS Compensator. Upper/Lower Receivers: 7075 T6 billet aluminum, DPMS Pattern High, Type III anodizing with forward assist and dust cover. Stock: Mission First Tactical Minimalist. Sights: None, full length top rail. Weight: NA. Trigger: Mil-Std. Length: 33-37.5 in. Features: Mid-length gas system, M-LOK Thin Rail Handguard, 15 in.
Price: 18- and 20-in. barrel................................ **$1,050.00**
Price: 24-in. barrel.. **$1,100.00**
Price: 20- and 24-in. barrel, 6.5 CM **$1,100.00**

ROCK RIVER ARMS LAR SERIES
Calibers: 204 Ruger, .223/5.56, .243 Win., 6.5 Creedmoor, .300 AAC Blackout, 7.62x39mm, .308/7.62, 6.8 SPC, .450 Bushmaster, .458 SOCOM, 9mm and .40 S&W. Features: These AR-15 type rifles and carbines are available with a very wide range of options. Virtually any AR configuration is offered including tactical, hunting and competition models. Some models are available in left-hand versions.
Price: .... **$760.00–$2,200.00**

ROCK RIVER ARMS LAR SERIES
Chamberings in .350 Legend were added in 2020. RRAGE 3G Rifles and Carbines with skeletonized handguards were added in 2020.
Price: RRAGE 3G Rifle **$820.00**
Price: RRAGE 3G Carbine................................ **$760.00**

ROCK RIVER ARMS PRECISION RIFLE BT-3
Similar to Enhanced Mid-Length A4. Barrel: 18 in. Weight: 8.5 lbs. Length: 36.5 to 39 in. Introduced 2020.
Price: Starting at **$1,550.00**

ROCK RIVER ARMS VARMINT RIFLE BT-3
Similar to Enhanced Mid-Length A4. Barrel: 20 in., 1:10 twist, fluted stainless steel heavy, cryogenically treated. Stock: RRA 6-position NSP-2 CAR. Grip: Hogue Rubber. Sights: None, optics-ready full-length top rail. Weight: 9.8 lbs. Trigger: RRA Two Stage. Length: 37 to 39.75 in. Features: RRA lightweight free-float rail, 17-in. extended, M-LOK compatible. Introduced 2020.
Price: Starting at.. **$1,500.00**

ROCK RIVER ARMS 20-INCH SELECT TARGET RIFLE BT-3
Similar to Enhanced Mid-Length A4. Barrel: 20 in. Weight: 8.6 lbs. Length: 42 in. Stock: Magpul Gen3 Precision Rifle. Hogue Grip. Introduced 2020.
Price: Starting at.. **$1,800.00**

RUGER AR-556
Caliber: 5.56 NATO, .350 Legend, .450 Bushmaster. Capacity: 30-round magazine (5.56), 5 rounds (.350 and .450). Features: Basic AR M4-style Modern Sporting Rifle with direct impingement operation, forged aluminum upper and lower receivers, and cold hammer-forged chrome-moly steel barrel with M4 feed ramp cuts. Other features include Ruger Rapid Deploy folding rear sight, milled F-height gas block with post front sight, telescoping 6-position stock and one 30-round Magpul magazine. Introduced in 2015. MPR (Multi Purpose Rifle) model has 18-in. barrel with muzzle brake, flat-top upper, 15-in. free-floating handguard with Magpul M-LOK accessory slots, Magpul MOE SL collapsible buttstock and MOE grip.
Price: **$799.00**
Price: MPR (5.56) **$899.00**
Price: MPR (.350 Legend, .450 Bushmaster) **$1,099.00**

ROCK RIVER ARMS BT-6
Caliber: .338 Lapua Magnum. Capacity: two 10-round magazines. Barrel: 24 in., 1:10 twist, black-nitride stainless steel. Upper/Lower Receivers: BT-6 billet aluminum. Stock: Magpul Gen3 Precision Rifle. RRA Overmolded A2 pistol grip. Sights: None, optics-ready full-length top rail. Weight: 13.5 lbs. Trigger: RRA Ultra Match Two Stage. Length: 48 in. Introduced 2020.
Price: **$5,050.00**

SAVAGE MSR 15/MSR 10
Calibers: AR-style series chambered in 5.56 NATO (Patrol and Recon), 6.5 Creedmoor or .308 Win. (MSR 10 Hunter and Long Range). Barrels: 16.1 in. (Patrol and Recon), 16 or 18 in. (Hunter), 20 or 22 in. (Long Range). Wylde chamber on Patrol and Recon models. Hunter and Long Range models have muzzle brake.
Price: Patrol **$869.00**
Price: Recon (shown) **$994.00**
Price: MSR 10 Long Range **$2,284.00**
Price: MSR 10 Hunter.................................**$1,481.00**

SIG SAUER M400 TREAD
Caliber: 5.56 NATO/.223 Rem. Capacity: one 30-round magazine, compatible with AR-15 types. Barrel: 16 in., 1:8 RH twist, stainless steel. Upper/Lower Receivers: Forged aluminum, hard-coat anodized finish. Stock: Magpul SL-K 6-position telescoping stock. Sights: None, optics ready. Weight: 7 lbs. Trigger: Single-stage, polished hard-coat trigger. Overall Length: 30.8 in. Features: Direct-impingement operating system, integral QD mount, ambi safety selector, charging handle, free-floating 15-in. MLOK handguard, mid-length gas system.
Price: **$799.00**

SIG SAUER 716i TREAD
Caliber: .308 Win. Capacity: one 20-round magazine, compatible with SR-25 magazines. Barrel: 16 in., 1:10 RH twist, stainless steel. Upper/Lower Receivers: Forged aluminum, hard-coat anodized finish. Stock: Magpul SL-K 6-position telescoping stock. Sights: None, optics ready. Weight: 8.5 lbs. Trigger: Two-stage match. Overall Length: 33.8 to 37 in. Features: Direct-impingement operating system, integral QD mount, ambi safety selector, charging handle, free-floating 15-in. M-LOK handguard.
Price: **$1,299.00**

Prices given are believed to be accurate at time of publication however, many factors affect retail pricing **so exact** prices are not possible.

76TH EDITION, 2022 ⬦ **401**

SIG 516 PATROL

Caliber: 5.56 NATO. Features: AR-style rifle with included 30-round magazine, 16-in. chrome-lined barrel with muzzle brake; free-floating, aluminum quad Picatinny rail, Magpul MOE adjustable stock, black anodized or Flat Dark Earth finish, various configurations available.
Price: $1,888.00

SIG-SAUER SIG716 TACTICAL PATROL

Caliber: 7.62 NATO/.308 Win., 6.5 Creedmoor. Features: AR-10 type rifle. Gas-piston operation with 3-round-position (4-position optional) gas valve; 16-, 18- or 20-in. chrome-lined barrel with threaded muzzle and nitride finish; free-floating aluminum quad rail fore-end with four M1913 Picatinny rails; telescoping buttstock; lower receiver is machined from a 7075-T6 Aircraft grade aluminum forging; upper receiver, machined from 7075-T6 aircraft grade aluminum with integral M1913 Picatinny rail. DMR has free-floating barrel, two-stage match-grade trigger, short-stroke pushrod operating system.
Price: $2,385.00
Price: Designated Marksman (DMR) $3,108.00

SIG-SAUER M400

Caliber: 5.56 NATO. AR-style rifle with Direct Impingement system, 20-in. chrome-lined barrel with muzzle brake; free-floating M-LOK handguard with lightening cuts, 3-chamber compensator, Magpul SLK 6-position adjustable stock, various configurations available.
Price: $900.00

SIG-SAUER MCX VIRTUS PATROL

Calibers: 5.56 NATO, 7.62x39mm or .300 Blackout. Features: AR-style rifle. Modular system allows switching between calibers with conversion kit. Features include a 16 in. barrel, aluminum KeyMod handguards, ambi controls and charging handle, choice of side-folding or telescoping stock, auto-regulating gas system to all transition between subsonic and supersonic loads.
Price: $2,233.00

SMITH & WESSON M&P15

Caliber: 5.56mm NATO/.223. Capacity: 30-shot steel magazine. Barrel: 16 in., 1:9 in. twist. Weight: 6.74 lbs., w/o magazine. Lengths: 32–35 in. overall. Stock: Black synthetic. Sights: Adjustable post front sight, adjustable dual aperture rear sight. Features: 6-position telescopic stock, thermo-set M4 handguard. 14.75 in. sight radius. 7-lbs. (approx.) trigger pull. 7075 T6 aluminum upper, 4140 steel barrel. Chromed barrel bore, gas key, bolt carrier. Hard-coat black-anodized receiver and barrel finish. OR (Optics Ready) model has no sights. TS model has Magpul stock and folding sights. Made in USA by Smith & Wesson.
Price: Sport Model...$739.00
Price: OR Model...$1,069.00
Price: TS model $1,569.00

SMITH & WESSON M&P15-300

Calibers: .300 Whisper/.300 AAC Blackout. Features: Other specifications the same of 5.56 models.
Price: $1,119.00

SMITH & WESSON MODEL M&P15 VTAC II

Caliber: .223 Remington/5.56 NATO. Capacity: 30-round magazine. Barrel: 16 in. Weight: 6.5 lbs. Length: 35 in. extended, 32 in. collapsed, overall.

Features: Six-position stock. Surefire flash-hider and G2 light with VTAC light mount; VTAC/JP handguard; Geissele Super-V trigger; three adjustable Picatinny rails; VTAC padded two-point adjustable sling.
Price: $1,949.00

SMITH & WESSON M&P15PC CAMO

Caliber: 223 Rem/5.56 NATO, A2 configuration. Capacity: 10-round magazine. Barrel: 20 in. stainless with 1:8 in. twist. Weight: 8.2 lbs. Length: 38.5 in. overall. Features: AR-style, no sights but integral front and rear optics rails. Two-stage trigger, aluminum lower. Finished in Realtree Advantage Max-1 camo.
Price: $1,589.00

SMITH & WESSON M&P10

Caliber: .308 Win., 6.5 Creedmoor. Capacity: 10 rounds. Barrel: 18-20 in. Weight: 7.7 pounds. Features: Magpul MOE stock with MOE Plus grip, 15-in. free-float Troy M-LOK handguard, black hard anodized finish. Camo finish hunting model available w/5-round magazine.
Price: .308 ....$1,619.00
Price: 6.5 Creedmoor..$2,035.00

SPRINGFIELD ARMORY SAINT

Caliber: 5.56 NATO. Capacity: 30-round magazine. Barrel: 16 in., 1:8 twist. Weight: 6 lbs., 11 oz. Sights: AR2-style fixed post front, flip-up aperture rear. Features: Mid-length gas system, BCM 6-position stock, Mod 3 grip PMT KeyMod handguard 7075 T6 aluminum receivers. Springfield Armory's first entry into AR category. Introduced 2016. In 2020, several models with M-LOK handguards were added. The Bravo Company handguards have an internal aluminum heat shield.
Price: $899.00
Price: ST916556BM..$972.00

SPRINGFIELD ARMORY SAINT VICTOR RIFLES

Caliber: 5.56 NATO. Capacity: Includes one 30-round Magpul PMAG Gen M3. Barrel: 16-in., CMV, 1:8 twist, Melonite-finished barrels, Springfield Armory proprietary muzzle brake. Upper/Lower Receivers: Lowers are Accu-Tite tension-bonded to a flat-top forged upper receiver with Melonite finish. Stock: BCMGUNFIGHTER Mod 0. Pistol Grip: BCMGUNFIGHTER Mod 3. Sights: Spring-loaded, flip-up iron sights adjustable for windage and elevation. Weight: 6.9 lbs. Trigger: Enhanced nickel-boron-coated, single-stage flat trigger. Overall Length: 32.25 to 35.5 in. Features: Introduced 2019. Direct-impingement mid-length gas system. M16 bolt carrier group that is also Melonite finished, HPT/MPI tested, shot peened, and houses a 9310 steel bolt. 15-in. M-LOK free-float handguard, pinned, low-profile gas block. QD mounts built into the end plate and stock.
Price: Starting at..$1,073.00

SPRINGFIELD ARMORY SAINT VICTOR RIFLE .308

Caliber: .308 Win. Capacity: one 20-round Magpul Gen M3. Barrel: 16 in., 1:10 twist, lightweight profile, CMV Melonite finish, SA muzzle brake. Upper/Lower Receivers: Forged Type III hard-coat anodized, 7075 T6 Aluminum. Lower has Accu-Tite Tension System. Stock: Bravo Company 6-Position. Pistol Grip: Bravo Company Mod. 3. Sights: Spring-loaded, flip-ups. Weight: 7.8 lbs. Trigger: Enhanced nickel-boron-coated, single-stage flat trigger. Overall Length: 34.5 to 37.5 in. Features: Introduced 2019. Gas system is direct-impingement, mid-length, pinned gas block. Bolt carrier group is MPT, Melonite finish with a 9310 steel bolt; handguard is 15-in. M-LOK aluminum free-float with SA locking tabs.
Price: $1,399.00

STAG ARMS AR-STYLE RIFLES

Calibers: 5.56 NATO/.223, 6.8 SPC II. Capacities: 20- or 30-round magazine. Features: This manufacturer offers many AR-style rifles or carbines with many optional features including barrel length and configurations, stocks, sights, rail systems and both direct-impingement and gas-piston operating systems. Left-hand models are available on some products.

Price: Stag 15 Tactical 16 .... **$1,000.00**
Price: Stag 15 M4 .... **$900.00**
Price: Stag 15 Retro **$950.00**
Price: Stag 15 Bones **$800.00**
Price: Stag 15 O.R.C. **$760.00**
Price: Stag 15 Super Varminter (6.8) **$1,050.00**
Price: Stag 15 LEO **$1,050.00**
Price: Stag 15 Tactical SBR 10.5 .... **$900.00**
Price: Stag 15 3Gun Elite **$1,400.00**

STAG ARMS AR-10 STYLE RIFLES

Similar to AR-15 models, but chambered in .308 Win. or 6.5 Creedmoor.
Price: Stag 10 Creedmoor Bones **$1,575.00**
Price: Stag 10 LR **$2,050.00**
Price: Stag 10 Creedmoor S **$1,950.00**
Price: Stag 10 .308 M-LOK **$1,800.00**
Price: Stag 10 Creedmoor **$2,200.00**

STONER SR-15 MOD2 LPR

Caliber: .223. Capacity: 30-round magazine. Barrel: 18 in., free-floated inside M-LOK URSx handguard. Weight: 7.6 lbs. Length: 38 in. overall. Stock: Mag-Pul MOE. Sights: Post front, fully adjustable rear (300-meter sight). Features: URX-4 upper receiver; two-stage trigger, 30-round magazine. Black finish. Made in USA by Knight's Mfg.
Price: **$2,700.00**

STONER SR-25 ACC E2

Caliber: 7.62 NATO. Capacities: 10- or 20-shot steel magazine. Barrel: 16 in. with flash hider. Weight: 8.5 lbs. Features: Shortened, non-slip handguard; drop-in two-stage match trigger, removable carrying handle, ambidextrous controls, matte black finish. Made in USA by Knight's Mfg. Co.
Price: **$4,900.00**

WILSON COMBAT TACTICAL

Caliber: .204 Ruger, 5.56mm NATO, .223 Wylde, .22 Nosler, .260 Rem., 6.8 SPC, .300 Blackout, .300 Ham'r, 7.62x40mm WT, .338 Federal, .358 Win. Capacity: Accepts all M-16/AR-15 Style Magazines, includes one 20-round magazine. Barrel: 16.25 in., 1:9 in. twist, match-grade fluted. Weight: 6.9 lbs. Length: 36.25 in. overall. Stock: Fixed or collapsible. Features: Free-float ventilated aluminum quad-rail handguard, Mil-Spec Parkerized barrel and steel components, anodized receiver, precision CNC-machined upper and lower receivers, 7075 T6 aluminum forgings. Single-stage JP Trigger/ Hammer Group, Wilson Combat Tactical muzzle brake, nylon tactical rifle case. Made in USA by Wilson Combat.
Price: Protector, Ranger **$2,000.00**
Price: Recon Tactical **$2,225.00**
Price: Hunter **$2,365.00**
Price: Ultimate, Ultralight Hunter **$3,210.00**
Price: Super Sniper **$3,020.00**
Price: Urban Sniper.................................. **$2,200.00Price:** Ultralight Ranger

WINDHAM WEAPONRY 20 VARMINT

Caliber: .223 Rem./5.56mm NATO. Capacity: 5+1, ships with one 5-round magazine (accepts all standard AR-15 sizes). Barrel: 20 in., 1:8 RH twist, fluted 416R stainless steel, matte finish. Upper/Lower Receivers: A4-type flattop upper receiver, forged 7075 T6 aircraft aluminum with aluminum triggerguard. Electroless nickel-plated finish. Forend: 15-in. Windham Weaponry Aluminum M-LOK Free Float. Pistol Grip: Hogue OverMolded rubber pistol grip. Sights: None, optics ready, Picatinny top rail. Weight: 8.4 lbs. Length: 38.1875 in. Features: Gas-impingement system, Carpenter 158 steel bolt. Compass Lake chamber specification with matched bolt. LUTH MBA-1 stock. Comes with hard-plastic gun case with black web sling.
Price: R20FSSFTTL **$1,432.00**

WINDHAM WEAPONRY A1 GOVERNMENT

Caliber: .223 Rem./5.56mm NATO. Capacity: 30+1, ships with one 30-round magazine (accepts all standard AR-15 sizes). Barrel: 20-in., A2 profile, chrome-lined with A1 flash suppressor, 4150 chrome-moly-vanadium 11595E steel with M4 feed ramps. Rifling: 1:7 RH twist. Receivers: A1 upper with brass deflector and teardrop forward assist. Forend: Rifle-length triangular handguard with A1 Delta Ring. Pistol Grip: A1 Black Plastic Grip. Rear Sight: A1 dual aperture rear sight. Front Sight: Adjustable-height square post in A2 standard base. Trigger: Standard Mil-Spec Trigger. Stock: A2 Solid Stock with Trapdoor Storage Compartment. Weight: 7.45 lbs. Length: 39.5 in.

0

WINDHAM WEAPONRY DISSIPATOR M4

Caliber: .223 Rem./5.56mm NATO. Similar to Superlight SRC. Barrel: 16 in., M4 profile, chrome lined with A2 flash suppressor. Flattop-type upper receiver with A4 detachable carry handle. Rifle-length heat-shielded handguards. A2 black plastic grip. Rear Sight: A4 dual-aperture elevation and windage adjustable for 300–600m. Front Sight: adjustable-height square post in A2 standard base. Six-position telescoping buttstock. Weight: 7.2 lbs. Length: 32.375-36.125 in.
Price: R16M4DA4T **$1,192.00**

WINDHAM WEAPONRY SRC-308

Caliber: .308 Win. Capacity: 20+1, ships with one 20-round Magpul PMag magazine. Barrel: 16.5-in., medium profile, chrome lined with A2 flash suppressor; 4150M chrome-moly-vanadium 11595E steel; 1:10 right-hand-twist rifling, 6 lands and grooves. Upper/Lower Receivers: A4-type flattop upper receiver, forged 7075 T6 aircraft aluminum with aluminum trigger guard. Fore-end: Midlength tapered shielded handguards. Pistol Grip: Hogue OverMolded rubber pistol grip. Sights: None, optics ready, Picatinny top rail. Weight: 7.55 lbs. Length: 34.1875-38 in. Features: Gas-impingement system, Carpenter 158 steel bolt. Compass Lake chamber specification with matched bolt. Six-position telescoping buttstock. Comes with hard-plastic gun case with black web sling.
Price: R16FTT-308.. **$1,413.00**

BIG HORN ARMORY MODEL 89 RIFLE AND CARBINE

Caliber: .500 S&W Mag. Capacities: 5- or 7-round magazine. Features: Lever-action rifle or carbine chambered for .500 S&W Magnum. 22- or 18-in. barrel; walnut or maple stocks with pistol grip; aperture rear and blade front sights; recoil pad; sling swivels; enlarged lever loop; magazine capacity 5 (rifle) or 7 (carbine) rounds.

Price: $2,424.00

BIG HORN ARMORY MODEL 90 SERIES

Calibers: .460 S&W, .454 Casull. Features similar to Model 89. Several wood and finish upgrades available.

Price: .460 S&W $2,849.00
Price: .454 Casull, .45 Colt $3,049.00
Price: .500 Linebaugh $3,699.00

BROWNING BLR

Features: Lever action with rotating bolt head, multiple-lug breech bolt with recessed bolt face, side ejection. Rack-and-pinion lever. Flush-mounted detachable magazines, with 4+1 capacity for magnum cartridges, 5+1 for standard rounds. Barrel: Button-rifled chrome-moly steel with crowned muzzle. Stock: Buttstocks and fore-ends are American walnut with grip and forend checkering. Recoil pad installed. Trigger: Wide-groove design, trigger travels with lever. Half-cock hammer safety; fold-down hammer. Sights: Gold bead on ramp front; low-profile square-notch adjustable rear. Features: Blued barrel and receiver, high-gloss wood finish. Receivers are drilled and tapped for scope mounts, swivel studs included. Action lock provided. Introduced 1996. Imported from Japan by Browning.

BROWNING BLR GOLD MEDALLION

Calibers: .243 Win., 6.5 Creedmoor, .308 Win., .270 Win., .30-06 Spfld., .300 Win. Mag. Capacity: 3–5 round magazine, depending on caliber. Barrel: 20, 22, or 24 in. Length: 40–45 in. Weight: 6 lbs. 8 oz.–7 lbs. 4 oz. Stock: Grade III/IV Walnut stock with Schnabel forearm and brass spacers and rosewood caps. Features: High Grade lever action centerfire limited edition. Gloss finish engraved receiver built of lightweight aluminum. Gloss blued barrel drilled and tapped for optic mounts. Detachable box magazine. Iron sights. Pachmayr Decelerator recoil pad. Gold-plated trigger and gold inlay receiver branding.

Price: Short actions $1,540.00
Price: Long actions $1,630.00

CHIAPPA MODEL 1892 RIFLE

Calibers: .38 Special/357 Magnum, .38-40, .44-40, .44 Mag., .45 Colt. Barrels: 16 in. (Trapper), 20 in. round and 24 in. octagonal (Takedown). Weight: 7.7 lbs. Stock: Walnut. Sights: Blade front, buckhorn. Trapper model has interchangeable front sight blades. Features: Finishes are blue/case colored. Magazine capacity is 12 rounds with 24 in. bbl.; 10 rounds with 20 in. barrel; 9 rounds in 16 in. barrel. Mare's Leg models have 4-shot magazine, 9- or 12-in. barrel.

Price: $1,329.00
Price: Takedown...$1,435.00
Price: Trapper $1,329.00
Price: Mare's Leg $1,288.00

CHIAPPA MODEL 1886

Caliber: .45-70. Barrels: 16, 18.5, 22, 26 in. Replica of famous Winchester model offered in several variants.

Price: Rifle..$1,709.00
Price: Carbine $1,629.00

CHIAPPA 1892 LEVER-ACTION WILDLANDS

Caliber: .44 Mag. Capacity: 5. Barrel: 16.5 in., stainless steel, Cerakote dark gray or color case finish, heavy. Stock: Wood laminate or hand-oiled walnut. Sights: Fixed fiber-optic front, Skinner peep rear. Weight: 6.3 lbs. Features: Takedown and solid-frame configurations, mag tube fed.

Price: ....$1,434.00-$1,689.00

CIMARRON 1873 SHORT RIFLE

Calibers: .357 Magnum, .38 Special, .32 WCF, .38 WCF, .44 Special, .44 WCF, .45 Colt. Barrel: 20 in. tapered octagon. Weight: 7.5 lbs. Length: 39 in. overall. Stock: Walnut. Sights: Bead front, adjustable semi-buckhorn rear. Features: Has half "button" magazine. Original-type markings, including caliber, on barrel and elevator and "Kings" patent. Trapper Carbine (.357 Mag., .44 WCF, .45 Colt). From Cimarron F.A. Co.

Price: $1,299.00
Price: Trapper Carbine 16-in. bbl. $1,352.00

CIMARRON 1873 DELUXE SPORTING

Similar to the 1873 Short Rifle except has 24-in. barrel with half-magazine.

Price: $1,485.00

CIMARRON 1873 LONG RANGE SPORTING

Calibers: .44 WCF, .45 Colt. Barrel: 30 in., octagonal. Weight: 8.5 lbs. Length: 48 in. overall. Stock: Walnut. Sights: Blade front, semi-buckhorn ramp rear. Tang sight optional. Features: Color casehardened frame; choice of modern blued-black or charcoal blued for other parts. Barrel marked "Kings Improvement." From Cimarron F.A. Co.

Price: $1,385.00

EMF 1866 YELLOWBOY LEVER ACTIONS

Calibers: .38 Special, .44-40, .45 LC. Barrels: 19 in. (carbine), 24 in. (rifle). Weight: 9 lbs. Length: 43 in. overall (rifle). Stock: European walnut. Sights: Bead front, open adjustable rear. Features: Solid brass frame, blued barrel, lever, hammer, buttplate. Imported from Italy by EMF.

Price: Rifle...$1,175.00

EMF MODEL 1873 LEVER-ACTION

Calibers: .32/20, .357 Magnum, .38/40, .44-40, .45 Colt. Barrels: 18 in., 20 in., 24 in., 30 in. Weight: 8 lbs. Length: 43.25 in. overall. Stock: European walnut. Sights: Bead front, rear adjustable for windage and elevation. Features: Color casehardened frame (blued on carbine). Imported by EMF.

Price: $1,250.00

HENRY NEW ORIGINAL RIFLE

Calibers: .44-40 Win, .45 Colt. Capacity: 13-round tubular magazine. Barrel: 24-in. octagonal blued steel. Weight: 9 lbs. Length: 43 in. Stock: Fancy-grade American Walnut with straight-grip buttstock. Sights: Folding ladder rear with blade front. Features: Hardened brass receiver finished in high polish. Essentially identical to the 1860 original, except for caliber. Serial numbers begin with "BTH" prefix in honor of Benjamin Tyler Henry, inventor of the lever action repeating rifle that went on to become the most legendary firearm in American history. Made in the USA. Only this standard model New Original is available in the .45 Colt chambering; all other New Original Models below are .44-40 Win. only.

Price: $2,590.00
Price: New Original Deluxe Engraved $3,810.00
Price: New Original B.T. Henry 200th Anniv. Edition $4,286.00
Price: New Original Rare Carbine $2,590.00
Price: New Original Iron Framed $3,023.00
Price: New Original Silver Deluxe Engraved $4,078.00

Prices given are believed to be accurate at time of publication however, many factors affect retail pricing so exact prices are not possible.

HENRY SIDE GATE MODELS

Beginning in 2020, Henry began building the centerfire lever actions listed below with a side loading gate in addition to the tubular magazine charging port. These are not to be confused with the specific Henry Side Gate Model H024. NOTE: All previous Henry centerfire models without the side gate are now discontinued and considered "Legacy" models with slightly lower value at time of publication.

Price: Big Boy Color Case Hardened Side Gate **$1,141.00**
Price: Big Boy Steel Side Gate, Carbine or Rifle **$969.00**
Price: Big Boy Steel Side Gate, Large Loop **$986.00**
Price: Color Case Hardened Side Gate .30-30 and .45-70 ....**$1,141.00**
Price: Steel .30-30 Side Gate **$969.00**
Price: Steel .30-30 Side Gate Large Loop **$986.00**
Price: Steel .45-70 Side Gate **$969.00**
Price: Steel Wildlife Edition Side Gate **$1,618.00**

HENRY MODEL H024 SIDE GATE LEVER ACTION

Calibers: .38-55 Win., .30-30 Win., .45-70 Govt, .35 Rem. Capacity: 4 or 5-round tubular magazine. Barrel: 20-in. round blued steel. Weight: 7.5 lbs. Length: 38.3 in. Stock: American Walnut straight style with special deep checkering including floral scroll and Henry logo wood detail not found on any other models. Sights: Fully adjustable semi-buckhorn diamond-insert rear. Front ramp with 0.62-in. ivory bead. Drilled and tapped. Features: This H024 is the debut model using Henry's side loading gate design in addition to the standard tubular loading port. These hardened brass receiver centerfires are instantly recognizable with the special engraved and checkered stocks. Polished brass buttplate, barrel band, and swivel stud. Standard-size lever loop. Transfer bar safety.
Price: **$1,100.00**

HENRY BIG BOY X MODEL

Calibers: .45 Colt, .357/.38 Spl, .44 Mag/.44 Spl. Capacity: 7. Barrel: 17.4 in., round blue steel. Stock: Synthetic. Sights: Fiber optic. Weight: 7.3 lbs. Features: Robust and versatile, solid rubber buttpad, M-LOK Picatinny rail optional.
Price: **$970.00**

HENRY LONG RANGER

Calibers: .223 Rem., .243 Win., 6.5 Creedmoor, .308 Win. Capacity: 4 (.243, 6.5CM, .308) or 5 (.223) box magazine. Barrel: 20 or 22 in. (6.5 Creedmoor) round blued steel. Weight: 7 lbs. Length: 40.5–42.5 in. Stock: Straight-grip, checkered, oil-finished American Walnut. Sights: Two models, one sighted with folding fully adjustable rear and ramp ivory bead front. The other does not have iron sights but includes scope bases and hammer extension instead. Both are drilled and tapped. Features: Geared action with side ejection port. Chromed steel bolt with six lugs. Flush-fit box magazine with side push-button release. Sling studs, rubber recoil pad. Transfer bar safety.
Price: **$1,138.00**
Price: Long Ranger Wildlife Editions **$1,973.00**
Price: Long Ranger Deluxe Engraved............................**$1,973.00**

HENRY X-MODELS

Calibers: .30-30 Win., .45-70 Govt., .45 Colt, .44 Mag., .38 Spl./.357 Mag. Capacity: 4 (.45-70), 5 (.30-30), or 7 (Big Boys) tubular magazine Barrel: 17.4-, 19.8-, 21.375-in. round blued steel. Weight: 7.3–8.07 lbs. Length: 36.3–40.375 in. Stock: Black synthetic with M-LOK attachment points and lower Picatinny rail. Sights: Fully adjustable fiber-optic front and rear. Also drilled and tapped for Weaver 63B base. Features: Blacked-out lever actions built around several of Henry's existing family lines of long guns. Large loop lever. Barrel threaded at 5/8x24 for easy suppressor or brake attachment. Transfer bar safety. Solid rubber recoil pad. Sling studs. Matte blued steel metalwork.

Price: Big Boy X-Model..**$1,000.00**
Price: X-Model .30-30 ....**$1,019.00**
Price: X-Model .45-70 ....**$1,000.00**

MARLIN MODEL 336C LEVER-ACTION CARBINE

Calibers: .30-30 or .35 Rem. Capacity: 6-shot tubular magazine. Barrel: 20 in. Micro-Groove. Weight: 7 lbs. Length: 38.5 in. overall. Stock: Checkered American black walnut, capped pistol grip. Mar-Shield finish; rubber buttpad; swivel studs. Sights: Ramp front with wide-scan hood, semi-buckhorn folding rear adjustable for windage and elevation. Features: Hammer-block safety. Receiver tapped for scope mount, offset hammer spur; top of receiver sandblasted to prevent glare. Includes safety lock. The latest variation of Marlin's classic lever gun that originated in 1937.
Price: **$635.00**
Price: Curly Maple stock..**$899.00**

MARLIN MODEL 1894 COWBOY

Calibers: .357 Magnum, .44 Magnum, .45 Colt. Capacity: 10-round magazine. Barrel: 20 in. tapered octagon, deep cut rifling. Weight: 7.5 lbs. Length: 41.5 in. overall. Stock: Straight grip American black walnut, hard rubber buttplate, Mar-Shield finish. Sights: Marble carbine front, adjustable Marble semi-buckhorn rear. Features: Squared finger lever; straight grip stock; blued steel fore-end tip. Designed for Cowboy Shooting events. Introduced 1996. Includes safety lock. Made in USA by Marlin.
Price: **$1,093.00**

MARLIN 1894 SBL

Caliber: .44 Magnum. Capacity: 6-round tubular magazine. Features: 16.5-in. barrel, laminated stock, stainless finish, large lever, accessory rail, XS Ghost Ring sights.
Price: **$1,146.00**

MARLIN MODEL 1895 LEVER-ACTION

Caliber: .45-70 Govt. Capacity: 4-shot tubular magazine. Barrel: 22 in. round. Weight: 7.5 lbs. Length: 40.5 in. overall. Stock: Checkered American black walnut, full pistol grip. Mar-Shield finish; rubber buttpad; quick detachable swivel studs. Sights: Bead front with Wide-Scan hood, semi-buckhorn folding rear adjustable for windage and elevation. Features: Hammer-block safety. Solid receiver tapped for scope mounts or receiver sights; offset hammer spur. Includes safety lock.
Price: **$745.00**

MARLIN MODEL 1895 DARK SERIES

Similar to Model 1895 with deep-cut Ballard-type rifling; pistol-grip synthetic stock with large-loop lever, matte stainless finish, full length magazine. Barrel: 16.25 in. Overall length: 34.5 in. Weight: 7.65 lbs. Sights: XS lever rail with ghost-ring receiver sight.
....**$949.00**

Prices given are believed to be accurate at time of publication however, many factors affect retail pricing so exact prices are not possible.

76TH EDITION, 2022 ✦ **405**

MARLIN 1895GBL

Caliber: .45-70 Govt. Features: Lever-action rifle with 6-shot, full-length tubular magazine; 18.5-in. barrel with deep-cut Ballard-type rifling (6 grooves); big-loop finger lever; side ejection; solid-top receiver; deeply blued metal surfaces; hammer block safety; pistol-grip two-tone brown laminate stock with cut checkering; ventilated recoil pad; Mar-Shield finish, swivel studs.
Price: **$786.00**

NAVY ARMS 1873 RIFLE

Calibers: .357 Magnum, .45 Colt. Capacity: 12-round magazine. Barrels: 20 in., 24.25 in., full octagonal. Stock: Deluxe checkered American walnut. Sights: Gold bead front, semi-buckhorn rear. Features: Turnbull color case-hardened frame, rest blued. Full-octagon barrel. Available exclusively from Navy Arms. Made by Winchester.
Price: **$2,500.00**

NAVY ARMS 1892 SHORT RIFLE

Calibers: .45 Colt, .44 Magnum. Capacity: 10-round magazine. Barrel: 20 in. full octagon. Stock: Checkered Grade 1 American walnut. Sights: Marble's Semi-Buckhorn rear and gold bead front. Finish: Color casehardened.
Price: **$2,300.00**

ROSSI R92 LEVER-ACTION CARBINE

Calibers: .38 Special/.357 Magnum, .44 Magnum., .44-40 Win., .45 Colt. Barrels: 16or 20 in. with round barrel, 20 or 24 in. with octagon barrel. Weight: 4.8–7 lbs. Length: 34–41.5 in. Features: Blued or stainless finish. Various options available in selected chamberings (large lever loop, fiber-optic sights, cheekpiece).
Price: R92 Blued Rifle **$730.00**
Price: R92 Stainless Rifle **$770.00**
Price: R92 Carbine **$725.00**
Price: R92 Stainless Carbine **$770.00**
Price: R92 Octagonal Barrel ....**$830.00–$875.00**
Price: R92 Gold **$810.00**
Price: R92 Triple Black **$925.00**
Price: R92 .454 Casull **$950.00**

UBERTI 1873 SPORTING RIFLE

Calibers: .357 Magnum, .44-40, .45 Colt. Barrels: 16.1 in. round, 19 in. round or 20 in., 24.25 in. octagonal. Weight: Up to 8.2 lbs. Length: Up to 43.3 in. overall. Stock: Walnut, straight grip and pistol grip. Sights: Blade front adjustable for windage, open rear adjustable for elevation. Features: Color casehardened frame, blued barrel, hammer, lever, buttplate, brass elevator. Imported by Stoeger Industries.
Price: Carbine 19-in. bbl. **$1,309.00**
Price: Trapper 16.1-in. bbl. **$1,329.00**
Price: Carbine 18-in. half oct. bbl. **$1,379.00**
Price: Short Rifle 20-in. bbl. **$1,339.00**
Price: Sporting Rifle, 24.25-in. bbl. **$1,339.00**
Price: Special Sporting Rifle, A-grade walnut **$1,449.00**

UBERTI 1866 YELLOWBOY CARBINE, SHORT, RIFLE

Calibers: .38 Special, .44-40, .45 Colt. Barrel: 24.25 in. octagonal. Weight: 8.2 lbs. Length: 43.25 in. overall. Stock: Walnut. Sights: Blade front adjustable for windage, rear adjustable for elevation. Features: Frame, buttplate, fore-end cap of polished brass, balance charcoal blued. Imported by Stoeger Industries.
Price: 1866 Yellowboy Carbine, 19-in. round barrel.....................**$1,269.00**
Price: 1866 Yellowboy Short Rifle, 20-in. octagonal barrel **$1,269.00**
Price: 1866 Yellowboy Rifle, 24.25-in. octagonal barrel **$1,269.00**

UBERTI 1860 HENRY

Calibers: .44-40, .45 Colt. Barrel: 24.25 in. half-octagon. Weight: 9.2 lbs. Length: 43.75 in. overall. Stock: American walnut. Sights: Blade front, rear adjustable for elevation. Imported by Stoeger Industries.
Price: 1860 Henry Trapper, 18.5-in. barrel, brass frame................**$1,499.00**
Price: 1860 Henry Rifle Iron Frame, 24.25-in. barrel **$1,499.00**

WINCHESTER MODEL 94 SHORT RIFLE

Calibers: .30-30, .38-55, .32 Special. Barrel: 20 in. Weight: 6.75 lbs. Sights: Semi-buckhorn rear, gold bead front. Stock: Walnut with straight grip. Fore-end has black grip cap. Also available in Trail's End takedown design in .450 Marlin or .30-30.
Price: **$1,230.00**
Price: (Takedown) **$1,460.00**

WINCHESTER MODEL 94 SPORTER

Calibers: .30-30, .38-55. Barrel: 24 in. Weight: 7.5 lbs. Features: Same features of Model 94 Short Rifle except for crescent butt and steel buttplate, 24 in. half-round, half-octagon barrel, checkered stock.
Price: **$1,400.00**

WINCHESTER 1873 SHORT RIFLE

Calibers: .357 Magnum, .44-40, .45 Colt. Capacities: Tubular magazine holds 10 rounds (.44-40, .45 Colt), 11 rounds (.38 Special). Barrel: 20 in. Weight: 7.25 lbs. Sights: Marble semi-buckhorn rear, gold bead front. Tang is drilled and tapped for optional peep sight. Stock: Satin finished, straight-grip walnut with steel crescent buttplate and steel fore-end cap. Tang safety. A modern version of the "Gun That Won the West."
Price: **$1,300.00**
Price: Deluxe Sporting Rifle.............................**$1,800.00**

ARMALITE AR-30A1 TARGET
Calibers: .300 Win. Mag., .338 Lapua. Capacity: 5 rounds. Barrel: 26 in., target-grade chrome moly. Weight: 12.8 lbs. Length: 46 in. Stock: Standard fixed with adjustable cheek piece. Sights: None. Accessory top rail included. Features: Bolt-action rifle. Muzzle brake, ambidextrous magazine release, large ejection port makes single loading easy, V-block patented bedding system, bolt-mounted safety locks firing pin. AR-31 is in .308 Win., accepts AR-10 double-stack magazines, has adjustable pistol grip stock.
Price: **$3,460.00**
Price: AR-31..**$3,460.00**

ARMALITE AR-50A1
Caliber: .50 BMG, .416 Barrett. Capacity: Bolt-action single-shot. Barrel: 30 in. with muzzle brake. National Match model (shown) has 33-in. fluted barrel. Weight: 34.1 lbs. Stock: Three-section. Extruded fore-end, machined vertical grip, forged and machined buttstock that is vertically adjustable. National Match model (.50 BMG only) has V-block patented bedding system, Armalite Skid System to ensure straight-back recoil.
Price: **$3,359.00**

ANSCHUTZ 1782
Calibers: .243 Win., 6.5 Creedmoor, .308 Win., .30-06, 8x57, 9.3x62. Capacity: 3. Barrel: 20.5 to 23.8 in., blued, threaded. Stock: Walnut. Sights: Integrated Picatinny rail. Weight: 8 lbs. Features: Solid-steel milled action, 60-degree bolt lift, sliding safety catch.
Price: **$2,795.00**

BENELLI LUPO
Calibers: .243 Win., 6.5 Creedmoor, .308 Win., .30-06 Spfld., .270 Win, .300 Win. Mag. Capacity: 4 or 5-round box magazine Barrel: 22- and 24-in. Crio-treated, free-floating, threaded barrel with thread cover. Length: 44.225–46.625 in. Stock: Black Synthetic. Sights: None. Includes two-piece Picatinny rail. Weight: 6.9–7.1 lbs. Features: Shims allow stock adjustment. Matte blued metalwork. Progressive comfort recoil reduction system. Sub-MOA guarantee. CombTech cheek pad. Ambidextrous safety. Integral swivel mounts.
Price: **$1,700.00**

BARRETT FIELDCRAFT HUNTING RIFLE
Calibers: .22-250 Rem., .243 Win., 6mm Creedmoor, .25-06, 6.5 Creedmoor, 6.5x55, 7mm-08 Rem., .308 Win. .270 Win., .30-06. Capacity: 4-round magazine. Barrel: 18 (threaded), 21 or 24 inches. Weight: 5.2-5.6 lbs. Features: Two-position safety, Timney trigger. Receiver, barrels and bolts are scaled for specific calibers. Barrels and action are made from 416 stainless steel and are full-length hand bedded.
Price: ....**$1,879.00-$1,929.00**

BARRETT MRAD
Calibers: .260 Rem., 6.5 Creedmoor, .308 Win., .300 Win. Mag., .338 Lapua Magnum. Capacity: 10-round magazine. Barrels: 20 in., 24 in. or 26 in. fluted or heavy. Features: User-interchangeable barrel system, folding stock, adjustable cheekpiece, 5-position length of pull adjustment button, match-grade trigger, 22-in. optics rail.
Price: ....**$5,850.00–$6,000.00**

BERGARA B-14 SERIES
Calibers: 6.5 Creedmoor, .270 Win., 7mm Rem. Mag., .308 Win., .30-06, .300 Win. Mag. Barrels: 22 or 24 in. Weight: 7 lbs. Features: Synthetic with Soft touch finish, recoil pad, swivel studs, adjustable trigger, choice of detachable mag or hinged floorplate. Made in Spain.
Price: **$825.00**
Price: Walnut Stock (Shown, Top) **$945.00**
Price: Premier Series **$2,190.00**
Price: Hunting and Match Rifle (HMR)(Shown, Bottom)................**$1,150.00**

BERGARA BCR SERIES
Calibers: Most popular calibers from .222 Rem. to .300 Win. Mag Barrels: 18, 22, 24 or 26 in. Various options available.
Price: BCR23 Sport Hunter **$3,950.00**
Price: BCR24 Varmint Hunter **$4,100.00**
Price: BCR25 Long Range Hunter **$4,350.00**
Price: BCR27 Competition **$4,950.00**

BERGARA MOUNTAIN 2.0
Calibers: 6.5 Creedmoor, 6.5 PRC, .308 Win., 28 Nosler, .300 Win. Mag., .300 PRC. Capacity: 2 to 4. Barrel: 22 to 24-in. No. 3 stainless steel. Stock: Carbon fiber. Sights: None, drilled and tapped. Features: Trigger tech trigger, two-lug action, Cerakote finished metal.
Price: **$2,250.00**

BERGARA PREMIER HIGHLANDER
Calibers: 6.5 Creedmoor, 6.5 PRC, .308 Win., 7mm Rem. Mag., 28 Nosler, .300 Win. Mag., .300 PRC. Capacity: 4-standard, 3-magnum, 2-PRC with hinged floorplate. Barrel: 20–26-in. No. 5 taper, fluted. Weight: 7.3–7.8 lbs. Length: 38.5–45 in. Stock: Grayboe Fiberglass. Sights: Drilled and tapped for Remington 700 bases with 8-40 screws. Features: TriggerTech frictionless release trigger. Threaded muzzle with Omni Muzzle Brake. Sniper Grey Cerakote metalwork finish. Guaranteed MOA accuracy.
Price: ....**$1,885.00–$1,985.00**

BLASER R-8 SERIES
Calibers: Available in virtually all standard and metric calibers from .204 Ruger to .500 Jeffery. Straight-pull bolt action. Barrels: 20.5, 23, or 25.75 in. Weights: 6.375–8.375 lbs. Lengths: 40 in. overall (22 in. barrel). Stocks: Synthetic or Turkish walnut. Sights: None furnished; drilled and tapped for scope mounting. Features: Thumb-activated safety slide/cocking mechanism; interchangeable barrels and bolt heads. Many optional features. Imported from Germany by Blaser USA. *Note, Blaser R8 bolt action series adds a .22 LR rimfire conversion system.*
Price: **$3,787.00**

BROWNING AB3 COMPOSITE STALKER
Calibers: .243, 6.5 Creedmoor, .270 Win., .270 WSM, 7mm-08, 7mm Rem. Mag., .30-06, .300 Win. Mag., .300 WSM or .308 Win. Barrels: 22 in, 26 in. for magnums. Weights: 6.8–7.4 lbs. Stock: Matte black synthetic. Sights: None. Picatinny rail scope mount included.
Price: **$600.00**
Price: Micro Stalker **$600.00**
Price: Hunter..**$670.00**

BROWNING X-BOLT HUNTER
Calibers: .223, .22-250, .243 Win., 6mm Creedmoor, 6.5 Creedmoor, .25-06 Rem., .270 Win., .270 WSM, .280 Rem., 7mm Rem. Mag., 7mm WSM, 7mm-08 Rem., .308 Win., .30-06, .300 Win. Mag., .300 WSM, .325 WSM, .338 Win. Mag., .375 H&H Mag, 6.8 Western. Barrels: 22 in., 23 in., 24 in., 26 in., varies by model. Matte blued or stainless free-floated barrel, recessed muzzle crown. Weights: 6.3–7 lbs. Stocks: Hunter and Medallion models have black walnut stocks; Composite Stalker and Stainless Stalker models have composite stocks. Inflex Technology recoil pad. Sights: None, drilled and tapped receiver, X-Lock scope mounts. Features: Adjustable three-lever Feather Trigger system, polished hard-chromed steel components, factory pre-set at 3.5 lbs., alloy trigger housing. Bolt unlock button, detachable rotary magazine, 60-degree bolt lift, three locking lugs, top-tang safety, sling swivel studs. Introduced 2008.
Price: Standard calibers **$900.00**
Price: Magnum calibers **$950.00**
Price: Left-hand models......................**$940.00–$980.00**

BROWNING X-BOLT WESTERN HUNTER LONG RANGE
Calibers: 6.5 Creedmoor, 6.5 PRC, 7mm Rem. Mag., 28 Nosler, .280 Ackley Improved, .300 Win. Mag., 30 Nosler, .300 Rem. Ultra Mag., .300 PRC, 6.8 Western. Capacity: 3 or 4-round removeable rotary magazine Barrel: 26-in. heavy sporter contour with removeable muzzle brake. Length: 46–46.75 in. Weight: 7 lbs. 7 oz.–7 lbs. 12 oz. Stock: Composite with new adjustable comb system, A-TACS AU camo finish, and textured grip panels. Features: Top tang thumb safety. Extended bolt handle. Feather Trigger, InFlex recoil pad. X-Lock scope mount system. Gold-plated trigger. Sling studs.
Price: ....**$1,099.00–$1,219.00**

BROWNING X-BOLT HUNTER LONG RANGE
Calibers: 6.5 Creedmoor, 6.5 PRC, .308 Win., .270 Win., .30-06, 7MM Rem. Mag., .300 Win. Mag., 6.8 Western. Capacity: 3 to 4. Barrel: 22 to 26 in., blued sporter, heavy. Stock: Satin finish checkered walnut. Sights: None, drilled and tapped. Weight: 7.6 to 8 lbs. Features: Ambidextrous adjustable comb, muzzle brake with suppressor threads.
Price: **$1,300.00**

BROWNING X-BOLT MAX LONG RANGE
Calibers: 6mm Creedmoor, 6.5 Creedmoor, .308 Win., .300 WSM, 7MM Rem. Mag., 28 Nosler, .300 Win.Mag., .300 RUM, 6.5 PRC, 30 Nosler, .300 PRC, 6.8 Western. Capacity: 3 to 4. Barrel: 26 in., satin gray stainless steel sporter, heavy. Stock: Composite black, gray splatter. Sights: None, drilled and tapped. Weight: 8.2 to 8.6 lbs. Features: Adjustable comb, extended bolt handle, three swivel studs for sling and bipod use.
Price: ....**$1,300.00–$1,340.00**

BROWNING X-BOLT MEDALLION
Calibers: Most popular calibers from .223 Rem. to .375 H&H, 6.8 Western. Barrels: 22, 24 or 26 in. free-floated. Features: Engraved receiver with polished blue finish, gloss finished and checkered walnut stock with rosewood grip and fore-end caps, detachable rotary magazine. Medallion Maple model has AAA-grade maple stock.
Price: **$1,040.00**
Price: Medallion Maple **$1,070.00**

BROWNING X-BOLT HELL'S CANYON
Calibers: .22 Nosler, 6mm Creedmoor, .243 Win., 26 Nosler, 6.5 Creedmoor, .270 Win., .270 WSM, 7mm-08 Rem., 7mm Rem. Mag., .308 Win., .30-06, .300 Win. Mag., .300 WSM, 6.8 Western. Barrels: 22–26-in. fluted and free-floating with muzzle brake or thread protector. Stock: A-TACS AU Camo composite with checkered grip panels. Features: Detachable rotary magazine, adjustable trigger, Cerakote Burnt Bronze finish on receiver and barrel.
Price: ....**$1,260.00–$1,320.00**

BROWNING X-BOLT HELLS CANYON MAX LONG RANGE
Calibers: 6.5 Creedmoor, 6.5 PRC, 7mm Rem. Mag., 28 Nosler, .280 Ackley Improved, .300 Win. Mag., 30 Nosler, .300 Rem Ultra Mag., .300 PRC, 6.8 Western. Capacity: 3 or 4-round box magazine. Barrel: 26-in. heavy sporter contour. Weight: 8–8 lbs. 7 oz. Length: 46-3/4 in. Stock: Composite Max in A-TACS AU camo with adjustable comb, LOP spacers, and vertical pistol grip. Features: Long-range bolt-action platform with steel receiver. Cerakote Burnt Bronze finish. Removeable Browning Recoil Hawg muzzle brake. Top tang thumb safety. Extended bolt handle. Three swivel studs. FeatherTrigger, InFlex recoil pad. Gold-plated trigger and branding detail.
Price: ....**$1,430.00–$1,560.00**

BROWNING X-BOLT PRO SERIES
Calibers: 6mm Creedmoor, 6.5 Creedmoor, 26 Nosler, 28 Nosler, .270 Win., 7mm Rem. Mag., .308 Win., .30-06, 6.8 Western. Detachable rotary magazine. Barrels: 22–26 in. Stainless steel, fluted with threaded/removable muzzle brake. Weights: 6–7.5 lbs. Finish: Cerakote Burnt Bronze. Stock: Second generation carbon fiber with palm swell, textured gripping surfaces. Adjustable trigger, top tang safety, sling swivel studs. Long Range has heavy sporter-contour barrel, proprietary lapping process.
Price: X-Bolt Pro.........................**$2,070.00–$2,130.00**
Price: X-Bolt Pro Long Range ....**$2,100.00–$2,180.00**
Price: X-Bolt Pro Tungsten ....**$2,070.00–$2,130.00**

CHEYTAC M-200
Calibers: .357 CheyTac, .408 CheyTac. Capacity: 7-round magazine. Barrel: 30 in. Length: 55 in. stock extended. Weight: 27 lbs. (steel barrel); 24 lbs. (carbon-fiber barrel). Stock: Retractable. Sights: None, scope rail provided. Features: CNC-machined receiver, attachable Picatinny rail M-1913, detachable barrel, integral bipod, 3.5-lb. trigger pull, muzzle brake. Made in USA by CheyTac, LLC.
Price: **$11,700.00**

CHRISTENSEN ARMS MESA TITANIUM EDITION
Calibers: 6.5 Creedmoor, 6.5 PRC, .308 Win., .300 Win. Mag. Capacity: 3 to 4 Barrel: 22 to 24 in., 416R stainless steel, threaded. Stock: Carbon-fiber

Prices given are believed to be accurate at time of publication however, many factors affect retail pricing so exact prices are not possible.

composite, sporter style. Sights: None, drilled and tapped. Weight: 6.1 lbs. Features: LimbSaver recoil pad, nitride-treated bolt, match-grade trigger.
Price: **$1,795.00**

CHRISTENSEN ARMS RIDGELINE TITANIUM EDITION
Calibers: 6.5 Creedmoor, 6.5 PRC, .308 Win., .300 Win. Mag. Capacity: 3 to 4. Barrel: 22 to 24 in., 416R stainless steel, carbon-fiber wrapped. Stock: Carbon-fiber composite, sporter style. Sights: Picatinny rail. Weight: 5.8 lbs. Features: Titanium radial brake, M16-style extractor, LimbSaver recoil pad.
Price: **$2,495.00**

COOPER MODEL 21
Calibers: Virtually any factory or wildcat chambering in the .223 Rem. family is available including: .17 Rem., .19-223, Tactical 20, .204 Ruger, .222 Rem, .222 Rem. Mag., .223 Rem, .223 Rem AI, 6x45, 6x47. Single shot. Barrels: 22–24 in. for Classic configurations, 24–26 in. for Varminter configurations. Weights: 6.5–8.0 lbs., depending on type. Stock: AA-AAA select claro walnut, 20 LPI checkering. Sights: None furnished. Features: Three front locking-lug, bolt-action, single-shot. Action: 7.75 in. long, Sako extractor. Button ejector. Fully adjustable single-stage trigger. Options include wood upgrades, case-color metalwork, barrel fluting, custom LOP, and many others.
Price: Classic **$2,495.00**
Price: Custom Classic **$2,995.00**
Price: Western Classic. **$3,795.00**
Price: Varminter **$2,495.00**
Price: Mannlicher **$4,395.000**

COOPER MODEL 52
Calibers: .30-06, .270 Win., .280 Rem, .25-06, .284 Win., .257 Weatherby Mag., .264 Win. Mag., .270 Weatherby Mag., 7mm Remington Mag., 7mm Weatherby Mag., 7mm Shooting Times Westerner, .300 Holland & Holland, .300 Win. Mag., .300 Weatherby Mag., .308 Norma Mag., 8mm Rem. Mag., .338 Win. Mag., .340 Weatherby V. Three-shot magazine. Barrels: 22 in. or 24 in. in Classic configurations, 24 in. or 26 in. in Varminter configurations. Weight: 7.75–8 lbs. depending on type. Stock: AA-AAA select claro walnut, 20 LPI checkering. Sights: None furnished. Features: Three front locking-lug bolt-action single shot. Action: 7 in. long, Sako style extractor. Button ejector. Fully adjustable single-stage trigger. Options include wood upgrades, case-color metalwork, barrel fluting, custom LOP, and many others.
Price: Classic. **$2,495.00**
Price: Custom Classic. **$3,335.00**
Price: Western Classic. **$3,995.00**
Price: Jackson Game **$2,595.00**
Price: Jackson Hunter **$2,595.00**
Price: Excalibur. **$2,595.00**
Price: Mannlicher **$4,755.00**
Price: Open Country Long Range **$3,795.00-4,155.00**
Price: Timberline, Synthetic Stock **$2,595.00**
Price: Raptor, Synthetic tactical stock **$2,755.00**

CVA CASCADE
Calibers: .243 Win., 6.5 Creedmoor, 7mm-08 Rem., .308 Win., .350 Legend, .450 Bushmaster, .22-250 Rem., 6.5 PRC, 7mm Rem. Mag., .300 Win. Mag. Capacity: 3 or 4-round flush-fit detachable magazine Barrel: 22-in. 4140 carbon steel in either matte blue or Cerakote FDE. Weight: 6.85–7.25 lbs. Length: 42.5–45.5 in. Stock: Synthetic, fiber-glass reinforced with SoftTouch finish. Available in either charcoal gray or Veil Wideland camo. Sights: Drilled and tapped for Savage 110 mounts; aftermarket CVA 20-MOA one-piece base available. Features: Bolt designed with 70-degree throw. Two-position safety. Threaded muzzle. Dual front swivel studs. Buttstock

has adjustable LOP with removeable spacer. MOA guarantee.
Price: .... **$567.00–$658.00**
Price: Cascade SB (Short Barrel) Series **$670.00**

CZ 527 LUX BOLT-ACTION
Calibers: .17 Hornet, .204 Ruger, .22 Hornet, .222 Rem., .223 Rem. Capacity: 5-round magazine. Barrels: 23.5 in. standard or heavy. Weight: 6 lbs., 1 oz. Length: 42.5 in. overall. Stock: European walnut with Monte Carlo. Sights: Hooded front, open adjustable rear. Features: Improved mini-Mauser action with non-rotating claw extractor; single set trigger; grooved receiver. Imported from the Czech Republic by CZ-USA.
Price: Brown laminate stock **$733.00**
Price: Model FS, full-length stock, cheekpiece **$827.00**

CZ 527 AMERICAN BOLT-ACTION
Similar to the CZ 527 Lux except has classic-style stock with 18 LPI checkering; free-floating barrel; recessed target crown on barrel. No sights furnished. Introduced 1999. Imported from the Czech Republic by CZUSA.
Price: **$733.00**

CZ 550 SAFARI MAGNUM/AMERICAN SAFARI MAGNUM
Similar to CZ 550 American Classic. Calibers: .375 H&H Mag., .416 Rigby, .458 Win. Mag., .458 Lott. Overall length is 46.5 in. Barrel: 25 in. Weight: 9.4 lbs., 9.9 lbs (American). Features: Hooded front sight, express rear with one standing, two folding leaves. Imported from the Czech Republic by CZ-USA.
Price: Safari Magnum **$1,215.00**
Price: American Safari Field .... **$1,215.00–$1,348.00**

CZ 557
Calibers: .243 Win., 6.5x55, .270 Win., .308 Win., .30-06. Capacity: 5+1. Barrel: 20.5 in. Stock: Satin finished walnut or Manners carbon fiber with textured grip and fore-end. Sights: None on Sporter model. Features: Forged steel receiver has integral scope mounts. Magazine has hinged floorplate. Trigger is adjustable. Push-feed action features short extractor and plunger style ejector. Varmint model (.243, .308) has 25.6-in. barrel, detachable box magazine.
Price: Sporter, walnut stock **$832.00**
Price: Synthetic stock **$779.00**
Price: Varmint model **$865.00**

CZ 557 ECLIPSE
Calibers: 6.5 Creedmoor, .308 Win., .30-06 Spfld. Capacity: 5-round internal magazine with hinged floorplate. Barrel: 20.5-in. blued steel. Sights: No iron sights. Integral 19mm dovetails. Length: 41.5 in. Weight: 7.9 lbs. Stock: Black synthetic American-style. Features: Built on a precision, push-feed bolt action for both reliability and affordability. CNC'ed from steel billet and mated to a CZ cold hammer forged and lapped barrel. Fully adjustable trigger. Two-position safety. LOP 13.75 in. Two forward sling studs and one rear. Rubber recoil pad. The 6.5 Creedmoor model features a threaded barrel.
Price: **$659.00**

Prices given are believed to be accurate at time of publication however, many factors affect retail pricing so exact prices are not possible.

76TH EDITION, 2022 ✦ **409**

FIERCE FIREARMS CARBON FURY

Calibers: .300 PRC, 6.5 Creedmoor, 6.5 PRC, 7MM Rem. Mag, .300 Win. Mag, .300 RUM, .300 WSM, 28 Nosler. Capacity: 4 to 5. Barrel: 24 to 26 in., stainless steel liner, carbon-fiber overlay. Stock: Carbon-fiber Monte Carlo. Sights: None, drilled and tapped. Weight: 6.6 lbs. Features: Guaranteed half-inch three-shot group at 100 yards; target crown for accuracy.
Price: **$2,740.00**

FIERCE FIREARMS RIVAL

Calibers: 6.5 Creedmoor, 6.5 PRC, 7mm Rem., 28 Nosler, .300 Win., .300 PRC, .300 RUM. Capacity: 4 to 5. Barrel: 20 to 26 in., spiral-fluted, match-grade stainless steel or carbon fiber. Stock: Fierce Tech C3 carbon fiber. Sights: None, drilled and tapped. Weight: 6.4 to 7 lbs. Features: Cerakote finish, Trigger Tech trigger, built-in bipod rail.
Price: .... **$2,295.00-$2,795.00**

FRANCHI MOMENTUM

Calibers: .243 Win., 6.5 Creedmoor, .270 Win., .308 Win., .30-06, .300 Win. Mag. Barrels: 22 or 24 in. Weights: 6.5–7.5 lbs. Stock: Black synthetic with checkered gripping surface, recessed sling swivel studs, TSA recoil pad. Sights: None. Features: Available with Burris Fullfield II 3-9X40mm scope.
Price: Varminter **$609.00**
Price: With Burris 3-9X scope **$729.00**

FRANCHI MOMENTUM ELITE

Calibers: .223 Rem., 6.5 Creedmoor, 6.5 PRC, .308 Win., .300 Win. Mag., .350 Legend. Capacity: 3 or 4-round box magazine. Barrel: 22- or 24-in. free floating, cold hammer forged with threaded muzzle brake. Weight: 7.1–7.5 lbs. Stock: Synthetic in True Timber Strata, Realtree Excape, and now also available with Sitka Optifade Elevation II camouflage. Sights: Picatinny rail. Features: TSA recoil pad absorbs up to 50 percent of felt recoil. Sling attachment points recessed into stock. One-piece spiral fluted bolt with three locking lugs and 60-degree throw. Two-position safety. RELIA trigger adjustable from 2 to 4 pounds. Cobalt Cerakote metalwork on the Sitka camo models.
Price: **$899.00**

FRANCHI MOMENTUM ELITE VARMINT

Calibers: .223 Rem., .22-250 Rem., .224 Valkyrie. Capacity: 3–4-round flush magazines or 7–8-round extended magazines. Barrel: 24-in. free-floating, heavy, spiral-fluted, threaded. Weight: 9.4 lbs. Length: 46.75 in. Stock: EVOLVED EGONOM-X synthetic with removeable cheek rest and checkered-polymer grip, finished in Sitka OptiFade Subalpine camo. Sights: One-piece Picatinny rail. Features: New for 2021 Varmint addition to the Momentum Elite family. Stock designed specifically for varmint hunting. Midnight Bronze Cerakote metalwork. RELIA-Trigger adjustable from 2 to 4 pounds. MOA accuracy guarantee. Bolt with three locking lugs and 60-degree throw.
Price: **$999.00**

HEYM EXPRESS BOLT-ACTION RIFLE

Calibers: .375 H&H Mag., .416 Rigby, .404 Jeffery, .458 Lott, .450 Rigby. Capacity: 5. Barrel: 24 in., Krupp steel, hammer-forged. Stock: Custom select European walnut. Sights: Iron, barrel-banded front. Weight: 9 to 10.5 lbs. Features: Caliber-specific action and magazine box, classic English sporting rifle, three-position safety.
Price: **$12,000.00**

HOWA MINI ACTION FULL DIP

Calibers: .223 Rem., 6.5 Grendel, 7.62x39. Capacity: 5. Barrel: 20 in., threaded, heavy. Stock: Hogue pillar-bedded. Sights: 3.5-10x44 scope. Weight: 10 lbs. Features: Full-dipped camo, forged, one-piece bolt with locking lugs.
Price: **$769.00**

HOWA HS CARBON FIBER

Caliber: 6.5 Creedmoor. Capacity: 4. Barrel: 24 in., carbon-fiber wrapped. Stock: Synthetic, CNC-machined aluminum bedding block. Sights: None, drilled and tapped. Weight: 7.8 lbs. Features: Lightweight, hand-finished stock, scope optional.
Price: **$1,819.00**

HOWA CARBON STALKER

Calibers: .223 Rem., 6.5 Grendel, 7.62x39, .350 Legend. Capacity: Extended detachable magazine standard. Barrel: 16.25 in. (.350 Legend) 22 in. (standard calibers) Weight: from 4 lbs. 10 oz. Length: 34.75–40.5 in. Stock: Custom carbon-fiber super lightweight design. Sights: No sights. Drilled and tapped. Scoped options available with Nikko Stirling optic. Features: Built on the Howa 1500 Mini Action. Three-position safety. Sub-MOA accuracy assurance. Two-stage match trigger. LimbSaver buttpad
Price: **$999.00**

HOWA ALPINE MOUNTAIN RIFLE

Calibers: .243 Win., 6.5 Creedmoor, 7mm-08, .308 Win. Barrel: 20 in. Weight: 5.7 lbs. Stock: OD Green synthetic. Features: Two-stage HACT trigger, Cerakote finish on barrel and action, Pachmyr Decelerator pad.
Price: Stainless **$1,188.00**

H-S PRECISION PRO-SERIES 2000

Calibers: 30 different chamberings including virtually all popular calibers. Made in hunting, tactical and competition styles with many options. Barrels: 20 in., 22 in., 24 in. or 26 in. depending on model and caliber. Hunting models include the Pro-Hunter Rifle (PHR) designed for magnum calibers with built-in recoil reducer and heavier barrel; Pro-Hunter Lightweight (PHL) with slim, fluted barrel; Pro-Hunter Sporter (SPR) and Pro-Hunter Varmint (VAR). Takedown, Competition and Tactical variations are available. Stock: H-S Precision synthetic stock in many styles and colors with full-length bedding block chassis system. Made in USA
Price: PHR **$3,795.00**
Price: PHL **$3,895.00**
Price: PLC Long Range Carbon Fiber **$4,750.00**
Price: PLR Pro Long Range **$3,799.00**
Price: SPR **$3,495.00**
Price: SPL Sporter **$3,595.00**
Price: VAR **$3,595.00**
Price: PTD Hunter Takedown **$3,595.00**
Price: TTD Tactical Take Down **$6,499.00**
Price: STR Short Tactical **$3,895.00**
Price: HTR Heavy Tactical **$3,895.00**
Price: Competition **$3,895.00**

J.P. SAUER & SOHN 404 SYNCHRO XTC
Calibers: .243 Win., .270 Win., 6.5 Creedmoor, 6.5x55, .308 Win., .30-06 Spfld., 7x64, 8x57IS, 9.3x62, 7mm Rem. Mag., .300 Win. Mag., .338 Win. Mag., .404 Jeffery, 10.3x60R. Barrel: 22-in. fluted, cold-hammer forged. Sights: Integral scope bases. Length: 42 in. Weight: 6.1 lbs. Stock: Carbon-fiber XTC thumbhole style with Green/Black/Grey carbon-fiber camo and adjustable comb. Features: Fully modular concept rifle. Adjustable trigger blade and trigger pull, from 1.2–2.7 lbs. Manual cocking. Threaded muzzle. MagLock magazine safety. Matte black hard anodized aluminum receiver. Engineered for changing bolt heads and barrels. SUS combination tool integrated into front sling swivel. Miniature universal tool integrated into rear sling swivel.
Price: **$8,199.00**

KIMBER HUNTER PRO
Calibers: 6.5 Creedmoor, .308 Win., .280 Ackley Improved. Capacity: 3-round box magazine. Barrel: 22 or 24 in. sporter with satin finish and muzzle brake. Weight: 5 lbs. 7oz.–5 lbs. 12 oz. Length: 41.25 in. Stock: Fiber-reinforced polymer in Desolve Blak pattern with pillar bedding. Sights: No iron sights. Drilled and tapped. Features: Full stainless build based on 84M action with Mauser claw extraction. Three-position wing safety. Sling studs. One-inch rubber recoil pad. Match-grade chamber. Factory adjustable trigger set at 3.5–4 lbs. Sub-MOA guarantee.
Price: **$1,006.00**

KENNY JARRETT RIFLES
Calibers: Custom built in virtually any chambering including .223 Rem., .243 Improved, .243 Catbird, 7mm-08 Improved, .280 Remington, .280 Ackley Improved, 7mm Rem. Mag., .284 Jarrett, .30-06 Springfield, .300 Win. Mag., .300 Jarrett, .323 Jarrett, .338 Jarrett, .375 H&H, .416 Rem., .450 Rigby, other modern cartridges. Numerous options regarding barrel type and weight, stock styles and material. Features: Tri-Lock receiver. Talley rings and bases. Accuracy guarantees and custom loaded ammunition. Newest series is the Shikar featuring 28-year aged American Black walnut hand-checkered stock with Jarrett-designed stabilizing aluminum chassis. Accuracy guaranteed to be .5 MOA with standard calibers, .75 MOA with magnums.
Price: Shikar Series **$10,320.00**
Price: Signature Series **$8,320.00**
Price: Long Ranger Series **$8,320.00**
Price: Ridge Walker Series **$8,320.00**
Price: Wind Walker **$8,320.00**
Price: Original Beanfield (customer's receiver) **$6,050.00**
Price: Professional Hunter **$11,070.00**
Price: SA/Custom **$7,000.00**

KIMBER MODEL 8400
Calibers: .25-06 Rem., .270 Win., 7mm, .30-06, .300 Win. Mag., .338 Win. Mag., or .325 WSM. Capacity: 4. Barrel: 24 in. Weights: 6 lbs., 3 oz.–6 lbs., 10 oz. Length: 43.25 in. Stocks: Claro walnut or Kevlar-reinforced fiberglass. Sights: None; drilled and tapped for bases. Features: Mauser claw extractor, two-position wing safety, action bedded on aluminum pillars and fiberglass, free-floated barrel, match-grade adjustable trigger set at 4 lbs., matte or polished blue or matte stainless finish. Introduced 2003. Sonora model (2008) has brown laminated stock, hand-rubbed oil finish, chambered in .25-06 Rem., .30-06, and .300 Win. Mag. Weighs 8.5 lbs., measures 44.50 in. overall length. Front swivel stud only for bipod. Stainless steel bull barrel, 24 in. satin stainless steel finish. Made in USA by Kimber Mfg. Inc.
Price: Classic **$1,223.00**
Price: Classic Select Grade, French walnut stock (2008) **$1,427.00**
Price: SuperAmerica, AAA walnut stock **$2,240.00**
Price: Patrol Tactical **$2,447.00**
Price: Montana **$1,427.00**

KIMBER MODEL 84L CLASSIC
Calibers: .270 Win., .30-06. Capacity: 5-round magazine. Features: Bolt-action rifle. 24-in. sightless matte blue sporter barrel; hand-rubbed A-grade walnut stock with 20 LPI panel checkering; pillar and glass bedding; Mauser claw extractor; 3-position M70-style safety; adjustable trigger.
Price: **$1,427.00**

KIMBER ADVANCED TACTICAL SOC/SRC II
Calibers: 6.5 Creedmoor, .308 Win. SRC chambered only in .308. Capacity: 5-round magazine. Barrel: 22-in. (SOC) stainless steel, (18 in. (SRC) with threaded muzzle. Stock: Side-folding aluminum with adjustable comb. Features: Stainless steel action, matte black or Flat Dark Earth finish. 3-position Model 70-type safety.
Price: **$2,449.00**

KIMBER OPEN RANGE PRO CARBON
Calibers: 6.5 Creedmoor, .308 Win. Capacity: 4. Barrel: 24 in., carbon-fiber wrapped, Proof Research. Stock: Carbon fiber. Sights: None, drilled and tapped. Weight: 6 lbs. Features: Sub-MOA accuracy, 84M stainless controlled-round-feed action, three-position safety.
Price: **$3,099.00**

MAUSER M-12 PURE
Calibers: .22-250, .243, 6.5x55SE, .270 Win., 7x64mm, 7mm Rem. Mag., .308 Win., .30-06, .300 Win Mag., 8x57mm IS, .338 Win. Mag. 9.3x62mm. Capacity: 5-round magazine. Barrel: 22 in. Sights: Adjustable rear, blade front. Stock: Walnut with ebony fore-end tip.
Price: **$1,971.00**

MAUSER M-18
Calibers: .223 Rem., .243 Win., 6.5x55, 6.5 PRC, 6.5 Creedmoor, .270 Win., .308 Win., .30-06 Spfld., 8x57IS, 9.3x62, 7mm Rem. Mag., .300 Win. Mag. Capacity: 5-round box magazine. Barrel: 21.75 or 24.5 in. Weight: 6.5–6.8 lbs. Length: 41.7–44.0 in. Stock: Polymer with softgrip inlays. Sights: No iron sights. Drilled and tapped. Features: Adjustable trigger. Three-position safety. Removeable recoil pad section with interior buttstock storage. Budget-priced option tagged "The People's Rifle."
Price: **$699.00**

MOSSBERG MVP SERIES
Caliber: .223/5.56 NATO. Capacity: 10-round AR-style magazines. Barrels: 16.25-in. medium bull, 20-in. fluted sporter. Weight: 6.5–7 lbs. Stock: Classic black textured polymer. Sights: Adjustable folding rear, adjustable blade front. Features: Available with factory mounted 3-9x32 scope, (4-16x50 on Varmint model). FLEX model has 20-in. fluted sporter barrel, FLEX AR-style 6-position adjustable stock. Varmint model has laminated stock, 24-in. barrel. Thunder Ranch model has 18-in. bull barrel, OD Green synthetic stock.
Price: Patrol Model **$732.00**
Price: Patrol Model w/scope **$863.00**
Price: FLEX Model **$764.00**
Price: FLEX Model w/scope **$897.00**
Price: Thunder Ranch Model **$755.00**
Price: Predator Model **$732.00**
Price: Predator Model w/scope **$872.00**
Price: Varmint Model **$753.00**
Price: Varmint Model w/scope **$912.00**
Price: Long Range Rifle (LR) **$974.00**

Prices given are believed to be accurate at time of publication however, many factors affect retail pricing so exact prices are not possible.

76TH EDITION, 2022 ✦ **411**

MOSSBERG PATRIOT

Calibers: .22-250, .243 Win., .25-06, .270 Win., 7mm-08, .7mm Rem., .308 Win., .30-06, .300 Win. Mag., .38 Win. Mag., .375 Ruger, 350 Legend. Capacities: 4- or 5-round magazine. Barrels: 22-in. sporter or fluted. Stock: Walnut, laminate, camo or synthetic black. Weights: 7.5–8 lbs. Finish: Matte blued. Sights: Adjustable or none. Some models available with 3-9x40 scope. Other features include patented Lightning Bolt Action Trigger adjustable from 2 to 7 pounds, spiral-fluted bolt. Not all variants available in all calibers. Introduced in 2015.

Price: Walnut stock..$559.00
Price: Walnut with premium Vortex Crossfire scope $649.00
Price: Synthetic stock..$396.00
Price: Synthetic stock with standard scope $436.00
Price: Laminate stock w/iron sights $584.00
Price: Deer THUG w/Mossy Oak Infinity Camo stock $500.00

MOSSBERG PATRIOT LONG RANGE HUNTER

Calibers: 6.5 Creedmoor, 6.5 PRC, .308 Win., .300 Win. Mag. Capacity: 3–5-round box magazine. Barrel: 22 or 24 in., blued and fluted. Weight: 6.5–7.5 lbs. Length: 44.25–44.75 in. Stock: Polymer-coated Spider Gray synthetic, Monte Carlo style. Sights: Picatinny rail. Features: Fluted bolt. LBA adjustable trigger. Dual forward swivel studs. Aluminum pillar bedding. Flat-bottomed benchrest fore-end. Oversized bolt handle.
Price: $766.00

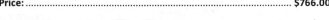

NESIKA SPORTER RIFLE

Calibers: .260 Rem., 6.5x284, 7mm-08, .280 Rem., 7mm Rem. Mag., 308 Win., .30-06, .300 Win. Mag. Barrels: 24 or 26 in. Douglas air-gauged stainless. Stock: Composite with aluminum bedding block. Sights: None, Leupold QRW bases. Weight: 8 lbs. Features: Timney trigger set at 3 pounds, receiver made from 15-5 stainless steel, one-piece bolt from 4340 CM steel. Guaranteed accuracy at 100 yards.
Price: $3,499.00
Price: Long Range w/heavy bbl., varmint stock $3,999.00
Price: Tactical w/28î bbl., muzzle brake, adj. stock $4,499.00

NEW ULTRA LIGHT ARMS

Calibers: Custom made in virtually every current chambering. Barrel: Douglas, length to order. Weights: 4.75–7.5 lbs. Length: Varies. Stock: Kevlar graphite composite, variety of finishes. Sights: None furnished; drilled and tapped for scope mounts. Features: Timney trigger, hand-lapped action, button-rifled barrel, hand-bedded action, recoil pad, sling-swivel studs, optional Jewell trigger. Made in USA by New Ultra Light Arms.
Price: Model 20 Ultimate Mountain Rifle $3,500.00
Price: Model 20 Ultimate Varmint Rifle $3,500.00
Price: Model 24 Ultimate Plains Rifle $3,600.00
Price: Model 28 Ultimate Alaskan Rifle $3,900.00
Price: Model 40 Ultimate African Rifle.................................$3,900.00

NOSLER M48 MOUNTAIN CARBON

Calibers: 6mm Creedmoor, 6.5 Creedmoor, 6.5 PRC, 26 Nosler, 27 Nosler, .280 Ackley Improved, 28 Nosler, .300 Win. Mag., 30 Nosler, 33 Nosler. Capacity: 3 or 4-round hinged aluminum floorplate. Barrel: 24-in. light Sendero contour, carbon-fiber wrapped with cut rifling. Sights: No iron sights; contoured to accept any standard two-piece scope base that would otherwise fit a Remington 700. Weight: 6.0 lbs. Length: 44.4–45 in. Stock: Carbon-fiber Mountain Hunter stock

in either Granite Green or Shale Gray with textured finish. Features: Built around a Model 48 action. Match-grade, cut-rifled, carbon-wrapped, fully free-floating barrel with guaranteed sub-MOA accuracy. Glass and aluminum pillar bedded into ultra-light Mountain Hunter stock. Steel surfaces coated in Tungsten Grey Cerakote for weather resistance. Timney trigger with two-position safety. Threaded muzzle with knurled thread protector. *Note, Nosler has discontinued all rifles except the Mountain Carbon and Long Range Carbon. Liberty and Heritage are no longer in current production.*
Price: $3,140.00

NOSLER LONG RANGE CARBON

Calibers: 6.5 Creedmoor, 6.5 PRC, 26 Nosler, 27 Nosler, 28 Nosler, .300 Win. Mag., 30 Nosler, 33 Nosler. Capacity: 3 or 4 rounds with hinged floorplate. Barrel: 26-in. PROOF, light Sendero contour, carbon-fiber wrapped, fully free-floating. Weight: 7.0 lbs. Length: 48 in. Stock: Manners MCS-T Elite Tac 100 percent carbon-fiber stock in Elite Midnight Camo with textured finish. Sights: No iron sights; contoured to accept any standard two-piece scope base that would otherwise fit a Remington 700. Features: Custom Nosler Model 48 action. Timney trigger with two-position safety. Threaded muzzle with knurled thread protector. Glass and aluminum pillar bedding. Action and bottom metal Cerakoted in Sniper Grey. Dual fore-end sling swivels. Guaranteed MOA accuracy. *Note, Nosler has discontinued all rifles except the Mountain Carbon and Long Range Carbon. Liberty and Heritage are no longer in current production.*
Price: $3,190.00

RUGER GUIDE GUN

Calibers: .30-06, .300 Win. Mag., .338 Win. Mag., .375 Ruger, .416 Ruger. Capacities: 3 or 4 rounds. Barrel: 20 in. with barrel band sling swivel and removable muzzle brake. Weights: 8–8.12 pounds. Stock: Green Mountain laminate. Finish: Hawkeye matte stainless. Sights: Adjustable rear, bead front. Introduced 2013.
Price: $1,269.00

RUGER HAWKEYE

Calibers: .204 Ruger, .223 Rem., .243 Win., .270 Win., 6.5 PRC, 6.5 Creedmoor, 7mm/08, 7mm Rem. Mag., .308 Win., .30-06, .300 Win. Mag., .338 Win. Mag., .375 Ruger, .416 Ruger. Capacities: 4-round magazine, except 3-round magazine for magnums; 5-round magazine for .204 Ruger and .223 Rem. Barrels: 22 in., 24 in. Weight: 6.75–8.25 lbs. Length: 42–44.4 in. overall. Stock: American walnut, laminate or synthetic. FTW has camo stock, muzzle brake. Long Range Target has adjustable target stock, heavy barrel. Sights: None furnished. Receiver has Ruger integral scope mount base, Ruger 1 in. rings. Features: Includes Ruger LC6 trigger, new red rubber recoil pad, Mauser-type controlled feeding, claw extractor, 3-position safety, hammer-forged steel barrels, Ruger scope rings. Walnut stocks have wrap-around cut checkering on the forearm, and more rounded contours on stock and top of pistol grips. Matte stainless all-weather version features synthetic stock. Hawkeye African chambered in .375 Ruger, .416 Ruger and has 23-in. blued barrel, checkered walnut stock, windage-adjustable shallow V-notch rear sight, white bead front sight. Introduced 2007. *(Note: VT Varmint Target and Compact Magnum are no longer currently produced)*
Price: Standard, right- and left-hand....................................$939.00
Price: Compact $939.00
Price: Laminate Compact $999.00
Price: Compact Magnum $969.00
Price: Hawkeye Hunter $1,099.00
Price: VT Varmint Target $1,139.00
Price: Predator $1,139.00
Price: Alaskan..$1,279.00

Price: Long Range Hunter **$1,279.00**
Price: African with muzzle brake.................................. **$1,279.00**
Price: FTW Hunter **$1,279.00**
Price: Long Range Target **$1,279.00**

SAKO TRG-22 TACTICAL RIFLE

Calibers: 6.5 Creedmoor, .308 Winchester (TRG-22). For TRG-22A1 add .260 Rem. TRG-42 only available in .300 Win. Mag., or .338 Lapua. Features: Target-grade Cr-Mo or stainless barrels with muzzle brake; three locking lugs; 60-degree bolt throw; adjustable two-stage target trigger; adjustable or folding synthetic stock; receiver-mounted integral 17mm axial optics rails with recoil stop-slots; tactical scope mount for modern three-turret tactical scopes (30 and 34 mm tube diameter); optional bipod. 22A1 has folding stock with two-hinge design, M-LOK fore-end, full aluminum middle chassis.

Price: TRG-22 .... **$3,495.00**
Price: TRG-22A1 .... **$6,725.00**
Price: TRG-42 .... **$4,550.00**

SAKO MODEL 85

Calibers: .22-250 Rem., .243 Win., .25-06 Rem., .260 Rem., 6.5x55mm, .270 Win., .270 WSM, 7mm-08 Rem., 7x64, .308 Win., .30-06; 7mm WSM, .300 WSM, .338 Federal, 8x57IS, 9.3x62. Barrels: 22.4 in., 22.9 in., 24.4 in. Weight: 7.75 lbs. Length: NA. Stock: Polymer, laminated or high-grade walnut, straight comb, shadow-line cheekpiece. Sights: None furnished. Features: Controlled-round feeding, adjustable trigger, matte stainless or nonreflective satin blue. Offered in a wide range of variations and models. Introduced 2006. Imported from Finland by Beretta USA.

Price: Grey Wolf.. **$1,725.00**
Price: Black Bear **$1,850.00**
Price: Kodiak **$1,950.00**
Price: Varmint Laminated **$2,025.00**
Price: Classic **$2,275.00**
Price: Bavarian .... **$2,200.00–$2,300.00**
Price: Bavarian carbine, Full-length stock **$2,400.00**
Price: Brown Bear **$2,175.00**

SAKO S20

Calibers: .243 Win., 6.5 Creedmoor, 6.5 PRC, .270 Win., .308 Win., .30-06 Spfld., 7mm Rem. Mag., .300 Win. Mag. Capacity: 5 (3 Magnum), and 10 (7 magnum) double-stacked magazines, glass-reinforced composite. Barrel: 20- to 24-in. cold-hammer forged, fluted, threaded. Weight: 7.3–8.8 lbs. Length: 42.9–46.9 in. Stock: Choice of two interchangeable injection-molded synthetic stock types — tactical precision or ergonomic hunting thumbhole. Sights: Picatinny rail integral to receiver. Features: Designed as a hybrid rifle for both hunters and precision shooters. Full aluminum rifle chassis. Takedown-style stock design allows user configuration. Adjustable recoil pad for LOP and adjustable cheek piece. QD sling attachments. Two-stage multi-adjustable trigger. Five-shot sub MOA guarantee.

Price: **$1,598.00**

SAVAGE IMPULSE BIG GAME

Calibers: .243 Win., .308 Win., 6.5 Creedmoor, .308 Win., .300 Win. Mag., .300 WSM. Capacity: 2, 3, or 4-round flush-fit detachable box magazine. Barrel: 22- or 24-in. medium contour, carbon steel, fluted, and threaded. Sights: Single piece 20 MOA rail machined into receiver. Length: 43.5–45.5 in. Weight: 8.8–8.9 lbs. Stock: Sporter-style AccuStock with AccuFit user-

adjustable system and Kuiu Verde 2.0 camouflage finish. Features: New straight-pull bolt action uses HexLock bolt system. Ambidextrous rotary bolt handle. Tang safety. Free-floating, tool-free, interchangeable bolt head. Four-bolt barrel clamp system. Adjustable AccuTrigger. Hazel Green Cerakote aluminum receiver. Removeable and user-adjustable round bolt knob handle.

Price: **$1,449.00**

SAVAGE IMPULSE PREDATOR

Calibers: .22-250 Rem., .243 Win., 6.5 Creedmoor, .308 Win. Capacity: 10-round AICS-style magazine with ambidextrous release. Barrel: 20-in. medium contour, threaded. Sights: Single-piece 20 MOA rail machined into receiver. Length: 41.25 in. Weight: 8.75 lbs. Stock: Mossy Oak Terra Gila camouflage AccuStock with AccuFit user-adjustable system. Features: New straight-pull bolt action like the Impulse Big Game.

Price: **$1,379.00**

SAVAGE IMPULSE PREDATOR

Calibers: .243 Win., 6.5 Creedmoor, .308 Win., 7mm-08 Rem., .270 Win., 7mm Rem. Mag., .30-06 Spfld., .300 Win. Mag., .300 WSM. Capacity: 2, 3, or 4-round detachable flush-fit box magazine. Barrel: 22- or 24-in. medium-contour carbon steel with straight fluting. Length: 42.375–45.25 in. Weight: 8.1–8.5 lbs. Stock: Synthetic AccuFit system for LOP and comb height adjustment finished in Realtree Excape camo. Features: Model 110 bolt action built specifically for distance hunting. AccuStock internal chassis system secures the action three-dimensionally along its entire length. User-adjustable AccuTrigger. OD Green Cerakote barrel, receiver, and internal parts. Factory blueprinted action. Threaded barrel with omni-port muzzle brake and target crown. Available in both left- and right-hand configurations.

Price: **$1,199.00**

SAVAGE MODEL 110 ULTRALITE

Calibers: 6.5 Creedmoor, 6.5 PRC, .308 Win., .270 Win., 28 Nosler, .280 Ackley Improved, .30-06 Spfld., .300 WSM. Capacity: 2–4-round box magazine. Barrel: 22- or 24-in. PROOF Research carbon-wrapped stainless. Weight: 5.8–6 lbs. Length: 42.5–44.5 in. Stock: Grey Synthetic AccuStock with AccuFit system of comb height and LOP adjustment. Sights: Drilled and tapped. Features: Factory blueprinted action. Spiral-fluted bolt. Melonite-finished skeletonized receiver. Cut-rifled barrel with threaded muzzle and flush-fit cap. User-adjustable AccuTrigger. Textured grip panels.

Price: **$1,595.00**

SAVAGE 110 ULTRALITE CAMO

Calibers: 6.5 Creedmoor, 6.5 PRC, .308 Win., .270 Win., 28 Nosler, .280 Ackley Improved, .30-06 Spfld., .300 WSM. Capacity: 2–4-round box magazine. Barrel: 22- or 24-in. PROOF Research carbon-wrapped stainless. Weight: 5.8–6 lbs. Length: 42.5–44.5 in. Stock: Synthetic AccuStock with AccuFit system of comb height and LOP adjustment finished in Kuiu Verde 2.0 camo. Sights: Drilled and tapped. Features: Savage partnered with PROOF Research for this bolt-action hunting lightweight. Factory blueprinted action. Melonite-skeletonized receiver minimizes weight. Overmold surfaces. User-adjustable AccuTrigger. Cut-rifled barrel. Threaded muzzle with flush fit cap. Spiral fluted bolt.

Price: **$1,639.00**

SAVAGE MODEL 110 PRECISION
Calibers: .308 Win., .300 Win. Mag, .338 Lapua, 6.5 Creedmoor. Capacity: 5, 8/10. Barrel: 20 to 24 in., carbon steel, heavy, threaded. Stock: Aluminum chassis. Sights: Picatinny rail. Weight: 8.9 lbs. Features: BA muzzle brake, skeletonized stock with adjustable comb height and LOP.
Price: **$1,499.00**

SAVAGE AXIS II PRECISION
Calibers: .243 Win., .223 Rem, .270 Win., .30-06, .308 Win., 6.5 Creedmoor. Capacity: 5 to 10. Barrel: 22 in., carbon steel, button-rifled heavy, threaded w/cap. Stock: Aluminum MDT chassis. Sights: Picatinny rail. Weight: 9.9 lbs. Features: AccuTrigger, adjustable comb height and LOP spacers, AICS magazine.
Price: **$949.00**

SAVAGE AXIS SERIES
Calibers: .243 Win., 6.5 Creedmoor, 7mm-08 Rem., .308 Win., .25-06 Rem., .270 Win, .30-06, .223 Rem., .22-250 Rem. Barrel: 22 in. Weight: 6.5 lbs. Length: 43.875 in. Stock: Black synthetic or camo, including pink/black Muddy Girl. Sights: Drilled and tapped for scope mounts. Several models come with factory mounted Weaver Kaspa 3-9x40 scope. Features: Available with black matte or stainless finish

Price: Axis XP	**$439.00**
Price: Axis XP Compact	**$439.00**
Price: Axis XP Compact Camo	**$529.00**
Price: Axis XP Camo	**$529.00**
Price: Axis II XP Stainless	**$609.00**
Price: Axis II XP Hardwood	**$639.00**
Price: Axis II XP Overwatch	**$559.00**

SAVAGE CLASSIC SERIES MODEL 14/114
Calibers: .243 Win., 7mm-08 Rem., .308 Win., .270 Win., 7mm Rem. Mag., .30-06, .300 Win. Mag. Capacities: 3- or 4-round magazine. Barrels: 22 in. or 24 in. Weight: 7–7.5 lbs. Length: 41.75–43.75 in. overall (Model 14 short action); 43.25–45.25 in. overall (Model 114 long action). Stock: Satin lacquer American walnut with ebony fore-end, wraparound checkering, Monte Carlo comb and cheekpiece. Sights: None furnished. Receiver drilled and tapped for scope mounting. Features: AccuTrigger, matte blued barrel and action, hinged floorplate.
Price: **$979.00**

SAVAGE MODEL 12 VARMINT/TARGET SERIES
Calibers: .204 Ruger, .223 Rem., .22-250 Rem. Capacity: 4-shot magazine. Barrel: 26 in. stainless barreled action, heavy fluted, free-floating and button-rifled barrel. Weight: 10 lbs. Length: 46.25 in. overall. Stock: Dual pillar bedded, low profile, black synthetic or laminated stock with extra-wide beavertail fore-end. Sights: None furnished; drilled and tapped for scope mounting. Features: Recessed target-style muzzle. AccuTrigger, oversized bolt handle, detachable box magazine, swivel studs. Model 112BVSS has heavy target-style prone laminated stock with high comb, Wundhammer palm swell, internal box magazine. Model 12VLP DBM has black synthetic stock, detachable magazine, and additional chamberings in .243, .308 Win., .300 Win. Mag. Model 12FV has blued receiver. Model

12BTCSS has brown laminate vented thumbhole stock. Made in USA by Savage Arms, Inc.

Price: 12 FCV	**$780.00**
Price: 12 BVSS	**$1,146.00**
Price: 12 Varminter Low Profile (VLP)	**$1,181.00**
Price: 12 Long Range Precision	**$1,288.00**
Price: 12 BTCSS Thumbhole stock	**$1,293.00**
Price: 12 Long Range Precision Varminter	**$1,554.00**
Price: 12 F Class	**$1,648.00**
Price: 12 Palma	**$2,147.00**

SAVAGE MODEL 10FP/110FP LAW ENFORCEMENT SERIES
Calibers: .223 Rem., .308 Win. (Model 10), 4-round magazine; .25-06 Rem., .300 Win. Mag., (Model 110), 3- or 4-round magazine. Barrel: 24 in.; matte blued free-floated heavy barrel and action. Weight: 6.5–6.75 lbs. Length: 41.75–43.75 in. overall (Model 10); 42.5–44.5 in. overall (Model 110). Stock: Black graphite/fiberglass composition, pillar-bedded, positive checkering. Sights: None furnished. Receiver drilled and tapped for scope mounting. Features: Black matte finish on all metal parts. Double swivel studs on the fore-end for sling and/or bipod mount. Right- or left-hand. Model 110FP introduced 1990. Model 10FP introduced 1998. Model 10FCP HS has HS Precision black synthetic tactical stock with molded alloy bedding system, Leupold 3.5-10x40 black matte scope with Mil Dot reticle, Farrell Picatinny Rail Base, flip-open lens covers, 1.25-in. sling with QD swivels, Harris bipod, Storm heavy-duty case. Made in USA by Savage Arms, Inc.

Price: Model 10FCP McMillan, McMillan fiberglass tactical stock..	**$1,591.00**
Price: Model 10FCP-HS HS Precision, HS Precision tactical stock ...	**$1,315.00**
Price: Model 10FCP	**$925.00**
Price: Model 10FLCP, left-hand model, standard stock or Accu-Stock	**$975.00**
Price: Model 10FCP SR	**$785.00**
Price: Model 10 Precision Carbine	**$952.00**

SAVAGE 110 BA STEALTH
Calibers: .300 win, Mag., or .338 Lapua Mag. Capacities: Detachable 5- or 6-round box magazine. Barrel: 24 in. with threaded muzzle. Stock: Fab Defense GLR Shock buttstock, M-LOK fore-end. Weight: 11.125 lbs. Features: Adjustable AccuTrigger, Picatinny rail. Stealth Evolution has fluted heavy barrel, 10-round magazine, adjustable length of pull stock, Flat Dark Earth finish.

Price: Stealth	**$1,484.00**
Price: Stealth, .338 Lapua	**$1,624.00**
Price: Evolution	**$1,999.00**
Price: Evolution, .338 Lapua	**$2,149.00**

SAVAGE MODEL 110 PREDATOR
Calibers: .204 Ruger. .223, .22-250, .243, .260 Rem., 6.5 Creedmoor. Capacity: 4-round magazine. Barrels: 22 or 24 in. threaded heavy contour. Weight: 8.5 lbs. Stock: AccuStock with Mossy Oak Max-1 camo finish, soft grip surfaces, adjustable length of pull.
Price: **$899.00**

SAVAGE MODEL 110 TACTICAL
Caliber: .308 Win. Capacity: 10-round magazine. Barrels: 20 or 24 in. threaded and fluted heavy contour. Weight: 8.65 lbs. Stock: AccuStock with soft-grip surfaces, AccuFit system. Features: Top Picatinny rail, right- or left-hand operation.
Price: **$784.00**
Price: Tactical Desert (6mm, 6.5 Creedmoor, FDE finish **$769.00**

SAVAGE MODEL 12 PRECISION TARGET SERIES BENCHREST
Calibers: .308 Win., 6.5x284 Norma, 6mm Norma BR. Barrel: 29-in. ultra-heavy. Weight: 12.75 lbs. Length: 50 in. overall. Stock: Gray laminate. Features: New Left-Load, Right-Eject target action, Target AccuTrigger adjustable from approx. 6 oz. to 2.5 lbs. oversized bolt handle, stainless extra-heavy free-floating and button-rifled barrel.
Price: **$1,629.00**

Prices given are believed to be accurate at time of publication however, many factors affect retail pricing so exact prices are not possible.

SAVAGE MODEL 12 PRECISION TARGET PALMA

Similar to Model 12 Benchrest but in .308 Win. only, 30-in. barrel, multi-adjustable stock, weighs 13.3 lbs.
Price: **$2,147.00**

SAVAGE MODEL 12 F/TR TARGET RIFLE

Similar to Model 12 Benchrest but in .308 Win. only, 30-in. barrel, weighs 12.65 lbs.
Price: **$1,538.00**

SAVAGE MODEL 112 MAGNUM TARGET

Caliber: .338 Lapua Magnum. Single shot. Barrel: 26-in. heavy with muzzle brake. Stock: Wood laminate. Features: AccuTrigger, matte black finish, oversized bolt handle, pillar bedding.
Price: **$1,177.00**

SEEKINS PRECISION HAVAK ELEMENT

Calibers: 28 Nosler, 6mm Creedmoor, 6.5 Creedmoor, .308 Win., 6.5 PRC, .300 Win. Mag., .300 PRC. Capacity: 3 or 5-round detachable Magpul PMAG or carbon-fiber magazine, depending on caliber. Barrel: 21- or 22-in. Mountain Hunter spiral fluted, built of 5R 416 stainless steel. Sights: 20 MOA rail. Weight: 5.5 lbs. short actions; long actions at 6.0 lbs. Stock: Element camouflage Carbon Composition stock. Features: Drawing on years of precision AR-rifle experience comes the bolt action, hybrid, ultra-lightweight Havak Element. Aerospace-grade 7075 aluminum encases stainless steel on a Mountain Hunter barrel. Four locking lugs on 90-degree bolt with removable head. ATC muzzle brake on long actions. M-16-style extractor. Muzzle threaded at 5/8x24. Integrated recoil lug, and bubble level.
Price: **$2,795.00**

SEEKINS PRECISION HAVAK PRO HUNTER PH2

Calibers: 6mm Creedmoor, 6.5 Creedmoor, 6.5 PRC, .308 Win., 28 Nosler, 7mm Rem. Mag., .300 Win. Mag., 300 PRC, .338 Win. Mag. Capacity: 5, short action; 3, long action detachable magazine. Barrel: 24 in. short action; 26 in. long action built of 5R 416 stainless steel. Weight: 6.9–7.2 lbs. Stock: Seekins carbon composite in Charcoal Gray. Sights: 20 MOA Picatinny rail with 8-32 screws. Features: Timney Elite Hunter trigger set at 2.5 lbs. Bead-blasted barreled action. Threaded muzzle. Integrated recoil lug and M16-style extractor. Bolt with four locking lugs and 90-degree throw. Removable bolt head. Extended cartridge overall length with Seekins carbon-fiber magazines.
Price: **$1,895.00**

SPRINGFIELD ARMORY 2020 WAYPOINT

Calibers: 6mm Creedmoor, 6.5 Creedmoor, .308 Win., 6.5 PRC. Capacity: 3 or 5-round AICS-pattern magazine. Barrel: 20, 22, or 24 in. Option of steel or carbon fiber. Weight: 6 lbs. 10 oz.–7 lbs. 6 oz. Length: 41.5–45.5 in. Stock: Choice of two stock configurations, premium AG Composites carbon fiber with custom camo in Evergreen or Ridgeline. Features: Stainless steel receiver. Dual locking lugs on a fluted bolt. Picatinny rail. 90-degree bolt handle with removeable knob. Enlarged ejection port and sliding extractor. Hybrid dual-plane feed ramp. Adjustable Trigger Tech trigger. Five QD stock mounts. SA Radial muzzle brake. Cerakote metalwork in Desert Verde or Mil-Spec Green. Pachmayr Decelerator recoil pad. Available in two stock configurations, one with three-axis adjustable cheek comb and two barrel choices. Accuracy guarantee of .75 MOA.
Price: Steel barrel, standard stock **$1,699.00**

Price: Steel barrel, adjustable stock..................................**$1,825.00**
Price: Carbon-fiber barrel, standard stock **$2,275.00**
Price: Carbon-fiber barrel, adjustable stock **$2,399.00**

STEYR PRO HUNTER II

Calibers: .223 Rem., 7mm-08 Rem., 6.5 Creedmoor, .308 Win. Capacity: 4 to 5. Barrel: 20 in., hammer-forged stainless steel. Stock: Wood laminate, Boyds. Sights: None, drilled and tapped. Weight: 7 lbs. Features: Three-position safety, crisp 3-lb. trigger.
Price: **$1,199.00**

STEYR SSG08

Calibers: .243 Win., 7.62x51 NATO (.308Win), 7.62x63B (.300 Win Mag)., .338 Lapua Mag. Capacity: 10-round magazine. Barrels: 20, 23.6 or 25.6 in. Stock: Dural aluminum folding stock black with .280 mm long UIT-rail and various Picatinny rails. Sights: Front post sight and rear adjustable. Features: High-grade aluminum folding stock, adjustable cheekpiece and buttplate with height marking, and an ergonomical exchangeable pistol grip. Versa-Pod, muzzle brake, Picatinny rail, UIT rail on stock and various Picatinny rails on fore-end, and a 10-round HC-magazine. SBS rotary bolt action with four frontal locking lugs, arranged in pairs. Cold-hammer-forged barrels are available in standard and compact lengths.
Price: **$5,899.00**

STEYR SM 12

Calibers: .243, 6.5x55SE, .270 Win., 7mm-08 Rem., .308 Win., .30-06, .300 Win. Mag, .300 WSM, 9.3x62mm. Barrels: 20-in. blue or 25-in. stainless. Stock: Walnut with checkered grip and fore-end. Available in half or full-length configurations. Sights: Adjustable rear, ramp front with bead. Stainless barrel has no sights. Features: Sling swivels, Bavarian cheekpiece, hand-cocking system operated by thumb manually cocks firing mechanism.
Price: Standard-length stock..**$2,545.00**
Price: Full length (Mannlicher) **$2,750.00**

STRASSER RS 14 EVOLUTION STANDARD

Calibers: .222 Rem., .223 Rem., .300 AAC Blackout, .22-250 Rem., .243 Win., 6 XC, 6.5 Creedmoor, .284 Norma, 6.5x55SE, 6.5x65RWS, .270 Win., 7x64, 7mm-08 Rem, .308 Win., .30-06, 8x57 IS, 8.5x63, 9.3x62, 9.3x57, 7mm Rem. Mag., .300 Win. Mag., .375 Ruger, .338 Win. Mag., .458 Win. Mag., 10.3x68. Capacity: 3 to 7. Barrel: 22 to 24 in., blued. Stock: Grade-1 wood, grade-2 wood, standard or thumbhole. Sights: Integrated Picatinny rail. Weight: 6.75 to 7.725 lbs. Features: Barrel-exchange system, adjustable trigger with trigger set, plasma-hardened bolt.
Price: ....**$3,452.00-$4,033.00**

THOMPSON/CENTER COMPASS II

Calibers: .223 Rem., 5.56 NATO, .243 Win., .270 Win., .300 Win. Mag., .308 Win., .30-06, 6.5 Creedmoor, 7mm Rem. Mag. Capacity: 5 to 6. Barrel: 21.625 to 24 in., blued. Stock: Composite. Sights: Weaver bases or Crimson Trace scope combo. Weight: 8 lbs. Features: Threaded muzzle, three-lug bolt design, three-position safety.
Price: ....**$405.00 to $575.00**

Prices given are believed to be accurate at time of publication however, many factors affect retail pricing so exact prices are not possible.

76TH EDITION, 2022 ◈ **415**

THOMSON/CENTER COMPASS II COMPACT
Calibers: .223 Rem., 5.56 NATO, .243 Win., .308 Win., 6.5 Creedmoor. Capacity: 6. Barrel: 16.5 in., blued. Stock: Composite. Sights: Weaver bases or Crimson Trace scope combo. Weight: 6.5 lbs. Features: 5R rifling, compact size, Generation II trigger.
Price: ....$405.00 to $575.00

THOMPSON/CENTER COMPASS UTILITY
Calibers: .223 Rem., 5.56 NATO, .243 Win., .270 Win., 6.5 Creedmoor, .308 Win., .30-06. Capacity: 6. Barrel: 21.625 in., blued. Stock: Composite. Sights: Weaver bases or T/C scope combo. Weight: 8 lbs. Features: 5R rifling, flush-fit rotary magazine, three-stage trigger.
Price: ....$359.00 to $459.00

THOMPSON/CENTER VENTURE II
Calibers: .223 Rem., 5.56 NATO, .243 Win., .270 Win., 6.5 Creedmoor, .308 Win., .30-06, 7mm Rem. Mag., .300 Win. Mag., .350 Legend. Capacity: 4. Barrel: 22 to 24 in., Weather-Shield stainless steel. Stock: Composite with Hogue panels. Sights: None. Weight: 7.3 lbs. Features: American made, Generation II trigger.
Price: $525.00

THOMPSON/CENTER VENTURE MEDIUM ACTION
Calibers: .204, .22-250, .223, .243, 7mm-08, .308 and 30TC. Capacity: 3+1 detachable nylon box magazine. Features: Bolt-action rifle with a 24-in. crowned medium weight barrel, classic-styled composite stock with inlaid traction grip panels, adjustable 3.5- to 5-pound trigger along with a drilled and tapped receiver (bases included). Weight: 7 lbs. Length: 43.5 in.
Price: $537.00

THOMPSON/CENTER VENTURE PREDATOR PDX
Calibers: .204, .22-250, .223, .243, .308. Weight: 8 lbs. Length: 41.5 in. Features: Bolt-action rifle similar to Venture medium action but with heavy, deep-fluted 22-in. barrel and Max-1 camo finish overall.
Price: $638.00

THOMPSON/CENTER LONG RANGE RIFLE
Calibers: .243 Win., 6.5 Creedmoor, .308 Win. Capacity: 10-round magazine. Barrel: 20 in. (.308), 22 in. (6.5), 24 in. (.243). Fluted and threaded with muzzle brake. Weight: 11-12 lbs. Stock: Composite black with adjustable cheek piece and buttplate, built-in Magpul M-LOK accessory slots. Finish: Black or Flat Dark Earth. Features: Picatinny-style rail, adjustable trigger, Caldwell Pic Rail XLA bipod. From the T/C Performance Center.
Price: $1,211.00

THOMPSON/CENTER COMPASS
Calibers: .204 Ruger, .223 Rem, .22-250 Rem., .243 Win., 6.5 Creedmoor, .270 Win., 7mm-08 Rem., 7mm Rem. Mag., .308 Win., .30-06, .300 Win. Mag. Capacity: 4-5-round detachable magazine. Barrel: Match-grade 22 in., (24 in. magnums.) with threaded muzzle. Weight: 7 ¼-7 1/2 lbs. Stock: Composite black with textured grip panels.
Price: $399.00

TIKKA T3X SERIES
Calibers: Virtually any popular chambering including .204 Ruger .222 Rem., .223 Rem., .243 Win., .25-06, 6.5x55 SE, .260 Rem, .270 Win., .260 WSM, 7mm-08, 7mm Rem. Mag., .308 Win., .30-06, .300 Win. Mag., .300 WSM. Barrels: 20, 22.4, 24.3 in. Stock: Checkered walnut, laminate or modular synthetic with interchangeable pistol grips. Newly designed recoil pad. Features: Offered in a variety of different models with many options. Left-hand models available. One minute-of-angle accuracy guaranteed. Introduced in 2016. Made in Finland by Sako. Imported by Beretta USA.
Price: Hunter $875.00
Price: Lite (shown) $725.00
Price: Varmint $950.00
Price: Laminate stainless $1,050.00
Price: Forest $1,000.00
Price: Tac A1 (shown)...$1,899.00
Price: Compact Tactical Rifle $1,150.00

WEATHERBY MARK V
This classic action goes back more than 60 years to the late '50s. Several significant changes were made to the original design in 2016. Stocks have a slimmer fore-end and smaller grip, which has an added palm swell. The new LXX trigger is adjustable down to 2.5 lbs. and has precision ground and polished surfaces and a wider trigger face. All new Mark V rifles come with sub-MOA guarantee. Range Certified (RC) models are range tested and come with a certified ballistic data sheet and RC engraved floorplate. Calibers: Varies depending on model. Barrels: 22 in., 24 in., 26 in., 28 in. Weight: 5 3/4 to 10 lbs. Stock: Varies depending on model. Sights: None furnished. Features: Deluxe version comes in all Weatherby calibers plus .243 Win., .270 Win., 7mm-08 Rem., .30-06, .308 Win. Lazermark same as Mark V Deluxe except stock has extensive oak leaf pattern laser carving on pistol grip and fore-end; chambered in Wby. Magnums .257, .270 Win., 7mm., .300, .340, with 26 in. barrel. Sporter is same as the Mark V Deluxe without the embellishments. Metal has low-luster blue, stock is Claro walnut with matte finish, Monte Carlo comb, recoil pad. Chambered for these Wby. Mags: .257, .270 Win., 7mm, .300, .340. Other chamberings: 7mm Rem. Mag., .300 Win. Introduced 1993. Six Mark V models come with synthetic stocks. Ultra Lightweight rifles weigh 5.75 to 6.75 lbs.; 24 in., 26 in. fluted stainless barrels with recessed target crown; Bell & Carlson stock with CNC-machined aluminum bedding plate and tan "spider web" finish, skeletonized handle and sleeve. Available in .243 Win., .25-06 Rem., .270 Win., 7mm-08 Rem., 7mm Rem. Mag., .280 Rem., .308 Win., .30-06, .300 Win. Mag. Wby. Mag chamberings: .240, .257, .270 Win., 7mm, .300. Accumark uses Mark V action with heavy-contour 26 in. and 28 in. stainless barrels with black oxidized flutes, muzzle diameter of .705 in. No sights, drilled and tapped for scope mounting. Stock is composite with matte gel-coat finish, full-length aluminum bedding block. Weighs 8.5 lbs. Chambered for these Wby. Mags: .240, .257, .270, 7mm, .300, .340, .338-378, .30-378. Other chamberings: 6.5 Creedmoor, .270 Win., .308 Win., 7mm Rem. Mag., .300 Win. Mag. Altitude has 22-, 24-, 26-, 28-in. fluted stainless steel barrel, Monte Carlo carbon fiber composite stock with raised comb, Kryptek Altitude camo. Tacmark has 28-in. free floated fluted barrel with Accubrake, fully adjustable stock, black finish. Safari Grade has fancy grade checkered French walnut stock with ebony fore-end and grip cap, adjustable express rear and hooded front sights, from the Weatherby Custom Shop. Camilla series is lightweight model designed to fit a woman's anatomy. Offered in several variations chambered for .240 Wby. Mag., 6.5 Creedmoor, .270 Win., .308 Win., .30-06. Arroyo is available in Weatherby Magnums from .240 to .338-378, plus 6.5 Creedmoor, .300 Win.

Prices given are believed to be accurate at time of publication however, many factors affect retail pricing so exact pricing not possible.

Mag., and .338 Lapua Mag. Finish is two-tone Cerakote with Brown Sand and FDE added flutes. Carbonmark has 26in. Proof Research carbon fiber threaded barrel and is chambered for .257 and .300 Wby. Mags. Outfitter is chambered for .240-.300 Wby. Magnums plus most popular calibers. Stock has Spiderweb accents. KCR model comes with Krieger Custom Match-grade barrel in .257, 6.5-300, .300 and .30-378 Wby. Magnums. Altitude is lightweight model (5 ¾-6 ¾ lbs.) and comes in Wby. Magnums from .240 to.300, plus 6.5 Creedmoor, .270 Win., .308, .30-06. Dangerous Game Rifle is offered in all Wby. Magnums from .300 to .450, plus .375 H&H. Hand laminated Monte Carlo composite stock. *Note: Most Mark V rifles are available in 6.5 Wby. RPM and 6.5-300 Wby. Mag. chamberings.* All Weatherby Mark V rifles are made in Sheridan, Wyoming.

Price: Mark V Backcountry $2,499.00
Price: Mark V Backcountry Ti .... $3,349.00–$3,449.00
Price: Mark V Deluxe $2,700.00
Price: Mark V Lazermark $2,800.00
Price: Mark V Sporter $1,800.00
Price: Mark V Ultra Lightweight $2,300.00
Price: Mark V Accumark .... $2,300.00–$2,700.00
Price: Mark V Altitude .... $3,000.00–$3,700.00
Price: Mark V Safari Grade Custom .... $6,900.00–$7,600.00
Price: Mark V Tacmark $4,100.00
Price: Mark V Camilla Series .... $2,300.00–$2,700.00
Price: Mark V Arroyo $2,800.00
Price: Mark V Carbonmark $4,100.00
Price: Mark V Outfitter .... $2,600-$2,800.00*
Price: Mark V Krieger Custom Rifle (KCR) .... $3,600-$4,100.00*
Price: Mark V Altitude $2,700.00*
Price: Mark V Dangerous Game Rifle $3,600.00
Price: Mark V Weathermark .... $1,549.00–$1,749.00
Price: Mark V Weathermark Bronze .... $1,549.00–$1,749.00
Price: Mark V Carbonmark Pro .... $2,999.00–$3,099.00
Price: Mark V Carbonmark Elite .... $3,299.00–$3,399.00

*Add .... $500 for optional Range Certified (RC) model with guaranteed sub-MOA accuracy certificate and target.

WEATHERBY VANGUARD II SERIES

Calibers: Varies depending on model. Most Weatherby Magnums and many standard calibers. Barrels: 20, 24, or 26 in. Weights: 7.5–8.75 lbs. Lengths: 44–46.75 in. overall. Stock: Raised comb, Monte Carlo, injection-molded composite stock. Sights: None furnished. Features: One-piece forged, fluted bolt body with three gas ports, forged and machined receiver, adjustable trigger, factory accuracy guarantee. Vanguard Stainless has 410-Series stainless steel barrel and action, bead blasted matte metal finish. Vanguard Deluxe has raised comb, semi-fancy-grade Monte Carlo walnut stock with maplewood spacers, rosewood fore-end and grip cap, polished action with high-gloss blued metalwork. Sporter has Monte Carlo walnut stock with satin urethane finish, fineline diamond point checkering, contrasting rosewood fore-end tip, matte-blued metalwork. Sporter SS metalwork is 410 Series bead-blasted stainless steel. Vanguard Youth/Compact has 20 in. No. 1 contour barrel, short action, scaled-down nonreflective matte black hardwood stock with 12.5-in. length of pull, and full-size, injection-molded composite stock. Chambered for .223 Rem., .22-250 Rem., .243 Win., 7mm-08 Rem., .308 Win. Weighs 6.75 lbs.; OAL 38.9 in. Sub-MOA Matte and Sub-MOA Stainless models have pillar-bedded Fiberguard composite stock (Aramid, graphite unidirectional fibers and fiberglass) with 24-in. barreled action; matte black metalwork, Pachmayr Decelerator recoil pad. Sub-MOA Stainless metalwork is 410 Series bead-blasted stainless steel. Sub-MOA Varmint guaranteed to shoot 3-shot group of .00 in. or less when used with specified Weatherby factory or premium (non-Weatherby calibers) ammunition. Hand-laminated, tan Monte Carlo composite stock with black spiderwebbing; CNC-machined aluminum bedding block, 22 in. No. 3 contour barrel, recessed target crown. Varmint Special has tan injection-molded Monte Carlo composite stock, pebble grain finish, black spiderwebbing. 22 in. No. 3 contour barrel (.740-in. muzzle dia.), bead blasted matte black finish, recessed target crown. Back Country has two-stage trigger, pillar-bedded Bell & Carlson stock, 24-in. fluted barrel, three-position safety.

Price: Vanguard Synthetic $649.00
Price: Vanguard Stainless $799.00
Price: Vanguard Deluxe, 7mm Rem. Mag., .300 Win. Mag. $1,149.00
Price: Vanguard Sporter $849.00
Price: Laminate Sporter $849.00
Price: Vanguard Youth/Compact $599.00
Price: Vanguard S2 Back Country $1,399.00
Price: Vanguard RC (Range Certified) $1,199.00

Price: Vanguard Varmint Special $849.00
Price: Camilla (designed for women shooters) $849.00
Price: Camilla Wilderness $899.00
Price: Lazerguard (Laser carved AA-grade walnut stock) $1,199.00
Price: H-Bar (tactical series) .... $1,149.00–$1,449.00
Price: Weatherguard $749.00
Price: Modular Chassis $1,519.00
Price: Dangerous Game Rifle (DGR) .375 H&H $1,299.00
Price: Safari (.375 or .30-06) $1,199.00
Price: First Lite Fusion Camo $1,099.00
Price: Badlands Camo $849.00
Price: Accuguard $1,099.00
Price: Select $599.00
Price: Wilderness $999.00
Price: High Country $999.00

WINCHESTER MODEL 70 SUPER GRADE

Calibers: .270 Win., .270 WSM, 7mm Rem. Mag., .30-06, .300 Win Mag., .300 WSM, .338 Win. Mag. Capacities: 5 rounds (short action) or 3 rounds (long action). Barrels: 24 in. or 26 in. blued. Weights: 8–8.5 lbs. Features: Full fancy Grade IV/V walnut stock with shadow-line cheekpiece, controlled round feed with claw extractor, Pachmayr Decelerator pad. No sights but drilled and tapped for scope mounts.
Price: .... $1,440.00–$1,480.00

WINCHESTER MODEL 70 ALASKAN

Calibers: .30-06, .300 Win. Mag., .338 Win. Mag., .375 H&H Magnum. Barrel: 25 in. Weight: 8.8 lbs. Sights: Folding adjustable rear, hooded brass bead front. Stock: Satin finished Monte Carlo with cut checkering. Features: Integral recoil lug, Pachmayr Decelerator recoil pad.
Price: $1,400.00

WINCHESTER MODEL 70 COYOTE LIGHT SUPRESSOR READY

Calibers: .22-250, .243 Win., .308 Win., .270 WSM, .300 WSM and .325 WSM. Capacities: 5-round magazine (3-round mag. in .270 WSM, .300 WSM and .325 WSM). Barrel: 22-in. fluted stainless barrel (24 in. in .270 WSM, .300 WSM and .325 WSM). Threaded for suppressor or other muzzle device. Weight: 7.5 lbs. Length: NA. Features: Composite Bell and Carlson stock, Pachmayr Decelerator pad. Controlled round feeding. No sights but drilled and tapped for mounts.
Price: .... $1,270.00–$1,310.00

WINCHESTER MODEL 70 FEATHERWEIGHT

Calibers: .22-250, .243, 6.5 Creedmoor, 7mm-08, .308, .270 WSM, 7mm WSM, .300 WSM, .325 WSM, .25-06, .270, .30-06, 7mm Rem. Mag., .300 Win. Mag., .338 Win. Mag. Capacities: 5 rounds (short action) or 3 rounds (long action). Barrels: 22-in. blued (24 in. in magnum chamberings). Weights: 6.5–7.25 lbs. Length: NA. Features: Satin-finished checkered Grade I walnut stock, controlled round feeding. Pachmayr Decelerator pad. No sights but drilled and tapped for scope mounts.
Price: $1,010.00
Price: Magnum calibers $1,050.00
Price: Featherweight Stainless .... $1,210.00-$1,250.00

WINCHESTER MODEL 70 SPORTER

Calibers: .270 WSM, 7mm WSM, .300 WSM, .325 WSM, .25-06, .270, .30-06, 7mm Rem. Mag., .300 Win. Mag., .338 Win. Mag., 6.8 Western. Capacities: 5 rounds (short action) or 3 rounds (long action). Barrels: 22 in., 24 in. or 26 in. blued. Weights: 6.5–7.25 lbs. Length: NA. Features: Satin-finished checkered Grade I walnut stock with sculpted cheekpiece, controlled round feeding. Pachmayr Decelerator pad. No sights but drilled and tapped for scope mounts.
Price: $1,010.00

WINCHESTER MODEL 70 SAFARI EXPRESS

Calibers: .375 H&H Magnum, .416 Remington, .458 Win. Mag. Barrel: 24 in. Weight: 9 lbs. Sights: Fully adjustable rear, hooded brass bead front. Stock: Satin finished Monte Carlo with cut checkering, deluxe cheekpiece. Features: Forged steel receiver with double integral recoil lugs bedded front and rear, dual steel crossbolts, Pachmayr Decelerator recoil pad.
Price: $1,560.00

Prices given are believed to be accurate at time of publication however, many factors affect retail pricing so exact prices are not possible.

76TH EDITION, 2022 ✦ **417**

WINCHESTER MODEL 70 LONG RANGE MB
Calibers: .22-250 Rem., .243 Win., 6.5 Creedmoor, .308 Win., 6.5 PRC, .270 WSM, .300 WSM, 6.8 Western. Capacity: 3, 4, or 5-round internal magazine with hinged floorplate. Barrel: 24-in. matte blued, light varmint contour, fluted with muzzle brake. Weight: 7 lbs. 8oz. Length: 44 in. Stock: Bell & Carlson composite with tan/black spider web and Pachmayr Decelerator recoil pad. Sights: Drilled and tapped. Features: Bolt-action short action designed for long-range hunting and target shooting. Aluminum bedding block. Matte black finish. Controlled round feed with claw extractor. Three-position safety. Flat, bench-rest style fore-end with dual sling studs. Jeweled bolt. Recessed target crown.
Price: **$1,589.00**

WINCHESTER MODEL 70 EXTREME WEATHER MB
Calibers: .243 Win, 6.5 Creedmoor, 7mm-08 Rem., .308 Win., 6.5 PRC, .270 WSM, .300 WSM, .25-06 Rem., .270 Win., .30-06 Spfld., .264 Win. Mag., 7mm Rem. Mag., .300 Win. Mag., 6.8 Western. Capacity: 3, 4, or 5, internal magazine with hinged floorplate. Barrel: 22-, 24-, or 26-in. sporter contour stainless, fluted, with muzzle brake. Weight: 6 lbs. 12 oz.–7 lbs. 4 oz. Length: 42.25 – 46.75 in. Stock: Bell & Carlson lay-up composite with textured charcoal gray matte finish. Pachmayr Decelerator recoil pad. Sights: Drilled and tapped. Features: Bolt-action hunting rifle designed for adverse conditions. Controlled-round feed with claw extractor. Three position safety. Stainless steel sling studs.
Price: **$1,649.00**

WINCHESTER RENEGADE LONG RANGE SR
Calibers: .243 Win., 6.5 Creedmoor, 7mm-08 Rem, .308 Win., .270 WSM, .300 WSM, 6.5 PRC. Capacity: 3. Barrel: 22 to 24 in., stainless steel, sporter. Stock: Composite Grayboe. Sights: None, drilled and tapped. Weight: 8.5 lbs. Features: Recessed target crown, Inflex Technology recoil pad, enlarged bolt knob.
Price: **$1,069.00**

WINCHESTER XPR HUNTER TRUE TIMBER STRATA
Calibers: .243 Win., 6.5 Creedmoor, 7mm-08 Rem., .308 Win., .270 WSM, .300 WSM, .325 WSM, .270 Win., .30-06, 7mm Rem. Mag., .300 Win. Mag., .338 Win. Mag., .350 Legend, .223 Rem., 6.5 PRC. Capacity: 3 to 5. Barrel: 22 to 26 in., steel sporter, with Permacote finish. Stock: Composite, True Timber Strata camo. Sights: None, drilled and tapped. Weight: 6.75 to 7 lbs. Features: Inflex Technology recoil pad, sling swivel studs.
Price: **$599.00**

WINCHESTER XPR
Calibers: .243, 6.5 Creedmoor, 270 Win., .270 WSM, 7mm-08, 7mm Rem. Mag., .308 Win., .30-06, .300 Win. Mag., .300 WSM, .325 WSM, .338 Win. Mag.,.350 Legend, 6.8 Western. Capacities: Detachable box magazine holds 3 to 5 rounds. Barrels: 24 or 26 in. Stock: Black polymer with Inflex Technology recoil pad. Weight: Approx. 7 lbs. Finish: Matte blue. Features: Bolt unlock button, nickel coated Teflon bolt.
Price: **$549.00**
Price: Mossy Oak Break-Up Country camo stock..............**$600.00**
Price: With Vortex II 3-9x40 scope.................................**$710.00**
Price: XPR Hunter Camo (shown) **$600.00**
Price: Sporter w/Grade 1 walnut stock..........................**$600.00**
Price: True Timber Strata Camo **$600.00**
Price: Thumbhole Varmint Suppressor Ready **$800.00**
Price: Stealth SR...**$669.00**

WINCHESTER XPC
Caliber: .243, 6.5 Creedmoor, 308 Winchester. Capacity: 3. Barrel: 20 in., free floating with target crown, threading for suppressor or muzzle brake. Stock: Cerakote fully machined alloy chassis frame, Magpul PRS Gen III fully adjustable buttstock. Weight: 10 lbs. Length: 40 in. Features: MOA Trigger System, two-position thumb safety. Full length Picatinny rail, M-LOK on fore-end and buttstock for attaching accessories.
Price: **$1,600.00**

BALLARD 1875 1 1/2 HUNTER
Caliber: Various calibers. Barrel: 26–30 in. Weight: NA Length: NA. Stock: Hand-selected classic American walnut. Sights: Blade front, Rocky Mountain rear. Features: Color casehardened receiver, breechblock and lever. Many options available. Made in USA by Ballard Rifle & Cartridge Co.
Price: $3,250.00

BALLARD 1875 #3 GALLERY SINGLE SHOT
Caliber: Various calibers. Barrel: 24–28 in. octagonal with tulip. Weight: NA. Length: NA. Stock: Hand-selected classic American walnut. Sights: Blade front, Rocky Mountain rear. Features: Color casehardened receiver, breechblock and lever. Many options available. Made in USA by Ballard Rifle & Cartridge Co.
Price: $3,300.00

BALLARD 1875 #4 PERFECTION
Caliber: Various calibers. Barrels: 30 in. or 32 in. octagon, standard or heavyweight. Weights: 10.5 lbs. (standard) or 11.75 lbs. (heavyweight bbl.) Length: NA. Stock: Smooth walnut. Sights: Blade front, Rocky Mountain rear. Features: Rifle or shotgun-style buttstock, straight grip action, single- or double-set trigger, "S" or right lever, hand polished and lapped Badger barrel. Made in USA by Ballard Rifle & Cartridge Co.
Price: $3,950.00

BALLARD MODEL 1885 LOW WALL SINGLE SHOT RIFLE
Calibers: Various calibers. Barrels: 24–28 in. Weight: NA. Length: NA. Stock: Hand-selected classic American walnut. Sights: Blade front, sporting rear. Features: Color casehardened receiver, breechblock and lever. Many options available. Made in USA by Ballard Rifle & Cartridge Co.
Price: $3,300.00

BALLARD MODEL 1885 HIGH WALL STANDARD SPORTING SINGLE SHOT
Calibers: Various calibers. Barrels: Lengths to 34 in. Weight: NA. Length: NA. Stock: Straight-grain American walnut. Sights: Buckhorn or flattop rear, blade front. Features: Faithful copy of original Model 1885 High Wall; parts interchange with original rifles; variety of options available. Introduced 2000. Made in USA by Ballard Rifle & Cartridge Co.
Price: $3,300.00

BALLARD MODEL 1885 HIGH WALL SPECIAL SPORTING SINGLE SHOT
Calibers: Various calibers. Barrels: 28–30 in. octagonal. Weight: NA. Length: NA. Stock: Hand-selected classic American walnut. Sights: Blade front, sporting rear. Features: Color casehardened receiver, breechblock and lever. Many options available. Made in USA by Ballard Rifle & Cartridge Co.
Price: $3,600.00

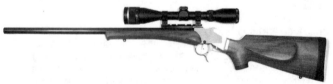

BROWN MODEL 97D SINGLE SHOT
Calibers: Available in most factory and wildcat calibers from .17 Ackley Hornet to .375 Winchester. Barrels: Up to 26 in., air-gauged match grade. Weight: About 5 lbs., 11 oz. Stock: Sporter style with pistol grip, cheekpiece and Schnabel fore-end. Sights: None furnished; drilled and tapped for scope mounting. Features: Falling-block action gives rigid barrel-receiver matting; polished blue/black finish. Hand-fitted action. Standard and custom made-to-order rifles with many options. Made in USA by E. Arthur Brown Co., Inc.
Price: Standard model $1,695.00

C. SHARPS ARMS 1874 BRIDGEPORT SPORTING
Calibers: .38-55 to .50-3.25. Barrel: 26 in., 28 in., 30-in. tapered octagon. Weight: 10.5 lbs. Length: 47 in. Stock: American black walnut; shotgun butt with checkered steel buttplate; straight grip, heavy fore-end with Schnabel tip. Sights: Blade front, buckhorn rear. Drilled and tapped for tang sight. Features: Double-set triggers. Made in USA by C. Sharps Arms.
Price: $1,995.00

C. SHARPS ARMS NEW MODEL 1885 HIGHWALL
Calibers: .22 LR, .22 Hornet, .219 Zipper, .25-35 WCF, .32-40 WCF, .38-55 WCF, .40-65, .30-40 Krag, .40-50 ST or BN, .40-70 ST or BN, .40-90 ST or BN, .45-70 Govt. 2-1/10 in. ST, .45-90 2-4/10 in. ST, .45-100 2-6/10 in.

ST, .45-110 2-7/8 in. ST, .45-120 3-1/4 in. ST. Barrels: 26 in., 28 in., 30 in., tapered full octagon. Weight: About 9 lbs., 4 oz. Length: 47 in. overall. Stock: Oil-finished American walnut; Schnabel-style fore-end. Sights: Blade front, buckhorn rear. Drilled and tapped for optional tang sight. Features: Single trigger; octagonal receiver top; checkered steel buttplate; color casehardened receiver and buttplate, blued barrel. Many options available. Made in USA by C. Sharps Arms Co.
Price: $1,975.00

C. SHARPS ARMS 1885 HIGHWALL SCHUETZEN RIFLE
Calibers: .30-30, .32-40, .38-55, .40-50. Barrels: 24, 26, 28 or 30 in. Full tapered octagon. Stock: Straight grain American walnut with oil finish, pistol grip, cheek rest. Sights: Globe front with aperture set, long-range fully adjustable tang sight with Hadley eyecup. Finish: Color casehardened receiver group, buttplate and bottom tang, matte blue barrel. Single set trigger.
Price: $2,875.00

CIMARRON BILLY DIXON 1874 SHARPS SPORTING
Calibers: .45-70, .45-90, .50-70. Barrel: 32-in. tapered octagonal. Weight: NA. Length: NA. Stock: European walnut. Sights: Blade front, Creedmoor rear. Features: Color casehardened frame, blued barrel. Hand-checkered grip and fore-end; hand-rubbed oil finish. Made by Pedersoli. Imported by Cimarron F.A. Co.
Price: $2,141.70
Price: Officer's Trapdoor Carbine w/26-in. round barrel.................$2,616.00

CIMARRON ADOBE WALLS ROLLING BLOCK
Caliber: .45-70 Govt. Barrel: 30-in. octagonal. Weight: 10.33 lbs. Length: NA. Stock: Hand-checkered European walnut. Sights: Bead front, semi-buckhorn rear. Features: Color casehardened receiver, blued barrel. Curved buttplate. Double-set triggers. Made by Pedersoli. Imported by Cimarron F.A. Co.
Price: $1,740.00

DAKOTA ARMS SHARPS
Calibers: Virtually any caliber from .17 Ackley Hornet to .30-40 Krag. Features: 26-in. octagon barrel, XX-grade walnut stock with straight grip and tang sight. Many options and upgrades are available.
Price: $4,490.00

EMF PREMIER 1874 SHARPS
Calibers: .45-70, .45-110, .45-120. Barrel: 32 in., 34 in.. Weight: 11–13 lbs. Length: 49 in., 51 in. overall. Stock: Pistol grip, European walnut. Sights: Blade front, adjustable rear. Features: Superb quality reproductions of the 1874 Sharps Sporting Rifles; casehardened locks; double-set triggers; blue barrels. Imported from Pedersoli by EMF.
Price: Business Rifle...$1,585.00
Price: Down Under Sporting Rifle, Patchbox, heavy barrel $2,405.00
Price: Silhouette, pistol-grip..................................$1,899.90
Price: Super Deluxe Hand Engraved $3,600.00
Price: Competition Rifle.......................................$2,200.00

Prices given are believed to be accurate at time of publication however, many factors affect retail pricing so exact prices are not possible.

76TH EDITION, 2022 ✛ 419

H&R BUFFALO CLASSIC

Calibers: .45 Colt or .45-70 Govt. Barrel: 32 in. heavy. Weight: 8 lbs. Length: 46 in. overall. Stock: Cut-checkered American black walnut. Sights: Williams receiver sight; Lyman target front sight with 8 aperture inserts. Features: Color casehardened Handi-Rifle action with exposed hammer; color casehardened crescent buttplate; 19th-century checkering pattern. Introduced 1995. Made in USA by H&R 1871, Inc.
Price: Buffalo Classic Rifle...**$479.00**

HENRY SINGLE SHOT BRASS

Calibers: .44 Mag./.44 Spl., .357 Mag./.38 Spl., .45-70 Govt. Capacity: Single shot. Barrel: 22-in. round blued steel. Weight: 7.01–7.14 lbs. Length: 37.5 in. Stock: American Walnut with English-style straight buttstock. Sights: Fully adjustable folding leaf rear and brass bead front. Also drilled and tapped. Features: Polished brass receiver single-shot break actions built in a limited number of calibers. Sling studs. Brass buttplate. Rebounding hammer safety. Break-action lever can be moved either left or right to open, making it friendly for lefties.
Price: **$646.00**

HENRY SINGLE SHOT STEEL

Calibers: .223 Rem., .243 Win., .308 Win., .357 Mag./.38 Spl., .44 Mag., .30-30 Win., .45-70 Govt., .350 Legend, .450 Bushmaster. Capacity: Single-shot. Barrel: 22-in. round blued steel. Weight: 6.73–6.96 lbs. Length: 37.5 in. Stock: Checkered American Walnut, pistol grip style. Sights: Fully adjustable folding leaf rear and brass bead front. Also drilled and tapped. Features: Blued steel receiver single-shot rifles. Solid rubber recoil pad. Rebounding hammer safety. Sling studs. Break-action lever can be moved either left or right to open, making it friendly for lefties. Youth model uses shorter 13-inch LOP, standard model LOP is 14 inches.
Price: **$525.00**
Price: Youth Single Shot .243 Win. **$525.00**

KRIEGHOFF HUBERTUS SINGLE-SHOT

Calibers: .222, .22-250, .243 Win., .270 Win., .308 Win., .30-06, 5.6x50R Mag., 5.6x52R, 6x62R Freres, 6.5x57R, 6.5x65R, 7x57R, 7x65R, 8x57JRS, 8x75RS, 9.3x74R, 7mm Rem. Mag., .300 Win. Mag. Barrels: 23.5 in. Shorter lengths available. Weight: 6.5 lbs. Length: 40.5 in. Stock: High-grade walnut. Sights: Blade front, open rear. Features: Break-open loading with manual cocking lever on top tang; takedown; extractor; Schnabel forearm; many options. Imported from Germany by Krieghoff International Inc.
Price: Hubertus single shot **$7,295.00**
Price: Hubertus, magnum calibers **$8,295.00**

MERKEL K1 MODEL LIGHTWEIGHT STALKING

Calibers: .243 Win., .270 Win., 7x57R, .308 Win., .30-06, 7mm Rem. Mag., .300 Win. Mag., 9.3x74R. Barrel: 23.6 in. Weight: 5.6 lbs. unscoped. Stock: Satin-finished walnut, fluted and checkered; sling-swivel studs. Sights: None (scope base furnished). Features: Franz Jager single-shot break-open action, cocking/uncocking slide-type safety, matte silver receiver, selectable trigger pull weights, integrated, quick detach 1 in. or 30mm optic mounts (optic not included). Extra barrels are an option. Imported from Germany by Merkel USA.
Price: Jagd Stalking Rifle **$3,795.00**
Price: Jagd Stutzen Carbine **$4,195.00**
Price: Extra barrels **$1,195.00**

MILLER ARMS

Calibers: Virtually any caliber from .17 Ackley Hornet to .416 Remington. Falling block design with 24-in. premium match-grade barrel, express sights, XXX-grade walnut stock and fore-end with 24 LPI checkering. Made in several styles including Classic, Target and Varmint. Many options and upgrades are available. From Dakota Arms.
Price: **$5,590.00**

ROSSI SINGLE-SHOT SERIES

Calibers: .223 Rem., .243 Win., .44 Magnum. Barrel: 22 in. Weight: 6.25 lbs. Stocks: Black Synthetic Synthetic with recoil pad and removable cheek piece. Sights: Adjustable rear, fiber optic front, scope rail. Some models have scope rail only. Features: Single-shot break open, positive ejection, internal transfer bar mechanism, manual external safety, trigger block system, Taurus Security System, Matte blue finish.
Price: **$238.00**

RUGER NO. 1 SERIES

This model is currently available only in select limited editions and chamberings each year. Features common to most variants of the No. 1 include a falling block mechanism and under lever, sliding tang safety, integral scope mounts machined on the steel quarter rib, sporting-style recoil pad, grip cap and sling swivel studs. Chamberings for 2018 and 2019 were .450 Bushmaster and .450 Marlin. In addition, many calibers are offered by Ruger distributors Lipsey's and Talo, usually limited production runs of approximately 250 rifles, including .204 Ruger, .22 Hornet, 6.5 Creedmoor, .250 Savage, .257 Roberts, .257 Weatherby Mag. and .30-30. For availability of specific variants and calibers contact www.lipseysguns.com or www.taloinc.com.
Price: ....**$1,899.00-$2,115.00**

SHILOH CO. SHARPS 1874 LONG RANGE EXPRESS

Calibers: .38-55, .40-50 BN, .40-70 BN, .40-90 BN, .40-70 ST, .40-90 ST, .45-70 Govt. ST, .45-90 ST, .45-110 ST, .50-70 ST, .50-90 ST. Barrel: 34-in. tapered octagon. Weight: 10.5 lbs. Length: 51 in. overall. Stock: Oil-finished walnut (upgrades available) with pistol grip, shotgun-style butt, traditional cheek rest, Schnabel fore-end. Sights: Customer's choice. Features: Re-creation of the Model 1874 Sharps rifle. Double-set triggers. Made in USA by Shiloh Rifle Mfg. Co.
Price: **$2,059.00**
Price: Sporter Rifle No. 1 (similar to above except with 30-in. barrel, blade front, buckhorn rear sight) **$2,059.00**
Price: Sporter Rifle No. 3 (similar to No. 1 except straight-grip stock, standard wood) **$1,949.00**

SHILOH CO. SHARPS 1874 QUIGLEY

Calibers: .45-70 Govt., .45-110. Barrel: 34-in. heavy octagon. Stock: Military-style with patch box, standard-grade American walnut. Sights: Semi-buckhorn, interchangeable front and midrange vernier tang sight with windage. Features: Gold inlay initials, pewter tip, Hartford collar, case color or antique finish. Double-set triggers.
Price: **$3,533.00**

SHILOH CO. SHARPS 1874 SADDLE

Calibers: .38-55, .40-50 BN, .40-65 Win., .40-70 BN, .40-70 ST, .40-90 BN, .40-90 ST, .44-77 BN, .44-90 BN, .45-70 Govt. ST, .45-90 ST, .45-100 ST, .45-110 ST, .45-120 ST, .50-70 ST, .50-90 ST. Barrels: 26 in. full or half octagon. Stock: Semi-fancy American walnut. Shotgun style with cheek rest. Sights: Buckhorn and blade. Features: Double-set trigger, numerous custom features can be added.

Price: **$2,044.00**

SHILOH CO. SHARPS 1874 MONTANA ROUGHRIDER

Calibers: .38-55, .40-50 BN, .40-65 Win., .40-70 BN, .40-70 ST, .40-90 BN, .40-90 ST, .44-77 BN, .44-90 BN, .45-70 Govt. ST, .45-90 ST, .45-100 ST, .45-110 ST, .45-120 ST, .50-70 ST, .50-90 ST. Barrels: 30 in. full or half octagon. Stock: American walnut in shotgun or military style. Sights: Buckhorn and blade. Features: Double-set triggers, numerous custom features can be added.

Price: **$2,059.00**

SHILOH CO. SHARPS CREEDMOOR TARGET

Calibers: .38-55, .40-50 BN, .40-65 Win., .40-70 BN, .40-70 ST, .40-90 BN, .40-90 ST, .44-77 BN, .44-90 BN, .45-70 Govt. ST, .45-90 ST, .45-100 ST, .45-110 ST, .45-120 ST, .50-70 ST, .50-90 ST. Barrel: 32 in. half round-half octagon. Stock: Extra fancy American walnut. Shotgun style with pistol grip. Sights: Customer's choice. Features: Single trigger, AA finish on stock, polished barrel and screws, pewter tip.

Price: **$3,105.00**

THOMPSON/CENTER ENCORE PRO HUNTER PREDATOR RIFLE

Calibers: .204 Ruger, .223 Remington, .22-250 and .308 Winchester. Barrel: 28-in. deep-fluted interchangeable. Length: 42.5 in. Weight: 7.75 lbs. Stock: Composite buttstock and fore-end with non-slip inserts in cheekpiece, pistol grip and fore-end. Realtree Advantage Max-1 camo finish overall. Scope is not included.

Price: **$882.00**

THOMPSON/CENTER G2 CONTENDER

Calibers: .204 Ruger, .223 Rem., 6.8 Rem. 7-30 Waters, .30-30 Win. Barrel: 23-in. interchangeable with blued finish. Length: 36.75 in. Stock: Walnut. Sights: None. Weight: 5.5 pounds. Reintroduced in 2015. Interchangeable barrels available in several centerfire and rimfire calibers.

Price: **$769.00**

UBERTI 1874 SHARPS SPORTING

Caliber: .45-70 Govt. Barrels: 30 in., 32 in., 34 in. octagonal. Weight: 10.57 lbs. with 32 in. barrel. Lengths: 48.9 in. with 32 in. barrel. Stock: Walnut. Sights: Dovetail front, Vernier tang rear. Features: Cut checkering, case-colored finish on frame, buttplate, and lever. Imported by Stoeger Industries.

Price: Standard Sharps **$1,919.00**
Price: Special Sharps **$2,019.00**

Price: Deluxe Sharps **$3,269.00**
Price: Down Under Sharps... **$2,719.00**
Price: Long Range Sharps **$2,719.00**
Price: Buffalo Hunter Sharps **$2,620.00**
Price: Sharps Cavalry Carbine **$2,020.00**
Price: Sharps Extra Deluxe... **$5,400.00**
Price: Sharps Hunter.. **$1,699.00**

UBERTI 1885 HIGH-WALL SINGLE-SHOT

Calibers: .45-70 Govt., .45-90, .45-120. Barrels: 28–32 in. Weights: 9.3–9.9 lbs. Lengths: 44.5–47 in. overall. Stock: Walnut stock and fore-end. Sights: Blade front, fully adjustable open rear. Features: Based on Winchester High-Wall design by John Browning. Color casehardened frame and lever, blued barrel and buttplate. Imported by Stoeger Industries.

Price: .... **$1,079.00–$1,279.00**

UBERTI 1885 COURTENEY STALKING RIFLE

Calibers: .303 British, .45-70 Gov't. Capacity: Single shot. Barrel: 24-in. round blued steel. Weight: 7.1 lbs. Length: 37.5 in. Stock: A-Grade Walnut, Prince of Wales buttstock and slim fore-end with African heartwood. Sights: Hooded front and V-style express rear with quarter-rib slot for Weaver rings. Features: Named after English hunter Courteney Selous, this single shot shows traditional British style. Casehardened receiver. Checkered pistol grip. Rubber buttpad. Sling swivels including barrel-mounted front.

Price: **$1,689.00**

UBERTI SPRINGFIELD TRAPDOOR RIFLE/CARBINE

Caliber: .45-70 Govt., single shot Barrel: 22 or 32.5 in. Features: Blued steel receiver and barrel, casehardened breechblock and buttplate. Sights: Creedmoor style.

Price: Springfield Trapdoor Carbine, 22 in. barrel **$1,749.00**
Price: Springfield Trapdoor Army, 32.5 in. barrel **$2,019.0**

Prices given are believed to be accurate at time of publication however, many factors affect retail pricing so exact prices are not possible.

76TH EDITION, 2022 ⬩ 421

BERETTA S686/S689 O/U RIFLE SERIES
Calibers: .30-06, 9.3x74R. Barrels: 23 in. O/U boxlock action. Single or double triggers. EELL Grade has better wood, moderate engraving.
Price: ....**$4,200.00–$9,000.00**
Price: EELL Diamond Sable grade **$12,750.00**

BRNO MODEL 802 COMBO GUN
Calibers/Gauges: .243 Win., .308 or .30-06/12 ga. Over/Under. Barrels: 23.6 in. Weight: 7.6 lbs. Length: 41 in. Stock: European walnut. Features: Double trigger, shotgun barrel is improved-modified chokes. Imported by CZ USA.
Price: **$2,087.00**

BRNO EFFECT
Caliber: .30-06 Single Shot.................................**$1,585.00**

BRNO STOPPER
Caliber: .458 Win. Over/Under **$5,554.00**
Caliber: .458 Win. Over/Under hand engraved **$8,072.00**

FAUSTI CLASS EXPRESS
Calibers: .30-06, .30R Blaser, 8x57 JRS, 9.3x74R, .444 Marlin, .45-70 Govt. Over/Under. Barrels: 24 in. Weight: 7.5 lbs. Length: 41 in. Stock: Oil-finished Grade A walnut. Pistol grip, Bavarian or Classic. Sights: Folding leaf rear, fiber optic front adjustable for elevation. Features: Inertia single or double trigger, automatic ejectors. Made in Italy and imported by Fausti USA.
Price: **$4,990.00**
Price: SL Express w/hand engraving, AA wood................**$7,600.00**

HEYM MODEL 88B SXS DOUBLE RIFLE
Calibers/Gauge: .22 Hornet, .300 Win. Mag., .375 H&H Belted Mag., .375 H&H Flanged Mag., .416 Rigby, .416/500 NE, .450/400 NE 3-in., .450 NE 3.25-in., .470 NE, .500 NE, .577 NE, .600 NE, 20 gauge, and more. Barrel: Up to 26 in., Krupp steel, hammer-forged. Stock: Custom select European walnut. Sights: V rear, bead front. Weight: 9 to 13 lbs. Features: Automatic ejectors, articulated front trigger, stocked-to-fit RH or LH, cocking indicators, engraving available.
Price: **$18,000.00**

HEYM MODEL 89B SXS DOUBLE RIFLE
Calibers/Gauge: .22 Hornet, .300 Win. Mag., .375 H&H Belted Mag., .375 H&H Flanged Mag., .416 Rigby, .416/500 NE, .450/400 NE 3-in., .450 NE 3.25-in., .470 NE, .500 NE, .577 NE, .600 NE, 20 gauge, and more. Barrel: Up to 26 in., Krupp steel, hammer-forged. Stock: Custom select European walnut. Sights: V rear, bead front. Weight: 9-13 lbs. Features: Five frame sizes, automatic ejectors, intercepting sears, stocked-to-fit RH or LH, engraving available.
Price: **$23,000.00**

HOENIG ROTARY ROUND ACTION DOUBLE
Calibers: Most popular calibers. Over/Under design. Barrels: 22–26 in. Stock: English Walnut; to customer specs. Sights: Swivel hood front with button release (extra bead stored in trap door grip cap), express-style rear on quarter-rib adjustable for windage and elevation; scope mount. Features: Round action opens by rotating barrels, pulling forward. Inertia extractor system, rotary safety blocks strikers. Single lever quick-detachable scope mount. Simple takedown without removing fore-end. Introduced 1997. Custom rifle made in USA by George Hoenig.
Price: **$22,500.00**

HOENIG ROTARY ROUND ACTION COMBINATION
Calibers: Most popular calibers and shotgun gauges. Over/Under design with rifle barrel atop shotgun barrel. Barrel: 26 in. Weight: 7 lbs. Stock: English Walnut to customer specs. Sights: Front ramp with button release blades. Foldable aperture tang sight windage and elevation adjustable. Quarter-rib with scope mount. Features: Round action opens by rotating barrels, pulling forward. Inertia extractor; rotary safety blocks strikers. Simple takedown without removing forend. Custom rifle made in USA by George Hoenig.
Price: **$27,500.00**

HOENIG VIERLING FOUR-BARREL COMBINATION
Calibers/gauges: Two 20-gauge shotgun barrels with one rifle barrel chambered for .22 Long Rifle and another for .223 Remington. Custom rifle made in USA by George Hoenig.
Price: **$50,000.00**

KRIEGHOFF CLASSIC DOUBLE
Calibers: 7x57R, 7x65R, .308 Win., .30-06, 8x57 JRS, 8x75RS, 9.3x74R, .375NE, .500/.416NE, .470NE, .500NE. Barrel: 23.5 in. Weight: 7.3–11 lbs. Stock: High grade European walnut. Standard model has conventional rounded cheekpiece, Bavaria model has Bavarian-style cheekpiece. Sights: Bead front with removable, adjustable wedge (.375 H&H and below), standing leaf rear on quarter-rib. Features: Boxlock action; double triggers; short opening angle for fast loading; quiet extractors; sliding, self-adjusting wedge for secure bolting; Purdey-style barrel extension; horizontal firing pin placement. Many options available. Introduced 1997. Imported from Germany by Krieghoff International.
Price: **$10,995.00**
Price: Engraved sideplates, add **$4,000.00**
Price: Extra set of rifle barrels, add.....................**$6,300.00**
Price: Extra set of 20-ga., 28 in. shotgun barrels, add....**$4,400.00**

KRIEGHOFF CLASSIC BIG FIVE DOUBLE RIFLE
Similar to the standard Classic except available in .375 H&H, .375 Flanged Mag. N.E., .416 Rigby, .458 Win., 500/416 NE, 470 NE, 500 NE. Has hinged front trigger, nonremovable muzzle wedge, Universal Trigger System, Combi Cocking Device, steel trigger guard, specially weighted stock bolt for weight and balance. Many options available. Introduced 1997. Imported from Germany by Krieghoff International.
Price: **$13,995.00**
Price: Engraved sideplates, add **$4,000.00**
Price: Extra set of 20-ga. shotgun barrels, add...........**$5,000.00**
Price: Extra set of rifle barrels, add.....................**$6,300.00**

MERKEL BOXLOCK DOUBLE
Calibers: 5.6x52R, .243 Winchester, 6.5x55, 6.5x57R, 7x57R, 7x65R, .308 Win., .30-06, 8x57 IRS, 9.3x74R. Barrel: 23.6 in. Weight: 7.7 oz. Length: NA. Stock: Walnut, oil finished, pistol grip. Sights: Fixed 100 meter. Features: Anson & Deeley boxlock action with cocking indicators, double triggers, engraved color casehardened receiver. Introduced 1995. Imported from Germany by Merkel USA.
Price: Model 140-2 ....**$13,255.00**
Price: Model 141 Small Frame SXS Rifle; built on smaller frame, chambered for 7mm Mauser, .30-06, or 9.3x74R **$11,825.00**
Price: Model 141 Engraved; fine hand-engraved hunting scenes on silvered receiver. **$13,500.00**

BROWNING BUCK MARK SEMI-AUTO

Caliber: .22 LR. Capacity: 10+1. Action: A rifle version of the Buck Mark Pistol; straight blowback action; machined aluminum receiver with integral rail scope mount; manual thumb safety. Barrel: Recessed crowns. Stock: Stock and forearm with full pistol grip. Features: Action lock provided. Introduced 2001. Four model name variations for 2006, as noted below. Sights: FLD Target, FLD Carbon, and Target models have integrated scope rails. Sporter has Truglo/Marble fiber-optic sights. Imported from Japan by Browning.

Price: FLD Target, 5.5 lbs., bull barrel, laminated stock......................$720.00
Price: Target, 5.4 lbs., blued bull barrel, wood stock $700.00
Price: Sporter, 4.4 lbs., blued sporter barrel w/sights $700.00

BROWNING SA-22 SEMI-AUTO 22

Caliber: .22 LR. Capacity: Tubular magazine in buttstock holds 11 rounds. Barrel: 19.375 in. Weight: 5 lbs. 3 oz. Length: 37 in. overall. Stock: Checkered select walnut with pistol grip and semi-beavertail fore-end. Sights: Gold bead front, folding leaf rear. Features: Engraved receiver with polished blue finish; crossbolt safety; easy takedown for carrying or storage. The Grade VI is available with either grayed or blued receiver with extensive engraving with gold-plated animals: right side pictures a fox and squirrel in a woodland scene; left side shows a beagle chasing a rabbit. On top is a portrait of the beagle. Stock and fore-end are of high-grade walnut with a double-bordered cut checkering design. Introduced 1956. Made in Belgium until 1974. Currently made in Japan by Miroku.

Price: Grade I, scroll-engraved blued receiver $700.00
Price: Grade II, octagon barrel $1,000.00
Price: Grade VI BL, gold-plated engraved blued receiver $1,640.00

CITADEL M-1 CARBINE

Caliber: .22LR. Capacity: 10-round magazine. Barrel: 18 in. Weight: 4.8 lbs. Length: 35 in. Stock: Wood or synthetic in black or several camo patterns. Features: Built to the exacting specifications of the G.I. model used by U.S. infantrymen in both WWII theaters of battle and in Korea. Used by officers as well as tankers, drivers, artillery crews, mortar crews, and other personnel. Weight, barrel length and OAL are the same as the "United States Carbine, Caliber .30, M1," its official military designation. Made in Italy by Chiappa. Imported by Legacy Sports.

Price: Synthetic stock, black. $316.00
Price: Synthetic stock, camo. $368.00
Price: Wood stock. $400.00

CZ MODEL 512

Calibers: .22 LR/.22 WMR. Capacity: 5-round magazines. Barrel: 20.5 in. Weight: 5.9 lbs. Length: 39.3 in. Stock: Beech. Sights: Adjustable. Features: The modular design is easily maintained, requiring only a coin as a tool for field stripping. The action of the 512 is composed of an aluminum alloy upper receiver that secures the barrel and bolt assembly and a fiberglass reinforced polymer lower half that houses the trigger mechanism and detachable magazine. The 512 shares the same magazines and scope rings with the CZ 455 bolt-action rifle.

Price: .22 LR $495.00
Price: .22 WMR $526.00

H&K 416-22

Caliber: .22 LR. Capacity: 10- or 20-round magazine. Features: Blowback semi-auto rifle styled to resemble H&K 416 with metal upper and lower receivers; rail interface system; retractable stock; pistol grip with storage compartment; on-rail sights; rear sight adjustable for wind and elevation; 16.1-in. barrel. Also available in pistol version with 9-in. barrel. Made in Germany by Walther under license from Heckler & Koch and imported by Umarex.

Price: $599.00

H&K MP5 A5

Caliber: .22 LR. Capacity: 10- or 25-round magazine Features: Blowback semi-auto rifle styled to resemble H&K MP5 with metal receiver; compensator; bolt catch; NAVY pistol grip; on-rail sights; rear sight adjustable for wind and elevation; 16.1-in. barrel. Also available in pistol version with 9-in. barrel. Also available with SD-type fore-end. Made in Germany by Walther under license from Heckler & Koch. Imported by Umarex.

Price: $499.00
Price: MP5 SD..$599.00

HENRY AR-7 SURVIVAL RIFLE

Caliber: .22 LR. Capacity: 8, detachable steel magazine. Barrel: 16.125-in. steel covered with ABS plastic. Weight: 3.5 lbs. Length: 35 in. Stock: ABS plastic, floating, hollow design allowing rifle to be disassembled and packed inside buttstock. Choice of Black, True Timber Kanati, or Viper Western camo. Sights: Peep rear with blaze orange blade front. Also 3/8-in. grooved receiver. Features: Henry's version of the AR-7 takedown rifle issued to U.S. Air Force pilots. Receiver, barrel, and spare mags stow inside the buttstock. Rubber buttpad. 14-inch LOP. Two 8-round magazines included. The US Survival Pack includes a black synthetic AR-7 rifle, zippered soft case, and a wide variety of survival gear, including a Henry-branded Buck knife.

Price: AR-7 Black $319.00
Price: AR-7 Camo $388.00
Price: AR-7 Survival Pack $577.00

HOWA GAMEPRO RIMFIRE

Calibers: .22 LR, .22 WMR, .17 HMR. Capacity: 10. Barrel: 18 in., threaded, blued. Stock: Composite Hogue over-molded. Sights: Picatinny rail. Weight: 9.35 lbs. Features: Guaranteed sub-MOA, two-stage HACT trigger.

Price: $699.00

KEL-TEC SU-22CA

Caliber: .22 LR. Capacity: 26-round magazine. Barrel: 16.1 in. Weight: 4 lbs. Length: 34 in. Features: Blowback action, crossbolt safety, adjustable front and rear sights with integral Picatinny rail. Threaded muzzle.

Price: $547.00

MAGNUM RESEARCH MAGNUM LITE RIMFIRE

Calibers: .22 LR or .22 WMR Capacity: 10 (.22 LR), 9 (.22 WMR) rotary magazine. Barrel: 17-, 18-, 18.5-, or 19-in. lengths with options of carbon, aluminum-tensioned, threaded, and integrally suppressed TTS-22. Weight: 4 lbs.–4 lbs. 8 oz. Length: 36-5/8–38-5/8 in. Stock: Multiple options including Hogue Overmolded and laminated Barracuda style. Sights: Integral scope base. Features: The Magnum Lite Rimfire (MLR) uses a one-piece forged 6061-T6 receivers that are black hardcoat anodized. Custom barrels. Integral Picatinny rail for easy optics mounting. Upgraded trigger. Multiple stock style and material options, as well as barrel types and lengths. Crossbolt safety and manual bolt hold-open catch. Made in the USA.

Price: Hogue Overmolded $764.00
Price: MLR .22 LR w/ aluminum-tensioned barrel $641.00
Price: MLR .22 WMR w/ Barracuda stock $935.00
Price: MLR .22 LR with Ultra barrel..$596.00
Price: MLR .22 LR with TTS-22 suppressed barrel $860.00

MAGNUM RESEARCH SWITCHBOLT

Caliber: .22 LR. Capacity: 10-round rotary magazine. Barrel: 17-in. carbon. Weight: 4.25 lbs. Length: 35-1/8–35-1/2 in. Stock: Two models, one with Hogue Overmolded Black and the other with colored Ambidextrous Evolution laminate. Sights: Integral scope base. Features: Unique gas-assisted blowback operation. An extension of the lightweight MLR rifles, the Switchbolt was tested and perfected on the professional speed shooting circuit. Built in the USA. Integral Picatinny rail. Machined from 6061-T6, hardcoat anodized. Equipped with a bolt handle on the left side of a right-handed bolt, built for right-handed shooters so the trigger hand never has to leave the stock. Custom-designed Switchbolts are available from the Magnum Research Custom Shop.

Price: Hogue overmolded black stock $731.00
Price: Ambidextrous Evolution laminate stock $893.00

MARLIN MODEL 60

Caliber: .22 LR. Capacity: 14-round tubular magazine. Barrel: 19 in. round tapered. Weight: About 5.5 lbs. Length: 37.5 in. overall. Stock: Press-checkered, laminated Maine birch with Monte Carlo, full pistol grip; black synthetic or Realtree Camo. Sights: Ramp front, open adjustable rear. Matted receiver is grooved for scope mount. Features: Last-shot bolt hold-open. Available with factory mounted 4x scope.

Price: Laminate $209.00
Price: Model 60C camo $246.00
Price: Synthetic $201.00

MARLIN MODEL 60SS SELF-LOADING RIFLE

Same as the Model 60 except breech bolt, barrel and outer magazine tube are made of stainless steel; most other parts are either nickel-plated or coated to match the stainless finish. Monte Carlo stock is of black/gray Maine birch laminate, and has nickel-plated swivel studs, rubber buttpad. Introduced 1993.

Price: $315.00

MARLIN MODEL 795

Caliber: .22. Capacity: 10-round magazine. Barrel: 18 in. with 16-groove Micro-Groove rifling. Sights: Ramp front sight, adjustable rear. Receiver grooved for scope mount. Stock: Black synthetic, hardwood, synthetic thumbhole, solid pink, pink camo, or Mossy Oak New Break-up camo finish. Features: Last shot hold-open feature. Introduced 1997. SS is similar to Model 795 except stainless steel barrel. Most other parts nickel-plated. Adjustable folding semi-buckhorn rear sights, ramp front high-visibility post and removable cutaway wide scan hood. Made in USA by Marlin Firearms Co.

Price: $183.00
Price: Stainless $262.00

MOSSBERG BLAZE SERIES

Caliber: .22 LR. Capacities: 10 or 25 rounds. Barrel: 16.5 in. Sights: Adjustable. Weights: 3.5–4.75 lbs. Features: A series of lightweight polymer rifles with several finish options and styles. Green Dot Combo model has Dead Ringer greet dot sight. Blaze 47 has AK-profile with adjustable fiber optic rear and raised front sight, ambidextrous safety, and a choice of wood or synthetic stock.

Price: $210.00
Price: Muddy Girl camo $269.00
Price: Green Dot Combo $281.00
Price: Wildfire camo $269.00
Price: Kryptek Highlander camo $283.00
Price: Blaze 47 wood stock $420.00

MOSSBERG MODEL 702 PLINKSTER

Caliber: .22 LR. Capacity: 10-round magazine. Barrel: 18 in. free-floating. Weights: 4.1–4.6 lbs. Sights: Adjustable rifle. Receiver grooved for scope mount. Stock: Wood or black synthetic. Features: Ergonomically placed magazine release and safety buttons, crossbolt safety, free gun lock. Made in USA by O.F. Mossberg & Sons, Inc.

Price: From...$190.00

MOSSBERG MODEL 715T SERIES

Caliber: .22 LR. Capacity: 10- or 25-round magazine. Barrel: 16.25 or 18 in. with A2-style muzzle brake. Weight: 5.5 lbs. Features: AR style offered in several models. Flattop or A2 style carry handle.

Price: Black finish $326.00
Price: Black finish, Red Dot sight $375.00
Price: Muddy Girl camo $438.00

REMINGTON MODEL 552 BDL DELUXE SPEEDMASTER

Calibers: .22 Short (20 rounds), Long (17) or LR (15) tubular magazine. Barrel: 21-in. round tapered. Weight: 5.75 lbs. Length: 40 in. overall. Stock: Walnut. Checkered grip and fore-end. Sights: Adjustable rear, ramp front. Features: Positive crossbolt safety in trigger guard, receiver grooved for tip-off mount. Operates with .22 Short, Long or Long Rifle cartridges. Classic design introduced in 1957.

Price: $707.00

ROSSI RS22

Caliber: .22 LR. Capacity: 10-round detachable magazine. Barrel: 18 in. Weight: 4.1 lbs. Length: 36 in. Stock: Black synthetic with impressed checkering. Sights: Adjustable fiber optic rear, hooded fiber optic front. Made in Brazil, imported by Rossi USA.

Price: Standard model, synthetic stock $139.00

RUGER 10/22 AUTOLOADING CARBINE

Caliber: .22 LR. Capacity: 10-round rotary magazine. Barrel: 18.5 in. round tapered (16.12 in. compact model). Weight: 5 lbs. (4.5, compact). Length: 37.25 in., 34 in. (compact) overall. Stock: American hardwood with pistol grip and barrel band, or synthetic. Sights: Brass bead front, folding leaf rear adjustable for elevation. Features: Available with satin black or stainless finish on receiver and barrel. Detachable rotary magazine fits flush into stock, crossbolt safety, receiver tapped and grooved for scope blocks or tip-off mount. Scope base adaptor furnished with each rifle. Made in USA by Sturm, Ruger & Co.

Price: Wood stock...$309.00
Price: Synthetic stock $309.00
Price: Stainless, synthetic stock $339.00
Price: Compact model, fiber-optic front sight $359.00
Price: Go Wild Rockstar Camo $399.00
Price: Collector's Series Man's Best Friend $399.00
Price: Weaver 3-9x Scope $399.00

RUGER 10/22 TAKEDOWN RIFLE

Caliber: .22 LR. Capacity: 10-round rotary magazine. Barrels: 18.5 in. stainless, or 16.6 in. satin black threaded with suppressor. Easy takedown feature enables quick separation of the barrel from the action by way of a recessed locking lever, for ease of transportation and storage. Stock: Black synthetic. Sights: Adjustable rear, gold bead front. Weight: 4.66 pounds. Comes with backpack carrying bag.

Price: Stainless..$439.00
Price: Satin black w/flash suppressor.........................$459.00
Price: Threaded barrel..$629.00
Price: With Silent-SR suppressor.............................$1,078.00

RUGER 10/22 SPORTER

Same specifications as 10/22 Carbine except has American walnut stock with hand-checkered pistol grip and fore-end, straight buttplate, sling swivels, 18.9-in. barrel, and no barrel band.

Price: $419.00

RUGER 10/22 TARGET LITE

Features a 16 1/8-in. heavy, hammer-forged threaded barrel with tight chamber dimensions, black or red/black laminate stock with thumbhole and adjustable length-of-pull, BX Trigger with 2.5-3 lbs. pull weight, minimal overtravel and positive reset.

Price: $649.00

SAVAGE A17 SERIES
Calibers: .17 HMR, . Capacity: 10-round rotary magazine. Barrel: 22 in. Weight: 5.4–5.6 lbs. Features: Delayed blowback action, Savage AccuTrigger, synthetic or laminated stock. Target model has heavy barrel, sporter or thumbhole stock. Introduced in 2016.
Price: Standard model $473.00
Price: Sporter (Gray laminate stock) $574.00
Price: Target Sporter...$571.00
Price: Target Thumbhole $631.00

SAVAGE A22 SERIES
Caliber: .22 LR, .22 WMR. Capacity 10-round magazine. Similar to A17 series except for caliber.
Price: $284.00
Price: A22 SS stainless barrel $419.00
Price: Target Thumbhole stock, heavy barrel $449.00
Price: Pro Varmint w/Picatinny rail, heavy bbl., target stock $409.00
Price: 22 WMR $479.00

SAVAGE A22 BNS-SR
Caliber: .22 LR. Capacity: 10. Barrel: 18 in., carbon steel. Stock: Laminated wood. Sights: Two-piece Weaver bases, no scope included. Weight: 6.6 lbs. Features: Ergonomic stock, AccuTrigger, straight blowback semi-auto.
Price: $479.00

SMITH & WESSON M&P15-22 SERIES
Caliber: .22 LR. Capacities: 10- or 25-round magazine. Barrel: 15.5 in., 16 in. or 16.5 in. Stock: 6-position telescoping or fixed. Features: A rimfire version of AR-derived M&P tactical autoloader. Operates with blowback action. Quad-mount Picatinny rails, plain barrel or compensator, alloy upper and lower, matte black metal finish. Kryptek Highlander or Muddy Girl camo finishes available.
Price: Standard $449.00
Price: Kryptek Highlander or Muddy Girl camo $499.00
Price: MOE Model with Magpul sights, stock and grip......................$609.00
Price: Performance Center upgrades, threaded barrel $789.00
Price: M&P 15 Sport w/Crimson Trace Red Dot sight.......................$759.00

THOMPSON/CENTER T/CR22
Caliber: .22 LR. Capacities: 10-round rotary magazine. Barrel: 20 in. stainless steel, threaded muzzle. Stock: Hogue overmolded sculpted and ambidextrous thumbhole. Features: Picatinny top rail, sling swivel studs, push-button safety, fully machined aluminum receiver with hole to allow cleaning from rear. From the Smith & Wesson Performance Center.
Price: $497.00

VOLQUARTSEN CLASSIC
Calibers: .22 LR, .22 WMR, .17 HMR. Capacity: 10-round rotary magazine. Barrel: .920-in. stainless bull barrel threaded into receiver. Weight: from 5 lbs. 5oz. Stock: Choice of multiple options, including black Hogue or colored laminate wood sporter style. Sights: Integral Picatinny rail Features: Classic semi-automatic is the foundation of all subsequent models. Match bore and chamber tolerances for bolt-action accuracy from a repeater. Stainless steel CNC-machined receiver. TG2000 for crisp 2.25-lb. trigger pull.
Price: $1,504.00

VOLQUARTSEN ULTRALITE MODSHOT
Caliber: .22 LR. Capacity: 10. Barrel: Forward blow comp, anodized aluminum. Stock: Modshot. Sights: Picatinny rail. Weight: 3.8 lbs. Features: Ultralight design, 2.25-lb. trigger pull, uses Ruger magazines, made in the USA.
Price: $1,769.00

VOLQUARTSEN VF-ORYX
Caliber: 22 LR Capacity: 10-round magazine. Barrel: 18.5-in. free-floating, snake-fluted. Weight: 9 lbs. 3 oz. Stock: MDT Oryx one-piece aluminum chassis. Sights: Integral 20 MOA rail. Features: CNC-machined stainless steel receiver. Barrel threaded into receiver for rigidity. CNC'ed bolt with round titanium firing pin and tuned extractor. TG2000 trigger group with crisp 2.25-lb. pull. Stock tailored for bench, bipod, and prone shooting. Adjustable cheek riser, overmolded pistol grip, and LOP spacer.
Price: $1,944.00
Price: VF-ORYX-S package with Zeiss Conquest............................$3,269.00

WINCHESTER WILDCAT 22 SR (SUPPRESSOR READY)
Caliber: .22 LR. Capacity: 10-round rotary magazine. Barrel: 16.5-in. precision button-rifled chromoly steel with threaded muzzle, thread protector, and recessed target crown. Weight: 4.0 lbs. Length: 34.75 in. Stock: Black polymer ambidextrous skeletonized buttstock with textured grip panels. Sights: Fully adjustable ghost ring rear and ramped post front. Also, integral Picatinny rail. Features: Suppressor-ready version of the company's lightweight repeating rimfire. Rotary magazine system with last round bolt hold open. Dual ambidextrous magazine releases. Reversible manual safety button. Suppressor not included.
Price: $299.00
Price: Wildcat SR True Timber Strata $329.0

Prices given are believed to be accurate at time of publication however, many factors affect retail pricing so exact prices are not possible.

76TH EDITION, 2022 ✦ 425

ANSCHUTZ MODEL 64 MP

Caliber: .22 LR. Capacity: 5-round magazine. Barrel: 25.6-in. heavy match. Weight: 9 lbs. Stock: Multipurpose hardwood with beavertail fore-end. Sights: None. Drilled and tapped for scope or receiver sights. Features: Model 64S BR (benchrest) has 20-in. heavy barrel, adjustable two-stage match-grade trigger, flat beavertail stock. Imported from Germany by Steyr Arms.

Price: $1,399.00

ANSCHUTZ 1416D/1516D CLASSIC

Calibers: .22 LR (1416D888), .22 WMR (1516D). Capacity: 5-round magazine. Barrel: 22.5 in. Weight: 6 lbs. Length: 41 in. overall. Stock: European hardwood with walnut finish; classic style with straight comb, checkered pistol grip and fore-end. Sights: Hooded ramp front, folding leaf rear. Features: Uses Match 64 action. Adjustable single-stage trigger. Receiver grooved for scope mounting. Imported from Germany by Steyr Arms.

Price: 1416D .22 LR $1,199.00
Price: 1416D Classic left-hand $1,249.00
Price: 1516D .22 WMR...$1,249.00
Price: 1416D, thumbhole stock $1,649.00

ANSCHUTZ 1710D CUSTOM

Caliber:.22 LR. Capacity: 5-round magazine. Barrels: 23.75- or 24.25-in. heavy contour. Weights: 6.5–7.375 lbs. Length: 42.5 in. overall. Stock: Select European walnut. Sights: Hooded ramp front, folding leaf rear; drilled and tapped for scope mounting. Features: Match 54 action with adjustable single-stage trigger; roll-over Monte Carlo cheekpiece, slim fore-end with Schnabel tip, Wundhammer palm swell on pistol grip, rosewood grip cap with white diamond insert; skip-line checkering on grip and fore-end. Introduced 1988. Imported from Germany by Steyr Arms.

Price: $2,195.00

BERGARA B-14 RIMFIRE

Caliber: .22 LR. Capacity: 10. Barrel: 18 in., 4140 Bergara. Stock: HMR composite. Sights: None. Weight: 9.25 lbs. Features: Threaded muzzle, B-14R action, Remington 700 accessories compatible.

Price: $1,150.00

BROWNING BL-22

Caliber: .22 LR. Capacity: Tubular magazines, 15+1. Action: Short-throw lever action, side ejection. Rack-and-pinion lever. Barrel: Recessed muzzle. Stock: Walnut, two-piece straight-grip Western style. Trigger: Half-cock hammer safety; fold-down hammer. Sights: Bead post front, folding-leaf rear. Steel receiver grooved for scope mount. Weight: 5–5.4 lbs. Length: 36.75–40.75 in. overall. Features: Action lock provided. Introduced 1996. FLD Grade II Octagon has octagonal 24-in. barrel, silver nitride receiver with scroll engraving, gold-colored trigger. FLD Grade I has satin-nickel receiver, blued trigger, no stock checkering. FLD Grade II has satin-nickel receivers with scroll engraving; gold-colored trigger, cut checkering. Both introduced 2005. Grade I has blued receiver and trigger, no stock checkering. Grade II has gold-colored trigger, cut checkering, blued receiver with scroll engraving. Imported from Japan by Browning.

Price: BL-22 Grade I/II, From ....$620.00–$700.00
Price: BL-22 FLD Grade I/II, From ....$660.00–$750.00
Price: BL-22 FLD, Grade II Octagon $980.00

BROWNING T-BOLT RIMFIRE

Calibers: .22 LR, .17 HMR, .22 WMR. Capacity: 10-round rotary box double helix magazine. Barrel: 22-in. free-floating, semi-match chamber, target muzzle crown. Weight: 4.8 lbs. Length: 40.1 in. overall. Stock: Walnut, maple or composite. Sights: None. Features: Straight-pull bolt action, three-lever trigger adjustable for pull weight, dual action screws, sling swivel studs. Crossbolt lockup, enlarged bolt handle, one-piece dual extractor with integral spring and red cocking indicator band, gold-tone trigger. Top-tang, thumb-operated two-position safety, drilled and tapped for scope mounts. Varmint model has raised Monte Carlo comb, heavy barrel, wide forearm. Introduced 2006. Imported from Japan by Browning. Left-hand models added in 2009.

Price: .22 LR, From..$750.00–$780.00
Price: Composite Target ....$780.00–$800.00
Price: .17 HMR/.22 WMR, From ....$790.00–$830.00

BROWNING T-BOLT TARGET W/ MUZZLE BRAKE

Calibers: .22 LR, .22 WMR, .17 HMR. Capacity: 10-round Double Helix box magazine. Barrel: 16.5-in. heavy bull. Sights: No iron sights. Drilled and tapped. Length: 34.75 in. Weight: 6 lbs. 2 oz. Stock: Black Walnut with satin-finish, checkered, Monte Carlo style. Features: Precision straight-pull bolt-action rimfire. Extra-wide fore-end. Free floating heavy bull target barrel threaded at 1/2x28. Includes removeable muzzle brake. Steel receiver with blued finish. Semi-match chamber and target crown. Top tang safety. Adjustable trigger. Sling studs. Plastic buttplate. Cut checkering at 20 LPI. Gold-plated trigger.

Price: ....$699.00–$739.00

CHIPMUNK SINGLE SHOT

Caliber: .22 Short, Long and Long Rifle or .22 WMR. Manually cocked single-shot bolt-action youth gun. Barrel: 16.125 in. blued or stainless. Weight: 2.6 lbs. Length: 30 in., LOP 11.6 in. Stock: Synthetic, American walnut or laminate. Barracuda model has ergonomic thumbhole stock with raised comb, accessory rail. Sights: Adjustable rear peep, fixed front. From Keystone Sporting Arms.

Price: Synthetic...$163.00-$250.00
Price: Walnut ....$209.00-$270.00
Price: Barracuda ....$258.00-$294.00

COOPER MODEL 57-M REPEATER

Calibers: .22 LR, .22 WMR, .17 HMR, .17 Mach. Barrel: 22 in. or 24 in. Weight: 6.5–7.5 lbs. Stock: Claro walnut, 22 LPI hand checkering. Sights: None furnished. Features: Three rear locking lug, repeating bolt-action with 5-round magazine for .22 LR; 4-round magazine for .22 WMR and 17 HMR. Fully adjustable trigger. Left-hand models add ....$150 to base rifle price. 0.250-in. group rimfire accuracy guarantee at 50 yards; 0.5-in. group centerfire accuracy guarantee at 100 yards. Options include wood upgrades, case-color metalwork, barrel fluting, custom LOP, and many others.

Price: Classic $2,495.00
Price: Custom Classic..$2,995.00
Price: Western Classic $3,795.00
Price: Schnabel $2,595.00
Price: Jackson Squirrel $2,595.00
Price: Jackson Hunter $2,455.00
Price: Mannlicher $4,755.00

Prices given are believed to be accurate at time of publication however, many factors affect retail pricing so exact prices are not possible.

CZ 457 AMERICAN

Calibers: .17 HMR, .22 LR, .22 WMR. Capacity: 5-round detachable magazine. Barrel: 24.8 in. Weight: 6.2 lbs. Stock: Turkish walnut American style with high flat comb. Sights: None. Integral 11mm dovetail scope base. Features: Adjustable trigger, push-to-fire safety, interchangeable barrel system.

Price: $476.00
Price: .17 HMR .22 WMR $496.00
Price: Varmint model..................................$660.00-$762.00

CRICKETT SINGLE SHOT

Caliber: .22 Short, Long and Long Rifle or .22 WMR. Manually cocked single-shot bolt-action. Similar to Chipmunk but with more options and models. Barrel: 16.125 in. blued or stainless. Weight: 3 lbs. Length: 30 in., LOP 11.6 in. Stock: Synthetic, American walnut or laminate. Available in wide range of popular camo patterns and colors. Sights: Adjustable rear peep, fixed front. Drilled and tapped for scope mounting using special Chipmunk base. Alloy model has AR-style buttstock, XBR has target stock and bull barrel, Precision Rifle has bipod and fully adjustable thumbhole stock.

Price: Alloy $300.00
Price: XBR...$380.00-$400.00
Price: Precision Rifle ....$316.00-$416.00
Price: Adult Rifle ....$240.00-$280.00

HENRY LEVER-ACTION RIFLES

Caliber: .22 Long Rifle (15 shot), .22 Magnum (11 shots), .17 HMR (11 shots). Barrel: 18.25 in. round. Weight: 5.5–5.75 lbs. Length: 34 in. overall (.22 LR). Stock: Walnut. Sights: Hooded blade front, open adjustable rear. Features: Polished blue finish; full-length tubular magazine; side ejection; receiver grooved for scope mounting. Introduced 1997. Made in USA by Henry Repeating Arms Co.

Price: H001 Carbine .22 LR $378.00
Price: H001L Carbine .22 LR, Large Loop Lever....................$394.00
Price: H001Y Youth model (33 in. overall, 11-round .22 LR) $378.00
Price: H001M .22 Magnum, 19.25 in. octagonal barrel, deluxe
    walnut stock $525.00
Price: H001V .17 HMR, 20 in. octagonal barrel,
    Williams Fire Sights $578.00
Price: Frontier Threaded Barrel, Suppressor-Ready .22 LR $552.00
Price: Frontier Threaded Barrel, Suppressor-Ready .22 WMR $656.00

HENRY MAGNUM EXPRESS

Caliber: .22 WMR. Capacity: 11-round tubular magazine. Barrel: 19.25-in. round blued steel. Weight: 5.5 lbs. Length: 37.5 in. Stock: American Walnut with Monte Carlo style and checkering. Sights: No iron sights. Includes Picatinny rail for easy optics mounting. Features: Lever-action rifle designed specifically for use with a scope. Quarter-cock safety. Solid rubber recoil pad.

Price: H001 Carbine .22 LR $622.00

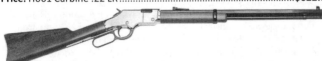

HENRY LEVER-ACTION OCTAGON FRONTIER MODEL

Same as lever rifles except chambered in .17 HMR, .22 Short/Long/LR, .22 Magnum. Barrel: 20 in. octagonal. Sights: Marble's fully adjustable semi-buckhorn rear, brass bead front. **Weight:** 6.25 lbs. Made in USA by Henry Repeating Arms Co.

Price: H001T Lever Octagon .22 S/L/R $473.00
Price: H001TM Lever Octagon .22 Magnum, .17 HMR $578.00

HENRY GOLDEN BOY SERIES

Calibers: .17 HMR, .22 LR (16-shot), .22 Magnum. Barrel: 20 in. octagonal. Weight: 6.25 lbs. Length: 38 in. overall. Stock: American walnut. Sights: Blade front, open rear. Features: Brasslite receiver, brass buttplate, blued barrel and lever. Introduced 1998. Made in USA from Henry Repeating Arms Co.

Price: H004 .22 LR.............................$578.00
Price: H004M .22 Magnum $625.00
Price: H004V .17 HMR $641.00
Price: H004DD .22 LR Deluxe, engraved receiver..........$1,575.00-1,654.00

HENRY SILVER BOY

Calibers: 17 HMR, .22 S/L/LR, .22 WMR. Capacities: Tubular magazine. 12 rounds (.17 HMR and .22 WMR), 16 rounds (.22 LR), 21 rounds (.22 Short). Barrel: 20 in. Stock: American walnut with curved buttplate. Finish: Nickel receiver, barrel band and buttplate. Sights: Adjustable buckhorn rear, bead front. Silver Eagle model has engraved scroll pattern from early original Henry rifle. Offered in same calibers as Silver Boy. Made in USA from Henry Repeating Arms Company.

Price: .22 S/L/LR $630.00
Price: .22 WMR $682.00
Price: .17 HMR $709.00
Price: Silver Eagle.....................$892.00–$945.00

HENRY PUMP ACTION

Caliber: .22 LR. Capacity: 15 rounds. Barrel: 18.25 in. Weight: 5.5 lbs. Length: NA. Stock: American walnut. Sights: Bead on ramp front, open adjustable rear. Features: Polished blue finish; receiver grooved for scope mount; grooved slide handle; two barrel bands. Introduced 1998. Made in USA from Henry Repeating Arms Co.

Price: H003T .22 LR.......................$578.00
Price: H003TM .22 Magnum $620.00

HENRY MINI BOLT YOUTH RIFLE

Caliber: .22 LR, single-shot youth gun. Barrel: 16 in. stainless, 8-groove rifling. Weight: 3.25 lbs. Length: 30 in., LOP 11.5 in. Stock: Synthetic, pistol grip, wraparound checkering and beavertail forearm. Available in black finish or bright colors. Sights: William Fire sights. Features: One-piece bolt configuration manually operated safety.

Price: $289.00

MARLIN MODEL XT-17 SERIES

Caliber: .17 HRM. Capacity: 4- and 7-round, two magazines included. Barrel: 22 in. Weight: 6 lbs. Stock: Black synthetic with palm swell, stippled grip areas, or walnut-finished hardwood with Monte Carlo comb. Laminated stock available. Sights: Adjustable rear, ramp front. Drilled and tapped for scope mounts. Features: Adjustable trigger. Blue or stainless finish.

Price: ....$269.00–$429.00

Prices given are believed to be accurate at time of publication however, many factors affect retail pricing so exact prices are not possible.

76TH EDITION, 2022 ✦ **427**

MARLIN MODEL XT-22 SERIES

Calibers: .22 Short, .22 Long, .22 LR. Capacities: Available with 7-shot detachable box magazine or tubular magazine (17 to 22 rounds). Barrels: 22 in. Varmint model has heavy barrel. Weight: 6 lbs. Stock: Black synthetic, walnut-finished hardwood, walnut or camo. Tubular model available with two-tone brown laminated stock. Finish: Blued or stainless. Sights: Adjustable rear, ramp front. Some models have folding rear sight with a hooded or high-visibility orange front sight. Features: Pro-Fire Adjustable Trigger, Micro-Groove rifling, thumb safety with red cocking indicator. The XT-22M series is chambered for .22 WMR. Made in USA by Marlin Firearms Co.

Price: .... $221.00–$340.00
Price: XT-22M .... $240.00–$270.00

MEACHAM LOW-WALL

Calibers: Any rimfire cartridge. Barrels: 26–34 in. Weight: 7-15 lbs. Sights: none. Tang drilled for Win. base, .375 in. dovetail slot front. Stock: Fancy eastern walnut with cheekpiece; ebony insert in forearm tip. Features: Exact copy of 1885 Winchester. With most Winchester factory options available including double-set triggers. Introduced 1994. Made in USA by Meacham T&H Inc.

Price: From $4,999.00

MOSSBERG MODEL 464 RIMFIRE

Caliber: .22 LR. Capacity: 14-round tubular magazine. Barrel: 20-in. round blued. Weight: 5.6 lbs. Length: 35.75 in. overall. Features: Adjustable sights, straight grip stock, plain hardwood straight stock and fore-end. Lever-action model.

Price: $503.00
Price: SPX Tactical model, adjustable synthetic stock $525.00

MOSSBERG MODEL 817

Caliber: .17 HMR. Capacity: 5-round magazine. Barrel: 21-in. free-floating bull barrel, recessed muzzle crown. Weight: 4.9 lbs. (black synthetic), 5.2 lbs. (wood). Stock: Black synthetic or wood; length of pull, 14.25 in. Sights: Factory-installed Weaver-style scope bases. Features: Blued or brushed chrome metal finishes, crossbolt safety, gun lock. Introduced 2008. Made in USA by O.F. Mossberg & Sons, Inc.

Price: .... $230.00–$274.00

MOSSBERG MODEL 801/802

Caliber: .22 LR Capacity: 10-round magazine. Barrel: 18 in. free-floating. Varmint model has 21-in. heavy barrel. Weight: 4.1–4.6 lbs. Sights: Adjustable rifle. Receiver grooved for scope mount. Stock: Black synthetic. Features: Ergonomically placed magazine release and safety buttons, crossbolt safety, free gun lock. 801 Half Pint has 12.25-in. LOP, 16-in. barrel and weighs 4 lbs. Hardwood stock; removable magazine plug.

Price: Plinkster $242.00
Price: Half Pint $242.00
Price: Varmint $242.00

NEW ULTRA LIGHT ARMS 20RF

Caliber: .22 LR, single-shot or repeater. Barrel: Douglas, length to order. Weight: 5.25 lbs. Length: Varies. Stock: Kevlar/graphite composite, variety of finishes. Sights: None furnished; drilled and tapped for scope mount. Features: Timney trigger, hand-lapped action, button-rifled barrel, hand-bedded action, recoil pad, sling-swivel studs, optional Jewell trigger. Made in USA by New Ultra Light Arms.

Price: 20 RF single shot $1,800.00
Price: 20 RF repeater $1,850.00

ROSSI GALLERY

Caliber: 22 LR. Capacity: 15-round tubular magazine. Barrel: 18-in. round. Weight: 5.3 lbs. Length: 36 in. Stock: Choice of either German Beechwood or black synthetic. Sights: Traditional Buckhorn iron sights on wood model; fiber optics on synthetic model. Features: Pump action reminiscent of classic gallery guns of the 1890s. Polished black metalwork. Hammer fired with cross-bolt safety. Sling studs.

Price: German Beechwood $360.00
Price: Black Polymer $315.00

ROSSI RIO BRAVO

Caliber: 22 LR. Capacity: 15-round tubular magazine. Barrel: 18-in. round. Weight: 5.5 lbs. Length: 36 in. Stock: Choice of either German Beechwood or black synthetic. Sights: Traditional Buckhorn iron sights on wood model; fiber optics on synthetic model. Features: Lever action rimfire based on the company's R92 centerfires. Polished black metal finish. Hammer fired with cross-bolt safety. Sling studs.

Price: German Beechwood $370.00
Price: Black Polymer $370.00

REMINGTON 572 BDL DELUXE FIELDMASTER PUMP

Calibers: .22 Short (20), .22 Long (17) or .22 LR (15), tubular magazine. Barrel: 21 in. round tapered. Weight: 5.5 lbs. Length: 40 in. overall. Stock: Walnut with checkered pistol grip and slide handle. Sights: Big game. Features: Crossbolt safety; removing inner magazine tube converts rifle to single shot; receiver grooved for tip-off scope mount. Another classic rimfire, this model has been in production since 1955.

Price: $723.00

RUGER AMERICAN RIMFIRE RIFLE

Calibers: .17 HMR, .22 LR, .22 WMR. Capacity: 10-round rotary magazine. Barrels: 22-in., or 18-in. threaded. Sights: Williams fiber optic, adjustable. Stock: Composite with interchangeable comb adjustments, sling swivels. Adjustable trigger.

Price: $359.00

RUGER PRECISION RIMFIRE RIFLE

Calibers: .17 HMR, .22 LR, .22 HMR. Capacity: 9 to 15-round magazine. Barrel: 18 in. threaded. Weight: 6.8 lbs. Stock: Quick-fit adjustable with AR-pattern pistol grip, free-floated handguard with Magpul M-LOK slots. Features: Adjustable trigger, oversized bolt handle, Picatinny scope base.

Price: $529.00

SAVAGE MARK II BOLT-ACTION

Calibers: .22 LR, .17 HMR. Capacity: 10-round magazine. Barrel: 20.5 in. Weight: 5.5 lbs. Length: 39.5 in. overall. Stock: Camo, laminate, thumbhole or OD Green stock available Sights: Bead front, open adjustable rear. Receiver grooved for scope mounting. Features: Thumb-operated rotating safety. Blue finish. Introduced 1990. Made in Canada, from Savage Arms, Inc.

Price: .... $228.00–$280.00
Price: Varmint w/heavy barrel $242.00
Price: Camo stock $280.00
Price: OD Green stock $291.00
Price: Multi-colored laminate stock $529.00
Price: Thumbhole laminate stock $469.00

SAVAGE MARK II-FSS STAINLESS RIFLE

Similar to the Mark II except has stainless steel barreled action and black synthetic stock with positive checkering, swivel studs, and 20.75-in. free-floating and button-rifled barrel with magazine. Weighs 5.5 lbs. Introduced 1997. Imported from Canada by Savage Arms, Inc.

Price: $336.00

SAVAGE MODEL 93G MAGNUM BOLT ACTION

Caliber: .22 WMR. Capacity: 5-round magazine. Barrel: 20.75 in. Weight: 5.75 lbs. Length: 39.5 in. overall. Stock: Walnut-finished hardwood with Monte Carlo-type comb, checkered grip and fore-end. Sights: Bead front, adjustable open rear. Receiver grooved for scope mount. Features: Thumb-operated rotary

Prices given are believed to be accurate at time of publication however, many factors affect retail pricing so exact prices are not possible.

safety. Blue finish. Introduced 1994. Made in Canada, from Savage Arms.
Price: Model 93G $285.00
Price: Model 93F (as above with black graphite/fiberglass stock) $364.00
Price: Model 93 BSEV, thumbhole stock $646.00

SAVAGE MODEL 93FSS MAGNUM RIFLE
Similar to Model 93G except stainless steel barreled action and black synthetic stock with positive checkering. Weighs 5.5 lbs. Introduced 1997. Imported from Canada by Savage Arms, Inc.
Price: $353.00

SAVAGE MODEL 93FVSS MAGNUM
Similar to Model 93FSS Magnum except 21-in. heavy barrel with recessed target-style crown, satin-finished stainless barreled action, black graphite/fiberglass stock. Drilled and tapped for scope mounting; comes with Weaver-style bases. Introduced 1998. Imported from Canada by Savage Arms, Inc.
Price: $364.00

SAVAGE B-MAG
Caliber: .17 Win. Super Magnum. Capacity: 8-round rotary magazine. Stock: Synthetic. Weight: 4.5 pounds. Chambered for new Winchester .17 Super Magnum rimfire cartridge that propels a 20-grain bullet at approximately 3,000 fps. Features: Adjustable AccuTrigger, rear locking lugs, new and different bolt-action rimfire design that cocks on close of bolt. New in 2013.
Price: $402.00
Price: Stainless steel receiver and barrel $440.00
Price: Heavy Bbl. Laminate stock $589.00

SAVAGE BRJ SERIES
Similar to Mark II, Model 93 and Model 93R17 rifles but features spiral fluting pattern on a heavy barrel, blued finish and Royal Jacaranda wood laminate stock.
Price: Mark II BRJ, .22 LR $519.00
Price: Model 93 BRJ, .22 Mag. $542.00
Price: Model 93 R17 BRJ, .17 HMR $542.00

SAVAGE TACTICAL RIMFIRE SERIES
Similar to Savage Model BRJ series semi-auto rifles but with matte finish and a tactical-style wood stock.
Price: Mark II TR, .22 LR $533.00
Price: Mark II TRR, .22 LR, three-way accessory rail $627.00
Price: Model 93R17 TR, .17 HMR $558.00
Price: Model 93R17 TRR, .17 HMR, three-way accessory rail $654.00

SAVAGE B SERIES
Calibers: .17 HMR, .22 LR, 22 WMR. Capacity: 10-round rotary magazine. Barrel: 21 in. (16.25 in. threaded heavy barrel on Magnum FV-SR Model). Stock: Black synthetic with target-style vertical pistol grip. Weight: 6 lbs. Features include top tang safety, Accutrigger. Introduced in 2017.
Price: ....$281.00–$445.00

SAVAGE MODEL 42
Calibers/Gauges: Break-open over/under design with .22 LR or .22 WMR barrel over a .410 shotgun barrel. Under-lever operation. Barrel: 20 in. Stock: Synthetic black matte. Weight: 6.1 lbs. Sights: Adjustable rear, bead front. Updated variation of classic Stevens design from the 1940s.
Price $509.00

SAVAGE RASCAL
Caliber: .22 LR. Capacity: Single shot. Barrel: 16.125-in. carbon steel. Weight: 2.71 lbs. Length: 30.6 in. Stock: Synthetic sporter. Upgraded models available with different stock options. Sights: Adjustable peep sights. Features: Micro-rimfire bolt action with short 11.25-inch length of pull for the smallest framed shooters. Cocks by lifting the bolt and unloads without pulling the trigger. User-adjustable AccuTrigger. Feed ramp. Manual safety.
Price $199.00

Price Rascal FV-SR Left Hand $249.00
Price Rascal Target $339.00
Price Rascal Target XP $429.00

SAVAGE RASCAL MINIMALIST
Caliber: .22 LR. Capacity: Single shot. Barrel: 16.125-in. carbon steel, threaded, with protector. Length: 30.625 in. Weight: 3.5 lbs. Stock: Minimalist hybrid laminate design in two color options. Features: Addition to the micro-sized Rascal single shot, bolt-action family. Blued carbon steel receiver. Manual safety. Cocks by lifting the bolt. Unloads without pulling the trigger. 11-degree target crown. Adjustable peep sight. Sling studs. User-adjustable AccuTrigger. Feed ramp. ChevCore Laminate technology with Boyd's stock in two color options: Pink/Purple or Teal/Gray. Short 11.5-in length of pull. Package includes ear plugs and firearms lock.
Price $289.00

STEYR ZEPHYR II
Calibers: .22 LR, .22 WMR, .17 HMR. Capacity: 5-round detachable magazine. Barrel: 19.7 in cold-hammer forged with Mannox finish. Option of standard or threaded. Weight: 5.8 lbs. Length: 39.2 in. Stock: European Walnut with Bavarian cheekpiece and fish scale checkering. Sights: No iron sights. 11mm receiver dovetail. Features: Rebirth of the original Zephyr rifle produced from 1955–1971. Single-stage trigger. Tang safety. Sling swivels. Gold trigger. Pistol grip features inset Steyr logo. Recessed target crown. Dual extractors.
Price $1,099.00

TIKKA T1x MTR
Calibers: .22 LR or .17 HMR. Capacity: 10-round polymer magazine. Barrel: 20-in. cold hammer forged, crossover profile. Weight: 5.7 lbs. Length: 39.6 in. Stock: Modular Black synthetic. Sights: No iron sights. Dovetailed and tapped. Features: Stainless steel bolt for smooth movement and weather resistance. Compatible with most T3x accessories. Action shares same bedding surfaces and inlay footprint with the T3x centerfire rifles. Threaded muzzle. Adjustable single-stage trigger.
Price $529.00

VOLQUARTSEN SUMMIT
Calibers: .22 LR or .17 Mach2. Capacity: 10-round rotary magazine. Barrel: 16.5-in. lightweight carbon fiber with threaded muzzle. Stainless steel tapered barrel also available. Weight: 4 lbs. 13 oz.–7 lbs. 11 oz. Stock: Available with multiple stock options, including black Hogue, colored Magpul, McMillan Sporter, or Laminated Silhouette Wood sporter. Sights: Integral 20 MOA Picatinny rail. Features: Unique straight-pull bolt-action rimfire inspired by the 10/22 platform. Built for both competition shooting and small game hunting. CNC-machined receiver with integral rail. Suppressor ready. Accepts 10/22-style magazines. Crisp 1.75-lb. trigger pull. Made in the USA.
Price $1,252.00

Prices given are believed to be accurate at time of publication however, many factors affect retail pricing so exact prices are not possible.

76TH EDITION, 2022 ✦ 429

ANSCHUTZ 1903 MATCH
Caliber: .22 LR. Capacity: Single-shot. Barrel: 21.25 in. Weight: 8 lbs. Length: 43.75 in. overall. Stock: Walnut-finished hardwood with adjustable cheekpiece; stippled grip and fore-end. Sights: None furnished. Features: Uses Anschutz Match 64 action. A medium weight rifle for intermediate and advanced Junior Match competition. Available from Champion's Choice.
Price: Right-hand **$1,195.00**

ANSCHUTZ 1912 SPORT
Caliber: .22 LR. Barrel: 26 in. match. Weight: 11.4 lbs. Length: 41.7 in. overall. Stock: Non-stained thumbhole stock adjustable in length with adjustable buttplate and cheekpiece adjustment. Flat fore-end raiser block 4856 adjustable in height. Hook buttplate. Sights: None furnished. Features: in. Free rifle in. for women. Smallbore model 1907 with 1912 stock: Match 54 action. Delivered with: Hand stop 6226, fore-end raiser block 4856, screwdriver, instruction leaflet with test target. Available from Champion's Choice.
Price: **$2,995.00**

ANSCHUTZ 1913 SUPER MATCH RIFLE
Same as the Model 1911 except European walnut International-type stock with adjustable cheekpiece, or color laminate, both available with straight or lowered fore-end, adjustable aluminum hook buttplate, adjustable hand stop, weighs 13 lbs., 46 in. overall. Stainless or blued barrel. Available from Champion's Choice.
Price: Right-hand, blued, no sights, walnut stock............ **$3,799.00**

ANSCHUTZ 1907 STANDARD MATCH RIFLE
Same action as Model 1913 but with 0.875-in. diameter 26-in. barrel (stainless or blues). Length: 44.5 in. overall. Weight: 10.5 lbs. Stock: Choice of stock configurations. Vented fore-end. Designed for prone and position shooting ISU requirements; suitable for NRA matches. Also available with walnut flat-forend stock for benchrest shooting. Available from Champion's Choice.
Price: Right-hand, blued, no sights.................................... **$2,385.00**

ARMALITE M15 A4 CARBINE 6.8 & 7.62X39
Calibers: 6.8 Rem., 7.62x39. Barrel: 16 in. chrome-lined with flash suppressor. Weight: 7 lbs. Length: 26.6 in. Features: Front and rear picatinny rails for mounting optics, two-stage tactical trigger, anodized aluminum/phosphate finish.
Price: **$1,107.00**

CZ 457 VARMINT PRECISION CHASSIS
Caliber: .22 LR. Capacity: 5. Barrel: 16.5 or 24 in., suppressor ready, cold hammer-forged, heavy. Stock: Aluminum chassis. Sights: None, integral 11mm dovetail. Weight: 7 lbs. Features: Fully adjustable trigger, receiver mounted push-to-fire safety, swappable barrel system.
Price: **$999.00**

CZ 457 VARMINT PRECISION TRAINER MTR
Caliber: .22 LR. Capacity: 5-round detachable polymer box magazine. Barrel: 16.5-in. cold-hammer forged varmint weight. Sights: No iron sights, integral 11mm dovetail. Length: 42 in. Weight: 7.1 lbs. Stock: Manners carbon-fiber with orange highlights to denote the stock as an upgraded version with special CZ color scheme. Features: Barrel borrowed from the Match Target Rifle (MTR). Match chamber. Heavy barrel threaded at 1/2x28. Designed to provide the same look and feel as a full-size tactical rifle. American-style push-to-fire safety. 60-degree bolt rotation. Fully adjustable trigger. Same swappable barrel system as the Model 455.
Price: **$1,449.00**

HEYM HIGH PERFORMANCE PRECISION RIFLE (HPPR)
Calibers: Standard: .308 Win., 7mm Rem. Mag., .300 Win. Mag. Additional calibers available in 6.5 Creedmoor, 6.5x55, .270 Win., 7x64, .30-06 Spfld., and 8.5x63. Capacity: Detachable box magazine, varies by caliber. Barrel: 26-in. Krupp Steel, hammer forged, threaded, with protector. Sights: Top rail; available paired with Schmidt & Bender Precision Hunter scope. Weight: 8.0 lbs. Stock: PSE Carbon Precision with adjustable comb. Features: Precision shooting bolt actions from Heym built around two models, one SR21 with three-locking-lug turn bolt and the other SR30 straight pull. Single-stage trigger set at 3-lbs. with no creep or overtravel. Guaranteed 5-shot 20mm groups at 100 meters. Sling studs. Rubber recoil pad.
Price: **$4,750.00**

MASTERPIECE ARMS MPA BA PMR COMPETITION RIFLE
Calibers: .308 Win., 6mm Creedmoor, 6.5 Creedmoor. Capacity: 10. Barrel: 26 in., M24 stainless steel, polished. Stock: Aluminum chassis. Sights: None, optional package with MPA 30mm mount and Bushnell scope. Weight: 11.5 lbs. Features: Built-in inclinometer, MPA/Curtis action, match-grade chamber.
Price: .... **$2,999.00-$3,459.00**

REMINGTON 40-XB RANGEMASTER TARGET
Calibers: 15 calibers from .22 BR Remington to .300 Win. Mag. Barrel: 27.25 in. Weight: 11.25 lbs. Length: 47 in. overall. Stock: American walnut, laminated thumbhole or Kevlar with high comb and beavertail fore-end stop. Rubber nonslip buttplate. Sights: None. Scope blocks installed. Features: Adjustable trigger. Stainless barrel and action. Receiver drilled and tapped for sights. Model 40-XB Tactical (2008) chambered in .308 Win., comes with guarantee of 0.75-in. maximum 5-shot groups at 100 yards. Weight: 10.25 lbs. Includes Teflon-coated stainless button-rifled barrel, 1:14 in. twist, 27.25-in. long, three longitudinal flutes. Bolt-action repeater, adjustable 40-X trigger and precision machined aluminum bedding block. Stock is H-S Precision Pro Series synthetic tactical stock, black with green web finish, vertical pistol grip. From Remington Custom Shop.
Price: 40-XB KS, aramid fiber stock, single shot **$2,863.00**
Price: 40-XB KS, aramid fiber stock, repeater **$3,014.00**
Price: 40-XB Tactical .308 Win. **$2,992.00**

REMINGTON 40-XBBR KS
Calibers: Five calibers from .22 BR to .308 Win. Barrel: 20 in. (light varmint class), 24 in. (heavy varmint class). Weight: 7.25 lbs. (light varmint class); 12 lbs. (heavy varmint class). Length: 38 in. (20-in. bbl.), 42 in. (24-in. bbl.). Stock: Aramid fiber. Sights: None. Supplied with scope blocks. Features: Unblued benchrest with stainless steel barrel, trigger adjustable from 1.5 lbs. to 3.5 lbs. Special 2-oz. trigger extra cost. Scope and mounts extra. From Remington Custom Shop.
Price: Single shot **$3,950.00**

REMINGTON 700 PCR ENHANCED
Calibers: .308 Win., .260 Rem., 6.5 Creedmoor. Capacity: 5. Barrel: 24 in., cold hammer-forged, 5R rifling, threaded. Stock: Anodized aluminum chassis, Magpul Gen 3 PRS. Sights: Picatinny rail. Weight: 11 lbs. Features: Aluminum handguard with square drop, X-Mark Pro adjustable trigger, tactical bolt knob.
Price: **$1,199.00**

ROCK RIVER ARMS RBG-1S

Calibers: .308 Win./7.62X51 NATO or 6.5 Creedmoor. Capacity: AICS/Magpul compatible box magazine. Barrel: 20-, 22-, or 24-in. stainless steel air-gauged, cryo-treated. Weight: 10.2 lbs. Length: 39.5–43.5 in. Stock: KRG adjustable chassis in tan, black or green. Sights: 20 MOA rail. Also has standard scope base holes drilled for use with conventional ring mounts. Features: Rock River's first precision bolt-action rifles series. Precision aluminum bedding. One-piece, interchangeable two-lug bolt. Oversized knurled handle. TriggerTech trigger standard, with option of Timney upgrade. Toolless field adjustability. Guaranteed sub-MOA accuracy.

Price: **$4,235.00**

SAVAGE 110 ELITE PRECISION

Calibers: .223 Rem., 6mm Creedmoor, 6.5 Creedmoor, .308 Win., .300 Win. Mag., .300 PRC, .338 Lapua. Capacity: 5- or 10-round AICS pattern detachable box magazine. Barrel: 26- or 30-in. stainless steel. Weight: 12.6–14.95 lbs. Stock: Modular Driven Technologies (MDT) Adjustable Core Competition aluminum chassis with Grey Cerakote finish. Sights: 20 MOA rail. Features: Factory blueprinted action. ARCA Rail along entire length of chassis. Titanium Nitride bolt body. User-adjustable AccuTrigger. MDT vertical grip. Self-timing taper aligned muzzle brake on short action calibers only.

Price: ....**$1,999.00–$2,199.00**

SEEKINS PRECISION HAVAK BRAVO

Calibers: 6mm Creedmoor, 6.5 Creedmoor, 6.5 PRC, .308 Win. Capacity: 5-round box magazine. Barrel: 24-in. 5R 416 stainless steel with threaded muzzle. Weight: 9.8 lbs. Stock: KRG Bravo Chassis in Black. OD Green, FDE, or Stealth Gray. Sights: 20 MOA Picatinny rail with five 8-32 screws. Features: Specialty bolt-action rifle built for hard-running, from SWAT to precision shooting. Matte black Cerakoted barreled action. Integrated recoil lug and M16-style extractor. Bolt with four locking lugs and 90-degree throw. Removeable bolt head. Extended magazine release.

Price: TRG-22 ....**$1,950.00**

SEEKINS PRECISION HAVAK ELEMENT

Calibers: .308 Win., 6mm Creedmoor, 6.5 PRC, 6.5 Creedmoor. Capacity: 3 to 5. Barrel: 21 in., Mountain Hunter contour, spiral fluted, threaded. Stock: Carbon composite. Sights: 20 MOA picatinny rail. Weight: 5.5 lbs. Features: Timney Elite Hunter trigger, M16-style extractor, 7075 aerospace aluminum/stainless steel body.

Price: **$2,795.00**

SIG SAUER CROSS RIFLE

Calibers: .277 Sig Fury, .308 Win., 6.5 Creedmoor. Capacity: 5. Barrel: 16 to 18 in., stainless steel. Stock: Sig precision, polymer/alloy, folding. Sights: Picatinny rail. Weight: 6.5 to 6.8 lbs. Features: M-LOK rail, two-stage match trigger.

Price: **$1,779.00**

SAKO TRG-22 BOLT-ACTION

Calibers: .308 Win., .260 Rem, 6.5 Creedmoor, .300 Win Mag, .338 Lapua. Capacity: 5-round magazine. Barrel: 26 in. Weight: 10.25 lbs. Length: 45.25 in. overall. Stock: Reinforced polyurethane with fully adjustable cheekpiece and buttplate. Sights: None furnished. Optional quick-detachable, one-piece scope mount base, 1 in. or 30mm rings. Features: Resistance-free bolt, free-floating heavy stainless barrel, 60-degree bolt lift. Two-stage trigger is adjustable for length, pull, horizontal or vertical pitch. TRG-42 has similar features but has long action and is chambered for .338 Lapua. Imported from Finland by Beretta USA.

Price: TRG-22 ....**$3,495.00**
Price: TRG-22 with folding stock **$6,400.00**
Price: TRG-42 ....**$4,445.00**
Price: TRG-42 with folding stock **$7,400.00**

SPRINGFIELD ARMORY M1A/M-21 TACTICAL MODEL

Similar to M1A Super Match except special sniper stock with adjustable cheekpiece and rubber recoil pad. Weighs 11.6 lbs. From Springfield Armory.

Price: **$3,619.00**
Price: Krieger stainless barrel...........................**$4,046.00**

Prices given are believed to be accurate at time of publication however, many factors affect retail pricing so exact prices are not possible.

76TH EDITION, 2022 ⊕ **431**

ACCU-TEK AT-380 II ACP
Caliber: 380 ACP. Capacity: 6-round magazine. Barrel: 2.8 in. Weight: 23.5 oz. Length: 6.125 in. overall. Grips: Textured black composition. Sights: Blade front, rear adjustable for windage. Features: Made from 17-4 stainless steel, has an exposed hammer, manual firing-pin safety block and trigger disconnect. Magazine release located on the bottom of the grip. American made, lifetime warranty. Comes with two 6-round stainless steel magazines and a California-approved cable lock. Introduced 2006. Made in USA by Excel Industries.
Price: Satin stainless **$289.00**

ACCU-TEK HC-380
Similar to AT-380 II except has a 13-round magazine.
Price: **$330.00**

ACCU-TEK LT-380
Similar to AT-380 II except has a lightweight aluminum frame. Weight: 15 ounces.
Price: **$324.00**

AMERICAN CLASSIC 1911-A1 II SERIES
Caliber: .45 ACP, 9mm, .38 Super. Capacity: 8+1 magazine Barrel: 5 in. Grips: Checkered walnut. Sights: Novak-style rear, fixed front. Finish: Blue or hard chromed. Other variations include Trophy model with checkered mainspring housing, fiber optic front sight, hard-chrome finish.
Price: .... **$627-$700.00**

AMERICAN CLASSIC AMIGO SERIES
Caliber: .45 ACP. Capacity: 7+1. Same features as Commander size with 3.6-in. bull barrel and Officer-style frame.
Price: .... **$714.00-$813.00**

AMERICAN CLASSIC BX SERIES
Calibers: .45 ACP, 9mm. Capacity: 14- or 17-round magazine. Barrel: 5 in. Grips: Checkered aluminum. Sights: Mil-Spec style. Finish: Blue.
Price: **$774.00**

AMERICAN CLASSIC COMMANDER
Caliber: .45 ACP. Same features as 1911-A1 model except is Commander size with 4.25-in. barrel.
Price: .... **$624.00–$795.00**

AMERICAN CLASSIC COMPACT COMMANDER SERIES
Caliber: .45 ACP. Capacity: 7-round magazine. Barrel: 4.25 in. Grips: Textured hardwood. Sights: Fixed Novak style. Finish: Blue, hard chrome, two-tone.
Price: .... **$714.00-$812.00**

AMERICAN CLASSIC TROPHY
Caliber: .45 ACP. Capacity: 8-round magazine. Barrel: 5 in. Grips: Textured hardwood. Sights: Fixed, fiber-optic front/Novak rear. Finish: Hard chrome. Features: Front slide serrations, ambidextrous thumb safety.
Price: **$819.00**

AMERICAN TACTICAL IMPORTS MILITARY 1911
Caliber: .45 ACP. Capacity: 7+1 magazine. Barrel: 5 in. Grips: Textured mahogany. Sights: Fixed military style. Finish: Blue. Also offered in Commander and Officer's sizes and Enhanced model with additional features.
Price: .... **$500.00–$899.00**

AMERICAN TACTICAL IMPORTS GSG 1911
Caliber: .22 LR. Capacity: 10+1 magazine. Weight: 34 oz. Other features and dimensions similar to centerfire 1911.
Price: **$299.00**

AUTO-ORDNANCE 1911A1
Caliber: 45 ACP. Capacity: 7-round magazine. Barrel: 5 in. Weight: 39 oz. Length: 8.5 in. overall. Grips: Brown checkered plastic with medallion. Sights: Blade front, rear drift-adjustable for windage. Features: Same specs as 1911A1 military guns-parts interchangeable. Frame and slide blued; each radius has non-glare finish. Introduced 2002. Made in USA by Kahr Arms.
Price: 1911BKO Parkerized, plastic grips **$673.00**
Price: 1911BKOW Black matte finish, wood grips **$689.00**
Price: 1911BKOWWC1 Victory Girls Special **$750.00**

BAER 1911 BOSS .45
Caliber: .45 ACP. Capacity: 8+1 capacity. Barrel: 5 in. Weight: 37 oz. Length: 8.5 in. overall. Grips: Premium Checkered Cocobolo Grips. Sights: Low-Mount LBC Adj. Sight, Red Fiber Optic Front. Features: Speed Trigger, Beveled Mag Well, Rounded for Tactical. Rear cocking serrations on the slide, Baer fiber optic front sight (red), flat mainspring housing, checkered at 20 LPI, extended combat safety, Special tactical package, chromed complete lower, blued slide, (2) 8-round premium magazines.
Price: **$2,636.00**

BAER 1911 CUSTOM CARRY
Caliber: .45 ACP. Capacity: 7- or 10-round magazine. Barrel: 5 in. Weight: 37 oz. Length: 8.5 in. overall. Grips: Checkered walnut. Sights: Baer improved ramp-style dovetailed front, Novak low-mount rear. Features: Baer forged NM frame, slide and barrel with stainless bushing. Baer speed trigger with 4-lb. pull. Partial listing shown. Made in USA by Les Baer Custom, Inc.
Price: Custom Carry 5, blued **$2,190.00**
Price: Custom Carry 5, stainless **$2,290.00**
Price: Custom Carry 5, 9mm or .38 Super **$2,625.00**
Price: Custom Carry 4 Commanche-length, blued **$2,190.00**
Price: Custom Carry 4 Commanche-length, .38 Super **$2,550.00**

Prices given are believed to be accurate at time of publication however, many factors affect retail pricing so exact prices are not possible.

BAER 1911 PREMIER II

Calibers: .38 Super, .45 ACP. Capacity: 7- or 10-round magazine. Barrel: 5 in. Weight: 37 oz. Length: 8.5 in. overall. Grips: Checkered rosewood, double diamond pattern. Sights: Baer dovetailed front, low-mount Bo-Mar rear with hidden leaf. Features: Baer NM forged steel frame and barrel with stainless bushing, deluxe Commander hammer and sear, beavertail grip safety with pad, extended ambidextrous safety; flat mainspring housing; 30 LPI checkered front strap. Made in USA by Les Baer Custom, Inc.

Price: 5 in. .45 ACP **$2,2,245.00**
Price: 5 in. .38 Super, 9mm **$2,968.00**
Price: 6 in. .45 ACP, .38 Super, 9mm .... $2,461.00-**$2,925.00**
Price: Super-Tac, .45 ACP, .38 Super $2,729.00-**3,917.00**
Price: 6-in Hunter 10mm **$3090.00**

BAER 1911 S.R.P.

Caliber: .45 ACP. Barrel: 5 in. Weight: 37 oz. Length: 8.5 in. overall. Grips: Checkered walnut. Sights: Trijicon night sights. Features: Similar to the F.B.I. contract gun except uses Baer forged steel frame. Has Baer match barrel with supported chamber, complete tactical action. Has Baer Ultra Coat finish. Introduced 1996. Made in USA by Les Baer Custom, Inc.
Price: Government or Commanche Length **$2,925.00**

BAER 1911 STINGER

Calibers: .45 ACP or .38 Super. Capacity: 7-round magazine. Barrel: 5 in. Weight: 34 oz. Length: 8.5 in. overall. Grips: Checkered cocobolo. Sights: Baer dovetailed front, low-mount Bo-Mar rear with hidden leaf. Features: Baer NM frame. Baer Commanche slide, Officer's style grip frame, beveled mag well. Made in USA by Les Baer Custom, Inc.
Price: .45 ACP .... **$2,307.00–$2,379.00**
Price: .38 Super **$2,925.00**

BAER HEMI 572

Caliber: .45 ACP. Based on Les Baer's 1911 Premier I pistol and inspired by Chrysler 1970 Hemi Cuda muscle car. Features: Double serrated slide, Baer fiber optic front sight with green insert, VZ black recon grips with hex-head screws, hard chrome finish on all major components, Dupont S coating on barrel, trigger, hammer, ambi safety and other controls.
Price: **$2,770.00**

BAER ULTIMATE MASTER COMBAT

Calibers: .45 ACP or .38 Super. A full house competition 1911 offered in 8 variations including 5 or 6-inch barrel, PPC Distinguished or Open class, Bullseye Wadcutter class and others. Features include double serrated slide, fitted slide to frame, checkered front strap and trigger guard, serrated rear of slide, extended ejector, tuned extractor, premium checkered grips, blued finish and two 8-round magazines.
Price: Compensated .45 .... **$3,131.00**
Price: Compensated .38 Super **$3,234.00**

BAER 1911 MONOLITH S

Calibers: .45 ACP, .38 Super, 9mm, .40 S&W. A full house competition 1911 offered in 14 variations. Unique feature is extra-long dust cover that matches the length of the slide and reduces muzzle flip. Features include flat-bottom double serrated slide, low mount LBC adjustable sight with hidden rear leaf, dovetail front sight, flat serrated mainspring housing, premium checkered grips, blued finish and two 8-round magazines.
Price: .45 .... From **$2,419.00**
Price: .38 Super, .40 S&W .... From **$2,790.00**

BAER KENAI SPECIAL

Caliber: 10mm. Capacity: 9-round magazine. Barrel: 5 in. Features: Hard-chrome finish, double serrated slide, Baer fiber optic front sight with green or red insert, low-mount LBC adjustable rear sight, Baer black recon grips, special bear paw logo, flat serrated mainspring housing, lowered and flared ejection port, extended safety.
Price: **$3,630.00**

BAER GUNSITE PISTOL

Calibers: .45 ACP. Capacity: 8-round magazine. Barrel: 5 in. Features: double serrated slide, fitted slide to frame, flat serrated mainspring housing, flared and lowered ejection port, extended tactical thumb safety, fixed rear sight, dovetail front sight with night sight insert, all corners rounded, extended ejector, tuned extractor, premium checkered grips, blued finish and two 8-round magazines. Gunsite Raven logo on grips and slide.
Price: **$2,255.00**

BERETTA M92/96 A1 SERIES

Calibers: 9mm, .40 S&W. Capacities: 15-round magazine; .40 S&W, 12 rounds (M96 A1). Barrel: 4.9 in. Weight: 33-34 oz. Length: 8.5 in. Sights: Fiber optic front, adjustable rear. Features: Same as other models in 92/96 family except for addition of accessory rail.
Price: **$775.00**

BERETTA MODEL 92FS

Caliber: 9mm. Capacity: 10-round magazine. Barrels: 4.9 in., 4.25 in. (Compact). Weight: 34 oz. Length: 8.5 in. overall. Grips: Checkered black plastic. Sights: Blade front, rear adjustable for windage. Tritium night sights available. Features: Double action. Extractor acts as chamber loaded indicator, squared trigger guard, grooved front and backstraps, inertia firing pin. Matte or blued finish. Introduced 1977. Made in USA
Price: **$699.00**
Price: Inox **$850.00**

BERETTA MODEL 92G ELITE

Calibers: 9mm. Capacities: 15-round magazine. Barrel: 4.7 in. Weight: 33 oz. Length: 8.5 in. Sights: Fiber optic front, square notch rear. Features: M9A1 frame with M9A3 slide, front and rear serrations, ultra-thin VZ/LTT G10 grips, oversized mag release button, skeletonized trigger, ships with three magazines.
Price: **$1,100.00**

BERETTA M9 .22 LR

Caliber: .22 LR. Capacity: 10 or 15-round magazine. Features: Black Brunitron finish, interchangeable grip panels. Similar to centerfire 92/M9 with same operating controls, lighter weight (26 oz.).
Price: **$430.00**

Prices given are believed to be accurate at time of publication however, many factors affect retail pricing so exact prices are not possible.

76TH EDITION, 2022 ✦ **433**

BERETTA MODEL PX4 STORM

Calibers: 9mm, 40 S&W. Capacities: 17 (9mm Para.); 14 (40 S&W). Barrel: 4 in. Weight: 27.5 oz. Grips: Black checkered w/3 interchangeable backstraps. Sights: 3-dot system coated in Superluminova; removable front and rear sights. Features: DA/SA, manual safety/hammer decocking lever (ambi) and automatic firing pin block safety. Picatinny rail. Comes with two magazines (17/10 in 9mm Para. and 14/10 in 40 S&W). Removable hammer unit. American made by Beretta. Introduced 2005.

Price: 9mm or .40 .... **$650.00**
Price: .45 ACP **$700.00**
Price: .45 ACP SD (Special Duty) **$1,150.00**

BERETTA MODEL PX4 STORM SUB-COMPACT

Calibers: 9mm, 40 S&W. Capacities: 13 (9mm); 10 (40 S&W). Barrel: 3 in. Weight: 26.1 oz. Length: 6.2 in. overall. Grips: NA. Sights: NA. Features: Ambidextrous manual safety lever, interchangeable backstraps included, lock breech and tilt barrel system, stainless steel barrel, Picatinny rail.

Price: **$650.00**

BERETTA MODEL APX SERIES

Calibers: 9mm, 40 S&W. Capacities: 10, 17 (9mm); 10, 15 (40 S&W). Barrel: 4.25 or 3.7 in. (Centurion). Weight: 28, 29 oz. Length: 7.5 in. Sights: Fixed. Features: Striker fired, 3 interchangeable backstraps included, reversible mag release button, ambidextrous slide stop. Centurion is mid-size with shorter grip and barrel. Magazine capacity is two rounds shorter than standard model.

Price: **$575.00**

BERETTA MODEL M9

Caliber: 9mm. Capacity: 15. Barrel: 4.9 in. Weights: 32.2-35.3 oz. Grips: Plastic. Sights: Dot and post, low profile, windage adjustable rear. Features: DA/SA, forged aluminum alloy frame, delayed locking-bolt system, manual safety doubles as decocking lever, combat-style trigger guard, loaded chamber indicator. Comes with two magazines (15/10). American made by Beretta. Introduced 2005.

Price: **$675.00**

BERETTA MODEL M9A1

Caliber: 9mm. Capacity: 15. Barrel: 4.9 in. Weights: 32.2-35.3 oz. Grips: Plastic. Sights: Dot and post, low profile, windage adjustable rear. Features: Same as M9, but also includes integral Mil-Std-1913 Picatinny rail, has checkered front and backstrap. Comes with two magazines (15/10). American made by Beretta. Introduced 2005.

Price: **$775.00**

BERETTA M9A3

Caliber: 9mm. Capacity: 10 or 15. Features: Same general specifications as M9A1 with safety lever able to be converted to decocker configuration. Flat Dark Earth finish. Comes with three magazines, Vertec-style thin grip.

Price: **$1,100.00**

BERETTA BU9 NANO

Caliber: 9mm. Capacity: 6- or 8-round magazine. Barrel: 3.07 in. Weight: 17.7 oz. Length: 5.7 in. overall. Grips: Polymer. Sights: 3-dot low profile. Features: Double-action only, striker fired. Replaceable grip frames. Polymer frames offered in black, RE Blue, FDE, Rosa or Sniper Grey colors.

Price: **$450.00**

BERETTA PICO

Caliber: .380 ACP. Capacity: 6-round magazine. Barrel: 2.7 in. Weight: 11.5 oz. Length: 5.1 in. overall. Grips: Integral with polymer frame. Interchangeable backstrap. Sights: White outline rear. Features: Adjustable, quick-change. Striker-fired, double-action only operation. Ambidextrous magazine release and slide release. Available with Black, RE Blue, FDE or Lavender frame. Ships with two magazines, one flush, one with grip extension. Made in the USA.

Price: **$300.00**

BERSA THUNDER 45 ULTRA COMPACT

Caliber: .45 ACP. Barrel: 3.6 in. Weight: 27 oz. Length: 6.7 in. overall. Grips: Anatomically designed polymer. Sights: White outline rear. Features: Double action; firing pin safeties, integral locking system. Available in matte or duo-tone. Introduced 2003. Imported from Argentina by Eagle Imports, Inc.

Price: Thunder 45, matte blue **$500.00**

BERSA THUNDER 380 SERIES

Caliber: .380 ACP. Capacity: 7 rounds. Barrel: 3.5 in. Weight: 23 oz. Length: 6.6 in. overall. Features: Otherwise similar to Thunder 45 Ultra Compact. 380 DLX has 9-round capacity. 380 Concealed Carry has 8-round capacity. Imported from Argentina by Eagle Imports, Inc.

Price: Thunder Matte **$335.00**
Price: Thunder Satin Nickel **$355.00**
Price: Thunder Duo-Tone **$355.00**
Price: Thunder Duo-Tone with Crimson Trace Laser Grips **$555.00**
Price: Thunder CC Duo-Tone with aluminum frame **$346.00**

BERSA THUNDER 9 ULTRA COMPACT/40 SERIES
Calibers: 9mm, 40 S&W. Barrel: 3.5 in. Weight: 24.5 oz. Length: 6.6 in. overall. Features: Otherwise similar to Thunder 45 Ultra Compact. 9mm Para. High Capacity model has 17-round capacity. 40 High Capacity model has 13-round capacity. Imported from Argentina by Eagle Imports, Inc.
Price: **$500.00**

BERSA THUNDER 22
Caliber: .22 LR. Capacity: 10-round magazine. Weight: 19 oz. Features: Similar to Thunder .380 Series except for caliber. Alloy frame and slide. Finish: Matte black, satin nickel or duo-tone.
Price: **$320.00**

BERSA THUNDER PRO XT
Caliber: 9mm. Capacity: 17-round magazine. Barrel: 5 in. Weight: 34 oz. Grips: Checkered black polymer. Sights: Adjustable rear, dovetail fiber optic front. Features: Available with matte or duo-tone finish. Traditional double/single action design developed for competition. Comes with five magazines.
Price: **$923.00**

BROWNING 1911-22 COMPACT
Caliber: .22 LR Capacity: 10-round magazine. Barrel: 3.625 in. Weight: 15 oz. Length: 6.5 in. overall. Grips: Brown composite. Sights: Fixed. Features: Slide is machined aluminum with alloy frame and matte blue finish. Blowback action and single action trigger with manual thumb and grip safeties. Works, feels and functions just like a full-size 1911. It is simply scaled down and chambered in the best of all practice rounds: .22 LR for focus on the fundamentals.
Price: **$600.00**

BROWNING 1911-22 A1
Caliber: .22 LR, Capacity: 10-round magazine. Barrel: 4.25 in. Weight: 16 oz. Length: 7.0625 in. overall. Grips: Brown composite. Sights: Fixed. Features: Slide is machined aluminum with alloy frame and matte blue finish. Blowback action and single action trigger with manual thumb and grip safeties. Works, feels and functions just like a full-size 1911. It is simply scaled down and chambered in the best of all practice rounds: .22 LR for focus on the fundamentals.
Price: **$600.00**

BROWNING 1911-22 BLACK LABEL
Caliber: .22 LR. Capacity: 10-round magazine. Barrels: 4.25 in. or 3.625 in. (Compact model). Weight: 14 oz. overall. Features: Other features are similar to standard 1911-22 except for this model's composite/polymer frame, extended grip safety, stippled black laminated grip, skeleton trigger and hammer. Available with accessory rail (shown). Suppressor Ready model has threaded muzzle protector, 4.875-inch barrel.
Price: **$640.00**
Price: With Rail **$720.00**
Price: Suppressor Ready model.. **$800.00**

BROWNING 1911-22 POLYMER DESERT TAN
Caliber: .22 LR. Capacity: 10-round magazine. Barrels: 4.25 in. or 3.625 in. Weight: 13–14 oz. overall. Features: Other features are similar to standard 1911-22 except for this model's composite/polymer frame. Also available with pink composite grips.
Price: **$580.00**

BROWNING 1911-380
Caliber: .380 ACP. Capacity: 8-round magazine. Barrels: 4.25 in. or 3.625 in. (Compact). Weight: 16 to 17.5 oz. Features: Aluminum or stainless slide, polymer frame with or without rail. Features are virtually identical to those on the 1911-22. 1911-380 Pro has three-dot combat or night sights, G10 grips, accessory rail. Medallion Pro has checkered walnut grips.
Price: **$670.00**
Price: Pro, Medallion Pro.. **$800.00–$910.00**

BROWNING BUCK MARK CAMPER UFX

Caliber: .22 LR. Capacity: 10-round magazine. Barrel: 5.5-in. tapered bull. Weight: 34 oz. Length: 9.5 in. overall. Grips: Overmolded Ultragrip Ambidextrous. Sights: Pro-Target adjustable rear, ramp front. Features: Matte blue receiver, matte blue or stainless barrel.
Price: Camper UFX.. $390.00
Price: Camper UFX stainless $430.00

BROWNING BUCK MARK HUNTER

Caliber: .22 LR. Capacity: 10-round magazine. Barrel: 7.25-in. heavy tapered bull. Weight: 38 oz. Length: 11.3 in. overall. Grips: Cocobolo target. Sights: Pro-Target adjustable rear, Tru-Glo/Marble's fiber-optic front. Integral scope base on top rail. Scope in photo not included. Features: Matte blue.
Price: $500.00

BROWNING BUCK PRACTICAL URX

Caliber: .22 LR. Capacity: 10-round magazine. Barrels: 5.5-in. tapered bull or 4-in. slab-sided (Micro). Weight: 34 oz. Length: 9.5 in. overall. Grips: Ultragrip RX Ambidextrous. Sights: Pro-Target adjustable rear, Tru-Glo/Marble's fiber-optic front. Features: Matte gray receiver, matte blue barrel.
Price: $479.00
Price: Stainless $470.00
Price: Micro $470.00

BROWNING BUCK MARK MEDALLION ROSEWOOD

Caliber: .22 LR. Capacity: 10-round magazine. Barrel: 5.5-in. Grips: Laminate rosewood colored with gold Buckmark. Sights: Pro-Target adjustable rear, TruGlo/Marble's fiber-optic front. Finish: Matte black receiver, blackened stainless barrel with polished flats. Gold-plated trigger.
Price: $510.00

BROWNING BUCK MARK CONTOUR STAINLESS URX

Caliber: .22 LR. Capacity: 10-round magazine. Barrel: 5.5 or 7.25-in. special contour. Grips: Checkered, textured. Sights: Pro-Target adjustable rear, Pro-Target front. Integral scope base on top rail. Finish: Matte black receiver, blackened stainless barrel with polished flats. Gold-plated trigger.
Price: $550.00

BROWNING BUCK MARK FIELD TARGET SUPPRESSOR READY

Caliber: .22 LR. Capacity: 10-round magazine. Barrel: 5.5-in. heavy bull, suppressor ready. Grips: Cocobolo target. Sights: Pro-Target adjustable rear, Tru-Glo/Marble's fiber-optic front. Integral scope base on top rail. Scope in photo not included. Features: Matte blue.
Price: $600.00

CHIAPPA 1911-22

Caliber: .22 LR. Capacity: 10-round magazine. Barrel: 5 in. Weight: 33.5 oz. Length: 8.5 in. Grips: Two-piece wood. Sights: Fixed. Features: A faithful replica of the famous John Browning 1911A1 pistol. Fixed barrel design. Available in black, OD green or tan finish. Target and Tactical models have adjustable sights.
Price: From .... $269.00–$408.00

CHIAPPA M9-22 STANDARD

Caliber: .22 LR. Barrel: 5 in. Weight: 2.3 lbs. Length: 8.5 in. Grips: Black molded plastic or walnut. Sights: Fixed front sight and windage adjustable rear sight. Features: The M9 9mm has been a U.S. standard-issue service pistol since 1990. Chiappa's M9-22 is a replica of this pistol in 22 LR. The M9-22 has the same weight and feel as its 9mm counterpart but has an affordable 10-shot magazine for the .22 Long Rifle cartridge, which makes it a true rimfire reproduction. Comes standard with steel trigger, hammer assembly and a 1/2x28 threaded barrel.
Price: $339.00

Prices given are believed to be accurate at time of publication however, many factors affect retail pricing so exact prices are not possible.

CHIAPPA M9-22 TACTICAL

Caliber: .22 LR. Barrel: 5 in. Weight: 2.3 lbs. Length: 8.5 in. Grips: Black molded plastic. Sights: Fixed front sight and Novak-style rear sights. Features: The M9-22 Tactical model comes with a faux suppressor (this ups the "cool factor" on the range and extends the barrel to make it even more accurate). It also has a 1/2x28 thread adaptor that can be used with a legal suppressor.
Price: $419.00

CHRISTENSEN ARMS 1911 SERIES

Calibers: .45 ACP, 9mm. Barrels: 4.25 in., 5 or 5.5 in. Features: Models are offered with aluminum, stainless steel or titanium frame with hand-fitted slide, match-grade barrel, tritium night sights and G10 Operator grip panels.
Price: Aluminum frame... $1,995.00
Price: Stainless $2,895.00
Price: Titanium.................................... $4,795.00–$5,095.00

CITADEL M-1911

Calibers: .45 ACP, 9mm. Capacity: 7 (.45), 8 (9mm). Barrels: 5 or 3.5 in. Weight: 2.3 lbs. Length: 8.5 in. Grips: Cocobolo. Sights: Low-profile combat fixed rear, blade front. Finish: Matte black. Features: Extended grip safety, lowered and flared ejection port, beveled mag well, Series 70 firing system. Built by Armscor (Rock Island Armory) in the Philippines and imported by Legacy Sports.
Price: $599.00

CIMARRON MODEL 1911

Caliber: .45 ACP. Barrel: 5 in. Weight: 37.5 oz. Length: 8.5 in. overall. Grips: Checkered walnut. Features: A faithful reproduction of the original pattern of the Model 1911 with Parkerized finish and lanyard ring. Polished or nickel finish available.
Price: $571.00
Price: Polished blue or nickel.............................. $800.00

CIMARRON MODEL 1911 WILD BUNCH

Caliber: .45 ACP. Barrel: 5 in. Weight: 37.5 oz. Length: 8.5 in. overall. Grips: Checkered walnut. Features: Original WWI 1911 frame with flat mainspring housing, correct markings, polished blue finish, comes with tanker shoulder holster.
Price: $956.00

COBRA ENTERPRISES FS32, FS380

Calibers: .32 ACP or .380 ACP. Capacity: 7 rounds. Barrel: 3.5 in. Weight: 2.1 lbs. Length: 6.375 in. overall. Grips: Black molded synthetic integral with frame. Sights: Fixed. Made in USA by Cobra Enterprises of Utah, Inc.
Price: .... $138.00–$250.00

COBRA ENTERPRISES PATRIOT SERIES

Calibers: .380, 9mm or .45 ACP. Capacities: 6-, 7- or 10-round magazine. Barrel: 3.3 in. Weight: 20 oz. Length: 6 in. overall. Grips: Black polymer. Sights: Fixed. Features: Bright chrome, satin nickel or black finish. Made in USA by Cobra Enterprises of Utah, Inc.
Price: .... $349.00–$395.00

COBRA DENALI

Caliber: .380 ACP. Capacity: 5 rounds. Barrel: 2.8 in. Weight: 22 oz. Length: 5.4 in. Grips: Black molded synthetic integral with frame. Sights: Fixed. Features: Made in USA by Cobra Enterprises of Utah, Inc.
Price: $179.00

COLT 1903 RE-ISSUE SERIES

Caliber: .32 ACP. Capacity: 8-round magazine. Barrel: 3.9 in. Grips: Checkered walnut. Sights: Fixed, round front/retro rear. Finish: Parkerized, Royal Blue, Blued or Chrome. Features: Reproduction of Colt 1903 pistol, marked "U.S. PROPERTY" on right side of frame.
Price: (Blued) $1,338.00
Price: (Chrome) $1,647.00
Price: (Parkerized)... $1,211.00
Price: (Royal Blue)... $1,544.00

COLT 1911 CLASSIC

Caliber: .45 ACP. Capacity: 7-round magazine. Barrel: 5 in. Grips: Double diamond checkered rosewood. Sights: Fixed-post front/retro rear. Finish: Blue. Features: Series 70 firing system.
Price: $799.00

COLT 1911 BLACK ARMY

Caliber: .45 ACP. Capacity: 7-round magazine. Barrel: 5 in. Grips: Double diamond checkered rosewood. Sights: Fixed, round front/retro rear. Finish: Matte blue. Features: Series 70 firing system, lanyard loop, reproduction of WWI U.S. Military model.
Price: $999.00

COLT MODEL 1991 MODEL O

Caliber: .45 ACP. Capacity: 7-round magazine. Barrel: 5 in. Weight: 38 oz. Length: 8.5 in. overall. Grips: Checkered black composition. Sights: Ramped blade front, fixed square notch rear, high profile. Features: Matte finish. Continuation of serial number range used on original G.I. 1911A1 guns. Comes with one magazine and molded carrying case. Introduced 1991. Series 80 firing system.
Price: Blue $799.00
Price: Stainless $879.00

COLT XSE SERIES MODEL O COMBAT ELITE

Caliber: .45 ACP. Capacity: 8-round magazine. Barrel: 5 in. Grips: Checkered, double-diamond rosewood. Sights: Three white-dot Novak. Features: Brushed stainless receiver with blued slide; adjustable, two-cut aluminum trigger; extended ambidextrous thumb safety; upswept beavertail with palm swell; elongated slot hammer.
Price: $1,100.00

COLT LIGHTWEIGHT COMMANDER

Calibers: .45 ACP, 8-shot, 9mm (9 shot). Barrel: 4.25 in. Weight: 26 oz. alloy frame, 33 oz. (steel frame). Length: 7.75 in. overall. Grips: G10 Checkered Black Cherry. Sights: Novak White Dot front, Low Mount Carry rear. Features: Blued slide, black anodized frame. Aluminum alloy frame.
Price: $999.00
Price: Combat Commander w/steel frame... $949.00

COLT DEFENDER

Caliber: .45 ACP (7-round magazine), 9mm (8-round). Barrel: 3 in. Weight: 22.5 oz. Length: 6.75 in. overall. Grips: Pebble-finish rubber wraparound with finger grooves. Sights: White dot front, snag-free Colt competition rear. Features: Stainless or blued finish; aluminum frame; combat-style hammer; Hi-Ride grip safety, extended manual safety, disconnect safety. Introduced 1998. Made in USA by Colt's Mfg. Co., Inc.
Price: Stainless $999.00
Price: Blue $999.00

COLT SERIES 70

Caliber: .45 ACP. Barrel: 5 in. Weight: 37.5 oz. Length: 8.5 in. Grips: Rosewood with double diamond checkering pattern. Sights: Fixed. Features: Custom replica of the Original Series 70 pistol with a Series 70 firing system, original roll marks. Introduced 2002. Made in USA by Colt's Mfg. Co., Inc.
Price: Blued $899.00
Price: Stainless $979.00

COLT 38 SUPER CUSTOM SERIES

Caliber: .38 Super. Barrel: 5 in. Weight: 36.5 oz. Length: 8.5 in. Grips: Wood with double diamond checkering pattern. Finish: Bright stainless. Sights: 3-dot. Features: Beveled magazine well, standard thumb safety and service-style grip safety, flat mainspring housing. Introduced 2003. Made in USA. by Colt's Mfg. Co., Inc.
Price: $1,549.00

COLT MUSTANG POCKETLITE

Caliber: .380 ACP. Capacity: 6-round magazine. Barrel: 2.75 in. Weight: 12.5 oz. Length: 5.5 in. Grips: Black composite. Finish: Brushed stainless. Features: Thumb safety, firing-pin safety block. Introduced 2012.
Price: $699.00

COLT MUSTANG LITE

Caliber: .380 ACP. Similar to Mustang Pocketlite except has black polymer frame.
Price: $599.00

COLT MUSTANG XSP

Caliber: .380 ACP. Features: Similar to Mustang Pocketlite except has polymer frame, black diamond or bright stainless slide, squared trigger guard, accessory rail, electroless nickel finished controls.
Price: Bright Stainless... $528.00
Price: Black Diamond-Like Carbon finish............................. $672.00

COLT RAIL GUN

Caliber: .45 ACP. Capacity: (8+1). Barrel: 5 in. Weight: 40 oz. Length: 8.5 in. Grips: Rosewood double diamond. Sights: White dot front and Novak rear. Features: 1911-style semi-auto. Stainless steel frame and slide, front and rear slide serrations, skeletonized trigger, integral accessory rail, Smith & Alexander upswept beavertail grip palm swell safety, tactical thumb safety, National Match barrel.
Price: $1,199.00

COLT M45A1 MARINE PISTOL

Caliber: .45 ACP. Variant of Rail Gun series with features of that model plus Decobond Brown Coating, dual recoil springs system, Novak tritium front and rear 3-dot sights. Selected by U.S. Marine Corps as their Close Quarters Battle Pistol (CQBP).
Price: $1,699.00

COLT DELTA ELITE

Caliber: 10 mm. Capacity: 8+1. Barrel: 5 in. Grips: Black composite with Delta Medallions. Sights: Novak Low Mount Carry rear, Novak White Dot front. Finish: Two-tone stainless frame, black matte slide. Features: Upswept beavertail safety, extended thumb safety, 3-hole aluminum trigger.
Price: $1,199.00

COLT SPECIAL COMBAT GOVERNMENT CARRY MODEL

Calibers: .45 ACP (8+1), .38 Super (9+1). Barrel: 5 in. Weight: NA. Length: 8.5 in. Grips: Black/silver synthetic. Sights: Novak front and rear night sights. Features: 1911-style semi-auto. Skeletonized three-hole trigger, slotted hammer, Smith & Alexander upswept beavertail grip palm swell safety and extended magazine well, Wilson tactical ambidextrous safety. Available in blued, hard chrome, or blued/satin-nickel finish, depending on chambering. Marine pistol has desert tan Cerakote stainless steel finish, lanyard loop.

Price: **$2,095.00**

COLT GOVERNMENT MODEL 1911A1 .22

Caliber: .22 LR. Capacity: 12-round magazine. Barrel: 5 in. Weight: 36 oz. Features: Made in Germany by Walther under exclusive arrangement with Colt Manufacturing Company. Blowback operation. All other features identical to original, including manual and grip safeties, drift-adjustable sights.

Price: **$399.00**

COLT COMPETITION PISTOL

 Calibers: .45 ACP, .38 Super or 9mm Para. Full-size Government Model with 5-inch national match barrel, dual-spring recoil operating system, adjustable rear and fiber optic front sights, custom G10 Colt logo grips blued or stainless steel finish.

Price: Blued finish **$949.00**
Price: Stainless steel **$999.00**
Price: 38 Super **$1,099.00**

COLT SERIES 70 NATIONAL MATCH GOLD CUP

Caliber: .45 ACP. Barrel: 5 in. national match. Weight: 37 oz. Length: 8.5 in. Grips: Checkered walnut with gold medallions. Sights: Adjustable Bomar rear, target post front. Finish: blued. Features: Flat top slide, flat mainspring housing. Wide three-hole aluminum trigger.

Price: **$1,299.00**

COLT GOLD CUP TROPHY

Calibers: .45 ACP or 9mm. Updated version of the classic Colt target and service pistol first introduced in the late 1950s to give shooters a serious competition pistol out of the box. Features include an undercut trigger guard, upswept beavertail grip safety and dual-spring recoil system. Checkering on the front and rear of the grip strap is 25 LPI with blue G10 grips. The new Gold Cup Trophy is built on the Series 70 firing system. Re-introduced to the Colt catalog in 2017.

Price: **$1,699.00**

CZ 75 B

Calibers: 9mm, .40 S&W. Capacity: 16-round magazine (9mm), 10-round (.40). Barrel: 4.7 in. Weight: 34.3 oz. Length: 8.1 in. overall. Grips: High impact checkered plastic. Sights: Square post front, rear adjustable for windage; 3-dot system. Features: Single action/double action; firing pin block safety; choice of black polymer, matte or high-polish blue finishes. All-steel frame. B-SA is a single action with a drop-free magazine. Imported from the Czech Republic by CZ-USA.

Price: 75 B **$625.00**
Price: 75 B, stainless **$783.00**
Price: 75 B-SA **$661.00**

CZ 75B 45TH ANNIVERSARY

Caliber: 9mm. Capacity: 16-round magazine. Barrel: 4.6 in. Grips: Engraved wood. Sights: Fixed, 3-dot tritium. Length: 8.1 in. overall. Weight: 35.2 oz. unloaded. Finish: Blued. Features: Limited edition pistol, only 1,000 produced. Engraved frame and slide.

Price: **$1,720.00**

CZ 75 BD DECOCKER

Similar to the CZ 75B except has a decocking lever in place of the safety lever. All other specifications are the same. Introduced 1999. Imported from the Czech Republic by CZ-USA.

Price: 9mm, black polymer **$612.00**

Prices given are believed to be accurate at time of publication however, many factors affect retail pricing so exact prices are not possible.

76TH EDITION, 2022 ✦ **439**

CZ 75 B COMPACT

Similar to the CZ 75 B except has 14-round magazine in 9mm, 3.9-in. barrel and weighs 32 oz. Has removable front sight, non-glare ribbed slide top. Trigger guard is squared and serrated; combat hammer. Introduced 1993. Imported from the Czech Republic by CZ-USA.

Price: 9mm, black polymer $631.00
Price: 9mm, dual tone or satin nickel $651.00
Price: 9mm. D PCR Compact, alloy frame $651.00

CZ P-07

Calibers: .40 S&W, 9mm. Capacity: 15 (9mm), 12 (.40). Barrel: 3.8 in. Weight: 27.2 oz. Length: 7.3 in. overall. Grips: Polymer black Polycoat. Sights: Blade front, fixed groove rear. Features: The ergonomics and accuracy of the CZ 75 with a totally new trigger system. The new Omega trigger system simplifies the CZ 75 trigger system, uses fewer parts and improves the trigger pull. In addition, it allows users to choose between using the handgun with a decocking lever (installed) or a manual safety (included) by a simple parts change. The polymer frame design and a new sleek slide profile (fully machined from bar stock) reduce weight, making the P-07 a great choice for concealed carry.

Price: $524.00

CZ P-09 DUTY

Calibers: 9mm, .40 S&W. Capacity: 19 (9mm), 15 (.40). Features: High-capacity version of P-07. Accessory rail, interchangeable grip backstraps, ambidextrous decocker can be converted to manual safety.

Price: $544.00
Price: Suppressor ready $629.00

CZ P-10 F

Caliber: 9mm. Capacity: 19-round magazine. Barrel: 4.5 in. Weight: 26 oz. Length: 8 in. overall. Grips: Textured polymer. Sights: Fixed, 3-dot. Features: Striker fire.

Price: $524.00

CZ 75 SP-01

Similar to NATO-approved CZ 75 Compact P-01 model. Features an integral 1913 accessory rail on the dust cover, rubber grip panels, black Polycoat finish, extended beavertail, new grip geometry with checkering on front and back straps, and double or single action operation. Introduced 2005. The Shadow variant designed as an IPSC "production" division competition firearm. Includes competition hammer, competition rear sight and fiber-optic front sight, modified slide release, lighter recoil and mainspring for use with "minor power factor" competition ammunition. Includes Polycoat finish and slim walnut grips. Finished by CZ Custom Shop. Imported from the Czech Republic by CZ-USA.

Price: SP-01 Standard $680.00
Price: SP-01 Shadow Target II $1,638.00

CZ 97 B

Caliber: .45 ACP. Capacity: 10-round magazine. Barrel: 4.85 in. Weight: 40 oz. Length: 8.34 in. overall. Grips: Checkered walnut. Sights: Fixed. Features: Single action/double action; full-length slide rails; screw-in barrel bushing; linkless barrel; all-steel construction; chamber loaded indicator; dual transfer bars. Introduced 1999. Imported from the Czech Republic by CZ-USA.

Price: Black polymer $707.00
Price: Glossy blue $727.00

CZ 97 BD DECOCKER

Similar to the CZ 97 B except has a decocking lever in place of the safety lever. Tritium night sights. Rubber grips. All other specifications are the same. Introduced 1999. Imported from the Czech Republic by CZ-USA.

Price: $816.00

CZ 2075 RAMI

Calibers: 9mm. Barrel: 3 in. Weight: 25 oz. Length: 6.5 in. overall. Grips: Rubber. Sights: Blade front with dot, white outline rear drift adjustable for windage. Features: Single action/double action; alloy frame, steel slide; has laser sight mount. Rami BD has decocking system. Imported from the Czech Republic by CZ-USA.

Price: Rami Standard $632.00
Price: Rami Decocker version $699.00

CZ P-01

Caliber: 9mm. Capacity: 14-round magazine. Barrel: 3.85 in. Weight: 27 oz. Length: 7.2 in. overall. Grips: Checkered rubber. Sights: Blade front with dot, white outline rear drift adjustable for windage. Features: Based on the CZ 75, except with forged aircraft-grade aluminum alloy frame. Hammer forged barrel, decocker, firing-pin block, M3 rail, dual slide serrations, squared trigger guard, re-contoured trigger, lanyard loop on butt. Serrated front and backstrap. Introduced 2006. Imported from the Czech Republic by CZ-USA.

Price: CZ P-01 .... $680.00

CZ SCORPION EVO

Caliber: 9mm. Capacity: 20-round magazine. Features: Semi-automatic version of CZ Scorpion Evo submachine gun. Ambidextrous controls, adjustable sights, accessory rails.

Price: $849.00

Prices given are believed to be accurate at time of publication however, many factors affect retail pricing so exact prices are not possible.

DAN WESSON DWX FULL SIZE

Calibers: 9mm, .40 S&W. **Capacity:** 19-round magazine (9mm), 15-round magazine (.40 S&W). **Barrel:** 5 in. **Grips:** Checkered red aluminum. **Sights:** Fixed fiber-optic front/adjustable rear. **Length:** 8.52 in. overall. **Weight:** 43 oz. unloaded. **Finish:** Black Duty Coat. **Features:** Hybrid pistol built using the single-action fire control group of a Dan Wesson 1911 and frame of a CZ 75 pistol. Compatible with CZ P-09 and CZ P-10 F magazines. Bull barrel and full dust cover with accessory rail. Flat red aluminum trigger. Oversized controls.
Price: $1,799.00

DAN WESSON DWX COMPACT

Caliber: 9mm. **Capacity:** 15-round magazine. **Barrel:** 5 in. **Grips:** Checkered red aluminum. **Sights:** Fixed, night-sight front/U-notch rear. **Length:** 7.47 in. overall. **Weight:** 28.5 oz. unloaded. **Finish:** Black Duty Coat. **Features:** Hybrid pistol built using the single-action fire control group of a Dan Wesson 1911 and frame of a CZ 75 pistol. With or without accessory rail. Full dust cover. Flat red aluminum trigger. Oversized controls.
Price: $1,799.00

DAN WESSON DW RZ-45 HERITAGE

Caliber: .45 ACP. **Capacity:** 7-round magazine. **Weight:** 36 oz. **Length:** 8.8 in. overall. Similar to the RZ-10 Auto except in .45 ACP.
Price: 10mm, 8+1 .... $1,428.00

DAN WESSON KODIAK

Caliber: 10mm. **Capacity:** 8-round magazine. **Barrel:** 6.03 in. **Grips:** Textured G10. **Sights:** Fixed, fiber-optic front/adjustable rear. **Length:** 9.7 in. overall. **Weight:** 47.1 oz. unloaded. **Finish:** Black or tri-tone. **Features:** 1911 platform with coarse slide serrations, mag well and ambidextrous safety. Black version has bronzed controls and barrel, and tri-tone with a matte gray slide.
Price: (tri-tone)... $2,349.00

DAN WESSON SPECIALIST

Caliber: .45 ACP. **Capacity:** 8-round magazine. **Barrel:** 5 in. **Grips:** G10 VZ Operator II. **Sights:** Single amber tritium dot rear, green lamp with white target ring front sight. **Features:** Integral Picatinny rail, 25 LPI frontstrap checkering, undercut trigger guard, ambidextrous thumb safety, extended mag release and detachable two-piece mag well.
Price: $1,701.00

DAN WESSON V-BOB

Caliber: .45 ACP. **Capacity:** 8-round magazine. **Barrel:** 4.25 in. **Weight:** 34 oz. **Length:** 8 in. **Grips:** Slim Line G10. **Sights:** Heinie Ledge Straight-Eight Night Sights. **Features:** Black matte or stainless finish. Bobtail forged grip frame with 25 LPI checkering front and rear.
Price: $2,077.00

DAN WESSON POINTMAN

Calibers: 9mm, .38 Super, .45 ACP. **Capacity:** 8 or 9-round magazine. **Barrel:** 5 in. **Length:** 8.5 in. **Grips:** Double-diamond cocobolo. **Sights:** Adjustable rear and fiber optic front. **Features:** Undercut trigger guard, checkered front strap, serrated rib on top of slide.
Price: .45, .38 Super $1,597.00
Price: 9mm $1,558.00

DAN WESSON A2

Caliber: .45 ACP. **Capacity:** 8-round magazine capacity. Limited production model based on traditional 1911A1 design. **Features:** Modern fixed combat sights, lowered/flared ejection port, double-diamond walnut grips. Introduced 2017.
Price: $1,363.00

DAN WESSON VALOR

Caliber: .45 ACP. **Capacity:** 8-round magazine. **Barrel:** 5 in. **Grips:** Textured G10. **Sights:** Fixed, night-sight front/U-notch rear. **Length:** 8.75 in. overall. **Weight:** 39.7 oz. unloaded. **Finish:** Matte stainless or black Duty Coat. **Features:** 1911 platform with GI style slide serrations, Stan Chen SI mag well, tapered grip and tactical ambidextrous safety.
Price: (stainless) $1,864.00

DAN WESSON VIGIL

Calibers: 9mm, .45 ACP. **Capacity:** 8 (.45) or 9 (9mm). **Barrel:** 4.25 or 5 in. **Features:** Forged aluminum frame with stainless round-top slide, serrated tactical rear and tritium front sight, checkered frontstrap and backstrap, walnut grips with rounded butt.
Price: $1,298.00

DAN WESSON WRAITH

Calibers: .45 ACP, 9m, 10mm. **Capacity:** 8 (.45), 9 (.40), 10 (9mm). **Barrel:** 5.75, threaded. **Finish:** Distressed Duty. **Features:** High profile fixed combat sights, lowered/flared ejection port, G10 grips, extended controls and grip safety.
Price: $2,077.00

Prices given are believed to be accurate at time of publication however, many factors affect retail pricing so exact prices are not possible.

76TH EDITION, 2022 ⬦ **441**

DESERT EAGLE 1911 G

Caliber: .45 ACP. Capacity: 8-round magazine. Barrels: 5 in. or 4.33 in. (DE1911C Commander size), or 3.0 in. (DE1911U Undercover). Grips: Double diamond checkered wood. Features: Extended beavertail grip safety, checkered flat mainspring housing, skeletonized hammer and trigger, extended mag release and thumb safety, stainless full-length guide road, enlarged ejection port, beveled mag well and high-profile sights. Comes with two 8-round magazines.
Price: **$904.00**
Price: Undercover.. **$1,019.00**

DESERT EAGLE MARK XIX

Calibers: .357 Mag., 9 rounds; .44 Mag., 8 rounds; .50 AE, 7 rounds. Barrels: 6 in., 10 in., interchangeable. Weight: 62 oz. (.357 Mag.); 69 oz. (.44 Mag.); 72 oz. (.50 AE) Length: 10.25-in. overall (6-in. bbl.). Grips: Polymer; rubber available. Sights: Blade-on-ramp front, combat-style rear. Adjustable available. Features: Interchangeable barrels; rotating three-lug bolt; ambidextrous safety; adjustable trigger. Military epoxy finish. Satin, bright nickel, chrome, brushed, matte or black-oxide finishes available. 10-in. barrel extra. Imported from Israel by Magnum Research, Inc.
Price: .... **$1,572.00–$2,060.00**

BABY DESERT EAGLE III

Calibers: 9mm, .40 S&W, .45 ACP. Capacities: 10-, 12- or 15-round magazines. Barrels: 3.85 in. or 4.43 in. Weights: 28–37.9 oz. Length: 7.25–8.25 overall. Grips: Ergonomic polymer. Sights: White 3-dot system. Features: Choice of steel or polymer frame with integral rail; slide-mounted decocking safety. Upgraded design of Baby Eagle II series.
Price: .... **$646.00–$691.00**

DESERT EAGLE L5/L6

Caliber: .357 Magnum, .44 Magnum, .50 AE. Capacity: 7, 8 or 9+1. Barrel: 5 in. or 6 in (L6). Weight: 50 to 70 oz. Length: 9.7 in. (L5), 10.8, (L6). Features: Steel barrel, aluminum frame and stainless steel slide with full Weaver-style accessory rail and integral muzzle brake. Gas-operated rotating bolt, single-action trigger, fixed sights.
Price: From **$1,790.00**

DIAMONDBACK DB380

Caliber: .380 ACP. Capacity: 6+1. Barrel: 2.8 in. Weight: 8.8 oz. Features: ZERO-Energy striker firing system with a mechanical firing pin block, steel magazine catch, windage-adjustable sights. Frames available with several color finish options.
Price: .... **$290.00–$350.00**

DIAMONDBACK DB9

Caliber: 9mm. Capacity: 6+1. Barrel: 3 in. Weight: 11 oz. Length: 5.60 in. Features: Other features similar to DB380 model.
Price: .... **$290.00–$350.00**

DIAMONDBACK DB FS NINE

Caliber: 9mm. Capacity: 15+1. Barrel: 4.75 in. Weight: 21.5 oz. Length: 7.8 in. Features: Double-action, striker-fired model with polymer frame and stainless steel slide. Flared mag well, extended magazine base pad, ergonomically contoured grip, fixed 3-dot sights, front and rear slide serrations, integral MIL-STD 1913 Picatinny rail.
Price: **$483.00**

DIAMONDBACK FIREARMS DBX

Caliber: 5.7x28mm. Capacity: 20-round magazine. Barrel: 8 in. Grips: Magpul MOE-K. Sights: Optic-ready, Picatinny rail. Length: 16.9 in. overall, brace folded. Weight: 3 lbs. unloaded. Finish: Black hard coat anodized. Features: DBX muzzle brake, compatible with FN Five-seveN, side-folding brace. Uses AR15 Mil-Spec trigger.
Price: **$1,299.00**

DIAMONDBACK FIREARMS DBAM29
Caliber: 9mm. Capacity: 12- or 17-round magazine. Barrel: 3.5 in. Grips: Textured grip. Sights: Fixed, 3-dot. Length: 6.6 in. overall. Weight: 21 oz. unloaded. Finish: Black.
Price: **$350.00**

DOUBLESTAR 1911 SERIES
Caliber: .45 ACP. Capacity: 8-round magazine. Barrels: 3.5 in., 4.25 in., 5 in. Weights: 33–40 oz. Grips: Cocobolo wood. Sights: Novak LoMount 2 white-dot rear, Novak white-dot front. Features: Single action, M1911-style with forged frame and slide of 4140 steel, stainless steel barrel machined from bar stock by Storm Lake, funneled mag well, accessory rail, black Nitride finish. Optional features include bobtail grip frame, accessory rail.
Price: .... **$1,364.00–$2,242.00**

EAA WITNESS FULL SIZE
Calibers: 9mm, .38 Super. Capacity: 18-round magazine; .40 S&W, 10mm, 15-round magazine; .45 ACP, 10-round magazine. Barrel: 4.5 in. Weight: 35.33 oz. Length: 8.1 in. overall. Grips: Checkered rubber. Sights: Undercut blade front, open rear adjustable for windage. Features: Double-action/single-action trigger system; round trigger guard; frame-mounted safety. Available with steel or polymer frame. Also available with interchangeable .45 ACP and .22 LR slides. Steel frame introduced 1991. Polymer frame introduced 2005. Imported from Italy by European American Armory.
Price: Steel frame **$699.00**
Price: Polymer frame **$589.00**

EAA WITNESS COMPACT
Caliber: 9mm. Capacity: 14-round magazine; .40 S&W, 10mm, 12-round magazine; .45 ACP, 8-round magazine. Barrel: 3.6 in. Weight: 30 oz. Length: 7.3 in. overall. Features: Available with steel or polymer frame (shown). All polymer frame Witness pistols are capable of being converted to other calibers. Otherwise similar to full-size Witness. Imported from Italy by European American Armory.
Price: Polymer frame **$589.00**
Price: Steel frame **$699.00**

EAA WITNESS-P CARRY
Caliber: 9mm. Capacity: 17-round magazine; 10mm, 15-round magazine; .45 ACP, 10-round magazine. Barrel: 3.6 in. Weight: 27 oz. Length: 7.5 in. overall. Features: Otherwise similar to full-size Witness. Polymer frame introduced 2005. Imported from Italy by European American Armory.
Price: **$711.00**

EAA WITNESS PAVONA COMPACT POLYMER
Calibers: .380 ACP (13-round magazine), 9mm (13) or .40 S&W (9). Barrel: 3.6 in. Weight: 30 oz. Length: 7 in. overall. Features: Designed primarily for women with fine-tuned recoil and hammer springs for easier operation, a polymer frame with integral checkering, contoured lines and in black, charcoal, blue, purple or magenta with silver or gold sparkle.
Price: .... **$476.00–$528.00**

EAA WITNESS ELITE 1911
Caliber: .45 ACP. Capacity: 8-round magazine. Barrel: 5 in. Weight: 32 oz. Length: 8.58 in. overall. Features: Full-size 1911-style pistol with either steel or polymer frame. Also available in Commander or Officer's models with 4.25- or 3.5-in. barrel, polymer frame.
Price: **$580.00**
Price: Commander or Officer's Model... **$627.00**
Price: Steel frame **$895.00**

Prices given are believed to be accurate at time of publication however, many factors affect retail pricing so exact prices are not possible.

76TH EDITION, 2022 ⊕ 443

EAA SAR B6P

Caliber: 9mm. Based on polymer frame variation of CZ 75 design. Manufactured by Sarsilmaz in Turkey. Features similar to Witness series.
Price: .... **$407.00–$453.00**

EAA SAR K2-45

Caliber: .45 ACP. Barrel: 4.7 in. Weight: 2.5 lbs. Features: Similar to B6P with upgraded features. Built by Sarsilmaz for the Turkish military. Features include a cocked and locked carry system, ergonomically designed grip, steel frame and slide construction, adjustable rear sight, extended beaver tail, serrated trigger guard and frame, removable dove-tail front sight, auto firing pin block and low barrel axis for reduced felt recoil.
Price: **$849.00**

EAA MC 1911 SERIES

Caliber: .45 ACP, 9mm. Capacity: 8-round magazine, 9+1 (9mm). Barrel: 5, 4.4, or 3.4 in. Weight: 26-39 oz. Sights: Novak-style rear, fixed front. Features: 1911-style pistol with either steel or polymer frame, ambidextrous safety, extended beavertail. Available in full-size, Commander or Officer's models. Manufactured by Girsan in Turkey.
Price: .... **$572.00-$694.00**

ED BROWN CLASSIC CUSTOM

Caliber: .45 ACP, 9mm, .38 Super. Capacity: 7-round magazine. Barrel: 5 in. Weight: 40 oz. Grips: Cocobolo wood. Sights: Bo-Mar adjustable rear, dovetail front. Features: Single action, M1911 style, custom made to order, stainless frame and slide available. Special mirror-finished slide.
Price: From **$3,695.00**

ED BROWN KOBRA CARRY

Caliber: .45 ACP. Capacity: 7-round magazine. Barrels: 4.25 in. Weight: 34 oz. Grips: Hogue exotic wood. Sights: Ramp, front; fixed Novak low-mount night sights, rear. Features: Snakeskin pattern serrations on forestrap and mainspring housing, dehorned edges, beavertail grip safety.
Price: .45 ACP From **$2,995.00**
Price: 9 mm From **$3,095.00**
Price: .38 Super From **$3,095.00**

ED BROWN KOBRA CARRY LIGHTWEIGHT

Caliber: .45 ACP, 9mm, .38 Super. Capacity: 7-round magazine. Barrel: 4.25 in. (Commander model slide). Weight: 27 oz. Grips: Hogue exotic wood. Sights: 10-8 Performance U-notch plain black rear sight with .156-in. notch for fast acquisition of close targets. Fixed dovetail front night sight with high-visibility white outlines. Features: Aluminum frame and bobtail housing. Matte finished Gen III coated slide for low glare, with snakeskin on rear of slide only. Snakeskin pattern serrations on forestrap and mainspring housing, dehorned edges, beavertail grip safety. LW insignia on slide, which stands for Lightweight.
Price: Kobra Carry Lightweight **$3,495.00**

ED BROWN EXECUTIVE SERIES

Similar to other Ed Brown products, but with 25-LPI checkered frame and mainspring housing. Various finish, sight and grip options.
Price: .... **$3,170.00-$3,880.00**

ED BROWN SPECIAL FORCES

Similar to other Ed Brown products, but with ChainLink treatment on forestrap and mainspring housing. Entire gun coated with Gen III finish. Square cut serrations on rear of slide only. Dehorned. Introduced 2006. Available with various finish, sight and grip options.
Price: From .... **$2,770.00–$4,775.00**

ED BROWN CCO SERIES

Caliber: .45 ACP, 9mm, .38 Super. Capacity: 7-round magazine. Barrel: 4.25 in. Built on Officer's size frame with Commander slide. Features: Snakeskin metal treatment on mainspring housing, front strap and slide, round butt housing, concealed-carry beavertail grip safety, fixed black rear sight, high visibility fiber optic front. Lightweight aluminum version available.
Price: From .... **$3,070.00–$3,585.00**

HANDGUNS Autoloaders, Service & Sport

EXCEL ARMS MP-22
Caliber: .22 WMR. Capacity: 9-round magazine. Barrel: 8.5-in. bull barrel. Weight: 54 oz. Length: 12.875 in. overall. Grips: Textured black composition. Sights: Fully adjustable target sights. Features: Made from 17-4 stainless steel, comes with aluminum rib, integral Weaver base, internal hammer, firing pin block. American made, lifetime warranty. Comes with two 9-round stainless steel magazines and a California-approved cable lock. .22 WMR Introduced 2006. Made in USA by Excel Arms.
Price: **$477.00**

EXCEL ARMS MP-5.7
Caliber: 5.7x28mm. Capacity: 9-round magazine. Features: Blowback action. Other features similar to MP-22. Red-dot optic sights, scope and rings are optional.
Price: **$615.00**
Price: With optic sights.. **$685.00**
Price: With scope and rings.................................... **$711.00**

FIRESTORM 380
Caliber: .380 ACP. Capacity: 7+1. Barrel: 3.5 in. Weight: 20 oz. Length: 6.6 in. Sights: Fixed, white outline system. Grips: Rubber. Finish: Black matte. Features: Traditional DA/SA operation.
Price: **$270.00**

FMK 9C1 G2
Caliber: 9mm. Capacity: 10+1 or 14+1. Barrel: 4 in. Overall length: 6.85 in. Weight: 23.45 oz. Finish: Black, Flat Dark Earth or pink. Sights: Interchangeable Glock compatible. Features: Available in either single action or double action only. Polymer frame, high-carbon steel slide, stainless steel barrel. Very low bore axis and shock absorbing backstrap are said to result in low felt recoil. DAO model has Fast Action Trigger (FAT) with shorter pull and reset. Made in the USA.
Price: **$409.00**

FN 509 COMPACT MRD
Caliber: 9mm. Capacity: 10-, 12- or 15-round magazine. Barrel: 3.7 in. Grips: Textured grip, interchangeable backstraps. Sights: Fixed, tall co-witness; FN Low Profile Optics Mounting System. Length: 6.8 in. overall. Weight: 25.5 oz. unloaded. Finish: Black or FDE.
Price: **$799.00**

FN FNS SERIES
Caliber: 9mm. Capacity: 17-round magazine, .40 S&W (14-round magazine). Barrels: 4 in. or 3.6 in. (Compact). Weights: 25 oz. (9mm), 27.5 oz. (.40). Length: 7.25 in. Grips: Integral polymer with two interchangeable backstrap inserts. Features: Striker fired, double action with manual safety, accessory rail, ambidextrous controls, 3-dot night sights.
Price: **$599.00**

FN FNX SERIES
Calibers: 9mm, .40 S&W. Capacities: 17-round magazine, .40 S&W (14 rounds), .45 ACP (10 or 14 rounds). Barrels: 4 in. (9mm and .40), 4.5 in. .45. Weights: 22–32 oz. (.45). Lengths: 7.4, 7.9 in. (.45). Features: DA/SA operation with decocking/manual safety lever. Has external extractor with loaded-chamber indicator, front and rear cocking serrations, fixed 3-dot combat sights.
Price: 9mm, .40 .... **$699.00**
Price: .45 ACP **$824.00**

FN FNX .45 TACTICAL
Similar to standard FNX .45 except with 5.3-in. barrel with threaded muzzle, polished chamber and feed ramp, enhanced high-profile night sights, slide cut and threaded for red-dot sight (not included), MIL-STD 1913 accessory rail, ring-style hammer.
Price: **$1,349.00**

FN FIVE-SEVEN
Caliber: 5.7x28mm. Capacity: 10- or 20-round magazine. Barrel: 4.8 in. Weight: 23 oz. Length: 8.2 in. Features: Adjustable three-dot system. Single-action polymer frame, chambered for low-recoil 5.7x28mm cartridge.
Price: **$1,435.00**

GLOCK 17/17C

Caliber: 9mm. Capacities: 17/19/33-round magazines. Barrel: 4.49 in. Weight: 22.04 oz. (without magazine). Length: 7.32 in. overall. Grips: Black polymer. Sights: Dot on front blade, white outline rear adjustable for windage. Features: Polymer frame, steel slide; double-action trigger with Safe Action system; mechanical firing pin safety, drop safety; simple takedown without tools; locked breech, recoil operated action. ILS designation refers to Internal Locking System. Adopted by Austrian armed forces 1983. NATO approved 1984. Model 17L has 6-inch barrel, ported or non-ported, slotted and relieved slide, checkered grip with finger grooves, no accessory rail. Imported from Austria by Glock, Inc. USA.

Price: From	**$599.00**
Price: 17L	**$750.00**
Price: 17 Gen 4	**$649.00**
Price: 17 Gen 5	**$699.00**

GLOCK GEN4 SERIES

In 2010, a new series of Generation 4 pistols was introduced with several improved features. These included a multiple backstrap system offering three different size options, short, medium or large frame; reversible and enlarged magazine release; dual recoil springs; and RTF (Rough Textured Finish) surface. Some recent models are only available in Gen 4 configuration.

GEN 5 SERIES

A new frame design was introduced in 2017 named Generation 5. The finger grooves were removed for more versatility and the user can customize the grip by using different backstraps, as with the Gen 4 models. A flared mag well and a cutout at the front of the frame give the user more speed during reloading. There is a reversible and enlarged magazine catch, changeable by users, as well as the ambidextrous slide stop lever to accommodate left- and right-handed operators. The rifling and crown of the barrel are slightly modified for increased precision. As of 2019, Gen 5 variants are available in Glock Models 17, 19, 26, 34 and 45.

GLOCK 19/19C

Caliber: 9mm. Capacities: 15/17/19/33-round magazines. Barrel: 4.02 in. Weight: 20.99 oz. (without magazine). Length: 6.85 in. overall. Compact version of Glock 17. Imported from Austria by Glock, Inc.

Price:	**$599.00**
Price: 19 Gen 4	**$649.00**
Price: 19 Gen 5	**$749.00**

GLOCK 20/20C 10MM

Caliber: 10mm. Capacity: 15-round magazine. Barrel: 4.6 in. Weight: 27.68 oz. (without magazine). Length: 7.59 in. overall. Features: Otherwise similar to Model 17. Imported from Austria by Glock, Inc. Introduced 1990.

Price: From	**$637.00**
Price: 20 Gen 4	**$687.00**

GLOCK MODEL 20 SF SHORT FRAME

Caliber: 10mm. Barrel: 4.61 in. with hexagonal rifling. Weight: 27.51 oz. Length: 8.07 in. overall. Sights: Fixed. Features: Otherwise similar to the Model 20 but with short-frame design, extended sight radius.

Price:	**$637.00**

GLOCK 21/21C

Caliber: .45 ACP. Capacity: 13-round magazine. Barrel: 4.6 in. Weight: 26.28 oz. (without magazine). Length: 7.59 in. overall. Features: Otherwise similar to the Model 17. Imported from Austria by Glock, Inc. Introduced 1991. SF version has tactical rail, smaller diameter grip, 10-round magazine capacity. Introduced 2007.

Price: From	**$637.00**
Price: 21 Gen 4	**$687.00**

GLOCK 22/22C

Caliber: .40 S&W. Capacities: 15/17-round magazine. Barrel: 4.49 in. Weight: 22.92 oz. (without magazine). Length: 7.32 in. overall. Features: Otherwise similar to Model 17, including pricing. Imported from Austria by Glock, Inc. Introduced 1990.

Price: From	**$599.00**
Price: 22C	**$649.00**
Price: 22 Gen 4	**$649.00**

GLOCK 23/23C

Caliber: .40 S&W. Capacities: 13/15/17-round magazine. Barrel: 4.02 in. Weight: 21.16 oz. (without magazine). Length: 6.85 in. overall. Features: Otherwise similar to the Model 22, including pricing. Compact version of Glock 22. Imported from Austria by Glock, Inc. Introduced 1990.

Price:	**$599.00**
Price: 23C Compensated	**$621.00**
Price: 23 Gen 4	**$649.00**

GLOCK 24/24C

Caliber: .40 S&W. Capacities: 10/15/17 or 22-round magazine. Features: Similar to Model 22 except with 6.02-inch barrel, ported or non-ported, trigger pull recalibrated to 4.5 lbs.

Price: From	**$750.00**

GLOCK 26

Caliber: 9mm. Capacities: 10/12/15/17/19/33-round magazine. Barrel: 3.46 in. Weight: 19.75 oz. Length: 6.29 in. overall. Subcompact version of Glock 17. Imported from Austria by Glock, Inc.

Price:	**$599.00**
Price: 26 Gen 4	**$649.00**
Price: 26 Gen 5	**$749.00**

GLOCK 27
Caliber: .40 S&W. Capacities: 9/11/13/15/17-round magazine. Barrel: 3.46 in. Weight: 19.75 oz. (without magazine). Length: 6.29 overall. Features: Otherwise similar to the Model 22, including pricing. Subcompact version of Glock 22. Imported from Austria by Glock, Inc. Introduced 1996.
Price: From **$599.00**
Price: 27 Gen 4 .... **$649.00**

GLOCK 29 GEN 4
Caliber: 10mm. Capacities: 10/15-round magazine. Barrel: 3.78 in. Weight: 24.69 oz. (without magazine). Length: 6.77 in. overall. Features: Otherwise similar to the Model 20, including pricing. Subcompact version of the Glock 20. Imported from Austria by Glock, Inc. Introduced 1997.
Price: Fixed sight **$637.00**

GLOCK MODEL 29 SF SHORT FRAME
Caliber: 10mm. Barrel: 3.78 in. with hexagonal rifling. Weight: 24.52 oz. Length: 6.97 in. overall. Sights: Fixed. Features: Otherwise similar to the Model 29 but with short-frame design, extended sight radius.
Price: **$637.00**

GLOCK 30 GEN 4
Caliber: .45 ACP. Capacities: 9/10/13-round magazines. Barrel: 3.78 in. Weight: 23.99 oz. (without magazine). Length: 6.77 in. overall. Features: Otherwise similar to the Model 21, including pricing. Subcompact version of the Glock 21. Imported from Austria by Glock, Inc. Introduced 1997. SF version has tactical rail, octagonal rifled barrel with a 1:15.75 rate of twist, smaller diameter grip, 10-round magazine capacity. Introduced 2008.
Price: **$637.00**
Price: 30 SF (short frame) **$637.00**

GLOCK 30S
Caliber: .45 ACP. Capacity: 10-round magazine. Barrel: 3.78 in. Weight: 20 oz. Length: 7 in. Features: Variation of Glock 30 with a Model 36 slide on a Model 30SF frame (short frame).
Price: **$637.00**

GLOCK 31/31C
Caliber: .357 Auto. Capacities: 15/17-round magazine. Barrel: 4.49 in. Weight: 23.28 oz. (without magazine). Length: 7.32 in. overall. Features: Otherwise similar to the Model 17. Imported from Austria by Glock, Inc.
Price: From **$599.00**
Price: 31 Gen 4 .... **$649.00**

GLOCK 32/32C
Caliber: .357 Auto. Capacities: 13/15/17-round magazine. Barrel: 4.02 in. Weight: 21.52 oz. (without magazine). Length: 6.85 in. overall. Features: Otherwise similar to the Model 31. Compact. Imported from Austria by Glock, Inc.
Price: **$599.00**
Price: 32 Gen 4 .... **$649.00**

GLOCK 33
Caliber: .357 Auto. Capacities: 9/11/13/15/17-round magazine. Barrel: 3.46 in. Weight: 19.75 oz. (without magazine). Length: 6.29 in. overall. Features: Otherwise similar to the Model 31. Subcompact. Imported from Austria by Glock, Inc.
Price: From **$599.00**
Price: 33 Gen 4 .... **$614.00**

GLOCK 34
Caliber: 9mm. Capacities: 17/19/33-round magazine. Barrel: 5.32 in. Weight: 22.9 oz. Length: 8.15 in. overall. Features: Competition version of Glock 17 with extended barrel, slide, and sight radius dimensions. Available with MOS (Modular Optic System).
Price: From **$679.00**
Price: MOS **$840.00**
Price: 34 Gen 4 .... **$729.00**
Price: 34 Gen 5 .... **$899.00**

GLOCK 35
Caliber: .40 S&W. Capacities: 15/17-round magazine. Barrel: 5.32 in. Weight: 24.52 oz. (without magazine). Length: 8.15 in. overall. Sights: Adjustable. Features: Otherwise similar to the Model 22. Competition version of the Glock 22 with extended barrel, slide and sight radius dimensions. Available with MOS (Modular Optic System). Introduced 1996.
Price: From **$679.00**
Price: MOS... **$840.00**
Price: 35 Gen 4 .... **$729.00**

GLOCK 36
Caliber: .45 ACP. Capacity: 6-round magazine. Barrel: 3.78 in. Weight: 20.11 oz. (without magazine). Length: 6.77 overall. Sights: Fixed. Features: Single-stack magazine, slimmer grip than Glock 21/30. Subcompact. Imported from Austria by Glock, Inc. Introduced 1997.
Price: **$637.00**

GLOCK 37
Caliber: .45 GAP. Capacity: 10-round magazine. Barrel: 4.49 in. Weight: 25.95 oz. (without magazine). Length: 7.32 overall. Features: Otherwise similar to the Model 17. Imported from Austria by Glock, Inc. Introduced 2005.
Price: **$614.00**
Price: 37 Gen 4 .... **$664.00**

GLOCK 38
Caliber: .45 GAP. Capacities: 8/10-round magazine. Barrel: 4.02 in. Weight: 24.16 oz. (without magazine). Length: 6.85 overall. Features: Otherwise similar to the Model 37. Compact. Imported from Austria by Glock, Inc.
Price: **$614.00**

GLOCK 39
Caliber: .45 GAP. Capacities: 6/8/10-round magazine. Barrel: 3.46 in. Weight: 19.33 oz. (without magazine). Length: 6.3 overall. Features: Otherwise similar to the Model 37. Subcompact. Imported from Austria by Glock, Inc.
Price: **$614.00**

GLOCK 40 GEN 4
Caliber: 10mm. Features: Similar features as the Model 41 except for 6.01-in. barrel. Includes MOS optics.
Price: **$840.00**

Prices given are believed to be accurate at time of publication however, many factors affect retail pricing so exact prices are not possible.

76TH EDITION, 2022 ✦ **447**

GLOCK 41 GEN 4
Caliber: .45 ACP. **Capacity:** 13-round magazine. **Barrel:** 5.31 in. **Weight:** 27 oz. **Length:** 8.9 in. overall. **Features:** This is a long-slide .45 ACP Gen4 model introduced in 2014. Operating features are the same as other Glock models. Available with MOS (Modular Optic System).
Price: **$749.00**
Price: MOS **$840.00**

GLOCK 42 GEN 4
Caliber: .380 ACP. **Capacity:** 6-round magazine. **Barrel:** 3.25 in. **Weight:** 13.8 oz. **Length:** 5.9 in. overall. **Features:** This single-stack, slimline sub-compact is the smallest pistol Glock has ever made. This is also the first Glock pistol made in the USA.
Price: **$499.00**

GLOCK 43 GEN 4
Caliber: 9mm. **Capacity:** 6+1. **Barrel:** 3.39 in. **Weight:** 17.95 oz. **Length:** 6.26 in. **Height:** 4.25 in. **Width:** 1.02 in. **Features:** Newest member of Glock's Slimline series with single-stack magazine.
Price: **$599.00**

GLOCK 43X
Caliber: 9mm. **Capacity:** 17+1. **Barrel:** 4.02 in. **Weight:** 24.5 oz. **Length:** 7.4 in. **Height:** 5.5 in. **Width:** 1.3 in. Combines compact slide with full-size frame.
Price: **$580.00**

GLOCK G44
Caliber: .22 LR. **Capacity:** 10-round magazine. **Barrel:** 4.02 in. **Grips:** Textured grip, interchangeable backstraps. **Sights:** Fixed, dot front/notch rear. **Length:** 7.28 in. overall. **Weight:** 14.6 oz. unloaded. **Finish:** Black. **Features:** Same size as Glock G19, hybrid slide of polymer and steel.
Price: **$430.00**

GLOCK 45
Caliber: 9mm. **Capacity:** 10+1. **Barrel:** 3.41 in. **Weight:** 18.7 oz. **Length:** 6.5 in. **Height:** 5.04 in. **Width:** 1.1 in. Combines Glock 43 short and slim dimensions with extended frame size of G48.
Price: **$580.00**

GLOCK 48 GEN 4
Caliber: 9mm. **Capacity:** 10. **Barrel:** 3.41 in. **Weight:** 18.7 oz. **Length:** 6.05 in. **Height:** 5.04 in. **Width:** 1.1 in. **Features:** Silver-colored PVD coated slide with front serrations. Similar length and height as Model 19 with width reduced to 1.1 inch.
Price: **$580.00**

GRAND POWER P-1 MK7
Caliber: 9mm. **Capacity:** 15+1 magazine. **Barrel:** 3.7 in. **Weight:** 26 oz. **Features:** Compact DA/SA pistol featuring frame-mounted safety, steel slide and frame and polymer grips. Offered in several variations and sizes. Made in Slovakia
Price: **$449.00**

GUNCRAFTER INDUSTRIES
Calibers: 9mm, .38 Super, .45 ACP or .50 GI. **Capacity:** 7- or 8-round magazine. **Features:** 1911-style series of pistols best known for the proprietary .50 GI chambering. Offered in approximately 30 1911 variations. No. 1 has 5-inch heavy match-grade barrel, Parkerized or hard chrome finish, checkered grips and frontstrap, numerous sight options. Other models include Commander-style, Officer's Model, Long Slide w/6-inch barrel and several 9mm and .38 Super versions.
Price: .... **$2,795.00–$5,195.00**

Prices given are believed to be accurate at time of publication however, many factors affect retail pricing so exact prices are not possible.

HECKLER & KOCH USP

Calibers: 9mm, .40 S&W, .45 ACP. Capacities: 15-round magazine; .40 S&W, 13-shot magazine; 45 ACP, 12-shot magazine. Barrels: 4.25–4.41 in. Weight: 1.65 lbs. Length: 7.64–7.87 in. overall. Grips: Non-slip stippled black polymer. Sights: Blade front, rear adjustable for windage. Features: New HK design with polymer frame, modified Browning action with recoil reduction system, single control lever. Special "hostile environment" finish on all metal parts. Available in SA/DA, DAO, left- and right-hand versions. Introduced 1993. .45 ACP Introduced 1995. Imported from Germany by Heckler & Koch, Inc.

Price: USP .45 .... **$1,199.00**
Price: USP .40 and USP 9mm **$952.00**

HECKLER & KOCH USP COMPACT

Calibers: 9mm, .357 SIG, .40 S&W, .45 ACP. Capacities: 13-round magazine; .40 S&W and .357 SIG, 12-shot magazine; .45 ACP, 8-shot magazine. Features: Similar to the USP except the 9mm, .357 SIG and .40 S&W have 3.58-in. barrels, measure 6.81 in. overall and weigh 1.47 lbs. (9mm). Introduced 1996. .45 ACP measures 7.09 in. overall. Introduced 1998. Imported from Germany by Heckler & Koch, Inc.

Price: USP Compact .45 .... **$1,040.00**
Price: USP Compact 9mm, .40 S&W **$992.00**

HECKLER & KOCH USP45 TACTICAL

Calibers: .40 S&W, .45 ACP. Capacities: 13-round magazine; .45 ACP, 12-round magazine. Barrels: 4.90-5.09 in. Weight: 1.9 lbs. Length: 8.64 in. overall. Grips: Non-slip stippled polymer. Sights: Blade front, fully adjustable target rear. Features: Has extended threaded barrel with rubber O-ring; adjustable trigger; extended magazine floorplate; adjustable trigger stop; polymer frame. Introduced 1998. Imported from Germany by Heckler & Koch, Inc.

Price: USP Tactical .45 .... **$1,352.00**
Price: USP Tactical .40 .... **$1,333.00**

HECKLER & KOCH USP COMPACT TACTICAL

Caliber: .45 ACP. Capacity: 8-round magazine. Features: Similar to the USP Tactical except measures 7.72 in. overall, weighs 1.72 lbs. Introduced 2006. Imported from Germany by Heckler & Koch, Inc.

Price: USP Compact Tactical **$1,352.00**

HECKLER & KOCH HK45

Caliber: .45 ACP. Capacity: 10-round magazine. Barrel: 4.53 in. Weight: 1.73 lbs. Length: 7.52 in. overall. Grips: Ergonomic with adjustable grip panels. Sights: Low profile, drift adjustable. Features: Polygonal rifling, ambidextrous controls, operates on improved Browning linkless recoil system. Available in Tactical and Compact variations. Tactical models come with threaded barrel, adjustable TruGlo high-profile sights, Picatinny rail.

Price: HK45 .... **$819.00**
Price: HK45 Tactical **$919.00-999.00**

HECKLER & KOCH MARK 23 SPECIAL OPERATIONS

Caliber: .45 ACP. Capacity: 12-round magazine. Barrel: 5.87 in. Weight: 2.42 lbs. Length: 9.65 in. overall. Grips: Integral with frame; black polymer. Sights: Blade front, rear drift adjustable for windage; 3-dot. Features: Civilian version of the SOCOM pistol. Polymer frame; double action; exposed hammer; short recoil, modified Browning action. Introduced 1996. Imported from Germany by Heckler & Koch, Inc.

Price: **$2,299.00**

HECKLER & KOCH P30 AND P30L

Calibers: 9mm, .40 S&W. Capacities: 13- or 15-round magazines. Barrels: 3.86 in. or 4.45 in. (P30L) Weight: 26–27.5 oz. Length: 6.95, 7.56 in. overall. Grips: Interchangeable panels. Sights: Open rectangular notch rear sight with contrast points. Features: Ergonomic features include a special grip frame with interchangeable backstrap inserts and lateral plates, allowing the pistol to be individually adapted to any user. Browning-type action with modified short recoil operation. Ambidextrous controls include dual slide releases, magazine release levers and a serrated decocking button located on the rear of the frame (for applicable variants). A Picatinny rail molded into the front of the frame. The extractor serves as a loaded-chamber indicator.

Price: P30 .... **$1,099.00**
Price: P30L Variant 2 Law Enforcement Modification (LEM) enhanced DAO **$1,149.00**
Price: P30L Variant 3 Double Action/Single Action (DA/SA) with Decocker **$1,108.00**

HECKLER & KOCH P2000

Calibers: 9mm, .40 S&W. Capacities: 13-round magazine; .40 S&W, 12-shot magazine. Barrel: 3.62 in. Weight: 1.5 lbs. Length: 7 in. overall. Grips: Interchangeable panels. Sights: Fixed Patridge style, drift adjustable for windage, standard 3-dot. Features: Incorporates features of HK USP Compact pistol, including Law Enforcement Modification (LEM) trigger, double-action hammer system, ambidextrous magazine release, dual slide-release levers, accessory mounting rails, recurved, hook trigger guard, fiber-reinforced polymer frame, modular grip with exchangeable backstraps, nitro-carburized finish, lock-out safety device. Introduced 2003. Imported from Germany by Heckler & Koch, Inc.
Price: **$799.00**

HECKLER & KOCH P2000 SK

Calibers: 9mm, .357 SIG, .40 S&W. Capacities: 10-round magazine; .40 S&W and .357 SIG, 9-round magazine. Barrel: 3.27 in. Weight: 1.3 lbs. Length: 6.42 in. overall. Sights: Fixed Patridge style, drift adjustable. Features: Standard accessory rails, ambidextrous slide release, polymer frame, polygonal bore profile. Smaller version of P2000. Introduced 2005. Imported from Germany by Heckler & Koch, Inc.
Price: **$799.00**

HECKLER & KOCH VP9/VP 40

Calibers: 9mm, .40 S&W. Capacities: 10- or 15-round magazine. .40 S&W (10 or 13). Barrel: 4.09 in. Weight: 25.6 oz. Length: 7.34 in. overall. Sights: Fixed 3-dot, drift adjustable. Features: Striker-fired system with HK enhanced light pull trigger. Ergonomic grip design with interchangeable backstraps and side panels. VP9SK is compact model with 3.4-in. barrel.
Price: **$719.00**

HI-POINT FIREARMS MODEL 9MM COMPACT

Caliber: 9mm. Capacity: 8-round magazine. Barrel: 3.5 in. Weight: 25 oz. Length: 6.75 in. overall. Grips: Textured plastic. Sights: Combat-style adjustable 3-dot system; low profile. Features: Single-action design; frame-mounted magazine release; polymer frame offered in black or several camo finishes. Scratch-resistant matte finish. Introduced 1993. Comps are similar except they have a 4-in. barrel with muzzle brake/compensator. Compensator is slotted for laser or flashlight mounting. Introduced 1998. Made in USA by MKS Supply, Inc.
Price: C-9 9mm **$199.00**

HI-POINT FIREARMS MODEL 380 POLYMER

Caliber: .380 ACP. Capacities: 10- and 8-round magazine. Weight: 25 oz. Features: Similar to the 9mm Compact model except chambered for adjustable 3-dot sights. Polymer frame with black or camo finish. Action locks open after last shot. Trigger lock.
Price: CF-380 .... **$179.00**

HI-POINT FIREARMS 40 AND 45 SW/POLYMER

Calibers: .40 S&W, .45 ACP. Capacities: .40 S&W, 8-round magazine; .45 ACP, 9 rounds. Barrel: 4.5 in. Weight: 32 oz. Length: 7.72 in. overall. Sights: Adjustable 3-dot. Features: Polymer frames, offered in black or several camo finishes, last round lock-open, grip-mounted magazine release, magazine disconnect safety, integrated accessory rail, trigger lock. Introduced 2002. Made in USA by MKS Supply, Inc.
Price: **$219.00**

ITHACA 1911

Caliber: .45 ACP. Capacity: 7-round capacity. Barrels: 4.25 or 5 in. Weight: 35 or 40 oz. Sights: Fixed combat or fully adjustable target. Grips: Checkered cocobolo with Ithaca logo. Classic 1911A1 style with enhanced features including match-grade barrel, lowered and flared ejection port, extended beavertail grip safety, hand-fitted barrel bushing, two-piece guide rod, checkered front strap.
Price: **$1,575.00**
Price: Hand fit **$2,375.00**

IVER JOHNSON EAGLE

Calibers: 9mm, .45 ACP, 10mm. Features: Series of 1911-style pistols made in typical variations including full-size (Eagle), Commander (Hawk), Officer's (Thrasher) sizes.
Price: .... **$532.00–$959.00**

Prices given are believed to be accurate at time of publication however, many factors affect retail pricing so exact prices are not possible.

KAHR 25TH ANNIVERSARY K9

Caliber: 9mm. Capacity: 7-round magazine. Barrel: 4.02 in. Grips: Hogue textured and engraved aluminum. Sights: Fixed, TruGlo tritium. Length: 6 in. overall. Weight: 23.1 oz. unloaded. Finish: Sniper Grey Cerakote. Features: Limited 25th year anniversary edition includes custom 1791 leather holster and three magazines. Ported slide with "25 Years" engraving.
Price: **$1,649.00**

KAHR CM SERIES

Calibers: 9mm, .40 S&W, .45 ACP. Capacities: 9mm (6+1), .40 S&W (6+1). .45 ACP (5+1). CM45 Model is shown. Barrels: 3 in., 3.25 in. (45) Weights: 15.9–17.3 oz. Length: 5.42 in. overall. Grips: Textured polymer with integral steel rails molded into frame. Sights: CM9093, Pinned in polymer sight; PM9093, drift-adjustable, white bar-dot combat. Features: A conventional rifled barrel instead of the match-grade polygonal barrel on Kahr's PM series; the CM slide stop lever is MIM (metal-injection-molded) instead of machined; the CM series slide has fewer machining operations and uses simple engraved markings instead of roll marking. The CM series are shipped with one magazine instead of two. The slide is machined from solid 416 stainless with a matte finish, each gun is shipped with one 6-round stainless steel magazine with a flush baseplate. Magazines are U.S.-made, plasma welded, tumbled to remove burrs and feature Wolff springs. The magazine catch in the polymer frame is all metal and will not wear out on the stainless steel magazine after extended use.
Price: **$460.00**

KAHR CT 9/40/45 SERIES

Calibers: 9mm, .40 S&W, .45 ACP. Capacities: 9mm (8+1), .40 S&W (6+1) .45 ACP (7+1). Barrel: 4 in. Weights: 20–25 oz. Length: 5.42 in. overall. Grips: Textured polymer with integral steel rails molded into frame. Sights: Drift adjustable, white bar-dot combat. Features: Same as Kahr CM Series.
Price: **$460.00**

KAHR CT 380

Caliber: .380 ACP. Capacity: (7+1). Barrel: 3 in. Weight: 14 oz. Other features similar to CT 9/40/45 models.
Price: **$419.00**

KAHR K SERIES

Calibers: K9: 9mm, 7-shot; K40: .40 S&W, 6-shot magazine. Barrel: 3.5 in. Weight: 25 oz. Length: 6 in. overall. Grips: Wraparound textured soft polymer. Sights: Blade front, rear drift adjustable for windage; bar-dot combat style. Features: Trigger-cocking double-action mechanism with passive firing pin block. Made of 4140 ordnance steel with matte black finish. Contact maker for complete price list. Introduced 1994. Made in USA by Kahr Arms.
Price: K9093C K9, matte stainless steel **$855.00**
Price: K9093NC K9, matte stainless steel w/tritium
    night sights **$985.00**
Price: K9094C K9 matte blackened stainless steel **$891.00**
Price: K9098 K9 Elite 2003, stainless steel **$932.00**
Price: K4043 K40, matte stainless steel **$855.00**
Price: K4043N K40, matte stainless steel w/tritium
    night sights **$985.00**
Price: K4044 K40, matte blackened stainless steel **$891.00**
Price: K4048 K40 Elite 2003, stainless steel **$932.00**

KAHR MK SERIES MICRO

Similar to the K9/K40 except is 5.35 in. overall, 4 in. high, with a 3.08 in. barrel. Weighs 23.1 oz. Has snag-free bar-dot sights, polished feed ramp, dual recoil spring system, DAO trigger. Comes with 5-round flush baseplate and 6-shot grip extension magazine. Introduced 1998. Made in USA by Kahr Arms.
Price: M9093 MK9, matte stainless steel **$911.00**
Price: M9093N MK9, matte stainless steel, tritium
    night sights **$1,017.00**
Price: M9098 MK9 Elite 2003, stainless steel **$991.00**
Price: M4043 MK40, matte stainless steel **$911.00**
Price: M4043N MK40, matte stainless steel, tritium
    night sights **$1,115.00**
Price: M4048 MK40 Elite 2003, stainless steel **$991.00**

KAHR P SERIES

Calibers: .380 ACP, 9mm, .40 S&W, 45 ACP. Capacity: 7-shot magazine. Features: Similar to K9/K40 steel frame pistol except has polymer frame, matte stainless steel slide. Barrel length 3.5 in.; overall length 5.8 in.; weighs 17 oz. Includes two 7-shot magazines, hard polymer case, trigger lock. Introduced 2000. Made in USA by Kahr Arms.
Price: KP9093 9mm **$762.00**
Price: KP4043 .40 S&W **$762.00**
Price: KP4543 .45 ACP **$829.00**
Price: KP3833 .380 ACP (2008) **$667.00**

KAHR KP GEN 2 PREMIUM SERIES

Calibers: 9mm, .45 ACP. Capacities: KP9 9mm (7-shot magazine), KP45 .45 ACP (6 shots). Barrel: 3.5 in. Features: Black polymer frame, matte stainless slide, Tru-Glo Tritium fiber optic sights, short trigger, accessory rail.
Price: .... **$833.00-$1,101.00**

KAHR TP GEN 2 PREMIUM SERIES

Calibers: 9mm, .45 ACP. Capacities: TP9 9mm (8-shot magazine), TP45 .45 ACP (7 or 8 shots). Barrels: 4, 5, or 6 in. Features: Model with 4-inch barrel has features similar to KP GEN 2. The 5-inch model has front and rear slide serrations, white 3-dot sights, mount for reflex sights. The 6-inch model has the same features plus comes with Leupold Delta Point Reflex sight.
Price: **$976.00**
Price: 5-inch bbl **$1,015.00**
Price: 6-inch bbl **$1,566.00**

Prices given are believed to be accurate at time of publication however, many factors affect retail pricing so exact prices are not possible.

76TH EDITION, 2022 **451**

KAHR PM SERIES

Calibers: 9mm, .40 S&W, .45 ACP. Capacity: 7-round magazine. Features: Similar to P-Series pistols except has smaller polymer frame (Polymer Micro). Barrel length 3.08 in.; overall length 5.35 in.; weighs 17 oz. Includes two 7-shot magazines, hard polymer case, trigger lock. Introduced 2000. Made in USA by Kahr Arms.

Price: PM9093 PM9 .... **$810.00**
Price: PM4043 PM40 .... **$810.00**
Price: PM4543 PM45 .... **$880.00**

KAHR T SERIES

Calibers: 9mm, .40 S&W. Capacities: T9: 9mm, 8-round magazine; T40: .40 S&W, 7-round magazine. Barrel: 4 in. Weight: 28.1–29.1 oz. Length: 6.5 in. overall. Grips: Checkered Hogue Pau Ferro wood grips. Sights: Rear: Novak low-profile 2-dot tritium night sight, front tritium night sight. Features: Similar to other Kahr makes, but with longer slide and barrel upper, longer butt. Trigger cocking DAO; locking breech; Browning-type recoil lug; passive striker block; no magazine disconnect. Comes with two magazines. Introduced 2004. Made in USA by Kahr Arms.

Price: KT9093 T9 matte stainless steel **$857.00**
Price: KT9093-NOVAK T9, "Tactical 9," Novak night sight **$980.00**
Price: KT4043 40 S&W **$857.00**

KAHR CW SERIES

Caliber: 9mm, .40 S&W, .45 ACP. Capacities: 9mm, 7-round magazine; .40 S&W and .45 ACP, 6-round magazine. Barrels: 3.5 and 3.64 in. Weight: 17.7–18.7 oz. Length: 5.9–6.36 in. overall. Grips: Textured polymer. Similar to P-Series, but CW Series have conventional rifling, metal-injection-molded slide stop lever, no front dovetail cut, one magazine. CW40 introduced 2006. Made in USA by Kahr Arms. Several optional finishes available.

Price: .... **$449.00-$495.00**

KAHR P380

Caliber: .380 ACP. Capacity: 6+1. Features: Very small DAO semi-auto pistol. Features include 2.5-in. Lothar Walther barrel; black polymer frame with stainless steel slide; drift adjustable white bar/dot combat/sights; optional tritium sights; two 6+1 magazines. Overall length 4.9 in., weight 10 oz. without magazine.

Price: Standard sights **$667.00**
Price: Night sights... **$792.00**

KAHR CW380

Caliber: .380 ACP. Capacity: 6-round magazine. Barrel: 2.58 in. Weight: 11.5 oz. Length: 4.96 in. Grips: Textured integral polymer. Sights: Fixed white-bar combat style. Features: DAO. Black or purple polymer frame, stainless slide.

Price: **$419.00**

KAHR TIG SPECIAL EDITION

Caliber: 9mm. Capacity: 8 rounds. Weight: 18.5 oz. Barrel: 4 in. (Sub-compact model). Features: Limited Special Edition to support Beyond the Battlefield Foundation founded by John "Tig" Tiegen and his wife to provide support for wounded veterans. Tiegen is one of the heroes of the Benghazi attack in 2012. Kryptek Typhon finish on frame, black Teracote finish on slide engraved with Tiegen signature, Tig logo and BTB logo. Production will be limited to 1,000 pistols. Part of the proceeds from the sale of each firearm will be donated to the Beyond the Battlefield Foundation by Kahr Firearms Group.

Price: **$541.00**

Prices given are believed to be accurate at time of publication however, many factors affect retail pricing so exact prices are not possible.

KEL-TEC P-11
Caliber: 9mm. Capacity: 10-round magazine. Barrel: 3.1 in. Weight: 14 oz. Length: 5.6 in. overall. Grips: Checkered black polymer. Sights: Blade front, rear adjustable for windage. Features: Ordnance steel slide, aluminum frame. DAO trigger mechanism. Introduced 1995. Made in USA by Kel-Tec CNC Industries, Inc.
Price: From **$340.00**

KEL-TEC PF-9
Caliber: 9mm. Capacity: 7 rounds. Weight: 12.7 oz. Sights: Rear sight adjustable for windage and elevation. Barrel: 3.1 in. Length: 5.85 in. Features: Barrel, locking system, slide stop, assembly pin, front sight, recoil springs and guide rod adapted from P-11. Trigger system with integral hammer block and the extraction system adapted from P-3AT. Mil-Std-1913 Picatinny rail. Made in USA by Kel-Tec CNC Industries, Inc.
Price: From **$356.00**

KEL-TEC P17
Caliber: .22 LR. Capacity: 16-round magazine. Barrel: 3.8 in. Grips: Textured polymer. Sights: Fixed. Length: 6.7 in. overall. Weight: 11.2 oz. unloaded. Finish: Matte black.
Price: **$199.00**

KEL-TEC P-32
Caliber: .32 ACP. Capacity: 7-round magazine. Barrel: 2.68. Weight: 6.6 oz. Length: 5.07 overall. Grips: Checkered composite. Sights: Fixed. Features: Double-action-only mechanism with 6-lb. pull; internal slide stop. Textured composite grip/frame.
Price: From **$326.00**

KEL-TEC P-3AT
Caliber: .380 ACP. Capacity: 7-round magazine Weight: 7.2 oz. Length: 5.2. Features: Lightest .380 ACP made; aluminum frame, steel barrel.
Price: From **$331.00**

KEL-TEC PLR-16
Caliber: 5.56mm NATO. Capacity: 10-round magazine. Weight: 51 oz. Sights: Rear sight adjustable for windage, front sight is M-16 blade. Barrel: 9.2 in. Length: 18.5 in. Features: Muzzle is threaded 1/2x28 to accept standard attachments such as a muzzle brake. Except for the barrel, bolt, sights and mechanism, the PLR-16 pistol is made of high-impact glass fiber reinforced polymer. Gas-operated semi-auto. Conventional gas-piston operation with M-16 breech locking system. MIL-STD-1913 Picatinny rail. Made in USA by Kel-Tec CNC Industries, Inc.
Price: Blued **$682.00**

KEL-TEC PLR-22
Caliber: .22 LR. Capacity: 26-round magazine. Length: 18.5 in. overall. 40 oz. Features: Semi-auto pistol based on centerfire PLR-16 by same maker. Blowback action. Open sights and Picatinny rail for mounting accessories; threaded muzzle.
Price: **$400.00**

KEL-TEC PMR-30
Caliber: .22 Magnum (.22WMR). Capacity: 30 rounds. Barrel: 4.3 in. Weight: 13.6 oz. Length: 7.9 in. overall. Grips: Glass reinforced Nylon (Zytel). Sights: Dovetailed aluminum with front & rear fiber optics. Features: Operates on a unique hybrid blowback/locked-breech system. It uses a double-stack magazine of a new design that holds 30 rounds and fits completely in the grip of the pistol. Dual opposing extractors for reliability, heel magazine release to aid in magazine retention, Picatinny accessory rail under the barrel, Urethane recoil buffer, captive coaxial recoil springs. The barrel is fluted for light weight and effective heat dissipation. PMR30 disassembles

Prices given are believed to be accurate at time of publication however, many factors affect retail pricing so exact prices are not possible.

76TH EDITION, 2022 ✛ **453**

KIMBER COLLECTOR EDITION RAPTOR

Calibers: 9mm (Micro 9 and EVO), .45 ACP (1911) Capacity: 7- or 8-round magazine. Barrels: 3.15, 3.16 or 5 in. Weight: 15.6–38 oz. Grips: G10 smooth/scaled texture. Sights: Low profile, tritium. Finish: Two-tone bronze. Features: Scale-style slide serrations. Made in the Kimber Custom Shop.

Price: (1911 model) **$1,524.00**
Price: (Micro 9 model) **$951.00**
Price: (EVO SP model) **$999.00**

KIMBER MICRO CDP

Caliber: .380 ACP. Capacity: 6-round magazine. Barrel: 2.75 in. Weight: 17 oz. Grips: Double diamond rosewood. Mini 1911-style single action with no grip safety.

Price: **$869.00**

KIMBER MICRO CRIMSON CARRY

Caliber: .380 ACP. Capacity: 6-round magazine. Barrel: 2.75 in. Weight: 13.4 oz. Length: 5.6 in Grips: Black synthetic, double diamond. Sights: Fixed low profile. Finish: Matte black. Features: Aluminum frame with satin silver finish, steel slide, carry-melt treatment, full-length guide rod, rosewood Crimson Trace Lasergrips.

Price: **$839.00**

KIMBER MICRO TLE

Caliber: .380 ACP. Features: Similar to Micro Crimson Carry. Features: Black slide and frame. Green and black G10 grips.

Price: **$734.00**

KIMBER MICRO RAPTOR

Caliber: .380 ACP Capacity: 6-round magazine. Sights: Tritium night sights. Finish: Stainless. Features: Variation of Micro Carry with Raptor-style scalloped "feathered" slide serrations and grip panels.

Price: **$842.00**

KIMBER COVERT SERIES

Caliber: .45 ACP Capacity: 7-round magazine. Barrels: 3, 4 or 5 in. Weight: 25–31 oz. Grips: Crimson Trace laser with camo finish. Sights: Tactical wedge 3-dot night sights. Features: Made in the Kimber Custom Shop. Finish: Kimber Gray frame, matte black slide, black small parts. Carry Melt treatment. Available in three frame sizes: Custom, Pro and Ultra.

Price: **$1,457.00**

KIMBER CUSTOM II

Caliber: 9mm, .45 ACP. Barrel: 5 in. Weight: 38 oz. Length: 8.7 in. overall. Grips: Checkered black rubber, walnut, rosewood. Sights: Dovetailed front and rear, Kimber low profile adjustable or fixed sights. Features: Slide, frame and barrel machined from steel or stainless steel. Match-grade barrel, chamber and trigger group. Extended thumb safety, beveled magazine well, beveled front and rear slide serrations, high ride beavertail grip safety, checkered flat mainspring housing, kidney cut under trigger guard, high cut grip, match-grade stainless steel barrel bushing, polished breechface, Commander-style hammer, lowered and flared ejection port, Wolff springs, bead blasted black oxide or matte stainless finish. Introduced in 1996. Made in USA by Kimber Mfg., Inc.

Price: Custom II **$871.00**
Price: Two-Tone **$1,136.00**

KIMBER CUSTOM TLE II

Caliber: .45 ACP or 10mm. Features: TLE (Tactical Law Enforcement) version of Custom II model plus night sights, frontstrap checkering, threaded barrel, Picatinny rail.

Price: .45 ACP **$1,007.00**
Price: 10mm **$1,028.00**

KIMBER MICRO 9

Caliber: 9mm. Capacity: 7-round magazine. Barrel: 3.15 in. Weight: 15.6 oz. Features: The easily concealed Micro 9 features mild recoil, smooth trigger pull and the intuitive operation of a 1911 platform. Micro 9 slides are made to the tightest allowable tolerances, with barrels machined from stainless steel for superior resistance to moisture. All Micro 9 frames are shaped from the finest aluminum for integrity and strength. Lowered and flared ejection ports for flawless ejection and a beveled magazine well for fast, positive loading. In 2020, Kimber offered 15 different Micro 9 models with a total of 26 variations.

Prices: .... **$654.00-$1,061.00**

KIMBER STAINLESS II

Same features as Custom II except has stainless steel frame.
Price: Stainless II .45 ACP **$998.00**
Price: Stainless II 9mm **$1,016.00**
Price: Stainless II .45 ACP w/night sights.................................. **$1,141.00**
Price: Stainless II Target .45 ACP (stainless, adj. sight) **$1,108.00**

KIMBER PRO CARRY II

Calibers: 9mm, .45 ACP. Features: Similar to Custom II, has aluminum frame, 4-in. bull barrel fitted directly to the slide without bushing. Introduced 1998. Made in USA by Kimber Mfg., Inc.
Price: Pro Carry II, .45 ACP **$837.00**
Price: Pro Carry II, 9mm **$857.00**
Price: Pro Carry II w/night sights **$977.00**
Price: Two-Tone **$1,136.00**

KIMBER SAPPHIRE PRO II

Caliber: 9mm. Capacity: 9-round magazine. Features: Similar to Pro Carry II, 4-inch match-grade barrel. Striking two-tone appearance with satin silver aluminum frame and high polish bright blued slide. Grips are blue/black G-10 with grooved texture. Fixed Tactical Edge night sights. From the Kimber Custom Shop.
Price: **$1,652.00**

KIMBER RAPTOR II

Caliber: .45 ACP. Capacities: .45 ACP (8-round magazine, 7-round (Ultra and Pro models). Barrels: 3, 4 or 5 in. Weight: 25–31 oz. Grips: Thin milled rosewood. Sights: Tactical wedge 3-dot night sights. Features: Made in the Kimber Custom Shop. Matte black or satin silver finish. Available in three frame sizes: Custom (shown), Pro and Ultra.
Price: .... **$1,192.00–$1,464.00**

KIMBER ULTRA CARRY II

Calibers: 9mm, .45 ACP. Features: Lightweight aluminum frame, 3-in. match-grade bull barrel fitted to slide without bushing. Grips 0.4-in. shorter. Light recoil spring. Weighs 25 oz. Introduced in 1999. Made in USA by Kimber Mfg., Inc.
Price: Stainless Ultra Carry II .45 ACP **$919.00**
Price: Stainless Ultra Carry II 9mm **$1,016.00**
Price: Stainless Ultra Carry II .45 ACP with night sights **$1,039.00**
Price: Two-Tone... **$1,177.00**

KIMBER GOLD MATCH II

Caliber: .45 ACP. Features: Similar to Custom II models. Includes stainless steel barrel with match-grade chamber and barrel bushing, ambidextrous thumb safety, adjustable sight, premium aluminum trigger, hand-checkered double diamond rosewood grips. Barrel hand-fitted for target accuracy. Made in USA by Kimber Mfg., Inc.
Price: Gold Match II .45 ACP... **$1,393.00**
Price: Gold Match Stainless II .45 ACP **$1,574.00**

KIMBER CDP II SERIES

Calibers: 9mm, .45 ACP. Features: Similar to Custom II but designed for concealed carry. Aluminum frame. Standard features include stainless steel slide, fixed Meprolight tritium 3-dot (green) dovetail-mounted night sights, match-grade barrel and chamber, 30 LPI frontstrap checkering, two-tone finish, ambidextrous thumb safety, hand-checkered double diamond rosewood grips. Introduced in 2000. Made in USA by Kimber Mfg., Inc.
Price: Ultra CDP II 9mm (2008) **$1,359.00**
Price: Ultra CDP II .45 ACP **$1,318.00**
Price: Compact CDP II .45 ACP **$1,318.00**
Price: Pro CDP II .45 ACP **$1,318.00**
Price: Custom CDP II (5-in. barrel, full length grip) **$1,318.00**

KIMBER CDP

Calibers: 9mm, .45 ACP. Barrel: 3, 4 or 5 in. Weight: 25–31 oz. Features: Aluminum frame, stainless slide, 30 LPI checkering on backstrap and trigger guard, low profile tritium night sights, Carry Melt treatment. Sights: Hand checkered rosewood or Crimson Trace Lasergrips. Introduced in 2017.
Price: **$1,173.00**
Price: With Crimson Trace Lasergrips... **$1,473.00**

KIMBER ECLIPSE II SERIES

Calibers: .38 Super, 10 mm, .45 ACP. Features: Similar to Custom II and other stainless Kimber pistols. Stainless slide and frame, black oxide, two-tone finish. Gray/black laminated grips. 30 LPI frontstrap checkering. All models have night sights; Target versions have Meprolight adjustable Bar/Dot version. Made in USA by Kimber Mfg., Inc.
Price: Eclipse Ultra II (3-in. barrel, short grip) **$1,350.00**
Price: Eclipse Pro II (4-in. barrel, full-length grip) **$1,350.00**
Price: Eclipse Custom II 10mm **$1,350.00**
Price: Eclipse Target II (5-in. barrel, full-length grip, adjustable sight) **$1,393.00**

KIMBER TACTICAL ENTRY II

Caliber: 45 ACP. Capacity: 7-round magazine. Barrel: 5 in. Weight: 40 oz. Length: 8.7 in. overall. Features: 1911-style semi-auto with checkered frontstrap, extended magazine well, night sights, heavy steel frame, tactical rail.
Price: **$1,490.00**

KIMBER TACTICAL CUSTOM HD II

Caliber: .45 ACP. Capacity: 7-round magazine. Barrel: 5 in. match-grade. Weight: 39 oz. Length: 8.7 in. overall. Features: 1911-style semiauto with night sights, heavy steel frame.
Price: **$1,387.00**

KIMBER ULTRA CDP II

Calibers: 9mm, .45 ACP. Capacities: 7-round magazine (9 in 9mm). Features: Compact 1911-style pistol; ambidextrous thumb safety; carry melt profiling; full-length guide rod; aluminum frame with stainless slide; satin silver finish; checkered frontstrap; 3-inch barrel; rosewood double diamond Crimson Trace laser grips; tritium 3-dot night sights.
Price: **$1,603.00**

KIMBER STAINLESS ULTRA TLE II

Caliber: .45 ACP. Capacity: 7-round magazine. Features: 1911-style semi-auto pistol. Features include full-length guide rod; aluminum frame with stainless slide; satin silver finish; checkered frontstrap; 3-in. barrel; tactical gray double diamond grips; tritium 3-dot night sights.
Price: **$1,136.00**

KIMBER ROYAL II

Caliber: .45 ACP. Capacity: 7-round magazine. Barrel: 5 in. Weight: 38 oz. Length: 8.7 in. overall. Grips: Solid bone-smooth. Sights: Fixed low profile. Features: A classic full-size pistol wearing a charcoal blue finish complimented with solid bone grip panels. Front and rear serrations. Aluminum match-grade trigger with a factory setting of approximately 4–5 pounds.
Price: **$1,785.00**

KIMBER MASTER CARRY SERIES

Caliber: .45 ACP. Capacity: 8-round magazine, 9mm (Pro only). Barrels: 5 in. (Custom), 4 in. (Pro), 3 in. (Ultra) Weight: 25–30 oz. Grips: Crimson Trace Laser. Sights: Fixed low profile. Features: Matte black KimPro slide, aluminum round heel frame, full-length guide rod.
Price: **$1,497.00**

KIMBER WARRIOR SOC

Caliber: .45 ACP. Capacity: 7-round magazine. Barrel: 5 in threaded for suppression. Sights: Fixed Tactical Wedge tritium. Finish: Dark Green frame, Flat Dark Earth slide. Features: Full-size 1911 based on special series of pistols made for USMC. Service melt, ambidextrous safety.
Price: **$1,392.00**

KIMBER SUPER JAGARE

Caliber: 10mm. Capacity: 8+1. Barrel: 6 in, ported. Weight: 42 oz. Finish: Stainless steel KimPro, Charcoal gray frame, diamond-like carbon coated slide. Slide is ported. Sights: Delta Point Pro Optic. Grips: Micarta. Frame has rounded heel, high cut trigger guard. Designed for hunting.
Price: **$2,688.00**

KIMBER KHX SERIES

Calibers: .45 ACP, 9mm. Capacity: 8+1. Features: This series is offered in Custom, Pro and Ultra sizes. Barrels: 5-, 4- or 3-inch match-grade stainless steel. Weights: 25–38 oz. Finishes: Stainless steel frame and slide with matte black KimPro II finish. Stepped hexagonal slide and top-strap serrations. Sights: Green and red fiber optic and Hogue Laser Enhanced MagGrip G10 grips and matching mainspring housings. Pro and Ultra models have rounded heel frames. Optics Ready (OR) models available in Custom and Pro sizes with milled slide that accepts optics plates for Vortex, Trijicon and Leupold red-dot sights.
Price: Custom OR .45 ACP **$1,087.00**
Price: Custom OR 9mm **$1,108.00**
Price: Custom, Pro or Ultra .45 .... **$1,259.00**
Price: Custom, Pro or Ultra 9mm **$1,279.00**

KIMBER AEGIS ELITE SERIES

Calibers: 9mm, .45 ACP. Features: Offered in Custom, Pro and Ultra sizes with 5-, 4.25- or 3-in. barrels. Sights: Green or red fiber optic or Vortex Venom red dot on OI (Optics Installed) models (shown). Grips: G10. Features: Satin finish stainless steel frame, matte black or gray slide, front and rear AEX slide serrations.
Price: .45 ACP **$1,021.00**
Price: 9mm **$1,041.00**
Price: .45 OI **$1,375.00**
Price: 9mm OI **$1,395.00**

KIMBER EVO SERIES

Caliber: 9mm. Capacity: 7 rounds. Barrel: 3.16 in. Sights: Tritium night sights. Weight: 19 oz. Grips: G10. Features: Offered in TLE, CDP, Two Tone variants with stainless slide, aluminum frame.
Price: TLE **$925.00**
Price: CDP **$949.00**
Price: Two Tone **$856.00**

LIONHEART LH9 MKII

Caliber: 9mm. Capacities: 15-round magazine. LH9C Compact, 10 rounds. Barrel: 4.1 in. Weight: 26.5 oz. Length: 7.5 in Grips: One-piece black polymer with textured design. Sights: Fixed low profile. Novak LoMount sights available. Finish: Cerakote Graphite Black or Patriot Brown. Features: Hammer-forged heat-treated steel slide, hammer-forged aluminum frame. Double-action PLUS action.
Price: $695.00
Price: Novak sights .... $749.

LLAMA MAX-1

Calibers: .38 Super, .45 ACP. Barrel: 5 in. Weight: 37 oz. Sights: Mil-spec. fixed. Features: Standard size and features of the 1911A1 full-size model. Lowered ejection port, matte blue or hard chrome finish. Imported from the Philippines by Eagle Imports. Introduced in 2016.
Price: $565.00

LLAMA MICRO MAX

Caliber: .380 ACP. Capacity: 7-round magazine. Weight: 23 oz. Sights: Novak style rear, fiber optic front. Grips: Wood or black synthetic. Features: A compact 1911-style pistol with 3.75-in. barrel. Skeletonized hammer and trigger, double slide serrations, comes with two 7-shot magazines. Imported from the Philippines by Eagle Imports.
Price: $468.00

MAC 1911 BOB CUT

Caliber: .45 ACP. Capacity: 8+1 magazine. Barrel: 4.25 in. Commander-size 1911 design. Sights: Novak-type fully adjustable rear, dovetail front. Weight: 34.5 oz. Finish: Blue or hard chrome. Grips: Custom hardwood. Features: Stippled frontstrap, skeletonized trigger and hammer, flared and lowered ejection port, bobtail grip frame. Imported from the Philippines by Eagle Imports.
Price: $902.00

MAC 1911 BULLSEYE

Caliber: .45 ACP Capacity: 8+1 magazine. Barrel: 6-in. match-grade bull. Sights: Bomar-type fully adjustable rear, dovetail front. Weight: 46 oz. Finish: Blue or hard chrome. Grips: Hardwood. Features: Checkered frontstrap, skeletonized trigger and hammer, flared and lowered ejection port, wide front and rear slide serrations. Imported from the Philippines by Eagle Imports.
Price: $1,219.00

MAC 1911 CLASSIC

Caliber: .45 ACP. Capacity: 8-round magazine. Barrel: 5-in., match-grade bull. Sights: Bomar-type fully adjustable rear, fiber-optic front. Weight: 40.5 oz. Finish: Blue, black chrome or hard chrome. Grips: Hardwood. Features: Checkered frontstrap, skeletonized trigger and hammer, flared and lowered ejection port, wide front and rear slide serrations. Imported from the Philippines by Eagle Imports.
Price: $1,045.00

MAC 3011 SLD TACTICAL

Calibers: 9mm, .40 S&W, .45 ACP. Capacity: 14-, 15- or 17-round magazines. Barrel: 5 in.-, match-grade bull. Sights: Bomar-type fully adjustable rear, fiber-optic front. Weight: 46.5 oz. Finish: Blue. Grips: Aluminum. Features: Checkered frontstrap serrations, skeletonized trigger and hammer, flared and lowered ejection port, ambidextrous safety, full dust cover. Imported from the Philippines by Eagle Imports.
Price: $1,136.00

Prices given are believed to be accurate at time of publication however, many factors affect retail pricing so exact prices are not possible.

76TH EDITION, 2022 ✦ 457

MOSSBERG MC1SC

Caliber: 9mm Capacity: 6+1 magazine. Barrel: 3.4 in. Sights: Three white-dot, snag free. TruGlo tritium Pro sights or Viridian E-Series Red Laser available as option. Grips: Integral with aggressive texturing and with palm swell. Features: Glass-reinforced polymer frame, stainless steel slide with multi-angle front and rear serrations, flat-profile trigger with integrated blade safety, ships with one 6-round and one 7-round magazine. Optional cross-bolt safety. Centennial Limited Edition (1,000 units) has 24k gold accents, tritium nitride finish on barrel, polished slide.

Price:	....	**$421.00**
Price:	Viridian laser sight........................	**$514.00**
Price:	TruGlo tritium sights.....................	**$526.00**
Price:	Centennial Limited Edition	**$686.00**
Price:	FDE	**$428.00**
Price:	Two-Tone......................................	**$421.00**

MOSSBERG MC2C

Caliber: 9mm. Capacity: 13- or 15-round magazine. Barrel: 3.9 in. Grips: Textured polymer. Sights: Fixed, 3-dot. Length: 7.1 in. overall. Weight: 21 oz. unloaded. Finish: Matte black. Features: Accessory rail, forward-slide serrations.

Price: **$490.00**

NIGHTHAWK CUSTOM AGENT2 COMMANDER

Calibers: 9mm, .45 ACP. Capacity: 10-round magazine. Barrel: 4.25 in. Grips: G10 Railscale texture. Sights: Fixed, Heinie Ledge Black rear/gold-bead front. Length: 7.85 in. overall. Weight: 38.6 oz. unloaded. Finish: Smoke Cerakote. Features: Accessory rail, faceted slide with side windows, one-piece mainspring housing/mag well, ultra-high-cut front grip strap.

Price: **$4,499.00**

NIGHTHAWK CUSTOM BULL OFFICER

Caliber: 9mm. Capacity: 8-round magazine. Barrel: 3.8 in. Grips: Textured carbon fiber. Sights: Fixed, Heinie Ledge Black rear/fiber-optic front. Length: 7.85 in. overall. Weight: 38.2 oz. unloaded. Finish: Black nitride. Features: Bull nose and French border on slide, ultra-high-cut front grip strap, dehorned.

Price: **$3,699.00**

NIGHTHAWK CUSTOM COLT SERIES 70

Caliber: .45 ACP. Capacity: 7-round magazine. Barrel: 5 in. Grips: Textured linen micarta. Sights: Fixed, retro rear/gold-bead front. Length: 8.75 in. overall. Weight: 39 oz. unloaded. Finish: Smoked nitride. Features: Match-grade solid short trigger, fully machined disconnector, retro hammer, Nighthawk Custom beavertail grip safety, mainspring housing and match barrel bushing.

Price: **$2,599.00**

NIGHTHAWK CUSTOM GRP

Calibers: 9mm, 10mm, .45 ACP. Capacity: 8-round magazine. Features: Global Response Pistol (GRP). Black, Sniper Gray, green, Coyote Tan or Titanium Blue finish. Match-grade barrel and trigger, choice of Heinie or Novak adjustable night sights.

Price: **$3,095.00**

NIGHTHAWK CUSTOM T4

Calibers: 9mm, .45 ACP Capacities: .45 ACP, 7- or 8-round magazine; 9mm, 9 or 10 rounds; 10mm, 9 or 10 rounds. Barrels: 3.8, 4.25 or 5 in. Weights: 28–41 ounces, depending on model. Features: Manufacturer of a wide range of 1911-style pistols in Government Model (full-size), Commander and Officer's frame sizes. Shown is T4 model, introduced in 2013 and available only in 9mm.

Price: From ....**$3,495.00–$3,695.00**

NIGHTHAWK CUSTOM THUNDER RANCH

Caliber: 9mm, .45 ACP. Capacity: 8-round (.45 ACP), 10-round (9mm) magazine. Barrel: 5 in. Grips: Textured linen micarta. Sights: Fixed, Heinie Black Ledge rear/gold-bead front. Length: 8.6 in. overall. Weight: 41.3 oz. unloaded. Finish: Smoked nitride. Features: Custom front- and rear-cocking serrations, lanyard-loop mainspring housing, GI-Style nub thumb safety and custom engraving.

Price: **$3,399.00**

NIGHTHAWK CUSTOM SHADOW HAWK

Caliber: 9mm. Barrels: 5 in. or 4.25 in. Features: Stainless steel frame with black Nitride finish, flat-faced trigger, high beavertail grip safety, checkered frontstrap, Heinie Straight Eight front and rear titanium night sights.

Price: **$3,795.00**

NIGHTHAWK CUSTOM VICE PRESIDENT

Caliber: 9mm. Capacity: 10-round magazine. Barrel: 4.25 in. Grips: G10 Railscale Ascend texture. Sights: Fixed, Heinie Straight Eight Ledge rear/tritium front. Length: 7.4 in. overall. Weight: 32 oz. unloaded. Finish: Black DLC. Features: Gold titanium nitride barrel, heavy angle slide-lightening cuts, one-piece mainspring housing/mag well, ultra-high-cut front grip strap, dehorned.

Price: **$4,199.00**

NIGHTHAWK CUSTOM WAR HAWK

Caliber: .45 ACP. Barrels: 5 in. or 4.25 in. Features: One-piece mainspring housing and mag well, Everlast Recoil System, Hyena Brown G10 grips.

Price: **$3,895.00**

NIGHTHAWK CUSTOM BOB MARVEL 1911

Calibers: 9mm or .45 ACP. Barrel: 4.25-in. bull barrel. Features: Everlast Recoil System, adjustable sights, match trigger, black Melonite finish.

Price: **$4,395.00**

NIGHTHAWK CUSTOM DOMINATOR

Caliber: .45 ACP. Capacity: 8-round magazine. Features: Stainless frame, black Perma Kote slide, cocobolo double-diamond grips,, front and rear slide serrations, adjustable sights.

Price: **$3,699.00**

NIGHTHAWK CUSTOM SILENT HAWK
Caliber: .45 ACP. Capacity: 8-round magazine. Barrel: 4.25 in. Features: Commander recon frame, G10 black and gray grips. Designed to match Silencerco silencer, not included with pistol.
Price: **$4,295.00**

NIGHTHAWK CUSTOM HEINIE LONG SLIDE
Calibers: 10mm, .45 ACP. Barrel: Long slide 6-in. Features: Cocobolo wood grips, black Perma Kote finish, adjustable or fixed sights, frontstrap checkering.
Price: **$3,895.00**

NIGHTHAWK CUSTOM BORDER SPECIAL
Caliber: .45 ACP Capacity: 8+1 magazine. Barrel: 4.25-in. match grade. Weight: 34 oz. Sights: Heinie Black Slant rear, gold bead front. Grips: Cocobolo double diamond. Finish: Cerakote Elite Midnight black. Features: Commander-size steel frame with bobtail concealed carry grip. Scalloped frontstrap and mainspring housing. Serrated slide top. Rear slide serrations only. Crowned barrel flush with bushing.
Price: **$3,699.00**

NIGHTHAWK VIP BLACK
Caliber: .45 ACP. Capacity: 8+1 magazine. Hand built with all Nighthawk 1911 features plus deep hand engraving throughout, black DLC finish, custom vertical frontstrap and mainspring serrations, 14k solid gold bead front sight, crowned barrel, giraffe bone grips, custom walnut hardwood presentation case.
Price: **$7,999.00**

NORTH AMERICAN ARMS GUARDIAN DAO
Calibers: .25 NAA, .32 ACP, .380 ACP, .32 NAA. Capacity: 6-round magazine. Barrel: 2.49 in. Weight: 20.8 oz. Length: 4.75 in. overall. Grips: Black polymer. Sights: Low-profile fixed. Features: DAO mechanism. All stainless steel construction. Introduced 1998. Made in USA by North American Arms. The .25 NAA is based on a bottle-necked .32 ACP case, and the .32 NAA is on a bottle-necked .380 ACP case. Custom model has roll-engraved slide, high-polish features, choice of grips.
Price: .25 NAA, .32 ACP **$409.00**
Price: .32 NAA, .380 ACP **$486.00**
Price: Engraved Custom Model .... **$575.00-$625.00**

PHOENIX ARMS HP22, HP25
Calibers: .22 LR, .25 ACP. Capacities: .22 LR, 10-shot (HP22), .25 ACP, 10-shot (HP25). Barrel: 3 in. Weight: 20 oz. Length: 5.5 in. overall. Grips: Checkered composition. Sights: Blade front, adjustable rear. Features: Single action, exposed hammer; manual hold-open; button magazine release. Available in satin nickel,matte blue finish. Introduced 1993. Made in USA by Phoenix Arms.
Price: With gun lock **$162.00**
Price: HP Range kit with 5-in. bbl., locking case and
accessories (1 Mag) **$207.00**
Price: HP Deluxe Range kit with 3- and 5-in. bbls., 2 mags, case **$248.00**

REPUBLIC FORGE 1911
Calibers: .45 ACP, 9mm, .38 Super, .40 S&W, 10mm. Features: A manufacturer of custom 1911-style pistols offered in a variety of configurations, finishes and frame sizes, including single- and double-stack models with many options. Made in Texas.
Price: From **$2,795.00**

ROBERTS DEFENSE 1911 SERIES
Caliber: .45 ACP. Capacity: 8-round magazine. Barrels: 5, 4.25 or 3.5 in. Weights: 26–38 oz. Sights: Novak-type drift-adjustable rear, tritium-dot or fiber optic front sight. Features: Skeletonized trigger. Offered in four model variants with many custom features and options. Made in Wisconsin by Roberts Defense.
Price: Recon.. **$2,370.00**
Price: Super Grade **$2,270.00**
Price: Operator... **$2,350.00**

ROCK ISLAND ARMORY 1911A1-45 FSP
Calibers: 9mm, .38 Super, .45 ACP. Capacities:.45 ACP (8 rounds), 9mm Parabellum, .38 Super (9 rounds). Features: 1911-style semi-auto pistol. Hard rubber grips, 5-inch barrel, blued, Duracoat or two-tone finish, drift-adjustable sights. Nickel finish or night sights available.
Price: From **$592.00**

ROCK ISLAND ARMORY 1911A1-FS MATCH
Caliber: .45 ACP. Barrels: 5 in. or 6 in. Features: 1911 match-style pistol. Features fiber optic front and adjustable rear sights, skeletonized trigger and hammer, extended beavertail, double diamond checkered walnut grips.
Price: **$877.00**

ROCK ISLAND ARMORY 1911A1-.22 TCM
Caliber: .22 TCM. Capacity: 17-round magazine. Barrel: 5 in. Weight: 36 oz. Length: 8.5 in. Grips: Polymer. Sights: Adjustable rear. Features: Chambered for high velocity .22 TCM rimfire cartridge. Comes with interchangeable 9mm barrel.
Price: From **$806.00**

ROCK ISLAND ARMORY PRO MATCH ULTRA "BIG ROCK"
Caliber: 10mm. Capacity: 8- or 16-round magazine. Barrel: 6 in. Weight: 40 oz. Length: 8.5 in. Grips: VZ G10. Sights: Fiber optic front, adjustable rear. Features: Two magazines, upper and lower accessory rails, extended beavertail safety.
Price: **$1,187.00**
Price: High capacity model.. **$1,340.00**

ROCK ISLAND ARMORY MAP & MAPP
Caliber: 9mm, .22 TCM. Capacity: 16-round magazine. Barrel: 3.5 (MAPP) or 4 in (MAP). Browning short recoil action-style pistols with: integrated front sight; snag-free rear sight; single- & double-action trigger; standard or ambidextrous rear safety; polymer frame with accessory rail.
Price: From **$429.00**

ROCK ISLAND ARMORY XT22
Calibers: .22 LR, .22 Magnum. Capacities: 10- or 15-round magazine. Barrel: 5 in. Weight: 38 oz. Features: The XT-22 is the only .22 1911 with a forged 4140 steel slide and a one piece 4140 chrome moly barrel. Available as a .22/.45 ACP combo.
Price: **$600.00**
Price: .22 LR/.45 combo **$900.00**

Prices given are believed to be accurate at time of publication however, many factors affect retail pricing so exact prices are not possible.

76TH EDITION, 2022 ✦ **459**

HANDGUNS Autoloaders, Service & Sport

ROCK ISLAND ARMORY BABY ROCK 380
Caliber: .380 ACP. Capacity: 7-round magazine. Features: Blowback operation. An 85 percent-size version of 1911-A1 design with features identical to full-size model.
Price: **$460.00**

ROCK RIVER ARMS LAR-15/LAR-9
Calibers: .223/5.56mm NATO, 9mm. Barrels: 7 in., 10.5 in. Wilson chrome moly, 1:9 twist, A2 flash hider, 1/2x28 thread. Weights: 5.1 lbs. (7-in. barrel), 5.5 lbs. (10.5-in. barrel). Length: 23 in. overall. Stock: Hogue rubber grip. Sights: A2 front. Features: Forged A2 or A4 upper, single stage trigger, aluminum free-float tube, one magazine. Similar 9mm Para. LAR-9 also available. From Rock River Arms, Inc.
Price: LAR-15 7 in. A2 AR2115... **$1,175.00**
Price: LAR-15 10.5 in. A4 AR2120....................................... **$1,055.00**
Price: LAR-9 7 in. A2 9mm2115... **$1,320.00**

ROCK RIVER ARMS TACTICAL PISTOL
Caliber: .45 ACP. Features: Standard-size 1911 pistol with rosewood grips, Heinie or Novak sights, Black Cerakote finish.
Price: **$2,200.00**

ROCK RIVER ARMS LIMITED MATCH
Calibers: .45 ACP, 40 S&W, .38 Super, 9mm. Barrel: 5 in. Sights: Adjustable rear, blade front. Finish: Hard chrome. Features: National Match frame with beveled magazine well, front and rear slide serrations, Commander Hammer, G10 grips.
Price: **$3,600.00**

ROCK RIVER ARMS CARRY PISTOL
Caliber: .45 ACP. Barrel: 5 in. Sights: Heinie. Finish: Parkerized. Grips: Rosewood. Weight: 39 oz.
Price: **$1,600.00**

ROCK RIVER ARMS 1911 POLY
Caliber: .45 ACP. Capacity: 7-round magazine. Barrel: 5 in. Weight: 33 oz. Sights: Fixed. Features: Full-size 1911-style model with polymer frame and steel slide.
Price: **$925.00**

RUGER-57
Caliber: 5.7x28mm. Capacity: 20-round magazine. Barrel: 4.94 in. Grips: Textured polymer. Sights: Adjustable rear/fiber-optic front, optic ready. Length: 8.65 in. overall. Weight: 24.5 oz. unloaded. Finish: Black oxide. Features: 1911-style ambidextrous manual safety, Picatinny-style accessory rail, drilled and tapped for optics with optic-adapter plate. Made in the USA.
Price: **$799.00**

RUGER AR-556 PISTOL
Calibers: 5.56 NATO, .350 Legend, .300 BLK. Capacity: .350 Legend (5-round magazine), 5.56 NATO or .300 BLK (30-round magazine). Barrels: 9.5 - 10.5 in. Weight: 6.2 lbs. Sights: Optic-ready, Picatinny rail. Grips: AR15 A2 style. Features: SB Tactical SBA3 brace.
Price: .... **$899.00-$949.00**

RUGER AMERICAN PISTOL
Calibers: 9mm, .45 ACP. Capacities: 10 or 17 (9mm), 10 (.45 ACP). Barrels: 4.2 in. (9), 4.5 in. (.45). Lengths: 7.5 or 8 in. Weights: 30–31.5 oz. Sights: Novak LoMount Carry 3-Dot. Finish: Stainless steel slide with black Nitride finish. Grip: One-piece ergonomic wrap-around module with adjustable palm swell and trigger reach. Features: Short take-up trigger with positive re-set, ambidextrous mag release and slide stop, integrated trigger safety, automatic sear block system, easy takedown. Introduced in 2016.
Price: **$579.00**

RUGER AMERICAN COMPACT PISTOL
Caliber: 9mm. Barrel: 3.5 in. Features: Compact version of American Pistol with same general specifications.
Price: **$579.00**

RUGER LITE RACK LCP II
Caliber: .22 LR. Capacity: 10-round magazine. Barrel: 2.75 in. Grips: Textured polymer. Sights: Integral-notch rear/post front. Length: 5.2 in. overall. Weight: 11.2 oz. unloaded. Finish: Black. Features: A good training/practice pistol for anyone who carries a Ruger LCP or LCP II. Lite Rack system with refined slide serrations, cocking ears and lighter recoil spring. Made in the USA.
Price: **$349.00**

RUGER PC CHARGER
Caliber: 9mm. Capacity: 17-round magazine. Barrel: Threaded 6.5 in. Grips: AR15 A2 style. Sights: Optic-ready, Picatinny-style rail. Length: 16.5 in. overall. Weight: 5.2 lbs. unloaded. Finish: Blued. Features: Pistol version of the Ruger PC Carbine with a glass-filled polymer chassis system and M-LOK rail. Easy takedown system separates barrel/fore-end assembly from the action, and interchangeable magazine wells for Ruger American, Ruger Security-9 or Glock magazines. Made in the USA.
Price: **$799.00**

RUGER SECURITY-9 PRO
Caliber: 9mm. Capacity: 15-round magazine. Barrel: 4 in. Grips: Textured polymer. Sights: Fixed-steel tritium. Length: 7.24 in. overall. Weight: 23.8 oz. unloaded. Finish: Black oxide. Features: Rugged construction with black oxide, through-hardened, alloy-steel slide and barrel and high-performance, glass-filled nylon grip frame. Made in the USA.
Price: **$549.00**

RUGER SECURITY-9 COMPACT PRO
Caliber: 9mm. Capacity: 10-round magazine. Barrel: 3.42 in. Grips: Textured polymer. Sights: Fixed-steel tritium. Length: 6.52 in. overall. Weight: 21.9 oz. unloaded. Finish: Black oxide. Features: Similar to Ruger Security-9 Pro. Precision-machined, hard-coat, anodized-aluminum chassis with full-length guide rails. Made in the USA.
Price: **$549.00**

Prices given are believed to be accurate at time of publication however, many factors affect retail pricing so exact prices are not possible.

RUGER SR9 /SR40

Calibers: 9mm, .40 S&W. Capacities: 9mm (17-round magazine), .40 S&W (15). Barrel: 4.14 in. Weights: 26.25, 26.5 oz. Grips: Glass-filled nylon in two color options — black or OD Green, w/flat or arched reversible backstrap. Sights: Adjustable 3-dot, built-in Picatinny-style rail. Features: Semi-auto in six configurations, striker-fired, through-hardened stainless steel slide brushed or blackened stainless slide with black grip frame or blackened stainless slide with OD Green grip frame, ambidextrous manual 1911-style safety, ambi. mag release, mag disconnect, loaded chamber indicator, Ruger cam block design to absorb recoil, comes with two magazines. 10-shot mags available. Introduced 2008. Made in USA by Sturm, Ruger & Co.
Price: SR9 (17-Round), SR9-10 (SS) **$569.00**

RUGER SR9C/SR40C COMPACT

Calibers: 9mm, .40 S&W. Capacities: 10- and 17-round magazine. Barrels: 3.4 in. (SR9C), 3.5 in. (SR40C). Weight: 23.4 oz. Features: Features include 1911-style ambidextrous manual safety; internal trigger bar interlock and striker blocker; trigger safety; magazine disconnector; loaded chamber indicator; two magazines, one 10-round and the other 17-round; 3.5-in. barrel; 3-dot sights; accessory rail; brushed stainless or blackened allow finish.
Price: **$569.00**

RUGER SR45

Caliber: .45 ACP. Capacity: 10-round magazine. Barrel: 4.5 in. Weight: 30 oz. Length: 8 in. Grips: Glass-filled nylon with reversible flat/arched backstrap. Sights: Adjustable 3-dot. Features: Same features as SR9.
Price: **$569.00**

RUGER LC9S

Caliber: 9mm. Capacity: 7+1. Barrel: 3.12 in. Grips: Glass-filled nylon. Sights: Adjustable 3-dot. Features: Brushed stainless slide, black glass-filled grip frame, blue alloy barrel finish. Striker-fired operation with smooth trigger pull. Integral safety plus manual safety. Aggressive frame checkering with smooth "melted" edges. Slightly larger than LCS380. LC9S Pro has no manual safety.
Price: **$479.00**

RUGER LC380

Caliber: .380 ACP. Other specifications and features identical to LC9.
Price: **$479.00**
Price: LaserMax laser grips **$529.00**
Price: Crimson Trace Laserguard **$629.00**

RUGER SECURITY-9

Caliber: 9mm. Capacity: 10- or 15-round magazine. Barrel: 4 or 3.4 in. Weight: 21 oz. Sights: Drift-adjustable 3-dot. Viridian E-Series Red Laser available. Striker-fired polymer-frame compact model. Uses the same Secure Action as LCP II. Bladed trigger safety plus external manual safety.
Price: **$379.00**
Price: Viridian Laser sight **$439.00**

RUGER LCP

Caliber: .380. Capacity: 6-round magazine. Barrel: 2.75 in. Weight: 9.4 oz. Length: 5.16 in. Grips: Glass-filled nylon. Sights: Fixed, drift adjustable or integral Crimson Trace Laserguard.
Price: Blued **$259.00**
Price: Stainless steel slide... **$289.00**
Price: Viridian-E Red Laser sight.. **$349.00**
Price: Custom w/drift adjustable rear sight............................ **$269.00**

Prices given are believed to be accurate at time of publication however, many factors affect retail pricing so exact prices are not possible.

76TH EDITION, 2022 ⊕ **461**

RUGER LCP II

Caliber: .380. Capacity: 6-round magazine. Barrel: 2.75 in. Weight: 10.6 oz. Length: 5.16 in. Grips: Glass-filled nylon. Sights: Fixed. Features: Last round fired holds action open. Larger grip frame surface provides better recoil distribution. Finger grip extension included. Improved sights for superior visibility. Sights are integral to the slide, hammer is recessed within slide.
Price: **$349.00**

RUGER EC9S

Caliber: 9mm. Capacity: 7-shot magazine. Barrel: 3.125 in. Striker-fired polymer frame. Weight: 17.2 oz.
Price: **$299.00**

RUGER CHARGER

Caliber: .22 LR. Capacity: 15-round BX-15 magazine. Features: Based on famous 10/22 rifle design with pistol grip stock and fore-end, scope rail, bipod. Black laminate stock. Silent-SR Suppressor available. Add $449. NFA regulations apply. Reintroduced with improvements and enhancements in 2015.
Price: Standard **$309.00**
Price: Takedown **$419.00**

RUGER MK IV COMPETITION

RUGER MARK IV SERIES

Caliber: .22 LR. Capacity: 10-round magazine. Barrels: 5.5 in, 6.875 in. Target model has 5.5-in. bull barrel, Hunter model 6.88-in. fluted bull, Competition model 6.88-in. slab-sided bull. Weight: 33–46 oz. Grips: Checkered or target laminate. Sights: Adjustable rear, blade or fiber-optic front (Hunter). Features: Updated design of Mark III series with one-button takedown. Introduced 2016. Modern successor of the first Ruger pistol of 1949.
Price: Standard **$449.00**
Price: Target (blue) **$529.00**
Price: Target (stainless) **$689.00**
Price: Hunter .... **$769.00–$799.00**
Price: Competition **$749.00**

RUGER 22/45 MARK IV PISTOL

Caliber: .22 LR. Features: Similar to other .22 Mark IV autos except has Zytel grip frame that matches angle and magazine latch of Model 1911 .45 ACP pistol. Available in 4.4-, 5.5-in. bull barrels. Comes with extra magazine, plastic case, lock. Molded polymer or replaceable laminate grips. Weight: 25–33 oz. Sights: Adjustable. Updated design of Mark III with one-button takedown. Introduced 2016.
Price: **$409.00**
Price: 4.4-in. bull threaded barrel w/rails **$529.00**
Price: Lite w/aluminum frame, rails **$549.00**

RUGER SR22

Caliber: .22 LR. Capacity: 10-round magazine. Barrel: 3.5 in. Weight: 17.5 oz. Length: 6.4 in. Sights: Adjustable 3-dot. Features: Ambidextrous manual safety/decocking lever and mag release. Comes with two interchangeable rubberized grips and two magazines. Black or silver anodize finish. Available with threaded barrel.
Price: Black **$439.00**
Price: Silver **$459.00**
Price: Threaded barrel **$479.00**

RUGER SR1911

Caliber: .45. Capacity: 8-round magazine. Barrel: 5 in. (3.5 in. Officer Model) Weight: 39 oz. Length: 8.6 in., 7.1 in. Grips: Slim checkered hardwood. Sights: Novak LoMount Carry rear, standard front. Features: Based on Series 70 design. Flared and lowered ejection port. Extended mag release, thumb safety and slide-stop lever, oversized grip safety, checkered backstrap on the flat mainspring housing. Comes with one 7-round and one 8-round magazine.
Price: **$939.00**

Prices given are believed to be accurate at time of publication however, many factors affect retail pricing so exact pricing is not possible.

RUGER SR1911 CMD

Caliber: .45 ACP. Barrel: 4.25 in. Weight: 29.3 (aluminum), 36.4 oz. (stainless). Features: Commander-size version of SR1911. Other specifications and features are identical to SR1911. Lightweight Commander also offered in 9mm.

Price: Low glare stainless **$939.00**
Price: Anodized aluminum two-tone.................................. **$979.00**

RUGER SR1911 TARGET

Calibers: 9mm, 10mm, .45 ACP. Capacities: .45 and 10mm (8-round magazine), 9mm (9 shot). Barrel: 5 in. Weight: 39 oz. Sights: Bomar adjustable. Grips: G10 Deluxe checkered. Features: Skeletonized hammer and trigger, satin stainless finish. Introduced in 2016.

Price: **$1,019.00**

RUGER SR1911 COMPETITION

Calibers: 9mm. Capacities: .10+1. Barrel: 5 in. Weight: 39 oz. Sights: Fiber optic front, adjustable target rear. Grips: Hogue Piranha G10 Deluxe checkered. Features: Skeletonized hammer and trigger, satin stainless finish, hand-fitted frame and slide, competition trigger, competition barrel with polished feed ramp. From Ruger Competition Shop. Introduced in 2016.

Price: **$2,499.00**

RUGER SR1911 OFFICER

Caliber: .45 ACP, 9mm. Capacity: 8-round magazine. Barrel: 3.6 in. Weight: 27 oz. Features: Compact variation of SR1911 Series. Black anodized aluminum frame, stainless slide, skeletonized trigger, Novak 3-dot Night Sights, G10 deluxe checkered G10 grips.

Price: **$979.00**

SCCY CPX

Caliber: 9mm. Capacity: 10-round magazine. Barrel: 3.1 in. Weight: 15 oz. Length: 5.7 in. overall. Grips: Integral with polymer frame. Sights: 3-dot

system, rear adjustable for windage. Features: Zytel polymer frame, steel slide, aluminum alloy receiver machined from bar stock. DAO with consistent 9-pound trigger pull. Concealed hammer. Available with (CPX-1) or without (CPX-2) manual thumb safety. Introduced 2014. CPX-3 is chambered for .380 ACP. Made in USA by SCCY Industries.

Price: CPX-1 .... **$284.00**
Price: CPX-2 .... **$270.00**
Price: CPX-3 .... **$305.00**

SEECAMP LWS 32/380 STAINLESS DA

Calibers: .32 ACP, .380 ACP. Capacity: 6-round magazine. Barrel: 2 in., integral with frame. Weight: 10.5 oz. Length: 4.125 in. overall. Grips: Glass-filled nylon. Sights: Smooth, no-snag, contoured slide and barrel top. Features: Aircraft quality 17-4 PH stainless steel. Inertia-operated firing pin. Hammer fired DAO. Hammer automatically follows slide down to safety rest position after each shot, no manual safety needed. Magazine safety disconnector. Polished stainless. Introduced 1985. From L.W. Seecamp.

Price: .32 .... **$446.25**
Price: .380 .... **$795.00**

SIG SAUER 1911

Calibers: .45 ACP, .40 S&W. Capacities: .45 ACP, .40 S&W. 8- and 10-round magazine. Barrel: 5 in. Weight: 40.3 oz. Length: 8.65 in. overall. Grips: Checkered wood grips. Sights: Novak night sights. Blade front, drift adjustable rear for windage. Features: Single-action 1911. Hand-fitted dehorned stainless steel frame and slide; match-grade barrel, hammer/sear set and trigger; 25-LPI front strap checkering, 20-LPI mainspring housing checkering. Beavertail grip safety with speed bump, extended thumb safety, firing pin safety and hammer intercept notch. Introduced 2005. XO series has contrast sights, Ergo Grip XT textured polymer grips. STX line available from Sig Sauer Custom Shop; two-tone 1911, non-railed, Nitron slide, stainless frame, burled maple grips. Polished cocking serrations, flat-top slide, mag well. Carry line has Siglite night sights, lanyard attachment point, gray diamondwood or rosewood grips, 8+1 capacity. Compact series has 6+1 capacity, 7.7 OAL, 4.25-in. barrel, slim-profile wood grips, weighs 30.3 oz. Ultra Compact in 9mm or .45 ACP has 3.3-in. barrel, low-profile night sights, slim-profile gray diamondwood or rosewood grips. 6+1 capacity. 1911 C3 is a 6+1 compact .45 ACP, rosewood custom wood grips, two-tone and Nitron finishes. Weighs 30 oz. unloaded, lightweight alloy frame. Length is 7.7 in. Now offered in more than 30 different models with numerous options for frame size, grips, finishes, sight arrangements and other features. From SIG Sauer, Inc.

Price: Nitron **$1,174.00**
Price: Tacops.. **$1,221.00**
Price: XO Black **$1,010.00**
Price: STX **$1,244.00**
Price: Nightmare **$1,244.00**
Price: Carry Nightmare **$1,195.00**
Price: Compact C3 .... **$1,010.00**
Price: Ultra Compact **$1,119.00**
Price: Max **$1,663.00**
Price: Spartan **$1,397.00**
Price: Super Target **$1,609.00**
Price: Traditional Stainless Match Elite **$1,164.00**
Price: We the People... **$1,481.00**
Price: Select **$1,234.00**
Price: Stand Commemorative (Honored Veterans, C.O.P.S.)........... **$1,279.00**

Prices given are believed to be accurate at time of publication however, many factors affect retail pricing so exact prices are not possible.

76TH EDITION, 2022 ✛ **463**

SIG SAUER P210 CARRY

Caliber: 9mm. Capacity: 8-round magazine. Barrel: 4.1 in. Grip: Checkered G10. Sights: SIGLITE night sights. Length: 7.5 in. overall. Weight: 32 ozs. unloaded. Finish: Nitron. Features: Conceal carry version of iconic P210.
Price: **$1,299.00**

SIG SAUER P220

Caliber: .45 ACP, 10mm. Capacity: 7- or 8-round magazine. Barrel: 4.4 in. Weight: 27.8 oz. Length: 7.8 in. overall. Grips: Checkered black plastic. Sights: Blade front, drift adjustable rear for windage. Optional Siglite night sights. Features: Double action. Stainless steel slide, Nitron finish, alloy frame, M1913 Picatinny rail; safety system of decocking lever, automatic firing pin safety block, safety intercept notch, and trigger bar disconnector. Squared combat-type trigger guard. Slide stays open after last shot. Introduced 1976. P220 SAS Anti-Snag has dehorned stainless steel slide, front Siglite night sight, rounded trigger guard, dust cover, Custom Shop wood grips. Equinox line is Custom Shop product with Nitron stainless slide with a black hard-anodized alloy frame, brush-polished flats and nickel accents. Truglo tritium fiber-optic front sight, rear Siglite night sight, gray laminated wood grips with checkering and stippling. From SIG Sauer, Inc.
Price: **$1,087.00**
Price: P220 Elite Stainless **$1,450.00**
Price: Hunter SAO.. **$1,629.00**
Price: Legion 45 ACP.. **$1,413.00**
Price: Legion 10mm.. **$1,904.00**

SIG SAUER P220 ELITE

Caliber: .45 ACP. Capacity: 8-round magazine. Barrel: 4.4 in. Grip: Textured polymer. Sights: SIGLITE night sights. Length: 7.7 in. overall. Weight: 30.4 ozs. unloaded. Finish: Nitron. Features: Accessory rail, extended beavertail.
Price: **$1,174.00**

SIG SAUER P225 A-1

Caliber: 9mm. Capacity: 8-round magazine. Barrels: 3.6 or 5 in. Weight: 30.5 oz. Features: Shorter and slim-profile version of P226 with enhanced short reset trigger, single-stack magazine.
Price: **$1,122.00**
Price: Night sights.. **$1,236.00**

SIG SAUER P226

Calibers: 9mm, .40 S&W. Barrel: 4.4 in. Length: 7.7 in. overall. Features: Similar to the P220 pistol except has 4.4-in. barrel, measures 7.7 in. overall, weighs 34 oz. DA/SA or DAO. Many variations available. Snap-on modular grips. Legion series has improved short reset trigger, contoured and shortened beavertail, relieved trigger guard, higher grip, other improvements. From SIG Sauer, Inc.
Price: From **$1,087.00**
Price: Elite Stainless... **$1,481.00**
Price: Legion **$1,428.00**
Price: Legion RX w/Romeo 1 Reflex sight........................ **$1,685.00**
Price: MK25 Navy Version **$1,187.00**

SIG SAUER P226 ELITE

Caliber: 9mm. Capacity: 15-round magazine. Barrel: 4.4 in. Grip: Textured polymer. Sights: SIGLITE night sights. Length: 7.7 in. overall. Weight: 34 ozs. unloaded. Finish: Nitron. Features: Accessory rail, extended beavertail.
Price: **$800.00**

SIG SAUER P227

Caliber: .45 ACP. Capacity: 10-round magazine. Features: Same general specifications and features as P226 except chambered for .45 ACP and has double-stack magazine.
Price: .... **$1,087.00–$1,350.00**

SIG SAUER P229 DA

Caliber: Similar to the P220 except chambered for 9mm (10- or 15-round magazines), .40 S&W, (10- or 12-round magazines). Barrels: 3.86-in. barrel, 7.1 in. overall length and 3.35 in. height. Weight: 32.4 oz. Features: Introduced 1991. Snap-on modular grips. Frame made in Germany, stainless steel slide assembly made in U.S.; pistol assembled in U.S. Many variations available. Legion series has improved short reset trigger, contoured and shortened beavertail, relieved trigger guard, higher grip, other improvements. Select has Nitron slide, Select G10 grips, Emperor Scorpion has accessory rail, FDE finish, G10 Piranha grips.
Price: P229, From **$1,085.00**
Price: P229 Emperor Scorpion **$1,282.00**
Price: P229 Legion **$1,413.00**
Price: P229 Select... **$1,195.00**

SIG SAUER P229 ELITE

Caliber: 9mm. Capacity: 15-round magazine. Barrel: 3.9-in. Grip: Textured polymer. Sights: SIGLITE night sights. Length: 7.1 in. overall. Weight: 32 ozs. unloaded. Finish: Nitron. Features: Accessory rail, extended beavertail.
Price: **$800.00**

SIG SAUER SP2022

Calibers: 9mm, .40 S&W. Capacities: 10-, 12-, or 15-round magazines. Barrel: 3.9 in. Weight: 30.2 oz. Length: 7.4 in. overall. Grips: Composite and rubberized one-piece. Sights: Blade front, rear adjustable for windage. Features: Polymer frame, stainless steel slide; integral frame accessory rail; replaceable steel frame rails; left- or right-handed magazine release, two interchangeable grips.
Price: **$642.00**

SIG SAUER P238

Caliber: .380 ACP. Capacity: 6-round magazine. Barrel: 2.7 in. Weight: 15.4 oz. Length: 5.5 in. overall. Grips: Hogue G-10 and Rosewood grips. Sights: Contrast/Siglite night sights. Features: All-metal beavertail-style frame.
Price: **$723.00**
Price: Desert Tan **$738.00**
Price: Polished **$798.00**
Price: Rose Gold **$932.00**
Price: Emperor Scorpion **$801.00**

SIG SAUER P320

Calibers: 9mm, .357 SIG, .40 S&W, .45 ACP. Capacities: 15 or 16 rounds (9mm), 13 or 14 rounds (.357 or .40). Barrels: 3.6 in. (Subcompact), 3.9 in. (Carry model) or 4.7 in. (Full size). Weights: 26–30 oz. Lengths: 7.2 or 8.0 in overall. Grips: Interchangeable black composite. Sights: Blade front, rear adjustable for windage. Optional Siglite night sights. Features: Striker-fired DAO, Nitron finish slide, black polymer frame. Frame size and calibers are interchangeable. Introduced 2014. Made in USA by SIG Sauer, Inc.
Price: Full size **$679.00**
Price: Carry (shown) **$679.00**

SIG SAUER P320 SUBCOMPACT

Calibers: 9mm, .40 S&W. Barrel: 3.6 in. Features: Accessory rail. Other features similar to Full-Size and Carry models.
Price: **$679.00**

SIG SAUER MODEL 320 RX

Caliber: 9mm. Capacity: 17-round magazine. Barrels: 4.7 in. or 3.9 in. Features: Full and Compact size models with ROMEO1 Reflex sight, accessory rail, stainless steel frame and slide. XFive has improved control ergonomics, bull barrel, 21-round magazines.
Price: **$952.00**
Price: XFive **$1,005.00**

SIG SAUER P365

Caliber: 9mm. Barrel: 3.1 in. Weight: 17.8 oz. Features: Micro-compact striker-fired model with 10-round magazine, stainless steel frame and slide, XRAY-3 day and night sights fully textured polymer grip.
Price: **$599.00**

SIG SAUER P365 XL

Caliber: 9mm. Capacity: 12-round magazine. Barrel: 3.7 in. Grips: Textured

polymer. Sights: Optic-ready, Day/Night sights. Length: 6.6 in. overall. Weight: 20.7 oz. unloaded. Finish: Nitron. Features: Grip with integrated carry mag well and extended beavertail, flat trigger and optic-ready slide.
Price: **$605.00**

SIG SAUER P365 XL ROMEOZERO

Caliber: 9mm. Capacity: 12-round magazine. Barrel: 3.7 in. Grips: Textured polymer. Sights: RomeoZero red dot, Xray3 front sight. Length: 6.6 in. overall. Weight: 20.7 oz. unloaded. Finish: Nitron. Features: Grip with integrated carry mag well and extended beavertail, and flat trigger.
Price: **$749.00**

SIG SAUER P365SAS

Caliber: 9mm. Capacity: 10-round magazine. Barrel: 3.1 in. Grips: Textured polymer. Sights: Flush-mounted FT Bullseye fiber-tritium night sight. Length: 5.8 in. overall. Weight: 17.8 oz. unloaded. Finish: Nitron. Features: Ported slide and barrel, Sig Anti Snag (SAS) treatment.
Price: **$599.00**

SIG SAUER P320-M18

Caliber: 9mm. Capacity: 17-round magazine. Barrel: 3.9 in. Grips: Textured polymer. Sights: Siglite front/night rear, optic ready. Length: 7.2 in. overall. Weight: 28.1 oz. unloaded. Finish: Coyote tan. Features: Commercial version of U.S. Military M18, manual thumb safety.
Price: **$679.00**

SIG SAUER P320 RXP FULL-SIZE

Caliber: 9mm. Capacity: 17-round magazine. Barrel: 4.7 in. Grips: Textured polymer. Sights: Romeo1Pro red dot, suppressor contrast 3-dot. Length: 8 in. overall. Weight: 30 oz. unloaded. Finish: Nitron.
Price: **$899.00**

Prices given are believed to be accurate at time of publication however, many factors affect retail pricing **so exact** prices are not possible.

76TH EDITION, 2022 ◈ **465**

SIG SAUER P320 LEGION XCARRY
Caliber: 9mm. Capacity: 15-round magazine. Barrel: 3.6 in. Grip: TXG heavy XCARRY grip. Sights: XRAY3 day/night sights. Length: 7.0 in. overall. Weight: 40 ozs. unloaded. Finish: Matte black. Features: Threaded barrel.
Price: .... **Not available at press time**

SIG SAUER P320 X MAX
Caliber: 9mm. Capacity: 21-round magazine. Barrel: 5 in. Grip: TXG heavy XCARRY grip. Sights: XRAY3 day/night sights, ROMEO red dot. Length: 8.5 in. overall. Weight: 40 ozs. unloaded. Finish: Matte black. Features: Flat trigger.
Price: **$1,658.00**

SIG SAUER CUSTOM WORKS AXG SCORPION
Caliber: 9mm. Capacity: 17-round magazine. Barrel: 3.9 in. Grip: Hogue Scorpion G10 grips. Sights: XRAY3 day/night sights, optic ready. Length: 7.4 in. overall. Weight: 31.3 ozs. unloaded. Finish: Cerakote FDE. Features: Accessory rail, extended beavertail, striker-fired, metal frame, flat trigger.
Price: **$1,299.00**

SIG SAUER P320 RXP COMPACT
Caliber: 9mm. Capacity: 15-round magazine. Barrel: 3.9 in. Grips: Textured polymer. Sights: Romeo1Pro red dot, suppressor contrast 3-dot. Length: 7.2 in. overall. Weight: 26 oz. unloaded. Finish: Nitron.
Price: **$899.00**

SIG SAUER P320 RXP XFULL-SIZE
Caliber: 9mm. Capacity: 17-round magazine. Barrel: 4.7 in. Grips: Textured polymer. Sights: Romeo1Pro red dot, suppressor contrast 3-dot. Length: 8 in. overall. Weight: 30 oz. unloaded. Finish: Nitron.
Price: **$899.00**

SIG SAUER MPX
Calibers: 9mm, .357 SIG, .40 S&W. Capacities: 10, 20 or 30 rounds. Barrel: 8 in. Weight: 5 lbs Features: Semi-auto AR-style gun with closed, fully locked short-stroke pushrod gas system.
Price: From **$2,016.00**

SIG SAUER P938
Calibers: 9mm, .22 LR. Capacities: 9mm (6-shot mag.), .22 LR (10-shot mag.). Barrel: 3.0 in. Weight: 16 oz. Length: 5.9 in. Grips: Rosewood, Blackwood, Hogue Extreme, Hogue Diamondwood. Sights: Siglite night sights or Siglite rear with Tru-Glo front. Features: Slightly larger version of P238.
Price: .... **$760.00–$1,195.00**
Price: .22 LR.. **$656.00**

SMITH & WESSON M&P SERIES
Calibers: .22 LR, 9mm, .40 S&W. Capacities, full-size models: 12 rounds (.22), 17 rounds (9mm), 15 rounds (.40). Compact models: 12 (9mm), 10 (.40). Barrels: 4.25, 3.5 in. Weights: 24, 22 oz. Lengths: 7.6, 6.7 in. Grips: Polymer with three interchangeable palm swell grip sizes. Sights: 3 white-dot system with low-profile rear. Features: Zytel polymer frame with stainless steel slide, barrel and structural components. VTAC (Viking Tactics) model has Flat Dark Earth finish, VTAC Warrior sights. Compact models available with Crimson Trace Lasergrips. Numerous options for finishes, sights, operating controls.
Price: **$569.00**
Price: (VTAC)... **$799.00**
Price: (Crimson Trace) .... **$699.00–$829.00**
Price: M&P 22 .... **$389.00–$419.00**

SMITH & WESSON M&P 45
Caliber: .45 ACP. Capacity: 8 or 10 rounds. Barrel length: 4 or 4.5 in. Weight: 26, 28 or 30 oz. Features: Available with or without thumb safety. Finish: Black or Dark Earth Brown. Features: M&P model offered in three frame sizes.
Price: .... **$599.00–$619.00**
Price: Threaded barrel kit.. **$719.00**

SMITH & WESSON M&P M2.0 SERIES
Calibers: 9mm, .40 S&W, .45 ACP. Capacities: 17 rounds (9mm), 15 rounds (.40), 10 rounds (.45). Barrels: 4.0 (Compact), 4.25, 4.5 or 4.6 in. (.45 only). Weights: 25 –27 oz. Finishes: Armornite Black or Flat Dark Earth. Grip: Textured polymer with 4 interchangeable modular inserts. Second Generation of M&P Pistol series. Introduced in 2017.
Price: **$599.00**
Price: Compact.. **$569.00**

SMITH & WESSON M&P 9/40 SHIELD
Calibers: 9mm, .40 S&W. Capacities: 7- and 8-round magazine (9mm);

6-round and 7-round magazine (.40). Barrel: 3.1 in. Length: 6.1 in. Weight: 19 oz. Sights: 3-white-dot system with low-profile rear. Features: Ultra-compact, single-stack variation of M&P series. Available with or without thumb safety. Crimson Trace Green Laserguard available.

Price: **$449.00**
Price: CT Green Laserguard **$589.00**

SMITH & WESSON M&P 45 SHIELD
Caliber: .45 ACP. Barrel: 3.3 in. Ported model available. Weight: 20–23 oz. Sights: White dot or tritium night sights. Comes with one 6-round and one 7-round magazine.

Price: **$479.00**
Price: Tritium night sights **$579.00**
Price: Ported barrel **$609.00**

SMITH & WESSON MODEL SD9 VE/SD40 VE
Calibers: .40 S&W, 9mm. Capacities: 10+1, 14+1 and 16+1 Barrel: 4 in. Weight: 39 oz. Length: 8.7 in. Grips: Wood or rubber. Sights: Front: Tritium Night Sight, Rear: Steel Fixed 2-Dot. Features: SDT (Self Defense Trigger) for optimal, consistent pull first round to last, standard Picatinny-style rail, slim ergonomic textured grip, textured finger locator and aggressive front and backstrap texturing with front and rear slide serrations.

Price: **$389.00**

SMITH & WESSON MODEL SW1911
Calibers: .45 ACP, 9mm. Capacities: 8 rounds (.45), 7 rounds (subcompact .45), 10 rounds (9mm). Barrels: 3, 4.25, 5 in. Weights: 26.5–41.7 oz. Lengths: 6.9–8.7 in. Grips: Wood, wood laminate or synthetic. Crimson Trace Lasergrips available. Sights: Low-profile white dot, tritium night sights or adjustable. Finish: Black matte, stainless or two-tone. Features: Offered in three different frame sizes. Skeletonized trigger. Accessory rail on some models. Compact models have round-butt frame. Pro Series have 30 LPI checkered frontstrap, oversized external extractor, extended mag well, full-length guide rod, ambidextrous safety.

Price: Standard Model E Series, From **$979.00**
Price: Crimson Trace grips **$1,149.00**
Price: Pro Series .... **$1,459.00–$1,609.00**
Price: Scandium Frame E Series **$1,449.00**

SMITH & WESSON BODYGUARD 380
Caliber: .380 Auto. Capacity: 6+1. Barrel: 2.75 in. Weight: 11.85 oz. Length: 5.25 in. Grips: Polymer. Sights: Integrated laser plus drift-adjustable front and rear. Features: The frame of the Bodyguard is made of reinforced polymer, as is the magazine base plate and follower, magazine catch and trigger. The slide, sights and guide rod are made of stainless steel, with the slide and sights having a Melonite hardcoating.

Price: **$449.00**

SMITH & WESSON PERFORMANCE CENTER M&P380 SHIELD EZ
Caliber: .380 ACP. Capacity: 8-round magazine. Barrel: 3.67 in. Grips: Textured polymer. Sights: Fixed, HI-VIZ Litewave H3 Tritium/Litepipe. Length: 6.8 in. overall. Weight: 23 oz. unloaded. Finish: Black Armornite frame and black, silver or gold accents. Features: Easy to rack slide, grip safety, manual thumb safety, accessory rail, reversible magazine release, ported barrel and lightening cuts in slide.

Price: **$517.00**

SMITH & WESSON PERFORMANCE CENTER M&P9 AND M&P40 M2.0 C.O.R.E. PRO SERIES
Calibers: 9mm, .40 S&W. Capacity: 17-round (9mm) or 15-round (.40 S&W) magazine. Barrel: 4.25 or 5 in. Grips: Four interchangeable palm-swell inserts. Sights: Fixed, tall 3-dot/C.O.R.E. optics-ready system. Length: 7.5-8.5 in. overall. Weight: 23-27.2 oz. unloaded. Finish: Black Armornite. Features: Accessory rail, reversible magazine release and tuned action with audible trigger reset.

Price: (4.25-in. barrel) **$700.00**
Price: (5-in. barrel) **$721.00**

SMITH & WESSON PERFORMANCE CENTER M&P9 AND M&P40 M2.0 PORTED SERIES
Calibers: 9mm, .40 S&W. Capacity: 17-round (9mm) or 15-round (.40 S&W) magazine. Barrel: 4.25 or 5 in. Grips: Four interchangeable palm-swell inserts. Sights: Fixed, fiber-optic front and rear. Length: 8.5 in. overall. Weight: 23 oz. unloaded. Finish: Black Armornite. Features: Accessory rail, reversible magazine release, ported barrel and slide and tuned action with audible trigger reset.

Price: (4.25-in. barrel) **$700.00**
Price: (5-in. barrel) **$721.00**

SMITH & WESSON PERFORMANCE CENTER M&P9 AND M&P40 M2.0 PORTED C.O.R.E. SERIES
Calibers: 9mm, .40 S&W. Capacity: 17-round (9mm) or 15-round (.40 S&W) magazine. Barrel: 4.25 or 5 in. Grips: Four interchangeable palm-swell inserts. Sights: Fixed, tall 3-dot/C.O.R.E. optics-ready system. Length: 8.5 in. overall. Weight: 23 oz. unloaded. Finish: Black Armornite. Features: Accessory rail, reversible magazine release, oversized slide release, ported barrel and slide, and tuned action with audible trigger reset.

Price: (4.25-in. barrel) **$714.00**
Price: (5-in. barrel) **$735.00**

Prices given are believed to be accurate at time of publication however, many factors affect retail pricing so exact prices are not possible.

76TH EDITION, 2022 ✛ **467**

SMITH & WESSON M&P9 SHIELD EZ M2.0
Caliber: 9mm. Capacity: 8-round magazine. Barrel: 3.67 in. Grips: Textured polymer. Sights: Fixed, 3-dot. Length: 6.8 in. overall. Weight: 23.2 oz. unloaded. Finish: Black Armornite. Features: Accessory rail and reversible magazine release, with or without manual thumb safety.
Price: **$479.00**
Price: (Crimson Trace Laserguard)................................. **$575.00**

SMITH & WESSON M&P9 M2.0 COMPACT
Caliber: 9mm. Capacity: 15-round magazine. Barrel: 4 in. Grips: Four interchangeable palm-swell inserts. Sights: Fixed, steel 3-dot. Length: 7.3 in. overall. Weight: 26.6 oz. unloaded. Finish: FDE. Features: Accessory rail, with or without manual thumb safety.
Price: **$569.00**

SPHINX SDP
Caliber: 9mm. Capacity: 15-shot magazine. Barrel: 3.7 in. Weight: 27.5 oz. Length: 7.4 in. Sights: Defiance Day & Night Green fiber/tritium front, tritium 2-dot red rear. Features: DA/SA with ambidextrous decocker, integrated slide position safety, aluminum MIL-STD 1913 Picatinny rail, Blued alloy/steel or stainless. Aluminum and polymer frame, machined steel slide. Offered in several variations. Made in Switzerland and imported by Kriss USA.
Price: From **$999.00**

SPRINGFIELD ARMORY EMP ENHANCED MICRO
Calibers: 9mm, 40 S&W. Capacity: 9-round magazine. Barrel: 3-inch stainless steel match grade, fully supported ramp, bull. Weight: 26 oz. Length: 6.5 in. overall. Grips: Thinline cocobolo hardwood. Sights: Fixed low-profile combat rear, dovetail front, 3-dot tritium. Features: Two 9-round stainless steel magazines with slam pads, long aluminum match-grade trigger adjusted to 5 to 6 lbs., forged aluminum alloy frame, black hardcoat anodized finish; dual spring full-length guide rod, forged satin-finish stainless steel slide. Introduced 2007. Champion has 4-inch barrel, fiber optic front sight, three 10-round magazines, Bi-Tone finish.
Price: .... **$1,104.00–$1,249.00**
Price: Champion **$1,179.00**

SPRINGFIELD ARMORY XD SERIES
Calibers: 9mm, .40 S&W, .45 ACP. Barrels: 3, 4, 5 in. Weights: 20.5-31 oz. Lengths: 6.26-8 overall. Grips: Textured polymer. Sights: Varies by model; Fixed sights are dovetail front and rear steel 3-dot units. Features: Three sizes in X-Treme Duty (XD) line: Sub-Compact (3-in. barrel), Service (4-in. barrel), Tactical (5-in. barrel). Three ported models available. Ergonomic polymer frame, hammer-forged barrel, no-tool disassembly, ambidextrous magazine release, visual/tactile loaded chamber indicator, visual/tactile striker status indicator, grip safety, XD gear system included. Compact is shipped with one extended magazine (13) and one compact magazine (10). XD Mod.2 Sub-Compact has newly contoured slide and redesigned serrations, stippled grip panels, fiber-optic front sight. OSP has Vortex Venom Red Dot sight, and suppressor-height sights that co-witness with red dot. Non-threaded barrel is also included.
Price: Sub-Compact OD Green 9mm/40 S&W, fixed sights **$508.00**
Price: Compact .45 ACP, 4 barrel, Bi-Tone finish **$607.00**
Price: Service Black 9mm/.40 S&W, fixed sights **$541.00**
Price: Service Black .45 ACP, external thumb safety **$638.00**
Price: V-10 Ported Black 9mm/.40 S&W **$608.00**
Price: XD Mod.2 .... **$565.00**
Price: XD OSP w/Vortex Venom Red Dot Sight **$958.00**

SPRINGFIELD ARMORY XD(M) SERIES
Calibers: 9mm, .40 S&W, .45 ACP. Barrels: 3.8 or 4.5 in. Sights: Fiber optic front with interchangeable red and green filaments, adjustable target rear.

Grips: Integral polymer with three optional backstrap designs. Features: Variation of XD design with improved ergonomics, deeper and longer slide serrations, slightly modified grip contours and texturing. Black polymer frame, forged steel slide. Black and two-tone finish options.
Price: .... $623.00–$779.00

SPRINGFIELD ARMORY MIL-SPEC 1911A1

Caliber: .45 ACP. Capacity: 7-round magazine. Barrel: 5 in. Weights: 35.6–39 oz. Lengths: 8.5–8.625 in. overall. Finish: Stainless steel. Features: Similar to Government Model military .45.
Price: Mil-Spec Parkerized, 7+1, 35.6 oz. $785.00
Price: Mil-Spec Stainless Steel, 7+1, 36 oz. $889.00

SPRINGFIELD ARMORY 1911 LOADED

Caliber: .45 ACP. Capacity: 7-round magazine. Barrel: 5 in. Weight: 34 oz. Length: 8.6 in. overall. Similar to Mil-Spec 1911A1 with the following additional features: Lightweight Delta hammer, extended and ergonomic beavertail safety, ambidextrous thumb safety, and other features depending on the specific model. MC, Marine, LB and Lightweight models have match-grade barrels, low-profile 3-dot combat sights.
Price: Parkerized.. $950.00
Price: Stainless $1,004.00
Price: MC Operator (shown)... $1,308.00
Price: Marine Operator $1,308.00
Price: LB Operator $1,409.00
Price: Lightweight Operator $1,210.00
Price: 10mm TRP (Trijicon RMR Red Dot sight $2,238.00

SPRINGFIELD ARMORY TACTICAL RESPONSE

Caliber: .45 ACP, 10mm. Features: Similar to 1911A1, except checkered frontstrap and main-spring housing, Novak Night Sight combat rear sight and matching dove-tailed front sight, tuned, polished extractor, oversize barrel link; lightweight speed trigger and combat action job, match barrel and bushing, extended ambidextrous thumb safety and fitted beavertail grip safety. Checkered Cocobolo wood grips, comes with two Wilson 7-shot magazines. Frame is engraved "Tactical" both sides of frame with "TRP" Introduced 1998. TRP-Pro Model meets FBI specifications for SWAT Hostage Rescue Team.
Price: $1,646.00
Price: Operator with adjustable Trijicon night sights......................... $1,730.00

SPRINGFIELD ARMORY RANGE OFFICER

Calibers: 9mm, .45 ACP. Barrels: 5-in. stainless match grade. Compact model has 4 in. barrel. Sights: Adjustable target rear, post front. Grips: Double diamond checkered walnut. Weights: 40 oz., 28 oz. (compact). Features: Operator model has fiber optic sights.
Price: $936.00
Price: Compact $899.00
Price: Stainless finish.. $1,045.00
Price: Operator $1,029.00
Price: Elite Operator... $1,145.00

SPRINGFIELD ARMORY RONIN OPERATOR

Calibers: 9mm, .45 ACP. Capacity: 7-round (.45 ACP) or 9-round (9mm) magazine. Barrel: 5 in. Grips: Checkered wood. Sights: Fiber-optic front, tactical-rack, white-dot rear. Length: 8.6 in. overall. Weight: 40 oz. unloaded. Finish: Two-tone, black slide/stainless frame.
Price: $849.00

SPRINGFIELD ARMORY CHAMPION OPERATOR LIGHTWEIGHT

Caliber: .45 ACP. Barrel: 4-in. stainless match-grade bull barrel. Sights: 3-dot Tritium combat profile. Grips: Double diamond checkered cocobolo with Cross Cannon logo. Features: Alloy frame with integral rail, extended ambi thumb safety and trigger, lightweight Delta hammer.
Price: $1,050.00

SPRINGFIELD ARMORY 911

Caliber: .380 ACP. Barrel: 2.7-in. stainless steel. Sights: 3-dot Tritium combat profile. Viridian Green Laser available. Weight: 12.6 oz. Length: 6.5 in. Grips: Grooved Hogue G10. Features: Alloy frame, stainless steel slide.
Price: $599.00
Price: Viridian Laser $809.00

SPRINGFIELD ARMORY 911 9MM

Caliber: 9mm. Barrel: 3-in. stainless steel. Sights: Pro-Glo Tritium/ luminescent front, white-dot outlined Tritium rear. Weight: 15.3 oz. Length: 5.9 in. Grips: Thin-line G10. Features: Alloy frame, stainless steel slide.
Price: $659.00
Price: Viridian Laser $849.00

Prices given are believed to be accurate at time of publication however, many factors affect retail pricing so exact prices are not possible.

76TH EDITION, 2022 ⊕ **469**

STANDARD MANUFACTURING 1911 SERIES
Caliber: .45 ACP. Capacity: 7-round magazine. Barrel: 5-inch stainless steel match grade. Weight: 38.4 oz. Length: 8.6 in. Grips: Checkered rosewood double diamond. Sights: Fixed, Warren Tactical blade front/U-notch rear. Finish: Blued, case color, or nickel. Features: Forged frame and slide, beavertail grip safety, extended magazine release and thumb safety, checkered mainspring housing and front grip strap.

Price: (blued) $1,295.00
Price: (blued, engraved) $1,579.00
Price: (case color) $1,599.00
Price: (case color, engraved) $1,899.00
Price: (nickel) $1,499.00

STEYR M-A1 SERIES
Calibers: 9mm, .40 S&W. Capacities: 9mm (15 or 17-round capacity) or .40 S&W (10-12). Barrels: 3.5 in. (MA-1), 4.5 in. (L-A1), 3 in. (C-A1). Weight: 27 oz. Sights: Fixed with white outline triangle. Grips: Black synthetic. Ergonomic low-profile for reduced muzzle lift. Features: DAO striker-fired operation.

Price: M-A1... $575.00
Price: C-A1 compact model $575.00
Price: L-A1 full-size model $575.00
Price: S-A1 subcompact model.................................... $575.00

STOEGER STR-9 COMPACT
Caliber: 9mm. Capacity: 13-round magazine. Barrel: 3.8 in. Grips: Three interchangeable backstraps. Sights: 3-dot sights or tritium night sights. Length: 6.9 in. overall. Weight: 24 oz. unloaded. Finish: Matte black. Features: Compact version of the STR-9 striker-fire pistol. Aggressive forward and rear slide serrations and accessory rail. Made in Turkey.
Price: (depending on configuration).....................................$329.00-$449.00

STOEGER COMPACT COUGAR
Caliber: 9mm. Capacity: 13+1. Barrel: 3.6 in. Weight: 32 oz. Length: 7 in. Grips: Wood or rubber. Sights: Quick read 3-dot. Features: DA/SA with a

matte black finish. The ambidextrous safety and decocking lever is easily accessible to the thumb of a right- or left-handed shooter.
Price: $469.00

STI FIREARMS STACCATO SERIES
Calibers: 9mm, .40 S&W, .38 Super. Capacity: 9-, 17- or 21-round magazine. Barrels: 3.9- or 5-in., match-grade. Sights: Optic-ready, Dawson Precision Perfect Impact. Weight: 38 - 46.5 oz. Finish: Carbon black. Grips: Textured polymer. Features: 4-lb. trigger pull, ambidextrous safety levers, single- or double-stack magazine.
Price: .... $1,699.00-$4,299.00

TAURUS CURVE
Caliber: .380 ACP. Capacity: 6+1. Barrel: 2.5 in. Weight: 10.2 oz. Length: 5.2 in. Features: Unique curved design to fit contours of the body for comfortable concealed carry with no visible "printing" of the firearm. Double-action only. Light and laser are integral with frame.
Price: $404.00

TAURUS G2S
Caliber: 9mm. Capacity: 6+1. Barrel: 3.2 in. Weight: 20 oz. Length: 6.3 in. Sights: Adjustable rear, fixed front. Features: Double/Single Action, polymer frame in blue with matte black or stainless slide, accessory rail, manual and trigger safeties.
Price: $317.00
Price: Two tone with stainless slide...................................... $333.00

TAURUS TH9
Caliber: 9mm. Capacity: 16+1. Barrel: 4.3 in. Weight: 28 oz. Length: 7.7 in. Sights: Novak drift adjustable. Features: Full-size 9mm double-stack model with SA/DA action. Polymer frame has integral grips with finger grooves and stippling panels. Compact model has 3.8-in barrel, 6.8-in overall length.
Price: $377.00

TAURUS MODEL 1911
Calibers: 9mm, .45 ACP. Capacities: .45 ACP 8+1, 9mm 9+1. Barrel: 5 in. Weight: 33 oz. Length: 8.5 in. Grips: Checkered black. Sights: Heinie straight 8. Features: SA. Blued, stainless steel, duotone blue and blue/gray finish. Standard/Picatinny rail, standard frame, alloy frame and alloy/Picatinny rail. Introduced in 2007. Imported from Brazil by Taurus International.
Price: 1911B, Blue $633.00
Price: 1911B, Walnut grips $685.00
Price: 1911SS, Stainless Steel $752.00
Price: 1911SS-1, Stainless Steel w/rail.................................... $769.00
Price: 1911 DT, Duotone Blue $727.00

Prices given are believed to be accurate at time of publication however, many factors affect retail pricing so exact prices are not possible.

TAURUS MODEL 92

Caliber: 9mm. Capacity: 10- or 17-round magazine. Barrel: 5 in. Weight: 34 oz. Length: 8.5 in. overall. Grips: Checkered rubber, rosewood, mother of pearl. Sights: Fixed notch rear. 3-dot sight system. Also offered with micrometer-click adjustable night sights. Features: DA, ambidextrous 3-way hammer drop safety, allows cocked and locked carry. Blued, stainless steel, blued with gold highlights, stainless steel with gold highlights, forged aluminum frame, integral key-lock. .22 LR conversion kit available. Imported from Brazil by Taurus International.
Price: 92B **$433.00**
Price: 92SS **$550.00**

TAURUS SPECTRUM

Caliber: .380. Barrel: 2.8 in. Weight: 10 oz. Length: 5.4 in. Sights: Low-profile integrated with slide. Features: Polymer frame with stainless steel slide. Many finish combinations with various bright colors. Made in the USA. Introduced in 2017.
Price: .... **$289.00–$305.00**

TRISTAR 100 /120 SERIES

Calibers: 9mm, .40 S&W (C-100 only). Capacities: 15 (9mm), 11 (.40). Barrels: 3.7–4.7 in. Weights: 26–30 oz. Grips: Checkered polymer. Sights: Fixed. Finishes: Blue or chrome. Features: Alloy or steel frame. SA/DA. A series of pistols based on the CZ 75 design. Imported from Turkey.
Price: From .... **$460.00–$490.00**

TURNBULL MODEL 1911

Caliber: .45 ACP. Features: An accurate reproduction of 1918-era Model 1911 pistol. Forged slide with appropriate shape and style. Late-style sight with semi-circle notch. Early-style safety lock with knurled undercut thumb piece. Short, wide checkered spur hammer. Hand-checkered double-diamond American Black Walnut grips. Hand polished with period correct Carbonia charcoal bluing. Custom made to order with many options. Made in the USA by Doug Turnbull Manufacturing Co.
Price: From **$2,625.00**

WALTHER P99 AS

Calibers: 9mm, .40 S&W. Capacities: 15 or 10 rounds (9mm), 10 or 8 rounds (.40). Barrels: 3.5 or 4 in. Weights: 21–26 oz. Lengths: 6.6–7.1 in. Grips: Polymer with interchangeable backstrap inserts. Sights: Adjustable rear, blade front with three interchangeable inserts of different heights. Features: Offered in two frame sizes, standard and compact. DA with trigger safety, decocker, internal striker safety, loaded chamber indicator. Made in Germany.
Price: **$629.00**

WALTHER PK380

Caliber: .380 ACP. Capacity: 8-round magazine. Barrel: 3.66 in. Weight: 19.4 oz. Length: 6.5 in. Sights: Three-dot system, drift adjustable rear. Features: DA with external hammer, ambidextrous mag release and manual safety. Picatinny rail. Black frame with black or nickel slide.
Price: **$399.00**
Price: Nickel slide **$449.00**

WALTHER PDP FULL SIZE

Caliber: 9mm. Capacity: 18-round magazine. Barrel: 4 in. Grip: Textured polymer, modular backstrap. Sights: 3-dot, optics ready. Length: 8 in. overall. Weight: 25.4 ozs. unloaded. Finish: Black. Features: Accessory rail.
Price: **$649.00**

WALTHER PDP COMPACT

Caliber: 9mm. Capacity: 15-round magazine. Barrel: 4 in. Grip: Textured polymer, modular backstrap. Sights: 3-dot, optic ready. Length: 7.5 in. overall. Weight: 24.4 ozs. unloaded. Finish: Black. Features: Accessory rail.
Price: **$649.00**

Prices given are believed to be accurate at time of publication however, many factors affect retail pricing so exact prices are not possible.

76TH EDITION, 2022 ◆ 471

WALTHER PPK, PPK/S
Caliber: .380 ACP. Capacities: 6+1 (PPK), 7+1 (PPK/s). Barrel: 3.3 in. Weight: 21-26 oz. Length: 6.1 in. Grips: Checkered plastic. Sights: Fixed. New production in 2019. Made in Fort Smith, AR with German-made slide.
Price: **$749.00**

WALTHER PPQ M2
Calibers: 9mm, .40 S&W, .45 ACP, .22 LR. Capacities: 9mm, (15-round magazine), .40 S&W (11). .45 ACP, 22 LR (PPQ M2 .22). Barrels: 4 or 5 in. Weight: 24 oz. Lengths: 7.1, 8.1 in. Sights: Drift-adjustable. Features: Quick Defense trigger, firing pin block, ambidextrous slidelock and mag release, Picatinny rail. Comes with two extra magazines, two interchangeable frame backstraps and hard case. Navy SD model has threaded 4.6-in. barrel. M2 .22 has aluminum slide, blowback operation, weighs 19 ounces.
Price: 9mm, .40 .... **$649.00–$749.00**
Price: M2 .22 .... **$429.00**
Price: .45 .... **$699.00–$799.00**

WALTHER CCP
Caliber: 9mm. Capacity: 8-round magazine. Barrel: 3.5 in. Weight: 22 oz. Length: 6.4 in. Features: Thumb-operated safety, reversible mag release, loaded chamber indicator. Delayed blowback gas-operated action provides less recoil and muzzle jump, and easier slide operation. Available in all black or black/stainless two-tone finish.
Price: From .... **$469.00–$499.00**

WALTHER PPS M2 SERIES
Caliber: 9mm. Capacity: 6-, 7- or 8-round magazine. Barrel: 3.2 in. Sights: Optic-ready, fixed 3-dot, fixed 3-dot tritium or Crimson Trace Laserguard. Weight: 19.4 oz. Length: 6.3 in. Finish: Carbon black. Grips: Textured polymer. Features: Striker-fire, 6.1-lb. trigger pull.
Price: .... **$469.00-$560.00**

WALTHER P22
Caliber: .22 LR. Barrels: 3.4, 5 in. Weights: 19.6 oz. (3.4), 20.3 oz. (5). Lengths: 6.26, 7.83 in. Sights: Interchangeable white dot, front, 2-dot adjustable, rear. Features: A rimfire version of the Walther P99 pistol, available in nickel slide with black frame, Desert Camo or Digital Pink Camo frame with black slide.
Price: From **$379.00**
Price: Nickel slide/black frame, or black slide/camo frame **$449.00**

WALTHER Q4 STEEL FRAME
Caliber: 9mm. Capacity: 15-round magazine. Barrel: 4 in. Grips: Textured polymer, wrap around. Sights: 3-dot night. Length: 7.4 in. overall. Weight: 39.7 oz. unloaded. Finish: Matte black Tenifer. Features: Duty optimized beaver tail, Quick Defense trigger, accessory rail, oversized controls.
Price: **$1,399.00**
Price: (optic-ready model) **$1,499.00**

WILSON COMBAT ELITE SERIES
Calibers: 9mm, .38 Super, .40 S&W; .45 ACP. Barrel: Compensated 4.1-in. hand-fit, heavy flanged cone match grade. Weight: 36.2 oz. Length: 7.7 in. overall. Grips: Cocobolo. Sights: Combat Tactical yellow rear tritium inserts, brighter green tritium front insert. Features: High-cut frontstrap, 30 LPI checkering on frontstrap and flat mainspring housing, High-Ride Beavertail grip safety. Dehorned, ambidextrous thumb safety, extended ejector, skeletonized ultra light hammer, ultralight trigger, Armor-Tuff finish on frame and slide. Introduced 1997. Made in USA by Wilson Combat. This manufacturer offers more than 100 different 1911 models ranging in price from about $2,800 to $5,000. XTAC and Classic 6-in. models shown. Prices show a small sampling of available models.
Price: Classic, From **$3,300.00**
Price: CQB, From **$2,865.00**
Price: Hackathorn Special **$3,750.00**
Price: Tactical Carry **$3,750.00**
Price: Tactical Supergrade **$5,045.00**
Price: Bill Wilson Carry Pistol **$3,850.00**
Price: Ms. Sentinel **$3,875.00**
Price: Hunter 10mm, .460 Rowland **$4,100.00**
Price: Beretta Brigadier Series, From **$1,195.00**
Price: X-Tac Series, From **$2,760.00**
Price: Texas BBQ Special, From **$4,960.00**

Prices given are believed to be accurate at time of publication however, many factors affect retail pricing so exact prices are not possible.

BAER 1911 ULTIMATE MASTER COMBAT

Calibers: .38 Super, 400 Cor-Bon, .45 ACP (others available). Capacity: 10-shot magazine. Barrels: 5, 6 in. Baer National Match. Weight: 37 oz. Length: 8.5 in. overall. Grips: Checkered cocobolo. Sights: Baer dovetail front, low-mount Bo-Mar rear with hidden leaf. Features: Full-house competition gun. Baer forged NM blued steel frame and double serrated slide; Baer triple port, tapered cone compensator; fitted slide to frame; lowered, flared ejection port; Baer reverse recoil plug; full-length guide rod; recoil buff; beveled magazine well; Baer Commander hammer, sear; Baer extended ambidextrous safety, extended ejector, checkered slide stop, beavertail grip safety with pad, extended magazine release button; Baer speed trigger. Made in USA by Les Baer Custom, Inc.

Price: .45 ACP Compensated	**$3,240.00**
Price: .38 Super Compensated	**$3,390.00**
Price: 5-in. Standard barrel	**$3,040.00**
Price: 5-in. barrel .38 Super or 9mm	**$3,140.00**
Price: 6-in. barrel	**$3,234.00**
Price: 6-in. barrel .38 Super or 9mm	**$3,316.00**

BAER 1911 NATIONAL MATCH HARDBALL

Caliber: .45 ACP. Capacity: 7-round magazine. Barrel: 5 in. Weight: 37 oz. Length: 8.5 in. overall. Grips: Checkered walnut. Sights: Baer dovetail front with under-cut post, low-mount Bo-Mar rear with hidden leaf. Features: Baer NM forged steel frame, double serrated slide and barrel with stainless bushing; slide fitted to frame; Baer match trigger with 4-lb. pull; polished feed ramp, throated barrel; checkered frontstrap, arched mainspring housing; Baer beveled magazine well; lowered, flared ejection port; tuned extractor; Baer extended ejector, checkered slide stop; recoil buff. Made in USA by Les Baer Custom, Inc.

Price: **$2,379.00**

BAER 1911 PPC OPEN CLASS

Caliber: .45 ACP, 9mm. Barrel: 6 in, fitted to frame. Sights: Adjustable PPC rear, dovetail front. Grips: Checkered Cocobola. Features: Designed for NRA Police Pistol Combat matches. Lowered and flared ejection port, extended ejector, polished feed ramp, throated barrel, frontstrap checkered at 30 LPI, flat serrated mainspring housing, Commander hammer, front and rear slide serrations. 9mm has supported chamber.

Price:	**$2,775.00**
Price: 9mm w/supported chamber	**$3,187.00**

BAER 1911 BULLSEYE WADCUTTER

Similar to National Match Hardball except designed for wadcutter loads only. Polished feed ramp and barrel throat; Bo-Mar rib on slide; full-length recoil rod; Baer speed trigger with 3.5-lb. pull; Baer deluxe hammer and sear; Baer beavertail grip safety with pad; flat mainspring housing checkered 20 LPI. Blue finish; checkered walnut grips. Made in USA by Les Baer Custom, Inc.

Price: From **$2,461.00**

COLT GOLD CUP NM SERIES

Caliber: .45 ACP, 9mm, .38 Super. Capacity: 8-round magazine. Barrel: 5-inch National Match. Weight: 37 oz. Length: 8.5. Grips: Checkered wraparound rubber composite with silver-plated medallions or checkered walnut grips with gold medallions. Sights: Target post dovetail front, Bomar fully adjustable rear. Features: Adjustable aluminum wide target trigger, beavertail grip safety, full-length recoil spring and target recoil spring, available in blued finish or stainless steel.

Price: (blued)	**$1,299.00**
Price: (stainless)	**$1,350.00**
Price: Gold Cup Lite	**$1,199.00**
Price: Gold Cup Trophy	**$1,699.00**

COLT COMPETITION PISTOL

Calibers: .45 ACP, 9mm or .38 Super. Capacities: 8 or 9-shot magazine. Barrel: 5 in. National Match. Weight: 39 oz. Length: 8.5 in. Grips: Custom Blue Colt G10. Sights: Novak adjustable rear, fiber optic front. A competition-ready pistol out of the box at a moderate price. Blue or satin nickel finish. Series 80 firing system. O Series has stainless steel frame and slide with Cerakote gray frame and black slide, competition trigger, gray/black G-10 grips, front and rear slide serrations.

Price:	**$949.00–$1,099.00**
Price: Competition O series	**$2,499.00**

CZ 75 TS CZECHMATE

Caliber: 9mm. Capacity: 20-round magazine. Barrel: 130mm. Weight: 1360 g Length: 266mm overall. Features: The handgun is custom built, therefore the quality of workmanship is fully comparable with race pistols built directly to IPSC shooters' wishes. Individual parts and components are excellently match fitted, broke-in and tested. Every handgun is outfitted with a four-port compensator, nut for shooting without a compensator, the slide stop with an extended finger piece, the slide stop without a finger piece, ergonomic grip panels from aluminum with a new type pitting and side mounting provision with the C-More red-dot sight. For shooting without a red-dot sight there is included a standard target rear sight of Tactical Sports type, package contains also the front sight.

Price: **$3,416.00**

CZ 75 TACTICAL SPORTS

Calibers: 9mm,.40 S&W. Capacities: 17-20-round magazines. Barrel: 114mm. Weight: 1270 g Length: 225mm overall. Features: Semi-automatic handgun with a locked breech. This model is designed for competition shooting in accordance with world IPSC (International Practical Shooting Confederation) rules and regulations. The CZ 75 TS pistol model design stems from the standard CZ 75 model. However, this model features a number of special modifications, which are usually required for competitive handguns: SA trigger mechanism, match trigger made of plastic featuring option for trigger travel adjustments before discharge (using upper screw), and for overtravel (using bottom screw). The adjusting screws are set by the manufacturer — sporting hammer specially adapted for a reduced trigger pull weight, an extended magazine catch, grip panels made of walnut, guiding funnel made of plastic for quick inserting of the magazine into pistol's frame. Glossy blued slide, silver Polycoat frame. Packaging includes 3 magazines.

Price: **$1,837.00**

Prices given are believed to be accurate at time of publication however, many factors affect retail pricing so exact prices are not possible.

76TH EDITION, 2022 ✛ **473**

CZ SHADOW 2 SA
Caliber: 9mm. Capacity: 17-round magazine. Barrel: 4.89 in. Grips: Textured blue aluminum. Sights: Fiber-optic front, HAJO rear. Length: 8.53 in. overall. Weight: 46.5 oz. unloaded. Finish: Nitride black. Features: Single-action-only trigger. Swappable magazine release with adjustable, extended button with three settings. Ambidextrous manual thumb safety.
Price: $1,349.00

DAN WESSON CHAOS
Caliber: 9mm. Capacity: 21-round magazine. Barrel: 5 in. Weight: 3.20 lbs. Length: 8.75 in. overall. Features: A double-stack 9mm designed for 3-Gun competition.
Price: $3,829.00

DAN WESSON HAVOC
Calibers: 9mm, .38 Super. Capacity: 21-round magazine. Barrel: 4.25 in. Weight: 2.20 lbs. Length: 8 in. overall. Features: The Havoc is based on an "All Steel" Hi-capacity version of the 1911 frame. It comes ready to compete in Open IPSC/USPSA division. The C-more mounting system offers the lowest possible mounting configuration possible, enabling extremely fast target acquisition. The barrel and compensator arrangement pair the highest level of accuracy with the most effective compensator available.
Price: $4,299.00

DAN WESSON MAYHEM
Caliber: .40 S&W. Capacity: 18-round magazine. Barrel: 6 in. Weight: 2.42 lbs. Length: 8.75 in. overall. Features: The Mayhem is based on an "All-Steel" Hi-capacity version of the 1911 frame. It comes ready to compete in Limited IPSC/USPSA division or fulfill the needs of anyone looking for a superbly accurate target-grade 1911. The 6-in. bull barrel and tactical rail add to the static weight, or "good weight." A 6-in. long slide for added sight radius and enhanced pointability, but that would add to the "bad weight" so the 6-in. slide has been lightened to equal the weight of a 5 in. The result is a 6 in. long slide that balances and feels like a 5 in. but shoots like a 6 in. The combination of the all-steel frame with industry leading parts delivers the most well-balanced, softest shooting 6-in. limited gun on the market.
Price: $3,899.00

DAN WESSON TITAN
Caliber: 10mm. Capacity: 21-round magazine. Barrel: 4.25 in. Weight: 1.62 lbs. Length: 8 in. overall. Features: The Titan is based on an "All Steel" Hi-capacity version of the 1911 frame. The rugged HD night sights are moved forward and recessed deep into the slide yielding target accuracy and extreme durability. The Snake Scale serrations' aggressive 25 LPI checkering, and the custom competition G-10 grips ensure controllability even in the harshest of conditions. The combination of the all-steel frame, bull barrel and tactical rail enhance the balance and durability of this formidable target-grade Combat handgun.
Price: $3,829.00

DAN WESSON DISCRETION
Caliber: .45 ACP. Capacity: 8-round magazine. Barrel: 5.75 in. Match-grade stainless extended and threaded. Weight: 2.6 lbs. Features: Ported slide, serrated trigger, competition hammer, high tritium sights for sighting over the top of most suppressors.
Price: $2,142.00

EAA WITNESS ELITE GOLD TEAM
Calibers: 9mm, 9x21, .38 Super, .40 S&W, .45 ACP. Barrel: 5.1 in. Weight: 44 oz. Length: 10.5 in. overall. Grips: Checkered walnut, competition-style. Sights: Square post front, fully adjustable rear. Features: Triple-chamber cone compensator; competition SA trigger; extended safety and magazine release; competition hammer; beveled magazine well; beavertail grip. Hand-fitted major components. Hard chrome finish. Match-grade barrel. From EAA Custom Shop. Introduced 1992. Limited designed for IPSC Limited Class competition. Features include full-length dust-cover frame, funneled magazine well, interchangeable front sights. Stock (2005) designed for IPSC Production Class competition. Match introduced 2006. Made in Italy, imported by European American Armory.
Price: Gold Team $2,406.00
Price: Stock, 4.5 in. barrel, hard-chrome finish $1,263.00
Price: Limited Custom Xtreme... $2,502.00
Price: Witness Match Xtreme... $2,335.00
Price: Witness Stock III Xtreme $2,252.00

FREEDOM ARMS MODEL 83 .22 FIELD GRADE SILHOUETTE CLASS
Caliber: .22 LR. Capacity: 5-round cylinder. Barrel: 10 in. Weight: 63 oz. Length: 15.5 in. overall. Grips: Black Micarta. Sights: Removable Patridge front blade; Iron Sight Gun Works silhouette rear click-adjustable for windage and elevation (optional adj. front sight and hood). Features: Stainless steel, matte finish, manual sliding-bar safety system; dual firing pins, lightened hammer for fast lock time, pre-set trigger stop. Introduced 1991. Made in USA by Freedom Arms.
Price: Silhouette Class $2,762.00

FREEDOM ARMS MODEL 83 CENTERFIRE SILHOUETTE MODELS
Calibers: 357 Mag., .41 Mag., .44 Mag. Capacity: 5-round cylinder. Barrel: 10 in., 9 in. (.357 Mag. only). Weight: 63 oz. (41 Mag.). Length: 15.5 in., 14.5 in. (.357 only). Grips: Pachmayr Presentation. Sights: Iron Sight Gun Works silhouette rear sight, replaceable adjustable front sight blade with hood. Features: Stainless steel, matte finish, manual sliding-bar safety system. Made in USA by Freedom Arms.
Price: Silhouette Models, From $2,460.00

KIMBER SUPER MATCH II

Caliber: .45 ACP. Capacity: 8-round magazine. Barrel: 5 in. Weight: 38 oz. Length: 8.7 in. overall. Grips: Rosewood double diamond. Sights: Blade front, Kimber fully adjustable rear. Features: Guaranteed to shoot 1-in. groups at 25 yards. Stainless steel frame, black KimPro slide; two-piece magazine well; premium aluminum match-grade trigger; 30 LPI frontstrap checkering; stainless match-grade barrel; ambidextrous safety; special Custom Shop markings. Introduced 1999. Made in USA by Kimber Mfg., Inc.
Price: **$2,313.00**

MAC RAPIDO

Calibers: 9mm, .38 Super. Capacity: 17-round magazine. Barrels: 5- or 5.5-in., match-grade with compensator. Sights: Optic ready. Weight: 46.5 oz. Finish: Blue. Grips: Aluminum. Features: Checkered frontstrap serrations, combat trigger and hammer, flared and lowered ejection port, ambidextrous safety. Imported from the Philippines by Eagle Imports.
Price: **$1,725.00**

RUGER AMERICAN COMPETITION

Caliber: 9mm. Capacity: 17-round magazine. Barrel: 5 in. Grips: Three interchangeable grip inserts. Sights: Adjustable rear, fiber-optic front, optic ready. Length: 8.3 in. overall. Weight: 34.1 oz. unloaded. Finish: Black Nitrite. Features: Slide is drilled and tapped for mounting red-dot reflex optics, ported stainless steel slide. Made in the USA.
Price: **$579.00**

RUGER MARK IV TARGET

Caliber: .22 LR. Capacity: 10-round magazine. Barrel: 5.5-in. heavy bull. Weight: 35.6 oz. Grips: Checkered synthetic or laminate. Sights: .125 blade front, micro-click rear, adjustable for windage and elevation. Features: Loaded Chamber indicator; integral lock, magazine disconnect. Plastic case with lock included.
Price: (blued) **$529.00**
Price: (stainless) **$689.00**

SMITH & WESSON MODEL 41 TARGET

Caliber: .22 LR. Capacity: 10-round magazine. Barrels: 5.5 in., 7 in. Weight: 41 oz. (5.5-in. barrel). Length: 10.5 in. overall (5.5-in. barrel). Grips: Checkered walnut with modified thumb rest, usable with either hand. Sights: .125 in. Patridge on ramp base; micro-click rear-adjustable for windage and elevation. Features: .375 in. wide, grooved trigger; adjustable trigger stop drilled and tapped.
Price: .... **$1,369.00–$1,619.00**

SIG SAUER P320 XFIVE LEGION

Caliber: 9mm. Capacity: 17-round magazine. Barrel: 5 in. Grips: Textured polymer. Sights: Dawson Precision adjustable rear, fiber-optic front, optic ready. Length: 8.5 in. overall. Weight: 43.5 oz. unloaded. Finish: Legion gray. Features: TXG tungsten infused heavy XGrip module, slide has lightening cuts, Henning Group aluminum magazine basepads.
Price: **$999.00**

S.P.S. VISTA

Calibers: 9mm, .38 Super. Capacity: 17-round magazine. Barrels: 5- or 5.5-in., match-grade with compensator. Sights: Optic ready. Weight: 43 oz. Finish: Black chrome. Grips: Aluminum. Features: Polymer frame, checkered frontstrap serrations, skeletonized trigger and hammer, flared and lowered ejection port, ambidextrous safety, wide mag well. Imported from Spain by Eagle Imports.
Price: **$2,450.00**

S.P.S. PANTERA

Calibers: 9mm, .40 S&W, .45 ACP. Capacity: 12-, 16- or 18-round magazine. Barrel: 5-in., match-grade. Sights: Bomar-type, fully adjustable rear, fiber-optic front. Weight: 36.6 oz. Finish: Black, black chrome, chrome. Grips: Polymer. Features: Polymer frame, checkered frontstrap serrations, skeletonized trigger and hammer, flared and lowered ejection port, ambidextrous safety, wide mag well, full dust cover. Imported from Spain by Eagle Imports.
Price: **$1,730.00**

STI APEIRO

Calibers: 9mm, .40 S&W, .45 ACP. Features: 1911-style semi-auto pistol with Schuemann "Island" barrel; patented modular steel frame with polymer grip; high capacity double-stack magazine; stainless steel ambidextrous thumb safeties and knuckle relief high-rise beavertail grip safety; unique sabertooth rear cocking serrations; 5-inch fully ramped, fully supported "Island" bull barrel, with the sight milled in to allow faster recovery to point of aim; custom engraving on the polished sides of the (blued) stainless steel slide; stainless steel mag well; STI adjustable rear sight and Dawson fiber optic front sight; blued frame.
Price: **$2,999.00**

STI DVC P

Calibers: 9mm, .45 ACP. Barrel: 5.0 in., compensated. Sights: HOST rear with Fiber Optic front. Grip: Gen II 2011 Double Stack. Features: Diamond Like Carbon Black finish, Dawson Precision Tool-Less guide rod, railed frame.
Price: **$3,999.00**

STI DVC O

Calibers: 9mm, .38 Super. Barrel: 5.4 in., TX2 Compensated, TiN coated. Sights: Frame mounted C-More RTS2. Grip: Gen II 2011. Finish: Hard chrome with Black DLC Barrel. Features: 2.5-lb trigger, ambidextrous safety, Dawson Precision Tool-Less guide rod.
Price: **$3,999.00**

STI DVC S

Calibers: 9mm, .38 Super. Barrel: 4.15 in., TX1 Compensated. Sights: Frame mounted C-More RTS2. Grip: Gen II 2011. Finish: Hard chrome or Black DLC with TiN or DLC Barrel. Features: 2.5-lb trigger, ambidextrous safety, Dawson Precision Tool-Less guide rod.
Price: **$3,999.00**

STI TROJAN

Calibers: 9mm, .45 ACP. Barrel: 5 in. Weight: 36 oz. Length: 8.5 in. Grips: Rosewood. Sights: STI front with STI adjustable rear. Features: Stippled frontstrap, flat-top slide, one-piece steel guide rod.
Price: (Trojan 5) **$1,499.00**

Prices given are believed to be accurate at time of publication however, many factors affect retail pricing so exact prices are not possible.

76TH EDITION, 2022 ⊕ **475**

CHARTER ARMS BOOMER
Caliber: .44 Special. Capacity: 5-round cylinder. Barrel: 2 in., ported. Weight: 20 oz. Grips: Full rubber combat. Sights: Fixed.
Price: Blued **$443.00**

CHARTER ARMS POLICE BULLDOG
Caliber: .38 Special. Capacity: 6-round cylinder. Barrel: 4.2 in. Weight: 26 oz. Sights: Blade front, notch rear. Large frame version of Bulldog design.
Price: Blued **$408.00**

CHARTER ARMS CHIC LADY & CHIC LADY DAO
Caliber: .38 Special. Capacity: 5-round cylinder. Barrel: 2 in. Weight: 12 oz. Grip: Combat. Sights: Fixed. Features: 2-tone pink or lavender & stainless with aluminum frame. American made by Charter Arms.
Price: Chic Lady **$473.00**
Price: Chic Lady DAO **$483.00**

CHARTER ARMS CRIMSON UNDERCOVER
Caliber: .38 Special +P. Capacity: 5-round cylinder. Barrel: 2 in. Weight: 16 oz. Grip: Crimson Trace. Sights: Fixed. Features: Stainless finish and frame. American made by Charter Arms.
Price: **$577.00**

CHARTER ARMS OFF DUTY
Caliber: .38 Special. Barrel: 2 in. Weight: 12.5 oz. Sights: Blade front, notch rear. Features: 5-round cylinder, aluminum casting, DAO with concealed hammer. Also available with semi-concealed hammer. American made by Charter Arms.
Price: Aluminum **$404.00**
Price: Crimson Trace Laser grip **$657.00**

CHARTER ARMS MAG PUG
Caliber: .357 Mag. Capacity: 5-round cylinder. Barrel: 2.2 in. Weight: 23 oz. Sights: Blade front, notch rear. Features: American made by Charter Arms.
Price: Blued or stainless **$400.00**
Price: 4.4-in. full-lug barrel **$470.00**
Price: Crimson Trace Laser Grip **$609.00**

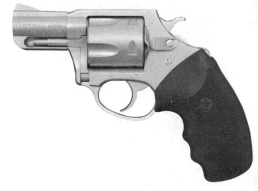

CHARTER ARMS PITBULL
Calibers: 9mm, 40 S&W, .45 ACP. Capacity: 5-round cylinder. Barrel: 2.2 in. Weights: 20–22 oz. Sights: Fixed rear, ramp front. Grips: Rubber. Features: Matte stainless steel frame or Nitride frame. Moon clips not required for 9mm, .45 ACP.
Price: 9mm **$502.00**
Price: .40 S&W **$489.00**
Price: .45 ACP **$489.00**
Price: 9mm Black Nitride finish **$522.00**
Price: .40, .45 Black Nitride finish **$509.00**

CHARTER ARMS PATHFINDER
Calibers: .22 LR or .22 Mag. Capacity: 6-round cylinder. Barrel: 2 in., 4 in. Weights: 20 oz. (12 oz. Lite model). Grips: Full. Sights: Fixed or adjustable (Target). Features: Stainless finish and frame.
Price .22 LR **$365.00**
Price .22 Mag **$367.00**
Price: Lite **$379.00**
Price: Target **$409.00**

CHARTER ARMS SOUTHPAW
Caliber: .38 Special +P. Capacity: 5-round cylinder. Barrel: 2 in. Weight: 12 oz. Grips: Rubber Pachmayr style. Features: Snubnose, matte black aluminum alloy frame with stainless steel cylinder. Cylinder latch and crane assembly are on right side of frame for convenience of left-hand shooters.
Price: **$419.00**

CHARTER ARMS THE PINK LADY
Caliber: .38 Special. Capacity: 6-round cylinder. Barrel: 2.2 in. Grips: Full. Sights: Fixed rear, LitePipe front. Weight: 12 oz. Features: As the name indicates, the Pink Lady has a pink and stainless steel finish. This is an aluminum-framed revolver from the Undercover Lite series.
Price: **$357.00**

Prices given are believed to be accurate at time of publication however, many factors affect retail pricing so exact prices are not possible.

CHARTER ARMS TARGET MAGNUM

Caliber: .357 Magnum. Capacity: 6-round cylinder. Barrel: 6 in. Grips: Full. Sights: Fully adjustable rear, fixed front. Features: This revolver of the Mag Pug series is built on Charter's XL frame. The 6-inch barrel and fully adjustable sights make this a great target piece that can also be used for hunting. Like all Charters, this one is made in the USA.

Price: $476.00

CHARTER ARMS THE PROFESSIONAL II

Caliber: .357 Magnum. Capacity: 6-round cylinder. Barrel: 3 in. Grips: Wood. Sights: Fixed rear, LitePipe front. Features: Built on Charter's large frame, the PROFESSIONAL II is a member of the PROFESSIONAL series of revolvers that is finished in a tough and attractive Blacknitride finish.

Price: $406.00

CHARTER ARMS THE PROFESSIONAL III

Caliber: .357 Magnum. Capacity: 6-round cylinder. Barrel: 4.2 in. Grips: Wood. Sights: Fixed rear, LitePipe front. Features: The PROFESSIONAL III is also a member of the PROFESSIONAL series of American-made revolvers from Charter Arms. This one, however, is built on Charter's XL frame, with a wood grip and a Blacknitride finish.

Price: $470.00

CHARTER ARMS THE PROFESSIONAL IV

Caliber: .32 Magnum. Capacity: 7-round cylinder. Barrel: 3 in. Grips: Wood. Sights: Fixed rear, LitePipe front. Features: A member of the PROFESSIONAL series, the PROFESSIONAL IV is manufactured on the large frame and features a 7-shot cylinder chambered in .32 Magnum. The finish is stainless steel.

Price: $420.00

CHARTER ARMS THE PROFESSIONAL V

Caliber: .357 Magnum. Capacity: 6-round cylinder. Barrel: 3 in. Grips: Wood. Sights: Fixed rear, LitePipe front. Features: A member of the PROFESSIONAL series, the PROFESSIONAL V is manufactured on the large frame and features a 6-shot cylinder chambered in .357 Magnum. The finish is stainless steel.

Price: $399.00

CHARTER ARMS THE PROFESSIONAL VI

Caliber: .357 Magnum. Capacity: 6-round cylinder. Barrel: 4.2 in. Grips: Wood. Sights: Fixed rear, LitePipe front. Features: The final model in the PROFESSIONAL series, the PROFESSIONAL VI is manufactured on Charter Arms' XL frame and features a 6-shot cylinder. The finish is stainless steel.

Price: $420.00

CHARTER ARMS UNDERCOVER

Caliber: .38 Special +P. Capacity: 6-round cylinder. Barrel: 2 in. Weight: 12 oz. Sights: Blade front, notch rear. Features: American made by Charter Arms.

Price: Blued $346.00

CHARTER ARMS UNDERCOVER LITE

Caliber: .38 Special. Capacity: 6-round cylinder. Barrel: 2.2 in. Grips: Full. Sights: Fixed rear, LitePipe front. Weight: 12 oz. Features: Aluminum-framed lightweight revolver with anodized finish. Lots of power in a feather-weight package.

Price: $357.00

CHARTER ARMS UNDERCOVER SOUTHPAW

Caliber: .38 Spec. +P. Capacity: 5-round cylinder. Barrel: 2 in. Weight: 12 oz. Sights: NA. Features: Cylinder release is on the right side and the cylinder opens to the right side. Exposed hammer for both SA and DA. American made by Charter Arms.

Price: $419.00

CHIAPPA RHINO

Calibers: .357 Magnum, 9mm, .40 S&W. Features: 2-, 4-, 5- or 6-inch barrel; fixed or adjustable sights; visible hammer or hammerless design. Weights: 24–33 oz. Walnut or synthetic grips with black frame; hexagonal-shaped cylinder. Unique design fires from bottom chamber of cylinder.

Price: From .... $1,090.00-$1,465.00

COBRA SHADOW

Caliber: .38 Special +P. Capacity: 5 rounds. Barrel: 1.875 in. Weight: 15 oz. Aluminum frame with stainless steel barrel and cylinder. Length: 6.375 in. Grips: Rosewood, black rubber or Crimson Trace Laser. Features: Black anodized, titanium anodized or custom colors including gold, red, pink and blue.

Price: $369.00
Price: Rosewood grips $434.00
Price: Crimson Trace Laser grips $625.00

Prices given are believed to be accurate at time of publication however, many factors affect retail pricing so exact prices are not possible.

76TH EDITION, 2022 ✦ **477**

COLT COBRA

Caliber: .38 Special. Capacity: 6 rounds. Sights: Fixed rear, fiber optic red front. Grips: Hogue rubbed stippled with finger grooves. Weight: 25 oz. Finish: Matte stainless. Same name as classic Colt model made from 1950–1986 but totally new design. Introduced in 2017. King Cobra has a heavy-duty frame and 3-inch barrel.

Price: **$699.00**
Price: King Cobra **$899.00**

COLT NIGHT COBRA

Caliber; .38 Special. Capacity: 6 rounds. Grips: Black synthetic VC G10. Sight: Tritium front night sight. DAO operation with bobbed hammer. Features a linear leaf spring design for smooth DA trigger pull.

Price: **$899.00**

COLT PYTHON

Caliber: .357 Magnum. Capacity: 6-round cylinder. Barrels: 4.25 and 6 in. Grips: Walnut. Sights: Fully adjustable rear, fixed red ramp interchangeable front. Weights: 42 oz. (4.25 in.), 46 oz. (6 in.). Features: New and improved and available only in stainless steel. Has recessed target crown and user-interchangeable front sight.

Price: **$1,499.00**

COLT ANACONDA

Caliber: .44 Magnum. Capacity: 6 rounds. Barrel: 6 and 8 in. Grip: Hogue Overmolded. Sights: Fully adjustable rear, fixed red ramp interchangeable front. Weight: 53 oz. (6 in.), 59 oz. (8 in.) Features: New and improved and available in stainless steel only. Has recessed target crown and user-interchangeable front sight.

Price: **$1,499.00**

COMANCHE II-A

Caliber: .38 Special. Capacity: 6-round cylinder. Barrels: 3 or 4 in. Weights: 33, 35 oz. Lengths: 8, 8.5 in. overall. Grips: Rubber. Sights: Fixed. Features: Blued finish, alloy frame. Distributed by SGS Importers.

Price: **$220.00**

DAN WESSON 715

Caliber: .357 Magnum. Capacity: 6-round cylinder. Barrel: 6-inch heavy barrel with full lug. Weight: 38 oz. Lengths: 8, 8.5 in. overall. Grips: Hogue rubber with finger grooves. Sights: Adjustable rear, interchangeable front blade. Features: Stainless steel. Interchangeable barrel assembly. Reintroduced in 2014. 715 Pistol Pack comes with 4-, 6- and 8-in. interchangeable barrels.

Price: From **$1,558.00**
Price: Pistol Pack... **$1,999.00**

EAA WINDICATOR

Calibers: .38 Special, .357 Mag Capacity: 6-round cylinder. Barrels: 2 in., 4 in. Weight: 30 oz. (4 in.). Length: 8.5 in. overall (4 in. bbl.). Grips: Rubber with finger grooves. Sights: Blade front, fixed rear. Features: Swing-out cylinder; hammer block safety; blue or nickel finish. Introduced 1991. Imported from Germany by European American Armory.

Price: .38 Spec. from **$354.00**
Price: .357 Mag, steel frame from **$444.00**

Prices given are believed to be accurate at time of publication however, many factors affect retail pricing so exact prices are not possible.

KIMBER K6S

Caliber: .357 Magnum. Capacity: 6-round cylinder. Barrel: 2-inch full lug. Grips: Gray rubber. Finish: Satin stainless. Kimber's first revolver, claimed to be world's lightest production 6-shot .357 Magnum. DAO design with non-stacking match-grade trigger. Introduced 2016. CDP model has laminated checkered rosewood grips, Tritium night sights, two-tone black DLC/brushed stainless finish, match grade trigger.

Price:	$878.00
Price: 3-in. Barrel	$899.00
Price: Deluxe Carry w/Medallion grips	$1,088.00
Price: Custom Defense Package	$1,155.00
Price: Crimson Trace Laser Grips	$1,177.00
Price: TLE	$999.00
Price: DA/SA	$949.00

KIMBER K6s DASA TARGET

Caliber: .357 Magnum. Capacity: 6-round cylinder. Barrel: 4 in. Grips: Walnut laminate, oversized. Sights: Fully adjustable rear, fiber-optic front. Features: The DASA is the next evolution of the K6s. The DASA is outfitted with a double- and single-action trigger mechanism. Kimber's K6s revolvers feature the purportedly smallest cylinder capable of housing 6 rounds of .357 Magnum at 1.39-inch diameter, making for a very slim and streamlined package.

Price: $989.00

KIMBER K6s DASA COMBAT

Caliber: .357 Magnum. Capacity: 6-round cylinder. Barrel: 4 in. Grips: Walnut laminate, oversized with finger grooves. Sights: Fixed front and rear with white dots. Features: The DASA Combat is outfitted with a double- and single-action trigger mechanism. Kimber's K6s DASA revolvers have a smooth no-stack double-action trigger and a crisp 3.25- to 4.25-lb. single-action pull. The K6s DASA revolvers are equipped with knurled hammer spur.

Price: $989.00

KIMBER K6s DASA TEXAS EDITION

Caliber: .357 Magnum. Capacity: 6-round cylinder. Barrel: 2 in. Grips: Ivory G10. Sights: Fixed front and rear with white dots. Features: The Texas Edition is adorned with ivory G10 grips with the state moto, name and flag on this special edition. The satin finish has American Western cut scroll engraving on the barrel, frame and cylinder. The K6s DASA Texas Edition revolvers are equipped with knurled hammer spur.

Price: $1,359.00

KIMBER K6s ROYAL

Caliber: .357 Magnum. Capacity: 6-round cylinder. Barrel: 2 in. Grips: Walnut. Sights: Fixed brass-bead front and rear with white dots. Features: The K6s Royal features a 2-inch barrel for easy concealment. The dovetailed white-dot rear sight complements the brass-bead front sight. The Royal's stainless steel is hand polished to a high shine and a Dark Oil DLC is applied for a unique look.

Price: $1,699.00

Prices given are believed to be accurate at time of publication however, many factors affect retail pricing so exact prices are not possible.

76TH EDITION, 2022 ✛ **479**

KORTH USA
Calibers: .22 LR, .22 WMR, .32 S&W Long, .38 Special, .357 Mag., 9mm. Capacity: 6-shot. Barrels: 3, 4, 5.25, 6 in. Weights: 36–52 oz. Grips: Combat, Sport: Walnut, Palisander, Amboina, Ivory. Finish: German Walnut, matte with oil finish, adjustable ergonomic competition style. Sights: Adjustable Patridge (Sport) or Baughman (Combat), interchangeable and adjustable rear w/Patridge front (Target) in blue and matte. Features: DA/SA, 3 models, over 50 configurations, externally adjustable trigger stop and weight, interchangeable cylinder, removable wide-milled trigger shoe on Target model. Deluxe models are highly engraved editions. Available finishes include high polish blued finish, plasma coated in high polish or matte silver, gold, blue or charcoal. Many deluxe options available. From Korth USA.
Price: From **$8,000.00**
Price: Deluxe Editions, from **$12,000.00**

KORTH SKYHAWK
Caliber: 9mm. Barrels: 2 or 3 in. Sights: Adjustable rear with gold bead front. Grips: Hogue with finger grooves. Features: Polished trigger, skeletonized hammer. Imported by Nighthawk Custom.
Price: **$1,699.00**

NIGHTHAWK CUSTOM/KORTH-WAFFEN NXR
Caliber: .44 Magnum. Capacity: 6-round cylinder Barrel: 6 in. Grips: Ivory G10. Sights: Adjustable rear, fast-changeable front. Weight: 3.05 lbs. Features: The NXR is a futuristic looking stainless steel double-action revolver that is black DLC finished. Comes equipped with a removable under-barrel balancing lug/weight. Picatinny rail on top of barrel and underneath for easy accessory mounting.
Price: **$5,299.00**

RUGER (CUSTOM SHOP) SUPER GP100 COMPETITION REVOLVER
Calibers: .357 Magnum, 9mm. Capacity: 8-round cylinder. Barrels: 5.5 and 6 in. Grips: Hogue hand-finished hardwood. Sights: Adjustable rear, fiber-optic front. Weights: 47 oz., 45.6 oz. Features: Designed for competition, the new Super GP100 is essentially a Super Redhawk with the frame extension removed and replaced by a shrouded, cold hammer-forged barrel. The Super GP utilizes the superior action of the Super Redhawk. The high-strength stainless steel cylinder has a PVD finish and is extensively fluted for weight reduction. Comes with high-quality, impact-resistant case.
Price: **$1,549.00**

RUGER GP-100
Calibers: .357 Mag., .327 Federal Mag, .44 Special Capacities: 6- or 7-round cylinder, .327 Federal Mag (7-shot), .44 Special (5-shot), .22 LR, (10-shot). Barrels: 3-in. full shroud, 4-in. full shroud, 6-in. full shroud. (.44 Special offered only with 3-in. barrel.) Weights: 36–45 oz. Sights: Fixed; adjustable on 4- and 6-in. full shroud barrels. Grips: Ruger Santoprene Cushioned Grip with Goncalo Alves inserts. Features: Uses action, frame features of both the Security-Six and Redhawk revolvers. Full-length, short ejector shroud. Satin blue and stainless steel.
Price: Blued **$769.00**
Price: Satin stainless **$799.00**
Price: .22 LR **$829.00**
Price: .44 Spl... **$829.00**
Price: 7-round cylinder, 327 Fed or .357 Mag **$899.00**

RUGER GP-100 MATCH CHAMPION
Calibers: 10mm Magnum, .357 Mag. Capacity: 6-round cylinder. Barrel: 4.2-in. half shroud, slab-sided. Weight: 38 oz. Sights: Fixed rear, fiber optic front. Grips: Hogue Stippled Hardwood. Features: Satin stainless steel finish.
Price: Blued **$969.00**

RUGER LCR

Calibers: .22 LR (8-round cylinder), .22 WMR, .327 Fed. Mag, .38 Special and .357 Mag., 5-round cylinder. Barrel: 1.875 in. Weights: 13.5–17.10 oz. Length: 6.5 in. overall. Grips: Hogue Tamer or Crimson Trace Lasergrips. Sights: Pinned ramp front, U-notch integral rear. Features: The Ruger Lightweight Compact Revolver (LCR), a 13.5 ounce, small frame revolver with a smooth, easy-to-control trigger and highly manageable recoil.

Price: .22 LR, .22 WMR, .38 Spl., iron sights **$579.00**
Price: 9mm, .327, .357, iron sights **$669.00**
Price: .22 LR, .22WMR, .38 Spl. Crimson Trace Lasergrip **$859.00**
Price: 9mm, .327, .357, Crimson Trace Lasergrip **$949.00**

RUGER LCRX

Calibers: .38 Special +P, 9mm, .327 Fed. Mag., .22 WMR. Barrels: 1.875 in. or 3 in. Features: Similar to LCR except this model has visible hammer, adjustable rear sight. The 3-inch barrel model has longer grip. 9mm comes with three moon clips.

Price: **$579.00**
Price: .327 Mag., .357 Mag., 9mm **$669.00**

RUGER SP-101

Calibers: .22 LR (8 shot); .327 Federal Mag. (6-shot), 9mm, .38 Spl, .357 Mag. (5-shot). Barrels: 2.25, 3 1/16, 4.2 in (.22 LR, .327 Mag., .357 Mag). Weights: 25–30 oz. Sights: Adjustable or fixed, rear; fiber-optic or black ramp front. Grips: Ruger Cushioned Grip with inserts. Features: Compact, small frame, double-action revolver. Full-length ejector shroud. Stainless steel only.

Price: Fixed sights **$719.00**
Price: Adjustable rear, fiber optic front sights **$769.00**
Price: .327 Fed Mag 3-in bbl **$769.00**
Price: .327 Fed Mag **$749.00**

RUGER REDHAWK

Calibers: .44 Rem. Mag., .45 Colt and .45 ACP/.45 Colt combo. Capacity: 6-round cylinder. Barrels: 2.75, 4.2, 5.5, 7.5 in. (.45 Colt in 4.2 in. only.) Weight: 54 oz. (7.5 bbl.). Length: 13 in. overall (7.5-in. barrel). Grips: Square butt cushioned grip panels. TALO Distributor exclusive 2.75-in. barrel stainless model has round butt, wood grips. Sights: Interchangeable Patridge-type front, rear adjustable for windage and elevation. Features: Stainless steel, brushed satin finish, blued ordnance steel. 9.5 sight radius. Introduced 1979.

Price: **$1,079.00**
Price: Hunter Model 7.5-in. bbl. **$1,159.00**
Price: TALO 2.75 in. model **$1,069.00**

RUGER SUPER REDHAWK

Calibers: 10mm, .44 Rem. Mag., .454 Casull, .480 Ruger. Capacities: 5- or 6-round cylinder. Barrels: 2.5 in. (Alaskan), 5.5 in., 6.5 in. (10mm) 7.5 in. or 9.5 in. Weight: 44–58 oz. Length: 13 in. overall (7.5-in. barrel). Grips: Hogue Tamer Monogrip. Features: Similar to standard Redhawk except has heavy extended frame with Ruger Integral Scope Mounting System on wide topstrap. Wide hammer spur lowered for better scope clearance. Incorporates mechanical design features and improvements of GP-100. Ramp front sight base has Redhawk-style interchangeable insert sight blades, adjustable rear sight. Alaskan model has 2.5-inch barrel. Satin stainless steel and low-glare stainless finishes. Introduced 1987.

Price: .44 Magnum, 10mm **$1,159.00**
Price: .454 Casull, .480 Ruger **$1,199.00**
Price: Alaskan, .44 Mag, .454 Casull, .480 Ruger **$1,189.00**

SMITH & WESSON GOVERNOR

Calibers: .410 Shotshell (2.5 in.), .45 ACP, .45 Colt. Capacity: 6 rounds. Barrel: 2.75 in. Length: 7.5 in., (2.5 in. barrel). Grip: Synthetic. Sights: Front: Dovetailed tritium night sight or black ramp, rear: fixed. Grips: Synthetic. Finish: Matte black or matte silver (Silver Edition). Weight: 29.6 oz. Features: Capable of chambering a mixture of .45 Colt, .45 ACP and .410 gauge 2.5-inch shotshells, the Governor is suited for both close and distant encounters, allowing users to customize the load to their preference. Scandium alloy frame, stainless steel cylinder. Packaged with two full moon clips and three 2-shot clips.

Price: $869.00
Price: w/Crimson Trace Laser Grip $1,179.00

SMITH & WESSON J-FRAME

The J-frames are the smallest Smith & Wesson wheelguns and come in a variety of chamberings, barrel lengths and materials as noted in the individual model listings.

SMITH & WESSON 60LS/642LS LADYSMITH

Calibers: .38 Special +P, .357 Mag. Capacity: 5-round cylinder. Barrels: 1.875 in. (642LS); 2.125 in. (60LS) Weights: 14.5 oz. (642LS); 21.5 oz. (60LS); Length: 6.6 in. overall (60LS). Grips: Wood. Sights: Black blade, serrated ramp front, fixed notch rear. 642 CT has Crimson Trace Laser Grips. Features: 60LS model has a Chiefs Special-style frame. 642LS has Centennial-style frame, frosted matte finish, smooth combat wood grips. Introduced 1996. Comes in a fitted carry/storage case. Introduced 1989. Made in USA by Smith & Wesson.

Price: (642LS) $499.00
Price: (60LS) $759.00
Price: (642 CT) $699.00

SMITH & WESSON MODEL 63

Caliber: .22 LR Capacity: 8-round cylinder. Barrel: 3 in. Weight: 26 oz. Length: 7.25 in. overall. Grips: Black synthetic. Sights: Hi-Viz fiber optic front sight, adjustable black blade rear sight. Features: Stainless steel construction throughout. Made in USA by Smith & Wesson.

Price: $769.00

SMITH & WESSON MODEL 442/637/638/642 AIRWEIGHT

Caliber: .38 Special +P. Capacity: 5-round cylinder. Barrels: 1.875 in., 2.5 in. Weight: 15 oz. Length: 6.375 in. overall. Grips: Soft rubber. Sights: Fixed, serrated ramp front, square notch rear. Features: A family of J-frame .38

Special revolvers with aluminum-alloy frames. Model 637; Chiefs Special-style frame with exposed hammer. Introduced 1996. Models 442, 642; Centennial-style frame, enclosed hammer. Model 638, Bodyguard style, shrouded hammer. Comes in a fitted carry/storage case. Introduced 1989. Made in USA by Smith & Wesson.

Price: From $469.00
Price: Laser Max Frame Mounted Red Laser sight $539.00

SMITH & WESSON MODELS 637 CT/638 CT

Similar to Models 637, 638 and 642 but with Crimson Trace Laser Grips.
Price: $699.00

SMITH & WESSON MODEL 317 AIRLITE

Caliber: .22 LR. Capacity: 8-round cylinder. Barrel: 1.875 in. Weight: 10.5 oz. Length: 6.25 in. overall (1.875-in. barrel). Grips: Rubber. Sights: Serrated ramp front, fixed notch rear. Features: Aluminum alloy, carbon and stainless steels, Chiefs Special-style frame with exposed hammer. Smooth combat trigger. Clear Cote finish. Model 317 Kit Gun has adjustable rear sight, fiber optic front. Introduced 1997.

Price: $759.00

SMITH & WESSON MODEL 340/340PD AIRLITE SC CENTENNIAL

Calibers: .357 Mag., 38 Special +P. Capacity: 5-round cylinder. Barrel: 1.875 in. Weight: 12 oz. Length: 6.375 in. overall (1.875-in. barrel). Grips: Rounded butt rubber. Sights: Black blade front, rear notch Features: Centennial-style frame, enclosed hammer. Internal lock. Matte silver finish. Scandium alloy frame, titanium cylinder, stainless steel barrel liner. Made in USA by Smith & Wesson.

Price: $1,019.00

SMITH & WESSON MODEL 351PD

Caliber: .22 Mag. Capacity: 5-round cylinder. Barrel: 1.875 in. Weight: 10.6 oz. Length: 6.25 in. overall (1.875-in. barrel). Sights: HiViz front sight, rear notch. Grips: Wood. Features: 7-shot, aluminum-alloy frame. Chiefs Special-style frame with exposed hammer. Nonreflective matte-black finish. Internal lock. Made in USA by Smith & Wesson.
Price: **$759.00**

SMITH & WESSON MODEL 360/360PD AIRLITE CHIEF'S SPECIAL

Calibers: .357 Mag., .38 Special +P. Capacity: 5-round cylinder. Barrel: 1.875 in. Weight: 12 oz. Length: 6.375 in. overall (1.875-in. barrel). Grips: Rounded butt rubber. Sights: Red ramp front, fixed rear notch. Features: Chief's Special-style frame with exposed hammer. Internal lock. Scandium alloy frame, titanium cylinder, stainless steel barrel. Model 360 has unfluted cylinder. Made in USA by Smith & Wesson.
Price: 360 .... **$770.00**
Price: 360PD **$1,019.00**

SMITH & WESSON BODYGUARD 38

Caliber: .38 Special +P. Capacity: 5-round cylinder. Barrel: 1.9 in. Weight: 14.3 oz. Length: 6.6 in. Grip: Synthetic. Sights: Front: Black ramp, Rear: fixed, integral with backstrap. Plus: Integrated laser sight. Finish: Matte black. Features: The first personal protection series that comes with an integrated laser sight.
Price: **$539.00**

SMITH & WESSON MODEL 640 CENTENNIAL DA ONLY

Calibers: .357 Mag., .38 Special +P. Capacity: 5-round cylinder. Barrel: 2.125 in. Weight: 23 oz. Length: 6.75 in. overall. Grips: Uncle Mike's Boot grip. Sights: Tritium Night Sights. Features: Stainless steel. Fully concealed hammer, snag-proof smooth edges. Internal lock.
Price: **$839.00**

SMITH & WESSON MODEL 649 BODYGUARD

Caliber: .357 Mag., .38 Special +P. Capacity: 5-round cylinder. Barrel: 2.125 in. Weight: 23 oz. Length: 6.625 in. overall. Grips: Uncle Mike's Combat. Sights: Black pinned ramp front, fixed notch rear. Features: Stainless steel construction, satin finish. Internal lock. Bodyguard style, shrouded hammer. Made in USA by Smith & Wesson.
Price: **$729.00**

SMITH & WESSON K-FRAME/L-FRAME

The K-frame series are mid-size revolvers and the L-frames are slightly larger.

SMITH & WESSON MODEL 10 CLASSIC

Caliber: .38 Special. Capacity: 6-round cylinder. Features: Bright blued steel frame and cylinder, checkered wood grips, 4-inch barrel and fixed sights. The oldest model in the Smith & Wesson line, its basic design goes back to the original Military & Police Model of 1905.
Price: **$739.00**

SMITH & WESSON MODEL 17 MASTERPIECE CLASSIC

Caliber: .22 LR. Capacity: 6-round cylinder. Barrel: 6 in. Weight: 40 oz. Grips: Checkered wood. Sights: Pinned Patridge front, micro-adjustable rear. Updated variation of K-22 Masterpiece of the 1930s.
Price: **$989.00**

SMITH & WESSON MODEL 19 CLASSIC

Caliber: .357 Magnum. Capacity: 6-round cylinder Barrel: 4.25 in. Weight: 37.2 oz. Grips: Walnut. Sights: Adjustable rear, red ramp front. Finish: Polished blue. Classic-style thumbpiece. Reintroduced 2019.
Price: **$826.00**

Prices given are believed to be accurate at time of publication however, many factors affect retail pricing so exact prices are not possible.

76TH EDITION, 2022 ✦ **483**

SMITH & WESSON MODEL 48 CLASSIC

Same specifications as Model 17 except chambered in .22 Magnum (.22 WMR) and is available with a 4- or 6-inch barrel.
Price: .... **$949.00–$989.00**

SMITH & WESSON MODEL 64/67

Caliber: .38 Special +P. Capacity: 6-round cylinder Barrel: 3 in. Weight: 33 oz. Length: 8.875 in. overall. Grips: Soft rubber. Sights: Fixed, .125-in. serrated ramp front, square notch rear. Model 67 is similar to Model 64 except for adjustable sights. Features: Satin finished stainless steel, square butt.
Price: From .... **$689.00–$749.00**

SMITH & WESSON MODEL 66

Caliber: .357 Magnum. Capacity: 6-round cylinder. Barrel: 4.25 in. Weight: 36.6 oz. Grips: Synthetic. Sights: White outline adjustable rear, red ramp front. Features: Return in 2014 of the famous K-frame "Combat Magnum" with stainless finish.
Price: **$849.00**

SMITH & WESSON MODEL 69

Caliber: .44 Magnum. Capacity: 5-round cylinder. Barrel: 4.25 in. Weight: 37 oz. Grips: Checkered wood. Sights: White outline adjustable rear, red ramp front. Features: L-frame with stainless finish, 5-shot cylinder, introduced in 2014.
Price: **$989.00**

SMITH & WESSON MODEL 610

Caliber: 10mm. Capacity: 6-round cylinder. Barrels: 4.25 and 6 in. Grips: Walnut. Sights: Fully adjustable rear, fixed red ramp interchangeable front. Weights: 42.6 oz. (4.25 in.), 50.1 oz (6 in.). Features: Built on Smith & Wesson's large N-frame in stainless steel only. Will also fire .40 S&W ammunition. Comes with three moon clips.
Price: **$987.00**

SMITH & WESSON MODEL 617

Caliber: .22 LR. Capacity: 10-round cylinder. Barrel: 6 in. Weight: 44 oz. Length: 11.125 in. Grips: Soft rubber. Sights: Patridge front, adjustable rear. Drilled and tapped for scope mount. Features: Stainless steel with satin finish. Introduced 1990.
Price: From **$829.00**

SMITH & WESSON MODEL 648

Caliber: .22 Magnum. Capacity: 8-round cylinder. Barrel: 6 in. Grips: Walnut. Sights: Fully adjustable rear, Patridge front. Weight: 46.2 oz. Features: This reintroduction was originally released in 1989 and produced until 2005. Ideal for target shooting or small-game hunting.
Price: **$752.00**

SMITH & WESSON MODEL 686/686 PLUS

Caliber: .357 Mag/.38 Special. Capacity: 6 (686) or 7 (Plus). Barrels: 6 in. (686), 3 or 6 in. (686 Plus), 4 in. (SSR). Weight: 35 oz. (3 in. barrel). Grips: Rubber. Sights: White outline adjustable rear, red ramp front. Features: Satin stainless frame and cylinder. Stock Service Revolver (SSR) has tapered underlug, interchangeable front sight, high-hold ergonomic wood grips, chamfered charge holes, custom barrel w/recessed crown, bossed mainspring.
Price: 686 .... **$829.00**
Price: Plus **$849.00**
Price: SSR **$999.00**

Prices given are believed to be accurate at time of publication however, many factors affect retail pricing so exact prices are not possible.

SMITH & WESSON MODEL 986 PRO
Caliber: 9mm. Capacity: 7-round cylinder Barrel: 5-in. tapered underlug. Features: SA/DA L-frame revolver chambered in 9mm. Features similar to 686 PLUS Pro Series with 5-inch tapered underlug barrel, satin stainless finish, synthetic grips, adjustable rear and Patridge blade front sight.
Price: **$1,149.00**

SMITH & WESSON M&P R8
Caliber: .357 Mag. Capacity: 8-round cylinder. Barrel: 5-in. half lug with accessory rail. Weight: 36.3 oz. Length: 10.5 in. Grips: Black synthetic. Sights: Adjustable v-notch rear, interchangeable front. Features: Scandium alloy frame, stainless steel cylinder.
Price: **$1,329.00**

SMITH & WESSON N-FRAME
These large-frame models introduced the .357, .41 and .44 Magnums to the world.

SMITH & WESSON MODEL 25 CLASSIC
Calibers: .45 Colt or .45 ACP. Capacity: 6-round cylinder. Barrel: 6.5 in. Weight: 45 oz. Grips: Checkered wood. Sights: Pinned Patridge front, micro-adjustable rear.
Price: **$1,019.00**

SMITH & WESSON MODEL 27 CLASSIC
Caliber: .357 Magnum. Capacity: 6-round cylinder. Barrels: 4 or 6.5 in. Weight: 41.2 oz. Grips: Checkered wood. Sights: Pinned Patridge front, micro-adjustable rear. Updated variation of the first magnum revolver, the .357 Magnum of 1935.
Price: (4 in.) **$1,019.00**
Price: (6.5 in.) **$1,059.00**

SMITH & WESSON MODEL 29 CLASSIC
Caliber: .44 Magnum Capacity: 6-round cylinder. Barrel: 4 or 6.5 in. Weight: 48.5 oz. Length: 12 in. Grips: Altamont service walnut. Sights: Adjustable white-outline rear, red ramp front. Features: Carbon steel frame, polished-blued or nickel finish. Has integral key lock safety feature to prevent accidental discharges. Original Model 29 made famous by "Dirty Harry" character played in 1971 by Clint Eastwood.
Price: .... **$999.00–$1,169.00**

SMITH & WESSON MODEL 57 CLASSIC
Caliber: .41 Magnum. Capacity: 6-round cylinder. Barrel: 6 in. Weight: 48 oz. Grips: Checkered wood. Sights: Pinned red ramp, micro-adjustable rear.
Price: **$1,009.00**

SMITH & WESSON MODEL 329PD ALASKA BACKPACKER
Caliber: .44 Magnum. Capacity: 6-round cylinder. Barrel: 2.5 in. Weight: 26 oz. Length: 9.5 in. Grips: Synthetic. Sights: Adj. rear, HiViz orange-dot front. Features: Scandium alloy frame, blue/black finish, stainless steel cylinder.
Price: From **$1,159.00**

SMITH & WESSON MODEL 625/625JM
Caliber: .45 ACP. Capacity: 6-round cylinder. Barrels: 4 in., 5 in. Weight: 43 oz. (4-in. barrel). Length: 9.375 in. overall (4-in. barrel). Grips: Soft rubber; wood optional. Sights: Patridge front on ramp, S&W micrometer click rear adjustable for windage and elevation. Features: Stainless steel construction with .400-in. wide semi-target hammer, .312-in. smooth combat trigger; full lug barrel. Glass beaded finish. Introduced 1989. Jerry Miculek Professional (JM) Series has .265-in. wide grooved trigger, special wooden Miculek Grip, five full moon clips, gold bead Patridge front sight on interchangeable front sight base, bead blast finish. Unique serial number run. Mountain Gun has 4-in. tapered barrel, drilled and tapped, Hogue Rubber Monogrip, pinned black ramp front sight, micrometer click-adjustable rear sight, satin stainless frame and barrel weighs 39.5 oz.
Price: 625 or 625JM **$1,074.00**

SMITH & WESSON MODEL 629
Calibers: .44 Magnum, .44 S&W Special. Capacity: 6-round cylinder. Barrels: 4 in., 5 in., 6.5 in. Weight: 41.5 oz. (4-in. bbl.). Length: 9.625 in. overall (4-in. bbl.). Grips: Soft rubber; wood optional. Sights: .125-in. red ramp front, white outline rear, internal lock, adjustable for windage and elevation. Classic similar to standard Model 629, except Classic has full-lug 5-in. barrel, chamfered front of cylinder, interchangeable red ramp front sight with adjustable white outline rear, Hogue grips with S&W monogram, drilled and tapped for scope mounting. Factory accurizing and endurance packages. Introduced 1990. Classic Power Port has Patridge front sight and adjustable rear sight. Model 629CT has 5-in. barrel, Crimson Trace Hoghunter Lasergrips, 10.5 in. OAL, 45.5 oz. weight. Introduced 2006.
Price: From **$949.00**

SMITH & WESSON X-FRAME
These extra-large X-frame S&W revolvers push the limits of big-bore handgunning.

Prices given are believed to be accurate at time of publication however, many factors affect retail pricing so exact prices are not possible.

76TH EDITION, 2022 ⊕ **485**

SMITH & WESSON MODEL 500
Caliber: 500 S&W Magnum. Capacity: 5-round cylinder. Barrels: 4 in., 6.5 in., 8.375 in. Weight: 72.5 oz. Length: 15 in. (8.375-in. barrel). Grips: Hogue Sorbothane Rubber. Sights: Interchangeable blade, front, adjustable rear. Features: Recoil compensator, ball detent cylinder latch, internal lock. 6.5-in.-barrel model has orange-ramp dovetail Millett front sight, adjustable black rear sight, Hogue Dual Density Monogrip, .312-in. chrome trigger with overtravel stop, chrome tear-drop hammer, glass bead finish. 10.5-in.-barrel model has red ramp front sight, adjustable rear sight, .312-in. chrome trigger with overtravel stop, chrome teardrop hammer with pinned sear, hunting sling. Compensated Hunter has .400-in. orange ramp dovetail front sight, adjustable black blade rear sight, Hogue Dual Density Monogrip, glass bead finish w/black clear coat. Made in USA by Smith & Wesson.
Price: From **$1,299.00**

SMITH & WESSON MODEL 460V
Caliber: 460 S&W Magnum (Also chambers .454 Casull, .45 Colt). Capacity: 5-round cylinder. Barrels: 7.5 in., 8.375-in. gain-twist rifling. Weight: 62.5 oz. Length: 11.25 in. Grips: Rubber. Sights: Adj. rear, red ramp front. Features: Satin stainless steel frame and cylinder, interchangeable compensator. 460XVR (X-treme Velocity Revolver) has black blade front sight with interchangeable green Hi-Viz tubes, adjustable rear sight. 7.5-in.-barrel version has Lothar-Walther barrel, 360-degree recoil compensator, tuned Performance Center action, pinned sear, integral Weaver base, non-glare surfaces, scope mount accessory kit for mounting full-size scopes, flashed-chromed hammer and trigger, Performance Center gun rug and shoulder sling. Interchangeable Hi-Viz green dot front sight, adjustable black rear sight, Hogue Dual Density Monogrip, matte-black frame and shroud finish with glass-bead cylinder finish, 72 oz. Compensated Hunter has teardrop chrome hammer, .312-in. chrome trigger, Hogue Dual Density Monogrip, satin/matte stainless finish, HiViz interchangeable front sight, adjustable black rear sight. XVR introduced 2006.
Price: 460V **$1,369.00**
Price: 460XVR, fr **$1,369.00**

STANDARD MANUFACTURING S333 THUNDERSTRUCK
Caliber: .22 Magnum. Capacity: 8-round cylinder. Barrel: 1.25 in. Grips: Polymer. Sights: Fixed front and rear. Weight: 18 oz. Features: Designed to be the ultimate in personal protection and featuring two-barrels that fire simultaneously with each trigger pull. The DA revolver has an 8-round, .22 Magnum capacity. Frame is constructed of 7075 aircraft-grade aluminum with anodized finish.
Price: **$429.00**

SUPER SIX CLASSIC BISON BULL
Caliber: .45-70 Government. Capacity: 6-round cylinder. Barrel: 10in. octagonal with 1:14 twist. Weight: 6 lbs. Length: 17.5 in. overall. Grips: NA. Sights: Ramp front sight with dovetailed blade, click-adjustable rear. Features: Manganese bronze frame. Integral scope mount, manual cross-bolt safety.
Price: **$1,500.00**

TAURUS 942
Caliber: .22 LR. Capacity: 8-round cylinder. Barrels: 2 and 3 in. Grips: Soft rubber. Sights: Drift-adjustable rear, serrated-ramp front. Weight: 17.8, 25 oz. Features: The 942 is based closely on the Taurus 856 revolver, but chambered in .22 LR with an 8-shot cylinder. Eight models are available: 2- and 3-inch-barrel models with a steel-alloy frame and cylinder in matte-black finish, 2- and 3-inch-barrel models with an ultralight aluminum-alloy frame in hard-coat, black-anodized finish, 2- and 3-inch-barrel models with a stainless steel frame and cylinder in a matte finish, and 2- and 3-inch-barrel models with an ultralight aluminum-alloy frame in a stainless-matte finish. Imported by Taurus International.
Prce: ....**$369.52 - $384.97**

TAURUS DEFENDER 856

Caliber: .38 Special +P. Capacity: 6-round cylinder. Barrel: 3 in. Grips: Hogue rubber, VZ black/gray, walnut. Sights: Fixed rear, tritium night sight with bright orange outline. Features: The Defender 856 is built on Taurus' small frame, making for a compact defensive revolver. Four standard models are available to include a stainless steel frame with matte finish, an ultralight aluminum-alloy frame with matte finish, stainless steel frame with black Tenifer finish, and an aluminum-alloy frame with hard-coat, black-anodized finish. Two upgrade versions are available with special grips and finish treatments. Imported by Taurus International.
Price: ....$429.00 - $477.00

TAURUS MODEL 17 TRACKER

Caliber: .17 HMR. Capacity: 7-round cylinder. Barrel: 6.5 in. Weight: 45.8 oz. Grips: Rubber. Sights: Adjustable. Features: Double action, matte stainless, integral key-lock.
Price: From $539.00

TAURUS MODEL 992 TRACKER

Calibers: .22 LR with interchangeable .22 WMR cylinder. Capacity: 9-round cylinder. Barrel: 4 or 6.5 in with ventilated rib. Features: Adjustable rear sight, blued or stainless finish.
Price: Blue $640.00
Price: Stainless $692.00

TAURUS MODEL 44SS

Caliber: .44 Magnum. Capacity: 5-round cylinder. Barrel: Ported, 4, 6.5, 8.4 in. Weight: 34 oz. Grips: Rubber. Sights: Adjustable. Features: Double action. Integral key-lock. Introduced 1994. Finish: Matte stainless. Imported from Brazil by Taurus International Manufacturing, Inc.
Price: From ....$648.00-$664.00

TAURUS MODEL 65

Caliber: .357 Magnum. Capacity: 6-round cylinder. Barrel: 4-in. full underlug. Weight: 38 oz. Length: 10.5 in. overall. Grips: Soft rubber. Sights: Fixed. Features: Double action, integral key-lock. Matte blued or stainless. Imported by Taurus International.
Price: Blued $539.00
Price: Stainless $591.00

TAURUS MODEL 66

Similar to Model 65, 4 in. or 6 in. barrel, 7-round cylinder, adjustable rear sight. Integral key-lock action. Imported by Taurus International.
Price: Blue $599.00
Price: Stainless $652.00

TAURUS MODEL 82 HEAVY BARREL

Caliber: .38 Special. Capacity: 6-round cylinder. Barrel: 4 in., heavy. Weight: 36.5 oz. Length: 9.25 in. overall. Grips: Soft black rubber. Sights: Serrated ramp front, square notch rear. Features: Double action, solid rib, integral key-lock. Imported by Taurus International.
Price: From $521.00

TAURUS MODEL 85FS

Caliber: .38 Special. Capacity: 5-round cylinder. Barrel: 2 in. Weights: 17–24.5 oz., titanium 13.5–15.4 oz. Grips: Rubber, rosewood or mother of pearl. Sights: Ramp front, square notch rear. Features: Spurred hammer. Blued, matte stainless, blue with gold accents, stainless with gold accents; rated for +P ammo. Integral keylock. Some models have titanium frame. Introduced 1980. Imported by Taurus International.
Price: From $379.00

TAURUS MODEL 856 ULTRALIGHT

Caliber: .38 Special. Capacity: 6-round cylinder. Barrel: 2 in. Matte black or stainless. Weights: 15.7 oz., titanium 13.5–15.4 oz. Grips: Rubber, rosewood or mother of pearl. Sights: Serrated ramp front, square notch rear. Features: Aluminum frame, matte black or stainless cylinder, azure blue, bronze, burnt orange or rouge finish.
Price: .... $364.00-$461.00

TAURUS 380 MINI

Caliber: .380 ACP. Capacity: 5-round cylinder w/moon clip. Barrel: 1.75 in. Weight: 15.5 oz. Length: 5.95 in. Grips: Rubber. Sights: Adjustable rear, fixed front. Features: DAO. Available in blued or stainless finish. Five Star (moon) clips included.
Price: Blued $478.00
Price: Stainless $514.00

TAURUS MODEL 45-410 JUDGE

Calibers: 2.5-in. .410/.45 Colt, 3-in. .410/.45 Colt. Barrels: 3 in., 6.5 in. (blued finish). Weights: 35.2 oz., 22.4 oz. Length: 7.5 in. Grips: Ribber rubber. Sights: Fiber Optic. Features: DA/SA. Matte stainless and ultra-lite stainless finish. Introduced in 2007. Imported from Brazil by Taurus International.
Price: From $511.00

Prices given are believed to be accurate at time of publication however, many factors affect retail pricing so exact prices are not possible.

76TH EDITION, 2022 ✦ **487**

TAURUS JUDGE PUBLIC DEFENDER POLYMER

Caliber: .45 Colt/.410 (2.5 in.). Capacity: 5-round cylinder. Barrel: 2.5-in. Weight: 27 oz. Features: SA/DA revolver with 5-round cylinder; polymer frame; Ribber rubber-feel grips; fiber-optic front sight; adjustable rear sight; blued or stainless cylinder; shrouded hammer with cocking spur; blued finish.
Price: From **$469.00**

TAURUS RAGING HUNTER

Calibers: .357 Magnum, .44 Magnum, .454 Casull, .460 Smith & Wesson Magnum. Capacity: 7 (.357), 6 (.44) and 5 (.454) rounds. Barrels: 5.12, 6.75, 8.37 in. Grips: Cushioned rubber. Sights: Adjustable rear, fixed front. Weight: 49 - 59.2 oz. Features: This is a DA/SA big-game-hunting revolver, available in three calibers and three barrel lengths, each featuring a Picatinny rail for easy optic mounting without removing the iron sights. All Raging Hunter models come with factory porting and cushioned rubber grips. Two finishes are available: matte black and two-tone matte stainless. Imported by Taurus International.
Prce: Black **$968.00**
Prce: Two Tone **$983.00**

TAURUS MODEL 627 TRACKER

Caliber: .357 Magnum. Capacity: 7-round cylinder. Barrels: 4 or 6.5 in. Weights: 28.8, 41 oz. Grips: Rubber. Sights: Fixed front, adjustable rear. Features: Double-action. Stainless steel, Shadow Gray or Total Titanium; vent rib (steel models only); integral key-lock action. Imported by Taurus International.
Price: From **$577.00**

TAURUS MODEL 444 ULTRA-LIGHT

Caliber: .44 Magnum. Capacity: 5-round cylinder. Barrels: 2.5 or 4 in. Weight: 28.3 oz. Grips: Cushioned inset rubber. Sights: Fixed red-fiber optic front, adjustable rear. Features: UltraLite titanium blue finish, titanium/alloy frame built on Raging Bull design. Smooth trigger shoe, 1.760-in. wide, 6.280-in. tall. Barrel rate of twist 1:16, 6 grooves. Introduced 2005. Imported by Taurus International.
Price: **$944.00**

TAURUS MODEL 444/454 RAGING BULL SERIES

Calibers: .44 Magnum, .454 Casull. Barrels: 2.25 in., 5 in., 6.5 in., 8.375 in. Weight: 53–63 oz. Length: 12 in. overall (6.5 in. barrel). Grips: Soft black rubber. Sights: Patridge front, adjustable rear. Features: DA, ventilated rib, integral key-lock. Most models have ported barrels. Introduced 1997. Imported by Taurus International.
Price: 444 .... **$900.00**
Price: 454 .... **$1,204.00.**

TAURUS MODEL 605 PLY

Caliber: .357 Magnum. **Capacity:** 5-round cylinder. **Barrel:** 2 in. **Weight:** 20 oz. **Grips:** Rubber. **Sights:** Fixed. **Features:** Polymer frame steel cylinder. Blued or stainless. Introduced 1995. Imported by Taurus International.
Price: Blued **$393.00**
Price: Stainless **$410.00**

TAURUS MODEL 905

Caliber: 9mm. **Capacity:** 5-round cylinder. **Barrel:** 2 in. **Features:** Small-frame revolver with rubber boot grips, fixed sights, choice of exposed or concealed hammer. Blued or stainless finish.
Price: Blued **$531.00**
Price: Stainless **$583.00**

TAURUS MODEL 692

Calibers: .38 Special/.357 Magnum or 9mm. **Capacity:** 7-round cylinder. **Barrels:** 3 or 6.5 in, ported. **Sights:** Adjustable rear, fixed front. **Grip:** "Ribber" textured. **Finish:** Matte blued or stainless. **Features:** Caliber can be changed with a swap of the cylinders which are non-fluted.
Price: **$659.00**

CIMARRON 1872 OPEN TOP

Calibers: .38, .44 Special, .44 Colt, .44 Russian, .45 LC, .45 S&W Schofield. Barrels: 5.5 in. and 7.5 in. Grips: Walnut. Sights: Blade front, fixed rear. Features: Replica of first cartridge-firing revolver. Blued finish; Navy-style brass or steel Army-style frame. Introduced 2001 by Cimarron F.A. Co.
Price: Navy model $529.00
Price: Army $550.00

CIMARRON 1875 OUTLAW

Calibers: .357 Magnum, .38 Special, .44 W.C.F., .45 Colt, .45 ACP. Barrels: 5.5 in. and 7.5 in. Weight: 2.5–2.6 lbs. Grip: 1-piece walnut. Features: Standard blued finish with color casehardened frame. Replica of 1875 Remington model. Available with dual .45 Colt/.45 ACP cylinder.
Price: $578.00
Price: Dual Cyl. $686.00

CIMARRON MODEL 1890

Caliber: .357 Magnum, .38 Special, .44 W.C.F., .45 Colt, .45 ACP. Barrel: 5.5 in. Weight: 2.4-2.5 lbs. Grip: 1-piece walnut. Features: Standard blued finish with standard blue frame. Replica of 1890 Remington model. Available with dual .45 Colt/.45 ACP cylinder.
Price: $606.00
Price: Dual Cylinder $702.00

CIMARRON BISLEY MODEL SINGLE-ACTION

Calibers: .357 Magnum, .44 WCF, .44 Special, .45. Features: Similar to Colt Bisley, special grip frame and trigger guard, knurled wide-spur hammer, curved trigger. Introduced 1999. Imported by Cimarron F.A. Co.
Price: From $636.00

CIMARRON LIGHTNING SA

Calibers: .22 LR, .32-20/32 H&R dual cyl. combo, .38 Special, .41 Colt. Barrels: 3.5 in., 4.75 in., 5.5 in. Grips: Smooth or checkered walnut. Sights: Blade front. Features: Replica of the Colt 1877 Lightning DA. Similar to Cimarron Thunderer, except smaller grip frame to fit smaller hands. Standard blued, charcoal blued or nickel finish with forged, old model, or color casehardened frame. Dual cylinder model available with .32-30/.32 H&R chambering. Introduced 2001. From Cimarron F.A. Co.
Price: From .... $503.00–$565.00
Price: .32-20/.32 H&R dual cylinder $649.00

CIMARRON MODEL P SAA

Calibers: .32 WCF, .38 WCF, .357 Magnum, .44 WCF, .44 Special, .45 Colt and .45 ACP. Barrels: 4.75, 5.5, 7.5 in. Weight: 39 oz. Length: 10 in. overall (4.75-in. barrel). Grips: Walnut. Sights: Blade front. Features: Old model black-powder frame with Bullseye ejector, or New Model frame. Imported by Cimarron F.A. Co.
Price: From $550.00

CIMARRON MODEL "P" JR.

Calibers: .22 LR, .32-20, .32 H&R, 38 Special Barrels: 3.5, 4.75, 5.5 in. Grips: Checkered walnut. Sights: Blade front. Features: Styled after 1873 Colt Peacemaker, except 20 percent smaller. Blue finish with color case-hardened frame; Cowboy action. Introduced 2001. From Cimarron F.A. Co.
Price: From $480.00

CIMARRON ROOSTER SHOOTER

Calibers: .357, .45 Colt and .44 W.C.F. Barrel: 4.75 in. Weight: 2.5 lbs. Grip: 1-piece orange finger grooved. Features: A replica of John Wayne's Colt Single Action Army model used in many of his great Westerns including his Oscar-winning performance in "True Grit," where he brings the colorful character Rooster Cogburn to life.
Price: $909.00

CIMARRON THUNDERER

Calibers: .357 Magnum, .44 WCF, .45 Colt. Capacity: 6-round cylinder. Features: Doc Holiday combo comes with leather shoulder holster, ivory handled dagger. Gun and knife have matching serial numbers. Made by Uberti.
Price: From .... $575.00–$948.00
Price: Combo $1,559.00

CIMARRON FRONTIER

Calibers: .357 Magnum, .44 WCF, .45 Colt. Barrels: 3.5, 4.75, 5.5 or 7.5 in. Features: Basic SAA design. Choice of Old Model or Pre-War frame. Blued or stainless finish. Available with Short Stroke action.
Price: Blued $530.00
Price: Stainless $723.00
Price: Short Stroke Action $598.00

Prices given are believed to be accurate at time of publication however, many factors affect retail pricing so exact prices are not possible.

76TH EDITION, 2022 ◈ **489**

CIMARRON U.S.V. ARTILLERY MODEL SINGLE-ACTION
Caliber: .45 Colt. Barrel: 5.5 in. Weight: 39 oz. Length: 11.5 in. overall. Grips: Walnut. Sights: Fixed. Features: U.S. markings and cartouche, casehardened frame and hammer. Imported by Cimarron F.A. Co.
Price: Blued finish... $594.00
Price: Original finish $701.00

CIMARRON BAD BOY
Calibers: .44 Magnum, 10mm. Capacity: 6-round cylinder. Barrel: 8 in. Grips: Walnut. Sights: Fully adjustable rear, fixed front. Features: Built on a replica Single Action Army Pre-War frame with an 1860 Army-style, one-piece walnut grip. The carbon-alloy steel frame is covered in a classic blue finish and it is fitted with an 8-inch octagon barrel and adjustable sights, and chambered in the popular semi-auto 10mm round in 2020.
Price: $726.05

COLT NEW FRONTIER
Calibers: .357 Magnum, .44 Special and .45 Colt. Barrels: 4.75 in., 5.5 in., and 7.5 in. Grip: Walnut. Features: From 1890 to 1898, Colt manufactured a variation of the venerable Single Action Army with a uniquely different profile. The "Flattop Target Model" was fitted with an adjustable leaf rear sight and blade front sights. Colt has taken this concept several steps further to bring shooters a reintroduction of a Colt classic. The New Frontier has that sleek flattop design with an adjustable rear sight for windage and elevation and a target ready ramp-style front sight. The guns are meticulously finished in Colt Royal Blue on both the barrel and cylinder, with a case-colored frame. Additional calibers available through Colt Custom Shop.
Price: $1,899.00

COLT SINGLE ACTION ARMY
Calibers: .357 Magnum, .45 Colt. Capacity: 6-round cylinder. Barrels: 4.75, 5.5, 7.5 in. Weight: 40 oz. (4.75-in. barrel). Length: 10.25 in. overall (4.75-in. barrel). Grips: Black Eagle composite. Sights: Blade front, notch rear. Features: Available in full nickel finish with nickel grip medallions, or Royal Blue with color casehardened frame. Reintroduced 1992. Additional calibers available through Colt Custom Shop.
Price: Blued $1,599.00
Price: Nickel.. $1,799.00

EAA BOUNTY HUNTER SA
Calibers: .22 LR/.22 WMR, .357 Mag., .44 Mag., .45 Colt. Capacities: 6. 10-round cylinder available for .22LR/.22WMR. Barrels: 4.5 in., 7.5 in. Weight: 2.5 lbs. Length: 11 in. overall (4.625 in. barrel). Grips: Smooth walnut. Sights: Blade front, grooved topstrap rear. Features: Transfer bar safety; 3-position hammer; hammer-forged barrel. Introduced 1992. Imported by European American Armory
Price: Centerfire, blued or case-hardened $478.00
Price: Centerfire, nickel $515.00
Price: .22 LR/.22 WMR, blued $343.00
Price: .22LR/.22WMR, nickel $380.00
Price: .22 LR/.22WMR, 10-round cylinder $465.00

EMF 1875 OUTLAW
Calibers: .357 Magnum, .44-40, .45 Colt. Barrels: 7.5 in., 9.5 in. Weight: 46 oz. Length: 13.5 in. overall. Grips: Smooth walnut. Sights: Blade front, fixed groove rear. Features: Authentic copy of 1875 Remington with firing pin in hammer; color casehardened frame, blued cylinder, barrel, steel backstrap and trigger guard. Also available in nickel, factory engraved. Imported by E.M.F. Co.
Price: All calibers $520.00
Price: Laser Engraved $800.00

Prices given are believed to be accurate at time of publication however, many factors affect retail pricing so exact prices are not possible.

EMF 1873 GREAT WESTERN II

Calibers: .357 Magnum, .45 Colt, .44/40. Barrels: 3.5 in., 4.75 in., 5.5 in., 7.5 in. Weight: 36 oz. Length: 11 in. (5.5-in. barrel). Grips: Walnut. Sights: Blade front, notch rear. Features: Authentic reproduction of the original 2nd Generation Colt single-action revolver. Standard and bone casehardening. Coil hammer spring. Hammer-forged barrel. Alchimista has case-hardened frame, brass backstrap, longer and wider 1860 grip.

Price: 1873 Californian .... **$545.00–$560.00**
Price: 1873 Custom series, bone or nickel, ivory-like grips **$689.90**
Price: 1873 Stainless steel, ivory-like grips **$589.90**
Price: 1873 Paladin **$560.00**
Price: Deluxe Californian with checkered walnut grips stainless.......... **$780.00**
Price: Buntline **$605.00**
Price: Alchimista.. **$675.00**

EMF 1873 DAKOTA II

Caliber: .357 Magnum, 45 Colt. Barrel: 4.75 in. Grips: Walnut. Finish: black.
Price: **$460.00**

FREEDOM ARMS MODEL 83 PREMIER GRADE

Calibers: .357 Magnum, 41 Magnum, .44 Magnum, .454 Casull, .475 Linebaugh, .500 Wyo. Exp. Capacity: 5-round cylinder. Barrels: 4.75 in., 6 in., 7.5 in., 9 in. (.357 Mag. only), 10 in. (except .357 Mag. and 500 Wyo. Exp.) Weight: 53 oz. (7.5-in. bbl. in .454 Casull). Length: 13 in. (7.5 in. bbl.). Grips: Impregnatedhardwood. Sights: Adjustable rear with replaceable front sight. Fixed rear notch and front blade. Features: Stainless steel construction with brushed finish; manual sliding safety bar. Micarta grips optional. 500 Wyo. Exp. Introduced 2006. Lifetime warranty. Made in USA by Freedom Arms, Inc.
Price: From **$2,738.00**

FREEDOM ARMS MODEL 83 FIELD GRADE

Calibers: .22 LR, .357 Magnum, .41 Magnum, .44 Magnum, .454 Casull, .475 Linebaugh, .500 Wyo. Exp. Capacity: 5-round cylinder. Barrels: 4.75 in., 6 in., 7.5 in., 9 in. (.357 Mag. only), 10 in. (except .357 Mag. and .500 Wyo. Exp.) Weight: 56 oz. (7.5-in. bbl. in .454 Casull). Length: 13.1 in. (7.5 in. bbl.). Grips: Pachmayr standard, impregnated hardwood or Micarta optional. Sights: Adjustable rear with replaceable front sight. Model 83 frame. All stainless steel. Introduced 1988. Made in USA by Freedom Arms Inc.
Price: From **$2,332.00**

FREEDOM ARMS MODEL 97 PREMIER GRADE

Calibers: .17 HMR, .22 LR, .32 H&R, .327 Federal, .357 Magnum, 6 rounds; .41 Magnum, .44 Special, .45 Colt. Capacity: 5-round cylinder. Barrels: 4.25 in., 5.5 in., 7.5 in., 10 in. (.17 HMR, .22 LR, .32 H&R). Weight: 40 oz. (5.5 in. .357 Mag.). Length: 10.75 in. (5.5 in. bbl.). Grips: Impregnated hardwood; Micarta optional. Sights: Adjustable rear, replaceable blade front. Fixed rear notch and front blade. Features: Stainless steel construction, brushed finish, automatic transfer bar safety system. Introduced in 1997. Lifetime warranty. Made in USA by Freedom Arms.
Price: From **$2,148.00**

HERITAGE ROUGH RIDER

Calibers: .22 LR, 22 LR/22 WMR combo, .357 Magnum .44-40, .45 Colt. Capacity: 6-round cylinder. Barrels: 3.5 in., 4.75 in., 5.5 in., 7.5 in. Weights: 31–38 oz. Grips: Exotic cocobolo laminated wood or mother of pearl; bird's head models offered. Sights: Blade front, fixed rear. Adjustable sight on 4.75 in. and 5.5 in. models. Features: Hammer block safety. Transfer bar with Big Bores. High polish blue, black satin, silver satin, casehardened and stainless finish. Introduced 1993. Made in USA by Heritage Mfg., Inc.
Price: Rimfire calibers, From **$200.00**
Price: Centerfire calibers, From.. **$450.00**

HERITAGE MANUFACTURING BARKEEP REVOLVER

Caliber: .22 LR. Capacity: 6 rounds. Barrel: 2, 3 in. Grip: Custom scroll wood or gray pearl. Sights: Fixed front and rear. Weight: 2.2 lbs. Features: Heritage Manufacturing's take on the 19th-Century "Storekeeper" single-action revolver. The new Barkeep is chambered in the economical .22 LR but is compatible with an optional interchangeable .22 WMR six-shot cylinder. Available with a black oxide or case-hardened finish. Two grips are also available — custom scroll wood or gray pearl.
Price: Custom wood scroll grips **$180.00**
Price: Gray pearl grips **$189.00**

Prices given are believed to be accurate at time of publication however, many factors affect retail pricing so exact prices are not possible.

76TH EDITION, 2022 ✛ **491**

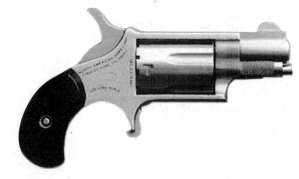

MAGNUM RESEARCH BFR SINGLE ACTION

Calibers: .44 Magnum, .444 Marlin, .45-70, .45 Colt/.410, .450 Marlin, .454 Casull, .460 S&W Magnum, .480 Ruger/.475 Linebaugh, .500 Linebaugh, .500 JRH, .500 S&W, .30-30. Barrels: 6.5 in., 7.5 in. and 10 in. Weights: 3.6–5.3 lbs. Grips: Black rubber. Sights: Rear sights are the same configuration as the Ruger revolvers. Many aftermarket rear sights will fit the BFR. Front sights are machined by Magnum in four heights and anodized flat black. The four heights accommodate all shooting styles, barrel lengths and calibers. All sights are interchangeable with each BFR's. Features: Crafted in the USA, the BFR single-action 5-shot stainless steel revolver frames are CNC machined inside and out from a pre-heat treated investment casting. This is done to prevent warping and dimensional changes or shifting that occurs during the heat treat process. Magnum Research designed the frame with large calibers and substantial recoil in mind, built to close tolerances to handle the pressure of true big-bore calibers. The BFR is equipped with a transfer bar safety feature that allows the gun to be carried safely with all five chambers loaded.
Price: .... **$1,218.00-$1,302.00**

NORTH AMERICAN ARMS MINI

Calibers: .22 Short, 22 LR, 22 WMR. Capacity: 5-round cylinder. Barrels: 1.125 in., 1.625 in. Weight: 4–6.6 oz. Length: 3.625 in., 6.125 in. overall. Grips: Laminated wood. Sights: Blade front, notch fixed rear. Features: All stainless steel construction. Polished satin and matte finish. Engraved models available. From North American Arms.
Price: .22 Short, .22 LR **$226.00**
Price: .22 WMR **$236.00**

MAGNUM RESEARCH BFR SHORT FRAME

Caliber: .357 Magnum, .44 Magnum. Capacity: 6-round cylinder. Barrels: 5 and 7.5 in. Grips: Standard rubber, Bisley, white polymer or black micarta. Sights: Adjustable rear, fixed front. Weights: 3.5, 3.65 lbs. Features: Made entirely of super tough 17-4PH stainless steel, BFRs are made in the United States and were designed from the outset to handle powerful revolver cartridges. The pre-eminent single-action hunting revolver. Two grip frame options available: a standard plow handle with rubber grip, and Magnum Research iteration of a Bisley with white polymer or black micarta grips.
Price: **$1,302.00**

NORTH AMERICAN ARMS MINI-MASTER

Calibers: .22 LR, .22 WMR. Capacity: 5-round cylinder. Barrel: 4 in. Weight: 10.7 oz. Length: 7.75 in. overall. Grips: Checkered hard black rubber. Sights: Blade front, white outline rear adjustable for elevation, or fixed. Features: Heavy vented barrel; full-size grips. Non-fluted cylinder. Introduced 1989.
Price: .... **$284.00–$349.00**

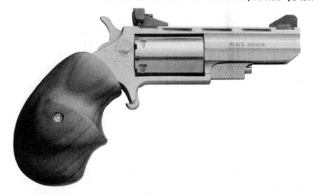

MAGNUM RESEARCH BFR LONG FRAME

Caliber: .350 Legend. Capacity: 6-round cylinder. Barrels: 7.5 and 10 in. Grips: Standard rubber, Bisley, white polymer or black micarta. Sights: Adjustable rear, fixed front. Weights: 4.8, 5 lbs. Features: Built on Magnum Research's long frame and made entirely of 17-4PH stainless steel. The first long frame in six-shot configuration. Two grip frame options available: a standard plow handle with rubber grip, and Magnum Research iteration of a Bisley with white polymer or black micarta grips.
Price:... ....$1,302.00**

NORTH AMERICAN ARMS BLACK WIDOW

Similar to Mini-Master, 2-in. heavy vent barrel. Built on .22 WMR frame. Non-fluted cylinder, black rubber grips. Available with Millett low-profile fixed sights or Millett sight adjustable for elevation only. Overall length 5.875 in., weighs 8.8 oz. From North American Arms.
Price: Adjustable sight, .22 LR or .22 WMR **$352.00**
Price: Fixed sight, .22 LR or .22 WMR **$288.00**

NORTH AMERICAN ARMS "THE EARL" SINGLE-ACTION

Calibers: .22 Magnum with .22 LR accessory cylinder. Capacity: 5-round cylinder. Barrel: 4 in. octagonal. Weight: 6.8 oz. Length: 7.75 in. overall. Grips: Wood. Sights: Barleycorn front and fixed notch rear. Features: Single-action mini-revolver patterned after 1858-style Remington percussion revolver. Includes a spur trigger and a faux loading lever that serves as cylinder pin release.
Price: .... **$298.00,$332.00 (convertible)**

Prices given are believed to be accurate at time of publication however, many factors affect retail pricing so exact prices are not possible.

RUGER NEW MODEL SINGLE-SIX SERIES

Calibers: .22 LR, .17 HMR. Convertible and Hunter models come with extra cylinder for .22 WMR. Capacity: 6. Barrels: 4.62 in., 5.5 in., 6.5 in. or 9.5 in. Weight: 35–42 oz. Finish: Blued or stainless. Grips: Black checkered hard rubber, black laminate or hardwood (stainless model only). Single-Six .17 Model available only with 6.5-in. barrel, blue finish, rubber grips. Hunter Model available only with 7.5-in. barrel, black laminate grips and stainless finish.
Price: (blued) **$629.00**
Price: (stainless) **$699.00**

RUGER SINGLE-TEN AND RUGER SINGLE-NINE SERIES

Calibers: .22 LR, .22 WMR. Capacities: 10 (.22 LR Single-Ten), 9 (.22 Mag Single-Nine). Barrels: 5.5 in. (Single-Ten), 6.5 in. (Single-Nine). Weight: 38–39 oz. Grips: Hardwood Gunfighter. Sights: Williams Adjustable Fiber Optic.
Price: **$699.00**

RUGER NEW MODEL BLACKHAWK/ BLACKHAWK CONVERTIBLE

Calibers: .30 Carbine, .357 Magnum/.38 Special, .41 Magnum, .44 Special, .45 Colt. Capacity: 6-round cylinder. Barrels: 4.625 in., 5.5 in., 6.5 in., 7.5 in. (.30 carbine and .45 Colt). Weights: 36–45 oz. Lengths: 10.375 in. to 13.5 in. Grips: Rosewood or black checkered. Sights: .125-in. ramp front, micro-click rear adjustable for windage and elevation. Features: Rosewood grips, Ruger transfer bar safety system, independent firing pin, hardened chrome-moly steel frame, music wire springs through-out. Case and lock included. Convertibles come with extra cylinder.
Price: (blued) **$669.00**
Price: (Convertible, .357/9mm) **$749.00**
Price: (Convertible, .45 Colt/.45 ACP) **$749.00**
Price: (stainless, .357 only) **$799.00**

RUGER BISLEY SINGLE ACTION

Calibers: .44 Magnum. and .45 Colt. Barrel: 7.5-in. barrel. Length: 13.5 in. Weight: 48–51 oz. Similar to standard Blackhawk, hammer is lower with smoothly curved, deeply checkered wide spur. The trigger is strongly curved with wide smooth surface. Longer grip frame. Adjustable rear sight, ramp-style front. Unfluted cylinder and roll engraving, adjustable sights. Plastic lockable case. Orig. fluted cylinder introduced 1985; discontinued 1991. Unfluted cylinder introduced 1986.
Price: **$899.00**

RUGER NEW MODEL SUPER BLACKHAWK

Caliber: .44 Magnum/.44 Special. Capacity: 6-round cylinder. Barrel: 4.625 in., 5.5 in., 7.5 in., 10.5 in. bull. Weight: 45–55 oz. Length: 10.5 in. to 16.5 in. overall. Grips: Rosewood. Sights: .125-in. ramp front, micro-click rear adjustable for windage and elevation. Features: Ruger transfer bar safety system, fluted or unfluted cylinder, steel grip and cylinder frame, round or square back trigger guard, wide serrated trigger, wide spur hammer. With case and lock.
Price: **$829.00**

RUGER NEW MODEL SUPER BLACKHAWK HUNTER

Caliber: .44 Magnum. Capacity: 6-round cylinder. Barrel: 7.5 in., full-length solid rib, unfluted cylinder. Weight: 52 oz. Length: 13.625 in. Grips: Black laminated wood. Sights: Adjustable rear, replaceable front blade. Features: Reintroduced Ultimate SA revolver. Includes instruction manual, high-impact case, set of medium scope rings, gun lock, ejector rod as standard. Bisley-style frame available.
Price: (Hunter, Bisley Hunter) **$959.00**

RUGER NEW VAQUERO SINGLE-ACTION

Calibers: .357 Magnum, .45 Colt. Capacity: 6-round cylinder. Barrel: 4.625 in., 5.5 in., 7.5 in. Weight: 39–45 oz. Length: 10.5 in. overall (4.625 in. barrel). Grips: Rubber with Ruger medallion. Sights: Fixed blade front, fixed notch rear. Features: Transfer bar safety system and loading gate interlock. Blued model color casehardened finish on frame, rest polished and blued. Engraved model available. Gloss stainless. Introduced 2005.
Price: **$829.00**

Prices given are believed to be accurate at time of publication however, many factors affect retail pricing so exact prices are not possible.

76TH EDITION, 2022 493

RUGER NEW MODEL BISLEY VAQUERO

Calibers: .357 Magnum, .45 Colt. Capacity: 6-round cylinder. Barrel: 5.5-in. Length: 11.12 in. Weight: 45 oz. Features: Similar to New Vaquero but with Bisley-style hammer and grip frame. Simulated ivory grips, fixed sights.
Price: **$899.00**

RUGER NEW BEARCAT SINGLE-ACTION

Caliber: .22 LR. Capacity: 6-round cylinder. Barrel: 4 in. Weight: 24 oz. Length: 9 in. overall. Grips: Smooth rosewood with Ruger medallion. Sights: Blade front, fixed notch rear. Distributor special edition available with adjustable sights. Features: Reintroduction of the Ruger Bearcat with slightly lengthened frame, Ruger transfer bar safety system. Available in blued finish only. Rosewood grips. Introduced 1996 (blued), 2003 (stainless). With case and lock.
Price: SBC-4, blued **$639.00**
Price: KSBC-4, satin stainless **$689.00**

RUGER WRANGLER

Caliber: .22 LR. Capacity: 6-round cylinder. Barrel: 4.62 in. Grips: Checkered synthetic. Sights: Fixed front and rear. Weight: 30 oz. Features: Inexpensive to own and inexpensive to shoot, this SA revolver is built on an aluminum-alloy frame and fitted with a cold hammer-forged barrel. Available in three models with three different finishes: Black Cerakote, Silver Cerakote or Burnt Bronze Cerakote. Equipped with transfer-bar mechanism and a free-wheeling pawl, allowing for easy loading and unloading.
Price: **$249.00**

STANDARD MANUFACTURING NICKEL SINGLE ACTION

Calibers: .38 Special, .45 Colt. Capacity: 6-round cylinder. Barrels: 4.75, 5.5 and 7.5 in. Grips: Walnut. Sights: Fixed front and rear. Weight: 40 oz. Features: This is one of the finest Single Action Army reproductions ever built, with great attention to detail. Made entirely from 4140 steel, the new nickel-plated revolvers are available in .38 special and the iconic .45 Colt. You can also opt for C-coverage engraving, making for a truly remarkable firearm. One- or two-piece walnut grips available.
Price: .... **$1,995.00 - $3,495.00**

TAYLOR'S CATTLEMAN SERIES

Calibers: .357 Magnum or 45 Colt. Barrels: 4.75 in., 5.5 in., or 7.5 in. Features: Series of Single Action Army-style revolvers made in many variations.
Price: Gunfighter w/blued & color case finish **$556.00**
Price: Stainless **$720.00**
Price: Nickel **$672.00**
Price: Charcoal blued **$647.00**
Price: Bird's Head 3.5- or 4.5-in. bbl., walnut grips **$603.00**
Price: Engraved (shown) **$925.00**

TAYLOR'S & COMPANY GUNFIGHTER

Caliber: .357 Magnum, .45 Colt. Capacity: 6 rounds. Barrel: 4.75, 5.5 in. Grip: Walnut. Checkered or smooth. Sights: Fixed front and rear. Weight: 2.4 lbs. Features: This 1873 Colt Single Action Army replica features an Army-sized grip for users with large hands. Casehardened finish. Available with Taylor Tuned action for additional cost.
Price: Smooth grip **$599.00**
Price: Checkered grip **$629.00**

TAYLOR'S & COMPANY SODBUSTER

Caliber: .44 Caliber. Capacity: 6 rounds. Barrel: 8 in. Grip: Polymer ivory. Sights: Fixed front and rear. Weight: 2.82 lbs. Features: 1858 Remington replica blackpowder revolver. Forged steel frame with blued finish topped off with faux ivory grips. A conversion cylinder is available to fire .45 Colt smokeless ammunition. Made for Taylor's exclusively by Uberti.
Price: **$619.00**

TAYLOR'S & COMPANY DEVIL ANSE

Caliber: .357 Magnum, .45 Colt. Capacity: 6 rounds. Barrel: 4.75 in. Grip: Matte black wood. Sights: Fixed front and rear. Weight: 2.43 lbs. Features: 1873 Colt Single Action Army replica featuring a blue finish with a casehardened hammer and matte black wood grips. Available with Taylor Tuned action for additional cost. Manufactured exclusively by Uberti for Taylor's & Company.
Price: **$599.00**

Prices given are believed to be accurate at time of publication however, many factors affect retail pricing so exact prices are not possible.

TAYLOR'S & COMPANY 1860 ARMY SNUB NOSE
Caliber: .36 Caliber, .44 Caliber. Capacity: 6 rounds. Barrel: 3 in. Grip: Checkered flattop birdshead grip. Sights: Fixed front and rear. Weight: 2.3 lbs. Features: 1860 Army Snub Nose blackpowder percussion replica revolver. It features a steel frame, shoulder stock frame cuts and screws, and a round barrel. Barrel and cylinder are blued while the frame is casehardened. A conversion cylinder is available to shoot smokeless ammunition. Manufactured exclusively by Pietta for Taylor's & Company.
Price: **$379.00**

UBERTI 1851–1860 CONVERSION
Calibers: .38 Special, .45 Colt. Capacity: 6-round engraved cylinder. Barrels: 4.75 in., 5.5 in., 7.5 in., 8 in. Weight: 2.6 lbs. (5.5-in. bbl.). Length: 13 in. overall (5.5-in. bbl.). Grips: Walnut. Features: Brass backstrap, trigger guard; color casehardened frame, blued barrel, cylinder. Introduced 2007.
Price: 1851 Navy **$569.00**
Price: 1860 Army **$589.00**

UBERTI 1871–1872 OPEN TOP
Calibers: .38 Special, .45 Colt. Capacity: 6-round engraved cylinder. Barrels: 4.75 in., 5.5 in., 7.5 in. Weight: 2.6 lbs. (5.5-in. bbl.). Length: 13 in. overall (5.5-in. bbl.). Grips: Walnut. Features: Blued backstrap, trigger guard; color casehardened frame, blued barrel, cylinder. Introduced 2007.
Price: .... **$539.00–$569.00**

UBERTI 1873 CATTLEMAN SINGLE-ACTION
Caliber: .45 Colt. Capacity: 6-round cylinder. Barrels: 4.75 in., 5.5 in., 7.5 in. Weight: 2.3 lbs. (5.5-in. bbl.). Length: 11 in. overall (5.5-in. bbl.). Grips: Styles: Frisco (pearl styled); Desperado (buffalo horn styled); Chisholm (checkered walnut); Gunfighter (black checkered), Cody (ivory styled), one-piece walnut. Sights: Blade front, groove rear. Features: Steel or brass backstrap, trigger guard; color casehardened frame, blued barrel, cylinder. NM designates New Model plunger-style frame; OM designates Old Model screw cylinder pin retainer.
Price: 1873 Cattleman Frisco **$869.00**
Price: 1873 Cattleman Desperado (2006) **$889.00**
Price: 1873 Cattleman Chisholm (2006) **$599.00**
Price: 1873 Cattleman NM, blued 4.75 in. barrel **$669.00**
Price: 1873 Cattleman NM, Nickel finish, 7.5 in. barrel **$689.00**
Price: 1873 Cattleman Cody **$899.00**

UBERTI 1873 CATTLEMAN BIRD'S HEAD SINGLE ACTION
Calibers: .357 Magnum, .45 Colt. Capacity: 6-round cylinder. Barrels: 3.5 in., 4 in., 4.75 in., 5.5 in. Weight: 2.3 lbs. (5.5-in. bbl.). Length: 10.9 in. overall (5.5-in. bbl.). Grips: One-piece walnut. Sights: Blade front, groove rear. Features: Steel or brass backstrap, trigger guard; color casehardened frame, blued barrel, fluted cylinder.
Price: **$569.00**

UBERTI CATTLEMAN .22
Caliber: .22 LR. Capacity: 6- or 12-round cylinder. Barrel: 5.5 in. Grips: One-piece walnut. Sights: Fixed. Features: Blued and casehardened finish, steel or brass backstrap/trigger guard.
Price: (brass backstrap, trigger guard) **$539.00**
Price: (steel backstrap, trigger guard) **$559.00**
Price: (12-round model, steel backstrap, trigger guard) **$589.00**

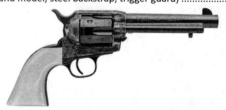

UBERTI DALTON REVOLVER
Caliber: .45 Colt. Capacity: 6-round cylinder. Barrel: 5.5 in. Grips: Simulated pearl. Sights: Fixed front and rear. Weight: 2.3 lbs. Features: Uberti USA expands its Outlaws & Lawmen Series of revolvers with the addition of the Dalton Revolver, a faithful reproduction of the Colt Single Action Army revolver used by Dalton Gang leader Bob Dalton. Features hand-chased engraving from famed Italian engraving company, Atelier Giovanelli, on the receiver, grip frame and cylinder.
Price: **$1,109.00**

UBERTI 1873 BISLEY SINGLE-ACTION
Calibers: .357 Magnum, .45 Colt (Bisley); .22 LR and .38 Special. (Stallion), both with 6-round fluted cylinder. Barrels: 4.75 in., 5.5 in., 7.5 in. Weight: 2–2.5 lbs. Length: 12.7 in. overall (7.5-in. barrel). Grips: Two-piece walnut. Sights: Blade front, notch rear. Features: Replica of Colt's Bisley Model. Polished blued finish, color casehardened frame. Introduced 1997.
Price: 1873 Bisley, 7.5-in. barrel **$619.00**

UBERTI 1873 BUNTLINE AND REVOLVER CARBINE SINGLE-ACTION
Caliber: .357 Magnum, .44-40, .45 Colt. Capacity: 6. Barrel: 18 in. Length: 22.9–34 in. Grips: Walnut pistol grip or rifle stock. Sights: Fixed or adjustable.
Price: 1873 Revolver Carbine, 18-in. bbl., 34 in. OAL **$729.00**
Price: 1873 Cattleman Buntline Target, 18-in. bbl. 22.9 in. OAL **$639.00**

UBERTI OUTLAW, FRONTIER, AND POLICE

Caliber: .45 Colt. Capacity: 6-round cylinder. Barrels: 5.5 in., 7.5 in. Weight: 2.5–2.8 lbs. Length: 10.8 in. to 13.6 in. overall. Grips: Two-piece smooth walnut. Sights: Blade front, notch rear. Features: Cartridge version of 1858 Remington percussion revolver. Nickel and blued finishes. Fluted cylinder.
Price: 1875 Outlaw, nickel finish **$609.00**
Price: 1875 Frontier, blued finish **$609.00**
Price: 1890 Police, blued finish **$599.00**

UBERTI 1870 SCHOFIELD-STYLE TOP BREAK

Calibers: .38 Special, .44 Russian, .44-40, .45 Colt. Capacity: 6-round cylinder. Barrels: 3.5 in., 5 in., 7 in. Weight: 2.4 lbs. (5-in. barrel) Length: 10.8 in. overall (5-in. barrel). Grips: Two-piece smooth walnut or pearl. Sights: Blade front, notch rear. Features: Replica of Smith & Wesson Model 3 Schofield. Single-action, top break with automatic ejection. Polished blued finish (first model). Introduced 1994.
Price: .... **$1,189.00-$1,599.00**

UBERTI STAINLESS STEEL SHORT STROKE CMS PRO

Caliber: .45 Colt. Capacity: 6-round cylinder. Barrel: 3.5 in. Grips: Synthetic traditional. Sights: Fixed front and rear. Weight: 2.1 lbs. Features: Made specifically for the rigors of Cowboy Mounted Shooting competition, and built entirely of stainless steel. Good for quick, one-handed shooting while riding a horse. Features low-profile, short-stroke hammer with 20-percent less travel. Extra-wide, deeply grooved hammer, and chambered in the classic .45 Colt.
Price: **$909.00**

UBERTI STAINLESS STEEL SHORT STROKE CMS KL PRO

Caliber: .45 Colt. Capacity: 6-round cylinder. Barrel: 3.5 in. Grips: Synthetic bird's head. Sights: Fixed front and rear. Weight: 2.1 lbs. Features: Made specifically for the rigors of Cowboy Mounted Shooting competition, and built entirely of stainless steel. This model is the result of the partnership between Uberti USA and legendary Cowboy Mounted Shooter competitor Kenda Lenseigne, winner of multiple world and national mounted shooting championships. It features a modified bird's-head grip with Lenseigne's brand on the grip and her signature engraved on the barrel. Features low-profile, short-stroke hammer with 20-percent less travel. Extra-wide, deeply grooved hammer, and chambered in the classic .45 Colt.
Price: **$909.00**

UBERTI USA DALTON

Caliber: .357 Magnum. Capacity: 6 rounds. Barrel: 5.5 in. Grip: Simulated pearl. Sights: Fixed front and rear. Weight: 2.3 lbs. Features: Uberti USA Outlaw & Lawmen Series of revolvers adds the Dalton — a faithful reproduction of the Colt Single Action Army revolver used by Dalton Gang leader Bob Dalton. Features hand-chased engraving from famed Italian engraving company, Atelier Giovanelli on the receiver, grip frame, and cylinder. This new version is chambered in .357 Magnum.
Price: **$1,109.00**

UBERTI USA FRANK

Caliber: .357 Magnum. Capacity: 6 rounds. Barrel: 7.5 in. Grip: Simulated ivory. Sights: Fixed front and rear. Weight: 2.3 lbs. Features: Uberti USA Outlaw & Lawmen Series of revolvers adds a .357 Magnum version of the Frank revolver, a faithful reproduction of the outlaw Frank James' 1875 Remington. Finished in nickel plating, the grip is simulated ivory with a lanyard loop.
Price: **$949.00**

UBERTI USA HARDIN

Caliber: .45 Colt. Capacity: 6 rounds. Barrel: 7 in. Grip: Simulated bison horn. Sights: Fixed front and rear. Weight: 2.6 lbs. Features: Uberti USA Outlaw & Lawmen Series adds the Hardin, a faithful reproduction of the Smith & Wesson Top-break revolver used by John Wesley Hardin. Features a case-colored frame and charcoal blue barrel and cylinder along with simulated bison-horn grip, chambered in .45 Colt.
Price: **$1,479.00**

UBERTI USA TEDDY

Caliber: .45 Colt. Capacity: 6 rounds. Barrel: 5.5 in. Grip: Simulated ivory. Sights: Fixed front and rear. Weight: 2.3 lbs. Features: Replica of the revolver Theodore Roosevelt carried on many of his adventures. A replica 1873 Colt, this one is chambered in .45 Colt, and features a nickel finish, full laser engraving along the frame, cylinder, and barrel, and simulated ivory grips.
Price: **$1,249.00**

AMERICAN DERRINGER MODEL 1
Calibers: All popular handgun calibers plus .45 Colt/.410 Shotshell. Capacity: 2, (.45-70 model is single shot). Barrel: 3 in. Overall length: 4.82 in. Weight: 15 oz. Features: Manually operated hammer-block safety automatically disengages when hammer is cocked. Texas Commemorative has brass frame and is available in .38 Special, .44-40. or .45 Colt.
Price: .... **$635.00–$735.00**
Price: Texas Commemorative **$835.00**

AMERICAN DERRINGER MODEL 8
Calibers: .45 Colt/.410 shotshell. Capacity: 2. Barrel: 8 in. Weight: 24 oz.
Price: **$915.00**
Price: High polish finish **$1,070.00**

AMERICAN DERRINGER DA38
Calibers: .38 Special, .357 Magnum, 9mm Luger. Barrel: 3.3 in. Weight: 14.5 oz. Features: DA operation with hammer-block thumb safety. Barrel, receiver and all internal parts are made from stainless steel.
Price: ....**$690.00–$740.00**

BOND ARMS TEXAS DEFENDER DERRINGER
Calibers: Available in more than 10 calibers, from .22 LR to .45 LC/.410 shotshells. Barrel: 3 in. Weight: 20 oz. Length: 5 in. Grips: Rosewood. Sights: Blade front, fixed rear. Features: Interchangeable barrels, stainless steel firing pins, cross-bolt safety, automatic extractor for rimmed calibers. Stainless steel construction, brushed finish. Right or left hand.
Price: **$543.00**
Price: Interchangeable barrels, .22 LR thru .45 LC, 3 in. **$139.00**
Price: Interchangeable barrels, .45 LC, 3.5 in. ....**$159.00–$189.00**

BOND ARMS RANGER II
Caliber: .45 LC/.410 shotshells or .357 Magnum/.38 Special. Barrel: 4.25 in. Weight: 23.5 oz. Length: 6.25 in. Features: This model has a trigger guard. Intr. 2011. From Bond Arms.
Price: **$673.00**

BOND ARMS CENTURY 2000 DEFENDER
Calibers: .45 LC/.410 shotshells. or .357 Magnum/.38 Special. Barrel: 3.5 in. Weight: 21 oz. Length: 5.5 in. Features: Similar to Defender series.
Price: **$517.00**

BOND ARMS COWBOY DEFENDER
Calibers: From .22 LR to .45 LC/.410 shotshells. Barrel: 3 in. Weight: 19 oz. Length: 5.5 in. Features: Similar to Defender series. No trigger guard.
Price: **$493.00**

BOND ARMS GRIZZLY
Calibers: .45 Colt/.410 bore. Capacity: 2 rounds. Barrel: 3 in. Grips: Rosewood. Sights: Fixed front and rear. Features: Similar to other Bond Arms derringers, this model is chambered in .45 Colt and 2.5-inch, .410-bore shotshells. Vibrant rosewood grips with grizzly-bear artwork adorn the Grizzly. It includes a matching leather holster embossed with a grizzly bear.
Price: **$377.00**

BOND ARMS SNAKE SLAYER
Calibers: .45 LC/.410 shotshell (2.5 in. or 3 in.). Barrel: 3.5 in. Weight: 21 oz. Length: 5.5 in. Grips: Extended rosewood. Sights: Blade front, fixed rear. Features: Single-action; interchangeable barrels; stainless steel firing pin. Introduced 2005.
Price: **$603.00**

BOND ARMS ROUGHNECK
Calibers: 9mm, .357 Magnum, .45 ACP. Capacity: 2 rounds. Barrel: 2.5 in. Grips: Textured rubber. Sights: Fixed front and rear. Weight: 22 oz. Features: A member of the new Bond Arms Rough series of derringers that includes the premium features found in all Bond guns, including stainless steel barrel, cross-bolt safety, retracting firing pin, spring-loaded, cam-lock lever and rebounding hammer. Each gun of the new series undergoes a quick clean up and deburring and then is bead-blasted, giving it a rough finish. This lightweight tips the scales at 22 ounces.
Price: **$269.00**

BOND ARMS ROUGH N ROWDY
Calibers: .45 Colt/.410 bore. Capacity: 2 rounds. Barrel: 3 in. Grips: Black rubber. Sights: Fixed front and rear. Features: Similar to Bond Arms Roughneck, this model is chambered in .45 Colt and 2.5-inch, .410 bore shotshells.
Price: $299.00

BOND ARMS SNAKE SLAYER IV
Calibers: .45 LC/.410 shotshell (2.5 in. or 3 in.). Barrel: 4.25 in. Weight: 22 oz. Length: 6.25 in. Grips: Extended rosewood. Sights: Blade front, fixed rear. Features: Single-action; interchangeable barrels; stainless steel firing pin. Introduced 2006.
Price: **$648.00**

BOND ARMS STINGER
Calibers: 9mm, .38 Special. Capacity: 2 rounds. Barrel: 2.5 in. Grips: Black rubber. Sights: Fixed front and rear. Weight: 12 oz. Features: An all-new offering from Bond Arms that redefines the term lightweight, the Stinger is a slim-line derringer with an aluminum frame and stainless steel barrels that tips the scales at a whopping 12 oz.
Price: $299.00

Calibers: .22 WMR, .32 H&R Mag., .38 Special, 9mm Para., .380 ACP. Barrel: 2.75 in. Weight: 14 oz. Length: 4.65 in. overall. Grips: Textured black or white synthetic or laminated rosewood. Sights: Blade front, fixed notch rear. Features: Alloy frame, steel-lined barrels, steel breechblock. Plunger-type safety with integral hammer block. Black, chrome or satin finish. Introduced 2002. Made in USA by Cobra Enterprises of Utah, Inc.
Price: **$187.00**

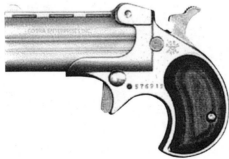

COBRA STANDARD SERIES DERRINGERS
Calibers: .22 LR, .22 WMR, .25 ACP, .32 ACP. Barrel: 2.4 in. Weight: 9.5 oz. Length: 4 in. overall. Grips: Laminated wood or pearl. Sights: Blade front, fixed notch rear. Features: Choice of black powder coat, satin nickel or chrome finish. Introduced 2002. Made in USA by Cobra Enterprises of Utah, Inc.
Price: **$169.00**

COBRA LONG-BORE DERRINGERS
Calibers: .22 WMR, .38 Special, 9mm. Barrel: 3.5 in. Weight: 16 oz. Length: 5.4 in. overall. Grips: Black or white synthetic or rosewood. Sights: Fixed. Features: Chrome, satin nickel, or black Teflon finish. Introduced 2002. Made in USA by Cobra Enterprises of Utah, Inc.
Price: **$187.00**

COBRA TITAN .45 LC/.410 DERRINGER
Calibers: .45 LC, .410 or 9mm, 2-round capacity. Barrel: 3.5 in. Weight: 16.4 oz. Grip: Rosewood. Features: Standard finishes include: satin stainless, black stainless and brushed stainless. Made in USA by Cobra Enterprises of Utah, Inc.
Price: **$399.00**

COMANCHE SUPER SINGLE-SHOT
Calibers: .45 LC/.410 Barrel: 10 in. Sights: Adjustable. Features: Blue finish, not available for sale in CA, MA. Distributed by SGS Importers International, Inc.
Price: **$240.00**

DOUBLETAP DERRINGER
Calibers: .45 Colt or 9mm Barrel: 3 in. Weight: 12 oz. Length: 5.5 in. Sights: Adjustable. Features: Over/under, two-barrel design. Rounds are fired individually with two separate trigger pulls. Tip-up design, aluminum frame.
Price: **$499.00**

Prices given are believed to be accurate at time of publication however, many factors affect retail pricing so exact prices are not possible.

HEIZER PAK1
Caliber: 7.2x39. Similar to Pocket AR but chambered for 7.62x39mm. Single shot. Barrel: 3.75 in., ported or unported. Length: 6.375 in. Weight: 23 oz.
Price: **$339.00**

HEIZER PS1 POCKET SHOTGUN
Calibers: .45 Colt or .410 shotshell. Single-shot. Barrel: Tip-up, 3.25 in. Weight: 22 oz. Length: 5.6 in. Width: .742 in Height: 3.81 in. Features: Available in several finishes. Standard model is matte stainless or black. Also offered in Hedy Jane series for the women in pink or in two-tone combinations of stainless and pink, blue, green, purple. Includes interchangeable AR .223 barrel. Made in the USA by Heizer Industries.
Price: **$499.00**

HEIZER POCKET AR
Caliber: .223 Rem./5.56 NATO. Single shot. Barrel: 3.75 in., ported or non-ported. Length: 6.375 in. Weight: 23 oz. Features: Similar to PS1 pocket shotgun but chambered for .223/5.56 rifle cartridge.
Price: **$339.00**

HENRY MARE'S LEG
Calibers: .22 LR, .22 WMR, .357 Magnum, .44 Magnum, .45 Colt. Capacities: 10 rounds (.22 LR), 8 rounds (.22 WMR), 5 rounds (others). Barrel: 12.9 in. Length: 25 in. Weight: 4.5 lbs. (rimfire) to 5.8 lbs. (centerfire calibers). Features: Lever-action operation based on Henry rifle series and patterned after gun made famous in Steve McQueen's 1950s TV show, "Wanted: Dead or Alive." Made in the USA.
Price: .22 LR...**$462.00**
Price: .22 WMR **$473.00**
Price: Centerfire calibers **$1,024.00**

MAXIMUM SINGLE-SHOT
Calibers: .22 LR, .22 Hornet, .22 BR, .22 PPC, 223 Rem., .22-250, 6mm BR, 6mm PPC, .243, .250 Savage, 6.5mm-35M, .270 MAX, .270 Win., 7mm TCU, 7mm BR, 7mm-35, 7mm INT-R, 7mm-08, 7mm Rocket, 7mm Super-Mag., .30 Herrett, .30 Carbine, .30-30, .308 Win., 30x39, .32-20, .350 Rem. Mag., .357 Mag., .357 Maximum, .358 Win., .375 H&H, .44 Mag., .454 Casull. Barrel: 8.75 in., 10.5 in., 14 in. Weight: 61 oz. (10.5-in. bbl.); 78 oz. (14-in. bbl.). Length: 15 in., 18.5 in. overall (with 10.5- and 14-in. bbl., respectively). Grips: Smooth walnut stocks and fore-end. Also available with 17-finger-groove grip. Sights: Ramp front, fully adjustable open rear. Features: Falling block action; drilled and tapped for M.O.A. scope mounts; integral grip frame/receiver; adjustable trigger; Douglas barrel (interchangeable). Introduced 1983. Made in USA by M.O.A. Corp.
Price: **$1,062.00**

ROSSI MATCHED PAIR, "DUAL THREAT PERFORMER"
Calibers: .22LR, .44 Magnum, .223, .243, .410, 20 gauge, single shot. Interchangeable rifle and shotgun barrels in various combinations. Sights: Fiber optic front sights, adjustable rear. Features: Two-in-one pistol system with single-shot simplicity. Removable choke and cushioned grip with a Taurus Security System.
Price: .22/.410 from **$345.00**

Prices given are believed to be accurate at time of publication however, many factors affect retail pricing so exact prices are not possible.

76TH EDITION, 2022 ⊕ 499

THOMPSON/CENTER ENCORE PRO HUNTER
Calibers: .223, .308. Single shot, break-open design. Barrel: 15 in. Weight: 4.25–4.5 lbs. Grip: Walnut on blued models, rubber on stainless. Matching fore-end. Sights: Adjustable rear, ramp front. Features: Interchangeable barrels, adjustable trigger. Pro Hunter has "Swing Hammer" to allow reaching the hammer when the gun is scoped. Other Pro Hunter features include fluted barrel.
Price: From $779.00

THOMPSON/CENTER G2 CONTENDER
Calibers: .22 LR or .357 Magnum. A second generation Contender pistol maintaining the same barrel interchangeability with older Contender barrels and their corresponding forends (except Herrett fore-end). The G2 frame will not accept old-style grips due to the change in grip angle. Incorporates an automatic hammer block safety with built-in interlock. Features include trigger adjustable for overtravel, adjustable rear sight; ramp front sight blade, blued steel finish.
Price: From $729.00

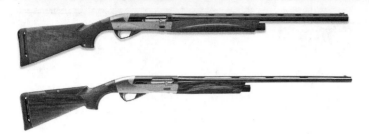

BENELLI ETHOS

Gauges: 12 ga., 20 ga., 28 ga. 3 in. Capacity: 4+1. Barrel: 26 in. or 28 in. (Full, Mod., Imp. Cyl., Imp. Mod., Cylinder choke tubes). Weights: 6.5 lbs. (12 ga.), 5.3–5.7 (20 & 28 ga.). Length: 49.5 in. overall (28 in. barrel). Stock: Select AA European walnut with satin finish. Sights: Red bar fiber optic front, with three interchangeable inserts, metal middle bead. Features: Utilizes Benelli's Inertia Driven system. Recoil is reduced by Progressive Comfort recoil reduction system within the buttstock. Twelve and 20-gauge models cycle all 3-inch loads from light 7/8 oz. up to 3-inch magnums. Also available with nickel-plated engraved receiver. Imported from Italy by Benelli USA, Corp.

Price: **$1,999.00**
Price: Engraved nickel-plated (shown) **$2,149.00**
Price: 20 or 28 ga. (engraved, nickel plated only) **$2,149.00**

BENELLI ETHOS BE.S.T.

Benelli expands its Ethos line with the new BE.S.T. model, so named for the Benelli Surface Treatment, a proprietary coating that protects steel from rust and corrosion and was tested over several months in saltwater with no signs of corrosion. Parts treated with BE.S.T. are backed with a 25-year warranty against rust and corrosion.

Price: **$2,199.00**

BENELLI ETHOS CORDOBA BE.S.T.

Gauge: 12 ga. 3in., 20ga. 3in, 28ga. 3in. Barrel: 28 in. or 30 in. ventilated wide rib. Length: 49.5 –51.5 in. Weight: 5.4–7.0 lbs. Stock: Black Synthetic. Features: Benelli expands their Ethos line of Inertia-Driven semi-autos with the new BE.S.T. (Benelli Surface Treatment). This Cordoba version is designed for high-volume shooting like that of dove hunting in Argentina — the gun's namesake location. Specialty features include ported barrels, ComforTech recoil-reducing system, and lighter weight. Fiber optic front sight with mid-rib bead on a wide broadway sight channel. Shell View system places small windows in the magazine tube for quickly visualizing remaining shell count. Advertised to handle 3-inch magnum rounds down to the lightest 7/8-ounce loads. Ships with five extended Crio chokes (C, IC, M, IM, F).

Price: $2,349.00

BENELLI ETHOS SPORT

Gauges: 12 ga., 20 ga., 28 ga. 3 in. Capacity: 4+1. Barrel: Ported, 28 in. or 30 in. (12 ga. only). Full, Mod., Imp. Cyl., Imp. Mod., Cylinder extended choke tubes. Wide rib. Other features similar to Ethos model.

Price: **$2,269.00**

BENELLI ETHOS SUPER SPORT

Gauge: 12 ga. 3in., 20ga. 3in. Barrel: 26 in. or 28 in. ventilated wide rib. Length: 49.5–51.5 in. Weight: 5.4–7.0 lbs. Stock: Carbon-fiber finish composite stock and fore-end. Features: Benelli expands their Ethos semi-automatic line with the Super Sport competition-ready model. Light-weight, weather-resistant carbon-fiber finish furniture. Inertia-Driven semi-automatic with ComforTech recoil-reducing system. Ported Crio barrel. Fiber optic front sight and mid-barrel bead. Nickel-plated receiver. Capacity of 4+1 rounds. Ships with five extended Crio chokes (C, IC, M, IM, F).

Price: **$2,299.00**

BENELLI M2 FIELD

Gauges: 20 ga., 12 ga., 3 in. chamber. Barrels: 21 in., 24 in., 26 in., 28 in. Weights: 5.4–7.2 lbs. Length: 42.5–49.5 in. overall. Stock: Synthetic, Advantage Max-4 HD, Advantage Timber HD, APG HD. Sights: Red bar. Features: Uses the Inertia Driven bolt mechanism. Vent rib. Comes with set of five choke tubes. Imported from Italy by Benelli USA.

Price: Synthetic stock 12 ga. **$1,499.00**
Price: Camo stock 12 ga. **$1,549.00**
Price: Synthetic stock 20 ga. **$1,499.00**
Price: Camo stock 20 ga. **$1,599.00**
Price: Rifled slug ....**$1,469.00–$1,589.00**
Price: Left-hand 12 ga. **$1,409.00**
Price: Left-hand model 20 ga. **$1,519.00**
Price: Tactical **$1,249.00**

BENELLI M2 TURKEY EDITION

Gauges: 12 ga. and 20 ga., Full, Imp. Mod., Mod., Imp. Cyl., Cyl. choke tubes. Barrel: 24 in. Weight: 6-7 lbs. Stock: 12 ga. model has ComfortTech with pistol grip, Bottomland/Cerakote finish. 20 ga. has standard stock with Realtree APG finish. Features: From the Benelli Performance Shop.

Price: 20 ga. standard stock **$3,199.00**
Price: 12 ga. pistol grip stock **$3,399.00**

BENELLI MONTEFELTRO

Gauges: 12 ga. and 20 ga. Full, Imp. Mod., Mod., Imp. Cyl., Cyl. choke tubes. Barrels: 24 in., 26 in., 28 in., 30 in. (Sporting). Weights: 5.3–7.1 lbs. Stock: Checkered walnut with satin finish. Lengths: 43.6–49.5 in. overall. Features: Burris FastFire II sight. Uses the Inertia Driven rotating bolt system with a simple inertia recoil design. Finish is blued. Introduced 1987.

Price: Standard Model **$1,129.00**
Price: Silver **$1,779.00**
Price: Sporting **$1,329.00**

BENELLI SUPER BLACK EAGLE III

Gauge: 12 ga. 3in., 20ga. 3in., 28ga. 3in Barrel: 28 in. or 30 in. ventilated rib. Length: 47.5–49.5 in. Weight: 5.8–6.9 lbs. Stock: Synthetic with multiple finish choices. Features: Benelli expands their SBE III line by adding three-inch chamber models in both 12 and 20 gauge. Models available in Black synthetic, Realtree MAX-5, Gore OptiFade Timber, and Mossy Oak Bottomland.

Price: **$1,699.00**

BENELLI SUPER BLACK EAGLE III BE.S.T.

Benelli expands its SBE III line with the new BE.S.T. model, so named for the Benelli Surface Treatment, a proprietary coating that protects steel from rust and corrosion and was tested over several months in saltwater with no signs of corrosion. Parts treated with BE.S.T. are backed with a 25-year warranty against rust and corrosion. The BE.S.T. package will be available on select SBE III models.

Price: **$2,199.00**

BENELLI SUPERSPORT & SPORT II

Gauges: 20 ga., 12 ga., 3-in. chamber. Capacity: 4+1. Barrels: 28 in., 30 in., ported, 10mm sporting rib. Weight: 7.2–7.3 lbs. Lengths: 49.6–51.6 in. Stock: Carbon fiber, ComforTech (Supersport) or walnut (Sport II). Sights: Red bar front, metal midbead. Sport II is similar to the Legacy model except has nonengraved dual tone blued/silver receiver, ported wide-rib barrel, adjustable buttstock, and functions with all loads. Walnut stock with satin finish. Introduced 1997. Features: Designed for high-volume sporting clays. Inertia-driven action, Extended CrioChokes. Ported. Imported from Italy by Benelli USA.

Price: SuperSport $2,199.00
Price: Sport II $1,899.00

BENELLI VINCI

Gauge: 12 ga., 3-in. Barrels: 26- or 28-inch ribbed. Tactical model available with 18.5-in. barrel. Finishes: Black, MAX-4HD or APG HD; synthetic contoured stocks; optional Steady-Grip model. Weight: 6.7–6.9 lbs. Features: Gas-operated action. Modular disassembly; interchangeable choke tubes. Picatinny rail, pistol grip, ghost ring sight.
Price: ....$1,349.00–$1,469.00

BENELLI SUPER VINCI

Gauge: 12 ga.. 2 3/4 in., 3 in. and 3 1/2 in. Capacity: 3+1. Barrels: 26 in., 28 in. Weights: 6.9–7 lbs. Lengths: 48.5–50.5 in. Stock: Black synthetic, Realtree Max4 and Realtree APG. Features: Crio Chokes: C,IC,M,IM,F. Length of Pull: 14.375 in. Drop at Heel: 2 in. Drop at Comb: 1.375 in. Sights: Red bar front sight and metal bead mid-sight. Minimum recommended load: 3-dram, 1 1/8 oz. loads (12 ga.). Receiver drilled and tapped for scope mounting. Imported from Italy by Benelli USA., Corp.
Price: Black Synthetic Comfortech $1,799.00
Price: Camo $1,899.00

BROWNING A5

Gauges: 12 ga., 3 or 3 1/2; 16 ga., 2 3/4 in. (Sweet Sixteen). Barrels: 26 in., 28 in. or 30 in. Weights: 5 3/4 to 7 lbs. Lengths: 47.25–51.5 in. Stock: Gloss finish walnut with 22 LPI checkering, black synthetic or camo. Adjustable for cast and drop. Features: Operates on Kinematic short-recoil system, totally different than the classic Auto-5 long-recoil action manufactured from 1903–1999. Lengthened forcing cone, three choke tubes (IC, M, F), flat ventilated rib, brass bead front sight, ivory middle bead. Available in Mossy Oak Duck Blind or Break-up Infinity camo. Ultimate Model has satin finished aluminum alloy receiver with light engraving of pheasants on left side, mallards on the right. Gloss blued finish, Grade III oil-finished walnut stock. Wicked Wing has Cerakote Burnt Bronze finish on receiver and barrel, Mossy Oak Shadow Grass Blades camo on stock.
Price: A5 Hunter $1,670.00
Price: A5 Hunter 3 1/2 in. $1,800.00
Price: A5 Stalker (synthetic) $1,540.00
Price: A5 Stalker 3 1/2 in. $1,670.00
Price: A5 Ultimate $2,030.00
Price: A5 Sweet Sixteen $1,740.00
Price: A5 Wicked Wing $1,870.00
Price: A5 Wicked Wing 3 1/2 in. $2,000.00

BROWNING MAXUS HUNTER

Gauges: 12 ga., 3 in. and 3 1/2 in. Barrels: 26 in., 28 in. and 30 in. Flat ventilated rib with fixed cylinder choke; stainless steel; matte finish. Weight: 7 lbs. 2 oz. Length: 40.75 in. Stock: Gloss finish walnut stock with close radius pistol grip, sharp 22 LPI checkering, Speed Lock Forearm, shim adjustable for length of pull, cast and drop. Features: Vector Pro-lengthened forcing cone, three Invector-Plus choke tubes, Inflex Technology recoil pad, ivory front bead sight, One 1/4 in. stock spacer. Strong, lightweight aluminum alloy receiver with durable satin nickel finish & laser engraving (pheasant on the right, mallard on the left). All-Purpose Hunter has Mossy Oak Break-Up Country Camo, Duratouch coated composite stock. Wicked Wing has Cerakote Burnt Bronze finish on receiver and barrel, Mossy Oak Shadow Grass Blades camo on stock.
Price: 3 in. $1,590.00
Price: 3 1/2 in. $1,740.00
Price: All-Purpose Hunter..$1,780.00
Price: Maxus Wicked Wing..$1,900.00

BROWNING MAXUS SPORTING

Gauge: 12 ga., 3 in. Barrels: 28 in., 30 in. flat ventilated rib. Weight: 7 lbs. 2 oz. Length: 49.25 in.–51.25 in. Stock: Gloss finish high grade walnut stock with close radius pistol grip, Speed Lock forearm, shim adjustable for length of pull, cast and drop. Features: Laser engraving of game birds transforming into clay birds on the lightweight alloy receiver. Quail are on the right side, and a mallard duck on the left. The Power Drive Gas System reduces recoil and cycles a wide array of loads. It's available in a 28 in. or 30 in. barrel length. The high-grade walnut stock and forearm are generously checkered, finished with a deep, high gloss. The stock is adjustable and one .250-in. stock spacer is included. For picking up either clay or live birds quickly, the HiViz Tri-Comp fiber-optic front sight with mid-bead ivory sight does a great job, gathering light on the most overcast days. Vector Pro-lengthened forcing cone, five Invector-Plus choke tubes, Inflex Technology recoil pad, HiViz Tri-Comp fiber-optic front sight, ivory mid-bead sight, one .250-in. stock spacer.
Price: $1,800.00
Price: Golden Clays..$2,100.00

BROWNING MAXUS SPORTING CARBON FIBER

Gauge: 12 ga., 3 in. Barrels: 28 in., 30 in. flat ventilated rib. Weights: 6 lbs. 15 oz.–7 lbs. Length: 49.25–51.25 in. Stock: Composite stock with close radius pistol grip, Speed Lock forearm, textured gripping surfaces, shim adjustable for length of pull, cast and drop, carbon fiber finish, Dura-Touch Armor Coating. Features: Strong, lightweight aluminum alloy, carbon fiber finish on top and bottom. The stock is finished with Dura-Touch Armor Coating for a secure, non-slip grip when the gun is wet. It has the Browning exclusive Magazine Cut-Off, a patented Turn-Key Magazine Plug and Speed Load Plus. Deeply finished look of carbon fiber and Dura-Touch Armor Coating. Vector Pro-lengthened forcing cone, five Invector-Plus choke tubes, Inflex Technology recoil pad, HiViz Tri-Comp fiber-optic front sight, ivory mid-bead sight, one .250-in. stock spacer.
Price: $1,590.00

BROWNING MAXUS II

Gauge: 12 ga. Choice of 3 or 3.5-in. models. Barrel: 26, 28, or 30 in. Weight: 7.0 lbs.–7.3 lbs. Stock: Dependent on model, but current listings include black synthetic and camouflaged variants. Features: Builds on Browning's Power Drive gas-operated Maxus autoloader in a II version with enhancements. Chrome chamber and bore. Ramped triggerguard for easier loading. Composite stock can be trimmed and is shim adjustable for cast, drop, and LOP. Rubber overmolding on the stock, including SoftFlex cheek pad and Inflex recoil pad. Oversized controls. New screw-on magazine cap design. Includes Invector-Plus choke tubes, extended on most models, as well as an ABS hard case.
Price: Mossy Oak Shadow Grass Habitat (MOSGH) **$1,789.00**
Price: Wicked Wing in MOSGH................................**$1,939.00**
Price: All-Purpose Hunter in MOBU **$1,979.00**
Price: Sporting Carbon Fiber **$1,859.00**
Price: Stalker **$1,589.00**

BROWNING GOLD LIGHT 10 GAUGE

Gauge: 10 ga. 3 1/2 in. Capacity: 4 rounds. Barrels: 24 (NWTF), 26 or 28 in. Stock: Composite with Dura-Cote Armor coating. Mossy Oak camo (Break-Up Country or Shadow Grass Blades). Weight: Approx. 9.5 pounds. Gas operated action, aluminum receiver, three standard Invector choke tubes. Receiver is drilled and tapped for scope mount. National Wild Turkey Foundation model has Hi-Viz 4-in-1 fiber optic sight, NWTF logo on buttstock.
Price: Mossy Oak Camo finishes.........................**$1,780.00**
Price: NWTF Model................................**$1,900.00**

BROWNING GOLD 10 GAUGE FIELD

Gauge: 10 ga. 3.5 in. Barrel: 26 in. or 28 in. with ventilated rib. Weight: 9 lbs. 9 oz.–9 lbs. 10 oz. Length: 48.0–50.0 in. Stock: Composite with camouflage coverage in either Mossy Oak Shadow Grass Habitat or Mossy Oak Break-Up Country. Features: Browning's autoloading Gold Light 10-gauge shotgun is redesigned as the Gold 10 Gauge Field. The new style composite stock and forearm wear textured gripping surfaces with the buttstock able to be trimmed up to ¾-inch to shorten LOP. Added Inflex recoil pad. Silver bead front sight. Integral sling swivel studs. Capacity of 4+1 magnum shells. Standard Invector-style flush-mount interchangeable choke tubes with three included (F, M, IC).
Price: **$1,859.00**

BROWNING SILVER

Gauges: 12 ga., 3 in. or 3 1/2 in.; 20 ga., 3 in. chamber. Barrels: 26 in., 28 in., 30 in. Invector Plus choke tubes. Weights: 7 lbs., 9 oz. (12 ga.), 6 lbs., 7 oz. (20 ga.). Stock: Satin finish walnut or composite. Features: Active Valve gas system, semi-humpback receiver. Invector Plus choke system, three choke tubes. Imported by Browning.
Price: Silver Field, 12 ga.................................**$1,070.00**
Price: Silver Field, 20 ga.................................**$1,140.00**
Price: Black Lightning, 12 ga.................................**$1,140.00**
Price: Silver Field Composite, 12 ga., 3 in.................................**$1,000.00**
Price: Silver Field Composite, 12 ga., 3 1/2 in.................................**$1,070.00**
Price: Silver Field Rifled Deer Matte, 20 ga...................................**$1,200.00**

CHARLES DALY MODEL 600

Gauges: 12 ga. or 20 ga. (3 in.) or 28 ga. (2 3/4 in.). Capacity: 5+1. Barrels: 26 in., 28 in. (20 and 28 ga.), 26 in., 28 in. or 30 in. (12 ga.). Three choke tubes provided (Rem-Choke pattern). Stock: Synthetic, wood or camo. Features: Comes in several variants including Field, Sporting Clays, Tactical and Trap. Left-hand models available. Uses gas-assisted recoil operation. Imported from Turkey.
Price: Field 12, 20 ga..**$480.00**
Price: Field 28 ga..**$531.00**
Price: Sporting **$858.00**
Price: Tactical..**$685.00**

CZ MODEL 712/720

Gauges: 12 ga., 20 ga. Capacity: 4+1. Barrel: 26 in. Weight: 6.3 lbs. Stock: Turkish walnut with 14.5 in. length of pull. Features: Chrome-lined barrel with 3-inch chamber, ventilated rib, five choke tubes. Matte black finish.
Price: 712 12 ga. ....**$499.00–$699.00**
Price: 720 20 ga..**$516.00–$599.00**

CZ 1012

Gauge: 12 ga., 3 in. Capacity: 4+1. Barrel: 28 in., 8mm flat ventilated rib. Weight: 6.5-6.9 lbs. Length: 47 in. Stock: Options in either Turkish walnut or black synthetic. Features: The company's first gas-less, inertia-driven semi-automatic wears a gloss-black chrome barrel finish along with a choice of three receiver finishes: standard blued, bronze or gray. Oversized controls ideal for use when wearing gloves. Cross-bolt safety located at front of trigger guard. Addition of 26-inch barreled models to the existing 1012 inertia-driven repeater lineup. Includes two camouflaged synthetic stock options as well as checkered Walnut, consistent with the existing 1012 family. Includes five chokes (F, IM, M, IC, C).
Price: **$645.00**

EUROPEAN AMERICAN ARMORY (EAA) MC312 GOBBLER

Gauge: 12 ga., 3.5 in. Barrel: 24 in., with ventilated turkey rib. Length: 50 in. Stock: Synthetic camouflage with either straight or pistol-grip options. Features: The MC312 inertia-driven semi-auto produced by Girsan gets a turkey upgrade with a shorter barrel, mid-bead, Picatinny rail cut into the receiver, Cerakote finish receiver and barrel, cross-bolt safety, sling studs, rubber buttpad, fiber-optic front sight, and field-tested reflex optic. Includes flush mount choke tubes.
Price: **$600.00**

EUROPEAN AMERICAN ARMORY (EAA) AKKAR CHURCHILL 220

Gauge: 20 ga. Barrel: 18.5 in. Length: 37.5 in. Weight: 5.0 lbs. Stock: Black synthetic pistol grip style. Features: This Turkish-made semi-automatic springs from the Churchill 220 series of gas-driven repeaters is now re-vamped for home defense and tactical use. Optics rail machined into receiver for easy target acquisition with included red-dot optic on quick-release mount. Semi-enhanced loading port. Accessible controls. 5+1 round capacity. Checkered pistol grip stock. Black rubber recoil pad, sling swivels. Door-breaching choke tube and shrouded red fiber-optic front sight.
Price: **$561.00**

FABARM XLR5 VELOCITY AR

Gauge: 12 ga. 3 in. Barrel: 28 or 30 in. with flat rib. Stock: All-Terrain camouflage composite with soft-touch finish. Both right- and left-handed option available for each model. Features: The Italian-made, gas-operated,

semi-automatic XLR Chesapeake springs from Fabarm's XLR5 family of repeaters and is built for hunters. Pulse Pistol system acts as a brake, eliminating the valve system to cycle varying ammo types. Cerakote Midnight Bronze finish on action and barrel. Red fiber-optic bar front sight. Soft comb insert and rubberized buttpad. TriBore XP barrel with tapered bore for improved patterns and lower recoil. Inner HP extended choke tubes come standard.

Price: **$1,875.00**

FABARM XLR CHESAPEAKE

Gauge: 12 ga. Barrels: 30 or 32 in. Weight: 8.25 lbs. Features: Gas-operated model designed for competition shooting. Unique adjustable rib that allows a more upright shooting position. There is also an adjustable trigger shoe, magazine cap adjustable weight system. Five interchangeable choke tubes. Imported from Italy by Fabarm USA.

Price:	**$2,755.00–$3,300.00**
Price: FR Sporting	**$1,990.00–$2,165.00**
Price: LR (Long Rib)	**$2,260.00–$2,800.00**

FRANCHI AFFINITY

Gauges: 12 ga., 20 ga. Three-inch chamber also handles 2 3/4-inch shells. Barrels: 26 in., 28 in., 30 in. (12 ga.), 26 in. (20 ga.). 30-in. barrel available only on 12-ga. Sporting model. Weights: 5.6–6.8 pounds. Stocks: Black synthetic or Realtree Camo. Left-hand versions available. Catalyst model has stock designed for women.

Price: Synthetic	**$789.00**
Price: Synthetic left-hand action	**$899.00**
Price: Camo	**$949.00**
Price: Compact	**$849.00**
Price: Catalyst	**$969.00**
Price: Sporting	**$1,149.00**
Price: Companion	**$1,599.00**

FRANCHI AFFINITY ELITE

Gauges: 12ga. 3 in., 12ga. 3.5in., 20ga. 3 in. Barrel: 26 or 28 in. ventilated rib. Length: 48.5–50.75 in. Weight: 6.0–7.1 lbs. Stock: Synthetic with OptiFade Marsh or OptiFade Timber camo. Features: The Affinity Elite lineup offers semi-customized features building on the Affinity Italian-made family of Inertia-Drive semi-autos. Cerakote and OptiFade camo finishes. Oversized controls, lengthened forcing cone, TruGlo front sight. Oversized loading port, ambidextrous safety, chrome lined barrel. Drilled and tapped for optics mounting. Twin Shock Absorber (TSA) recoil pad allows for LOP adjustments. Capacity of 4+1 rounds. Includes shims for fitting drop and cast. Ships with three extended waterfowl chokes (Close, Mid, Long-Range).

Price: Synthetic **$1,249.00**

FRANCHI AFFINITY TURKEY

Gauge: 12 ga. 3.5 in, 20ga. 3in. Barrel: 24 in. ventilated rib. Length: 40.0 in. Weight: 6.7–7.5 lbs. Stock: Synthetic pistol grip style with Mossy Oak Bottomland camo. Features: Italian-made inertia-drive semi-auto for turkey hunters. Oversized controls, enlarged loading port, sling attachments. Drilled and tapped for optics mounting. Adjustable rear sight, hooded fiber-optic front sight. Capacity of 4+1 rounds. Modular trigger assembly removes quickly for cleaning. Ships with extended Turkey and Turkey XF chokes.

Price: **$959.00**

FRANCHI AFFINITY ELITE TURKEY

Gauge: 12 ga. 3 in., 20 ga. 3 in. Barrel: 24 in. ventilated rib. Length: 41.0–41.4 in. Weight: 6.8– 7.7 lbs. Stock: Synthetic pistol grip style with OptiFade SubAlpine camo. Features: Built on the Affinity Italian-made Inertia-Drive semi-automatic action. Midnight Bronze Cerakote metalwork finish. Oversized controls, lengthened forcing cone. Adjustable, fiber-optic rear sight and hooded fiber-optic front. Oversized loading port, sling attachments. Picatinny rail for optics mounting. Capacity of 4+1 rounds. Ships with two gobbler-specific ported and extended chokes (Rhino Turkey and Rhino Extra-Full Turkey).

Price: **$1,249.00**

MOSSBERG 930

Gauge: 12 ga. 3 in. Capacity: 4-shell magazine. Barrels: 24 in., 26 in., 28 in., over-bored to 10-gauge bore dimensions; factory ported, Accu-Choke tubes. Weight: 7.5 lbs. Length: 44.5 in. overall (28-in. barrel). Stock: Walnut or synthetic. Adjustable stock drop and cast spacer system. Sights: Turkey Taker fiber-optic, adjustable windage and elevation. Front bead fiber-optic front on waterfowl models. Features: Self-regulating gas system, dual gas-vent system and piston, EZ-Empty magazine button, cocking indicator. Interchangeable Accu-Choke tube set (IC, Mod, Full) for waterfowl and field models. XX-Full turkey Accu-Choke tube included with turkey models. Ambidextrous thumb-operated safety, Uni-line stock and receiver. Receiver drilled and tapped for scope base attachment, free gun lock. Introduced 2008. From O.F. Mossberg & Sons, Inc.

Price: Turkey	**$630.00**
Price: Waterfowl	**$619.00**
Price: Combo	**$693.00**
Price: Field	**$560.00**
Price: Slugster,	**$678.00**
Price: Turkey Pistolgrip; Mossy Oak Infinity Camo	**$735.00**
Price: Tactical; 18.5-in. tactical barrel, black synthetic stock and matte black finish	**$878.00**
Price: SPX; no muzzle brake, M16-style front sight, ghost ring rear sight, pistol grip stock, 8-shell extended magazine	**$1,046.00**
Price: Home Security/Field Combo; 18.5 in. Cylinder bore barrel and 28 in. ported Field barrel; black synthetic stock and matte black finish	**$693.00**
Price: High Performance (13-round magazine)	**$974.00**

MOSSBERG MODEL 935 MAGNUM

Gauge: 12 ga. 3 in. and 3 1/2-in., interchangeable. Barrels: 22 in., 24 in., 26 in., 28in. Weights: 7.25–7.75 lbs. Lengths: 45–49 in. overall. Stock: Synthetic. Features: Gas-operated semi-auto models in blued or camo finish. Fiber-optics sights, drilled and tapped receiver, interchangeable Accu-Mag choke tubes.

Price: 935 Magnum Turkey Pistol grip; full pistol grip stock	**$924.00**
Price: 935 Magnum Grand Slam: 22 in. barrel	**$756.00**
Price: 935 Magnum Waterfowl: 26 in. or 28 in. barrel	**$660.00–$735.00**
Price: 935 Pro Series Waterfowl	**$875.00**

MOSSBERG 940 JM PRO

Gauge: 12 ga. 3 in. Capacity: 9+1. Barrel: 24 in., ventilated rib. Weight: 7.75 lbs. Length: 44.75 in. Stock: Choice of either black synthetic or Black Multicam. Features: Created in conjunction with speed shooter Jerry Miculek, the new 940 JM Pro uses a redesigned gas system built for fast-cycling competition. Adjustable for length of pull, cast and drop. Hi-Viz green front fiber-optic sight, oversized controls. Nickel-boron coated internal parts and anodized receivers in either tungsten gray or black. Competition-level loading port allows for quad loading, elongated pinch-free elevator, and anodized bright orange follower. Black synthetic model uses gold finish appointments and a tungsten-gray receiver. Multicam model wears black-anodized receiver. Ships with Briley Extended choke tube set.

Price: **$1,015.00**

MOSSBERG SA-20

Gauge: 20 or 28 ga. Barrels: 20 in. (Tactical), 26 in. or 28 in. Weight: 5.5–6 lbs. Stock: Black synthetic. Gas operated action, matte blue finish. Tactical model has ghost-ring sight, accessory rail.

Price: 20 ga.	**$592.00–$664.00**
Price: 28 ga.	**$588.00–$675.00**

MOSSBERG SA-410 FIELD
Gauge: .410 bore, 3 in. Capacity: 4+1. Barrel: 26 in., ventilated rib. Weight: 6.5 lbs. Length: 46 in. Stock: Black synthetic. Features: Mossberg offers the baby bore for small-game and field hunters as well as light recoiling plinking with this lightweight gas-driven autoloader. Metalwork is finished in matte blue. Brass front bead, fixed 13.75 in. length of pull, ventilated rubber buttpad. Cross-bolt safety, easy-load elevator. Includes Sport Set flush fit chokes (F, IM, M, IC, C).
Price: **$616.00**

MOSSBERG SA-410 TURKEY
Gauge: .410 bore, 3 in. Capacity: 4+1. Barrel: 26 in., ventilated rib. Weight: 6.5 lbs. Length: 46 in. Stock: Synthetic stock with Mossy Oak Bottomland camouflage. Features: Mossberg expands its baby-bore turkey lineup with this gas-driven semi-automatic. Both the stocks and metalwork wear full camouflage coverage. Rear fiber-optic ghost-ring sight and front green fiber-optic. Top Picatinny rail for easy optics mounting. Cross-bolt safety, easy-load elevator. Ships with an XX-Full Extended Turkey choke.
Price: **$735.00**

RETAY GORDION
Gauge: 12 ga., 3 in. Barrels: 26 in., 28 in., ventilated rib. Weight: 6.5-6.75 lbs. Stock: Choice of black synthetic, several Realtree camo patterns, or Turkish walnut. Features: The Turkish-made Gordion line of semi-automatics uses an inertia-plus action and bolt system. Oversized SP controls, quick unload system, TruGlo red front sight. Choice of matte or polished black receiver and barrel, or full camouflage coverage. Easy-Load port as well as Easy Unload system that allows the magazine tube to be emptied without racking the action. Includes a stock adjustment ship kit, TSA airline-approved hard case, and five flush choke tubes (F, IM, M, IC, S).
Price: .... **$799.00-$899.00**
Price: Gordion Turkey 24-in. barrel, Realtree or Mossy Oak camo ... **$925.00**

RETAY MASAI MARA
Gauges: 12 ga., 3.5 in., 20 ga., 3 in. Barrels: 26 in., 28 in., ventilated rib. Weight: 6.5-6.75 lbs. Stock: Choice of synthetic in black or numerous camouflage patterns or two grades of Turkish walnut. Features: The Turkish-made Masai Mara line of semi-automatics uses an inertia-plus action and bolt system. Oversized controls, Easy Unload system, TruGlo red fiber-optic front sight. Options in Cerakote metalwork or anodized finishes. Push-button removeable trigger group for both safety and easy field cleaning. Microcell rubber recoil pad. Includes a TSA airline-approved hard case and ships with five flush choke tubes (F, IM, M, IC, S).
Price: **$1,099.00**
Price: Upland Grade 2.. **$1,399.00**
Price: Upland Grade 3.. **$1,900.00**
Price: Comfort Grade 2.. **$1,399.00**
Price: Comfort Grade 4.. **$1,999.00**
Price: SP Air King Waterfowl Camo/Cerakote................ **$1,600.00**
Price: SP Air King Waterfowl Cerakote........................... **$1,600.00**

SAVAGE RENEGAUGE FIELD
Gauges: 12 ga. 3 in. Barrel: 26 or 28 in. fluted carbon steel with ventilated rib. Weight: 7.9–8.0 lbs. Length: 47.5–49.5 in. Stock: Grey synthetic stock with Monte Carlo-style cheekpiece. Adjustable for length of pull, comb height, drop and cast with included inserts. Features: American-made D.R.I.V. (Dual Regulating Inline Valve) gas system. Single-piece, chrome-plated action bar assembly and chrome-plated reciprocating components. Melonite-finished external metalwork. Stock rod buffer to reduce felt recoil. Red fiber-optic sight, competition-ready easy-loading port, oversized controls. 4+1 round capacity. Includes three Beretta/Benelli style chokes (IC, M, F) and hard case.
Price: **$1,489.00**

SAVAGE RENEGAUGE TURKEY
Gauge: 12 ga. 3 in. Barrel: 24-in. fluted carbon steel with ventilated rib. Weight: 7.8 lbs. Length: 49.5 in. Stock: Camo synthetic stock with Monte Carlo-style cheekpiece, adjustable for length of pull, comb height, drop and cast with included inserts. Choice of Mossy Oak Bottomland or Mossy Oak Obsession camouflage finishes. Features: American-made D.R.I.V. (Dual Regulating Inline Valve) gas system. Single-piece, chrome-plated action bar assembly

and chrome-plated reciprocating components. Stock rod buffer to reduce felt recoil. Red fiber-optic front sight, competition-ready loading port, oversized controls. 4+1 round capacity. Includes four Beretta/Benelli style chokes (EF, F, IC, M) and hard case.
Price: **$1,599.00**

SAVAGE RENEGAUGE WATERFOWL
Gauge: 12 ga. 3 in. Barrel: 26- or 28-in. fluted carbon steel with ventilated rib. Weight: 7.8 lbs. Lengths: 47.5–49.5 in. Stock: Camouflage synthetic stock with Monte Carlo-style cheekpiece, adjustable for length of pull, comb height, drop and cast with included inserts. Mossy Oak Shadow Grass Blades camouflage. Features: American-made D.R.I.V. (Dual Regulating Inline Valve) gas system. Single-piece, chrome-plated action bar assembly and chrome-plated reciprocating components. Stock rod buffer to reduce felt recoil. Red fiber-optic sight, competition-ready easy loading port, oversized controls. 4+1 round capacity. Includes three Beretta/Benelli style chokes (IC, M, F) and hard case.
Price: **$1,959.00**

SAVAGE RENEGAUGE COMPETITION
Gauge: 12 ga. 3in. Barrel: 24-in. fluted carbon steel with ventilated rib. Weight: 8.2 lbs. Length: 46.2 in. Stock: Black synthetic Monte Carlo style, adjustable for length of pull, comb height, drop and cast. Features: American-made D.R.I.V. (Dual Regulating Inline Valve) gas system. Single-piece, chrome-plated action bar assembly and chrome-plated reciprocating components. Stock rod buffer to reduce felt recoil. Extended magazine tube with 9+1 capacity. Melonite finished barrel and Red Cerakote receiver. Hi-Viz Tri-Comp front sight. Competition-ready loading port, oversized controls. Extended Skeet2 Light Mod (.015-in.) choke tube of Beretta/Benelli-style.
Price: **$1,959.00**

SAVAGE RENEGAUGE PRAIRIE
Gauge: 12 ga. 3 in. Barrel: 28 in. fluted carbon steel with ventilated rib. Weight: 7.9 lbs. Length: 49.5 in. Stock: Camo synthetic sporter style, adjustable for length of pull, comb height, drop and cast with included inserts. Features: American-made D.R.I.V. (Dual Regulating Inline Valve) gas system. Single-piece, chrome plated action bar assembly and chrome-plated reciprocating components. True Timber Prairie camouflage stock finish with Brown Sand Cerakote metalwork. Stock rod buffer to reduce felt recoil. Red fiber-optic sight, competition-ready easy-loading port, oversized controls. 4+1 round capacity. Includes three Beretta/Benelli style chokes (IC, M, F) and hard case.
Price: **$1,599.00**

STANDARD MANUFACTURING SKO-12
Gauge: 12 ga., 3 in. Capacity: 5-round magazine. Barrel: 18-7/8-in. Weight: 7 lbs., 10 oz. Length: 38 in. Stock: Synthetic with six-position buttstock and will accept any Mil-Spec buttstock. Features: Gas-operated semi-automatic. Receivers machined from aircraft-grade aluminum and Mil-Spec hard anodized. Extended 22-inch Picatinny rail. Ambidextrous safety, AR-style mag and bolt release. MOE slots on fore-end. Tru-Choke thread pattern.
Price: **$1,100.00**

STANDARD MANUFACTURING SKO SHORTY
Gauge: 12 ga., 3 in. Capacity: 5-round magazine. Barrel: 18-7/8-in. Weight: 7.14 lbs. Length: 28.75 in. Stock: Black synthetic with forward vertical grip, but without a buttstock. Features: Gas-operated semi-automatic. Receivers machined from aircraft-grade aluminum and Mil-Spec hard anodized. Ambidextrous safety, AR-style mag and bolt release. MOE slots on fore-end. No sights or top rail. Tru-Choke thread pattern. Buttstock conversion kit available from manufacturer.
Price: **$599.00**

STOEGER M3500 PREDATOR/TURKEY

Gauge: 12 ga., 3.5 in. Capacity: 4+1. Barrel: 24 in., ventilated rib. Length: 46 in. Weight: 7.5 lbs. Stock: Synthetic Mossy Oak Overwatch. Features: Stoeger expands its M3500 line of inertia-driven autoloaders with a predator- and turkey-specific model with a shorter barrel and rubber pistol grip. Red bar fiber-optic front sight. Receiver drilled and tapped for optics mounting. Ships with a paracord sling and five extended chokes, including MOJO Predator and MOJO Turkey tubes.

Price: **$929.00**

STOEGER M3500 WATERFOWL

Gauge: 12 ga. 3.5 in. Barrel: 28 in. ventilated rib. Length: 50 in. Weight: 8.2 lbs. Stock: Synthetic with distressed white Cerakote finish. Features: Stoeger combines the M3500 Waterfowl semi-auto with the 922R-compliant extended magazine Freedom Series to create the higher-capacity M3500 Snow Goose. Full 10+1 capacity. Inertia-driven autoloader with oversized controls. Beveled loading port. Distressed white Cerakote finish on stock, fore-end, receiver, and barrel act as winter camo. Red bar front sight. Includes paracord sling and shim kit for adjusting drop and cast. Ships with five extended choke tubes (IC, M, XFT, Close Range, Mid Range).

Price: **$899.00**

STOEGER MODEL 3000

Gauge: 12 ga., 2 3/4- and 3-in. loads. Minimum recommended load 3-dram, 1 1/8 ounces. Capacity: 4+1 magazine. Inertia-driven operating system. Barrels: 26 or 28 in. with 3 choke tubes IC, M, XF. Weights: 7.4–7.5 lbs. Finish: Black synthetic or camo (Realtree APG or Max-4). M3K model is designed for 3-Gun competition and has synthetic stock, 24-in. barrel, modified loading port.

Price: Synthetic **$599.00**
Price: Walnut or Camo **$649.00**
Price: M3K **$699.00**
Price: 3000R rifled slug model **$649.00**

STOEGER MODEL 3020

Gauge: 20 ga., 2 3/4- or 3-in. loads. Features: This model has the same general specifications as the Model 3000 except for its chambering and weight of 5.5 to 5.8 pounds.

Price: Synthetic **$599.00**
Price: Camo **$649.00**

STOEGER MODEL 3500

Gauge: 12 ga. 2 3/4-, 3- and 3 1/2-in. loads. Minimum recommended load 3-dram, 1-1/8 ounces. Barrels: 24 in., 26 in. or 28 in. Choke tubes for IC, M, XF. Weights: 7.4–7.5 pounds. Finish: Satin walnut, black synthetic or camo (Realtree APG or Max-4). Features: Other features similar to Model 3000.

Price: Synthetic **$679.00**
Price: Camo **$799.00**
Price: Satin Walnut (shown) **$769.00**

TRISTAR VIPER G2

Gauges: 12 ga., 20 ga. 2 3/4 in. or 3 in. interchangeably. Capacity: 5-round magazine. Barrels: 26 in., 28 in. (carbon fiber only offered in 12-ga. 28 in. and 20-ga. 26 in.). Stock: Wood, black synthetic, Mossy Oak Duck Blind camouflage, faux carbon fiber finish (2008) with the new Comfort Touch technology. Features: Magazine cutoff, vent rib with matted sight plane, brass front bead (camo models have fiber-optic front sight), shot plug included, and 3 Beretta-style choke tubes (IC, M, F). Viper synthetic, Viper camo have swivel studs. Five-year warranty. Viper Youth models have shortened length of pull and 24 in. barrel. Sporting model has ported barrel, checkered walnut stock with adjustable comb. Imported by Tristar Sporting Arms Ltd.

Price: **$549.00**
Price: Camo models **$640.00**
Price: Silver Model .... **$670.00–$715.00**
Price: Youth Model **$565.00**
Price: Sporting Model **$825.00**

TRISTAR VIPER MAX

Gauge: 12. 3 1/2 in. Barrel: 24–30 in., threaded to accept Benelli choke tubes. Gas-operated action. Offered in several model variants. Introduced in 2017.

Price: .... **$630.00–$730.00**

WEATHERBY SA-SERIES

Gauges: 12 ga., 20 ga., 3 in. Barrels: 26 in., 28 in. flat ventilated rib. Weight: 6.5 lbs. Stock: Wood and synthetic. Features: The SA-08 is a reliable workhorse that lets you move from early season dove loads to late fall's heaviest waterfowl loads in no time. Available with wood and synthetic stock options in 12- and 20-gauge models, including a scaled-down youth model to fit 28 ga. Comes with 3 application-specific choke tubes (SK/IC/M). Made in Turkey.

Price: SA-08 Synthetic **$649.00**
Price: SA-08 Synthetic Youth **$649.00**
Price: SA-08 Deluxe **$849.00**

WEATHERBY 18-I

Gauges: 12 ga., 20 ga., 3 in. Capacities: 4+1. Barrels: 26 or 28 in. Stock: Synthetic, camo or walnut. Features: Inertia-operated system. Mossy Oak Shadow Grass or Realtree Max-5 camo full coverage.

Price: Synthetic **$1,099.00**
Price: Waterfowler camo **$1,199.00**
Price: Deluxe model walnut stock **$1,899.00**

WEATHERBY ELEMENT

Gauges: 12 ga. 3 in., 20 ga. 3 in. Barrel: 26- or 28-in. ventilated rib. Weight: 6.25–6.75 lbs. Length: 46.75–48.75 in. Stock: Gray/black synthetic stock. Features: Addition to the Weatherby Element line of semi-automatic inertia-driven shotguns. The Element Tungsten Synthetic brings Tungsten Cerakote on all metalwork. Weatherby Griptonite stock with pistol grip and fore-end inserts. Ships with three chokes (F, M, and IC.) The 12-gauge model also includes a Long Range Steel choke.

Price: **$599.00**

WINCHESTER SUPER X3

Gauge: 12 ga., 3 in. and 3 1/2 in. Barrels: 26 in., 28 in., .742-in. back-bored; Invector Plus choke tubes. Weights: 7–7.25 lbs. Stock: Composite, 14.25 in. x 1.75 in. x 2 in. Mossy Oak New Break-Up camo with Dura-Touch Armor Coating. Pachmayr Decelerator buttpad with hard heel insert, customizable length of pull. Features: Alloy magazine tube, gunmetal grey Perma-Cote UT finish, self-adjusting Active Valve gas action, lightweight recoil spring system. Electroless nickel-plated bolt, three choke tubes, two length-of-pull stock spacers, drop and cast adjustment spacers, sling swivel studs. Introduced 2006. Made in Belgium, assembled in Portugal.

Price: Field **$1,140.00**
Price: Sporting, adj. comb **$1,700.00**
Price: Long Beard, pistol grip camo stock **$1,270.00**
Price: Composite Sporting **$1,740.00**

WINCHESTER SUPER X4

Gauge: 12 ga., 3 in. and 3 1/2 in. Capacity: 4-round magazine. Barrels: 22 in., 24 in., 26 in. or 28 in. Invector Plus Flush choke tubes. Weight: 6 lbs. 10 oz. Stock: Synthetic with rounded pistol grip and textured gripping surfaces, or satin finished checkered grade II/III Turkish walnut. Length-of-pull spacers. Several camo finishes available. Features: TruGlo fiber optic front sight, Inflex Technology recoil pad, active valve system, matte blue barrel, matte black receiver. Offered in Standard, Field, Compact, Waterfowl, Cantilever Buck, Cantilever Turkey models.

Price: Synthetic **$940.00**
Price: Field .... **$940.00–$1,070.00**
Price: Upland Field **$1,100.00**
Price: Waterfowl Hunter .... **$940.00–$1,070.00**
Price: Waterfowl Hunter in Mossy Oak Shadow Grass Habitat **$1,099.00**
Price: Waterfowl Hunter Compact in Mossy Oak Shadow Grass Habitat ... **$959.00**
Price: Hybrid Hunter **$1,040.00**
Price: Hybrid Hunter in Mossy Oak Shadow Grass Habitat **$1,079.00**
Price: NWTF Cantilever Turkey, Mossy Oak Obsession **$1,070.00**
Price: 20-gauge, 3-inch models **$939.00**
Price: Universal Hunter in MOBU camo **$1,069.00**

Prices given are believed to be accurate at time of publication however, many factors affect retail prices so exact prices are not possible.

BENELLI SUPERNOVA
Gauge: 12 ga. 3 1/2 in. Capacity: 4-round magazine. Barrels: 24 in., 26 in., 28 in. Lengths: 45.5–49.5 in. Stock: Synthetic; Max-4, Timber, APG HD (2007). Sights: Red bar front, metal midbead. Features: 2 3/4 in., 3 in. chamber (3 1/2 in. 12 ga. only). Montefeltro rotating bolt design with dual action bars, magazine cutoff, synthetic trigger assembly, adjustable combs, shim kit, choice of buttstocks. Introduced 2006. Imported from Italy by Benelli USA.
Price: **$549.00**
Price: Camo stock **$669.00**
Price: Rifle slug model ....**$829.00–$929.00**
Price: Tactical model...**$519.00–$549.00**

BENELLI NOVA
Gauges: 12 ga., 20 ga. Capacity: 4-round magazine. Barrels: 24 in., 26 in., 28 in. Stock: Black synthetic, Max-4, Timber and APG HD. Sights: Red bar. Features: 2 3/4 in., 3 in. (3 1/2 in. 12 ga. only). Montefeltro rotating bolt design with dual action bars, magazine cut-off, synthetic trigger assembly. Introduced 1999. Field & Slug Combo has 24 in. barrel and rifled bore; open rifle sights; synthetic stock; weighs 8.1 lbs. Imported from Italy by Benelli USA.
Price: Field Model...**$449.00**
Price: Max-5 camo stock **$559.00**
Price: H20 model, black synthetic, matte nickel finish **$669.00**
Price: Tactical, 18.5-in. barrel, Ghost Ring sight **$459.00**
Price: Black synthetic youth stock, 20 ga. **$469.00**

BROWNING BPS
Gauges: 10 ga., 12 ga., 3 1/2 in.; 12 ga., 16 ga., or 20 ga., 3 in. (2 3/4 in. in target guns), 28 ga., 2 3/4 in., 5-shot magazine, .410, 3 in. chamber. Barrels: 10 ga. 24 in. Buck Special, 28 in., 30 in., 32 in. Invector; 12 ga., 20 ga. 22 in., 24 in., 26 in., 28 in., 30 in., 32 in. (Imp. Cyl., Mod. or Full), .410 26 in. (Imp. Cyl., Mod. and Full choke tubes.) Also available with Invector choke tubes, 12 or 20 ga. Upland Special has 22-in. barrel with Invector tubes. BPS 3 in. and 3 1/2 in. have back-bored barrel. Weight: 7 lbs., 8 oz. (28 in. barrel). Length: 48.75 in. overall (28 in. barrel). Stock: 14.25 in. x 1.5 in. x 2.5 in. Select walnut, semi-beavertail fore-end, full pistol grip stock. Features: All 12 ga. 3 in. guns except Buck Special and game guns have back-bored barrels with Invector Plus choke tubes. Bottom feeding and ejection, receiver top safety, high post vent rib. Double action bars eliminate binding. Vent rib barrels only. All 12 and 20 ga. guns with 3 in. chamber available with fully engraved receiver flats at no extra cost. Each gauge has its own unique game scene. Introduced 1977. Stalker is same gun as the standard BPS except all exposed metal parts have a matte blued finish and the stock has a black finish with a black recoil pad. Available in 10 ga. (3 1/2 in.) and 12 ga. with 3 in. or 3 1/2 in. chamber, 22 in., 28 in., 30 in. barrel with Invector choke system. Introduced 1987. Rifled Deer Hunter is similar to the standard BPS except has newly designed receiver/magazine tube/barrel mounting system to eliminate play, heavy 20.5-in. barrel with rifle-type sights with adjustable rear, solid receiver scope mount, "rifle" stock dimensions for scope or open sights, sling swivel studs. Gloss or matte finished wood with checkering, polished blue metal. Medallion model has additional engraving on receiver, polished blue finish, AA/AAA grade walnut stock with checkering. All-Purpose model has Realtree AP camo on stock and fore-end, HiVis fiber optic sights. Introduced 2013. Imported from Japan by Browning.
Price: Field, Stalker models ....**$600.00–$700.00**
Price: Camo coverage **$820.00**
Price: Deer Hunter **$830.00**
Price: Deer Hunter Camo...**$870.00**
Price: Field Composite Field Composite in Mossy Oak Shadow
  Grass Habitat..**$799.00**
Price: Field Composite in Mossy Oak Shadow Grass Habitat 10 ga. ..**$899.00**
Price: Field Composite in Mossy Oak Break-Up Country 10 ga. **$899.00**
Price: Field Composite Camo **$779.00**
Price: Magnum Hunter (3 1/2 in.)......................**$800.00–$1,030.00**
Price: Medallion..**$830.00**
Price: Trap **$840.00**

BROWNING BPS 10 GAUGE SERIES
Similar to the standard BPS except completely covered with Mossy Oak Shadow Grass camouflage. Available with 26- and 28-in. barrel. Introduced 1999. Imported by Browning
Price: Mossy Oak camo **$950.00**
Price: Synthetic stock, Stalker **$800.00**

BROWNING BPS MICRO MIDAS
Gauges: 12 ga, 20 ga., 28 ga. or .410 bore. Barrels: 24 or 26 in. Three Invector choke tubes for 12 and 20 ga., standard tubes for 28 ga. and .410. Stock: Walnut with pistol grip and recoil pad. Satin finished and scaled down to fit smaller statured shooters. Length of pull is 13.25 in. Two spacers included for stock length adjustments. Weights: 7–7.8 lbs.
Price: ....**$700.00–$740.00**

CZ 612
Gauge: 12 ga. Chambered for all shells up to 3 1/2 in. Capacity: 5+1, magazine plug included with Wildfowl Magnum. Barrels: 18.5 in. (Home Defense), 20 in. (HC-P), 26 in. (Wildfowl Mag). Weights: 6–6.8 pounds. Stock: Polymer. Finish: Matte black or full camo (Wildfowl Mag.) HC-P model has pistol grip stock, fiber optic front sight and ghost-ring rear. Home Defense Combo comes with extra 26-in. barrel.
Price: Wildfowl Magnum **$428.00**
Price: Home Defense ....**$304.00–$409.00**
Price: Target **$549.00**

CZ MODEL 620/628 Field Select
Gauges: 20 ga. or 28 ga. Barrel: 28 inches. Weight: 5.4 lbs. Features: Similar to Model 612 except for chambering. Introduced in 2017.
Price: **$429.00**

ESCORT FIELDHUNTER TURKEY
Gauges: 12 ga., 3 in., 20 ga., 3 in., .410 bore, 3 in. Capacity: 4+1. Barrels: 22 in., 24 in., 26 in., ventilated rib. Length: 42-46 in. Weight: 6.0-6.9 lbs. Stock: Synthetic with camo finish. Features: The pump-action Turkey model addition to the FieldHunter family is built of aircraft alloy with a black chrome-finished steel barrel that is camo coated. Cantilever Weaver optics rail, fully adjustable green rear fiber-optic sight with windage-adjustable front red fiber-optic sight. Cross-bolt safety, rubber butt pad, sling studs. Includes three chokes (Ext Turkey, F, IM).
Price: **$399.00**

ESCORT SLUGGER
Gauge: 12 ga., 3 in. Capacity: 5+1. Barrels: 26 in., 28 in., ventilated rib. Length: 38 in. Weight: 6.4-6.5 lbs. Stock: Black synthetic. Slugger Tactical has pistol grip. Features: The pump-action Slugger is built of black-anodized aircraft alloy with a black chrome-finished steel barrel. Fixed cylinder bore choke, cross-bolt safety, fiber-optic front sight, rubber butt pad, sling studs.

Price: ....**$209.00–$219.00**

EUROPEAN AMERICAN ARMORY (EAA) AKKAR CHURCHILL 620
Gauge: 20 ga. Barrel: 18.5 in. Length: 37.5 in. Weight: 5.0 lbs. Stock: Black Synthetic pistol grip style. Features: This Turkish-made pump builds on the Churchill 620 series of slide actions now re-vamped for home defense and tactical use. Optics rail machined into receiver for easy target acquisition with included red-dot optic on quick-release mount. Semi-enhanced loading port. Accessible controls. Checkered pistol grip stock. Black rubber recoil pad, sling swivels. Door-breaching choke tube and shrouded red fiber-optic front sight.
Price: **$427.00**

HARRINGTON & RICHARDSON (H&R) PARDNER PUMP
Gauges: 12 ga., 20 ga. 3 in. Barrels: 21–28 in. Weight: 6.5–7.5 lbs. Stock: Synthetic or hardwood. Ventilated recoil pad and grooved fore-end. Features: Steel receiver, double action bars, cross-bolt safety, easy takedown, ventilated rib, screw-in choke tubes.
Price: ....**$231.00–$259.00**

Prices given are believed to be accurate at time of publication however, many factors affect retail pricing so exact prices are not possible.

76TH EDITION, 2022 ✦ **507**

IAC MODEL 97T TRENCH GUN
Gauge: 12 ga., 2 3/4 in. Barrel: 20 in. with cylinder choke. Stock: Hand rubbed American walnut. Features: Replica of Winchester Model 1897 Trench Gun. Metal handguard, bayonet lug. Imported from China by Interstate Arms Corp.
Price: **$465.00**

IAC HAWK SERIES
Gauge: 12, 2 3/4 in. Barrel: 18.5 in. with cylinder choke. Stock: Synthetic. Features: This series of tactical/home defense shotguns is based on the Remington 870 design. 981 model has top Picatinny rail and bead front sight. 982 has adjustable ghost ring sight with post front. 982T has same sights as 982 plus a pistol grip stock. Imported from China by Interstate Arms Corporation.
Price: 981 ....**$275.00**
Price: 982 ....**$285.00**
Price: 982T **$300.00**

ITHACA MODEL 37 FEATHERLIGHT
Gauges: 12 ga., 20 ga., 16 ga., 28 ga. Capacity: 4+1. Barrels: 26 in., 28 in. or 30 in. with 3-in. chambers (12 and 20 ga.), plain or ventilated rib. Weights: 6.1–7.6 lbs. Stock: Fancy-grade black walnut with Pachmayr Decelerator recoil pad. Checkered fore-end made of matching walnut. Features: Receiver machined from a single block of steel or aluminum. Barrel is steel shot compatible. Three Briley choke tubes provided. Available in several variations including turkey, home defense, tactical and high-grade.
Price: 12 ga., 16 ga. or 20 ga. From **$895.00**
Price: 28 ga. **$1,149.00**
Price: Turkey Slayer w/synthetic stock **$925.00**
Price: Trap Series 12 ga...**$1,020.00**
Price: Waterfowl **$885.00**
Price: Home Defense 18- or 20-in. bbl......................**$784.00**

ITHACA DEERSLAYER III SLUG
Gauges: 12 ga., 20 ga. 3 in. Barrel: 26 in. fully rifled, heavy fluted with 1:28 twist for 12 ga. 1:24 for 20 ga. Weights: 8.14–9.5 lbs. with scope mounted. Length: 45.625 in. overall. Stock: Fancy black walnut stock and fore-end. Sights: NA. Features: Updated, slug-only version of the classic Model 37. Bottom ejection, blued barrel and receiver.
Price: **$1,350.00**

KEYSTONE SPORTING ARMS 4200 MY FIRST SHOTGUN
Gauges: .410 bore. 3 in. Barrel: 18.5 in. Length: 37 in. Stock: Turkish Walnut. Features: Marketed as a Crickett "My First Shotgun," this pump-action baby bore holds 5+1 rounds of 2.75-inch shells or 4+1 rounds of 3 inch. Aluminum receiver with matte blue metalwork. MC-1 choke. Blade-style front sight. Checkered stocks with rubber recoil pad. Length of pull built for small-frame shooters at only 12 in.
Price: **$399.00**

MOSSBERG MODEL 835 ULTI-MAG
Gauge: 12 ga., 3 1/2 in. Barrels: Ported 24 in. rifled bore, 24 in., 28 in., Accu-Mag choke tubes for steel or lead shot. Combo models come with interchangeable second barrel. Weight: 7.75 lbs. Length: 48.5 in. overall. Stock: 14 in. x 1.5 in. x 2.5 in. Dual Comb. Cut-checkered hardwood or camo synthetic; both have recoil pad. Sights: White bead front, brass mid-bead; fiber-optic rear. Features: Shoots 2 3/4-, 3- or 3 1/2-in. shells. Back-bored

and ported barrel to reduce recoil, improve patterns. Ambidextrous thumb safety, twin extractors, dual slide bars. Mossberg Cablelock included. Introduced 1988.
Price: Turkey ....**$601.00–$617.00**
Price: Waterfowl ....**$518.00–$603.00**
Price: Turkey/Deer combo.....................................**$661.00–$701.00**
Price: Turkey/Waterfowl combo **$661.00**
Price: Tactical Turkey...**$652.00**

MOSSBERG MODEL 500 SPORTING SERIES
Gauges: 12 ga., 20 ga., .410 bore, 3 in. Barrels: 18.5 in. to 28 in. with fixed or Accu-Choke, plain or vent rib. Combo models come with interchangeable second barrel. Weight: 6.25 lbs. (.410), 7.25 lbs. (12). Length: 48 in. overall (28-in. barrel). Stock: 14 in. x 1.5 in. x 2.5 in. Walnut-stained hardwood, black synthetic, Mossy Oak Advantage camouflage. Cut-checkered grip and fore-end. Sights: White bead front, brass mid-bead; fiber-optic. Features: Ambidextrous thumb safety, twin extractors, disconnecting safety, dual action bars. Quiet Carry fore-end. Many barrels are ported. FLEX series has many modular options and accessories including barrels and stocks. From Mossberg. Left-hand versions (L-series) available in most models.
Price: Turkey **$486.00**
Price: Waterfowl **$537.00**
Price: Combo **$593.00**
Price: FLEX Hunting...**$702.00**
Price: FLEX All Purpose **$561.00**
Price: Field **$419.00**
Price: Slugster **$447.00**
Price: FLEX Deer/Security combo................................**$787.00**
Price: Home Security 410 ....**$477.00**
Price: Tactical...**$486.00–$602.00**

MOSSBERG MODEL 500 SUPER BANTAM PUMP
Same as the Model 500 Sporting Pump except 12 or 20 ga., 22-in. vent rib Accu-Choke barrel with choke tube set; has 1 in. shorter stock, reduced length from pistol grip to trigger, reduced fore-end reach. Introduced 1992.
Price: **$419.00**
Price: Combo with extra slug barrel, camo finish **$549.00**

MOSSBERG 510 MINI BANTAM
Gauges: 20 ga., .410 bore, 3 in. Barrel: 18.5 in. vent-rib. Weight: 5 lbs. Length: 34.75 in. Stock: Synthetic with optional Mossy Oak Break-Up Infinity, Muddy Girl pink/black camo. Features: Available in either 20 ga. or .410 bore, the Mini features an 18.5-in. vent-rib barrel with dual bead sights. Parents don't have to worry about their young shooter growing out of this gun too quick, the adjustable classic stock can be adjusted from 10.5 to 11.5-in. length of pull so the Mini can grow with your youngster. This adjustability also helps provide a proper fit for young shooters and allowing for a more safe and enjoyable shooting experience.
Price: ....**$419.00–$466.00**

Prices given are believed to be accurate at time of publication however, many factors affect retail pricing so exact prices are not possible.

MOSSBERG SHOCKWAVE SERIES

Gauges: 12, 20 ga. or .410 cylinder bore, 3-inch chamber. Barrel: 14 3/8, 18.5 in. Weight: 5 – 5.5 lbs. Length: 26.4 - 30.75 in. Stock: Synthetic or wood. Raptor bird's-head type pistol grip. Nightstick has wood stock and fore-end.

Price:	$455.00
Price: CTC Laser Saddle Model	$613.00
Price: Ceracote finish	$504.00
Price: Nightstick (shown	$539.00
Price: Mag-Fed	$721.00
Price: SPX w/heatshield	$560.00

$710.00

RETAY GPS

Gauges: 12 ga. 3 in. Barrel: 18.5 in. Weight: 6 lbs. 9 oz. Stock: Black ABS synthetic. Features: Retay's first pump-action shotgun is the GPS, short for Geometric Pump System. Extra-short travel pump action. Anodized aluminum receiver. 5+1-round capacity. Chrome-lined barrel with elongated, back-bored forcing cones. Crossbolt safety. Milled aluminum trigger housing and guard. Integral sling swivel mounts. Beavertail adapter for optics mounting. High visibility front blade sight. Comfort rubber recoil pad. Ships with removeable MaraPro chokes (S, M, F).

Price: $349.00

RETAY GPS

Gauges: 12 ga. 3 in. Barrel: 18.5 in. Weight: 6 lbs. 9 oz. Stock: Black ABS synthetic. Features: Retay's first pump-action shotgun is the GPS, short for Geometric Pump System. Extra-short travel pump action. Anodized aluminum receiver. 5+1-round capacity. Chrome-lined barrel with elongated, back-bored forcing cones. Crossbolt safety. Milled aluminum trigger housing and guard. Integral sling swivel mounts. Beavertail adapter for optics mounting. High visibility front blade sight. Comfort rubber recoil pad. Ships with removeable MaraPro chokes (S, M, F).

Price: $349.00

STEVENS MODEL 320

Gauges: 12 ga., or 20 ga. with 3-in. chamber. Capacity: 5+1. Barrels: 18.25 in., 20 in., 22 in., 26 in. or 28 in. with interchangeable choke tubes. Features include all-steel barrel and receiver; bottom-load and ejection design; black synthetic stock.

Price: Security Model	$276.00
Price: Field Model 320 with 28-inch barrel	$251.00
Price: Combo Model with Field and Security barrels	$307.00

STEVENS 320 SECURITY THUMBHOLE

Gauges: 12 ga. 3 in., or 20 ga. 3in. Barrel: 18.5-in. chrome alloy steel matte black. Weight: 7.0–7.3 lbs. Length: 39.1 in. Stock: Black matte synthetic with thumbhole cutout. Features: Pump action with dual slide bars and rotary bolt. Thumbhole stock design with ambidextrous cheek riser and grip texture. Swivel studs. Bottom-loading tubular magazine with 5+1-round capacity. Black rubber recoil pad. Ghost Ring Sight or Front Bead Sight models available in both chamberings.

Price: 12-ga. Front Bead Sight Model	$275.00
Price: 12-ga. Ghost Ring Sight Model	$305.00
Price: 20-ga. Front Bead Sight Model	$275.00
Price: 20-ga. Ghost Ring Sight Model	$305.00

STEVENS 320 TURKEY THUMBHOLE

Gauges: 12 ga. 3 in., or 20 ga. 3 in. Barrel: 22-in. chrome alloy steel matte black with ventilated rib. Weight: 7.6 lbs. Length: 43.4 in. Stock: Olive drab green matte synthetic with thumbhole cutout. Features: Pump action with dual slide bars and rotary bolt. Thumbhole stock design with ambidextrous cheek riser and grip texture. Swivel studs. Bottom-loading tubular magazine with 5+1-round capacity. Black rubber recoil pad. Adjustable fiber-optic turkey sights. Extended Win-Choke-style Extra Full choke tube.

Price: 12-ga. Front Bead Sight Model $323.00

STOEGER P3000

Gauge: 12 ga. 3-in. Barrels: 18.5 in., 26 in., 28 in., with ventilated rib. Weight: 6.5–7 lbs. Stock: Black synthetic. Camo finish available. Defense Model available with or without pistol grip.

Price:	$299.00
Price: Camo finish	$399.00
Price: Defense model w/pistol grip	$349.00

TRISTAR COBRA III FIELD

Gauges: 12 ga., 3 in., 20 ga., 3 in. Barrels: 26 in., 28 in., ventilated rib. Weight: 6.7-7.0 lbs. Length: 46.5-48.5 in. Stock: Field models available with either Turkish walnut or black synthetic furniture. Features: Third model upgrade to the Cobra pump-action line with extended fore-end. Rubber buttpad, cross-bolt safety, chrome-lined barrel, high-polish blue metalwork, sling studs. Includes three Beretta Mobil-style choke tubes (IC, M, F).

Price: .... $305.00—$335.00

TRISTAR COBRA III YOUTH

Gauge: 20 ga., 3 in. Barrel: 24 in., ventilated rib. Weight: 5.4-6.5 lbs. Length: 37.7 in. Stock: Version III youth models available with black synthetic, Realtree Max-5 camo or Turkish-walnut furniture. Features: Third iteration of the Cobra pump-action with extended fore-end. Ventilated rubber buttpad, cross-bolt safety, chrome-lined barrel, sling studs. Shorter length of pull on Youth model. Includes three Beretta Mobil-style choke tubes (IC, M, F).

Price: .... $305.00—$365.00

WINCHESTER SUPER X (SXP)

Gauges: 12 ga., 3 in. or 3 1/2 in. chambers; 20 ga., 3 in. Barrels: 18 in., 26 in., 28 in. Barrels .742-in. back-bored, chrome plated; Invector Plus choke tubes. Weights: 6.5–7 lbs. Stocks: Walnut or composite. Features: Rotary bolt, four lugs, dual steel action bars. Walnut Field has gloss-finished walnut stock and forearm, cut checkering. Black Shadow Field has composite stock and forearm, non-glare matte finish barrel and receiver. SXP Defender has composite stock and forearm, chromed plated, 18-in. cylinder choked barrel, non-glare metal surfaces, five-shot magazine, grooved forearm. Some models offered in left-hand versions. Reintroduced 2009. Made in USA by Winchester Repeating Arms Co.

Price: Black Shadow Field, 3 in.	$380.00
Price: Black Shadow Field, 3 1/2 in.	$430.00
Price: SXP Defender	$350.00–$400.00
Price: Hybrid Hunter in Mossy Oak Shadow Grass Habitat	$449.00
Price: Waterfowl Hunter 3 in.	$460.00
Price: Waterfowl Hunter 3 1/2 in.	$500.00
Price: Waterfowl Hunter in Mossy Oak Shadow Grass Habitat	$499.00
Price: Turkey Hunter 3 1/2 in.	$520.00
Price: Black Shadow Deer	$520.00
Price: Trap	$480.00
Price: Field, walnut stock	$400.00–$430.00
Price: 20-ga., 3-in. models	$379.00
Price: Extreme Defender FDE	$549.00

Prices given are believed to be accurate at time of publication however, many factors affect retail pricing so exact prices are not possible.

76TH EDITION, 2022 ✦ **509**

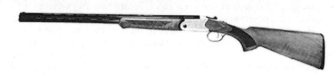

AMERICAN TACTICAL INC (ATI) CRUSADER

Gauges: 12 ga., 3 in., 20 ga., 3 in., 28 ga., 2.75 in., .410 bore, 3 in. Barrels: 26 in., 28 in., 30 in., ventilated rib. Weight: 6.0-6.5 lbs. Stock: Turkish walnut with oil finish. Features: ATI's new O/U line has both Field and Sport models. Made from 7075 aluminum with laser engraving on the receiver. Single selective trigger, fiber-optic front sight, extractors, chrome-moly steel barrel. Ships with five chokes: flush on the Field, extended on the Sport.

Price: Crusader Field **$499.00**
Price: Crusader Sport **$549.00**

BENELLI 828U

Gauges: 12 ga. 3 in. Barrels: 26 in., 28 in. Weights: 6.5–7 lbs. Stock: AA-grade satin walnut, fully adjustable for both drop and cast. Features: New patented locking system allows use of aluminum frame. Features include carbon fiber rib, fiber-optic sight, removable trigger group, and Benelli's Progressive Comfort recoil reduction system.

Price: Matte black..**$2,699.00**
Price: Nickel **$3,199.00**
Price: 20-gauge Nickel **$3,199.00**

BERETTA 694

Gauge: 12 ga., 3 in. Barrels: 28 in., 30 in., 32 in., with either 10x8 or 10x10 ventilated rib. Weight: 7.8-8.1 lbs. Stock: Walnut with 35/50 and 35/55 B-Fast options. Features: Designed specifically for competition shooting, the 694 has a slim, modern design. Steelium Plus barrels for dense, uniform patterns. Fore-end iron system with adjustable opening. MicroCore 18mm recoil pad, single centrally positioned adjustable trigger, 1.5 pitch checkering, 2.5-plus grade wood. Matte gray Nistan finish with blue inlay trim. Balance weights of 20g and 40g available separately. Both Sporting and Trap models available.

Price: **$4,500.00**

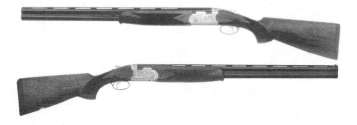

BERETTA 686/687 SILVER PIGEON SERIES

Gauges: 12 ga., 20 ga., 28 ga., 3 in. (2 3/4 in. 28 ga.). .410 bore, 3 in. Barrels: 26 in., 28 in. Weight: 6.8 lbs. Stock: Checkered walnut. Features: Interchangeable barrels (20 ga. and 28 ga.), single selective gold-plated trigger, boxlock action, auto safety, Schnabel fore-end.

Price: 686 Silver Pigeon Grade I **$2,350.00**
Price: 686 Silver Pigeon Grade I, Sporting **$2,400.00**
Price: 687 Silver Pigeon Grade III **$3,430.00**
Price: 687 Silver Pigeon Grade V **$4,075.00**

BERETTA 687 SILVER PIGEON III

Gauges: 12 ga. 3 in., 20 ga. 3 in., 28 ga. 2.75 in., .410 bore, 3 in. Barrels: 26, 28, 30 in. with 6x6 windowed rib. Stock: Class 2.5 Walnut with gloss finish. Features: The 687 Silver Pigeon III stems from the 680 series design. Trapezoid shoulders and dual conical locking lugs. Fine engraving with game scenes and floral motif done with 5-axis laser. MicroCore 20mm buttpad. The 28-gauge and .410-bore doubles are built on a smaller frame. Gold-colored single selective trigger. Tang safety selector. Steelium barrels. The 12, 20, and 28 gauges use 70mm Optima HP choke tubes while the .410 is equipped with 50mm Mobil Chokes.

Price: **$2,699.00**

BERETTA MODEL 687 EELL

Gauges: 12 ga., 20 ga., 28 ga., 410 bore. Features: Premium-grade model with decorative sideplates featuring lavish hand-chased engraving with a classic game scene enhanced by detailed leaves and flowers that also cover the trigger guard, trigger plate and fore-end lever. Stock has high-grade, specially selected European walnut with fine-line checkering. Offered in three action sizes with scaled-down 28 ga. and .410 receivers. Combo models are available with extra barrel sets in 20/28 or 28/.410.

Price: **$7,995.00**
Price: Combo model **$9,695.00**

BERETTA MODEL 690

Gauge: 12 ga. 3 in. Barrels: 26 in., 28 in., 30 in. with OptimaChoke HP system. Features: Similar to the 686/687 series with minor improvements. Stock has higher grade oil-finished walnut. Re-designed barrel/fore-end attachment reduces weight.

Price: ....**$2,650.00–$3,100.00**

BERETTA MODEL 692 SPORTING

Gauge: 12 ga., 3 in. Barrels: 30 in. with long forcing cones of approximately 14 in.. Skeet model available with 28- or 30-in. barrel, Trap model with 30 in or 32 in. Receiver is .50-in. wider than 682 model for improved handling. Stock: Hand rubbed oil finished select walnut with Schnabel fore-end. Features include selective single adjustable trigger, manual safety, tapered 8mm to 10mm rib.

Price: **$4,800.00**
Price: Skeet **$5,275.00**
Price: Trap **$5,600.00**

BERETTA DT11

Gauge: 12 ga. 3 in. Barrels: 30 in., 32 in., 34 in. Top rib has hollowed bridges. Stock: Hand-checkered buttstock and fore-end. Hand-rubbed oil, Tru-Oil or wax finish. Adjustable comb on skeet and trap models. Features: Competition model offered in Sporting, Skeet and Trap models. Newly designed receiver, top lever, safety/selector button.

Price: Sporting **$8,650.00**
Price: Skeet **$8,650.00**
Price: Trap **$8,999.00**

BLASER F3 SUPERSPORT

Gauge: 12 ga., 3 in. Barrel: 32 in. Weight: 9 lbs. Stock: Adjustable semi-custom, Turkish walnut wood grade: 4. Features: The latest addition to the F3 family is the F3 SuperSport. The perfect blend of overall weight, balance and weight distribution make the F3 SuperSport the ideal competitor. Briley Spectrum-5 chokes, free-floating barrels, adjustable barrel hanger system on o/u, chrome plated barrels full length, revolutionary ejector ball system, barrels finished in a powder coated nitride, selectable competition trigger.

Price: SuperSport..**$9,076.00**
Price: Competition Sporting..**$7,951.00**
Price: Superskeet..**$9,076.00**
Price: American Super Trap **$9,530.00**

Prices given are believed to be accurate at time of publication however, many factors affect retail pricing so exact prices are not possible.

BROWNING CYNERGY

Gauges: .410 bore, 12 ga., 20 ga., 28 ga. Barrels: 26 in., 28 in., 30 in., 32 in. Stocks: Walnut or composite. Sights: White bead front most models; HiViz Pro-Comp sight on some models; mid bead. Features: Mono-Lock hinge, recoil-reducing interchangeable Inflex recoil pad, silver nitride receiver; striker-based trigger, ported barrel option. Imported from Japan by Browning.

Price:		
Price: Field Grade Model, 12 ga.		$1,910.00
Price: CX composite		$1,710.00
Price: CX walnut stock		$1,780.00
Price: Field, small gauges		$1,940.00
Price: Ultimate Turkey, Mossy Oak Breakup camo		$2,390.00
Price: Micro Midas		$1,979.00
Price: Feather		$2,269.00
Price: Wicked Wing		$2,339.00

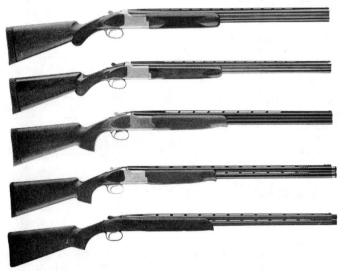

BROWNING CITORI SERIES

Gauges: 12 ga., 20 ga., 28 ga., .410 bore. Barrels: 26 in., 28 in. in 28 ga. and .410 bore. Offered with Invector choke tubes. All 12- and 20-ga. models have back-bored barrels and Invector Plus choke system. Weights: 6 lbs., 8 oz. (26 in. .410) to 7 lbs., 13 oz. (30 in. 12 ga.). Length: 43 in. overall (26-in. bbl.). Stock: Dense walnut, hand checkered, full pistol grip, beavertail fore-end. Field-type recoil pad on 12 ga. field guns and trap and skeet models. Sights: Medium-raised beads, German nickel silver. Features: Barrel selector integral with safety, automatic ejectors, three-piece takedown. Imported from Japan by Browning.

Price: White Lightning		$2,670.00
Price: Feather Lightning		$2,870.00
Price: Gran Lightning		$3,300.00
Price: Crossover (CX)		$2,140.00
Price: Crossover (CX) w/adjustable comb		$2,560.00
Price: Crossover (CXS)		$2,140.00
Price: Crossover Target (CXT)		$2,260.00
Price: Crossover Target (CXT) w/adjustable comb		$2,660.00
Price: Crossover (CXS)		$2,190.00
Price: Crossover (CXS) w/adjustable comb		$2,590.00
Price: Crossover (CXS Micro)		$2,140.00
Price: White Lightning .410 bore and 28 ga.		$2,669.00–$2,739.00
Price: CX White		$2,379.00
Price: CX White Adjustable		$2,939.00
Price: CX Micro		$2,469.00
Price: CXS 20/28 Ga. Combo		$3,939.00
Price: CXS White		$2,439.00
Price: CXT White		$2,499.00

BROWNING CITORI FIELD SPORTING GRADE VII

Gauge: 12 ga. 3 in., 20 ga. 3 in., 28 ga. 2.75 in., .410 bore 3 in. Barrels: 30 or 32 in., steel with ventilated rib. Weight: 7 lbs. 7oz.–8 lbs. 2 oz. Length: 47.5–49.5 in. Stock: Grade VI / VII Black Walnut with gloss oil finish and nameplate inlay

for owner's initials. **Features:** Browning expands its high-end O/U with the addition of sub-gauge offerings. This shotgun comes from the Browning High Grade Program and shows silver bird and dog engraving. Triple Trigger System with three trigger shoes and gold-plated trigger, and triggerguard engraving. Silver Nitride receiver finish. Cut checkering at 20 LPI. Polished blued barrels with chrome plated chambers. Hi-Viz Pro Comp sight and ivory mid bead. Inflex recoil pad. Includes five extended Black Midas Grade choke tubes (F, IM, M, IC, SK).

Price: 12 ga.		$6,269.00
Price: 20 ga.		$6,459.00
Price: 28 ga. and .410 bore		$6,539.00

BROWNING CITORI TRAP MAX

Gauge: 12 ga., 2.75 in. Barrels: 30 in., 32 in., ported with 5/16 to 7/16 adjustable ventilated rib. Weight: 9.0-9.2 lbs. Length: 47.75-49.75 in. Stock: Grade V/VI black walnut with gloss-oil finish. Features: Graco adjustable Monte Carlo comb. Buttplate adjusts for location and angle. GraCoil recoil reduction system increases comfort and offers length-of-pull adjustment. Adjustable rib allows for 50/50 or 90/10 POI. Semi-beavertail forearm with finger grooves, Pachmayr Decelerator XLT recoil pad. Close radius grip and palm swell. Triple Trigger System with three trigger shoes, gold-plated trigger, Hi-Viz Pro Comp sight, ivory mid-bead, polished blue barrels, Silver-Nitride receiver, chrome-plated chamber. Five Invector DS Extended choke tubes ideal for trap (F, LF, M, IM, IM).

Price:		$5,859.00

BROWNING 725 CITORI

Gauges: 12 ga., 20 ga., 28 ga. or .410 bore. Barrels: 26 in., 28 in., 30 in. Weights: 5.7–7.6 lbs. Length: 43.75–50 in. Stock: Gloss oil finish, grade II/III walnut. Features: New receiver that is significantly lower in profile than other 12-gauge Citori models. Mechanical trigger, Vector Pro lengthened forcing cones, three Invector-DS choke tubes, silver nitride finish with high relief engraving.

Price: 725 Field (12 ga. or 20 ga.)		$2,560.00
Price: 725 Field (28 ga. or .410 bore)		$2,590.00
Price: 725 Field Grade VI		$6,000.00
Price: 725 Feather (12 ga. or 20 ga.)		$2,670.00
Price: 725 Sporting		$3,270.00
Price: 725 Sporting w/adjustable comb		$3,600.00
Price: 725 Sporting Golden Clays		$5,440.00
Price: 725 Trap		$3,400.00

BROWNING 725 FEATHER

Gauges: 12 ga., 3 in., 20 ga., 3 in. Barrels: 26 in., 28 in., with 0.25-in. ventilated rib. Weight: 5 lbs., 12 oz.-6 lbs., 9 oz. Length: 43.75-45.75 in. Stock: Grade II/III walnut with gloss-oil finish. Features: Lightweight aluminum-alloy receiver with steel breech face and hinge pin, Silver-Nitride finish. New accented engraving. Inflex recoil pad, ivory bead sight, gold-plated trigger. Ideal for hunting and sporting clays. Includes three Invector DS flush-mount choke tubes (F, M, IC).

Price:		$2,739.00

CAESAR GUERINI

Gauges: 12 ga., 20 ga., 28 ga., also 20/28 gauge combo. Some models are available in .410 bore. Barrels: All standard lengths from 26–32 inches. Weights: 5.5–8.8 lbs. Stock: High-grade walnut with hand-rubbed oil finish. Features: A wide range of over/under models designed for the field, sporting clays, skeet and trap shooting. The models listed below are representative of some of the different models and variants. Many optional features are offered including high-grade wood and engraving, and extra sets of barrels. Made it Italy and imported by Caesar Guerini USA.

Price: Summit Sporting		$3,995.00
Price: Summit Limited		$4,895.00
Price: Summit Ascent		$5,135.00
Price: Tempio		$4,325.00
Price: Ellipse		$4,650.00
Price: Ellipse Curve		$7,500.00
Price: Ellipse EVO Sporting		$6,950.00

Price: Magnus $5,075.00
Price: Maxum $6,825.00
Price: Forum $11,500.00
Price: Woodlander $3,795.00
Price: Invictus Sporting $7,400.00
Price: Maxum Trap $9,295.00
Price: Maxum Sporting $7,150.00

CAESAR GUERINI REVENANT

Addition of a new combo set to the high-grade 2019 Revenant O/U with a tapered, solid rib and highly engraved maple leaf and branch design receiver. Now with a 20/28-gauge combo barrel set.
Price: $13,495.00

CAESAR GUERINI REVENANT SPORTING

Gauge: 20 ga. 3 in. 28 ga. 2.75 in. Barrels: 28 or 30 in. with non-ventilated center rib, tapered from 8–6mm. Weight: 6 lbs. 6 oz.–6 lbs. 11 oz. Stock: Extra-deluxe wood grade with hand-rubbed oil finish. Left-hand stock option available by special order. Features: Fine-grade over-under Sporting version of the Revenant. Hand-polished coin finish with Invisalloy protective finish. Long-tang triggerguard. Anson rod fore-end escutcheon. Intricate engraving and gold inlay that takes over 40-hours to produce each Revenant action. Wood butt plate. Silver front bead. Checkered at 26 LPI. Premium Revenant gun case included. Ships with five nickel-plated flush-fitting chokes.
Price: $14,750.00

CAESAR GUERINI SYREN JULIA SPORTING

Gauges: 12 ga. 2.75 in. Barrels: 30 in. ventilated rib tapered from 10–8mm. Weight: 7 lbs. 15 oz. Stock: Deluxe Turkish Walnut with hand-rubbed, semi-gloss oil finish. Left-hand stock option and adjustable comb (RH) available by special order Features: Named after Julia, daughter of Julius Caesar, as a top-tier, competition-grade target gun in the Syren line of shotguns for women. Fantasy-style receiver engraving depicting a woman's face evolving from floral scrollwork. Rich case color hardened finish. Checking cut at 26 LPI. Black rubber recoil pad. DuoCon forcing cones. White Bradley style front sight and silver center bead. DTS trigger system with take-up, over-travel, and LOP adjustments. Manual safety. Includes six MAXIS competition chokes as well as plastic hard case, combination locks, and velvet sleeves.
Price: $6,050.00

CHARLES DALY 202

Gauges: 12 ga., 3 in., 20 ga., 3 in., .410 bore, 3 in. Barrels: 26 in., 28 in., ventilated rib. Length: 43-45 in. Weight: 6.2-7.3 lbs. Stock: Checkered walnut. Features: The new Charles Daly 202 line of O/U shotguns are built of aluminum alloy. Silver receivers are engraved with a dog scene. Single selective mechanical reset trigger, fixed fiber-optic front sight, extractors, rubber buttpad. Includes five extended Mobil style chokes (SK, IC, M, IM, F).
Price: $499.00

CONNECTICUT SHOTGUN A10 AMERICAN

Gauges: 12 ga., 20 ga., 28 ga., .410 bore. 2 3/4, 3 in. Sidelock design. Barrels: 26 in., 28 in., 30 in. or 32 in. with choice of fixed or interchangeable chokes. Weight: 6.3 lbs. Stock: Hand rubbed oil finish, hand checkered at 24 LPI. Black, English or Turkish walnut offered in numerous grades. Pistol or Prince of Wales grip, short or long tang. Features: Low-profile, shallow frame full sidelock. Single-selective trigger, automatic ejectors. Engraved models available. Made in the USA by Connecticut Shotgun Mfg. Co.
Price: 12 ga. $9,999.00
Price: Smaller ga. $11,900.00
Price: Sporting Clays $14,950.00

CONNECTICUT SHOTGUN MODEL 21 O/U

Gauge: 20 ga., 3 in. Barrels: 26–32 in. chrome-lined, back-bored with extended forcing cones. Weight: 6.3 lbs. Stock: A Fancy (2X) American walnut, standard point checkering, choice of straight or pistol grip. Higher grade walnut is optional. Features: The over/under version of

Conn. Shotgun's replica of the Winchester Model 21 side-by-side, built using the same machining, tooling, techniques and finishes. Low-profile shallow frame with blued receiver. Pigeon and Grand American grades are available. Made in the USA by Connecticut Shotgun Mfg. Co.
Price: $4,545.00

CZ ALL TERRAIN SERIES

Gauges: 12 ga., 3 in., 20 ga., 3 in. Barrels: 28 in., 30 in. Stock: Walnut, various styles. Features: CZ's new All-Terrain series encompasses five existing shotgun models. The new package includes upgraded wood, OD Green Cerakote finish on all metalwork, as well as a set of rare earth magnets added to the extractor/ejectors of the SxS and O/U models to keep shells from dropping out while handling a dog or working in the blind.
Price: Upland Ultralight All-Terrain 12 ga. or 20 ga. $890.00
Price: Redhead Premier All-Terrain 12 ga. or 20 ga. $1,123.00
Price: Drake All-Terrain 12 ga. or 20 ga. $791.00

CZ REDHEAD PREMIER

Gauges: 12 ga., 20 ga., (3 in. chambers), 28 ga. (2 3/4 in.). Barrel: 28 in. Weight: 7.4 lbs. Length: NA. Stock: Round-knob pistol grip, Schnabel fore-end, Turkish walnut. Features: Single selective triggers and extractors (12 & 20 ga.), screw-in chokes (12 ga., 20 ga., 28 ga.) choked IC and Mod (.410), coin-finished receiver, multi chokes. From CZ-USA.
Price: Deluxe $953.00
Price: Mini (28 ga., .410 bore) $1,057.00
Price: Target $1,389.00
Price: 16 ga., 28 in. barrel $988.00

FABARM ELOS 2 ELITE

Gauge: 12 ga. 3 in., 20 ga. 3 in. Barrels: 28 in. ventilated rib. Stock: Deluxe-grade European Walnut with matte oil finish and pistol grip design. Features: Left-handed stock option available by special order. Rich case-colored action with gold inlay of sporting birds. Hand-cut checkering. Brass front bead. Single gold-plated trigger. TriBore HP barrel and Inner HP flush-fitting chokes. Ships with Integrale case.
Price: $3,325.00

FABARM ELOS N2 ALLSPORT COMBO

Gauge: 12 ga. Barrels: 30 in. O/U with 34 in. Unsingle combo; 32 in. O/U with 34 in. Unsingle combo. Stock: Turkish Walnut with TriWood enhanced finish. Available with left-hand stock option or Modified Compact Stock with shorter LOP. Features: The Elos N2 Allsport Type T Combo is built for competition shooting. Microcell 22mm recoil pad. Quick Release Rib (QRR) rib on O/U barrels. Adjustable competition trigger. Adjustable comb. TriBore HP barrel. Hand-cut checkering. Single trigger. Includes five EXIS HP Competition extended choke tubes. Ships with hard case.
Price: $3,325.00

FAUSTI CLASS ROUND BODY

Gauges: 16 ga., 20 ga., 28 ga.. Barrels: 28 or 30 in. Weights: 5.8–6.3 lbs. Lengths: 45.5–47.5 in. Stock: Turkish walnut Prince of Wales style with oil finish. Features include automatic ejectors, single selective trigger, laser-engraved receiver.
Price: $4,199.00

FAUSTI CALEDON
Gauges: 12 ga., 16 ga., 20 ga., 28 ga. and .410 bore. Barrels: 26 in., 28 in., 30 in. Weights: 5.8–7.3 lbs. Stock: Turkish walnut with oil finish, round pistol grip. Features: Automatic ejectors, single selective trigger, laser-engraved receiver. Coin finish receiver with gold inlays.

Price: 12 ga. or 20 ga. **$1,999.00**
Price: 16 ga., 28 ga., .410 bore **$2,569.00**

FRANCHI INSTINCT SERIES
Gauges: 12 ga., 16 ga., 20 ga., 28 ga., .410 bore, 2 1/5 in. 2 3/4 in, 3 in." Barrels: 26 in., 28 in. Weight: 5.3–6.4 lbs. Lengths: 42.5–44.5 in. Stock: AA-grade satin walnut (LS), A-grade (L) with rounded pistol grip and recoil pad. Single trigger, automatic ejectors, tang safety, choke tubes. L model has steel receiver, SL has aluminum alloy receiver. Sporting model has higher grade wood, extended choke tubes. Catalyst model is designed for women, including stock dimensions for cast, drop, pitch, grip and length of pull.

Price: L **$1,299.00**
Price: SL **$1,599.00**
Price: Sporting **$1,999.00**
Price: Catalyst **$1,469.00**
Price: SL 28 ga. and .410 bore **$1,699.00**

FRANCHI INSTINT SLX
Gauges: 12 ga., 3 in., 16 ga., 2.75 in., 20 ga., 3 in. Barrel: 28 in., ventilated rib. Length: 46.25 in. Weight: 5.6-6.3 lbs. Stock: AA-grade walnut. Features: Similar to the SL family of O/Us, but with both reduced weight and the addition of deluxe aesthetics. Floral engraving on the receiver along with a gold trigger and inlays. Upgraded wood, Prince of Wales grip and Schnabel fore-end. Auto ejectors, barrel select switch, red fiber-optic front sight, gloss-blued barrels, tang safety. Includes five extended choke tubes and a hard case.

Price: 28 ga. 3 in. **$1,799.00**

KOLAR SPORTING CLAYS
Gauge: 12 ga., 2 3/4 in. Barrels: 30 in., 32 in., 34 in.; extended choke tubes. Stock: 14.625 in. x 2.5 in. x 1.875 in. x 1.375 in. French walnut. Four stock versions available. Features: Single selective trigger, detachable, adjustable for length; overbored barrels with long forcing cones; flat tramline rib; matte blue finish. Made in U.S. by Kolar.

Price: Standard **$11,995.00**
Price: Prestige **$14,190.00**
Price: Elite Gold **$16,590.00**
Price: Legend **$17,090.00**
Price: Select **$22,590.00**
Price: Custom .... **Price on request**

KOLAR AAA COMPETITION TRAP
Gauge: 12 ga. Similar to the Sporting Clays gun except has 32 in. O/U 34 in. Unsingle or 30 in. O/U 34 in. Unsingle barrels as an over/under, unsingle, or combination set. Stock dimensions are 14.5 in. x 2.5 in. x 1.5 in.; American or French walnut; step parallel rib standard. Contact maker for full listings. Made in USA by Kolar.

Price: Single bbl. **$8,495.00**
Price: O/U **$11,695.00**

KOLAR AAA COMPETITION SKEET
Similar to the Sporting Clays gun except has 28 in. or 30 in. barrels with Kolarite AAA sub-gauge tubes; stock of American or French walnut with matte finish; flat tramline rib; under barrel adjustable for point of impact. Many options available. Contact maker for complete listing. Made in USA by Kolar.

Price: Max Lite **$13,995.00**

KRIEGHOFF K-80 SPORTING CLAYS
Gauge: 12 ga. Barrels: 28 in., 30 in., 32 in., 34 in. with choke tubes. Weight: About 8 lbs. Stock: #3 Sporting stock designed for gun-down shooting. Features: Standard receiver with satin nickel finish and classic scroll engraving. Selective mechanical trigger adjustable for position. Choice of tapered flat or 8mm parallel flat barrel rib. Free-floating barrels. Aluminum case. Imported from Germany by Krieghoff International, Inc.

Price: Standard grade with five choke tubes **$12,395.00**

KRIEGHOFF K-80 SKEET
Gauge: 12 ga., 2 3/4 in. Barrels: 28 in., 30 in., 32 in., (skeet & skeet), optional choke tubes. Weight: About 7.75 lbs. Stock: American skeet or straight skeet stocks, with palm-swell grips. Walnut. Features: Satin gray receiver finish. Selective mechanical trigger adjustable for position. Choice of ventilated 8mm parallel flat rib or ventilated 8–12mm tapered flat rib. Introduced 1980. Imported from Germany by Krieghoff International, Inc.

Price: Standard, skeet chokes **$11,795.00**

KRIEGHOFF K-80 TRAP
Gauge: 12 ga., 2 3/4 in. Barrels: 30 in., 32 in. (Imp. Mod. & Full or choke tubes). Weight: About 8.5 lbs. Stock: Four stock dimensions or adjustable stock available; all have palm-swell grips. Checkered European walnut. Features: Satin nickel receiver. Selective mechanical trigger, adjustable for position. Ventilated step rib. Introduced 1980. Imported from Germany by Krieghoff International, Inc.

Price: K-80 O/U (30 in., 32 in., Imp. Mod. & Full **$11,795.00**
Price: K-80 Unsingle (32 in., 34 in., Full), standard **$13,995.00**
Price: K-80 Combo (two-barrel set), standard **$17,995.00**

KRIEGHOFF K-20
Similar to the K-80 except built on a 20-ga. frame. Designed for skeet, sporting clays and field use. Offered in 20 ga., 28 ga. and .410; Barrels: 28 in., 30 in. and 32 in. Imported from Germany by Krieghoff International Inc.

Price: K-20, 20 ga. **$11,695.00**
Price: K-20, 28 ga. **$12,395.00**
Price: K-20, .410 .... **$12,395.00**
Price: K-20 Sporting or Parcours **$12,395.00**
Price: K-20 Victoria **$12,395.00**

MERKEL MODEL 2001EL O/U
Gauges: 12 ga., 20 ga., 3 in., 28 ga. 2-3/4 in. chambers. Barrels: 12 ga. 28 in.; 20 ga., 28 ga. 26.75 in. Weight: About 7 lbs. (12 ga.). Stock: Oil-finished walnut; English or pistol grip. Features: Self-cocking Blitz boxlock action with cocking indicators; Kersten double cross-bolt lock; silver-grayed receiver with engraved hunting scenes; coil spring ejectors; single selective or double triggers. Imported from Germany by Merkel USA.

Price: **$13,255.00**

MERKEL MODEL 2000CL
Similar to Model 2001EL except scroll-engraved casehardened receiver; 12 ga., 20 ga., 28 ga. Imported from Germany by Merkel USA.

Price: **$12,235.00**

MOSSBERG SILVER RESERVE II
Gauge: 12 ga., 3 in. Barrels: 28 in. with ventilated rib, choke tubes. Stock: Select black walnut with satin finish. Sights: Metal bead. Available with extractors or automatic ejectors. Also offered in Sport model with ported barrels with wide rib, fiber optic front and middle bead sights. Super Sport has extra wide high rib, optional adjustable comb.

Price: Field **$773.00**
Price: Sport **$950.00**
Price: Sport w/ejectors **$1,070.00**
Price: Super Sport w/ejectors **$1,163.00**
Price: Super Sport w/ejectors, adj. comb **$1,273.00**

MOSSBERG INTERNATIONAL SILVER RESERVE FIELD SERIES
Gauge: Options depend on model, but include 12 ga. 3 in., 20 ga. 3 in., 28 ga. 2.75 in., and .410 bore 3 in., as well as a 20-ga. Youth. Barrels: 26- or 28-in. ventilated rib. Weight: 6.5–7.5 lbs. Length: 42.25–45 in. Stock: Choice of black synthetic or satin Black Walnut, depending upon model, as well as a Youth-sized model with shorter LOP. Features: Matte blue barrel finish. Satin silver receiver on all except the synthetic model with a matte

Prices given are believed to be accurate at time of publication however, many factors affect retail pricing so exact prices are not possible.

76TH EDITION, 2022 ✦ 513

blue receiver. Dual shell extractors. Tang-mounted safety/barrel selector. Includes flush-mount Field set of five chokes (Cyl, IC, M, IM, F).

Price: Eventide Black Synthetic 12-ga. **$636.00**
Price: Black Walnut Price 12, 20, 28 ga., .410 and 20-ga. Youth **$692.00**

MOSSBERG INTERNATIONAL GOLD RESERVE SPORTING SERIES

Gauge: 12 ga. 3 in., 20 ga. 3 in., and .410 bore 3 in. Barrels: 28 or 30 in. ventilated rib. Weight: 6.5–7.5 lbs. Length: 45.0–48.0 in. Stock: Grade-A Satin Black Walnut. Adjustable stock on Super Sport model. Features: Dual locking lugs and Jeweled action. Chrome-lined bores and chambers. Competition-ready dual shell ejectors. Tang-mounted safety/barrel selector with scroll engraving. Polished silver receiver with scroll-engraved receiver with 24-Karat gold inlay on the underside receiver. Black Label variants wear polished black receiver with same embellishments. Includes set of five Extended Sport chokes (SK, IC, M, IM, F).

Price: Black Walnut 12 or 20 ga., .410 ....**$983.00**
Price: Black Label 12 ga. **$983.00**
Price: Super Sport in 12 ga with fully adjustable stock **$1,221.00**

PERAZZI HIGH TECH 2020

Gauge: 12 ga., 3 in. Barrels: 27-9/16 in., 28-3/8 in., 29-1/2 in., 30-3/4 in., 31-1/2 in., flat ramped stepped 9/32 x 3/8 in. rib. Weight: 8 lbs.-8 lbs., 8 oz. Stock: Oil-finish, high-grade walnut, HT design standard or custom adjustable. Features: The competition grade High Tech 2020 is made in Italy. Logo engraving across silver-finish receiver. Hand-cut checkering, blued-steel barrels. Removeable trigger group with coil or flat springs and selector. Ventilated mid-rib. Interchangeable chokes available on demand.

Price: **$21,075.00**

PERAZZI MX8/MX8 TRAP/SKEET

Gauge: 12 ga., 20 ga. 2 3/4 in. Barrels: Trap: 29.5 in. (Imp. Mod. & Extra Full), 31.5 in. (Full & Extra Full). Choke tubes optional. Skeet: 27.625 in. (skeet & skeet). Weights: About 8.5 lbs. (trap); 7 lbs., 15 oz. (skeet). Stock: Interchangeable and custom made to customer specs. Features: Has detachable and interchangeable trigger group with flat V springs. Flat .4375 in. vent rib. Many options available. Imported from Italy by Perazzi USA, Inc.

Price: Trap **$11,760.00**
Price: Skeet **$11,760.00**

PERAZZI MX8

Gauge: 12 ga., 20 ga. 2 3/4 in. Barrels: 28.375 in. (Imp. Mod. & Extra Full), 29.50 in. (choke tubes). Weight: 7 lbs., 12 oz. Stock: Special specifications. Features: Has single selective trigger; flat .4375 in. x .3125 in. vent rib. Many options available. Imported from Italy by Perazzi USA, Inc.

Price: Standard **$11,760.00**
Price: Sporting **$11,760.00**
Price: SC3 Grade (variety of engraving patterns) **$21,000.00**
Price: SCO Grade (more intricate engraving/inlays) **$36,000.00**

PERAZZI MX12 HUNTING

Gauge: 12 ga., 2 3/4 in. Barrels: 26.75 in., 27.5 in., 28.375 in., 29.5 in. (Mod. & Full); choke tubes available in 27.625 in., 29.5 in. only (MX12C). Weight: 7 lbs., 4 oz. Stock: To customer specs; interchangeable. Features: Single selective trigger; coil springs used in action; Schnabel fore-end tip. Imported from Italy by Perazzi USA, Inc.

Price: $12,700.00
Price: MX12C (with choke tubes) $12,700.00

PERAZZI MX20 HUNTING

Gauges: 20 ga., 28 ga., .410 with 2 3/4 in. or 3 in. chambers. Barrel: 26 in. standard barrel choked Mod. & Full. Weight: 6 lbs., 6 oz. Features: Similar to the MX12 except 20 ga. frame size. Non-removable trigger group. Imported from Italy by Perazzi USA, Inc.

Price: $12,700.00
Price: MX20C (with choke tubes) $13,700.00

PERAZZI MX2000S

Gauges: 12 ga., 20 ga. Barrels: 29.5 in., 30.75 in., 31.5 in. with fixed I/M and Full chokes, or interchangeable. Competition model with features similar to MX8.

Price: $13,200.00

PERAZZI MX15 UNSINGLE TRAP

Gauge: 12 ga. Barrel: 34 in. with fixed Full choke. Features: Bottom single barrel with 6-notch adjustable rib, adjustable stock, drop-out trigger or interchangeable. Competition model with features similar to MX8.

Price: $9,175.00

PIOTTI BOSS

Gauges: 12 ga., 16 ga., 20 ga., 28 ga., .410 bore. Barrels: 26–32 in., chokes as specified. Weight: 6.5–8 lbs. Stock: Dimensions to customer specs. Best quality figured walnut. Features: Essentially a custom-made gun with many options. Introduced 1993. SportingModel is production model with many features of custom series Imported from Italy by Wm. Larkin Moore.

Price: $78,000.00
Price: Sporting Model...$27,200.00

RIZZINI AURUM

Gauges: 12 ga., 16 ga., 20 ga., 28 ga., .410 bore. Barrels: 26, 28, 29 and 30, set of five choke tubes. Weight: 6.25 to 6.75 lbs. (Aurum Light 5.5 to 6.5 lbs.) Stock: Select Turkish walnut with Prince of Wales grip, rounded fore-end. Hand checkered with polished oil finish. Features: Boxlock low-profile action, single selective trigger, automatic ejectors, engraved game scenes in relief, light coin finish with gold inlay. Aurum Light has alloy receiver.

Price: 12, 16, 20 ga..$3,425.00
Price: 28, .410 bore..$3,625.00
Price: Aurum Light 12, 16, 20 ga...$3,700.00
Price: Aurum Light 28, .410 bore...$3,900.00

RIZZINI ARTEMIS

Gauges: 12 ga., 16 ga., 20 ga., 28 ga., .410 bore. Same as Upland EL model except dummy sideplates with extensive game scene engraving. Fancy European walnut stock. Fitted case. Introduced 1996. Imported from Italy by Fierce Products and by Wm. Larkin Moore & Co.

Price: $3,975.00
Price: Artemis Light $4,395.00

RIZZINI BR 460

Gauge: 12 ga., 3 in. Barrels: 30 in., 32 in., with 10mm x 6mm ventilated rib. Length: 43-45 in. Weight: 8.3 lbs. Stock: Walnut with hand-rubbed oil finish and adjustable comb. Features: These Rizzini O/U Competition guns are produced in Skeet, Sporting, Trap, and Double Trap, each with different characteristics. Choice of fixed or interchangeable chokes and fixed, adjustable or ramped rib. Stock checkered at 28 LPI. White rounded style front sight with silver mid-bead. Rubber buttpad. Either standard or long forcing cones depending on model. Ships with hard case and velvet stock sleeve.

Price: $7,045.00

RIZZINI FIERCE 1 COMPETITION

Gauges: 12 ga., 20 ga., 28 ga. Barrels: 28, 30 and 32 in. Five extended completion choke tubes. Weight: 6.6 to 8.1 lbs. Stock: Select Turkish walnut, hand checkered with polished oil finish. Features: Available in trap, skeet or sporting models. Adjustable stock and rib available. Boxlock low-profile action, single selective trigger, automatic ejectors, engraved game scenes in relief, light coin finish with gold inlay. Aurum Light has alloy receiver.

Price: $4,260.00

Prices given are believed to be accurate at time of publication however, many factors affect retail pricing so exact prices are not possible.

SKB 90TSS

Gauges: 12 ga., 20 ga., 2 3/4 in. Barrels: 28 in., 30 in., 32 in. Three SKB Competition choke tubes (SK, IC, M for Skeet and Sporting Models; IM, M, F for Trap). Lengthened forcing cones. Stock: Oil finished walnut with Pachmayr recoil pad. Weight: 7.1–7.9 lbs. Sights: Ventilated rib with target sights. Features: Boxlock action, bright blue finish with laser engraved receiver. Automatic ejectors, single trigger with selector switch incorporated in thumb-operated tang safety. Sporting and Trap models have adjustable comb and buttpad system. Imported from Turkey by GU, Inc.
Price: Skeet **$1,470.00**
Price: Sporting Clays, Trap..**$1,800.00**

STEVENS MODEL 555

Gauges: 12 ga., 20 ga., 28 ga., .410; 2 3/4 and 3 in. Barrels: 26 in., 28 in. Weights: 5.5–6 lbs. Features: Five screw-in choke tubes with 12 ga., 20 ga., and 28 ga.; .410 has fixed M/IC chokes. Turkish walnut stock and Schnabel fore-end. Single selective mechanical trigger with extractors.
Price: **$705.00**
Price: Enhanced Model..**$879.00**

STOEGER CONDOR

Gauge: 12 ga., 20 ga., 2 3/4 in., 3 in.; 16 ga., .410. Barrels: 22 in., 24 in., 26 in., 28 in., 30 in. Weights: 5.5–7.8 lbs. Sights: Brass bead. Features: IC, M, or F screw-in choke tubes with each gun. Oil finished hardwood with pistol grip and fore-end. Auto safety, single trigger, automatic extractors.
Price: ....**$449.00–$669.00**
Price: Combo with 12 and 20 ga. barrel sets **$899.00**
Price: Competition..**$669.00**

STOEGER CONDOR

Gauge: 12 ga. 3 in. Barrels: 28 in. ventilated rib. Length: 44.0 in. Weight: 7.3 lbs. Stock: Black synthetic. Features: Stoeger expands the Condor family of budget-priced O/U shotguns with the most affordable yet. Single trigger, tang-mounted safety/selector. Bead front sight. Shell extractors. Matte black metalwork. Black rubber buttpad. Ships with two interchangeable chokes (Mod and IC).
Price: **$349.00**

TRISTAR HUNTER MAG CAMO

Gauge: 12 ga., 3.5 in. Barrels: 26 in., 28 in., 30 in., ventilated rib. Length: 44-48 in. Weight: 7.3-7.9 lbs. Stock: Synthetic, with choice of black or numerous Mossy Oak patterns. Features: The 3.5-inch magnum chambered Hunter Mag O/U expands with the addition of Cerakote/Mossy Oak combination models. Steel mono-block construction, extractors, rubber recoil pad, fiber-optic front sight, single selective trigger, chrome-lined barrel, swivel studs. Includes five Mobil-style choke tubes (SK, IC, M, IM, F).
Price: ....**$655.00-$760.00**

TRISTAR SETTER

Gauge: 12 ga., 20 ga., 3-in. Barrels: 28 in. (12 ga.), 26 in. (20 ga.) with ventilated rib, three Beretta-style choke tubes. Weights: 6.3–7.2 pounds. Stock: High gloss wood. Single selective trigger, extractors.
Price: ....**$535.00-$565.00**
Price: Sporting Model...**$824.00-$915.00**

TRISTAR TT-15 FIELD

Gauges: 12 ga., 3 in., 20 ga., 3 in., 28 ga., 2.75 in., .410 bore, 3 in. Barrel: 28 in., ventilated rib. Length: 45 in. Weight: 5.7-7.0 lbs. Stock: Turkish walnut. Features: Field hunting O/U model with steel mono-block construction, mid-rib, top-tang barrel selector and safety. Chrome-lined barrel and chamber, engraved silver receiver, single selective trigger, fiber-optic front sight, auto ejectors. Includes five Mobil-style extended, color-coded chokes (SK, IC, M, IM, F).
Price: **$855.00**

TRISTAR TRINITY

Gauges: 12 ga., 3 in., 16 ga., 2.75 in., 20 ga., 3 in. Barrels: 26 in., 28 in., steel ventilated rib. Weight: 6.3-6.9 lbs. Length: 43.5-45.5 in. Stock: Oil-finished Turkish walnut with checkering. Features: The CNC-machined all-steel receiver Trinity wears 24-karat gold inlay on the silver-finish engraved receiver. Barrels are blued steel. Single selective trigger, red fiber-optic front sight, rubber buttpad, dual extractors. Includes five Beretta Mobil-style chokes (SK, IC, M, IM, F).
Price: **$685.00**

TRISTAR TRINITY LT

Gauges: 12 ga., 3 in., 20 ga., 3 in., 28 ga., 2.75 in., .410 bore, 3 in. Barrels: 26 in., 28 in, ventilated rib. Weight: 5.3-6.3 lbs. Length: 43.5-45.5 in. Stock: Oil-finished Turkish walnut with checkering. Features: The CNC-machined lightweight aluminum-alloy receiver Trinity LT is engraved and wears a silver finish. Barrels are blued steel. Single selective trigger, red fiber-optic front sight, rubber buttpad, dual extractors. Includes five Beretta Mobil-style chokes (SK, IC, M, IM, F).
Price: ....**$685.00–$700.00**

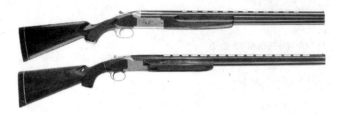

WINCHESTER MODEL 101

Gauge: 12 ga., 2 3/4 in., 3 in. Barrels: 28 in., 30 in., 32 in., ported, Invector Plus choke system. Weights: 7 lbs. 6 oz.–7 lbs. 12. oz. Stock: Checkered high-gloss grade II/III walnut stock, Pachmayr Decelerator sporting pad. Features: Chrome-plated chambers; back-bored barrels; tang barrel selector/safety; Signature extended choke tubes. Model 101 Field comes with solid brass bead front sight, three tubes, engraved receiver. Model 101 Sporting has adjustable trigger, 10mm runway rib, white mid-bead, Tru-Glo front sight, 30 in. and 32 in. barrels. Model 101 Pigeon Grade Trap has 10mm steel runway rib, mid-bead sight, interchangeable fiber-optic front sight, porting and vented side ribs, adjustable trigger shoe, fixed raised comb or adjustable comb, Grade III/IV walnut, 30 in. or 32 in. barrels, molded ABS hard case. Reintroduced 2008. Made in Belgium by FN. Winchester 150th Anniversary Commemorative model has grade IV/V stock, deep relief scrolling on a silver nitride finish receiver.
Price: Field **$1,900.00**
Price: Sporting **$2,380.00**
Price: Pigeon Grade Trap **$2,520.00**
Price: Pigeon Grade Trap w/adj. comb..**$2,680.00**

WINCHESTER 101 LIGHT

Gauge: 12 ga., 3 in. Barrels: 26 in., 28 in., ventilated rib. Length: 43-45 in. Weight: 6 lbs.-6 lbs., 4 oz. Stock: Grade II/III Turkish walnut. Features: Similar to the Model 101, but weighs 1 pound less with its aluminum-alloy receiver; adorned with quail on the right and flushing pheasants on the left. Pachmayr Decelerator buttpad with white-line spacer, chrome-plated back-bored barrels, cut checkering, steel grip cap, brass front bead. Includes three Invector Plus chokes (F, M, IC).
Price: **$1,869.00**

WINCHESTER 101 DELUXE FIELD

Gauge: 12 ga., 3 in. Barrels: 26 in., 28 in., ventilated rib. Length: 43-45 in. Weight: 6 lbs., 12 oz. Stock: Grade III European walnut. Features: Classic field gun design on the proven 101 line of O/U shotguns. Detailed engraving on the sides of the steel receiver. Blued metalwork. Pachmayr Decelerator recoil pad, hard-chrome-plated chamber and bore, steel grip cap, brass bead front, white mid-bead. Includes three Invector Plus chokes (F, M, IC).
Price: **$1,999.00**
Price: Deluxe Field Maple..**$1,999.00**

ARRIETA SIDELOCK DOUBLE

Gauges: 12 ga., 16 ga., 20 ga., 28 ga., .410 bore. Barrels: Length and chokes to customer specs. Weight: To customer specs. Stock: To customer specs. Straight English with checkered butt (standard), or pistol grip. Select European walnut with oil finish. Features: Essentially custom gun with myriad options. H&H pattern hand-detachable sidelocks, selective automatic ejectors, double triggers (hinged front) standard. Some have self-opening action. Finish and engraving to customer specs. Imported from Spain by Quality Arms, Wm. Larking Moore and others.

Price: Model 557	$6,970.00
Price: Model 570	$7,350.00
Price: Model 578	$12,200.00
Price: Model 600 Imperial	$14,125.00
Price: Model 803	$17,000.00
Price: Model 931	$40,000.00

BERETTA 486 PARALELLO

Gauges: 12 ga., 20 ga., 3 in., or 28 ga. 2 3/4 in. Barrels: 26 in., 28 in., 30 in. Weight: 7.1 lbs. Stock: English-style straight grip, splinter fore-end. Select European walnut, checkered, oil finish. Features: Round action, Optima-Choke Tubes. Automatic ejection or mechanical extraction. Firing-pin block safety, manual or automatic, open top-lever safety. Imported from Italy by Beretta USA

Price: $5,350.00

CHARLES DALY 500

Gauge: .410 bore, 3 in. Barrel: 28 in. Length: 43.25 in. Weight: 4.4 lbs. Stock: Checkered walnut English-style buttstock. Features: Charles Daly's new pair of baby-bore SxS Model 500 includes two versions, both steel, one with a black engraved receiver and the other black engraved with gold accents. Double triggers, extractors, manual safety, brass front bead. Includes five Mobil-style chokes (SK, IC, M, IM, F).

Price: $725.00–$875.00

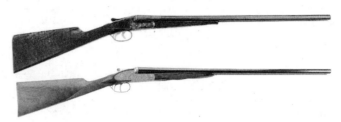

CIMARRON 1878 COACH GUN

Gauge: 12 ga. 3 in. Barrels: 20 in., 26 in. Weights: 8–9 lbs. Stock: Hardwood. External hammers, double triggers. Finish: Blue, Cimarron "USA", Cimarron "Original."

Price: Blue $597.00 (20 in.)–$623.00 (26 in.)

CIMARRON DOC HOLLIDAY MODEL

Gauge: 12 ga. Barrels: 20 in., cylinder bore. Stock: Hardwood with rounded pistol grip. Features: Double triggers, hammers, false sideplates.

Price: $1,581.00

CONNECTICUT SHOTGUN MANUFACTURING CO. RBL

Gauges: 12 ga., 16 ga., 20 ga.. Barrels: 26 in., 28 in., 30 in., 32 in. Weight: NA. Length: NA. Stock: NA. Features: Round-action SxS shotguns made in the USA. Scaled frames, five TruLock choke tubes. Deluxe fancy grade walnut buttstock and fore-end. Quick Change recoil pad in two lengths. Various dimensions and options available depending on gauge.

Price: 12 ga.	$3,795.00
Price: 16 ga.	$3,795.00
Price: 20 ga. Special Custom Model	$7,995.00

CONNECTICUT SHOTGUN MANUFACTURING CO. MODEL 21

Gauges: 12 ga., 16 ga., 20 ga., 28 ga., .410 bore. Features: A faithful re-creation of the famous Winchester Model 21. Many options and upgrades are available. Each frame is machined from specially produced proof steel. The 28 ga. and .410 guns are available on the standard frame or on a newly engineered small frame. These are custom guns and are made to order to the buyer's individual specifications, wood, stock dimensions, barrel lengths, chokes, finishes and engraving.

Price: 12 ga., 16 ga. or 20 ga	$15,000.00
Price: 28 ga. or .410	$18,000.00

CZ ALL TERRAIN SERIES

Gauges: 12 ga., 3 in., 20 ga., 3 in. Barrels: 28 in., 30 in. Stock: Walnut, various styles. Features: CZ's new All-Terrain series encompasses five existing shotgun models. The new package includes upgraded wood, OD Green Cerakote finish on all metalwork, as well as a set of rare earth magnets added to the extractor/ejectors of the SxS and O/U models to keep shells from dropping out while handling a dog or working in the blind.

Price: Bobwhite G2 All-Terrain 12 ga. or 20 ga. $828.00

CZ SHARP-TAIL

Gauges: 12 ga., 20 ga., 28 ga., .410. (5 screw-in chokes in 12 and 20 ga. and fixed chokes in IC and Mod in .410). Barrels: 26 in. or 28 in. Weight: 6.5 lbs. Stock: Hand-checkered Turkish walnut with straight English-style grip and single selective trigger.

Price: Sharp-Tail	$1,022.00
Price: Sharp-Tail Target	$1,298.00

CZ HAMMER COACH

Gauge: 12 ga., 3 in. Barrel: 20 in. Weight: 6.7 lbs. Features: Following in the tradition of the guns used by the stagecoach guards of the 1880s, this cowboy gun features double triggers, 19th-century color casehardening and fully functional external hammers.

Price:	$922.00
Price: Classic model w/30-in. bbls.	$963.00

EMF MODEL 1878 WYATT EARP

Gauge: 12. Barrel: 20 in.. Weight: 8 lbs. Length: 37 in. overall. Stock: Smooth walnut with steel butt place. Sights: Large brass bead. Features: Colt-style exposed hammers rebounding type; blued receiver and barrels; cylinder bore. Based on design of Colt Model 1878 shotgun. Made in Italy by Pedersoli.

Price:	$1,590.00
Price: Hartford Coach Model	$1,150.00

EUROPEAN AMERICAN ARMORY (EAA) CHURCHILL 512

Gauges: 12 ga., 3in., 20 ga., 3 in., 28 ga., 3 in., .410 bore. Barrels: 26 in., 28 in. Length: 45-47 in. Stock: Standard Turkish walnut. Features: These Turkish made Akkar side-by-sides have a Nitride-silver receiver, rubber buttpad, checkered stock, single selective gold-plated trigger, front bead, manual safety, chrome-lined barrels, extractors. Ships with three choke tubes.

Price: $1,355.00

FABARM AUTUMN

Gauges: 20 ga. 3 in. Barrels: 28 or 30 in. with textured top rib. Weight: 5 lbs. 9 oz.–6 lbs. 2 oz. Stock: Deluxe Turkish Walnut with hand-oiled matte finish. Available in either English-style straight stock or standard pistol grip style. Left-hand option available by special order. Features: Fine grade side-by-side built in Italy. Color casehardened receiver finish with ornamental scroll engraving. Four lug locking system. Monolithic action design machined from steel forging. Splinter fore-end with English stock or Semi-beavertail with pistol-grip stock. Hand-fit walnut buttplate. Single trigger, tang-mounted safety/selector, auto-ejectors. Ships with Integrale case. Includes five INNER HP long choke tubes.

Price: $4,095.00

FAUSTI DEA SERIES

Gauges: 12 ga., 16 ga., 20 ga., 28 ga., .410. Barrels: 26 in., 28 in., 30 in. Weight: 6–6.8 lbs. Stock: AAA walnut, oil finished. Straight grip, checkered butt, classic fore-end. Features: Automatic ejectors, single non-selective trigger. Duetto model is in 28 ga. with extra set of .410 barrels. Made in Italy and imported by Fausti, USA.

Price: 12 ga. or 20 ga. **$5,590.00**
Price: 16 ga., 28 ga., .410 ....**$6,260.00**
Price: Duetto **$5,790.00**

FOX, A.H.

Gauges: 16 ga., 20 ga., 28 ga., .410. Barrels: Length and chokes to customer specifications. Rust-blued Chromox or Krupp steel. Weight: 5.5–6.75 lbs. Stock: Dimensions to customer specifications. Hand-checkered Turkish Circassian walnut with hand-rubbed oil finish. Straight, semi or full pistol grip; splinter, Schnabel or beavertail fore-end; traditional pad, hard rubber buttplate or skeleton butt. Features: Boxlock action with automatic ejectors; double or Fox single selective trigger. Scalloped, rebated and color case-hardened receiver; hand finished and hand-engraved. Grades differ in engraving, inlays, grade of wood, amount of hand finishing. Introduced 1993. Made in U.S. by Connecticut Shotgun Mfg.

Price: CE Grade **$19,500.00**
Price: XE Grade **$22,000.00**
Price: DE Grade **$25,000.00**
Price: FE Grade..**$30,000.00**
Price: 28 ga./.410 CE Grade **$21,500.00**
Price: 28 ga./.410 XE Grade **$24,000.00**
Price: 28 ga./.410 DE Grade **$27,000.00**
Price: 28 ga./.410 FE Grade............................**$32,000.00**

MERKEL MODEL 147SL

H&H style sidelock action with cocking indicators, ejectors. Silver-grayed receiver and sideplates have arabesque engraving, fine hunting scene engraving. Limited edition. Imported from Germany by Merkel USA.
Price: Model 147SL **$13,255.00**

MERKEL MODEL 280EL, 360EL

Similar to Model 47E except smaller frame. Greener crossbolt with double under-barrel locking lugs, fine engraved hunting scenes on silver-grayed receiver, luxury-grade wood, Anson and Deeley boxlock action. H&H ejectors, single-selective or double triggers. Introduced 2000. Imported from Germany by Merkel USA.
Price: Model 280EL (28 ga., 28 in. barrel, Imp. Cyl.
and Mod. chokes) **$8,870.00**
Price: Model 360EL (.410, 28 in. barrel, Mod. and Full chokes).......**$8,870.00**

MERKEL MODEL 280SL AND 360SL

Similar to Model 280EL and 360EL except has sidelock action, double triggers, English-style arabesque engraving. Introduced 2000. Imported from Germany by Merkel USA.
Price: Model 280SL (28 ga., 28 in. barrel, Imp. Cyl.
and Mod. chokes) **$13,255.00**
Price: Model 360SL (.410, 28 in. barrel, Mod. and Full chokes) **$13,255.00**

MERKEL MODEL 1620

Gauge: 16 ga. Features: Greener crossbolt with double under-barrel locking lugs, scroll-engraved casehardened receiver, Anson and Deeley boxlock action, Holland & Holland ejectors, English-style stock, single selective or double triggers, or pistol grip stock with single selective trigger. Imported from Germany by Merkel USA.
Price: Model 1620EL **$8,870.00**
Price: Model 1620EL Combo; 16- and 20-ga. two-barrel set **$13,255.00**

MERKEL MODEL 40E

Gauges: 12 ga., 20 ga. Barrels: 28 in. (12 ga.), 26.75 in. (20 ga.). Weight: 6.2 lbs. Features: Anson & Deeley locks, Greener-style crossbolt, automatic ejectors, choice of double or single trigger, blue finish, checkered walnut stock with cheekpiece.
Price: **$4,795.00**

PIOTTI KING NO. 1

Gauges: 12 ga., 16 ga., 20 ga., 28 ga., .410. Barrels: 25–30 in. (12 ga.), 25–28 in. (16 ga., 20 ga., 28 ga., .410). To customer specs. Chokes as specified. Weight: 6.5–8 lbs. (12 ga. to customer specs.). Stock: Dimensions to customer specs. Finely figured walnut; straight grip with checkered butt with classic splinter fore-end and hand-rubbed oil finish standard. Pistol grip, beavertail fore-end. Features: Holland & Holland pattern sidelock action, automatic ejectors. Double trigger; non-selective single trigger optional. Coin finish standard; color case-hardened optional. Top rib; level, file-cut; concave, ventilated optional. Very fine, full coverage scroll engraving with small floral bouquets. Imported from Italy by Wm. Larkin Moore.
Price: **$42,800.00**

PIOTTI LUNIK SIDE-BY-SIDE SHOTGUN

Similar to the Piotti King No. 1 in overall quality. Has Renaissance-style large scroll engraving in relief. Best quality Holland & Holland-pattern sidelock ejector double with chopper lump (demi-bloc) barrels. Other mechanical specifications remain the same. Imported from Italy by Wm. Larkin Moore.
Price: **$46,000.00**

PIOTTI PIUMA

Gauges: 12 ga., 16 ga., 20 ga., 28 ga., .410. Barrels: 25–30 in. (12 ga.), 25–28 in. (16 ga., 20 ga., 28 ga., .410). Weights: 5.5–6.25 lbs. (20 ga.). Stock: Dimensions to customer specs. Straight grip stock with walnut checkered butt, classic splinter fore-end, hand-rubbed oil finish are standard; pistol grip, beavertail fore-end, satin luster finish optional. Features: Anson & Deeley boxlock ejector double with chopper lump barrels. Level, file-cut rib, light scroll and rosette engraving, scalloped frame. Double triggers; single non-selective optional. Coin finish standard, color case-hardened optional. Imported from Italy by Wm. Larkin Moore.
Price: **$25,000.00**

SAVAGE FOX A-GRADE

Gauge: 12 or 20. Barrels: 26 or 28 in. with solid rib and IC, M, and F choke tubes. Features: Straight-grip American walnut stock with splinter fore-end, oil finish and cut checkering. Anson & Deeley-style boxlock action, Holland & Holland-style ejectors, double triggers and brass bead sight. A re-creation of the famous Fox double gun, presented by Savage and made at the Connecticut Shotgun Manufacturing Co. plant.
Price: **$5,375.00**

SKB 200 SERIES

Gauges: 12 ga., 20 ga., .410, 3 in.; 28 ga., 2 3/4 in. Barrels: 26 in., 28 in. Five choke tubes provided (F, IM, M, IC, SK). Stock: Hand checkered and oil finished Turkish walnut. Prince of Wales grip and beavertail fore-end. Weight: 6–7 lbs. Sights: Brass bead. Features: Boxlock with platform lump barrel design. Polished bright blue finish with charcoal color case hardening on receiver. Manual safety, automatic ejectors, single selective trigger. 200 HR target model has high ventilated rib, full pistol grip. 250 model has decorative color casehardened sideplates. Imported from Turkey by GU, Inc.
Price: 12 ga., 20 ga.......................................**$2,100.00**
Price: 28 ga., .410..**$2,250.00**
Price: 200 28 ga./.410 Combo **$3,300.00**
Price: 200 HR 12 ga., 20 ga. **$2,500.00**
Price: 200 HR 28 ga., .410...............................**$2,625.00**
Price: 200 HR 28 ga./.410 combo **$3,600.00**
Price: 250 12 ga., 20 ga..................................**$2,600.00**
Price: 250 28 ga., .410...................................**$2,725.00**
Price: 250 28 ga./.410 Combo..........................**$3,700.00**

SKB 7000SL SIDELOCK

Gauges: 12 ga., 20 ga. Barrels: 28 in., 30 in. Five choke tubes provided (F, IM, M, IC, SK). Stock: Premium Turkish walnut with hand-rubbed oil finish, fine-line hand checkering, Prince of Wales grip and beavertail fore-end. Weights: 6–7 lbs. Sights: Brass bead. Features: Sidelock design with Holland & Holland style seven-pin removable locks with safety sears. Bison Bone Charcoal casehardening, hand engraved sculpted sidelock receiver. Manual safety, automatic ejectors, single selective trigger. Available by special order only. Imported from Turkey by GU, Inc.
Price: **$6,500.00**

Prices given are believed to be accurate at time of publication however, many factors affect retail pricing so exact prices are not possible.

76TH EDITION, 2022 ✛ **517**

STOEGER UPLANDER

Gauges: 12 ga., 20 ga., .410, 3 in.; 28 ga., 2 3/4. Barrels: 22 in., 24 in., 26 in., 28 in. Weights: 6.5–7.3 lbs. Sights: Brass bead. Features: Double trigger, IC & M choke tubes included with gun. Other choke tubes available. Tang auto safety, extractors, black plastic buttplate. Imported by Benelli USA.

Price: Standard **$449.00**
Price: Supreme (single trigger, AA-grade wood) **$549.00**
Price: Longfowler (12 ga., 30-in. bbl.) **$449.00**
Price: Home Defense (20 or 12 ga., 20-in. bbl., tactical sights) **$499.00**
Price: Double Defense (20 ga.) fiber-optic sight, accessory rail **$499.00**

YILDIZ ELEGANT

Gauge: .410 bore, 3 in. Barrels: 26 in., 28 in., 30 in., with 7mm or 8mm rib. Weight: 4.8-6.0 lbs. Stock: Oil-finish selected walnut from standard through Grades 3 and 5, some pistol grip and others straight English-style. Features: Built of 4140 Steel, with varying degrees of receiver engraving. Manual or automatic safety, extractors or ejectors, depending on model. Single selective trigger, front bead, full black rubber recoil pad. Models include: A1, A3, A4, A5, and Special Lux. Includes five Mobil chokes. Manufactured in Turkey and imported/sold through Academy.

Price: **$479.00**

STOEGER COACH GUN

Gauges: 12 ga., 20 ga., 2 3/4 in., 3 in., .410 bore, Barrel: 20 in. Weight: 6.5 lbs. Stock: Brown hardwood, classic beavertail fore-end. Sights: Brass bead. Features: Double or single trigger, IC & M choke tubes included, others available. Tang auto safety, extractors, black plastic buttplate. Imported by Benelli USA.

Price: **$549.00**
Price: **$449.00**
Price: .410 bore, 3-inch, 20-in. barrel **$449.00**
Price: Black-finished hardwood/polished-nickel model **$549.00**

TRISTAR BRISTOL

Gauges: 12 ga. 3 in., 20 ga. 3 in., 28 ga. 2.75 in., .410 bore 3 in. Barrels: 28 in. Weight: 5.08–6.74 lbs. Stock: Select Turkish Walnut with oil finish, English style. Features: Side-by-side double available in four gauges, each built on a true steel frame. Laser-engraved detail. Features an English-style straight stock paired with case colored receiver. Dual-purpose tang safety/barrel selector. Auto-ejectors, brass front sight, single selective trigger. Chrome-lined chamber and barrel. Includes five Beretta-style choke tubes (SK, IC, M, IM, F).

Price: .... **$1,065.00–$1,100.00**

TRISTAR BRISTOL SILVER

Gauges: 12 ga. 3 in., 20 ga. 3 in., 28 ga. 2.75 in., .410 bore 3in. Barrels: 28 in. Weight: 5.08–6.74 lbs. Stock: Select Turkish Walnut with oil finish, pistol grip style. Features: Side-by-side double available in four gauges, each built on a true steel frame. Laser-engraved detail. Features a nickel-finished receiver with 24-Karat gold inlay on the bottom of the receiver, and semi-pistol grip-style stock. Dual-purpose tang safety-barrel selector. Auto-ejectors, brass front sight, single selective trigger. Chrome-lined chamber and barrel. Includes five Beretta-style choke tubes (SK, IC, M, IM, F).

Price: .... **$1,000.00–$1,040.00**

BROWNING BT-99 TRAP

Gauge: 12 ga. Barrels: 30 in., 32 in., 34 in. Stock: Walnut; standard or adjustable. Weights: 7 lbs. 11 oz.–9 lbs. Features: Back-bored single barrel; interchangeable chokes; beavertail forearm; extractor only; high rib.
Price: BT-99 w/conventional comb, 32- or 34-in. barrel.................**$1,470.00**
Price: BT-99 w/adjustable comb, 32- or 34-in. barrel.......................**$1,840.00**
Price: BT-99 Max High Grade w/adjustable comb, 32- or
    34-in. barrel..**$5,340.00**
Price: Micro Adjustable LOP Model...................................... **$1,669.00**

CHARLES DALY 101

Gauges: 12 ga., 3 in., 20 ga., 3in., .410 bore. Barrels: 26 in., 28 in. Weight: 5.0-8.1 lbs. Length: 41.75-43.75 in. Stock: Choice of either checkered walnut or black synthetic stocks. Features: These updated break-action single shots have become more affordable than ever. Though built of steel, they're still quite light. Brass front bead, manual safety, single trigger, extractor, rubber butt pad. Includes a Modified Beretta/Benelli Mobil choke tube.
Price: ....**$119.00-$129.00**

HENRY .410 LEVER-ACTION SHOTGUN

Gauge: .410, 2 1/2 in. Capacity: 5. Barrels: 20 or 24 in. with either no choke (20 in.) or full choke (24 in.). Stock: American walnut. Sights: Gold bead front only. Finish: Blued. Introduced in 2017. Features: Design is based on the Henry .45-70 rifle.
Price: 20-in. bbl..**$893.00**
Price: 24-in. bbl.. **$947.00**

HENRY SINGLE-SHOT SHOTGUN

Gauges: 12 ga., 20 ga. or .410 bore, 3 1/2 in. (12 ga.), 3 in. (20 ga. and 410). Barrels: 26 or 28 in. with either modified choke tube (12 ga., 20 ga., compatible with Rem-Choke tubes) or fixed full choke (.410). Stock: American walnut, straight or pistol grip. Sights: Gold bead front only. Weight: 6.33 lbs. Finish: Blued or brass receiver. Features: Break-open single-shot design. Introduced in 2017.
Price: **$448.00**
Price: Brass receiver, straight grip..**$576.00**

HENRY SINGLE SHOT SLUG

Gauges: 12 ga. 3 in. Barrel: 24-in. round blued steel. Weight: 6.88 lbs. Length: 39.5 in. Stock: American Walnut. Features: The company's first slug-hunting shotgun, with a fully-rifled 1:35 twist barrel. This single shot is finished in traditional blued steel and checkered walnut with a black rubber recoil pad. Buttstock has a 14-inch LOP. Sling studs. Rebounding hammer safety. Fiber optic sights. Drilled and tapped for a Weaver 82 base.
Price: $560.00

HENRY SINGLE SHOT TURKEY

Gauges: 12 ga. 3.5 in. Barrel: 24-in. round. Weight: 6.78 lbs. Length: 39.5 in. Stock: American Walnut covered in Mossy Oak Obsession camo. Features: The company's first dedicated turkey-hunting shotgun wears full-coverage Mossy Oak Obsession, the official camouflage pattern of the National Wild Turkey Federation. Fiber-optic front and rear sights. Drilled and tapped for a Weaver 82 base. Black solid rubber recoil pad creates a 14-inch LOP. Swivel studs. Rebounding hammer safety. Includes an extended Turkey choke.
Price: $687.00

KEYSTONE SPORTING ARMS 4100 My First Shotgun

Gauges: .410 bore 3 in. Barrel: 18.5 in. Length: 32 in. Weight: 4.2 lbs. Stock: Turkish Walnut. Features: Marketed as a Crickett "My First Shotgun," this single-shot baby bore uses a folding design. Recoil reducing chamber and soft rubber recoil pad. Aluminum receiver with matte blue metalwork. Blade-style front sight. Checkered stock. Length of pull built for small-frame shooters at 11 inches. Fixed modified choke.
Price: **$179.00**

KRIEGHOFF K-80 SINGLE BARREL TRAP GUN

Gauge: 12 ga., 2 3/4 in. Barrel: 32 in., 34 in. Unsingle. Fixed Full or choke tubes. Weight: About 8.75 lbs. Stock: Four stock dimensions or adjustable stock available. All hand-checkered European walnut. Features: Satin nickel finish. Selective mechanical trigger adjustable for finger position. Tapered step vent rib. Adjustable point of impact.
Price: Standard Grade Full Unsingle................................**$12,995.00**

KRIEGHOFF KX-6 SPECIAL TRAP GUN

Gauge: 12 ga., 2 3/4 in. Barrel: 32 in., 34 in.; choke tubes. Weight: About 8.5 lbs. Stock: Factory adjustable stock. European walnut. Features: Ventilated tapered step rib. Adjustable position trigger, optional release trigger. Fully adjustable rib. Satin gray electroless nickel receiver. Fitted aluminum case. Imported from Germany by Krieghoff International, Inc.
Price: **$5,995.00**

LJUTIC MONO GUN SINGLE BARREL

Gauge: 12 ga. Barrel: 34 in., choked to customer specs; hollow-milled rib, 35.5-in. sight plane. Weight: Approx. 9 lbs. Stock: To customer specs. Oil finish, hand checkered. Features: Custom gun. Pull or release trigger; removable trigger guard contains trigger and hammer mechanism; Ljutic pushbutton opener on front of trigger guard. From Ljutic Industries.
Price: Std., med. or Olympic rib, custom bbls., fixed choke. **$7,495.00**
Price: Stainless steel mono gun... **$8,495.00**

LJUTIC LTX PRO 3 DELUXE MONO GUN

Deluxe, lightweight version of the Mono gun with high-quality wood, upgrade checkering, special rib height, screw-in chokes, ported and cased.
Price: **$8,995.00**
Price: Stainless steel model..**$9,995.00**

ROSSI CIRCUIT JUDGE

Revolving shotgun chambered in .410 (2 1/2- or 3-in./.45 Colt. Based on Taurus Judge handgun. Features include 18.5-in. barrel; fiber-optic front sight; 5-round cylinder; hardwood Monte Carlo stock.
Price: **$689.00**

ROSSI TUFFY SINGLE SHOT 410 TURKEY

Gauge: .410 bore 3 in. Barrel: 26 in. Length: 41 in. Weight: 58.80 oz. Stock: Olive drab green polymer thumbhole-style with integral buttstock shell holders. Features: Part of Rossi's single-shot, break-action Tuffy family, the new 410 Turkey has an extended barrel length and gobbler-specific choke. Polymer receiver with steel frame structure. Matte black finish metalwork. Bead front sight. Picatinny top rail for easy optics mounting. Sling swivels. Black rubber buttpad. Transfer bar safety. Extended Extra Full Turkey choke.
Price: Standard Grade Full Unsingle **$220.00**

SAVAGE 212/220

Gauges: 12 ga., 3 in., 20 ga., 3 in. Barrel: 22 in., carbon steel. Weight: 7.34-7.75 lbs. Length: 43 in. Stock: Synthetic AccuFit stock with included LOP and comb inserts. Thumbhole model uses gray wood laminate. Features: The bolt-action Savage models 212 and 220, so named for their chamberings, are available in Slug, Slug Camo, Thumbhole, Left-Handed and Turkey models. Choice of button-rifled slug barrels or smoothbore. Detachable box magazine, thread-in barrel headspacing. User adjustable AccuTrigger and AccuStock internal chassis. Oversized bolt handle, Picatinny optics rail, sling studs, rubber buttpad.
Price: ....**$629.00–$799.00**
Price: 212 Turkey w/extended X-Full choke.......................... **$779.00**
Price: 220 Turkey w/extended X-Full choke.......................... **$695.00**

Prices given are believed to be accurate at time of publication however, many factors affect retail pricing so exact prices are not possible.

76TH EDITION, 2022 ✛ **519**

STEVENS 301 TURKEY XP
Gauges: 20 ga., 3 in., .410 bore, 3 in. Barrel: 26 in., black matte. Weight: 5.07 lbs. Length: 41.5 in. Stock: Camouflage synthetic stock and fore-end with either Mossy Oak Obsession or Mossy Oak Bottomland pattern. Features: Single-shot break action with removable one-piece rail. XP variant includes mounted and bore-sighted 1x30 red-dot optic. Barrel optimized for Federal Premium TSS Heavyweight turkey loads. Swivel studs, front bead, manual hammer block safety, rubber recoil pad. Includes Winchoke pattern Extra Full turkey choke.
Price: **$239.00**

STEVENS 301 TURKEY THUMBHOLE
Gauges: .410 bore 3 in. Barrel: 26 in. chrome alloy steel black matte. Weight: 5.07 lbs. Length: 41.5 in. Stock: Olive drab green matte synthetic thumbhole style. Features: Continuation of the 301 single-shot break-action line with a removeable one-piece rail and gobbler-specific features. Ambidextrous cheek riser. Barrel optimized for Federal Premium Heavyweight TSS turkey loads. Swivel studs, front bead sight, manual hammer block safety, rubber recoil pad. Includes Win-Choke pattern Extra Full turkey choke.
Price: **$229.00**

STEVENS 555 TRAP
Gauges: 12 ga., 3 in., 20 ga., 3 in. Barrel: 30 in., raised ventilated rib. Weight: 6.6-6.8 lbs. Length: 47.5 in. Stock: Turkish walnut stock and fore-end with adjustable comb and oil finish. Features: Lightweight silver aluminum receiver scaled to gauge with steel breech reinforcement. Top single barrel with shell extractor. Manual tang safety, front bead, chrome-lined barrel, semi-gloss metalwork finish. Includes three chokes.
Price: **$689.00**

STEVENS 555 TRAP COMPACT
Gauges: 12 ga., 3 in., 20 ga., 3 in. Barrel: 26 in., raised ventilated rib. Weight: 7.3-7.5 lbs. Length: 42.5 in. Stock: Turkish walnut stock and fore-end with adjustable comb and oil finish. Features: Lightweight silver aluminum receiver scaled to gauge with steel breech reinforcement. Top single barrel with shell extractor. Manual tang safety, front bead, chrome-lined barrel, semi-gloss metalwork finish. Compact 13.5 in. length of pull. Includes three chokes.
Price: **$689.00**

TAR-HUNT RSG-12 PROFESSIONAL RIFLED SLUG GUN
Gauge: 12 ga., 2 3/4 in., 3 in., Capacity: 1-round magazine. Barrel: 23 in., fully rifled with muzzle brake. Weight: 7.75 lbs. Length: 41.5 in. overall. Stock: Matte black McMillan fiberglass with Pachmayr Decelerator pad. Sights: None furnished; comes with Leupold windage or Weaver bases. Features: Uses rifle-style action with two locking lugs; two-position safety; Shaw barrel; single-stage, trigger; muzzle brake. Many options available. All models have area-controlled feed action. Introduced 1991. Made in U.S. by Tar-Hunt Custom Rifles, Inc.
Price: 12 ga. Professional model **$3,495.00**
Price: Left-hand model **$3,625.00**

TAR-HUNT RSG-20 MOUNTAINEER SLUG GUN
Similar to the RSG-12 Professional except chambered for 20 ga. (2 3/4 in. and 3 in. shells); 23 in. Shaw rifled barrel, with muzzle brake; two-lug bolt; one-shot blind magazine; matte black finish; McMillan fiberglass stock with Pachmayr Decelerator pad; receiver drilled and tapped for Rem. 700 bases. Right- or left-hand versions. Weighs 6.5 lbs. Introduced 1997. Made in USA by Tar-Hunt Custom Rifles, Inc.
Price: **$3,495.00**

HENRY SIDE GATE LEVER ACTION 410 MODEL H018G-410R
Gauge: .410 bore 2.5in. Barrel: 19.75 in. smoothbore, round blued steel. Weight: 7.09 lbs. Length: 38.1 in. Stock: American Walnut with checkering. Features: This model launches as a blued steel companion to Henry's polished brass version last year. This is the more compact of the pair of lever action 410's. Has Henry's new side-loading gate in addition to the tubular loading port and magazine capacity of six rounds. Adjustable semi-buckhorn rear sight with diamond insert and brass bead front post sight. Black ventilated rubber recoil pad, transfer bar safety, sling swivel studs. Fixed cylinder bore choke.
Price: **$969.00**

HENRY SIDE GATE LEVER ACTION 410 Model H018G-410
Gauges: .410 bore, 2.5 in. Barrel: 24 in. smoothbore, round blued steel. Weight: 7.54 lbs. Length: 42.75 in. Stock: American Walnut with checkering. Features: The new-for-2021 model is blued steel instead of polished brass. Has Henry's side loading gate in addition to the tubular loading port and magazine capacity of six rounds. Brass bead front sight. Black ventilated rubber recoil pad, sling swivel studs. Transfer bar safety. LOP of 14-inches. Drilled and tapped for a Weaver 63B optics base. Threaded for Invector-style chokes with a Full choke supplied.
Price: **$1,012.00**

HENRY SIDE GATE LEVER ACTION 410 Model H024-410
Gauge: .410 bore 2.5 in. Barrel: 19.8 in. smoothbore, round blued steel. Weight: 7.09 lbs. Length: 38.1 in. Stock: American walnut with intricate floral and Henry logo checkering appointments. Features: Polished brass receiver with Henry's new side loading gate in addition to the tubular loading port. Magazine capacity of six rounds. Fully adjustable semi-buckhorn rear sight with diamond insert and ramp front with 0.62-inch ivory bead. Polished brass buttplate, transfer bar safety, sling swivel studs. Fixed cylinder bore choke.
Price: **$1,100.00**

HENRY X-MODEL 410
Gauges: .410 bore 2.5 in. Barrel: 19.8 in. smoothbore, round blued steel. Weight: 7.5 lbs. Length: 38.6 in. Stock: Black synthetic with textured panels. Features: Henry's first blacked-out model with matte blued steel receiver. Side loading gate in addition to tubular port with magazine capacity of 6+1 rounds. Black solid rubber recoil pad. Green fiber-optic front sight, transfer bar safety, swivel studs, large loop lever. Tactical features include lower Picatinny rail and M-LOK attachment points at fore-end. Drilled and tapped for a Weaver 63B optics mount. Includes Invector choke.
Price: **$1,000.00**

BENELLI M2 TACTICAL
Gauge: 12 ga., 2 3/4 in., 3 in. Capacity: 5-round magazine. Barrel: 18.5 in. IC, M, F choke tubes. Weight: 6.7 lbs. Length: 39.75 in. overall. Stock: Black polymer. Standard or pistol grip. Sights: Rifle type ghost ring system, tritium night sights optional. Features: Semi-auto inertia recoil action. Cross-bolt safety; bolt release button; matte-finish metal. Introduced 1993. Imported from Italy by Benelli USA.
Price: .... **$1,239.00–$1,359.00**

BENELLI M3 TACTICAL
Gauge: 12 ga., 3 in. Barrel: 20 in. Stock: Black synthetic w/pistol grip. Sights: Ghost ring rear, ramp front. Convertible dual-action operation (semi-auto or pump).
Price: **$1,599.00**

BENELLI M4 TACTICAL
Gauge: 12 ga., 3 in. Barrel: 18.5 in. Weight: 7.8 lbs. Length: 40 in. overall. Stock: Synthetic. Sights: Ghost Ring rear, fixed blade front. Features: Auto-regulating gas-operated (ARGO) action, choke tube, Picatinny rail, standard and collapsible stocks available, optional LE tactical gun case. Introduced 2006.
Price: **$1,999.00**
Price: M4 H20 Cerakote Finish **$2,269.00**

BENELLI NOVA TACTICAL
Gauge: 12 ga., 3 in. Barrel: 18.5 in. Stock: Black synthetic standard or pistol grip. Sights: Ghost ring rear, ramp front. Pump action.
Price: **$439.00**

BENELLI VINCI TACTICAL
Gauge: 12 ga., 3 in. Barrel: 18.5 in. Semi-auto operation. Stock: Black synthetic. Sights: Ghost ring rear, ramp front.
Price: **$1,349.00**
Price: ComforTech stock **$1,469.00**

CHARLES DALY AR 410 UPPER
Gauge: .410 bore 2.5 in. Barrel: 19 in. Length: 26.75 in. Weight: 4.9 lbs. Stock: Upper only with quad Picatinny rail fore-end. Features: Charles Daly enters the AR market with a .410 bore shotgun upper. Built of black anodized aluminum. Auto-ejection, gas-operated system. Windage-adjustable rear sight and elevation adjustable rear flip-up sights. Ships with a five-round magazine but compatible with 10 and 15 rounders. This upper must be used with a Mil-Spec lower and carbine-length buffer tube.
Price: **$415.00**

IVER JOHNSON STRYKER-12
Gauge: 12 ga., 3 in. Barrel: 20 in., smoothbore with muzzle brake. Length: 43 in. Stock: Black synthetic two-piece, pistol-grip stock. Features: This AR15-style semi-auto shotgun uses a standard AR15 bolt and mag release. A2-style detachable carry handle with adjustable sight, fiber-optic front sight. Light rails on both sides and bottom of fore-end. Push button releases the stock and leaves the pistol grip for a modular platform. Cross-bolt safety, thick rubber buttpad. Ships with two MKA 1919 5-round box magazines.
Price: **$495.00**

KALASHNIKOV KOMP12
Gauge: 12 ga. 3 in. Barrel: 18.25 in. with external threading. Weight: 17 lbs. Stock: Synthetic skeleton-style, collapsible. Features: The Kalashnikov USA x Dissident Arms KOMP12 is an American-made semi-automatic based on the Russian Saiga series. Adjustable gas system. Extended charging handle, aluminum handguard rail, enhanced safety lever. Flared magazine well, tuned trigger. Top Picatinny rail for optics. Threaded flash suppressor. Magpul AK pistol grip. Zinc phosphate parkerized undercoat with Dissident Arms Black, Red, and Sniper Grey color scheme. Ships with Dissident SGM 12-round magazine.
Price: **$1,499.00**

KEL-TEC KSG BULL-PUP TWIN-TUBE
Gauge: 12 ga. Capacity: 13+1. Barrel: 18.5 in. Overall Length: 26.1 in. Weight: 8.5 lbs. (loaded). Features: Pump-action shotgun with two magazine tubes. The shotgun bears a resemblance to the South African designed Neostead pump-action gun. The operator is able to move a switch located near the top of the grip to select the right or left tube, or move the switch to the center to eject a shell without chambering another round. Optional accessories include a factory installed Picatinny rail with flip-up sights and a pistol grip. KSG-25 has 30-in. barrel and 20-round capacity magazine tubes.
Price: **$990.00**
Price: KSG-25 .... **$1400.00**

KEL-TEC KS7 BULLPUP
Gauge: 12 ga., 3 in. Capacity: 6+1. Barrel: 18.5 in. Length: 26.1 in. Weight: 5.9 lbs. Stock: Black synthetic bullpup. Features: The pump-action KS7 Bullpup is a compact self-defense shotgun. Carry handle, Picatinny rail, M-LOK mounting points. Rear loading, downward ejection, ambidextrous controls. Cylinder choke.
Price: **$495.00**

MOSSBERG MAVERICK 88 CRUISER
Gauges: 12 ga., 3 in., 20 ga., 3in. Capacity: 5+1 or 7+1 capacity. Barrels: 18.5 in., 20 in. Length: 28.125-30.375 in. Weight: 5.5-6.0 lbs. Stock: Black synthetic pistol grip. Features: Fixed cylinder bore choke, blued metalwork, bead front sight, cross-bolt safety.
Price: **$231.00**

MOSSBERG MODEL 500 SPECIAL PURPOSE
Gauges: 12 ga., 20 ga., .410, 3 in. Barrels: 18.5 in., 20 in. (Cyl.). Weight: 7 lbs. Stock: Walnut-finished hardwood or black synthetic. Sights: Metal bead front. Features: Slide-action operation. Available in 6- or 8-round models. Top-mounted safety, double action slide bars, swivel studs, rubber recoil pad. Blue, Parkerized, Marinecote finishes. Mossberg Cablelock included. The HS410 Home Security model chambered for .410 with 3 in. chamber; has pistol grip fore-end, thick recoil pad, muzzle brake and has special spreader choke on the 18.5-in. barrel. Overall length is 37.5 in. Blued finish; synthetic field stock. Mossberg Cablelock and video included. Mariner model has Marinecote metal finish to resist rust and corrosion. Synthetic field stock; pistol grip kit included. 500 Tactical 6-shot has black synthetic tactical stock. Introduced 1990.
Price: 500 Mariner **$636.00**
Price: HS410 Home Security **$477.00**
Price: Home Security 20 ga. **$631.00**
Price: FLEX Tactical **$672.00**
Price: 500 Chainsaw pistol grip only; removable top handle **$547.00**
Price: JIC (Just In Case) **$500.00**
Price: Thunder Ranch **$553.00**

Prices given are believed to be accurate at time of publication however, many factors affect retail pricing so exact prices are not possible.

76TH EDITION, 2022 ✦ 521

MOSSBERG MODEL 590 SPECIAL PURPOSE

Gauges: 12 ga., 20 ga., .410 3 in. Capacity: 9-round magazine. Barrel: 20 in. (Cyl.). Weight: 7.25 lbs. Stock: Synthetic field or Speedfeed. Sights: Metal bead front or Ghost Ring. Features: Slide action. Top-mounted safety, double slide action bars. Comes with heat shield, bayonet lug, swivel studs, rubber recoil pad. Blue, Parkerized or Marinecote finish. Shockwave has 14-inch heavy walled barrel, Raptor pistol grip, wrapped fore-end and is fully BATFE compliant. Magpul model has Magpul SGA stock with adjustable comb and length of pull. Mossberg Cablelock included. From Mossberg.

Price: **$559.00**
Price: Flex Tactical **$672.00**
Price: Tactical Tri-Rail Adjustable **$879.00**
Price: Mariner **$756.00**
Price: Shockwave .... **$455.00–$721.00**
Price: MagPul 9-shot **$836.00**

MOSSBERG 930 SPECIAL PURPOSE SERIES

Gauge: 12 ga., 3 in. Barrel: 18.5-28 in. flat ventilated rib. Weight: 7.3 lbs. Length: 49 in.. Stock: Composite stock with close radius pistol grip; Speed Lock forearm; textured gripping surfaces; shim adjustable for length of pull, cast and drop; Mossy Oak Bottomland camo finish; Dura-Touch Armor Coating. Features: 930 Special Purpose shotguns feature a self-regulating gas system that vents excess gas to aid in recoil reduction and eliminate stress on critical components. All 930 autoloaders chamber both 2 3/4 inch and 3-in. 12-ga. shotshells with ease — from target loads, to non-toxic magnum loads, to the latest sabot slug ammo. Magazine capacity is 7+1 on models with extended magazine tube, 4+1 on models without. To complete the package, each Mossberg 930 includes a set of specially designed spacers for quick adjustment of the horizontal and vertical angle of the stock, bringing a custom-feel fit to every shooter. All 930 Special Purpose models feature a drilled and tapped receiver, factory-ready for Picatinny rail, scope base or optics installation. 930 SPX models conveniently come with a factory-mounted Picatinny rail and LPA/M16-Style Ghost Ring combination sight right out of the box. Other sighting options include a basic front bead, or white-dot front sights. Mossberg 930 Special Purpose shotguns are available in a variety of configurations; 5-round tactical barrel, 5-round with muzzle brake, 8-round pistol-grip, and even a 5-round security/field combo.

Price: Tactical 5-Round **$612.00**
Price: Home Security **$662.00**
Price: Standard Stock **$787.00**
Price: Pistol Grip 8-Round **$1,046.00**
Price: 5-Round Combo w/extra 18.5-in. barrel **$693.00**
Price: Chainsaw **$564.00**

REMINGTON 870 DM SERIES

Gauge: 12 ga. (2 3/4 in., 3 in. interchangeably) **Barrel:** 18.5-in. cylinder bore. Detachable 6-round magazine. **Stock:** Hardwood or black synthetic with textured gripping surfaces. Tac-14 DM model features short pistol grip buttstock and 14-in. barrel.

Price: **$529.00**

REMINGTON MODEL 870 PUMP TACTICAL SHOTGUNS

Gauges: 12 ga., 2 3/4 or 3 in. Barrels: 18 in., 20 in., 22 in. (Cyl or IC). Weight: 7.5–7.75 lbs. Length: 38.5–42.5 in. overall. Stock: Black synthetic, synthetic Speedfeed IV full pistol-grip stock, or Knoxx Industries SpecOps stock w/ recoil-absorbing spring-loaded cam and adjustable length of pull (12 in. to 16 in., 870 only). Sights: Front post w/dot. Features: R3 recoil pads,

LimbSaver technology to reduce felt recoil, 2-, 3- or 4-round extensions based on barrel length; matte-olive-drab barrels and receivers. Standard synthetic-stocked version is equipped with 22-in. barrel and four-round extension. Introduced 2006. From Remington Arms Co.

Price: 870 Express Tactical Knoxx 20 ga. **$555.00**
Price: 870 Express Magpul **$898.00**
Price: 870 Special Purpose Marine (nickel) **$841.00**

REMINGTON 870 EXPRESS TACTICAL

Gauge: 12 ga., 2 3/4 and 3 in. Features: Pump-action shotgun; 18.5-in. barrel; extended ported Tactical RemChoke; SpeedFeed IV pistol-grip stock with SuperCell recoil pad; fully adjustable XS Ghost Ring Sight rail with removable white bead front sight; 7-round capacity with factory-installed 2-shot extension; drilled and tapped receiver; sling swivel stud.

Price: **$600.00**

REMINGTON 887 NITRO MAG TACTICAL

Gauge: 12 ga., 2 3/4 to 3 1/2 in. Features: Pump-action shotgun,18.5-in. barrel with ported, extended tactical RemChoke; 2-shot magazine extension; barrel clamp with integral Picatinny rails; ArmorLokt coating; synthetic stock and fore-end with specially contour grip panels.

Price: **$534.00**

REMINGTON V3 TACTICAL

Addition of two tactical models to the V3 lineup with the same VersaPort self-regulating gas system that works with any shotshell from 2.75 in. to 3 in. Capacity: 6+1. Both wear an 18.5 in. barrel and oversized controls. One model with rifle sights, the other with a vent rib and bead sights.

Price: .... **$1,024.00–$1,076.00**

REMINGTON V3 COMPETITION TACTICAL

Addition of competition tactical model to the exiting V3 lineup. This 12 ga. uses the same Versa-Port technology to self-regulate for any shotshell from 2.75 in. to 3in. Capacity: 8+1. Features: 22-inch barrel with Hi-Viz front sight and low-profile, dovetail-rib mounting rear sight and oversized controls.

Price: **$1,128.00**

RETAY MASAI MARA WARDEN

Gauge: 12 ga., 3 in. Barrel: 18.5 in. Weight: 6.6 lbs. Stock: Black Synthetic. Features: The Turkish-made Masai Mara line of semi-automatics uses an inertia-plus action and bolt system. Oversized controls, quick unload system, Picatinny rail, extended charging handle, ghost-ring sights. Push-button removeable trigger group. Microcell rubber recoil pad. Includes a hard case and ships with five MaraPro choke tubes.

Price: **$1,099.00**

ROCK ISLAND ARMORY/ARMSCOR VRBP-100

Gauge: 12 ga., 3 in. Capacity: 5+1. Barrel: 20 in. contoured. Length: 32 in. Weight: 7.94 lbs. Stock: Black polymer bullpup design with pistol grip. Features: Semi-automatic bullpup design. Compatible with all VR Series magazines. Matte-black anodized finish. Includes rubber spacers to adjust length of pull. Full length top rail with flip-up sights, right-sided Picatinny accessory rail. Ships with three interchangeable chokes.

Price: **$774.00**

Prices given are believed to be accurate at time of publication however, many factors affect retail pricing so exact prices are not possible.

ROCK ISLAND ARMORY/ARMSCOR VRPA-40
Gauge: 12 ga., 3 in. Capacity: 5+1. Barrel: 20 in., contoured. Length: 55.11 in. Weight: 6.9 lbs. Stock: Black synthetic. Features: The VRPA40 marks the more affordable pump action addition to the VR family of shotguns. Magazine fed, aluminum heat shield, fiber-optic front sight, adjustable rear sight, Picatinny rail. Marine black anodized, compatible with VR series 9-round magazines. Mobil chokes.
Price: **$399.00**

ROCK ISLAND ARMORY/ARMSCOR VR82
Gauge: 20 ga. 3 in. Barrel: 18 in. contoured. Length: 38 in. Weight: 7.5 lbs. Stock: Black polymer thumbhole style. Features: The semi-automatic VR82 is the little brother of the VR80. Built of 7075 T6 aluminum for lighter weight. Magazine fed with 5+1 capacity but also accepts VR-series 10- and 20-round mags. Ambidextrous controls, flip-up sights, barrel shroud. Fore-end accepts most aftermarket accessories. Compatible with most buffer tube stocks and pistol grips. Black anodized finish. Mobil choke.
Price: **$729.00**

STANDARD MANUFACTURING DP-12 PROFESSIONAL
Gauge: 12 ga. 3 in. Barrels: 18-7/8 in. Length: 29.5 in. Weight: 9 lb. 12 oz. Stock: Synthetic with anodized aluminum. Features: Upgraded Professional version of the pump-action DP-12 high-capacity defense shotgun. Additions include an aluminum rail with front grip, which wears an integral laser and flashlight. Precision-honed bores and chambers finished with hand-lapping. PVD coating on all critical wear areas. Mil-spec hard anodized finish with accents in either Blue or OD Green. Includes Reflex Sight with multiple brightness levels. Ships with both soft and hard cases
Price: **$3,250.00**

TACTICAL RESPONSE STANDARD MODEL
Gauge: 12 ga., 3 in. Capacity: 7-round magazine. Barrel: 18 in. (Cyl.). Weight: 9 lbs. Length: 38 in. overall. Stock: Fiberglass-filled polypropylene with non-snag recoil absorbing butt pad. Nylon tactical fore-end houses flashlight. Sights: Trak-Lock ghost ring sight system. Front sight has Tritium insert. Features: Highly modified Remington 870P with Parkerized finish. Comes with nylon three-way adjustable sling, high visibility non-binding follower, high-performance magazine spring, Jumbo Head safety, and Side Saddle extended 6-shotshell carrier on left side of receiver. Introduced 1991. From Scattergun Technologies, Inc.
Price: Standard model **$1,540.00**
Price: Border Patrol model **$1,135.00**
Price: Professional Model 13-in. bbl. (Law enf., military only)........**$1,550.00**

WINCHESTER SXP EXTREME DEFENDER
Gauge: 12 ga., 3 in. Barrel: 18 in., with Heat Shield. Length: 38.5 in. Weight: 7.0 lbs. Stock: Flat Dark Earth composite with textured grip panels and pistol grip. Features: Aluminum-alloy receiver, hard-chrome chamber and bore, Picatinny rail with ghost-ring sight, blade front sight. Two interchangeable comb pieces and two quarter-inch length-of-pull spacers for custom fit. Side-mounted Picatinny accessory rails, sling studs, Inflex recoil pad. Includes one Invector Plus cylinder choke and one Door Breacher choke.
Price: **$529.00**

Prices given are believed to be accurate at time of publication however, many factors affect retail pricing so exact prices are not possible.

76TH EDITION, 2022 ⨁ **523**

CHIAPPA LE PAGE PERCUSSION DUELING PISTOL

Caliber: .45. Barrel: 10 in. browned octagon, rifled. Weight: 2.5 lbs. Length: 16.6 in. overall. Stock: Walnut, rounded, fluted butt. Sights: Blade front, open-style rear. Features: Double set trigger. Bright barrel, silver-plated brass furniture. External ramrod. Made by Chiappa.
Price: Chiappa 940.001 .... **$779.00**

CVA OPTIMA PISTOL

Caliber: .50. Barrel: 14 in., 1:28-in. twist, Cerakote finish. Weight: 3.7 lbs. Length: 19 in. Stock: Black synthetic, Realtree Xtra Green. Sights: Scope base mounted. Features: Break-open action, all stainless construction, aluminum ramrod, quick-removal breech plug for 209 primer. From CVA.
Price: PP222SM Stainless/Realtree Xtra, rail mount **$354.00**
Price: PP221SM Stainless/black, rail mount **$307.00**

DIXIE MURDOCK SCOTTISH HIGHLANDER'S PISTOL

Caliber: .352. Barrel: 7.5 in., blued steel finish, round. Weight: 3.75 lbs. Length: 18.25 in. overall. Stock: Steel frame. Sights: None. Features: Flintlock, steel ramrod. An exact copy of an Alexander Murdock Scottish pistol of the 1770s. Made in India. Imported by Dixie Gun Works.
Price: Dixie Gun Works FH1040 .... **$425.00**

DIXIE MODEL 1855 U.S. DRAGOON PISTOL

Caliber: .58. Barrel: 12 in., bright finish, round. Weight: 2.25 lbs. Length: 16.75 in. overall. Stock: Walnut. Sights: Fixed rear and front sights. Features: Percussion, swivel-style, steel ramrod. Made by Palmetto Arms. Imported by Dixie Gun Works.
Price: Dixie Gun Works PH1000 .... **$650.00**

LYMAN PLAINS PISTOL

Caliber: .50 or .54. Barrel: 8 in.; 1:30-in. twist, both calibers. Weight: 3.1 lb. Length: 15 in. overall. Stock: Walnut. Sights: Blade front, square-notch rear adjustable for windage. Features: Polished brass triggerguard and ramrod tip, color case-hardened coil spring lock, spring-loaded trigger, stainless steel nipple, blackened iron furniture. Hooked patent breech, detachable belt hook. Introduced 1981. From Lyman Products.
Price: 6010608 .50-cal.. **$426.00**
Price: 6010609 .54-cal.. **$426.00**
Price: 6010610 .50-cal Kit **$349.00**
Price: 6010611 .54-cal. Kit... **$349.00**

PEDERSOLI CARLETON UNDERHAMMER MATCH PERCUSSION PISTOL

Caliber: .36. Barrel: 9.5 in., browned octagonal, rifled. Weight: 2.25 lbs. Length: 16.75 in. overall. Stock: Walnut. Sights: Blade front, open rear, adjustable for elevation. Features: Percussion, under-hammer ignition, adjustable trigger, no half cock. No ramrod. Made by Pedersoli. Imported by Dixie Gun Works.
Price: Dixie Gun Works FH0332... **$925.00**

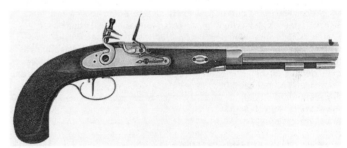

PEDERSOLI CHARLES MOORE ENGLISH DUELING PISTOL

Caliber: .45. Barrel: 11 in., 1:18 twist Weight: 2.5 lbs. Length: 16.5 in. overall. Stock: Walnut. Sights: Fixed. Features: Flintlock or percussion. Single set, adjustable trigger. Blued barrel and lock, steel furniture left in the white. Wooden ramrod. Replica of a fine British dueling pistol made by Charles Moore in London. Made by Pedersoli. Imported by Dixie Gun Works.
Price: Dixie Gun Works Flintlock FH0237 .... **$795.00**
Price: Dixie Gun Works Percussion PH0501 .... **$610.00**

PEDERSOLI FRENCH AN IX NAPOLEONIC PISTOL

Caliber: .69. Barrel: 8.25 in. Weight: 3 lbs. Length: 14 in. overall. Stock: Walnut. Sights: None. Features: Flintlock, case-hardened lock, brass furniture, buttcap, lock marked "Imperiale de S. Etienne." Steel ramrod. Made by Pedersoli. Imported by Dixie Gun Works.
Price: Dixie Gun Works FH0890... **$740.00**

PEDERSOLI FRENCH AN IX GENDARMERIE NAPOLEONIC PISTOL

Caliber: .69. Barrel: 5.25 in. Weight: 3 lbs. Length: 14 in. overall. Stock: Walnut. Sights: None. Features: Flintlock, case-hardened lock, brass furniture, buttcap, lock marked "Imperiale de S. Etienne." Steel ramrod. Imported by Dixie Gun Works.
Price: Dixie Gun Works Gendarmerie FHO954................................... **$725.00**

PEDERSOLI FRENCH AN XIII NAPOLEONIC PISTOL
Caliber: .69. Barrel: 8.25 in. Weight: 3 lbs. Length: 14 in. overall. Stock: Walnut half-stock. Sights: None. Features: Flintlock, case-hardened lock, brass furniture, butt cap, lock marked "Imperiale de S. Etienne." Steel ramrod. Made by Pedersoli. Imported by Dixie Gun Works.
Price: Dixie Gun Works AN XIII FHO895 .... **$725.00**

PEDERSOLI HARPER'S FERRY 1805 PISTOL
Caliber: .58. Barrel: 10 in. Weight: 2.5 lbs. Length: 16 in. overall. Stock: Walnut. Sights: Fixed. Features: Flintlock or percussion. Case-hardened lock, brass-mounted German silver-colored barrel. Wooden ramrod. Replica of the first U.S. government made flintlock pistol. Made by Pedersoli. Imported by Dixie Gun Works.
Price: Dixie Gun Works Flint RH0225 .... **$565.00**
Price: Dixie Gun Works Flint Kit RH0411 .... **$450.00**
Price: Dixie Gun Works Percussion RH0951 .... **$565.00**
Price: Dixie Gun Works Percussion Kit RH0937 .... **$395.00**

PEDERSOLI HOWDAH HUNTER PISTOLS
Caliber: .50, 20 gauge, .58. Barrels: 11.25 in., blued, rifled in .50 and .58 calibers. Weight: 4.25 to 5 lbs. Length: 17.25 in. Stock: American walnut with checkered grip. Sights: Brass bead front sight. Features: Blued barrels, swamped barrel rib, engraved, color case-hardened locks and hammers, captive steel ramrod. Available with detachable shoulder stock, case, holster and mold. Made by Pedersoli. Imported by Dixie Gun Works, Cabela's, Taylor's and others.
Price: Dixie Gun Works, 50X50, PH0572 .... **$895.00**
Price: Dixie Gun Works, 58XD58, PH09024 .... **$895.00**
Price: Dixie Gun Works, 20X20 gauge, PH0581 .... **$850.00**
Price: Dixie Gun Works, 50X20 gauge, PH0581 .... **$850.00**
Price: Dixie Gun Works, 50X50, Kit, PK0952 .... **$640.00**
Price: Dixie Gun Works, 50X20, Kit, PK1410 .... **$675.00**
Price: Dixie Gun Works, 20X20, Kit, PK0954 .... **$640.00**

PEDERSOLI KENTUCKY PISTOL
Caliber: .45, .50, .54. Barrel: 10.33 in. Weight: 2.5 lbs. Length: 15.4 in. overall. Stock: Walnut with smooth rounded birds-head grip. Sights: Fixed. Features: Available in flint or percussion ignition in various calibers. Case-hardened lock, blued barrel, drift-adjustable rear sights, blade front. Wooden ramrod. Kit guns of all models available from Dixie Gun Works. Made by Pedersoli. Imported by Dixie Gun Works, EMF and others.
Price: Dixie Gun Works .45 Percussion, PH0440 .... **$395.00**
Price: Dixie Gun Works.45 Flint, PH0430 .... **$437.00**
Price: Dixie Gun Works .45 Flint, Kit FH0320 .... **$325.00**

Price: Dixie Gun Works .50 Flint, PH0935 .... **$495.00**
Price: Dixie Gun Works .50 Percussion, PH0930 .... **$450.00**
Price: Dixie Gun Works 54 Flint, PH0080 .... **$495.00**
Price: Dixie Gun Works .54 Percussion, PH0330 .... **$450.00**
Price: Dixie Gun Works .54 Percussion, Kit PK0436 .... **$325.00**
Price: Dixie Gun Works .45, Navy Moll, brass buttcap, Flint PK0436 ...... **$650.00**
Price: .45, Navy Moll, brass buttcap, Percussion PK0903 .... **$595.00**

PEDERSOLI LE PAGE PERCUSSION DUELING PISTOL
Caliber: .44. Barrel: 10 inches, browned octagon, rifled. Weight: 2.5 lbs. Length: 16.75 inches overall. Stock: Walnut, rounded checkered butt. Sights: Blade front, open-style rear. Features: Single set trigger, external ramrod. Made by Pedersoli. Imported by Dixie Gun Works.
Price: Dixie, Pedersoli, PH0431 .... **$950.00**
Price: Dixie, International, Pedersoli, PH0231 .... **$1,250.00**

PEDERSOLI MAMELOUK
Caliber: .57. Barrel: 7-5/8 in., bright. Weight: 1.61 lbs. Length: 13 in. overall. Stock: Walnut, with brass end cap and medallion. Sights: Blade front. Features: Flint, lanyard ring, wooden ramrod. Made by Pedersoli. Available on special order from IFG (Italian Firearms Group)
Price: .... **TBD at time of order**

PEDERSOLI MANG TARGET PISTOL
Caliber: .38. Barrel: 11.5 in., octagonal, browned; 1:15-in. twist. Weight: 2.5 lbs. Length: 17. in. overall. Stock: Walnut with fluted grip. Sights: Blade front, open rear adjustable for windage. Features: Browned barrel, polished breech plug, remainder color case-hardened. Made by Pedersoli. Imported by Dixie Gun Works.
Price: PH0503 .... **$1,795.00**

PEDERSOLI MORTIMER TARGET PISTOL

Caliber: .44. Barrel: 10 in., bright octagonal on Standard, browned on Deluxe, rifled. Weight: 2.55 lbs. Length: 15.75 in. overall. Stock: Walnut, checkered saw-handle grip on Deluxe. Sights: Blade front, open-style rear. Features: Percussion or flint, single set trigger, sliding hammer safety, engraved lock on Deluxe. Wooden ramrod. Made by Pedersoli. Imported by Dixie Gun Works.

Price: Dixie, Flint, FH0316 ....**$1,175.00**
Price: Dixie, Percussion, PH0231......................................**$1,095.00**
Price: Dixie, Deluxe, FH0950 ....**$2,220.00**

PEDERSOLI PHILADELPHIA DERRINGER

Caliber: .45. Barrel: 3.1 in., browned, rifled. Weight: 0.5 lbs. Length: 6.215 in. Stock: European walnut checkered. Sights: V-notch rear, blade front. Features: Back-hammer percussion lock with engraving, single trigger. Made by Pedersoli. Imported by Dixie Gun Works.

Price: Dixie, PH0913 .... **$550.00**
Price: Dixie, Kit PK0863 .... **$385.00**

PEDERSOLI QUEEN ANNE FLINTLOCK PISTOL

Caliber: .50. Barrel: 7.5 in., smoothbore. Stock: Walnut. Sights: None. Features: Flintlock, German silver-colored steel barrel, fluted brass triggerguard, brass mask on butt. Lockplate left in the white. No ramrod. Introduced 1983. Made by Pedersoli. Imported by Dixie Gun Works.

Price: Dixie, RH0211 .... **$495.00**
Price: Dixie, Kit, FH0421 .... **$375.00**

PEDERSOLI REMINGTON RIDER DERRINGER

Caliber: 4.3 mm (BB lead balls only). Barrel: 2.1 in., blued, rifled. Weight: 0.25 lbs. Length: 4.75 in. Grips: All-steel construction. Sights: V-notch rear, bead front. Features: Fires percussion cap only – no powder. Available as case-hardened frame or polished white. Made by Pedersoli. Imported by Dixie Gun Works.

Price: Dixie, Case-hardened PH0923.................................... **$210.00**

PEDERSOLI SCREW BARREL PISTOL

Caliber: .44. Barrel: 2.35 in., blued, rifled. Weight: 0.5 lbs. Length: 6.5 in. Grips: European walnut. Sights: None. Features: Percussion, boxlock with center hammer, barrel unscrews for loading from rear, folding trigger, external hammer, combination barrel and nipple wrench furnished. Made by Pedersoli. Imported by Dixie Gun Works.

Price: Dixie, PH0530. .... **$225.00**
Price: Dixie, PH0545. .... **$175.00**

TRADITIONS KENTUCKY PISTOL

Caliber: .50. Barrel: 10 in., 1:20 in. twist. Weight: 2.75 lbs. Length: 15 in. Stock: Hardwood full stock. Sights: Brass blade front, square notch rear adjustable for windage. Features: Polished brass finger spur-style trigger guard, stock cap and ramrod tip, color case-hardened leaf spring lock, spring-loaded trigger, No. 11 percussion nipple, brass furniture. From Traditions, and as kit from Bass Pro and others.

Price: P1060 Finished **$244.00**
Price: KPC50602 Kit **$209.00**

TRADITIONS TRAPPER PISTOL

Caliber: .50. Barrel: 9.75 in., octagonal, blued, hooked patent breech, 1:20 in. twist. Weight: 2.75 lbs. Length: 15.5 in. Stock: Hardwood, modified saw-handle style grip, halfstock. Sights: Brass blade front, rear sight adjustable for windage and elevation. Features: Percussion or flint, double set triggers, polished brass triggerguard, stock cap and ramrod tip, color case-hardened leaf spring lock, spring-loaded trigger, No. 11 percussion nipple, brass furniture. From Traditions and as a kit from Bass Pro and others.

Price: P1100 Finished, percussion.. **$329.00**
Price: P1090 Finished, flint **$369.00**
Price: KPC51002 Kit, percussion **$299.00**
Price: KPC50902 Kit, flint **$359.00**

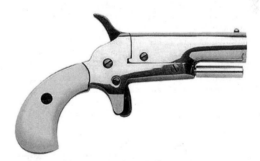

TRADITIONS VEST POCKET DERRINGER

Caliber: .31. Barrel: 2.35 in., round brass, smoothbore. Weight: .75 lbs. Length: 4.75 in. Grips: Simulated ivory. Sights: Front bead. Features: Replica of riverboat gambler's derringer. No. 11 percussion cap nipple, brass frame and barrel, spur trigger, external hammer. From Traditions.

Price: P1381, Brass **$194.00**
Price: Dixie, White, PH0920. .... **$175.00**

Prices given are believed to be accurate at time of publication however, many factors affect retail pricing so exact prices are not possible.

DANCE AND BROTHERS PERCUSSION REVOLVER
Caliber: .44. Barrel: 7.4 in., round. Weight: 2.5 lbs. Length: 13 in. overall. Grips: One-piece walnut. Sights: Brass blade front, hammer notch rear. Features: Reproduction of the C.S.A. revolver. Brass trigger guard. Color case-hardened frame Made by Pietta. Imported by Dixie Gun Works and others.
Price: Dixie Gun Works RH0344 .... **$350.00**

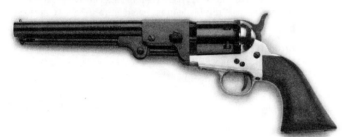

GRISWOLD AND GUNNISON PERCUSSION REVOLVER
Caliber: .36. Barrel: 7.5 in., round. Weight: 2.5 lbs. Length: 13.25 in. Grips: One-piece walnut. Sights: Fixed. Features: Reproduction of the C.S.A. revolver. Brass frame and triggerguard. Made by Pietta. Imported by EMF, Cabela's and others.
Price: EMF PF51BRGG36712 .... **$235.00**

NORTH AMERICAN COMPANION PERCUSSION REVOLVER
Caliber: .22. Barrel: 1-1/8 in. Weight: 5.1 oz. Length: 4 in. overall. Grips: Laminated wood. Sights: Blade front, notch rear. Features: All stainless steel construction. Uses No. 11 percussion caps. Comes with bullets, powder measure, bullet seater, leather clip holster, gun rag. Long Rifle frame. Introduced 1996. Made in U.S. by North American Arms.
Price: NAA-22LR-CB Long Rifle frame.................................. **$251.00**

NORTH AMERICAN SUPER COMPANION PERCUSSION REVOLVER
Caliber: .22. Barrel: 1-5/8 in. Weight: 7.2 oz. Length: 5-1/8 in. Grips: Laminated wood. Sights: Blade font, notched rear. Features: All stainless steel construction. No. 11 percussion caps. Comes with bullets, powder measure, bullet seater, leather clip holster, gun rag. Introduced 1996. Larger "Magnum" frame. Made in U.S. by North American Arms.
Price: NAA-Mag-CB Magnum frame..................................... **$296.00**

PEDERSOLI REMINGTON PATTERN TARGET REVOLVER
Caliber: .44. Barrel: 8 in., tapered octagon progressive twist. Weight: 2.75 lbs. Length: 13-3/4 in. overall. Grips: One-piece hardwood. Sights: V-notch on top strap, blued steel blade front. Features: Brass trigger guard, Non-reflective coating on the barrel and a wear resistant coating on the cylinder, blued steel frame, case-hardened hammer, trigger and loading lever. Made by Pedersoli. Imported by EMF, Dixie Gun Works, Cabela's and others.
Price: EMF Steel Frame PF58ST448................................... **$1,010.00**

PIETTA TEXAS PATTERSON PERCUSSION REVOLVER
Caliber: .36. Barrel: 9 in. tapered octagon. Weight: 2.75 lbs. Length: 13.75 in. Grips: One-piece walnut. Sights: Brass pin front, hammer notch rear. Features: Folding trigger, blued steel furniture, frame and barrel; engraved scene on cylinder. Ramrod: Loading tool provided. Made by Pietta. Imported by E.M.F, Dixie Gun Works.
Price: EMF PF36ST36712.. **$610.00**

PIETTA 1851 NAVY MODEL PERCUSSION REVOLVER
Caliber: .36, .44, 6-shot. Barrel: 7.5 in. Weight: 44 oz. Length: 13 in. overall. Grips: Walnut. Sights: Post front, hammer notch rear. Features: Available in brass-framed and steel-framed models. Made by Pietta. Imported by EMF, Dixie Gun Works, Cabela's, Cimarron, Taylor's, Traditions and others.
Price: Brass frame EMF PF51BR36712 ....**$230.00**
Price: Steel frame EMF PF51CH36712................................**$275.00**

PIETTA 1851 NAVY LONDON MODEL PERCUSSION REVOLVER
Caliber: .36, 6-shot. Barrel: 7.5 in. Weight: 44 oz. Length: 13 in. overall. Grips: Walnut. Sights: Post front, hammer notch rear. Features: steel frame and steel trigger guard and back strap. Available with oval trigger guard or squared back trigger guard. Made by Pietta. Imported by EMF, Dixie, Gun Works, Cabela's, Cimarron, Taylor's, Traditions and others.
Price: EMF PF51CHS36712 ....**$275.00**

PIETTA 1851 NAVY SHERIFF'S MODEL PERCUSSION REVOLVER

Caliber: .44, 6-shot. Barrel: 5.5 in. Weight: 40 oz. Length: 11 in. overall. Grips: Walnut. Sights: Post front, hammer notch rear. Features: Available in brass-framed and steel-framed models. Made by Pietta. Imported by EMF, Dixie, Gun Works, Cabela's.
Price: Brass frame EMF PF51BR44512 ....**$235.00**
Price: Steel frame EMF PF51CH44512................................**$275.00**

PIETTA 1851 NAVY CAPTAIN SCHAEFFER MODEL PERCUSSION REVOLVER

Caliber: .36, 6-shot. Barrel: 4 in. Weight: 40 oz. Length: 9.5 in. overall. Grips: Grips Ultra-ivory (polymer). Sights: Post front, hammer notch rear. Features: Polished steel finish, completely laser engraved. Made by Pietta. Imported by EMF
Price: EMF PF51LESS36312UI..**$395.00**

PIETTA 1851 NAVY YANK PEPPERBOX MODEL PERCUSSION REVOLVER

Caliber: .36, 6-shot. Barrel: No Barrel. Weight: 36 oz. Length: 7 in. overall. Grips: One-piece walnut. Sights: Post front, hammer notch rear. Features: There is no barrel. Rounds fire directly out of the chambers of the elongated cylinder. Made by Pietta. Imported by EMF, Dixie Gun Works and Taylor's & Co.
Price: EMF PF51PEPPER36 ....**$235.00**

PIETTA 1851 NAVY BUNTLINE MODEL PERCUSSION REVOLVER

Caliber: .44, 6-shot. Barrel: 12 in. Weight: 36 oz. Length: 18.25 in. overall. Grips: Walnut. Sights: Post front, hammer notch rear. Features: Available in brass-framed and steel-framed models. Made by Pietta. Imported by EMF, Dixie Gun Works (Brass only).
Price: Brass frame EMF PF51BR4412 ....**$245.00**
Price: Steel frame EMF PF51CH4412...................................**$295.00**

PIETTA 1851 NAVY SNUBNOSE MODEL PERCUSSION REVOLVER

Caliber: .44, 6-shot. Barrel: 3 in. Weight: 36 oz. Length: 8.25 in. overall. Grips: Birds-head grip frame, one-piece checkered walnut. Sights: Post front, hammer notch rear. Features: Color case-hardened, steel-frame. Made by Pietta. Imported by Dixie Gun Works.
Price: Dixie SS1249..**$395.00**

PIETTA 1858 GENERAL CUSTER

Caliber: .44, 6-shot. Barrel: 8 in., blued. Grips: Two-piece wood. Sights: Open. Weight: 2.7 lbs. Features: Nickel-plated trigger guard, color case-hardened hammer, laser engraving.
Price: **$360.00**

PIETTA 1860 ARMY MODEL PERCUSSION REVOLVER

Caliber: .44. Barrel: 8 in. Weight: 2.75 lbs. Length: 13.25 in. overall. Grips: One-piece walnut. Sights: Brass blade front, hammer notch rear. Features: Models available with either case-hardened, steel frame, brass trigger guard, or brass frame, trigger guard and backstrap. EMF also offers a model with a silver finish on all the metal. Made by Pietta. Imported by EMF, Cabela's, Dixie Gun Works, Taylor's and others.
Price: EMF Brass Frame PF60BR448..................................... **$260.00**
Price: EMF Steel Frame PF60CH448................................... **$295.00**
Price: EMF Steel Frame Old Silver finish PF60OS448 .... **$325.00**
Price: EMF Steel Frame Old Silver finish Deluxe Engraved PF60CHES448 ....**$350.00**

PIETTA 1860 ARMY SHERIFF'S MODEL PERCUSSION REVOLVER

Caliber: .44. Barrel: 5.5in. Weight: 40 oz. Length: 11.5 in. overall. Grips: One-piece walnut. Sights: Brass blade front, hammer notch rear. Features: Case-hardened, steel frame, brass trigger guard. Made by Pietta. Imported by EMF, Cabela's, Dixie Gun Works and others.
Price: EMF PF60CH44512... **$295.00**

PIETTA 1860 ARMY SNUBNOSE MODEL PERCUSSION REVOLVER

Caliber: .44. Barrel: 3 in. Weight: 36 oz. Length: 8.25 in. overall. Grips: Birds-head grip frame, one-piece, checkered walnut. Sights: Brass blade front, hammer notch rear. Features: Fluted cylinder, case-hardened, steel frame, brass trigger guard, Made by Pietta. Imported by EMF.
Price: EMF PF51CHLG44212CW **$385.00**

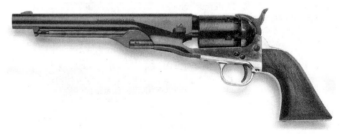

PIETTA NAVY 1861 PERCUSSION REVOLVER

Caliber: .36. Barrel: 8 in. Weight: 2.75 lbs. Length: 13.25 in. overall. Grips: One-piece walnut. Sights: Brass blade front, hammer notch rear. Features: Steel, case-hardened frame, brass-grip frame, or steel-grip frame (London Model), case-hardened creeping loading lever. Made by Pietta. Imported by EMF, Dixie Gun Works, Cabela's and others.
Price: EMF with brass triggerguard PF61CH368CIV **$300.00**
Price: EMF with steel triggerguard PF61CH368................................... **$300.00**

Prices given are believed to be accurate at time of publication however, many factors affect retail pricing so exact prices are not possible.

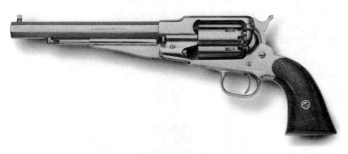

PIETTA 1858 REMINGTON ARMY REVOLVER
Caliber: .44. Barrel: 8 in., tapered octagon. Weight: 2.75 lbs. Length: 13.5 in. overall. Grips: Two-piece walnut. Sights: V-notch on top strap, blued steel blade front. Features: Brass triggerguard, blued steel backstrap and frame, case-hardened hammer and trigger. Also available, a brass-framed model, and an all stainless steel model. Made by Pietta. Imported by EMF, Dixie Gun Works, Cabela's and others.
Price: EMF Steel Frame PF58ST448 .... **$290.00**
Price: EMF Brass Frame PF58BR448 .... **$250.00**
Price: EMF Stainless Steel PF58SS448 .... **$430.00**

PIETTA 1858 REMINGTON TARGET REVOLVER
Caliber: .44. Barrel: 8 in., tapered octagon. Weight: 2.75 lbs. Length: 13.5 in. overall. Grips: Two-piece walnut. Sights: Adjustable rear, ramped blade front. Features: Brass triggerguard, blued steel frame, case-hardened hammer, and trigger. Also available, a brass-framed model. Made by Pietta. Imported by EMF, Dixie Gun Works, Cabela's and others.
Price: EMF PF58STT448 .... **$350.00**

PIETTA 1858 REMINGTON SHIRIFF'S MODEL REVOLVER
Caliber: .36 and .44. Barrel: 5.5in., tapered octagon. Weight: 2.75 lbs. Length: 11.5 in. overall. Grips: Two-piece checkered walnut. Sights: V-notch on top strap, blued steel blade front. Features: Brass triggerguard, blued steel backstrap and frame, case-hardened hammer and trigger. Also available in a color case-hardened-framed model, and in an all stainless steel model. Made by Pietta. Imported by EMF, and others.
Price: EMF Blued Steel Frame PF58ST36612 .... **$290.00**
Price: EMF Color Case-Hardened frame PF58CH44512CW **$395.00**
Price: EMF Stainless Steel PF58SS44512CW **$490.00**

PIETTA 1858 REMINGTON BUFFALO BILL COMMEMORATIVE REVOLVER
Caliber: .44. Barrel: 8 in., tapered octagon. Weight: 2.75 lbs. Length: 13-3/4 in. overall. Grips: Two-piece walnut. Sights: V-notch on top strap, blued steel blade front. Features: Gold-filled engraving over dark blue steel. A higher-grade gun commemorating the life of Buffalo Bill Cody. Made by Pietta. Imported by EMF.
Price: EMF PF58BB448 .... **$695.00**

PIETTA REMINGTON BELT MODEL REVOLVER
Caliber: .36. Barrel: 6.5 in., octagon. Weight: 44 oz. Length: 12.5 in. overall. Grips: Two-piece walnut. Sights: V-notch on top strap, blued steel blade front. Features: Brass triggerguard, blued steel backstrap and frame, case-hardened hammer and trigger. Made by Pietta. Imported by Dixie Gun Works.
Price: Dixie RH0214 .... **$295.00**

PIETTA 1863 REMINGTON POCKET MODEL REVOLVER
Caliber: .31, 5-shot. Barrel: 3.5 in. Weight: 1 lb. Length: 7.6 in. Grips: Two-piece walnut. Sights: Pin front, groove-in-frame rear. Features: Spur trigger, iron-, brass- or nickel-plated frame. Made by Pietta. Imported by EMF (Steel Frame), Dixie Gun Works, Taylor's and others.
Price: Brass frame, Dixie PH0407 .... **$260.00**
Price: Steel frame, Dixie PH0370 .... **$295.00**
Price: Nickel-plated, Dixie PH0409 .... **$315.00**

PIETTA LEMATT REVOLVER
Caliber: .44/20 Ga. Barrel: 6.75 in. (revolver); 4-7/8 in. (single shot). Weight: 3 lbs., 7 oz. Length: 14 in. overall. Grips: Hand-checkered walnut. Sights: Post front, hammer notch rear. Features: Exact reproduction with all-steel construction; 44-cal., 9-shot cylinder, 20-gauge single barrel; color case-hardened hammer with selector; spur triggerguard; ring at butt; lever-type barrel release. Made by Pietta. Imported by EMF, Dixie Gun Works and others.
Price: EMF Navy PFLMSTN44634 .... **$1,075.00**
Price: EMF Cavalry PFLMST44712 .... **$1,100.00**
Price: EMF Army PFLMSTA44634 .... **$1,100.00**

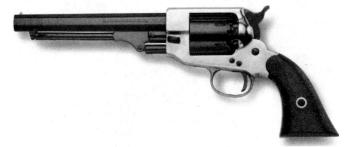

PIETTA SPILLER & BURR PERCUSSION REVOLVER
Caliber: .36. Barrel: 7 in., octagon. Weight: 2.5 lbs. Length: 12.5 in. overall. Grips: Two-piece walnut. Sights: V-notch on top strap, blued steel blade front. Features: Reproduction of the C.S.A. revolver. Brass frame and trigger guard. Also available as a kit. Made by Pietta. Imported by Dixie Gun Works, Traditions, Midway USA and others.
Price: Dixie RH0120 .... **$275.00**
Price: Dixie kit RH0300 .... **$235.00**

PIETTA STARR DOUBLE-ACTION ARMY REVOLVER
Caliber: .44. Barrel: 6 in. tapered round. Weight: 3 lbs. Length: 11.75 in. Grips: One-piece walnut. Sights: Hammer notch rear, dovetailed front. Features: Double-action mechanism, round tapered barrel, all blued frame and barrel. Made by Pietta. Imported by Dixie Gun Works and others.
Price: Dixie RH460 .... **$565.00**

PIETTA STARR SINGLE-ACTION ARMY REVOLVER
Caliber: .44. Barrel: 8 in. tapered round. Weight: 3 lbs. Length: 13.5 in. Grips: One-piece walnut. Sights: Hammer notch rear, dovetailed front. Features: Single-action mechanism, round tapered barrel, all blued frame and barrel. Made by Pietta. Imported by Cabela's, Dixie Gun Works and others.
Price: Dixie RH460 .... **$550.00**

PIETTA 1873 PERCUSSION REVOLVER
Caliber: .44. Barrel: 5.5 in. Weight: 40 oz. Length: 11.25 in. overall. Grips: One-piece walnut. Sights: V-notch on top strap, blued steel blade front. Features: A cap-and-ball version of the Colt Single Action Army revolver. Made by Pietta. Imported by EMF, Cabela's, Dixie Gun Works and others.
Price: EMF PF73CHS434NM **$360.00**

TRADITIONS U.S. MARSHAL
Caliber: .36, 6-shot. Barrel: 8 in., blued. Grips: One-piece walnut. Sights: Open, hammer/blade. Weight: 2.61 lbs. Features: Case-hardened frame, single action, U.S. Marshal logo on grips.
Price: **$351.00**

Prices given are believed to be accurate at time of publication however, many factors affect retail pricing so exact prices are not possible.

76TH EDITION, 2022 ⊕ **529**

TRADITIONS WILDCARD
Caliber: .36, 6-shot. Barrel: 7.375 in., blued octagon. Grips: Simulated stag. Sights: Open, hammer/blade. Weight: 2.5 lbs. Features: 1851 "Gunfighter," 13.5-in. overall length, case-hardened frame.
Price: **$409.00**

UBERTI 1847 WALKER PERCUSSION REVOLVER
Caliber: .44. Barrel: 9 in. Weight: 4.5 lbs. Length: 15.7 in. overall. Grips: One-piece hardwood. Sights: Brass blade front, hammer notch rear. Features: Copy of Sam Colt's first U.S. contract revolver. Engraved cylinder, case-hardened hammer and loading lever. Blued finish. Made by Uberti. Imported by Cabela's, Cimarron, Dixie Gun Works, EMF, Taylor's, Uberti U.S.A. and others.
Price: Uberti USA, standard model, blued steel 340200 .... **$429.00**

UBERTI DRAGOON PERCUSSION REVOLVERS
Caliber: .44. Barrel: 7.5 in. Weight: 4.1 lbs. Grips: One-piece walnut. Sights: Brass blade front, hammer notch rear. Features: Four models of the big .44 caliber revolvers that followed the massive Walker model and pre-dated the sleek 1860 Army model. Blued barrel, backstrap and trigger guard. Made by Uberti. Imported by Uberti USA, Dixie Gun Works, Taylor's and others.
Price: Uberti USA, Whitneyville Dragoon 340830 .... **$429.00**
Price: Uberti USA, First Model Dragoon 340800 .... **$429.00**
Price: Uberti USA, Second Model Dragoon 340810 .... **$429.00**
Price: Uberti USA, Third Model Dragoon 340860 .... **$429.00**

UBERTI 1849 POCKET MODEL WELLS FARGO PERCUSSION REVOLVER
Caliber: .31. Barrel: 4 in., seven-groove, RH twist. Weight: About 24 oz. Grips: One-piece walnut. Sights: Brass pin front, hammer notch rear. Features: Unfluted cylinder with stagecoach holdup scene, cupped cylinder pin, no grease grooves, one safety pin on cylinder and slot in hammer face. Made by Uberti. Imported by Uberti USA, Cimarron, Dixie Gun Works and others.
Price: Uberti USA 340350 .... **$349.00**

UBERTI 1849 WELLS FARGO PERCUSSION REVOLVER
Caliber: .31. Barrel: 4 in.; seven-groove; RH twist. Weight: About 24 oz. Grips: One-piece walnut. Sights: Brass pin front, hammer notch rear. Features: No loading lever, Unfluted cylinder with stagecoach holdup scene, cupped cylinder pin, no grease grooves, one safety pin on cylinder and slot in hammer face. Made by Uberti. Imported by Uberti USA, Cimarron, Dixie Gun Works and others.
Price: Uberti USA 340380 .... **$349.00**

UBERTI NAVY MODEL 1851 PERCUSSION REVOLVER
Caliber: .36, 6-shot. Barrel: 7.5 in. Weight: 44 oz. Length: 13 in. overall. Grips: One-piece walnut. Sights: Post front, hammer notch rear. Features: Brass backstrap and trigger guard, or steel backstrap and trigger guard (London Model), engraved cylinder with navy battle scene; case-hardened hammer, loading lever. Made by Uberti and Pietta. Imported by Uberti USA, Cabela's, Cimarron, and others.
Price: Uberti USA Brass grip assembly 340000 .... **$329.00**
Price: Uberti USA London Model 340050 .... **$369.00**

UBERTI 1860 ARMY REVOLVER
Caliber: .44. Barrel: 8 in. Weight: 44 oz. Length: 13.25 in. overall. Grips: One-piece walnut. Sights: Brass blade front, hammer notch rear. Features: Steel or case-hardened frame, brass triggerguard, case-hardened creeping loading lever. Many models and finishes are available for this pistol. Made by Uberti. Imported by Cabela's, Cimarron, Dixie Gun Works, EMF, Taylor's, Uberti U.S.A. and others.
Price: Uberti USA, roll engraved cylinder 340400 .... **$349.00**
Price: Uberti USA, full fluted cylinder 340410 .... **$369.00**

UBERTI 1861 NAVY PERCUSSION REVOLVER
Caliber: .36 Barrel: 7.5 in. Weight: 44 oz. Length: 13.25 in. overall. Grips: One-piece walnut. Sights: Brass blade front, hammer notch rear. Features: Brass backstrap and trigger guard, or steel backstrap and trigger guard (London Model), engraved cylinder with navy battle scene; case-hardened hammer, loading lever. Made by Uberti USA, Cabela's, Cimarron, Dixie Gun Works, Taylor's and others.
Price: Uberti USA Brass grip assembly 340630 .... **$349.00**
Price: Uberti USA London Model 340500 .... **$349.00**

Prices given are believed to be accurate at time of publication however, many factors affect retail pricing so exact prices are not possible.

UBERTI 1862 POLICE PERCUSSION REVOLVER
Caliber: .36, 5-shot. Barrel: 5.5 in., 6.5 in., 7.5 in. Weight: 26 oz. Length: 12 in. overall (6.5 in. bbl.). Grips: One-piece walnut. Sights: Fixed. Features: Round tapered barrel; half-fluted and rebated cylinder; case-hardened frame, loading lever and hammer; brass trigger guard and backstrap. Made by Uberti. Imported by Cimarron, Dixie Gun Works, Taylor's, Uberti U.S.A. and others.
Price: Uberti USA 340700... **$369.00**

UBERTI 1862 POCKET NAVY PERCUSSION REVOLVER
Caliber: .36, 5-shot. Barrel: 5.5 in., 6.5 in. Weight: 26 oz. Length: 12 in. overall (6.5 in. bbl.). Grips: One-piece walnut. Sights: Fixed. Features: Octagon barrel; case-hardened frame, loading lever and hammer; silver or brass trigger guard and backstrap; also available in an all stainless steel version. Made by Uberti. Imported by Uberti USA, Cimarron, Dixie Gun Works, Taylor's and others.
Price: Uberti USA 340750... **$369.00**

UBERTI LEACH AND RIGDON PERCUSSION REVOLVER
Caliber: .36. Barrel: 7.5 in., octagon to round. Weight: 2.75 lbs. Length: 13 in. Grips: One-piece walnut. Sights: Hammer notch and pin front. Features: Steel frame. Reproduction of the C.S.A. revolver. Brass backstrap and trigger guard. Made by Uberti. Imported by Uberti USA, Dixie Gun Works and others.
Price: Uberti USA 340030... **$349.00**

UBERTI NEW ARMY REMINGTON PERCUSSION REVOLVER
Caliber: .44, 6-shot. Barrel: Tapered octagon 8 in. Weight: 32 oz. Length: Standard 13.5 in. Grips: Two-piece walnut. Sights: Standard blade front, groove-in-frame rear; adjustable on some models. Features: Many variations of this gun are available. Target Model (Uberti U.S.A.) has fully adjustable target rear sight, target front, .36 or .44. Made by Uberti. Imported by Uberti USA, Cimarron F.A. Co., Taylor's and others.
Price: Uberti USA Steel frame, 341000 .... **$369.00**
Price: Uberti USA Stainless, 341020.. **$449.00**

Prices given are believed to be accurate at time of publication however, many factors affect retail pricing so exact prices are not possible.

76TH EDITION, 2022 ✛ **531**

ARMI SPORT ENFIELD THREE-BAND P1853 RIFLE

Caliber: .58. Barrel: 39 in. Weight: 10.25 lbs. Length: 52 in. overall. Stock: European walnut. Sights: Blade front, flip-up rear with elevator marked to 800 yards. Features: Reproduction of the original three-band rifle. Percussion musket-cap ignition. Blued barrel with steel barrelbands, brass furniture. Case-hardened lock. Lockplate marked "London Armory Co. and Crown." Made by Euro Arms, Armi Sport (Chiappa). Imported by Dixie Gun Works and others.

Price: Dixie Gun Works rifled bore PR1130 ....**$895.00**
Price: Dixie Gun Work smooth bore PR1052.....................................**$750.00**

CVA ACCURA IN-LINE BREAK-ACTION RIFLE

Caliber: .50. Barrel: 28 in. fluted. Weight: 7.5 lbs. Length: Standard 45 in. Stock: Ambidextrous solid composite in standard or thumbhole. Sights: Adj. fiber-optic. Features: Break-action, quick-release breech plug, aluminum loading rod, cocking spur, lifetime warranty. By CVA.

Price: CVA PR3120NM (Accura MR Nitride with Black Stocks
      and Scope Mount)..**$493.00**

CVA ACCURA V2 LR NITRIDE "SPECIAL EDITION" IN-LINE BREAK-ACTION RIFLE

Caliber: .50. Barrel: 30 in. fluted. Weight: 7.5 lbs. Length: Standard 45 in. Stock: Ambidextrous solid composite. Sights: Adj. fiber-optic. Features: Break-action, quick-release breech plug, aluminum loading rod, cocking spur, equipped with a genuine, Nitride treated, 30-inch Bergara Barrel, and a deep pistol grip stock decorated in APG camo. Lifetime warranty. By CVA.

Price: CVA PR6124NM **$449.00**

CVA ACCURA LR

Caliber: .45, .50. Barrel: 30 in., Nitride-treated, 416 stainless steel Bergara. Stock: Ambidextrous thumbhole camo. Sights: DuraSight Dead-On one-piece scope mount, scope not included. Weight: 6.75 lbs. Features: Reversible hammer spur, CrushZone recoil pad, quick-release breech plug.

Price: **$605.00**

CVA ACCURA MR (MOUNTAIN RIFLE) IN-LINE BREAK-ACTION RIFLE

Caliber: .50. Barrel: 25 in. Weight: 6.35 lbs. Length: Standard 45 in. Stock: Ambidextrous solid composite. Sights: DuraSight DEAD-ON One-Piece Scope Mount. Features: Break-action, quick-release breech plug, aluminum loading rod, cocking spur, and a deep pistol grip stock decorated in Realtree APG camo. Lifetime warranty. By CVA.

Price: CVA PR3121SNM **$546.00**

CVA ACCURA LRX

Caliber: .45 and .50. Barrel: 30 in. Nitride-treated stainless steel Bergara barrel. Comes with a carbon-fiber collapsible field rod, which you carry on your hip, a configuration that allows the barrel to be completely free-floated. The stock also wears a height-adjustable comb. Utilizes CVA's screw-in/out breech plug system.

Price: **$675.00**

CVA PLAINS RIFLE

Caliber: .50. Barrel: 28 in., Nitride, fluted, stainless steel Bergara. Stock: Ambidextrous composite Realtree MAX-1 XT. Sights: DuraSight Dead-On one-piece scope mount, scope not included. Weight: 7.2 lbs. Features: Solid aluminum PalmSaver ramrod, reversible cocking spur, Quake Claw sling.

Price: **$593.00**

CVA PARAMOUNT PRO

Caliber: .45, magnum. Barrel: Fluted Bergara free-floating, Cerakote/Nitride stainless steel/camo. Stock: Grayboe fiberglass. Sights: Threaded 3/4x20, scope not included. Weight: 8.75 lbs. Features: TriggerTech trigger, VariFlame breech plug, accessory trap door, self-deploying ramrod.

Price: **$1,667.00**

CVA PARAMOUNT PRO COLORADO

Caliber: .50, magnum. Barrel: Fluted Bergara free-floating, Cerakote/Nitride stainless steel/camo. Stock: Grayboe fiberglass. Sights: Williams peep sight. Weight: 8.75 lbs. Features: TriggerTech trigger, VariFlame breech plug, accessory trap door, self-deploying ramrod.

Price: **$1,667.00**

CVA PARAMOUNT HTR LONG RANGE MUZZLELOADER

Caliber: .40 and .45. Barrel: 26 in. Threaded 3/4x20 for muzzle brake. Twist rate: 1:20 (.40 cal.), 1:22 (.45 cal.). Weight: 9.6 lbs. Comes with a collapsible carbon-fiber ram rod. Features: Designed to handle "super-magnum" charges of Blackhorn 209 and capable of producing muzzle velocities comparable to centerfire rifles — eclipsing 2,700 fps.The HTR has a more hunting-focused stock design than the original Paramount model, featuring an adjustable comb and an internal aluminum chassis that provides a consistent shot-to-shot foundation for the action and free-floating barrel.

Price: **$1,225.00**

CVA OPTIMA IN-LINE BREAK-ACTION RIFLE

Caliber: .50. Barrel: 26 in., stainless steel. Weight: 6.65 lbs. Length: 41in. Stock: Ambidextrous solid composite. Available in pistol grip or thumbhole configurations. Sights: DuraSight DEAD-ON One-Piece Scope Mount. Features: Ambidextrous with rubber grip panels in black or Realtree APG camo, crush-zone recoil pad, reversible hammer spur, quake claw sling. Lifetime warranty. By CVA.

Price: CVA PR2020SM.. **$371.00**

CVA WOLF IN-LINE BREAK-ACTION RIFLE

Caliber: .50 Barrel: 24 in. Weight: 6.23 lbs. Stock: Ambidextrous composite. Sights: Dead-On Scope Mounts or Fiber Optic. Features: Break-action, quick-release breech plug for 209 primer, aluminum loading road, cocking spur. Lifetime warranty. By CVA.

Price: CVA PR2112SM (.50-cal, stainless/Realtree Hardwoods HD,
      scope mount)...**$289.50**
Price: CVA PR2112S (50-cal, stainless/Realtree Hardwoods HD,
      fib. opt. sight) **$289.50**
Price: CVA PR2110SM (.50-cal, stainless/black, scope mount) **$240.50**

DIXIE DELUXE CUB RIFLE

Caliber: .32, .36. Barrel: 28 in. octagonal. Weight: 6.5 lbs. Length: 44 in. overall. Stock: Walnut. Sights: Fixed. Features: Each gun available in either flint or percussion ignition. Short rifle for small game and beginning shooters. Brass patchbox and furniture. Made by Pedersoli for Dixie Gun Works.

Price: Dixie Gun Works (.32-cal. flint) PR3130....................................**$890.00**
Price: Dixie Gun Works (.36-cal. flint) FR3135.....................................**$890.00**
Price: Dixie Gun Works (.32-cal. Percussion kit) PK3360 ....**$690.00**
Price: Dixie Gun Works (.36-cal. Percussion kit) PK3365 ....**$690.00**
Price: Dixie Gun Works (.32-cal. Flint kit) PK3350 ....**$710.00**
Price: Dixie Gun Works (.36-cal. Flint kit) PK335 ....**$710.00**
Price: Dixie Gun Works (.32-cal. percussion) PR3140........................**$850.00**
Price: Dixie Gun Works (.36-cal. percussion) PR3145........................**$850.00**

Prices given are believed to be accurate at time of publication however, many factors affect retail pricing so exact prices are not possible.

DIXIE PENNSYLVANIA RIFLE

Caliber: .45 and .50. Barrel: 41.5 in. octagonal, .45/1:48, .50/1:56 in. twist. Weight: 8.5, 8.75 lbs. Length: 56 in. overall. Stock: European walnut, full-length stock. Sights: Notch rear, blade front. Features: Flintlock or percussion, brass patchbox, double-set triggers. Also available as kit guns for both calibers and ignition systems. Made by Pedersoli for Dixie Gun Works.
Price: Dixie Gun Works (.45-cal. flint) FR1060 .... $1,100.00
Price: Dixie Gun Works (.50-cal. flint) FR3200 .... $1,100.00
Price: Dixie Gun Works (.45-cal. Percussion kit) PR1075 .... $910.00
Price: Dixie Gun Works (.50-cal. Percussion kit) PK3365 .... $910.00
Price: Dixie Gun Works (.45-cal. Flint kit) FR1065 .... $910.00
Price: Dixie Gun Works (.50-cal. Flint kit) FK3420 .... $910.00
Price: Dixie Gun Works (.45-cal. percussion) FR1070 .... $1,050.00
Price: Dixie Gun Works (.50-cal. percussion) PR3205 .... $1,050.00

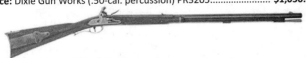

EUROARMS 1803 HARPER'S FERRY FLINTLOCK RIFLE

Caliber: .54. Barrel: 35.5 in., smoothbore. Weight: 9.5 lbs. Length: 50.5 in. overall. Stock: Half-stock, walnut w/oil finish. Sights: Blade front, notched rear. Features: Color case-hardened lock, browned barrel, with barrel key. Made by Euroarms. Imported by Dixie Gun Works.
Price: Dixie Gun Works FR0171 .... $795.00

EUROARMS J.P. MURRAY ARTILLERY CARBINE

Caliber: .58. Barrel: 23.5 in. Weight: 8 lbs. Length: 39.5 in. Stock: European walnut. Sights: Blade front, fixed notch rear. Features: Percussion musket-cap ignition. Reproduction of the original Confederate carbine. Lock marked "J.P. Murray, Columbus, Georgia." Blued barrel. Made by Euroarms. Imported by Dixie Gun Works and others.
Price: Dixie, Gun Works PR0173 .... $1,100.00

EUROARMS ENFIELD MUSKETOON P1861

Caliber: .58. Barrel: 24 in. Weight: 9 lbs. Length: 40 in. overall. Stock: European walnut. Sights: Blade front, flip-up rear with elevator marked to 700 yards. Features: Reproduction of the original cavalry version of the Enfield rifle. Percussion musket-cap ignition. Blued barrel with steel barrelbands, brass furniture. Case-hardened lock. Euroarms version marked London Armory with crown. Pedersoli version has Birmingham stamp on stock and Enfield and Crown on lockplate. Made by Euroarms. Imported by Dixie Gun Works and others.
Price: Dixie Gun Works PR0343 .... $1,050.00

KNIGHT 500 IN-LINE RIFLE

Caliber: .50. Barrel: 28 in., custom Green Mountain. Weight: 10 lbs. Length: 46 in. overall. Stock: Boyd's custom stock with integrated aluminum bedding Sights: Not included. Features: Competition-grade muzzleloader that can be used as hunting rifle, handcrafted Green Mountain barrel, the stock also features an adjustable cheek piece that gives you a clear view down range. Made in U.S. by Knight Rifles.
Price: Muzzleloaders.com MMTE758TAR .... Starting at $2,080.00

KNIGHT BIGHORN IN-LINE RIFLE

Caliber: .50. Barrel: 26 in., 1:28 in. twist. Weight: 7 lbs. 3 oz. Length: 44.5 in. overall. Stock: G2 straight or thumbhole, Carbon Knight straight or thumbhole or black composite thumbhole with recoil pad, sling swivel studs. Ramrod: Carbon core with solid brass extendable jag. Sights: Fully adjustable metallic fiber optic. Features: Uses four different ignition systems (included): #11 nipple, musket nipple, bare 208 shotgun primer and 209 Extreme shotgun primer system (Extreme weatherproof full plastic jacket system); vented breech plug, striker fired with one-piece removable hammer assembly. With recommended loads, guaranteed to have 4-inch, three-shot groups at 200 yards. Also available as Western gun with exposed ignition. Made in U.S. by Knight Rifles.
Price: Muzzleloaders.com MBH706C $646.00

KNIGHT DISC EXTREME

Caliber: .50, .52. Barrel: 26 in., fluted stainless, 1:28 in. twist. Weight: 7 lbs. 14 oz. to 8 lbs. Length: 45 in. overall. Stock: Carbon Knight straight or thumbhole with blued or SS; G2 thumbhole; left-handed Nutmeg thumbhole. Ramrod: Solid brass extendable jag. Sights: Fully adjustable metallic fiber optics. Features: Bolt-action rifle, full plastic jacket ignition system, #11 nipple, musket nipple, bare 208 shotgun primer. With recommended loads, guaranteed to have 4-inch, three-shot groups at 200 yards. Also available as Western gun with exposed ignition. Made in U.S. by Knight Rifles.
Price: Muzzleloaders.com MDE706SMX .... Starting at $721.00

KNIGHT LITTLEHORN IN-LINE RIFLE

Caliber: .50. Barrel: 22 in., 1:28 in. twist. Weight: 6.7 lbs. Length: 39 in. overall. Stock: 12.5-in. length of pull, G2 straight or pink Realtree AP HD. Ramrod: Carbon core with solid brass extendable jag. Sights: Fully adjustable Williams fiber optic. Features: Uses four different ignition systems (included): Full Plastic Jacket, #11 nipple, musket nipple or bare 208 shotgun primer; vented breech plug, striker-fired with one-piece removable hammer assembly. Finish: Stainless steel. With recommended loads, guaranteed to have 4-inch, three-shot groups at 200 yards. Also available as Western gun with exposed ignition. Made in U.S. by Knight Rifles.
Price: Muzzleloaders.com MLHW702C .... Starting at $390.00

KNIGHT MOUNTAINEER IN-LINE RIFLE

Caliber: .45, .50, .52. Barrel: 27 in. fluted stainless steel, free floated. Weight: 8 lbs. (thumbhole stock), 8.3 lbs. (straight stock). Length: 45.5 inches. Sights: Fully adjustable metallic fiber optic. Features: Bolt-action rifle, adjustable match-grade trigger, aluminum ramrod with carbon core, solid brass extendable jag, vented breech plug. Ignition: Full plastic jacket, #11 nipple, musket nipple, bare 208 shotgun primer. With recommended loads, guaranteed to have 4-inch, three-shot groups at 200 yards. Also available as Western gun with exposed ignition. Made in U.S. by Knight Rifles.
Price: Muzzleloaders.com MMT707SNMNT .... Starting at $1,016.00

KNIGHT TK-2000 IN-LINE SHOTGUN

Gauge: 12. Barrel: 26 inches. Choke: Extra-full and improved cylinder available. Stock: Realtree Xtra Green straight or thumbhole. Weight: 7.7 pounds. Sights: Williams fully adjustable rear, fiber-optic front. Features: Striker-fired action, receiver is drilled and tapped for scope, adjustable trigger, removable breech plug, double-safety system. Ignition: #209 primer with Full Plastic Jacket, musket cap or No. 11. Striker-fired with one-piece removable hammer assembly. Made in U.S. by Knight Rifles.
Price: Muzzleloaders.com MTK2000SXG .... Starting at $742.00

KNIGHT ULTRA-LITE IN-LINE RIFLE

Caliber: .45 or .50. Barrel: 24 in. Stock: Black, tan or olive-green Kevlar spider web. Weight: 6 lbs. Features: Bolt-action rifle. Ramrod: Carbon core with solid brass extendable jag. Sights: With or without Williams fiber-optic sights, drilled and tapped for scope mounts. Finish: Stainless steel. Ignition: 209 Primer with Full Plastic Jacket, musket cap or #11 nipple, bare 208 shotgun primer; vented breech plug. With recommended loads, guaranteed to have 4-inch, three-shot groups at 200 yards. Also available as Western version with exposed ignition. Made in U.S. by Knight Rifles.
Price: Muzzleloaders.com MULE704TNT .... Starting at $1,217.00

KNIGHT VISION IN-LINE RIFLE

Caliber: .50. Barrel: 24 in. Length: 44 in. Stock: Black composite. Weight: 7.9 lbs. Features: Break-open rifle with carbon-steel barrel and all-new machined steel action. With recommended loads, guaranteed to have 4-inch, three-shot groups at 200 yards. Ramrod: Carbon core with solid brass extendable jag. Ignition: Full Plastic Jacket. Sights: Weaver sight bases attached, and Williams fiber-optic sights provided. Finish: Blued steel. Made in U.S. by Knight Rifles.
Price: Muzzleloaders.com MKVE04XT ... . Starting at $346.00

Prices given are believed to be accurate at time of publication however, many factors affect retail pricing so exact prices are not possible.

76TH EDITION, 2022 ✛ 533

KNIGHT WOLVERINE IN-LINE RIFLE

Caliber: .50. Barrel: 22 in. stainless steel, 1:28 in. twist. Weight: 6.9 lbs. Length: 40.5 overall. Stock: Realtree Hardwoods straight, CarbonKnight straight. Ramrod: Carbon core with solid brass extendable jag. Sights: Fully adjustable Williams fiber optic. Features: Ignition systems (included): #11 nipple, musket nipple, bare 208 shotgun primer; vented breech plug, striker-fired with one-piece removable hammer assembly. Finish: Stainless steel. With recommended loads, guaranteed to have 4-inch, three-shot groups at 200 yards. Also available as Western gun with exposed ignition. Made in U.S. by Knight Rifles.
Price: Muzzleloaders.com MWS702XT.............................**Starting at $395.00**

LYMAN DEERSTALKER RIFLE

Caliber: .50, .54. Barrel: 28 in. octagon, 1:48 in. twist. Weight: 10.8 lbs. Length: 45 in. overall. Stock: European walnut with black rubber recoil pad. Sights: Lyman's high visibility, fiber-optic sights. Features: Fast-twist rifling for conical bullets. Blackened metal parts to eliminate glare, stainless steel nipple. Hook breech, single trigger, coil spring lock. Steel barrel rib and ramrod ferrules. From Lyman.
Price: Muzzleloaders.com 6033146/7. 50-cal /.54-cal. flint **$448.00**
Price: Muzzleloaders.com 6033140/7 .50-cal /.54-cal. percussion **$398.00**

LYMAN GREAT PLAINS RIFLE

Caliber: .50, .54. Barrel: 32 in., 1:60 in. twist. Weight: 11.6 lbs. Stock: Walnut. Sights: Steel blade front, buckhorn rear adjustable for windage and elevation, and fixed notch primitive sight included. Features: Percussion or flint ignition. Blued steel furniture. Stainless steel nipple. Coil spring lock, Hawken-style triggerguard and double-set triggers. Round thimbles recessed and sweated into rib. Steel wedge plates and toe plate. Introduced 1979. From Lyman.
Price: 6031102/3 .50-cal./.54-cal percussion **$784.00**
Price: 6031105/6 .50-cal./.54-cal flintlock **$839.00**
Price: 6031125/6 .50-ca./.54-cal left-hand percussion **$824.00**
Price: 6031137 .50-cal. left-hand flintlock **$859.00**
Price: 6031111/2 .50/.54-cal. percussion kit.. **$639.00**
Price: 6031114/5 .50/.54-cal. flintlock kit... **$689.00**

LYMAN GREAT PLAINS HUNTER MODEL

Similar to Great Plains model except 1:32 in. twist, shallow-groove barrel for conicals or sabots, and comes drilled and tapped for Lyman 57GPR peep sight.
Price: 6031120/1 .50-cal./.54-cal percussion **$791.00**
Price: 6031148/9 .50-cal./.54-cal flintlock **$839.00**
Price: 6031112 .50-cal/.54-cal percussion kit **$669.00**
Price: 6031115 .50-cal/.54-cal flintlock kit.. **$729.00**

LYMAN TRADE RIFLE

Caliber: .50, .54. Barrel: 28 in. octagon, 1:48 in. twist. Weight: 10.8 lbs. Length: 45 in. overall. Stock: European walnut. Sights: Blade front, open rear adjustable for windage, or optional fixed sights. Features: Fast-twist rifling for conical bullets. Polished brass furniture with blue steel parts, stainless steel nipple. Hook breech, single trigger, coil spring percussion lock. Steel barrel rib and ramrod ferrules. Introduced 1980. From Lyman.
Price: 6032125/6 .50-cal./.54-cal. percussion **$565.00**
Price: 6032129/30 .50-cal./.54-cal. flintlock **$583.00**

PEDERSOLI 1777 CHARLEVILLE MUSKET

Caliber: .69. Barrel: 44.75 in. round, smoothbore. Weight: 10.5 lbs. Length: 57 in. Stock: European walnut, fullstock. Sights: Steel stud on upper barrelband. Features: Flintlock using one-inch flint. Steel parts all polished armory bright, brass furniture. Lock marked Charleville. Made by Pedersoli. Imported by Cabela's, Dixie Gun Works, others.
Price: Dixie Gun Works FR0930 .... **$1,450.00**

PEDERSOLI 1795 SPRINGFIELD MUSKET

Caliber: .69. Barrel: 44.75 in., round, smoothbore. Weight: 10.5 lbs. Length: 57.25 in. Stock: European walnut, fullstock. Sights: Brass stud on upper barrelband. Features: Flintlock using one-inch flint. Steel parts all polished armory bright, brass furniture. Lock marked US Springfield. Made by Pedersoli. Imported by Cabela's, Dixie Gun Works, others.
Price: Dixie Gun Works FR3210 .... **$1,495.00**

PEDERSOLI POTSDAM 1809 PRUSSIAN MUSKET

Caliber: .75. Barrel: 41.2 in. round, smoothbore. Weight: 9 lbs. Length: 56 in. Stock: European walnut, fullstock. Sights: Brass lug on upper barrelband. Features: Flintlock using one-inch flint. Steel parts all polished armory bright, brass furniture. Lock marked "Potsdam over G.S." Made by Pedersoli. Imported by Dixie Gun Works.
Price: Dixie Gun Works FR3175 .... **$1,575.00**

PEDERSOLI 1816 FLINTLOCK MUSKET

Caliber: .69. Barrel: 42 in., smoothbore. Weight: 9.75 lbs. Length: 56-7/8 in. overall. Stock: Walnut w/oil finish. Sights: Blade front. Features: All metal finished in "National Armory Bright," three barrel bands w/springs, steel ramrod w/ button-shaped head. Made by Pedersoli. Imported by Dixie Gun Works.
Price: Dixie Gun Works PR3180, Percussion conversion **$1,495.00**

PEDERSOLI 1841 MISSISSIPPI RIFLE

Caliber: .54, .58. Barrel: 33 inches. Weight: 9.5 lbs. Length: 48.75 in. overall. Stock: European walnut. Sights: Blade front, notched rear. Features: Percussion musket-cap ignition. Reproduction of the original one-band rifle with large brass patchbox. Color case-hardened lockplate with browned barrel. Made by Pedersoli. Imported by Dixie Gun Works, Cabela's and others.
Price: Dixie Gun Works PR0870 (.54 caliber)..................................... **$1,200.00**
Price: Dixie Gun Works PR3470 (.58 caliber)..................................... **$1,100.00**

PEDERSOLI 1854 LORENZ RIFLE

Caliber: .54. Barrel: 37 in. Weight: 9 lbs. Length: 49 in. overall. Stock: European walnut. Sights: Blade front, rear steel open, flip-up style. Features: Percussion musket-cap ignition. Armory bright lockplate marked "Konigi. Wurt Fabrik." Armory bright steel barrel. Made by Pedersoli. Imported by Dixie Gun Works.
Price: Dixie Gun Works PR3156... **$1,500.00**

PEDERSOLI 1857 MAUSER RIFLE

Caliber: .54. Barrel: 39.75 in. Weight: 9.5 lbs. Length: 52 in. overall. Stock: European walnut. Sights: Blade front, rear steel adjustable for windage and elevation. Features: Percussion musket-cap ignition. Color case-hardened lockplate marked "Konigi. Wurt Fabrik." Armory bright steel barrel. Made by Pedersoli. Imported by Dixie Gun Works.
Price: Dixie Gun Works PR1330... **$1,695.00**

PEDERSOLI 1861 RICHMOND MUSKET

Caliber: .58. Barrel: 40 inches. Weight: 9.5 lbs. Length: 55.5 in. overall. Stock: European walnut. Sights: Blade front, three-leaf military rear. Features: Reproduction of the original three-band rifle. Percussion musket-cap ignition. Lock marked C. S. Richmond, Virginia. Armory bright. Made by Pedersoli. Imported by Dixie Gun Works and others.
Price: Dixie Gun Works PR4095... **$1,150.00**

PEDERSOLI 1861 SPRINGFIELD RIFLE

Caliber: .58. Barrel: 40 inches. Weight: 10 lbs. Length: 55.5 in. overall. Stock: European walnut. Sights: Blade front, three-leaf military rear. Features: Reproduction of the original three-band rifle. Percussion musket-cap ignition. Lockplate marked 1861 with eagle and U.S. Springfield. Armory bright steel. Made by Armi Sport/Chiappa, Pedersoli. Imported by Cabela's, Dixie Gun Works, others.
Price: Cabela's **$1,199.00**

PEDERSOLI BAKER CAVALRY SHOTGUN

Gauge: 20. Barrels: 11.25 inches. Weight: 5.75 pounds. Length: 27.5 in. overall. Stock: American walnut. Sights: Bead front. Features: Reproduction of shotguns carried by Confederate cavalry. Single non-selective trigger, back-action locks. No. 11 percussion musket-cap ignition. Blued barrel with steel furniture. Case-

Prices given are believed to be accurate at time of publication however, many factors affect retail pricing so exact prices are not possible.

hardened lock. Pedersoli also makes a 12-gauge coach-length version of this back-action-lock shotgun with 20-inch barrels, and a full-length version in 10, 12 and 20 gauge. Made by Pedersoli. Imported by Cabela's and others.
Price: Cabela's $1,099.00

PEDERSOLI BRISTLEN MORGES AND WAADTLANDER TARGET RIFLES
Caliber: .44, .45. Barrel: 29.5 in. tapered octagonal, hooked breech. Weight: 15.5 lbs. Length: 48.5 in. overall. Stock: European walnut, halfstock with hooked buttplate and detachable palm rest. Sights: Creedmoor rear on Morges, Swiss Diopter on Waadtlander, hooded front sight notch. Features: Percussion back-action lock, double set, double-phase triggers, one barrel key, muzzle protector. Specialized bullet molds for each gun. Made by Pedersoli. Imported by Dixie Gun Works and others.
Price: Dixie Gun Works, .44 Bristlen Morges PR0165 .... $2,995.00
Price: Dixie Gun Works, .45 Waadtlander PR0183 .... $2,995.00

PEDERSOLI BROWN BESS
Caliber: .75. Barrel: 42 in., round, smoothbore. Weight: 9 lbs. Length: 57.75 in. Stock: European walnut, fullstock. Sights: Steel stud on front serves as bayonet lug. Features: Flintlock using one-inch flint with optional brass flash guard (SCO203), steel parts all polished armory bright, brass furniture. Lock marked Grice, 1762 with crown and GR. Made by Pedersoli. Imported by Cabela's, Dixie Gun Works, others.
Price: Dixie Gun Works Complete Gun FR0810 .... $1,350.00
Price: Dixie Gun Works Kit Gun FR0825 .... $1,050.00
Price: Dixie Gun Works Trade Gun, 30.5-in. barrel FR0665 .... $1,495.00
Price: Dixie Gun Works Trade Gun Kit FR0600 .... $975.00

PEDERSOLI COOK & BROTHER CONFEDERATE CARBINE/ARTILLERY/RIFLE
Caliber: .58 Barrel: 24/33/39 inches. Weight: 7.5/8.4/8.6 lbs. Length: 40.5/48/54.5 in. Stock: Select oil-finished walnut. Features: Percussion musket-cap ignition. Color case-hardened lock, browned barrel. Buttplate, triggerguard, barrelbands, sling swivels and nose cap of polished brass. Lock marked with stars and bars flag on tail and Athens, Georgia. Made by Pedersoli. Imported by Dixie Gun Works, others.
Price: Dixie Gun Works Carbine PR0830 ....$995.00
Price: Dixie Gun Works Artillery/Rifle PR32165 .... $995.00

PEDERSOLI COUNTRY HUNTER
Caliber: .50. Barrel: 26 in. octagonal. Weight: 6 lbs. Length: 41.75 in. overall. Stock: European walnut, halfstock. Sights: Rear notch, blade front. Features: Percussion, one barrel key. Made by Pedersoli. Imported by Dixie Gun Works.
Price: Cherry's Fine Guns Percussion, .50 .... $675.00
Price: Cherry's Fine Guns Flint, .50.. $688.00

PEDERSOLI ENFIELD MUSKETOON P1861
Caliber: .58. Barrel: 33 in. Weight: 9 lbs. Length: 35 in. overall. Stock: European walnut. Sights: Blade front, flip-up rear with elevator marked to 700 yards. Features: Reproduction of the original cavalry version of the Enfield rifle. Percussion musket-cap ignition. Blued barrel with steel barrelbands, brass furniture. Case-hardened lock. Euroarms version marked London Armory with crown. Pedersoli version has Birmingham stamp on stock and Enfield and Crown on lockplate. Made by Euroarms, Pedersoli. Imported by Cabela's and others.
Price: Cabela's $1,099.00

PEDERSOLI FRONTIER RIFLE
Caliber: .32, .36, .45, .50, .54. Barrel: 39 in., octagon, 1:48 twist. Weight: 7.75 lbs. Length: 54.5 in. overall. Stock: American black walnut. Sights: Blade front, rear drift adjustable for windage. Features: Color case-hardened lockplate and cock/hammer, brass triggerguard and buttplate; double set, double-phased triggers. Made by Pedersoli. Imported by Dixie Gun Works, and by Cabela's (as the Blue Ridge Rifle).
Price: Cabela's Percussion $599.00
Price: Cabela's Flintlock $649.00

PEDERSOLI ENFIELD THREE-BAND P1853 RIFLE
Caliber: .58. Barrel: 39 in. Weight: 10.25 lbs. Length: 52 in. overall. Stock: European walnut. Sights: Blade front, flip-up rear with elevator marked to 800 yards. Features: Reproduction of the original three-band rifle. Percussion

musket-cap ignition. Blued barrel with steel barrelbands, brass furniture. Case-hardened lock. Lockplate marked "London Armory Co. and Crown." Made by Pedersoli. Imported by Cabela's.
Price: Cabela's $1,149.00

PEDERSOLI INDIAN TRADE MUSKET
Gauge: 20. Barrel: 36 in., octagon to round, smoothbore. Weight: 7.25 lbs. Length: 52 in. overall. Stock: American walnut. Sights: Blade front sight, no rear sight. Features: Flintlock. Kits version available. Made by Pedersoli. Imported by Dixie Gun Works.
Price: Dixie Gun Works, FR3170 .... $1,095.00
Price: Dixie Gun Works Kit, FK3370 .... $995.00

PEDERRSOLI JAEGER RIFLE
Caliber: .54. Barrel: 27.5 in. octagon, 1:24 in. twist. Weight: 8.25 lbs. Length: 43.5 in. overall. Stock: American walnut; sliding wooden patchbox on butt. Sights: Notch rear, blade front. Features: Flintlock or percussion. Conversion kits available, and recommended converting percussion guns to flintlocks using kit LO1102 at $209.00. Browned steel furniture. Made by Pedersoli. Imported by Dixie Gun Works.
Price: Dixie Gun Works Percussion, PR0835....................................$1,350.00
Price: Dixie Gun Works Flint, PR0835 ....$1,450.00
Price: Dixie Gun Works Percussion, kit gun, PK0146 ....$1,075.00
Price: Dixie Gun Works Flint, kit gun, PKO143.................................$1,100.00

PEDERSOLI KENTUCKY RIFLE
Caliber: .32, .45 and .50. Barrel: 35.5 in. octagonal. Weight: 7.5 (.50 cal.) to 7.75 lbs. (.32 cal.) Length: 51 in. overall. Stock: European walnut, full-length stock. Sights: Notch rear, blade front. Features: Flintlock or percussion, brass patchbox, double-set triggers. Also available as kit guns for all calibers and ignition systems. Made by Pedersoli. Imported by Dixie Gun Works.
Price: Dixie Gun Works Percussion, .32, PR3115................................. $750.00
Price: Dixie Gun Works Flint, .32, FR3100 .... $775.00
Price: Dixie Gun Works Percussion, .45, FR3120 .... $750.00
Price: Dixie Gun Works Flint, .45, FR3105 .... $775.00
Price: Dixie Gun Works Percussion, .50, FR3125 .... $750.00
Price: Dixie Gun Works Flint, .50, FR3110 .... $775.00

PEDERSOLI KODIAK DOUBLE RIFLES AND COMBINATION GUN.
Caliber: .50, .54 and .58. Barrel: 28.5 in.; 1:24/1:24/1:48 in. twist. Weight: 11.25/10.75/10 lbs. Stock: Straight grip European walnut. Sights: Two adjustable rear, steel ramp with brass bead front. Features: Percussion ignition, double triggers, sling swivels. A .72-caliber express rifle and a .50-caliber/12-gauge shotgun combination gun are also available. Blued steel furniture. Stainless steel nipple. Made by Pedersoli. Imported by Dixie Gun Works and some models by Cabela's and others.
Price: Dixie Gun Works Rifle 50X50 PR0970......................................$1,525.00
Price: Dixie Gun Works Rifle 54X54 PR0975 ....$1,525.00
Price: Dixie Gun Works Rifle 58X58 PR0980.....................................$1,525.00
Price: Dixie Gun Works Combo 50X12 gauge PR0990 ....$1,350.00
Price: Dixie Gun Works Express Rifle .72 caliber PR0916 ....$1,550.00

PEDERSOLI MAGNUM PERCUSSION SHOTGUN & COACH GUN
Gauge: 10, 12, 20 Barrel: Chrome-lined blued barrels, 25.5 in. Imp. Cyl. and Mod. Weight: 7.25, 7, 6.75 lbs. Length: 45 in. overall. Stock: Hand-checkered walnut, 14-in. pull. Features: Double triggers, light hand engraving, case-hardened locks, sling swivels. Made by Pedersoli. From Dixie Gun Works, others.
Price: Dixie Gun Works 10-ga. PS1030 .... $1,250.00
Price: Dixie Gun Works 10-ga. kit PS1040 .... $975.00
Price: Dixie Gun Works 12-ga. PS0930 .... $1,175.00
Price: Dixie Gun Works 12-ga. Kit PS0940 .... $875.00
Price: Dixie Gun Works 12-ga. Coach gun, CylXCyl, PS0914 ....$1,150.00
Price: Dixie Gun Works 20-ga. PS0334 .... $1,175.00

Prices given are believed to be accurate at time of publication however, many factors affect retail pricing so exact prices are not possible.

PEDERSOLI MORTIMER RIFLE & SHOTGUN

Caliber: .54, 12 gauge. Barrel: 36 in., 1:66 in. twist, and cylinder bore. Weight: 10 lbs. rifle, 9 lbs. shotgun. Length: 52.25 in. Stock: Halfstock walnut. Sights: Blued steel rear with flip-up leaf, blade front. Features: Percussion and flint ignition. Blued steel furniture. Single trigger. Lock with hammer safety and "waterproof pan" marked Mortimer. A percussion .45-caliber target version of this gun is available with a peep sight on the wrist, and a percussion shotgun version is also offered. Made by Pedersoli. Imported by Dixie Gun Works.
Price: Dixie Gun Works Flint Rifle, FR0151 .... **$1,575.00**
Price: Dixie Gun Works Flint Shotgun FS0155 .... **$1,525.00**

PEDERSOLI OLD ENGLISH SHOTGUN

Gauge: 12 Barrels: Browned, 28.5 in. Cyl. and Mod. Weight: 7.5 lbs. Length: 45 in. overall. Stock: Hand-checkered American maple, cap box, 14-in. pull. Features: Double triggers, light hand engraving on lock, cap box and tang, swivel studs for sling attachment. Made by Pedersoli. From Dixie Gun Works, others.
Price: Dixie Gun Works PR4090 .... **$1,750.00**

PEDERSOLI ROCKY MOUNTAIN & MISSOURI RIVER HAWKEN RIFLES

Caliber: .54 Rocky Mountain, .45 and .50 in Missouri River. Barrel: 34.75 in. octagonal with hooked breech; Rocky Mountain 1:65 in. twist; Missouri River 1:47 twist in .45 cal., and 1:24 twist in .50 cal. Weight: 10 lbs. Length: 52 in. overall. Stock: Maple or walnut, halfstock. Sights: Rear buckhorn with push elevator, silver blade front. Features: Available in Percussion, with brass furniture and double triggers. Made by Pedersoli. Imported by Dixie Gun Works and others.
Price: Dixie Gun Works Rocky Mountain, Maple PR3430 .... **$1,395.00**
Price: Dixie Gun Works Rocky Mountain, Walnut PR3435 .... **$1,195.00**
Price: Dixie Gun Works Missouri River, .50 Walnut PR3415 .... **$1,275.00**
Price: Dixie Gun Works Missouri River, .45 Walnut PR3405 .... **$1,275.00**

PEDERSOLI PENNSYLVANIA RIFLE

Caliber: .32, .45 and .50. Barrel: 41.5 in. browned, octagonal, 1:48 in. twist. Weight: 8.25 lbs. Length: 56 in. overall. Stock: American walnut. Sights: Rear semi-buckhorn with push elevator, steel blade front. Features: Available in flint or percussion, with brass furniture, and double triggers. Also available as a kit. Made by Pedersoli. Imported by Dixie Gun Works and others.
Price: Dixie Gun Works Flint .32 FR3040 .... **$950.00**
Price: Dixie Gun Works Percussion .32 PR3055 .... **$900.00**
Price: Dixie Gun Works Flint .45 PR3045 .... **$950.00**
Price: Dixie Gun Works Percussion .45 PR3060 .... **$900.00**
Price: Dixie Gun Works Flint .50 PR3050 .... **$950.00**
Price: Dixie Gun Works Percussion .50 PR3065 .... **$900.00**
Price: Dixie Gun Works Flint Kit .32 FK3260 .... **$750.00**
Price: Dixie Gun Works Percussion kit .32 PK3275 .... **$695.00**
Price: Dixie Gun Works Flint kit .45 FK3265 .... **$750.00**
Price: Dixie Gun Works Percussion kit .45 PR3280 .... **$695.00**
Price: Dixie Gun Works Flint kit .50 FK3270 .... **$750.00**
Price: Dixie Gun Works Percussion kit .50 PK3285 .... **$695.00**

PEDERSOLI SHARPS NEW MODEL 1859 MILITARY RIFLE AND CARBINE

Caliber: .54. Barrel: 30 in., 6-groove, 1:48 in. twist. Weight: 9 lbs. Length: 45.5 in. overall. Stock: Oiled walnut. Sights: Blade front, ladder-style rear. Features: Blued barrel, color case-hardened barrelbands, receiver, hammer, nose cap, lever, patchbox cover and buttplate. Introduced in 1995. Rifle made by Pedersoli. Rifle imported from Italy by Dixie Gun Works and others.
Price: Dixie Gun Work Rifle PR0862 .... **$1,650.00**
Price: Dixie Gun Work Carbine (22-in. barrel) PR0982 .... **$1,400.00**

PEDERSOLI SHARPS MODEL 1863 SPORTING RIFLE

Caliber: .45. Barrel: 32 in., octagon, 6-groove, 1:18 in. twist. Weight: 10.75 lbs. Length: 49 in. overall. Stock: Oiled walnut. Sights: Silver blade front, flip-up rear. Features: Browned octagon barrel, color case-hardened receiver, hammer and buttplate. Rifle made by Pedersoli. Imported by Dixie Gun Works and others.
Price: Dixie Gun Work Rifle PR5001 .... **$1,500.00**

PEDERSOLI SHARPS CONFEDERATE CARBINE

Caliber: .54. Barrel: 22 in., 6-groove, 1:48 in. twist. Weight: 8 lbs. Length: 39 in. overall. Stock: Oiled walnut. Sights: Blade front, dovetailed rear. Features: Browned barrel, color case-hardened receiver, hammer, and lever. Brass buttplate and barrel bands. Rifle made by Pedersoli. Imported by Dixie Gun Works and others.
Price: Dixie Gun Work Carbine PR3380 .... **$1,395.00**

PEDERSOLI TRADITIONAL HAWKEN TARGET RIFLE

Caliber: .50 and .54. Barrel: 29.5 in. octagonal, 1:48 in. twist. Weight: 9 or 8.5 lbs. Length: 45.5 in. overall. Stock: European walnut, halfstock. Sights: Rear click adjustable for windage and elevation, blade front. Features: Percussion and flintlock, brass patchbox, double-set triggers, one barrel key. Flint gun available for left-handed shooters. Both flint and percussion guns available as kit guns. Made by Pedersoli. Imported by Dixie Gun Works.
Price: Dixie Gun Works Percussion, .50 PR0502 .... **$650.00**
Price: Dixie Gun Works Percussion, .54 PR0507 .... **$650.00**
Price: Dixie Gun Works Flint, .50 FR1332 .... **$725.00**
Price: Dixie Gun Works Flint, .54 FR3515 .... **$725.00**

PEDERSOLI TRYON RIFLE

Caliber: .50. Barrel: 32 in. octagonal, 1:48 in. twist. Weight: 9.5 lbs. Length: 49 in. overall. Stock: European walnut, halfstock. Sights: Elevation-adjustable rear with stair-step notches, blade front. Features: Percussion, brass patchbox, double-set triggers, two barrel keys. Made by Pedersoli. Imported by Dixie Gun Works.
Price: Percussion, PR0860 .... **$1,100.00**

PEDERSOLI VOLUNTEER RIFLE

Caliber: .451. Barrel: 33 in., round interior bore 1:21 in. twist. Weight: 9.5 lbs. Length: 49 in. Stock: Oiled Grade 1 American walnut. Sights: Blade front, ladder-style rear. Features: Checkered stock wrist and fore-end. Blued barrel, steel ramrod, bone charcoal case-hardened receiver and hammer. Designed for .451 conical bullets. Compare to hexagonal-bored Whitworth Rifle below. Hand-fitted and finished.
Price: Dixie Gun Works PR3150...... .... **$1,295.00**

PEDERSOLI WHITWORTH RIFLE

Caliber: .451. Barrel: 36 in., hexagonal interior bore 1:20 in. twist. Weight: 9.6 lbs. Length: 52.5 in. Stock: Oiled Grade 1 American walnut. Sights: Blade front, ladder-style rear. Features: Checkered stock wrist and fore-end. Blued barrel, steel ramrod, bone charcoal case-hardened receiver and hammer. Designed for .451 conical hexagonal bullet. Compare to round-bored Volunteer Rifle above. Hand-fitted to original specifications using original Enfield arsenal gauges.
Price: Dixie Gun Works PR3256...... .... **$1,750.00**

PEDERSOLI ZOUAVE RIFLE

Caliber: .58 percussion. Barrel: 33 inches. Weight: 9.5 lbs. Length: 49 inches. Stock: European walnut. Sights: Blade front, three-leaf military rear. Features: Percussion musket-cap ignition. One-piece solid barrel and bolster. Brass-plated patchbox. Made in Italy by Pedersoli. Imported by Dixie Gun Works, others.
Price: Dixie Gun Works PF0340. .... **$975.00**

REMINGTON MODEL 700 ULTIMATE MUZZLELOADER

Caliber: .50 percussion. Barrel: 26 in., 1:26 in. twist, satin stainless steel, fluted. Length: 47 in. Stock: Bell & Carlson black synthetic. Sights: None on synthetic-stocked model. Ramrod: Stainless steel. Weight: 8.5 lbs. Features: Remington single shot Model 700 bolt action, re-primable cartridge-case ignition using Remington Magnum Large Rifle Primer, sling studs.
Price: 86960 Starting at **$1,015.00**

Prices given are believed to be accurate at time of publication however, many factors affect retail pricing so exact pricing is not possible.

THOMPSON/CENTER IMPACT MUZZLELOADING RIFLE
Caliber: .50. Barrel: 26 in., 1:28 twist, Weather Shield finish. Weight: 6.5 lbs. Length: 41.5 in. Stock: Straight Realtree Hardwoods HD or black composite. Features: Sliding-hood, break-open action, #209 primer ignition, removable breech plug, synthetic stock adjustable from 12.5 to 13.5 in., adjustable fiber-optic sights, aluminum ramrod, camo, QLA relieved muzzle system.
Price: .50-cal Stainless/Realtree Hardwoods, Weather Shield **$324.00**
Price: .50-cal Blued/Black/scope, case.......................... ....**$263.00**

THOMPSON/CENTER PRO HUNTER FX
Caliber: .50 as muzzleloading barrel. Barrel: 26 in., Weather Shield with relieved muzzle on muzzleloader; interchangeable with 14 centerfire calibers. Weight: 7 lbs. Length: 40.5 in. overall. Stock: Interchangeable American walnut butt and fore-end, black composite, FlexTech recoil-reducing camo stock as thumbhole or straight, rubber over-molded stock and fore-end. Ramrod: Solid aluminum. Sights: Tru-Glo fiber-optic front and rear. Features: Blue or stainless steel. Uses the frame of the Encore centerfire pistol; break-open design using triggerguard spur; stainless steel universal breech plug; uses #209 shotshell primers. Made in U.S. by Thompson/Center Arms.
Price: .50-cal Stainless/Black FlexTech Stock Model 5800...................**$649.00**
Price: .50-cal Stainless/Engraved frame FlexTech RT-AP camo.............**$709.00**

THOMPSON/CENTER TRIUMPH BONE COLLECTOR
Caliber: .50. Barrel: 28 in., Weather Shield coated. Weight: 6.5 lbs. Overall: 42 in. Stock: FlexTech recoil-reducing. Black composite or Realtree AP HD camo straight, rubber over-molded stock and fore-end. Sights: Fiber optic. Ramrod: Solid aluminum. Features: Break-open action. Quick Detachable Speed Breech XT plug, #209 shotshell primer ignition, easy loading QLA relieved muzzle. Made in U.S. by Thompson/Center Arms. Available from Cabela's, Bass Pro.
Price: .50-cal Synthetic Realtree AP, fiber optics.... .... **$720.00**
Price: .50-cal Synthetic/Weather Shield Black.......................................**$638.00**
Price: .50-cal. Weather Shield/AP Camo...**$679.00**
Price: .50 cal. Silver Weather Shield/AP Camo.......................................**$689.00**

THOMPSON/CENTER STRIKE
Caliber: .50. Barrel: 24 or 20 in., nitride finished, tapered barrel. Weight: 6.75 or 6.25 lbs. Length: 44 in. or 40 in. Stock: Walnut, black synthetic, G2-Vista Camo. Finish: Armornite nitride. Features: Break-open action, sliding hammerless cocking mechanism, optional pellet or loose powder primer holders, easily removable breech plugs retained by external collar, aluminum frame with steel mono-block to retain barrel, recoil pad. Sights: Williams fiber-optic sights furnished, drilled and tapped for scope. Made in the U.S. by Thompson/Center.
Price: .50 cal. 24-in. barrel, black synthetic stock **$499.00**
Price: .50 cal. 24-in. barrel, walnut stock **$599.00**
Price: .50 cal. 24-in. barrel, G2 camo stock **$549.00**

TRADITIONS BUCKSTALKER IN-LINE RIFLE
Caliber: .50. Barrel: 24 in., Cerakote finished, Accelerator Breech Plug. Weight: 6 lbs. Length: 40 in. Stock: Synthetic, G2 Vista camo or black. Sights: Fiber-optic rear. Features: Break-open action, matte-finished action and barrel. Ramrod: Solid aluminum. Imported by Traditions.
Price: R72003540 .50-cal. Youth Synthetic stock/blued........................**$219.00**
Price: R72103540 .50-cal. Synthetic stock/Cerakote **$329.00**
Price: R5-72003540 .50-cal. Synthetic stock/blued, scope.................**$294.00**
Price: R5-72103547 .50-cal. Synthetic stock/Cerakote, scope **$369.00**

TRADITIONS BUCKSTALKER XT
Caliber: .50. Barrel: 24 in. Twist rate: 1:28 in. Ignition: 209 primer. Features: Upgraded premium-grade Chromoly steel barrel, Elite XT trigger system upgrade. Uses the Dual Safety System, Accelerator Breech Plug (the plug is removable by hand and allows the use of loose or pelletized powder), and what Traditions calls its Speed Load System. Variants include a G2 Vista camo or black stock, various finish options, and scoped and non-scoped versions. For Idaho and Oregon, the Buckstalker XT Northwest Magnum features the musket ignition, open breech, and open-sights.
Price: **$229.00**

TRADITIONS CROCKETT RIFLE
Caliber: .32. Barrel: 32 in., 1:48 in. twist. Weight: 6.75 lbs. Length: 49 in. overall. Stock: Beech, inletted toe plate. Sights: Blade front, fixed rear. Features: Set triggers, hardwood halfstock, brass furniture, color case-hardened lock. Percussion. Imported by Traditions.
Price: R26128101 .32-cal. Percussion, finished **$543.00**
Price: RK52628100 .32-cal. Percussion, kit....................................**$479.00**

TRADITIONS EVOLUTION BOLT-ACTION BLACKPOWDER RIFLE
Caliber: .50 percussion. Barrel: 26 in., 1:28 in. twist, Cerakote finished barrel and action. Length: 39 in. Sights: Steel Williams fiber-optic sights. Weight: 7 to 7.25 lbs. Length: 45 in. overall. Features: Bolt action, cocking indicator, thumb safety, shipped with adaptors for No. 11 caps, musket caps and 209 shotgun-primer ignition, sling swivels. Ramrod: Aluminum, sling studs. Available with exposed ignition as a Northwest gun. Imported by Traditions.
Price: R67113350 .50-cal. synthetic black, Cerakote..........................**$250.00**
Price: R67113353 .50-cal. synthetic Realtree AP camo...... ....**$299.00**

TRADITIONS HAWKEN WOODSMAN RIFLE
Caliber: .50. Barrel: 28 in., blued, 15/16 in. flats. Weight: 7 lbs., 11 oz. Length: 44.5 in. overall. Stock: Walnut stained hardwood. Sights: Beaded blade front hunting-style open rear adjustable for windage and elevation. Features: Brass patchbox and furniture. Double-set triggers. Flint or percussion. Imported by Traditions.
Price: R2390801 .50-cal. Flintlock **$544.00**
Price: R24008 .50-cal. Percussion **$499.00**

TRADITIONS KENTUCKY DELUXE
Caliber: .50. Barrel: 33.5 in., blued octagon. Stock: Walnut-finished select hardwood. Sights: Fixed blade. Weight: 7 lbs. Features: Double set trigger, brass patch box, available as a kit, authentic wooden ramrod.
Price: ....**$379.00-$485.00**

TRADITIONS KENTUCKY RIFLE
Caliber: .50. Barrel: 33.5 in., 7/8 in. flats, 1:66 in. twist. Weight: 7 lbs. Length: 49 in. overall. Stock: Beech, inletted toe plate. Sights: Blade front, fixed rear. Features: Full-length, two-piece stock; brass furniture; color case-hardened lock. Flint or percussion. Imported by Traditions.
Price: R2010 .50-cal. Flintlock,1:66 twist **$509.00**
Price: R2020 .50-cal. Percussion, 1:66 twist.......................................**$449.00**
Price: KRC52206 .50-cal. Percussion, kit..**$343.00**

TRADITIONS MOUNTAIN RIFLE
Caliber: .50. Barrel: 32 in., octagon with brown Cerakote finish. Stock: Select hardwoods. Sights: Primitive, adjustable rear. Weight: 8.25 lbs. Features: Available in percussion or flintlock, case-hardened lock, wooden ramrod, available as a kit.
Price: .... **$494.00-$649.00**

TRADITIONS NITROFIRE
Caliber: .50. Barrel: 26 in., ultralight chromoly steel, tapered and fluted, premium Cerakote finish. Stock: Synthetic black or camo. Sights: Drilled and tapped, optional 3-9x40 scope. Weight: 6.5 lbs. Features: Several stock color options, Federal FireStick ignition system, no breech plug required, aluminum ramrod, sling swivel studs.
Price: .... **$549.00-$699.00**

TRADITIONS PA PELLET FLINTLOCK
Caliber: .50. Barrel: 26 in., blued, 1:28 in. twist., Cerakote. Weight: 7 lbs. Length: 45 in. Stock: Hardwood, synthetic and synthetic break-up, sling swivels. Fiber-optic sights. Features: New flintlock action, removable breech plug, available as left-hand model with hardwood stock. Imported by Traditions.
Price: R3800501 .50-cal. Hardwood, blued, fib. opt **$519.00**
Price: R3890501 .50-cal. Hardwood, left-hand, blued **$529.00**
Price: R3800550 .50-cal. Synthetic/blued, fib. opt............. **$497.00**

TRADITIONS PENNSYLVANIA RIFLE
Caliber: .50. Barrel: 40.25 in., 7/8 in. flats, 1:66 in. twist, octagon. Weight: 9 lbs. Length: 57.5 in. overall. Stock: Walnut. Sights: Blade front, adjustable rear. Features: Single-piece walnut stock, brass patchbox and ornamentation. Double-set triggers. Flint or percussion. Imported by Traditions.
Price: R2090 .50-cal. Flintlock **$865.00**
Price: R2100 .50-cal. Percussion........................... **$834.00**

TRADITIONS PURSUIT ULTRALIGHT MUZZLELOADER
Caliber: .50. Barrel: 26 in., chromoly tapered, fluted barrel with premium Cerakote finish, Accelerator Breech Plug. Weight: 5.5 lbs. Length: 42 in. Stock: Rubber over-molded Soft Touch camouflage, straight and thumbhole stock options. Sights: Optional 3-9x40 scope with medium rings and bases, mounted and bore-sighted by a factory-trained technician. Features: Break-open action, Williams fiber-optic sights. Imported by Traditions.
Price: Pursuit G4 Ultralight .50 Cal. Select Hardwoods/
  Cerakote R741101NS...**$469.00**
Price: Pursuit G4 Ultralight .50 Cal. Mossy Oak Break Up Country Camo/
  Cerakote R7411416.......................................**$404.00**
Price: Pursuit G4 Ultralight .50 Cal. Mossy Oak Break Up Country/Cerakote/
  Scope/Carrying Case.... .... **$479.00**

TRADITIONS TRACKER IN-LINE RIFLE
Caliber: .50. Barrel: 24 in., blued or Cerakote, 1:28 in. twist. Weight: 6 lbs., 4 oz. Length: 43 in. Stock: Black synthetic. Ramrod: Synthetic, high-impact polymer. Sights: Lite Optic blade front, adjustable rear. Features: Striker-fired action, thumb safety, adjustable trigger, rubber buttpad, sling swivel studs. Takes 150 grains of Pyrodex pellets, one-piece musket cap and 209 ignition systems. Drilled and tapped for scope. Legal for use in Northwest. Imported by Traditions.
Price: R44003470 .50-cal. Synthetic/blued **$184.00**

TRADITIONS VORTEK STRIKERFIRE
Caliber: .50. Barrel: 28 in., chromoly, tapered, fluted barrel. Weight: 6.25 lbs. Length: 44 in. Stock: Over-molded soft-touch straight stock, removable buttplate for in-stock storage. Finish: Premium Cerakote and Realtree Xtra. Features: Break-open action, sliding hammerless cocking mechanism, drop-out trigger assembly, speed load system, Accelerator Breech Plug, recoil pad. Sights: Optional 3-9x40 muzzleloader scope. Imported by Traditions. Recently upgraded with a VAPR twist barrel, 1:24-in-twist configuration. This faster twist rate stabilizes long bullets, increases accuracy, and expands the range of bullet options fueling the current long-range muzzleloading trends.
Price: Vortek StrikerFire with Nitride Coating Mossy Oak
  Break-Up Country Camo..... ....**$450.00**
Price: Vortek StrikerFire with 3-9x40 Sig Sauer Whisky 3 Scope,
  Sling & Case..**$756.00**

TRADITIONS VORTEK STRIKERFIRE LDR
Caliber: .50. Barrel: 30 in., chromoly, tapered, fluted barrel. Weight: 6.8 lbs. Length: 46 in. Stock: Over-molded soft-touch straight stock, removable buttplate for in-stock storage. Finish: Premium Cerakote and Realtree Xtra. Features: Break-open action, sliding hammerless cocking mechanism, drop-out trigger assembly, speed load system, Accelerator Breech Plug, recoil pad. Sights: Optional 3-9x40 muzzleloader scope. Imported by Traditions.
Price: R491140WA Synthetic/black Hogue Over-mold,
  Cerakote barrel, no sights...**$499.00**

WOODMAN ARMS PATRIOT
Caliber: .45, .50. Barrel: 24 in., nitride-coated, 416 stainless, 1:24 twist in .45, 1:28 twist in .50. Weight: 5.75 lbs. Length: 43-in. Stocks: Laminated, walnut or hydrographic dipped, synthetic black, over-molded soft-touch straight stock. Finish: Nitride black and black anodized. Features: Break-open action, hammerless cocking mechanism, match-grade patented trigger assembly, speed load system, recoil pad. Sights: Picatinny rail with built-in rear and 1-inch or 30 mm scope mounts, red fiber-optic front bead.
Price: Patriot .45 or .50-cal...**$899.00**

UBERTI 1858 NEW ARMY REMINGTON TARGET CARBINE REVOLVER
Caliber: .44, 6-shot. Barrel: Tapered octagon, 18 in. Weight: 70.4 oz. Length: Standard 35.3 in. Stock: Walnut. Sights: Standard blade front, adjustable rear. Features: Replica of Remington's revolving rifle of 1866. Made by Uberti. Imported by Uberti USA, Cimarron F.A. Co., Taylor's and others.
Price: Uberti USA, 341200.. **$559.00**

Prices given are believed to be accurate at time of publication however, many factors affect retail pricing so exact prices are not possible.

AIRFORCE TALON P PCP AIR PISTOL
Caliber: .25. Barrel: Rifled 12.0 in. Weight: 3.5 lbs. Length: 24.2 in. Sights: None, grooved for scope. Features: Quick-detachable air tank with adjustable power. Match-grade Lothar Walther, massive power output in a highly compact size, two-stage trigger. Velocity: 400-900 fps.
Price: $479.00

Air Venturi v10 Match air pistol
Caliber: .177 pellets. Barrel: Rifled. Weight: 1.95 lbs. Length: 12.6 in. Power: Single stroke pneumatic. Sights: Front post, fully adjustable rear blade, Features: 10-Meter competition class pistol, fully adjustable trigger, 1.5-lb. trigger pull Velocity: 400 fps.
Price: $299.00

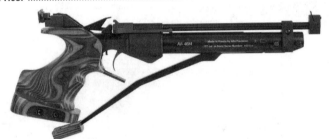

AIR VENTURI AV-46M MATCH AIR PISTOL
Caliber: .177 pellets. Barrel: Rifled. Weight: 2.6 lbs. Length: 16.5 in. Power: Single stroke pneumatic. Sights: Front post, fully adjustable rear blade. Features: Bolt action, 18 lb. cocking effort, red and black laminate grip, two-stage adjustable trigger, adjustable/removable palm shelf, made by Alpha Precision, entry level 10 meter competition pistol, can be dry fired. Velocity: 480 fps.
Price: $649.00

ALFA PROJ COMPETITION PCP PISTOL
Caliber: .177 pellets. Barrel: Rifled, 9.5 in. Weight: 2 lbs. Length: 15.5 inches. Power: Precharged pneumatic. Sights: Front adjustable width post, fully adjustable rear blade. Features: Single shot, 10-Meter competition class pistol, highly adjustable trigger, adjustable velocity, factory trigger pull set to 8 oz., ambidextrous grip. Velocity: 500 fps.
Price: $989.00

ASG STI DUTY ONE CO2 BB PISTOL
Caliber: .177 steel BBs. Barrel: Smoothbore Weight: 1.82 lbs. Length: 8.66 in. Power: CO2. Sights: Fixed. Features: Blowback, accessory rail, and metal slide. Velocity: 383 fps.
Price: $120.00

ATAMAN AP16 REGULATED COMPACT AIR PISTOL
Caliber: .177, .22 pellets. Barrel: Rifled Match Barrel Weight: 1.76 lbs. Length: 12.0 in. Power: Pre-Charged Pneumatic. Sights: Fixed Front Ramp, Adjustable Rear Notch. Features: 7-round Rotary Magazine, 300 Bar Max Fill, Regulated for hunting power, exceptional build quality, available in satin and blued finishes Velocity: 590 fps.
Price: $1,049.00

ATAMAN AP16 REGULATED STANDARD AIR PISTOL
Caliber: .177, .22 pellets. Barrel: Rifled Match Barrel Weight: 2.2 lbs. Length: 14.37 in. Power: Pre-Charged Pneumatic. Sights: Fixed Front Ramp, Adjustable Rear Notch. Features: 7-round Rotary Magazine, 300 Bar Max Fill, Regulated for hunting power, exceptional build quality, Velocity: 656 fps.
Price: $1,049.00

BEEMAN P17 AIR PISTOL
Caliber: .177 pellets. Barrel: Rifled. Weight: 1.7 lbs. Length: 9.6 in. Power: Single stroke pneumatic. Sights: Front and rear fiber-optic sights, rear sight fully adjustable. Features: Exceptional trigger, grooved for scope mounting with dry-fire feature for practice. Velocity: 410 fps.
Price: $45.00

BEEMAN P1 MAGNUM AIR PISTOL
Caliber: .177, .20, .22. pellets. Barrel: Rifled. Weight: 2.5 lbs. Length: 11 in. Power: Single stroke, spring-piston. Grips: Checkered walnut. Sights: Blade front, square notch rear with click micrometer adjustments for windage and elevation. Grooved for scope mounting. Features: Dual power for .177 and 20 cal.; Compatible with all Colt 45 auto grips. Dry-firing feature for practice. Velocity: varies by caliber and power setting.
Price: ....$455.00–$549.00

BEEMAN P3 PNEUMATIC AIR PISTOL
Caliber: .177. pellets. Barrel: Rifled Weight: 1.7 lbs. Length: 9.6 in. Power: Single-stroke pneumatic. Sights: Front and rear fiber-optic sights, rear sight fully adjustable. Features: Grooved for scope mounting, exceptional trigger, automatic safety. Velocity: 410 fps.
Price: $249.00

BEEMAN P11 AIR PISTOL
Caliber: .177, .22. Barrel: Rifled. Weight: 2.6 lbs. Length: 10.75 in. Power: Single-stroke pneumatic with high and low settings. Sights: Front ramp sight, fully adjustable rear sight. Features: 2-stage adjustable trigger and automatic safety. Velocity: Up to 600 fps in .177 caliber and Up to 460 fps in .22 caliber.
Price: ....$524.00–$634.00

BEEMAN 2027 PCP PISTOL
Caliber: .177 Barrel: Rifled. Weight: 1.7 lbs. Length: 9.25 in. Power: Single stroke pneumatic. Sights: Adjustable open sights. Features: Textured grip, 12-round magazine, adjustable velocity, 60 shots per fill (at 600 fps), adjustable trigger. Velocity: 600 fps.
Price: $169.00

BENJAMIN MARAUDER PCP PISTOL
Caliber: .22 Barrel: Rifled. Weight: 2.7-3 lbs. Length: Pistol length 18 in./ Carbine length 29.75 in. Power: Pre-charged pneumatic Sights: None. Grooved for optics. Features: Multi-shot (8-round rotary magazine) bolt action, shrouded steel barrel, two-stage adjustable trigger, includes both pistol grips and a carbine stock and is built in America. Velocity: 700 fps.
Price: $419.00

BENJAMIN MARAUDER WOODS WALKER PCP PISTOL
Caliber: .22 Barrel: Rifled. Weight: 2.7 lbs. Length: Pistol length 18 in./Carbine length 29.75 in. Power: Pre-charged pneumatic Sights: Includes CenterPoint Multi-TAC Quick Aim Sight. Features: Multi-shot (8-round rotary magazine) bolt action, shrouded steel barrel, two-stage adjustable trigger, includes both pistol grips and a carbine stock and is built in America. Velocity: 700 fps.
Price: $549.00

BERETTA APX BLOWBACK AIR PISTOL
Caliber: .177 steel BBs. Barrel: Smoothbore. Weight: 1.47 lbs. Length: 7.48 in. Power: CO2. Sights: Fixed. Features: Highly accurate replica action pistol, 19-shot capacity, front accessory rail, metal and ABS plastic construction. Velocity: 400 fps.
Price: $69.00

BERETTA M84FS AIR PISTOL
Caliber: .177 steel BBs. Barrel: Smoothbore Weight: 1.4 lbs. Length: 7 in. Power: CO2. Sights: Fixed. Features: Highly realistic replica action pistol, blowback operation, full metal construction. Velocity: To 360 fps.
Price: $119.00

BERETTA PX4 Storm CO2 PISTOL
Caliber: .177 pellet /.177 steel BBs. Barrel: Rifled Weight: 1.6 lbs. Length: 7.6 in. Power: CO2. Sights: Blade front sight and fixed rear sight. Features: Semi-automatic, 16-shot capacity with maximum of 40-shots per fill, dual ammo capable. Velocity: To 380 fps.
Price: $119.00

BERETTA M9A3 FULL AUTO BB PISTOL
Caliber: .177 steel BBs. Barrel: Smoothbore Weight: NA. Length: NA. Power: CO2. Sights: Blade front sight and fixed rear sight. Features: Can operate as semi-automatic or fully automatic, full size 18-shot magazine, blowback slide, single/double action, ambidextrous safety. Velocity: To 380 fps.
Price: $124.00

BERETTA 92A1 CO2 FULL AUTO BB PISTOL
Caliber: .177 steel BBs. Barrel: Smoothbore Weight: 2.4 lbs. Length: 8.5 in. Power: CO2. Sights: Fixed. Features: Highly realistic replica action pistol, 18-shot semi-automatic, full metal construction, selectable fire semi-automatic & full-automatic. Velocity: To 330 fps.
Price: $139.00

BERETTA 92FS CO2 PELLET GUN
Caliber: .177 pellets. Barrel: Rifled Weight: 2.75 lbs. Length: 8.0 in. Power: CO2. Sights: Fixed front sight, rear adjustable for windage. Features: Highly realistic replica-action pistol, 8-shot semi-automatic, full metal construction, available in various finishes and grips. Velocity: To 425 fps.
Price: ....$225.00-$289.00

BERSA THUNDER 9 PRO BB PISTOL
Caliber: .177 steel BBs. Barrel: Smoothbore. Weight: 1.17 lbs. Length: 7.56 in. Power: CO2. Sights: Fixed, three-white-dot system. Features: Highly realistic replica action pistol, 19-shot semi-automatic, composite/synthetic construction. Velocity: To 400 fps.
Price: $64.00

BERSA BP9CC BLOWBACK AIR PISTOL
Caliber: .177 steel BBs. Barrel: Smoothbore Weight: 1.35 lbs. Length: 6.61 in. Power: CO2. Sights: Fixed 3-dot system. Features: Blowback, metal slide, weaver accessory rail, is also available in a non-blowback version. Velocity: 350 fps.
Price: $104.00

BROWNING 800 EXPRESS AIR PISTOL
Caliber: .177 pellets. Barrel: Rifled Weight: 3.9 lbs. Length: 18 in. Power: Single cock, spring-piston. Sights: Fiber-optic front sight and adjustable fiber-optic rear sight. Features: Automatic safety, 11mm dovetail rail scope mounting possible. Velocity: 700 fps.
Price: $168.00

BROWNING BUCK MARK URX

BROWNING BUCK MARK AIR PISTOL
Caliber: .177 pellets. Barrel: Rifled Weight: 1.5 lbs. Length: 12.0 in. Power: Single cock, spring-piston. Sights: Front ramp sight, fully adjustable rear notch sight. Features: Weaver rail for scope mounting, light cocking force. Velocity: 360 fps.
Price: $49.00

CHIAPPA AG92 CO2 PISTOL
Caliber: .177 pellets. Barrel: Rifled, 4.8 in. Weight: 1.3 lbs. Length: 8.6 in. Power: CO2. Sights: Adjustable rear. Features: Powered by two 12 gram CO2 cylinders, holds two 7-round pellet cylinders, single/double action, polymer frame reinforced with fiberglass. Velocity: 330 fps.
Price: $138.00

CHIAPPA FAS 6004 PNEUMATIC PISTOL
Caliber: .177 pellets. Barrel: Rifled. Weight: 2 lbs. Length: 11.0 in. Power: Single stroke pneumatic. Sights: Fully adjustable target rear sight. Features: Walnut ambidextrous grip, fully adjustable trigger. Velocity: 330 fps.
Price: $442.00

CHIAPPA RHINO 50DS CO2 REVOLVER
Caliber: .177 BBs. Barrel: Smoothbore, 5 in. Weight: 2.5 lbs. Length: 9.5 in. Power: CO2. Sights: Adjustable rear sight. Features: Single/double action, 6-shot capacity, black or silver frame, under barrel accessory rail. Velocity: 330 fps.
Price: ....$159.00–$179.00

COBRAY INGRAM M11 CO2 BB SUBMACHINE GUN
Caliber: .177 BBs. Barrel: Smoothbore. Weight: 1.2 lbs. Length: 10.0 in. Power: CO2. Sights: Fixed sights. Features: Semiautomatic, 39-shot capacity, folding metal stock. Velocity: 394 fps.
Price: $59.00

COLT PYTHON

COLT PYTHON CO2 PISTOL
Caliber: .177 steel BBs. Barrel: Smoothbore Weight: 2.6 lbs. Length: 11.25 in. Power: CO2. Sights: Fixed. Features: High-quality replica, swing-out cylinder, removable casings and functioning ejector, multiple finishes. Velocity: To 400 fps.
Price: $149.00

COLT DEFENDER BB PISTOL
Caliber: .177 steel BBs. Barrel: Smoothbore Weight: 1.6 lbs. Length: 6.75 in. Power: CO2. Sights: Fixed with blade ramp front sight. Features: Semi-automatic, 16-shot capacity, all metal construction, realistic weight and feel. Velocity: 410 fps.
Price: $74.00

COLT 1911 SPECIAL COMBAT CLASSIC BB PISTOL
Caliber: .177 steel BBs. Barrel: Smoothbore. Weight: 2.05 lbs. Length: 8.58 in. Power: CO2. Sights: Blade front sight and adjustable rear sight. Features: Semi-automatic, 20-shot capacity, realistic action, weight and feel. Velocity: 400 fps.
Price: $120.00

COLT 1911 A1 CO2 PELLET PISTOL
Caliber: .177 pellets. Barrel: Rifled Weight: 2.4 lbs. Length: 9.0 in. Power: CO2. Sights: Blade ramp front sight and adjustable rear sight. Features: Semi-automatic, 8-shot capacity, all metal construction, realistic weight and feel. Velocity: 425 fps.
Price: $279.00

COLT COMMANDER CO2 PISTOL
Caliber: .177 steel BBs. Barrel: Smoothbore. Weight: 2.1 lbs. Length: 8.5 in. Power: CO2. Sights: Blade front sight and fixed rear sight. Features: Semi-automatic, blowback action, 18-shot capacity, highly realistic replica pistol. Velocity: 325 fps.
Price: $119.00

COLT SAA CO2 PELLET REVOLVER

Caliber: .177 pellets. Barrel: Rifled. Weight: 2.1 lbs. Length: 11 in. Power: CO2. Sights: Blade front sight and fixed rear sight. Features: Full metal revolver with manual safety, realistic loading, 6 individual shells, highly accurate, full metal replica pistol, multiple finishes and grips available. Velocity: 380 fps.
Price: $179.00

COMETA INDIAN AIR PISTOL

Caliber: .177 pellets. Barrel: Rifled. Weight: 2.43 lbs. Length: 10.43 in. Power: Spring Powered. Sights: Blade front sight and adjustable rear sight. Features: Single shot, cold-hammered forged barrel, textured grips. Velocity: 492 fps.
Price: .... $199.00–$219.00

CROSMAN 2240 CO2 PISTOL

Caliber: .22. Barrel: Rifled. Weight: 1.8 lbs. Length: 11.13 in. Power: CO2. Sights: Blade front, rear adjustable. Features: Single shot bolt action, ambidextrous grip, all metal construction. Velocity: 460 fps.
Price: $79.00

CROSMAN 2300S TARGET PISTOL

Caliber: .177 pellets. Barrel: Rifled. Weight: 2.66 lbs. Length: 16 in. Power: CO2. Sights: Front fixed sight and Williams notched rear sight. Features: Meets IHMSA rules for Production Class Silhouette Competitions. Lothar Walter match-grade barrel, adjustable trigger, adjustable hammer, stainless steel bolt, 60 shots per CO2 cartridge. Velocity: 520 fps.
Price: $339.00

CROSMAN 2300T CO2 PISTOL

Caliber: .177 pellets. Barrel: Rifled. Weight: 2.66 lbs. Length: 13.25 in. Power: CO2. Sights: fixed front sight and LPA rear sight. Features: Single-shot, bolt action, adjustable trigger, designed for shooting clubs and organizations that teach pistol shooting and capable of firing 40 shots per CO2 cartridge. Velocity: 420 fps.
Price: $229.00

CROSMAN 1701P SILHOUETTE PCP AIR PISTOL

Caliber: .177 pellets. Barrel: Rifled Lothar Walther Match. Weight: 2.5 lbs. Length: 14.75 in. Power: Pre-charged Pneumatic. Sights: fixed front sight rear sight not included Features: Adjustable trigger, designed for shooting silhouette competition, 50 shots per fill. Velocity: 450 fps.
Price: $429.00

CROSMAN 1720T PCP TARGET PISTOL

Caliber: .177 pellets. Barrel: Rifled Lothar Walther Match. Weight: 2.96 lbs. Length: 18.00 in. Power: Pre-charged Pneumatic. Sights: Not included Features: Adjustable trigger, designed for shooting silhouettes, fully shrouded barrel, 50 shots per fill. Velocity: 750 fps.
Price: $559.00

CROSMAN SR.357S DUAL AMMO CO2 REVOLVER

Caliber: .177 steel BBs/.177 pellets. Barrel: Smoothbore Weight: 2.00 lbs. Length: 11.73 in. Power: CO2. Sights: Adjustable rear sight, Fixed Front Blade. Features: Full metal revolver in "stainless steel" finish. Comes with shells for BBs and .177 lead pellets Velocity: 400 fps. with steel BBs.
Price: $99.00

CROSMAN FULL AUTO A4P PISTOL

Caliber: .177 steel BBs. Barrel: Smoothbore Weight: NA. Length: NA. Power: CO2. Sights: None, comes with red-dot sight. Features: Tactical-style AR full-/semi-auto pistol, blowback action, AR compatible pistol grip, quad rail forearm for accessory mounting, 25-round removable magazine. Velocity: NA.
Price: ....$NA

CROSMAN FULL AUTO P1 PISTOL
Caliber: .177 steel BBs. Barrel: Smoothbore Weight: 2.5 lbs. Length: 8.5 in. Power: CO_2. Sights: Fixed, rail-mounted laser included. Features: Full-/semi-auto pistol, blowback action, metal frame and slide, single/double action, 20-round removable magazine, Picatinny rail. Velocity: 400 fps.
Price: $179.00

CROSMAN TRIPLE THREAT CO2 REVOLVER
Caliber: .177 steel BBs/.177 pellets. Barrel: Rifled. Weight: Variable. Length: Variable. Power: CO_2. Sights: Adjustable rear sight. Features: Comes with three barrels (3 in., 6 in., and 8 in.) and six-shot BB clip and 10-shot .177 lead pellet clip, single/double action, die cast full metal frame. Velocity: Up to 425 fps. with steel BBs.
Price: $84.00

CROSMAN C11 CO2 BB GUN
Caliber: .177 steel BBs. Barrel: Smoothbore Weight: 1.4 lbs. Length: 7.0 in. Power: CO_2. Sights: Fixed. Features: Compact semi-automatic BB pistol, front accessory rail. Velocity: 480 fps.
Price: $49.00

CROSMAN MK45 BB PISTOL
Caliber: .177 steel BBs. Barrel: Smoothbore. Weight: 1.1 lbs. Length: 7.5 in. Power: CO_2. Sights: Fixed. Features: 20-round drop-out magazine, accessory rail. Velocity: 480 fps.
Price: $49.00

CROSMAN CM9B MAKO BB PISTOL
Caliber: .177 BBs. Barrel: Smoothbore. Weight: 1.7 lbs. Length: 8.6 in. Power: CO_2. Sights: Fiber optic. Blowback action, tricolor, accessory rail. Velocity: 425 fps.
Price: $79.00

CROSMAN AMERICAN CLASSIC P1377/1322 AIR PISTOL
Caliber: .177 or .22. Barrel: Rifled Weight: 2 lbs. Length: 13.63 in. Power: Multi-pump pneumatic. Sights: Front Blade & Ramp, adjustable rear. Features: Single shot, bolt action, available with brown (.177 only) or black grips, pistol grip shoulder stock available separately. Velocities: To 695 fps (.177); to 460 fps (.22).
Price: $79.00

CROSMAN VIGILANTE CO2 REVOLVER
Caliber: .177 steel BBs/.177 pellets. Barrel: Rifled. Weight: 2 lbs. Length: 11.38 in. Power: CO_2. Sights: Blade front, rear adjustable. Features: Single- and double-action revolver (10-shot pellet/6-shot BBs) synthetic frame and finger-molded grip design. Velocity: 465 fps.
Price: $79.00

CROSMAN GI MODEL 1911 CO2 BLOWBACK BB PISTOL
Caliber: .177 steel BBs. Barrel: Smoothbore. Weight: 1.88 lbs. Length: 8.63 in. Power: CO_2. Sights: Rear Fixed sights Front Blade. Features: Full metal replica with realistic blowback, 20-round capacity, double-action only. Velocity: 450 fps.
Price: $99.00

CZ P-09 DUTY CO2 PISTOL
Caliber: .177 BBs/.177 flat-head pellets. Barrel: Rifled. Weight: 1.6 lbs. Length: 8.2 in. Power: CO_2. Sights: Three-dot fixed sights. Features: Blowback action, manual safety, double-action-only trigger, 16-round capacity in a 2x8 shot stick magazine, Weaver-style accessory rail, threaded muzzle, blue or two-tone finish, ambidextrous safety with decocker. Velocity: 492 fps.
Price: $104.00

CZ-75 CO2 PISTOL
Caliber: .177 BBs. Barrel: Smooth. Weight: 2.1 lbs. Length: 8.2 in. Power: CO_2. Sights: Fixed sights. Features: Blowback action, manual safety, full metal construction, single-action trigger, removable 17-round BB magazine, Weaver-style accessory rail, also available as a non-blowback compact version. Velocity: 312 fps.
Price: $159.00

CZ 75 SP-01 SHADOW CO2 BB PISTOL
Caliber: .177 steel BBs. Barrel: Smoothbore threaded for barrel extension. Power: CO_2. Weight: 1.3 lbs. Length: 8.4 in. Sights: Fiber-optic front and rear. Features: Non-blowback, double action, accessory rail, 21-round capacity, also available in a heavier-weight, blowback version. Velocity: 380 fps.
Price: $59.00

Prices given are believed to be accurate at time of publication however, many factors affect retail pricing so exact prices are not possible.

76TH EDITION, 2022 ✛ **543**

CZ SHADOW 2 CO2 BB PISTOL
Caliber: .177 steel BBs. Barrel: Smoothbore. Weight: 2.7 lbs. Length: 8.5 in. Power: CO2. Sights: Fiber optic, adjustable rear. Features: Full metal construction, adjustable travel trigger, adjustable hop up, double action, checkered grip, individual serial number, blowback, 18-round dropout magazine, uses one 12-gram CO2 cylinder, under barrel accessory rail, adjustable magazine release. Velocity: 285 fps.
Price: $179.00

CZ 75 P-07 DUTY PISTOL
Caliber: .177 steel BBs. Barrel: Smoothbore. Weight: 1.81 lbs. Length: 7.5 in. Power: CO2. Sights: Fixed. Features: Full metal construction, accessory rail, blowback, 20-round dropout magazine, threaded barrel, blue or two-tone finish, also available in a non-blowback, lower-priced version. Velocity: 342 fps.
Price: $109.00

CZ 75D COMPACT CO2 BB PISTOL
Caliber: .177 steel BBs. Barrel: Smoothbore. Weight: 1.5 lbs. Length: 7.4 in. Power: CO2. Sights: Adjustable rear sight and blade front sight. Features: Compact design, non-blowback action, blue or two-tone finish, accessory rail. Velocity: 380 fps.
Price: $79.00

DAISY POWERLINE 340 AIR PISTOL
Caliber: .177 steel BBs. Barrel: Smoothbore. Weight: 1.0 lbs. Length: 8.5 in. Power: Single cock, spring-piston. Sights: Rear sight Fixed Front blade. Features: Spring-air action, 200-shot BB reservoir with a 13-shot Speed-load Clip located in the grip. Velocity: 240 fps.
Price: $24.00

DAISY 408 CO2 PISTOL
Caliber: .177 steel BBs. Barrel: Rifled. Weight: 1.3 lbs. Length: 7.75 in. Power: CO2. Sights: Front blade, fixed open rear. Features: Semi-automatic, 8-shot removable clip, lower accessory rail. Velocity: 485 fps.
Price: $64.00

DAISY POWERLINE 415 CO2 BB PISTOL
Caliber: .177 steel BBs. Barrel: Smoothbore. Weight: 1 lb. Length: 8.6 in. Power: CO2. Sights: Front blade, fixed open rear. Features: Semi-automatic 21-shot BB pistol. Velocity: 500 fps.
Price: $35.00

DAISY POWERLINE 5501 CO2 PISTOL
Caliber: .177 steel BBs. Barrel: Smoothbore. Weight: 1.0 lbs. Length: 6.8 in. Power: CO2. Sights: Blade and ramp front, Fixed rear. Features: CO2 semi-automatic blowback action. 15-shot clip. Velocity: 430 fps.
Price: $79.00

DAN WESSON 2.5 in./4 in./6 in./8 in. PELLET REVOLVER
Caliber: .177 BBs or .177 pellets. Barrel: Smoothbore (BB version) or Rifled (Pellet version). Weights: 1.65–2.29 lbs. Lengths: 8.3–13.3 in. Power: CO2. Sights: Blade front and adjustable rear sight. Features: Highly realistic replica revolver with swing-out, six-shot cylinder, Weaver-style scope rail, multiple finishes and grip configurations, 6 realistic cartridges, includes a speed loader. Velocities: 318–426 fps.
Price: ....$149.00–$199.00

DAN WESSON 715 2.5 in./4 in./6 in. REVOLVER
Caliber: .177 BBs or .177 pellets. Barrel: Smoothbore (BB Version) or Rifled (Pellet version). Weights: 2.2–2.7 lbs. Lengths: 8.3–11.7 in. Power: CO2. Sights: Blade front and adjustable rear sight. Features: Highly realistic replica revolver, accessory rail, multiple finishes and grip configurations, six realistic cartridges, includes a speed loader. Velocities: 318–426 fps.
Price: ....$159.00–$199.00

DAN WESSON VALOR 1911 PISTOL
Caliber: .177 pellets. Barrel: Rifled. Weight: 2.2 lbs. Length: 8.7 in. Power: CO2. Sights: Fixed. Features: Non-blowback, full metal construction, 12-round capacity in two six-round drum magazines. Velocities: 332 fps.
Price: $99.00

DIANA AIRBUG CO2 PISTOL
Caliber: .177, .22 pellets. Barrel: Rifled, 8.3 in. Weight: 2 lbs. Length: 14 in. Power: CO2. Sights: Front post, adjustable rear. Features: Hardwood, ambidextrous grip, bolt action, 9 shot (.117), 7 shot (.22), or single shot, comes with a soft-sided case. Velocities: 525 fps (.177), 460 fps (.22).
Price: $139.00

DIANA BANDIT PCP PISTOL
Caliber: .177, .22 pellets. Barrel: Rifled, 9.5 in. Weight: 2.2 lbs. Length: 20.1 in. Power: Precharged pneumatic. Sights: Front post, adjustable rear, 11 mm dovetail under rear sight. Features: Hardwood, ambidextrous grip, bolt action, 9 shot (.117), 7 shot (.22), or single shot, two stage adjustable Diana Improved Trigger (DIT), comes with a soft-sided case. Velocities: 725 fps (.177), 630 fps (.22).
Price: $199.00

Prices given are believed to be accurate at time of publication however, many factors affect retail pricing so exact prices are not possible.

DIANA LP 8 PISTOL
Caliber: .177 pellets. Barrel: Rifled. Weight: 3.20 lbs. Length: 7.00 in. Power: Spring powered. Sights: Fixed front sight with fully adjustable rear sight. Features: Powerful spring powered air pistol, single cock delivers full power, exceptional design and build quality. Velocity: 700 fps.
Price: **$349.00**

FEINWERKBAU P11 PICCOLO AIR PISTOL
Caliber: .177 pellets. Barrel: Rifled. Weight: 1.6 lbs. Length: 13.58 in. Power: Pre-charged pneumatic. Sights: Front post, fully adjustable rear blade, Features: 10-Meter competition class pistol, meets ISSF requirements, highly adjustable match trigger, Velocity: 492 fps.
Price: **$1,599.00**

FEINWERKBAU P8X PCP 10-METER AIR PISTOL
Caliber: .177 pellets. Barrel: Rifled. Weight: 2.09 lbs. Length: 16.33 in. Power: Pre-charged pneumatic. Sights: Front post, fully adjustable rear blade. Features: 10-Meter competition class pistol with highly customizable grip system, meets ISSF requirements, highly adjustable match trigger. Velocity: 508 fps.
Price: **$2,399.00**

GAMO C-15 BONE COLLECTOR CO2 PISTOL
Caliber: .177 BB/.177 pellets. Barrel: Smooth. Weight: 1.5 lbs. Length: 10 in. Power: CO2. Sights: Fixed. Features: Blowback action, approximately 80 shots per CO2 cylinder, single/double action, manual safety, has two side-by-side eight-shot magazines Velocity: 450 fps with PBA pellets.
Price: **$118.00**

GAMO GP-20 COMBAT CO2 BB PISTOL
Caliber: .177 BBs. Barrel: Smooth. Weight:1 lb. Length: 10 in. Power: CO2. Sights: Fixed with fiber optic rear. Features: Single/double action, manual safety, 20 BB magazine. Velocity: 400 fps.
Price: **$39.00**

GAMO P-900 IGT AIR PISTOL
Caliber: .177 pellets. Barrel: Rifled. Weight: 1.3 lbs. Length: 12.6 in. Power: Single cock, gas-pistol. Sights: Fiber-optic front and fully adjustable fiber-optic rear sight. Features: Break-barrel single-shot, ergonomic design, rubberized grip. Velocity: 508 fps.
Price: **$79.00**

GAMO P-900 IGT AIR PISTOL
Caliber: .177 pellets. Barrel: Rifled. Weight: 1.3 lbs. Length: 12.6 in. Power: Single-cock, gas-pistol. Sights: Fiber-optic front and fully adjustable fiber-optic rear. Features: Break-barrel single-shot, ergonomic design, rubberized grip. Velocity: 508 fps.
Price: **$79.00**

GAMO P-25 AIR PISTOL
Caliber: .177 pellets. Barrel: Rifled. Weight: 1.5 lbs. Length: 7.75 in. Power: CO2. Sights: Fixed. Features: Semi-automatic, 16-shot capacity, realistic blowback action. Velocity: 450 fps.
Price: **$109.00**

GAMO P-27 AIR PISTOL
Caliber: .177 BB/.177 pellets. Barrel: Smooth. Weight: 1.5 lbs. Length: 7 in. Power: CO2. Sights: Fixed with white dots. Features: Single/double action, Semi-automatic, 16-shot capacity in two 8-round clips, non-blowback action, rail under barrel. Velocity: 400 fps.
Price: **$69.00**

GAMO PR-776 CO2 REVOLVER
Caliber: .177 pellets. Barrel: Rifled. Weight: 2.29 lbs. Length: 11.5 in. Power: CO2. Sights: Fixed front sight with fully adjustable rear sight. Features: All metal frame, comes with two 8-shot clips, double- and single-action Velocity: 438 fps.
Price: **119.00**

GAMO PT-85 CO2 PISTOL
Caliber: .177 pellets. Barrel: Rifled. Weight: 1.5 lbs. Length: 7.8 in. Power: CO2. Sights: Fixed. Features: Semi-automatic, 16-shot capacity, realistic blowback action Velocity: 450 fps.
Price: **$119.00**

GLETCHER STECHKIN APS GOLD BLOWBACK CO2 BB PISTOL
Caliber: .177 steel BBs. Barrel: Smoothbore. Weight: 2.3 lbs. Length: 8.88 in. Power: CO2. Sights: Fixed Features: Full metal gold-colored frame, highly realistic replica of the Soviet Stechkin pistol, 22-round magazine, double action and single action. Velocities: 361 fps.
Price: **$259.00**

GLETCHER NGT F CO2 BB REVOLVER
Caliber: .177 steel BBs. Barrel: Smoothbore. Weight: 1.54 lbs. Length: 9.00 in. Power: CO2. Sights: Fixed Features: Full metal frame, highly realistic replica, 7-shot cylinder with realistic "shells," double action and single action, available in blued and polished silver finishes. Velocity: 403 fps..
Price: ....**$134.00-$179.00**

Prices given are believed to be accurate at time of publication however, many factors affect retail pricing so exact prices are not possible.

76TH EDITION, 2022 ⊕ **545**

GLOCK 17 GEN3/GEN 4 CO2 PISTOL
Caliber: .177 BBs. Barrel: Smoothbore. Weight: 1.6 lbs. Length: 7.75 in. Power: CO2. Sights: Fixed Features: Blowback action, metal slide and magazine, 18 BB capacity, manual safety, double-action trigger, replica of the Glock 17 firearm. Velocity: 365 fps..
Price: $109.00-149.00

GLOCK 19 GEN3 CO2 PISTOL
Caliber: .177 BBs. Barrel: Smoothbore. Weight: 1.6 lbs. Length: 7.25 in. Power: CO2. Sights: Fixed Features: Non-blowback action, manual safety, 16 BB capacity, integrated Weaver-style accessory rail, double-action trigger, replica of the Glock 19 firearm. Velocity: 410 fps.
Price: $79.00

HAMMERLI AP-20 AIR PISTOL
Caliber: .177 pellets. Barrel: Rifled. Weight: 1.92 lbs. Length: 16.34 in. Power: Pre-charged pneumatic. Sights: Fully adjustable micrometer. Features: 2-stage adjustable trigger factory set to 500 grams pull weight, single shot, bolt action, up to 120 shots per fill. Velocity: 492 fps.
Price: $999.00

HATSAN MODEL 25 SUPERCHARGER VORTEX AIR PISTOL
Caliber: .177 or .22 pellets. Barrel: Rifled. Weight: 3.9 lbs. Length: 20 in. Power: Single cock, air-piston Sights: Fiber-optic front and fully adjustable fiber-optic rear sight. Features: Molded right-handed grips, left-handed grips available, fully adjustable "Quattro" trigger, integrated anti-recoil system, threaded muzzle. Velocity: 700 fps with lead pellets.
Price: $189.00

HATSAN USA AT P1 QUIET ENERGY PCP PISTOL

HATSAN USA AT P1 QUIET ENERGY PCP PISTOL
Calibers: .177, .22, .25. Barrel: Rifled. Weight: 4.7 lbs. Length: 23.2 in. Power: Pre-charged pneumatic. Sights: N/A. Grooved for scope mounting. Features: Multi-shot magazine feed, integrated suppressor, muzzle energy suitable for pest control and small game hunting. Velocity: .177, 870 fps/.22, 780 fps/.25, 710 fps.
Price: $479.00

HATSAN SORTIE AIR PISTOL
Caliber: .177, .22, or .25 pellets. Barrel: Rifled. Weight: 4.4 lbs. Length: 15.5 in. Power: Pre-charged pneumatic. Sights: Fiber-optic front and fully adjustable rear sight. Features: Polymer grips, semi-automatic action, fully shrouded barrel, rotary magazine, Picatinny rail. Velocity with lead pellets: 850 fps (.177), 700 fps (.22), 625 fps (.25).
Price: $649.00

H&K VP9 BB CO2 PISTOL
Caliber: .177 steel BBs. Barrel: Smoothbore. Weight: 1.42 lbs. Length: 7.2 in. Power: CO2. Sights: Fixed. Features: Highly realistic replica, blowback action, integrated front weaver accessory rail, 18-round magazine. Velocity: 350 fps.
Price: $89.00

H&K P30 BB CO2 Pistol
Caliber: .177 BB/.177 pellet. Barrel: Rifled. Weight: 1.7 lbs. Length: 7.1 in. Power: CO2. Sights: Front and rear windage adjustable. Features: Highly realistic replica, blowback action, integrated front weaver accessory rail, eight-pellet rotary magazine, drop out 15-BB magazine, double/single action. Velocity: 360 fps.
Price: $249.00

H&K USP CO2 BB PISTOL
Caliber: .177 steel BBs. Barrel: Smoothbore. Weight: 1.35 lbs. Length: 7.5 in. Power: CO2. Sights: Fixed Features: Highly realistic replica, integrated front weaver accessory rail, 22-round magazine, double action only, also available as a higher-priced blowback version. Velocity: 360 fps.
Price: $60.00

H&K HK45 CO2 BB PISTOL
Caliber: .177 steel BBs. Barrel: Smoothbore. Weight: 1.4 lbs. Length: 8.0 in. Power: CO2. Sights: Fixed. Features: Highly realistic replica, integrated front weaver accessory rail, 20-shot capacity, double-action only. Velocity: 400 fps.
Price: $54.00

Prices given are believed to be accurate at time of publication however, many factors affect retail pricing so exact prices are not possible.

MORINI MOR-162EL AIR PISTOL
Caliber: .177 pellets. Barrel: Rifled. Weight: 2.25 lbs. Length: 16.14 in. Power: Precharged pneumatic. Sights: Front post, rear adjustable for windage. Features: Adjustable electronic trigger, single-shot bolt action, extreme match grade accuracy, over 200 regulated shots per 200 bar fill, available with different grip sizes. Velocity: 500 fps.
Price: $2,199.00

MORINI CM 200EI AIR PISTOL
Caliber: .177 pellets. Barrel: Rifled, Lothar Walther. Weight: 2.17 lbs. Length: 15.75 in. Power: Pre-charged pneumatic. Sights: Front post, rear diopter/micrometer adjustable. Features: Adjustable electronic trigger, single-shot bolt action, digital manometer, battery life of 15,000 shots, match-grade accuracy, available with medium or large grip size, muzzle compensator, 150 regulated shots per 200 bar fill, comes with two air cylinders. Velocity: 492 fps.
Price: $2,439.00

SCHOFIELD NO. 3 REVOLVER, FULL METAL
Caliber: .177 steel BBs or .177 pellets. Barrel: Smoothbore. Weight: 2.4 lbs. Length: 12.5 in. Power: CO2. Sights: Fixed. Features: Highly detailed replica top-break revolver, 6-shot capacity, realistic reusable cartridges, available in distressed black with imitation wood grips and plated steel with imitation ivory grips. Velocity: Up to 430 fps.
Price: .... $159.00–$169.00

SIG SAUER X-FIVE ASP .177 CO2 PISTOL
Caliber: .177 pellets. Barrel: Smoothbore. Weight: 2.75 lbs. Length: 9.75 in. Power: CO2. Sights: Fixed. Features: Realistic replica action pistol, 18-shot capacity, front accessory rail, full metal construction, metal slide with blowback action. Velocity: 300 fps.
Price: $139.00

SIG SAUER 1911 METAL BLOWBACK CO2 BB PISTOL
Caliber: .177 steel BBs. Barrel: Smoothbore. Weight: 2.0 lbs. Length: 8.75 in. Power: CO2. Sights: Adjustable. Features: Extremely Realistic replica action pistol, 20-shot capacity, front accessory rail, black or silver finish, full metal construction, metal slide with blowback action. Velocity: 430 fps.
Price: $149.00

SIG SAUER P226 CO2 PELLET PISTOL
Caliber: .177 pellets. Barrel: Rifled. Weight: 2.35 lbs. Length: 8.25 in. Power: CO2. Sights: Fixed. Features: Highly detailed replica action pistol, 16-shot capacity, front accessory rail, full metal construction, metal slide with blowback action, available in dark earth and black. Velocity: 450 fps.
Price: $109.00

SIG SAUER P320 CO2 PISTOL
Caliber: .177 BBs/.177 pellets. Barrel: Rifled. Weight: 2.2 lbs. Length: 9.6 in. Power: CO2. Sights: Fixed, white dot. Features: 30-round belt-fed magazine, front accessory rail, polymer frame, metal slide with blowback action, black or coyote tan finish. Velocity: 430 fps.
Price: $119.00

SMITH & WESSON MODEL 29 CO2 REVOLVER
Caliber: .177 BBs. Barrel: Smoothbore, 8.375 in. Weight: 2.65 lbs. with cartridges. Length: 12.14 in. Power: CO2. Sights: Fixed front, adjustable rear. Features: Brown faux wood grip, single/double action, approximately 60 shots per 12 gram cartridge, removable bullet casings. Velocity: 425 fps.
Price: $149.00

SMITH & WESSON 586 & 686 CO2 PISTOL
Caliber: .177 pellets. Barrel: Rifled. Weights: Model 586 4 in. 2.50 lbs. / Model 586 & 686 6 in. 2.8 lbs. Length: Model 586 4-in. barrel - 9.5 in. - Model 586, 6 in. barrel - 11.50 in. / Model 686 6 in. barrel - 11.5 in. Power: CO2. Sights: Fixed front, adjustable rear Features: Extremely accurate, full metal, replica revolvers.
Price: 586 4-in. barrel. Velocity - 400 fps $299.00
Price: 586 6-in. barrel. Velocity - 425 fps $295.00
Price: 686 6-in. barrel. Velocity - 425 fps $329.00

Prices given are believed to be accurate at time of publication however, many factors affect retail pricing so exact prices are not possible.

76TH EDITION, 2022 ⊕ 547

SMITH & WESSON M&P CO2 PISTOL
Caliber: .177 steel BBs. Barrel: Smoothbore. Weight: 1.5 lbs. Lengths: 7.5 in. Power: CO2. Sights: Blade front and ramp rear fiber optic. Features: Integrated accessory rail, removable 19-shot BB magazine, double-action only, synthetic frame available in dark earth brown or black color. Velocity: 300–480 fps.
Price: $50.00

SMITH & WESSON M&P 45 CO2 PISTOL
Caliber: .177 steel BBs, .177 pellets. Barrel: Rifled. Weight: 1.35 lbs. Length: 8.1 in. Power: CO2. Sights: Fixed front sight, fully adjustable rear sight. Features: Double and single action, 8-shot semi-automatic. Velocity: 370 fps.
Price: $79.00

SPRINGFIELD ARMORY 1911 MIL-SPEC CO2 BB PISTOL
Caliber: .177 BBs. Barrel: Smoothbore, 4.1 in. Weight: 2.0 lbs. Length: 8.6 in. Power: CO2. Sights: Fixed 3-dot. Features: Full metal construction, blow-back slide, 18-round magazine, single action, checkered grips, approximately 65 shots per fill, slide locks back after last shot, functioning grip safety. Velocity: 320 fps.
Price: $119.00

SPRINGFIELD ARMORY XDE CO2 BB PISTOL
Caliber: .177 BBs. Barrel: Smoothbore, 4.3 in. Weight: 1.95 lbs. Length: 7.75 in. Power: CO2. Sights: Fixed fiber optic. Features: Full metal construction, blow-back slide, 18-round drop-free magazine, double/single action, functional takedown lever, ambidextrous safety and magazine release, checkered grips, single slot Picatinny rail, front and rear slide serrations. Velocity: 380 fps.
Price: $119.00

STEYR M9-A1 PISTOL
Caliber: .177 BBs. Barrel: Smoothbore. Weight: 1.2 lbs. Length: 7.5 in. Power: CO2. Sights: Fixed. Features: Non-blowback, accessory rail, metal slide, two-tone or blue finish, 19-round capacity. Velocity: 449 fps.
Price: Blue $59.00
Price: Two-tone..$99.00

STI DUTY ONE CO2 BB PISTOL
Caliber: .177 steel BBs. Barrel: Smoothbore. Weight: 1.8 lbs. Length: 8.8 in. Power: CO2. Sights: Fixed. Features: Blowback, accessory rail, metal slide, threaded barrel, 20-round magazine. Velocity: 397 fps.
Price: $99.00

STEYR M9-A1 CO2 PISTOL
Caliber: .177 steel BBs. Barrel: Smoothbore. Weight: 2.4 lbs. Length: 7.4 in. Power: CO2. Sights: Fixed. Features: Non-blowback, accessory rail, metal slide, removable 19-round magazine. Velocity: 449 fps.
Price: $99.00

SWISS ARMS P92 CO2 PISTOL
Caliber: .177 steel BBs. Barrel: Smoothbore. Weight: 2.4 lbs. Length: 8.5 in. Power: CO2. Sights: Fixed. Features: Blowback, accessory rail, includes BBs, hex wrench, CO2 cartridge cap, 20-round magazine. Velocity: 312 fps.
Price: $14.00

TANFOGLIO WITNESS 1911 CO2 BB PISTOL, BROWN GRIPS
Caliber: .177 steel BBs. Barrel: Smoothbore. Weight: 1.98 lbs. Length: 8.6 in. Power: CO2. Sights: Fixed. Features: Often recognized as the "standard" for 1911 replica action pistols, 18-shot capacity, full metal construction with metal slide with blowback action. Velocity: 320 fps.
Price: $119.00

UMAREX LEGENDS MAKAROV ULTRA BLOWBACK CO2 BB PISTOL
Caliber: .177 steel BBs. Barrel: Smoothbore. Weight: 1.40 lbs. Length: 6.38 in. Power: CO2. Sights: Fixed. Features: Highly realistic replica, all-metal construction with blowback action, semi-automatic and fully-automatic capable, 16-round capacity. Velocity: 350 fps.
Price: $90.00

UMAREX LEGENDS M712 BROOM HANDLE FULL-AUTO CO2 BB PISTOL
Caliber: .177 steel BBs. Barrel: Smoothbore. Weight: 3.10 lbs. Length: 12.00 in. Power: CO2. Sights: Fixed front sight with rear sight adjustable for elevation. Features: Highly realistic replica that functions as the original, all-metal construction with blowback action, semi-automatic and fully-automatic capable, 18-round capacity. Velocity: 360 fps.
Price: $149.00

Prices given are believed to be accurate at time of publication however, many factors affect retail pricing so exact prices are not possible.

UMAREX LEGENDS P08 BLOWBACK CO2 BB PISTOL
Caliber: .177 steel BBs. Barrel: Smoothbore. Weight: 1.90 lbs. Length: 8.75 in. Power: CO2. Sights: Fixed. Features: Highly realistic replica that functions as the original, all-metal construction with blowback action, 21-round capacity. Velocity: 300 fps.
Price: $149.00

UMAREX BRODAX BB
Caliber: .177 steel BBs. Barrel: Smoothbore. Weight: 1.52 lbs. Length: 10.0 in. Power: CO2. Sights: Fixed. Features: Aggressively styled BB revolver, 10-shot capacity, top accessory rail, front accessory rail, synthetic construction. Velocity: 375 fps.
Price: $42.00

UMAREX SA10 CO2 PISTOL
Caliber: .177 pellet or steel BBs. Barrel: Rifled. Weight: 2.05 lbs. Length: 9.25 in. Power: CO2. Sights: Fixed. Features: Full metal slide with polymer grips, blowback action, ported slide with gold-look barrel and breech block, threaded muzzle, magazine holds the CO2 cylinder, an 8-shot rotary clip, and three additional clips, under-muzzle accessory rail. Velocity: 420 fps.
Price: $129.00

UMAREX STEEL STORM CO2 PISTOL
Caliber: .177 steel BBs. Barrel: Smooth, 7.5 in. Weight: 2.7 lbs. Length: 15 in. Power: CO2. Sights: Fixed, Picatinny accessory rail. Features: Submachine gun styling, blowback action, uses two 12-gram CO2 cylinders, 30-round nonremovable magazine, 300 round reservoir, full or semiautomatic modes, six-shot bursts in full auto mode, up to 300 shots per fill, CO2 housed in a drop-out magazine, can be bulk filled with an adapter (not included). Velocity: 430 fps.
Price: $119.00

UMAREX STRIKE POINT PELLET MULTI-PUMP AIR PISTOL
Caliber: .177 pellets. Barrel: Rifled. Weight: 2.6 lbs. Length: 14.00 in. Power: Multi-pump pneumatic. Sights: Adjustable rear sight, fixed fiber-optic front sight. Features: Variable power based on number of pumps, bolt action, includes integrated "silenceair" moderator for quite shooting. Velocity: Up to 650 fps.
Price: $59.00

UMAREX TREVOX AIR PISTOL
Caliber: .177 pellets. Barrel: Rifled. Weight: 3.5 lbs. Length: 18.25 in. Power: Gas Piston. Sights: Adjustable rear sight, fixed fiber-optic front sight. Features: full power from a single cock, suitable for target practice and plinking, includes integrated "silenceair" moderator for quite shooting. Velocity: 540 fps.
Price: $89.00

UZI MINI CARBINE
Caliber: .177 steel BBs. Barrel: Smoothbore. Weight: 2.45 lbs. Length: 23.5 in. Power: CO2. Sights: Fixed. Features: Realistic replica airgun, 28-shot capacity, foldable stock, semi-automatic with realistic blowback system, heavy bolt provides realistic "kick" when firing. Velocity: 390 fps.
Price: $120.00

UZI CO2 BB SUBMACHINE GUN
Caliber: .177 steel BBs. Barrel: Smoothbore. Weight: 4.85 lbs. Length: 23.5 in. Power: CO2. Sights: Fixed. Features: Realistic replica airgun, 25-shot capacity, foldable stock, semi-automatic and fully-automatic selectable fire, realistic blowback system. Velocity: 360 fps.
Price: $199.00

WALTHER CP88, BLUED, 4-INCH BARREL
Caliber: .177 pellets. Barrel: Rifled. Weight: 2.3 lbs. Length: 7 in. Power: CO_2. Sights: Blade ramp front sight and adjustable rear sight. Features: Manual safety, semi-auto repeater, single or double action, available in multiple finishes and grip materials, 8-shot capacity. Velocity: 400 fps.
Price: $229.00

WALTHER CP88 PISTOL
Caliber: .177 pellets. Barrel: Rifled. Weight: 2.5 lbs. Length: 9 in. Power: CO_2. Sights: Blade ramp front sight and adjustable rear sight. Features: Manual safety, Semi-auto repeater, single or double action, available in multiple finishes and grip materials, 8-shot capacity. Velocity: 450 fps.
Price: $229.00

WALTHER CP99 CO2 PISTOL
Caliber: .177 pellets. Barrel: Rifled Weight: 1.6 lbs. Length: 7.1 in. Power: CO_2. Sights: Fixed front and fully adjustable rear sight. Features: Extremely realistic replica pistol, single and double action, 8-shot rotary magazine. Velocity: 360 fps.
Price: $200.00

WALTHER CP99 COMPACT

WALTHER CP99 COMPACT PISTOL
Caliber: .177 steel BBs. Barrel: Smoothbore. Weight: 1.7 lbs. Length: 6.6 in. Power: CO_2. Sights: Fixed front and rear. Features: Extremely realistic replica pistol, semi-automatic 18-shot capacity, available in various configurations including a nickel slide. Velocity: 345 fps.
Price: ....$99.00–$105.00

WALTHER PPQ

WALTHER PPQ / P99 Q CO2 PISTOL
Caliber: .177 steel BBs, .177 pellets. Barrel: Rifled Weight: 1.37 lbs. Length: 7.0 in. Power: CO_2. Sights: Fixed front and fully adjustable rear sight. Features: Extremely realistic replica pistol, semi-automatic 8-shot rotary magazine. Velocity: 360 fps.
Price: $70.00

WALTHER P38 CO2 BB PISTOL
Caliber: .177 steel BBs. Barrel: Smoothbore. Weight: 1.9 lbs. Length: 8.5 in. Power: CO_2. Sights: Fixed. Features: Authentic replica action pistol, blowback action, semi-automatic 20-shot magazine. Velocity: 400 fps.
Price: $120.00

WALTHER PPK/S CO2 PISTOL
Caliber: .177 steel BBs. Barrel: Smoothbore. Weight: 3.7 lbs. Length: 6.1 in. Power: CO_2. Sights: Fixed. Features: Authentic replica action pistol, blowback slide locks back after last shot, stick-style magazine with 15-shot capacity. Velocity: 295 fps.
Price: $129.00

WALTHER PPS

WALTHER PPS M blowback compact co2 PISTOL
Caliber: .177 steel BBs. Barrel: Smoothbore. Weight: 1.2 lbs. Length: 6.38 in. Power: CO_2. Sights: Fixed. Features: Authentic replica action pistol, blowback action, semi-automatic 18-shot capacity. Velocity: 390 fps.
Price: $99.00

WEBLEY AND SCOTT MKVI REVOLVER
Caliber: .177 pellets. Barrel: Rifled. Weight: 2.4 lbs. Length: 11.25 in. Power: CO_2. Sights: Fixed. Features: Authentic replica pistol, single/double action, can be field-stripped, full metal construction, six-shot capacity, available in silver or distressed finish. Velocity: 430 fps.
Price: $199.00

WEIHRAUCH HW 40 AIR PISTOL
Caliber: .177, .20, .22. Barrel: Rifled. Weight: 1.7 lbs. Length: 9.5 in. Power: Single-stroke spring piston. Sights: Fiber-optic, fully adjustable. Features: Automatic safety, two-stage trigger, single shot. Velocity: 400 fps..
Price: $252.00

WEIHRAUCH HW 44 AIR PISTOL, FAC VERSION

Caliber: .177, .22. Barrel: Rifled. Weight: 2.9 lbs. Length: 19 in. Power: Pre-charged pneumatic. Sights: None. Features: Ambidextrous safety, two-stage adjustable match trigger, built in suppressor, Weaver-style scope rail, 10-shot magazine, built-in air cartridge with quick fill, internal pressure gauge. Velocity: 750 (.177), 570 (.22) fps.

Price: **$1,049.00**

WEIHRAUCH HW 45 AIR PISTOL

Caliber: .177, .20, .22. Barrel: Rifled. Weight: 2.5 lbs. Length: 10.9 in. Power: Single-stroke spring piston. Sights: Fiber-optic, fully adjustable. Features: Automatic safety, two-stage trigger, single shot, two power levels, blued or two tone. Velocity: 410/558 (.177), 394/492 (.20), 345/427 (.22) fps.

Price: **$515.00**

WEIHRAUCH HW 75 AIR PISTOL

Caliber: .177. Barrel: Rifled. Weight: 2.3 lbs. Length: 11 in. Power: Single-stroke spring piston. Sights: Micrometer adjustable rear. Features: Ambidextrous, adjustable match-type trigger, single shot. Velocity: 410 fps.

Price: **$482.00**

WINCHESTER MODEL 11

WINCHESTER MODEL 11 bb pistol

Caliber: .177 steel BBs. Barrel: Smoothbore. Weight: 1.9 lbs. Length: 8.5 in. Power: CO2. Sights: Fixed. Features: All-metal replica action pistol, blowback action, 4-lb. 2-stage trigger, semi-automatic 15-shot capacity. Velocity: 410 fps.

Price: **$149.00**

Prices given are believed to be accurate at time of publication however, many factors affect retail pricing so exact prices are not possible.

76TH EDITION, 2022 ⊕ **551**

AIR ARMS TX200 MKIII AIR RIFLE
Calibers: .177, .22. Barrel: Rifled, Lothar Walter match-grade, 13.19 in. Weight: 9.3 lbs. Length: 41.34 in. Power: Single cock, spring-piston. Stock: Various; right- and left-handed versions, multiple wood options. Sights: 11mm dovetail. Features: Fixed barrel, heirloom quality craftsmanship, holds the record for the most winning spring powered airgun in international field target competitions. Velocities: .177, 930 fps/.22, 755 fps.
Price: ....$699.00–$829.00

AIR ARMS PRO-SPORT RIFLE
Calibers: .177, .22. Barrel: Rifled, Lothar Walter match-grade, 9.5 in. Weight: 9.03 lbs. Length: 40.5 in. Power: Single cock, spring-piston Stock: Various; right-and left-handed versions, multiple wood options. Sights: 11mm dovetail. Features: Fixed barrel, Heirloom quality craftsmanship, unique inset cocking arm. Velocities: .177, 950 fps/.22, 750 fps.
Price: $824.00–879.00

AIR ARMS S510 XTRA FAC PCP AIR RIFLE
Calibers: .177, .22, .25. Barrel: Rifled, Lothar Walter match-grade, 19.45 in. Weight: 7.55 lbs. Length: 43.75 in. Power: Pre-charged pneumatic. Stock: Right-handed, multiple wood options. Sights: 11mm dovetail. Features: Side-lever action, 10-round magazine, shrouded barrel, variable power, Heirloom quality craftsmanship Velocities: .177, 1,050 fps/.22, 920 fps/.25, 850 fps.
Price: $1,299.00

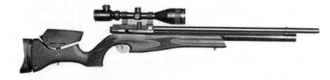

AIR ARMS S510 ULTIMATE SPORTER
Calibers: .177, .22, .25. Barrel: Rifled, Lothar Walter match-grade, 19.5 in. Weight: 8.6 lbs. Length: 44.25 in. Power: Pre-charged pneumatic. Stock: Fully adjustable, ambidextrous laminate stock. Sights: 11mm dovetail. Features: Side-lever action, 10-shot magazine, integrated suppressor, variable power, Heirloom quality craftsmanship. Velocities: .177, 1,050 fps/.22, 920 fps/.25, 850 fps.
Price: $1,699.00

AIR ARMS S510 TDR
Calibers: .177, .22. Barrel: Rifled, Lothar Walter match-grade, 15.55 in. Weight: 6.2 lbs. Length: 40.55 in. Power: Precharged pneumatic. Stock: Fully adjustable, ambidextrous walnut fore end with removable buttstock. Sights: 11mm dovetail. Features: Take down rifle breaks down in seconds, comes with a hard case with custom cut foam, side-lever action, 10-shot magazine, integrated suppressor, variable power, built-in manometer, adjustable two-stage trigger. Velocities: .177, 1,035 fps/.22, 950 fps.
Price: $1,499.00

AIR ARMS T200 SPORTER
Caliber: .177 pellets. Barrel: Hammer-forged, rifled 19.1 in. Weight: 6.6 lbs. Length: 35.5 in. Power: Pre-charged pneumatic. Stock: Hardwood. Sights: Globe front sight, fully adjustable diopter rear sight. Features: Aluminum muzzle brake, two-stage adjustable trigger, removable air tank, single shot, grooved receiver, made by CZ. Velocity: 575 fps.
Price: $650.00

AIR ARMS FTP 900 FIELD TARGET PCP AIR RIFLE
Caliber: .177. Barrel: Rifled, Lothar Walter match-grade, 19.0 in. Weight: 11.00 lbs. Length: 42.50 in. Power: Pre-charged pneumatic Stock: Fully adjustable competition style, available in right- or left-handed laminate stock. Sights: 11mm dovetail. Features: Side-lever action, single shot for maximum accuracy, integrated muzzle break, heirloom quality craftsmanship, regulated for supreme shot consistency, delivers up to 100 shots per fill. Velocity: 800 fps.
Price: $3,029.00

AIR ARMS GALAHAD RIFLE REG FAC
Calibers: .22, .25. Barrel: Rifled, Lothar Walter match-grade, 19.4 in. Weight: 8.6 lbs. Length: 35.5 in. Power: Pre-charged pneumatic. Stock: Ambidextrous bullpup stock available in "soft touch" synthetic over beech or walnut. Sights: 11mm dovetail. Features: Moveable side-lever action, 10-shot magazine, available with integrated moderator, variable power with integrated regulator, Heirloom quality craftsmanship. Velocity: .22, 900 fps/.25, 800 fps.
Price: ....$1699.00–$1849.00

AIRFORCE CONDOR/CONDOR SS RIFLE
Calibers: .177, .20, .22, .25. Barrel: Rifled, Lothar Walther match-grade, 18 or 24 in. Weight: 6.1 lbs. Length: 38.1-38.75 in. Power: Pre-charged pneumatic. Stock: Synthetic pistol grip, tank acts as buttstock. Sights: Grooved for scope mounting. Features: Single shot, adjustable power, automatic safety, large 490cc tank volume, extended scope rail allows easy mounting of the largest air-gun scopes, optional CO2 power system available, manufactured in the USA by AirForce Airguns. Velocities: .177, 1,450 fps/.20, 1,150 fps/.22, 1,250 fps/.25, 1,100 fps.
Price: $744.00

AIRFORCE EDGE 10-METER AIR RIFLE
Caliber: .177. Barrel: Rifled, Lothar Walther match-grade, 12 in. Weight: 6.1 lbs. Length: 40.00 in. Power: Pre-charged pneumatic. Stock: Synthetic pistol grip, tank acts as buttstock. Sights: Front sight only or match front globe and rear micrometer adjustable diopter sight. Features: Single shot, automatic safety, two-stage adjustable trigger, accepted by CMP for completive shooting, available in multiple colors and configurations, manufactured in the USA. Velocity: .530 fps.
Price: ....$639.00-$799.00

AIRFORCE ESCAPE/SS/UL AIR RIFLE
Calibers: .22, .25. Barrel: Rifled, Lothar Walther match-grade, 12, 18 or 24 in. Weight: 4.3-5.3 lbs. Length: 32.3-39.00 in. Power: Pre-charged pneumatic. Stock: Synthetic pistol grip, tank acts as buttstock. Sights: Grooved for scope mounting. Features: Single shot, adjustable power, automatic safety, extended scope rail allows easy mounting of the largest airgun scopes, manufactured in the USA by AirForce Airguns. Velocities: .22, 1,300 fps/.25, 1,145 fps.
Price: ....$642.00-$694.00

AIRFORCE TALON P PCP CARBINE
Caliber: .25. Barrel: Rifled, Lothar Walther match-grade, 12 in. Weight: 4.3 lbs. Length: 27.75-32.35 in. Power: Pre-charged pneumatic. Stock: Synthetic pistol grip. Sights: Grooved for scope mounting. Features: Single shot, removable moderator to reduce noise, adjustable power, can be easily broken down for compact transport, automatic safety, two-stage adjustable trigger, 213cc air tank, up to 50 foot-pounds of energy. Velocity: 500-900 fps.
Price: $749.00

AIRFORCE TEXAN .50-CF AIR RIFLE
Calibers: .510. Barrel: Rifled Lothar Walther, 34 in. Weight: 8 lbs. Length: 48.00 in. Power: Precharged pneumatic. Stock: Synthetic pistol grip, tank acts as buttstock. Sights: None, grooved for scope mounting. Features: Carbon fiber tank, pressure relief device, 800+ foot-pounds of energy, two-stage non-adjustable trigger, low effort side cocking, manufactured in the USA. Velocity: 1,100 fps.
Price: **$1.229.00**

AIRFORCE INTERNATIONAL LYNX V10 AIR RIFLE
Calibers: .177, .22. Barrel: Rifled, hammer forged barrel, 18.5 in. Weight: 7.25 lbs. Length: 41.30 in. Power: Pre-charged pneumatic. Stock: Natural or black hardwood stock. Sights: 11mm dovetail for scope mounting. Features: Multi-shot magazine varies on caliber, side-lever action, adjustable power and adjustable trigger, Spanish made. Velocities: .177, 1,000 fps/.22, 700 fps.
Price: **$599.00**

AIRFORCE INTERNATIONAL ORION AIR RIFLE
Calibers: .177, .22, .25. Barrel: Hammer forged barrel, 18.5 in. Weight: 7.25 lbs. Length: 41.00 in. Power: Pre-charged pneumatic. Stock: Right-handed hardwood stock with adjustable cheek riser. Sights: 11mm dovetail for scope mounting. Features: Multi-shot magazine varies on caliber, side-lever action, adjustable power and adjustable trigger. Velocities: .177, 1,000 fps/.22, 800 fps/.25, 600 fps.
Price: **$629.00**

AIRFORCE INTERNATIONAL MODEL 94 SPRING AIR RIFLE
Calibers: .177, .22, 25. Barrel: Rifled, hammer forged, 18.75 in. Weight: 7.5 lbs. Length: 44.9 in. Power: Spring piston. Stock: Synthetic with textured grip and forearm. Sights: Fixed fiber-optic front and fully adjustable fiber-optic rear. Features: Single shot, adjustable two-stage trigger, 32-pound cocking effort, integral muzzle brake. Velocities: 1100 fps (.177)/900 fps (.22)/700 fps (.25).
Price:.. **$249.00**

AIRFORCE INTERNATIONAL MODEL 95 SPRING AIR RIFLE
Calibers: .177, .22. Barrel: Rifled, hammer forged. Weight: 7.25 lbs. Length: 44.9 in. Power: Spring piston. Stock: Hardwood stock with checkering on grip and forearm. Sights: None, 11mm dovetail for scope mounting. Features: Single shot, adjustable trigger, 32-pound cocking effort. Velocities: .177, 980 fps/.22, 835 fps.
Price: **$315.00**

AIRGUN TECHNOLOGY URAGAN KING RIFLE
Calibers: .25 or .30. Barrel: 19.6 in. Weight: 8 to 10 lbs. Length: 36 in. Power: Precharged pneumatic. Stock: Ambidextrous walnut or synthetic bullpup stock. Sights: None, Picatinny rail for scope mounting. Features: Has a reversible biathlon side lever, 10-shot (.25) or 9-shot (.30) magazine, dual air cylinders, bullpup design, sound moderator, approximately 100 shots per fill. Velocities: NA.
Price: ....**$1,899.00–$1,999.00**

AIRGUN TECHNOLOGY VULCAN 2 BULLPUP RIFLE
Calibers: .22 or .25. Barrel: 19.6 in. Weight: 7.25 lbs. Length: 29.75 in. Power: Precharged pneumatic. Stock: Ambidextrous walnut bullpup stock with polymer cheekpiece. Sights: Picatinny rail for scope mounting. Features: Has a biathlon side lever, comes with two 12-shot magazines, includes a hard case, side-lever action, shrouded barrel with M14 adapter, up to 60 shots per fill. Velocities: .22, 800 fps/.25, 600 fps.
Price: **$1,799.00**

AIR VENTURI AVENGER RIFLE
Caliber: .50. Barrel: Smoothbore 22.5 in. Weight: 7.4 lbs. Length: 43.0 in. Power: Pre-charged pneumatic. Stock: Ambidextrous wood stock. Sights: Fixed bead shotgun-style sight. Features: 244cc reservoir delivers several powerful shots, shoots shot cartridges and round balls, exceptionally reliable. Use as a shotgun to hunt birds or small game or as a slug gun to hunt larger game. Velocity: 760 fps (with slug), 1,130 fps.
Price: **$849.00**

AIR VENTURI TR5 RIFLE
Caliber: .177. Barrel: Rifled, 18.75 in. Weight: 5.0 lbs. Length: 32.5-34.5 in. Power: Spring piston. Stock: Black or green synthetic stock. Sights: Fully adjustable rear sight, globe front sight, 11 mm dovetail. Features: Two-stage adjustable trigger, adjustable trigger blade position, five-position adjustable buttstock, includes two 5 round magazine, UIT accessory rail on underside of fore end. Velocity: 500 fps.
Price: **$139.00**

AIR VENTURI WING SHOT II SHOTGUN
Caliber: .50. Barrel: Smoothbore 22.5 in. Weight: 7.4 lbs. Length: 43.0 in. Power: Pre-charged pneumatic. Stock: Ambidextrous wood stock. Sights: Fixed bead shotgun-style sight. Features: 244cc reservoir delivers several powerful shots, shoots shot cartridges and round balls, exceptionally reliable. Use as a shotgun to hunt birds or small game or as a slug gun to hunt larger game. Velocity: 760 fps (with slug), 1,130 fps.
Price: **$849.00**

AMERICAN AIR ARMS EVOL CLASSIC CARBINE
Calibers: .22, .25, or .30. Barrel: Hammer forged, rifled, threaded, 15 in. (.22), 18 in (.25 or .30). Weight: 7-7.2 lbs. Length: 36-39 in with moderator. Power: Precharged pneumatic. Stock: Walnut. Sights: None, Picatinny rail. Features: Upper and lower chassis made from aluminum, titanium air cylinder, Picatinny underside accessory rail, adjustable two-stage trigger set to 10 ounces, 9-13 shot rotary magazine, Magpul stock and grip, manufactured in very limited quantities. Velocity: Adjustable.
Price: **$2,895.00**

AMERICAN AIR ARMS SLAYER HI-POWER BULLPUP RIFLE
Calibers: .308 or .357. Barrel: Rifled, threaded, 24 in (.357) or 26 in. (.308). Weight: 7.2 lbs. Length: 36-40 in with moderator. Power: Precharged pneumatic. Stock: Synthetic adjustable length stock. Sights: None, Picatinny rail. Features: Titanium reservoir, three pound cocking effort, 6 (.357 caliber) or 7 (.308 caliber) round magazine, adjustable two-stage trigger, underside accessory rail, rear velocity adjuster, available in right or left hand, manufactured in very limited quantities. Velocity: 950 fps.
Price: **$2,795.00**

Prices given are believed to be accurate at time of publication however, many factors affect retail pricing so exact prices are not possible.

76TH EDITION, 2022 ✛ 553

ANSCHUTZ 9015 AIR RIFLE
Caliber: .177. Barrel: Rifled, 16.5 in. Weight: Variable from 8.1 to 11 pounds. Length: Variable from 39.0 to 47 in. Power: Pre-charged pneumatic. Stock: Fully adjustable variable composition. Sights: Fully adjustable target sights with interchangeable inserts. Features: Single shot, ambidextrous grip, adjustable match trigger, exchangeable air cylinder with integrated manometer, approximately 200 shots per fill, available with a bewildering array of options. Velocity: 560 fps.
Price: .... $2,545.00 - $5,350.00

ASG TAC-4.5 CO2 BB RIFLE
Caliber: .177 steel BBs. Barrel: Smoothbore. Weight: 3.5 lbs. Length: 36.0 in. Power: CO2 Stock: Synthetic thumbhole stock. Sights: Fixed fiber-optic front sight and fully adjustable fiber-optic rear sight/weaver rail for optics. Features: Semi-automatic action, includes bi-pod, 21-shot capacity. Velocity: 417 fps.
Price: $119.00

ATAMAN M2R TACT CARBINE AIR RIFLE
Calibers: .177, .22, .25, .30, .35. Barrel: Lothar Walther rifled match-grade, 20.47 in. Weight: 8.82 lbs. Length: 43.31 in. Power: Pre-charged pneumatic. Stock: Ambidextrous stock available in various configurations and finishes. Sights: weaver rails for scope mounting. Features: Multi-shot side-lever action, shot capacity varies on caliber, adjustable match trigger, finely tuned regulator matched to optimal velocity in each caliber for maximum accuracy. Velocities: .177, 980 fps/.22, 980 fps/.25, 980 fps/.30, 984 fps/.35, 900 fps.
Price: .... $1,599.00-$1,999.00

ATAMAN M2R BULLPUP AIR RIFLE
Calibers: .22, .25, .35. Barrel: Lothar Walther rifled match-grade free-floating, 20.47 in. Weight: 8.81 lbs. Length: 32.12 in. Power: Precharged pneumatic. Stock: Ambidextrous bullpup stock available in walnut or "soft touch" synthetic. Sights: Integrated Picatinny rails for scope mounting. Features: Multi-shot side level action, shot capacity varies on caliber, adjustable match trigger, side-lever action, finely tuned regulator matched to optimal velocity in each caliber for maximum accuracy. Velocities: .22, 980 fps/.25, 980 fps/.35, 900 fps.
Price: $1,429.00–1,899.00

ATAMAN M2R CARBINE ULTRA COMPACT AIR RIFLE
Caliber: .22. Barrel: Lothar Walther rifled match-grade, 15.39 in. Weight: 6.17 lbs. Length: 36.48 in. Power: Pre-charged pneumatic. Stock: Ambidextrous adjustable/foldable stock available in walnut or "soft touch" synthetic. Sights: Weaver rails for scope mounting. Features: Multi-shot side-lever action, 10-shot capacity, adjustable match trigger, finely tuned regulator matched to optimal velocity. Velocity: 850 fps.
Price: $1,319.00

BEEMAN R9 AIR RIFLE
Calibers: .177, .20, .22. Barrel: Rifled 16.33 in. Weight: 7.3 lbs. Length: 43 in. Power: Break-barrel, spring-piston. Stock: Ambidextrous walnut-stained beech, cut-checkered pistol grip, Monte Carlo comb and rubber buttpad. Sights: None, grooved for scope. Features: German quality, limited lifetime warranty, highly adjustable match-grade trigger, extremely accurate. Velocities: .177, 935 fps/.20, 800 fps/.22, 740 fps.
Price: $479.00

BEEMAN AR2078A CO2 RIFLE
Calibers: .177, .22 pellets. Barrel: Rifled, 21.50 in. Weight: 7.5 lbs. Length: 38 in. Power: CO2. Stock: Beech. Sights: Competition diopter peep sight, 11 mm dovetail. Features: Bolt action, single shot, operates on two standard 12 gram CO2 cylinders or with tank adapter and connector, adjustable trigger, approximately 60 shots per fill. Velocities: .177, 650/.22, 500 fps.
Price: $239.00

BEEMAN AR2079A CO2 RIFLE
Calibers: .177, .22 pellets. Barrel: Rifled, 21.5 in. Weight: 6.8 lbs. Length: 38 in. Power: CO2. Stock: Beech. Sights: Competition diopter peep sight, 11 mm dovetail. Features: Filled from tank by standard G2 1/2 tank filling device, does not include CO2 cylinder, adjustable trigger. Velocities: .177, 650/.22, 500 fps.
Price: $229.00

BEEMAN COMMANDER PCP RIFLE
Calibers: .177, .22 pellets. Barrel: Rifled. Weight: 8 lbs. Length: 43 in. Power: Precharged pneumatic. Stock: Hardwood thumbhole. Sights: Adjustable fiber optic, comes with a 4x32 scope. Features: Up to 100 shots per fill, 10-shot magazine, built in noise suppressor. Velocities: .177, 1100/.22, 1000 fps.
Price: $298.00

BEEMAN COMPETITION PCP RIFLE
Caliber: .177 pellets. Barrel: Rifled. Weight: 8.8 lbs. Length: 41.7 in. Power: Precharged pneumatic. Stock: Adjustable hardwood. Sights: None, dovetail grooves. Features: Side lever cocking, up to 200 shots per fill, single shot, built-in noise suppressor, 10-meter competition, adjustable trigger, adjustable pistol grip, comb, and buttplate. Velocity: 550 fps.
Price: $959.00

BEEMAN GAS RAM DUAL CALIBER AIR RIFLE COMBO
Calibers: .177, .22. Barrel: Rifled. Weight: 8.5 lbs. Length: 45.5 in. Power: Break-barrel, gas-piston. Stock: Ambidextrous hardwood stock. Sights: Fiber optic with adjustable rear, includes 4x32 scope with mount. Features: Single-shot, adjustable two-stage trigger, 35-40 lb. cocking effort, comes with both .177 and .22 caliber barrels. Velocities: .177, 1,000 fps/.22, 850 fps.
Price: $179.00

BEEMAN NEW CHIEF PCP RIFLE
Calibers: .177, .22 pellets. Barrel: Rifled. Weight: 6.8 lbs. Length: 39 in. Power: Precharged pneumatic. Stock: Synthetic. Sights: Adjustable fiber optic. Features: Up to 100 shots per fill, 10 shot magazine, built in noise suppressor. Velocities: .177, 1000/.22, 830 fps.
Price: $269.00

BEEMAN PCP UNDER LEVER RIFLE
Calibers: .177, .22 pellets. Barrel: Rifled. Weight: 7.3 lbs. Length: 32 in. Power: Precharged pneumatic. Stock: Bullpup style wood. Sights: Adjustable fiber optic. Features: 10 shot magazine, unique front under level cocking system, built in noise suppressor. Velocity: .177, 1000/.22, 830 fps.
Price: $369.00

BEEMAN QB II MODEL 1085 CO2 RIFLE
Calibers: .177, .22 pellets. Barrel: Rifled. Weight: 6.5 lbs. Length: 38.6 in. Power: CO2. Stock: Synthetic thumbhole. Sights: Fiber optic, 11 mm dovetail. Features: Uses two 12 g CO2 cartridges, 10 shot magazine, accessory rail under fore end. Velocities: .177, 650/.22, 500 fps.
Price: $139.00

BEEMAN SILVER KODIAK X2 COMBO AIR RIFLE
Calibers: .177, .22. Barrel: Rifled. Weight: 9 lbs. Length: 45.5 in. Power: Break-barrel, gas ram piston. Stock: Ambidextrous hardwood stock. Sights: Open includes 4x32 scope and rings. Features: Satin finish nickel plated receiver and barrels, single-shot, easily exchangeable .177 and .22 cal. barrels, two-stage trigger. Velocities: .177, 1,200 fps/.22, 830 fps.
Price: **$169.00**

BENJAMIN 392 / 397 AIR RIFLE
Calibers: .177, .22. Barrel: Rifled 19.25 in. Weight: 5.5 lbs. Length: 36.25 in. Power: Multi-pump Pneumatic. Stock: Ambidextrous wood or synthetic stock. Sights: Front ramp and adjustable rear sight. Features: Multi-pump system provides variable power, single-shot bolt action. Velocities: .177, 800 fps/.20, 685 fps.
Price: **$172.00**

BENJAMIN ARMADA, BASE, TACTICAL, & MAGPUL EDITION AIR RIFLE

BENJAMIN ARMADA
Calibers: .177, .22, .25. Barrel: Rifled, 20 in. Weight: 7.3 lbs. (10.3 lbs. with scope and bipod). Length: 42.8 in. Power: Precharged pneumatic. Stock: Adjustable mil-spec AR-15-style buttstock, all metal M-LOK compatible handguard with 15 in. of Picatinny rail space. Sights: None, Weaver/Picatinny rail for scope mounting. Features: Fully shrouded barrel with integrated suppressor, dampener device, bolt action, multi shot, choked barrel for maximum accuracy. Velocities: .177, 1,100 fps/.22, 1,000 fps/.25, 900 fps.
Price: **$649.00**

BENJAMIN AKELA PCP AIR RIFLE
Calibers: .22. Barrel: Rifled. Weight: 7.7 lbs. Length: 32.9 in. Power: Precharged pneumatic. Stock: Bullpup style Turkish walnut stock. Sights: None, Picatinny rail for scope mounting. Features: Side cocking lever, adjustable trigger shoe, 3,000 psi pressure, up to 60 shots per fill, 12-shot rotary magazine. Velocity: 1,000 fps.
Price: **$649.00**

BENJAMIN BULLDOG .357 BULLPUP
Caliber: .357. Barrel: Rifled 28 in. Weight: 7.7 lbs. Length: 36 in. Power: Precharged pneumatic. Stock: Synthetic bullpup stock with pistol grip, black or Realtree camo. Sights: Full top Picatinny rail. Features: Innovative bullpup design, massive power output of up to 180 ft-lbs, 5-shot magazine, shrouded barrel for noise reduction, large cylinder delivers up to 10 usable shots, available in multiple bundled configurations and stock finishes. Velocity: Up to 900 fps based on the weight of the projectile.
Price: ....**$849.00-$1,099.00**

BENJAMIN CAYDEN PCP AIR RIFLE
Calibers: .22. Barrel: Rifled. Weight: 7.95 lbs. Length: 40.8 in. Power: Precharged Pneumatic. Stock: Turkish walnut stock with adjustable cheekpiece. Sights: None, grooved 11mm dovetail for scope mounting. Features: Side cocking lever, adjustable trigger shoe, 3,000 psi pressure, up to 60 shots per fill, 12-shot rotary magazine. Velocity: 1000 fps.
Price: **$599.00**

BENJAMIN FORTITUDE GEN 2 PCP RIFLE
Calibers: .177 or .22. Barrel: Rifled 24.25 in. Weight: 5.3 lbs. Length: 42.6 in. Power: Precharged Pneumatic. Stock: Synthetic, ambidextrous. Sights: None, grooved 11mm dovetail for scope mounting. Features: Shrouded barrel with integrated suppressor, 10-shot rotary magazine, 3,000 PSI pressure gauge with regulator, 60-200 shots per fill, adjustable hammer spring. Velocity: 950 fps (.177), 850 fps (.22).
Price: **$319.00**

BENJAMIN IRONHIDE AIR RIFLE
Caliber: .177 or .22. Barrel: 15.75 in rifled. Weight: 7.8 lbs. Length: 45.5 in. Power: Nitro Piston Elite break barrel. Stock: Synthetic thumbhole stock. Sights: Fixed front and adjustable rear, includes CenterPoint 4x32 scope and mounts. Features: Single shot, sound suppression, adjustable two-stage trigger. Velocity: 1,400 fps (.177), 1,100 fps (.22).
Price: **$199.00**

BENJAMIN KRATOS PCP AIR RIFLE
Calibers: .22, .25. Barrel: Rifled. Weight: 8.26 lbs. Length: 43.35 in. Power: Precharged Pneumatic. Stock: Turkish walnut stock with adjustable cheekpiece. Sights: None, Picatinny rail for scope mounting. Features: Side cocking lever, adjustable trigger shoe, 3,000 psi pressure, up to 60 shots per fill, 12-shot rotary magazine in .22, 10-shot rotary magazine in .25. Velocities: 1,000 fps (.22), 900 fps (.25).
Price: **$699.00**

BENJAMIN MARAUDER PCP AIR RIFLE
Caliber: .177, .22, .25. Barrel: Rifled 20 in. Weight: Synthetic 7.3 lbs/Hardwood 8.2 lbs. Length: 42.8 in. Power: Precharged pneumatic. Stock: Ambidextrous stock available in hardwood or synthetic, adjustable cheek riser. Sights: None, grooved for scope mounting. Features: Multi-shot bolt action, 10-shot in .177 and .22, 8-shot in .25, user-adjustable performance settings for power and shot count, reversible bolt handle. Also available with options such as an integrated regulator for shot-to-shot consistency, a Picatinny rail, and Lothar Walther barrel. Velocities: .177, 1,100 fps/.22, 1,000 fps/.25, 900 fps.
Price: ....**$579.00-$599.00**

BENJAMIN TRAIL STEALTH NITRO PISTON 2 (NP2) BREAK BARREL AIR RIFLE
Calibers: .177, .22. Barrel: Rifled 15.75 in. Weight: 8.3 lbs. Length: 46.25 in. Power: Break-barrel, 2nd generation gas-piston. Stock: Ambidextrous thumbhole stock available in wood and synthetic options as well as multiple finishes and patterns. Sights: None, Picatinny rail for scope mounting, multiple CenterPoint scope options available as factory bundles. Features: Very quiet due to the shrouded barrel with integrated suppressor, extremely easy cocking, single-shot, advanced adjustable two-stage trigger, innovative sling mounts for optional Benjamin break-barrel rifle sling. Velocities: .177, 1,400 fps/.22, 1,100 fps.
Price: ....**$295.00-$349.00**

BENJAMIN TRAIL NITRO PISTON 2 (NP2) SBD BREAK BARREL AIR RIFLE

Calibers: .177, .22. Barrel: Rifled 15.75 in. Weight: 8.3 lbs. Length: 45.6 in. Power: Break-barrel, 2nd generation gas-piston. Stock: Ambidextrous thumbhole stock available in wood and synthetic options as well as multiple finishes and patterns. Sights: None, Picatinny rail for scope mounting, multiple Crosman CenterPoint scope options available as factory bundles. Features: Newly introduced SBD integrated suppressor does not interfere with scope sight picture, extremely easy cocking, single-shot, advanced adjustable two-stage trigger, innovative sling mounts for optional Benjamin break-barrel rifle sling. Velocities: .177, 1,400 fps/.22, 1,100 fps.
Price: ....$299.00–$339.00

BENJAMIN MAXIMUS PCP AIR RIFLE

Calibers: .177, .22. Barrel: Rifled 26.25 in. Weight: 5.0 lbs. Length: 41.7 in. Power: Precharged Pneumatic. Stock: Ambidextrous synthetic stock. Sights: Front Fiber-optic and adjustable rear fiber-optic sight/grooved 11mm dovetail for scope mounting. Features: HPA required only 2,000 psi to operate, built in pressure gauge. Velocities: .177, 1,000 fps/.22, 850 fps.
Price: $219.00

BENJAMIN VARMINT POWER PACK

Caliber: .22. Barrel: Rifled. Weight: 7.38 lbs. Length: 44.5 in. Power: Break-barrel, gas-piston. Stock: Ambidextrous synthetic stock. Sights: none, Weaver rail for scope mounting, includes a Crosman CenterPoint 4x32 scope with laser and light attachments complete with intermittent pressure switches. Features: Shrouded barrel, easy cocking, single-shot, adjustable two-stage trigger. Velocity: 950 fps.
Price: $249.00

BENJAMIN WILDFIRE SEMI-AUTOMATIC PCP AIR RIFLE

Caliber: .177. Barrel: Rifled 20.39 in. Weight: 3.69 lbs. Length: 36.88 in. Power: Precharged Pneumatic. Stock: Ambidextrous synthetic stock. Sights: Front fiber-optic and adjustable rear sight/grooved 11mm dovetail for scope mounting. Features: HPA required only 2,000 psi to operate, built in pressure gauge, 12-shot semi-automatic system, double-action only. Velocity: 800 fps.
Price: $149.00

BERETTA CX4 STORM AIR RIFLE

Caliber: .177 pellets. Barrel: Rifled 17.5 in. Weight: 5.25 lbs. Length: 30.75 in. Power: CO2. Stock: Synthetic thumbole. Sights: Adjustable front and rear. Features: Multi-shot semi-automatic with 30-round belt-fed magazine, highly realistic replica, utilizes large 88/90 gram disposable CO2 canisters for high shot count and uninterrupted shooting sessions. Available bundled with a Walther red-dot optics. Velocity: 600 fps.
Price: ....$375.00–$399.00

BLACK OPS TACTICAL SNIPER GAS-PISTON AIR RIFLE

Calibers: .177, .22. Barrel: Rifled. Weight: 9.6 lbs. Length: 44.0 in. Power: Break-barrel, gas-piston. Stock: Ambidextrous pistol grip synthetic stock. Sights: none, Weaver rail for scope mounting, includes a 4x32 scope. Features: Muzzle brake helps with cocking force, single-shot, single cock delivers maximum power, adjustable single-stage trigger. Velocities: .177, 1,250 fps/.22, 1,000 fps.
Price: ....$179.00–$199.00

BROCOCK BANTAM HI-LITE PCP RIFLE

Caliber: .25. Barrel: Rifled, Lothar Walther barrel. Weight: 6.4 lbs. Length: 34 in. Power: Pre-charged pneumatic. Stock: Semi-bullpup, beech wood. Sights: None, grooved for scope mounting. Features: 10-shot magazine, 480cc carbon-fiber air bottle, adjustable cheek piece and buttpad, three-step power adjuster. Velocities: NA.
Price: $1,553.00

BROWNING LEVERAGE AIR RIFLE

Calibers: .177, .22. Barrel: Rifled 18.9 in. Weight: 8.6 lbs. Length: 44.8 in. Power: Under-lever cock, spring-piston Stock: Hardwood right handed with raised cheekpiece. Sights: Front fiber-optic sight and fully adjustable rear fiber-optic sight, Weaver/Picatinny rail for scope mounting, includes 3-9x40 scope. Features: Fixed barrel accuracy, easy cocking, two-stage trigger. Velocities: .177, 1,000 fps/.22, 800 fps.
Price: $229.00

BSA R-10 SE PCP AIR RIFLE

Calibers: .177, .22. Barrel: Rifled, BSA-made cold hammer forged precision barrel, 19 in. Weight: 7.3 lbs. Length: 44 in. Power: Precharged pneumatic. Stock: Available right- or left-hand, walnut, laminate, camo or black synthetic. Sights: None, grooved for scope mounting. Features: Multi-shot bolt action, 10-shot magazine (8-shot for .25 caliber), fully regulated valve for maximum accuracy and shot consistency, free-floating, shrouded barrel, also available with lower power/velocity and as a shorter carbine. Velocities: 1,000 fps (.177)/980 fps (.22).
Price: 1,299.00-1,495.00

BSA BUCCANEER SE AIR RIFLE

Calibers: .177, .22. Barrel: Rifled, BSA-made cold hammer forged precision barrel, 24 in. Weight: 7.7 lbs. Length: 42.5 in. Power: Pre-charged pneumatic. Stock: Ambidextrous beech stock or hardwood stock wrapped in innovative black soft-touch. Sights: None, grooved for scope mounting. Features: Multi-shot bolt action, 10-shot magazine, enhanced valve system for maximum shot count and consistency, integrated suppressor, adjustable two-stage trigger. Velocities: .177, 1,000 fps/.22, 800 fps.
Price: ....$649.00–$749.00

BSA DEFIANT BULLPUP AIR RIFLE

Calibers: .177, .22. Barrel: Rifled, cold hammer forged precision barrel, 18.5 in. Weight: 9 lbs. Length: 31 in. Power: Pre-charged pneumatic. Stock: Ambidextrous walnut, black soft-touch or black pepper laminate with adjustable buttpad. Sights: None, grooved for scope mounting. Features: Multi-shot bolt action, two 10-shot magazines, enhanced valve system for maximum shot count and consistency, integrated suppressor, adjustable two-stage trigger. Velocities: .177, 825 fps /.22. 570 fps.
Price: ....$1,599.00–$1,699.00

BSA GOLD STAR SE HUNTER FIELD TARGET PCP AIR RIFLE

Caliber: .177. Barrel: Rifled, BSA-made enhanced cold hammer forged precision barrel, 15.2 in. Weight: 7 lbs. Length: 35.8 in. Power: Pre-charged pneumatic. Stock: Highly adjustable gray laminate field target competition stock. Sights: None, grooved for scope mounting. Features: Multi-shot boltaction, 10-shot magazine, fully regulated valve for maximum accuracy and shot consistency, 70 consistent shots per charge, free-floating barrel with 1/2 UNF threaded muzzle, includes adjustable air stripper, adjustable match-grade trigger. Velocity: 800 fps.
Price: $1,499.00

BSA SCORPION PCP AIR RIFLE
Calibers: .177. Barrel: Rifled, free-floated match grade barrel, 18.5 in. Weight: 7.7 lbs. Length: 36.5 in. Power: Precharged pneumatic. Stock: Monte Carlo wood stock with checkered grip and forearm. Sights: None, 11 mm scope rail. Features: Single-shot bolt action, bolt can be swapped from right hand to left hand, swing swivel studs, approximately 25 shots per fill, two-stage adjustable trigger. Velocity: 1,000 fps.
Price: $899.00

BSA ULTRA XL AIR RIFLE
Calibers: .177, .22. Barrel: Rifled, BSA-made cold hammer forged precision barrel, 15.2 in. Weight: 7.3 lbs. Length: 35.4 in. Power: Precharged pneumatic. Stock: Ambidextrous, thumbhole, adjustable cheek piece, wood. Sights: None, grooved for scope mounting. Features: 10-shot magazine, fully regulated valve for maximum accuracy and shot consistency, free-floating, shrouded barrel, single-stage adjustable trigger, removable muzzle brake, also available as the JSR version for smaller framed shooters. Velocities: .177, 700 fps/.22, 570 fps.
Price: $749.00

BSA ULTRA JSR AIR RIFLE
Calibers: .177, .22. Barrel: Rifled, BSA-made cold hammer forged precision barrel, 12 in. Weight: 4.95 lbs. Length: 27 in. Power: Precharged pneumatic. Stock: Beech. Sights: None, grooved for scope mounting. Features: Built for younger or smaller framed shooters, 10-shot magazine, fully regulated valve for maximum accuracy and shot consistency, free-floating, shrouded barrel, two-stage adjustable trigger, threaded muzzle, .177 available in two power configurations. Velocities: 560 or 800 fps (.177)/600 fps (.22).
Price: $699.00

CROSMAN CHALLENGER PCP COMPETITION AIR RIFLE
Caliber: .177. Barrel: Match-grade Lothar Walther rifled barrel. Weight: 7.3 lbs. Length: 41.75 in. Power: Precharged pneumatic. Stock: Highly adjustable synthetic competition stock. Sights: Globe front sight and Precision Diopter rear sight. Features: Up to 200 shots per fill, single-shot, adjustable two-stage match-grade trigger with adjustable shoe, approved by the Civilian Marksmanship Program (CMP) for 3-position air rifle Sporter Class competition, swappable side-lever cocking handle. Velocity: 580 fps.
Price: ....$699.00–$899.00

CROSMAN GENESIS NP AIR RIFLE
Caliber: .22. Barrel: Rifled. Weight: 7.44 lbs. Length: 44.5 in. Power: Break-barrel, gas-piston. Stock: Ambidextrous wood stock with dual raised cheekpieces and checkered grip and forearm. Sights: None, Weaver/Picatinny rail for scope mounting, includes 4x32 scope and rings. Features: Shrouded barrel with integrated suppressor, extremely easy cocking, single-shot, adjustable two-stage trigger, innovative sling mounts for optional Benjamin break-barrel rifle sling. Velocity: 950 fps
Price: $229.00

CROSMAN FULL AUTO AK1 RIFLE
Caliber: .177 BBs. Barrel: Smoothbore. Weight: 8 lbs. Length: 34.5 in. Power: CO2. Stock: Synthetic adjustable/folding 5-position buttstock. Sights: Open, Picatinny rail. Features: Releasable magazine holds two CO2 cartridges and spring feeds 28 BBs, shoots full- or semi-auto with blowback, AK compatible pistol grip, quad rail forearm for accessory mounting. Velocity: 430 fps.
Price: $229.00

CROSMAN FULL AUTO R1 CO2 RIFLE
Caliber: .177 BBs. Barrel: Smooth, 10 in. Weight: 6 lbs. Length: 26.25-29.5 in. Power: CO2. Stock: Synthetic 6 position adjustable buttstock. Sights: None, Picatinny rail, comes with a red dot sight. Features: 25 round drop free magazine, full or semi-auto with blowback, powered by two CO2 cartridges, AR compatible buffer tube and pistol grip, quad rail forearm for accessory mounting, speedloader included. Velocity: 430 fps.
Price: $259.00

CROSMAN M4-177

CROSMAN M4-177 RIFLE (various styles and kits available)
Caliber: .177 steel BBs, .177 pellets. Barrel: Rifled 17.25 in. Weight: 3.75 lbs. Length: 33.75 in. Power: Multi-pump pneumatic. Stock: M4-style adjustable plastic stock. Sights: Weaver/Picatinny rail for scope mounting and flip-up sights. Bundled packages include various included sighting options. Features: Single-shot bolt action, lightweight and very accurate, multiple colors available. "Ready to go" kits available complete with ammo, safety glasses, targets and extra 5-shot pellet magazines. Velocity: 660 fps.
Price: ....$89.00-$149.00

CROSMAN MODEL 760 PUMPMASTER AIR RIFLE
Caliber: .177 steel BBs, .177 pellets. Barrel: Rifled 16.75 in. Weight: 2.75 lbs. Length: 33.5 in. Power: Multi-pump pneumatic. Stock: Ambidextrous plastic stock. Sights: Blade and ramp, rear sight adjustable for elevation, grooved for scope mounting. Features: Single-shot pellet, BB repeater, bolt action, lightweight, accurate and easy to shoot. Multiple colors available and configurations available. "Ready to go" kits available complete with ammo, safety glasses, targets and extra 5-shot pellet magazines. Velocity: 625 fps.
Price: ....$49.00–$69.00

CROSMAN DIAMONDBACK SBD AIR RIFLE
Caliber: .22. Barrel: Rifled. Weight: 8.5 lbs. Length: 46.5 in. Power: Break-barrel, Nitro-piston. Stock: Synthetic with pistol grip. Sights: Open sights, dovetail for scope mounting, includes CenterPoint 4x32 scope and rings. Features: SBD sound-suppression system, sling mounts, single-shot, adjustable two-stage trigger. Velocities: 1,100 fps.
Price: $189.00

CROSMAN FIRE NITRO PISTON AIR RIFLE
Caliber: .177. Barrel: Rifled. Weight: 6.0 lbs. Length: 43.5 in. Power: Break-barrel, Nitro-piston. Stock: Synthetic thumbhole style. Sights: None, dovetail for scope mounting, includes CenterPoint 4x32 scope and rings. Features: Integrated muzzle brake for reduced recoil and noise, single-shot, adjustable two-stage trigger. Velocities: 1,200 fps.
Price: $149.00

CROSMAN MAG-FIRE EXTREME/ULTRA/MISSION BREAK BARREL AIR RIFLES
Caliber: .177, .22. Barrel: Rifled. Weight: 6.5 lbs. Length: 43 in. Power: Break-barrel. Stock: Ambidextrous synthetic. Sights: Adjustable rear sight, Picatinny rail for scope mounting, includes 3-9x40 scope and rings. Features: Extreme has a tactical-style stock with adjustable cheekpiece and pistol grip, Ultra has an all-weather stock with soft-touch inserts, Mission has a thumbhole-style stock, 12-shot magazine, QuietFire sound suppression, adjustable two-stage trigger, sling mount. Velocities: 1,300 fps (.177)/975 fps (.22).
Price: $199.00

Prices given are believed to be accurate at time of publication however, many factors affect retail pricing so exact prices are not possible.

76TH EDITION, 2022 ⊕ 557

CROSMAN OPTIMUS AIR RIFLE COMBO
Caliber: .177, .22. Barrel: Rifled. Weight: 6.5 lbs. Length: 43 in. Power: Break-barrel. Stock: Ambidextrous wood. Sights: Fiber-optic with adjustable rear sight, dovetail for scope mounting, includes CenterPoint 4x32 scope and rings. Features: Single-shot, adjustable two-stage trigger. Velocities: 1,200 fps (.177)/950 fps (.22).
Price: **$149.00**

CROSMAN REPEATAIR 1077/1077 FREESTYLE CO2 RIFLE
Caliber: .177 pellets. Barrel: Rifled 20.38 in. Weight: 3.75 lbs. Length: 36.88 in. Power: CO2. Stock: Ambidextrous plastic stock. Sights: Blade and ramp, rear sight adjustable for windage and elevation, grooved for scope mounting. Features: Multi-shot, semi-automatic, 12-shot magazine, lightweight, fun and easy to shoot. "Ready to go" kits available complete with ammo, CO2, targets, target trap, etc. Velocity: 625 fps.
Price: ....**$94.00-$129.00**

CROSMAN TYRO AIR RIFLE
Calibers: .177. Barrel: Rifled. Weight: 4.9 lbs. Length: 37.5 in. Power: Break-barrel, spring-piston. Stock: Synthetic thumbhole with spacers to adjust length of pull. Sights: Front fiber-optic sight and adjustable rear sight. Features: Single shot, sized for smaller shooters. Velocities: 720 fps with alloy pellet.
Price: **$105.00**

DAISY 1938 RED RYDER AIR RIFLE
Caliber: .177 steel BBs. Barrel: Smoothbore 10.85 in. Weight: 2.2 lbs. Length: 35.4 in. Power: Single-cock, lever action, spring-piston. Stock: Solid wood stock and fore-end. Sights: Blade front sight, adjustable rear sight. Features: 650 BB reservoir, single-stage trigger, designed for all day fun and backyard plinking, exceptional first airgun for young shooters. Velocity: 350 fps.
Price: **$56.00**

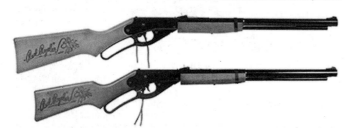

DAISY ADULT RED RYDER BB RIFLE
Caliber: .177 steel BBs. Barrel: Smoothbore, 10.85 in. Weight: 2.95 lbs. Length: 36.75 in. Power: Single-cock, lever-action, spring-piston. Stock: Solid wood stock and fore-end. Sights: Blade front sight, adjustable rear sight. Features: A larger, adult-size version of the classic youth Red Ryder with 650-shot reservoir. 18-pound cocking effort. Velocity: 350 fps.
Price: **$52.00**

DAISY AVANTI MODEL 887 GOLD MEDALIST COMPETITION
Caliber: .177 pellets. Barrel: Rifled, match-grade Lothar Walther barrel, 20.88 in. Weight: 6.9 lbs. Length: 38.5 in. Power: CO2. Stock: Ambidextrous laminated wood stock. Sights: Globe front sight and Precision Diopter rear sight. Features: Precision bored and crowned barrel for match accuracy, bulk fill CO2 is capable of up to 300 shots, additional inserts available for front sight, ideal entry level rifle for all 10-meter shooting disciplines. Velocity: 500 fps.
Price: **$563.00**

DAISY MODEL 499B CHAMPION COMPETITION RIFLE
Caliber: .177 BBs. Barrel: Smoothbore, 20.88 in. Weight: 3.1 lbs. Length: 36.25. Power: Lever action spring piston. Stock: Hardwood. Sights: Hooded front with aperture inserts and adjustable rear peep sight. Features: Single shot, 5-meter competition rifle. Velocity: 240 fps.
Price: **$164.00**

DAISY MODEL 599 COMPETITION AIR RIFLE
Caliber: .177 pellets. Barrel: Rifled, cold hammer forged BSA barrel, 20.88 in. Weight: 7.1 lbs. Length: 34.35-37.25 in. Power: Pre-charged pneumatic. Stock: Ambidextrous beech wood stock with vertical and length-of-pull adjustment, adjustable comb. Sights: Hooded front and diopter rear sight. Features: Trigger weight adjustable down to 1.5 lbs., rotating trigger adjustment for positioning right or left, straight pull T-bolt handle, removable power cylinder. Velocity: 520 fps.
Price: **$595.00**

DAISY MODEL 25 PUMP GUN
Caliber: .177 steel BBs. Barrel: Smoothbore. Weight: 3 lbs. Length: 37 in. Power: pump action, spring-air. Stock: Solid wood buttstock. Sights: Fixed front and rear sights. Features: 50 shot BB reservoir, removable screw out shot tube, decorative engraving on receiver, rear sight can be flipped over to change from open to peep sight. Velocity: 350 fps.
Price: **$47.00**

DAISY MODEL 105 BUCK AIR RIFLE
Caliber: .177 steel BBs. Barrel: Smoothbore 7.97 in. Weight: 1.6 lbs. Length: 29.8 in. Power: Single-cock, lever action, spring-piston. Stock: Solid wood buttstock. Sights: Fixed front and rear sights. Features: 400 BB reservoir, single-stage trigger, designed for all day fun and backyard plinking. Velocity: 275 fps.
Price: **$35.00**

DAISY AVANTI MODEL 753S MATCH GRADE AVANTI
Caliber: .177 pellets. Barrel: Rifled, Lothar Walther, 19.5 in. Weight: 7.3 lbs. Length: 38.5 in. Power: Single-stroke pneumatic. Stock: Ambidextrous wood stock & Synthetic stock available Sights: Globe front sight and Precision Diopter rear sight. Features: Full-size wood stock, additional inserts available for front sight, fully self-contained power system, excellent "first" rifle for all 10-meter shooting disciplines. Velocity: 495 fps.
Price: ....**$299.00–$469.00**

DAISY PINK 1999 BB GUN
Caliber: .177, steel BBs. Barrel: Smoothbore 10.85 in. Weight: 2.2 lbs. Length: 35.4 in. Power: Single-cock, lever action, spring-piston. Stock: Solid wood stock and forearm painted pink. Sights: Blade front sight, adjustable rear sight. Features: 650 BB reservoir, single-stage trigger, designed for all day fun and backyard plinking, great option for young ladies just starting out. Velocity: 350 fps.
Price: **$47.00**

DAISY POWERLINE MODEL 880 AIR RIFLE
Caliber: .177 steel BBs, .177 pellets. Barrel: Rifled, 21 in. Weight: 3.1 lbs. Length: 37.6 in. Power: Multi-pump pneumatic. Stock: Synthetic. Sights: Fiber-optic front sight, rear sight adjustable for elevation, grooved for scope mounting. Features: Single-shot pellet, 50 shot BB, lightweight, accurate and easy to shoot. Velocity: 800 fps (BBs), 665 fps (pellets).
Price: $54.00

DAISY POWERLINE MODEL 35 AIR RIFLE
Caliber: .177 steel BBs, .177 pellets. Barrel: Smoothbore. Weight: 2.25 lbs. Length: 34.5 in. Power: Multi-pump pneumatic. Stock: Ambidextrous plastic stock, available in black and pink camo. Sights: Blade and ramp, rear sight adjustable for elevation, grooved for scope mounting. Features: Single-shot pellet, BB rep, lightweight, accurate and easy to shoot. Velocity: 625 fps.
Price: ....$41.00-$69.00

DAISY POWERLINE 901 AIR RIFLE
Caliber: .177 steel BBs, .177 pellets. Barrel: Rifled 20.8 in. Weight: 3.2 lbs. Length: 37.75 in. Power: Multi-pump pneumatic Stock: Ambidextrous black wood grain plastic stock. Sights: Front fiber-optic sight, rear blade sight adjustable for elevation, grooved for scope mounting. Features: Full-size adult airgun, single-shot pellet, BB repeater, bolt action, lightweight, accurate and easy to shoot. "Ready to go" kit available complete with ammo, safety glasses, shatterblast targets, 4x15 scope and mounts. Velocity: 750 fps.
Price: ....$71.00–$95.00

DAYSTATE DELTA WOLF RIFLE
Calibers: .177, .22, .25, .30. Barrel: Rifled 43 cm (.177 or .22) or 60 cm (.177, .22, .25, .30). Weight: 6.8 lbs. Length: 34 in. Power: Precharged pneumatic. Stock: AR style. Sights: None, 22mm Picatinny rail. Features: Advanced Velocity Technology with display touch screen, multi-caliber with fast-change barrel system, factory set power profiles for each caliber, built-in chronoscope that allows the shooter to dial in their preferred velocity, OEM Huma-Air regulated, large capacity (813-shot) magazine, Bluetooth connectivity, switchable side lever action, carbon-fiber shroud and optional silencer, removable air tank. Velocity: Adjustable.
Price: $2,999.00

DAYSTATE HUNTSMAN REGAL XL AIR RIFLE
Calibers: .177, .22, .25. Barrel: Rifled 17 in. Weight: 6.17 lbs. Length: 40.0 in. Power: Pre-charged pneumatic. Stock: Right-handed Monte Carlo hardwood. Sights: None, 11mm grooved dovetail for scope mounting. Features: Features the exceptional pedigree of the finest European airguns, 10-shot rotary magazine, rear bolt action, adjustable trigger, fully moderated barrel. Velocity: (not provided).
Price: $1,499.00

DAYSTATE RED WOLF RIFLE
Calibers: .177, .22, .25. Barrel: Match grade rifled Lothar Walther 17 in. Weight: 7.5 lbs. Length: 39 in. Power: Pre-charged pneumatic. Stock: Fully adjustable walnut. Sights: None, 11mm grooved dovetail for scope mounting. Features: Three individual programmed energy and velocity settings, computer controlled state-of-the-art MCT firing system, LCD screen displays air pressure, battery state, number of shots fired. Ten-shot magazine, fully adjustable trigger from ounces to pounds, stock provides cheek-piece adjustments for height, left and right canting as well as buttpad adjustment for up, down, left and right. Velocity: NA.
Price: $2,899.00

DAYSTATE RED WOLF SAFARI HIGH POWER RIFLE
Calibers: .177, .22, .25, .30. Barrel: Match grade rifled Lothar Walther, 23 in. Weight: 8.5 lbs. Length: 45 in. Power: Precharged pneumatic. Stock: Ambidextrous textured wood. Sights: None, 11mm grooved dovetail for scope mounting. Features: Three individual programmed energy and velocity settings, computer controlled state of the art MCT firing system, LCD screen displays air pressure, battery state, number of shots fired, 10-shot magazine or single shot tray, fully adjustable trigger from ounces to pounds, stock provides cheek piece adjustments for height, left and right canting as well as butt pad adjustment for up, down, left, and right, right or left hand reversible side cocking, carbon fiber shroud. Velocity: NA.
Price: $2,999.00

DAYSTATE TSAR TARGET RIFLE
Calibers: .177 pellet. Barrel: Match grade rifled Lothar Walther 20.5 in. Weight: 9.9 lbs. Length: 39 in. Power: Pre-charged pneumatic. Stock: Laminate. Sights: None, 11mm grooved dovetail for scope mounting. Features: Adjustable cheek rest and buttpad, five-level adjustable multi-sear trigger, fully moderated barrel, designed for field target competition, side lever cocking system allows for dry-firing practice. Velocity: (not provided).
Price: $2,935.00

DIANA MAUSER K98 AIR RIFLE
Calibers: .177, .22. Barrel: Rifled 18.0 in. Weight: 9.5 lbs. Length: 44 in. Power: Break-barrel, spring-piston. Stock: Authentic Mauser K98 hardwood stock. Sights: Front post and fully adjustable rear sight, 11mm dovetail grooved for scope mounting. Features: European quality, fixed barrel with underlever cocking, exceptional two-stage adjustable match trigger, single-shot, German manufactured to stringent quality control and testing, limited lifetime warranty. Velocities: .177, 1,150 fps/.22, 850 fps.
Price: $469.00

Prices given are believed to be accurate at time of publication however, many factors affect retail pricing so exact prices are not possible.

76TH EDITION, 2022 ⊕ 559

DIANA CHASER CO2 AIR RIFLE/PISTOL KIT

Caliber: .177, .22. Barrel: Rifled, 17.7. in. Weight: 3.1 lbs. Length: 38.4 in. Power: CO2. Stock: Ambidextrous synthetic. Sights: Front fiber-optic sight and adjustable rear sight, 11 mm dovetail for scope mounting. Features: Shrouded barrel, two-stage adjustable trigger, single-shot (can use indexing 7-9 shot magazines from the Stormrider), approximately 50 shots per CO2 cylinder, kit includes soft case, Chaser pistol, buttstock, and rifle barrel. Velocities: 642 fps (.177 rifle), 500 fps (.22 rifle).
Price: **$139.00**

DIANA 34 EMS BREAK BARREL AIR RIFLE

Caliber: .177, .22. Barrel: Rifled, 19.5 in. Weight: 7.85 lbs. Length: 46.3 in. Power: Break-barrel, spring-piston, convertible to N-TEC gas piston. Stock: Ambidextrous thumbhole synthetic. Sights: Front fiber-optic sight and micrometer adjustable rear sight, 11 mm dovetail. Features: Two-stage adjustable trigger, single-shot, removable ½ in UNF threaded barrel, EMS (easy modular system) allows for easy changing of barrels, adjustable barrel alignment, changeable front and rear sights, two piece cocking lever. Velocities: 890 fps (.177), 740 fps (.22).
Price: **$367.00**

DIANA 54 AIRKING PRO LAMINATE AIR RIFLE

Caliber: .177, .22. Barrel: Rifled, 17.3 in. Weight: 10.25 lbs. Length: 44in. Power: Spring piston side lever. Stock: Red and black laminated. Sights: Adjustable rear sight, 11 mm dovetail. Features: Two-stage adjustable trigger, single-shot, forearm swivel stud to attach a bipod, adjustable barrel weight, checkered grip and forearm. Velocities: 1100 fps (.177), 990 fps (.22).
Price: **$749.00**

DIANA 340 N-TEC PREMIUM AIR RIFLE

Calibers: .177, .22. Barrel: Rifled 19.5 in. Weight: 7.9 lbs. Length: 46 in. Power: Break-barrel, German gas-piston. Stock: Ambidextrous beech stock. Sights: Front fiber-optic sight and fully adjustable rear fiber-optic sight, grooved for scope mounting. Features: European quality, exceptional two-stage adjustable match trigger, single-shot, German manufactured to stringent quality control and testing, limited lifetime warranty. The new N-TEC gas-piston power plant boasts smoother cocking and shooting, making the N-TEC line of Diana guns the most refined Diana airguns to date. Various bundled configurations available. Velocities: .177, 1,000 fps/.22, 800 fps.
Price: **$449.00**

DIANA 350 N-TEC MAGNUM PREMIUM AIR RIFLE

Calibers: .177, .22. Barrel: Rifled 19.5 in. Weight: 6.7 lbs. Length: 48.5 in. Power: Break-barrel, German gas-piston. Stock: Ambidextrous stock, available in beech and synthetic options. Sights: Front post and fully adjustable rear sight, grooved for scope mounting. Features: European quality, exceptional two-stage adjustable match trigger, single-shot, German manufactured to stringent quality control and testing, limited lifetime warranty. The new N-TEC gas-piston power plant boasts smoother cocking and shooting, making the N-TEC line of Diana guns the most refined Diana airguns to date. Velocities: .177, 1,250 fps/.22, 1,000 fps.
Price: **$499.00**

DIANA MODEL RWS 48 AIR RIFLE, T06 TRIGGER

Calibers: .177, .22. Barrel: Rifled 17 in. Weight: 8.5 lbs. Length: 42.13 in. Power: Single-cock, side-lever, spring-piston. Stock: Ambidextrous beech thumbhole stock. Sights: Blade front sight, fully adjustable rear sight, grooved for scope mounting. Features: European quality, exceptional two-stage match trigger, single-shot, German manufactured to stringent quality control and testing, limited lifetime warranty. Velocities: .177, 1,100 fps/.22, 900 fps.
Price: **$398.00**

DIANA RWS 460 MAGNUM AIR RIFLE

Calibers: .177, .22. Barrel: Rifled 18.44 in. Weight: 8.3 lbs. Length: 45 in. Power: Under-lever, spring-piston. Stock: Right-hand hardwood stock with grip and fore-end checkering. Sights: Post front sight and fully adjustable rear sight, grooved for scope mounting. Features: European quality, exceptional two-stage adjustable match trigger, single-shot, German manufactured to stringent quality control and testing, limited lifetime warranty. Various bundled configurations available. Velocity: .177, 1,200 fps/.22, 1,000 fps.
Price: **$419.00**

DIANA STORMRIDER GEN 2 PCP RIFLE

Calibers: .177, .22. Barrel: Rifled 19 in. Weight: 5.0 lbs. Length: 40.5 in. Power: Pre-charged pneumatic. Stock: Checkered beech stock. Sights: Blade front, fully adjustable rear, 11 mm dovetail grove. Features: Entry level PCP rifle, nine-shot (.177) or seven-shot (.22) capacity, adjustable two-stage trigger, built-in muzzle brake, integrated pressure gauge. Velocities: 1,050 fps (.177)/900 fps (.22).
Price: **$219.00**

DIANA TRAILSCOUT CO2 RIFLE

Caliber: .177, .22 pellet. Barrel: Rifled, 19 in. Weight: 4.6 lbs. Length: 38.9 in. Power: CO2. Stock: Synthetic. Sights: Adjustable rear. Features: Uses three 12 g CO2 cylinders, can be used single shot or with a 7 (.22) or 9 (.177) shot magazine, bolt action, adjustable trigger, approximately 100 shots per fill. Velocities: 660 fps (.177), 560 fps (.22).
Price: **$179.00**

DPMS CLASSIC A4 NITRO PISTON AIR RIFLE

Caliber: .177 pellets. Barrel: Rifled 15 in. Weight: 7 lbs. Length: 40 in. Power: Break-barrel, gas-piston. Stock: Ambidextrous AR-15-styled stock. Sights: none, Weaver/Picatinny rail for flip-up sights and scope mounting, includes 4x32 scope and rings. Features: Aggressive and realistic AR-15 styling. Sling mounts, single-shot, adjustable two-stage trigger. Velocity: 1,200 fps.
Price: **$229.00**

EDGUN LESHIY GEN2 PCP RIFLE

Calibers: .177, .22, .25. Barrel: Rifled, Lothar Walther, 10-14 in. Weight: 4.25 lbs. Length: 25 in., (without moderator) overall. Power: Pre-charged pneumatic. Stock: Ambidextrous adjustable. Sights: None, Weaver-style rail for scope mounting. Features: Single shot, folds in the center to cock the action, can be stored while folded making it compact to carry, chassis CNC machined out of aluminum, easily switchable between calibers with replacement barrels, up to 40 shots per fill depending on caliber. Velocities: Approximately 950 fps (adjustable).
Price: **$1,395.00**

Prices given are believed to be accurate at time of publication however, many factors affect retail pricing so exact prices are not possible.

EDGUN MATADOR R5M STANDARD PCP RIFLE
Calibers: .177, .22, or .25. Barrel: Rifled, Lothar Walther, 18.75 in. Weight: 6.75 lbs. Length: 27.5 in. Power: Precharged pneumatic. Stock: Ambidextrous walnut thumbhole or synthetic. Sights: None, Weaver rail for scope mounting. Features: Adjustable trigger, adjustable hammer spring tension, designed and manufactured in Russia, 40-60 shots per fill depending on caliber, also available with a longer barrel, ambidextrous safety. Velocities: 950 fps (.177), 920 fps (.22 and .25)
Price: **$1,704.00**

EVANIX RAINSTORM II PCP AIR RIFLE
Calibers: .22, .25, .30, .35 (9mm). Barrel: Rifled, 17.00 in. Weight: 7.2 lbs. Length: 39.00 in. overall. Power: Pre-charged Pneumatic. Stock: Ambidextrous beech thumbhole stock. Sights: None, grooved 11mm dovetail for scope mounting Features: Multi-shot side-lever action, shot count varies based on caliber, very well made and versatile hunting airgun. Velocities: .22, 1,176 fps/.25, 910 fps/.30, 910 fps/.35, 800 fps.
Price: **$799.00-999.00**

EVANIX REX AIR RIFLE
Calibers: .22, .25, .35 (9mm), .45. Barrel: Rifled, 19.68 in. Weight: 5.51 lbs. Length: 35.82 in. overall. Power: Precharged Pneumatic. Sights: weaver rail for scope mounting Features: Lightweight, compact and massively powerful, single shot, capable of putting out well over 200 ft-lbs at the muzzle in .45 caliber, truly effective hunting power in a compact package Velocities: .22, 1,080 fps/.25, 970 fps/.35, 860 fps/.45, 700 fps.
Price: **$699.00-799.00**

FEINWERKBAU 500 AIR RIFLE
Caliber: .177. Barrel: Rifled 13.8 in. Weight: 7.05 lbs. Length: 43.7 in. Power: Pre-charged pneumatic. Stock: Ambidextrous beech stock with adjustable cheekpiece and buttstock. Sights: Globe front sight and diopter rear. Features: Meets requirements for ISSF competition, trigger-pull weight adjusts from 3.9 to 7.8 ounces, bolt action, competition grade airgun. Velocity: 574 fps.
Price: **$1,649.00**

FEINWERKBAU 800X FIELD TARGET AIR RIFLE
Caliber: .177. Barrel: Rifled 16.73 in. Weight: 11.7–15.05 lbs. Length: 49.76 in. Power: Pre-charged pneumatic. Stock: Highly adaptable field target competition stock Sights: None, 11mm grooved for scope mounting. Features: Designed from airguns featuring Olympic accuracy, this field target variant is designed to win., 5-way adjustable match trigger, bolt action, competition grade airgun Velocity: 825 fps.
Price: **$3,799.00**

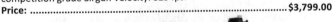

FEINWERKBAU P75 BIATHLON AIR RIFLE
Caliber: .177. Barrel: Rifled 16.73 in. Weight: 9.26 lbs. Length: 42.91 in. Power: Pre-charged pneumatic. Stock: Highly adaptable laminate wood competition stock Sights: Front globe with aperture inserts and diopter micrometer rear. Features: 5-shot bolt action, competition grade airgun, inspired from airguns featuring Olympic accuracy, 5-way adjustable match trigger. Velocity: 564 fps.
Price: **$3,254.00**

FEINWERKBAU SPORT AIR RIFLE
Caliber: .177. Barrel: Rifled 18.31 in. Weight: 8.27 lbs. Length: 44.84 in. Power: Spring-piston break barrel. Stock: Ambidextrous wood stock with dual raised cheekpieces. Sights: Front globe, fully adjustable rear sight, grooved for scope mounting. Features: Lightweight, single-shot, easy cocking, adjustable two-stage trigger. Velocity: .177, 850 fps.
Price: **$999.00**

FX CROWN AIR RIFLE
Calibers: .177, .22, .25, .30. Barrel: Rifled 19-23.5 in. Weight: 6.5-7.5 lbs. Length: 38.5-43 in. Power: Precharged pneumatic. Stock: Ambidextrous stock in walnut, laminate, or synthetic. Sights: None, 11mm grooved for scope mounting. Features: Smooth Twist X barrels can be swapped to change not only caliber but also twist rate, adjustable 15 ounce two-stage trigger, externally adjustable regulator, adjustable power wheel and hammer spring, removable carbon fiber tank, dual air pressure gauges, multiple-shot magazine (14-18 shots depending on caliber). Velocities: .177, 1,000 fps/.22, 920 fps/.25, 900 fps/.30, 870 fps.
Price: **$1,799.00-2,199.00**

FX IMPACT AIR RIFLE
Calibers: .25, .30. Barrel: Rifled 24.4 in. Weight: 7.0 lbs. Length: 34.0 in. Power: Pre-charged pneumatic. Stock: Compact bullpup stock in various materials and finishes Sights: None, 11mm grooved for scope mounting. Features: Premium airgun brand known for exceptional build quality and accuracy, regulated for consistent shots, adjustable two-stage trigger, FX smooth twist barrel, multi-shot side lever action, fully moderated barrel, highly adjustable and adaptable air rifle system. Velocities: .25, 900 fps/.30, 870 fps.
Price: **$2,198.00**

FX MAVERICK SNIPER PCP AIR RIFLE
Calibers: .22, .25, .30. Barrel: Rifled 27.6 in. Weight: 7.2 lbs. Length: 36.0 in. Power: Precharged pneumatic. Stock: Tactical style with AR style grip. Sights: None, Picatinny rail with 20 MOA tilt for scope mounting. Features: Three Picatinny rails for accessories, adjustable match trigger, threaded barrel shroud, side lever action, dual AMP regulators, 580 cc carbon fiber air cylinder, dual manometers, 90 (.30), 170 (.25), 270 (.22) maximum shots per fill, 18 (.22), 16 (.25), 13 (.30) shot magazine, includes one magazine and a hard case, also available in a compact version. Velocities: .22, 1000 fps/.25, 1000 fps/.30, 900 fps.
Price: **$1,899.00**

FX WILDCAT AIR RIFLE
Calibers: .22, .25. Barrel: Rifled 19.7 in. Weight: 6.1 lbs. Length: 26.5 in. Power: Pre-charged pneumatic. Stock: Compact bullpup stock in various materials and finishes. Sights: None, 11mm grooved for scope mounting. Features: Premium airgun brand known for exceptional build quality and accuracy, regulated for consistent shots, adjustable two-stage trigger, FX smooth twist barrel, multi-shot side lever action, fully moderated barrel. Velocity: .22, 1,200 fps/.25, 900 fps.
Price: **$1,499.00–1,899.00**

FX .30 BOSS AIR RIFLE
Caliber: .30. Barrel: Rifled 24.4 in. Weight: 7.0 lbs. Length: 47.5 in. Power: Pre-charged pneumatic. Stock: Right-handed Monte Carlo Stock available in various materials and finishes. Sights: None. 11mm grooved for scope mounting. Features: Premium airgun brand known for exceptional build quality and accuracy, regulated for consistent shots, adjustable two-stage trigger, FX smooth twist barrel, multi-shot side lever action, fully moderated barrel. Velocities: .22, 1,200 fps/.25, 900 fps.
Price: ....**$1,949.00–$2,399.00**

Prices given are believed to be accurate at time of publication however, many factors affect retail pricing so exact prices are not possible.

76TH EDITION, 2022 ✛ 561

FX ROYALE 400 AIR RIFLE

Caliber: .177, .22. Barrel: Rifled 19.5 in. Weight: 7.5 lbs. Length: 40.25 in. Power: Precharged pneumatic. Stock: Ambidextrous laminated thumbhole. Sights: None. 11mm dovetailed for scope mounting. Features: FX smooth twist barrel, removable carbon fiber air cylinder, fully shrouded barrel, adjustable power, up to 100 shots per fill, side lever action, two-stage adjustable trigger, adjustable buttplate, 12-shot rotary magazine. Velocities: .177, 950 fps/.22, 950 fps.
Price: $1,899.00

GAMO COYOTE WHISPER PCP AIR RIFLE

Calibers: .177, .22. Barrel: Cold hammer-forged match-grade rifled barrel, 24.5 in. Weight: 6.6 lbs. Length: 42.9 in. Power: Pre-charged pneumatic. Stock: Ambidextrous hardwood stock. Sights: None, grooved for scope mounting, Features: European class airgun, highly accurate and powerful, adjustable two-stage trigger, integrated moderator, 10-shot bolt action. Velocities: .177, 1,200 fps/.22, 1,000 fps.
Price: $559.00

GAMO WILDCAT WHISPER BREAK BARREL AIR RIFLE

Calibers: .177, .22. Barrel: Rifled barrel, 19.1 in. Weight: 5.6 lbs. Length: 44.5 in. Power: Gas piston, break barrel. Stock: Ambidextrous synthetic stock. Sights: Fixed, grooved for scope mounting, includes a 4x32 scope. Features: Single shot, Inert Gas Technology (IGS), 30 pound cocking effort, Whisper noise suppression. Velocities: .177, 1,350 fps/.22, 975 fps.
Price: $149.00

GAMO SWARM MAXXIM GEN2 MULTI-SHOT AIR RIFLE

Calibers: .177, .22. Barrel: Rifled 19.9 in. Weight: 5.64 lbs. Length: 45.3 in. Power: Break-barrel, gas-piston. Stock: Ambidextrous glass-filled nylon stock. Sights: None, grooved for scope mounting, includes recoil-reducing rail, 3-9x32 scope and mounts. Features: 10-shot multi-shot system allows for automatic loading with each cock of the barrel, easy cocking, adjustable two-stage trigger, all-weather fluted barrel, features integrated suppressor technology. Velocities: .177, 1,300 fps/.22, 1,000 fps.
Price: $249.00

GAMO SWARM MAGNUM MULTI-SHOT AIR RIFLE

Caliber: .22. Barrel: Rifled 21.3 in. Weight: 6.88 lbs. Length: 49.2 in. Power: Break-barrel, gas-piston. Stock: Ambidextrous lightweight composite stock. Sights: None, grooved for scope mounting, includes recoil-reducing rail, 3-9x32 scope and mounts. Features: New for 2018, loaded with patented features including an ingenious 10-shot multi-shot system allows for automatic loading with each cock of the barrel, easy cocking, adjustable two-stage trigger, steel barrel, features integrated suppressor technology. Velocity: 1,300 fps.
Price: $279.00

GAMO URBAN PCP AIR RIFLE

Caliber: .22. Barrel: Cold hammer forged match grade rifled barrel. Weight:

6.7 lbs. Length: 42.0 in. Power: Pre-charged pneumatic. Stock: Ambidextrous composite thumbhole stock. Sights: None, grooved for scope mounting, Features: European class airgun, highly accurate and powerful, adjustable two-stage trigger, integrated moderator, 10-shot bolt action. Velocity: 800 fps.
Price: $449.00

GAMO BIG BORE TC35 AIR RIFLE

Caliber: .35. Barrel: rifled, 14.96 in. Weight: 6.0 lbs. Length: 35.88 in. Power: Pre-charged pneumatic. Stock: Ambidextrous. Sights: None, weaver rail for scope mounting, Features: Very light and yet very powerful producing up to 170 ft-lbs of muzzle energy, adjustable trigger, two power settings, shrouded barrel, single-shot action allows for an extremely wide range of ammo choices.
Price: $1,099.00

GAMO BIG BORE TC45 AIR RIFLE

Caliber: .45. Barrel: rifled, 24.24 in. Weight: 8.0 lbs. Length: 47.13 in. Power: Pre-charged pneumatic. Stock: Ambidextrous. Sights: None, weaver rail for scope mounting. Features: Very light and yet very powerful producing over 400 ft-lbs of muzzle energy shooting 350-grain cast slugs, adjustable trigger, two power settings, shrouded barrel, single shot action allows for an extremely wide range of ammo choices.
Price: $1,099.00

GAMO WHISPER FUSION MACH 1 AIR RIFLE, IGT

Calibers: .177, .22. Barrel: Rifled, 20.5 in. Weight: 6.6 lbs. Length: 46 in. Power: Break-barrel, Inert Gas Technology gas-piston. Stock: Lightweight composite stock with ambidextrous cheek piece. Sights: Globe fiber-optic front sight and fully adjustable fiber-optic rear sight, grooved for scope mounting, includes Shock Wave Absorber recoil reducing pad, 3-9x40 scope and heavy-duty mount. Features: Integrated Gamo "Whisper" noise-dampening system and bull barrel noise-suppression system for maximum stealth, single-shot, 32-pound cocking effort, adjustable two-stage trigger. Velocities: .177, 1,420 fps/.22, 1,020 fps.
Price: $299.00

GLETCHER M1891 CO2 BB RIFLE

Caliber: .177 BBs. Barrel: Smooth, 16 in. Weight: 5.6 lbs. Length: 22.44 in. Power: CO2. Stock: Imitation wood. Sights: Adjustable rear with removable front globe. Features: Reproduction of the Mosin-Nagant sawed off rifle, working sliding metal bolt action, built in hex wrench for changing CO2 cylinders, 16 BB capacity, approximately 120 shots per fill. Velocity: 427 fps.
Price: $199.00

GLETCHER M1944 CO2 BB RIFLE

Caliber: .177 BBs. Barrel: Smooth, 16 in. Weight: 8.21 lbs. Length: 40.5 in with bayonet folded. Power: CO2. Stock: Imitation wood. Sights: Adjustable rear with removable front globe. Features: Reproduction of the Russian Mosin-Nagant rifle, working sliding metal bolt action, built in hex wrench for changing CO2 cylinders, 16 BB capacity, approximately 120 shots per fill, integral folding bayonet, reproduction sling included. Velocity: 427 fps.
Price: $329.00

Prices given are believed to be accurate at time of publication however, many factors affect retail pricing so exact prices are not possible.

HAMMERLI 850 AIR MAGNUM RIFLE

Calibers: .177, .22. Barrel: Rifled 23.62 in. Weight: 5.65 lbs. Length: 41 in. Power: CO2. Stock: Ambidextrous lightweight composite stock with dual raised cheekpieces. Sights: Globe fiber-optic front sight and fully adjustable fiber-optic rear sight, grooved for scope mounting. Features: Multi-shot bolt action, 8-shot rotary magazine, utilizes 88-gram disposable CO2 canisters delivering up to 200 shots per cartridge. Extremely accurate, very easy to shoot. German manufacturing. Velocities: .177, 760 fps/.22, 655 fps.
Price: $349.00

HAMMERLI AR20 SILVER AIR RIFLE

Calibers: .177. Barrel: Rifled Lothar Walther 19.7 in. Weight: 8.75 lbs. Length: 41.65-43.66 in. Power: Pre-charged pneumatic. Stock: Ambidextrous aluminum stock with vertically adjustable buttpad and spacers for adjusting length. Sights: Globe front sight and fully adjustable diopter rear sight, grooved for scope mounting. Features: Single shot, ambidextrous cocking piece, removable aluminum air cylinder, meets ISSF requirements, stock is available in several colors. Velocity: 557 fps.
Price: $995.00

HATSAN USA EDGE CLASS AIRGUNS

Calibers: .177, .22, .25. Barrel: Rifled 17.7 in. Weight: 6.4–6.6 lbs. Length: 43 in. Power: Break-barrel, spring-piston and gas-spring variations. Stock: Multiple synthetic and synthetic skeleton stock options. Available in different colors such as black, muddy girl camo, moon camo, etc. Sights: Fiber-optic front sight and fully adjustable fiber-optic rear sight, grooved for scope mounting, includes 3-9x32 scope and mounts. Features: European manufacturing with German steel, single-shot, adjustable two-stage trigger, performance tested at the factory with lead pellets for accurate velocity specifications. Velocities: .177, 1,000 fps/.22, 800 fps/.25, 650 fps.
Price: ....$150.00–$180.00

HATSAN USA AIRMAX PCP AIR RIFLE

Calibers: .177, .22, .25. Barrel: Rifled 23.0 in. Weight: 10.8 lbs. Length: 37 in. Power: Precharged pneumatic. Stock: Ambidextrous wood bullpup stock Sights: None, combination Picatinny rail and 11mm dovetail for scope mounting. Features: Multi-shot side-lever action, 10-shot .177 and .22 magazines/9-shot .25 magazine, "Quiet Energy" barrel shroud with integrated suppressor, removable air cylinder, fully adjustable two-stage "Quattro" trigger, "EasyAdjust" elevation comb, sling swivels, includes two magazines. Velocities: .177, 1,170 fps/.22, 1,070 fps/.25, 970 fps.
Price: $799.00

HATSAN USA BULLBOSS QE AIR RIFLE

Calibers: .177, .22, .25. Barrel: Rifled 23.0 in. Weight: 8.6 lbs. Length: 36.8 in. Power: Pre-charged pneumatic. Stock: Ambidextrous synthetic or hardwood bullpup stock Sights: None, innovative dual rail 11mm dovetail and Weaver compatible for scope mounting. Features: Multi-shot side-lever action, 10-shot .177 and .22 magazines/9-shot .25 magazine, "Quiet Energy" barrel shroud with integrated suppressor, European manufacturing with German steel, removable air cylinder, fully adjustable two-stage "Quattro" trigger, performance tested at the factory with lead pellets for accurate velocity specifications. Velocities: .177, 1,170 fps/.22, 1,070 fps/.25, 970 fps.
Price: ....$649.00–$799.00

HATSAN USA BARRAGE SEMI-AUTOMATIC PCP AIR RIFLE

Calibers: .177, .22 .25. Barrel: Rifled, 19.7 in. Weight: 10.1 lbs. Length: 40.9 in. Power: Precharged pneumatic. Stock: Ambidextrous adjustable synthetic thumbhole stock with integrated magazine storage. Sights: None, innovative dual rail 11mm dovetail and Weaver compatible for scope mounting. Features: Air-driven true semi-automatic action, 14 shots in .177 and 12 shots in .22, "Quiet Energy" barrel shroud with integrated suppressor, 500cc cylinder with 250-BAR capacity, European manufacturing with German steel, performance tested at the factory with lead pellets for accurate velocity specifications. Velocities: .177, 1,100 fps/.22, 1,000 fps/.25, 900 fps.
Price: ....$1,099.00–$1,199.00

HATSAN USA BULLMASTER SEMI-AUTOMATIC PCP AIR RIFLE

Calibers: .177, .22, .25. Barrel: Rifled, 19.7 in. Weight: 10.3 lbs. Length: 30.9 in. Power: Pre-charged pneumatic. Stock: Ambidextrous adjustable synthetic bullpup stock with integrated magazine storage. Sights: None, innovative dual rail 11mm dovetail and Weaver compatible for scope mounting. Features: Air-driven true semi-automatic action, 14 shots in .177 and 12 shots in .22, "Quiet Energy" barrel shroud with integrated suppressor, 500 cc cylinder with 250BAR capacity, European manufacturing with German steel, performance tested at the factory with lead pellets for accurate velocity specifications. Velocities: .177, 1,100 fps/.22, 1,000 fps/.25 900 fps.
Price: $1,099.00–1,199.00

HATSAN USA HERCULES BULLY PCP AIR RIFLE

Calibers: .177, .22, .25, .30, .35, .45. Barrel: Rifled 23 in. Weight: 13 lbs. Length: 48.4 in. Power: Pre-charged pneumatic. Stock: Adjustable synthetic all-weather bullpup stock with, sling mounts. Sights: None, innovative dual rail 11mm dovetail and Weaver compatible for scope mounting. Features: Available in 6 calibers, 500cc of air via carbon fiber reservoir, multi-shot side-lever action, 17-shot .177 magazine, 14-shot .22 magazine, 13-shot .25 magazine, 10-shot .30 magazine, 9-shot .35 magazine, 7-shot .45 magazine. "Quiet Energy" barrel shroud with integrated suppressor, European manufacturing with German steel, fully adjustable two-stage "Quattro" trigger, performance tested at the factory with lead pellets for accurate velocity specifications. Velocities: .177, 1,450 fps/.22, 1,300 fps/.25, 1,200 fps/.30, 1,070 fps/.35, 910 fps/.45, 850 fps.
Price: $899.00

HATSAN USA FLASH QE PCP

Calibers: .177, .22, .25. Barrel: Rifled, 17.7 in. Weight: 5.9 lbs. Length: 42.3 in. Power: Pre-charged pneumatic. Stock: Ambidextrous synthetic or hardwood thumbhole stock Sights: None, innovative dual rail 11mm dovetail and Weaver compatible for scope mounting. Features: Very lightweight, multi-shot side-lever action, multi-shot magazine (shot count varies by caliber). "Quiet Energy" barrel shroud with integrated suppressor, European manufacturing with German steel, fully adjustable two-stage "Quattro" trigger, performance tested at the factory with lead pellets for accurate velocity specifications. Velocities: .177, 1,250 fps/.22, 1,100 fps/.25, 900 fps.
Price: ....$329.00-$399.00

HATSAN USA FLASHPUP QE PCP

Calibers: .177, .22, .25. Barrel: Rifled, 19.4 in. Weight: 6.1 lbs. Length: 32.0 in. Power: Pre-charged pneumatic. Stock: Ambidextrous hardwood bullpup stock Sights: None, innovative dual rail 11mm dovetail and Weaver compatible for scope mounting. Features: Very lightweight, multi-shot side-lever action, multi-shot magazine (shot count varies by caliber). "Quiet Energy" barrel shroud with integrated suppressor, European manufacturing with German steel, fully adjustable two-stage "Quattro" trigger, performance tested at the factory with lead pellets for accurate velocity specifications. Velocity: .177, 1,250 fps/.22, 1,100 fps/.25, 900 fps.
Price: ....$399.00-$439.00

Prices given are believed to be accurate at time of publication however, many factors affect retail pricing so exact prices are not possible.

76TH EDITION, 2022 ⊕ 563

HATSAN USA GLADIUS AIRGUN

Calibers: .177, .22, .25. Barrel: Rifled, 23.0 in. Weight: 10.6 lbs. Length: 38 in. Power: Pre-charged pneumatic. Stock: Ambidextrous adjustable synthetic bullpup stock with integrated magazine storage Sights: None, innovative dual rail 11mm dovetail and Weaver compatible for scope mounting. Features: 6 way variable power, multi-shot side-lever action, 10-shot .177 and .22 magazines / 9-shot .25 magazine, "Quiet Energy" barrel shroud with integrated suppressor, European manufacturing with German steel, removable air cylinder, fully adjustable two-stage "Quattro" trigger, performance tested at the factory with lead pellets for accurate velocity specifications. Velocities: .177, 1,070 fps/.22, 970 fps/.25, 870 fps.
Price: $999.00

HATSAN USA MOD 87 QE VORTEX AIR RIFLE

Calibers: .22 Barrel: Rifled 10.6 in. Weight: 7.4 lbs. Length: 44.5 in. Power: Break-barrel, gas-spring. Stock: Synthetic all-weather stock with adjustable cheekpiece. Sights: Fiber-optic front sight and fully adjustable fiber-optic rear sight, grooved for scope mounting, includes 3-9x32 scope and mounts. Features: "Quiet Energy" barrel shroud with integrated suppressor, European manufacturing with German steel, single-shot, fully adjustable two-stage "Quattro" trigger, performance tested at the factory with lead pellets for accurate velocity specifications. Velocities: .177, 1,000 fps/.22, 800 fps/.25, 650 fps.
Price: $219.00

HATSAN USA MOD 135
QE VORTEX AIRGUN

HATSAN USA MOD 135 QE VORTEX AIR RIFLE

Calibers: .177, .22, .25, .30. Barrel: Rifled 10.6 in. Weight: 9.9 lbs. Length: 47.2 in. Power: Break-barrel, gas-spring. Stock: Turkish walnut stock with grip and fore-end checkering, adjustable buttplate and cheekpiece. Sights: Fiber-optic front sight and fully adjustable fiber-optic rear sight, innovative dual rail 11mm dovetail and Weaver compatible for scope mounting. Features: The most powerful break barrel in the world. Worlds first "big-bore" break-barrel airgun, "Quiet Energy" barrel shroud with integrated suppressor, European manufacturing with German steel, single-shot, fully adjustable two-stage "Quattro" trigger, performance tested at the factory with lead pellets for accurate velocity specifications. Velocities: .177, 1,250 fps/.22, 1,000 fps/.25, 750 fps/.30, 550 fps.
Price: $329.00

HATSAN USA AT44 QE PCP AIRGUN

HATSAN USA AT44S-10 QE PCP AIRGUN

Calibers: .177, .22, .25. Barrel: Rifled 19.5 in. Weight: 8 lbs. Length: 45.4 in. Power: Pre-charged pneumatic. Stock: Various configurations, synthetic all-weather stock with front accessory rail and sling mounts. Turkish hardwood with sling mounts, full tactical stock with soft rubber grip inserts, adjustable buttstock and cheek riser. Sights: None, innovative dual rail 11mm dovetail and Weaver compatible for scope mounting. Features: Multi-shot side-lever action, 10-shot .177 and .22 magazines / 9-shot .25 magazine. "Quiet Energy" barrel shroud with integrated suppressor, European manufacturing with German steel, removable air cylinder, fully adjustable two-stage "Quattro" trigger, performance tested at the factory with lead pellets for accurate velocity specifications. Velocities: .177, 1,070 fps/.22, 970 fps/.25, 870 fps.
Price: $459.00

HATSAN USA ALPHA YOUTH QE AIR RIFLE

Caliber: .177. Barrel: Rifled, 15.4 in. Weight: 5.3 lbs. Length: 37.8 in. Power: Spring piston. Stock: Synthetic ambidextrous. Sights: Fiber-optic front sight and fully adjustable fiber-optic rear sight, dual-rail 11mm dovetail and Weaver compatible for scope mounting. Features: Easy cocking, designed for smaller, younger shooters, single-shot, integrated Quiet Energy sound-reducing moderator, adjustable trigger. Velocity: 600 fps with lead-free pellet.
Price: $99.00

HATSAN USA BT BIG BORE CARNIVORE QE AIR RIFLE

Calibers: .30, .35. Barrel: Rifled 23 in. Weight: 9.3 lbs. Length: 48.9 in. Power: Pre-charged pneumatic. Stock: Synthetic all-weather stock with sling mounts, front accessory rail, adjustable cheekpiece and buttpad. Sights: None, innovative dual rail 11mm dovetail and Weaver compatible for scope mounting. Features: Multi-shot bolt action, 6-shot .35 magazine / 7-shot .30 magazine. "Quiet Energy" barrel shroud with integrated suppressor, European manufacturing with German steel, removable air cylinder, fully adjustable two-stage "Quattro" trigger, performance tested at the factory with lead pellets for accurate velocity specifications. Velocities: .30, 860 fps/.35, 730 fps.
Price: $599.00

HATSAN USA HERCULES QE AIR RIFLE

Calibers: .177, .22, .25, .30, .35, .45. Barrel: Rifled 23 in. Weight: 13 lbs. Length: 48.4 in. Power: Pre-charged pneumatic. Stock: Fully adjustable synthetic all-weather stock with, sling mounts. Sights: None, innovative dual rail 11mm dovetail and Weaver compatible for scope mounting. Features: Available in 6 calibers, 1000cc of air on board provides industry leading shot count and energy on target. Multi-shot side-lever action, 17-shot .177 magazine, 14-shot .22 magazine, 13-shot .25 magazine, 10-shot .30 magazine, 9-shot .35 magazine, 7-shot .45 magazine. "Quiet Energy" barrel shroud with integrated suppressor, European manufacturing with German steel, fully adjustable two-stage "Quattro" trigger, performance tested at the factory with lead pellets for accurate velocity specifications. Velocities: .177, 1,300 fps/.22, 1,230 fps/.25, 1,200 fps/.30, 1,070 fps/.35, 930 fps/.45, 810 fps.
Price: $1,399.00

HATSAN USA HYDRA QE AIR RIFLE

Calibers: .177, .22, .25. Barrel: Rifled, 17.7 in. Weight: 6.8 lbs. Length: 42.7 in. Power: Pre-charged pneumatic. Stock: Turkish walnut. Sights: None, dual-rail 11mm dovetail and Weaver compatible for scope mounting. Features: Multi-caliber platform with Versi-Cal technology, swap calibers with a single thumb screw, extra barreled receivers sold separately, Quiet Energy fully shrouded barrel, fully adjustable two-stage "Quattro" trigger, multishot (14 rounds, .177; 12 rounds, .22; 10 rounds, .25). Velocities: .177, 1,250 fps/.22, 1,120 fps/.25, 900 fps (with lead-free pellets).
Price: $449.00

HATSAN USA INVADER AUTO AIR RIFLE

Calibers: .22, .25. Barrel: Rifled 19.7 in. Weight: 8.2 lbs. Length: 40.5 in. Power: Precharged pneumatic. Stock: Black ambidextrous thumbhole tactical style. Sights: Adjustable on removable carry handle, Picatinny rail for scope mounting. Features: Approximately 50 shots per fill, adjustable cheekpiece, built in magazine storage, three Picatinny rails for accessories, Quiet Energy fully shrouded barrel, multishot (12 rounds, .22; 10 rounds, .25). Velocities: .22, 1,100 fps/.25, 900 fps.
Price: $609.00

HATSAN USA NEUTRONSTAR PCP AIR RIFLE

Calibers: .177, .22, .25. Barrel: Rifled, 23 in. Weight: 8.4 lbs. Length: 43.5 in. Power: Precharged pneumatic. Stock: Turkish walnut. Sights: None, dual rail 11mm dovetail and Weaver compatible for scope mounting. Features: Adjustable cheekpiece and buttpad, shrouded barrel with threaded muzzle cap, fully adjustable two-stage "Quattro" trigger, arm accessory rail, lever action, single shot tray and multishot (14 rounds, .177; 12 rounds, .22; 10 rounds, .25). Velocities: .177, 1,400 fps/.22, 1,250 fps/.25, 1,050 fps (with lead-free pellets).
Price: $889.00

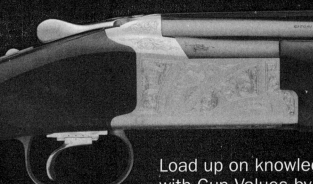

AIRGUNS Long Guns

HATSAN USA PILEDRIVER BIG BORE PCP AIR RIFLE
Calibers: .45, .50. Barrel: Rifled 33 in. Weight: 10 lbs. Length: 46.5 in. Power: Precharged pneumatic. Stock: Bullpup style synthetic thumbhole stock with adjustable cheekpiece. Sights: None, dual rail 11mm dovetail and Weaver compatible for scope mounting. Features: 480 cc carbon fiber tank, long sidelever for easy cocking, three Picatinny accessory rails, 4-6 shots in .45 caliber, 3-5 shots in 50 caliber, fully adjustable two-stage "Quattro" trigger. Velocities: .45, 900 fps/.50, 850 fps.
Price: **$1,199.00**

HATSAN USA PROXIMA MULTISHOT UNDERLEVER AIR RIFLE
Calibers: .177, .22, .25. Barrel: Rifled, 15.5 in. Weight: 9.3 lbs. Length: 45.4 in. Power: Gas piston. Stock: Turkish walnut ambidextrous stock with thumbhole and elevation-adjustable comb. Sights: Hooded TruGlo fiber-optic front sight, micro-adjustable rear sight. Features: Fixed barrel, underlever cocking system, shock-absorber system, fully adjustable two-stage "Quattro" trigger, 45-pound cocking effort. Velocities: .177, 820 fps/.22, 720 fps/.25, 620 fps.
Price: **$449.00**

HATSAN USA VECTIS LEVER ACTION PCP AIR RIFLE
Calibers: .177, .22, .25. Barrel: Rifled 17.7 in. Weight: 7.1 lbs. Length: 41.3 in. Power: Pre-charged pneumatic. Stock: Synthetic all-weather stock. Sights: Fiber-optic front and rear, combination dual 11mm dovetail and Weaver compatible for scope mounting. Features: Multi-shot lever action, 14-shot .177 magazine, 12-shot .22 magazine, 10-shot .25 magazine. "Quiet Energy" barrel shroud with integrated suppressor, fully adjustable two-stage "Quattro" trigger, Picatinny under barrel accessory rail. Velocities: .177, 1,150 fps/.22, 1,000 fps/.25, 900 fps.
Price: **$399.00**

HELLRAISER HELLBOY RIFLE
Caliber: .177 BB. Barrel: 14.5 in. Weight: 5.2 lbs. Length: 30-33.5 in. Power: CO2 cartridge. Stock: Synthetic, tactical style. Sights: Open sights adjustable for windage and elevation, Picatinny rail for scope mounting. Features: Based on the M4 carbine, full-metal construction of barrel, magazine, and receiver, stock adjustable for length of pull, semiautomatic, 18 round magazine, removable carry handle, integrated sling swivels. Velocity: 495 fps.
Price: **$159.00**

KALIBR CRICKET BULLPUP PCP AIR RIFLE
Caliber: .22. Barrel: Rifled 17.5 in. Weight: 6.95 lbs. Length: 27.0 in. Power: Pre-charged pneumatic. Stock: Ambidextrous bullpup stock available in various materials. Sights: None, weaver rail for scope mounting. Features: Multi-shot side-lever action, 14-shot magazine, shrouded barrel with integrated suppression technology, adjustable two-stage trigger. Velocity: .22, 925 fps.
Price: ....**$1,629.00–$1,835.00**

KRAL ARMS PUNCHER MEGA WALNUT SIDELEVER PCP AIR RIFLE
Calibers: .177, .22, .25. Barrel: Rifled 21.0 in. Weight: 8.35 lbs. Length: 42.0 in. Power: Pre-charged pneumatic. Stock: Ambidextrous stock available in synthetic with adjustable cheek piece, and Turkish walnut. Sights: None, 11mm grooved dovetail for scope mounting. Features: Multi-shot side-lever action, 14-shot .177 magazine, 12-shot .22 magazine, 10-shot .25 magazine, half shrouded barrel with integrated suppression technology, available in blue and satin marine finish, adjustable two-stage trigger. Velocities: .177, 1,070 fps/.22, 975 fps/.25, 825 fps.
Price: **$599.00**

KRAL ARMS PUNCHER PRO PCP AIR RIFLE
Calibers: .177, .22, .25. Barrel: Rifled 22.8 in. Weight: 8.6 lbs. Length: 41.3 in. Power: Pre-charged pneumatic. Stock: Monte Carlo hardwood right-handed stock. Sights: None, 11mm grooved dovetail for scope mounting. Features: Multi-shot rear bolt action, 14-shot .177 magazine, 12-shot .22 magazine, 10-shot .25 magazine, half shrouded barrel with integrated suppression technology, two-stage adjustable trigger. Velocities: .177, 1,070 fps/.22, 975 fps/.25, 825 fps.
Price: **$599.00**

KRAL ARMS PUNCHER BREAKER SILENT SYNTHETIC SIDELEVER PCP AIR RIFLE
Calibers: .177, .22, .25. Barrel: Rifled 21.0 in. Weight: 7.4 lbs. Length: 29.0 in. Power: Pre-charged pneumatic. Stock: Ambidextrous bullpup stock available in synthetic and Turkish walnut. Sights: None, 11mm grooved dovetail for scope mounting. Features: Multi-shot side-lever action, 14-shot .177 magazine, 12-shot .22 magazine, 10-shot .25 magazine, half shrouded barrel with integrated suppression technology, available in blue and satin marine finish, adjustable two-stage trigger. Velocities: .177, 1,100 fps/.22, 975 fps/.25, 825 fps.
Price: **$549.00**

KRAL ARMS PUNCHER BIG MAX PCP AIR RIFLE
Calibers: .177, .22, .25. Barrel: Rifled 22.0 in. Weight: 9.5 lbs. Length: 42.1 in. Power: Pre-charged pneumatic. Stock: Ambidextrous Turkish walnut pistol grip. Sights: None, 11mm grooved dovetail for scope mounting. Features: Multi-shot side-lever action, 14-shot .177 magazine, 12-shot .22 magazine, 10-shot .25 magazine, shrouded barrel, adjustable two-stage trigger, massive dual air reservoirs with total of 850 CC. Velocities: .177, 1,070 fps/.22, 975 fps/.25, 825 fps.
Price: **$779.00**

KRAL ARMS PUNCHER PITBULL PCP AIR RIFLE
Calibers: .177, .22, .25. Barrel: Rifled 23.0 in. Weight: 8.65 lbs. Length: 42.3 in. Power: Pre-charged pneumatic. Stock: Ambidextrous Turkish walnut pistol grip. Sights: None, 11mm grooved dovetail for scope mounting. Features: Multi-shot side-lever action, 14-shot .177 magazine, 12-shot .22 magazine, 10-shot .25 magazine, shrouded barrel, adjustable two-stage trigger, massive dual air reservoirs with total of 755 CC. Velocities: .177, 1,070 fps/.22, 975 fps/.25, 825 fps.
Price: **$749.00**

LCS AIR ARMS SK19 FULL AUTO AIRGUN
Calibers: .22, .25. Barrel: Lothar Walther match grade, 23 in. Weight: 7.75 lbs. Length: 35.0 in. Power: Precharged pneumatic. Stock: Laminate with adjustable cheek piece. Sights: None, Picatinny rail for scope mounting. Features: Made in USA, selector for semi-auto or full-auto rate of fire, tunable regulated action, carbon fiber barrel shroud, 480 cc removable tank, optional 580cc tank available, hard case, 19-shot magazine. Velocity: 890-910 fps.
Price: $2,089.00

RAPID AIR WEAPONS RAW HM1000X LRT RIFLE
Calibers: .22, .25, .30, .357. Barrel: Lothar Walther match grade with polygonal rifling, 24 in. Weight: 7 lbs., 13 oz. Length: 45.4 in. Power: Pre-charged pneumatic. Stock: Laminate with adjustable cheek piece. Sights: Grooved for scope mounting. Features: Picatinny rail and M-LOK mounting slots, match-grade trigger, multi-shot rotary magazine, adjustable power, side-lever cocking, regulated, quick-fill system, available in right- or left-hand actions. Velocities: .22, 950 fps/.25, 900 fps/.30, NA/.357, NA.
Price: $2,199.00

RAPID AIR WEAPONS RAW HM1000X CHASSIS RIFLE
Calibers: .22, .25. Barrel: Lothar Walther match grade with polygonal rifling, 24 in. Weight: 7 lbs., 13 oz. Length: 43-47 in. Power: Pre-charged pneumatic. Stock: Synthetic AR-15 style. Sights: Grooved for scope mounting. Features: Chassis constructed from aluminum, designed to accept all AR-15 buttstocks, buffer tubes and pistol grips, Picatinny rail and M-LOK mounting slots, match-grade trigger, 12-shot rotary magazine, adjustable power, side-lever cocking, regulated, quick-fill system. Velocities: .22, 950 fps/.25, 920 fps.
Price: $2,199.00

RAPID AIR WEAPONS RAW TM1000 BENCHREST RIFLE
Calibers: .177, .22. Barrel: Lothar Walther match grade with polygonal rifling, 24 in. Weight: 9.2 - 10.5 lbs. Length: 44 in. Power: Precharged pneumatic. Stock: Walnut or black laminate. Sights: Grooved for scope mounting. Features: Built to specifications, target model, internally fitted regulator, fixed bottle, quick fill coupling, approximately 80 shots depending on settings and caliber, Picatinny rail and M-LOK mounting slots, stainless steel ported shroud, adjustable cheek piece and buttpad, match grade trigger, single shot, 10 inch long accessory rail under barrel, side-lever cocking, right- or left-handed action. Velocities: Dependent on settings and caliber.
Price: $2,199.00

RUGER 10/22 CO2 RIFLE
Calibers: .177 pellets. Barrel: Rifled 18 in. Weight: 4.5 lbs. Length: 37.1 in. Power: Two 12-gram CO_2 cylinders. Stock: Synthetic stock. Sights: Rear sight adjustable for elevation, accepts aftermarket rail. Features: 10-shot Ruger-style rotary magazine, bolt cocks rifle, 3-pound single-action trigger pull, sling attachments. Velocity: 650 fps.
Price: $149.00

RUGER AIR MAGNUM COMBO

RUGER AIR MAGNUM COMBO
Calibers: .177, .22. Barrel: Rifled 19.5 in. Weight: 9.5 lbs. Length: 48.5 in. Power: Break-barrel, spring-piston. Stock: Ambidextrous Monte Carlo synthetic stock with textured grip and fore-end. Sights: Fiber-optic front sight and fully adjustable fiber-optic rear sight, Weaver scope rail, includes 4x32 scope and mounts. Features: Single-shot, two-stage trigger. Velocities: .177, 1,400 fps/.22, 1,200 fps.
Price: $219.00

RUGER EXPLORER RIFLE
Caliber: .177 pellets. Barrel: Rifled 15 in. Weight: 4.45 lbs. Length: 37.12 in. Power: Break-barrel, spring-piston Stock: Ambidextrous synthetic skeleton stock. Sights: Fiber-optic front sight and fully adjustable fiber-optic rear sight, grooved for scope mounting. Features: Designed as an entry level youth break-barrel rifle, easy to shoot and accurate, single-shot, two-stage trigger. Velocity: 495 fps.
Price: $89.00

RUGER TARGIS HUNTER MAX AIR RIFLE COMBO
Caliber: .22. Barrel: Rifled 18.7 in. Weight: 9.85 lbs. Length: 44.85 in. Power: Break-barrel, spring-piston. Stock: Ambidextrous synthetic stock with texture grip and fore-end, includes rifle sling. Sights: Fiber-optic front sight and fully adjustable fiber-optic rear sight, Picatinny optics rail, includes scope and mounts. Features: Integrated "SilencAIR" suppressor, single-shot, two-stage trigger. Velocity: 1,000 fps.
Price: $229.00

SENECA BIG BORE 44 909 LIGHT HUNTER 500CC TANK
Caliber: .45. Barrel: Rifled 21.65 in. Weight: 8.5 lbs. Length: 42.1 in. Power: Pre-charged pneumatic. Stock: Right-handed wood stock. Sights: Fixed front sight with fully adjustable rear sight. Features: Massive 500cc reservoir delivers several powerful shots, delivers well over 200 ft-lbs at the muzzle, long-range hunting accuracy, exceptionally reliable. Velocity: 730 fps.
Price: $729.00

SENECA DOUBLE SHOT .50 CAL DOUBLE BARREL AIR SHOTGUN
Caliber: .50. Barrel: Smooth, double barrel, 20.9 in. Weight: 8.55 Length: 43.5 in. Power: Precharged pneumatic. Stock: Ambidextrous wood stock. Sights: Front bead with no rear sight. Features: Up to five shots per fill, shoots shotshells, airbolts, or roundballs, thread on chokes, optional dovetail rail, two-stage nonadjustable trigger. Velocity: Up to 1,130 fps with shotshells.
Price: $999.00

SENECA DRAGON CLAW PCP AIR RIFLE
Caliber: .50. Barrel: Rifled, 21.65 in. Weight: 8.5 lbs. Length: 42.1 in. Power: Pre-charged pneumatic. Stock: Right-handed wood stock. Sights: Fixed front sight with fully adjustable rear sight. Features: Massive 500cc reservoir delivers several powerful shots, 230 ft-lbs energy at the muzzle on high setting, two power levels, dual air chambers, built-in manometer, 11mm scope rail. Velocity: 639 fps.
Price: $729.00

SENECA DRAGON FLY MULTI-PUMP AIR RIFLE
Calibers: .177, .22. Barrel: Rifled 21.7 in. Weight: 6.65 lbs. Length: 38.5 in. Power: Multi-Pump pneumatic. Stock: Ambidextrous wood stock. Sights: Fixed front sight with fully adjustable rear sight. Features: No recoil for maximum precision, variable power based on number of pumps, bolt action, single shot and multi-shot capability. Velocities: .177, 800 fps/.22 630 fps.
Price: **$219.00**

SENECA RECLUSE AIR RIFLE
Caliber: .35 (9mm). Barrel: Rifled 21.60 in. Weight: 7.5 lbs. Length: 42.1 in. Power: Pre-charged pneumatic. Stock: Right-handed wood stock. Sights: Fixed front sight with fully adjustable rear sight. Features: Massive 500cc reservoir delivers several powerful shots, delivers well over 150 ft-lbs at the muzzle, long-range hunting accuracy, exceptionally reliable. Velocity: 983 fps.
Price: **$699.00**

SIG SAUER MCX CO2 RIFLE & SCOPE, BLACK
Caliber: .177. Barrel: Rifled 17.7 in. Weight: 7.9 lbs. Length: 34.7 in. Power: CO2. Stock: Synthetic stock, various color options. Sights: Varies with model, weaver rail system for iron sight systems, red dot systems, and traditional scope mounting. Features: 30-round semi-auto, reliable belt fed magazine system, available in various colors and sighting combination, very realistic replica. Velocity: 700 fps.
Price: $269.00

SIG SAUER MPX CO2 RIFLE, DOT SIGHT, BLACK
Caliber: .177. Barrel: Rifled 8 in. Weight: 6.6 lbs. Length: 25.8 in. Power: CO2. Stock: Synthetic stock, various color options. Sights: Varies with model, weaver rail system for iron sight systems, red dot systems, and traditional scope mounting. Features: 30-round semi-auto, reliable belt fed magazine system, available in various colors and sighting combination, very realistic replica. Velocity: 575 fps.
Price: $245.00

SIG SAUER ASP20 RIFLE
Caliber: .177 or .22 pellets. Barrel: Rifled 13.8 in. Weight: 8.5 pounds. Length: 45.6 in. Power: Break barrel. Stock: Black synthetic or black-stained beech wood. Sights: None, Picatinny rail. Features: Two-stage Matchlite trigger adjustable from 2.5-4 lbs., integrated suppressor, 33-lb. cocking effort. Velocity: 1,021 fps (.177), 841 fps (.22).
Price: ....$399.00-$489.00

SPRINGFIELD ARMORY M1A UNDERLEVER RIFLE
Calibers: .177, .22. Barrel: Rifled, 18.9 in. Weight: 9.9 lbs. Length: 45.6 in. Power: Spring-piston underlever. Stock: Ambidextrous wood. Sights: Fixed front sight, rear peep sight adjustable for windage and elevation. Features: Fixed barrel, single shot, realistic replica of the National Match firearm, threaded holes on the left-hand side accept a traditional M1A/M14 mount for a scope, 35-pound cocking effort, two-stage nonadjustable trigger. Velocity: 1,000 fps (.177), 750 fps (.22).
Price: $219.00

STOEGER XM1 PCP RIFLE
Caliber: .177 or .22 pellets. Barrel: Rifled, 22 in. Weight: 5.7 lbs. Length: 39 in. Power: Precharged pneumatic. Stock: Black or camo thumbhole synthetic. Sights: Adjustable fiber optic, 11 mm dovetail. Features: Approximately 50 shots per charge, 9-shot (.177) or 7-shot (.22) removable rotary magazine, available as a kit with a 4x32 scope, checkered stock, interchangeable cheekpiece, pistol grip, and buttpad, adjustable trigger, available as a suppressed model, Picatinny rails on each side, bolt action. Velocities: 1,200 fps (.177), 1,000 fps (.22).
Price: **$199.00**

UMAREX EMBARK AIR RIFLE
Caliber: .177. Barrel: Rifled 15 in. Weight: 4.45 Length: 37.25 in. Power: Spring piston. Stock: Ambidextrous neon green thumbhole synthetic. Sights: Fully adjustable micrometer rear, grooved 11mm dovetail for scope mounting. Features: Official air rifle for the Student Air Rifle program, 12-inch length of pull, muzzle brake, 16.5-pound cocking effort, 4.25-pound trigger pull, automatic safety. Velocity: 510 fps.
Price: **$109.00**

UMAREX FUSION 2 CO2 RIFLE
Calibers: .177 pellets. Barrel: Rifled, 18.5 in. Weight: 5.95 lbs. Length: 40.55 in. Power: CO2. Stock: Ambidextrous, synthetic, thumbhole. Sights: None, Picatinny rail for scope mounting. Features: SilencAir noise dampening, uses two 12-gram cylinders or one 88-gram cylinder, 9-shot rotary magazine, bolt action, M-LOK slots on both sides, single-stage trigger. Velocity: 700 fps.
Price: **$139.00**

UMAREX GAUNTLET PCP AIR RIFLE, SYNTHETIC STOCK
Caliber: .22, .25. Barrel: Rifled 23.5 in. Weight: 8.5 Length: 46 in. Power: Precharged pneumatic. Stock: Ambidextrous synthetic. Sights: None, grooved 11mm dovetail for scope mounting. Features: Removable regulated bottle, multi-shot bolt action, fully shrouded and moderated, adjustable two-stage trigger, first production PCP with these high-end features at this low price point. Velocities: .177, 1,000 fps/.22, 900 fps.
Price: **$329.00**

UMAREX HAMMER AIR RIFLE
Caliber: .50 Barrel: Rifled 29.5 in. Weight: 8.5 Length: 43.75 in. Power: Precharged pneumatic. Stock: Nymax synthetic. Sights: None, Picatinny rail for scope mounting. Features: Fires three full-power shots, two pound straight-pull bolt cocks the rifle and advances the magazine, 4,500 psi built-in carbon-fiber tank with quick disconnect Foster fitting, trigger-block safety, will not fire without magazine, Magpul AR grip, full-length composite barrel shroud, comes with two double chamber magazines. Velocities: 1,130 fps (180-gr. non-lead bullet), 760 fps (550-gr. lead slug).
Price: **$849.00**

UMAREX LEGENDS COWBOY LEVER ACTION RIFLE
Caliber: .177 BBs. Barrel: Smoothbore, 19.25 in. Weight: 7.75 lbs. Length: 38 in. Power: CO2. Stock: Faux wood polymer. Sights: Blade front sight with rear sight adjustable for elevation. Features: Lever-action, 10-shot capacity, ejectable cartridges, full metal frame, powered by two CO2 capsules, saddle ring. Velocity: 600 fps.
Price: **$219.00**

UMAREX LEGENDS M1A1 FULL AUTO BB GUN

Calibers: .177 BBs. Barrel: Smoothbore, 12.0 in. Weight: 7.75 lbs. Length: 31.75 in. Power: CO2. Stock: Synthetic. Sights: Fixed. Features: Semi-auto and full auto fire capability, 30-round drop free magazine with two CO2 cartridges, full metal frame, faux-wood polymer stock, blowback action, sling mounts. Velocity: 435 fps.
Price: **$249.00**

UMAREX LEGENDS M3 GREASE GUN

Calibers: .177 BBs. Barrel: Smoothbore. Weight: NA lbs. Length: NA in. Power: CO2. Stock: Synthetic with collapsible wire butt. Sights: Fixed. Features: Semi-auto and full-auto fire capability, operates on two 12-gram CO2 cylinders, 30-round drop-free magazine with 2 CO2 cartridges, full metal frame, blowback action, sling mounts. Velocity: 435 fps.
Price: **$219.00**

UMAREX MORPH 3X CO2 PISTOL & RIFLE COMBO

Calibers: .177 BBs. Barrel: 4.5 in (pistol), 12 in. (rifle) rifled. Weight: 1.5 lbs (pistol), 25 lbs (rifle). Length: 11.5 in (pistol), 38.5 in. (rifle). Power: CO2. Stock: Synthetic. Sights: Fixed, fiber optic. Features: Converts from pistol, to carbine, to rifle, nonremovable 30-round BB magazine, double-action only, integral Weaver/Picatinny rail, includes detachable skeletonized shoulder stock, forearm, and barrel extender. Velocity: 380 fps (pistol), 600 fps (rifle).
Price: **$90.00**

UMAREX SYNERGIS UNDER LEVER AIR RIFLE, COMBO

Calibers: .177, .22 pellets. Barrel: 18.5 in rifled. Weight: 8.3 lbs. Length: 45.3 in. Power: Gas piston under lever. Stock: Synthetic. Sights: None, Picatinny rail for scope mounting. Features: 3-9x32 scope, 2 magazines, 10-shot (.22) or 12-shot (.177) repeater, fixed barrel, removable magazine, integrated suppressor, two-stage nonadjustable trigger. Velocities: 1,000 fps (.177), 900 fps (.22).
Price: **$189.00**

UMAREX THROTTLE AIR RIFLE COMBO, GAS PISTON

Calibers: .177, .22. Barrel: Rifled 15.9 in. Weight: 8.3 lbs. Length: 45.3 in. Power: Break-barrel, gas-piston. Stock: Ambidextrous synthetic. Sights: None, Weaver rail for scope mounting, includes 3-9x32 AO scope and mounts. Features: Single shot, includes integrated suppressor, features new "STOPSHOX" anti-recoil feature. Velocities: .177, 1,200 fps/.22, 1,000 fps.
Price: **$229.00**

WALTHER LG400 UNIVERSAL AIR RIFLE, AMBI GRIP

Caliber: .177. Barrel: Advanced match-grade rifled barrel 16.53 in. Weight: 8.6 lbs. Length: 43.7 in. Power: Pre-charged pneumatic. Stock: Ambidextrous competition, highly adjustable wood stock. Sights: Olympic-grade, match Diopter/Micrometer adjustable sights. Features: True professional class 10-meter target rifle, meets ISSF requirements. Velocity: 557 fps.
Price: **$1,799.00**

WALTHER MAXIMATHOR AIR RIFLE

Calibers: .22, .25. Barrel: Advanced match-grade rifled barrel, 23.5 in. Weight: 9.6 lbs. Length: 41.75 in. Power: Pre-charged pneumatic. Stock: Ambidextrous wood stock. Sights: None, grooved 11mm dovetail for scope mounting. Features: Bolt action 8-shot magazine, pure hunting PCP with range and accuracy. Velocities: .22, 1,260 fps/.25, 1,000 fps.
Price: **$799.00**

WALTHER LEVER ACTION CO2 RIFLE, BLACK

Caliber: .177. Barrel: Rifled 18.9 in. Weight: 6.2 lbs. Length: 39.2 in. Power: CO2 Stock: Ambidextrous wood stock. Sights: Blade front sight, adjustable rear sight. Features: Lever-action repeater, 8-shot rotary magazine, great wild west replica airgun. Velocity: 600 fps.
Price: **$499.00**

WALTHER LG400 JUNIOR AIR RIFLE

Caliber: .177. Barrel: Advanced match-grade rifled barrel, 16.53 in. Weight: 7.7 lbs. Length: 39.8 in. Power: Pre-charged pneumatic. Stock: Ambidextrous highly adjustable competition laminate wood stock. Sights: Olympic-grade, match Diopter/Micrometer adjustable sights. Features: 10-meter competition target rifle, meets ISSF requirements, removable air cylinder delivers up to 400 shots per fill. Velocity: 570 fps.
Price: **$1,799.00**

WALTHER REIGN UXT PCP BULLPUP RIFLE

Caliber: .22, .25. Barrel: Rifled, 23.6 in. Weight: 5.5 lbs. Length: 34 in. Power: Precharged pneumatic. Stock: Ambidextrous bullpup synthetic. Sights: None, Picatinny rail. Features: 10-shot (.22) or 9-shot (.25) auto indexing magazine, 40-60 shots per fill, adjustable trigger, ambidextrous cocking level, quick detach sling mount, muzzle shroud. Velocities: 975 fps (.22), 840 fps (.25).
Price: **$599.00**

WALTHER ROTEK AIR RIFLE

Calibers: .177, .22. Barrel: Rifled Lothar Walther 19.7 in. Weight: 8 lbs. Length: 41 in. Power: Pre-charged pneumatic. Stock: Ambidextrous Minelli beech with checkered forearm and grip. Sights: None, 11 mm dovetail grooved for scope mounting. Features: 1/2 UNF threaded muzzle, eight-shot rotary clip, vibration reduction system, two-stage adjustable match trigger. Velocities: 1,000 fps (.177)/900 fps (.22).
Price: **449.00**

WALTHER TERRUS AIR RIFLE
Calibers: .177, .22. Barrel: Rifled 17.75 in. Weight: 7.52 lbs. Length: 44.25 in. Power: Single-cock, spring-piston. Stock: Ambidextrous beech and synthetic stock options available. Sights: Front fiber-optic sight and fully adjustable rear fiber-optic sight, grooved for scope mounting. Features: German engineered and manufactured, very easy cocking and shooting, 1/2 UNF threaded muzzle, single-shot, two-stage target trigger, limited lifetime warranty. Velocities: .177, 1,050 fps /.22, 800 fps.
Price: $299.00

WEIHRAUCH HW50S SPRING PISTON RIFLE
Caliber: .177, .22. Barrel: Rifled, 15.5 in. Weight: 6.8 lbs. Length: 40.5 in. Power: Spring-piston. Stock: Checkered beech wood. Sights: Front globe and adjustable rear. Features: Single shot, 24-lb. cocking effort, two-stage adjustable Rekord trigger. Velocity: 820 fps (.177), 574 fps (.22).
Price: $367.00

WEIHRAUCH HW90 SPRING PISTON RIFLE
Caliber: .177, .22, .25. Barrel: Rifled, 19.7 in. Weight: 6.8 lbs. Length: 45.3 in. Power: Spring-piston. Stock: Checkered beech wood. Sights: Front globe and adjustable rear, 11mm dovetail for scope mounting. Features: Single shot, 46-lb. cocking effort, 2-stage adjustable Rekord trigger. Velocity: 1,050 fps (.177), 853 fps (.22), 625 fps (.25).
Price: $682.00

WEIHRAUCH HW97K/KT AIR RIFLE
Calibers: .177, .20, .22, Barrel: Rifled, 11.81 in. Weight: 8.8 lbs. Length: 40.1 in. Power: Under-lever, spring-piston. Stock: Various, beech wood, blue-gray laminated, or synthetic, with or without thumbhole. Sights: None, grooved for scope. Features: Silver or blue finish, highly adjustable match-grade trigger. Extremely accurate fixed-barrel design. Velocity: 820 fps (.177), 755 fps (.22).
Price: .... $629.00–$661.00

WEIHRAUCH HW100 SK PCP RIFLE
Calibers: .177, .22. Barrel: Rifled, 16.2 in. Weight: 7.65 lbs. Length: 38.4 in. Power: Pre-charged pneumatic. Stock: Monte Carlo walnut stock with raised cheek piece. Sights: Grooved for scope mounting. Features: Multi-shot side lever, includes two 14-round magazines, shrouded barrel, two-stage adjustable match trigger. Velocity: 1,135 fps (.177), 870 fps (.22).
Price: $1,699.00

WEIHRAUCH HW110 TK CARBINE PCP RIFLE
Caliber: .177, .20, .22. Barrel: Rifled 16.1 in. Weight: 7.5 lbs. Length: 36.2 in. Power: Precharged pneumatic. Stock: Laminated thumbhole. Sights: None, Picatinny rail grooved for scope mounting. Features: 10-shot capacity, built-in air tank, internal pressure gauge, available left handed, built in muzzle brake, two-stage adjustable match trigger, adjustable buttplate, 30-40 shots per fill. Velocities: 1,050 fps (.177), 965 fps (.20), 1,025 fps (.22).
Price: $1,299.00

WESTERN BIG BORE BUSHBUCK PCP RIFLE
Calibers: .45. Barrel: Rifled, 30 in. Weight: 10.25 lbs. Length: 49.5 in. Power: Precharged pneumatic. Stock: Walnut or laminate. Sights: None, Picatinny rail for scope mounting. Features: One-piece aluminum receiver and Picatinny rail, all-steel air cylinder, accuracy tested to 250 yards, two 600 ft-lbs or four 400 ft lb shots per fill, accommodates extra-long bullets, approximately three pound trigger pull, sling studs, single shot, made in USA.
Price: .... $1,895.00–$2,154.00

WINCHESTER MODEL 12 YOUTH PUMP ACTION BB GUN
Caliber: .177 steel BBs. Barrel: Smooth. Weight: 3.2 lbs. Length: 34.25 in. Power: Spring piston, pump action. Stock: Synthetic brown wood-look stock. Sights: Modeled after the famous Winchester Model 12 shotgun, adjustable for windage and elevation. Features: Single pump per shot, 250-round BB reservoir, 14 inch length of pull. Velocity: 350fps.
Price: $39.00

WINCHESTER 1977XS MULTI-PUMP AIR RIFLE
Caliber: .177 steel BBs, .177 Pellet. Barrel: Rifled 20.8 in. Weight: 3.1 lbs. Length: 37.6 in. Power: Multi-pump pneumatic. Stock: Ambidextrous synthetic thumbhole stock. Sights: Blade front sight, adjustable rear sight, grooved for scope mounting, includes 4x32 scope and mounts. Features: Single-shot pellet, 50-round BB repeater, bolt action, lightweight, accurate and easy to shoot. Velocity: 800 fps.
Price: $95.00

WINCHESTER MODEL 70 PCP RIFLE

Calibers: .35, .45. Barrel: Rifled, 20.87 in. Weight: 9.0 lbs. Length: 41.75 in. Power: Pre-charged pneumatic. Stock: Right handed hardwood. Sights: None, grooved for scope mounting. Features: Multi-Shot big bore (6 shots .35 / 5 shots .45), highly stable shot strings for maximum accuracy, traditional Winchester styling, .35 produces up to 134 ft-lbs, .45 produces over 200 ft-lbs. Velocities: .35, 865 fps/.45, 803 fps.
Price: **$849.00**

ZBROIA HORTIZIA PCP RIFLE

Calibers: .177, .22. Barrel: Rifled. Weight: NA. Length: NA. Power: Precharged pneumatic. Stock: Black stained ash Monte-Carlo style wood stock. Sights: None, grooved for scope mounting. Features: Up to 100 shots per fill in .177 caliber or 60 shots in .22 caliber, free floated barrel with 12 grooves, two-stage adjustable trigger that is detachable, side-lever cocking, 10- or 12-shot repeater, built in manometer with 4,351 psi fill, made in the Ukraine. Velocities: .177, 1,000 fps/.22, 980 fps.
Price: **$849.00**

ZBROIA KOZAK TACTICAL PCP RIFLE

Calibers: .177, .22. Barrel: Rifled. Weight: NA. Length: NA. Power: Precharged pneumatic. Stock: Black stained ash wood stock semi-bullpup design with adjustable cheekpiece. Sights: None, grooved for scope mounting. Features: Up to 100 shots per fill (.22 caliber), free floated barrel with 12 grooves, two stage adjustable trigger, side-lever cocking, 10- or 12-shot repeater, built in manometer with 4,351 psi fill, made in the Ukraine. Velocities: .177, 1,000 fps/.22, 980 fps.
Price: **$869.00**

Many manufacturers do not supply suggested retail prices. Others did not get their pricing to us before press time. All pricing can vary dependent on the exact brand and style of ammo selected and/or the retail outlet from which you make your purchase. Pricing has been rounded to the nearest dollar and represents our best estimate of average pricing. An * after the cartridge means these loads are available with Nosler Partition or Swift A-Frame bullets. Listed pricing may or may not reflect this bullet type. ** = these are packed 50 to box, all others are 20 to box. Wea. Mag.= Weatherby Magnum. Spfd. = Springfield. A-Sq. = A-Square. N.E.=Nitro Express.

Cartridge	Bullet Wgt. Grs.	VELOCITY (fps)					ENERGY (ft. lbs.)					TRAJ. (in.)				Est. Price/box
		Muzzle	100 yds.	200 yds.	300 yds.	400 yds.	Muzzle	100 yds.	200 yds.	300 yds.	400 yds.	100 yds.	200 yds.	300 yds.	400 yds.	
17, 22																
17 Hornet	15.5	3860	2924	2159	1531	1108	513	294	160	81	42	1.4	0	-9.1	-33.7	NA
17 Hornet	20	3650	3078	2574	2122	1721	592	421	294	200	131	1.1	0	-6.4	-20.6	NA
17 Hornet	25	3375	2842	2367	1940	1567	632	448	311	209	136	1.4	0	24.8	56.3	NA
17 Remington Fireball	20	4000	3380	2840	2360	1930	710	507	358	247	165	1.6	1.5	-2.8	-13.5	NA
17 Remington Fireball	25	3850	3280	2780	2330	1925	823	597	429	301	206	0.9	0	-5.4	NA	NA
17 Remington	20	4200	3544	2978	2477	2029	783	558	394	272	183	0	-1.3	-6.6	-17.6	NA
17 Remington	25	4040	3284	2644	2086	1606	906	599	388	242	143	2	1.7	-4	-17	NA
4.6x30 H&K	30	2025	1662	1358	1135	1002	273	184	122	85	66	0	-12.7	-44.5	—	$17
4.6x30 H&K	40	1900	1569	1297	1104	988	320	218	149	108	86	0	-14.3	-39.3	—	NA
204 Ruger (Hor)	24	4400	3667	3046	2504	2023	1032	717	494	334	218	0.6	0	-4.3	-14.3	NA
204 Ruger (Fed)	32 Green	4030	3320	2710	2170	1710	1155	780	520	335	205	0.9	0	-5.7	-19.1	NA
204 Ruger	32	4125	3559	3061	2616	2212	1209	900	666	486	348	0	-1.3	-6.3	—	NA
204 Ruger	32	4225	3632	3114	2652	2234	1268	937	689	500	355	0.6	0	-4.2	-13.4	NA
204 Ruger	40	3900	3451	3046	2677	2336	1351	1058	824	636	485	0.7	0	-4.5	-13.9	NA
204 Ruger	45	3625	3188	2792	2428	2093	1313	1015	778	589	438	1	0	-5.5	-16.9	NA
5.45x39mm	60	2810	2495	2201	1927	1677	1052	829	645	445	374	1	0	-9.2	-27.7	NA
221 Fireball	40	3100	2510	1991	1547	1209	853	559	352	212	129	0	-4.1	-17.3	-45.1	NA
221 Fireball	50	2800	2137	1580	1180	988	870	507	277	155	109	0	-7	-28	0	$14
22 Hornet (Fed)	30 Green	3150	2150	1390	990	830	660	310	130	65	45	0	-6.6	-32.7	NA	NA
22 Hornet	34	3050	2132	1415	1017	852	700	343	151	78	55	0	-6.6	-15.5	-29.9	NA
22 Hornet	35	3100	2278	1601	1135	929	747	403	199	100	67	2.75	0	-16.9	-60.4	NA
22 Hornet	40	2800	2397	2029	1698	1413	696	510	366	256	177	0	-4.6	-17.8	-43.1	NA
22 Hornet	45	2690	2042	1502	1128	948	723	417	225	127	90	0	-7.7	-31	0	$27**
218 Bee	46	2760	2102	1550	1155	961	788	451	245	136	94	0	-7.2	-29	0	$46**
222 Rem.	35	3760	3125	2574	2085	1656	1099	759	515	338	213	1	0	-6.3	-20.8	NA
222 Rem.	50	3345	2930	2553	2205	1886	1242	953	723	540	395	1.3	0	-6.7	-20.6	NA
222 Remington	40	3600	3117	2673	2269	1911	1151	863	634	457	324	1.07	0	-6.13	-18.9	NA
222 Remington	50	3140	2602	2123	1700	1350	1094	752	500	321	202	2	-0.4	-11	-33	$11
222 Remington	55	3020	2562	2147	1773	1451	1114	801	563	384	257	2	-0.4	-11	-33	$12
222 Rem. Mag.	40	3600	3140	2726	2347	2000	1150	876	660	489	355	1	0	-5.7	-17.8	NA
222 Rem. Mag.	50	3340	2917	2533	2179	1855	1238	945	712	527	382	1.3	0	-6.8	-20.9	NA
222 Rem. Mag.	55	3240	2748	2305	1906	1556	1282	922	649	444	296	2	-0.2	-9	-27	$14
22 PPC	52	3400	2930	2510	2130	NA	1335	990	730	525	NA	2	1.4	-5	0	NA
223 Rem.	35	3750	3206	2725	2291	1899	1092	799	577	408	280	1	0	-5.7	-18.1	NA
223 Rem.	35	4000	3353	2796	2302	1861	1243	874	607	412	269	0.8	0	-5.3	-17.3	NA
223 Rem.	64	2750	2368	2018	1701	1427	1074	796	578	411	289	2.4	0	-11	-34.1	NA
223 Rem.	75	2790	2562	2345	2139	1943	1296	1093	916	762	629	1.5	0	-8.2	-24.1	NA
223 Remington	40	3650	3010	2450	1950	1530	1185	805	535	340	265	2	1	-6	-22	$14
223 Remington	40	3800	3305	2845	2424	2044	1282	970	719	522	371	0.84	0	-5.34	-16.6	NA
223 Remington (Rem)	45 Green	3550	2911	2355	1865	1451	1259	847	554	347	210	2.5	2.3	-4.3	-21.1	NA
223 Remington	50	3300	2874	2484	2130	1809	1209	917	685	504	363	1.37	0	-7.05	-21.8	NA
223 Remington	52/53	3330	2882	2477	2106	1770	1305	978	722	522	369	2	0.6	-6.5	-21.5	$14
223 Remington (Win)	55 Green	3240	2747	2304	1905	1554	1282	921	648	443	295	1.9	0	-8.5	-26.7	NA
223 Remington	55	3240	2748	2305	1906	1556	1282	922	649	444	296	2	-0.2	-9	-27	$12
223 Remington	60	3100	2712	2355	2026	1726	1280	979	739	547	397	2	0.2	-8	-24.7	$16
223 Remington	62	3000	2700	2410	2150	1900	1240	1000	800	635	495	1.6	0	-7.7	-22.8	NA
223 Remington	64	3020	2621	2256	1920	1619	1296	977	723	524	373	2	-0.2	-9.3	-23	$14
223 Remington	69	3000	2720	2460	2210	1980	1380	1135	925	750	600	2	0.8	-5.8	-17.5	$15
223 Remington	75	2790	2554	2330	2119	1926	1296	1086	904	747	617	2.37	0	-8.75	-25.1	NA
223 Rem. Super Match	75	2930	2694	2470	2257	2055	1429	1209	1016	848	703	1.2	0	-6.9	-20.7	NA
223 Remington	77	2750	2584	2354	2169	1992	1293	1110	948	804	679	1.93	0	-8.2	-23.8	NA
223 WSSM	55	3850	3438	3064	2721	2402	1810	1444	1147	904	704	0.7	0	-4.4	-13.6	NA
223 WSSM	64	3600	3144	2732	2356	2011	1841	1404	1061	789	574	1	0	-5.7	-17.7	NA
5.56 NATO	55	3130	2740	2382	2051	1750	1196	917	693	514	372	1.1	0	-7.3	-23	NA
5.56 NATO	75	2910	2676	2543	2242	2041	1410	1192	1002	837	693	1.2	0	-7	-21	NA
224 Wea. Mag.	55	3650	3192	2780	2403	2057	1627	1244	943	705	516	2	1.2	-4	-17	$32

Cartridge	Bullet Wgt. Grs.	VELOCITY (fps) Muzzle	100 yds.	200 yds.	300 yds.	400 yds.	ENERGY (ft. lbs.) Muzzle	100 yds.	200 yds.	300 yds.	400 yds.	TRAJ. (in.) 100 yds.	200 yds.	300 yds.	400 yds.	Est. Price/box
22 Nosler	55	3350	2965	2615	2286	1984	1370	1074	833	638	480	0	-2.5	-10.1	-24.4	
22 Nosler	77	2950	2672	2410	2163	1931	1488	1220	993	800	637	0	-3.4	-12.8	-29.7	
224 Valkyrie	90	2700	2542	2388	2241	2098	1457	1291	1140	1003	880	1.9	0	-8.1	-23.2	NA
224 Valkyrie	75	3000	2731	2477	2237	2010	1499	1242	1022	833	673	1.6	0	-7.3	-21.5	NA
224 Valkyrie	60	3300	2930	2589	2273	1797	1451	1144	893	688	522	1.3	0	-6.5	-19.8	NA
225 Winchester	55	3570	3066	2616	2208	1838	1556	1148	836	595	412	2	1	-5	-20	$19
22-250 Rem.	35	4450	3736	3128	2598	2125	1539	1085	761	524	351	6.5	0	-4.1	-13.4	NA
22-250 Rem.	40	4000	3320	2720	2200	1740	1420	980	660	430	265	2	1.8	-3	-16	$14
22-250 Rem.	40	4150	3553	3033	2570	2151	1530	1121	817	587	411	0.6	0	-4.4	-14.2	NA
22-250 Rem.	45 Green	4000	3293	2690	2159	1696	1598	1084	723	466	287	1.7	1.7	-3.2	-15.7	NA
22-250 Rem.	50	3725	3264	2641	2455	2103	1540	1183	896	669	491	0.89	0	-5.23	-16.3	NA
22-250 Rem.	50	3725	3264	2656	2222	1832	1654	1201	861	603	410	2	1.3	-4	-17	$13
22-250 Rem.	52/55	3680	3137	2656	2222	1832	1654	1201	861	603	410	2	1.3	-4	-17	$13
22-250 Rem.	60	3600	3195	2826	2485	2169	1727	1360	1064	823	627	2	2	-2.4	-12.3	$19
22-250 Rem.	64	3425	2988	2591	2228	1897	1667	1269	954	705	511	1.2	0	-6.4	-20	NA
220 Swift	40	4200	3678	3190	2739	2329	1566	1201	904	666	482	0.51	0	-4	-12.9	NA
220 Swift	50	3780	3158	2617	2135	1710	1586	1107	760	506	325	2	1.4	-4.4	-17.9	$20
220 Swift	50	3850	3396	2970	2576	2215	1645	1280	979	736	545	0.74	0	-4.84	-15.1	NA
220 Swift	50	3900	3420	2990	2599	2240	1688	1298	992	750	557	0.7	0	-4.7	-14.5	NA
220 Swift	55	3800	3370	2990	2630	2310	1765	1390	1090	850	650	0.8	0	-4.7	-14.4	NA
220 Swift	55	3650	3194	2772	2384	2035	1627	1246	939	694	506	2	2	-2.6	-13.4	$19
220 Swift	60	3600	3199	2824	2475	2156	1727	1364	1063	816	619	2	1.6	-4.1	-13.1	$19
22 Savage H.P.	70	2868	2510	2179	1874	1600	1279	980	738	546	398	0	-4.1	-15.6	-37.1	NA
22 Savage H.P.	71	2790	2340	1930	1570	1280	1225	860	585	390	190	2	-1	-10.4	-35.7	NA
6mm (24)																
6mm BR Rem.	100	2550	2310	2083	1870	1671	1444	1185	963	776	620	2.5	-0.6	-11.8	0	$22
6mm Norma BR	107	2822	2667	2517	2372	2229	1893	1690	1506	1337	1181	1.73	0	-7.24	-20.6	NA
6mm Creedmoor	108	2786	2618	2456	2299	2149	1861	1643	1446	1267	1106	1.5	0	-6.6	-18.9	$26
6mm PPC	70	3140	2750	2400	2070	NA	1535	1175	895	665	NA	2	1.4	-5	0	NA
6mm ARC	103	2800	2623	2452	2288	2130	1793	1573	1375	1197	1038	1.8	0	-7.6	-21.8	NA
6mm ARC	105	2750	2580	2417	2260	2108	1763	1552	1362	1190	1036	1.9	0	-7.8	-22.4	NA
6mm ARC	108	2750	2582	2421	2265	2115	1813	1599	1405	1230	1072	1.9	0	-7.8	-22.4	NA
243 Winchester	55	4025	3597	3209	2853	2525	1978	1579	1257	994	779	0.6	0	-4	-12.2	NA
243 Win.	58	3925	3465	3052	2676	2330	1984	1546	1200	922	699	0.7	0	-4.4	-13.8	NA
243 Winchester	60	3600	3110	2660	2260	1890	1725	1285	945	680	475	2	1.8	-3.3	-15.5	$17
243 Win.	70	3400	3020	2672	2350	2050	1797	1418	1110	858	653	0	-2.5	-9.7	—	NA
243 Winchester	70	3400	3040	2700	2390	2100	1795	1435	1135	890	685	1.1	0	-5.9	-18	NA
243 Winchester	75/80	3350	2955	2593	2259	1951	1993	1551	1194	906	676	2	0.9	-5	-19	$16
243 Win.	80	3425	3081	2763	2468	2190	2984	1686	1357	1082	852	1.1	0	-5.7	-17.1	NA
243 Win.	87	2800	2574	2359	2155	1961	1514	1280	1075	897	743	1.9	0	-8.1	-23.8	NA
243 Win.	95	3185	2908	2649	2404	2172	2140	1784	1480	1219	995	1.3	0	-6.3	-18.6	NA
243 W. Superformance	80	3425	3080	2760	2463	2184	2083	1684	1353	1077	847	1.1	0	-5.7	-17.1	$18
243 Winchester	85	3320	3070	2830	2600	2380	2080	1770	1510	1280	1070	2	1.2	-4	-14	NA
243 Winchester	90	3120	2871	2635	2411	2199	1946	1647	1388	1162	966	1.4	0	-6.4	-18.8	$16
243 Winchester*	100	2960	2697	2449	2215	1993	1945	1615	1332	1089	882	2.5	1.2	-6	-20	$21
243 Winchester	105	2920	2689	2470	2261	2062	1988	1686	1422	1192	992	2.5	1.6	-5	-18.4	NA
243 Light Mag.	100	3100	2839	2592	2358	2138	2133	1790	1491	1235	1014	1.5	0	-6.8	-19.8	NA
243 WSSM	55	4060	3628	3237	2880	2550	2013	1607	1280	1013	794	0.6	0	-3.9	-12	NA
243 WSSM	95	3250	3000	2763	2538	2325	2258	1898	1610	1359	1140	1.2	0	-5.7	-16.9	NA
243 WSSM	100	3110	2838	2583	2341	2112	2147	1789	1481	1217	991	1.4	0	-6.6	-19.7	$16
6mm Remington	80	3470	3064	2694	2352	2036	2139	1667	1289	982	736	2	1.1	-5	-17	NA
6mm R. Superformance	95	3235	2955	2692	2443	3309	2207	1841	1528	1259	1028	1.2	0	-6.1	-18	$16
6mm Remington	100	3100	2829	2573	2332	2104	2133	1777	1470	1207	983	2.5	1.6	-5	-17	$21
6mm Remington	105	3060	2822	2596	2381	2177	2105	1788	1512	1270	1059	2.5	1.1	-3.3	-15	$32
240 Wea. Mag.	87	3500	3202	2924	2663	2416	2366	1980	1651	1370	1127	2	2	-2	-12	NA
240 Wea. Mag.	100	3150	2894	2653	2425	2207	2202	1860	1563	1395	1082	1.3	0	-6.3	-18.5	$43
240 Wea. Mag.	100	3395	3106	2835	2581	2339	2559	2142	1785	1478	1215	2.5	2.8	-2	-11	$32**
25-20 Win.	86	1460	1194	1030	931	858	407	272	203	165	141	0	-23.5	0	0	$25
25-45 Sharps	87	3000	2677	2385	2112	1859	1739	1384	1099	862	668	1.1	0	-7.4	-22.6	$24
25-35 Win.	117	2230	1866	1545	1282	1097	1292	904	620	427	313	2.5	-4.2	-26	0	$17
250 Savage	100	2820	2504	2210	1936	1684	1765	1392	1084	832	630	2.5	0.4	-9	-28	$20
257 Roberts	100	2980	2661	2363	2085	1827	1972	1572	1240	965	741	2.5	-0.8	-5.2	-21.6	$21
257 Roberts	122	2600	2331	2078	1842	1625	1831	1472	1169	919	715	2.5	0	-10.6	-31.4	NA
257 Roberts+P	100	3000	2758	2529	2312	2105	1998	1689	1421	1187	984	1.5	0	-7	-20.5	NA

Cartridge	Bullet Wgt. Grs.	VELOCITY (fps)					ENERGY (ft. lbs.)					TRAJ. (in.)				Est. Price/box
		Muzzle	100 yds.	200 yds.	300 yds.	400 yds.	Muzzle	100 yds.	200 yds.	300 yds.	400 yds.	100 yds.	200 yds.	300 yds.	400 yds.	
257 Roberts+P	117	2780	2411	2071	1761	1488	2009	1511	1115	806	576	2.5	-0.2	-10.2	-32.6	$18
257 Roberts+P	120	2780	2560	2360	2160	1970	2060	1750	1480	1240	1030	2.5	1.2	-6.4	-23.6	$22
257 R. Superformance	117	2946	2705	2478	2265	2057	2253	1901	1595	1329	1099	1.1	0	-5.7	-17.1	NA
25-06 Rem.	87	3440	2995	2591	2222	1884	2286	1733	1297	954	686	2	1.1	-2.5	-14.4	$17
25-06 Rem.	90	3350	3001	2679	2378	2098	2243	1790	1434	1130	879	1.2	0	-6	-18.3	NA
25-06 Rem.	90	3440	3043	2680	2344	2034	2364	1850	1435	1098	827	2	1.8	-3.3	-15.6	$17
25-06 Rem.	100	3230	2893	2580	2287	2014	2316	1858	1478	1161	901	2	0.8	-5.7	-18.9	$17
25-06 Rem.	117	2990	2770	2570	2370	2190	2320	2000	1715	1465	1246	2.5	1	-7.9	-26.6	$17
25-06 Rem.*	120	2990	2730	2484	2252	2032	2382	1985	1644	1351	1100	2.5	1.2	-5.3	-19.6	$19
25-06 Rem.	122	2930	2706	2492	2289	2095	2325	1983	1683	1419	1189	2.5	1.8	-4.5	-17.5	$17
25-06 R. Superformance	117	3110	2861	2626	2403	2191	2512	2127	1792	1500	1246	1.4	0	-6.4	-18.9	$23
25 WSSM	85	3470	3156	2863	2589	2331	2273	1880	1548	1266	1026	1	0	-5.2	-15.7	NA
25 WSSM	115	3060	2844	2639	2442	2254	2392	2066	1778	1523	1398	1.4	0	-6.4	-18.6	NA
25 WSSM	120	2990	2717	2459	2216	1987	2383	1967	1612	1309	1053	1.6	0	-7.4	-21.8	NA
257 Wea. Mag.	87	3825	3456	3118	2805	2513	2826	2308	1870	1520	1220	2	2.7	-0.3	-7.6	$32
257 Wea. Mag.	90	3550	3184	2848	2537	2246	2518	2026	1621	1286	1008	1	0	-5.3	-16	NA
257 Wea. Mag.	100	3555	3237	2941	2665	2404	2806	2326	1920	1576	1283	2.5	3.2	0	-8	$32
257 Wea. Mag.	110	3330	3069	2823	2591	2370	2708	2300	1947	1639	1372	1.1	0	-5.5	-16.1	NA
257 Scramjet	100	3745	3450	3173	2912	2666	3114	2643	2235	1883	1578	2.1	2.77	0	-6.93	NA
6.5																
6.5 Grendel	123	2590	2420	2256	2099	1948	1832	1599	1390	1203	1037	1.8	0	-8.6	-25.1	NA
6.5x47 Lapua	123	2887	NA	2554	NA	2244	2285	NA	1788	NA	1380	NA	4.53	0	-10.7	NA
6.5x50mm Jap.	139	2360	2160	1970	1790	1620	1720	1440	1195	985	810	2.5	-1	-13.5	0	NA
6.5x50mm Jap.	156	2070	1830	1610	1430	1260	1475	1155	900	695	550	2.5	-4	-23.8	0	NA
6.5x52mm Car.	139	2580	2360	2160	1970	1790	2045	1725	1440	1195	985	2.5	0	-9.9	-29	NA
6.5x52mm Car.	156	2430	2170	1930	1700	1500	2045	1630	1285	1005	780	2.5	-1	-13.9	0	NA
6.5x52mm Carcano	160	2250	1963	1700	1467	1271	1798	1369	1027	764	574	3.8	0	-15.9	-48.1	NA
6.5x55mm Swe.	93	2625	2350	2090	1850	1630	1425	1140	905	705	550	2.4	0	-10.3	-31.1	NA
6.5x55mm Swe.	123	2750	2570	2400	2240	2080	2065	1810	1580	1370	1185	1.9	0	-7.9	-22.9	NA
6.5x55mm Swe.*	139/140	2850	2640	2440	2250	2070	2525	2170	1855	1575	1330	2.5	1.6	-5.4	-18.9	$18
6.5x55mm Swe.	140	2550	NA	NA	NA	NA	2020	NA	NA	NA	NA	0	0	0	0	$18
6.5x55mm Swe.	140	2735	2563	2397	2237	2084	2325	2041	1786	1556	1350	1.9	0	-8	-22.9	NA
6.5x55mm Swe.	156	2650	2370	2110	1870	1650	2425	1950	1550	1215	945	2.5	0	-10.3	-30.6	NA
260 Rem.	100	3200	2917	2652	2402	2165	2273	1889	1561	1281	1041	1.3	0	-6.3	-18.6	NA
260 Rem.	130	2800	2613	2433	2261	2096	2262	1970	1709	1476	1268	1.8	0	-7.7	-22.2	NA
260 Remington	125	2875	2669	2473	2285	2105	2294	1977	1697	1449	1230	1.71	0	-7.4	-21.4	NA
260 Remington	140	2750	2544	2347	2158	1979	2351	2011	1712	1448	1217	2.2	0	-8.6	-24.6	NA
6.5 Creedmoor	120	3020	2815	2619	2430	2251	2430	2111	1827	1574	1350	1.4	0	-6.5	-18.9	NA
6.5 Creedmoor	120	3050	2850	2659	2476	2300	2479	2164	1884	1634	1310	1.4	0	-6.3	-18.3	NA
6.5 Creedmoor	130	2875	2709	2550	2396	2247	2386	2119	1877	1657	1457	1.6	0	-6.9	-20	$46
6.5 Creedmoor	140	2550	2380	2217	2060	1910	2021	1761	1527	1319	1134	2.3	0	-9.4	-27	NA
6.5 Creedmoor	140	2710	2557	2410	2267	2129	2283	2033	1805	1598	1410	1.9	0	-7.9	-22.6	NA
6.5 Creedmoor	140	2820	2654	2494	2339	2190	2472	2179	1915	1679	1467	1.7	0	-7.2	-20.6	NA
6.5 C. Superformance	129	2950	2756	2570	2392	2221	2492	2175	1892	1639	1417	1.5	0	-6.8	-19.7	NA
6.5x52R	117	2208	1856	1544	1287	1104	1267	895	620	431	317	0	-8.7	-32.2	—	NA
6.5x57	131	2543	2295	2060	1841	1638	1882	1532	1235	986	780	0	-5.1	-18.5	-42.1	NA
6.5 PRC	143	2960	2808	2661	2519	2381	2782	2503	2248	2014	1800	1.5	0	-6.4	-18.2	NA
6.5 PRC	147	2910	2775	2645	2518	2395	2764	2514	2283	2069	1871	1.5	0	-6.5	-18.4	NA
6.5-284 Norma	142	3025	2890	2758	2631	2507	2886	2634	2400	2183	1982	1.13	0	-5.7	-16.4	NA
6.5-284 Norma	156	2790	2531	2287	2056	-	2697	2220	1812	1465	-	1.9	0	-8.6	-	NA
6.5 Weatherby RPM	127	3225	3011	2809	2615	2429	2933	2554	2224	1928	1664	3	3.7	0	-8.8	$65
6.5 Weatherby RPM	140	2975	2772	2579	2393	2215	2751	2389	2067	1780	1525	3.8	4.5	0	-10.6	$50
6.5 Weatherby RPM	140	3075	2885	2703	2529	2361	2939	2587	2272	1988	1766	3.4	4.1	0	-9.5	$65
6.71 (264) Phantom	120	3150	2929	2718	2517	2325	2645	2286	1969	1698	1440	1.3	0	-6	-17.5	NA
6.5 Rem. Mag.	120	3210	2905	2621	2353	2102	2745	2248	1830	1475	1177	2.5	1.7	-4.1	-16.3	Disc.
264 Win. Mag.	100	3400	3104	2828	2568	2322	2566	2139	1775	1464	1197	1.1	0	-5.4	-16.1	NA
264 Win. Mag.	125	3200	2978	2767	2566	2373	2841	2461	2125	1827	1563	1.2	0	-5.8	-16.8	NA
264 Win. Mag.	130	3100	2900	2709	2526	2350	2773	2427	2118	1841	1594	1.3	0	-6.1	-17.6	NA
264 Win. Mag.	140	3030	2782	2548	2326	2114	2854	2406	2018	1682	1389	2.5	1.4	-5.1	-18	$24
6.5 Nosler	129	3400	3213	3035	2863	2698	3310	2957	2638	2348	2085	0.9	0	-4.7	-13.6	NA
6.5 Nosler	140	3300	3118	2943	2775	2613	3119	2784	2481	2205	1955	1	0	-5	-14.6	NA
6.71 (264) Blackbird	140	3480	3261	3053	2855	2665	3766	3307	2899	2534	2208	2.4	3.1	0	-7.4	NA
6.8 REM SPC	90	2840	2444	2083	1756	1469	1611	1194	867	616	431	2.2	0	-3.9	-32	NA

Cartridge	Bullet Wgt. Grs.	VELOCITY (fps)					ENERGY (ft. lbs.)					TRAJ. (in.)				Est. Price/box
		Muzzle	100 yds.	200 yds.	300 yds.	400 yds.	Muzzle	100 yds.	200 yds.	300 yds.	400 yds.	100 yds.	200 yds.	300 yds.	400 yds.	
6.8 REM SPC	110	2570	2338	2118	1910	1716	1613	1335	1095	891	719	2.4	0	-6.3	-20.8	NA
6.8 REM SPC	120	2460	2250	2051	1863	1687	1612	1349	1121	925	758	2.3	0	-10.5	-31.1	NA
6.8mm Rem.	115	2775	2472	2190	1926	1683	1966	1561	1224	947	723	2.1	0	-3.7	-9.4	NA
27																
270 Win. (Rem.)	115	2710	2482	2265	2059	NA	1875	1485	1161	896	NA	0	4.8	-17.3	0	NA
270 Win.	120	2675	2288	1935	1619	1351	1907	1395	998	699	486	2.6	0	-12	-37.4	NA
270 Win.	140	2940	2747	2563	2386	2216	2865	2396	1993	1646	1348	1.3	0	-6.4	-18.9	NA
270 Win. Supreme	130	3150	2881	2628	2388	2161	2860	2416	2030	1693	1402	1.7	0	-7.4	-21.6	NA
270 Win. Supreme	150	2930	2693	2468	2254	2051	2860	2570	2228	1924	1653	1.2	0	-5.7	-16.7	NA
270 W. Superformance	130	3200	2984	2788	2582	2393	2955	2570	2228	1179	877	2	1	-4.9	-17.5	$17
270 Winchester	100	3430	3021	2649	2305	1988	2612	2027	1557	1472	1180	2.5	1.4	-5.3	-18.2	$17
270 Winchester	130	3060	2776	2510	2259	2022	2702	2225	1818	1472	1180	2.5	1.4	-6	-17.6	$23
270 Winchester	135	3000	2780	2570	2369	2178	2697	2315	1979	1682	1421	2.5	1.8	-4.6	-17.9	$20
270 Winchester*	140	2940	2700	2480	2260	2060	2685	2270	1905	1590	1315	2.5	1.8	-4.6	-17.9	$20
270 Winchester*	150	2850	2585	2336	2100	1879	2705	2226	1817	1468	1175	2.5	1.2	-6.5	-22	$17
277 Fury	140	3000														NA
270 WSM	130	3275	3041	2820	2609	2408	3096	2669	2295	1564	1673	1.1	0	-5.5	-16.1	NA
270 WSM	140	3125	2865	2619	2386	2165	3035	2559	2132	1769	1457	1.4	0	-6.5	-19	NA
270 WSM	150	3000	2795	2599	2412	2232	2997	2601	2250	1937	1659	1.5	0	-6.6	-19.2	NA
270 WSM	150	3120	2923	2734	2554	2380	3242	2845	2490	2172	1886	1.3	0	-5.9	-17.2	NA
6.8 Western	165	2970	2815	2667	2524	2385	3226	2902	2605	2333	2084	1.2	0	-6.3	-18.1	NA
6.8 Western	170	2920	2754	2593	2439	2289	3218	2862	2538	2244	1978	1.3	0	-6.7	-19.3	NA
6.8 Western	175	2835	2686	2541	2402	2266	3123	2803	2509	2241	1995	1.7	0	-7	-20.1	NA
270 Wea. Mag.	100	3760	3380	3033	2712	2412	3139	2537	2042	1633	1292	2	2.4	-1.2	-10.1	$32
270 Wea. Mag.	130	3375	3119	2878	2649	2432	3287	2808	2390	2026	1707	2.5	-2.9	-0.9	-9.9	$32
270 Wea. Mag.	130	3450	3194	2958	2732	2517	3435	2949	2525	2143	1828	1	0	-4.9	-14.5	NA
270 Wea. Mag.*	150	3245	3036	2837	2647	2465	3507	3070	2681	2334	2023	2.5	2.6	-1.8	-11.4	$47
27 Nosler	150	3300	3143	2983	2828	2676	3638	3289	2964	2663	2385	1	0	-4.9	-14.2	$81
7mm																
7mm BR	140	2216	2012	1821	1643	1481	1525	1259	1031	839	681	2	-3.7	-20	0	$23
275 Rigby	139	2680	2456	2242	2040	1848	2217	1861	1552	1284	1054	2.2	0	-9.1	-26.5	NA
275 Rigby	140	2680	2455	2242	2040	1848	2233	1874	1563	1292	1062	2.2	0	-9.1	-26.5	NA
7mm Mauser*	139/140	2660	2435	2221	2018	1827	2199	1843	1533	1266	1037	2.5	0	-9.6	-27.7	$17
7mm Mauser	139	2740	2556	2379	2209	2046	2317	2016	1747	1506	1292	1.9	0	-8.1	-23.3	NA
7mm Mauser	154	2690	2490	2300	2120	1940	2475	2120	1810	1530	1285	2.5	0.8	-7.5	-23.5	$17
7mm Mauser	175	2440	2137	1857	1603	1382	2313	1774	1340	998	742	2.5	-1.7	-16.1	0	$17
7x30 Waters	120	2700	2300	1930	1600	1330	1940	1405	990	685	470	2.5	-0.2	-12.3	0	$18
7x30 Waters	120	2700	2425	2167	1926	1702	1942	1567	1251	988	772	2.2	0	-9.7	-28.8	$36
7mm-08 Rem.	120	2675	2435	2207	1992	1790	1907	1579	1298	1057	854	2.2	0	-9.4	-27.5	NA
7mm-08 Rem.	120	3000	2725	2467	2223	1992	2398	1979	1621	1316	1058	2	0	-7.6	-22.3	$18
7mm-08 Rem.	139	2840	2608	2387	2177	1978	2489	2098	1758	1463	1207	1.8	0	-7.9	-23.2	NA
7mm-08 Rem.*	140	2860	2625	2402	2189	1988	2542	2142	1793	1490	1228	2.5	0.8	-6.9	-21.9	$18
7mm-08 Rem.	154	2715	2510	2315	2128	1950	2520	2155	1832	1548	1300	2.5	1	-7	-22.7	$23
7-08 R. Superformance	139	2950	2857	2571	2393	2222	2686	2345	2040	1768	1524	1.5	0	-6.8	-19.7	NA
7x64mm	173	2526	2260	2010	1777	1565	2452	1962	1552	1214	941	0	-5.3	-19.3	-44.4	NA
7x64mm Bren.	140	2950	2710	2483	2266	2061	2705	2283	1910	1597	1320	1.5	0	-2.9	-7.3	$24.50
7x64mm Bren.	154	2820	2610	2420	2230	2050	2720	2335	1995	1695	1430	2.5	1.4	-5.7	-19.9	NA
7x64mm Bren.*	160	2850	2669	2495	2327	2166	2885	2530	2211	1924	1667	2.5	1.6	-4.8	-17.8	$24
7x64mm Bren.	175	2650	2445	2248	2061	1883	2728	2322	1964	1650	1378	2.2	0	-9.1	-26.4	$24.50
7x65mmR	173	2608	2337	2082	1844	1626	2613	2098	1666	1307	1015	0	-4.9	-17.9	-41.9	NA
284 Winchester	150	2860	2595	2344	2108	1886	2724	2243	1830	1480	1185	2.5	0.8	-7.3	-23.2	$24
280 R. Superformance	139	3090	2890	2699	2516	2341	2946	2578	2249	1954	1691	1.3	0	-6.1	-17.7	NA
280 Rem.	139	3090	2891	2700	2518	2343	2947	2579	2250	1957	1694	1.3	0	-6.1	-17.7	NA
280 Remington	140	3000	2758	2528	2309	2102	2797	2363	1986	1657	1373	2.5	1.4	-5.2	-18.3	$17
280 Remington*	150	2890	2624	2373	2135	1912	2781	2293	1875	1518	1217	2.5	0.8	-7.1	-22.6	$17
280 Remington	160	2840	2637	2442	2556	2078	2866	2471	2120	1809	1535	2.5	0.8	-6.7	-21	$20
280 Remington	165	2820	2510	2220	1950	1701	2913	2308	1805	1393	1060	2.5	0.4	-8.8	-26.5	$17
280 Ack. Imp.	140	3150	2946	2752	2566	2387	3084	2698	2354	2047	1772	1.3	0	-5.8	-17	NA
280 Ack. Imp.	150	2900	2712	2533	2360	2194	2800	2450	2136	1855	1603	1.6	0	-7	-20.3	NA
280 Ack. Imp.	160	2950	2751	2561	2379	2205	3091	2686	2331	2011	1727	1.5	0	-6.9	-19.9	NA
7x61mm S&H Sup.	154	3060	2720	2400	2100	1820	3200	2520	1965	1505	1135	2.5	1.8	-5	-19.8	NA
7mm Dakota	160	3200	3001	2811	2630	2455	3637	3200	2808	2456	2140	2.1	1.9	-2.8	-12.5	NA
7mm Rem. Mag.	139	3190	2986	2791	2605	2427	3141	2752	2405	2095	1817	1.2	0	-5.7	-16.5	NA

Cartridge	Bullet Wgt. Grs.	VELOCITY (fps)					ENERGY (ft. lbs.)					TRAJ. (in.)				Est. Price/box
		Muzzle	100 yds.	200 yds.	300 yds.	400 yds.	Muzzle	100 yds.	200 yds.	300 yds.	400 yds.	100 yds.	200 yds.	300 yds.	400 yds.	
7mm Rem. Mag. (Rem.)	140	2710	2482	2265	2059	NA	2283	1915	1595	1318	NA	0	-4.5	-1.57	0	NA
7mm Rem. Mag.*	139/140	3150	2930	2710	2510	2320	3085	2660	2290	1960	1670	2.5	2.4	-2.4	-12.7	$21
7mm Rem. Mag.	150/154	3110	2830	2568	2320	2085	3221	2667	2196	1792	1448	2.5	1.6	-4.6	-16.5	$21
7mm Rem. Mag.*	160/162	2950	2730	2520	2320	2120	3090	2650	2250	1910	1600	2.5	1.8	-4.4	-17.8	$34
7mm Rem. Mag.	165	2900	2699	2507	2324	2147	3081	2669	2303	1978	1689	2.5	1.2	-5.9	-19	$28
7mm Rem Mag.	175	2860	2645	2440	2244	2057	3178	2718	2313	1956	1644	2.5	1	-6.5	-20.7	$21
7 R.M. Superformance	139	3240	3033	2836	2648	2467	3239	2839	2482	2163	1877	1.1	0	-5.5	-15.9	NA
7 R.M. Superformance	154	3100	2914	2736	2565	2401	3286	2904	2560	2250	1970	1.3	0	-5.9	-17.2	NA
7mm Rem. SA ULTRA MAG	140	3175	2934	2707	2490	2283	3033	2676	2277	1927	1620	1.3	0	-6	-17.7	NA
7mm Rem. SA ULTRA MAG	150	3110	2828	2563	2313	2077	3221	2663	2188	1782	1437	2.5	2.1	-3.6	-15.8	NA
7mm Rem. SA ULTRA MAG	160	2850	2676	2508	2347	2192	2885	2543	2235	1957	1706	1.7	0	-7.2	-20.7	NA
7mm Rem. SA ULTRA MAG	160	2960	2762	2572	2390	2215	3112	2709	2350	2029	1743	2.6	2.2	-3.6	-15.4	NA
7mm Rem. WSM	140	3225	3008	2801	2603	2414	3233	2812	2438	2106	1812	1.2	0	-5.6	-16.4	NA
7mm Rem. WSM	160	2990	2744	2512	2081	1883	3176	2675	2241	1864	1538	1.6	0	-7.1	-20.8	NA
7mm Wea. Mag.	139	3300	3091	2891	2701	2519	3361	2948	2580	2252	1958	1.1	0	-5.2	-15.2	NA
7mm Wea. Mag.	140	3225	2970	2729	2501	2283	3233	2741	2315	1943	1621	2.5	2	-3.2	-14	$35
7mm Wea. Mag.	140	3340	3127	2925	2732	2546	3467	3040	2659	2320	2016	0	-2.1	-8.2	-19	NA
7mm Wea. Mag.	150	3175	2957	2751	2553	2364	3357	2913	2520	2171	1861	0	-2.5	-9.6	-22	NA
7mm Wea. Mag.	154	3260	3023	2799	2586	2382	3539	3044	2609	2227	1890	2.5	2.8	-1.5	-10.8	$32
7mm Wea. Mag.*	160	3200	3004	2816	2637	2464	3637	3205	2817	2469	2156	2.5	2.7	-1.5	-10.6	$47
7mm Wea. Mag.	165	2950	2747	2553	2367	2189	3188	2765	2388	2053	1756	2.5	1.8	-4.2	-16.4	$43
7mm Wea. Mag.	175	2910	2693	2486	2288	2098	3293	2818	2401	2033	1711	2.5	1.2	-5.9	-19.4	$35
7.21(.284) Tomahawk	140	3300	3118	2943	2774	2612	3386	3022	2693	2393	2122	2.3	3.2	0	-7.7	NA
7mm STW	140	3300	3086	2889	2697	2513	3384	2966	2594	2261	1963	0	-2.1	-8.5	-19.6	NA
7mm STW	140	3325	3064	2818	2585	2364	3436	2918	2468	2077	1737	2.3	1.8	-3	-13.1	NA
7mm STW	150	3175	2957	2751	2553	2364	3357	2913	2520	2171	1861	0	-2.5	-9.6	-22	NA
7mm STW	175	2900	2760	2625	2493	2366	3267	2960	2677	2416	2175	0	-3.1	-11.2	-24.9	NA
7mm STW Supreme	160	3150	2894	2652	2422	2204	3526	2976	2499	2085	1727	1.3	0	-6.3	-18.5	NA
7mm Rem. Ultra Mag.	140	3425	3184	2956	2740	2534	3646	3151	2715	2333	1995	1.7	1.6	-2.6	-11.4	NA
7mm Rem. Ultra Mag.	160	3225	3035	2854	2680	2512	3694	3273	2894	2551	2242	0	-2.3	-8.8	-20.2	NA
7mm Rem. Ultra Mag.	174	3040	2896	2756	2621	2490	3590	3258	2952	2669	2409	0	-2.6	-9.9	-22.2	NA
7mm Firehawk	140	3625	3373	3135	2909	2695	4084	3536	3054	2631	2258	2.2	2.9	0	-7.03	NA
7.21 (.284) Firebird	140	3750	3522	3306	3101	2905	4372	3857	3399	2990	2625	1.6	2.4	0	-6	NA
.28 Nosler	160	3300	3114	2930	2753	2583	3883	3444	3049	2693	2371	1.1	0	-5.1	-14.9	$78
30																
300 ACC Blackout	110	2150	1886	1646	1432	1254	1128	869	661	501	384	0	-8.3	-29.6	-67.8	NA
300 AAC Blackout	125	2250	2031	1826	1636	1464	1404	1145	926	743	595	0	-7	-24.4	-54.8	NA
300 AAC Blackout	220	1000	968	-	-	-	488	457	-	-	-	0	-	-	-	-
30 Carbine	110	1990	1567	1236	1035	923	977	600	373	262	208	0	-13.5	0	0	$28**
30 Carbine	110	2000	1601	1279	1067	—	977	626	399	278	—	0	-12.9	-47.2	—	NA
300 Whisper	110	2375	2094	1834	1597	NA	1378	1071	822	623	NA	3.2	0	-13.6	NA	NA
300 Whisper	208	1020	988	959	NA	NA	480	451	422	NA	NA	0	-34.1	NA	NA	NA
303 Savage	190	1890	1612	1327	1183	1055	1507	1096	794	591	469	2.5	-7.6	0	0	$24
30 Remington	170	2120	1822	1555	1328	1153	1696	1253	913	666	502	2.5	-4.7	-26.3	0	$20
7.62x39mm Rus.	123	2360	2049	1764	1511	1296	1521	1147	850	623	459	3.4	0	-14.7	-44.7	NA
7.62x39mm Rus.	123/125	2300	2030	1780	1550	1350	1445	1125	860	655	500	2.5	-2	-17.5	0	$13
30-30 Win.	55	3400	2693	2085	1570	1187	1412	886	521	301	172	2	0	-10.2	-35	$18
30-30 Win.	125	2570	2090	1660	1320	1080	1830	1210	770	480	320	-2	-2.6	-19.9	0	$13
30-30 Win.	140	2500	2198	1918	1662	—	1943	1501	1143	858	—	2.9	0	-12.4	—	NA
30-30 Win.	150	2390	2040	1723	1447	1225	1902	1386	989	697	499	0	-7.5	-27	-63	NA
30-30 Win. Supreme	150	2480	2095	1747	1446	1209	2049	1462	1017	697	487	0	-6.5	-24.5	0	NA
30-30 Win.	160	2300	1997	1719	1473	1268	1879	1416	1050	771	571	2.5	-2.9	-20.2	0	$18
30-30 Win. Lever Evolution	160	2400	2150	1916	1699	NA	2046	1643	1304	1025	NA	3	0.2	-12.1	NA	NA
30-30 PMC Cowboy	170	1300	1198	1121	—	—	638	474	—	—	—	0	-27	0	0	NA
30-30 Win.*	170	2200	1895	1619	1381	1191	1827	1355	989	720	535	2.5	-5.8	-23.6	0	$13
300 Savage	150	2630	2354	2094	1853	1631	2303	1845	1462	1143	886	2.5	-0.4	-10.1	-30.7	$17
300 Savage	150	2740	2499	2272	2056	1852	2500	2081	1718	1407	1143	2.1	0	-8.8	-25.8	NA
300 Savage	180	2350	2137	1935	1754	1570	2207	1825	1496	1217	985	2.5	-1.6	-15.2	0	$17
30-40 Krag	180	2430	2213	2007	1813	1632	2360	1957	1610	1314	1064	2.5	-1.4	-13.8	0	$18
7.65x53mm Arg.	180	2590	2390	2200	2010	1830	2685	2280	1925	1615	1345	2.5	0	-27.6	0	NA
7.5x53mm Argentine	150	2785	2519	2269	2032	1814	2583	2113	1714	1376	1096	2	0	-8.8	-25.5	NA
308 Marlin Express	140	2800	2532	2279	2040	1818	2437	1992	1614	1294	1207	2	0	-8.7	-25.8	NA
308 Marlin Express	160	2660	2430	2226	2026	1836	2513	2111	1761	1457	1197	3	1.7	-6.7	-23.5	NA

Cartridge	Bullet Wgt. Grs.	VELOCITY (fps)					ENERGY (ft. lbs.)					TRAJ. (in.)				Est. Price/box
		Muzzle	100 yds.	200 yds.	300 yds.	400 yds.	Muzzle	100 yds.	200 yds.	300 yds.	400 yds.	100 yds.	200 yds.	300 yds.	400 yds.	
307 Winchester	150	2760	2321	1924	1575	1289	2530	1795	1233	826	554	2.5	-1.5	-13.6	0	Disc.
307 WInchester	160	2650	2386	2137	1904	1688	2494	2022	1622	1287	1688	2.3	0	-10	-29.6	NA
7.5x55 Swiss	180	2650	2450	2250	2060	1880	2805	2390	2020	1700	1415	2.5	0.6	-8.1	-24.9	NA
7.5x55mm Swiss	165	2720	2515	2319	2132	1954	2710	2317	1970	1665	1398	2	0	-8.5	-24.6	NA
30 Remington AR	123/125	2800	2465	2154	1867	1606	2176	1686	1288	967	716	2.1	0	-9.7	-29.4	NA
308 Winchester	55	3770	3215	2726	2286	1888	1735	1262	907	638	435	-2	1.4	-3.8	-15.8	$22
308 Win.	110	3165	2830	2520	2230	1960	2447	1956	1551	1215	938	1.4	0	-6.9	-20.9	NA
308 Win. PDX1	120	2850	2497	2171	NA	NA	2164	1662	1256	NA	NA	0	-2.8	NA	NA	NA
308 Winchester	150	2820	2533	2263	2009	1774	2648	2137	1705	1344	1048	2.5	0.4	-8.5	-26.1	$17
308 W. Superformance	150	3000	2772	2555	2348	1962	2997	2558	2173	1836	1540	1.5	0	-6.9	-20	NA
308 Win.	155	2775	2553	2342	2141	1950	2650	2243	1887	1577	1308	1.9	0	-8.3	-24.2	NA
308 Win.	155	2850	2640	2438	2247	2064	2795	2398	2047	1737	1466	1.8	0	-7.5	-22.1	NA
308 Winchester	165	2700	2440	2194	1963	1748	2670	2180	1763	1411	1199	2.5	0	-9.7	-28.5	$20
308 Winchester	168	2680	2493	2314	2143	1979	2678	2318	1998	1713	1460	2.5	0	-8.9	-25.3	$18
308 Win. Super Match	168	2870	2647	2462	2284	2114	3008	2613	2261	1946	1667	1.7	0	-7.5	-21.6	NA
308 Win. (Fed.)	170	2000	1740	1510	NA	NA	1510	1145	860	NA	NA	0	0	0	0	NA
308 Winchester	178	2620	2415	2220	2034	1857	2713	2306	1948	1635	1363	2.5	0	-9.6	-27.6	$23
308 Win. Super Match	178	2780	2609	2444	2285	2132	3054	2690	2361	2064	1797	1.8	0	-7.6	-21.9	NA
308 Winchester*	180	2620	2393	2178	1974	1782	2743	2288	1896	1557	1269	2.5	-0.2	-10.2	-28.5	$17
30-06 Spfd.	55	4080	3485	2965	2502	2083	2033	1483	1074	764	530	2	1.9	-2.1	-11.7	$22
30-06 Spfd. (Rem.)	125	2660	2335	2034	1757	NA	1964	1513	1148	856	NA	0	-5.2	-18.9	0	NA
30-06 Spfd.	125	2700	2412	2143	1891	1660	2023	1615	1274	993	765	2.3	0	-9.9	-29.5	NA
30-06 Spfd.	125	3140	2780	2447	2138	1853	2736	2145	1662	1279	953	2	1	-6.2	-21	$17
30-06 Spfd.	150	2910	2617	2342	2083	1853	2820	2281	1827	1445	1135	2.5	0.8	-7.2	-23.4	$17
30-06 Superformance	150	3080	2848	2617	2417	2216	3159	2700	2298	1945	1636	1.4	0	-6.4	-18.9	NA
30-06 Spfd.	152	2910	2654	2413	2184	1968	2858	2378	1965	1610	1307	2.5	1	-6.6	-21.3	$23
30-06 Spfd.*	165	2800	2534	2283	2047	1825	2872	2352	1909	1534	1220	2.5	0.4	-8.4	-25.5	$17
30-06 Spfd.	168	2710	2522	2346	2169	2003	2739	2372	2045	1754	1497	2.5	0.4	-8	-23.5	$18
30-06 M1 Garand	168	2710	2523	2343	2171	2006	2739	2374	2048	1758	1501	2.3	0	-8.6	-24.6	NA
30-06 Spfd. (Fed.)	170	2000	1740	1510	NA	NA	1510	1145	860	NA	NA	0	0	0	0	NA
30-06 Spfd.	178	2720	2511	2311	2121	1939	2924	2491	2111	1777	1486	2.5	0.4	-8.2	-24.6	$23
30-06 Spfd.*	180	2700	2469	2250	2042	1846	2913	2436	2023	1666	1362	-2.5	0	-9.3	-27	$17
30-06 Superformance	180	2820	2630	2447	2272	2104	3178	2764	2393	2063	1769	1.8	0	-7.6	-21.9	NA
30-06 Spfd.	220	2410	2130	1870	1632	1422	2837	2216	1708	1301	988	2.5	-1.7	-18	0	$17
30-06 High Energy	180	2880	2690	2500	2320	2150	3315	2880	2495	2150	1845	1.7	0	-7.2	-21	NA
30 T/C	150	2920	2696	2483	2280	2087	2849	2421	2054	1732	1450	1.7	0	-7.3	-21.3	NA
30 T/C Superformance	150	3000	2772	2555	2348	2151	2997	2558	2173	1836	1540	1.5	0	-6.9	-20	NA
30 T/C Superformance	165	2850	2644	2447	2258	2078	2975	2560	2193	1868	1582	1.7	0	-7.6	-22	NA
300 Rem SA Ultra Mag	150	3200	2901	2622	2359	2112	3410	2803	2290	1854	1485	1.3	0	-6.4	-19.1	NA
300 Rem SA Ultra Mag	165	3075	2792	2527	2276	2040	3464	2856	2339	1898	1525	1.5	0	-7	-20.7	NA
300 Rem SA Ultra Mag	180	2960	2761	2571	2389	2214	3501	3047	2642	2280	1959	2.6	2.2	-3.6	-15.4	NA
300 Rem. SA Ultra Mag	200	2800	2644	2494	2348	2208	3841	3104	2761	2449	2164	0	-3.5	-12.5	-27.9	NA
7.82 (308) Patriot	150	3250	2999	2762	2537	2323	3519	2997	2542	2145	1798	1.2	0	-5.8	-16.9	NA
300 RCM	150	3265	3023	2794	2577	2369	3550	3043	2600	2211	1870	1.2	0	-5.6	-16.5	NA
300 RCM Superformance	150	3310	3065	2833	2613	2404	3648	3128	2673	2274	1924	1.1	0	-5.4	-16	NA
300 RCM Superformance	165	3185	2964	2753	2552	2360	3716	3217	2776	2386	2040	1.2	0	-5.8	-17	NA
300 RCM Superformance	180	3040	2840	2649	2466	2290	3693	3223	2804	2430	2096	1.4	0	-6.4	-18.5	NA
300 WSM	150	3300	3061	2834	2619	2414	3628	3121	2676	2285	1941	1.1	0	-5.4	-15.9	NA
300 WSM	180	2970	2741	2524	2317	2120	3526	3005	2547	2147	1797	1.6	0	-7	-20.5	NA
300 WSM	180	3010	2923	2734	2554	2380	3242	2845	2490	2172	1886	1.3	0	-5.9	-17.2	NA
300 WSM	190	2875	2729	2588	2451	2319	3486	3142	2826	2535	2269	0	3.2	-11.5	-25.7	NA
308 Norma Mag.	180	2975	2787	2608	2435	2269	3536	3105	2718	2371	2058	0	-3	-11.1	-25	NA
308 Norma Mag.	180	3020	2820	2630	2440	2270	3645	3175	2755	2385	2050	2.5	2	-3.5	-14.8	NA
300 Dakota	200	3000	2824	2656	2493	2336	3996	3542	3131	2760	2423	2.2	1.5	-4	-15.2	NA
300 H&H Mag.	180	2870	2678	2494	2318	2148	3292	2866	2486	2147	1844	1.7	0	-7.3	-21.6	NA
300 H&H Magnum*	180	2880	2640	2412	2196	1990	3315	2785	2325	1927	1583	2.5	0.8	-6.8	-21.7	$24
300 H&H Mag.	200	2750	2596	2447	2303	2164	3357	2992	2659	2355	2079	1.8	0	-7.6	-21.8	NA
300 H&H Magnum	220	2550	2267	2002	1757	NA	3167	2510	1958	1508	NA	-2.5	-0.4	-12	0	NA
300 Win. Mag.	150	3290	2951	2636	2342	2068	3605	2900	2314	1827	1424	2.5	1.9	-3.8	-15.8	$22
300 WM Superformance	150	3400	3150	2914	2690	2477	3850	3304	2817	2409	2043	1	0	-5.1	-15	NA
300 Win. Mag.	165	3100	2877	2665	2462	2269	3522	3033	2603	2221	1897	2.5	2.4	-3	-16.9	$24
300 Win. Mag.	178	2900	2760	2568	2375	2191	3509	3030	2606	2230	1897	2.5	1.4	-5	-17.6	$29
300 Win. Mag.	178	2960	2770	2588	2413	2245	3463	3032	2647	2301	1992	1.5	0	-6.7	-19.4	NA

Cartridge	Bullet Wgt. Grs.	Velocity (fps)					Energy (ft. lbs.)					Traj. (in.)				Est. Price/box
		Muzzle	100 yds.	200 yds.	300 yds.	400 yds.	Muzzle	100 yds.	200 yds.	300 yds.	400 yds.	100 yds.	200 yds.	300 yds.	400 yds.	
300 WM Super Match	178	2960	2770	2587	2412	2243	3462	3031	2645	2298	1988	1.5	0	-6.7	-19.4	NA
300 Win. Mag.*	180	2960	2745	2540	2344	2157	3501	3011	2578	2196	1859	2.5	1.2	-5.5	-18.5	$22
300 WM Superformance	180	3130	2927	2732	2546	2366	3917	3424	2983	2589	2238	1.3	0	-5.9	-17.3	NA
300 Win. Mag.	190	2885	1691	2506	2327	2156	3511	3055	2648	2285	1961	2.5	1.2	-5.7	-19	$26
300 Win. Mag.	195	2930	2760	2596	2438	2286	3717	3297	2918	2574	2262	1.5	0	-6.7	-19.4	NA
300 Win. Mag.*	200	2825	2595	2376	2167	1970	3545	2991	2508	2086	1742	-2.5	1.6	-4.7	-17.2	$36
300 Win. Mag.	220	2680	2448	2228	2020	1823	3508	2927	2424	1993	1623	2.5	0	-9.5	-27.5	$23
300 Rem. Ultra Mag.	150	3450	3208	2980	2762	2556	3964	3427	2956	2541	2175	1.7	1.5	-2.6	-11.2	NA
300 Rem. Ultra Mag.	150	2910	2686	2473	2279	2077	2820	2403	2037	1716	1436	1.7	0	-7.4	-21.5	NA
300 Rem. Ultra Mag.	165	3350	3099	2862	2938	2424	4110	3518	3001	2549	2152	1.1	0	-5.3	-15.6	NA
300 Rem. Ultra Mag.	180	3250	3037	2834	2640	2454	4221	3686	3201	2786	2407	2.4	0	-3	-12.7	NA
300 Rem. Ultra Mag.	180	2960	2774	2505	2294	2093	3501	2971	2508	2103	1751	2.7	2.2	-3.8	-16.4	NA
300 Rem. Ultra Mag.	200	3032	2791	2562	2345	2138	4083	3459	2916	2442	2030	1.5	0	-6.8	-19.9	NA
300 Rem. Ultra Mag.	210	2920	2790	2665	2543	2424	3975	3631	3311	3015	2740	1.5	0	-6.4	-18.1	NA
30 Nosler	180	3200	3004	2815	2635	2462	4092	3606	3168	2774	2422	0	-2.4	-9.1	-20.9	NA
30 Nosler	210	3000	2868	2741	2617	2497	4196	3836	3502	3193	2906	0	-2.7	-10.1	-22.5	NA
300 Wea. Mag.	100	3900	3441	3038	2652	2305	3714	2891	2239	1717	1297	2	2.6	-0.6	-8.7	$32
300 Wea. Mag.	150	3375	3126	2892	2670	2459	3794	3255	2786	2374	2013	1	0	-5.2	-15.3	NA
300 Wea. Mag.	150	3600	3307	3033	2776	2533	4316	3642	3064	2566	2137	2.5	3.2	0	-8.1	$32
300 Wea. Mag.	165	3140	2921	2713	2515	2325	3612	3126	2697	2317	1980	1.3	0	-6	-17.5	NA
300 Wea. Mag.	165	3450	3210	3000	2792	2593	4360	3796	3297	2855	2464	2.5	3.2	0	-7.8	NA
300 Wea. Mag.	178	3120	2902	2695	2497	2308	3847	3329	2870	2464	2104	2.5	-1.7	-3.6	-14.7	$43
300 Wea. Mag.	180	3330	3110	2910	2710	2520	4430	3875	3375	2935	2540	1	0	-5.2	-15.1	NA
300 Wea. Mag.	190	3030	2830	2638	2455	2279	3873	3378	2936	2542	2190	2.5	1.6	-4.3	-16	$38
300 Wea. Mag.	220	2850	2541	2283	1964	1736	3967	3155	2480	1922	1471	2.5	0.4	-8.5	-26.4	$35
300 Pegasus	180	3500	3319	3145	2978	2817	4896	4401	3953	3544	3172	2.28	2.89	0	-6.79	NA
300 Norma Magnum	215	3017	2881	2748	2618	2491	4346	3963	3605	3272	2963	NA	NA	NA	NA	$85
300 Norma Magnum	230	2934	2805	2678	2555	2435	4397	4018	3664	3334	3028	NA	NA	NA	NA	$85
300 Norma Magnum	225	2850	2731	2615	2502	2392	4058	3726	3417	3128	2859	1.6	0	-6.7	-18.9	NA
300 PRC	212	2860	2723	2589	2849	2565	3850	3489	3156	2849	2565	1.6	0	-6.8	-19.3	na
300 PRC	225	2810	2692	2577	2465	2356	3945	3620	3318	3036	2773	1.7	0	-6.9	-19.5	na
31																
32-20 Win.	100	1210	1021	913	834	769	325	231	185	154	131	0	-32.3	0	0	$23**
303 British	150	2685	2441	2211	1993	1789	2401	1985	1628	1323	1066	2.2	0	-9.3	-27.4	NA
303 British	180	2460	2124	1817	1542	1311	2418	1803	1319	950	687	2.5	-1.8	-16.8	0	$18
303 Light Mag.	150	2830	2570	2325	2094	1884	2667	2199	1800	1461	1185	2	0	-8.4	-24.6	NA
7.62x54mm Rus.	146	2950	2730	2520	2320	NA	2820	2415	2055	1740	NA	2.5	2	-4.4	-17.7	NA
7.62x54mm Rus.	174	2800	2607	2422	2245	2075	3029	2626	2267	1947	1664	1.8	0	-7.8	-22.4	NA
7.62x54mm Rus.	180	2580	2370	2180	2000	1820	2650	2250	1900	1590	1100	2.5	0	-9.8	-28.5	NA
7.7x58mm Jap.	150	2640	2399	2170	1954	1752	2321	1916	1568	1271	1022	2.3	0	-9.7	-28.5	NA
7.7x58mm Jap.	180	2500	2300	2100	1920	1750	2490	2105	1770	1475	1225	2.5	0	-10.4	-30.2	NA
8mm																
8x56 R	205	2400	2188	1987	1797	1621	2621	2178	1796	1470	1196	2.9	0	-11.7	-34.3	NA
8x57mm JS Mau.	165	2850	2520	2210	1930	1670	2965	2330	1795	1360	1015	2.5	1	-7.7	0	NA
32 Win. Special	165	2410	2145	1897	1669	NA	2128	1685	1318	1020	NA	2	0	-13	-19.9	NA
32 Win. Special	170	2250	1921	1626	1372	1175	1911	1393	998	710	521	2.5	-3.5	-22.9	0	NA
8mm Mauser	170	2360	1969	1622	1333	1123	2102	1464	993	671	476	2.5	-3.1	-22.2	0	$14
8mm Mauser	196	2500	2338	2182	2032	1888	2720	2379	2072	1797	1552	2.4	0	-9.8	-27.9	$18
325 WSM	180	3060	2841	2632	2432	2242	3743	3226	2769	2365	2009	1.4	0	-6.4	-18.7	NA
325 WSM	200	2950	2753	2565	2384	2210	3866	3367	2922	2524	2170	1.5	0	-6.8	-19.8	NA
325 WSM	220	2840	2605	2382	2169	1968	3941	3316	2772	2300	1893	1.8	0	-8	-23.3	NA
8mm Rem. Mag.	185	3080	2761	2464	2186	1927	3896	3131	2494	1963	1525	2.5	1.4	-5.5	-19.7	$30
8mm Rem. Mag.	220	2830	2581	2346	2123	1913	3912	3254	2688	2201	1787	2.5	0.6	-7.6	-23.5	Disc.
33																
338 Federal	180	2830	2590	2350	2130	1930	3200	2670	2215	1820	1480	1.8	0	-8.2	-23.9	NA
338 Marlin Express	200	2565	2365	2174	1992	1820	2922	2484	2099	1762	1471	3	1.2	-7.9	-25.9	NA
338 Federal	185	2750	2550	2350	2160	1980	3105	2660	2265	1920	1615	1.9	0	-8.3	-24.1	NA
338 Federal	210	2630	2410	2200	2010	1820	3225	2710	2265	1880	1545	2.3	0	-9.4	-27.3	NA
338 Federal MSR	185	2680	2459	2230	2020	1820	2950	2460	2035	1670	1360	2.2	0	-9.2	-26.8	NA
338-06	200	2750	2553	2364	2184	2011	3358	2894	2482	2118	1796	1.9	0	-8.22	-23.6	NA
330 Dakota	250	2900	2719	2545	2378	2217	4668	4103	3595	3138	2727	2.3	1.3	-5	-17.5	NA
338 Lapua	250	2900	2685	2481	2285	2098	4668	4002	2416	2899	2444	1.7	0	-7.3	-21.3	NA
338 Lapua	250	2963	2795	2640	2493	NA	4842	4341	3881	3458	NA	1.9	0	-7.9	0	NA
338 Lapua	285	2745	2616	2491	2369	2251	4768	4331	3926	3552	3206	1.8	0	-7.4	-21	NA

Cartridge	Bullet Wgt. Grs.	VELOCITY (fps)					ENERGY (ft. lbs.)					TRAJ. (in.)				Est. Price/box
		Muzzle	100 yds.	200 yds.	300 yds.	400 yds.	Muzzle	100 yds.	200 yds.	300 yds.	400 yds.	100 yds.	200 yds.	300 yds.	400 yds.	
338 Lapua	300	2660	2544	2432	2322	-	4715	4313	3940	3592	-	1.9	0	-7.8	-	NA
338 RCM Superformance	185	2980	2755	2542	2338	2143	3647	3118	2653	2242	1887	1.5	0	-6.9	-20.3	NA
338 RCM Superformance	200	2950	2744	2547	2358	2177	3846	3342	2879	2468	2104	1.6	0	-6.9	-20.1	NA
338 RCM Superformance	225	2750	2575	2407	2245	2089	3778	3313	2894	2518	2180	1.9	0	-7.9	-22.7	NA
338 WM Superformance	185	3080	2850	2632	2424	2226	3896	3337	2845	2413	2034	1.4	0	-6.5	-18.9	NA
338 Win. Mag.	200	3030	2820	2620	2429	2246	4077	3532	3049	2621	2240	1.4	0	-6.5	-18.9	NA
338 Win. Mag.*	200	3030	2820	2620	2429	2246	4077	3532	3049	2621	2240	2.5	1.4	-6	-20.9	$33
338 Win. Mag.*	210	2830	2590	2370	2150	1940	3735	3130	2610	2155	1760	2.5	0.4	-8.5	-25.9	$27
338 Win. Mag.*	225	2785	2517	2266	2029	1808	3871	3165	2565	2057	1633	1.5	0	-6.8	-19.5	NA
338 WM Superformance	225	2840	2758	2582	2414	2252	4318	3798	3331	2911	2533	2.5	1.2	-6.3	-21	$40
338 Win. Mag.	230	2780	2573	2375	2186	2005	3948	3382	2881	2441	2054	2.5	0.2	-9	-26.2	$27
338 Win. Mag.*	250	2660	2456	2261	2075	1898	3927	3348	2837	2389	1999	1.7	0	-7.6	-22.1	NA
338 Ultra Mag.	250	2860	2645	2440	2244	2057	4540	3882	3303	2794	2347	1.5	0	-6.6	-18.8	NA
338 Lapua Match	250	2900	2760	2625	2494	2366	4668	4229	3825	3452	3108	1.8	0	-7.3	-20.8	NA
338 Lapua Match	285	2745	2623	2504	2388	2275	4768	4352	3966	3608	3275	0	-2.8	-10.4	-23.4	NA
33 Nosler	225	3025	2856	2687	2525	2369	4589	4074	3608	3185	2803	0	-3.4	-12.2	-26.8	NA
33 Nosler	265	2775	2661	2547	2435	2326	4543	4167	3816	3488	3183	0	-4.3	-15	-32.6	NA
33 Nosler	300	2550	2445	2339	2235	2134	4343	3981	3643	3327	3033	3	3.8	0	-9.3	NA
8.59(.338) Galaxy	200	3100	2899	2707	2524	2347	4269	3734	3256	2829	2446	2.5	1.9	-1.8	-11.8	$56
340 Wea. Mag.*	210	3250	2991	2746	2515	2295	4924	4170	3516	2948	2455	2.5	2	-3.5	-14.8	$56
340 Wea. Mag.*	250	3000	2806	2621	2443	2272	4995	4371	3812	3311	2864	2.5	2.7	-1.5	-10.5	NA
338 A-Square	250	3120	2799	2500	2220	1958	5403	4348	3469	2736	2128	3.1	3.8	0	-8.9	NA
338-378 Wea. Mag.	225	3180	2974	2778	2591	2410	5052	4420	3856	3353	2902	3.07	3.8	-8.95		NA
338 Titan	225	3230	3010	2800	2600	2409	5211	4524	3916	3377	2898	2.23	2.87	0	-6.99	NA
338 Excalibur	200	3600	3361	3134	2920	2715	5755	5015	4363	3785	3274	1.3	0	-6.35	-19.2	NA
338 Excalibur	250	3250	2922	2618	2333	2066	5863	4740	3804	3021	2370					NA

34, 35

Cartridge	Bullet Wgt. Grs.	Muzzle	100 yds.	200 yds.	300 yds.	400 yds.	Muzzle	100 yds.	200 yds.	300 yds.	400 yds.	100 yds.	200 yds.	300 yds.	400 yds.	Est. Price/box
348 Winchester	200	2520	2215	1931	1672	1443	2820	2178	1656	1241	925	2.5	-1.4	-14.7	0	$42
348 Winchester LeveRevolution	200	2560	2294	2044	1811	1597	2910	2336	1855	1456	1133	2.6	0	-10.9	-32.6	na
357 Magnum	158	1830	1427	1138	980	883	1175	715	454	337	274	0		-33.1	0	$25**
350 Legend	145	2350	1916	1539	1241	n/a	1778	1182	763	496	n/a	0	-8.1	-31.2	NA	na
350 Legend	150	2325	1968	1647	1373	na	4800	1289	903	628	na	0	-7.6	-28.1	na	na
350 Legend	160	2225	1843	1509	1243	na	1759	1206	809	548	na	0	-8.9	-33.2	na	na
350 Legend	180	2100	1762	1466	1230	na	1762	1240	859	604	na	0	-9.8	-36	na	na
350 Legend	265	1060	990	936	890	na	661	577	515	466	na	0	-34.1	-107.4	na	na
35 Remington	150	2300	1874	1506	1218	1039	1762	1169	755	494	359	2.5	-4.1	-26.3	0	$16
35 Remington	200	2080	1698	1376	1140	1001	1921	1280	841	577	445	2.5	-6.3	-17.1	-33.6	$16
35 Remington	200	2225	1963	1722	1505	—	2198	1711	1317	1006	—	3.8	0	-15.6	—	NA
35 Rem. Lever Evolution	200	2225	1963	1721	1503	NA	2198	1711	1315	1003	NA	3	-1.3	-17.5	NA	NA
356 Winchester	200	2460	2114	1797	1517	1284	2688	1985	1434	1022	732	2.5	-1.8	-15.1	0	$31
356 Winchester	250	2160	1911	1682	1476	1299	2591	2028	1571	1210	937	2.5	-3.7	-22.2	0	$31
358 Winchester	200	2475	2180	1906	1655	1434	2720	2110	1612	1217	913	2.9	0	-12.6	-37.9	NA
358 Winchester	200	2490	2171	1876	1619	1379	2753	2093	1563	1151	844	2.5	-1.6	-15.6	0	$31
358 STA	275	2850	2562	2292	2039	NA	4958	4009	3208	2539	NA	1.9	0	-8.6	0	$33
350 Rem. Mag.	200	2710	2410	2130	1870	1631	3261	2579	2014	1553	1181	2.5	-0.2	-10	-30.1	$20
35 Whelen	200	2675	2378	2100	1842	1606	3177	2510	1958	1506	1145	2.5	-0.2	-10.3	-31.1	NA
35 Whelen	200	2910	2585	2283	2001	1742	3760	2968	2314	1778	1347	1.9	0	-8.6	-25.9	NA
35 Whelen	225	2500	2300	2110	1930	1770	3120	2650	2235	1870	1560	2.6	0	-10.2	-29.9	$20
35 Whelen	250	2400	2197	2005	1823	1652	3197	2680	2230	1844	1515	2.5	-1.2	-13.7	0	NA
358 Norma Mag.	250	2800	2510	2230	1970	1730	4350	3480	2750	2145	1655	2.5	1	-7.6	-25.2	NA
358 STA	275	2850	2562	2292	2039	1764	4959	4009	3208	2539	1899	1.9	0	-8.58	-26.1	NA

9.3mm

Cartridge	Bullet Wgt. Grs.	Muzzle	100 yds.	200 yds.	300 yds.	400 yds.	Muzzle	100 yds.	200 yds.	300 yds.	400 yds.	100 yds.	200 yds.	300 yds.	400 yds.	Est. Price/box
9.3x57mm Mau.	232	2362	2058	1778	1528	NA	2875	2182	1630	1203	NA	0	-6.8	-24.6	NA	NA
9.3x57mm Mau.	286	2070	1810	1590	1390	1110	2710	2090	1600	1220	955	2.5	-2.6	-22.5	0	NA
370 Sako Mag.	286	3550	2370	2200	2040	2880	4130	3570	3075	2630	2240	2.4	0	-9.5	-27.2	NA
9.6x62mm	232	2625	2302	2002	1728	-	2551	2731	2066	1539	-	2.6	0	-11.3	-	NA
9.3x62mm	250	2550	2376	2208	2048	—	3609	3133	2707	2328	—	0	-5.4	-17.9	—	NA
9.3x62mm	286	2360	2155	1961	1778	1608	3537	2949	2442	2008	1642	0	-6	-21.1	-47.2	NA
9.3x62mm	286	2400	2163	1941	1733	—	3657	2972	2392	1908	—	0	-6.7	-22.6	—	NA
9.3x64mm	286	2700	2505	2318	2139	1968	4629	3984	3411	2906	2460	2.5	2.7	-4.5	-19.2	NA
9.3x72mmR	193	1952	1610	1326	1120	996	1633	1112	754	538	425	0	-12.1	-44.1	—	NA
9.3x74mmR	250	2550	2376	2208	2048	—	3609	3133	2707	2328	—	0	-5.4	-17.9	—	NA
9.3x74Rmm	286	2360	2136	1924	1727	1545	3536	2896	2351	1893	1516	0	-6.1	-21.7	-49	NA

375

Cartridge	Bullet Wgt. Grs.	Muzzle	100 yds.	200 yds.	300 yds.	400 yds.	Muzzle	100 yds.	200 yds.	300 yds.	400 yds.	100 yds.	200 yds.	300 yds.	400 yds.	Est. Price/box
375 Winchester	200	2200	1841	1526	1268	1089	2150	1506	1034	714	527	2.5	-4	-26.2	0	$27
375 Winchester	250	1900	1647	1424	1239	1103	2005	1506	1126	852	676	2.5	-6.9	-33.3	0	$27
376 Steyr	225	2600	2331	2078	1842	1625	3377	2714	2157	1694	1319	2.5	0	-10.6	-31.4	NA

| | | VELOCITY (fps) | | | | | ENERGY (ft. lbs.) | | | | | TRAJ. (in.) | | | | |
Cartridge	Bullet Wgt. Grs.	Muzzle	100 yds.	200 yds.	300 yds.	400 yds.	Muzzle	100 yds.	200 yds.	300 yds.	400 yds.	100 yds.	200 yds.	300 yds.	400 yds.	Est. Price/box
376 Steyr	270	2600	2372	2156	1951	1759	4052	3373	2787	2283	1855	2.3	0	-9.9	-28.9	NA
375 Dakota	300	2600	2316	2051	1804	1579	4502	3573	2800	2167	1661	2.4	0	-11	-32.7	NA
375 N.E. 2-1/2"	270	2000	1740	1507	1310	NA	2398	1815	1362	1026	NA	2.5	-6	-30	0	NA
375 Flanged	300	2450	2150	1886	1640	NA	3998	3102	2369	1790	NA	2.5	-2.4	-17	0	NA
375 Ruger	250	2890	2675	2471	2275	2088	4636	3973	3388	2873	2421	1.7	0	-7.4	-21.5	NA
375 Ruger	260	2900	2703	2514	2333	—	4854	4217	3649	3143	—	0	-4	-13.4	—	NA
375 Ruger	270	2840	2600	2372	2156	1951	4835	4052	3373	2786	2283	1.8	0	-8	-23.6	NA
375 Ruger	300	2660	2344	2050	1780	1536	4713	3660	2800	2110	1572	2.4	0	-10.8	-32.6	NA
375 H&H Magnum	250	2890	2675	2471	2275	2088	4636	3973	3388	2873	2421	1.7	0	-7.4	-21.5	NA
375 H&H Magnum	250	2670	2450	2240	2040	1850	3955	3335	2790	2315	1905	2.5	-0.4	-10.2	-28.4	NA
375 H&H Magnum	270	2690	2420	2166	1928	1707	4337	3510	2812	2228	1747	2.5	0	-10	-29.4	$28
375 H&H Mag.	270	2800	2562	2337	2123	1921	4700	3936	3275	2703	2213	1.9	0	-8.3	-24.3	NA
375 H&H Magnum*	300	2530	2245	1979	1733	1512	4263	3357	2608	2001	1523	2.5	-1	-10.5	-33.6	$28
375 H&H Mag.	300	2660	2345	2052	1782	1539	4713	3662	2804	2114	1577	2.4	0	-10.8	-32.6	NA
375 H&H Hvy. Mag.	270	2870	2628	2399	2182	1976	4937	4141	3451	2150	1845	1.7	0	-7.2	-21	NA
375 H&H Hvy. Mag.	300	2705	2386	2090	1816	1568	4873	3793	2908	2195	1637	2.3	0	-10.4	-31.4	NA
375 H&H Mag	350	2300	2052	1821	-	-	4112	3273	2578	-	-	0	-6.7	-	-	NA
375 Rem. Ultra Mag.	270	2900	2558	2241	1947	1678	5041	3922	3010	2272	1689	1.9	2.7	-8.9	-27	NA
375 Rem. Ultra Mag.	260	2950	2750	2560	2377	—	5023	4367	3783	3262	—	0	-3.8	-12.9	—	NA
375 Rem. Ultra Mag.	300	2760	2505	2263	2035	1822	5073	4178	3412	2759	2210	2	0	-8.8	-26.1	NA
375 Wea. Mag.	260	3000	2798	2606	2421	—	5195	4520	3920	3384	—	0	-3.6	-12.4	—	NA
375 Wea. Mag.	300	2700	2420	2157	1911	1685	4856	3901	3100	2432	1891	2.5	-0.04	-10.7	0	NA
378 Wea. Mag.	260	3100	2894	2697	2509	—	5547	4834	4199	3633	—	0	-4.2	-14.6	—	NA
378 Wea. Mag.	270	3180	2976	2781	2594	2415	6062	5308	4635	4034	3495	2.5	2.6	-1.8	-11.3	NA
378 Wea. Mag.	300	2929	2576	2252	1952	1680	5698	4419	3379	2538	1881	2.5	1.2	-7	-24.5	$71
375 A-Square	300	2920	2626	2351	2093	1850	5679	4594	3681	2917	2281	2.5	1.4	-6	-21	$77
38-40 Win.	180	1160	999	901	827	764	538	399	324	273	233	0	-33.9	0	0	$42**
40, 41																
400 A-Square DPM	400	2400	2146	1909	1689	NA	5116	2092	3236	2533	NA	2.98	0	-10	NA	NA
400 A-Square DPM	170	2980	2463	2001	1598	NA	3352	2289	1512	964	NA	2.16	0	-11.1	NA	NA
408 CheyTac	419	2850	2752	2657	2562	2470	7551	7048	6565	6108	5675	-1.02	0	1.9	4.2	NA
405 Win.	300	2200	1851	1545	1296		3224	2282	1589	1119		4.6	0	-19.5	0	NA
450/400-3"	400	2050	1815	1595	1402	NA	3732	2924	2259	1746	NA	0	NA	-33.4	NA	NA
416 Ruger	400	2400	2151	1917	1700	NA	5116	4109	3264	2568	NA	0	-6	-21.6	0	NA
416 Dakota	400	2450	2294	2143	1998	1859	5330	4671	4077	3544	3068	2.5	-0.2	-10.5	-29.4	NA
416 Taylor	375	2350	2021	1722	na	na	4600	3403	2470	NA	NA	0	-7	NA	NA	NA
416 Taylor	400	2350	2117	1896	1693	NA	4905	3980	3194	2547	NA	2.5	-1.2	15	0	NA
416 Hoffman	400	2380	2145	1923	1718	1529	5031	4087	3285	2620	2077	2.5	-1	-14.1	0	NA
416 Rigby	350	2600	2449	2303	2162	2026	5253	4661	4122	3632	3189	2.5	-1.8	-10.2	-26	NA
416 Rigby	400	2370	2210	2050	1900	NA	4990	4315	3720	3185	NA	2.5	-0.7	-12.1	0	NA
416 Rigby	400	2400	2115	1851	1611	—	5115	3973	3043	2305	—	0	-6.5	-21.8	—	NA
416 Rigby	400	2415	2156	1915	1691	—	5180	4130	3256	2540	—	0	-6	-21.6	—	NA
416 Rigby	410	2370	2110	1870	1640	NA	5115	4050	3165	2455	NA	2.5	-2.4	-17.3	0	$110
416 Rigby No. 2	400	2400	2115	1851	1611	—	5115	3973	3043	2305	—	0	-6.5	-21.8	—	NA
416 Rem. Mag.*	350	2520	2270	2034	1814	1611	4935	4004	3216	2557	2017	2.5	-0.8	-12.6	-35	$82
416 Rem. Mag.	400	2400	2142	1901	1679	—	5116	4076	3211	2504	—	3.1	0	-12.7	—	NA
416 Rem. Mag	450	2150	1925	1716	-	-	4620	3702	2942	-	-	0	-7.8	-	-	NA
416 Wea. Mag.*	400	2700	2397	2115	1852	1613	6474	5104	3971	3047	2310	2.5	0	-10.1	-30.4	$96
10.57 (416) Meteor	400	2730	2532	2342	2161	1987	6621	5695	4874	4147	3508	1.9	0	-8.3	-24	NA
500/416 N.E.	400	2300	2092	1895	1712	—	4697	3887	3191	2602	—	0	-7.2	-24	—	NA
404 Jeffrey	400	2150	1924	1716	1525	NA	4105	3289	2614	2064	NA	2.5	-4	-22.1	0	NA
404 Jeffrey	400	2300	2053	1823	1611	—	4698	3743	2950	2306	—	0	-6.8	-24.1	—	NA
404 Jeffery	400	2350	2020	1720	1458	—	4904	3625	2629	1887	—	0	-6.5	-21.8	—	NA
404 Jeffery	450	2150	1946	1755	-	-	4620	3784	3078	-	-	0	-7.6	-	-	NA
425, 44																
425 Express	400	2400	2160	1934	1725	NA	5115	4145	3322	2641	NA	2.5	-1	-14	0	NA
44-40 Win.	200	1190	1006	900	822	756	629	449	360	300	254	0	-33.3	0	0	$36**
44 Rem. Mag.	210	1920	1477	1155	982	880	1719	1017	622	450	361	0	-17.6	0	0	$14
44 Rem. Mag.	240	1760	1380	1114	970	878	1650	1015	661	501	411	0	-17.6	0	0	$13
444 Marlin	240	2350	1815	1377	1087	941	2942	1753	1001	630	472	2.5	-15.1	-31	0	$22
444 Marlin	265	2120	1733	1405	1160	1012	2644	1768	1162	791	603	2.5	-6	-32.2	0	Disc.
444 Mar. Lever Evolution	265	2325	1971	1652	1380	NA	3180	2285	1606	1120	NA	3	-1.4	-18.6	NA	NA
444 Mar. Superformance	265	2400	1976	1603	1298	NA	3389	2298	1512	991	NA	4.1	0	-17.8	NA	NA

Cartridge	Bullet Wgt. Grs.	VELOCITY (fps)					ENERGY (ft. lbs.)					TRAJ. (in.)				Est. Price/box
		Muzzle	100 yds.	200 yds.	300 yds.	400 yds.	Muzzle	100 yds.	200 yds.	300 yds.	400 yds.	100 yds.	200 yds.	300 yds.	400 yds.	
45																
45-70 Govt.	250	2025	1616	1285	1068	—	2276	1449	917	634	—	6.1	0	-27.2	—	NA
45-70 Govt.	300	1810	1497	1244	1073	969	2182	1492	1031	767	625	0	-14.8	0	0	$21
45-70 Govt. Supreme	300	1880	1558	1292	1103	988	2355	1616	1112	811	651	0	-12.9	-46	-105	NA
45-70 Govt.	325	2000	1685	1413	1197	—	2886	2049	1441	1035	—	5.5	0	-23		NA
45-70 Lever Evolution	325	2050	1729	1450	1225	NA	3032	2158	1516	1083	NA	3	-4.1	-27.8	NA	NA
45-70 Govt. CorBon	350	1800	1526	1296			2519	1810	1307			0	-14.6	0	0	NA
45-70 Govt.	405	1330	1168	1055	977	918	1590	1227	1001	858	758	0	-24.6	0	0	$21
45-70 Govt. PMC Cowboy	405	1550	1193	—	—	—	1639	1280	—	—	—	0	-23.9	0	0	NA
45-70 Govt. Garrett	415	1850	—	—	—	—	3150	—	—	—	—	3	-7	0	0	NA
45-70 Govt. Garrett	530	1550	1343	1178	1062	982	2828	2123	1633	1327	1135	0	-17.8	0	0	NA
450 Bushmaster	250	2200	1831	1508	1480	1073	2686	1860	1262	864	639	0	-9	-33.5	0	NA
450 Marlin	325	2225	1887	1587	1332	—	3572	2570	1816	1280	—	4.2	0	-18.1	—	NA
450 Marlin	350	2100	1774	1488	1254	1089	3427	2446	1720	1222	922	0	-9.7	-35.2	0	NA
450 Mar. Lever Evolution	325	2225	1887	1585	1331	NA	3572	2569	1813	1278	NA	3	-2.2	-21.3	NA	NA
457 Wild West Magnum	350	2150	1718	1348	NA	NA	3645	2293	1413	NA	NA	0	-10.5	NA	NA	NA
450/500 N.E.	400	2050	1820	1609	1420	—	3732	2940	2298	1791	—	0	-9.7	-32.8	—	NA
450 N.E. 3-1/4"	465	2190	1970	1765	1577	NA	4952	4009	3216	2567	NA	2.5	-3	-20	0	NA
450 N.E.	480	2150	1881	1635	1418	—	4927	3769	2850	2144	—	0	-8.4	-29.8	—	NA
450 N.E. 3-1/4"	500	2150	1920	1708	1514	NA	5132	4093	3238	2544	NA	2.5	-4	-22.9	0	NA
450 No. 2	465	2190	1970	1765	1577	NA	4952	4009	3216	2567	NA	2.5	-3	-20	0	NA
450 No. 2	500	2150	1920	1708	1514	NA	5132	4093	3238	2544	NA	2.5	-4	-22.9	0	NA
450 Ackley Mag.	465	2400	2169	1950	1747	NA	5947	4857	3927	3150	NA	2.5	-1	-13.7	0	NA
450 Ackley Mag.	500	2320	2081	1855	1649	NA	5975	4085	3820	3018	NA	2.5	-1.2	-15	0	NA
450 Rigby	500	2350	2139	1939	1752	—	6130	5079	4176	3408	—	0	-6.8	-22.9	—	NA
450 Rigby	550	2100	1866	1651	-	-	5387	4256	3330	-	-	-	-	-	-	
458 Win. Magnum	400	2380	2170	1960	1770	NA	5030	4165	3415	2785	NA	2.5	-0.4	-13.4	0	$73
458 Win. Magnum	465	2220	1999	1791	1601	NA	5088	4127	3312	2646	NA	2.5	-2	-17.7	0	$61
458 Win. Magnum	500	2040	1823	1623	1442	1237	4620	3689	2924	2308	1839	2.5	-3.5	-22	0	NA
458 Win. Mag.	500	2140	1880	1643	1432	—	5084	3294	2996	2276	—	0	-8.4	-29.8	—	$41
458 Win. Magnum	510	2040	1770	1527	1319	1157	4712	3547	2640	1970	1516	2.5	-4.1	-25	0	NA
458 Lott	465	2380	2150	1932	1730	NA	5848	4773	3855	3091	NA	2.5	-1	-14	0	NA
458 Lott	500	2300	2029	1778	1551	—	5873	4569	3509	2671	—	0	-7	-25.1	—	NA
458 Lott	500	2300	2062	1838	1633	NA	5873	4719	3748	2960	NA	2.5	-1.6	-16.4	0	NA
460 Short A-Sq.	500	2420	2175	1943	1729	NA	6501	5250	4193	3319	NA	2.5	-0.8	-12.8	0	NA
460 Wea. Mag.	500	2700	2404	2128	1869	1635	8092	6416	5026	3878	2969	2.5	0.6	-8.9	-28	$72
475																
500/465 N.E.	480	2150	1917	1703	1507	NA	4926	3917	3089	2419	NA	2.5	-4	-22.2	0	NA
470 Rigby	500	2150	1940	1740	1560	NA	5130	4170	3360	2695	NA	2.5	-2.8	-19.4	0	NA
470 Nitro Ex.	480	2190	1954	1735	1536	NA	5111	4070	3210	2515	NA	2.5	-3.5	-20.8	0	NA
470 N.E.	500	2150	1885	1643	1429	—	5132	3945	2998	2267	—	0	-8.9	-30.8	—	NA
470 Nitro Ex.	500	2150	1890	1650	1440	1270	5130	3965	3040	2310	1790	2.5	-4.3	-24	0	$177
475 No. 2	500	2200	1955	1728	1522	NA	5375	4243	3316	2573	NA	2.5	-3.2	-20.9	0	NA
50, 58																
50 Alaskan	450	2000	1729	1492	NA	NA	3997	2987	2224	NA	NA	0	-11.25	NA	NA	NA
500 Jeffery	570	2300	1979	1688	1434	—	6694	4958	3608	2604	—	0	-8.2	-28.6	—	NA
505 Gibbs	525	2300	2063	1840	1637	NA	6166	4922	3948	3122	NA	2.5	-3	-18	0	NA
505 Gibbs	570	2100	1893	1701	-	-	5583	4538	3664	-	-	0	-8.1	-	-	NA
505 Gibbs	600	2100	1899	1711	-	-	5877	4805	3904	-	-	0	-8.1	-	-	NA
500 N.E.	570	2150	1889	1651	1439	—	5850	4518	3450	2621	—	0	-8.9	-30.6	—	NA
500 N.E.-3"	570	2150	1928	1722	1533	NA	5850	4703	3752	2975	NA	2.5	-3.7	-22	0	NA
500 N.E.-3"	600	2150	1927	1721	1531	NA	6158	4947	3944	3124	NA	2.5	-4	-22	0	NA
495 A-Square	570	2350	2117	1896	1693	NA	5850	4703	3752	2975	NA	2.5	-1	-14.5	0	NA
495 A-Square	600	2280	2050	1833	1635	NA	6925	5598	4478	3562	NA	2.5	-2	-17	0	NA
500 A-Square	600	2380	2144	1922	1766	NA	7546	6126	4920	3922	NA	2.5	-3	-17	0	NA
500 A-Square	707	2250	2040	1841	1567	NA	7947	6530	5318	4311	NA	2.5	-2	-17	0	NA
500 BMG PMC	660	3080	2854	2639	2444	2248	13688	500 yd. zero				3.1	3.9	4.7	2.8	NA
577 Nitro Ex.	750	2050	1793	1562	1360	NA	6990	5356	4065	3079	NA	2.5	-5	-26	0	NA
577 Tyrannosaur	750	2400	2141	1898	1675	NA	9591	7633	5996	4671	NA	3	0	-12.9	0	NA
600, 700																
600 N.E.	900	1950	1680	1452	NA	NA	7596	5634	4212	NA	NA	5.6	0	0	0	NA
700 N.E.	1200	1900	1676	1472	NA	NA	9618	7480	5774	NA	NA	5.7	0	0	0	NA
50 BMG																
50 BMG	624	2952	2820	2691	2566	2444	12077	11028	10036	9125	8281	0	-2.9	-10.6	-23.5	NA
50 BMG Match	750	2820	2728	2637	2549	2462	13241	12388	11580	10815	10090	1.5	0	-6.5	-18.3	NA

Notes: Blanks are available in 32 S&W, 38 S&W and 38 Special. "V" after barrel length indicates test barrel was vented to produce ballistics similar to a revolver with a normal barrel-to-cylinder gap. Ammo prices are per 50 rounds except when marked with an ** which signifies a 20 round box; *** signifies a 25-round box. Not all loads are available from all ammo manufacturers. Listed loads are those made by Remington, Winchester, Federal, and others. DISC. is a discontinued load. Prices are rounded to the nearest whole dollar and will vary with brand and retail outlet.

Cartridge	Bullet Wgt. Grs.	VELOCITY (fps)			ENERGY (ft. lbs.)			Mid-Range Traj. (in.)		Bbl. Lgth. (in).	Est. Price/ box
		Muzzle	50 yds.	100 yds.	Muzzle	50 yds.	100 yds.	50 yds.	100 yds.		
22, 25											
221 Rem. Fireball	50	2650	2380	2130	780	630	505	0.2	0.8	10.5"	$15
25 Automatic	35	900	813	742	63	51	43	NA	NA	2"	$18
25 Automatic	45	815	730	655	65	55	40	1.8	7.7	2"	$21
25 Automatic	50	760	705	660	65	55	50	2	8.7	2"	$17
30											
7.5mm Swiss	107	1010	NA	NA	240	NA	NA	NA	NA	NA	
7.62x25 Tokarev	85	1647	1458	1295	512	401	317	0	-3.2	4.75	NEW
7.62mmTokarev	87	1390	NA	NA	365	NA	NA	0.6	NA	4.5"	NA
7.62 Nagant	97	790	NA	NA	134	NA	NA	NA	NA	NA	NA
7.63 Mauser	88	1440	NA	NA	405	NA	NA	NA	NA	NA	NEW
30 Luger	93	1220	1110	1040	305	255	225	NA	NA	NA	NEW
30 Carbine	110	1790	1600	1430	785	625	500	0.9	3.5	4.5"	$34
30-357 AeT	123	1992	NA	NA	1084	NA	NA	0.4	1.7	10"	$28
32										10"	NA
32 NAA	80	1000	933	880	178	155	137	NA	NA	4"	NA
32 S&W	88	680	645	610	90	80	75	2.5	10.5	3"	$17
32 S&W Long	98	705	670	635	115	100	90	2.3	10.5	4"	$17
32 Short Colt	80	745	665	590	100	80	60	2.2	9.9	4"	$19
32 H&R	80	1150	1039	963	235	192	165	NA	NA	4"	NA
32 H&R Magnum	85	1100	1020	930	230	195	165	1	4.3	4.5"	$21
32 H&R Magnum	95	1030	940	900	225	190	170	1.1	4.7	4.5"	$19
327 Federal Magnum	85	1400	1220	1090	370	280	225	NA	NA	4-V	NA
327 Federal Magnum	100	1500	1320	1180	500	390	310	-0.2	-4.5	4-V	NA
32 Automatic	60	970	895	835	125	105	95	1.3	5.4	4"	$22
32 Automatic	60	1000	917	849	133	112	96			4"	NA
32 Automatic	65	950	890	830	130	115	100	1.3	5.6	NA	NA
32 Automatic	71	905	855	810	130	115	95	1.4	5.8	4"	$19
8mm Lebel Pistol	111	850	NA	NA	180	NA	NA	NA	NA	NA	NEW
8mm Steyr	112	1080	NA	NA	290	NA	NA	NA	NA	NA	NEW
8mm Gasser	126	850	NA	NA	200	NA	NA	NA	NA	NA	NEW
9mm, 38											
380 Automatic	60	1130	960	NA	170	120	NA	1	NA	NA	NA
380 Automatic	75	950	NA	NA	183	NA	NA	NA	NA	3"	$33
380 Automatic	85/88	990	920	870	190	165	145	1.2	5.1	4"	$20
380 Automatic	90	1000	890	800	200	160	130	1.2	5.5	3.75"	$10
380 Automatic	95/100	955	865	785	190	160	130	1.4	5.9	4"	$20
38 Super Auto +P	115	1300	1145	1040	430	335	275	0.7	3.3	5"	$26
38 Super Auto +P	125/130	1215	1100	1015	425	350	300	0.8	3.6	5"	$26
38 Super Auto +P	147	1100	1050	1000	395	355	325	0.9	4	5"	NA
38 Super Auto +P	115	1130	1016	938	326	264	225	1	-9.5	-	NA
9x18mm Makarov	95	1000	930	874	211	182	161	NA	NA	4"	NEW
9x18mm Ultra	100	1050	NA	NA	240	NA	NA	NA	NA	NA	NEW
9x21	124	1150	1050	980	365	305	265	NA	NA	4"	NA
9x21 IMI	123	1220	1095	1010	409	330	281	-3.15	—	5	NA
9x23mm Largo	124	1190	1055	966	390	306	257	0.7	3.7	4"	NA
9x23mm Win.	125	1450	1249	1103	583	433	338	0.6	2.8	NA	NA
9mm Steyr	115	1180	NA	NA	350	NA	NA	NA	NA	NA	NEW
9mm Luger	88	1500	1190	1010	440	275	200	0.6	3.1	4"	$24
9mm Luger	90	1360	1112	978	370	247	191	NA	NA	4"	$26
9mm Luger	92	1325	1117	991	359	255	201	-3.2	—	4	NA
9mm Luger	95	1300	1140	1010	350	275	215	0.8	3.4	4"	NA
9mm Luger	100	1180	1080	NA	305	255	NA	0.9	NA	4"	NA
9mm Luger Guard Dog	105	1230	1070	970	355	265	220	NA	NA	4"	NA
9mm Luger	115	1155	1045	970	340	280	240	0.9	3.9	4"	$21
9mm Luger	123/125	1110	1030	970	340	290	260	1	4	4"	$23

Cartridge	Bullet Wgt. Grs.	VELOCITY (fps)			ENERGY (ft. lbs.)			Mid-Range Traj. (in.)		Bbl. Lgth. (in).	Est. Price/ box
		Muzzle	50 yds.	100 yds.	Muzzle	50 yds.	100 yds.	50 yds.	100 yds.		
9mm Luger	124	1150	1040	965	364	298	256	-4.5	—	4	NA
9mm Luger	135	1010	960	918	306	276	253	—	—	4	NA
9mm Luger	140	935	890	850	270	245	225	1.3	5.5	4"	$23
9mm Luger	147	990	940	900	320	290	265	1.1	4.9	4"	$26
9mm Luger +P	90	1475	NA	NA	437	NA	NA	NA	NA	NA	NA
9mm Luger +P	115	1250	1113	1019	399	316	265	0.8	3.5	4"	$27
9mm Federal	115	1280	1130	1040	420	330	280	0.7	3.3	4"V	$24
9mm Luger Vector	115	1155	1047	971	341	280	241	NA	NA	4"	NA
9mm Luger +P	124	1180	1089	1021	384	327	287	0.8	3.8	4"	NA
38											
38 S&W	146	685	650	620	150	135	125	2.4	10	4"	$19
38 S&W Short	145	720	689	660	167	153	140	-8.5	—	5	NA
38 Short Colt	125	730	685	645	150	130	115	2.2	9.4	6"	$19
39 Special	100	950	900	NA	200	180	NA	1.3	NA	4"V	NA
38 Special	110	945	895	850	220	195	175	1.3	5.4	4"V	$23
38 Special	110	945	895	850	220	195	175	1.3	5.4	4"V	$23
38 Special	130	775	745	710	175	160	120	1.9	7.9	4"V	$22
38 Special Cowboy	140	800	767	735	199	183	168			7.5" V	NA
38 (Multi-Ball)	140	830	730	505	215	130	80	2	10.6	4"V	$10**
38 Special	148	710	635	565	165	130	105	2.4	10.6	4"V	$17
38 Special	158	755	725	690	200	185	170	2	8.3	4"V	$18
38 Special +P	95	1175	1045	960	290	230	195	0.9	3.9	4"V	$23
38 Special +P	110	995	925	870	240	210	185	1.2	5.1	4"V	$23
38 Special +P	125	975	929	885	264	238	218	1	5.2	4"	NA
38 Special +P	125	945	900	860	250	225	205	1.3	5.4	4"V	#23
38 Special +P	129	945	910	870	255	235	215	1.3	5.3	4"V	$11
38 Special +P	130	925	887	852	247	227	210	1.3	5.5	4"V	NA
38 Special +P	147/150	884	NA	NA	264	NA	NA	NA	NA	4"V	$27
38 Special +P	158	890	855	825	280	255	240	1.4	6	4"V	$20
357											
357 SIG	115	1520	NA	NA	593	NA	NA	NA	NA	NA	NA
357 SIG	124	1450	NA	NA	578	NA	NA	NA	NA	NA	NA
357 SIG	125	1350	1190	1080	510	395	325	0.7	3.1	4"	NA
357 SIG	135	1225	1112	1031	450	371	319	—	—	4	NA
357 SIG	147	1225	1132	1060	490	418	367	—	—	4	NA
357 SIG	150	1130	1030	970	420	355	310	0.9	4	NA	NA
356 TSW	115	1520	NA	NA	593	NA	NA	NA	NA	NA	NA
356 TSW	124	1450	NA	NA	578	NA	NA	NA	NA	NA	NA
356 TSW	135	1280	1120	1010	490	375	310	0.8	3.5	NA	NA
356 TSW	147	1220	1120	1040	485	410	355	0.8	3.5	5"	NA
357 Mag., Super Clean	105	1650									NA
357 Magnum	110	1295	1095	975	410	290	230	0.8	3.5	4"V	$25
357 (Med.Vel.)	125	1220	1075	985	415	315	270	0.8	3.7	4"V	$25
357 Magnum	125	1450	1240	1090	585	425	330	0.6	2.8	4"V	$25
357 Magnum	125	1500	1312	1163	624	478	376	—	—	8	NA
357 (Multi-Ball)	140	1155	830	665	420	215	135	1.2	6.4	4"V	$11**
357 Magnum	140	1360	1195	1075	575	445	360	0.7	3	4"V	$25
357 Magnum FlexTip	140	1440	1274	1143	644	504	406	NA	NA	NA	NA
357 Magnum	145	1290	1155	1060	535	430	360	0.8	3.5	4"V	$26
357 Magnum	150/158	1235	1105	1015	535	430	360	0.8	3.5	4"V	$25
357 Mag. Cowboy	158	800	761	725	225	203	185				NA
357 Magnum	165	1290	1189	1108	610	518	450	0.7	3.1	8-3/8"	NA
357 Magnum	180	1145	1055	985	525	445	390	0.9	3.9	4"V	$25
357 Magnum	180	1180	1088	1020	557	473	416	0.8	3.6	8"V	NA
357 Mag. CorBon F.A.	180	1650	1512	1386	1088	913	767	1.66	0		NA
357 Mag. CorBon	200	1200	1123	1061	640	560	500	3.19	0		NA
357 Rem. Maximum	158	1825	1590	1380	1170	885	670	0.4	1.7	10.5"	$14**
40, 10mm											
40 S&W	120	1150	-	-	352	-	-	-	-	-	$38
40 S&W	125	1265	1102	998	444	337	276	-3	—	4	NA
40 S&W	135	1140	1070	NA	390	345	NA	0.9	NA	4"	NA

Cartridge	Bullet Wgt. Grs.	VELOCITY (fps)			ENERGY (ft. lbs.)			Mid-Range Traj. (in.)		Bbl. Lgth. (in).	Est. Price/ box
		Muzzle	50 yds.	100 yds.	Muzzle	50 yds.	100 yds.	50 yds.	100 yds.		
40 S&W Guard Dog	135	1200	1040	940	430	325	265	NA	NA	4"	NA
40 S&W	155	1140	1026	958	447	362	309	0.9	4.1	4"	$14***
40 S&W	165	1150	NA	NA	485	NA	NA	NA	NA	4"	$18***
40 S&W	175	1010	948	899	396	350	314	—	—	4	NA
40 S&W	180	985	936	893	388	350	319	1.4	5	4"	$14***
40 S&W	180	1000	943	896	400	355	321	4.52	—	4	NA
40 S&W	180	1015	960	914	412	368	334	1.3	4.5	4"	NA
400 Cor-Bon	135	1450	NA	NA	630	NA	NA	NA	NA	5"	NA
10mm Automatic	155	1125	1046	986	436	377	335	0.9	3.9	5"	$26
10mm Automatic	155	1265	1118	1018	551	430	357	—	—	5	NA
10mm Automatic	170	1340	1165	1145	680	510	415	0.7	3.2	5"	$31
10mm Automatic	175	1290	1140	1035	650	505	420	0.7	3.3	5.5"	$11**
10mm Auto. (FBI)	180	950	905	865	361	327	299	1.5	5.4	4"	$16**
10mm Automatic	180	1030	970	920	425	375	340	1.1	4.7	5"	$16**
10mm Auto H.V.	180	1240	1124	1037	618	504	430	0.8	3.4	5"	$27
10mm Auto	200	1100	1015	951	537	457	402	-1.1	-9.6	NA	NA
10mm Automatic	200	1160	1070	1010	495	510	430	0.9	3.8	5"	$14**
10.4mm Italian	177	950	NA	NA	360	NA	NA	NA	NA	NA	NEW
41 Action Exp.	180	1000	947	903	400	359	326	0.5	4.2	5"	$13**
41 Rem. Magnum	170	1420	1165	1015	760	515	390	0.7	3.2	4"V	$33
41 Rem. Magnum	175	1250	1120	1030	605	490	410	0.8	3.4	4"V	$14**
41 (Med. Vel.)	210	965	900	840	435	375	330	1.3	5.4	4"V	$30
41 Rem. Magnum	210	1300	1160	1060	790	630	535	0.7	3.2	4"V	$33
41 Rem. Magnum	240	1250	1151	1075	833	706	616	0.8	3.3	6.5V	NA
44											
44 S&W Russian	247	780	NA	NA	335	NA	NA	NA	NA	NA	NA
44 Special	210	900	861	825	360	329	302	5.57	—	6	NA
44 Special FTX	165	900	848	802	297	263	235	NA	NA	2.5"	NA
44 S&W Special	180	980	NA	NA	383	NA	NA	NA	NA	6.5"	NA
44 S&W Special	180	1000	935	882	400	350	311	NA	NA	7.5"V	NA
44 S&W Special	200	875	825	780	340	302	270	1.2	6	6"	$13**
44 S&W Special	200	1035	940	865	475	390	335	1.1	4.9	6.5"	$13**
44 S&W Special	240/246	755	725	695	310	285	265	2	8.3	6.5"	$26
44-40 Win.	200	722	698	676	232	217	203	-3.4	-23.7	4	NA
44-40 Win.	205	725	689	655	239	216	195	—	—	7.5	NA
44-40 Win.	210	725	698	672	245	227	210	-11.6	—	5.5	NA
44-40 Win.	225	725	697	670	263	243	225	-3.4	-23.8	4	NA
44-40 Win. Cowboy	225	750	723	695	281	261	242				NA
44 Rem. Magnum	180	1610	1365	1175	1035	745	550	0.5	2.3	4"V	$18**
44 Rem. Magnum	200	1296	1193	1110	747	632	548	-0.5	-6.2	6	NA
44 Rem. Magnum	200	1400	1192	1053	870	630	492	0.6	NA	6.5"	$20
44 Rem. Magnum	200	1500	1332	1194	999	788	633	—	—	7.5	NA
44 Rem. Magnum	210	1495	1310	1165	1040	805	635	0.6	2.5	6.5"	$18**
44 Rem. Mag. FlexTip	225	1410	1240	1111	993	768	617	NA	NA	NA	NA
44 (Med. Vel.)	240	1000	945	900	535	475	435	1.1	4.8	6.5"	$17
44 R.M. (Jacketed)	240	1180	1080	1010	740	625	545	0.9	3.7	4"V	$18**
44 R.M. (Lead)	240	1350	1185	1070	970	750	610	0.7	3.1	4"V	$29
44 Rem. Magnum	250	1180	1100	1040	775	670	600	0.8	3.6	6.5"V	$21
44 Rem. Magnum	250	1250	1148	1070	867	732	635	0.8	3.3	6.5"V	NA
44 Rem. Magnum	275	1235	1142	1070	931	797	699	0.8	3.3	6.5"	NA
44 Rem. Magnum	300	1150	1083	1030	881	781	706	—	—	7.5	NA
44 Rem. Magnum	300	1200	1100	1026	959	806	702	NA	NA	7.5"	$17
44 Rem. Magnum	330	1385	1297	1220	1406	1234	1090	1.83	0	NA	NA
44 Webley	262	850	—	—	—	—	—	—	—	—	NA
440 CorBon	260	1700	1544	1403	1669	1377	1136	1.58	NA	10"	NA
45, 50											
450 Short Colt/450 Revolver	226	830	NA	NA	350	NA	NA	NA	NA	NA	NEW
45 S&W Schofield	180	730	NA	NA	213	NA	NA	NA	NA	NA	NA
45 S&W Schofield	230	730	NA	NA	272	NA	NA	NA	NA	NA	NA
45 G.A.P.	165	1007	936	879	372	321	283	-1.4	-11.8	5	NA
45 G.A.P.	185	1090	970	890	490	385	320	1	4.7	5"	NA

Cartridge	Bullet Wgt. Grs.	VELOCITY (fps)			ENERGY (ft. lbs.)			Mid-Range Traj. (in.)		Bbl. Lgth. (in.)	Est. Price/ box
		Muzzle	50 yds.	100 yds.	Muzzle	50 yds.	100 yds.	50 yds.	100 yds.		
45 G.A.P.	230	880	842	NA	396	363	NA	NA	NA	NA	NA
45 Automatic	150	1050	NA	NA	403	NA	NA	NA	NA	NA	$40
45 Automatic	165	1030	930	NA	385	315	NA	1.2	NA	5"	NA
45 Automatic Guard Dog	165	1140	1030	950	475	390	335	NA	NA	5"	NA
45 Automatic	185	1000	940	890	410	360	325	1.1	4.9	5"	$28
45 Auto. (Match)	185	770	705	650	245	204	175	2	8.7	5"	$28
45 Auto. (Match)	200	940	890	840	392	352	312	2	8.6	5"	$20
45 Automatic	200	975	917	860	421	372	328	1.4	5	5"	$18
45 Automatic	230	830	800	675	355	325	300	1.6	6.8	5"	$27
45 Automatic	230	880	846	816	396	366	340	1.5	6.1	5"	NA
45 Automatic +P	165	1250	NA	NA	573	NA	NA	NA	NA	NA	NA
45 Automatic +P	185	1140	1040	970	535	445	385	0.9	4	5"	$31
45 Automatic +P	200	1055	982	925	494	428	380	NA	NA	5"	NA
45 Super	185	1300	1190	1108	694	582	504	NA	NA	5"	NA
45 Win. Magnum	230	1400	1230	1105	1000	775	635	0.6	2.8	5"	$14**
45 Win. Magnum	260	1250	1137	1053	902	746	640	0.8	3.3	5"	$16**
45 Win. Mag. CorBon	320	1150	1080	1025	940	830	747	3.47			NA
455 Webley MKII	262	850	NA	NA	420	NA	NA	NA	NA	NA	NA
45 Colt FTX	185	920	870	826	348	311	280	NA	NA	3"V	NA
45 Colt	200	1000	938	889	444	391	351	1.3	4.8	5.5"	$21
45 Colt	225	960	890	830	460	395	345	1.3	5.5	5.5"	$22
45 Colt + P CorBon	265	1350	1225	1126	1073	884	746	2.65	0		NA
45 Colt + P CorBon	300	1300	1197	1114	1126	956	827	2.78	0		NA
45 Colt	250/255	860	820	780	410	375	340	1.6	6.6	5.5"	$27
454 Casull	250	1300	1151	1047	938	735	608	0.7	3.2	7.5"V	NA
454 Casull	260	1800	1577	1381	1871	1436	1101	0.4	1.8	7.5"V	NA
454 Casull	300	1625	1451	1308	1759	1413	1141	0.5	2	7.5"V	NA
454 Casull CorBon	360	1500	1387	1286	1800	1640	1323	2.01	0		NA
460 S&W	200	2300	2042	1801	2350	1851	1441	0	-1.6	NA	NA
460 S&W	260	2000	1788	1592	2309	1845	1464	NA	NA	7.5"V	NA
460 S&W	250	1450	1267	1127	1167	891	705	NA	NA	8.375-V	NA
460 S&W	250	1900	1640	1412	2004	1494	1106	0	-2.75	NA	NA
460 S&W	300	1750	1510	1300	2040	1510	1125	NA	NA	8.4-V	NA
460 S&W	395	1550	1389	1249	2108	1691	1369	0	-4	NA	NA
475 Linebaugh	400	1350	1217	1119	1618	1315	1112	NA	NA	NA	NA
480 Ruger	325	1350	1191	1076	1315	1023	835	2.6	0	7.5"	NA
50 Action Exp.	300	1475	1251	1092	1449	1043	795	-	-	6"	NA
50 Action Exp.	325	1400	1209	1075	1414	1055	835	0.2	2.3	6"	$24**
500 S&W	275	1665	1392	1183	1693	1184	854	1.5	NA	8.375	NA
500 S&W	300	1950	1653	1396	2533	1819	1298	—	—	8.5	NA
500 S&W	325	1800	1560	1350	2340	1755	1315	NA	NA	8.4-V	NA
500 S&W	350	1400	1231	1106	1523	1178	951	NA	NA	10"	NA
500 S&W	400	1675	1472	1299	2493	1926	1499	1.3	NA	8.375	NA
500 S&W	440	1625	1367	1169	2581	1825	1337	1.6	NA	8.375	NA
500 S&W	500	1300	1178	1085	1876	1541	1308	—	—	8.5	NA
500 S&W	500	1425	1281	1164	2254	1823	1505	NA	NA	10"	NA

Note: The actual ballistics obtained with your firearm can vary considerably from the advertised ballistics.
Also, ballistics can vary from lot to lot with the same brand and type load.

Cartridge	Bullet Wt. Grs.	Velocity (fps) 22-1/2" Bbl.		Energy (ft. lbs.) 22-1/2" Bbl.		Mid-Range Traj. (in.)	Muzzle Velocity
		Muzzle	100 yds.	Muzzle	100 yds.	100 yds.	6" Bbl.
17 Aguila	20	1850	1267	NA	NA	NA	NA
17 Hornady Mach 2	15.5	2050	1450	149	75	NA	NA
17 Hornady Mach 2	17	2100	1530	166	88	0.7	NA
17 HMR Lead Free	15.5	2550	1901	NA	NA	0.9	NA
17 HMR TNT Green	16	2500	1642	222	96	NA	NA
17 HMR	17	2550	1902	245	136	NA	NA
17 HMR	17	2650	na	na	na	na	NA
17 HMR	20	2375	1776	250	140	NA	NA
17 Win. Super Mag.	15	3300	2496	363	207	0	NA
17 Win. Super Mag.	20 Tipped	3000	2504	400	278	0	NA
17 Win. Super Mag.	20 JHP	3000	2309	400	237	0	NA
17 Win. Super Mag.	25 Tipped	2600	2230	375	276	0	NA
5mm Rem. Rimfire Mag.	30	2300	1669	352	188	NA	24
22 Short Blank	—	—	—	—	—	—	—
22 Short CB	29	727	610	33	24	NA	706
22 Short Target	29	830	695	44	31	6.8	786
22 Short HP	27	1164	920	81	50	4.3	1077
22 Colibri	20	375	183	6	1	NA	NA
22 Super Colibri	20	500	441	11	9	NA	NA
22 Long CB	29	727	610	33	24	NA	706
22 Long HV	29	1180	946	90	57	4.1	1031
22 LR Pistol Match	40	1070	890	100	70	4.6	940
22 LR Shrt. Range Green	21	1650	912	127	NA	NA	NA
CCI Quiet 22 LR	40	710	640	45	36	NA	NA
22 LR Sub Sonic HP	38	1050	901	93	69	4.7	NA
22 LR Segmented HP	40	1050	897	98	72	NA	NA
22 LR Standard Velocity	40	1070	890	100	70	4.6	940
22 LR AutoMatch	40	1200	990	130	85	NA	NA
22 LR HV	40	1255	1016	140	92	3.6	1060
22 LR Silhoutte	42	1220	1003	139	94	3.6	1025
22 SSS	60	950	802	120	86	NA	NA
22 LR HV HP	40	1280	1001	146	89	3.5	1085
22 Velocitor GDHP	40	1435	0	0	0	NA	NA
22 LR Segmented HP	37	1435	1080	169	96	2.9	NA
22 LR Hyper HP	32/33/34	1500	1075	165	85	2.8	NA
22 LR Expediter	32	1640	NA	191	NA	NA	NA
22 LR Stinger HP	32	1640	1132	191	91	2.6	1395
22 LR Lead Free	30	1650	NA	181	NA	NA	NA
22 LR Hyper Vel	30	1750	1191	204	93	NA	NA
22 LR Shot #12	31	950	NA	NA	NA	NA	NA
22 WRF LFN	45	1300	1015	169	103	3	NA
22 Win. Mag. Lead Free	28	2200	NA	301	NA	NA	NA
22 Win. Mag.	30	2200	1373	322	127	1.4	1610
22 Win. Mag. V-Max BT	33	2000	1495	293	164	0.6	NA
22 Win. Mag. JHP	34	2120	1435	338	155	1.4	NA
22 Win. Mag. JHP	40	1910	1326	324	156	1.7	1480
22 Win. Mag. FMJ	40	1910	1326	324	156	1.7	1480
22 Win. Mag. Dyna Point	45	1550	1147	240	131	2.6	NA
22 Win. Mag. JHP	50	1650	1280	300	180	1.3	NA
22 Win. Mag. Shot #11	52	1000	—	NA	—	—	NA

NOTES: * = 10 rounds per box. ** = 5 rounds per box. Pricing variations and number of rounds per box can occur with type and brand of ammunition. Listed pricing is the average nominal cost for load style and box quantity shown. Not every brand is available in all shot size variations. Some manufacturers do not provide suggested list prices. All prices rounded to nearest whole dollar. The price you pay will vary dependent upon outlet of purchase. # = new load spec this year; "C" indicates a change in data.

10 Gauge 3-1/2" Magnum

Dram Equiv.	Shot Ozs.	Load Style	Shot Sizes	Brands	Avg. Price/box	Velocity (fps)
Max	2-3/8	magnum blend	5, 6, 7	Hevi-shot	NA	1200
4-1/2	2-1/4	premium	BB, 2, 4, 5, 6	Win., Fed., Rem.	$33	1205
Max	2	premium	4, 5, 6	Fed., Win.	NA	1300
4-1/4	2	high velocity	BB, 2, 4	Rem.	$22	1210
Max	18 pellets	premium	00 buck	Fed., Win.	$7**	1100
Max	1-7/8	Bismuth	BB, 2, 4	Bis.	NA	1225
Max	1-3/4	high density	BB, 2	Rem.	NA	1300
4-1/4	1-3/4	steel	TT, T, BBB, BB, 1, 2, 3	Win., Rem.	$27	1260
Mag	1-5/8	steel	T, BBB, BB, 2	Win.	$27	1285
Max	1-5/8	Bismuth	BB, 2, 4	Bismuth	NA	1375
Max	1-1/2	hypersonic	BBB, BB, 2	Rem.	NA	1700
Max	1-1/2	heavy metal	BB, 2, 3, 4	Hevi-Shot	NA	1500
Max	1-1/2	steel	T, BBB, BB, 1, 2, 3	Fed.	NA	1450
Max	1-3/8	steel	T, BBB, BB, 1, 2, 3	Fed., Rem.	NA	1500
Max	1-3/8	steel	T, BBB, BB, 2	Fed., Win.	NA	1450
Max	1-3/4	slug, rifled	slug	Fed.	NA	1280
Max	24 pellets	Buckshot	1 Buck	Fed.	NA	1100
Max	54 pellets	Super-X	4 Buck	Win.	NA	1150

12 Gauge 3-1/2" Magnum

Dram Equiv.	Shot Ozs.	Load Style	Shot Sizes	Brands	Avg. Price/box	Velocity (fps)
Max	2-1/4	premium	4, 5, 6	Fed., Rem., Win.	$13*	1150
Max	2	Lead	4, 5, 6	Fed.	NA	1300
Max	2	Copper plated turkey	4, 5	Rem.	NA	1300
Max	18 pellets	premium	00 buck	Fed., Win., Rem.	$7**	1100
Max	1-7/8	Wingmaster HD	4, 6	Rem.	NA	1225
Max	1-7/8	heavyweight	5, 6	Fed.	NA	1300
Max	1-3/4	high density	BB, 2, 4, 6	Rem.		1300
Max	1-7/8	Bismuth	BB, 2, 4	Bis.	NA	1225
Max	1-5/8	blind side	Hex, 1, 3	Win.	NA	1400
Max	1-5/8	Hevi-shot	T	Hevi-shot	NA	1350
Max	1-5/8	Wingmaster HD	T	Rem.	NA	1350
Max	1-5/8	high density	BB, 2	Fed.	NA	1450
Max	1-5/8	Blind side	Hex, BB, 2	Win.	NA	1400
Max	1-3/8	Heavyweight	2, 4, 6	Fed.	NA	1450
Max	1-3/8	steel	T, BBB, BB, 2, 4	Fed., Win., Rem.	NA	1450
Max	1-1/2	FS steel	BBB, BB, 2	Fed.	NA	1500
Max	1-1/2	Supreme H-V	BBB, BB, 2, 3	Win.	NA	1475
Max	1-3/8	H-speed steel	BB, 2	Rem.	NA	1550

12 Gauge 3-1/2" Magnum (cont.)

Dram Equiv.	Shot Ozs.	Load Style	Shot Sizes	Brands	Avg. Price/box	Velocity (fps)
Max	1-1/4	Steel	BB, 2	Win.	NA	1625
Max	24 pellets	Premium	1 Buck	Fed.	NA	1100
Max	54 pellets	Super-X	4 Buck	Win.	NA	1050

12 Gauge 3" Magnum

Dram Equiv.	Shot Ozs.	Load Style	Shot Sizes	Brands	Avg. Price/box	Velocity (fps)
Max	1-3/4	turkey	4, 5, 6	Fed., Fio.	$9*	1175
Win., Rem.	NA	1300	BB, 2, 4, 6	Win., Fed., Rem.	$19	1210
Max	1-3/4	high density	BB, 2, 4	Rem.	NA	1450
Max	1-5/8	high density	BB, 2	Fed.	NA	1450
Max	1-5/8	Wingmaster HD	4, 6	Rem.	NA	1227
Max	1-5/8	high velocity	4, 5, 6	Fed.	NA	1350
4	1-5/8	premium	2, 4, 5, 6	Win., Fed., Rem.	$18	1290
Max	1-1/2	Wingmaster HD	T	Rem.	NA	1300
Max	1-1/2	Hevi-shot	T	Hevi-shot	NA	1300
Max	1-1/2	high density	BB, 2, 4	Rem.	NA	1300
Max	1-1/2	slug	slug	Bren.	NA	1604
Max	1-5/8	Bismuth	BB, 2, 4, 5, 6	Bis.	NA	1250
4	24 pellets	buffered	1 buck	Win., Fed., Rem.	$5**	1040
4	15 pellets	buffered	00 buck	Win., Fed., Rem.	$6**	1210
4	10 pellets	buffered	000 buck	Win., Fed., Rem.	$6**	1225
4	41 pellets	buffered	4 buck	Win., Fed., Rem.	$6**	1210
Max	1-3/8	heavyweight	5, 6	Fed.	NA	1300
Max	1-3/8	high density	B, 2, 4, 6	Rem. Win.	NA	1450
Max	1-3/8	slug	slug	Bren.	NA	1476
Max	1-3/8	blind side	Hex, 1, 3, 5	Win.	NA	1400
Max	1-1/4	slug, rifled	slug	Fed.	NA	1600
Max	1-3/16	saboted	Hex, 1, 3, 5	Win.	NA	1400
slug	copper slug	Rem.	NA	1500	NA	1600
Max	7/8	slug, rifled	slug	Rem.	NA	1875
Max	1-1/8	low recoil	BB	Fed.	NA	850
Max	1-1/8	steel	BB, 2, 3, 4	Fed., Win., Rem.	NA	1550
Max	1-1/16	high density	2, 4	Win.	NA	1400
Max	1	steel	4, 6	Fed.	NA	1330
Max	1-3/8	buckhammer	slug	Rem.	NA	1500
Max	1	TruBall slug	slug	Fed.	NA	1700
Max	1	slug, rifled	slug, magnum	Win., Rem.	$5**	1760
Max	1	saboted slug	slug	Rem., Win., Fed.	$10**	1550

Dram Equiv.	Shot Ozs.	Load Style	Shot Sizes	Brands	Avg. Price/box	Velocity (fps)
12 Gauge 3" Magnum (cont.)						
Max	385 grs.	partition gold	slug	Win.	NA	2000
Max	1-1/8	Rackmaster	slug	Win.	NA	1700
Max	300 grs.	XP3	slug	Win.	NA	2100
3-5/8	1-3/8	steel	BBB, BB, 1, 2, 3, 4	Win., Fed., Rem.	$19	1275
Max	1-1/8	snow goose FS	BB, 2, 3, 4	Fed.	NA	1635
Max	1-1/8	steel	BB, 2, 4	Rem.	NA	1500
Max	1-1/8	steel	T, BBB, BB, 2, 4, 5, 6	Fed., Win.	NA	1450
Max	1-1/8	steel	BB, 2	Fed.	NA	1400
Max	1-1/8	FS lead	3, 4	Fed.	NA	1600
Max	1-3/8	Blind side	Hex, BB, 2	Win.	NA	1400
4	1-1/4	steel	T, BBB, BB, 1, 2, 3, 4, 6	Win., Fed., Rem.	$18	1400
Max	1-1/4	FS steel	BBB, BB, 2	Fed.	NA	1450
12 Gauge 2-3/4"						
Max	1-5/8	magnum	4, 5, 6	Win., Fed.	$8*	1250
Max	1-3/8	lead	4, 5, 6	Fiocchi	NA	1485
Max	1-3/8	turkey	4, 5, 6	Fio.	NA	1250
Max	1-3/8	steel	4, 5, 6	Fed.	NA	1400
Max	1-3/8	Bismuth	BB, 2, 4, 5, 6	Bis.	NA	1300
3-3/4	1-1/2	magnum	BB, 2, 4, 5, 6	Win., Fed., Rem.	$16	1260
Max	1-1/4	blind side	Hex, 2, 5	Win.	NA	1400
Max	1-1/4	Supreme H-V	4, 5, 6, 7-1/2	Win.	NA	1400
Rem.	NA	1400	BB, 2, 4, 5, 6, 7-1/2, 8, 9	Win., Fed., Rem., Fio.	$13	1330
3-3/4	1-1/4	high velocity	BB, 2, 4, 5, 6, 7-1/2, 8, 9	Win., Fed., Rem., Fio.	$13	1330
Max	1-1/4	high density	B, 2, 4	Win.	NA	1450
Max	1-1/4	high density	4, 6	Rem.	NA	1325
3-1/4	1-1/4	standard velocity	6, 7-1/2, 8, 9	Win., Fed.	$11	1220
Rem., Fio.	$11	1220	5	Hevi-shot	NA	1350
Max	1-1/8	Hevi-shot	5	Hevi-shot	NA	1350
3-1/4	1-1/8	standard velocity	4, 6, 7-1/2, 8, 9	Win., Fed., Rem., Fio.	$9	1255
Max	1-1/8	steel	2, 4	Rem.	NA	1390
Max	1	steel	BB, 2	Fed.	NA	1450
3-1/4	1	standard velocity	6, 7-1/2, 8	Rem., Fed., Fio., Win.	$6	1290
3-1/4	1-1/4	target	7-1/2, 8, 9	Win., Fed., Rem.	$10	1220
3	1-1/8	spreader	7-1/2, 8, 8-1/2, 9	Fio.	NA	1200
3	1-1/8	target	7-1/2, 8, 9, 7-1/2x8	Win., Fed., Rem., Fio.	$7	1200
2-3/4	1-1/8	target	7-1/2, 8, 8-1/2, 9, 7-1/2x8	Win., Fed., Rem., Fio.	$7	1145
2-3/4	1-1/8	low recoil	7-1/2, 8	Rem.	NA	1145

Dram Equiv.	Shot Ozs.	Load Style	Shot Sizes	Brands	Avg. Price/box	Velocity (fps)
12 Gauge 2-3/4" (cont.)						
2-1/2	26 grams	low recoil	8	Win.	NA	980
2-1/4	1-1/8	target	7-1/2, 8, 8-1/2, 9	Rem., Fed.	$7	1080
Max	1	spreader	7-1/2, 8, 8-1/2, 9	Fio.	NA	1300
3-1/4	28 grams(1 oz)	target	7-1/2, 8, 9	Win., Fed., Rem., Fio.	$8	1290
3	1	target	7-1/2, 8, 8-1/2, 9	Win., Fio.	NA	1235
2-3/4	1	target	7-1/2, 8, 8-1/2, 9	Fed., Rem., Fio.	NA	1180
3-1/4	24 grams	target	7-1/2, 8, 9	Fed., Win., Fio.	NA	1325
3	7/8	light	8	Fio.	NA	1200
3-3/4	8 pellets	buffered	000 buck	Win., Fed., Rem.	$4**	1325
4	12 pellets	premium	00 buck	Win., Fed., Rem.	$5**	1290
3-3/4	9 pellets	buffered	00 buck	Win., Fed., Rem., Fio.	$19	1325
3-3/4	12 pellets	buffered	0 buck	Win., Fed., Rem.	$4**	1275
4	20 pellets	buffered	1 buck	Win., Fed., Rem.	$4**	1075
3-3/4	16 pellets	buffered	1 buck	Win., Fed., Rem.	$4**	1250
4	34 pellets	premium	4 buck	Fed., Rem.	$5**	1250
3-3/4	27 pellets	buffered	4 buck	Win., Fed., Rem., Fio.	$4**	1325
		PDX1	1 oz. slug, 3-00 buck	Win.	NA	1150
Max	1 oz	segmenting, slug	slug	Win.	NA	1600
Max	1	saboted slug	slug	Win., Fed., Rem.	$10**	1450
Max	1-1/4	slug, rifled	slug	Fed.	NA	1520
Max	1-1/4	slug	slug	Lightfield		1440
Max	1-1/4	saboted slug	attached sabot	Rem.	NA	1550
Max	1	slug, rifled	slug, magnum	Rem., Fio.	$5**	1680
Max	1	slug, rifled	slug	Win., Fed., Rem.	$4**	1610
Max	1	sabot slug	slug	Sauvestre		1640
Max	7/8	slug, rifled	slug	Rem.	NA	1800
Max	400	plat. tip	sabot slug	Win.	NA	1700
Max	385 grains	Partition Gold Slug	slug	Win.	NA	1900
Max	385 grains	Core-Lokt bonded	sabot slug	Rem.	NA	1900
Max	325 grains	Barnes Sabot	slug	Fed.	NA	1900
Max	300 grains	SST Slug	sabot slug	Hornady	NA	2050
Max	3/4	Tracer	#8 + tracer	Fio.	NA	1150
Max	130 grains	Less Lethal	.73 rubber slug	Lightfield	NA	600
Max	3/4	non-toxic	zinc slug	Win.	NA	NA
3	1-1/8	steel target	6-1/2, 7	Rem.	NA	1200

12 Gauge 2-3/4" (cont.)

Dram Equiv.	Shot Ozs.	Load Style	Shot Sizes	Brands	Avg. Price/box	Velocity (fps)
2-3/4	1-1/8	steel target	7	Rem.	NA	1145
3	1#	steel	7	Win.	$11	1235
3-1/2	1-1/4	steel	T, BBB, BB, 1, 2, 3, 4, 5, 6	Win., Fed., Rem.	$18	1275
3-3/4	1-1/8	steel	BB, 1, 2, 3, 4, 5, 6	Win., Fed., Rem., Fio.	$16	1365
3-3/4	1	steel	2, 3, 4, 5, 6, 7	Win., Fed., Rem., Fio.	$13	1390
Max	7/8	steel	7	Fio.	NA	1440

16 Gauge 2-3/4"

Dram Equiv.	Shot Ozs.	Load Style	Shot Sizes	Brands	Avg. Price/box	Velocity (fps)
3-1/4	1-1/4	magnum	2, 4, 6	Fed., Rem.	$16	1260
3-1/4	1-1/8	high velocity	4, 6, 7-1/2	Win., Fed., Rem., Fio.	$12	1295
Max	1-1/8	Bismuth	4, 5	Bis.	NA	1200
2-3/4	1-1/8	standard velocity	6, 7-1/2, 8	Fed., Rem., Fio.	$9	1185
2-1/2	1	dove	6, 7-1/2, 8, 9	Fio., Win.	NA	1165
2-3/4	1		6, 7-1/2, 8	Fio.	NA	1200
Max	15/16	steel	2, 4	Fed., Rem.	NA	1300
Max	7/8	steel	2, 4	Win.	$16	1300
3	12 pellets	buffered	1 buck	Win., Fed., Rem.	$4**	1225
Max	4/5	slug, rifled	slug	Win., Fed., Rem.	$4**	1570
Max	.92	sabot slug	slug	Sauvestre	NA	1560

20 Gauge 3" Magnum

Dram Equiv.	Shot Ozs.	Load Style	Shot Sizes	Brands	Avg. Price/box	Velocity (fps)
3	1-1/4	premium	2, 4, 5, 6, 7-1/2	Win., Fed., Rem.	$15	1185
Max	1-1/4	Wingmaster HD	4, 6	Rem.	NA	1185
3	1-1/4	turkey	4, 6	Fio.	NA	1200
Max	1-1/4	Hevi-shot	2, 4, 6	Hevi-shot	NA	1250
Max	1-1/8	high density	4, 6	Rem.	NA	1300
Max	18 pellets	buck shot	2 buck	Fed.	NA	1200
Max	24 pellets	buffered	3 buck	Win.	$5**	1150
2-3/4	20 pellets	buck	3 buck	Rem.	$4**	1200
Max	1	hypersonic	2, 3, 4	Rem.	NA	Rem.
3-1/4	1	steel	1, 2, 3, 4, 5, 6	Win., Fed., Rem.	$15	1330
Max	1	blind side	Hex, 2, 5	Win.	NA	1300
Max	7/8	steel	2, 4	Win.	NA	1300
Max	7/8	FS lead	3, 4	Fed.	NA	1500
Max	1-1/16	high density	2, 4	Win.	NA	1400
Max	1-1/16	Bismuth	2, 4, 5, 6	Bismuth	NA	1250

20 Gauge 3" Magnum (cont.)

Dram Equiv.	Shot Ozs.	Load Style	Shot Sizes	Brands	Avg. Price/box	Velocity (fps)
Mag	5/8	saboted slug	275 gr.	Fed.	NA	1900
Max	3/4	TruBall slug	slug	Fed.	NA	1700

20 Gauge 2-3/4"

Dram Equiv.	Shot Ozs.	Load Style	Shot Sizes	Brands	Avg. Price/box	Velocity (fps)
2-3/4	1-1/8	magnum	4, 6, 7-1/2	Win., Fed., Rem.	$14	1175
2-3/4	1	high velocity	4, 5, 6, 7-1/2, 8, 9	Win., Fed., Rem., Fio.	$12	1220
Max	1	Bismuth	4, 6	Bis.	NA	1200
Max	1	Hevi-shot	5	Hevi-shot	NA	1250
Max	1	Supreme H-V	4, 6, 7-1/2	Win. Rem.	NA	1300
Max	1	FS lead	4, 5, 6	Fed.	NA	1350
Max	7/8	Steel	2, 3, 4	Fio.	NA	1500
2-1/2	1	standard velocity	6, 7-1/2, 8	Win., Rem., Fed., Fio.	$6	1165
2-1/2	7/8	clays	8	Rem.	NA	1200
2-1/2	7/8	promotional	6, 7-1/2, 8	Win., Rem., Fio.	$6	1210
2-1/2	1	target	8, 9	Win., Rem.	$8	1165
Max	7/8	clays	7-1/2, 8	Win.	NA	1275
2-1/2	7/8	target	8, 9	Win., Fed., Rem.	$8	1200
Max	3/4	steel	2, 4	Rem.	NA	1425
2-1/2	7/8	steel - target	7	Rem.	NA	1200
1-1/2	7/8	low recoil	8	Win.	NA	980
Max	1	buckhammer	slug	Rem.	NA	1500
Max	5/8	Saboted Slug	Copper Slug	Rem.	NA	1500
Max	20 pellets	buffered	3 buck	Win., Fed.	$4	1200
Max	5/8	slug, saboted	slug	Win.,	$9**	1400
2-3/4	5/8	slug, rifled	slug	Rem.	$4**	1580
Max	3/4	saboted slug	copper slug	Fed., Rem.	NA	1450
Max	3/4	slug, rifled	slug	Win., Fed., Rem., Fio.	$4**	1570
Max	.9	sabot slug	slug	Sauvestre		1480
Max	260 grains	Partition Gold Slug	slug	Win.	NA	1900
Max	260 grains	Core-Lokt Ultra	slug	Rem.	NA	1900

Dram Equiv.	Shot Ozs.	Load Style	Shot Sizes	Brands	Avg. Price/box	Velocity (fps)
20 Gauge 2-3/4" (cont.)						
Max	260 grains	saboted slug	platinum tip	Win.	NA	1700
Max	3/4	steel	2, 3, 4, 6	Win., Fed., Rem.	$14	1425
Max	250 grains	SST slug	slug	Hornady	NA	1800
Max	1/2	rifled, slug	slug	Rem.	NA	1800
Max	67 grains	Less lethal	2/.60 rubber balls	Lightfield	NA	900
28 Gauge 3"						
Max	7/8	tundra tungsten	4, 5, 6	Fiocchi	NA	TBD
28 Gauge 2-3/4"						
2	1	high velocity	6, 7-1/2, 8	Win.	$12	1125
2-1/4	3/4	high velocity	6, 7-1/2, 8, 9	Win., Fed., Rem., Fio.	$11	1295
2	3/4	target	8, 9	Win., Fed., Rem.	$9	1200
Max	3/4	sporting clays	7-1/2, 8-1/2	Win.	NA	1300
Max	5/8	Bismuth	4, 6	Bis.	NA	1250
Max	5/8	steel	6, 7	NA	NA	1300
Max	5/8	slug		Bren.	NA	1450

Dram Equiv.	Shot Ozs.	Load Style	Shot Sizes	Brands	Avg. Price/box	Velocity (fps)
410 Bore 3"						
Max	11/16	high velocity	4, 5, 6, 7-1/2, 8, 9	Win., Fed., Rem., Fio.	$10	1135
Max	9/16	Bismuth	4	Bis.	NA	1175
Max	3/8	steel	6	NA	NA	1400
		judge	5 pellets 000 Buck	Fed.	NA	960
		judge	9 pellets #4 Buck	Fed.	NA	1100
Max	Mixed	Per. Defense	3DD/12BB	Win.	NA	750
410 Bore 2-1/2"						
Max	1/2	high velocity	4, 6, 7-1/2	Win., Fed., Rem.	$9	1245
Max	1/5	slug, rifled	slug	Win., Fed., Rem.	$4**	1815
1-1/2	1/2	target	8, 8-1/2, 9	Win., Fed., Rem., Fio.	$8	1200
Max	1/2	sporting clays	7-1/2, 8, 8-1/2	Win.	NA	1300
Max		Buckshot	5-000 Buck	Win.	NA	1135
		judge	12-bb's, 3 disks	Win.	NA	TBD
Max	Mixed	Per. Defense	4DD/16BB	Win.	NA	750
Max	42 grains	Less lethal	4/.41 rubber balls	Lightfield	NA	1150